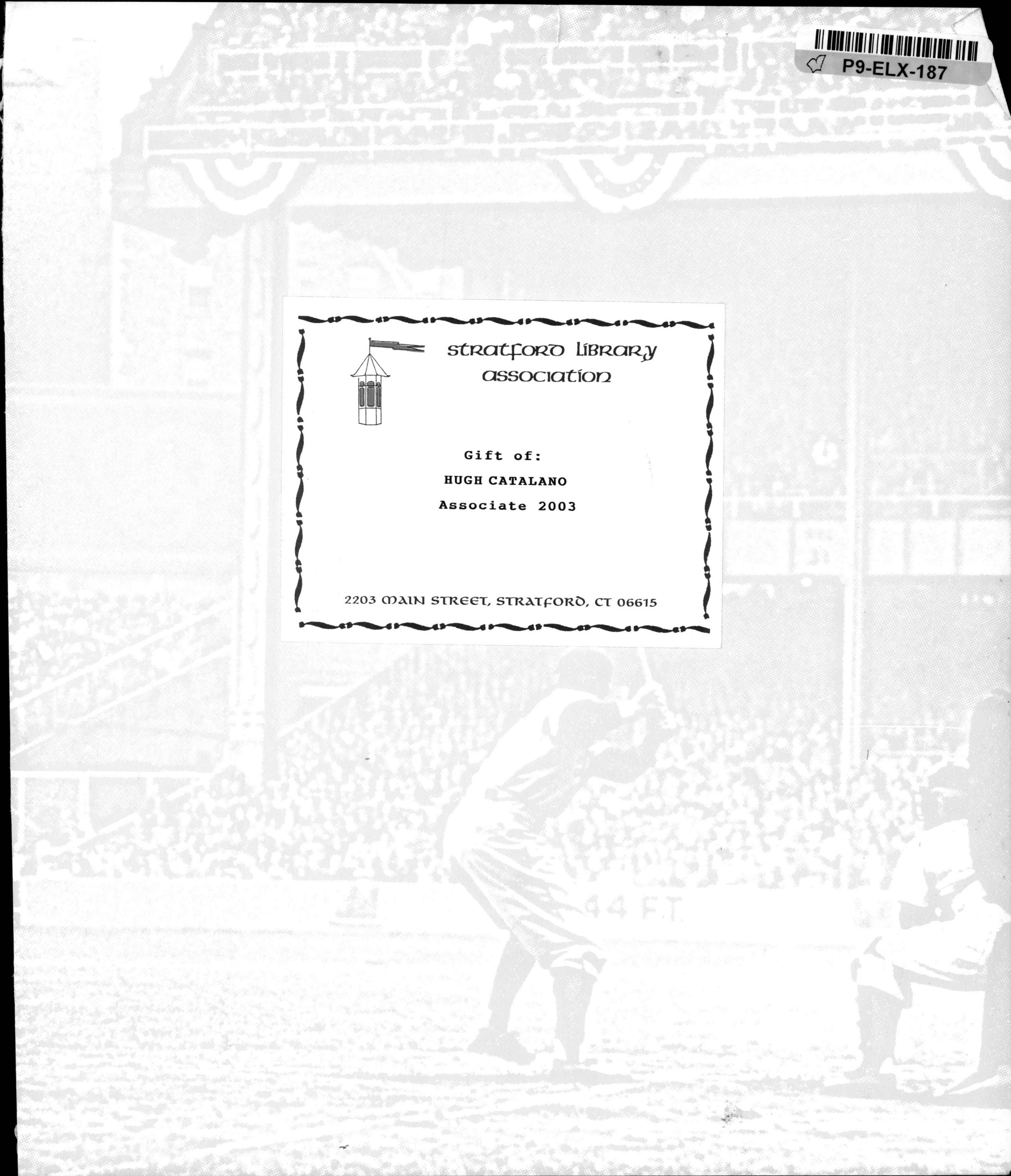

100 YEARS OF THE World Series

24

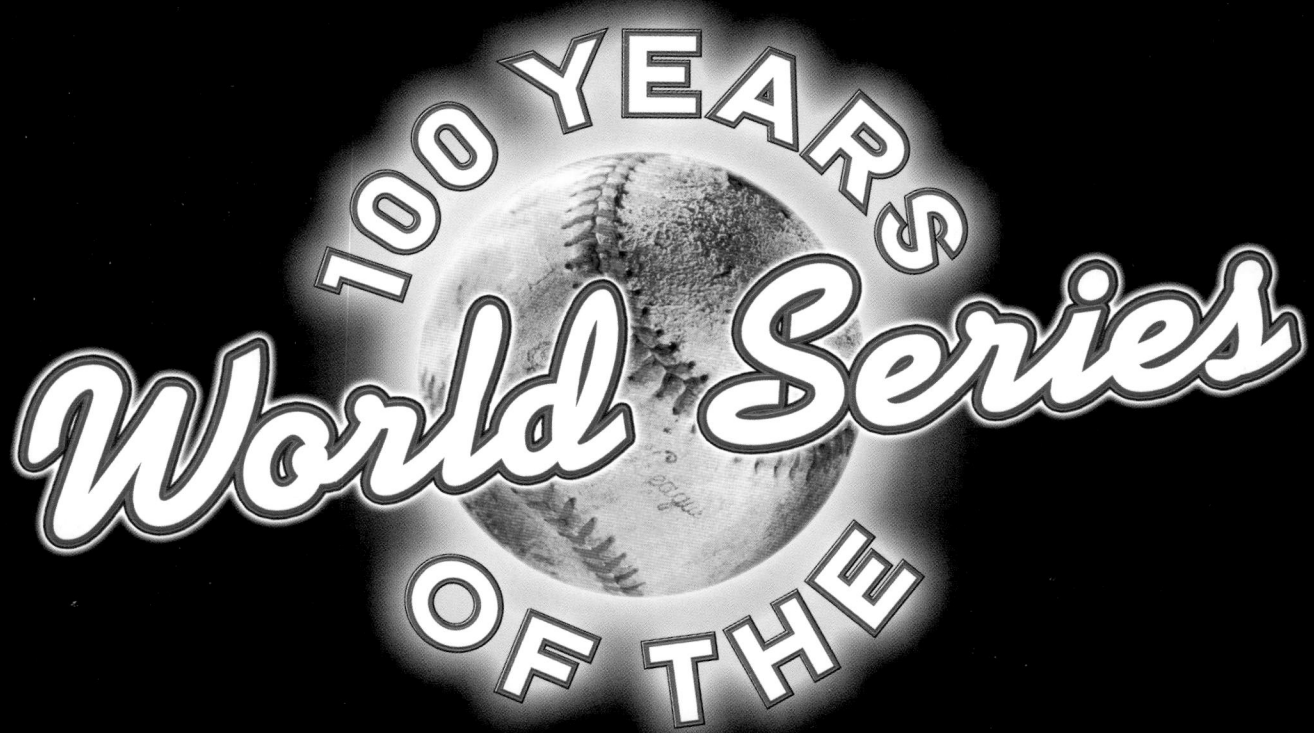

100 Years of the World Series

ERIC ENDERS

BARNES & NOBLE BOOKS

BARNES & NOBLE BOOK

ISBN 0-7607-4201-4

Project Editor: Nathaniel Marunas
Editor: Dan Heend
Art Director: Kevin Ullrich
Designer: Kevin Baier
Photography Editor: Janice Ackerman
Digital Imaging: Daniel J. Rutkowski
Production Manager: Richela Fabian Morgan

Color separations by Chroma Graphics (Overseas) PTE LTD
Printed in United Kingdom by Butler & Tanner

5 7 9 10 8 6 4

Dedication

For Penny Dillon, Robert Dahl, and Charles Murray—
three teachers who made a difference.

Acknowledgments

No baseball book can be written without utilizing the vast resources of the National Baseball Library in Cooperstown, where many of my friends and former colleagues were especially helpful. Special thanks to Bill Burdick, Claudette Burke, Sweet Willie Francis, Jeremy Jones, Rachael Kepner, Anne McFarland, Rob Pendell, Gabriel Schechter, Tom Shieber, Erik Strohl, Tim Wiles, Russell Wolinsky, and Andy Zides, who are Hall of Famers in every sense of the term.

In addition to sharing his expertise on the nineteenth-century World Series, my friend David Jones served as a sounding board for ideas. Thanks to everyone at Barnes & Noble Publishing, especially editor Dan Heend, for keeping me in line; editorial director Nathaniel Marunas, for developing the project; designer Kevin Baier, for doing such a terrific job with the layout; art director Kevin Ullrich, for shaping the look of the book; photography editor Janice Ackerman, whose research turned up some wonderful gems; digital imaging specialist Daniel Rutkowski, for cleaning up the images so beautifully; and production director Richela Morgan, who shepherded this large and complicated book through its many stages of growth. I am also grateful for the World Series ephemera provided by Brian Bielemeier, Jonathan Palmer, and Spike Vrusho. Mike McCormick, Erin Whiteside, and Paul Cunningham of MLB Properties were helpful, as always. So were many of the 7,000 members of the Society for American Baseball Research, who are always eager to share those obscure bits of information that make this such a wonderful game.

Special thanks to Sean Forman and David Smith, who maintain the two best baseball sites on the internet, Baseball-Reference.com and Retrosheet.org, respectively. Neither of them receives enough credit for providing a staggering amount of information to the public free of charge. I also salute the many hundreds of authors who have written about the World Series over the last century, particularly such people as Fred Lieb and Francis Richter, whose descriptions are vivid enough to get us excited about old baseball games nearly 100 years after the fact.

Lastly, I'd like to thank my family, particularly my parents, Steve and Sandra, and my brother, Mark (the real ballplayer in the family), for all their support.

Eric Enders
Cooperstown, New York
December 12, 2002

Baseball
Magazine
15¢
Gowdy
Maranville
Schmidt
BOSTON BRAVES ISSUE
THE WORK OF THE "MIRACLE MAN" :: GREAT WAGNER POSTER IN COLORS

ENDPAPERS: Pee Wee Reese, the (future Hall-of-Fame) shortstop for the Brooklyn Dodgers, takes the plate against the New York Yankees at the opening of the 1949 World Series. The setting is Yankee Stadium, one of the temples of baseball—and the Fall Classic.

PAGE 2: The sheer joy experienced by the winning team in any World Series is captured perfectly here by a jubilant bunch of New York Yankees. Pitcher John Wetteland raises his hand to the sky as he is himself hoisted aloft by his teammates. The 3-2 win in this Game 6 outing clinched the 1996 World Series for the Bronx Bombers.

LEFT: The 1914 Boston Braves—which included catcher Hank Gowdy, shortstop Rabbit Maranville, and first baseman Butch Schmidt, featured here on the cover of *Baseball Magazine*—were the surprise winners of that year's World Series. They faced Connie Mack's heavily favored Philadelphia Athletics, sweeping the A's in four games.

FOLLOWING PAGES: Seconds after this photo was taken, at the bottom of the ninth inning of Game 7—which the reigning world champion Yankees were winning, 2-1, as they took the field—the ball flew off the bat of Luis Gonzalez and over the infield to short center field, driving in the winning run. The expansion Diamondbacks, a team only four years old, had won the dramatic 2001 World Series.

jiffy lube
GONZAL

CONTENTS

Introduction

My first opportunity to tell others about the World Series was in the fifth grade. Knowing that I loved baseball and knowing that my favorite team, the Dodgers, were playing in the World Series, my teacher, Mrs. Dillon, set aside a bulletin board in the school hallway and asked me to keep track of the Series' progress. Each morning before class I stood on a stepstool with a marker in my hand and painstakingly recorded the events of the night before: definitely the winning team and the line score, and perhaps the winning and losing pitchers—to tell you the truth, I no longer remember exactly what I put on the board. What I do remember, though, is the excitement I felt at sharing the events with my classmates—in a way, it's the same feeling I have now in writing this book.

The history of the World Series is not only thrilling, but amazing in its breadth. In these pages you will read stories of passenger pigeons, a hen, and a Foxx. There are gamblers, tough guys, charmers, liars, gentlemen, con artists, and great ballplayers—and at least one man (Pete Rose) who is all of the above. There are ejections and mad dashes and drunken brawls. And there are plenty of heroes, some with names like Pepper, Bullet, Wildfire, and Home Run.

Why does the Fall Classic continue to capture our imagination so, despite baseball's current tendency to ruin it with late-night endings and tasteless MasterCard commercials? Well, for one thing, the World Series can change lives, as Joe Torre, Joe Jackson, and even Robin Williams' character in *Good Will Hunting* can attest. But I think the real reason for its popularity is that no other sporting event comes close to embodying the combination of history and excitement of the World Series. The NCAA Basketball Tournament is every bit as exciting, but has existed in its current form only since 1985. It has no Sandy Koufaxes, no Babe Ruths. The Super Bowl is young, too; it's been around only since the 1960s, and is usually lopsided anyway. The NHL, the NBA—neither has anything that can compare to baseball's championship, which now has a century of memorable games under its belt.

One way to measure its impact is to observe how deeply the term "World Series" has embedded itself in the American language. Once it referred only to the championship of Major League Baseball. Now there are a host of other baseball events that borrow the name, for instance, the Little League World Series, College World Series, and Wiffleball World Series—and a myriad of others in completely unrelated areas. There's the World Series of Poker, the World Series of Comedy, the World Series of Philately—even the World Series of Birding. (If the champions of all those events could somehow face off against each other, there could even be a World Series of World Series.)

Like all history, baseball history is best told by those who were there—but even those who were there often disagree on the facts. And, of course, no one observer could have been there for all of it. In addition, the game, with all its legends, lends itself to inaccuracies ranging from fanciful exaggeration to willful mistruth. I am sure that a few of those inaccuracies have crept into this book. Those "facts" I can identify as false, I have either omitted or refuted. For the ones I didn't catch, I apologize—I'll fix them in future editions.

And now, let's play ball. *Batter up!*

These three men—each from a different era, and representing both sides of the plate—all left their mark on greatest sports championship in the world with outstanding performances in highly scrutinized games performed under incredible pressure.

OPPOSITE TOP: In an era when the longball was still relatively rare, Frank Baker earned the nickname "Home Run" by hitting two game-winning drives over the fence during the 1911 World Series. For his career, Baker finished with a .363 batting average and three homers in six World Series.

OPPOSITE BOTTOM: Barry Bonds homers in his first career World Series at-bat, the first of four dingers he would hit in the 2002 Fall Classic. In his seventeenth major league season, Bonds finally removed himself from the list of greatest players who never made it to the World Series—a list headed by the great Ernie Banks, who played 2,528 games without ever making the postseason.

LEFT: The incomparable Sandy Koufax throws a pitch during the 1963 World Series, when, according to teammate Stan Williams, he "just took all the confidence away from the Yankee hitters...Sandy confirmed for a national television audience that he was the greatest pitcher who ever lived." In eight career World Series starts, Koufax allowed an average of less than one run per game.

CHAPTER 1
THE DEADBALL ERA
1903–1919

For baseball, the Deadball Era was a period of drastic change. In four short years, the baseball scene transformed from one major league to two warring leagues, then to two peaceful leagues. By the time the era ended, stability had set in. The number of major league teams had doubled, and almost all of them played in brand-new baseball palaces of steel and concrete—dependable sources of revenue that would keep each team in place until the 1950s. The cities and teams that played host to major league baseball stayed constant for fifty years, surviving two World Wars and the Great Depression. The World Series, almost an afterthought when it was first played, was on the brink of becoming the nation's premier sporting event by 1919.

Home teams enjoyed a significantly larger home-field advantage during the Deadball Era than they do today, with the home team winning about 55 percent of all games from 1903–1919. However, such was not the case in the World Series, as the home team posted only a 45–47 record in Series games. Part of the reason for this was undoubtedly the selection of a respected umpiring team representing both leagues to work the World Series, as opposed to the more easily influenced lone umpire who usually worked in-season games. Less afraid of violence from the crowd when working in pairs, the umpires brought a sense of law and order to World Series games that was often missing during the regular season.

During this era, the characteristics of a championship team were far different than they would be in subsequent years. Offensively, the question was not whether you could hit home runs, but whether you could get a bunt down and steal bases. Defensively, a catcher who could throw well was of paramount importance. The Detroit Tigers, without such a catcher, appeared in three consecutive World Series, from 1907–1909, but lost all three years because their opponents were able to steal 49 bases in 17 games. Outfielders who could run (such as Tris Speaker and Duffy Lewis) and shortstops with steady gloves (Joe Tinker and Honus Wagner) were also common components of Series-winning teams during the Deadball Era.

But one thing served as a harbinger of future years: the ability of one star pitcher to completely dominate a short series. During this era Bill Dineen, Christy Mathewson, Babe Adams, Red Faber, and other pitchers led their teams to victory nearly single-handedly, setting an example to be followed by the likes of Sandy Koufax, Orel Hershiser, Curt Schilling, and Randy Johnson.

THE TRIBUNE ALWAYS MAKES A HIT WITH ITS SPORTING

PREVIOUS PAGE: Cubs 20-game winner Jack Pfiester delivers a pitch in the sixth inning of Game 3 of the 1906 World Series, at Chicago's West Side Grounds. The bases are loaded and the infield is playing in, enabling baserunner Ed Walsh to take an enormous lead at second base. The game was still scoreless at this point, but all three baserunners eventually scored, giving the White Sox a 3-0 victory.

BOTTOM: The Boston Pilgrims, winners of the first modern World Series, in 1903, were led by player-manager Jimmy Collins, pictured at center.

1903

BOSTON PILGRIMS (5)
PITTSBURG PIRATES (3)

IT ALL STARTED WITH A WAR. FOR TWO YEARS after the American League declared itself a major league in 1901, it fought a bitter battle with the National League for the baseball supremacy of the United States. Contracts were broken, lawsuits were filed, the two sides bickered at each other in the press. The fledgling American League, in its quest for legitimacy, staged a full frontal assault on the National, signing away many of its best players and placing teams in New York and Philadelphia with intentions of driving their N.L. rivals there out of business. Both sides finally agreed that the bleeding was getting out of hand and they signed a peace agreement in January 1903. The two leagues still hated each other, but at least now each recognized the other's right to exist. They stopped stealing each other's players and each league stopped trying to run the other into the ground. The outcome of all this was that during the summer of 1903—with plenty of bad feelings left to go around, and with plenty of money to be made besides—the two leagues agreed to play their first postseason series. It was apparent who the pennant winners would be by mid-September. On September 16, 1903, Pittsburg Pirates owner Barney Dreyfuss and Boston Pilgrims owner Henry Killilea signed an agreement pledging their teams to meet after the season in a best-of-nine "World's Series." The name was a remnant from the postseason championships played between the National League and American Association in the 1880s; contrary to a popular legend, the moniker did not come about because the series was sponsored by the *New York World* newspaper. Although major league baseball was played in only one country—and even in that country, in only seven of the forty-five states—the owners did not think twice about calling it the World's Series.* Only one prominent sportswriter, William Rankin, even mentioned the irony. "Will [the Boston team] please inform me what foreign teams they defeated to become the World's Champions?" Rankin asked in *The Sporting News* after the 1903 Series. "Some people have a vague idea of how large the world is, and for the life of them can not see anything beyond the borders of the United States."

In 1902 the Pittsburg Pirates (whose hometown restored the 'h' to its name in 1911) enjoyed one of the best seasons in baseball history, going 103-36 and posting a .741 winning percentage that still ranks as the second-best since 1900. But in 1903 they were nowhere near as dominant. Their two best pitchers, Jack Chesbro and Jesse Tannehill, had jumped to the American League. Still, the Pirates won 91 games and the pennant in 1903, thanks largely to Honus Wagner, who won the batting title at .355 and fielded brilliantly in his first season as a full-time shortstop. The team's other stars included player-manager Fred Clarke, who led the league in doubles and slugging percentage, and center fielder Clarence "Ginger" Beaumont, the league's leader in runs, hits, and total bases. Their Series opponents, the Boston Pilgrims (who would change their name to the Red Sox a few years later) featured a bevy of stars recently lured away from the National League, including future Hall of Famers Jimmy Collins and Denton T. "Cy" Young. Their best hitter was left fielder John "Buck" Freeman. Freeman was the top power hitter in baseball, leading the junior circuit in home runs, runs batted in, and total bases.

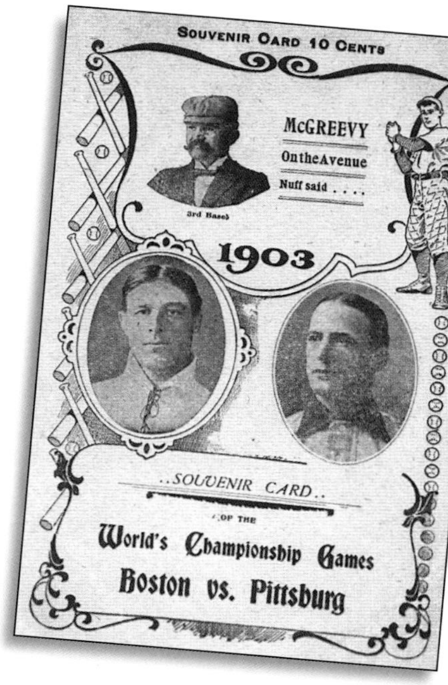

In Game 1 Boston started Cy Young, who on June 13 of that season had won his 361st game to become the winningest pitcher in baseball history. But that didn't impress the Pirates, who battered Young for seven runs. The Pirates won the first game 7-3 behind four hits by Tommy Leach, including a pair of triples, and the stellar pitching of Charles "Deacon" Phillippe. But the Pilgrims came back in Game 2, as Boston's Bill Dineen shut out the Pirates 3-0. With the Series tied 1-1, more than 19,000 fans packed Boston's Huntington Avenue Grounds, which normally held around 11,000, for Game 3. They watched in silence as the Pirates knocked Boston pitcher Tom Hughes out of the game in the third inning. Young relieved Hughes, but the Pirates had scored all the runs they would need, winning the game 4-2 behind Phillippe. (Young, who attended the game in street clothes because he wasn't expecting to pitch, had to be summoned from the Boston club office where he was helping to count gate receipts.)

After a train trip and a rain delay, play resumed at Pittsburg's Exposition Park for Game 4. Remarkably, Phillippe started again for the Pirates, his third start in four games.

Phillippe, pitching in the rain, won his third game of the Series, surviving a ninth-inning Boston rally to win, 5-4.

Game 5 the next day was played with unusual ground rules in effect. Fans who couldn't buy grandstand seats were roped into a standing-room area in what would normally be center field. Any ball hit into the throng was deemed a ground-rule triple. Five such hits disappeared into the mass of people during the game. One of them was by Young, who was impressive both at the plate and on the mound as he beat the host Pirates 11-2. Five Pilgrims collected at least two hits. Boston won again the next day, 6-3, behind Dineen. Now the Series was tied at three games apiece and Pirates owner Dreyfuss decided to postpone Game 7 for one day. The official reason was that it was too cold and rainy to play, but many suspected the real reason was to give Pirates' star pitcher, Phillippe, another day of rest. The move backfired as Phillippe lost the game to Young, 7-3.

The two teams now traveled back to Boston with the Pilgrims needing just one more win to wrap up the Series. Phillippe, after going the distance in games 1, 3, 4, and 7, was given yet another start for the Pirates. Though he performed admirably, Phillippe was outdone by Dineen, who wrapped up the Series for Boston with a three-hit shutout, his second shutout of the Series. The Pilgrims were "world" champs, and more importantly, the American League had triumphed in the first post-season series between the rival leagues.

** The World Series was actually called the "World's Series" until the 1920s, when the possessive form of the term began to fade out. However, for consistency's sake, the modern term World Series will be used throughout the text, except in quoted matter.*

TOP: Under the eye of watchful policemen, fans line up for World Series tickets outside the Polo Grounds.

BOTTOM: Cy Young was old and overweight by the time this photo was taken in 1908, but in 1903 he was the American League's best pitcher, posting five more wins than any other hurler.

FOLLOWING PAGES: Huntington Avenue Grounds during the 1903 World Series. At the time, the park's centerfield was the deepest in the major leagues, measuring a whopping 635 feet.

1903 WORLD SERIES

Huntington Ave. Grounds (Boston) ◆ 10.1.03

	1	2	3	4	5	6	7	8	9	R	H	E
Pitt.	4	0	1	1	0	0	1	0	0	7	12	2
Boston	0	0	0	0	0	0	2	0	1	3	6	4

WP–Phillippe LP–Young HR: PIT–Sebring ATT: 16,242

Huntington Avenue Grounds ◆ 10.2.03

	1	2	3	4	5	6	7	8	9	R	H	E
Pitt.	0	0	0	0	0	0	0	0	0	0	3	2
Boston	2	0	0	0	0	1	0	0	X	3	9	0

WP–Dineen LP–Leever HR: BOS–Dougherty (2) ATT: 9,415

Huntington Avenue Grounds ◆ 10.3.03

	1	2	3	4	5	6	7	8	9	R	H	E
Pitt.	0	1	2	0	0	0	0	1	0	4	7	0
Boston	0	0	0	1	0	0	0	1	0	2	4	2

WP–Phillippe LP–Hughes ATT: 18,801

Exposition Park (Pittsburg) ◆ 10.6.03

	1	2	3	4	5	6	7	8	9	R	H	E
Boston	0	0	0	0	1	0	0	0	3	4	9	1
Pitt.	1	0	0	0	1	0	3	0	X	5	12	1

WP–Phillippe LP–Dineen ATT: 7,600

Exposition Park ◆ 10.7.03

	1	2	3	4	5	6	7	8	9	R	H	E
Boston	0	0	0	0	0	6	4	1	0	11	14	2
Pitt.	0	0	0	0	0	0	0	2	0	2	6	4

WP–Young LP–Kennedy ATT: 12,322

Exposition Park ◆ 10.8.03

	1	2	3	4	5	6	7	8	9	R	H	E
Boston	0	0	3	0	2	0	1	0	0	6	10	1
Pitt.	0	0	0	0	0	0	3	0	0	3	10	3

WP–Dineen LP–Leever ATT:11,556

Exposition Park ◆ 10.10.03

	1	2	3	4	5	6	7	8	9	R	H	E
Boston	2	0	0	2	0	2	0	1	0	7	11	4
Pitt.	0	0	0	1	0	1	0	0	1	3	10	3

WP–Young LP–Phillippe Att: 17,038

Huntington Avenue Grounds ◆ 10.13.03

	1	2	3	4	5	6	7	8	9	R	H	E
Pitt.	0	0	0	0	0	0	0	0	0	0	4	3
Boston	0	0	0	2	0	1	0	0	X	3	8	0

WP–Dineen LP–Phillippe Att: 7,455

HOOT MON!
C.M.C.
GARTERS FOR MEN
HOSE
EMERSON
SHOE

HUNTINGT
AVENUE
AMERICAN LEAGUE
BASE BA
GROUNDS

RIGHT: Honus Wagner, star shortstop for the Pittsburg Pirates, warms up before a game. One of the first batch of inductees into the Hall of Fame, Wagner had an outstanding, 21-year career, including 17 seasons batting better than .300. Unfortunately, his talents were not enough to help the Pirates claim victory in the inaugural World Series in 1903.

1904

No Series

THE INAUGURAL WORLD SERIES HAD BEEN such a success that fans assumed it would become an annual event. But in July 1904, John McGraw, whose New York Giants were running away with the pennant, said there would be no such series as long as he was in charge of the team. He was backed up by Giants owner John T. Brush, who said his team had no obligation to play a post-season series against "a victorious club in a minor league."

Nobody truly considered the American League a minor league, but Brush and McGraw both had reasons to dislike the junior circuit. McGraw had been lured to the new league to become manager of Baltimore, but when the riches the American League promised never materialized, he bolted to the Giants. Brush disliked the American League because it had placed a rival team, the New York Highlanders, only minutes away from the Polo Grounds in an attempt to drive the Giants out of business. Both men despised A.L. president Ban Johnson and wanted no part of any scheme that would lend legitimacy to the American League. "We have gained all the glory there is to be acquired in baseball—winning the National League pennant," Brush said. "Some people say that it was understood that the champions of both leagues would play an after-season series. I was never a party to such an agreement or understanding." Johnson urged his National League counterpart, Harry Pulliam, to order the Giants to play the series. Pulliam declined, saying he had no authority to issue such orders.

One New York newspaper was so incensed that it produced a petition signed by 10,000 Giants fans who favored a World Series. Reporters and fans saw through the team's superficial reasons for avoiding a World Series. Rumors began to circulate that the Giants players were circumventing the owners and making their own arrangements for a series against Boston, forcing Brush to pay them off to abandon the plan. Brush denounced the allegation as "an outrageous lie." On October 8, McGraw tried

TOP: John T. Brush, owner of the New York Giants, refused to play a World Series in 1904 because the American League's New York Highlanders had tried to drive him out of business.

BOTTOM: Although John McGraw, the raucous manager of the New York Giants, declined to play the 1904 World Series, he relented the next year and allowed the Giants to face the Philadelphia Athletics in the World Series.

to take some of the heat off Brush, writing an open letter to baseball fans:

> *The blame should rest on my shoulders, not Mr. Brush's, for I and I alone am responsible for the club's actions.... Mr. Brush's only part in it is supporting me, as he has always done.*
>
> *When I came to New York, three years ago, the team was in last place. Since that time, on and off the field, I have worked to bring the pennant to New York. The result is known. Now that the New York team has won this honor I for one will not stand to see it tossed away like a rag. The pennant means something to me. It is the first I have ever won. It means something to our players, and they are with me in my stand. We are not a lot of grafters looking for box-office receipts at the expense of our club. ...*
>
> *Never while I am manager of the New York Club and while this club holds the pennant will I consent to enter into a haphazard box-office game with Ban Johnson & Company. ...*
>
> *If the National League should see fit to place post-season games on the same plane as championship games and surround them with the same protection and safeguards for square sport as championship games, then and not till then will I ever take part in them.*
>
> *We are here and here to stay; we will defend the pennant in 1905, and hope to for many years. We are willing to be judged by our patrons and the supporters of honest sport.*
>
> *John J. M'Graw.*

McGraw's claim that the players supported his decision was a lie. "We had a chance at a good bit of money, but what can we do," one of them said anonymously. "We must obey orders, and there you are." One of the most outspoken Giants, Mike Donlin, didn't even bother with anonymity. "There was a sore bunch of ballplayers around the clubhouse when McGraw refused to stand for the post-season games," Donlin told a reporter in Cleveland.

After the season, instead of a World Series, McGraw's champions played an exhibition game at the Polo Grounds against the 1889 New York Giants, the last Giants club to win the pennant. McGraw's men defeated the old-timers, 10-8. Meanwhile, as it became apparent that there would be no World Series involving the Giants, other schemes were hatched. Frank Selee, manager of the second-place Cubs, offered to pick a National League all-star team to play in the World Series against the Pilgrims. Joseph Gordon, president of the New York Highlanders—runners-up in the American League—offered to take the Giants' place and face Boston in the World Series. Neither series ever materialized.

In late October, even though most of the players had either gone home for the winter or embarked on barnstorming tours in warmer climes, hope for a World Series wasn't quite dead yet. Brush sent a letter to Pulliam on October 18 agreeing to let the Giants play a World Series against Boston the following spring if certain conditions were met. These conditions included a formal agreement regarding game sites, umpire selection, and distribution of gate receipts. The offer came too late for the 1904 season; as *Sporting Life* noted, "the time to play any world's championship is in the fall, when the issue is alive, public interest is keenest, and the contending teams are at their best." However, Brush's idea for a formal World Series agreement between the two leagues met with widespread approval and such an arrangement was put in place for the 1905 season.

1905

NEW YORK GIANTS (4)
PHILADELPHIA A'S (1)

A LANDMARK IN SEVERAL WAYS, THE 1905 World Series was most important for the stability it brought to the postseason championship. After a fairly tenuous Series in 1903 and no Series at all in 1904, the 1905 version went off without a hitch. In an era of rampant rowdyism, observers were pleasantly surprised by "the sportsmanlike conduct and exceptionally good deportment of the contestants." The continued existence of the World Series, which had been a shaky proposition before 1905, was now ensured.

Despite the Giants' thorough domination—according to *Sporting Life*'s Francis Richter, they "out-batted, out-fielded, out-pitched, out-maneuvered, and out-lucked the Athletics"—the series was a dramatic and entertaining one. It remains the only Series in which every game has been a shutout, and nine of the ten starters pitched complete games. It is remembered for the pitching of Christy Mathewson. His three shutouts in the five games still stands as the greatest individual performance in World Series history.

The Giants boasted the National League's best offense in 1905, scoring an average of more than five runs per game. Their specialty was getting on base, and except for pitchers, every Giant who batted more than fifty times had an on-base percentage of .322 or better.

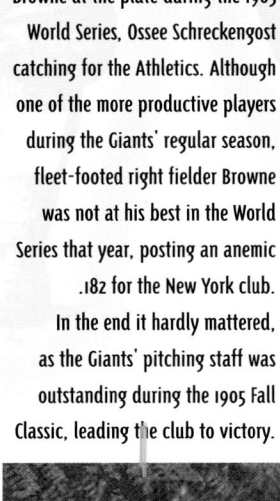

BOTTOM: New York Giant George Browne at the plate during the 1905 World Series, Ossee Schreckengost catching for the Athletics. Although one of the more productive players during the Giants' regular season, fleet-footed right fielder Browne was not at his best in the World Series that year, posting an anemic .182 for the New York club. In the end it hardly mattered, as the Giants' pitching staff was outstanding during the 1905 Fall Classic, leading the club to victory.

(The league average was .309.) The New York pitching staff was also outstanding, posting a 2.39 team ERA while using only six pitchers all year. Young Mathewson established himself as the best pitcher in the National League in 1905, leading the league with 31 wins and a 1.28 ERA. He was supported by four other outstanding starters—Joe McGinnity, Leon "Red" Ames, George "Hooks" Wiltse, and Luther "Dummy" Taylor—all of whom won at least 115 career games.

The Athletics were at a disadvantage, in part because they had to struggle to win the pennant while the Giants had clinched early and coasted. To make matters worse, the eccentric George "Rube" Waddell, the American League's best pitcher that year, was unavailable to the Athletics. He had injured himself in September in a fight with teammate Andy Coakley, who had ruined Waddell's favorite hat in a practical joke. Waddell denied rumors that he was malingering because gamblers had paid him to sit out the Series. He was one of two key Athletics sidelined for the Series, the other being center fielder Danny Hoffman, the team leader in stolen bases.

Seeking to intimidate the Athletics, McGraw trotted out his Giants in special new World Series uniforms—solid black with "World's Champions" stitched across the chest in gleaming white. (The fact that the Giants *weren't* world's champions at the time didn't seem to bother him.) The Athletics got their own dig in before the first game, too, as shortstop Lafayette "Lave" Cross presented McGraw—who had earlier dismissed the Athletics as "a bunch of white elephants"—with a statue of a white pachyderm. The white elephant remains the Athletics' team symbol almost a century later.

A crowd of 17,955, including thirty-eight reporters and a fifty-six-piece band that the Giants brought from New York, attended the first game at Philadelphia's Columbia Park. Mathewson was magnificent, shutting out the Athletics and beating Eddie Plank. Mathewson allowed four hits, all of them ground-rule doubles hit into the roped-off crowd standing in the outfield, and started the decisive rally himself with a fifth inning single. In the second game, Philadelphia hurler Charles Bender—a Native American who was given the derisive nickname "Chief" by newspapermen—pitched a four-hit shutout of his own, beating McGinnity 3-0.

A heavy rainstorm hit Philadelphia on the morning of Game 3. The rain postponement allowed McGraw to bring Mathewson back to pitch the next day. On a cold, wet Thursday afternoon, Mathewson pitched another gem before 10,991 Athletics fans, easily the smallest crowd of the series. This time it was no pitcher's duel, as the Giants battered Coakley

BOTTOM LEFT: Pictured here in 1911, Christy Mathewson (left) in 1905 put on the greatest pitching performance in World Series history, tossing three consecutive shutouts against the Philadelphia Athletics.

BOTTOM RIGHT: After his 1905 Philadelphia team was ridiculed as "a bunch of white elephants," manager Connie Mack (left) adopted the white elephant as his team's logo, and it remains on the Athletics' uniforms to this day. Pitcher Charles Albert "Chief" Bender (right) turned in the only win against the Giants in the 1905 World Series, a Game 2 shutout.

for nine runs and won 9-0, taking a 2-1 lead in the Series. In Game 4 back in New York, McGinnity and Plank squared off in what remains one of the best pitcher's duels in Series history. Each pitched a complete game without allowing an earned run, but the Giants scored an unearned run when Philadelphia's defense broke down in the fourth inning. The A's blew their best chance to score in the eighth when Tully "Topsy" Hartsel, on base with the tying run, was left stranded at third after Bristol "Bris" Lord failed to lay down a sacrifice bunt.

It was left to Mathewson to finish off the Athletics the next day at the Polo Grounds. He pitched his third masterful game of the Series, shutting out Philadelphia 2-0 on six hits. Chief Bender pitched well but struggled with his control, walking three batters, which led to the only two runs in the game. As soon as Bill Dahlen threw out Cross for the final out of the Series, the victorious Giants sprinted toward their center field clubhouse to escape the thousands of fans who rushed the field. "Hats, canes, umbrellas, everything at hand were thrown from every angle of the grand stand," one breathless writer reported. After the police restored order, a few Giants ventured onto the clubhouse balcony to greet the throng of admirers gathered below. Mike Donlin emerged first, struggled for something to say, and then—like the silent film star he would later become—simply smiled and ducked out of sight. McGinnity and McGraw followed, with the latter making a victory speech to the crowd. After all the controversy he'd caused a year earlier, McGraw finally had his undisputed world championship.

In 1905, the World Series hadn't yet acquired the mythic status it now enjoys, and the owners had created several financial safeguards to ensure the integrity of the Series and encourage players on both sides to try their hardest. It was decreed that members of the winning team would receive three times more money than the losers, providing a powerful incentive for players to try their best. (The victorious Giants took home $1,142 each, while the Athletics each got $382.) At the same time, the owners declared that the players' share would be drawn from a percentage of receipts from the first four games only, which would deter a team with a series lead from losing on purpose in order to force more games. It worked. Not only was the Series played on the level, but it was also a financial success with a reported gross of $68,437 for the five games. The 1905 World Series became, as Francis Richter wrote in *Sporting Life*, "a model for succeeding world's championship battles."

1905 WORLD SERIES

Columbia Park (Philadelphia) ◆ 10.9.05

	1	2	3	4	5	6	7	8	9	R	H	E
NYG	0	0	0	0	2	0	0	0	1	3	10	1
Phil.	0	0	0	0	0	0	0	0	0	0	4	0

WP–Mathewson LP–Plank ATT: 17,955

Polo Grounds III (New York) ◆ 10.10.05

	1	2	3	4	5	6	7	8	9	R	H	E
Phil.	0	0	1	0	0	0	0	2	0	3	6	2
NYG	0	0	0	0	0	0	0	0	0	0	4	2

WP–Bender LP–McGinnity ATT: 24,992

Columbia Park ◆ 10.12.05

	1	2	3	4	5	6	7	8	9	R	H	E
NYG	2	0	0	0	5	0	0	0	2	9	9	1
Phil.	0	0	0	0	0	0	0	0	0	0	4	5

WP–Mathewson LP–Coakley ATT: 10,991

Polo Grounds III ◆ 10.13.05

	1	2	3	4	5	6	7	8	9	R	H	E
Phil.	0	0	0	0	0	0	0	0	0	0	5	2
NYG	0	0	0	1	0	0	0	0	X	1	4	1

WP–McGinnity LP–Plank ATT: 13,598

Polo Grounds III ◆ 10.14.05

	1	2	3	4	5	6	7	8	9	R	H	E
Phil.	0	0	0	0	0	0	0	0	0	0	6	0
NYG	0	0	0	0	1	0	0	1	X	2	5	1

WP–Mathewson LP–Bender ATT: 14,187

BOTTOM: Because the Polo Grounds was built into the side of Coogan's Bluff in Manhattan, these fans were able to get a free view of Chief Bender and Joe McGinnity facing off in Game 2 of the 1905 World Series.

1906

Chicago White Sox (4)
Chicago Cubs (2)

The 1906 World Series was baseball's version of David vs. Goliath. It pitted the powerful Chicago Cubs—winners of 116 games, a total unmatched in the first 125 years of major league baseball—against their crosstown rivals, the Chicago White Sox, who had been in last place as late as June 21. The 22½-game difference between the Cubs and White Sox remains by far the greatest mismatch in World Series history. The 1906 World Series is still the only one ever played between the two Chicago teams.

The American League had no truly outstanding team in 1906. This enabled the White Sox, a fourth-place team most of the year, to capture the pennant with a nineteen-game winning streak in August. The press dubbed the Sox "hitless wonders" because they batted .230 on the year with a collective seven home runs, but in reality they were a capable offensive team. Even though they played in the best pitcher's park in the major leagues, they still ranked third in the American League with 567 runs scored. They were led by manager-center fielder Fielder Jones and shortstop George Davis, a 17-year veteran who was one of the A.L.'s top players in 1906.

In 1906 the Cubs were, as the *Spalding Guide* noted, "a perfected Base Ball machine that showed no weakness at any point." Their double-play trio of Joe Tinker, Johnny Evers, and Frank Chance, though they would not be immortalized in poetry until six years later, were all excellent players. The Cubs also boasted four of the league's top ten in slugging percentage: Chance, third baseman Harry Steinfeldt, catcher Johnny Kling, and right fielder Frank "Wildfire" Schulte. They were speedsters, too, as every Chicago regular except Kling had at least 25 stolen bases. But as good as the Cubs' offense was, it was no match for their pitching. The six-man staff posted a collective ERA of 1.75, almost a full run better than the league average, led by Mordecai "Three-Fingered" Brown, who was 26-6 with a 1.04 ERA.

The all-Chicago World Series aroused passion for baseball in the Windy City like never before. Two teenage fans, desperate for money so they could buy tickets from scalpers, were arrested for holding up a grocery store. City councilman Charles Martin, a White Sox fan, was arrested after brawling

BOTTOM: Although White Sox manager Fielder Jones is pictured here wearing a derby hat and bow tie, he was also the team's starting center fielder. George Davis, the team's best player, is second from left in the front row.

Postseason Pioneers

THE NINETEENTH-CENTURY WORLD SERIES

Baseball is famous for its adherence to tradition, but in its infancy, the grand old game liked to experiment. Pick a revolutionary change of the twentieth century—night baseball, integration, the designated hitter—and chances are that our nineteenth century ball-tossing brethren thought up the idea, and maybe even gave it a whirl. (This is the century, after all, that briefly tried to make four strikes an out.) Therefore, it should come as no surprise that the 1800s were also the first testing grounds for the World Series.

The first World Series game was played on October 23, 1884, before a shivering crowd of 2,500 at New York's Polo Grounds. Aside from its name, this inaugural Fall Classic bore little relation to the larger-than-life spectacle we have come to know in the television age. Neither participant of the 1884 World Series would go on to etch its name in the annals of the sport. The Providence Grays, champions of the eight-year-old National League, would disappear from the baseball map just one year later, while the New York Metropolitans, frontrunners of the two-year-old American Association, would last for just three more seasons. The Association, known also as the "Beer and Whisky League" for the beer barons that were attracted to its ownership ranks by the circuit's lax concessions policy (the staider National League barred alcohol from all ballparks), was the first serious challenger to the N.L.'s hegemony over the national pastime. By 1884, the Association even outdrew the National League at the box office. James Mutrie, owner of the Metropolitans, thought his club could compete with the senior circuit on the diamond as well, so he challenged the Grays to a three-game postseason series to settle the issue. Thus the World Series was born.

ABOVE: Charley Radbourn won 59 games during the 1884 season and three more in that year's fledgling World Series.

The Grays, led by their ace pitcher Charles "Old Hoss" Radbourn, made quick work of the Mets. Radbourn, winner of a major-league record 59 games that season, beat New York on three consecutive afternoons. The first two victories clinched the championship for Providence. The clubs agreed to play the third game anyway, because the players had been promised the profits from the final two games of the Series. Only three hundred fans showed up, Mets pitcher Tim Keefe umpired the contest, and Providence thumped New York 11-2.

Despite its billing as the first interleague championship, few newspapers treated the games as anything more than meaningless postseason exhibitions. It would take the emergence of two evenly matched rivals, a little controversy, and a healthy dose of bad blood to elevate the Series as the sport's premier showcase.

The 1886 Series between the National League champion Chicago White Stockings and the American Association champion St. Louis Browns proved to be just what the doctor ordered. The two clubs had met in the second World Series the previous year. That series was scheduled for twelve games but was abandoned in dispute after seven. One game ended in a tie because of darkness and another game concluded in a riot following an unpopular decision by an umpire. But if no one could agree who actually won the 1885 Series, the controversy only set the stage for the 1886 contest, a classic showdown between the two dominant teams of the era.

Both teams were managed by their star first basemen. The White Stockings, winners of five pennants in seven years, were led by Adrian "Cap" Anson, the strapping first baseman from Marshalltown, Iowa, who was arguably the century's most significant player, if not its best. The Browns were led by Charlie Comiskey, who would later achieve his greatest fame as owner of the Chicago White Sox. Soon after joining St. Louis in 1882, Comiskey set about building a pennant winner that captured four consecutive flags from 1885 to 1888.

The 1886 World Series was scheduled for seven games and would become a model for the modern Fall Classic. Chicago owner Albert Spalding was confident that his team would beat the upstart Browns. But any thoughts of an easy victory were quickly erased when St. Louis won three of the first five games. Game 6 in St. Louis would go down as one of the most exciting games of the era. The game was tied 3-3 in the bottom of the tenth inning. The Browns' Curt Welch singled. Another single and a sacrifice moved the fleet outfielder to third base, where the daring Welch began to dance off the bag, threatening to steal. The rattled White Stockings pitcher, John Clarkson, then unleashed a wild pitch and Welch dashed home with the championship. It was the most famous play of the century, and would come to be known as "Welch's $15,000 Slide," for the amount of gate receipts St. Louis took home as the winning team.

ABOVE: Cap Anson's Chicago White Stockings lost the hotly contested 1886 World Series to the St. Louis Browns.

St. Louis's improbable championship was the crowning achievement of the "Beer and Whisky League." The two leagues met in the World Series four more times, but the American Association never won again. Mounting debts forced the Association out of business after the 1891 season. The National League was once again the country's only major league. Without a natural postseason rival, the league spent much of the 1890s dreaming up different ways to fabricate interest in a postseason series—splitting the season into two halves, pitting the first place team against the second place team—but nothing worked. It would take the arrival of another upstart league, the American League, to bring back the unique thrills of postseason baseball first experienced by fans in the nineteenth century. —David Jones

David Jones is a freelance writer and baseball historian in Troy, New York.

with a drunken Cubs fan. The series began on October 9, 1906, the thirty-fifth anniversary of the Great Chicago Fire that had destroyed most of the city. Eight men were arrested for ticket scalping that day as snow flurries blew through West Side Park, the Cubs' home field. Brown pitched well but gave up two runs, one of which scored on his own miscue, a poor throw home on a squeeze bunt. The Cubs got a run back in the sixth inning and were looking for more, but spectacular back-to-back defensive plays by shortstop Lee Tannehill (subbing for the injured George Davis) and first baseman John "Jiggs" Donahue ended the inning and the threat. Nick Altrock shut down the Cubs the rest of the way and the Sox took the first game 2-1.

Game 2 was one-sided from the beginning. The Cubs jumped on pitcher Doc White (who spent his off-seasons writing parlor music tunes with Ring Lardner) for three runs in the second inning en route to a 7-1 victory. Ed Reulbach, the 23-year-old owner of a 19-4 record during the regular season, pitched a one-hitter and went all the way for the Cubs. The third game saw another masterful pitching performance, this time by White Sox spitballer Ed Walsh, who allowed the Cubs two hits in the first inning, then shut them down the rest of the way in a 3-0 victory. Midway through the game, a mother hen wandered onto the playing field and plopped down in right field next to the White Sox' Ed Hahn (whose surname meant "rooster" in German), where she stayed for much of the game. The hen must have brought bad luck, as Cubs pitcher Jack Pfiester broke Hahn's nose with a pitch in the sixth inning, loading the bases and sending Hahn to the hospital. Two batters later, the White Sox' George Rohe hit a ground-rule triple into the left field stands, driving in all three Sox runs and putting them up in the Series, two games to one.

Brown and Altrock staged their second dazzling pitcher's duel of the Series in Game 4. It was even better than the first, with the Cubs winning 1-0 and both pitchers going the distance. Brown saved the game with an exceptional defensive play in the bottom of the ninth, gloving a hard grounder that knocked him off his feet, then recovering to throw out Frank Isbell (who was playing with a lucky wishbone in the lining of his cap) at first for the game's final out.

The Series was now tied 2-2, and Chicago fans, who had expected the White Sox to be overmatched, looked to the remaining games with renewed interest. An overflowing crowd of 23,257 attended Game 5 at West Side Park. Thousands more gathered outside to listen as fans in the stands shouted the play-by-play down to them. The Cubs took the early lead, but Reulbach, who had pitched so brilliantly for them in Game 2, was knocked out in the third inning. In that inning, the Sox' Davis stole home to tie the game at 3. His two-run double in the fourth gave them a 6-3 lead. The White Sox led the rest of the way, as White relieved the struggling Walsh and saved the game with 2⅔ innings of scoreless relief.

Facing elimination in Game 6, the visiting Cubs turned to the best pitcher in baseball, Mordecai Brown, who started on one day's rest. The day began with a bad omen for the Cubs when the retired Adrian "Cap" Anson—who had collected almost 3,000 hits with the franchise and managed it to five National League pennants—was ejected from the Cubs bench by umpire Silk O'Loughlin. (O'Loughlin said only active players were allowed on the bench.) Meanwhile, the decision to start Brown on short rest turned out to be a disaster. The White Sox pounded him for three runs in the first inning and four more in the second. By the time Brown headed for the showers in the second inning, the World Series was effectively over. Doc White, after pitching in relief the day before, went the distance for the White Sox as they won easily, 8-3. David had beaten Goliath.

Beer had been banned from the grandstand for Game 6, but even so, after the game a mob of delirious Sox rooters set bonfires in the streets and surrounded manager Jones' house on Ellis Street, serenading him well into the night. White Sox owner Charles Comiskey was so pleased with the unexpected Series victory that he added $15,000 of his own money to the $25,401 in winnings that the White Sox divided between them. It was a handsome reward for a scrappy team that refused to give in.

1906 WORLD SERIES

WEST SIDE PARK II (CHICAGO CUBS) ◆ 10.9.06

	1	2	3	4	5	6	7	8	9	R	H	E
Sox	0	0	0	0	1	1	0	0	0	2	4	1
Cubs	0	0	0	0	0	1	0	0	0	1	4	2

WP–Altrock LP–Brown ATT: 12,693

SOUTH SIDE PARK II (CHICAGO W. SOX) ◆ 10.10.06

	1	2	3	4	5	6	7	8	9	R	H	E
Cubs	0	3	1	0	0	1	0	2	0	7	10	2
Sox	0	0	0	0	1	0	0	0	0	1	1	2

WP–Reulbach LP–White ATT: 9,415

WEST SIDE PARK II ◆ 10.11.06

	1	2	3	4	5	6	7	8	9	R	H	E
Sox	0	0	0	0	0	3	0	0	0	3	4	1
Cubs	0	0	0	0	0	0	0	0	0	0	2	1

WP–Walsh LP–Pfiester ATT: 13,667

SOUTH SIDE PARK II ◆ 10.12.06

	1	2	3	4	5	6	7	8	9	R	H	E
Cubs	0	0	0	0	0	0	1	0	0	1	7	1
Sox	0	0	0	0	0	0	0	0	0	0	2	1

WP–Brown LP–Altrock ATT: 18,385

WEST SIDE PARK II ◆ 10.13.06

	1	2	3	4	5	6	7	8	9	R	H	E
Sox	1	0	2	4	0	1	0	0	0	8	12	6
Cubs	3	0	0	1	0	2	0	0	0	6	6	0

WP–Walsh LP–Pfiester S–White ATT: 23,257

SOUTH SIDE PARK II ◆ 10.14.06

	1	2	3	4	5	6	7	8	9	R	H	E
Cubs	1	0	0	0	1	0	0	0	1	3	7	0
Sox	3	4	0	0	0	0	0	1	X	8	14	3

WP–White LP–Brown ATT: 19,249

BOTTOM: Nick Altrock became a noted baseball clown in his later years, but in 1906 he was nothing to laugh about. One of the White Sox' best pitchers that year, he posted a 20-13 record and won the first game of the World Series.

1907

CHICAGO CUBS (4)
DETROIT TIGERS (0)
(1 TIE)

After their bitter defeat in the 1906 Series, the Chicago Cubs got a quick chance at redemption when they faced the Detroit Tigers the next year. The Cubs were nowhere near the offensive force they had been in 1906, but they still posted an impressive 107-45 record and were heavily favored to win the series. The Tigers, winners of 92 games and a hard-fought pennant race against the Philadelphia Athletics, had a tired pitching staff, while the Cubs pitchers, having clinched long before, were well-rested. Still, the Tigers had what they hoped would be the Series' biggest weapon: 20-year-old center fielder Ty Cobb, who that year had established himself as the best player in the American League. Even though it was only his first full season, Cobb's temper had already won him the nickname "Terrible Ty."

The first game was played at Chicago's West Side Park. Forty carrier pigeons were on hand to carry inning-by-inning updates back to interested fans in Blue Island, Illinois. It was a pitcher's duel until the eighth inning, when the Tigers scored three runs thanks in part to Cubs pitcher Orval Overall, who botched a rundown play at home plate. The Cubs came back to tie the game in the ninth when Detroit catcher Charles "Boss" Schmidt let a strike three pitch go to the backstop. Shortly afterward, with the bases loaded and two outs in the bottom of the ninth, Johnny Evers tried a daring steal of home. Had he made it safely the game would have been over, but catcher Schmidt redeemed himself by tagging out Evers to send the game into extra innings. In the tenth, the Cubs' Jimmy Slagle scored what appeared to be the winning run on another passed ball by Schmidt, but umpire Hank O'Day ruled Slagle out because the batter, Harry Steinfeldt, had interfered with the play. The game continued deadlocked until the end of the twelfth inning, when play was stopped by darkness and the game declared a tie. It was the first of three tie games in World Series history, and was a bitter outcome for the Cubs, who would have won if even one of the three key plays at home plate had gone their way. But the Tigers should have felt lucky, too. They got away clean even though their catcher, Schmidt, turned in one of the worst defensive games in Series history. In addition to his two passed balls, Schmidt (who was playing with a broken bone in his throwing hand) had two throwing errors and allowed the Cubs to steal seven bases.

The highlight of Game 2 came in the first inning when third baseman Bill Coughlin pulled the hidden ball trick on Chicago's Slagle. This remains the only time the trick has ever worked in the World Series. It cost the Cubs a run, as the next batter, Frank Chance, singled. Still, the Cubs scored three runs in the game thanks to five stolen bases, as pitcher Jack Pfiester, using a deceptive pitch he called the "Hoodoo Snake," beat the Tigers 3-1. Chicago also took the next game easily, 5-1, as Ed Reulbach threw a complete game.

The teams traveled to freezing Detroit for Game 4, with the Cubs up 2-0 in the Series. Detroit struck first in the fourth inning when Cobb tripled and scored. But hampered by snow and sleet, the Tiger defense played miserably, giving the Cubs six runs. Chicago romped again behind the pitching of Overall. The next day, with their team on the brink

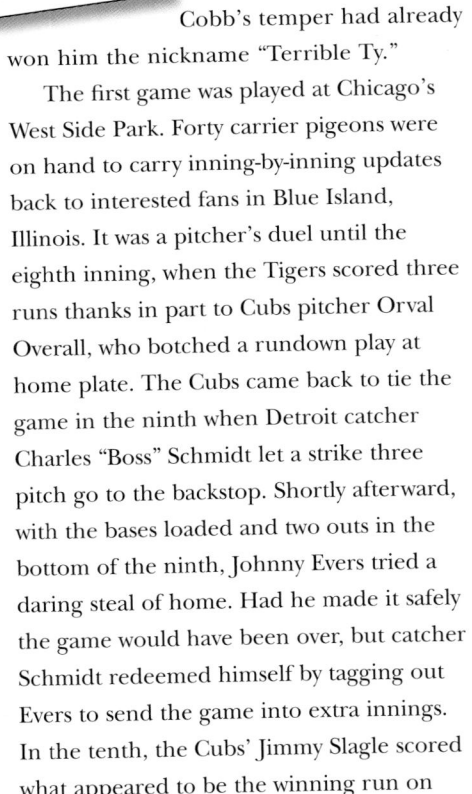

BOTTOM: Tigers catcher Boss Schmidt turned in one of the worst World Series performances ever in Game 1, committing two errors, two passed balls, and allowing seven stolen bases.

of elimination, a paltry crowd of 7,370 Detroiters braved the cold and snow to watch Game 5. It looked to be a great pitcher's duel, but the Cubs scored single runs off George Mullin in the first two innings, and that was all Mordecai Brown needed. The three-fingered pitcher made up for his poor World Series showing the previous year by blanking the Tigers for all nine innings. The Cubs won the game, 2-0, and the Series, 4-0-1.

The *Spalding Guide* placed the blame for losing the Series squarely on the Tigers' rookie manager Hughie Jennings. "He lost because of a devotion to his own ideas," Edward Westlake wrote in the *Guide*. "Think of only three bunts laid down by the Tigers in five games!" It is unlikely, though, that bunts would have helped the Tigers much, since two of their four losses were blowouts. Jennings was an attorney and a forward-thinking manager who that year had become one of the first managers to use a platoon system, alternating catchers Schmidt and Fred Payne depending on whether the opposing pitcher was right- or left-handed. It was not his fault that the Tigers lost the World Series. Instead the finger should have been pointed at Detroit's defense, which gave the Cubs eight unearned runs, and its offense, which scored only three runs in the four games that counted. The Tigers' two best hitters, Cobb and Sam Crawford, batted only .200 and .238, respectively. It was a great disappointment for Cobb, who during the regular season had become the youngest player ever to win a batting title. But in 1908, he would get a chance to redeem himself.

1907 WORLD SERIES

West Side Park II (Chicago Cubs) ◆ 10.8.07

	1	2	3	4	5	6	7	8	9	10	11	12	R	H	E
Det.	0	0	0	0	0	0	0	3	0	0	0	0	3	9	3
Chi.	1	0	0	0	0	2	0	0	0	0	0	0	3	10	5

WP–NONE LP–NONE ATT: 24,377

West Side Park II ◆ 10.9.07

	1	2	3	4	5	6	7	8	9	R	H	E
Det.	0	1	0	0	0	0	0	0	0	1	9	1
Chi.	0	1	0	2	0	0	0	0	X	3	9	1

WP–Pfiester LP–Mullin ATT: 21,901

West Side Park II ◆ 10.10.07

	1	2	3	4	5	6	7	8	9	R	H	E
Det.	0	0	0	0	0	1	0	0	0	1	6	1
Chi.	0	1	0	3	1	0	0	0	X	5	10	1

WP–Reulbach LP–Siever ATT: 13,114

Bennett Park (Detroit) ◆ 10.11.07

	1	2	3	4	5	6	7	8	9	R	H	E
Chi.	0	0	0	0	2	0	3	0	1	6	7	2
Det.	0	0	0	1	0	0	0	0	0	1	5	2

WP–Overall LP–Donovan ATT: 11,306

Bennett Park ◆ 10.12.07

	1	2	3	4	5	6	7	8	9	R	H	E
Chi.	1	1	0	0	0	0	0	0	0	2	7	1
Det.	0	0	0	0	0	0	0	0	0	0	7	2

WP–Brown LP–Mullin ATT: 7,370

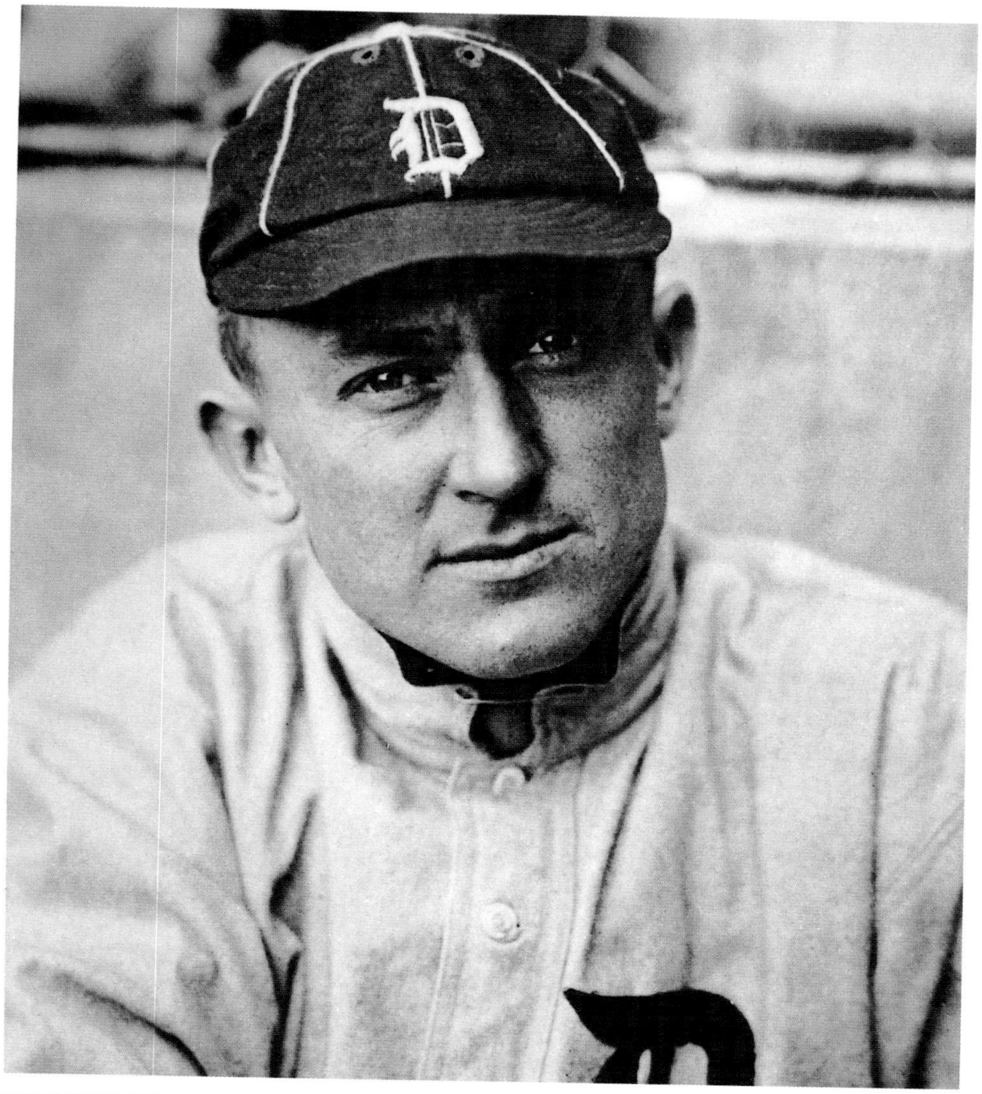

TOP: In 1907, his first full season in the major leagues, Ty Cobb collected 119 RBI, 27 more than the next-best player.

BOTTOM: For the Tigers, this was the 1907 World Series in microcosm: The Cubs' Frank Chance slides home safely while Detroit catcher Boss Schmidt has his back turned to the plate.

1908

Chicago Cubs	**(4)**
Detroit Tigers	**(1)**

BOTTOM LEFT: In the fifth game of the 1908 World Series, Orval Overall struck out four batters in the first inning, with one of them reaching base on a wild pitch. His three-hit shutout in that game clinched the Series for the Cubs.

BOTTOM RIGHT: Mordecai Brown—whose childhood mishap with a piece of farm machinery gave him a deformed hand and the moniker "Three-Fingered"—won two games for the Cubs in the 1908 Series.

THE 1908 WORLD SERIES WAS THE FIRST ever to feature a rematch of the previous year's teams. Neither participant was decided until the last day of the season, when the Cubs and Tigers prevailed over the Giants and White Sox, respectively, in two of the most exciting pennant races of all time.

The Series started on a rainy day in Detroit. Hughie Jennings provided the first surprise when he named southpaw Ed Killian, the Tigers' fifth-best pitcher that year, to start the first game. The move backfired as Chicago knocked out Killian with a four-run third inning. The Tigers came back and took the lead in the eighth, only to see the Cubs take it right back again in the top of the ninth when two ground balls went for infield hits after Tiger fielders slipped in the mud. The Cubs won the game 10-6.

The Series then moved to Chicago, where only 17,760 of a possible 25,000 fans were at West Side Park for Game 2. Cubs president Charles Murphy, who in past years had charged double the usual ticket price for World Series games, decided to raise prices even more for the 1908 Series. Adding insult to injury, he also clandestinely sold most of the available tickets directly to scalpers, causing many fans to stay home in protest. It didn't bother the Cubs on the field, though, as they breezed to a 6-1 victory behind the pitching of Orval Overall. In Game 3 Detroit finally beat the Cubs for the first time in eight Series games, thanks to a four hit, two stolen base performance from Ty Cobb. But Mordecai Brown shut down the Tigers in Game 4, beating them 3-0 and giving the Cubs a 3-1 advantage in the Series.

With Detroit facing elimination, only 6,210 Tiger fans—still the smallest crowd ever for a Series game—attended Game 5. The Tigers were overmatched once again, as Overall shut them out 2-0 to finish off the Series. In the final eighteen innings of the Series, all played at home, the Tigers had scored no runs and managed only seven hits. They were beaten convincingly on their own home turf for the second year in a row.

After the 1908 contest, the World Series was at the lowest point in its six-year history. Crowds were small and getting smaller. The press coverage was provided by sportswriters disgruntled at their treatment by the owners. Murphy's back-room deals with ticket scalpers not only discouraged Chicago fans, but also prompted disciplinary action by the National Commission. Even the competition in the Series was poor, with the American League

having been utterly humiliated twice in a row. And Cobb, the best player in that young league, had again failed to lead his team to victory. It was no fault of his own; according to Francis Richter, in the Series "Cobb proved himself the lone star for Detroit, his batting, base-running and run-producing work being first class." Amazingly, Cobb would get yet another chance at a world championship in 1909.

1908 WORLD SERIES

Bennett Park (Detroit Tigers) ◆ 10.10.08

	1	2	3	4	5	6	7	8	9	R	H	E
Chi.	0	0	4	0	0	0	1	0	5	10	14	2
Det.	1	0	0	0	0	0	3	2	0	6	10	4

WP–Brown LP–Summers ATT: 10,812

West Side Park II (Chicago Cubs) ◆ 10.11.08

	1	2	3	4	5	6	7	8	9	R	H	E
Det.	0	0	0	0	0	0	0	0	1	1	4	1
Chi.	0	0	0	0	0	0	0	6	X	6	7	1

WP–Overall LP–Donovan HR: CHC–Tinker ATT: 17,760

West Side Park II ◆ 10.12.08

	1	2	3	4	5	6	7	8	9	R	H	E
Det.	1	0	0	0	0	5	0	2	0	8	11	4
Chi.	0	0	0	3	0	0	0	0	0	3	7	2

WP–Mullin LP–Pfiester ATT: 14,543

West Side Park II ◆ 10.13.08

	1	2	3	4	5	6	7	8	9	R	H	E
Chi.	0	0	2	0	0	0	0	0	1	3	10	0
Det.	0	0	0	0	0	0	0	0	0	0	4	1

WP–Brown LP–Summers ATT: 12,907

Bennett Park ◆ 10.14.08

	1	2	3	4	5	6	7	8	9	R	H	E
Chi.	1	0	0	0	1	0	0	0	0	2	10	0
Det.	0	0	0	0	0	0	0	0	0	0	3	0

WP–Brown LP–Mullin ATT: 6,210

1909

Pittsburg Pirates (4)

Detroit Tigers (3)

BEFORE GEORGE HERMAN "BABE" RUTH ushered in the home run era in the 1920s, only two players could stake a legitimate claim to the title of greatest player in baseball history. One, Ty Cobb, was in just his third full season in 1909, but finished that year with three batting titles and three World Series appearances to his credit. The other, Honus Wagner, was a 35-year-old veteran who already had seven batting titles under his belt. In the 1909 World Series, these two outstanding players faced each other for the first and only time. Wagner's team prevailed in a Series that was, according to Francis Richter, "probably the most remarkable ever played."

The men were polar opposites in everything except playing ability. Wagner, the veteran, was a gentle man, loved and respected by almost everyone in baseball. Cobb, the young star, was brash, arrogant, and vulgar, and was almost universally disliked. When the Tigers traveled to Pittsburg for Game 1, Cobb had to travel separately from his teammates. He avoided Ohio because he had stabbed a night watchman there earlier in the season and a warrant was still out for his arrest. The press made much of the contrast between the two stars and could hardly contain their delight when Pittsburg dispatched the Tigers in seven games. Wagner batted .333 and stole six bases, while Cobb was held to .231 and only two steals. Cobb, according to Richter, "enjoyed one good day and then gradually faded away." His lone Series highlight was a steal of home in Game 2. Cobb also received his comeuppance in a tale that, although untrue, has become such a staple of baseball lore that its veracity hardly matters. Cobb reached first base, the story goes, and on the next pitch yelled at Wagner, "I'm coming down on the next pitch, Krauthead!" When Cobb did indeed run on the pitch, Wagner was waiting

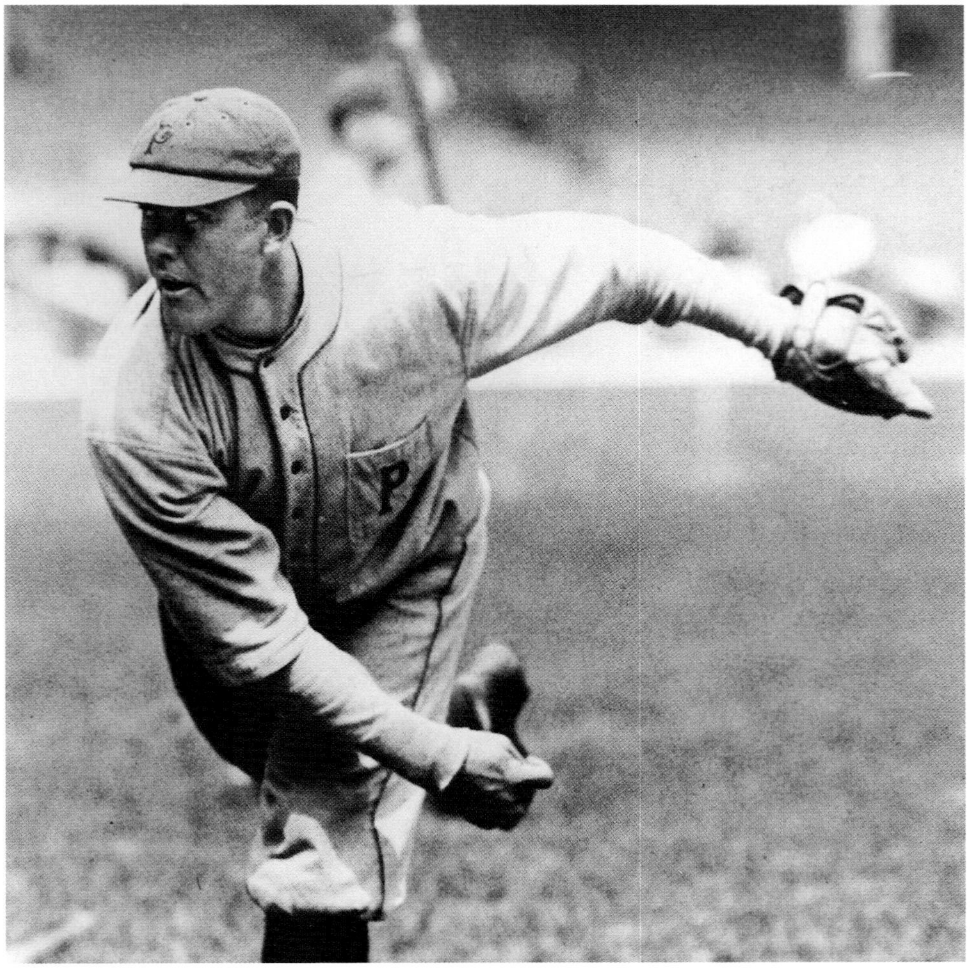

1909 WORLD SERIES

Forbes Field (Pittsburg Pirates) ◆ 10.8.09

	1	2	3	4	5	6	7	8	9	R	H	E
Det.	1	0	0	0	0	0	0	0	0	1	6	4
Pitt.	0	0	0	1	2	1	0	0	X	4	5	0

WP–Adams LP–Mullin HR: PIT–Clarke ATT: 29,264

Forbes Field ◆ 10.9.09

	1	2	3	4	5	6	7	8	9	R	H	E
Det.	0	2	3	0	2	0	0	0	0	7	9	3
Pitt.	2	0	0	0	0	0	0	0	0	2	5	1

WP–Donovan LP–Camnitz ATT: 30,915

Bennett Park (Detroit Tigers) ◆ 10.11.09

	1	2	3	4	5	6	7	8	9	R	H	E
Pitt.	5	1	0	0	0	0	0	0	2	8	10	3
Det.	0	0	0	0	0	0	4	0	2	6	10	5

WP–Maddox LP–Summers ATT: 18,277

Bennett Park ◆ 10.12.09

	1	2	3	4	5	6	7	8	9	R	H	E
Pitt.	0	0	0	0	0	0	0	0	0	0	5	6
Det.	0	2	0	3	0	0	0	0	X	5	8	0

WP–Mullin LP–Leifield ATT: 17,036

Forbes Field ◆ 10.13.09

	1	2	3	4	5	6	7	8	9	R	H	E
Det.	1	0	0	0	0	2	0	1	0	4	6	1
Pitt.	1	1	1	0	0	0	4	1	X	8	10	2

WP–Adams LP–Summers HR: DET–D. Jones, Crawford; PIT–Clarke ATT: 21,706

Bennett Park ◆ 10.14.09

	1	2	3	4	5	6	7	8	9	R	H	E
Pitt.	3	0	0	0	0	0	0	0	1	4	7	3
Det.	1	0	0	2	1	1	0	0	X	5	10	3

WP–Mullin LP–Willis ATT: 10,535

Bennett Park ◆ 10.16.09

	1	2	3	4	5	6	7	8	9	R	H	E
Pitt.	0	2	0	2	0	3	0	1	0	8	7	0
Det.	0	0	0	0	0	0	0	0	0	0	6	3

WP–Adams LP–Donovan ATT: 17,562

BOTTOM: Rookie Babe Adams went on one of the hottest streaks of all time in 1909, going 12-3 with a 1.11 ERA in half a season with the Pirates, then pitching three shutouts against the Tigers in the World Series.

with the ball and planted the tag emphatically in Cobb's face, loosening a few teeth.

The real hero of the World Series, however, turned out to be neither Cobb nor Wagner, but a 27-year-old rookie pitcher named Charles Adams. Better known as "Babe," Adams had posted a magnificent 1.11 ERA in half a season's work with the Pirates, though he was not expected to be a major factor in the Series. But according to sportswriter Fred Lieb, National League president John Heydler had seen a Washington pitcher named William "Dolly" Gray handcuff the pennant-bound Tigers in a late-season game. Feeling that Gray and Adams were similar pitchers, Heydler recommended that his league start Adams against the Tigers in the World Series. Adams won that opening game and two more, posting a 1.33 ERA while becoming the third pitcher to win three games in a single World Series.

For the first time in their three-year run, the Tigers made a respectable showing in the World Series, stretching it out to a seventh game. But in that decisive game at Detroit's Bennett Park, Adams pitched again for the Pirates, winning the game 8-0 and the series, four games to three. It was a hotly contested series, and six players were assessed fines for excessive arguing with the umpires. The Pirates won despite the dreadful play of their first baseman, Bill Abstein, who turned in perhaps the worst performance of any individual player in World Series history. Abstein set new Series records for strikeouts by a batter (ten) and errors by a first baseman (five). According to Fred Lieb, enraged Pirates owner Barney Dreyfuss released Abstein immediately following the championship celebration.

It was even worse for the Tigers. For the third year in a row they had lost the World Series, each time losing the final game in front of their home fans while failing to score even a single run. There was enough blame to spread around. Writing in *Sporting Life*, Francis Richter said manager Hughie Jennings' mistakes were "numerous and fatal," and accused him of "lack of moral courage." Others blamed the Tiger catchers, who had allowed opponents to steal 49 bases in seventeen World Series games. But most of the blame was heaped on Detroit's two sluggers, Sam Crawford and Ty Cobb, who had combined for a .252 average and 17 RBI in the three losing Series. For Cobb, who had played in the World Series in each of his three full major league seasons, the loss must have been tempered by the belief that he would soon get another chance. But as it turned out, the 22-year-old Cobb had played the final World Series game of his career. "I was an ambitious hustling kid in those days, just beginning to learn how to play baseball," Cobb said years later. "I had lots of speed, but I lacked experience."

BOTTOM LEFT: The Pirates' Honus Wagner, shown here in 1913, was not just the star of the 1909 World Series, but arguably the best player in the history of the National League.

BOTTOM RIGHT: Columbia alumnus Eddie Collins batted .429 and slugged .619 in the Athletics' five-game rout of the Cubs in 1910. It was the first of three World Series in which he batted over .400.

1910

PHILADELPHIA A'S (4)
CHICAGO CUBS (1)

MOST OBSERVERS CONSIDERED THE 1910 World Series to be one of the greatest mismatches in the Series' young history. Although the Philadelphia Athletics had won 102 games during the regular season, they were given little chance to prevail over the Chicago Cubs, who had won the Series two of the previous three years. Moreover, the American League had made such a poor showing in those three contests that the inexperienced Athletics seemed to be overmatched.

Connie Mack's A's were a mixture of untested youngsters, including 23-year-old Eddie Collins and 24-year-old Frank Baker, and unspectacular veterans such as first baseman Harry Davis and right fielder Danny Murphy. The Cubs, meanwhile, featured most of the same personnel that had won three straight pennants from 1906–1909, but with an average age of 29, they were now the oldest team in baseball. One of their youngest stars, 28-year-old Johnny Evers, was injured and unable to play, but still attended the games on crutches in order to bait the umpires.

Because the American League season ended a week earlier than the National, the Athletics had considerable idle time before Game 1. They filled the time by playing a series of exhibition games against a team of American League All-Stars including Ty Cobb, Tris Speaker, Walter Johnson, and Ed Walsh. Many thought these games helped prepare Philadelphia to face the mighty Cubs; as one writer noted, "the beatings they were given by the All-Stars roused their fighting spirit and brought them right up to the World's Series keyed up to a high pitch." Whatever the reason, the A's got off to a good start, as Chief Bender pitched a three-hitter in Game 1, winning 4-1. He got defensive help from Murphy, who tumbled into the right field stands to make a spectacular catch of a long drive.

A's pitcher Jack Coombs was plagued by control problems in Game 2, walking nine batters and throwing just 34 strikes in 105 pitches. But Cubs ace Mordecai Brown, perhaps shaken after being involved in an auto accident on his way to the game, pitched even worse, giving up nine runs in seven innings. Despite Coombs' wildness, the A's prevailed again, 9-3. Now down 2-0, the Cubs returned to Chicago in a deep hole. Their treatment by the home fans only made things worse. One fan on the street heckled manager Frank Chance so badly that Chance jumped out of his car and attacked him. The entire team was greeted with a chorus of boos as it took the field for Game 3 at West Side Park. Remarkably, Jack Coombs took the mound again for the A's after pitching nine innings in the previous game, and won again, 12-5.

At three games to none, the Series was now essentially over. The Cubs beat Bender in Game 4, but the Athletics closed it out in Game 5, as Coombs won to notch his third victory of the Series. Using only two pitchers in the five games, the Athletics thoroughly outclassed Chicago, outscoring them 35-15. The switch-hitting Coombs dominated both on the mound and at the plate, where his .385 Series average was higher than that of any Cubs batter. And for the two young Philadelphia stars, Baker and Collins, the Series was a coming out party, as they batted .409 and .429, respectively. The sensational Collins also stole four bases, leaving strong-armed Cubs catcher Johnny Kling in disbelief. "He gets the best leads I ever saw, and his slide is a beauty," Kling said.

Chicago White Sox owner Charles Comiskey, gleeful at the demise of his crosstown rivals, sent the Athletics players two cases of champagne and one thousand cigars in gratitude. It was a sign of things to come for the Athletics. Led by Baker and Collins, they developed into one of the juggernauts of early baseball. For the Cubs, meanwhile, it was the end of a great dynasty, as the core of the team—Brown, Chance, Evers, Joe Tinker, Jimmy Sheckard, Wildfire Schulte, Johnny Kling, Ed Reulbach, Orval

BOTTOM: Frank Chance, seen here sliding at the Polo Grounds, was perhaps the greatest player-manager in baseball history. He batted .296 in a 17-year career while also managing the Cubs to four National League pennants.

Overall, Jack Pfiester, and Harry Steinfeldt—would all be retired by the time the team won its next pennant. With those eleven remarkable players, the Cubs won four pennants and two World Series from 1906–1910; nearly a century after their departure, the team has yet to enjoy another World Championship.

1910 WORLD SERIES

Shibe Park (Philadelphia Athletics) ◆ 10.17.10 (Game 1)

	1	2	3	4	5	6	7	8	9	R	H	E
Chi.	0	0	0	0	0	0	0	0	1	1	3	1
Phil.	0	2	1	0	0	0	0	1	X	4	7	2

WP–Bender LP–Overall ATT: 26,891

Shibe Park ◆ 10.18.10 (Game 2)

	1	2	3	4	5	6	7	8	9	R	H	E
Chi.	1	0	0	0	0	0	1	0	1	3	8	3
Phil.	0	0	2	0	1	0	6	0	X	9	14	4

WP–Coombs LP–Brown ATT: 24,597

West Side Park II (Chicago Cubs) ◆ 10.20.10 (Game 3)

	1	2	3	4	5	6	7	8	9	R	H	E
Phil.	1	2	5	0	0	0	4	0	0	12	15	1
Chi.	1	2	0	0	0	0	0	2	0	5	6	5

WP–Coombs LP–McIntire HR: PHA–Murphy ATT: 26,210

West Side Park II ◆ 10.22.10 (Game 4)

	1	2	3	4	5	6	7	8	9	10	R	H	E
Phil.	0	0	1	2	0	0	0	0	0	0	3	11	3
Chi.	1	0	0	1	0	0	0	0	1	1	4	9	1

WP–Brown LP–Bender ATT: 19,150

West Side Park II ◆ 10.23.10 (Game 5)

	1	2	3	4	5	6	7	8	9	R	H	E
Phil.	1	0	0	0	1	0	0	5	0	7	9	1
Chi.	0	1	0	0	0	0	0	1	0	2	9	2

WP–Coombs LP–Brown ATT: 27,374

1911

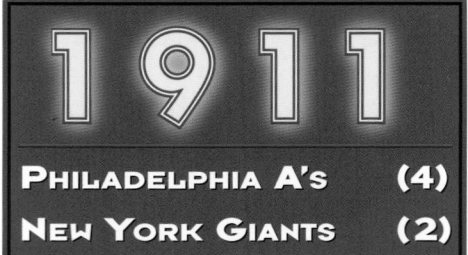

Philadelphia A's (4)
New York Giants (2)

At the time, the 1911 Series was considered by most to be the best World Series ever played. With classic pitcher's duels, dramatic home runs, a fresh young hero, controversial plays, and a bevy of colorful characters, it was the type of series that might have been imagined by an overzealous screenwriter. It was a rematch of the 1905 Series, with John McGraw's Giants again facing Connie Mack's Athletics. The first game, played on October 14, also featured a rematch between the two pitching aces of that Series, Christy Mathewson and Chief Bender. Six years earlier to the day, Mathewson had beaten Bender 2-0 to clinch the 1905 Series for New York. The two pitchers, now seasoned veterans, staged another classic duel in Game 1. Although Mathewson lacked his best fastball, he was able to tame the Athletics with a steady diet of curveballs as the Giants won, 2-1.

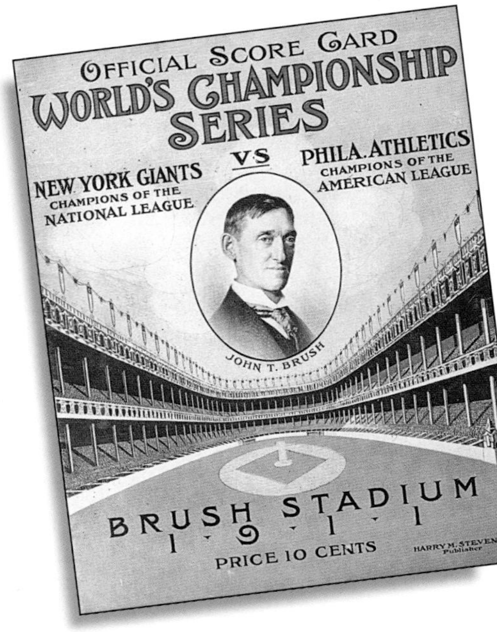

The second game was also a close contest. In the sixth inning Philadelphia's Frank Baker stepped to the plate with the teams tied 1-1. The promising young third baseman had led the American League with 11 home runs during the regular season, and he promptly sent a low fastball from Richard "Rube" Marquard over the right-field fence to give the A's a 3-1 lead. According to Francis Richter, who covered the Series for *Sporting Life*, the dramatic homer "sent the great multitude howling, cheering, and stamping for fully five minutes, in the conviction that the hit settled the game." That conviction turned out to be correct, as the Athletics won the game to even the Series.

Back at New York's Polo Grounds, the third game was even more exciting; indeed, Richter wrote that it "has had no equal in World's Series history." It was another remarkable pitcher's duel, this one between Mathewson and Jack Coombs. Mathewson had created some controversy earlier that day when a newspaper column with his name on it (but written by a ghostwriter) criticized his teammate Marquard's poor pitch selection to Baker in Game 2. Mathewson got a chance to prove his point when he pitched to Baker with a 1-0 lead and one out in the ninth inning of Game 3. Since Marquard had been stung on a fastball, Mathewson decided to throw Baker a two-strike curve. But Baker was expecting it, and when the pitch hung over the plate, he deposited it into the right-field stands to send the game into extra innings.

In addition to all the theatrics, Game 3 featured no less than six close calls by the umpiring crew, including one that became the most controversial play in the history of

BOTTOM: After getting off the streetcar, throngs of Giants fans wait for the Polo Grounds (also known as Brush Stadium, from 1911–1919) to open before the 1911 World Series.

TOP: In the most controversial play of the 1911 World Series, the Giants' Fred Snodgrass slides hard into third base. He was accused of intentionally spiking Frank Baker, the star of the Series for the Athletics.

BOTTOM: As Snodgrass stands alone on third base, Baker receives medical attention from the team trainer.

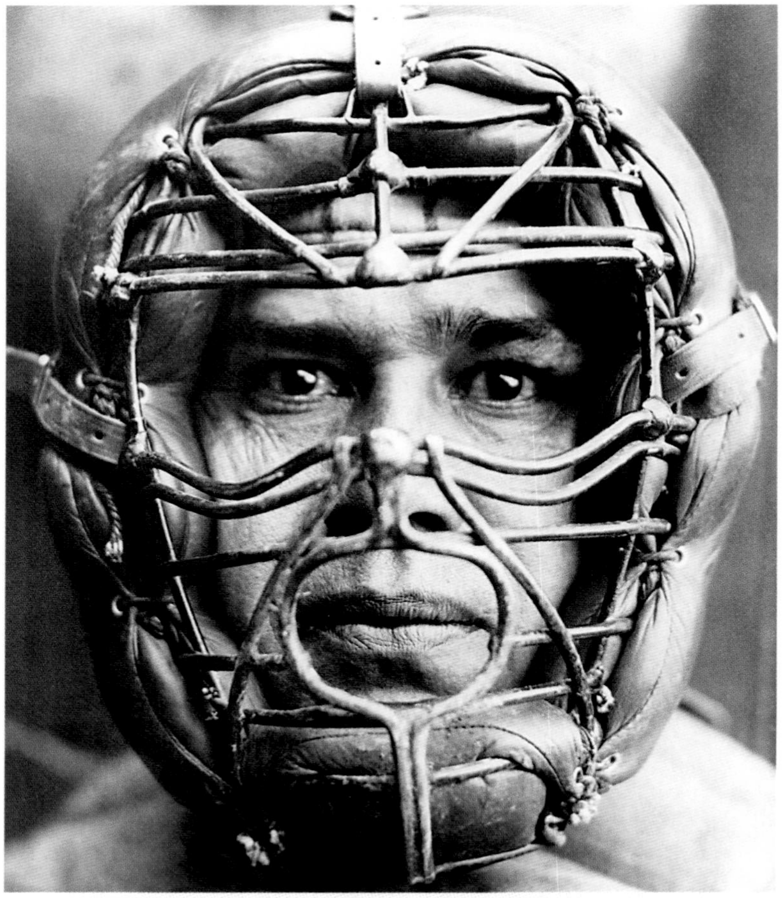

TOP LEFT: Like almost all Native American players of his day, the Giants' John Meyers was nicknamed "Chief." The best-hitting catcher of his era, Meyers finished third in the National League in 1911 with a .332 batting average.

TOP RIGHT: Frank Baker is shown here batting in 1911, the year he won the World Series for Philadelphia and acquired his famous nickname, "Home Run."

the young World Series. In the bottom of the tenth, Baker, the hero of the moment, was spiked at third base when New York's Fred Snodgrass slid in with his spikes high. "Before the Series began, we'd been told by friends that Baker was spike-shy, that he'd get out of your way at third base if the occasion arose," Snodgrass told writer Larry Ritter in *The Glory of Their Times*. "But Baker knew we had been told he was spike-shy, and he just had guts enough to try to block me off that base. So he was down on one knee in front of the bag, with the ball, waiting for me to slide. All I could do was go hard into him and try to upset him, which I did, and I was safe." Although Snodgrass always insisted the spiking was accidental, Connie Mack and most of the press corps accused him of hurting Baker deliberately. Snodgrass was even booed by his own home fans for the deed. The game, meanwhile, continued into the top of the eleventh, when the Athletics scored two runs, including one by Baker, to take a 3-1 lead. In the bottom of the inning, the Giants had a man on second when catcher John "Chief" Meyers hit what appeared to be a game-tying homer into the left field bleachers. But according to writer Fred Lieb's account, a gust of wind caught hold of the ball and blew it just a few inches foul. Given a second chance, Coombs was eventually able to get the final out on his 135th pitch of the game, as the A's won 3-2.

And then it rained. And rained. And rained. The A's and Giants sat idle while a raging storm battered the East Coast for six days. Finally, on October 24, the teams resumed play with their pitching staffs well-rested. After the layoff, Chief Bender—whose brother John, a minor league pitcher, had died on the pitching mound less than a month earlier—beat Mathewson 4-2 in Game 4 to give the A's a 3-1 Series lead.

Game 5 was another nail-biter. The Giants, only an out away from the end of their season, tied the game with two outs in the ninth on a single by Josh Devore. As darkness fell over Harlem, both teams knew the tenth inning would be the last. In the bottom of the inning the Giants threatened, placing Larry Doyle on third base with one out. Fred Merkle then hit a deep but catchable fly down the right field line, which presented Athletics right fielder Danny Murphy with a dilemma. If he caught the ball, Doyle would almost certainly tag and score the winning run; if he let it drop, it might fall for a harmless foul. Given only an instant to make his decision, Murphy decided to catch the ball and try to throw Doyle out at the plate. Doyle beat the throw easily and the game was over. The players rushed to the clubhouses one step ahead of the fans, who were streaming onto the field. But home plate umpire Bill Klem still stood silently at home plate without making a signal. Doyle had missed the plate, although neither he nor catcher Jack Lapp had noticed the miscue. Since the Athletics ran off the field, Klem had no choice but to count the run and declare a

1911 WORLD SERIES

Polo Grounds IV (New York Giants) ◆ 10.14.11

	1	2	3	4	5	6	7	8	9	R	H	E
Phil.	0	1	0	0	0	0	0	0	0	1	6	2
NYG	0	0	0	1	0	0	1	0	X	2	5	0

WP–Mathewson LP–Bender ATT: 38,281

Shibe Park (Philadelphia Athletics) ◆ 10.16.11

	1	2	3	4	5	6	7	8	9	R	H	E
NYG	0	1	0	0	0	0	0	0	0	1	5	3
Phil.	1	0	0	0	0	2	0	0	X	3	4	0

WP–Plank LP–Marquard HR: PHA–Baker
ATT: 26,286

Polo Grounds IV ◆ 10.17.11

	1	2	3	4	5	6	7	8	9	10	11	R	H	E
Phil.	0	0	0	0	0	0	0	0	1	0	2	3	9	2
NYG	0	0	1	0	0	0	0	0	0	0	1	2	3	5

WP–Coombs LP–Mathewson HR: PHA–Baker
ATT: 37,216

Shibe Park ◆ 10.24.11

	1	2	3	4	5	6	7	8	9	R	H	E
NYG	2	0	0	0	0	0	0	0	0	2	7	3
Phil.	0	0	0	3	1	0	0	0	X	4	11	1

WP–Bender LP–Mathewson ATT: 24,355

Polo Grounds IV ◆ 10.25.11

	1	2	3	4	5	6	7	8	9	10	R	H	E
Phil.	0	0	3	0	0	0	0	0	0	0	3	7	1
NYG	0	0	0	0	0	0	1	0	2	1	4	9	2

WP–Crandall LP–Plank HR: PHA–Oldring
ATT: 33,228

Shibe Park ◆ 10.26.11

	1	2	3	4	5	6	7	8	9	R	H	E
NYG	1	0	0	0	0	0	0	0	1	2	4	3
Phil.	0	0	1	4	0	1	7	0	X	13	13	5

WP–Bender LP–Ames ATT: 20,485

Giants victory. After the game, Connie Mack and several of his players said they had noticed Doyle's failure to touch home, but that they chose not to protest for fear of sparking a riot among the New York fans. "My players know that Doyle did not touch the plate," Mack said. "It was the most pleasing moment of my life when not one of them tried to take advantage of a technicality." While today it might seem like a foolish move for Mack to lose a World Series game on purpose, to Connie it was a matter of honor.

Game 6 was anticlimactic from the very beginning, as Philadelphia teed off on Giant pitching for an embarrassing 13-2 victory to end the Series. For the cocky Giants, the humiliation was complete. They batted a collective .175 and committed sixteen errors, and though they had stolen a major-league record 347 bases during the season, they ran the bases miserably during the Series, going 4-for-14 in steal attempts and making several more outs while trying for extra bases. Sportswriter Richter placed the blame on McGraw, saying the Giants lost because they were "lacking in resourcefulness and initiative, due probably to too much blind faith and dependence upon their manager."

It was the second championship in a row for Philadelphia and its famed "$100,000 Infield." The dollar amount may have been an overstatement, for the A's players only received a total of $76,746 in Series shares, but there would be more to come in future years. For Baker, meanwhile, the Series was a star-making turn. He was now a World Series hero, a national celebrity, and even had a new nickname, after the notation that seemed to appear so often in box scores: "Home Run—Baker."

1912

Boston Red Sox (4)
New York Giants (3)
(1 tie)

Though it was a hard-fought battle between two well-matched teams, the 1912 World Series is remembered today mostly for the theatrics of one extraordinary game. Nearly a century later, Game 8 in 1912 still ranks with Game 6 in 1975 and Game 6 in 1986 as one of the most exciting and dramatic contests ever played.

The Boston Red Sox interrupted Connie Mack's string of pennants in 1912, returning to the World Series for the first time since winning the inaugural one in 1903. They were opposed by the New York Giants, who once again were led by pitchers Christy Mathewson, Rube Marquard, and a fleet lineup in which eight players stole more than twenty bases.

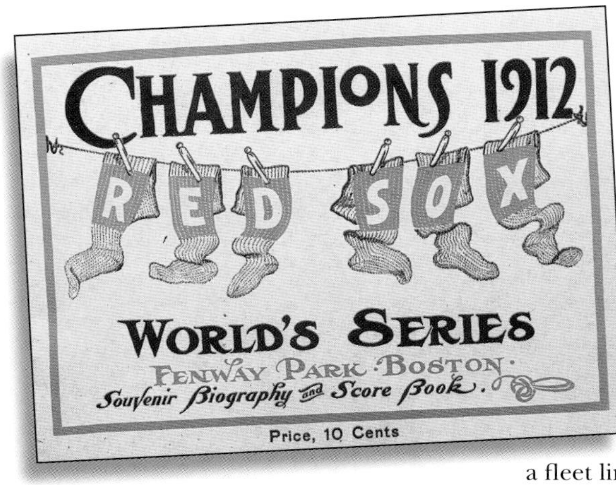

BOTTOM LEFT: Chief Meyers slides into third base during the 1912 World Series. The Red Sox player on the right, misidentified on the photograph as Everett Scott (who wasn't with the team yet in 1912), is probably Boston third baseman Larry Gardner. The late afternoon sun at Fenway Park is apparent from the long shadow thrown by third base coach John McGraw.

BOTTOM RIGHT: Fred Snodgrass made fourteen outfield errors during the 1912 regular season, plus another very costly one during the World Series.

The Series' first surprise came when John McGraw announced that Jeff Tesreau, not Mathewson, would start Game 1 at the Polo Grounds. Presumably this was so Mathewson would not have to face Smoky Joe Wood, the young Red Sox ace who that year posted one of the greatest pitching seasons in baseball history: 34-5 with a 1.91 ERA. Wood won the first game, and after Game 2 was called a tie on account of darkness, Marquard and the Giants captured Game 3 to even the Series. Wood pitched a masterpiece to win Game 4 and, in the upset of the Series, Boston rookie Hugh Bedient defeated Mathewson in Game 5. Now the Red Sox had a commanding 3-1 Series lead.

Boston manager Jake Stahl decided to hold back Wood in Game 6 to keep his ace in the hole for Game 7 if necessary. The move backfired as the Giants rocked replacement starter Thomas "Buck" O'Brien for five runs in the first inning, and went on to win the game easily. The pressure was now on a nervous Wood to finish out the Series in Game 7. "He couldn't speak," teammate Harry Hooper recalled. "Couldn't say a word. Well, what can you expect? I think he was only about twenty-two when all this was happening. Mighty young to be under such pressure for so many months." The pressure apparently got to Wood, as the Giants once again sealed up a victory by scoring six first inning runs on their way to an 11-4 win.

The momentum was in the Giants' favor as the teams prepared for the decisive Game 8. They had come back from a 3-1 deficit to tie the Series, they had beaten the world's best pitcher to a pulp, and they now had their own ace, Mathewson, ready for a rematch with the rookie Bedient in the final game.

The game was played before a tiny crowd of 17,034 on a clear afternoon at brand-new Fenway Park, with even Red Sox fans apparently convinced that the Giants were on their way to victory. Interest was high elsewhere in the country—as in Washington, D.C., where Supreme Court justices listening to oral arguments arranged for clerks to slip them inning-by-inning updates of the game. Early on it looked as if the Giants would prevail, as Mathewson mowed through the Boston lineup with little trouble. But his zeroes were matched by Bedient and later Wood, who entered in relief after getting knocked out of the box the day before. The Red Sox were aided defensively by right fielder Harry Hooper, who in the fifth inning made what *Sporting Life* declared "the most wonderful catch ever seen in a World's Series," robbing Larry Doyle of a home run and keeping Boston in the game. The score was tied 1-1 after nine innings, but the Giants took the lead in the top of the tenth on doubles by John "Red" Murray and Fred Merkle. They were now three outs away from the championship with their ace Mathewson still on the mound.

But the Giants never got the last out. With Wood scheduled to lead off the bottom of the tenth, Stahl sent up pinch hitter Clyde Engle instead. He lifted a high routine fly to Fred Snodgrass in center field. "I yelled that I'd take it and waved Murray off, and—well—I dropped the darn thing," Snodgrass later recalled. Snodgrass' mother, watching the game on a telegraph scoreboard in a California theater, reportedly fainted when the play came over the wires. The error put the tying run on second with nobody out. The Giants pulled their defense in, assuming that Hooper would bunt Engle to third. But, as Snodgrass told writer Larry Ritter, "Instead of bunting Hooper cracked a drive way over my head. I made one of the greatest plays of my life on it, catching the ball over my shoulder while on the dead run out in deep left center. They always forget about that play when they write about that inning." "Ninety-nine times out of one hundred no outfielder could have come close to that ball," Hooper recalled ruefully. "But in some way, I don't know how, Snodgrass ran like the wind and dang if he didn't catch it. I think he outran the ball. Robbed me of a sure triple." Snodgrass' great play more than canceled out his error. Instead of a man on third with one out, the Giants now had a man on second with one out. But because of what happened next, the error is the play that became famous.

After Mathewson walked Steve Yerkes, Tris Speaker, a dangerous .383 hitter that season, came up to bat. He took "a fierce swipe at the ball," but hit an easy popup into foul

BOTTOM: Smoky Joe Wood enjoyed one of the greatest pitching seasons ever in 1912, winning 37 games in the regular season and World Series combined. Although just 22 years old, he would never win more than 15 games in a season again.

1912 WORLD SERIES

Polo Grounds IV (New York Giants) ◆ 10.8.12 (GAME 1)

	1	2	3	4	5	6	7	8	9	R	H	E
Boston	0	0	0	0	0	1	3	0	0	4	6	1
NYG	0	0	2	0	0	0	0	0	1	3	8	1

WP–Wood LP–Tesreau ATT: 35,730

Fenway Park I (Boston Red Sox) ◆ 10.9.12 (GAME 2)

	1	2	3	4	5	6	7	8	9	10	11	R	H	E
NYG	0	1	0	1	0	0	0	3	0	1	0	6	11	5
Boston	3	0	0	0	1	0	0	1	0	1	0	6	10	1

WP–None LP–None ATT: 30,148

Fenway Park I ◆ 10.10.12 (GAME 3)

	1	2	3	4	5	6	7	8	9	R	H	E
NYG	0	1	0	0	1	0	0	0	0	2	7	1
Boston	0	0	0	0	0	0	0	0	1	1	7	0

WP–Marquard LP–O'Brien ATT: 34,624

Polo Grounds IV ◆ 10.11.12 (GAME 4)

	1	2	3	4	5	6	7	8	9	R	H	E
Boston	0	1	0	1	0	0	0	0	1	3	8	1
NYG	0	0	0	0	0	0	1	0	0	1	9	1

WP–Wood LP–Tesreau ATT: 36,502

Fenway Park I ◆ 10.12.12 (GAME 5)

	1	2	3	4	5	6	7	8	9	R	H	E
NYG	0	0	0	0	0	0	1	0	0	1	3	4
Boston	0	0	2	0	0	0	0	0	X	2	5	1

WP–Bedient LP–Mathewson ATT: 34,683

Polo Grounds IV ◆ 10.14.12 (GAME 6)

	1	2	3	4	5	6	7	8	9	R	H	E
Boston	0	2	0	0	0	0	0	0	0	2	7	2
NYG	5	0	0	0	0	0	0	0	X	5	11	2

WP–Marquard LP–O'Brien ATT: 30,622

Fenway Park I ◆ 10.15.12 (GAME 7)

	1	2	3	4	5	6	7	8	9	R	H	E
NYG	6	1	0	0	0	2	1	0	1	11	16	4
Boston	0	1	0	0	0	0	2	1	0	4	9	3

WP–Tesreau LP–Wood HR: NYG–Doyle; BOS–Gardner ATT: 32,694

Fenway Park I ◆ 10.16.12 (GAME 8)

	1	2	3	4	5	6	7	8	9	10	R	H	E
NYG	0	0	1	0	0	0	0	0	0	1	2	9	2
Boston	0	0	0	0	0	0	1	0	0	2	3	8	5

WP–Wood LP–Mathewson ATT: 17,034

ground near first base. It would have been an easy play for first baseman Fred Merkle, but Merkle, according to one sportswriter, "seemed to be in a trance." Mathewson also could have caught the ball easily himself, but instead he called for catcher Chief Meyers, who was too far away to reach the ball in time. "He kept hollering for the Chief to take it," Hooper remembered, "And poor Chief—he was never too fast to begin with—he lumbered down that line as fast as his big legs would carry him, stuck out his big catcher's mitt—and just missed it." Mathewson later claimed that he had called for Merkle to catch it, but whatever the mix-up, according to Fred Lieb, "Matty gave the two culprits a pained look and walked sadly to the mound." Given new life, Speaker promptly banged a single into right field to score the tying run. Later, with the winning run on third and only one out, the Giants brought their defense in hoping to cut off the runner at the plate, but Larry Gardner lifted a long fly to right field. Josh Devore, playing with a broken finger, ran back to catch it and made a perfunctory throw home, but Yerkes scored the winning run easily on the sacrifice fly. The Red Sox were world champions.

After the game "Snodgrass looked as if he had lost his last friend on earth," while, according to Fred Lieb, "Mathewson, after a few bitter remarks about his support, joined a card game." The New York press, in need of someone to skewer, singled out Snodgrass for his muff of Engle's fly. "For over half a century I've had to live with the fact that I dropped a fly ball in the World Series," Snodgrass recalled in the 1960s. "For years and years, whenever I'd be introduced to somebody, they'd start to say something and then stop, you know, afraid of hurting my feelings." After Snodgrass' baseball career ended he became a successful banker and politician, but he continued to be hounded by the memory of the dropped fly ball. When he died in 1974, the headline over his obituary in the *New York Times* read: FRED SNODGRASS, 86, DEAD; BALLPLAYER MUFFED 1912 FLY.

1913

PHILADELPHIA A's (4)
NEW YORK GIANTS (1)

THE AMERICAN LEAGUE HAD NOW WON three consecutive World Series contests. The New York Giants had a better regular-season record, but the Philadelphia Athletics, with two world titles already under their belt, were considered strong favorites in 1913. When a Giants player suggested that New York might actually win the Series, Home Run Baker scoffed. "Quit fooling yourself," he said. "By Monday I'll be down in Maryland shooting ducks."

More than 35,000 fans packed the Polo Grounds for Game 1, a contest which must have seemed like déjà vu for the Giants. As he had in 1912, McGraw skipped over Christy Mathewson in the opener, this time

BOTTOM: Sitting on overturned cases of Hires Root Beer, policemen keep the crowd under control during the 1913 World Series at Philadelphia's Shibe Park.

TOP: Fred Merkle watches his long drive bounce into the left field bleachers for a three-run homer in 1913, Game 4. Though it would be ruled a double today, the hit was a home run under the ground rules set for that Series. Watching are Athletics catcher Wally Schang and umpire Rip Egan.

BOTTOM: Fans stream onto the Polo Grounds field as players try to escape after a 1913 World Series game. At least four Athletics players are visible in the photo, including one just above the men in white suits.

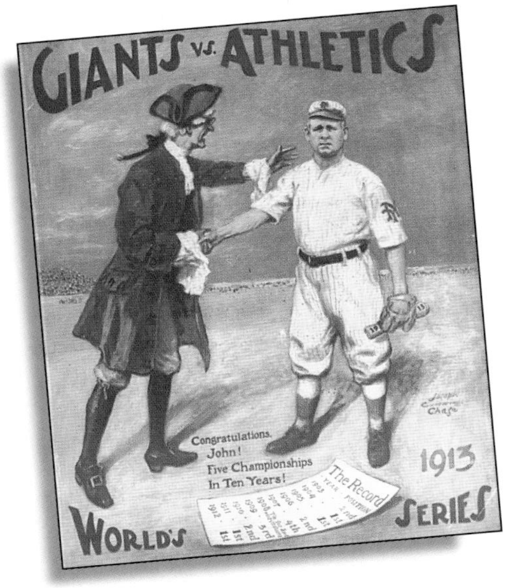

1913 WORLD SERIES

Polo Grounds IV (New York Giants) ◆ 10.7.13

	1	2	3	4	5	6	7	8	9	R	H	E
Phil.	0	0	0	3	2	0	0	1	0	6	11	1
NYG	0	0	1	0	3	0	0	0	0	4	11	0

WP–Bender LP–Marquard HR: PHA–Baker
ATT: 36,291

Shibe Park (Philadelphia Athletics) ◆ 10.8.13

	1	2	3	4	5	6	7	8	9	10	R	H	E
NYG	0	0	0	0	0	0	0	0	0	3	3	7	2
Phil.	0	0	0	0	0	0	0	0	0	0	0	8	2

WP–Mathewson LP–Plank ATT: 20,563

Polo Grounds IV ◆ 10.9.13

	1	2	3	4	5	6	7	8	9	R	H	E
Phil.	3	2	0	0	0	0	2	1	0	8	12	1
NYG	0	0	0	0	1	0	1	0	0	2	5	1

WP–Bush LP–Tesreau HR: PHA–Schang
ATT: 36,896

Shibe Park ◆ 10.10.13

	1	2	3	4	5	6	7	8	9	R	H	E
NYG	0	0	0	0	0	0	3	2	0	5	8	2
Phil.	0	1	0	3	2	0	0	0	X	6	9	0

WP–Bender LP–Demaree HR: NYG–Merkle
ATT: 20,568

Polo Grounds IV ◆ 10.11.13

	1	2	3	4	5	6	7	8	9	R	H	E
Phil.	1	0	2	0	0	0	0	0	0	3	6	1
NYG	0	0	0	0	1	0	0	0	0	1	2	2

WP–Plank LP–Mathewson ATT: 36,682

starting his third-best pitcher, Rube Marquard, instead. McGraw's decision backfired just as it had the previous year. For Marquard, meanwhile, it was a repeat of the 1911 Series, as Home Run Baker drove him from the game with a two-run homer in the fifth. The Athletics won 6-4, and to make matters worse for the Giants, two of their best players—Fred Merkle and Chief Meyers—sustained injuries that hampered the team for the rest of the Series.

Back at Shibe Park, Game 2 pitted Mathewson against Eddie Plank in what *Sporting Life* called "the most remarkable pitchers' duel in the record of modern World's Series." With 337 and 269 victories, respectively, Mathewson and Plank were the two winningest active pitchers in baseball. The last time they faced each other, Mathewson had beaten Plank 3-0 in Game 1 of the 1905 World Series. This time, the pitchers matched scoreless frames for nine tense innings. Philadelphia threatened in the bottom of the ninth, putting a runner on third with one out as Plank came to the plate. A's manager Connie Mack refused to pinch-hit for his pitcher, even with the game on the line. Plank grounded into a fielder's choice and the next batter, Danny Murphy, grounded out to end the inning. The scoreless tie remained. In the top of the tenth, Plank allowed a runner to reach second with one out. McGraw followed Mack's example and allowed Mathewson to hit, and Matty came through with an RBI single to break the scoreless tie. Mathewson retired the A's in order in the bottom of the tenth to cap off one of the greatest individual games in Series history: a 10-inning shutout and two hits, including the game-winner.

Mack surprised everyone with his choice to start Game 3. It was Joe Bush, a 20-year-old rookie whose 3.82 regular season ERA was a full run worse than the league average. But Bush pitched a creditable game, allowing just one earned run as the A's clobbered the Giants 8-2. In Game 4 Chief Bender pulled out a 6-5 Philadelphia win despite a late New York rally. The Athletics now held a commanding 3-1 lead in the Series.

With their backs against the wall, the Giants sent Mathewson to the mound in Game 5 for a rematch with Plank, who had announced that he would retire after the Series. Mathewson pitched valiantly, but allowed three early runs that gave the Athletics and Plank all they needed. After retiring the last batter in the top of the ninth, Mathewson, losing 3-1 and knowing he would be pinch hit for, made the long walk from the pitcher's mound to the center field clubhouse at the Polo Grounds. When the dejected New York crowd realized what was happening, they rose to their feet and applauded him until he disappeared into the clubhouse. It was the last World Series appearance of Christy Mathewson's career.

The Giants went quietly in the ninth, and the Series was over. A throng of A's fans descended on winning pitcher Plank, hoisted him onto their shoulders, and carried him around the field. They tried to do the same with the stately Connie Mack, but the manager outran them and jumped into a taxi. Before his escape, though, Mack had spoken briefly with John McGraw, who ran over to the A's bench to offer Mack his congratulations. With three World Series defeats in a row, McGraw had perfected the art of accepting defeat with grace and dignity—qualities the volatile manager rarely displayed during the regular season. McGraw's reputation as a good loser was so widespread that he even authored an article for *Baseball Magazine* titled, "My Unfortunate World's Series Record: How the Giants Under My Leadership Have Lost More World's Series Games than Any Other Club." But by the time he retired in 1932, McGraw would have more wins *and* losses than any other World Series manager.

1914

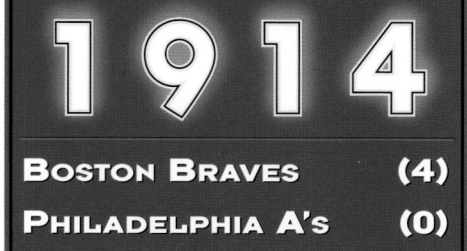

Boston Braves	**(4)**
Philadelphia A's	**(0)**

It was business as usual for the Athletics in 1914. They won the American League pennant easily behind the outstanding play of Home Run Baker, who led the junior circuit with nine home runs, and Eddie Collins, who had a .453 on-base percentage, 58 stolen bases, and won the Chalmers Award as the league's best player. The National League pennant race, on the other hand, was a jumbled mess. On July 18, the New York Giants occupied first place, followed closely by the Cubs, Cardinals, Reds, Phillies, and Dodgers. The Boston Braves, the perennial doormats who had finished last in four of the past five seasons, were in the cellar again with a 35-43 record. But the unheralded Braves soon began to win. By August 1, they had reached

BOTTOM: Two heroes of the 1914 World Series for the Braves were catcher Hank Gowdy, left, and shortstop Rabbit Maranville. This photograph was taken in 1933, nearly two decades later, when Gowdy was a coach and Maranville a 41-year-old second baseman.

.500 and fourth place. On August 23, scarcely a month after being in last place, the Braves moved into a first-place tie with the Giants. They had gone 24-5 in that span. The Braves and Giants battled back and forth for a few weeks, taking turns atop the standings until the Braves finally began to pull away in mid-September. Boston ended the season with a 94-59 record and won the National League by 10½ games.

So how did they do it? How did a mediocre team, late in the season, move from last place to first in only a month? There were many factors. First, the National League had tremendous parity in 1914 due in part to player raids by the outlaw Federal League. This made the journey from last to first easier than it might have been otherwise. As one writer put it, the Boston team was "composed of such little known, mediocre, and inexperienced players that its success was attributed more to all-round league deterioration than to individual superiority." Still, the Braves had to their credit an outstanding manager, George Stallings, whose innovative ideas helped propel them into contention. That year Stallings became the first National League manager to use platooning, a system that the Detroit Tigers had experimented with a few years earlier, but which remained a daring and unproven strategy. Boston had a plethora of weak outfielders—under Stallings' system, no Braves outfielder had as many as four hundred at bats, but eight of them batted more than one hundred times. As a result of the shuffling, Stallings got more out of his eight outfielders collectively than he could have from any of them individually. The Braves also had outstanding defense, sporting perhaps the best double play combination of all time in Johnny Evers and Walter "Rabbit" Maranville. They had a new young catcher, Hank Gowdy, who emerged as a solid regular. And finally, they got outstanding pitching from two unexpected sources: Dick Rudolph, a .500 pitcher over his three previous seasons in the majors, posted a 26-10 record in 1914, and Bill James, a 22-year-old spitballer who had gone 6-10 in his only prior major league season, suddenly emerged as the best pitcher in the National League with a 26-7 record and 1.90 ERA.

1914 WORLD SERIES

Shibe Park (Philadelphia Athletics) ◆ 10.9.14 — GAME 1

	1	2	3	4	5	6	7	8	9	R	H	E
Boston	0	2	0	0	1	3	0	1	0	7	11	2
Phil.	0	1	0	0	0	0	0	0	0	1	5	0

WP–Rudolph LP–Bender ATT: 20,562

Shibe Park ◆ 10.10.14 — GAME 2

	1	2	3	4	5	6	7	8	9	R	H	E
Boston	0	0	0	0	0	0	0	0	1	1	7	1
Phil.	0	0	0	0	0	0	0	0	0	0	2	1

WP–James LP–Plank ATT: 20,562

Fenway Park I (Boston Braves) ◆ 10.12.14 — GAME 3

	1	2	3	4	5	6	7	8	9	10	11	12	R	H	E
Phil.	1	0	0	1	0	0	0	0	0	2	0	0	4	8	2
Boston	0	1	0	1	0	0	0	0	0	2	0	1	5	9	1

WP–James LP–Bush HR: BSN–Gowdy ATT: 35,520

Fenway Park I ◆ 10.13.14 — GAME 4

	1	2	3	4	5	6	7	8	9	R	H	E
Phil.	0	0	0	0	1	0	0	0	0	1	7	0
Boston	0	0	0	1	2	0	0	0	X	3	6	0

WP–Rudolph LP–Shawkey ATT: 34,365

Despite the Braves' storybook climb to the pennant, gambling houses still offered three-to-one odds in favor of the mighty Athletics. The Braves just laughed. "I am perfectly confident," Evers said before the Series. "The Athletics are destined to receive the one biggest surprise of their lives." Boston manager Stallings was more blunt, declaring the Braves' intention to "knock Mack's head off."

The A's started Chief Bender, the hero of so many previous Series, in Game 1 at Shibe Park, but, as observed by the *Sporting Life*, Bender "pitched a poor game in all respects, lacking speed, judgment, and control." Boston won easily 7-1 with Rudolph pitching. Gowdy was the star of the game with a single, double, triple, walk, stolen base, RBI, and two runs scored. In Game 2, Bill James pitched a masterful game for Boston, using his spitball to hold the Athletics to two hits in a 1-0 win over Eddie Plank. The Braves scored the game's only run in the ninth inning when, after a misplayed fly ball and a botched rundown had placed a runner on third, part-time outfielder Herbie Moran poked a run-scoring single over the infield that barely grazed the outstretched glove of Collins. The underdog Braves now led the Series two games to none.

The Braves returned home for the next game, at brand-new Fenway Park, which they had arranged to borrow from the Red Sox because their own ballpark, the South End Grounds, was too small to accommodate all the fans who wanted to see the Series. Game 3 was, according to *Sporting Life*, "one of the most thrilling and wild-exciting games ever played." The score was tied 2-2 at the end of nine innings. Philadelphia scored in the top of the tenth when a hard shot by Baker deflected off Evers' shin, scoring one runner. When the apparently dazed Evers picked up the ball and held it at second base, another A's runner, Danny Murphy, came dashing home to make the score 4-2. Boston wasn't done, though. Gowdy led off the bottom of the tenth with a deep fly that bounced into the center field bleachers for a home run. Then Herbie Moran walked, Evers singled him over to third, and Joe Connolly brought him home with a game-tying sacrifice fly. When the game continued into the eleventh inning, Stallings brought James, who had pitched nine innings in the previous game, back in relief. The tie continued until the bottom of the twelfth, when Gowdy, again leading off the inning for the Braves, smashed a drive into the left field bleachers for a double. (Of course, Fenway Park has no left field bleachers. These were temporary seats erected for the World Series, which is why Gowdy's drive, though it entered the bleachers on the fly, was only a ground-rule double.) After an intentional walk, Moran attempted to bunt Gowdy over to third. A's pitcher Joe Bush fielded the ball and tried to force the runner at third, but the throw was wild and Gowdy scored, giving Game 3 to the Braves.

OPPOSITE: Hank Gowdy tripped over his catcher's mask in a famous play during the 1924 World Series, but he could do no wrong in 1914, leading the Braves to victory with a .545 Series batting average.

Rudolph, on the mound trying to make it a clean sweep for the Braves, did exactly that in Game 4. He allowed the Athletics just one run on seven hits, and Boston polished off Philadelphia, 3-1. The journey of the "Miracle Braves" was complete, and it ended with a sweep of the mightiest team in the country. But because a third major league, the Federal League, had entered the scene in 1914, the Braves were not undisputed champions of the world. Evers, the Braves' captain, turned down an offer from the Federal League champions, the Indianapolis Hoosiers, to face them in a seven-game series. Still, the Braves' place in history was secure. Their Series win, wrote the *Sporting Life*, "was the most amazing feat of the age, and the most stunning surprise ever dealt the base ball world."

RIGHT: This cover of *Baseball Magazine* from 1914 captures the spirit of contemporary World Series perfectly with its depiction of an excited crowd gathered around the scoreboard. At the time, fans not lucky enough to attend the game in person would congregate at designated locations to follow along as their team played. The action was telegraphed to the scoreboard operators, who would then announce the play-by-play through a speaking tube and manually update the score on the board. The growth of broadcast technology would quickly change how such information was disseminated, of course, but at the time it must have been great for fans to publicly band together like this in common cause.in common cause.

1915

BOSTON RED SOX (4)
PHILADELPHIA PHILLIES (1)

THE 1915 WORLD SERIES FEATURED BOSTON and Philadelphia once again—but this time it was the Red Sox and Phillies instead of the Braves and Athletics. Although it lasted only five games, the Series was an exciting one, with four of the five being one-run affairs, and three of those decided in the winning team's final at-bat.

The 1915 Phillies were the first World Series team to be built around power hitting. Aided by the Baker Bowl's 272-foot (83m) right field fence, Gavy Cravath and Fred Luderus combined for 31 homers and a .484 slugging percentage. That, along with the extraordinary performance of Grover Cleveland Alexander—who, with 31 wins and a 1.22 ERA, was far and away the best pitcher in baseball—propelled the Phils to the pennant. Still, the Phillies entered the Series as underdogs to the Red Sox, thanks mostly to the American League's reputation as a superior circuit.

The first game was played on a soggy field in Philadelphia and the conditions helped determine the outcome of the game. Alexander pitched effectively, but his counterpart, Boston's Ernie Shore, was even more dominant. Shore allowed only one clean hit in the game, but several routine grounders got stuck in the infield mud, resulting in Phillies hits. This, combined with walks and a key eighth inning error by Shore, helped Philadelphia win 3-1.

Game 2 in Philadelphia was the first World Series game ever attended by a U.S. President, as Woodrow Wilson threw out the first ball. But the day belonged to Boston's George "Rube" Foster, who allowed just three hits while collecting three himself, including a tie-breaking single in the ninth inning. Pitching in the bottom of the ninth, Foster needed one more out for a 2-1 victory when George "Dode" Paskert came to bat. Paskert slammed a drive to deep center field that looked like a game-tying homer. Although a swirling wind made it difficult to judge the ball, Tris Speaker was able to catch it with his glove outstretched over the center field bleachers, thus saving a home run and ending the game.

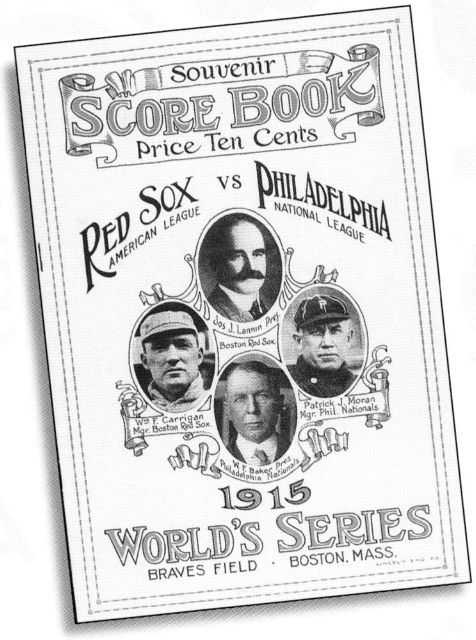

Game 3 took place in Boston, not at Fenway Park, but at the much more spacious Braves Field, which the Red Sox had arranged to rent for the duration of the Series. The decision to play there was an economic one—the brand-new Braves Field held 42,000 fans, the largest capacity in baseball—but it turned out to be fortunate

BOTTOM: Phillies centerfielder Dode Paskert is caught stealing in the third inning of Game 5 of the 1915 World Series. It was the third out of the inning, leaving Gavy Cravath, the Phillies' top slugger, standing at home with the bat in his hands.

TOP: After enjoying one of the greatest pitching seasons in baseball history, "Ol' Pete" Alexander (as he was known) was able to beat the Red Sox just once in the 1915 World Series.

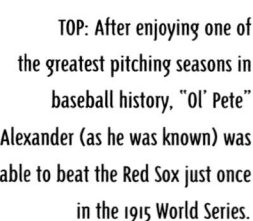

BOTTOM: Duffy Lewis put on one of the greatest World Series performances of all time in 1915, batting .444 and playing spectacular defense in left field. Normally a left-handed hitter, Lewis swings from the other side of the plate in this photograph.

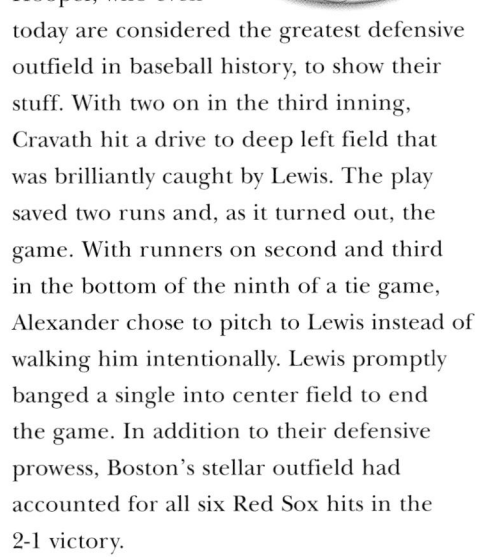

for on-the-field reasons as well. The vast outfield spaces provided plenty of room for George "Duffy" Lewis, Speaker, and Harry Hooper, who even today are considered the greatest defensive outfield in baseball history, to show their stuff. With two on in the third inning, Cravath hit a drive to deep left field that was brilliantly caught by Lewis. The play saved two runs and, as it turned out, the game. With runners on second and third in the bottom of the ninth of a tie game, Alexander chose to pitch to Lewis instead of walking him intentionally. Lewis promptly banged a single into center field to end the game. In addition to their defensive prowess, Boston's stellar outfield had accounted for all six Red Sox hits in the 2-1 victory.

The fourth game was episode two of the Duffy Lewis show. He made two running catches that, according to Francis Richter, were "seemingly impossible," and once again batted in the winning run, this time with a sixth-inning double. The Series headed back to the Baker Bowl with the Red Sox up three games to one. The Phillies' power-friendly ballpark had been made even more so with the addition of temporary bleachers in center field for the World Series, and this decision to grub for more money ended up costing the Phillies

1915 WORLD SERIES

Baker Bowl (Philadelphia Phillies) ◆ 10.8.15

	1	2	3	4	5	6	7	8	9	R	H	E
Boston	0	0	0	0	0	0	0	1	0	1	8	1
Phil.	0	0	0	1	0	0	0	2	X	3	5	1

WP–Alexander LP–Shore ATT: 19,343

Baker Bowl ◆ 10.9.15

	1	2	3	4	5	6	7	8	9	R	H	E
Boston	1	0	0	0	0	0	0	0	1	2	10	0
Phil.	0	0	0	0	1	0	0	0	0	1	3	0

WP–Foster LP–Mayer ATT: 20,306

Braves Field (Boston Red Sox) ◆ 10.11.15

	1	2	3	4	5	6	7	8	9	R	H	E
Phil.	0	0	1	0	0	0	0	0	0	1	3	0
Boston	0	0	0	1	0	0	0	0	1	2	6	1

WP–Leonard LP–Alexander ATT: 42,300

Braves Field ◆ 10.12.15

	1	2	3	4	5	6	7	8	9	R	H	E
Phil.	0	0	0	0	0	0	0	1	0	1	7	0
Boston	0	0	1	0	0	1	0	0	X	2	8	1

WP–Shore LP–Chalmers ATT: 41,096

Baker Bowl ◆ 10.13.15

	1	2	3	4	5	6	7	8	9	R	H	E
Boston	0	1	1	0	0	0	0	2	1	5	10	1
Phil.	2	0	0	2	0	0	0	0	0	4	9	1

WP–Foster LP–Rixey HR: BOS–Hooper (2), Lewis; PHI–Luderus ATT: 36,682 the Series. In Game 5 Boston players hit three homers into the temporary stands, all of which would have been doubles ordinarily. The Red Sox were batting in the eighth inning, down 4-2, when Lewis—who else?—stepped to the plate. He hit a long drive that bounced into the stands to tie the game. (Balls bouncing into the stands are doubles today, but in 1915 they were home runs.) Then, in the top of the ninth, Harry Hooper hit a ball that again bounced into the center field bleachers. It was Hooper's second such homer of the game, Boston's third, and it won the game and the Series for the Red Sox.

Perhaps more than any other series, the outcome of the 1915 World Series was determined by the parks in which it was played. The Phillies' offense, tailored to take advantage of the Baker Bowl, sputtered in Boston. Cravath, whose 24 home runs that year were the most any player had hit in the twentieth century, hit three balls that would have been homers at any park other than Braves Field. Had the ballparks been different, the outcome likely would have been also.

1916

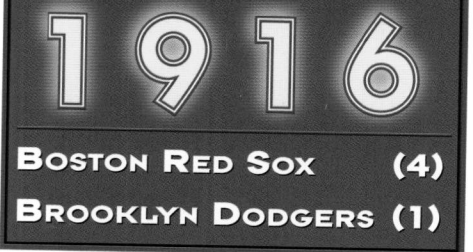

Boston Red Sox (4)
Brooklyn Dodgers (1)

Although the Red Sox won the 1915 championship, their best player, Tris Speaker, had what was for him a bad year. He batted only .322, lowest since his rookie year, and stole bases at a lackluster 54 percent success rate. But Speaker resisted when Boston owner Joseph Lannin tried to cut his salary at the end of the year. Lannin then shocked the baseball world by trading him to Cleveland for $50,000 and two prospects. Forced to play the 1916 season without their superstar, the Red Sox scored only 3.5 runs per game, one of the worst figures in the American League. But they still managed to win the weak A.L. thanks to their pitching staff of Babe Ruth, Ernie Shore, Hubert "Dutch" Leonard, and Carl Mays, all of whom posted ERAs under 2.70. Ruth, the 21-year-old southpaw, emerged as the league's best pitcher, leading the A.L. in both ERA (1.75) and shutouts (nine). The Red Sox' opponents in the World Series were the Brooklyn Dodgers, often called the "Robins" after their boisterous and rotund manager, Wilbert Robinson, who did a remarkable job of turning a team of castoffs and ne'er-do-wells into a pennant winner. Like the Red Sox, the Robins were a team of lackluster hitters, but they led the National League with a remarkable 2.12 team ERA, a figure that no team in baseball has matched

TOP: Babe Ruth had his best season as a pitcher in 1916, going 23-12 with a league-leading 1.75 ERA.

BOTTOM: Brooklyn Dodgers pitcher Rube Marquard (left) and manager Wilbert Robinson. In 1916, the Dodgers (nicknamed the "Robins" because of their manager's feisty personality) won the N.L. pennant thanks to the sturdy hurlers on the pitching staff, in particular Marquard, who posted a team-best regular-season ERA of 1.58. Interestingly, in 1916 the Robins became the only team ever to play in the World Series wearing checkered uniforms.

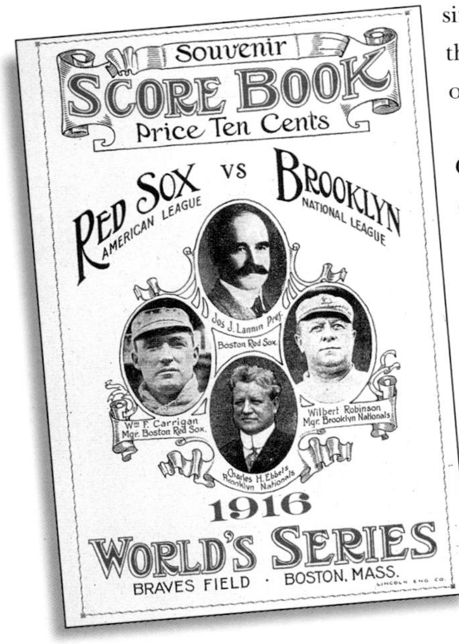

since. The 1916 World Series, then, was expected to be a string of pitcher's duels.

A steady Boston attack in Game 1 netted them a 6-1 lead entering the ninth inning with Shore pitching a fine game. But Brooklyn came back with what Francis Richter called "one of the most sensational ninth-inning rallies ever staged in a World's Series," as the Robins scored three runs in the ninth before loading the bases for Henry "Hy" Myers. With two outs, Boston manager Bill Carrigan replaced Shore with Mays. Myers' infield hit then made the score 6-5. Mays next faced first baseman Jake Daubert, a onetime National League MVP, with the bases still loaded. Daubert hit a sharp grounder to deep shortstop, where Everett Scott fielded it in the hole and made the long throw to first base. Daubert was out by half a step, and by that razor-thin margin the Red Sox won the first game. For years afterward, Dodger manager Robinson contended that Scott's play was the most important of the Series, and that if it had gone the other way, his Brooklyn team would have won the championship.

The next day the fans got the pitcher's duel they had been expecting. After each gave up a run in the early innings, left-handers Sherry Smith and Ruth traded zeroes for ten frames and the game went into the fourteenth inning tied 1-1. (Ruth drove in the Boston run himself with a groundout.) With it getting so dark that some players felt play should be stopped, the game continued into the bottom of the fourteenth. In that inning, a walk to Dick Hoblitzel, a sacrifice fly by Duffy Lewis, and a single by Del Gainer did Smith in, as Ruth and the Red Sox won 2-1 in what was then the longest World Series game ever played.

1916 WORLD SERIES

Braves Field (Boston Red Sox) ◆ 10.7.16

	1	2	3	4	5	6	7	8	9	R	H	E
B'klyn	0	0	0	1	0	0	0	0	4	5	10	4
Boston	0	0	1	0	1	0	3	1	X	6	8	1

WP–Shore LP–Marquard ATT: 36,117

Braves Field ◆ 10.8.16

	1	2	3	4	5	6	7	8	9	10	11	12	13	14	R	H	E
B'klyn	1	0	0	0	0	0	0	0	0	0	0	0	0	0	1	6	2
Boston	0	0	1	0	0	0	0	0	0	0	0	0	0	1	2	7	1

WP–Ruth LP–Smith HR: BKN–Myers ATT: 41,373

Ebbets Field (Brooklyn Dodgers) ◆ 10.10.16

	1	2	3	4	5	6	7	8	9	R	H	E
Boston	0	0	0	0	0	2	1	0	0	3	7	1
B'klyn	0	0	1	1	2	0	0	0	X	4	10	0

WP–Coombs LP–Mays HR: BOS–Gardner ATT: 21,087

Ebbets Field ◆ 10.11.16

	1	2	3	4	5	6	7	8	9	R	H	E
Boston	0	3	0	1	1	0	1	0	0	6	10	1
B'klyn	2	0	0	0	0	0	0	0	0	2	5	4

WP–Leonard LP–Marquard ATT: 21,662

Braves Field ◆ 10.12.16

	1	2	3	4	5	6	7	8	9	R	H	E
B'klyn	0	1	0	0	0	0	0	0	0	1	3	3
Boston	0	1	2	0	1	0	0	0	X	4	7	2

WP–Shore LP–Pfeffer ATT: 42,620

Game 3 was played with thousands of seats empty at Ebbets Field because Robins owner Charles Ebbets had upped the price for Series tickets to a scandalous five dollars. The 21,087 who attended went home happy, though, as the Dodgers pulled out a narrow 4-3 victory behind the pitching of Jack Coombs and Jeff Pfeffer. The Dodgers jumped out to a two-run lead in Game 4, but gave it right back when Boston's Larry Gardner hit a three-run, inside-the-park home run. In the eighth inning, losing 6-2, the Robins sent in lefty George "Nap" Rucker for a couple of mop-up innings. It was the first World Series appearance for Rucker, Brooklyn's best player over the previous decade, who had announced his intention to retire at the end of the season. Rucker pitched two scoreless innings in his final major league appearance, but the Dodgers lost and were now in the hole three games to one.

The Red Sox made quick work of Brooklyn in Game 5, wrapping up the Series with a 4-1 win behind Shore. Throughout the Series, the Boston players had been mercilessly taunting Robin shortstop Ivan "Ivy" Olson, who had committed 48 errors during the season. "When in doubt, hit to Ivy," they yelled from the bench. In Game 5 they did exactly that, and Olson committed two errors on one double-play ball as Boston scored the go-ahead runs. The Dodgers went down easily after that, managing only three hits against Shore. While Olson had committed four errors in the Series, there was plenty of blame for the other Brooklyn players to share. Pitcher Rube Marquard had been beaten to a pulp, and all but three Robins ended the Series with a batting average of .211 or lower. The vitriolic press criticized not only Brooklyn's play in the Series, but also the way in which the team divided their losing World Series shares: according to Fred Lieb, "coaches, clubhouse attendants, and other underlings were voted big chunks of Flatbush air." For Boston, meanwhile, Ruth, Shore, and Leonard had lived up to their billing as outstanding pitchers, and the entire city looked toward 1917 with hopes of a third consecutive World Series title.

BOTTOM: Larry Gardner slides in under the tag of Brooklyn catcher Chief Meyers for a three-run, inside-the-park home run in Game 4. It was the Vermont native's second homer of the Series. (The first, in Game 3, left the park.)

1917

Chicago White Sox (4)
New York Giants (2)

In 1917 the New York Giants, two years removed from last place, became the fourth different team in four years to capture the National League pennant. John McGraw's team, completely retooled since its last World Series appearance in 1913, featured Henry "Heinie" Zimmerman and Benny Kauff, talented sluggers of dubious moral reputation, batting in the middle of the lineup. (Both would later be banned from baseball for life, Zimmerman for throwing games and Kauff for his participation in a stolen car ring.) Though the Giants won 98 games, the most in the National League since 1913, they were considered underdogs against the Chicago White Sox, who were making their first appearance in the World Series since unexpectedly winning it in 1906. Eddie Collins and Joe Jackson, imports from the Philadelphia A's and Cleveland Indians, respectively, were among the half-dozen greatest players in the game. Both had disappointing seasons in 1917, but a cast of supporting characters, including center fielder Oscar "Happy" Felsch, third baseman George "Buck" Weaver, and catcher, Ray Schalk, helped the Sox win one game and the American League pennant. Chicago also had outstanding pitching, with Urban "Red" Faber, Eddie Cicotte, Ewell "Reb" Russell, and Jim Scott all posting ERAs under 2.00.

GIANTS VS WHITE SOX
NEW YORK
WORLDS SERIES 1917
CHICAGO
Brush Stadium
Polo Grounds
PRESIDENT WILSON THROWING OUT BALL AT THE OPENING OF THE AMERICAN LEAGUE SEASON AT WASHINGTON.
A BIG ENOUGH BOY TO ENJOY THE NATIONAL GAME—AND A MAN BIG ENOUGH TO GUIDE OUR COUNTRY THROUGH ITS GREATEST CRISIS.
PRICE 25 CENTS

Though both teams were plagued by mistakes during the Series, it was exciting in its way; as *Baseball Magazine* put it, "It was a horrible series, and yet the very absurdities and asininities kept the crowds stirred up and made it a thriller all the way."

The trio of Cicotte, Felsch, and Jackson combined to win the first game for the White Sox. Cicotte held the Giants to one run and seven hits, Felsch homered deep into the left field bleachers, and Jackson made a terrific diving catch with a runner in scoring position to preserve the 2-1 White Sox win. The second game was all White Sox, too, thanks to three hits apiece by Jackson and Weaver. Sox pitcher Urban Faber

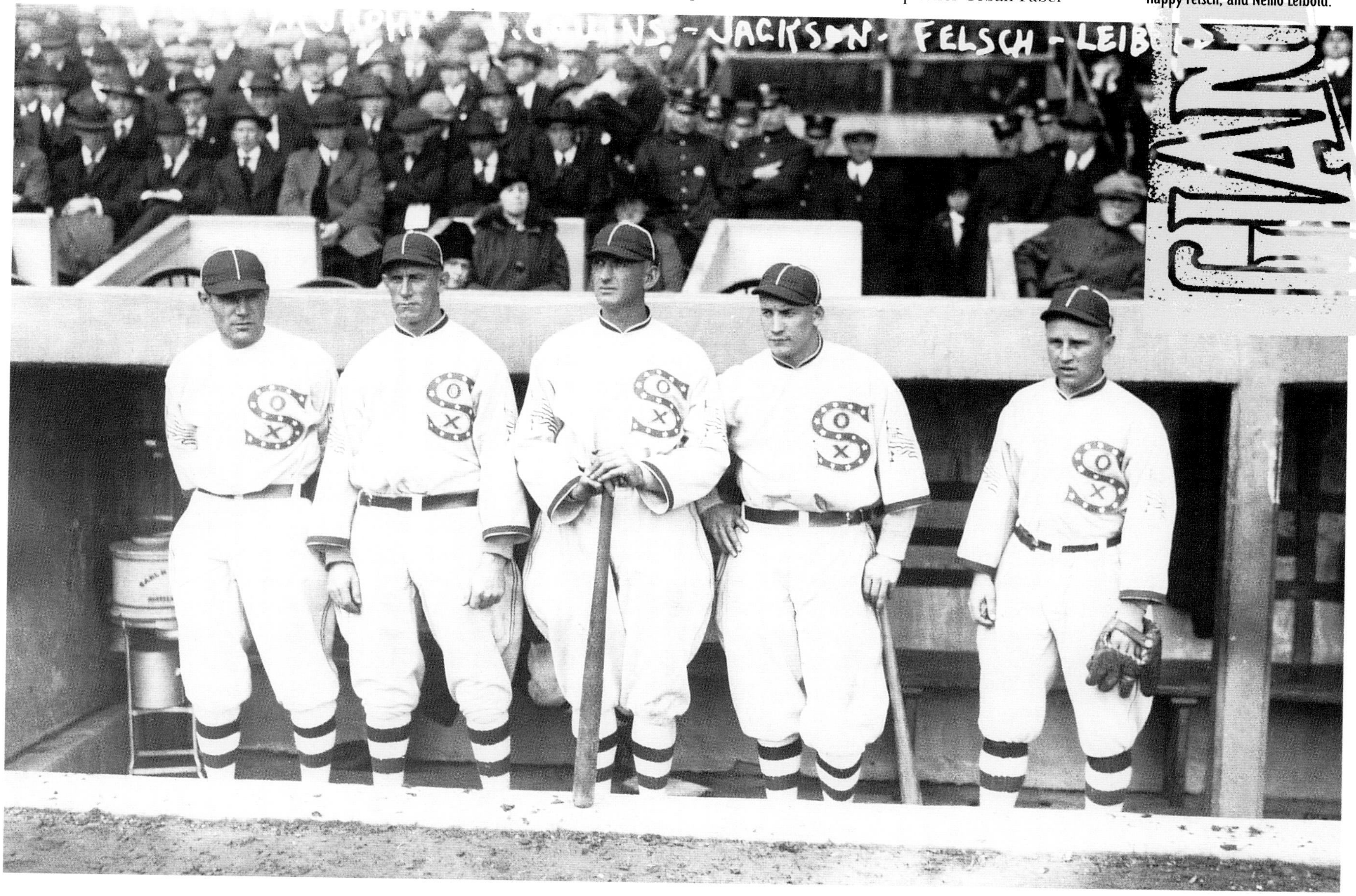

BOTTOM: The White Sox' vaunted outfield poses before the 1917 World Series at Comiskey Park. From left to right are Eddie Murphy, Shano Collins, Shoeless Joe Jackson, Happy Felsch, and Nemo Leibold.

TOP: Heinie Zimmerman was considered the villain of the 1917 World Series.

BOTTOM: Chicago's Red Faber won three games in the 1917 World Series using the spitball, a pitch that was banned after the 1919 season.

scattered eight hits in the 7-2 Chicago victory and also provided the Series' most comical moment when, in the fifth inning, he stole third base—only to find it already occupied by Weaver. Faber, to his humiliation, was tagged out.

The Series moved on to the Polo Grounds, where the Giants, down 2-0, suddenly began to dominate the Series. In Game 3, lefty John "Rube" Benton used his drop ball to beat Chicago 2-0; according to *Baseball Magazine*, Benton "pitched the game of his life, blanking Comiskey's men with almost pathetic ease." McGraw threw another left-hander at the White Sox in Game 4 and the result was the same. This time it was Ferdie Schupp, enjoying the best season of his ten-year major league career, who shut out Chicago 5-0. Most of the Giants' offense came from Kauff, who hit two home runs, one into the right field stands and the other an inside-the-park job over Felsch's head in center field. Game 5 was played the next day in cold and windy conditions at the Polo Grounds. The Giants seemed to have the game "sewed up, sealed, and clinched," leading 4-1 entering the sixth inning, but a tremendous White Sox comeback resulted in an 8-5 Chicago win. The damage was again done by the heart of the White Sox batting order—Collins, Jackson, and Felsch—who collected three hits apiece. McGraw was skewered by the press for leaving his starter, Harry "Slim" Sallee, in the game long enough to give up eight runs and thirteen hits. "When your pitcher is getting thumped steadily, savagely, and harder every inning," William Phelon asked, "why hold him when your lead is growing less every minute?"

The Series returned to the Polo Grounds with the White Sox leading three games to two. Faber, who had won Game 5 in relief, performed masterfully on short rest for Chicago, as the Giants could manage only two runs and six hits off his spitball. Chicago, meanwhile, scored three runs—all it would need—in the fourth inning thanks to New York defensive mistakes. Eddie Collins reached base on a throwing error by Heinie Zimmerman and went to third when right fielder Bill Robertson dropped Joe Jackson's fly ball. Felsch then grounded back to the pitcher, who threw to third base, trapping Collins in a rundown. Zimmerman, the third baseman, threw to catcher Bill Rariden, who threw it back to Zimmerman as Collins danced between them. But Collins, always known for his clever baserunning, managed to slip past the catcher Rariden and run toward home. With nobody covering the plate, the slow-footed Zimmerman had no choice but to run after Collins, chasing him right across the plate. The run gave the Sox a 1-0 lead that they would never relinquish. The White Sox had become world champions for the first time with a 4-2 victory.

The press placed the blame for the Giants' loss squarely on Zimmerman's shoulders. The *New York Times* called the botched rundown "one of the stupidest plays that has ever been seen in a world's series," while *Baseball Magazine* said it was "the greatest bone-play of all time." The play was not even Zimmerman's fault, since there was nobody for him to throw the ball to, but the rest of his Series performance—a .120 batting average and two errors—may have been bad enough for him to merit the goat horns anyway. There were heroes to be celebrated—Faber had won three games in the Series, while Collins had batted .409—but Zimmerman's "bone-play" was the only thing anyone talked about. It was a fitting coda for what one writer called "the worst played series in the history of the annual classic."

1917 WORLD SERIES

Comiskey Park (Chicago White Sox) ◆ 10.6.17

	1	2	3	4	5	6	7	8	9	R	H	E
NYG	0	0	0	0	1	0	0	0	0	1	7	1
Chi.	0	0	1	1	0	0	0	0	X	2	7	1

WP–Cicotte LP–Sallee HR: CHW–Felsch
ATT: 32,000

Comiskey Park ◆ 10.7.17

	1	2	3	4	5	6	7	8	9	R	H	E
NYG	0	2	0	0	0	0	0	0	0	2	8	1
Chi.	0	2	0	5	0	0	0	0	X	7	14	1

WP–Faber LP–Anderson ATT: 32,000

Polo Grounds IV (New York Giants) ◆ 10.10.17

	1	2	3	4	5	6	7	8	9	R	H	E
Chi.	0	0	0	0	0	0	0	0	0	0	5	3
NYG	0	0	0	2	0	0	0	0	X	2	8	2

WP–Benton LP–Cicotte ATT: 33,616

Polo Grounds IV ◆ 10.11.17

	1	2	3	4	5	6	7	8	9	R	H	E
Chi.	0	0	0	0	0	0	0	0	0	0	7	0
NYG	0	0	0	1	1	0	1	2	X	5	10	1

WP–Schupp LP–Faber HR: NYG–Kauff (2)
ATT: 27,746

Comiskey Park ◆ 10.13.17

	1	2	3	4	5	6	7	8	9	R	H	E
NYG	2	0	0	2	0	0	1	0	0	5	12	3
Chi.	0	0	1	0	0	1	3	3	X	8	14	6

WP–Faber LP–Sallee ATT: 27,323

Polo Grounds IV ◆ 10.15.17

	1	2	3	4	5	6	7	8	9	R	H	E
Chi.	0	0	0	3	0	0	0	0	1	4	7	1
NYG	0	0	0	0	2	0	0	0	0	2	6	3

WP–Faber LP–Benton ATT: 33,969

Making The Biggest Calls
World Series Umpires

In baseball's early days, Irving Sanborn wrote, "about the only chance a World's Series umpire has to break into the top of a sport page headline is to break his own head against a pop bottle." Such was the life of a baseball umpire, who risked life and limb to perform a job that usually went unappreciated.

Although regular season games had only one umpire in 1903, the World Series debuted with two: the American League's dignified Tom Connolly and the National's volatile Hank O'Day. Four-man umpiring crews were adopted for the Series in 1908. The number was upped to six in 1947. "Umpiring in a World's Series game is not so hard as at the average big league contest," umpire George Moriarty said in 1921, "for in a World's Series there are four umpires and therefore a greater distribution of work. This permits more careful umpiring and, of course, more accurate umpiring."

Umpires originally received $500 each for their postseason work, but their pay was raised to $750 in 1912. That year featured one of the finest umpiring crews ever to work a World Series: Billy Evans and Francis "Silk" O'Loughlin of the American League, and Bill Klem and Charles "Cy" Rigler of the National. The quartet was roundly praised for their fine work in that hair-raising Series. "From the viewpoint of good umpiring the Series just closed has proven the best in the history of these post-season games," *Sporting Life* wrote. "Not a complaint of any magnitude was made by a manager or player of either team." Klem would eventually umpire in a record 108 Series games.

Players have historically been on their best behavior during the World Series, but there have been a few ugly incidents. "Such kicks are inevitable," a *Baseball Magazine* writer noted, "in a series where everyone is keyed almost to the breaking point by the size of the stakes." White Sox catcher Ray Schalk, not knowing that his teammates were trying to throw the game, was ejected from Game 5 in 1919 after bumping Rigler while arguing a close play at the plate. Senators star Heinie Manush was ejected and fined $50 in 1933 for pushing an ump. After this incident, Commissioner Kenesaw Mountain Landis issued an edict that no player could be ejected from a future Series game without first consulting the commissioner. (This rule was later dropped.) Frank Crosetti got a thirty-game suspension and $250 fine in 1942 for shoving ump Bill Summers during the World Series. Although such physical contact has almost disappeared from modern baseball, Billy Martin, Whitey Herzog, and Joaquin Andujar have all been ejected from World Series games for excessive arguing.

TOP: The 1913 four-man World Series umpire squad—Tom Connolly, John Egan, Bill Klem, and Charles "Cy" Rigler—poses at center. Klem holds the records for working more World Series than any other umpire (18), the highest number of Series games (108), and the most consecutive Fall Classics (5, 1911–1915).

BOTTOM: Umpire Frank W. Umant, who worked four World Series, looks on during Game 4 of the 1972 Series to make sure Oakland A's catcher Gene Tenace—rounding the bases after walloping one of the four round-trippers that helped him win MVP honors during the Fall Classic that year—touches home plate.

At least two umpires have themselves been disciplined for inappropriate World Series conduct. Bill Klem and outfielder Goose Goslin got into a fight in a hotel elevator during the 1934 Series that resulted in a $50 fine for each. George Moriarty was reportedly fined $200 in 1935 for ejecting four men from Game 3 in violation of Landis' prior-approval rule.

The World Series has seen dozens of controversial decisions, including Sam Rice's disputed 1925 catch and the third game of 1922, which was called due to darkness at 4:46 p.m., although the sun was still shining brightly. One of the most famous blown calls in the history of umpiring was Don Denkinger's ruling on Jorge Orta's grounder in the 1985 Series. "I got myself caught in a position nobody likes," Denkinger told historian John Skipper. "I had to depend on watching the foot and listening for the sound of the ball in the glove, but the crowd was so loud I couldn't hear it...When I found out I missed it, I was just sick. But you have to leave it there. It can destroy you if you let it. No one ever missed one intentionally."

Denkinger umpired for thirteen more years, but he never lived down the notoriety of his missed call. For most umpires, working the World Series is an overwhelmingly positive experience, though. "You always remember your first World Series," Laurence "Dutch" Rennert said. "I remember stopping and thinking how this is the only baseball game being played right now, and millions of people are watching."

1918

Boston Red Sox (4)
Chicago Cubs (2)

BASEBALL WAS DEEMED A "NON-ESSENTIAL" industry after the United States entered World War I in 1917, and the U.S. government gave baseball teams until Labor Day to finish the 1918 season. After that, able-bodied players would have to either join the armed forces or get jobs in wartime industry. A few, including Red Sox player-manager Jack Barry and outfielder Duffy Lewis, joined the military during the season anyway. They weren't missed, though, thanks mostly to the 23-year-old Babe Ruth who enjoyed the most unique season in baseball history. With left-fielder Lewis in the Army, new manager Ed Barrow helped Ruth begin the transition from the pitcher's mound to the outfield. The 1918 season was the only one in which he saw significant playing time as both a pitcher and a batter, and the experiment was an unqualified success. Playing three-quarters of his games in the outfield, Ruth hit .300 with an outstanding .411 on-base percentage and tied for his first American League home run title with eleven. As a pitcher he started nineteen games, completing all but one, and finished with a 13-7 record and 2.22 ERA. The Red Sox were an otherwise mediocre team, but with a double threat that had no equal in baseball history, they didn't need much else to win the pennant.

Official Score Card
World's Series 1918
Fenway Park
Boston (Red Sox) American League vs. Chicago (Cubs) National League
Harry H. Frazee, President
Between the Acts
(All Tobacco)
Little Cigars
Price Ten Cents

Their opponents in the World Series were the Chicago Cubs, who in 1918 won their first pennant since the collapse of the Tinker-Evers-Chance dynasty of a decade earlier. Their franchise player, Grover Cleveland Alexander, had entered the Army after pitching only three games. The rest of the team, though hardly household names—their best players included the likes of Charlie Hollocher, Dode Paskert, Les Mann, and Claude Hendrix—thoroughly dominated the National League, leading it in both runs scored and fewest runs allowed.

BOTTOM LEFT: Babe Ruth in 1918 enjoyed the finest two-way season in baseball history, winning 13 games as a pitcher and tying for the league lead in homers as a batter.

BOTTOM RIGHT: Carl Mays, a submarine pitcher with a notoriously nasty disposition, defeated the Cubs twice in the 1918 World Series.

Making The Biggest Calls

WORLD SERIES UMPIRES

In baseball's early days, Irving Sanborn wrote, "about the only chance a World's Series umpire has to break into the top of a sport page headline is to break his own head against a pop bottle." Such was the life of a baseball umpire, who risked life and limb to perform a job that usually went unappreciated.

Although regular season games had only one umpire in 1903, the World Series debuted with two: the American League's dignified Tom Connolly and the National's volatile Hank O'Day. Four-man umpiring crews were adopted for the Series in 1908. The number was upped to six in 1947. "Umpiring in a World's Series game is not so hard as at the average big league contest," umpire George Moriarty said in 1921, "for in a World's Series there are four umpires and therefore a greater distribution of work. This permits more careful umpiring and, of course, more accurate umpiring."

TOP: The 1913 four-man World Series umpire squad—Tom Connolly, John Egan, Bill Klem, and Charles "Cy" Rigler—poses at center. Klem holds the records for working more World Series than any other umpire (18), the highest number of Series games (108), and the most consecutive Fall Classics (5, 1911–1915).

BOTTOM: Umpire Frank W. Umant, who worked four World Series, looks on during Game 4 of the 1972 Series to make sure Oakland A's catcher Gene Tenace—rounding the bases after walloping one of the four round-trippers that helped him win MVP honors during the Fall Classic that year—touches home plate.

Umpires originally received $500 each for their postseason work, but their pay was raised to $750 in 1912. That year featured one of the finest umpiring crews ever to work a World Series: Billy Evans and Francis "Silk" O'Loughlin of the American League, and Bill Klem and Charles "Cy" Rigler of the National. The quartet was roundly praised for their fine work in that hair-raising Series. "From the viewpoint of good umpiring the Series just closed has proven the best in the history of these post-season games," *Sporting Life* wrote. "Not a complaint of any magnitude was made by a manager or player of either team." Klem would eventually umpire in a record 108 Series games.

Players have historically been on their best behavior during the World Series, but there have been a few ugly incidents. "Such kicks are inevitable," a *Baseball Magazine* writer noted, "in a series where everyone is keyed almost to the breaking point by the size of the stakes." White Sox catcher Ray Schalk, not knowing that his teammates were trying to throw the game, was ejected from Game 5 in 1919 after bumping Rigler while arguing a close play at the plate. Senators star Heinie Manush was ejected and fined $50 in 1933 for pushing an ump. After this incident, Commissioner Kenesaw Mountain Landis issued an edict that no player could be ejected from a future Series game without first consulting the commissioner. (This rule was later dropped.) Frank Crosetti got a thirty-game suspension and $250 fine in 1942 for shoving ump Bill Summers during the World Series. Although such physical contact has almost disappeared from modern baseball, Billy Martin, Whitey Herzog, and Joaquin Andujar have all been ejected from World Series games for excessive arguing.

At least two umpires have themselves been disciplined for inappropriate World Series conduct. Bill Klem and outfielder Goose Goslin got into a fight in a hotel elevator during the 1934 Series that resulted in a $50 fine for each. George Moriarty was reportedly fined $200 in 1935 for ejecting four men from Game 3 in violation of Landis' prior-approval rule.

The World Series has seen dozens of controversial decisions, including Sam Rice's disputed 1925 catch and the third game of 1922, which was called due to darkness at 4:46 p.m., although the sun was still shining brightly. One of the most famous blown calls in the history of umpiring was Don Denkinger's ruling on Jorge Orta's grounder in the 1985 Series. "I got myself caught in a position nobody likes," Denkinger told historian John Skipper. "I had to depend on watching the foot and listening for the sound of the ball in the glove, but the crowd was so loud I couldn't hear it...When I found out I missed it, I was just sick. But you have to leave it there. It can destroy you if you let it. No one ever missed one intentionally."

Denkinger umpired for thirteen more years, but he never lived down the notoriety of his missed call. For most umpires, working the World Series is an overwhelmingly positive experience, though. "You always remember your first World Series," Laurence "Dutch" Rennert said. "I remember stopping and thinking how this is the only baseball game being played right now, and millions of people are watching."

1918

Boston Red Sox (4)
Chicago Cubs (2)

BASEBALL WAS DEEMED A "NON-ESSENTIAL" industry after the United States entered World War I in 1917, and the U.S. government gave baseball teams until Labor Day to finish the 1918 season. After that, able-bodied players would have to either join the armed forces or get jobs in wartime industry. A few, including Red Sox player-manager Jack Barry and outfielder Duffy Lewis, joined the military during the season anyway. They weren't missed, though, thanks mostly to the 23-year-old Babe Ruth who enjoyed the most unique season in baseball history. With left-fielder Lewis in the Army, new manager Ed Barrow helped Ruth begin the transition from the pitcher's mound to the outfield. The 1918 season was the only one in which he saw significant playing time as both a pitcher and a batter, and the experiment was an unqualified success. Playing three-quarters of his games in the outfield, Ruth hit .300 with an outstanding .411 on-base percentage and tied for his first American League home run title with eleven. As a pitcher he started nineteen games, completing all but one, and finished with a 13-7 record and 2.22 ERA. The Red Sox were an otherwise mediocre team, but with a double threat that had no equal in baseball history, they didn't need much else to win the pennant.

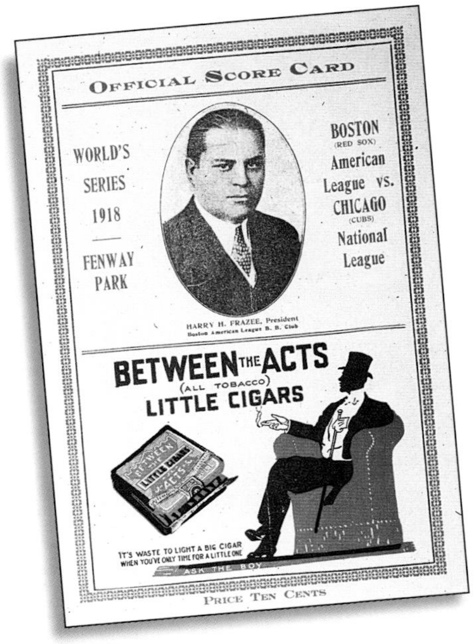

Their opponents in the World Series were the Chicago Cubs, who in 1918 won their first pennant since the collapse of the Tinker-Evers-Chance dynasty of a decade earlier. Their franchise player, Grover Cleveland Alexander, had entered the Army after pitching only three games. The rest of the team, though hardly household names—their best players included the likes of Charlie Hollocher, Dode Paskert, Les Mann, and Claude Hendrix—thoroughly dominated the National League, leading it in both runs scored and fewest runs allowed.

BOTTOM LEFT: Babe Ruth in 1918 enjoyed the finest two-way season in baseball history, winning 13 games as a pitcher and tying for the league lead in homers as a batter.

BOTTOM RIGHT: Carl Mays, a submarine pitcher with a notoriously nasty disposition, defeated the Cubs twice in the 1918 World Series.

Though Ruth was now arguably the best hitter in baseball—the only other candidate being Ty Cobb—the Red Sox chose to use him solely as a pitcher in the Series, which may have been prompted by the Cubs' decision to start only left-handed pitchers in the Series as protection against him. Ruth pitched a shutout in the first game, narrowly beating James "Hippo" Vaughn, 1-0, and the Cubs evened it up the next day as pitcher George "Lefty" Tyler silenced the Red Sox' bats while driving in two runs himself. In Game 3, Carl Mays' "curious, freakish underhand pitching had the Cubs crazy," as Boston beat the hard-luck Hippo Vaughn, 2-1. The difference in that game was made by 35-year-old rookie George Whiteman, who made a stunning catch of a would-be homer by Chicago's Dode Paskert. "Whiteman ran, and galloped, and, when tired of galloping, ran some more," *Baseball Magazine* wrote. "He had no more license to catch that ball than the Kaiser has to call himself a gentleman." The game ended when, with two outs in the ninth, little-used Cubs infielder Charlie Pick was thrown out trying to score from second on a passed ball.

It was Ruth's turn to start in the fourth game, though he was forced to pitch with an injured middle finger on his pitching hand, sustained when he got into a scuffle with teammate Walt Kinney on the team train to Boston. It didn't hurt him at the plate, as he used his black bat—a much-commented-on novelty—to smash a two-run triple. He also pitched well, holding Chicago scoreless until the eighth inning, when the Cubs tied it with a pair of runs. The tallies ended Ruth's World Series scoreless streak at 29⅔ innings, a record which stood for nearly half a century until broken by Edward "Whitey" Ford in 1961. The Red Sox took the lead back in the bottom of the eighth on a throwing error by pitcher Phil Douglas and won the game 3-2.

Vaughn, after two hard-luck losses, finally got a win in Game 5. He pitched a shutout as the Cubs won 3-0. The next day, with Chicago still facing elimination, they sent Tyler to the hill to face Mays. Both men performed brilliantly, but the Cubs' Max Flack dropped a fly ball in the third inning that allowed two Red Sox to score. Those turned out to be the only runs Boston scored in the game, but it was all they would need, as Mays won 2-1 to clinch the championship. Whiteman had made another remarkable catch in the final game, diving to snag a low line drive, and he was hailed as the hero of the Series despite batting only .250. It was a Series filled with great pitching performances and stunning defense by the Red Sox, who committed just one error in the six games, an unprecedented feat. The teams combined to score only nineteen runs in the Series, and the Red Sox' .186 team batting average was the worst ever for a World Series winner. It is tempting to speculate that Boston would have won even more convincingly had they used Ruth as a hitter, but it mattered little, as the Red Sox had their fifth world championship. They have yet to win another to this day.

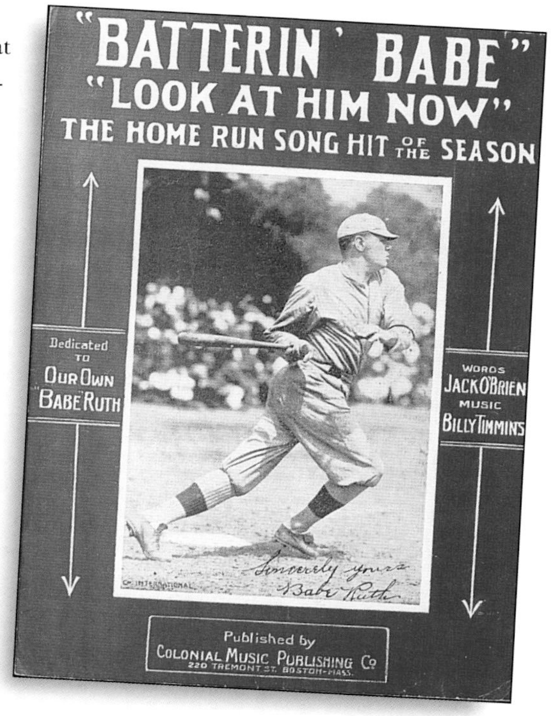

1918 WORLD SERIES

COMISKEY PARK (CHICAGO CUBS) ◆ 9.5.18

	1	2	3	4	5	6	7	8	9	R	H	E
Boston	0	0	0	1	0	0	0	0	0	1	5	0
Chi.	0	0	0	0	0	0	0	0	0	0	6	0

WP–Ruth LP–Vaughn ATT: 19,274

COMISKEY PARK ◆ 9.6.18

	1	2	3	4	5	6	7	8	9	R	H	E
Boston	0	0	0	0	0	0	0	0	1	1	6	1
Chi.	0	3	0	0	0	0	0	0	X	3	7	1

WP–Tyler LP–Bush ATT: 20,040

COMISKEY PARK ◆ 9.7.18

	1	2	3	4	5	6	7	8	9	R	H	E
Boston	0	0	0	2	0	0	0	0	0	2	7	0
Chi.	0	0	0	0	1	0	0	0	0	1	7	1

WP–Mays LP–Vaughn ATT: 27,054

FENWAY PARK I (BOSTON RED SOX) ◆ 9.9.18

	1	2	3	4	5	6	7	8	9	R	H	E
Chi.	0	0	0	0	0	0	0	2	0	2	7	1
Boston	0	0	0	2	0	0	0	1	X	3	4	0

WP–Ruth LP–Douglas S–Bush ATT: 22,183

FENWAY PARK I ◆ 9.10.18

	1	2	3	4	5	6	7	8	9	R	H	E
Chi.	0	0	1	0	0	0	0	2	0	3	7	0
Boston	0	0	0	0	0	0	0	0	0	0	5	0

WP–Vaughn LP–Jones ATT: 24,694

FENWAY PARK I ◆ 9.11.18

	1	2	3	4	5	6	7	8	9	R	H	E
Chi.	0	0	0	1	0	0	0	0	0	1	3	2
Boston	0	0	2	0	0	0	0	0	X	2	5	0

WP–Mays LP–Tyler ATT: 15,238

BOTTOM: The Cubs' Fred Merkle (in dark uniform) is called out at third base on an attempted sacrifice in Game 2 of the 1918 World Series.

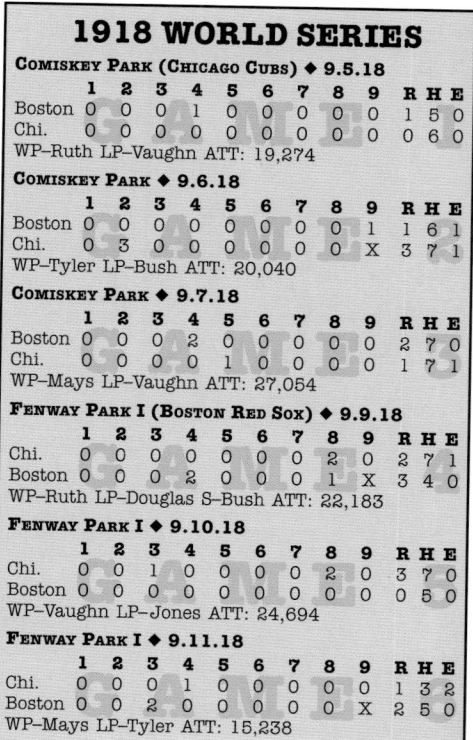

1919

Cincinnati Reds (5)

Chicago White Sox (3)

The story reads like a cheap dimestore novel—if the evidence hadn't been so overwhelming, nobody would have ever believed it. In the autumn of 1919, seven members of the American League champion Chicago White Sox conspired with a motley crew of gamblers, hoods, ex-players, and other shady characters to throw the best-of-nine World Series to the Cincinnati Reds. For more than a year, they managed to keep the truth more or less under wraps, until it erupted in September 1920 as the greatest scandal in the history of the sport.

The White Sox were owned by Charles Comiskey, a tyrant who regarded his players as chattel. He paid the lowest wages in the game, reneged on promises, and deducted nickel-and-dime expenses like laundry fees from their paychecks. When the team responded by refusing to wash their uniforms unless Comiskey paid for it, the press dubbed them the "Black Sox." Traditional baseball history tells that the White Sox were a juggernaut, a dominant team that would have swept the Series easily if only they had tried. In

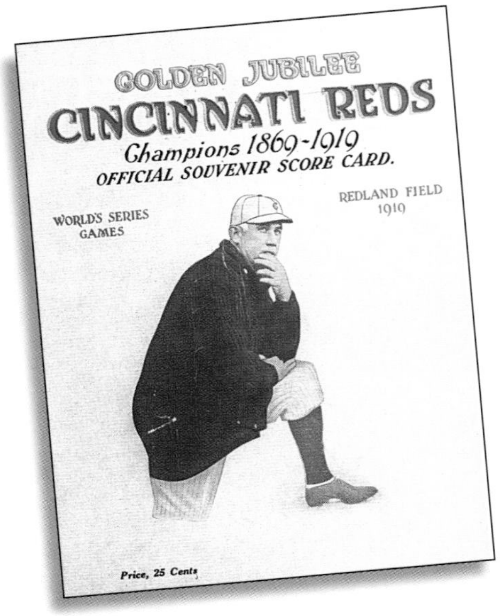

truth, the White Sox were far from a great team. They finished the regular season with a .629 winning percentage, a figure which in seven of the previous ten seasons would not even have been good enough to win the pennant. The White Sox were the favorites in the Series, at 8-5 odds, not because they were a great team, but simply because they played in the superior American League, whose teams had won eight of the last nine Series with only the unexpected 1914 Braves interrupting the streak.

To understand the fix, though, one must understand the era. In 1919, the World Series was not yet the *World Series.* It was not a sacrosanct, mythical event. It was not watched by millions on national television. It was simply a way for team owners to make a few extra bucks at the end of the season and for players to determine the next year's bragging rights. In addition, the idea of gamblers meddling in baseball was neither new nor shocking. In 1877, four Louisville players had been banned for life when they conspired to lose the National League pennant. In 1903, gamblers had supposedly tried to fix the first World Series ever played, although Cy Young and Lou Criger turned down their bribes. Every year, allegations of game fixing were made against someone, somewhere. It was simply part of the game.

Angry at Comiskey and longing to be paid what they were really worth, the White Sox decided to get their money another way. They made deals with two different gambling syndicates, one for $80,000 and the other for $100,000, to lose the World Series on purpose. One of the groups was bankrolled by Arnold Rothstein, the nation's most famous gambler, a man so notorious that he later ended up as a character in *The Great Gatsby.* Seven players agreed to throw the Series:

Eddie Cicotte, 35, best pitcher in the American League, whose "shine ball" helped him to a record of 29-7.

Arnold "Chick" Gandil, 32, slick-fielding first baseman, nothing special at the plate,

CLAUDE
WILLIAMS
Southpaw twirler of the Sox,

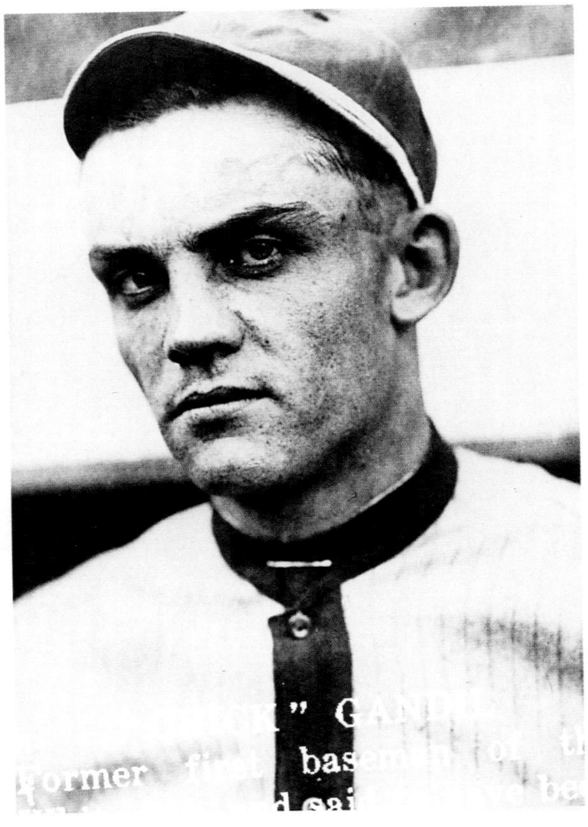

"BUCK"
WEAVER
Third baseman

who masterminded the scheme on the players' behalf.

"SHOELESS" JOE JACKSON, 30, one of the greatest sluggers in the game, whose .356 career batting average ranks third all-time.

OSCAR "HAPPY" FELSCH, 28, hard-hitting center fielder noted for his conspicuous lack of intelligence.

FRED MCMULLIN, 27, seldom-used utility infielder who found out about the fix and demanded to be included.

CLAUDE "LEFTY" WILLIAMS, 26, journeyman pitcher who enjoyed his best season in 1919.

CHARLES "SWEDE" RISBERG, 24, shortstop who was both a bad hitter and a bad fielder.

An eighth player, star third baseman Buck Weaver, sat in on the conspirators' meetings but declined to participate in the fix. The plot was a chaotic disaster from day one as gamblers double-crossed other gamblers, gamblers double-crossed players, players double-crossed gamblers, and players double-crossed players. It seemed as if everybody knew about the fix as the opening game approached. Gamblers told other gamblers, who told other gamblers. Players told their friends to bet on the Reds. Word quickly leaked back to the press, to Comiskey, and to the White Sox manager, William "Kid" Gleason, that something wasn't right. But nobody wanted to be the first to speak up.

Cicotte hit Morrie Rath with the second pitch of Game 1 as a signal to Rothstein that the fix was on. After that, Cicotte wasn't subtle about throwing the game. He threw high to second base on a double play in the fourth inning. He gave up a double to the pitcher, then another double, then a single. After retiring only eleven batters, Cicotte was removed from the game trailing 6-1. It was Williams' turn in Game 2. Though usually a master of pinpoint control, he walked three batters in the fourth inning, then hung a curveball to the Reds' Larry Kopf, who hit a triple. That alone was enough for the Reds, who won it 4-2.

The players had not received most of the money promised them after losing the first two games, so some of them resolved to play the Series honestly until the gamblers had paid them in full. Rookie Dickie Kerr started Game 3 at Comiskey Park. The 5′7″ lefty pitched the game of his life, holding the Reds to three hits as every ground ball seemed to find its way to a fielder. Even Gandil had a two-run single as the White Sox triumphed, 3-0.

The gamblers delivered $20,000 more before Game 4, and with Cicotte pitching, the fix was on again. With the game scoreless in the top of the fifth, it was time for Cicotte to go to work. He began with a wild throw to first on a comebacker. Then came a base hit to left field with a runner on second. Jackson made a strong throw to the plate that would have gotten the runner out, but Cicotte cut the ball off. The next batter hit a double over Jackson's head and the Reds had all the runs they would need as Cicotte gift-wrapped both runs in the 2-0 loss.

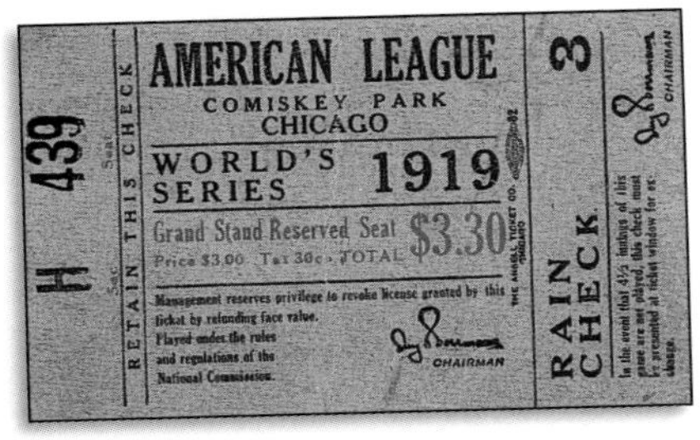

Williams pitched brilliantly in Game 5, allowing only one hit in the first five innings, but with the game still scoreless in the sixth, the White Sox set to work throwing the game. A fly ball fell between Jackson and Felsch, and Felsch made a poor throw back to the infield. Then Williams walked a batter. Next, Edd Roush hit a deep fly over Felsch's head in center field that Felsch pretended to have problems with, zigging and zagging before finally letting it hit his glove and drop to the ground. The triple scored two runs, and Roush himself scored a moment later on a sacrifice fly as Cincinnati won 5-0. The White Sox hadn't scored a run in their last 22 innings at the plate.

Kerr pitched Game 6 with the Series back in Cincinnati and the White Sox now facing elimination. And when the gamblers failed to come through with another payment, the rest of the White Sox played to

EDWARD CICOTTE,
Once premier pitcher of the White Sox, but now suspended from the team for crooked playing. He has confessed that he received $10,000

JOE JACKSON (right),
Sox outfielder,

THESE PAGES: Six of the eight men on the 1919 Chicago White Sox whose lack of judgment would make them the most notorious lineup in World Series history. When the scandal surrounding the 1919 fix finally broke nearly a year later, the eight players were drummed out of baseball for life by the newly appointed commissioner of baseball, Kenesaw Mountain Landis, despite the fact that a jury had acquitted the men in a court of law.

win, too. Kerr couldn't match the brilliance of his Game 3 performance, but he pitched well enough to keep the game tied 4-4 after nine innings. Weaver and Jackson then opened the tenth inning with hits and Gandil won the game with an RBI single.

Rumors of the fix, combined with considerable traffic problems in Cincinnati, led to Redland Field being less than half full for Game 7. This time the Reds looked as if they were the ones trying to throw the Series, committing four errors and making other less-than-stellar plays. The White Sox scored four runs, two of them earned, as Jackson, Felsch, Eddie Collins, and John "Shano" Collins all had multi-hit games. And Cicotte, pitching to win for the first time, pitched a complete game victory. Chicago won 4-1, and trailed in the Series by just four games to three.

Now, the gamblers were getting nervous, as it looked as if Chicago might come back to win the Series. There was every indication that Williams planned on pitching to win Game 8, too. Rothstein had to ensure otherwise, so he talked to Sport Sullivan, the man who was handling the fix for him. Sullivan, in turn, hired a man named Harry F. to visit Williams the night before the game and relay the message that unless Williams lost the game convincingly in the first inning, his wife would be harmed. Williams retired the first batter he faced, but then gave up a single to Jake Daubert. Then another single. Then a double. Then another double. Gleason had seen enough. He pulled Williams from the game after pitching to only five batters. It was too late, though. The game, and the Series, were already lost.

CHARLES COMISKEY
Owner of the White Sox, who promptly suspended the members of the team involved in the baseball scandal. He was

TOP LEFT: Kenesaw Mountain Landis, named after a Civil War battle in which his father had lost a leg, was hired as baseball commissioner after a long career as a publicity-seeking judge.

TOP RIGHT: Charles Comiskey, owner of the White Sox, had once been a star player himself, but by 1919 he was doing everything he could to take advantage of the ballplayers he employed.

BOTTOM: After laying down a sacrifice bunt in Game 1, Edd Roush was safe at first when the throw from Buck Weaver was dropped—probably on purpose—by first baseman Chick Gandil.

1919 WORLD SERIES

Redland Field (Cincinnati Reds) ◆ 10.1.19

	1	2	3	4	5	6	7	8	9	R	H	E
Chi.	0	1	0	0	0	0	0	0	0	1	6	1
Cin.	1	0	0	5	0	0	2	1	X	9	14	1

WP–Ruether LP–Cicotte ATT: 30,511

Redland Field ◆ 10.2.19

	1	2	3	4	5	6	7	8	9	R	H	E
Chi.	0	0	0	0	0	0	2	0	0	2	10	1
Cin.	0	0	0	3	0	1	0	0	X	4	4	2

WP–Sallee LP–Williams ATT: 29,690

Comiskey Park (Chicago White Sox) ◆ 10.3.19

	1	2	3	4	5	6	7	8	9	R	H	E
Cin.	0	0	0	0	0	0	0	0	0	0	3	1
Chi.	0	2	0	1	0	0	0	0	X	3	7	0

WP–Kerr LP–Fisher ATT: 29,126

Comiskey Park ◆ 10.4.19

	1	2	3	4	5	6	7	8	9	R	H	E
Cin.	0	0	0	0	2	0	0	0	0	2	5	2
Chi.	0	0	0	0	0	0	0	0	0	0	3	2

WP–Ring LP–Cicotte ATT: 34,363

Comiskey Park ◆ 10.6.19

	1	2	3	4	5	6	7	8	9	R	H	E
Cin.	0	0	0	0	0	4	0	0	1	5	4	0
Chi.	0	0	0	0	0	0	0	0	0	0	3	3

WP–Eller LP–Williams ATT: 34,379

Redland Field ◆ 10.7.19

	1	2	3	4	5	6	7	8	9	10	R	H	E
Chi.	0	0	0	0	1	3	0	0	0	1	5	10	3
Cin.	0	0	2	2	0	0	0	0	0	0	4	11	0

WP–Kerr LP–Ring ATT: 32,006

Redland Field ◆ 10.8.19

	1	2	3	4	5	6	7	8	9	R	H	E
Chi.	1	0	1	0	2	0	0	0	0	4	10	1
Cin.	0	0	0	0	0	1	0	0	0	1	7	4

WP–Cicotte LP–Sallee ATT: 13,923

Comiskey Park ◆ 10.9.19

	1	2	3	4	5	6	7	8	9	R	H	E
Cin.	4	1	0	0	1	3	0	1	0	10	16	2
Chi.	0	0	1	0	0	0	0	4	0	5	10	1

WP–Eller LP–Williams HR: CHW–Jackson
ATT: 32,930

The Series fix was the nation's worst-kept secret during the off-season. Sportswriter Hugh Fullerton accused the players of crookedness in a series of articles beginning in December 1919, but nobody took him seriously. Still, whispers were everywhere. Finally, in September 1920, nearly a year after it happened, several players admitted the Series fix to the press and the public. Eight players—the seven conspirators, plus Weaver—were indicted by a grand jury in Chicago, and were suspended for the remainder of the 1920 season. Comiskey, who was afraid that losing his best players to suspension would result in bankruptcy for his team, conducted a sham investigation of his own. He probably also tampered with the court proceedings, as the players' confessions to the grand jury mysteriously disappeared.

Defended at trial by Comiskey's lawyers, the eight players were acquitted by a jury. But the other team owners wanted to project a new image of law and order. They hired an independent-minded, authoritarian Federal judge named Kenesaw Mountain Landis to serve as the game's first commissioner, governing all aspects of major league baseball. Given a lifetime appointment to the office, Landis' first order of business was to announce that, "regardless of the verdict of juries," the eight players were guilty and would be banished for life. It was a harsh step, especially in Weaver's case, but it worked. Almost immediately, baseball regained the nation's trust and held on to its status as the nation's pastime.

Although films and books would later romanticize Jackson's role in the scandal, the facts are clear: He accepted money to throw the Series. He also confessed to throwing the Series. His supporters point to the fact that he batted .375, hit the only home run of the Series, and tied a record with his twelve hits. But eight of the twelve hits came in the games—3, 6, 7, and 8—that Jackson was presumably trying to win. In the games that the seven players agreed to fix, he went 4-for-16 and was involved in several questionable defensive plays. Although it is possible that Jackson was playing to win, the evidence does not support this idea.

In other words, it ain't so that it ain't so.

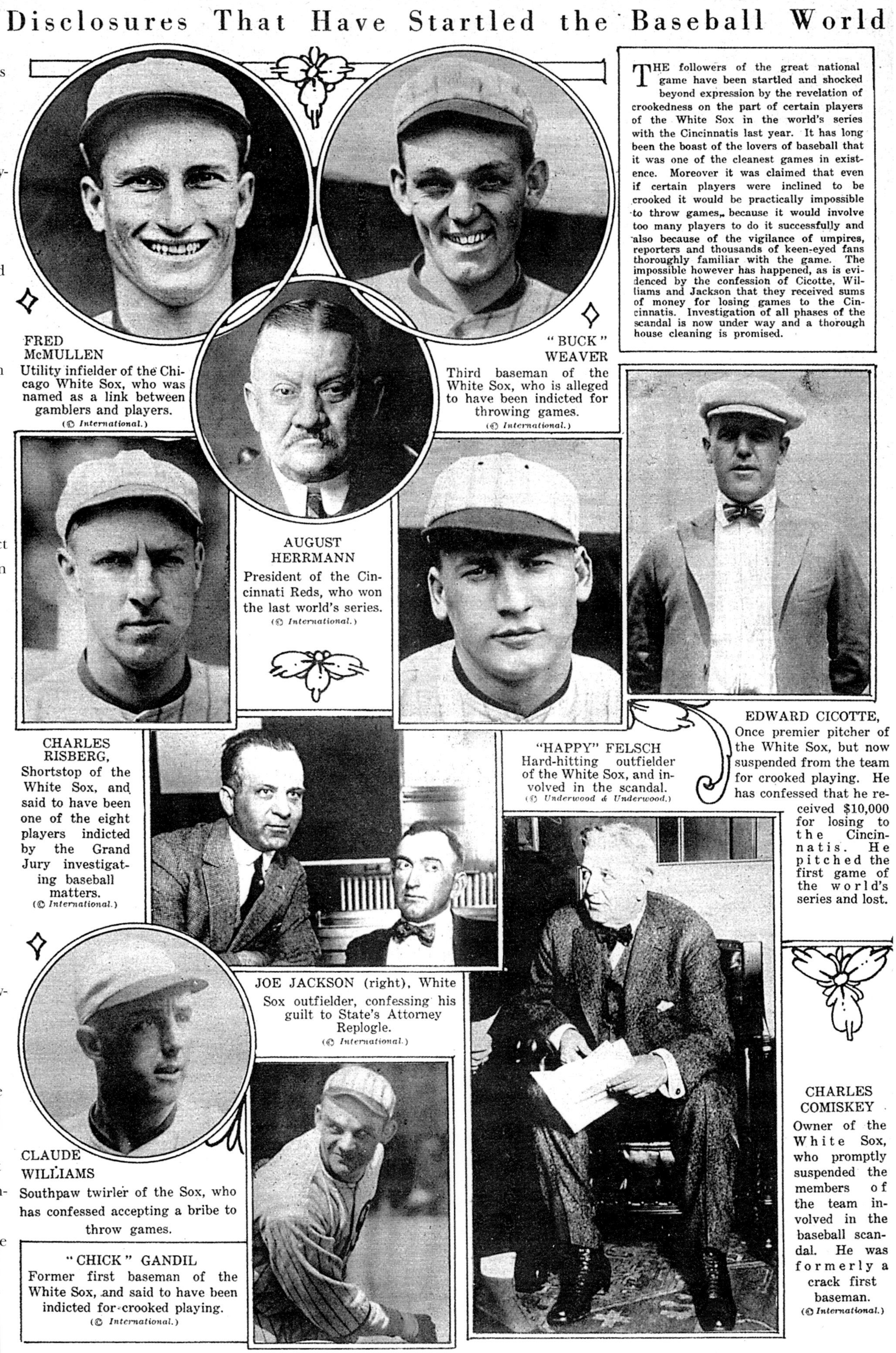

Disclosures That Have Startled the Baseball World

THE followers of the great national game have been startled and shocked beyond expression by the revelation of crookedness on the part of certain players of the White Sox in the world's series with the Cincinnatis last year. It has long been the boast of the lovers of baseball that it was one of the cleanest games in existence. Moreover it was claimed that even if certain players were inclined to be crooked it would be practically impossible to throw games, because it would involve too many players to do it successfully and also because of the vigilance of umpires, reporters and thousands of keen-eyed fans thoroughly familiar with the game. The impossible however has happened, as is evidenced by the confession of Cicotte, Williams and Jackson that they received sums of money for losing games to the Cincinnatis. Investigation of all phases of the scandal is now under way and a thorough house cleaning is promised.

FRED McMULLEN
Utility infielder of the Chicago White Sox, who was named as a link between gamblers and players.
(© International.)

"BUCK" WEAVER
Third baseman of the White Sox, who is alleged to have been indicted for throwing games.
(© International.)

AUGUST HERRMANN
President of the Cincinnati Reds, who won the last world's series.
(© International.)

CHARLES RISBERG,
Shortstop of the White Sox, and said to have been one of the eight players indicted by the Grand Jury investigating baseball matters.
(© International.)

"HAPPY" FELSCH
Hard-hitting outfielder of the White Sox, and involved in the scandal.
(© Underwood & Underwood.)

EDWARD CICOTTE,
Once premier pitcher of the White Sox, but now suspended from the team for crooked playing. He has confessed that he received $10,000 for losing to the Cincinnatis. He pitched the first game of the world's series and lost.

JOE JACKSON (right), White Sox outfielder, confessing his guilt to State's Attorney Replogle.
(© International.)

CLAUDE WILLIAMS
Southpaw twirler of the Sox, who has confessed accepting a bribe to throw games.

"CHICK" GANDIL
Former first baseman of the White Sox, and said to have been indicted for crooked playing.
(© International.)

CHARLES COMISKEY
Owner of the White Sox, who promptly suspended the members of the team involved in the baseball scandal. He was formerly a crack first baseman.
(© International.)

CHAPTER 2

BASEBALL BETWEEN THE WARS

1920–1945

THE WORLD SERIES CAME OF AGE BETWEEN 1920 AND 1945. IN 1920, MOST of the fans who cared about major league baseball were clustered in the northeastern sector of the United States. By the mid-1940s, millions of people across the country were listening to the World Series on the radio, and American soldiers were watching the highlights on film in places like Germany and Guam.

At the beginning of the era, the credibility of baseball in general, and the World Series in particular, was in doubt due to the Black Sox scandal. By the end of the period, it was so firmly entrenched as the National Pastime that it was declared an important part of the war effort by President Franklin D. Roosevelt. "If 300 teams use 5,000 or 6,000 players, these players are a definite recreational asset to at least 20,000,000 of their fellow citizens," Roosevelt wrote in a letter to commissioner Landis, "and that in my judgment is thoroughly worthwhile."

The period between the wars was the last era of successful player-managers in baseball, as twelve of the fifty-two World Series teams in the period were managed by active players. (On the other hand, nine were also managed by Joe McCarthy, who never played in the major leagues.)

Although it may seem as if the New York Yankees have thoroughly dominated the last eighty years of baseball, that is not really the case. There have actually been five distinct periods of Yankee dominance, with slight lulls in between each. Each period can be identified by its most prominent manager: the Miller Huggins period (1921–28); the Joe McCarthy period (1932–43); the Casey Stengel period (1947–64); the Billy Martin period (1976–81); and the Joe Torre period (1996–2002). Of these, the McCarthy period was arguably the most impressive. Over the eight-year period from 1936–43, McCarthy's Yankees averaged 100 wins per year while posting a remarkable 25-9 record in World Series play. The strength of the team was its hitting, arguably the best in baseball history. In 1939, for example, four Yankee outfielders—Joe DiMaggio, Tommy Henrich, Charlie Keller, and George Selkirk—split the playing time equally, batting a collective .328 with 367 RBI and a remarkable .433 on-base percentage. For much of the era between the wars, the question was not which teams would play in the World Series, but which team would lose to the Yankees in the World Series.

McQUAY-NORRIS
Greater St. Louis
WAR CHEST
October 5TH-31ST
HYDE PARK True Lager BEER
Courtesy of HYDE PARK BREWERIES ASS'N. INC. AND FALSTAFF BREWING CORPOR
GEM SINGLEDGE BLADES
BATTER
BALL STRIKE
OUT
UMPIRES
SOLD
GOOD TASTE SUGGESTS
Mavrakos Candies
7 STORES IN ST. LOUIS
Alpen Brau
IT'S THE TOPS-ENJOY IT...
COLD

1920

CLEVELAND INDIANS (5)
BROOKLYN DODGERS (2)

PREVIOUS PAGES: Seen here on October 4, opening day of the 1944 World Series, Sportsman's Park in St. Louis is packed with fans. Hurling for the Browns at the top of the first inning is Denny Galehouse, who faces Cardinals first baseman Ray Sanders at the plate. Baseball was still very much on the minds of Americans during World War II, despite the fact that many of the game's biggest stars were serving in their nation's military overseas.

BOTTOM LEFT: Indians player-manager Tris Speaker posted a .483 on-base percentage in 1920, which at the time ranked as the second-best mark in A.L. history.

BOTTOM RIGHT: Cleveland second baseman Bill Wambsganss (known to teammates as "Wamby") tags Otto Miller to complete the only unassisted triple play in World Series history.

WITH THE NATION AT LARGE GEARING UP for the Roaring '20s, baseball breathlessly entered a new era of its own in 1920, as sweeping and unprecedented events changed both the way the game was played and the way it was perceived. Outside the major league arena, a group of businessmen met at the Kansas City (Missouri) YMCA on February 13 to form the Negro National League, the first formally organized Negro league. The major leagues, meanwhile, formally banned the spitball, shine ball, emery ball, and other trick pitches, although each team was allowed to designate two pitchers who could continue using them. On July 19, new Yankee Babe Ruth became the first player in major league history to hit thirty home runs in a season. On August 16, he became the first ever to hit forty. On September 24, he became the first ever to hit fifty. Ruth ended the season with 54 homers, nearly doubling the previous record (which he also held) and ushering in a new era of power hitting. On August 16, with the Yankees facing the Indians at the Polo Grounds, Cleveland shortstop Ray Chapman was killed after being hit by a pitch from submarine pitcher Carl Mays, a notorious headhunter. It remains the only on-field death in major league history. In September, after nearly a year of being a poorly kept secret, news of the Black Sox scandal leaked to the press and the public. On September 28, with the White Sox half a game out of first place and only three games left in the season, the players who threw the 1919 Series were indicted. All were immediately suspended. On October 7, seeking to purify baseball's tainted public image, the owners hired Kenesaw Mountain Landis as commissioner.

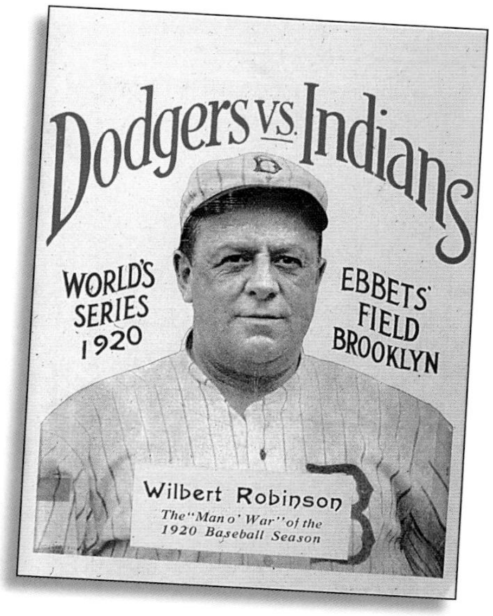

Dodgers vs. Indians
WORLD'S SERIES 1920
EBBETS' FIELD BROOKLYN
Wilbert Robinson
The "Man o' War" of the 1920 Baseball Season

Amidst the changing baseball world, the American League in 1920 featured one of the greatest three-way pennant races of all time, with Ruth's Yankees and the decimated Black Sox narrowly losing out to the Cleveland Indians. Despite losing their star shortstop in the middle of the pennant race, the Indians made it to the World Series anyway on the shoulders of two unlikely rookies. Joe Sewell, who had never even seen a major league game before, was purchased from the New Orleans Pelicans on September 11 to replace Chapman at shortstop. Although he fielded poorly, Sewell batted .329 with twelve RBI in his 22 games, ably filling Chapman's shoes. Walter Mails made an even bigger impact after the young left-handed pitcher was acquired from the Pacific Coast League in August. "Get me someone," manager Tris Speaker told the front office shortly after Chapman's death. "Get me anyone who wasn't here when Chappie got it. Get me that big Mails from Portland." Mails, nicknamed "Duster" for his frequent brushback pitches, posted a 7-0 record and 1.85 ERA during September, almost single-handedly winning the pennant for the Indians.

The two dazzling rookies were not all Cleveland had to offer, though. Their man-

Wambsganss, the second baseman of the Cleveland team, completing his wonderful triple play by touching out Miller near second base in the fifth inning of the fifth game of the world's series at Cleveland Oct. 10. A triple play is one of the rarest things in baseball, and it had never before been accomplished in a world's series game. Kilduff was on second and Miller on first, both having made clean hits. Mitchell sent a smoking drive that Wambsganss had to go

ager, Speaker, was also the league's best player outside of Ruth, batting .388 and throwing out 24 men from center field. The rest of the lineup was rock solid, with catcher Steve O'Neill, third baseman Larry Gardner, and outfielders Elmer Smith and Charlie Jamieson all batting over .300. The Indians worried that Sewell would not be eligible to play in the World Series because of a rule, still in existence today, that bars players who joined their club after September 1 from playing in the Series. But the Indians' Series opponents, the Brooklyn Robins, agreed to a special exception because of Chapman's death, and Sewell was allowed to play. The Robins, winners of 93 games on their way to the National League pennant, were nothing special offensively but boasted the best pitching staff in baseball, led by spitballer Burleigh Grimes and southpaw Sherry Smith. The Dodgers' team ERA of 2.62 was by far the best in baseball, but to everyone's surprise, manager Wilbert Robinson picked his worst pitcher, Rube Marquard, to start Game 1 of the best-of-nine World Series. It was an odd choice, and Marquard, who had been both hero and goat in three previous Series appearances, didn't help matters by getting arrested on the day of the opening after police caught him trying to scalp his complementary Series tickets for $350. He was released in time to pitch the game, but Brooklyn fans later wished he had stayed incarcerated, as he gave up two early runs en route to a 3-1 loss. Stan Coveleski, winner of 24 games during the regular season, picked up the win for the Indians.

The Dodgers bounced back in the second game, winning 3-0 thanks to Grimes, who pitched a shutout, and Zack Wheat, who made an outstanding catch to rob Wheeler "Doc" Johnston of an apparent homer. The Robins struck first the next day, too, as Indians starter Ray Caldwell was knocked out after getting only one out in the first inning. Duster Mails came in to pitch almost seven innings of shutout relief, but the damage had been done. Sherry Smith pitched a fine game for Brooklyn, winning 2-1.

Now down two games to one, the Indians returned home looking to tie the Series in Game 4 and did exactly that, as Coveleski won a 5-1 decision with help from Speaker and Sewell, who collected two hits apiece. Then came Game 5, one of the most unusual games in World Series history. In the first inning, the Indians loaded the bases for Elmer Smith, whose twelve home runs had ranked fifth in the league during the regular season. Grimes, the 23-game winner on the mound for Brooklyn, had two favored pitches: the fastball and the spitball. The Indians had noticed that second baseman Pete Kilduff was tipping the pitches, and every time Grimes was going to throw a spitball, Kilduff would grab a handful of dirt from the infield and then let it go, so that if the wet ball was hit to him it would not slip away. With two strikes, Smith watched Kilduff, and he knew a fastball was coming. Smith took his mightiest swing and sent the pitch over the right field fence for the first grand slam in World Series history. That wasn't all for the Indians, though. Cleveland pitcher Jim Bagby homered off Grimes in the fourth inning, becoming the first pitcher to ever hit a home run in the World Series.

Twice in the game, the Indians had done something never before accomplished in the World Series—but there was more to come. With men on first and second in the fifth inning, Brooklyn pitcher Clarence Mitchell, a .252 career hitter, came up to bat. The Indians knew he was a dead pull hitter and played him accordingly. The runners took off from their bases with the 3-2 pitch and Mitchell hit a line drive over the head of second baseman Bill Wambsganss, who leaped to his right and caught it. *One out.* With his momentum carrying him toward second base, Wambsganss stepped on the bag to double off Pete Kilduff. *Two outs.* Then Wambsganss turned around and looked to his left. "Well, Otto Miller, from first base, was just standing there with his mouth open, no more than a few feet away from me. I simply took a step or two over and touched him lightly on the right shoulder, and that was it." *Three outs.* Wambsganss had completed only the third unassisted triple play in baseball history, and the first in the World Series. "It took place so suddenly that most of the fans didn't know what had happened," Wambsganss told writer Larry Ritter. "They had to stop and figure out just how many were out. So there was dead silence for a few seconds. Then, as I approached the dugout, it began to dawn on them what they had just seen, and the cheer-

TOP: Tris Speaker, left, has some words of advice for Joe Sewell, who played 22 games filling in for the late Ray Chapman at the end of the 1920 season.

BOTTOM: In Game 5 of the 1920 Series, Bill Wambsganss (left) turned an unassisted triple play and Elmer Smith (right) hit a grand slam. Neither feat had been accomplished in the World Series before.

ing started and quickly got louder and louder and louder. By the time I got back to the bench it was bedlam, straw hats flying onto the field, people yelling themselves hoarse, my teammates pounding me on the back."

The Series was all but over after the Indians won Game 5. They triumphed again in Game 6 thanks to a three-hit shutout by Mails, and sent the spitballer Coveleski to the mound to try to clinch it in Game 7. Coveleski, whose wife had died earlier in the season, was cheered on from the stands by his young son. The Robins never had a chance as Coveleski shut them down on five hits, winning 3-0 and wrapping up the title for the Indians, five games to two.
The pitching of Coveleski, Bagby, and Mails limited Brooklyn to just two runs in the Series' last 44 innings. Coveleski was particularly brilliant, throwing three complete games and dispensing with the Robins while throwing an average of just 87 pitches per game. Coveleski's clinching shutout also marked the end of a World Series era. In future years, Series success would depend less on which team had the star pitcher, and more on which team had the sluggers who could drive the ball out of the park.

BOTTOM: Emil "Irish" Meusel, left, and his younger brother Bob were two of the best power hitters in baseball. They faced each other in the 1921 Series.

1920 WORLD SERIES

Ebbets Field (Brooklyn Dodgers) ◆ 10.5.20

	1	2	3	4	5	6	7	8	9	R	H	E
Clev.	0	2	0	1	0	0	0	0	0	3	5	0
B'klyn	0	0	0	0	0	0	1	0	0	1	5	1

WP–Coveleski LP–Marquard HR: CLE–Jackson ATT: 23,753

Ebbets Field ◆ 10.6.20

	1	2	3	4	5	6	7	8	9	R	H	E
Clev.	0	0	0	0	0	0	0	0	0	0	7	1
B'klyn	1	0	1	0	1	0	0	0	X	3	7	0

WP–Grimes LP–Bagby ATT: 22,559

Ebbets Field ◆ 10.7.20

	1	2	3	4	5	6	7	8	9	R	H	E
Clev.	0	0	0	1	0	0	0	0	0	1	3	1
B'klyn	2	0	0	0	0	0	0	0	X	2	6	1

WP–S. Smith LP–Caldwell ATT: 25,088

League Park II (Cleveland Indians) ◆ 10.9.20

	1	2	3	4	5	6	7	8	9	R	H	E
B'klyn	0	0	0	1	0	0	0	0	0	1	5	1
Clev.	2	0	2	0	0	1	0	0	X	5	12	2

WP–Coveleski LP–Cadore ATT: 25,734

League Park II ◆ 10.10.20

	1	2	3	4	5	6	7	8	9	R	H	E
B'klyn	0	0	0	0	0	0	0	0	1	1	13	1
Clev.	4	0	0	3	1	0	0	0	X	8	12	2

WP–Bagby LP–Grimes HR: CLE–E. Smith, Bagby ATT: 26,884

League Park II ◆ 10.11.20

	1	2	3	4	5	6	7	8	9	R	H	E
B'klyn	0	0	0	0	0	0	0	0	0	0	3	0
Clev.	0	0	0	0	0	1	0	0	X	1	7	3

WP–Mails LP–S. Smith ATT: 27,194

League Park II ◆ 10.12.20

	1	2	3	4	5	6	7	8	9	R	H	E
B'klyn	0	0	0	0	0	0	0	0	0	0	5	2
Clev.	0	0	0	1	1	0	1	0	X	3	7	3

WP–Coveleski LP–S. Grimes ATT: 27,525

1921

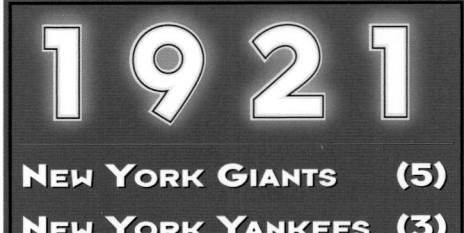

New York Giants (5)
New York Yankees (3)

The 1921 World Series between the Giants and Yankees is best remembered for being the first of the fourteen New York "Subway Series." (Of these, the Brooklyn Dodgers appeared in seven, the Giants six, the Mets one, and the Yankees all fourteen.) After the 1919 debacle, the best-of-nine 1921 Series was the second spectacularly exciting Series in a row, further putting baseball back into the good graces of the fans. It was also the first Series to be played entirely in the same stadium, since both the Yankees and Giants called the Polo Grounds home.

The Yankees thoroughly dominated the American League in 1921, winning the first pennant in team history thanks to an historic season from Babe Ruth, who broke his own record with 59 home runs and produced a .512 on-base percentage and an .846 slugging percentage. Not only did the Yankees lead

the American League in runs scored, but their pitchers also led in earned run average, thanks to the right arms of Carl Mays, Waite Hoyt, and Bob Shawkey. The Yankees put together their squad like a hungry vulture, plucking star players from the two decimated A.L. dynasties of the 1910s, Philadelphia (where they got Shawkey and Home Run Baker) and Boston (where they got Mays, Hoyt, catcher Wally Schang, and Ruth).

The Giants were much the same. Only one significant player, George Burns, remained from John McGraw's pennant-winning squad of four years earlier. McGraw prided himself on his ability to rejuvenate players deemed expendable by other teams, and he filled his 1921 squad with talented castoffs including catcher Frank Snyder, shortstop Dave Bancroft, left fielder Emil "Irish" Meusel, and the entire pitching staff of Art Nehf, Fred Toney, Jesse Barnes, and Phil Douglas. These players, combined with three homegrown young stars—Frankie Frisch, Ross Youngs, and George Kelly—gave the Giants the nucleus of a team that would win four consecutive National League pennants.

The Yankees jumped out to a quick lead in the Series, winning each of the first two games by the score of 3-0. In Game 1, Mays, according to *Baseball Magazine*, "had the Giants' bats waving like palm fronds in a hurricane." The offensive star was utility infielder Mike McNally, who had a single, a double, and a daring steal of home. The Yanks won the second game behind the shutout pitching of Hoyt, and for the second consecutive day they had a steal of home, this one by Emil's younger brother Bob Meusel. Ruth, trim and athletic at age 26, also stole second and third in the same inning.

Things looked bleak for the Giants midway through Game 3. Not only had no team ever come back from a 2-0 deficit in the World Series, but Giants starter Toney was battered around in Game 3, leaving after two miserable innings. But Barnes came in to pitch seven innings of magnificent relief, and also contributed hits to two key rallies. The Giants charged back into the lead with eight runs in the seventh inning, winning the game 13-5. The fourth game again started well for the Yankees as Mays held the Giants hitless into the sixth inning. But the Giants took the lead when Irish Meusel's triple started a seventh inning rally. Ruth homered in the ninth, but it wasn't enough as the Giants won 4-2. With the Series now tied, Hoyt pitched well in Game 5 and the Yankees won 3-1, scoring the winning run when Ruth started a rally with, of all things, a bunt single.

The Yankees suffered a huge blow before Game 6 when Ruth was forced to sit out the rest of the Series with a bad knee and an abscess on his left elbow. The Babe Ruth of 1921 was the single greatest offensive force in baseball history and his absence meant the Yankees, though leading the Series, were in deep trouble. McGraw brought back Toney, who had been bombed in Game 3, to start Game 6. Toney pitched even worse this time, as he was unable to even get out of the first inning. But once again, Barnes came to his rescue, pitching 8⅓ innings of solid relief as the Giants came back to win 8-5. The Giants won again the next day behind spitballer Douglas, who outpitched Mays in a 2-1 squeaker. Now the Giants held the upper hand, leading the Series 4-3 entering the Game 8 matchup between Nehf and Hoyt. Both pitched magnificently, as the only run of the game scored in the first inning when the Yankees' Roger Peckinpaugh let a grounder go through his legs. The Yankees, batting in the bottom of the ninth down by a run, put a man on first with one out. On a hit and run play, Frank Baker smashed a line drive that appeared headed toward right field, but second baseman Johnny Rawlings dove for the ball, knocked it down, and threw from the ground to get Baker out at first. Baserunner Aaron Ward tried to go to third on the play, and first baseman Kelly threw him out to complete a spectacular World Series–ending double play. Though they had played well in a hard-fought Series, the losing Yankees couldn't help but wonder what might have happened if they'd had Babe Ruth for the last three games.

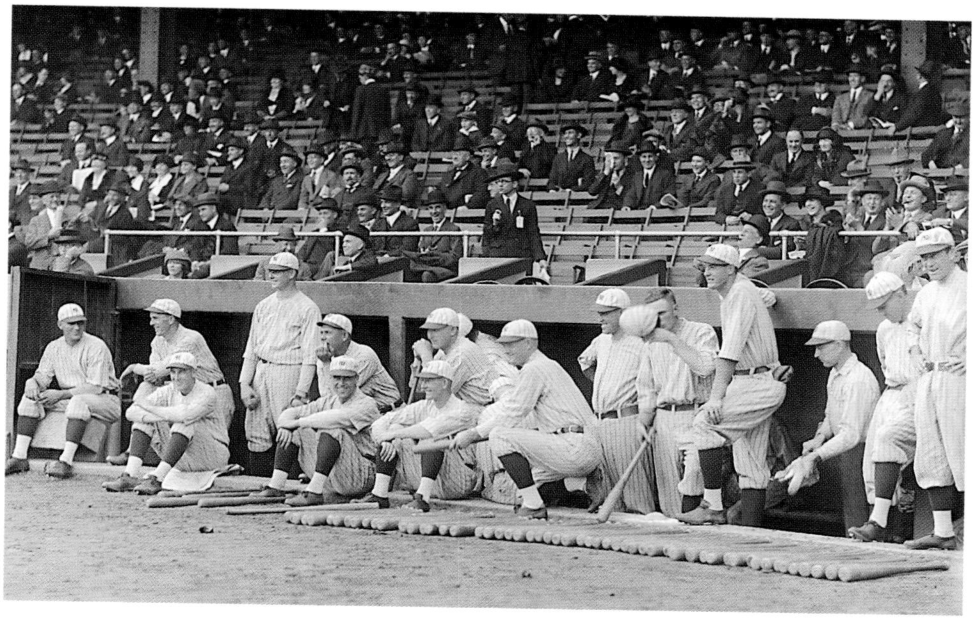

TOP: The New York Yankees, including Babe Ruth (fifth from left), enjoy a light-hearted moment in the dugout during Game 6 of the 1921 Series.

Exciting Moments in the First World Series Game Between Yankees and Giants

BOTTOM: Babe Ruth batting at the Polo Grounds. As this photo shows, Ruth was a slender and powerful athlete in the early 1920s, far from the reputation he would later acquire.

1921 WORLD SERIES

Polo Grounds IV (New York Giants) ◆ 10.5.21

	1	2	3	4	5	6	7	8	9	R	H	E
NYY	1	0	0	0	1	1	0	0	0	3	7	0
NYG	0	0	0	0	0	0	0	0	0	0	5	0

WP–Mays LP–Douglas ATT: 30,202

Polo Grounds IV (New York Yankees) ◆ 10.6.21

	1	2	3	4	5	6	7	8	9	R	H	E
NYG	0	0	0	0	0	0	0	0	0	0	2	3
NYY	0	0	0	1	0	0	0	2	X	3	3	0

WP–Hoyt LP–Nehf ATT: 34,939

Polo Grounds IV (New York Giants) ◆ 10.7.21

	1	2	3	4	5	6	7	8	9	R	H	E
NYY	0	0	4	0	0	0	0	1	0	5	8	0
NYG	0	0	4	0	0	0	8	1	X	13	20	0

WP–Barnes LP–Quinn ATT: 36,509

Polo Grounds IV (New York Yankees) ◆ 10.9.21

	1	2	3	4	5	6	7	8	9	R	H	E
NYG	0	0	0	0	0	0	0	3	1	4	9	1
NYY	0	0	0	0	1	0	0	0	1	2	7	1

WP–Douglas LP–Mays HR: NYY–Ruth ATT: 36,372

Polo Grounds IV (New York Giants) ◆ 10.10.21

	1	2	3	4	5	6	7	8	9	R	H	E
NYY	0	0	1	2	0	0	0	0	0	3	6	1
NYG	1	0	0	0	0	0	0	0	0	1	10	1

WP–Hoyt LP–Nehf ATT: 35,758

Polo Grounds IV (New York Yankees) ◆ 10.11.21

	1	2	3	4	5	6	7	8	9	R	H	E
NYG	0	3	0	4	0	1	0	0	0	8	13	0
NYY	3	2	0	0	0	0	0	0	0	5	7	2

WP–Barnes LP–Shawkey HR: NYG–Meusel, Snyder; NYY–Fewster ATT: 34,238

Polo Grounds IV (New York Giants) ◆ 10.12.21

	1	2	3	4	5	6	7	8	9	R	H	E
NYY	0	1	0	0	0	0	0	0	0	1	8	1
NYG	0	0	0	1	0	0	1	0	X	2	6	0

WP–Douglas LP–Mays ATT: 36,503

Polo Grounds IV (New York Yankees) ◆ 10.13.21

	1	2	3	4	5	6	7	8	9	R	H	E
NYG	1	0	0	0	0	0	0	0	0	1	6	0
NYY	0	0	0	0	0	0	0	0	0	0	4	1

WP–Nehf LP–Hoyt ATT: 25,410

1922

New York Giants (4)
New York Yankees (0)
(1 tie)

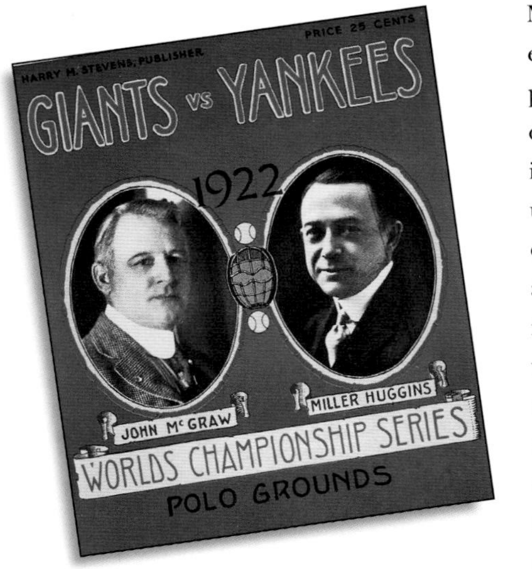

After their Series loss in 1921, the Yankees continued to plunder what few good players remained on the Red Sox roster, coming away with pitchers Sam Jones and Joe Bush, shortstop Everett Scott, and third baseman Joe Dugan. But New York was dealt a heavy blow when Commissioner Landis suspended the American League's two leading home run hitters, Babe Ruth and Bob Meusel, for the first 33 games of the 1922 season for embarking on a prohibited barnstorming tour after the World Series. (The theory was that fans would be less likely to attend World Series games if they knew they could see the same players elsewhere after the Series.) The Yankees were in first place with a 22-11 record when the sluggers returned, and went on to win the pennant narrowly over the St. Louis Browns. Although Ruth was still the best hitter in the league after his return, his final numbers—a .315 average, 35 homers, and 99 RBI—were such a letdown from the previous two years that he was considered a huge disappointment.

After the three-year experiment with a best-of-nine matchup, the World Series now returned to seven games for good. The Giants won the Series by simply pecking the Yankees to death, collecting 50 hits in the five games, 46 of them singles. The Yankees' power hitters, Ruth, Meusel, and Wally Pipp, were completely neutralized by Giants pitching, and their inability to score runs in other ways hurt them. The Yankees led the first game until the eighth inning, when consecutive hits by Dave Bancroft, Heinie Groh, Frankie Frisch, and Irish Meusel gave the Giants the lead and an eventual 3-2 victory. The next day the teams played to a 3-3 tie before the game was called due to darkness after ten innings, although it was only 4:46 p.m. and at least thirty minutes of daylight remained. The crowd rained down boos on umpire George Hildebrand and Commissioner Landis, who was watching from the first row of the stands. Fans and writers suspected that the game had been called early so the teams could make more money on an extra game, creating so much controversy that Landis was forced to announce that all proceeds from the tie game would be donated to charity. Back in action the next day, the Giants won Game 3 behind the brilliant pitching of Jack Scott, a Boston Braves castoff with a 40-44 career record whom Giants manager McGraw had rescued from the scrap heap at midseason. Scott blanked the Yankees on four hits while the Giants collected twelve themselves en route to a 3-0 win. Ruth angered the Giants during the game by sliding hard into the 5'8" Groh at third base, and the two benches jawed at each other the rest of the game, with the Giants challenging Ruth to a fight. Both Ruth and Meusel showed up at the Giants' clubhouse after the game, but were ejected by McGraw before anything serious happened.

Game 4 was played in a downpour at the Polo Grounds. The Giants unleashed a torrent of their own, again singling the Yankees to death, 4-3. The Yankees tried to stave off the Giants in Game 5, taking a 3-2 lead into the eighth inning, but the

BOTTOM: Heinie Groh, swinging his distinctive bottle-shaped bat, collected nine hits to lead all players during the 1922 World Series.

1922 WORLD SERIES

Polo Grounds IV (New York Giants) ◆ 10.4.22

	1	2	3	4	5	6	7	8	9	R	H	E
NYY	0	0	0	0	0	1	1	0	0	2	7	0
NYG	0	0	0	0	0	0	0	3	X	3	11	3

WP–Ryan LP–Bush ATT: 36,514

Polo Grounds IV (New York Yankees) ◆ 10.5.22

	1	2	3	4	5	6	7	8	9	10	R	H	E
NYG	3	0	0	0	0	0	0	0	0	0	3	8	1
NYY	1	0	0	1	0	0	0	1	0	0	3	8	0

WP–NONE LP–NONE HR: NYG–Meusel ATT: 37,020

Polo Grounds IV (New York Giants) ◆ 10.6.22

	1	2	3	4	5	6	7	8	9	R	H	E
NYY	0	0	0	0	0	0	0	0	0	0	4	1
NYG	0	0	2	0	0	0	1	0	X	3	12	1

WP–J. Scott LP–Hoyt ATT: 37,620

Polo Grounds IV (New York Yankees) ◆ 10.7.22

	1	2	3	4	5	6	7	8	9	R	H	E
NYG	0	0	0	0	4	0	0	0	0	4	9	1
NYY	2	0	0	0	0	0	1	0	0	3	8	0

WP–McQuillan LP–Mays HR: NYY–Ward
ATT: 36,242

Polo Grounds IV (New York Giants) ◆ 10.8.22

	1	2	3	4	5	6	7	8	9	R	H	E
NYY	1	0	0	0	1	0	1	0	0	3	5	0
NYG	0	2	0	0	0	0	0	3	X	5	10	0

WP–Nehf LP–Bush ATT: 38,551

Giants pounced on Joe Bush in the eighth, scoring three runs on well-timed and well-placed hits. It seemed an odd Series, with the Giants sweeping despite both hitting and pitching that was less than intimidating. John McGraw's theory of "scientific" baseball had proven superior to the power-hitting philosophy embodied by the Yankees, if only temporarily. It was a bitter loss for the Yankees, and two men bore the brunt of the blame: manager Miller Huggins, who was nearly fired despite winning two consecutive pennants, and Babe Ruth, who had only two hits in the Series. After enduring a winter of criticism, both men would find redemption in 1923.

1923

New York Yankees (4)
New York Giants (2)

The Yankees and Giants met for the third consecutive year in 1923, but it wasn't quite the same old song. After two World Series played entirely at the Polo Grounds, which both teams called home, the Yankees moved into a brand-new stadium in 1923. Both colossal and classy, Yankee Stadium, with a capacity of 58,000, was considerably larger than the Polo Grounds and able to hold all the people who wanted to see Babe Ruth play. And play he did, winning his only American League batting title with a .393 average and adding an astonishing 170 walks, enabling him to set a new modern record with a .545 on-base percentage (a figure since bested by Ted Williams and Barry Bonds). In 2002, baseball analyst Bill James rated Ruth's 1923 season the second-greatest of all time, behind only Honus Wagner's performance in 1908.

When Yankee first baseman Wally Pipp got hurt late in the season, they called on a young first baseman not long out of Columbia University, Lou Gehrig, to replace him. Gehrig played in only thirteen games, but what a thirteen games it was: a .423 batting average, .769 slugging percentage, and nine RBI. With Pipp still hurting, the Yankees petitioned to be allowed to carry Gehrig on their World Series roster, even though he had not been with the team on the September 1 deadline. Permission was denied after Giants manager John McGraw complained. With the regular season winding down, meanwhile, Babe Ruth prepared for the World Series in a decidedly unusual way: He played a game with the enemy. On October 3 the Giants played a benefit game against the Baltimore Orioles, then the most powerful minor league team in the country. Ruth agreed to play for the Giants in the exhibition and hit a homer off Robert "Lefty" Grove before returning to the team whose House he had built.

The World Series started a week later. Game 1 was tied 4-4 in the ninth inning when the Giants' Casey Stengel came up to bat and sent a ball into left center field, not

TOP: Irish Meusel connects for a three-run homer off Bob Shawkey in Game 2 of the 1922 Series. The game ended in a 3-3 tie after 10 innings, called due to darkness even though the sun still shone brightly.

BOTTOM: Hall of Fame managers Miller Huggins, left, and John McGraw opposed each other in three consecutive World Series, from 1921–23.

hit particularly hard, but placed brilliantly. Stengel circled the bases as outfielders Lawton "Whitey" Witt and Bob Meusel ran to the wall to retrieve it. Since Meusel had the most powerful throwing arm in baseball, other Yankee outfielders were in the habit of passing the ball to him whenever they could so he could throw it back in. So Witt fielded Stengel's hit and handed it off to Meusel, who relayed it to shortstop Everett Scott, who threw home. But by that time, Stengel had slid home safely with what proved to be a game-winning inside-the-park home run. Baseball lore has it that Stengel lost his shoe while rounding the bases and slid home barefoot, although archival film of the homer is inconclusive on that point. The homer was captured marvelously in print the next day by Damon Runyan:

This is the way Casey Stengel ran the bases yesterday afternoon...His mouth wide open. His warped old legs bending beneath him at every stride. His arms flying back and forth like those of a man swimming with a crawl stroke. His flanks heaving, his breath whistling, his head far back...The warped old legs, twisted and bent by many a year of baseball campaigning, just barely held out under Casey as he reached the plate, running his home run home.

Then they collapsed.

It was Ruth's turn to capture the spotlight in Game 2, as he slammed two home runs, to take the Yankees to a 4-2 victory. Stengel snatched that spotlight right back in Game 3. Before a crowd of 62,430—at the time the most people ever to witness a World Series game—the teams entered the seventh inning in a scoreless tie. Batting against Sam Jones, Stengel smacked a change-up into the right field stands for a homer, thumbing his nose at the Yankee bench as he rounded the bases with what turned out to be the only run of the game. Commissioner Landis later fined him $50 for the rude gesture, but even Landis had to admit, "Casey Stengel can't help being Casey Stengel."

The Yankees won the next two games with their big bats, beating the Giants 8-4 and 8-1. Joe Dugan was the star of Game 5, collecting four hits including a three-run inside-the-park homer. In Game 6, Ruth hit a first-inning homer, and the Yankees scored the decisive runs in the eighth when Giants pitchers walked two consecutive batters with the bases loaded. After two disheartening losses to the Giants, the New York Yankees had finally won their first World Series.

1923 WORLD SERIES

Yankee Stadium I (N.Y. Yankees) ◆ 10.10.23 (GAME 1)

	1	2	3	4	5	6	7	8	9	R	H	E
NYG	0	0	4	0	0	0	0	0	1	5	8	0
NYY	1	2	0	0	0	0	1	0	0	4	12	1

WP–Ryan LP–Bush HR: NYG–Stengel ATT: 55,307

Polo Grounds IV (N.Y. Giants) ◆ 10.11.23 (GAME 2)

	1	2	3	4	5	6	7	8	9	R	H	E
NYY	0	1	0	2	1	0	0	0	0	4	10	0
NYG	0	1	0	0	0	1	0	0	0	2	9	2

WP–Pennock LP–McQuillan HR: NYY–Ward, Ruth (2); NYG–Meusel ATT: 40,402

Yankee Stadium I ◆ 10.12.23 (GAME 3)

	1	2	3	4	5	6	7	8	9	R	H	E
NYG	0	0	0	0	0	0	1	0	0	1	4	0
NYY	0	0	0	0	0	0	0	0	0	0	6	1

WP–Nehf LP–Jones HR: NYG–Stengel ATT: 62,430

Polo Grounds IV ◆ 10.13.23 (GAME 4)

	1	2	3	4	5	6	7	8	9	R	H	E
NYY	0	6	1	1	0	0	0	0	0	8	13	1
NYG	0	0	0	0	0	0	0	3	1	4	13	1

WP–Shawkey LP–J. Scott S–Pennock HR: NYG–Youngs ATT: 46,302

Yankee Stadium I ◆ 10.14.23 (GAME 5)

	1	2	3	4	5	6	7	8	9	R	H	E
NYG	0	1	0	0	0	0	0	0	0	1	3	2
NYY	3	4	0	1	0	0	0	0	X	8	14	0

WP–Bush LP–Bentley HR: NYY–Dugan ATT: 62,817

Polo Grounds IV ◆ 10.15.23 (GAME 6)

	1	2	3	4	5	6	7	8	9	R	H	E
NYY	1	0	0	0	0	0	0	5	0	6	5	0
NYG	1	0	0	1	1	1	0	0	0	4	10	1

WP–Pennock LP–Nehf S–S. Jones HR: NYY–Ruth; NYG–Snyder ATT: 34,172

BOTTOM: All eyes at the Polo Grounds are on Casey Stengel, seen here sliding into home plate after hustling around the bases for an inside-the-park home run. Yankee pitcher Joe Bush watches as the throw from shortstop Everett Scott arrives too late in the glove of catcher Wally Schang, himself looking over his shoulder as the winning run slides past him.

1924

WASHINGTON SENATORS (4)
NEW YORK GIANTS (3)

THE 1924 WORLD SERIES PITTED THE New York Giants, playing in their fourth consecutive Fall Classic, against the Washington Senators, who had never played in one before. As with many great dramas, the two key figures were polar opposites: Walter Johnson, winner of 377 major league games and generally regarded as the best pitcher in baseball history, who was only now appearing in his first World Series; and Freddy Lindstrom, a fresh-faced Giants infielder who, at 18, remains the youngest player to ever appear in a Series, and who was one year old when Johnson pitched his first major league game back in 1907. Johnson, at 36, was so ancient that even his manager, so-called "Boy Wonder" Stanley Harris, also the Senators' shortstop, was only ten years old when Johnson had won his first game.

Johnson, though not the pitcher he had once been, had a fine season, going 23-7 with a 2.72 ERA. He was the man of the hour in the nation's capital, as Senators fans presented him with a new car before the first game of the Series, and President Calvin Coolidge (whose wife Grace was the real fan in the family) was on hand to throw out the first ball. Johnson's mother was also in the stands for her first major league game.

Johnson's hands were shaking as he signed autographs before the game. "I am doggone fidgety about my job this afternoon," he said. "Every last soul in the ballpark expects me to win, including the President of the United States." The Giants, though, did not share in that expectation, peppering Johnson for fourteen hits and two early runs. The game went into extra innings with starters Johnson and Art Nehf still pitching. New York scored two runs off Johnson in the twelfth. The Senators tried to come back in the bottom of the inning, but could only score one run, and the Giants won 4-3.

The Senators took a 3-1 lead into the ninth inning the next day but the Giants tied it on hits by George Kelly and Lewis "Hack" Wilson. Fred "Firpo" Marberry, the Senators pitcher who was baseball's first true relief ace, came in to strike out Travis Jackson and end the threat. In the bottom of the ninth, Roger Peckinpaugh smashed a double down the left field line, driving in Joe Judge with the winning run as the Senators tied the Series.

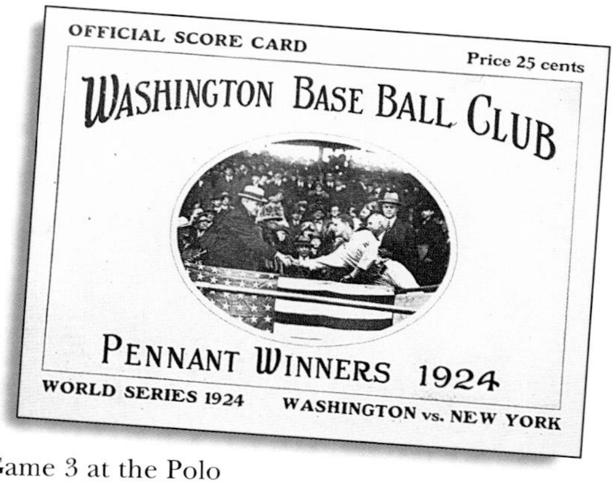

Marberry got a rare start for Washington in Game 3 at the Polo Grounds, but he lasted only three innings, giving up four runs to the Giants. Down 6-3 entering the ninth, Washington again tried to come back, loading the bases with one out. Giants manager John McGraw had to use three different pitchers to get out of the inning, but the Giants eventually escaped with a 6-4 win. Johnson had been scheduled to start Game 4, but because he had pitched twelve innings in the opener, manager Bucky Harris decided to give the hurler an extra day's rest. Instead, George Mogridge fended off the Giants attack for seven solid innings, and with the Senators leading 7-2, Marberry came in to close out the win. The game's hero was Leon "Goose" Goslin, who had four hits, including a three-run homer.

BOTTOM: Walter Johnson, legendary pitcher for the Washington Senators, hits a long fly ball to left field in Game 7 of the 1924 World Series. Johnson pitched three games in the Series, losing two. His Game 7 win, however, secured the Series for the Senators for the first time in the club's history. It was also the veteran hurler's first appearance in a World Series.

Finally, with the Series tied 2-2, it was Walter Johnson's turn to pitch again, this time in New York. Remarkably, the opposing fans gave him a sustained ovation as he walked to the mound. But the Giants were not kind to him, nicking him for a run in the third and two in the fifth before breaking out with three runs in the eighth inning, capped by Lindstrom's fourth hit of the game. Though Goslin hit another homer for Washington, it wasn't enough, as they lost 6-2. Johnson lost again, and the fans at the Polo Grounds watched silently with, the Associated Press wrote, "a spirit of the dying gladiator in the air." It seemed that Johnson's chance at World Series glory had passed. "What happened yesterday at the Polo Grounds was a shame," Fred Lieb wrote. "Walter Johnson's great moment came, and it will leave a lifetime of tragic recollections." Now the Series shifted back to Washington's Griffith Stadium. Tom Zachary pitched a good Game 6 for the Senators and Sam Rice made three fine catches in right field to preserve a 2-1 Washington victory.

It all came down to a deciding seventh game for only the second time in Series history. Harris began the game with a nifty bit of strategy. He sent a decoy pitcher, Warren "Curly" Ogden, out to the mound to start the game, and McGraw filled out his lineup accordingly. Then, after Ogden pitched to just two batters, Harris replaced him with his real pitcher, the left-handed George Mogridge, who had secretly been warming up under the stands. Now McGraw's lineup, designed to face a right-handed pitcher, would face a lefty for most of the game. Bill Terry, the lefty batter who was New York's best hitter in the Series, was forced out of the game for a pinch hitter in the fifth inning. Still, the Giants led 3-1 entering the eighth inning. Washington loaded the bases with two outs, and Harris, the shortstop/manager, hit a ground ball to Fred Lindstrom at third base that looked like the third out, but hit a pebble in the infield and bounced high over Lindstrom's head, scoring the tying runs.

With the game now likely to go into extra innings, Harris played his trump card, bringing Walter Johnson in to pitch on just one day's rest. Johnson allowed a one-out triple to Frankie Frisch in the bottom of the ninth, but pitched out of the jam. He then held the Giants scoreless in the tenth, eleventh, and twelfth innings. Finally, in the bottom of the twelfth, the Senators got two extraordinarily lucky breaks. First, catcher Hank Gowdy tripped over his own face

TOP: The Giants lost Game 7 of the 1924 World Series when two different ground balls took bad hops over the head of third baseman Fred Lindstrom.

BOTTOM: Leon "Goose" Goslin scores after hitting a two-run homer in Game 2 of the 1924 World Series at Griffith Stadium. It was the first of three homers in the Series for Goslin.

1924 WORLD SERIES

GRIFFITH STADIUM I (WASH. SENATORS) ◆ 10.4.24

	1	2	3	4	5	6	7	8	9	10	11	12	R	H	E
NYG	0	1	0	1	0	0	0	0	0	0	0	2	4	14	1
Wash.	0	0	0	0	0	1	0	0	1	0	0	1	3	10	1

WP–Nehf LP–Johnson HR: NYG–Kelly, Terry
ATT: 35,760

GRIFFITH STADIUM I ◆ 10.5.24

	1	2	3	4	5	6	7	8	9	R	H	E
NYG	0	0	0	0	0	0	1	0	2	3	6	0
Wash.	2	0	0	0	1	0	0	0	1	4	6	1

WP–Zachary LP–Bentley HR: WSH–Goslin, Harris
ATT: 35,922

POLO GROUNDS IV (NEW YORK GIANTS) ◆ 10.6.24

	1	2	3	4	5	6	7	8	9	R	H	E
Wash.	0	0	0	2	0	0	0	1	1	4	9	2
NYG	0	2	1	1	0	1	0	1	X	6	12	0

WP–McQuillan LP–Marberry S–Watson
HR: NYG–Ryan ATT: 47,608

POLO GROUNDS IV ◆ 10.7.24

	1	2	3	4	5	6	7	8	9	R	H	E
Wash.	0	0	3	0	2	0	0	2	0	7	13	3
NYG	0	0	1	1	0	1	0	1	X	4	6	1

WP–Mogridge LP–Barnes S–Marberry
HR: WSH–Goslin ATT: 49,243

POLO GROUNDS IV ◆ 10.8.24

	1	2	3	4	5	6	7	8	9	R	H	E
Wash.	0	0	0	1	0	0	0	1	0	2	9	1
NYG	0	0	1	0	2	0	0	3	X	6	13	0

WP–Bentley LP–Johnson S–McQuillan
HR: WSH–Goslin; NYG–Bentley ATT: 49,211

GRIFFITH STADIUM I ◆ 10.9.24

	1	2	3	4	5	6	7	8	9	R	H	E
NYG	1	0	0	0	0	0	0	0	0	1	7	1
Wash.	0	0	0	0	2	0	0	0	X	2	4	0

WP–Nehf LP–Zachary ATT: 34,254

GRIFFITH STADIUM I ◆ 10.10.24

	1	2	3	4	5	6	7	8	9	10	11	12	R	H	E
NYG	0	0	0	0	0	3	0	0	0	0	0	0	3	8	3
Wash.	0	0	0	1	0	0	0	2	0	0	0	1	4	10	4

WP–Johnson LP–Bentley HR: WSH–Harris
ATT: 31,667

mask while chasing a foul pop-up and the ball fell harmlessly to the ground. Given another chance, the Senators' Muddy Ruel doubled. Then Johnson, allowed to bat for himself, reached on an error. With runners now on first and second, Earl McNeely grounded to third, and lightning struck for the second time. "Well, it happened again," Lindstrom recalled. "The ball hit a pebble—maybe the same darned pebble that Harris' ball had hit—and took a big kangaroo hop over my head and went out into left field." Ruel scored from second to end both the game and the Series. Walter Johnson, standing on second base as Ruel lumbered home with the world championship, simply smiled. Nobody could believe it. "This is not fiction," Shirley Povich insisted in a *Washington Post* article. "It happened in 1924. I was there."

For the 18-year-old Lindstrom, it was a rude introduction to the Fall Classic, and one he never quite lived down. "If it hadn't been for that ball bouncing over my head a lot of people would have forgotten I ever existed," he said many years later. "You know the saying, 'That's the way the ball bounces'? Well, it was never more appropriate than in the seventh game of the 1924 World Series."

1925

Pittsburgh Pirates (4)
Washington Senators (3)

The Senators returned to defend their championship in 1925 against the Pittsburgh Pirates, appearing in their first World Series since the memorable Cobb-Wagner showdown in 1909. Remarkably, the star of that Series, Babe Adams, still pitched for the Pirates, and would throw one scoreless inning in the 1925 Series. But Pittsburgh had a new generation of stars. Running away with the pennant on the fleet feet of Max Carey and Hazen "Kiki" Cuyler, the Pirates stole far more bases, and were caught far less often, than any other team in baseball. Moreover, their stunning lineup had five players with on-base percentages over .370.

With Forbes Field decked out in red, white, and blue bunting for its first World Series since the days of Honus Wagner, the Senators sent Walter Johnson to the mound for Game 1. He was brilliant. "The Johnson who tied Pittsburgh batters into true lover's knots was not the nervous, high strung Johnson of a year ago who faced the Giants in his first world series test," Grantland Rice wrote. "He was the Johnson of 19 brilliant major league campaigns. They never had a chance." Johnson won the game, 4-1, as Sam Rice had two hits including a bases-loaded single. The next day started with sad news for both teams, as they learned of Christy Mathewson's death from tuberculosis at Saranac Lake, New York. The teams placed black armbands on their sleeves and lowered the flag to half-mast before beginning play in Game 2. For a while it looked as if Washington would win, but the Pirates scored two runs in the eighth inning when Washington shortstop Roger Peckinpaugh committed two errors and Cuyler hit a home run. The Pirates won, 3-2.

Washington was leading Game 3, 4-3 in the eighth inning, when one of the most controversial plays in Series history occurred. The Pirates' Earl Smith launched a deep fly ball toward the stands. Rice, playing right field for Washington, raced after it, leaped high in the air, and tumbled, head over heels, over the outfield wall and into the temporary bleachers. Then nothing.

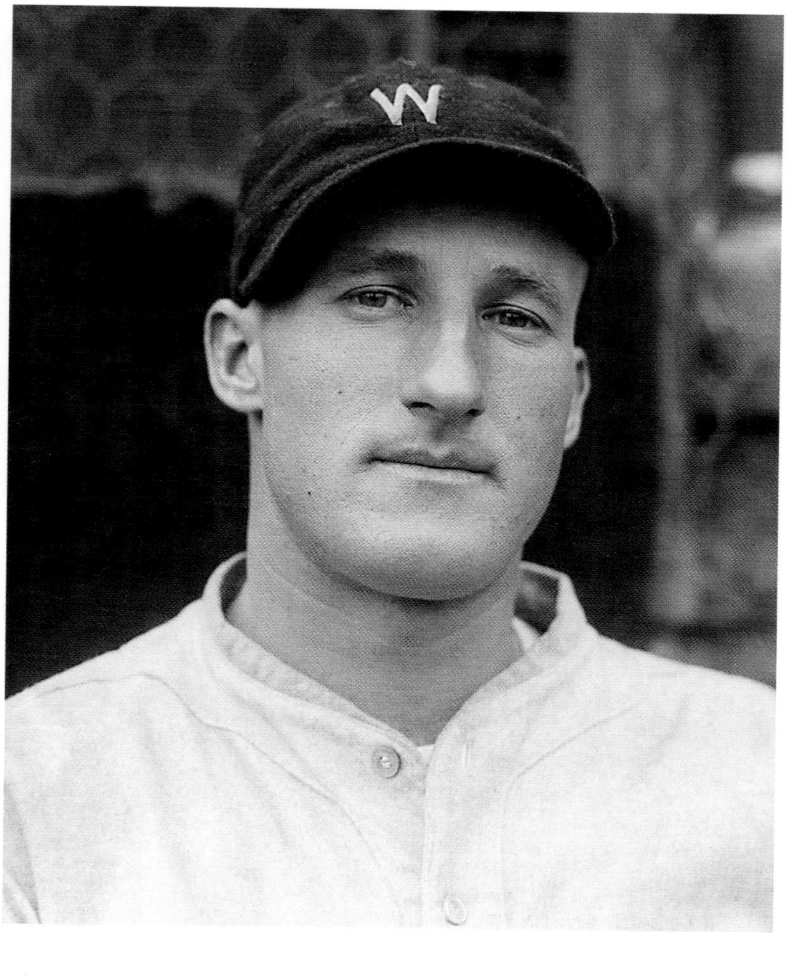

BOTTOM LEFT: Walter Johnson won 377 major league games before making his first World Series appearance, then pitched in two straight series in 1924–25.

BOTTOM RIGHT: Goose Goslin was the star of two consecutive World Series for the Senators, batting a combined .328 with six homers and 13 RBI in 1924–25.

After what seemed like an eternity—according to one witness, it was "longer than a TV station break with the eight consecutive commercials"—Rice emerged with the ball in his glove. Umpire Cy Rigler signaled an out. Many called it the greatest catch they had ever seen, and it did end up saving the game for the Senators, but the catch quickly became the center of the Series' biggest controversy. More than sixteen hundred Pirates fans wrote to Commissioner Landis stating that they, or someone they knew, saw Rice drop the ball, and that a fan had probably put it back into his glove. Some of them even sent notarized affidavits. "I have the names of a number of other people who say without the slightest qualification that Rice did not catch the ball," one fan wrote. "I don't know what you can do about the matter." Landis, taking the proper course, did nothing. When he asked Rice whether he had caught the ball, Rice replied coyly, "Well, the umpire said I did."

It was Johnson's turn to pitch before his home fans in Game 4. Despite an injured leg, he shut out the Pirates 4-0 with support from Goose Goslin, who hit a three-run homer. At 37, Johnson became the oldest pitcher to ever throw a World Series shutout, a record that stood until Randy Johnson broke it in 2001. Now, with a three games to one lead, Washington seemed on the verge of clinching the Series. But the Pirates pounded Stan Coveleski in Game 5 and beat Alex Ferguson in Game 6 to send the Series to a seventh game.

Johnson, though his arm was tired and his leg was sore, went to the mound for Washington in Game 7. The game was played in appalling conditions as a rainstorm brought torrents down on Forbes Field all afternoon. Landis refused to postpone it, saying that he didn't want to disappoint the fans. *The New York Times*' James Harrison called it:

> *The wettest, weirdest, and wildest game that 50 years of baseball has ever seen. Water, mud, fog, mist, sawdust, fumbles, muffs, wild throws, wild pitches, one near fistfight, impossible rallies—these were mixed up to make the best and the worst game of baseball ever played in this country. Players wallowing ankle deep in mud, pitchers slipping as they delivered the ball to the plate, athletes skidding and sloshing, falling full length, dropping soaked baseballs—there you have part of the picture that was unveiled at Forbes Field this dripping afternoon. It was a great day for water polo.*

The Senators pounded Pirates starter Vic Aldridge right away, and were winning 4-0

BOTTOM: Goose Goslin takes a mighty swing during the 1925 World Series at Pittsburgh's Forbes Field. The black armband on his left sleeve is for Christy Mathewson, who died the day the Series opened.

before Johnson even had to throw a pitch. With pitchers finding it difficult to throw the wet baseball with any kind of precision, the Pirates began to pound Johnson, too. Sawdust was brought in to soak up the puddles in the infield, and Johnson also put some in his baseball cap for the same reason. By the end of the day, according to his grandson and biographer Henry Thomas, "he looked like he was covered with oatmeal." After six innings, with the field even more unplayable than before, Landis turned to Senators owner Clark Griffith. "You're world champions," he said. "I'm calling this game." But Griffith refused to accept a tainted victory and the game plodded on. Visibility was so bad that the infielders couldn't see the outfielders.

The weather gave the Pirates two runs in the seventh when Peckinpaugh slipped while chasing a popup, and a foul drive by Carey was called fair because the umpires couldn't see that far away. The Pirates threatened in the eighth inning with Washington leading 7-6, as another error by Peckinpaugh loaded the bases with two outs and Cuyler, one of the most dangerous hitters in baseball, batting. Cuyler took a Johnson fastball over the heart of the plate for an apparent strike three, but the pitch was inexplicably called a ball. Then Cuyler hit a fly ball to right field that disappeared into the mist. None of the umpires really knew what happened, but after much discussion, they ruled that it had bounced into the stands for a ground-rule double. Two runs scored, putting the Pirates ahead, but Goslin, playing left field for Washington, always insisted it was a foul ball. "It wasn't fair at all," he said. "I know it was foul because the ball hit in the mud and *stuck* there. The umpires couldn't see it. It was too dark and foggy."

Foul or not, Cuyler's hit won the World Series for Pittsburgh, as Washington's batters went out meekly in the ninth inning. Ray Kremer was the winning pitcher in relief, and Johnson, after winning Game 7 the year before, was the loser this time. He pitched all nine innings, giving up fifteen hits and nine runs, though only five were earned. Still, there were two men who bore far more responsibility than Johnson for Washington's loss. One was shortstop Peckinpaugh, whose eight errors in the Series led to eight unearned runs, and were directly responsible for two of Washington's losses. ("Some of them were stinko calls by the scorer," Peckinpaugh later insisted.) The other man responsible for Washington's loss was Commissioner Landis, whose shameful decision to force the teams to play Game 7 in a downpour resulted in a championship decided not by baseball ability, but by rain, mud, and fog.

For the rest of his life, the mysterious Rice always refused to answer questions about whether he had really caught the ball in Game 3. "I never told a soul, and I haven't to this day," he said in 1964. After Rice was elected to the Hall of Fame, he gave a letter about the catch to Hall officials, to be opened only upon his death. The letter's contents were finally revealed when Rice died in 1974. "I had a death grip on it," he wrote. "I toppled over on my stomach into the first row of bleachers, I hit my Adam's apple on something which sort of knocked me out for a few seconds but McNeely arrived about that time and grabbed me by the shirt and pulled me out...At no time did I lose possession of the ball."

1925 WORLD SERIES

Forbes Field (Pittsburgh Pirates) ◆ 10.7.25

	1	2	3	4	5	6	7	8	9	R	H	E
Wash.	0	1	0	0	2	0	0	0	1	4	8	1
Pitt.	0	0	0	0	1	0	0	0	0	1	5	0

WP–Johnson LP–Meadows HR: WSH–J. Harris; PIT–Traynor ATT: 41,723

Forbes Field ◆ 10.8.25

	1	2	3	4	5	6	7	8	9	R	H	E
Wash.	0	1	0	0	0	0	0	0	1	2	8	2
Pitt.	0	0	0	1	0	0	0	2	X	3	7	0

WP–Aldridge LP–Coveleski HR: WSH–Judge; PIT–Wright, Cuyler ATT: 43,364

Griffith Stadium I (Wash. Senators) ◆ 10.10.25

	1	2	3	4	5	6	7	8	9	R	H	E
Pitt.	0	1	0	1	0	1	0	0	0	3	8	3
Wash.	0	0	1	0	0	1	2	0	X	4	10	1

WP–Ferguson LP–Kremer S–Marberry HR: WSH–Goslin ATT: 36,495

Griffith Stadium I ◆ 10.11.25

	1	2	3	4	5	6	7	8	9	R	H	E
Pitt.	0	0	0	0	0	0	0	0	0	0	6	1
Wash.	0	0	4	0	0	0	0	0	X	4	12	0

WP–Johnson LP–Yde HR: WSH–Goslin, J. Harris ATT: 38,701

Griffith Stadium I ◆ 10.12.25

	1	2	3	4	5	6	7	8	9	R	H	E
Pitt.	0	0	2	0	0	0	2	1	1	6	13	0
Wash.	1	0	0	1	0	0	1	0	0	3	8	1

WP–Aldridge LP–Coveleski HR: WSH–J. Harris ATT: 35,899

Forbes Field ◆ 10.13.25

	1	2	3	4	5	6	7	8	9	R	H	E
Wash.	1	1	0	0	0	0	0	0	0	2	6	2
Pitt.	0	0	2	0	1	0	0	0	X	3	7	1

WP–Kremer LP–Ferguson HR: WSH–Goslin ATT: 43,810

Forbes Field ◆ 10.15.25

	1	2	3	4	5	6	7	8	9	R	H	E
Wash.	4	0	0	2	0	0	0	1	0	7	7	2
Pitt.	0	0	3	0	1	0	2	3	X	9	15	2

WP–Kremer LP–Johnson S–Oldham HR: WSH–Peckinpaugh ATT: 42,856

1926

St. Louis Cardinals (4)
New York Yankees (3)

As it had for Walter Johnson two years earlier, the World Series in 1926 provided a golden opportunity for one of the game's greatest pitchers to shine for the last time. In this case it was Grover Cleveland Alexander, quite possibly the best pitcher in the history of the National League, and winner of 327 career games.

Alexander had lived a hard life. He was an alcoholic, as his father had been before him. Exploding artillery on the battlefields of World War I had damaged his hearing. He married the same woman twice, and divorced her twice. He suffered from epilepsy, never knowing when the next seizure might come. Rumor had it that he had shown up too drunk to pitch Game 5 of the 1915 World Series, forcing his team to start an inferior pitcher and lose the Series. (The story was

BOTTOM: By 1926 Grover Cleveland Alexander's life was in shambles due to alcoholism, but as it turned out, he still had one great moment left in him.

BOTTOM: After trying to swipe home on a double steal, Tony Lazzeri is caught in a rundown during Game 2 of the 1926 Series. Grover Alexander, shown here about to catch the ball, eventually made a throwing error that allowed Lazzeri to score.

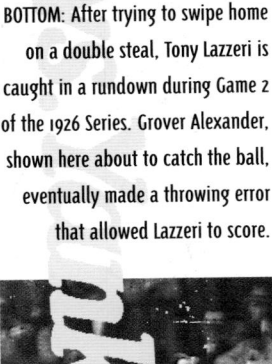

almost certainly false, but by 1926 it had become part of the Alexander legend.)

The 39-year-old Alexander was believed to be washed up by 1926. The Cubs, tired of the irresponsibility that came with his alcoholism, sold him to the Cardinals for just $6,000 in the middle of the season. He posted a 9-7 record and a fine 2.91 ERA for the Cardinals down the stretch, helping them to win the pennant by two games. Other than Alexander, the Cardinals were a fairly nondescript team, with mediocre pitching and a bunch of singles hitters. Player-manager Rogers Hornsby had a poor season at the plate, batting .317, the only time in a ten-year stretch that he dropped below .360. The Cardinals seemed colossally outmatched facing the Yankees in the World Series.

New York took the first game in a pitcher's duel, with lefty Herb Pennock beating Bill Sherdel, 2-1. The Cardinals evened the Series the next day thanks to Alexander, who struck out ten Yankees while allowing only four hits and one earned run. He won the game 6-2 behind a three-hit, three-RBI performance by Billy Southworth. Cardinal knuckleballer Jesse Haines had the day of his life in Game 3, shutting out the Yankees 4-0 and hitting a two-run homer. The much-ballyhooed Yankee offense finally showed up in Game 4, as they battered five Cardinals pitchers for ten runs. Most of the damage was done by Babe Ruth, who hit three towering home runs, two of which cleared the roof in the right field bleachers, exiting Sportsman's Park entirely. The Series was now tied 2-2.

Pennock pitched another fine game for the Yankees in Game 5, becoming a 3-2 winner when New York scored the winning run in the tenth on a sacrifice fly by Tony Lazzeri. Now down in the Series, the Cardinals turned to Alexander to start Game 6. St. Louis pounded Yankee starter Bob Shawkey, as Les Bell had four RBI on three hits, including a home run, and Southworth scored three runs. Alexander pitched another fine game, going the distance for the 10-2 victory.

Now, for a remarkable third year in a row, the World Series came down to a Game 7. And for the second year in a row, Game 7 was played in the rain, this time at Yankee Stadium. The pitchers were Haines, winner of Game 3 for the Cardinals, and Waite Hoyt, winner of Game 4 for the Yankees. New York scored first when Ruth hit a solo homer into the right-center field bleachers, but soon fumbled away their lead, with errors by Mark Koenig and Bob Meusel allowing the Cardinals to score three times. The Yankees scored again in the sixth inning when the Cards' Charles "Chick" Hafey barely missed a shoestring catch, allowing Joe Dugan to score.

Now down 3-2, the Yankee beast began to roar in the bottom of the seventh. Earle Combs walked and was sacrificed to second. Then Hornsby ordered Ruth intentionally walked. After a force play for the second out, Lou Gehrig was intentionally walked, even though there was a runner on first. The bases were now loaded with Tony Lazzeri due up, but Haines was unable to continue in the game. His fingers were bleeding from throwing too many knuckleballs and he could no longer grip the ball. With the game and the Series hanging in the balance, Hornsby called to the bullpen for Alexander. Bell, playing third base for the Cardinals that day, summed it up best:

> *He had gone nine the day before, and if he got out of this jam he still had two more innings to go today, and he was 40 years old* [sic]. *But doggone, there wasn't another man in the world I would have rather seen out there at that moment than Grover Cleveland Alexander.*
>
> *I can see him yet, to this day, walking in from the left-field bullpen through the gray mist. The Yankee fans recognized him right off, of course, but you didn't hear a sound from anywhere in that stadium....He just came straggling along, a lean old Nebraskan, wearing a Cardinal sweater, his face wrinkled, that cap sitting on top of his head and tilted to one side. That's the way he liked to wear it.*

Lazzeri, a second-year player, had batted .309 with 102 RBI during the season, and though dangerous, he was a more desirable foe than Ruth or Gehrig. It was the first time that Lazzeri and Alexander, the major leagues' two most prominent epileptics, had ever faced each other. At the mound, Alexander and Hornsby discussed how to pitch Lazzeri. Alexander wanted to start him with a fastball high and inside, believing that if Lazzeri made good contact, he would hit it foul anyway. The prediction came true, as Lazzeri launched a foul ball over the fence down the left field line. "Now for fifty years that ball has been traveling," Bell said. "It has been foul anywhere from an inch to twenty feet, depending on who you're listening to....But I was standing on third base, and let me tell you, it was foul all the way. All the way." After the narrow miss, Alexander had Lazzeri eating from his hand. The young Yankee waved at two breaking balls, both low and outside, and struck out to end the inning.

Although the big threat was over, Alexander still had two more innings to go. He breezed through them until walking Ruth with two outs in the bottom of the ninth. But as Alexander delivered a pitch to Combs, Ruth inexplicably took off for second base, and catcher Bob O'Farrell threw him out to end the game. It remains the only time a World Series has ended on a player caught stealing. Over the years, a persistent legend has held that Alexander, not expecting to have to pitch, had stayed out all night and gotten drunk the night before Game 7. "All a lot of bunk," Bell said. "Now in the first place, if you stop to think about it, no man could have done what Alex did if he was drunk or even a little soggy. Not the way his mind was working and not the way he pitched. It's true that he was a drinker and that he had a problem with it. Everybody knows that. But he was not drunk when he walked into the ball game that day. No way. No way at all, for heaven's sake."

BOTTOM: On October 5, Jesse Haines pitched a five-hit shutout against the Yankees in the Cardinals' first home game of the 1926 Series. The hometown enthusiasm in St. Louis was intense: the surging crowd pictured here gathered to welcome the team back from New York after Game 2—the day *before* Haines' shutout.

1926 WORLD SERIES

YANKEE STADIUM I (N.Y. YANKEES) ◆ 10.2.26

	1	2	3	4	5	6	7	8	9	R	H	E
St.L.	1	0	0	0	0	0	0	0	0	1	3	1
NYY	1	0	0	0	0	1	0	0	X	2	6	0

WP–Pennock LP–Sherdel ATT: 61,658

YANKEE STADIUM I ◆ 10.3.26

	1	2	3	4	5	6	7	8	9	R	H	E
St.L.	0	0	2	0	0	0	3	0	1	6	12	1
NYY	0	2	0	0	0	0	0	0	0	2	4	0

WP–Alexander LP–Shawkey HR: STL–Southworth, Thevenow ATT: 63,600

SPORTSMAN'S PARK IV (ST. LOUIS) ◆ 10.5.26

	1	2	3	4	5	6	7	8	9	R	H	E
NYY	0	0	0	0	0	0	0	0	0	0	5	1
St.L.	0	0	0	3	1	0	0	0	X	4	8	0

WP–Haines LP–Ruether HR: STL–Haines
ATT: 37,708

SPORTSMAN'S PARK IV ◆ 10.6.26

	1	2	3	4	5	6	7	8	9	R	H	E
NYY	1	0	1	1	4	2	1	0	0	10	14	1
St.L.	1	0	0	3	0	0	0	0	1	5	14	0

WP–Hoyt LP–Reinhart HR: NYY–Ruth (3)
ATT: 38,825

SPORTSMAN'S PARK IV ◆ 10.7.26

	1	2	3	4	5	6	7	8	9	10	R	H	E
NYY	0	0	0	0	0	1	0	0	1	1	3	9	1
St.L.	0	0	0	1	0	0	1	0	0	0	2	7	1

WP–Pennock LP–Sherdel ATT: 39,552

YANKEE STADIUM I ◆ 10.9.26

	1	2	3	4	5	6	7	8	9	R	H	E
St.L.	3	0	0	0	1	0	5	0	1	10	13	2
NYY	0	0	0	1	0	0	1	0	0	2	8	1

WP–Alexander LP–Shawkey HR: STL–L. Bell
ATT: 48,615

YANKEE STADIUM I ◆ 10.10.26

	1	2	3	4	5	6	7	8	9	R	H	E
St.L.	0	0	0	3	0	0	0	0	0	3	8	0
NYY	0	0	1	0	0	1	0	0	0	2	8	3

WP–Haines LP–Hoyt S–Alexander HR: NYY–Ruth
ATT: 38,093

1927

New York Yankees (4)
Pittburgh Pirates (0)

The 1927 Yankees are generally regarded as the greatest baseball team of all time. Likewise, Babe Ruth's record-breaking 60 homers that year have led many to assume that it was his best season. In reality, the former belief is probably false, while the latter is unquestionably false. Although there is no consensus among historians as to the greatest team of all time, the 1906 Cubs, 1902 Pirates, and 1939 and 1998 Yankees are often mentioned as candidates. In their book *Baseball Dynasties*, analysts Rob Neyer and Eddie Epstein concluded that the 1939 Yankees were superior to the 1927 version, and other experts have agreed. In addition, a variety of statistical measures have shown that Ruth, despite his record number of homers in 1927, was actually a significantly better player in 1920, 1921, and 1923.

But the 1927 Yankees were still a great team. They ran roughshod over the American League with a 110-44 record. Lou Gehrig, at age 24, turned in one of his very best seasons, with an astounding 117 extra-base hits: 52 doubles, 18 triples, and 47 home runs. Ruth had a Ruthian season, while Tony Lazzeri, Bob Meusel, and Earle Combs were all outstanding players. The pitching staff, while boasting no superstars, had a bevy of consistent, productive hurlers. The Yankees in 1927 were the class act of major league baseball.

The Pirates had mostly the same team they had won the 1925 pennant with, except for the two superstars—Kiki Cuyler, who was benched after a run-in with manager Owen "Donie" Bush, and Max Carey, who was sold to Brooklyn. The Pirates replaced them in the outfield with a pair of brothers from Oklahoma, Paul and Lloyd Waner. Though they looked alike and were close in age, the Waners were complete opposites as players. Paul, the eldest, was one of the best hitters in baseball. A line drive hitter, he batted .380 in 1927, his second year in the majors. He specialized in doubles and especially triples, collecting 40 of the latter in his first two seasons. Lloyd, meanwhile, was a diminutive man who batted .300, but who rarely hit anything but singles. He was also a fabulous defensive center fielder.

One story is often told to illustrate the might of the '27 Yankees. As the tale goes, the Pirates watched the Yankees take batting practice the day before the Series started. After seeing many a line drive leave the ballpark off the bats of Ruth, Gehrig, and Meusel, the Pirates knew they didn't have a chance. They were beaten before they even showed up. It is the only interesting story that has ever been told about the 1927 World Series, and it is false.

"According to the story, which I have read and heard so many times, Paul and me and the rest of us were sitting there watching those big New Yorkers knock ball after ball out of sight and became so discouraged that we just about threw in the towel," Lloyd Waner said. "Well, I don't know how that got started. If you want to know the truth, I never even saw the Yankees work out that day. We had our workout first and I dressed and was leaving the ball park just as they were coming out on the field. I don't know where that story came from. Somebody made it up out of thin air, that's all I can say."

BOTTOM: Lou Gehrig takes a practice swing before Game 2 of the 1927 World Series at Forbes Field.

1927 World Series

Forbes Field (Pittsburgh Pirates) ◆ 10.5.27 (Game 1)

	1	2	3	4	5	6	7	8	9	R	H	E
NYY	1	0	3	0	1	0	0	0	0	5	6	1
Pitt.	1	0	1	0	1	0	0	1	0	4	9	2

WP–Hoyt LP–Kremer S–Moore ATT: 41,467

Forbes Field ◆ 10.6.27 (Game 2)

	1	2	3	4	5	6	7	8	9	R	H	E
NYY	0	0	3	0	0	0	0	3	0	6	11	0
Pitt.	1	0	0	0	0	0	0	1	0	2	7	2

WP–Pipgras LP–Aldridge ATT: 41,634

Yankee Stadium I (N.Y. Yankees) ◆ 10.7.27 (Game 3)

	1	2	3	4	5	6	7	8	9	R	H	E
Pitt.	0	0	0	0	0	0	0	1	0	1	3	1
NYY	2	0	0	0	0	0	6	0	X	8	9	0

WP–Pennock LP–Meadows HR: NYY–Ruth
ATT: 60,695

Yankee Stadium I ◆ 10.8.27 (Game 4)

	1	2	3	4	5	6	7	8	9	R	H	E
Pitt.	1	0	0	0	0	0	2	0	0	3	10	1
NYY	1	0	0	0	2	0	0	0	1	4	12	2

WP–Moore LP–Miljus HR: NYY–Ruth ATT: 57,909

Although it was not true that the Pirates were beaten before they started, the Yankees were so dominant that the World Series was, frankly, boring. It was only the second four-game sweep in Series history, and the first sweep—by the 1914 Miracle Braves—had been much more entertaining.

The Yankees won Game 1 on three hits by Ruth and a triple by Gehrig. They won Game 2 with the pitching of George Pipgras, aided by Mark Koenig's three hits. Herb Pennock pitched well to beat the Pirates in Game 3, while Ruth had a three-run homer and Gehrig a double and a triple. And after a Ruth homer, they won Game 4 in the bottom of the ninth when Johnny Miljus' wild pitch scored Earle Combs with the Series-ending run. The Yankees, according to the *Spalding Guide*, did not celebrate much when it was over, but simply "shook hands sedately and disappeared." It was a fitting ending for what was probably the least interesting World Series ever played.

1928

New York Yankees (4)
St. Louis Cardinals (0)

The 1928 Series pitted the Yankees versus the Cardinals for the second time in three years. But unlike the 1926 Series, the outcome of this one was never in doubt. Although two key New York players, Herb Pennock and Earle Combs, were sidelined by injuries, the Yankees demolished the Cardinals, winning each of the four games easily while outscoring St. Louis 27-10.

The Yankees coasted in the first game behind three hits by Babe Ruth and two by Lou Gehrig, as Waite Hoyt pitched a gem to win 4-1. The Cardinals hoped to rebound in Game 2 behind 41-year-old Grover Cleveland Alexander, whose heroics had helped beat the Yankees two years earlier, but this time it was not to be. "You know how they always ask the starting pitchers to pose for pictures before a World Series game?" said George Pipgras, Alexander's mound opponent in Game 2. "Well, when I got together with Alex, I put my hand out for him to shake and I swear he missed it by a foot, he was so drunk." Alexander's performance was so bad that the *Reach Guide*, in its annual recap of the Series, called him "a pathetic and beaten star." He lasted only $2\frac{1}{3}$ innings, giving up four walks and six hits, including a three-run homer by Gehrig, as the Yankees won 9-3.

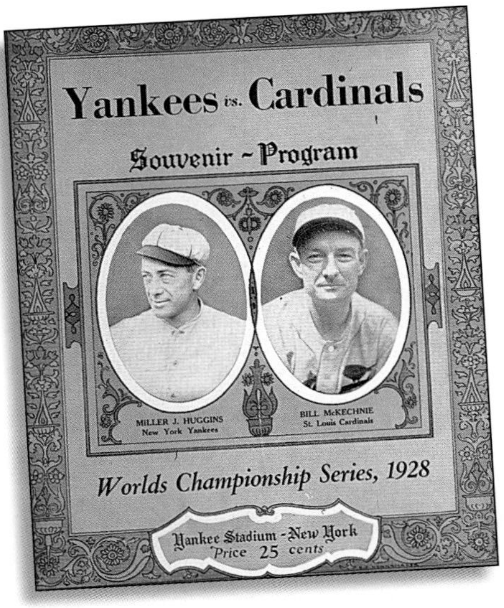

Now down 2-0, whatever slim hope the Cardinals had left rested on the fact that Game 3 would be played on their home turf at Sportsman's Park. Jesse Haines pitched well for St. Louis, but as the *Reach Guide* wrote, "errors of head and hand foiled him." Gehrig hit an inside-the-park homer in the fourth inning on a ball that was misplayed by center fielder Taylor Douthit. It was Gehrig's second homer of the game and his third of the Series. The Cardinals still managed to keep the game close, but were undone in the sixth inning when catcher Jimmie Wilson made two errors on one play, and the Yankees scored three runs to take the lead for good.

With New York now ahead three games to none, Game 4 was merely a formality. The score was close for a while, but the outcome was never really in doubt. In the fourth inning, Ruth hit a towering home run over the right field roof. In the seventh inning, after a pitch he had struck out on was ruled illegal, Ruth hit another homer over the right field roof. And in the eighth inning, he hit another homer onto the right field roof, his third of the game. Entering the bottom of the ninth, the Yankees led 7-2 on the strength of Ruth's homers. The Cardinals made an attempt to come back, scoring one run and putting two men on base with two outs, but Frankie Frisch hit a long foul fly to left field, and Ruth, playing with an injured ankle, made a spectacular running catch with his glove reaching over the fence to end the game and the Series. Ruth never broke stride after the putout, running all the way to

LEFT: Lou Gehrig and Babe Ruth combined for nine home runs and 24 RBI during the 1927 and 1928 World Series.

1928 WORLD SERIES

Yankee Stadium I (N.Y. Yankees) ◆ 10.4.28

	1	2	3	4	5	6	7	8	9	R	H	E
St.L.	0	0	0	0	0	0	1	0	0	1	3	1
NYY	1	0	0	2	0	0	0	1	X	4	7	0

WP–Hoyt LP–Sherdel HR: STL–Bottomley; NYY–Meusel ATT: 61,425

Yankee Stadium I ◆ 10.5.28

	1	2	3	4	5	6	7	8	9	R	H	E
St.L.	0	3	0	0	0	0	0	0	0	3	4	1
NYY	3	1	4	0	0	0	1	0	X	9	8	2

WP–Pipgras LP–Alexander HR: NYY–Gehrig ATT: 60,714

Sportsman's Park IV (St. Louis Cards) ◆ 10.7.28

	1	2	3	4	5	6	7	8	9	R	H	E
NYY	0	1	0	2	0	3	1	0	0	7	7	2
St.L.	2	0	0	0	1	0	0	0	0	3	9	3

WP–Zachary LP–Haines HR: NYY–Gehrig (2) ATT: 39,602

Sportsman's Park IV ◆ 10.9.28

	1	2	3	4	5	6	7	8	9	R	H	E
NYY	0	0	0	1	0	0	4	2	0	7	15	2
St.L.	0	0	1	1	0	0	0	0	1	3	11	0

WP–Hoyt LP–Sherdel HR: NYY–Ruth (3), Durst, Gehrig ATT: 37,331

the Yankees clubhouse with the ball that brought him his fifth World Series championship.

The Yankees set a record by winning eight consecutive World Series games with the victory. Gehrig tied the record for highest average ever in a Series with a .545 batting average. But Ruth topped even that, upping the record to .625, a mark that still stands today. Despite the brevity of the Series, Ruth also set new records with nine runs scored and six extra-base hits. Gehrig, not to be outdone, tied Ruth's 1926 record of four homers in a Series and set a new mark with nine RBI. After winning two straight Series in the most convincing fashion possible, the Ruth-Gehrig dynasty had reached its pinnacle.

1929

Philadelphia A's (4)
Chicago Cubs (1)

The 1929 World Series between the Cubs and Athletics was exciting in a myriad of ways, featuring late-inning comebacks in each of the last two games and, in the first game, what was probably the most brilliant strategic move in Series history. The Athletics, a young team on the cusp of a dynasty, were led to the series by 27-year-old outfielder Al Simmons, who drove in 157 runs; 26-year-old catcher Gordon "Mickey" Cochrane, who batted .331 and anchored the defense; and strapping 21-year-old first baseman Jimmie Foxx, who came into his own that season with a .354 average and 33 homers, and who admitted to being "as nervous as a hen on a hot griddle" at the prospect of playing in the World Series. The Cubs, meanwhile, were an offensive juggernaut, batting .303 as a team, including three regulars over .360.

In late August, Philadelphia manager Connie Mack intended to release one of his pitchers, 35-year-old Howard Ehmke, who had won 166 games in his career but looked to be finished as a major leaguer, throwing only 55 innings through early September. But Ehmke, who had never played for a pennant-winning team, talked Mack out of releasing him. Ehmke believed he had one more good game left in him, and he wanted it to be a World Series game. So Mack told him to leave the team for a couple of weeks to scout the Cubs, who were coasting to the National League pennant.

Although Mack had Lefty Grove, the best pitcher in the American League, and George Earnshaw, a 24-game winner, at his disposal,

OPPOSITE, BOTTOM LEFT: Jimmie Foxx, nicknamed "The Beast," had a spectacular season in 1929, batting .354 with 33 home runs. He was also the centerpiece of the A's offense in the World Series, batting .350 with 2 homers.

OPPOSITE, BOTTOM RIGHT: Mule Haas slides home after collecting perhaps the most important hit of the 1929 World Series, a three-run, inside-the-park homer that tied the game in the seventh inning of Game 4.

LEFT: In this stereopticon view, the Chicago Cubs congregate in their Wrigley Field dugout before the 1929 World Series, their first Series appearance in more than a decade.

he shocked the press and the public by selecting Ehmke to start the first game of the World Series at Wrigley Field. It was a brilliant strategic move by Mack. Not only had Ehmke been scouting the Cubs for two weeks, but Chicago's four outstanding hitters—Rogers Hornsby, Hack Wilson, Jackson "Riggs" Stephenson, and Kiki Cuyler—were all right-handed, and Mack wanted only right-handed pitchers to face them. The Cubs were also deadly fastball hitters and Mack believed they would be stymied by Ehmke's sidearm motion and his eclectic assortment of curves, sinkers, and change-ups. The strategy worked beautifully, as

1929 WORLD SERIES

Wrigley Field (Chicago Cubs) ◆ 10.8.29 (Game 1)

	1	2	3	4	5	6	7	8	9	R	H	E
Phil.	0	0	0	0	0	0	1	0	2	3	6	1
Chi.	0	0	0	0	0	0	0	0	1	1	8	2

WP–Ehmke LP–Root HR: PHA–Foxx ATT: 50,740

Wrigley Field ◆ 10.9.29 (Game 2)

	1	2	3	4	5	6	7	8	9	R	H	E
Phil.	0	0	3	3	0	0	1	2	0	9	12	0
Chi.	0	0	0	0	3	0	0	0	0	3	11	1

WP–Earnshaw LP–Malone S–Grove
HR: PHA–Simmons, Foxx ATT: 49,987

Shibe Park (Philadelphia Athletics) ◆ 10.11.29 (Game 3)

	1	2	3	4	5	6	7	8	9	R	H	E
Chi.	0	0	0	0	0	3	0	0	0	3	6	1
Phil.	0	0	0	0	1	0	0	0	0	1	9	1

WP–Bush LP–Earnshaw ATT: 29,921

Shibe Park ◆ 10.12.29 (Game 4)

	1	2	3	4	5	6	7	8	9	R	H	E
Chi.	0	0	0	2	0	5	1	0	0	8	10	2
Phil.	0	0	0	0	0	0	10	0	X	10	15	2

WP–Rommel LP–Blake S–Grove HR: CHC–Grimm; PHA–Haas, Simmons ATT: 29,921

Shibe Park ◆ 10.14.29 (Game 5)

	1	2	3	4	5	6	7	8	9	R	H	E
Chi.	0	0	2	0	0	0	0	0	0	2	8	1
Phil.	0	0	0	0	0	0	0	0	3	3	6	0

WP–Walberg LP–Malone HR: PHA–Haas
ATT: 29,921

Ehmke shut out the Cubs for eight innings and took a 3-0 lead into the ninth inning. He gave up an unearned run in the ninth but, with two men on base, Ehmke struck out pinch hitter Charles "Chick" Tolson to win, 3-1. It was Ehmke's thirteenth strikeout of the day, breaking a 23-year-old Series record. Howard Ehmke, the most unlikely postseason hero of all time, had given the A's a 1-0 lead in the Series.

Game 2, played on a cold and windy day at Wrigley Field, also went to the Athletics. Foxx—whose wife was listening to the game from her hospital bed after giving birth to Jimmie Foxx, Jr.—had three hits, including a three-run homer, and Grove pitched 4⅓ innings of shutout relief to preserve a 9-3 Philadelphia win. The teams then traveled to Philadelphia's Shibe Park with the A's up 2-0 in the Series. The Cubs won the next game, a pitcher's duel between Guy Bush and Earnshaw, after Earnshaw walked the pitcher leading off the seventh inning, setting up a two-run single by Cuyler that proved to be the difference in the game. Hack Wilson made two spectacular catches in center field to preserve the first World Series game won by a National League team since Game 7 of the 1926 Series.

The Cubs were also leading Games 4 and 5 in the late innings, but each time Philadelphia rallied to win. The A's were losing 8-0 entering the seventh inning of Game 4, but mounted what Fred Lieb called "the most spectacular rally in the entire history of the sport." The Athletics scored ten runs in the bottom of the seventh to take the lead, 10-8. Simmons and Foxx each had two hits in the inning, and the Cubs' Wilson, after making two fine catches the day before, lost a key fly ball in the sun. The A's went on to win as Grove shut down the Cubs for the last two innings.

With President Herbert Hoover and the first lady in attendance at Shibe Park two days later, Game 5 was more of the same. Ehmke started again for Philadelphia, but he didn't have the magic this time, giving up two runs before leaving the game in the fourth inning. Pat Malone was pitching masterfully for Chicago, and the Cubs had a 2-0 lead with one out in the bottom of the ninth. But Max Bishop singled for the A's and George "Mule" Haas homered to tie the game. Simmons doubled with two outs in the inning, and after an intentional walk to Foxx, right fielder Edmund "Bing" Miller doubled off the right-field scoreboard to end the game and the Series.

All of Mack's strategic moves paid off, including his use of right-handed starters exclusively, which relegated Grove—the only starting pitcher in baseball that season with an ERA under 3.00—to the bullpen. It worked, as right-handed starters Ehmke and Earnshaw stumped the Cubs batters, and Grove earned two saves (although saves wouldn't become an official statistic until 1969) in his bullpen role. "When danger beckoned thickest," Heywood Broun wrote, "it was always Grove who stood towering on the mound, whipping over strikes against the luckless Chicago batters." With their core of four superstars under the age of 30—Grove, Foxx, Simmons, and Cochrane—the Athletics believed the 1929 championship was only the beginning of a great dynasty.

1930

Philadelphia A's (4)
St. Louis Cardinals (2)

PHILADELPHIA CRUSHED THE REST OF THE American League again in 1930, cruising to the pennant with a 102-52 record. Offensively they were the same powerhouse as the previous year, with Mickey Cochrane batting .357, Al Simmons .381 with 165 RBI, and Jimmie Foxx .335 with 156 RBI. Lefty Grove had one of the best pitching seasons in baseball history, going 28-5 while leading the A.L. with nine saves and a 2.54 ERA, nearly a full run better than the second-place pitcher. Grove finally got a chance to make his first career World Series start in Game 1 against the St. Louis Cardinals, who had outlasted Chicago, the New York Giants, and Brooklyn in a tight National League race. The Cardinal players, though hardly household names, were an offensive wrecking crew, the only team in the twentieth century on which all eight regulars batted over .300. Even the top two reserves, George "Showboat" Fisher and Gus Mancuso, hit .374 and .366 respectively.

But the Cardinals' bats were no match for Lefty Grove in Game 1. Though not his usual overpowering self, Grove threw a 119-pitch complete game, beating the Cardinals 5-2. His offensive support came from Cochrane and Simmons, who each homered off of Burleigh Grimes, one of four pitchers still allowed to throw the spitball that year. The A's increased their Series lead to 2-0 the next day as George Earnshaw, who had been overshadowed by Grove despite winning 22 games during the regular season, scattered six hits and beat the Cardinals 6-1.

The Series moved to St. Louis, and it was the home team's turn for a masterful pitching performance. Wild Bill Hallahan, an erratic flame-throwing southpaw who had led the N.L. in both walks and strikeouts, completely dominated the world champs in an easy 5-0 victory. A's manager Connie

BOTTOM LEFT: Jimmie Foxx takes a monstrous swing at a Jesse Haines pitch during Game 4 of the 1930 Series. (He singled.) Foxx drove in 159 runs during the 1930 season, including three in the World Series.

BOTTOM RIGHT: After being reduced to a relief role in the previous year's Series, Lefty Grove dominated the 1930 Fall Classic, posting a 1.42 ERA in three games.

Mack sent Grove back to the mound for Game 4. A defensive miscue by A's third baseman Jimmy Dykes resulted in two unearned runs, and the Cardinals' Jesse Haines held the Athletics to four hits, beating Grove 3-1. The Cardinals' pitching, which had impressed few during the regular season, was now keeping them in the World Series. The teams entered Game 5 at Sportsman's Park tied at two games apiece.

The fifth game was another pitcher's duel, this one between Grimes and Earnshaw. The score was tied 0-0 after eight innings, but in the top of the ninth, with a runner on first, Grimes had to face Foxx. Though his repertoire was mostly fastballs and spitters, Grimes had struck Foxx out on a curveball in the seventh inning. He tried to sneak another curve past Foxx with his first pitch, but this time the 22-year-old slugger was ready and he hit the ball into the bleachers to give the A's a 2-0 lead. Grove, who had entered the game after Earnshaw was removed for a pinch hitter, held the Cardinals at bay for the last two innings to earn the victory.

Now the Athletics returned home with a chance to win the Series, and Mack tapped George Earnshaw, who had pitched so well for seven innings in the previous game, to start again. The game was never close as the A's pounded Cardinal pitchers Hallahan and

1930 WORLD SERIES

Shibe Park (Philadelphia Athletics) ◆ 10.1.30

	1	2	3	4	5	6	7	8	9	R	H	E
St.L.	0	0	2	0	0	0	0	0	0	2	9	0
Phil.	0	1	0	1	0	1	1	1	X	5	5	0

WP–Grove LP–Grimes HR: PHA–Cochrane, Simmons ATT: 32,295

Shibe Park ◆ 10.2.30

	1	2	3	4	5	6	7	8	9	R	H	E
St.L.	0	1	0	0	0	0	0	0	0	1	6	2
Phil.	2	0	2	2	0	0	0	0	X	6	7	2

WP–Earnshaw LP–Rhem HR: STL–Watkins; PHA–Cochrane ATT: 32,295

Sportsman's Park IV (St. Louis Cards) ◆ 10.3.30

	1	2	3	4	5	6	7	8	9	R	H	E
Phil.	0	0	0	0	0	0	0	0	0	0	7	0
St.L.	0	0	0	1	1	0	2	1	X	5	10	0

WP–Hallahan LP–Walberg HR: STL–Douthit ATT: 36,944

Sportsman's Park IV ◆ 10.5.30

	1	2	3	4	5	6	7	8	9	R	H	E
Phil.	1	0	0	0	0	0	0	0	0	1	4	1
St.L.	0	0	1	2	0	0	0	0	X	3	5	1

WP–Haines LP–Grove ATT: 39,946

Sportsman's Park IV ◆ 10.6.30

	1	2	3	4	5	6	7	8	9	R	H	E
Phil.	0	0	0	0	0	0	0	0	2	2	5	0
St.L.	0	0	0	0	0	0	0	0	0	0	3	1

WP–Grove LP–Grimes HR: PHA–Foxx ATT: 38,844

Shibe Park ◆ 10.8.30

	1	2	3	4	5	6	7	8	9	R	H	E
St.L.	0	0	0	0	0	0	0	0	1	1	5	1
Phil.	2	0	1	2	1	1	0	0	X	7	7	0

WP–Earnshaw LP–Hallahan HR: PHA–Dykes, Simmons ATT:32,295

TOP: As the cleanup hitter in the Philadelphia Athletics' fearsome lineup, Al Simmons batted .364 during the 1930 World Series.

BOTTOM: The 1930 St. Louis pitching staff featured such hurlers as Wild Bill Hallahan (far left), Jesse Haines (fifth from left), and Burleigh Grimes (far right). They posted a respectable 3.35 ERA during the Series, but still lost to the A's in six games.

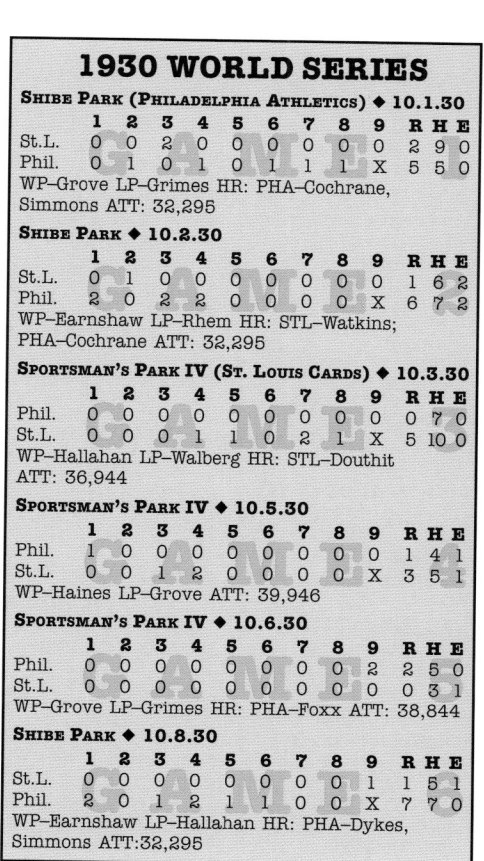

Sylvester Johnson for five doubles and two homers in the first six innings. Earnshaw managed to go the distance on short rest, holding St. Louis to one run and five hits in his third masterful pitching performance of the Series. After holding the best offensive team in baseball to an average of just two runs per game, the Athletics were world champions once again. St. Louis' .200 team batting average was higher than the Athletics' .197, but eighteen of Philadelphia's 35 hits went for extra bases, enabling them to outscore the Cardinals 21-12 for the Series. Simmons and Cochrane had two homers and four RBI each, but the real stars for Philadelphia were Grove and Earnshaw, who posted ERAs of 1.42 and 0.72, respectively, while pitching in three games each. "They were sure a great team," the Cards' Hallahan said of Philadelphia. "But we had a secret weapon waiting for them when we played them in the Series again the next year. The name of the weapon was Pepper Martin."

BOTTOM: The Cardinals' Burleigh Grimes, who flirted with a no-hitter in Game 3 of the 1931 World Series, greets Commissioner Kenesaw Mountain Landis. By the time Grimes retired, in 1934, he was the last of the legal spitballers.

1931

St. Louis Cardinals (4)
Philadelphia A's (3)

The 1931 World Series again featured the Athletics and Cardinals, the fourth rematch in Series history. The Philadelphia juggernaut was again considered the prohibitive favorite, especially after trouncing the American League competition with 107 wins, second most (after the 1927 Yankees) in A.L. history, to that date. Once again, Mickey Cochrane, Al Simmons, and Jimmie Foxx led the offense, while Lefty Grove enjoyed an even better season than in 1930. With a 31-4 record, a league-leading 175 strikeouts, and a 2.06 ERA—less than half the league average—Grove's 1931 performance is considered by some historians to be the greatest pitching season in baseball history. The Cardinals, meanwhile, had nowhere near the offensive firepower of the year before, but they did have a speedy new center fielder: John Leonard Martin, a brash, exuberant 27-year-old rookie from Oklahoma, nicknamed "Pepper" for the vitality he injected into every game he played. The 1931 World Series may have seemed a mismatch on paper, but by the time it was over, the Athletics' hopes for an unprecedented third consecutive title were dashed, and the cocky young rookie walked away with one of the greatest performances in the history of the Fall Classic.

At first it looked like déjà vu for the Cardinals, as Grove, pitching despite a blister on his finger, won a 6-2 decision over Paul Derringer, the Cards' other star rookie, who had posted an 18-8 record during the regular season. The lone bright spot for St. Louis was Martin, who stole a base and got three hits off Grove, including an RBI double. In the second game, Wild Bill Hallahan lived up to his nickname by walking seven Philadelphia batters, but he allowed them only three hits in the process, beating the previous year's hero, George Earnshaw, 2-0. Martin was again the batting star, manufacturing the game's two runs almost single-handedly. In the second inning he doubled, stole third, and scored on a sacrifice fly. In the seventh, he singled, stole second, went

to third on an infield hit, and scored on a squeeze bunt by Charlie Gelbert. The Series was tied 1-1 heading back to Philadelphia.

Spitballer Burleigh Grimes, loser of two games in the 1930 Series, flirted with a no-hitter in Game 3 at Shibe Park. He made it through seven innings without allowing the A's a hit, and in the top of the eighth, with the Cardinals well in front, even the Philadelphia crowd began cheering for Grimes to complete the unprecedented World Series no-hitter. But after Foxx walked

1931 World Series

Sportsman's Park IV (St. Louis Cards) ◆ 10.1.31

	1	2	3	4	5	6	7	8	9	R	H	E
Phil.	0	0	4	0	0	0	2	0	0	6	11	0
St.L.	2	0	0	0	0	0	0	0	0	2	12	0

WP–Grove LP–Derringer HR: PHA–Simmons
ATT: 38,529

Sportsman's Park IV ◆ 10.2.31

	1	2	3	4	5	6	7	8	9	R	H	E
Phil.	0	0	0	0	0	0	0	0	0	0	3	0
St.L.	0	1	0	0	0	0	1	0	X	2	6	1

WP–Hallahan LP–Earnshaw ATT: 35,947

Shibe Park (Philadelphia Athletics) ◆ 10.5.31

	1	2	3	4	5	6	7	8	9	R	H	E
St.L.	0	2	0	2	0	0	0	0	1	5	12	0
Phil.	0	0	0	0	0	0	0	0	2	2	2	0

WP–Grimes LP–Grove HR: PHA–Simmons
ATT: 32,295

Shibe Park ◆ 10.6.31

	1	2	3	4	5	6	7	8	9	R	H	E
St.L.	0	0	0	0	0	0	0	0	0	0	2	1
Phil.	1	0	0	0	0	2	0	0	X	3	10	0

WP–Earnshaw LP–Johnson HR: PHA–Foxx
ATT: 32,295

Shibe Park ◆ 10.7.31

	1	2	3	4	5	6	7	8	9	R	H	E
St.L.	1	0	0	0	0	2	0	1	1	5	12	0
Phil.	0	0	0	0	0	0	1	0	0	1	9	0

WP–Hallahan LP–Hoyt HR: STL–Martin
ATT: 32,295

Sportsman's Park IV ◆ 10.9.31

	1	2	3	4	5	6	7	8	9	R	H	E
Phil.	0	0	0	0	4	0	4	0	0	8	8	1
St.L.	0	0	0	0	0	1	0	0	0	1	5	2

WP–Grove LP–Derringer ATT: 39,401

Sportsman's Park IV ◆ 10.10.31

	1	2	3	4	5	6	7	8	9	R	H	E
Phil.	0	0	0	0	0	0	0	0	2	2	7	1
St.L.	2	0	2	0	0	0	0	0	X	4	5	0

WP–Grimes LP–Earnshaw HR: STL–Watkins
ATT: 20,805

leading off the eighth, Bing Miller cracked a clean single to center field. Grimes had lost his bid for immortality, but won the game, pitching a two-hitter and beating Grove 5-2. The hitting stars for St. Louis were Grimes himself, who had two hits and two RBI, and, once again, Martin, who doubled off the top of the right field scoreboard, missing a homer by inches. The next day the A's came back, as it was Earnshaw's turn to pitch a gem. The New York City native threw a two-hitter of his own, blanking the Cardinals 3-0. Foxx supported him with one of the longest homers in Shibe Park history, although once again, the ubiquitous Martin collected both Cardinal hits and stole a base.

Hallahan pitched another fine game to win Game 5 for the Cardinals, 5-1. The real story, however, was Martin. He had three hits and drove in four of the Cards' five runs, capped by a long home run to left field that earned him a standing ovation from the awed opposing crowd. When the teams returned to St. Louis, Martin, who had begun the Series batting sixth, was moved into the cleanup spot, but Grove accomplished the seemingly impossible feat of holding him hitless in Game 6. Grove also stymied the rest of the Cardinal lineup, giving up only five hits in an easy 8-1 win. His win evened the Series at 3-3, setting up the Game 7 matchup between veterans Grimes and Earnshaw. Each had already pitched a two-hitter in the Series, so a pitcher's duel was expected, but to the disappointment of the Athletics, Game 7 was a one-sided affair. Philadelphia self-destructed in the first inning, giving the Cardinals two runs on an error by Foxx, a wild pitch by Earnshaw, a passed ball by Cochrane, and two Texas League pop-ups that some felt should have been caught by Philadelphia's infielders. The Cardinals added two more in the third inning, which was more than enough for Grimes, who coasted until allowing a couple of runs in the ninth. With two outs, Hallahan came in to polish off the Athletics and preserve Grimes' second victory of the Series. As Martin caught Max Bishop's bases-loaded fly to center for the final out, the delirious St. Louis crowd rushed onto the field to congratulate their new hero. Martin had again been held hitless in Game 7, but it didn't matter. His Cardinals had toppled the mighty Athletics. Philadelphia, after slugging its way to two world championships, was held to a .282 team slugging percentage by Cardinal pitchers, although Foxx and Simmons performed admirably. Martin's final numbers, meanwhile, were among the greatest ever achieved in a single World Series: a .500 batting average, twelve hits, four doubles, five runs scored, five RBI, and five steals. Judge Kenesaw Mountain Landis, congratulating Martin after the game, told him, "Young man, I'd rather trade places with you than with any man in the country." Martin replied: "Why, that'll be fine, Judge, if we can trade salaries, too."

TOP: The tenacious Pepper Martin scores one of his five runs during the 1931 World Series, a total that led all Series players. A's catcher Mickey Cochrane is the unfortunate victim.

BOTTOM: Pepper Martin swings for one of his two hits in Game 4 of the 1931 World Series.

1932

New York Yankees (4)

Chicago Cubs (0)

BOTTOM: Babe Ruth, trying to suppress a grin, crosses the plate and shakes hands with Lou Gehrig after hitting one of his two homers in Game 3 of the 1932 World Series.

OPPOSITE, TOP: Charlie Root won 201 games in a 17-year major league career, but is best known for serving up Babe Ruth's "called shot" homer in the 1932 World Series.

OPPOSITE, BOTTOM: The 1932 Cubs outfield of (left to right) Riggs Stephenson, Johnny Moore, and Kiki Cuyler combined to bat .308 during the regular season and .302 during the World Series, but it wasn't enough for the Cubs to beat the Yankees.

Remembered today for a home run that sparked the longest-running controversy in baseball history, the 1932 World Series was, after 1927 and 1928, the third in a line of one-sided World Series demolitions for the Yankees of Babe Ruth and Lou Gehrig. "You hate to say it, but we were overmatched, strictly overmatched," Chicago Cubs second baseman Billy Herman said. "And we were a damn good ball club." Ruth, at age 37, was no longer the player he had once been—his 41 home runs and 137 RBI ranked only second and fourth, respectively, in the American League—and he missed the latter part of the season with what was believed to be appendicitis. But he still knew how put on a show and entertain a crowd. In the 1932 Series he cemented his already considerable legend by smashing the most-talked about hit in baseball history.

Both Series teams featured new managers: Joe McCarthy was in his second season as head of the Yankees, while Charlie Grimm had replaced the abrasive Rogers Hornsby as manager of the Chicago Cubs on August 4. With the club in second place when he took over, Grimm guided the Cubs to a 37-18 record the rest of the way, winning the pennant by four games. The Cubs were also aided by another late-season change, the recall of shortstop Mark Koenig from the Pacific Coast League, as he batted .353 down the stretch and played solid defense to help the Cubs secure the pennant. Despite his dazzling play, the Chicago players voted him only a half share of the Series proceeds. Koenig had previously been the Yankee shortstop for five seasons, and when the Series started, his old friends on the Yankees wasted no time in hurling insults at the Cub players for their stinginess. "Hey Mark," Ruth bellowed, "Who are those cheapskates you're with?" The two teams shot vulgar hoots and catcalls back and forth through-

out the Series, with Ruth the main target of the Cubs' wrath. "Once all that yelling starts back and forth, it's hard to stop it," Herman remembered. "And of course, the longer it goes on, the nastier it gets. What were jokes in the first game became personal insults by the third game."

The Yankees won the first two games easily behind Charles "Red" Ruffing and Lefty

Gomez. The Wrigley Field fans were more raucous than ever for Game 3, and even threw lemons at Ruth as he shagged flies in pre-game practice. He answered the jeers with a three-run homer in the first inning. The Cubs came back, though, scoring the tying run when Ruth made a comical and ill-timed attempt at a diving catch, which only increased the catcalls. With the score now 4-4, Ruth came to bat in the top of the fifth with fans heckling and the Cubs players calling him, among other names, "nigger." The first pitch from Charlie Root was a called strike. Ruth turned to the Cubs dugout and held up one finger, as if to signify that it was only one strike. After two balls, there was another called strike. The Cubs were hollering even louder now, especially idle pitcher Guy Bush, who ran several feet out from the dugout to heckle Ruth. Ruth then made some kind of gesture toward the pitcher's mound or toward center field, and according to Cubs catcher Charles "Gabby" Hartnett, he said "it only takes one to hit it." Gehrig, in the on-deck circle, later claimed that he heard Ruth boast, "I'm going to knock the next pitch right down your goddamned throat." But whatever he said, Ruth blasted the next pitch deep into the center field bleachers for his second home run of the game. He rounded the bases laughing and making more gestures toward the now silent Chicago dugout.

Eyewitnesses would forever disagree on what Ruth's famous gesture really was. Some thought he pointed toward the center field bleachers as if to call his shot; others insisted that he was only motioning toward pitcher Root, holding two fingers up to signify two strikes. "He didn't point," Herman insisted nearly fifty years later. "Don't kid yourself." The pitcher agreed: "If he had, I would have knocked him on his ass with the next pitch." To many, it was a non-story. Some newspapers reported nothing unusual about the home run in their stories the next day. The *Spalding Guide*, in its comprehensive review of the Series, made no mention of the alleged called shot. But some enthusiastic sportswriters reported in their game stories that Ruth had called his shot, although only one, Joe Williams of the *New York World-Telegram*, said specifically that he had pointed to the center field bleachers. The legend quickly spread as Lou Gehrig bought into it, enthusiastically declaring that the Babe had called his shot. Ruth's manager, Joe McCarthy, stayed steadfastly neutral. "I'm not going to say he didn't do it," McCarthy said. "Maybe I didn't see it. Maybe I was looking the other way. Anyway, I'm not going to say he didn't do it." Ruth himself was merely coy. When asked whether he'd called his shot, he replied, "It's in all the papers, isn't it?" In 1999, a grainy sixteen-millimeter home movie of the event surfaced, but it proved inconclusive. What really happened? Probably something like the scenario put forth by Ruth's biographer, Robert Creamer, who believes that Ruth did not specifically point toward the bleachers, but that with all his gestures and bravado, he did, in a way, call his shot.

When Ruth's drive left the park, the Series was effectively over. Gehrig followed immediately with another homer, and the Yankees won the game 7-5. The next day they clobbered the Cubs 13-6 to finish off the Series. Ironically, all the hoopla surrounding Ruth's homer obscured the fact that the real star of the Series was Gehrig, who batted .529 with three homers, nine runs scored, eight RBI, and a 1.118 slugging percentage, beating Ruth in every category. But still, all the press talked about was Ruth. For Gehrig, the 1932 World Series was a microcosm of his entire Yankee career.

1932 WORLD SERIES

Yankee Stadium I (N.Y. Yankees) ◆ 9.28.32

	1	2	3	4	5	6	7	8	9	R	H	E
Chi.	2	0	0	0	0	0	2	2	0	6	10	1
NYY	0	0	0	3	0	5	3	1	X	12	8	2

WP–Ruffing LP–Bush HR: NYY–Gehrig ATT: 41,459

Yankee Stadium I ◆ 9.29.32

	1	2	3	4	5	6	7	8	9	R	H	E
Chi.	1	0	1	0	0	0	0	0	0	2	9	0
NYY	2	0	2	0	1	0	0	0	X	5	10	1

WP–Gomez LP–Warneke ATT: 50,709

Wrigley Field (Chicago Cubs) ◆ 10.1.32

	1	2	3	4	5	6	7	8	9	R	H	E
NYY	3	0	1	0	2	0	0	0	1	7	8	1
Chi.	1	0	2	1	0	0	0	0	1	5	9	4

WP–Pipgras LP–Root S–Pennock HR: NYY–Ruth (2), Gehrig (2); CHC–Cuyler, Hartnett ATT: 49,986

Wrigley Field ◆ 10.2.32

	1	2	3	4	5	6	7	8	9	R	H	E
NYY	1	0	2	0	0	2	4	0	4	13	19	4
Chi.	4	0	0	0	0	1	0	0	1	6	9	1

WP–W. Moore LP–May S–Pennock HR: NYY–Lazzeri (2), Combs; CHC–Demaree ATT: 49,844

1933

New York Giants (4)
Washington Senators (1)

Both teams in the 1933 World Series were led by star player-managers. Bill Terry, in his first full season after inheriting the managerial reins of the New York Giants from John McGraw, batted .322 while guiding his team to its first pennant in nearly a decade. Meanwhile, 27-year-old Senators skipper Joe Cronin batted .309 with 118 RBI while leading his team to the league title. It was the third time in a decade that the Senators had been managed to the pennant by a twentysomething shortstop. The Giants, with a mediocre offense, won only 91 games, but managed to capture the flag on the strength of their pitching, in particular that of Carl Hubbell, the lefty screwballer who enjoyed the best season of his impressive career in 1933, going 23-12 with a league-leading 1.66 ERA. In contrast, the Senators' strength was a balanced offensive attack featuring Cronin, Goose Goslin, Heinie Manush, Joe Kuhel, Fred Schulte, and Charles "Buddy" Myer, all of whom batted at least .295. With the Great Depression at its lowest ebb, and two humdrum teams playing for the title, the 1933 World Series drew only 163,076 fans, the lowest attendance since World War I.

Hubbell got the Giants off to a good start in the first game at the Polo Grounds, striking out ten and giving up no earned runs in a 4-2 victory. Most of the offense came from the Giants' lone heavy hitter, Mel Ott, who had four hits, three RBI, and a home run. The Senators' Myer, shaken up after witnessing a fatal traffic accident on his way to the game, made three errors. In Game 2 the Giants got another fine pitching performance, this one a five-hitter by 22-year-old Hal Schumacher, who had graduated from St. Lawrence University only four months earlier. Every Giants starter except Ott collected at least one hit as they cruised to their second victory, 6-1.

The third game, played at Washington's Griffith Stadium, was attended by President Franklin Roosevelt, who had also been present at Ruth's called shot game in Chicago the year before. The pitching honors this time went to the Senator southpaw Earl Whitehill, a longtime Detroit Tiger who won 22 games in 1933, his first year with Washington. Whitehill shut out the Giants 4-0 with the aid of three hits from second baseman Myer. As it turned out, Game 3 would be the only Senators victory in the Series, and the last World Series win in the team's history.

Hubbell's name on the lineup card made the Giants heavy favorites in Game 4, but instead of an easy Giants victory, Hubbell and Monte Weaver put on an extended pitcher's duel that became the most exciting game of the Series. In the fourth inning Bill Terry put the Giants on the board with a solo homer into some temporary bleachers that had been erected for the Series in center field. With the tying run on second base for the Senators in the bottom of the sixth, Manush was called out on a close play at first by umpire Charles Moran, and the game was delayed for five minutes as Manush and several other Senators argued the call in vain. Manush had some more words for Moran as he ran out to right field in the top of the seventh, and this time the umpire ejected him, marking the first time since 1910 that a player was ejected from a Series game. Manush had to be restrained from punching Moran by his manager, Cronin, and the game was delayed again as hundreds of angry Washington fans threw glass soda bottles onto the field. The infuriated Senators managed to tie it in the bottom of the seventh, so the game continued into extra innings tied 1-1, with Hubbell and Weaver still exchanging zeroes. The Giants took a 2-1 lead in the top of the eleventh. Hubbell then went out to the mound to try and close it down in the bottom of the eleventh. The Senators refused to give up, though, loading the bases with only one out, and Cronin sent a quality pinch hitter to the plate: backup catcher Cliff Bolton, who had batted .410 that year. Bolton hit the ball sharply, but it was a grounder right to the shortstop, John "Blondy" Ryan, who turned it into a game-ending double play. Hubbell had an 11-inning, complete game victory, and the Senators had only one more chance to avoid elimination.

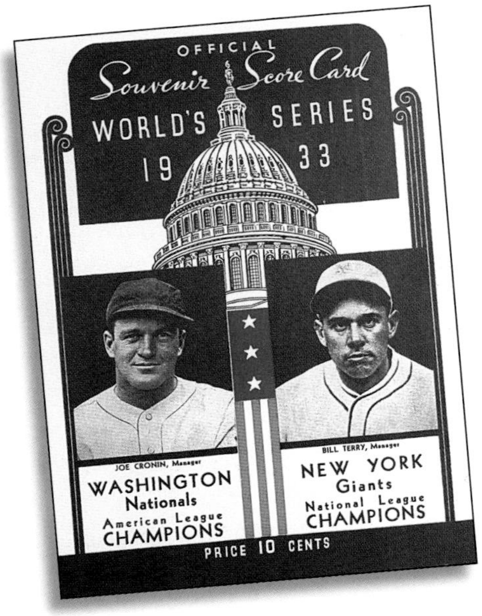

BOTTOM: The Giants won the 1933 World Series on the strength of their pitching staff. As a group, Hal Schumacher (left), Carl Hubbell (center), and Freddie Fitzsimmons combined for a 2.20 ERA during the season, and improved to 1.73 in the World Series.

Schumacher, starting his second game of the Series, gave the Giants the lead with a two-run single in the second inning of Game 5, and pitched well until the Senators' Schulte knocked him out of the game with a three-run homer in the sixth. Schumacher was relieved by 42-year-old Adolfo Luque, a career 189-game winner who two decades earlier had become the first Cuban pitcher in major league history. Luque shut down the Senators for three innings to send the game into extra innings for the second day in a row. This time the ending was even more dramatic, as Ott hit a deep fly toward the temporary bleachers in center with two out in the top of the tenth inning. Schulte, playing center field, raced back and lunged for the ball, getting a glove on it but deflecting the ball into the bleachers, to be followed moments later by Schulte himself, as his momentum caused him to topple head-first over the fence. At first the ball was ruled a ground-rule double, but after vociferous complaints from the Giants and a long conference between the umpires, the call was changed to a home run. The Giants had a 4-3 lead. The Senators threatened in the bottom of the inning, putting two on with two out, but Luque struck out Kuhel to end the Series. The Giants had their first championship since 1922. The Senators, meanwhile, would not appear in another World Series until 1965, after they had moved more than one thousand miles away and changed their name to the Minnesota Twins.

1933 WORLD SERIES

POLO GROUNDS IV (NEW YORK GIANTS) ◆ 10.3.33

	1	2	3	4	5	6	7	8	9	R	H	E
Wash.	0	0	0	1	0	0	0	0	1	2	5	3
NYG	2	0	2	0	0	0	0	0	X	4	10	2

WP–Hubbell LP–Stewart HR: NYG–Ott ATT: 46,672

POLO GROUNDS IV ◆ 10.4.33

	1	2	3	4	5	6	7	8	9	R	H	E
Wash.	0	0	1	0	0	0	0	0	0	1	5	0
NYG	0	0	0	0	0	6	0	0	X	6	10	0

WP–Schumacher LP–Crowder HR: WSH–Goslin ATT: 35,461

GRIFFITH STADIUM I (WASH. SENATORS) ◆ 10.5.33

	1	2	3	4	5	6	7	8	9	R	H	E
NYG	0	0	0	0	0	0	0	0	0	0	5	0
Wash.	2	1	0	0	0	0	1	0	X	4	9	1

WP–Whitehill LP–Fitzsimmons ATT: 25,727

GRIFFITH STADIUM I ◆ 10.6.33

	1	2	3	4	5	6	7	8	9	10	11	R	H	E
NYG	0	0	0	1	0	0	0	0	0	0	1	2	11	1
Wash.	0	0	0	0	0	0	1	0	0	0	0	1	8	0

WP–Hubbell LP–Weaver HR: NYG–Terry ATT: 26,726

GRIFFITH STADIUM I ◆ 10.7.33

	1	2	3	4	5	6	7	8	9	10	R	H	E
NYG	0	2	0	0	0	1	0	0	0	1	4	11	1
Wash.	0	0	0	0	0	3	0	0	0	0	3	10	0

WP–Luque LP–Russell HR: NYG–Ott; WSH–Schulte ATT: 28,454

1934

ST. LOUIS CARDINALS (4)
DETROIT TIGERS (3)

THE 1934 WORLD SERIES WAS A SHOWCASE not just of baseball, but of hyperbole, machismo, and vulgarity, thanks mostly to the boisterous St. Louis Cardinals. The rough-and-tumble Cards were known as the Gashouse Gang, and the team's greatest ego and greatest talent were both owned by Jay "Dizzy" Dean, an ignorant country boy from Arkansas who proclaimed himself the greatest pitcher on the planet, and probably was. The Cardinal roster also included Dean's more reserved brother Paul, a rookie who the press insisted on calling "Daffy"; Pepper Martin, the hustling hero of the 1931 Series who dabbled in auto racing as a hobby; Leo "The Lip" Durocher, a loudmouth and defensive whiz at shortstop who had been released by the Yankees for surreptitiously stealing from Babe Ruth's wallet; Joe Medwick, a strapping, hot-headed slugger who bore the non-sequitur nickname "Ducky Wucky"; and Frankie Frisch, a perennial .300 hitter who, as player-manager, was given the difficult task of keeping the rest of them in line. The Cardinals were a hard playing, hard drinking, trash talking, tobacco chewing, and brashly confident outfit. During spring training, before Paul Dean had ever pitched an inning in the major leagues, Dizzy predicted that "Me 'n' Paul will win fifty games between us this year." He was very nearly right, as Paul went 19-11 and Dizzy 30-7. The Cardinals battled the New York Giants for the pennant, and although they held first place for only thirteen days during the season, they won the race by two games. Their opponents in the World Series were the Detroit Tigers, who

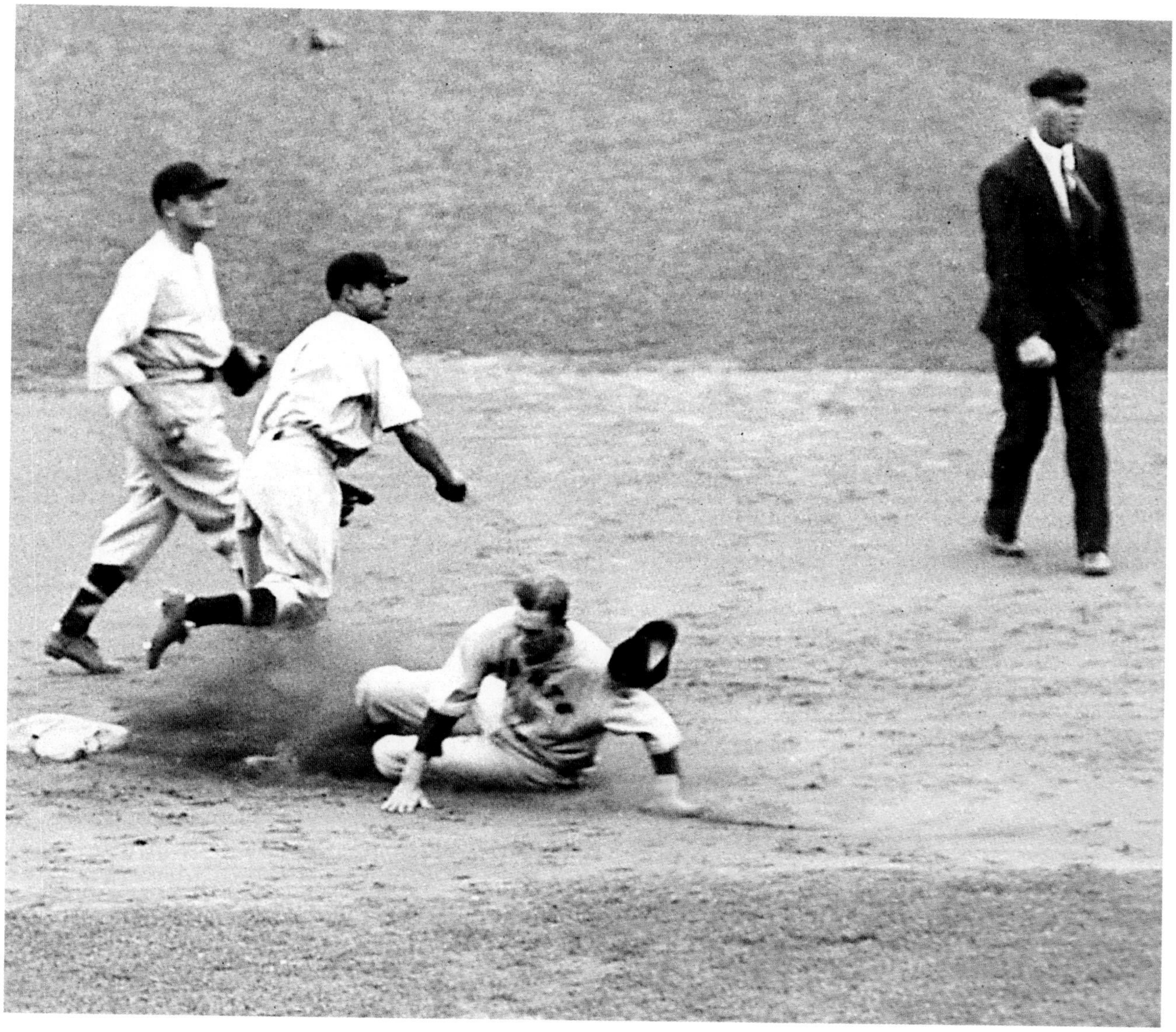

BOTTOM: Washington second baseman Buddy Myer completes a double play against the Giants in the 1933 Series.

bludgeoned American League pitching to the tune of a .300 team batting average. Every regular batted at least .285, including catcher-manager Mickey Cochrane, who became the first man to win both a pennant (as manager) and an MVP award (as a player) in the same season.

Dizzy Dean started the World Series the same way he had started the regular season: with braggadocio. "If Frankie Frisch wants me to pitch all four games, that's all right with me," Dean announced. "If he wants to save me to win the third and fourth, to save traveling expenses so we won't have to make another trip to Detroit, that's fine, too." Game 1 marked the first World Series game played in Detroit in nearly a quarter of a century, but Dean spoiled the occasion by beating the home team 8-3, thanks to four hits by Medwick and five errors by the Tigers. The Tigers threw their ace, 24-game winner Lynwood "Schoolboy" Rowe, at the Cardinals in Game 2 and came away with a 3-2 victory in twelve innings. The Cardinals were leading 2-1 entering the bottom of the ninth, but then came a scene reminiscent of the classic World Series Game 8 in 1912. Gerald "Gee" Walker hit an easy foul pop-up that either first baseman James "Ripper" Collins or catcher Bill DeLancey could have caught, but the ball somehow dropped between them. Walker, given new life, singled home the tying run exactly as Tris Speaker had done 22 years earlier, and the Tigers won it in the twelfth when Goose Goslin singled in Charlie Gehringer.

Now back in St. Louis with the Series tied at one game apiece, the Cardinals won Game 3, 4-1, thanks to the pitching of Paul Dean and the hitting of Pepper Martin, who knocked a double and a triple. Cochrane moved Hank Greenberg, the 23-year-old who was the Tigers' heaviest hitter during the regular season, from the cleanup spot down to sixth in the order for Game 4, after Greenberg struck out four times in key situations with men on base. He responded to the switch by getting four hits, including two doubles, and driving in three runs as the Tigers won 10-4. For the Cardinals, the

TOP: Bedlam erupted in Detroit during Game 7 of the 1934 World Series when fans began throwing objects at Cardinals left fielder Joe Medwick.

BOTTOM: After being knocked unconscious during Game 4 of the 1934 World Series, Dizzy Dean is carried off the field by a group of teammates that included his brother Paul (third from left in foreground).

1934 WORLD SERIES

Navin Field (Detroit Tigers) ◆ 10.3.34

	1	2	3	4	5	6	7	8	9	R	H	E
St.L.	0	2	1	0	1	4	0	0	0	8	13	2
Det.	0	0	1	0	0	1	0	1	0	3	8	5

WP–D. Dean LP–Crowder HR: STL–Medwick; DET–Greenberg ATT: 42,505

Navin Field ◆ 10.4.34

	1	2	3	4	5	6	7	8	9	10	11	12	R	H	E
St.L.	0	1	1	0	0	0	0	0	0	0	0	0	2	7	3
Det.	0	0	0	1	0	0	0	0	1	0	0	1	3	7	0

WP–Rowe LP–W. Walker ATT: 43,451

Sportsman's Park IV (St. Louis Cards) ◆ 10.5.34

	1	2	3	4	5	6	7	8	9	R	H	E
Det.	0	0	0	0	0	0	0	0	1	1	8	2
St.L.	1	1	0	0	2	0	0	0	X	4	9	1

WP–P. Dean LP–Bridges ATT: 34,073

Sportsman's Park IV ◆ 10.6.34

	1	2	3	4	5	6	7	8	9	R	H	E
Det.	0	0	3	1	0	0	1	5	0	10	13	1
St.L.	0	1	1	2	0	0	0	0	0	4	10	5

WP–Auker LP–W. Walker ATT: 37,492

Sportsman's Park IV ◆ 10.7.34

	1	2	3	4	5	6	7	8	9	R	H	E
Det.	0	1	0	0	0	2	0	0	0	3	7	0
St.L.	0	0	0	0	0	0	1	0	0	1	7	1

WP–Bridges LP–D. Dean HR: DET–Gehringer; STL–DeLancey ATT: 38,536

Navin Field ◆ 10.8.34

	1	2	3	4	5	6	7	8	9	R	H	E
St.L.	1	0	0	0	2	0	1	0	0	4	10	2
Det.	0	0	1	0	0	2	0	0	0	3	7	1

WP–P. Dean LP–Rowe ATT: 44,551

Navin Field ◆ 10.9.34

	1	2	3	4	5	6	7	8	9	R	H	E
St.L.	0	0	7	0	0	2	2	0	0	11	17	1
Det.	0	0	0	0	0	0	0	0	0	0	6	3

WP–D. Dean LP–Auker ATT: 40,902

game was marred by an incident involving Dizzy Dean. In the fourth inning, Frisch sent Dean in to pinch-run for catcher Virgil "Spud" Davis, not because Dean was fast, but because "he always seems to inspire the team." But as Dean was running to second with the Tigers trying to complete a double play, the throw from shortstop Billy Rogell hit Dean in the head and he dropped like a stone. His teammates carried him off the field and he was rushed to the hospital, a circumstance that led to the fabled newspaper headline the next day: "X-RAYS OF DEAN'S HEAD SHOW NOTHING." As it turned out, Dean was well enough to pitch the next game, and although he pitched well, he lost Game 5 to Tommy Bridges, 3-1.

The jubilant Tigers returned to Detroit needing only one win in two games for the championship. They never got it. On the brink of elimination, the Cardinals turned to Dizzy's brother Paul, who pitched a fine game and defeated Rowe by a score of 4-3. Now it all came down to the seventh game with Dizzy Dean facing Elden Auker. The drama was over quickly as the Cardinals busted out for seven runs in the third inning, thanks in part to two hits by Dean himself, which tied a Series record for hits in an inning. Detroit trotted out reliever after reliever, but the hits just kept on coming, and by the sixth inning the score stood at 9-0. That inning, the eighth run was driven in by Medwick, who hit a deep fly into the gap and hustled around to third, sliding into Detroit third sacker Marv Owen with his spikes high. Medwick and Owen nearly came to blows, but the situation cooled down. It flared up again when Medwick ran out to his position in left field for the bottom of the sixth. The Detroit fans, so full of hope as the game began, were now angry—partly at Medwick for his rough slide, but mostly because they knew the Tigers were about to lose the World Series. Those in the left field bleachers took out their frustrations on Medwick, pelting him with rolled up newspapers, fruit, bottles, and other sundry items. ("I don't know where they got all that produce from," Gehringer recalled years later. "It was fairly late in the game and you'd have thought they would have eaten most of it by then.") The game was delayed as groundskeepers cleaned up the mess, but as soon as Medwick returned to his position, the assault began anew. Commissioner Landis, after conferring with the umpires, called Medwick over to his box near the third-base dugout and ordered him banned from the game for his own safety. It was, of course, a patently unfair decision, and one that never would have been made had the outcome of the game and the Series still been in doubt. The last three innings passed uneventfully except for a couple more Cardinal runs, and Dizzy Dean finished with an 11-0 victory. The Dean brothers had accounted for all four Cardinal wins in the Series, putting their grand total for the year at 53 victories—outdoing even Dizzy's boastful prediction.

TOP: Three of the oustanding pitchers of the 1934 World Series: Dizzy Dean (left), Schoolboy Rowe (center), and Paul Dean.

BOTTOM: After winning the 1934 World Series, the Cardinals relax in the clubhouse with cigars and beer. The victors include Dizzy Dean (front row, far right) and player-manager Frankie Frisch (front row, second from right).

1935

DETROIT TIGERS (4)
CHICAGO CUBS (2)

THE DETROIT TIGERS REPEATED AS American League champs in 1935, led by the same cast of characters: manager-catcher Mickey Cochrane, who batted .319, second baseman Charlie Gehringer, who batted .330 with 108 RBI, and Hank Greenberg, now in his third full season, who was named the American League's MVP after driving in 170 runs. The Chicago Cubs, meanwhile, shot past the Giants and Cardinals with a 21-game September winning streak to clinch the National League pennant. The Cubs' balanced attack was led by second baseman Billy Herman, who batted .341, and stellar defensive catcher Gabby Hartnett, who was voted N.L. MVP after a .344 season. Both the Cubs and Tigers had lost in their last four World Series appearances, so something had to give. The Tigers were determined that this would be their year. "We came close in '34, losing in seven," Charlie Gehringer said. "And when you've come that close, well, you know what it is to *almost* win. That's a very itchy feeling."

TOP: After slugging the Senators to pennants in 1924, 1925, and 1933, Goose Goslin did the same for the Tigers in 1934 and 1935.

BOTTOM: In a collision of future Hall of Famers, Hank Greenberg slides into catcher Gabby Hartnett during Game 2 of the 1935 World Series. Not only was Greenberg out, but he worsened his wrist injury on the play and had to sit out the rest of the Series.

The first game took place at Navin Field (later called Tiger Stadium), the site of the ugly Game 7 display the year before. It was bad news again for Tiger fans, as the Cubs took the lead before they made a single out, and Chicago's Lon Warneke held the Tigers to four hits in a 3-0 shutout. The Tigers turned the tables the next day, scoring four runs themselves before they made an out, capped by Greenberg's homer into the left field stands. The Tigers cruised from there, winning 8-3, though the victory was not without its downside, as Greenberg injured his wrist when hit by a pitch in the seventh inning. He stayed in the game, but made the injury worse when he tried to score from second on a single and collided with Hartnett at the plate. An X-ray showed a broken bone in the wrist, putting Greenberg on the sidelines for the rest of the Series and for most of the next season as well.

The Tigers now traveled to Chicago with the Series tied, but without the league MVP. No matter, as they won 6-5 in eleven innings to take the Series lead. Detroit pitcher Schoolboy Rowe blew a two-run lead in the ninth, but the Tigers took it back in the eleventh on singles by Billy Rogell and Joyner "Jo-Jo" White, and an error by Freddy Lindstrom. Game 4 the next day was more good news for Detroit, as Alvin Crowder

1935 WORLD SERIES

GAME 1 — NAVIN FIELD (DETROIT TIGERS) ◆ 10.2.35

	1	2	3	4	5	6	7	8	9	R	H	E
Chi.	2	0	0	0	0	0	0	0	1	3	7	0
Det.	0	0	0	0	0	0	0	0	0	0	4	3

WP–Warneke LP–Rowe HR: CHC–Demaree
ATT: 47,391

GAME 2 — NAVIN FIELD ◆ 10.3.35

	1	2	3	4	5	6	7	8	9	R	H	E
Chi.	0	0	0	0	1	0	2	0	0	3	6	1
Det.	4	0	0	3	0	0	1	0	X	8	9	2

WP–Bridges LP–Root HR: DET–Greenberg
ATT: 46,742

GAME 3 — WRIGLEY FIELD (CHICAGO CUBS) ◆ 10.4.35

	1	2	3	4	5	6	7	8	9	10	11	R	H	E
Det.	0	0	0	0	0	1	0	4	0	0	1	6	12	2
Chi.	0	2	0	0	1	0	0	0	2	0	0	5	10	3

WP–Rowe LP–French HR: CHC–Demaree
ATT: 45,532

GAME 4 — WRIGLEY FIELD ◆ 10.5.35

	1	2	3	4	5	6	7	8	9	R	H	E
Det.	0	0	1	0	0	1	0	0	0	2	7	0
Chi.	0	1	0	0	0	0	0	0	0	1	5	2

WP–Crowder LP–Carleton HR: CHC–Hartnett
ATT: 49,350

GAME 5 — WRIGLEY FIELD ◆ 10.6.35

	1	2	3	4	5	6	7	8	9	R	H	E
Det.	0	0	0	0	0	0	0	0	1	1	7	1
Chi.	0	0	2	0	0	0	1	0	X	3	8	0

WP–Warneke LP–Rowe S–Lee HR: CHC–Klein
ATT: 49,237

GAME 6 — NAVIN FIELD ◆ 10.7.35

	1	2	3	4	5	6	7	8	9	R	H	E
Chi.	0	0	1	0	2	0	0	0	0	3	12	0
Det.	1	0	0	1	0	1	0	0	1	4	12	1

WP–Bridges LP–French HR: CHC–Herman
ATT: 48,420

pitched a fine game to defeat Chicago's James "Tex" Carleton, 2-1. It was the first time the Tigers had ever won three consecutive World Series games, and they now led the Cubs three games to one. Chicago stayed alive the next day, though, winning Game 5 on a homer into the Wrigley Field bleachers by Chuck Klein, and the teams returned to Detroit with the Tigers still needing just one more win for the championship.

Game 6 was the most exciting contest of the Series, as the teams were tied 3-3 after six innings, knowing that the next run would most likely decide the game. Things looked bleak for the Tigers when Stan Hack led off the ninth inning with a triple for the Cubs, but Detroit pitcher Tommy Bridges retired the next three batters on a strikeout, a grounder, and a fly ball to preserve the tie. "When I think back on the 1935 World Series," Billy Herman said many years later, "All I can see is Hack standing on third base, waiting for somebody to drive him in. Seems to me now he stood there for hours and hours." The Tigers threatened in the bottom of the ninth as Cochrane singled and moved to third when Gehringer hit a line drive off Phil Cavarretta's glove at first base. Goose Goslin then hit a sharp single to right field to drive in the winning run, and it was all over. The Tigers were world champions for the first time. "That was the thrill of a lifetime," Gehringer said. "You don't realize what the world championship means until you've won it. It was the first championship ever for Detroit, and the town really went wild. So did we."

1936

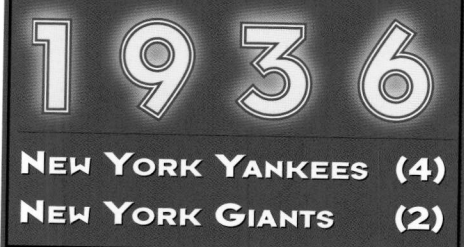

NEW YORK YANKEES (4)
NEW YORK GIANTS (2)

IN 1936 THE YANKEES PLAYED THEIR FIRST World Series without Babe Ruth, who the team had unceremoniously dumped two years earlier. New York rebuilt its lineup around Lou Gehrig, but the name of the game was the same: power hitting. Gehrig was named American League MVP after hitting a career-high 49 home runs and collecting 152 RBI, while Bill Dickey batted .362, still the best batting average ever posted by a catcher. In all, six of the eight New York regulars batted over .300, including rookie center fielder Joe DiMaggio. A much-ballyhooed prospect purchased from the San Francisco Seals for $25,000, DiMaggio enjoyed one of the greatest rookie seasons of all time, batting .323 with 29 homers and 125 RBI. The Yankees' opponents in the World Series were the crosstown New York Giants, who were pretty much a two-man team with Carl Hubbell and Mel Ott. Ott led the National League with 33 home runs and a .588 slugging percentage, while Hubbell went 26-6 with a 2.31 ERA to become the first-ever unanimous selection for N.L. MVP.

Game 1 was played on a rainy day at the Polo Grounds. Hubbell's screwball baffled the Bronx Bombers, and the Giants outfielders never even had to make a putout as they won 6-1. Game 2, however, was a different story, as the Yankees faced Hal Schumacher, who had pitched so well in the 1933 Series. The carnage started with the very first batter. Frankie Crosetti singled. Robert "Red" Rolfe walked. DiMaggio singled. Gehrig hit a sac fly. Dickey hit a sac fly. The Yankees led 2-0 at the end of the first inning. In the third, Crosetti singled. Rolfe walked. DiMaggio reached on an error. Gehrig singled. Dickey singled. Alvin "Jake" Powell walked. Tony Lazzeri hit a grand slam home run. And on and on it went. Although the Giants went through four relievers in an attempt to stem the tide of runs, nothing worked. By the time it was over,

BOTTOM LEFT: The Chicago Cubs won the 1935 pennant thanks to tough characters like catcher Gabby Hartnett (left), manager Charlie Grimm (center), and pitcher Lon Warneke.

BOTTOM RIGHT: The Yankees won 102 games in 1936 thanks in part to their star rookie, Joe DiMaggio, who batted .323 with 125 RBI.

the Yankees had bludgeoned the Giants, 18-4. The Series was now tied 1-1, but there was no question who had the momentum.

Game 3 was a low-scoring affair at Yankee Stadium. The Yankees got eight strong innings from Irving "Bump" Hadley and a solo homer from Gehrig as they won 2-1. They won again the next day, too, in front of a record Series crowd of 66,669, beating Hubbell 5-2 thanks to a double and a homer by Gehrig. With a chance to wrap up the Series in five games, the Yanks now prepared to face Schumacher, whom they had bombarded a few days earlier. But Schumacher got the better of them this time, pitching all ten innings of a 5-4 Giants win. A double by Moore and a sac fly by Bill Terry brought home the winning run in the tenth. The teams now moved back across the Harlem River to the Giants' turf.

The Giants' hopes rested on winning Game 6, so they could send a rested Carl Hubbell to the mound for Game 7. They took an early lead with two key hits from Mel Ott: a homer and a bases-loaded double. But pitcher Fred Fitzsimmons let the Yankees take the lead in the third inning, as the bottom of their order pounded out four singles. It was a close game from then on, but the Yankees made it a sure thing in the ninth, when they batted around and scored seven runs, with DiMaggio getting two hits in the inning. Now down 13-5, the Giants went meekly in the bottom of the ninth, and the Yankees were world champions. Even without Ruth in the lineup, they still batted .302 and slugged .447 as a team during the Series, setting a new record with 43 runs scored in the six games. Afterward, losing manager Terry was asked about DiMaggio's impact on the Series. "I've always heard that one player can make the difference between a winner and a loser, and I've never believed it," Terry said. "Now I know it's true." Terry was probably overstating his case—DiMaggio's .346 Series average was only third-highest on the Yankees—but when DiMaggio's train arrived back in his hometown of San Francisco, thousands of fans were waiting to greet him at the station. He was whisked away to City Hall, where the mayor gave him the key to the city. Twenty-one years old and a World Series hero, Joe DiMaggio was on top of the world.

RIGHT: The Yankees' "Murderers Row" of the late 1930s included (left to right) George Selkirk, Bill Dickey, Lou Gehrig, and Joe DiMaggio.

BOTTOM: Three reasons for the Yankees' success in 1936 were catcher Bill Dickey (left), pitcher Lefty Gomez (center), and Lou Gehrig. All were eventually elected to the Hall of Fame.

1936 WORLD SERIES

Polo Grounds IV (New York Giants) ◆ 9.30.36

	1	2	3	4	5	6	7	8	9	R	H	E
NYY	0	0	1	0	0	0	0	0	0	1	7	2
NYG	0	0	0	0	1	1	0	4	X	6	9	1

WP–Hubbell LP–Ruffing HR: NYY–Selkirk; NYG–Bartell ATT: 39,419

Polo Grounds IV ◆ 10.2.36

	1	2	3	4	5	6	7	8	9	R	H	E
NYY	2	0	7	0	0	1	2	0	6	18	17	0
NYG	0	1	0	3	0	0	0	0	0	4	6	1

WP–Gomez LP–Schumacher HR: NYY–Dickey, Lazzeri ATT: 43,543

Yankee Stadium I (N.Y. Yankees) ◆ 10.3.36

	1	2	3	4	5	6	7	8	9	R	H	E
NYG	0	0	0	0	1	0	0	0	0	1	11	0
NYY	0	1	0	0	0	0	0	1	X	2	4	0

WP–Hadley LP–Fitzsimmons HR: NYG–Ripple; NYY–Gehrig ATT: 64,842

Yankee Stadium I ◆ 10.4.36

	1	2	3	4	5	6	7	8	9	R	H	E
NYG	0	0	0	1	0	0	0	1	0	2	7	1
NYY	0	1	3	0	0	0	0	1	X	5	10	1

WP–Pearson LP–Hubbell HR: NYY–Gehrig ATT: 66,669

Yankee Stadium I ◆ 10.5.36

	1	2	3	4	5	6	7	8	9	10	R	H	E
NYG	3	0	0	0	0	1	0	0	0	1	5	8	3
NYY	0	1	1	0	0	2	0	0	0	0	4	10	1

WP–Schumacher LP–Malone HR: NYY–Selkirk ATT: 50,024

Polo Grounds IV ◆ 10.6.36

	1	2	3	4	5	6	7	8	9	R	H	E
NYY	0	2	1	2	0	0	0	1	7	13	17	2
NYG	2	0	0	0	1	0	1	1	0	5	9	1

WP–Gomez LP–Fitzsimmons S–Murphy HR: NYY–Powell; NYG–Moore, Ott ATT: 38,427

LEFT: Lou Gehrig tosses the ball during practice, one week before the beginning of the 1936 World Series. Some observers wondered whether the Yankees would struggle against the Giants now that Ruth was gone, but the 1936 Series was the beginning of four consecutive Series victories for the Pinstripes. Gehrig was his usual, excellent self in the Fall Classic that year, batting .292 with two homers, but third baseman Red Rolfe and outfielder Jake Powell were on fire: Rolfe got 10 hits in 25 at-bats (.400), all of them singles, and Powell got 10 hits in 22 at-bats (.455). As a team, in fact, the Yankees were an offensive juggernaut, outscoring the Giants in the Series 43-23.

1937

NEW YORK YANKEES (4)
NEW YORK GIANTS (1)

The Yankees and Giants returned for more of the same in 1937, playing a rematch with essentially the same personnel as the year before. Lou Gehrig had another fine season for the Yankees, but his title as the team's superstar was passed on to Joe DiMaggio, who surpassed Gehrig in nearly every facet of the game, batting .346 with 46 home runs and 167 RBI, while also winning raves for his graceful defense in center field. Otherwise, it was business as usual for the Yankees, who won 102 games and had five players—DiMaggio, Gehrig, Bill Dickey, Red Ruffing, and Lefty Gomez—finish among the top ten in MVP voting. The Giants' main stars, meanwhile, were still Mel Ott and Carl Hubbell, although the performance of both dropped considerably from their 1936 levels.

It wasn't much of a Series. The Yankees were supposed to win in a cakewalk, and they did. Game 1 was close until the sixth inning, when the Yankees, helped by some Giants defensive mistakes, unleashed their firepower on Carl Hubbell, scoring seven runs to knock him out of the game. The Yankees won 8-1 with Gomez pitching. It was the same in Game 2, as Red Ruffing pitched a solid game for the Yankees while their batters roughed up three Giants pitchers for a total of eight runs. Five Yankees—DiMaggio, Dickey, George Selkirk, Tony Lazzeri, and the pitcher Ruffing—had at least two hits in the second blowout win of the Series.

It was Hal Schumacher's turn to get bashed for the Giants in Game 3, as the Yankees scored in four of the first five innings en route to a 5-1 win. The Bombers led the Series three games to none, and by now there was no doubt which was the better team. But like a cat toying with a

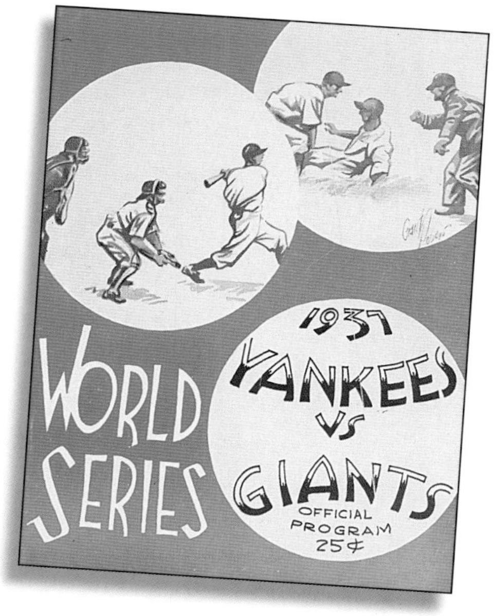

BOTTOM: Showing off his trademark high-step batting stance, Mel Ott bats against the Yankees during the 1937 World Series.

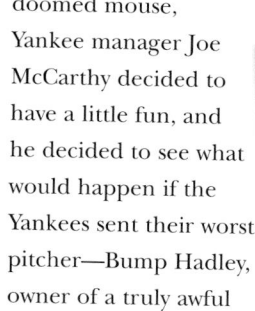

doomed mouse, Yankee manager Joe McCarthy decided to have a little fun, and he decided to see what would happen if the Yankees sent their worst pitcher—Bump Hadley, owner of a truly awful 5.30 ERA—to the mound. The Giants, to their credit, refused to fold, lighting up Hadley in a six-run second inning that featured two key hits by little-used outfielder Hank Leiber, and enabling Hubbell to fend off the Yankees 7-3. The Yankees stormed right back to win the Series the next day, though, as a homer by DiMaggio and a double and triple by Gehrig provided the margin of victory for Gomez. The Yankees were champs. Again.

Despite a spectacular hitting performance by the Giants' Jo-Jo Moore, who led all players with nine hits in the Series, the 1937 affair was one of the most lopsided ever. Even including Moore's heroics, the Giants were outscored 28-12. Not only did the Yankees have much better hitters, but they also had better pitching (a 2.45 team ERA, as opposed to 4.81 for the Giants) and vastly superior defense (the Giants made nine errors, the Yankees none). The baseball world looked forward to 1938 warily, knowing that another Yankee championship was all but inevitable.

1937 WORLD SERIES

Yankee Stadium I (N.Y. Yankees) ◆ 10.6.37 (GAME 1)

	1	2	3	4	5	6	7	8	9	R	H	E
NYG	0	0	0	0	1	0	0	0	0	1	6	2
NYY	0	0	0	0	0	7	0	1	X	8	7	0

WP–Gomez LP–Hubbell HR: NYY–Lazzeri
ATT: 60,573

Yankee Stadium I ◆ 10.7.37 (GAME 2)

	1	2	3	4	5	6	7	8	9	R	H	E
NYG	1	0	0	0	0	0	0	0	0	1	7	0
NYY	0	0	0	0	2	4	2	0	X	8	12	0

WP–Ruffing LP–Melton ATT: 57,675

Polo Grounds IV (New York Giants) ◆ 10.8.37 (GAME 3)

	1	2	3	4	5	6	7	8	9	R	H	E
NYY	0	1	2	1	1	0	0	0	0	5	9	0
NYG	0	0	0	0	0	0	1	0	0	1	5	4

WP–Pearson LP–Schumacher S–Murphy
ATT: 37,385

Polo Grounds IV ◆ 10.9.37 (GAME 4)

	1	2	3	4	5	6	7	8	9	R	H	E
NYY	1	0	1	0	0	0	0	0	1	3	6	0
NYG	0	6	0	0	0	0	1	0	X	7	12	3

WP–Hubbell LP–Hadley HR: NYY–Gehrig
ATT: 44,293

Polo Grounds IV ◆ 10.10.37 (GAME 5)

	1	2	3	4	5	6	7	8	9	R	H	E
NYY	0	1	1	0	2	0	0	0	0	4	8	0
NYG	0	0	2	0	0	0	0	0	0	2	10	0

WP–Gomez LP–Melton HR: NYY–DiMaggio, Hoag; NYG–Ott ATT: 38,216

TOP: Left-hander Carl Hubbell stymied the Yankees during the 1937 Series, going 1-1 with a 2.25 ERA.

BOTTOM: Joe DiMaggio watches his long fly reach the left field stands for a homer in the fifth game of the 1937 World Series.

Everlasting Infamy
WORLD SERIES LAST OUTS

Looking for an easy route to immortality? Just try making the last out of the World Series. The list of batters who have done so is a long and honorable one, featuring many of the game's greatest players. In fact, although less than 2 percent of all major leaguers make the Hall of Fame, nearly *15 percent* of the batters who have made the last out of a World Series have gone on to be enshrined in Cooperstown.

Twelve men in history, including Hall of Famers Honus Wagner, Jackie Robinson, and Goose Goslin, have ended their seasons in the most ignominious way possible—by striking out to end the World Series. As for pitchers, Mariano Rivera, the best reliever in postseason history, has been on the mound at the end of four World Series, twice as many as any other pitcher, though of course only three of those Series had happy endings for Rivera. From Jesse Orosco throwing his glove in the air (1986) to Orel Hershiser being lifted onto Rick Dempsey's shoulders (1988), the last pitch of a World Series often provides one of the baseball season's most memorable images.

Eighty-six World Series have ended when the losing team made an out, but only one has ended on an out made by the *winning team.* That occurred in 1912, when a sacrifice fly by the Red Sox' Larry Gardner brought an end to one of the most exciting games in baseball history. Boston had just tied the game in the bottom of the tenth, and Gardner came to plate with one out and the winning run on third. Giants manager John McGraw drew his infield and outfield in, but Gardner lofted a long fly ball to right fielder Josh Devore, a fast outfielder with a mediocre arm, whose throw home was not nearly in time. "I was disappointed at first because I thought the ball was going out," Gardner later said, "but when I saw Yerkes tag up, then score to end it, I realized it meant $4,024.68, just about double my earnings for the year."

In 1907 Detroit catcher Boss Schmidt, whose poor defensive play was one of the reasons the Tigers lost the World Series, fittingly made the last out. The next year he did so again, becoming the first player to make the last out in two consecutive World Series. The only other player to do so was Yankees second baseman Aaron Ward, who in 1921 made perhaps the strangest Series-ending out ever. With one out in the ninth inning of a 1-0 game, Ward drew a walk. The next batter, Frank Baker, smashed a hard grounder toward the hole at second base, but the Giants' Johnny Rawlings made a spectacular stop and threw out Baker for the second out of the inning. Ward, carrying the tying run, tried to advance from first to third on the play, but the alert Giants first baseman, George Kelly, threw him out. Not only did Ward commit the cardinal sin of making the final out at third base, but he ended the Yankees' season doing it. Ward ended their season the next year, too, flying out to end the fifth game of the 1922 World Series.

Another Yankee, Babe Ruth, was roundly criticized for showing poor judgment in getting caught stealing to end the 1926 Fall Classic. In his early twenties Ruth had been a tremendous all-around athlete with a supple physique, but by 1926 he was in his thirties and all those hot dogs had begun to take their toll. Always an aggressive baserunner, his 11 stolen bases during the regular season still ranked third on the Yankees, but his nine times caught stealing made it a poor percentage play. Still, when Ruth reached base as the tying run in the ninth inning of the seventh game, he tried to get himself into scoring position the old-fashioned way. With the Yankees down to their final out, he took off for second, hoping to take the Cardinals' defense by surprise. He did not, and was thrown out easily by catcher Bob O'Farrell. Stealing second with two outs in a one-run game was sound baseball strategy then as now, but with slugger Bob Meusel batting and rookie Lou Gehrig on deck, most viewed Ruth's gamble as an inexplicable blunder. Ed Barrow, the manager who had convinced Ruth to switch from pitching to hitting, called it "the only dumb play I ever saw Ruth make."

BOTTOM: In a showdown between potential Hall of Famers, Mike Piazza made the last out of the 2000 World Series against the Yankees' Mariano Rivera.

LAST PLAYS OF THE WORLD SERIES

YEAR	PITCHER	BATTER
1903	Bill Dineen, Boston A.L.	**Honus Wagner, Pittsburgh N.L. (struck out)**
1905	**Christy Mathewson, N.Y. N.L.**	Lave Cross, Phila. A.L. (grounded to short)
1906	Doc White, Chicago A.L.	Wildfire Schulte, Chi. N.L. (grounded to first)
1907	**Three-Fingered Brown, Chicago N.L.**	Boss Schmidt, Detroit (flied to left)
1908	Orval Overall, Chicago N.L.	Boss Schmidt, Detroit (grounded to catcher)
1909	Babe Adams, Pittsburgh	Tom Jones, Detroit (flied to left)
1910	Jack Coombs, Philadelphia A.L.	Johnny Kling, Chi. N.L. (force play to short)
1911	**Chief Bender, Philadelphia A.L.**	Art Wilson, N.Y. N.L. (grounded to third)
1912	**Christy Mathewson, N.Y. N.L.***	Larry Gardner, Boston A.L. (sac fly to right)
1913	**Eddie Plank, Philadelphia A.L.**	Larry Doyle, New York N.L. (fly to right)
1914	Dick Rudolph, Boston N.L.	Stuffy McInnis, Phila. A.L. (grounded to third)
1915	Rube Foster, Boston A.L.	Bill Killefer, Phila. N.L. (grounded to short)
1916	Ernie Shore, Boston A.L.	Mike Mowrey, Brooklyn (popped to short)
1917	**Red Faber, Chicago A.L.**	Lew McCarty, N.Y. N.L. (grounded to second)
1918	Carl Mays, Boston A.L.	Les Mann, Chicago N.L. (grounded to second)
1919	Hod Eller, Cincinnati	Joe Jackson, Chi. A.L. (grounded to second)
1920	**Stan Coveleski, Cleveland**	Ed Konetchy, Brooklyn (force to second)
1921	Art Nehf, New York N.L.	Aaron Ward, New York A.L. (out trying to go from first to third on Frank Baker's groundout)
1922	Art Nehf, New York N.L.	Aaron Ward, New York A.L. (flied to right)
1923	Sad Sam Jones, New York A.L.	Jack Bentley, N.Y. N.L. (grounded to second)
1924	Jack Bentley, New York N.L.*	Earl McNeely, Washington (RBI single)
1925	Red Oldham, Pittsburgh	**Goose Goslin, Wash. (struck out looking)**
1926	**Pete Alexander, St. Louis N.L.**	**Babe Ruth, N.Y. A.L. (caught stealing second)**
1927	Johnny Miljus, Pittsburgh N.L.*	**Tony Lazzeri, N.Y. A.L. (with an 0-1 count on Lazzeri, a wild pitch brought home Earl Combs with the winning run)**
1928	**Waite Hoyt, New York A.L.**	**Frankie Frisch, St. Louis N.L. (fouled out to right)**
1929	Pat Malone, Chicago N.L.*	Bing Miller, Philadelphia A.L. (RBI double)
1930	George Earnshaw, Phila. A.L.	Jimmie Wilson, St. Louis N.L. (flied to right)
1931	Wild Bill Hallahan, St. Louis N.L.	Max Bishop, Phila. A.L. (flied to center)
1932	**Herb Pennock, New York A.L.**	Riggs Stephenson, Chicago N.L. (flied to right)
1933	Adolfo Luque, New York N.L.	Joe Kuhel, Washington (struck out)
1934	**Dizzy Dean, St. Louis N.L.**	Marv Owen, Detroit (force to short)
1935	Larry French, Chicago N.L.*	**Goose Goslin, Detroit (RBI single)**
1936	Johnny Murphy, New York A.L.	Harry Danning, N.Y. N.L. (grounded to first)
1937	**Lefty Gomez, New York A.L.**	Jo-Jo Moore, New York N.L. (grounded to first)
1938	**Red Ruffing, New York A.L.**	**Billy Herman, Chicago N.L. (grounded to pitcher)**
1939	Johnny Murphy, New York A.L.	Wally Berger, Cincinnati (lined to short)
1940	Paul Derringer, Cincinnati	**Earl Averill, Detroit (grounded to second)**
1941	Ernie Bonham, New York A.L.	Jimmy Wasdell, Brooklyn (flied to center)
1942	Johnny Beazley, St. Louis N.L.	George Selkirk, N.Y. A.L. (grounded to 2nd)
1943	Spud Chandler, New York A.L.	Debs Garms, St. Louis N.L. (grounded to second)
1944	Ted Wilks, St. Louis N.L.	Mike Chartak, St. Louis A.L. (struck out)
1945	**Hal Newhouser, Detroit A.L.**	Don Johnson, Chicago N.L. (force to short)
1946	Harry Brecheen, St. Louis N.L.	Tom McBride, Boston A.L. (force to second)
1947	Joe Page, New York A.L.	Bruce Edwards, Brooklyn (6-4-3 double play)
1948	Gene Bearden, Cleveland	Tommy Holmes, Boston N.L. (flied to left)
1949	Joe Page, New York A.L.	Gil Hodges, Brooklyn (struck out)
1950	Allie Reynolds, New York A.L.	Stan Lopata, Philadelphia N.L. (struck out)
1951	Bob Kuzava, New York A.L.	Sal Yvars, New York N.L. (lined to right)
1952	Bob Kuzava, New York A.L.	**Pee Wee Reese, Brooklyn (flied to left)**
1953	Clem Labine, Brooklyn*	Billy Martin, New York A.L. (RBI single)
1954	Johnny Antonelli, New York N.L.	Dale Mitchell, Cleveland (fouled to third)
1955	Johnny Podres, Brooklyn	Elston Howard, N.Y. A.L. (grounded to short)
1956	Johnny Kucks, New York A.L.	**Jackie Robinson, Brooklyn (struck out, 2-3)**
1957	Lew Burdette, Milwaukee	Bill Skowron, New York A.L. (force to third)
1958	Bob Turley, New York A.L.	**Red Schoendienst, Milwaukee (lined to center)**
1959	Larry Sherry, New York A.L.	**Luis Aparicio, Chicago A.L. (flied to left)**
1960	Ralph Terry, New York A.L.*	**Bill Mazeroski, Pittsburgh (homer to left)**
1961	Bud Daley, New York A.L.	Vada Pinson, Cincinnati (flied to right)
1962	Ralph Terry, New York A.L.	**Willie McCovey, San Francisco (lined to second)**
1963	**Sandy Koufax, Los Angeles N.L.**	Hector Lopez, N.Y. A.L. (grounded to short)
1964	**Bob Gibson, St. Louis**	Bobby Richardson, N.Y. A.L. (pop to second)
1965	**Sandy Koufax, Los Angeles N.L.**	Bob Allison, Minnesota (struck out)
1966	Dave McNally, Baltimore	Lou Johnson, Los Angeles (flied to center)
1967	**Bob Gibson, St. Louis**	George Scott, Boston (struck out)
1968	Mickey Lolich, Detroit	Tim McCarver, St. Louis (fouled to catcher)
1969	Jerry Koosman, New York N.L.	Davey Johnson, Baltimore (flied to left)
1970	Mike Cuellar, Baltimore	Pat Corrales, Cincinnati (grounded to third)
1971	Steve Blass, Pittsburgh	Merv Rettenmund, Baltimore (grounded to short)
1972	**Rollie Fingers, Oakland**	Pete Rose, Cincinnati (flied to left)
1973	Darold Knowles, Oakland	Wayne Garrett, N.Y. N.L. (popped to short)
1974	**Rollie Fingers, Oakland**	Von Joshua, L.A. (grounded to pitcher)
1975	Will McEnaney, Cincinnati	**Carl Yastrzemski, Boston (flied to center)**
1976	Will McEnaney, Cincinnati	Roy White, New York A.L. (flied to left)
1977	Mike Torrez, New York A.L.	Lee Lacy, L.A. (popped up bunt to pitcher)
1978	Goose Gossage, New York A.L.	Ron Cey, Los Angleles (foul to catcher)
1979	Kent Tekulve, Pittsburgh	Pat Kelly, Baltimore (flied to center)
1980	Tug McGraw, Philadelphia	Willie Wilson, Kansas City (struck out)
1981	Steve Howe, Los Angeles	Bob Watson, N.Y. A.L. (flied to center)
1982	Bruce Sutter, St. Louis	Gorman Thomas, Milw. (struck out swinging)
1983	Scott McGregor, Baltimore	Garry Maddox, Philadelphia (lined to short)
1984	Guillermo Hernández, Detroit	Tony Gwynn, San Diego (flied to left)
1985	Bret Saberhagen, Kansas City	Andy Van Slyke, St. Louis (flied to right)
1986	Jesse Orosco, New York N.L.	Marty Barrett, Boston (struck out)
1987	Jeff Reardon, Minnesota	Willie McGee, St. Louis (grounded to third)
1988	Orel Hershiser, Los Angeles	Tony Phillips, Oakland (struck out swinging)
1989	Dennis Eckersley, Oakland	Brett Butler, San Francisco (grounded to second)
1990	Randy Myers, Cincinnati	Carney Lansford, Oakland (fouled to first)
1991	Alejandro Peña, Atlanta*	Gene Larkin, Minnesota (RBI single)
1992	Mike Timlin, Toronto	Otis Nixon, Atlanta (grounded to pitcher)
1993	Mitch Williams, Philadelphia*	Joe Carter, Toronto (homered to left)
1995	Mark Wohlers, Atlanta	Carlos Baerga, Cleveland (flied to center)
1996	John Wetteland, New York A.L.	Mark Lemke, Atlanta (fouled to third)
1997	Charles Nagy, Cleveland*	Edgar Renteria, Florida (RBI single to center)
1998	Mariano Rivera, New York A.L.	Mark Sweeney, San Diego (grounded to third)
1999	Mariano Rivera, New York A.L.	Keith Lockhart, Atlanta (flied to left)
2000	Mariano Rivera, New York A.L.	Mike Piazza, New York N.L. (flied to center)
2001	Mariano Rivera, New York A.L.*	Luis Gonzalez, Ariz. (RBI single to left center)
2002	Troy Percival, Anaheim A.L.	Kenny Lofton, San Francisco (flied to center)

Hall of Famers in boldface type. **denotes pitcher on losing team*

1938

New York Yankees (4)
Chicago Cubs (0)

The New York Yankees, to no one's surprise, were the American League champions again in 1938, winning the pennant easily for the third year in a row. The personnel this year was slightly different, as two talented young players—right fielder Tommy Henrich and second baseman Joe Gordon—moved into the starting lineup for the first time. Both were immediate successes, and both would become integral parts of the Yankee dynasty over the next several years. During the 1938 season Lou Gehrig played in his 2,000th consecutive game, and although his numbers were solid for anyone else—.295 with 29 home runs and 114 RBI—they were a step down from his established level of performance. At the time people thought the 35-year-old Gehrig was just showing the signs of normal aging, but now it is believed that his subpar performance in 1938 was the first manifestation of the disease that later took his life. Even with Gehrig not himself, the Yankees, with five men hitting more than twenty homers in the season, had more than enough firepower to handle the competition.

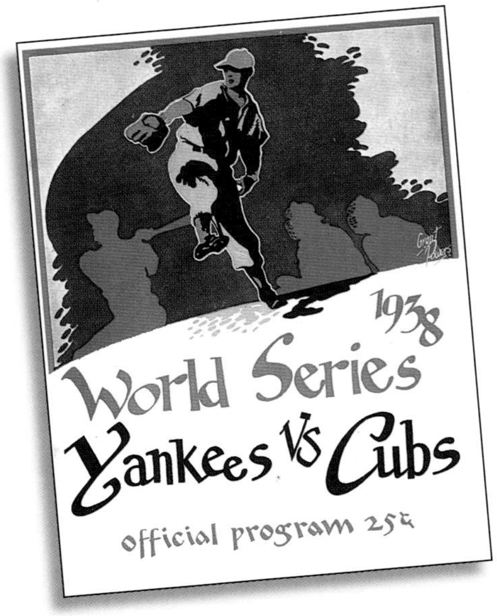

This year's Yankee fodder was the Chicago Cubs, champions of the National League despite winning only 89 games. For the second time in seven years, the Cubs had managed to win the pennant after changing managers in mid-season. On July 20 Charlie Grimm was fired and the team's veteran catcher, Gabby Hartnett, was named manager. One of the greatest backstops of all time, Hartnett's best years were clearly behind him, but on September 28, 1938, he provided perhaps the most dramatic moment in Cubs history. With two games left in the season and Chicago batting for the pennant with Pittsburgh, the two teams faced off at Wrigley Field. The game went into the bottom of the ninth tied 5-5, and with the sun going down, the umpires were prepared to call the game due to darkness after the inning ended. Hartnett didn't give them that chance, hitting a game-winning home run with two outs in the ninth that entered baseball lore as the "Homer in the Gloamin'." It all but clinched the pennant for the Cubs.

BOTTOM: The Yankees' Red Rolfe tries to push a first-inning drag bunt past pitcher Dizzy Dean during Game 2 of the 1938 World Series. Dean threw him out, but the Yankees won the game 6-3.

The Cubs were a good story, but the Yankees were the better team, and quickly set about proving it in the World Series. New York's Red Ruffing pitched a complete game victory in Game 1 at Wrigley Field, winning 3-1 behind four hits by Bill Dickey. The second game was a matchup between two slightly off-kilter heroes of previous Series, Dizzy Dean and Lefty Gomez. The Yankees got to Dean late in the game on homers by Frankie Crosetti and Joe DiMaggio, and won again, 6-3. In Game 3 the Cubs' Clay Bryant held the Yankees hitless until the fifth inning, when Gordon hit a homer. The young infielder also added a two-run single in the next inning as the Yankees won 5-2, taking a 3-0 lead in the Series. In Game 4, the Yankees wasted no time, scoring three second-inning runs on hits by Gordon, Ruffing, and Crosetti. They added four more insurance runs in the eighth and Ruffing went the distance, winning the clinching game 8-3. The experts had predicted that the Yankees would win the Series easily, and they were right. But if the result was the same as always, at least the style was new. Instead of bashing the Cubs to death, the Yankees won this Series with their pitching, holding Chicago to just nine runs while scoring 23 themselves. Gordon, the rookie second baseman, was the hitting star of the Series with a .400 batting average and .733 slugging percentage. Fans of other teams had to wonder: If the Yankees kept coming up with rookies like *this*, would their dynasty ever end?

1938 WORLD SERIES

Wrigley Field (Chicago Cubs) ◆ 10.5.38

	1	2	3	4	5	6	7	8	9	R	H	E
NYY	0	2	0	0	0	0	1	0	0	3	12	1
Chi.	0	0	1	0	0	0	0	0	0	1	9	1

WP–Ruffing LP–Lee ATT: 43,642

Wrigley Field ◆ 10.6.38

	1	2	3	4	5	6	7	8	9	R	H	E
NYY	0	2	0	0	0	0	0	2	2	6	7	2
Chi.	1	0	2	0	0	0	0	0	0	3	11	0

WP–Gomez LP–Dean S–Murphy HR: NYY–Crosetti, DiMaggio ATT: 42,108

Yankee Stadium I (N.Y. Yankees) ◆ 10.8.38

	1	2	3	4	5	6	7	8	9	R	H	E
Chi.	0	0	0	0	1	0	0	1	0	2	5	1
NYY	0	0	0	0	2	2	0	1	X	5	7	2

WP–Pearson LP–Bryant HR: CHC–Marty; NYY–Dickey, Gordon ATT: 55,236

Yankee Stadium I ◆ 10.9.38

	1	2	3	4	5	6	7	8	9	R	H	E
Chi.	0	0	0	1	0	0	0	2	0	3	8	1
NYY	0	3	0	0	0	1	0	4	X	8	11	1

WP–Ruffing LP–Lee S–none HR: CHC–O'Dea; NYY–Henrich ATT: 59,847

TOP: In much the same way DiMaggio had caused a sensation by being so terrific as a rookie in 1936, Joe Gordon, the Yankee's freshman second baseman in 1938, wowed observers by capping an excellent first major league season with a top-flight World Series performance.

BOTTOM: Four of the Yankees who went on to dismantle the Cubs in the 1938 World Series strike a relaxed pose in early September that year: the venerable Lou Gehrig, rookie phenom Joe Gordon, third baseman Red Rolfe, and speedy shortstop Frankie Crosetti (who led the league in steals in 1938).

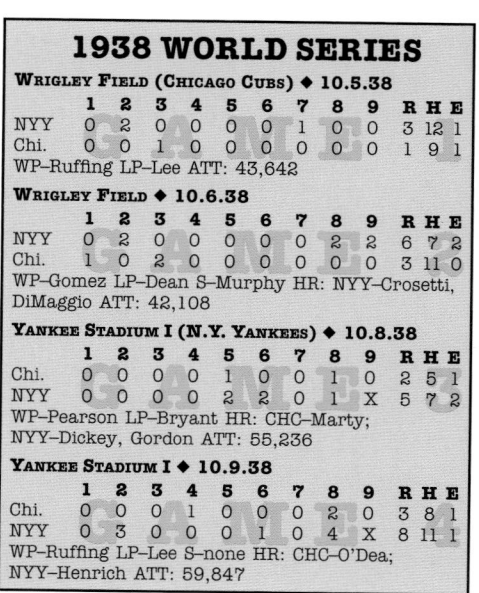

1939

New York Yankees (4)
Cincinnati Reds (0)

The year began with a bad blow for the Yankees. Lou Gehrig, after a spring training in which he could hardly field a ground ball, removed himself from the lineup on May 2 for the first time in fourteen years. Gehrig never played another major league game, but remained with the team for the rest of the season as a sort of team captain and father figure. But with or without Gehrig, the Yankees remained the best team in baseball. They had a star at every position except shortstop, where Frankie Crosetti performed poorly, and first base, where Ellsworth "Babe" Dahlgren couldn't come close to filling Gehrig's shoes. They put up a 106-45 record. Some historians have argued that this Yankee team, not the 1927 version, was the greatest in baseball history. With a healthy Gehrig in the lineup, they would almost certainly have broken the single-season record of 116 victories set by the 1906 Cubs.

The Yankees faced the Cincinnati Reds in the World Series. The Reds reached the Series by riding the right arms of William "Bucky" Walters and Paul Derringer, who became the two best pitchers in the National League after being cast off from other teams. Walters, a onetime Phillies third baseman, went 27-11 with a 2.29 ERA and was a near-unanimous selection for National League MVP, while Derringer, at 25-7, finished third. Although Walters was the MVP, Derringer started the first game of the World Series. He pitched to a 1-1 tie with Red Ruffing through eight innings, but in the bottom of the ninth, he gave up a triple to Charlie Keller, then intentionally walked Joe DiMaggio. Bill Dickey was the batter, and with George Selkirk on deck, many felt Dickey should have been intentionally walked as well. But the Reds decided to pitch to Dickey. "When I saw that," Tommy Henrich remembered, "I turned around and picked up my glove, because I knew the game was going to be over right now. And it was. Dickey singled into center field. One way or another, he was going to get that run in."

The Yankees got to Walters for four runs the next day, including an unlikely double and homer by the light-hitting Dahlgren. Remarkably, Monte Pearson, the Yankees' worst pitcher that year, held the Reds hitless until the eighth inning, when Ernie Lombardi hit a clean single to right-center. Pearson finished with a two-hitter, giving the Yankees a 2-0 lead in the Series.

Lefty Gomez, plagued by a sore arm most of the year, tried to pitch Game 3 for the Yankees, but had to come out of the game after only one inning. His replacement, Bump Hadley, pitched an impressive game, holding Cincinnati to two runs in eight innings. Reds starter Eugene "Junior" Thompson, meanwhile, gave up two home runs to Charlie Keller and one apiece to Dickey and DiMaggio as the Yankees romped 7-3. Now down 3-0 in the Series, the Reds sent Derringer back to the mound for Game 4 to try to delay the inevitable. Derringer pitched a good game for seven innings, and Walters came in to try to save the Reds' 4-2 lead, but Cincinnati shortstop Billy Myers dropped a double play ball in the ninth, enabling the Yankees to tie the game and send it into extra innings. In the tenth, another error by Myers brought DiMaggio to the plate with runners on first and third. He hit a single to score Crosetti, and when right fielder Ival Goodman bobbled the ball, Keller also headed for home, colliding with catcher Ernie Lombardi as the ball trickled away. DiMaggio noticed that the collision had left Lombardi dazed, and scored the third run of the inning as Lombardi lay helplessly on the ground. The Reds lost 7-4.

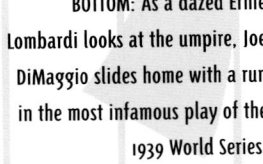

BOTTOM: As a dazed Ernie Lombardi looks at the umpire, Joe DiMaggio slides home with a run in the most infamous play of the 1939 World Series.

LEFT: Swinging with two outs in the ninth inning, Billy Werber connects for Cincinnati's second hit of Game 2 in 1939. Yankee pitcher Monte Pearson completed a two-hitter as the Bronx Bombers won, 4-0.

Lombardi was given an error on the DiMaggio play and was skewered by the sportswriters, who labeled the event "Lombardi's Snooze" or "Lombardi's Swoon" even though Lombardi had been, in his own words, "knocked senseless" by the collision, and the play had no bearing whatsoever on the outcome of the series. "Swoon, my neck," said Walters. "If you want to blame somebody you can start with yours truly—I should have been there backing up, because the ball was just lying there." But the press needed a scapegoat for the embarrassing Series loss, and Lombardi was a convenient target. The picture of him lying in the dirt while DiMaggio scored would be the lasting image of the 1939 World Series.

1939 WORLD SERIES

YANKEE STADIUM I (N.Y. YANKEES) ◆ 10.4.39

	1	2	3	4	5	6	7	8	9	R	H	E
Cin.	0	0	0	1	0	0	0	0	0	1	4	0
NYY	0	0	0	0	1	0	0	0	1	2	6	0

WP–Ruffing LP–Derringer ATT: 58,541

YANKEE STADIUM I ◆ 10.5.39

	1	2	3	4	5	6	7	8	9	R	H	E
Cin.	0	0	0	0	0	0	0	0	0	0	2	0
NYY	0	0	3	1	0	0	0	0	X	4	9	0

WP–Pearson LP–Walters HR: NYY–Dahlgren ATT: 59,791

CROSLEY FIELD (CINCINNATI REDS) ◆ 10.7.39

	1	2	3	4	5	6	7	8	9	R	H	E
NYY	2	0	2	0	3	0	0	0	0	7	5	1
Cin.	1	2	0	0	0	0	0	0	0	3	10	0

WP–Hadley LP–Thompson HR: NYY–Keller (2), Dimaggio, Dickey ATT: 32,723

CROSLEY FIELD ◆ 10.8.39

	1	2	3	4	5	6	7	8	9	10	R	H	E
NYY	0	0	0	0	0	0	2	0	2	3	7	7	1
Cin.	0	0	0	0	0	0	3	1	0	0	4	11	4

WP–Murphy LP–Walters HR: NYY–Keller, Dickey ATT: 32,794

1940

CINCINNATI REDS (4)

DETROIT TIGERS (3)

ONE THING WAS CERTAIN GOING INTO the 1940 World Series: The Yankees couldn't win it. After an unprecedented four straight world titles, the Yanks' pitching betrayed them in 1940, and the Detroit Tigers won a close three-way race for the American League pennant. The Tigers had lousy pitching, but they had the same two stars who had led them to their last pennant six years earlier: Hank Greenberg and Charlie Gehringer. Greenberg, with a .340 batting average and 150 RBI, was the league MVP, while Gehringer, nearing the end of his career, still managed a .428 on-base percentage.

The Tigers faced the Cincinnati Reds, who again won the National League pennant behind the pitching of Bucky Walters and Paul Derringer. The Reds also had National League MVP first baseman Frank McCormick. Their season was a tumultuous one, however, as their backup catcher, Willard Hershberger, committed suicide on August 3, blaming himself for calling the wrong pitches in a game lost by Walters. Meanwhile, Ernie Lombardi, the Reds' regular catcher and best hitter, severely sprained his ankle in mid-September, limiting him to mostly pinch-hitting duties in the World Series. With Lombardi hurt and Hershberger dead, the Reds were forced to bring Jimmie Wilson, their 40-year-old coach, out of retirement to catch in the World Series.

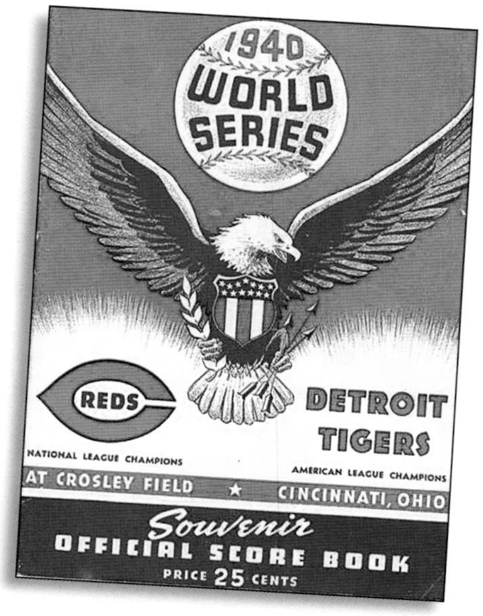

The Series opened at Crosley Field. Al Schacht, the famous baseball clown, put on a pre-game exhibition involving two giant baseball gloves. Oddly enough, the game itself was won by Detroit's Louis "Buck" Newsom, who outpitched Derringer for a 7-2 victory. Walters evened the Series the next day, winning 5-3 with the help of two hits from Wilson. The Tigers came back in Game 3, scoring six runs in the last two innings on homers by Preston "Rudy" York and Michael "Pinky" Higgins to win 7-4. Derringer, after losing the first game, came back on short rest to pitch Game 4, and won 5-2. The Series was now tied at two games apiece.

Newsom's father, who had been in the stands when his son won Game 1 of the Series, died of a heart attack a day later. Newsom took the mound for the Tigers in Game 5 promising to win the game for his father, and he did so by shutting the Reds out on three hits. One reporter said Newsom was "the first pitcher in history to work a World Series game with no heckling from opponents' bench jockeys and coaches." The Detroit bats also came alive in the game, as five Tigers had at least two hits, including Greenberg, who hit a three-run homer. The Series returned to Cincinnati with the Reds facing elimination and needing to win both games at Crosley Field to capture the title. Fortunately, they had Walters and Derringer waiting to pitch Games 6 and 7.

BOTTOM: The Yankees celebrate their sweep of the Reds in the 1939 World Series, with manager Joe McCarthy at far right.

TOP: Right-hander Schoolboy Rowe, a country boy from El Dorado, Arkansas, was one of Detroit's top pitchers in 1940.

BOTTOM LEFT: After a nail-biting Series, with the Reds and Tigers trading victories until the last game, when Cincinnati made it two in a row to take the championship, Reds manager Bill McKechnie (center) and his two star pitchers, Bucky Walters (left) and Paul Derringer (right), look mighty pleased. And why not? The two aces were instrumental not only in getting the Reds to the Series, but in winning it: each man won two games for their team in that year's Fall Classic.

BOTTOM RIGHT: The Tigers' Buck Newsom breaks into tears after pitching a three-hit shutout against the Reds in Game 5, three days after the death of his father.

Walters did his part in Game 6, pitching a five-hit shutout and hitting a homer to beat the Tigers 4-0. (An ex-third baseman, he was a .243 lifetime hitter.) That left it up to Derringer, who would face the Tigers' sentimental hero, Newsom, in Game 7. Both pitched brilliantly, though the Tigers got out to an early lead after scoring a run in the third on singles by Billy Sullivan (whose father, Billy Sullivan, Sr., had caught for the White Sox in the 1906 World Series) and Gehringer. But the Reds came back in the seventh, taking a 2-1 lead on consecutive doubles by McCormick and Jimmy Ripple. Derringer made the lead hold up, getting the Tigers out in the eighth and ninth to clinch the championship. Wilson ended up with a .353 batting average in the Series, but never played another major league game, instead accepting an offer to become manager of the Chicago Cubs. The World Series title was the second for the Reds franchise, but after 1919, it was the first time they'd won when the other team had been trying to win. Fans celebrated long into the night at Fountain Square in downtown Cincinnati.

1940 WORLD SERIES

Crosley Field (Cincinnati Reds) ◆ 10.2.40

	1	2	3	4	5	6	7	8	9	R	H	E
Det.	0	5	0	0	2	0	0	0	0	7	10	1
Cin.	0	0	0	1	0	0	0	1	0	2	8	3

WP–Newsom LP–Derringer S–none
HR: DET–Campbell ATT: 31,793

Crosley Field ◆ 10.3.40

	1	2	3	4	5	6	7	8	9	R	H	E
Det.	2	0	0	0	0	1	0	0	0	3	3	1
Cin.	0	2	2	1	0	0	0	0	X	5	9	0

WP–Walters LP–Rowe HR: CIN–Ripple ATT: 30,640

Tiger Stadium (Detroit Tigers) ◆ 10.4.40

	1	2	3	4	5	6	7	8	9	R	H	E
Cin.	1	0	0	0	0	0	0	1	2	4	10	1
Det.	0	0	0	1	0	0	4	2	X	7	13	1

WP–Bridges LP–Turner HR: DET–York, Higgins
ATT: 52,877

Tiger Stadium ◆ 10.5.40

	1	2	3	4	5	6	7	8	9	R	H	E
Cin.	2	0	1	1	0	0	0	1	0	5	11	1
Det.	0	0	1	0	0	1	0	0	0	2	5	1

WP–Derringer LP–Trout ATT: 54,093

Tiger Stadium ◆ 10.6.40

	1	2	3	4	5	6	7	8	9	R	H	E
Cin.	0	0	0	0	0	0	0	0	0	0	3	0
Det.	0	0	3	4	0	0	0	1	X	8	13	0

WP–Newsom LP–Thompson HR: DET–Greenberg
ATT: 55,189

Crosley Field ◆ 10.7.40

	1	2	3	4	5	6	7	8	9	R	H	E
Det.	0	0	0	0	0	0	0	0	0	0	5	0
Cin.	2	0	0	0	0	1	0	1	X	4	10	2

WP–Walters LP–Rowe HR: CIN–Walters
ATT: 30,481

Crosley Field ◆ 10.8.40

	1	2	3	4	5	6	7	8	9	R	H	E
Det.	0	0	1	0	0	0	0	0	0	1	7	0
Cin.	0	0	0	0	0	0	2	0	X	2	7	1

WP–Derringer LP–Newsom ATT: 26,854

1941

New York Yankees (4)
Brooklyn Dodgers (1)

Larry MacPhail took over as owner of the Brooklyn Dodgers in 1938 and immediately set about transforming the hapless Bums into contenders, brilliantly building a winning team from an unlikely collection of has-beens and never-would-bes. After nearly two decades of futility, new manager Leo Durocher took the Dodgers to third place in 1939, second in 1940, and finally to the pennant in 1941. It was the first flag to fly at Ebbets Field since the days of Zack Wheat. The Dodgers under Durocher functioned as an impressively cohesive machine despite being composed almost entirely of spare parts from other clubs. First baseman Dolph Camilli, an ex-pugilist purchased from the Phillies in 1938, drove in 120 runs and won the MVP award. Right fielder Fred "Dixie" Walker, rejected by three American League clubs, emerged as a star in Brooklyn, batting .311. Second baseman Billy Herman, acquired early in the season from the Cubs, batted .291, while ex-Cardinal Joe Medwick averaged .318. Kirby Higbe, owner of a 27-34 career record and 4.16 lifetime ERA with the Cubs and Phillies, went 22-9 in his first year with the Dodgers. And most impressively, Whitlow Wyatt—who had been a terrible pitcher for almost a decade, posting a 26-43 record and 5.22 ERA for three American League teams—transformed himself into the best pitcher in the National League, going 22-10 with a 2.34 ERA.

The Dodgers also had two youngsters playing their first full seasons in the big leagues. Harold "Pee Wee" Reese batted .229 and made 47 errors at shortstop, but showed enough promise to keep himself in the lineup on an everyday basis. And Harold "Pete" Reiser, a supremely talented center fielder, emerged at age 22 as one of the best players in the National League, winning the batting title with a .343 average while also leading the league in total bases, slugging percentage, doubles, triples, and runs scored. After winning one hundred games during the regular season, the Dodgers entered the World Series

BOTTOM: The Reds celebrate on the field after winning the seventh game of the 1940 World Series at Crosley Field. It was Cincinnati's first championship since 1919.

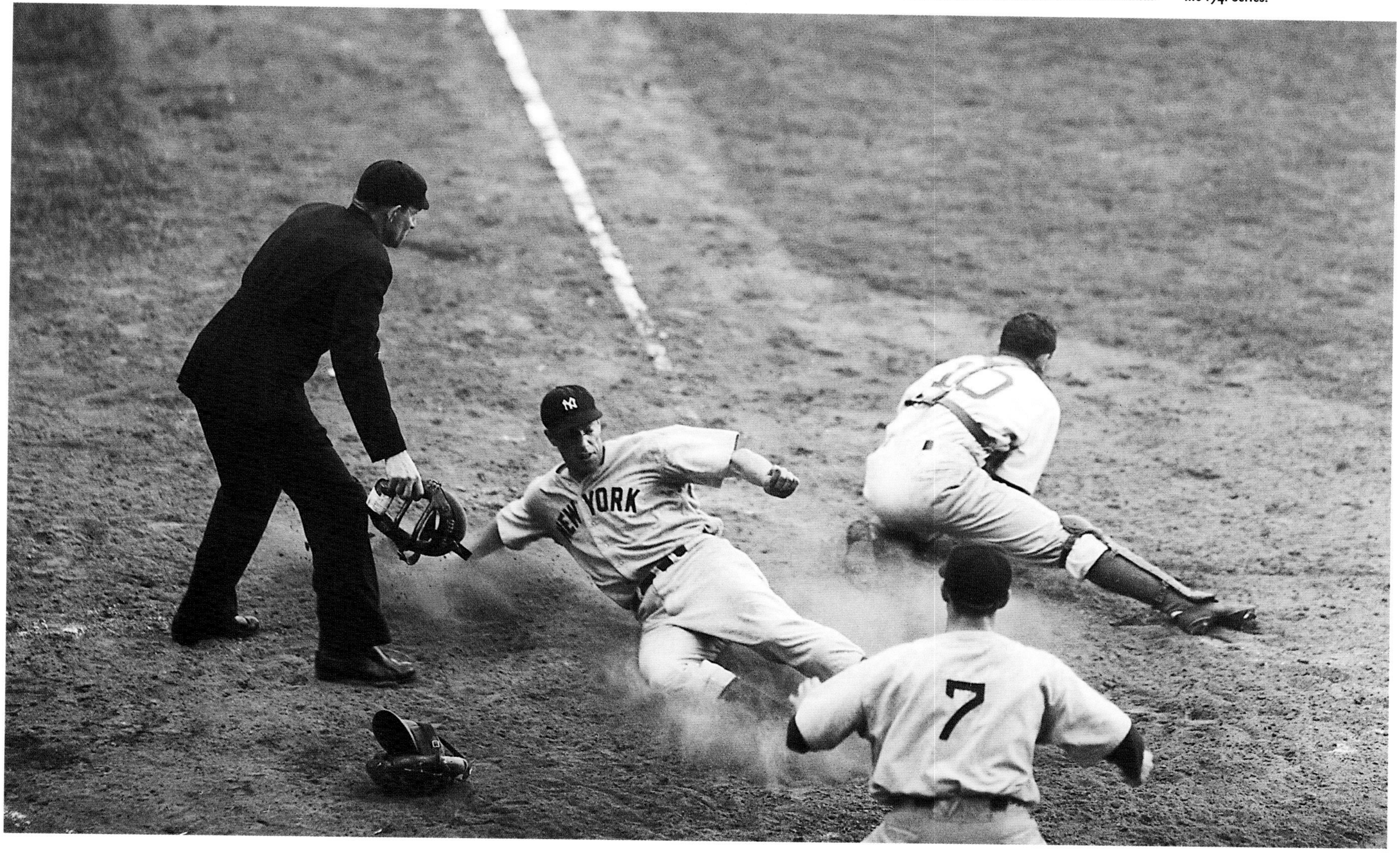

TOP: As umpire Larry Goetz raises his arm to indicate strike three, Brooklyn catcher Mickey Owen scrambles to retrieve a passed ball while Tommy Henrich runs toward first. It was the most infamous play of the 1941 World Series.

BOTTOM: Moments after Mickey Owen's passed ball, Joe DiMaggio slides home with the go-ahead run in the ninth inning of Game 4 of the 1941 Series.

Diamond Girls

THE WOMEN'S LEAGUE WORLD SERIES

During World War II, Cubs owner Phil Wrigley and a group of Midwestern businessmen founded the All-American Girls Professional Baseball League, a women's league intended to draw some attention away from the men's teams that had been decimated by the draft. Some mocked the idea, but the female players put to rest any criticism of their talents in the 1946 postseason. These were real ballplayers, and they played a top-notch World Series to prove it.

Because the league had a slightly larger ball and shorter basepaths than the major leagues, base stealing was the primary offensive weapon. Its best practitioner was Sophie Kurys, the five-foot-five, 115-pound second baseman of the Racine (Wisconsin) Belles, who spent her off-seasons working in a machine parts manufacturing plant. Kurys, 21, had led the league in stolen bases each of the previous two seasons, swiping an astonishing 281 bases in 221 games over that span. An adept sign stealer, she made a mockery of the running game in 1946, stealing 201 bases in 203 attempts while also setting new league records for walks (93) and runs scored (117). Her dominant play led the Belles into AAGPBL's version of the World Series, a best-of-seven affair dubbed the Shaughnessy Series, in which they faced the Rockford (Illinois) Peaches.

The first two games were played at Racine, and the hometown Belles won both, the second on a two-run single in the bottom of the ninth by Edythe Perlick. But Rockford took two of the next three games on its own home field, as pitcher Mildred Deegan held Racine to just one run in Game 3 and none in Game 5. With Racine leading the Series three games to two, the stage was set for Game 6, which turned out to be the most exciting ballgame in the twelve-year history of the AAGPBL.

The game was played at Racine's limestone-walled, ivy-covered Horlick Field. It was a classic duel between two sidearm pitchers. (League rules did not yet allow full-fledged overhand pitching, although that would change the next year.) Carolyn Morris, a right-hander with a 29-13 record, was on the hill for Rockford, while Racine countered with 21-year-old Joanne Winter, whose athletic prowess included not only baseball, but also swimming, volleyball, soccer, track, tennis, golf, and handball. The top pitcher in the league that year, Winter posted a 33-10 record that included a 63-inning scoreless streak.

For fourteen tense innings, the teams played to a draw. Carolyn Morris was simply dominating. Through nine innings she had still not allowed a hit, and the game went into extra innings as a scoreless tie. Rockford had a solid hitting attack the entire game, collecting 13 hits and putting 19 runners on base. But Winter, able to bear down when it counted, stranded all 19 to keep the game scoreless. In bottom of the fourteenth inning, Sophie Kurys led off with a single for Racine and promptly stole second base, her fifth steal of the game. The next batter, Betty Trezza, slapped a short single through the infield. Kurys, who had been running on the pitch, arrived at home plate at the same time as the ball. She barely eluded the catcher's tag with a hook slide, scoring the only run of the game and instantly giving Racine the Series victory. Fans swarmed onto the field and carried Kurys off on their shoulders. Even AAGPBL commissioner Max Carey, a Hall of Famer and star of the 1925 World Series for the Pittsburgh Pirates, was overwhelmed by the quality of play. "Barring none," he said, "even in the majors, it's the best game I've ever seen."

BOTTOM: In All-American Girls Professional Baseball League play, a Grand Rapids Chick—dressed, like all the other players, in a league-standard uniform (one-piece flared tunic, stockings, and baseball socks, shoes, and hat)—scores a run as the opposing catcher watches the rest of the play unfold. Originally called the Milwaukee Chicks, the team, which won the AAGPBL World Championship in 1947 and 1953, moved to Grand Rapids in 1945 and remained there until 1954, when the AAGPBL came to an end.

AAGPBL WORLD SERIES RESULTS

1943:	Racine Belles 3 Kenosha Comets 0 *MVP: Irene Hickson, Racine*
1944:	Milwaukee Chicks 4 Kenosha Comets 3 MVP: Connie Wisniewski, Milwaukee
1945:	Rockford Peaches 4 Fort Wayne Daisies 1 MVP: Carolyn Morris, Rockford
1946:	Racine Belles 4 Rockford Peaches 2 MVP: Joanne Winter, Racine
1947:	Grand Rapids Chicks 4 Racine Belles 3 MVP: Mildred Earp, Grand Rapids
1948:	Rockford Peaches 4 Fort Wayne Daisies 1 MVP: Dorothy Harrell, Rockford
1949:	Rockford Peaches 3 Grand Rapids Chicks 1 MVP: Eleanor Callow, Rockford
1950:	Rockford Peaches 4 Fort Wayne Daisies 3 MVP: Dottie Kamenshek, Rockford
1951:	South Bend Blue Sox 3 Rockford Peaches 2 MVP: Shirley Stovroff, South Bend
1952:	South Bend Blue Sox 3 Rockford Peaches 2 MVP: Jean Faut, South Bend
1953:	Grand Rapids Chicks 2 Kalamazoo Lassies 0 MVP: Joyce Ricketts, Grand Rapids
1954:	Kalamazoo Lassies 3 Fort Wayne Daisies 2 MVP: Fern Shollenberger, Kalamazoo

*MVPs selected by the author.

TOP: As umpire Larry Goetz raises his arm to indicate strike three, Brooklyn catcher Mickey Owen scrambles to retrieve a passed ball while Tommy Henrich runs toward first. It was the most infamous play of the 1941 World Series.

BOTTOM: Moments after Mickey Owen's passed ball, Joe DiMaggio slides home with the go-ahead run in the ninth inning of Game 4 of the 1941 Series.

convinced that their power-packed lineup could handle the mighty Yankees. "In the history of baseball, that is probably as close as any team has ever come to putting out a lineup of eight legitimate stars," historian Bill James wrote of the Dodgers.

The Yankees suggested that all seven games be held at Yankee Stadium in order to take advantage of its greater seating capacity. MacPhail declined the offer. About 33,000 fans spent the night of September 30 camping in the ticket line outside Yankee Stadium, many of them drinking hot coffee from thermoses and playing bridge by candlelight. The Series opened the next day with the Yankees' Red Ruffing defeating Brooklyn's Curt Davis in a close 3-2 game. In Game 2, however, Whit Wyatt ended the Yankees' ten-game World Series winning streak, beating them 3-2.

In Game 3 at Ebbets Field, Yankee pitcher Marius Russo, a Brooklyn native, defeated his hometown team by a 2-1 score. Dodgers' starter Freddie Fitzsimmons had to leave the game after being struck by a line drive, and reliever Hugh Casey gave up both Yankee runs in the top of the eighth inning. To make matters worse for Brooklyn, Herman was hurt while swinging his bat and was sidelined for the duration of the Series.

It was the fourth game of the Series, again played in Brooklyn, that Dodger fans would remember ruefully. It seemed to go well at first, as the Dodgers took a 4-3 lead into the ninth, scoring their runs on a double by pinch hitter Jimmy Wasdell and a towering homer by Reiser. But Casey ran into trouble in the ninth. He had been the Dodgers' relief ace during the regular season, going 14-11 with seven saves, a total that ranked second in the National League, but he had been pitching since the fifth inning and didn't have much left. Still, he got the first two Yankees to ground out in the ninth. The Dodgers were one out away from tying the Series. The next batter, Tommy Henrich, swung at strike three, but the ball glanced off catcher Mickey Owen's mitt, and Henrich dashed to first safely. That was all the Yankees needed. The next batter, Joe DiMaggio, singled. The next, Charlie Keller, waged a fierce battle with Casey, fouling off six pitches before finally launching a double off the right field wall to score both runners and give the Yankees the lead. They added two more runs in the

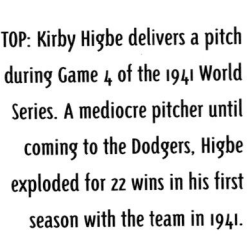

TOP: Kirby Higbe delivers a pitch during Game 4 of the 1941 World Series. A mediocre pitcher until coming to the Dodgers, Higbe exploded for 22 wins in his first season with the team in 1941.

BOTTOM: The Dodgers' Mickey Owen slides awkwardly into third here—his Game 1 triple drove in Pee Wee Reese with the Dodgers' first run of the 1941 World Series.

1941 WORLD SERIES

YANKEE STADIUM I (N.Y. YANKEES) ◆ 10.1.41

	1	2	3	4	5	6	7	8	9	R	H	E
B'klyn	0	0	0	0	1	0	1	0	0	2	6	0
NYY	0	1	0	1	0	1	0	0	X	3	6	1

WP–Ruffing LP–Davis HR: NYY–Gordon
ATT: 68,540

YANKEE STADIUM I ◆ 10.2.41

	1	2	3	4	5	6	7	8	9	R	H	E
B'klyn	0	0	0	0	2	1	0	0	0	3	6	2
NYY	0	1	1	0	0	0	0	0	0	2	9	1

WP–Wyatt LP–Chandler ATT: 66,248

EBBETS FIELD (BROOKLYN DODGERS) ◆ 10.4.41

	1	2	3	4	5	6	7	8	9	R	H	E
NYY	0	0	0	0	0	0	0	2	0	2	8	0
B'klyn	0	0	0	0	0	0	0	1	0	1	4	0

WP–Russo LP–Casey ATT: 33,100

EBBETS FIELD ◆ 10.5.41

	1	2	3	4	5	6	7	8	9	R	H	E
NYY	1	0	0	2	0	0	0	0	4	7	12	0
B'klyn	0	0	0	2	2	0	0	0	0	4	9	1

WP–Murphy LP–Casey HR: BKN–Reiser
ATT: 33,813

EBBETS FIELD ◆ 10.6.41

	1	2	3	4	5	6	7	8	9	R	H	E
NYY	0	2	0	0	1	0	0	0	0	3	6	0
B'klyn	0	0	1	0	0	0	0	0	0	1	4	1

WP–Bonham LP–Wyatt HR: NYY–Henrich
ATT: 34,072

inning, winning 7-4 after it looked like they had been defeated.

The heartbreaking loss all but ended the Series for the Dodgers. "We were licked before we went out on the field the next day," Billy Herman remembered. "We couldn't have beaten a girls' team." Yankee manager Joe McCarthy gave one of his little-used pitchers, the 6-foot-2 Ernest "Tiny" Bonham, a chance to start Game 5, and Bonham beat Whit Wyatt 3-1 to end the Series, with Henrich hitting a homer for the Yankees. The Dodger demise was blamed on Owen, who was lambasted as a goat for failing to catch the game-ending strikeout pitch in Game 4. But for more than fifty years, whispers have circulated that the pitch was a spitball so slippery that Owen couldn't hold on to it.

"Everybody says it was a spitter, but I don't buy that," Henrich told historian Donald Honig many years later. "I listened one time to Mickey Owen describe what he thought the pitch was, and he described it exactly as I remembered it. He said it was the best curveball Hugh Casey ever threw. Casey didn't have a good curveball, but this ball exploded....It looked like a fastball. Then when it broke, it broke so sharply that it was out of the strike zone. So I tried to hold up. But even as I was trying to hold up I was thinking that the ball had broken so fast that Owen might have trouble with it too....And I saw that little white jackrabbit ball bouncing, and I said, *Let's go.*"

"Casey swore it was a curveball," Herman said. "I think Owen might have nonchalanted the ball, putting his glove out for it instead of shifting his whole body to make the catch. Owen had a habit of doing that, and maybe that's what happened there. And the ball got away. But let's give the Yankees some credit, too. They jumped right in and took advantage of the break."

Casey, the losing pitcher in two of the Series games, continued to be an outstanding reliever until the late 1940s, when alcoholism and depression drove him from the major leagues. "He'd go back to his hotel room after a game," Higbe remembered, "and start drinking and not stop until he fell asleep." Casey killed himself in 1951 with a shotgun while talking to his wife on the phone.

1942

St. Louis Cardinals (4)
New York Yankees (1)

Nobody had beaten the Yankees in a World Series since 1926, when Grover Cleveland Alexander helped the Cardinals do it. In the fifteen years since, the Yankees had posted a phenomenal 32-4 record in Series play. Billy Southworth, who batted .317 for that '26 Cardinal team, was now the team's manager. He led them to the 1942 pennant in a hard-fought race with Brooklyn that lasted until the final day of the season. The Yankees, meanwhile, had won their pennant easily. Although they lost Tommy Henrich to military service just before the World Series started, New York was still expected to flatten the Cardinals.

But St. Louis was a spectacular team, winning 106 games. With an average age of just 26, the Cardinals' hallmark was team speed, which helped them excel both on the bases and in the field. Historian Bill James estimates that the Cardinals won seventeen games with their defense alone, making them one of the top defensive teams in history. They were led by the Cooper brothers of Atherton, Missouri. Mort Cooper was the National League MVP, winning 22 games with a 1.78 ERA. His younger brother, William "Walker" Cooper, was an outstanding defensive catcher who batted .281. Enos "Country" Slaughter, meanwhile, enjoyed a career year, batting .318 with seventeen triples. Shortstop Marty Marion and center fielder Terry Moore, two of the finest defensive players in baseball, anchored the team up the middle. And Stanley Musial, a promising rookie from Donora, Pennsylvania, posted a .397 on-base percentage in his first season.

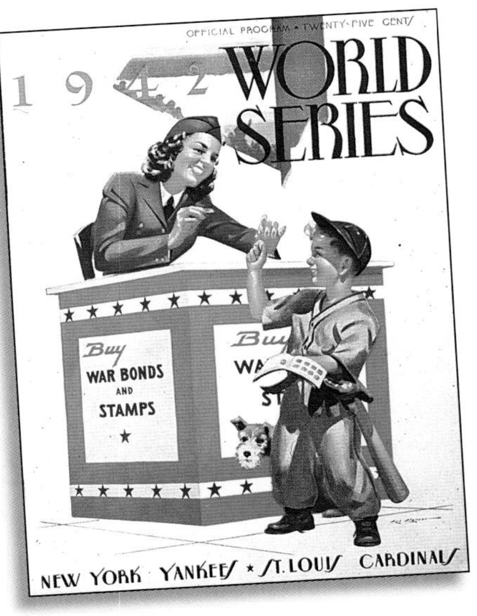

As expected, the Yankees began to pound the Cardinals from the very first pitch, knocking out Mort Cooper and taking a 7-0 lead into the bottom of the ninth in Game 1. Out of character, the Cardinals made four errors, and Red Ruffing held them hitless until the eighth inning. But then St. Louis began a furious comeback, scoring four runs in the ninth and loading the bases with two outs. Musial came to the plate as the potential winning run. Reliever Spurgeon "Spud" Chandler got Musial to ground out—Musial's second out of the

BOTTOM: The Cardinals celebrate their victory in Game 2 of the 1942 World Series. Clockwise from top left: Enos Slaughter, Stan Musial, winning pitcher Johnny Beazley, Whitey Kurowski, Walker Cooper, and manager Billy Southworth.

THE WOMEN'S LEAGUE WORLD SERIES

During World War II, Cubs owner Phil Wrigley and a group of Midwestern businessmen founded the All-American Girls Professional Baseball League, a women's league intended to draw some attention away from the men's teams that had been decimated by the draft. Some mocked the idea, but the female players put to rest any criticism of their talents in the 1946 postseason. These were real ballplayers, and they played a top-notch World Series to prove it.

Because the league had a slightly larger ball and shorter basepaths than the major leagues, base stealing was the primary offensive weapon. Its best practitioner was Sophie Kurys, the five-foot-five, 115-pound second baseman of the Racine (Wisconsin) Belles, who spent her off-seasons working in a machine parts manufacturing plant. Kurys, 21, had led the league in stolen bases each of the previous two seasons, swiping an astonishing 281 bases in 221 games over that span. An adept sign stealer, she made a mockery of the running game in 1946, stealing 201 bases in 203 attempts while also setting new league records for walks (93) and runs scored (117). Her dominant play led the Belles into AAGPBL's version of the World Series, a best-of-seven affair dubbed the Shaughnessy Series, in which they faced the Rockford (Illinois) Peaches.

The first two games were played at Racine, and the hometown Belles won both, the second on a two-run single in the bottom of the ninth by Edythe Perlick. But Rockford took two of the next three games on its own home field, as pitcher Mildred Deegan held Racine to just one run in Game 3 and none in Game 5. With Racine leading the Series three games to two, the stage was set for Game 6, which turned out to be the most exciting ballgame in the twelve-year history of the AAGPBL.

The game was played at Racine's limestone-walled, ivy-covered Horlick Field. It was a classic duel between two sidearm pitchers. (League rules did not yet allow full-fledged overhand pitching, although that would change the next year.) Carolyn Morris, a right-hander with a 29-13 record, was on the hill for Rockford, while Racine countered with 21-year-old Joanne Winter, whose athletic prowess included not only baseball, but also swimming, volleyball, soccer, track, tennis, golf, and handball. The top pitcher in the league that year, Winter posted a 33-10 record that included a 63-inning scoreless streak.

For fourteen tense innings, the teams played to a draw. Carolyn Morris was simply dominating. Through nine innings she had still not allowed a hit, and the game went into extra innings as a scoreless tie. Rockford had a solid hitting attack the entire game, collecting 13 hits and putting 19 runners on base. But Winter, able to bear down when it counted, stranded all 19 to keep the game scoreless. In bottom of the fourteenth inning, Sophie Kurys led off with a single for Racine and promptly stole second base, her fifth steal of the game. The next batter, Betty Trezza, slapped a short single through the infield. Kurys, who had been running on the pitch, arrived at home plate at the same time as the ball. She barely eluded the catcher's tag with a hook slide, scoring the only run of the game and instantly giving Racine the Series victory. Fans swarmed onto the field and carried Kurys off on their shoulders. Even AAGPBL commissioner Max Carey, a Hall of Famer and star of the 1925 World Series for the Pittsburgh Pirates, was overwhelmed by the quality of play. "Barring none," he said, "even in the majors, it's the best game I've ever seen."

BOTTOM: In All-American Girls Professional Baseball League play, a Grand Rapids Chick—dressed, like all the other players, in a league-standard uniform (one-piece flared tunic, stockings, and baseball socks, shoes, and hat)—scores a run as the opposing catcher watches the rest of the play unfold. Originally called the Milwaukee Chicks, the team, which won the AAGPBL World Championship in 1947 and 1953, moved to Grand Rapids in 1945 and remained there until 1954, when the AAGPBL came to an end.

AAGPBL WORLD SERIES RESULTS

1943:	Racine Belles 3 Kenosha Comets 0 *MVP: Irene Hickson, Racine*
1944:	Milwaukee Chicks 4 Kenosha Comets 3 MVP: Connie Wisniewski, Milwaukee
1945:	Rockford Peaches 4 Fort Wayne Daisies 1 MVP: Carolyn Morris, Rockford
1946:	Racine Belles 4 Rockford Peaches 2 MVP: Joanne Winter, Racine
1947:	Grand Rapids Chicks 4 Racine Belles 3 MVP: Mildred Earp, Grand Rapids
1948:	Rockford Peaches 4 Fort Wayne Daisies 1 MVP: Dorothy Harrell, Rockford
1949:	Rockford Peaches 3 Grand Rapids Chicks 1 MVP: Eleanor Callow, Rockford
1950:	Rockford Peaches 4 Fort Wayne Daisies 3 MVP: Dottie Kamenshek, Rockford
1951:	South Bend Blue Sox 3 Rockford Peaches 2 MVP: Shirley Stovroff, South Bend
1952:	South Bend Blue Sox 3 Rockford Peaches 2 MVP: Jean Faut, South Bend
1953:	Grand Rapids Chicks 2 Kalamazoo Lassies 0 MVP: Joyce Ricketts, Grand Rapids
1954:	Kalamazoo Lassies 3 Fort Wayne Daisies 2 MVP: Fern Shollenberger, Kalamazoo

*MVPs selected by the author.

TOP: Yankee left fielder Charlie Keller makes a spectacular catch of Terry Moore's long drive in Game 4 of the 1942 World Series, robbing Moore of an extra-base hit.

inning—and the Yankees won, 7-4. Still, as pitcher Max Lanier remembered, the ninth inning comeback "showed we could throw a scare into the Yankees. And then we did more than scare them." Game 1 was New York's only victory in the Series.

For Game 2 the Cardinals turned to Johnny Beazley, a rookie who had won 21 games during the regular season. With the game tied 3-3 in the bottom of the eighth, Musial singled in Slaughter with the go-ahead run. The Yankees tried to come back in the ninth. With George "Tuck" Stainback on first, John "Buddy" Hassett singled to right field, but Slaughter rushed over to cut off the ball and then unleashed a tremendous throw to nail Stainback at third base. The next batter, pinch hitter Red Ruffing, hit a fly ball that likely would have scored Stainback from third, but now it did the Yankees no good. They lost 4-3. The Cardinals' defense helped them win the third game, too, as Musial, Slaughter, and Moore all turned in impressive plays in the outfield. Ernie White, plagued most of the season by a sore arm, pitched a shutout as St. Louis won 2-0. The once dignified Yankees, perhaps sensing that the Series was slipping away, lost their cool completely in the game. Manager Joe McCarthy complained about everything from where the Cardinal batboy was standing to how White was using the rosin bag. Three close calls by the umpires drew bitter arguments from New York, capped by a play in which Joe DiMaggio tried to throw out Moore going from first to third on a single. When Moore was called safe, third baseman Frank Crosetti spiked the ball on the ground in disgust, then grabbed umpire Bill Summers and shoved him. Summers shoved right back. The Yankees, furious and frustrated, went into Game 4 behind two games to one in the Series.

The Cards won Game 4, too, 9-6, although Mort Cooper was knocked out of the game for the second time in the Series. Now leading the Series three games to one, the Cardinals turned again to Beazley. Both he and Ruffing pitched well in Game 5, and it was tied 2-2 in the top of the ninth when George "Whitey" Kurowski—a rookie with only nine home runs in his major league career—took Ruffing deep, hitting a two-run homer that landed just inside the foul pole. When it looked as if New York might come back in the ninth, Walker Cooper picked off the unsuspecting Joe Gordon at second base. St. Louis won the game, 4-2, and the Series, 4-1.

Most observers believed the Cardinals' baserunning was the key to their victory. Although they stole no bases in the Series, they took many an extra base on hits, and "just ran hell out of the Yankees on the bases," as one reporter wrote. Casey Stengel, watching the fifth game from the stands, remarked, "It isn't a ball club. It's a track team." Things were looking up in St. Louis. But scarcely a month after the World Series ended, Branch Rickey left the Cardinals to become president of the Brooklyn Dodgers. The Cardinal team he had assembled would win for a few more years, but Rickey's new team would eventually become the dynasty in the National League.

1942 WORLD SERIES

Sportsman's Park IV (St. Louis Cards) ◆ 9.30.42

	1	2	3	4	5	6	7	8	9	R	H	E
NYY	0	0	0	1	1	0	0	3	2	7	11	0
St.L.	0	0	0	0	0	0	0	0	4	4	7	4

WP–Ruffing LP–M. Cooper S–Chandler ATT: 34,769

Sportsman's Park IV ◆ 10.1.42

	1	2	3	4	5	6	7	8	9	R	H	E
NYY	0	0	0	0	0	0	0	3	0	3	10	2
St.L.	2	0	0	0	0	0	1	1	X	4	6	0

WP–Beazley LP–Bonham HR: NYY–Keller
ATT: 34,255

Yankee Stadium I (N.Y. Yankees) ◆ 10.3.42

	1	2	3	4	5	6	7	8	9	R	H	E
St.L.	0	0	1	0	0	0	0	0	1	2	5	1
NYY	0	0	0	0	0	0	0	0	0	0	6	1

WP–White LP–Chandler ATT: 69,123

Yankee Stadium I ◆ 10.4.42

	1	2	3	4	5	6	7	8	9	R	H	E
St.L.	0	0	0	6	0	0	2	0	1	9	12	1
NYY	1	0	0	0	0	5	0	0	0	6	10	1

WP–Lanier LP–Donald HR: NYY–Keller
ATT: 69,902

Yankee Stadium I ◆ 10.5.42

	1	2	3	4	5	6	7	8	9	R	H	E
St.L.	0	0	0	1	0	1	0	0	2	4	9	4
NYY	1	0	0	1	0	0	0	0	0	2	7	1

WP–Beazley LP–Ruffing HR: STL–Slaughter, Kurowski; NYY–Rizzuto ATT: 69,052

1943

New York Yankees (4)
St. Louis Cardinals (1)

After their embarrassing defeat in 1942 the Yankees again faced the Cardinals in 1943, the sixth rematch in World Series history. Despite losing Joe DiMaggio and several other players to the Army, the Yankees won the American League easily with 98 victories. The Cardinals were even more dominating in the National League, winning 105 games despite the absence of Enos Slaughter, Terry Moore, and Johnny Beazley, three key figures in the 1942 championship who were now serving in the military.

Each team was led by the MVP of its respective league. For the Yankees, late bloomer Spud Chandler, at age 35, posted a 20-4 record and a spectacular 1.64 ERA. For St. Louis, young Stan Musial enjoyed a breakout year, battering the decimated pitching staffs of the National League for a

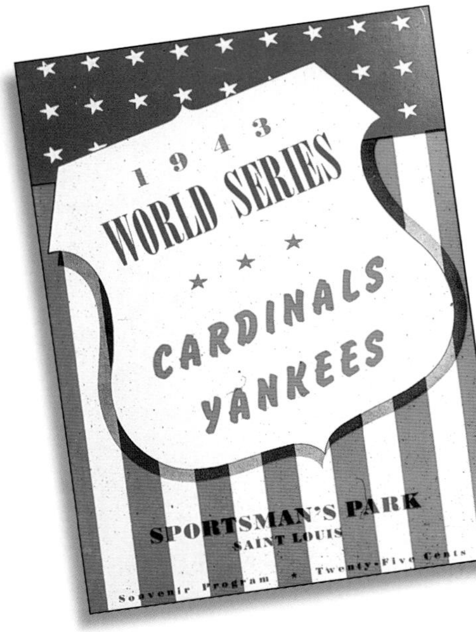

.357 average while leading the league in on-base percentage, slugging percentage, hits, doubles, triples, and total bases.

Chandler got New York off on the right foot by defeating Max Lanier in the first game at Yankee Stadium, 4-2. Lanier, who had posted a 1.90 ERA during the regular season, had nobody to blame for the loss but himself, as his error in the fourth inning and wild pitch in the sixth allowed all four Yankee runs to score. Mort Cooper, the scheduled pitcher in Game 2, received a telegram that morning informing him that his father had died back home in Missouri. Cooper talked things over with his brother Walker, who was also his catcher, and the pair decided that their father would have wanted them to continue with the game. So that afternoon, Mort pitched a complete game to defeat the Yankees, 4-3. After the game, the Cooper brothers boarded a homeward bound train to attend their father's funeral.

It looked as if the Cardinals would win Game 3, too, as they held a 2-1 lead entering the eighth inning. But the Yankees scored five runs in the eighth, three of them on a bases-clearing triple by rookie third baseman Billy Johnson. The Yankees won that game and the next one, too, prevailing by a narrow 2-1 score in Game 4 at Sportsman's Park. Marius Russo, the Brooklyn native who had helped beat the Dodgers in 1941, pitched a masterpiece for the Yankees. He allowed no earned runs while also hitting two doubles, the second of which resulted in the winning run.

BOTTOM LEFT: Yankee pitcher Spud Chandler was voted the American League MVP in 1943 after going 20-4 with a 1.64 ERA.

BOTTOM RIGHT: Mort (left) and Walker Cooper, the most famous brother battery in baseball history, helped beat the Yankees in Game 2 of the 1943 Series despite the death of their father that morning.

With the Cardinals on the ropes, the fifth game was a matchup between each team's best pitcher: Chandler for the Yankees and Mort Cooper for St. Louis. It was scoreless until the sixth inning, when Bill Dickey, the venerable Yankee catcher playing in his eighth and final World Series, launched a two-run homer. It was all the scoring the Yankees would need, as Chandler completed the 2-0 shutout to end the Series. Mort Cooper, still grieving his father's loss, was the hard-luck loser for St. Louis. "I wasn't what you'd call brilliant in that game," Chandler said. "I gave up ten base hits and a couple of walks. They left eleven men on base." The Cardinals' biggest threat had come in the fourth inning, when, with two men on base, Chandler ran the count to 3-2 on batter Johnny Hopp. "I made that three-and-two pitch to Hopp and I never will forget it as long as I live," Chandler told Donald Honig. "It was a fastball, and it had to be at least eight to ten inches outside—and he swung at it and missed. I got the next two men on ground balls and was out of the inning. When I went back to the bench, I was so elated I said, 'Fellows, there's no way I can lose today.'"

1943 WORLD SERIES

Yankee Stadium I (N.Y. Yankees) ◆ 10.5.43 (Game 1)

	1	2	3	4	5	6	7	8	9	R	H	E
St.L.	0	1	0	0	1	0	0	0	0	2	7	2
NYY	0	0	0	2	0	2	0	0	X	4	8	2

WP–Chandler LP–Lanier HR: NYY–Gordon ATT: 68,676

Yankee Stadium I ◆ 10.6.43 (Game 2)

	1	2	3	4	5	6	7	8	9	R	H	E
St.L.	0	0	1	3	0	0	0	0	0	4	7	2
NYY	0	0	0	1	0	0	0	0	2	3	6	0

WP–M. Cooper LP–Bonham HR: STL–Marion, Sander ATT: 68,578

Yankee Stadium I ◆ 10.7.43 (Game 3)

	1	2	3	4	5	6	7	8	9	R	H	E
St.L.	0	0	0	2	0	0	0	0	0	2	6	4
NYY	0	0	0	0	0	1	0	5	X	6	8	0

WP–Borowy LP–Brazle ATT: 69,990

Sportsman's Park IV (St. Louis Cards) ◆ 10.10.43 (Game 4)

	1	2	3	4	5	6	7	8	9	R	H	E
NYY	0	0	0	1	0	0	0	0	0	2	6	2
St.L.	0	0	0	0	0	0	1	0	0	1	7	1

WP–Russo LP–Brecheen ATT: 36,196

Sportsman's Park IV ◆ 10.11.43 (Game 5)

	1	2	3	4	5	6	7	8	9	R	H	E
NYY	0	0	0	0	0	2	0	0	0	2	7	1
St.L.	0	0	0	0	0	0	0	0	0	0	10	1

WP–Chandler LP–M. Cooper HR: NYY–Dickey ATT: 33,872

1944

St. Louis Cardinals (4)
St. Louis Browns (2)

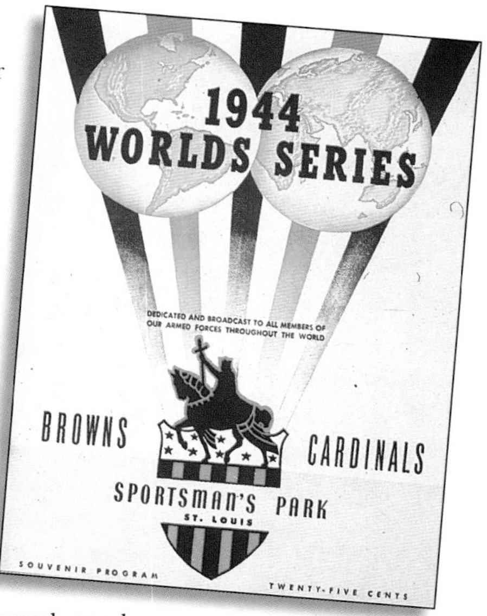

With the war in Europe and the Pacific raging worse than ever, 1944 saw major league baseball lose nearly all its able-bodied players to World War II. In the American League, the Yankees lost Joe DiMaggio, the Red Sox lost Ted Williams, the Indians lost Bob Feller, and the Tigers lost Hank Greenberg. With the top four teams each missing their best players, the pennant race turned into a free-for-all. When it was all over, the hapless St. Louis Browns sat atop the rubble heap with an 89-65 record, good enough for the first pennant in franchise history. The Browns swept the last four games of the season from the Yankees, enabling them to finish one game ahead of Detroit. Their only legitimate star was Vern Stephens, a 23-year-old who, with 20 homers and 109 RBI, was the best power-hitting shortstop in baseball. The rest of the roster was full of 4-Fs and journeymen. During the season sixteen different players over the age of 30 saw action for the Browns, making them one of the oldest pennant-winning teams in history.

The Browns were met in the Series by their crosstown rivals, the Cardinals, who had managed to keep more of their star players than any other team in baseball. Marty Marion posted a pedestrian .267 batting average with 63 RBI, but his tremendous defensive play at shortstop was enough to win him the N.L. MVP award. The award notwithstanding, the league's best player was actually Marion's teammate Stan Musial, who batted .347 while leading the league in a bevy of offensive categories. Musial, Marion, Mort and Walker Cooper, Max Lanier, Harry Brecheen, Whitey Kurowski, and Johnny Hopp—all contributors to St. Louis' previous two pennant winners—managed to stay out of the military during the season, enabling the Cardinals to make a

TOP: Bill Dickey is called out trying to go from first to third on a single during the 1943 World Series. The dusty third baseman is Whitey Kurowski.

mockery of the National League pennant race with 105 wins.

Not only did the two teams share Sportsman's Park, but the two managers, Billy Southworth and Luke Sewell, actually shared the same apartment in St. Louis. In the same respect, the World Series would take place in one ballpark for the third time in history. With servicemen eager to listen overseas, the radio broadcast was heard on six continents and in countless countries around the world. In Game 1 Mort Cooper was once again a hard-luck loser, falling 2-1 to the Browns' ace, Denny Galehouse, owner of an 81-88 career record. The Browns' runs came courtesy of a two-run homer by first baseman George McQuinn, who had spent eight years stuck in the Yankee farm system behind Lou Gehrig before the Browns finally gave him a chance to play.

Game 2 was tied 2-2 until the eleventh inning, when pinch hitter Ken O'Dea singled in the winning run for the Cardinals. Sylvester "Blix" Donnelly, pitching in relief of Max Lanier, threw four strong innings and helped kill off an eleventh inning Browns rally by pouncing on a bunt and throwing out the lead runner. The Browns came back to win Game 3 behind the strong pitching of Jack Kramer, discharged from the Navy a year earlier. They broke the game open in the third inning on five consecutive singles, and went on to win, 6-2. Now leading the World Series two games to one, the Browns, although they scarcely knew it, had reached the pinnacle of their franchise's history. Never before had they looked so likely to win a championship, and things would never look so good again.

Brecheen stymied the Browns in Game 4, winning 5-1 thanks to a homer and a double by Musial. The Cardinals won Game 5 as Mort Cooper pitched a 2-0 shutout and Ray Sanders and Danny Litwhiler hit solo home runs. Now the Cardinals were on the verge of clinching the Series, as the stout left-hander Lanier started for the Cardinals. He combined with reliever Ted Wilks to hold the Browns to three hits in the game. The Cardinals scored three times in the fourth inning on singles by Sanders, Emil Verban, and Lanier, and never relinquished the lead. The Browns played valiantly, but in the end, the Cardinals simply outclassed them. Browns batters struck out a series-record 49 times, including the last eight consecutive pinch hitters they sent to the plate. Their brief moment in the sun now over, the Browns would not win another pennant until 1966, when they were known as the Baltimore Orioles and led by two men named Robinson.

1944 WORLD SERIES

Sportsman's Park IV (St. Louis Cards) ◆ 10.4.44 (Game 1)

	1	2	3	4	5	6	7	8	9	R	H	E
St.L.B.	0	0	0	2	0	0	0	0	0	2	2	0
St.L.C.	0	0	0	0	0	0	0	0	1	1	7	0

WP–Galehouse LP–M. Cooper HR: SLB–McQuinn ATT: 33,242

Sportsman's Park IV (St. Louis Cards) ◆ 10.5.44 (Game 2)

	1	2	3	4	5	6	7	8	9	10	11	R	H	E
St.L.B.	0	0	0	0	0	0	2	0	0	0	0	2	7	4
St.L.C.	0	0	1	1	0	0	0	0	0	0	1	3	7	0

WP–Donnelly LP–Muncrief ATT: 35,076

Sportsman's Park IV (St. Louis Browns) ◆ 10.6.44 (Game 3)

	1	2	3	4	5	6	7	8	9	R	H	E
St.L.C.	1	0	0	0	0	0	1	0	0	2	7	0
St.L.B.	0	0	4	0	0	0	2	0	X	6	8	2

WP–Kramer LP–Wilks ATT: 34,737

Sportsman's Park IV (St. Louis Browns) ◆ 10.7.44 (Game 4)

	1	2	3	4	5	6	7	8	9	R	H	E
St.L.C.	2	0	2	0	0	1	0	0	0	5	12	0
St.L.B.	0	0	0	0	0	0	0	1	0	1	9	1

WP–Brecheen LP–Jakucki HR: STL–Musial ATT: 35,455

Sportsman's Park IV (St. Louis Browns) ◆ 10.8.44 (Game 5)

	1	2	3	4	5	6	7	8	9	R	H	E
St.L.C.	0	0	0	0	0	1	0	1	0	2	6	1
St.L.B.	0	0	0	0	0	0	0	0	0	0	7	1

WP–M. Cooper LP–Galehouse HR: STL–Sanders, Litwhiler ATT: 36,568

Sportsman's Park IV (St. Louis Cards) ◆ 10.9.44 (Game 6)

	1	2	3	4	5	6	7	8	9	R	H	E
St.L.B.	0	1	0	0	0	0	0	0	0	1	3	2
St.L.C.	0	0	0	3	0	0	0	0	X	3	10	0

WP–Lanier LP–Potter S–Wilks ATT: 31,630

1945

Detroit Tigers (4)
Chicago Cubs (3)

With World War II ending in mid-season and wholesale discharges allowing players to return home to their families and their teams, baseball began to resemble its old self again in 1945. The Detroit Tigers were energized by Hank Greenberg, their slugger who returned from a four-year stint in the Army to hit a homer in his first game back on July 1. Greenberg batted .311 and drove in 60 runs in half a season, and hit a stunning ninth-inning grand slam to win the pennant for the Tigers on the last day of the season. But the Tiger star for most of the year was pitcher Hal Newhouser, who won his second consecutive MVP award with a 25-9 record and 1.81 ERA. Detroit's record was just 88-65, but it was good enough to win the pennant by a nose over the Washington Senators. Like the St. Louis Browns the year before, the Tigers were one of the oldest pennant-winning teams in history, with an average age of 32.3. Their World Series opponents were the Chicago Cubs, with first baseman Phil Cavarretta and third baseman Stan

BOTTOM: Ray Sanders slides home with the Cardinals' second run of Game 2 in the 1944 World Series. The Browns' catcher is Myron Hayworth.

Hack the only holdovers from the last pennant-winning Cub team in 1938. Both had superb seasons. Hack got on base at a .420 clip and scored 110 runs, while Cavarretta was an easy choice for N.L. MVP with a league-leading .355 batting average.

The first three games took place at Detroit's Briggs Stadium. Newhouser, the best pitcher in baseball, was greeted rudely by the Cubs in Game 1. They hammered him 9-0, with Cavarretta and Andy Pafko collecting three hits and scoring three runs each, and Hank Borowy pitching the shutout. The Tigers bounced back in the second game, winning 4-1 thanks to two recently returned servicemen, as Greenberg hit a three-run homer, and Virgil Trucks, discharged from the Navy just in time for the World Series, pitched a seven-hitter in his second game back. The Cubs grabbed Game 3 as Claude Passeau fired a remarkable one-hit shutout in the first World Series start of his career. The only hit was a clean single to left by Rudy York.

With the teams now playing at Wrigley Field, Paul "Dizzy" Trout, pitching with a sore back, tied the Series for the Tigers with a 4-1 victory in Game 4. The Tigers chased Ray Prim, the N.L. ERA champion, from the game in the fourth inning on timely hits by Greenberg and Roy Cullenbine. Detroit won again the next day, pounding Borowy and four Cubs relievers in an 8-4 win, with Greenberg contributing three doubles. The Cubs tied the Series the day after that, winning 8-7 in what was at the time the longest game in World Series history. It looked as if the Cubs had the game well in hand until the top of the eighth when a four-run Detroit rally tied the game, capped by a Greenberg homer. The game went into extra innings with two relievers pitching, Dizzy Trout for Detroit and Borowy—who had started the day before—for the Cubs. In the twelfth inning, with a man on first, Hack hit an ordinary single that took a bad hop and sailed over the head of the charging Greenberg in left field. Pinch runner Bill Schuster scampered home with the winning run to force the Series to a seventh game.

Newhouser was the easy choice to pitch for Detroit in Game 7. Chicago manager Charlie Grimm nominated Hank Borowy to start for the Cubs, even though he would be pitching for the third consecutive day. The decision backfired, as Detroit unloaded on the exhausted Borowy for five quick runs, effectively ending the Series in the first inning. The key blow was a two-out, three-run double by catcher Paul Richards. The Cubs made a few halfhearted attempts to come back, but each was thwarted by Newhouser, who went the distance in the 9-3 victory. The Tigers were world champs. Although the quality of play in the wartime Series was ridiculed by many sportswriters, the Tigers didn't care. "In twenty years in the big leagues, that was my only world championship," remembered Roger "Doc" Cramer, who, at age 39, hit .379 in the Series. "It's a great feeling. You know you've done it all then. We drank champagne on the train all the way back to Detroit."

While the statistics might show that Greenberg won the Series for Detroit, many Cubs fans, to this day, point to a different reason. William "Billy Goat" Sianis, owner of a popular Chicago tavern, bought box seats to Game 4 for himself and his pet goat, Murphy. But ushers declined to admit Murphy into Wrigley Field, saying the goat smelled too bad to attend the game. Sianis and his goat left in anger, and Sianis placed a hex on the home team. The Cubs scoffed at first, but by 1950, after four consecutive losing seasons, team owner Philip Wrigley wrote to Sianis and pleaded with him to remove the hex. "Will you please extend to [Murphy] my most sincere and abject apologies, and ask him not only to remove the hex, but to reverse the flow and start pulling for wins?" Wrigley wrote. Sianis eventually removed the curse in 1969, shortly before he died. It has not helped the Cubs, who have never appeared in another World Series since banishing Sianis and his billy goat in 1945. The Billy Goat Tavern, meanwhile, became famous as the subject of a John Belushi skit on *Saturday Night Live* and still does a thriving business from the basement of the Tribune Tower in downtown Chicago.

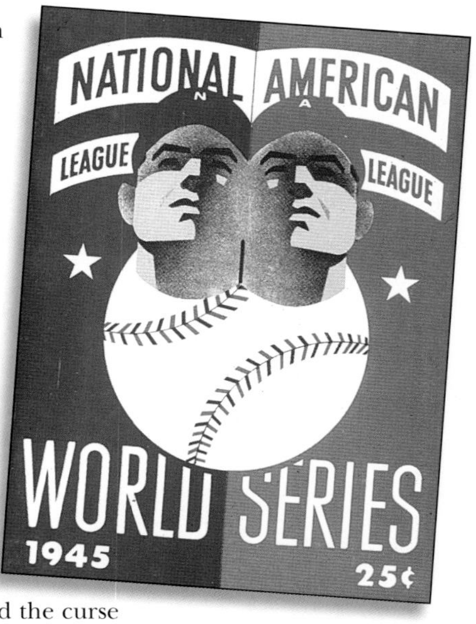

BOTTOM: Hank Greenberg is congratulated by teammates after hitting a three-run homer in Game 2 of the 1945 World Series. Greenberg's blast provided the margin of victory in a 4-1 Detroit win.

1945 WORLD SERIES

Briggs Stadium (Detroit Tigers) ◆ 10.3.45

	1	2	3	4	5	6	7	8	9	R	H	E
Chi.	4	0	3	0	0	0	2	0	0	9	13	0
Det.	0	0	0	0	0	0	0	0	0	0	6	0

WP–Borowy LP–Newhouser HR: CHC–Cavarretta
ATT: 54,637

Briggs Stadium ◆ 10.4.45

	1	2	3	4	5	6	7	8	9	R	H	E
Chi.	0	0	0	1	0	0	0	0	0	1	7	0
Det.	0	0	0	0	4	0	0	0	X	4	7	0

WP–Trucks LP–Wyse HR: DET–Greenberg
ATT: 53,636

Briggs Stadium ◆ 10.5.45

	1	2	3	4	5	6	7	8	9	R	H	E
Chi.	0	0	0	2	0	0	1	0	0	3	8	0
Det.	0	0	0	0	0	0	0	0	0	0	1	2

WP–Passeau LP–Overmire ATT: 55,500

Wrigley Field (Chicago Cubs) ◆ 10.6.45

	1	2	3	4	5	6	7	8	9	R	H	E
Det.	0	0	0	4	0	0	0	0	0	4	7	1
Chi.	0	0	0	0	0	1	0	0	0	1	5	1

WP–Trout LP–Prim ATT: 42,923

Wrigley Field ◆ 10.7.45

	1	2	3	4	5	6	7	8	9	R	H	E
Det.	0	0	1	0	0	4	1	0	2	8	11	0
Chi.	0	0	1	0	0	0	2	0	1	4	7	2

WP–Newhouser LP–Borowy ATT: 43,463

Wrigley Field ◆ 10.8.45

	1	2	3	4	5	6	7	8	9	10	11	12	R	H	E
Det.	0	1	0	0	0	0	2	4	0	0	0	0	7	13	1
Chi.	0	0	0	0	4	1	2	0	0	0	0	1	8	15	3

WP–Borowy LP–Trout HR: DET–Greenberg
ATT: 41,708

Wrigley Field ◆ 10.10.45

	1	2	3	4	5	6	7	8	9	R	H	E
Det.	5	1	0	0	0	0	1	2	0	9	9	1
Chi.	1	0	0	1	0	0	0	1	0	3	10	0

WP–Newhouser LP–Borowy ATT: 41,590

CHAPTER 3
BASEBALL IN TRANSITION
1946–1960

When stars like Ted Williams, Bob Feller, and Joe DiMaggio returned from World War II, they came back to a different kind of baseball than the one they had left. Baseball, like America, was in transition, and the primary reason was racial. Whites were moving out of cities and into suburbs, with blacks taking their place in cities. The changing neighborhoods made many white fans reluctant to attend games at inner-city ballparks like Ebbets Field and the Polo Grounds, and teams soon began searching for a way out. The first to find one was the Boston Braves, who packed their bags and headed for Milwaukee in 1953. It was the first franchise move in the National or American League in more than fifty years. The Dodgers and Giants soon followed. Most owners downplayed the racial motivations for their moves, but one who did not was Calvin Griffith, who transferred his team from Washington, D.C., to Minneapolis in 1961. "I'll tell you why we caame to Minnesota," he said. "It was when I found out you only had 15,000 blacks here....We came here because you've got good, hard-working white people here."

By the time Griffith's team became the Minnesota Twins, of course, black players were well-established stars in the National League. Jackie Robinson's debut in 1947 had changed the face of baseball, often in ways he could never have imagined. For instance, Robinson is at least partly responsible for the existence of the designated hitter. His early success in the National League encouraged other N.L. teams to employ black players, and by 1960, the Senior Circuit's best performers included Willie Mays, Henry Aaron, Frank Robinson, Roberto Clemente, Willie McCovey, Ernie Banks, Bob Gibson, and a bevy of other stars of color. Most American League teams, however, had resisted integration for many years, particularly the Yankees and Red Sox. By the early 1960s, then, the quality of play in the National League was vastly superior to the American. The Yankees were still winning the pennant every year, but they were usually losing the World Series to whoever won the National League pennant. Before the 1973 season, with the National League having outdrawn the American in attendance for the eleventh consecutive year, the desperate A.L. owners decided to address the problem. The solution they came up with was the designated hitter, the first fundamental change in the game's rules since 1903. At first an experiment intended to generate more fan interest, the DH has now become an established part of the game.

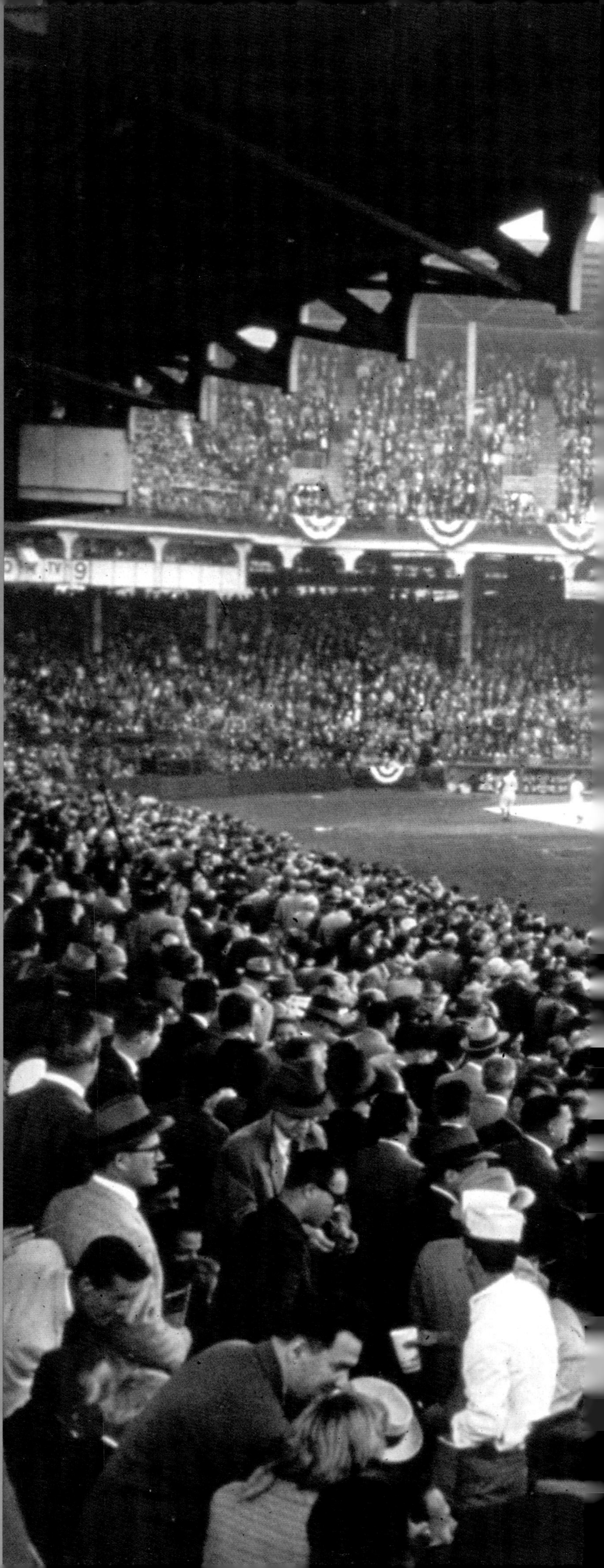

1946

ST. LOUIS CARDINALS (4)
BOSTON RED SOX (3)

PREVIOUS PAGES: Fans crowd Ebbets Field in 1956 as the Brooklyn Dodgers attempt to defend their World Series crown against perennial contenders (and cross-town rivals) the New York Yankees. After finally beating the Yankees the year before, the Dodgers (who entered the Series with home-field advantage) must have been hopeful that they could do it again. And after taking the first two games, things certainly looked good for the Brooklyn club. But the Yankees won the next three at Yankee Stadium, including a Game 5 no-hit masterpiece pitched by a hungover Don Larsen, setting the stage for the Yankees' eventual triumph.

IN 1946, THE BOSTON RED SOX WON THEIR first pennant since 1918, the year before they sold Babe Ruth to the Yankees. In the intervening 27 years, Boston had only seven winning seasons while finishing last eight times. The Red Sox won the pennant by averaging more than five runs per game with a lineup that included outstanding hitters Preston "Rudy" York, Johnny Pesky, Bobby Doerr, and Dom DiMaggio (Joe's brother). Ted Williams enjoyed one of his greatest seasons, winning the MVP award while leading the league in both on-base percentage and slugging percentage. The Red Sox won 104 games and were heavily favored in the World Series against the St. Louis Cardinals. The Cards had tied with the Dodgers during the regular season—the first such tie in baseball history—and won a best-of-three playoff to advance to the World Series.

The first game was played at Sportsman's Park, where the Cardinals took a 2-1 lead into the ninth behind Howie Pollet. With Pollet needing just one more strike to win the game, Tom McBride singled to tie it for Boston. The Red Sox completed their comeback in the tenth when York homered into a concession stand at the top of the left field bleachers to win the game.

Harry "The Cat" Brecheen, the diminutive lefty who had pitched so brilliantly in the 1944 Series, pitched a four-hit shutout for the Cardinals to win Game 2. But David "Boo" Ferriss, a righty who had won 25 games for the Red Sox during the regular season, returned the favor, pitching a shutout of his own in Game 3. The teams continued to swap victories, with the Cardinals winning Game 4, the Red Sox Game 5, and the Cardinals Game 6, taking the Series to a deciding seventh game.

In the decisive game, the Cardinals took a 3-1 lead into the seventh inning thanks to two miraculous catches by Terry Moore in center field. But Brecheen, pitching in relief of Murry Dickson, gave up a game-tying double to DiMaggio. DiMaggio, however, twisted his ankle rounding first and had to come out of the game—an injury that would

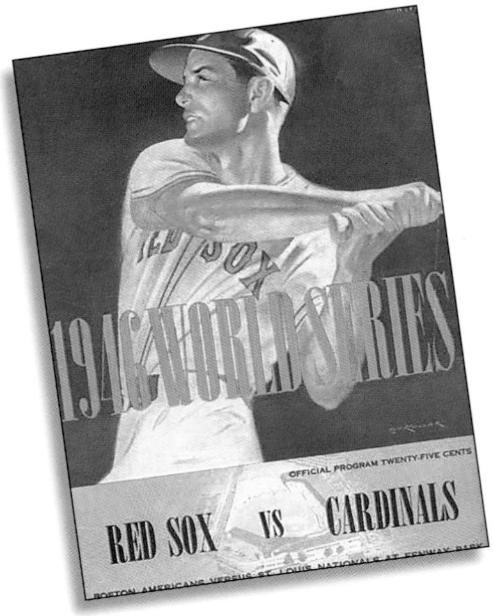

prove to be significant. Enos Slaughter walked to lead off the bottom of the eighth and Harry Walker lined a sharp hit into left-center field with two outs. Slaughter, who had been running on the pitch, glanced toward the outfield to assess the situation as he streaked from second to third, then ran through third base coach Mike González's stop sign and sprinted for home, sliding in safely with what proved to be the winning run. The Red Sox put two runners on in the

ninth, but Brecheen was able to get out of the trouble, and the Cardinals won their sixth world championship.

Slaughter was hailed as the hero of the Series for his "mad dash" home with the winning run, though the play was made possible by two fortuitous events earlier in the Series. In Game 1, Slaughter had been held up at third by González when he felt he could have scored. Discussing it afterward, manager Eddie Dyer gave Slaughter permission to trust his instincts if the situation came up again. The second key to the "mad dash" came when DiMaggio, one of the greatest defensive center fielders in baseball history, was injured in Game 7. Had he fielded the ball instead of Leon Culberson, Slaughter might have stopped at third.

Though it became perhaps the most famous baserunning play in baseball history, two pernicious myths persist about Slaughter's "mad dash." First, it is often said that he scored from first on a single, but Harry Walker's hit was actually ruled a double. (In fairness it was a very short double.) And for more than fifty years, Boston shortstop Johnny Pesky has been faulted by fans and the press for "holding the ball" on the play, hesitating as he decided what to do with the throw from the outfield. But film of the incident refutes this allegation. "Catch to throw takes less than a second," wrote Glenn Stout and Richard Johnson, who studied the footage while writing their book *Red Sox Century*. "He does not pause or freeze with the ball, although his body language exhibits surprise. Pesky, who got all the blame, simply made an average play in a situation that was already lost."

Ted Williams, meanwhile, had failed miserably in what would turn out to be the only World Series of his career. He batted just .200 with no extra-base hits and one RBI, a failure that would follow him the rest of his life. However, he had three extraordinary disadvantages facing him during the Series. First, he was injured. While waiting for the Cardinals-Dodgers playoff to finish, the Red Sox kept in shape by playing exhibition games against a team of American League all-stars. Williams was plunked on the elbow in one of those games by Senators southpaw Mickey Haefner, and the injury hampered him throughout the World Series. Second, Williams was facing a radical defensive shift in which the Cardinals concentrated their infielders on the right side of the diamond. Williams got one bunt hit in the Series, but most of the time the shift was effective in preventing base hits. And lastly, Williams played the entire World Series thinking he had been traded to the New York Yankees for Joe DiMaggio. Although Red Sox owner Tom Yawkey denied the rumors, Williams was convinced that a secret deal had been struck behind his back, and he could concentrate on little else throughout the Series. "I guess I'll miss Boston," he said after Game 1. "I know my way around there. What'll I do in New York on off days?"

1946 WORLD SERIES

Sportsman's Park IV (St. Louis Cards) ◆ 10.6.46 (GAME 1)

	1	2	3	4	5	6	7	8	9	10	R	H	E
Boston	0	1	0	0	0	0	0	0	1	1	3	9	2
St.L.	0	0	0	0	0	1	0	1	0	0	2	7	0

WP–D. Johnson LP–Pollet HR: BOS–York ATT: 36,218

Sportsman's Park IV ◆ 10.7.46 (GAME 2)

	1	2	3	4	5	6	7	8	9	R	H	E
Boston	0	0	0	0	0	0	0	0	0	0	4	1
St.L.	0	0	1	0	2	0	0	0	X	3	6	0

WP–Brecheen LP–Harris ATT: 35,815

Fenway Park II (Boston Red Sox) ◆ 10.9.46 (GAME 3)

	1	2	3	4	5	6	7	8	9	R	H	E
St.L.	0	0	0	0	0	0	0	0	0	0	6	1
Boston	3	0	0	0	0	0	0	1	X	4	8	0

WP–Ferriss LP–Dickson HR: BOS–York ATT: 34,500

Fenway Park II ◆ 10.10.46 (GAME 4)

	1	2	3	4	5	6	7	8	9	R	H	E
St.L.	0	3	3	0	1	0	1	0	4	12	20	1
Boston	0	0	0	1	0	0	0	2	0	3	9	4

WP–Munger LP–Hughson HR: STL–Slaughter; BOS–Doerr ATT: 35,645

Fenway Park II ◆ 10.11.46 (GAME 5)

	1	2	3	4	5	6	7	8	9	R	H	E
St.L.	0	1	0	0	0	0	0	0	2	3	4	1
Boston	1	1	0	0	0	1	3	0	X	6	11	3

WP–Dobson LP–Brazel HR: BOS–Culberson ATT: 35,982

Sportsman's Park IV ◆ 10.13.46 (GAME 6)

	1	2	3	4	5	6	7	8	9	R	H	E
Boston	0	0	0	0	0	0	1	0	0	1	7	0
St.L.	0	0	3	0	0	0	0	1	X	4	8	0

WP–Brecheen LP–Harris ATT: 35,768

Sportsman's Park IV ◆ 10.15.46 (GAME 7)

	1	2	3	4	5	6	7	8	9	R	H	E
Boston	1	0	0	0	0	0	0	2	0	3	8	0
St.L.	0	1	0	0	2	0	0	1	X	4	9	1

WP–Brecheen LP–Klinger ATT: 36,143

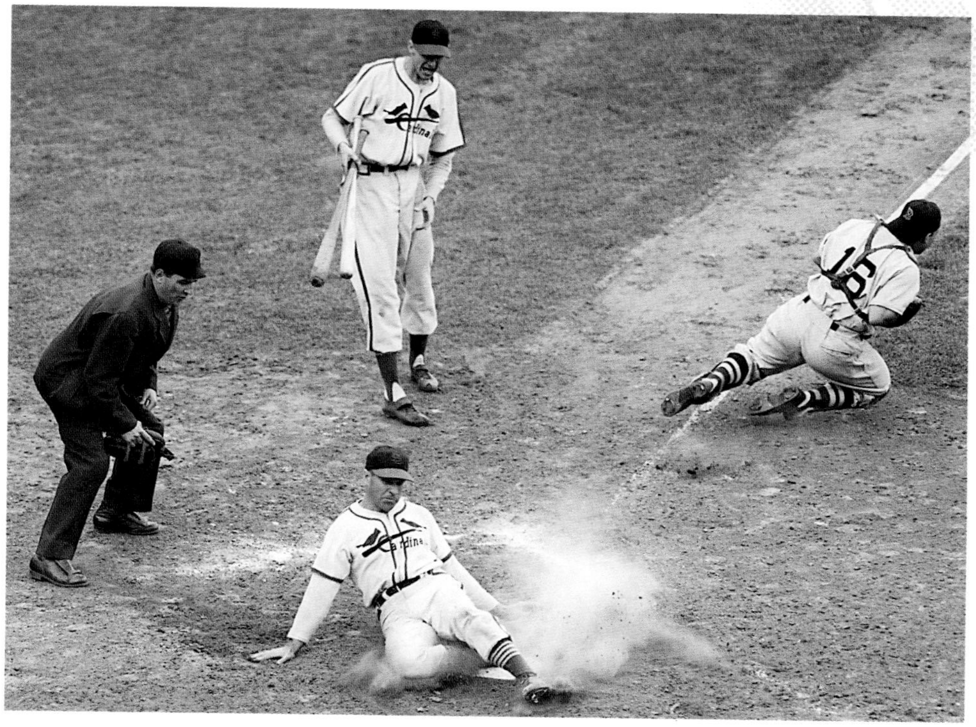

OPPOSITE: Fenway Park in 1946 was packed to the rafters with excited fans for the 1946 World Series. The crowd had every reason to be excited: the team was strong, Ted Williams had had a banner year (even for him), and it had been almost three decades since the Red Sox had last made it to the Fall Classic. Unfortunately, the Curse of the Bambino was in full effect, and the underdog Cardinals ultimately took the Series, 4-3.

BOTTOM LEFT: Enos Sluaghter slides across the plate after making one of the most famous baserunning plays in baseball history, his fabled "mad dash" from first to home.

BOTTOM RIGHT: Ted Williams, shown here in Yankee Stadium, was almost traded to the Yankees during the 1946 World Series.

1947

New York Yankees (4)
Brooklyn Dodgers (3)

The biggest story of the 1947 World Series, as for most of that season, was Jackie Robinson. After breaking the color barrier in April and leading the Dodgers to the pennant in September, Robinson became the first African-American ever to play in the World Series. "I was proud of that and yet I was uneasy," Robinson later wrote of his first World Series game. "There I was the black grandson of a slave, the son of a black sharecropper, part of an historic occasion, a symbolic hero to my people." His World Series debut brought about profoundly contradictory feelings for Robinson. He had finally made it as a black man in America, and yet, in many ways, he knew he never would make it.

Forty-five American League heroes of the past attended Game 1 at Yankee Stadium. These greats included Cy Young, Chief Bender, Tris Speaker, and Babe Ruth, who saw their league pull out a 5-3 victory. The Yankees shelled young Dodger pitcher Ralph Branca, who, with 21 victories that year, had won as many games as his age. It got even worse the next day for the Dodgers, as four Brooklyn pitchers gave up 15 hits in a 10-3 Yankee blowout. The Dodgers finally won one in Game 3. They jumped out to an early 6-0 lead, though they were barely able to fend off Yankee comebacks for the rest of the game. The key moment came in the bottom of the eighth when Joe DiMaggio ended a Yankee threat by grounding into a double play, and Brooklyn held on for a 9-8 win.

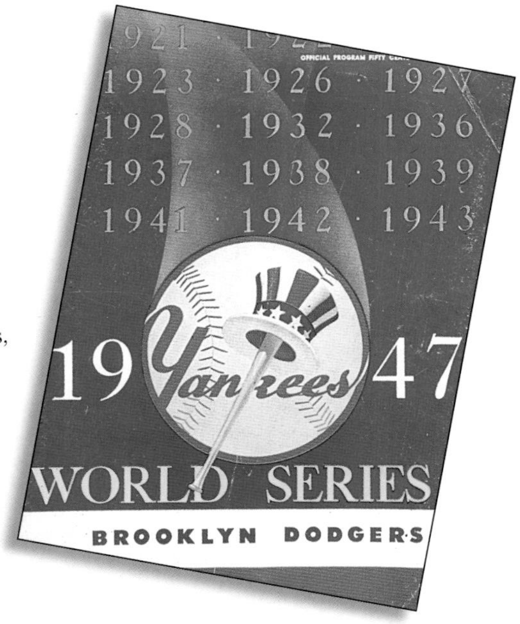

New York started Bill Bevens in Game 4. He posted a 7-13 record that year and was arguably the Yankees' worst pitcher. Bevens, a husky 30-year-old right-hander, struggled mightily with his control—but pitched the game of his life anyway. He entered the bottom of the ninth leading 2-1 with a no-hitter, but Carl Furillo drew a walk for the Dodgers in the ninth, and pinch runner Al Gionfriddo promptly stole second off inexperienced catcher Yogi Berra. ("Never in the World Series have I seen such awful catching," said Connie Mack, sitting in the stands.) With the tying run now in scoring position, Yankee manager Bucky Harris bucked conventional wisdom and ordered pinch hitter Pete Reiser intentionally walked. It was Bevens' tenth walk of the game. That brought up Eddie Stanky, but the little second baseman was called back to the dugout in favor of a pinch hitter. Harry "Cookie" Lavagetto, a solid third baseman since the mid-1930s but now an aging role player, stepped to the plate.

Lavagetto sent a screaming shot off the right field wall on the first pitch. Right fielder Tommy Henrich struggled to gain control of the ball and both baserunners scored. The game was over. Bevens had lost both his no-hitter and the game on one pitch.

BOTTOM LEFT: Bill Bevens winds up for a pitch during Game 7 of the 1947 World Series, a look of intense concentration on his face. He only pitched one inning, the seventh, in what would prove to be his last game as a major league ball player.

BOTTOM RIGHT: Jackie Robinson tries to break up a double play in Game 6 of the 1947 Series, but Phil Rizzuto was able to complete the twin killing.

OPPOSITE: Al Gionfriddo's momentum carries him into the fence after making a remarkable catch to rob Joe DiMaggio of an extra-base hit in Game 6.

415 FT.
OCT 4 1949
Al Gionfriddo looks back toward the plate after making a sensational catch of Joe DiMaggio's drive which was headed into the bull pen with two on and two out in the sixth inning of the sixth game of the 1947 series. The catch enabled the Dodgers to win 8-6 (Herald Tribune-Acme)

The Greatest Set of Games

THE NEGRO LEAGUE WORLD SERIES

THE GREATEST WORLD SERIES EVER PLAYED DID not take place in 1912, or 1975, or 1991. It was not shown on national television, nor broadcast on the radio, nor reviewed in *The Sporting News.* The vast majority of America's baseball fans did not know it was taking place. Even if they had, they'd never heard of most of the players anyway. You see, the greatest World Series was the first-ever Negro League World Series, played in 1924 between the Kansas City Monarchs and the Hilldale Daisies.

The genesis of the Negro League World Series has many parallels with its white counterpart. The first successful black baseball league was the Negro National League (N.N.L.). It was founded by Andrew "Rube" Foster and other Midwestern African-American businessmen in 1920. Three years later a rival league, the Eastern Colored League (E.C.L.), began on the East Coast, financed largely by white entrepreneurs. By mid-1923 fans and sportswriters were clamoring for a postseason World Series between the two leagues. Such a series would "make the white world series resemble a game of ping pong," the *Baltimore Afro-American* asserted. But Foster, impresario of the N.N.L., refused to allow his league to participate in such an event until the upstart E.C.L. agreed to quit stealing players from Foster's league. No World Series was played that first year. Foster and Ed Bolden, the man in charge of the E.C.L., met in September 1924 and agreed to respect each other's contracts and play an annual World Series.

As the Monarchs (N.N.L.) and the Daisies (E.C.L.) sewed up their pennants, it was decided that the best-of-nine 1924 World Series would take place in four cities: Philadelphia (the Daisies' home), Baltimore, Kansas City, and Chicago. Admission was $1.65 for box seats and $1.00 for general admission. Most observers felt the Monarchs, in their fifth season of existence, would prevail because of their outstanding defense, as they had an awe-inspiring double-play combination in Walter "Dobie" Moore and Newt Allen and a top-flight defensive catcher in Frank Duncan. The Monarchs' most important player was the incomparable Wilber "Bullet" Rogan, who ranks with Babe Ruth and Martín Dihigo as one of the greatest two-way threats in baseball history. Rudimentary statistics show Rogan led his league that year in both wins, at 16-5, and batting average, at .412. Many of Kansas City's best players, including Rogan, Moore, and Oscar "Heavy" Johnson, were World War I veterans. They had been recruited from Army teams by Monarchs owner J.L. Wilkinson.

The Daisies had their share of stars, too. Among them were third baseman William "Judy" Johnson, who batted .369, and utility man James Raleigh "Biz" Mackey, a switch hitter who batted .337. Mackey was one of the few players in baseball history able to play both shortstop and catcher. He would be shifted to third in the Series and Johnson to short because of an injury to Paul "Country Jake" Stephens, the team's regular shortstop. The World Series opened on October 3, 1924, as 5,366 Philadelphians—considered a good crowd for a weekday—watched Bullet Rogan collect two hits and pitch Kansas City to a 6-2 victory. "The Monarchs appeared in natty new suits," the *Chicago Defender* noted, "red, white, and blue stripes on blue hose, and new red sweater coats." Hilldale won the second game in an 11-0 blowout. The Series moved to Baltimore where fans witnessed a classic in Game 3.

The game was tied entering the ninth. Kansas City scored a run to make it 5-4, but Hilldale tied it in the bottom half. Kansas City took the lead again when Rogan singled in a run in the top of the eleventh. Hilldale tied it again in the bottom of the eleventh on a bases-loaded walk. With the game tied 6-6 and the bases still

BELOW: One of the most successful African-American teams of the century, the Kansas City Monarchs won the inaugural Negro League World Series in 1924.

loaded, Johnson tried to tag and score the winning run on a fly ball, but was thrown out by the Monarchs' Allen "Hurley" McNair to preserve the tie. Rogan pitched a scoreless thirteenth inning for Kansas City before the game was called due to darkness and officially declared a tie.

Hilldale won the next day on a bases-loaded throwing error in the ninth inning by Allen. They also beat Rogan in Game 5 thanks to a remarkable three-run, inside-the-park homer by Judy Johnson in the ninth inning. The sixth game was played in Kansas City and was the fourth dramatic contest in a row. Judy Johnson was having a tremendous series for Hilldale, and he tripled in two runs in the first inning. Kansas City tied it in the bottom of the first and scored the go-ahead run in the eighth. Monarch pitcher Bill Drake, a master of the emery ball and other trick pitches, entered in relief. Drake pitched in the ninth inning with the tying and winning runs on base but got out of the jam for a 6-5 win. Hilldale now led the Series three games to two.

The seventh game was tied as the eighth inning approached. Heavy Johnson, Kansas City's 250-pound slugger, untied it with a pinch hit single. Judy Johnson tied it again with a single in the ninth inning and Hilldale threatened to win the game right then by placing the winning run on second base. Then a remarkable thing happened. José Méndez, the 37-year-old manager of the Monarchs, put himself into the game at pitcher. The Cuban-born Méndez was one of the great pitchers in baseball history—he had shut out the Cincinnati Reds three times in one month in 1908—but was nearing the end as an active player. He struck out the first batter and retired the next man on a great catch in center field by Bullet Rogan to send the game into extra innings. Méndez pitched $3\frac{2}{3}$ scoreless innings, and was rewarded with a victory when a throw by Judy Johnson pulled the first baseman off the bag and allowed the winning run to score. The teams moved to Chicago for the final three games.

Rogan started Game 8 for Kansas City. He trailed 2-0 entering the bottom of the ninth, which historian John Holway later called "one of the legendary innings of blackball history." First, Hilldale center fielder Clint Thomas made an outstanding catch for the first out. Then Rogan

RIGHT: Wilber "Bullet" Rogan was not only a fantastic pitcher and hitter, but also served as an umpire in the Negro American League (N.A.L.) after his retirement.

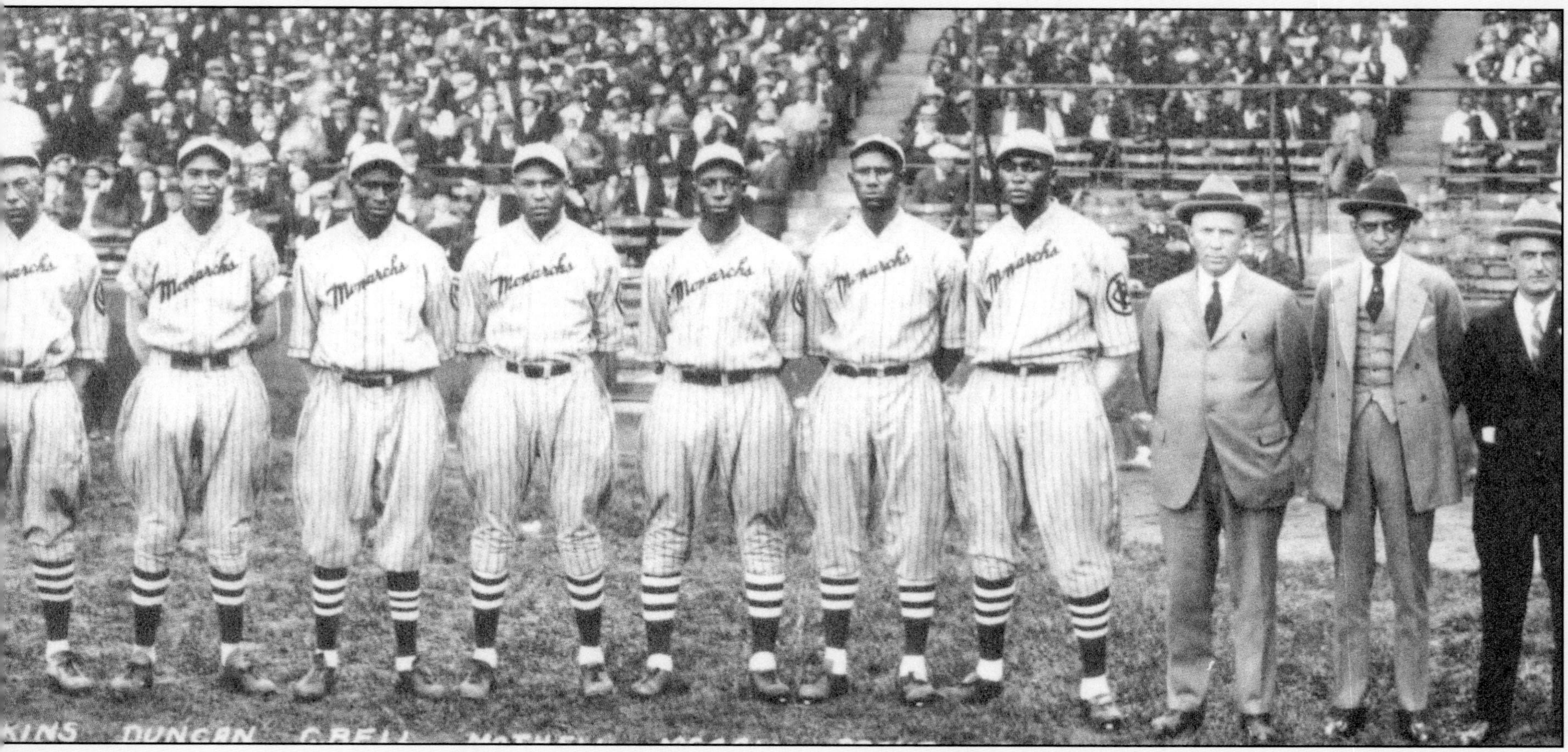

reached on an infield hit to Mackey, who was playing deep in the hole at third base. After another out, two more hits, and a hit batsman, the Monarchs had cut the lead to 2-1 and still had the bases loaded. Hilldale pitcher Reuben "Rube" Currie, an ex-Monarch, coaxed a foul pop-up from Duncan that should have ended the game—but it glanced off the mitt of Louis Santop, usually an excellent defensive catcher. Duncan was given new life and hit a hard grounder that handcuffed third baseman Mackey and rolled through his legs as the tying and winning runs scored for the Monarchs. Both Santop and Currie broke down in tears in the Hilldale dressing room after the game. Player-manager Frank Warfield—known to fans as "Weasel"—took the loss especially hard. He screamed viciously at Santop, the 16-year veteran, until his teammates silenced him.

In the ninth game, Hilldale started the same makeshift defensive lineup that had betrayed them the day before, with Mackey at third and Johnson at shortstop. It didn't matter this time, as left-handed curveball artist Jesse "Nip" Winters beat the Monarchs 5-3 for his third victory of the Series. Bullet Rogan ran in from left field to argue an umpire's call with the score tied in the eighth. He neglected to call time out, though, and Winters snuck home with the go-ahead run as Rogan gave the umpire an earful. The Monarchs tied it back up in their half of the eighth. Johnson scored the winning run for Hilldale in the ninth on a groundout. The remarkable Series had come down to a decisive tenth game.

Méndez picked himself as Kansas City's starting pitcher in the final game on Foster's advice. He was opposed by Holsey "Scrip" Lee, a 25-year-old submariner and onetime schoolmate of Duke Ellington's. "Oh, he was a tough man," Allen said. Although one writer described Méndez as "gaunt and gray," he pitched vibrantly as the teams battled to a scoreless tie after seven innings. Lee had only given up one hit through seven, but he fell apart in the eighth, as the Monarchs blistered him for five runs. Méndez retired Hilldale in the ninth to complete a mas-

TOP: Third baseman Judy Johnson was just beginning his distinguished Hall of Fame career when he starred in the 1924 World Series for Hilldale. Here, he poses in the uniform of the Pittsburgh Crawfords, which he joined in 1932.

BELOW: The Hilldale Daisies, based in a suburb of Philadelphia, were champions of the Eastern Colored League in 1924. In 1925, the mighty Daisies avenged their World Series loss to the Monarchs in 1924.

terful three-hit shutout, and the Kansas City Monarchs became champions of the first-ever Negro League World Series.

The debut Negro League World Championship had been an extraordinary Series by any standard. The ten games included one tie and four one-run contests, and the winning team scored the decisive runs in its final at-bat *in each of the last seven games.* It was not the pinnacle of artistry—the teams combined for 44 errors—but for excitement, the 1924 Negro League World Series is unmatched in all of baseball. None of the 98 "major league" World Series have come anywhere close to equaling it. Rube Foster had attended most of the 21 white World Series up to that point and called the final matches of the black World Series "eight of the best played games of ball I have ever witnessed." According to the *Kansas City Call*, the Series had importance beyond the sporting realm: it had "shown the world that a Negro can get attention for a good deed well done, and that publicity is no longer the exclusive mark of our criminals."

Even the losing Hilldale club returned home to a heroes' welcome in Philadelphia, as hundreds of fans met them at the train station and then marched down Broad Street in an impromptu parade. The irrepressible Johnson—an ex-longshoreman who had been cut by Hilldale as a teenager because they thought he was too small—had the Series of his life. He was the youngest player on the Hilldale club at 23 even though he was in his sixth season, and led all Series batters with a .364 batting average and .614 slugging percentage and seemed to be at the center of each of Hilldale's late-inning rallies.

Many black fans hoped the Series winner would eventually face the winner of the white World Series, but that never came to pass. In the end, a total of 45,857 fans attended the ten games—not bad for the Negro Leagues, but certainly not as many as the organizers had hoped. The gate receipts totaled $52,113. That left $30,000 in profits to be distributed among the owners and players, after expenses. It was not a smashing success, but neither was it a disaster. The World Series continued to function until 1927, when the Eastern Colored League collapsed. Despite no-hitters in 1926 and '27 by Bacharach Giants pitchers Claude "Red" Grier and Luther Farrell, the Series never again generated the sense of excitement it had in 1924. The Series started up again in 1942, but by then it had taken a back seat in prestige to the annual East-West All-Star Game in Chicago.

THE NEGRO LEAGUES SERIES RESULTS

1924	**Kansas City Monarchs (N.N.L.) 5**
	Hilldale Daisies (E.C.L.) 4, one tie
	MVP*: Judy Johnson, Hilldale
1925	**Hilldale Daisies (E.C.L.) 5**
	Kansas City Monarchs (N.N.L.) 1
	MVP: Rube Currie, Hilldale
1926	**Chicago American Giants (N.N.L.) 5**
	Atlantic City Bacharach Giants (E.C.L.) 4, two ties
	MVP: Willie Foster, Chicago
1927	**Chicago American Giants (N.N.L.) 5**
	Atlantic City Bacharach Giants (E.C.L.) 3, one tie
	MVP: Walter "Steel Arm" Davis, Chicago
1942	**Kansas City Monarchs (N.A.L.) 4**
	Homestead Grays (N.N.L.) 0
	MVP: William "Bonnie" Serrell, Kansas City
1943	**Homestead Grays (N.N.L.) 4**
	Birmingham Black Barons (N.A.L.) 3, one tie
	MVP: James "Cool Papa" Bell, Homestead
1944	**Homestead Grays (N.N.L.) 4**
	Birmingham Black Barons (N.A.L.) 1
	MVP: Josh Gibson, Homestead
1945	**Cleveland Buckeyes (N.A.L.) 4**
	Homestead Grays (N.N.L.) 0
	MVP: Quincy Trouppe, Cleveland
1946	**Newark Eagles (N.N.L.) 4**
	Kansas City Monarchs (N.A.L.) 3
	MVP: Monte Irvin, Newark
1947	**New York Cubans (N.N.L.) 4**
	Cleveland Buckeyes (N.A.L.) 1
	MVP: Orestes "Minnie" Miñoso, New York

*MVPs selected by the author

1947 WORLD SERIES

YANKEE STADIUM I (N.Y. YANKEES) ◆ 9.30.47

	1	2	3	4	5	6	7	8	9	R	H	E
B'klyn	1	0	0	0	0	1	1	0	0	3	6	0
NYY	0	0	0	0	5	0	0	0	X	5	4	0

WP–Shea LP–Branca S–Page ATT: 73,365

YANKEE STADIUM I ◆ 10.1.47

	1	2	3	4	5	6	7	8	9	R	H	E
B'klyn	0	0	1	1	0	0	0	0	1	3	9	2
NYY	1	0	1	1	2	1	4	0	X	10	15	1

WP–Reynolds LP–Lombardi HR: BKN–Walker; NYY–Henrich ATT: 69,865

EBBETS FIELD (BROOKLYN DODGERS) ◆ 10.2.47

	1	2	3	4	5	6	7	8	9	R	H	E
NYY	0	0	2	2	2	1	1	0	0	8	13	0
B'klyn	0	6	1	2	0	0	0	0	X	9	13	1

WP–Casey LP–Newsom HR: NYY–DiMaggio, Berra ATT: 33,098

EBBETS FIELD ◆ 10.3.47

	1	2	3	4	5	6	7	8	9	R	H	E
NYY	1	0	0	1	0	0	0	0	0	2	8	1
B'klyn	0	0	0	0	1	0	0	0	2	3	1	3

WP–Casey LP–Bevens ATT: 33,443

EBBETS FIELD ◆ 10.4.47

	1	2	3	4	5	6	7	8	9	R	H	E
NYY	0	0	0	1	1	0	0	0	0	2	5	0
B'klyn	0	0	0	0	0	1	0	0	0	1	4	1

WP–Shea LP–Barney HR: NYY–DiMaggio ATT: 34,379

YANKEE STADIUM I ◆ 10.5.47

	1	2	3	4	5	6	7	8	9	R	H	E
B'klyn	2	0	2	0	0	4	0	0	0	8	12	1
NYY	0	0	4	1	0	0	0	0	1	6	15	2

WP–Branca LP–Page S–Casey ATT: 74,065

YANKEE STADIUM I ◆ 10.6.47

	1	2	3	4	5	6	7	8	9	R	H	E
B'klyn	0	2	0	0	0	0	0	0	0	2	7	0
NYY	0	1	0	2	0	1	1	0	X	5	7	0

WP–Page LP–Gregg ATT: 71,548

Henrich had been forced to make a split-second decision: Try for the catch, or play the ball off the wall? He chose the former, and it cost the Yankees the game. "I would say that those were the toughest five seconds of my life," he later said. "It all happened in five seconds, and I won't second-guess myself. Not in that kind of situation. And I also say those are five seconds I could have lived without." The teams faced a similar situation the next day when pinch hitter Lavagetto strode to the plate with Brooklyn losing 2-1 and the tying run on base in the ninth inning. Joe DiMaggio, standing in center field, called over to Henrich: "For Christ's sake, say a prayer." But Frank Shea struck out Lavagetto to preserve the Yankee victory.

The Dodgers entered the bottom of the sixth with an 8-5 lead in Game 6 at Yankee Stadium when Dodgers manager Burt Shotton tapped Gionfriddo, a seldom-used outfielder who spent his offseasons working as a fireman on the Pennsylvania Railroad, as a defensive replacement for left fielder Eddie Miksis. DiMaggio came up with two Yankees on base and hit a long drive toward left, and Gionfriddo raced back toward the wall, stuck out his glove, and caught the ball just as it was about to bounce off the bullpen gate for a double or triple. DiMaggio, rounding the bases with what he thought was an extra-base hit, kicked the dirt in disgust. Though most newspaper accounts of the game said the hit would have been a homer, this was merely an example of the halo granted DiMaggio by the New York media. Film of the play clearly shows that it would not have left the park. Indeed, Gionfriddo caught the ball two full steps in front of the fence. Still, an extra-base hit would have put DiMaggio in scoring position with the tying run. Gionfriddo's remarkable catch helped preserve the game for Brooklyn.

The seventh game was something of an anticlimax after the excitement of Games 4 and 6, as New York won 5-2 thanks to five strong innings of relief pitching by Joe Page. "After all the delirious, exciting, and unbelievable baseball that has been displayed, this was just a routine, business-like job by a coldly efficient team," Arthur Daley wrote in *The New York Times*. Remarkably, none of the Series' three unlikely heroes—Bevens, Lavagetto, and Gionfriddo—would ever play major league baseball again. Meanwhile, Jackie Robinson, in his first World Series

BOTTOM LEFT: Phil Rizzuto scores during Game 7 of the 1947 Series as the throw goes over the head of catcher Allie Clark. The Yankees won 5-2 tobecome world champions.

BOTTOM RIGHT: Batting with two outs in the ninth inning of Game 4, Cookie Lavagetto breaks up pitcher Bill Bevens' no-hitter with a game-winning double to right field. It was one of the most famous hits in World Series history.

appearance, had batted .259 with three runs scored, three RBI, and two stolen bases. But as writer Wendell Smith noted, Robinson's accomplishments were overshadowed by those of Lavagetto, Gionfriddo, and DiMaggio, all Italian-Americans. "In short, it's been a great series," Smith wrote, "no matter who your parents were."

1948

Cleveland Indians (4)
Boston Braves (2)

The Cleveland Indians won their first pennant in nearly three decades in 1948, as shortstop Lou Boudreau became the second man in history (after Mickey Cochrane) to win an MVP award and manage his team to the pennant in the same season. The man many believe most responsible for the Indians' success, though, was their energetic 34-year-old owner Bill Veeck. He claimed to have aided the pennant drive by secretly moving the fences at Cleveland Municipal Stadium in or out, depending on whether the Indians were facing a power-hitting team.

Like their previous pennant-winning team in 1920, the 1948 Indians were led to the flag by two remarkable rookies. One was 42-year-old Satchel Paige, signed by Veeck in midseason to bolster the bullpen. On July 9 Paige debuted as the first African-American pitcher in the American League. He went on to post a 6-1 record with an outstanding 2.48 ERA. The other vital rookie was Henry "Gene" Bearden, a left-handed pitcher and career minor leaguer who, after developing a knuckleball, transformed himself into arguably the best pitcher in the American League. The 28-year-old Bearden posted a 20-7 record and league-leading 2.43 ERA. The Indians and Red Sox were tied at the end of the regular season and played a one-game playoff for the pennant, the first such playoff in American League history. Bearden, wearing a lucky sweatshirt that had brought him nine consecutive victories, won the game 8-3 to clinch the pennant for the Indians. The Indians advanced to face the Boston Braves in the World Series.

The first game was played at Braves Field and featured a classic duel between two outstanding pitchers. In Van Meter, Iowa, Bob Feller's hometown, children listened on the radio in the school auditorium as their former neighbor pitched. "When the game started, I was as ready as I've ever been in my life," wrote Feller, who pitched the tenth two-hitter in World Series history, but lost to curveball specialist Johnny Sain, 1-0. The game's lone run came in the bottom of the eighth inning when the habitually wild Feller—who seven years later would break the career record for walks by a pitcher—issued a free pass, and pinch runner Phil Masi was sacrificed to second base. Manager Lou Boudreau then made the controversial decision to walk the light-hitting Eddie Stanky intentionally. "I thought that was a mistake, and I told Lou so," Feller said later. "Stanky wasn't a good hitter, and I was confident I could get him out." After the walk to Stanky, Boudreau, managing from his shortstop position, covered his knee with his

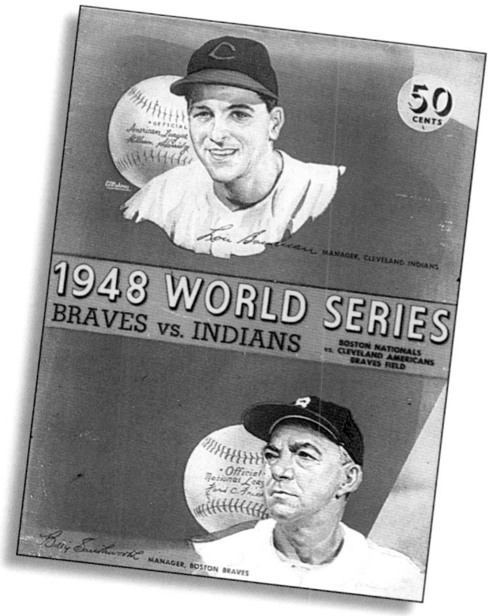

TOP: Cleveland owner Bill Veeck (in white shirt) congratulates Lou Boudreau after the Indians' 1948 Series victory.

BOTTOM: Boston pitcher Warren Spahn tracks the ball as it leaves the bat of Cleveland outfielder Dale Mitchell at the top of the first inning of Game 2 of the 1948 World Series.

TOP: In the key play of the 1948 Series, Boston's Phil Masi was called safe at second base on a pickoff play. Shortstop and manager Lou Boudreau argues the call with umpire Bill Stewart.

glove, the Indians' sign for a pickoff play. "It was a surprise play that we had been practicing for five years. We used it successfully several times that season," Feller wrote. "We caught Masi napping. Unfortunately, we caught the umpire, Bill Stewart of the National League, doing the same thing... Lou tagged Masi out by two feet. It wasn't even close. Everybody in the ballpark saw he was out—except one, the umpire." The next batter, Tommy Holmes, promptly punched a line drive down the left field line, bringing in what turned out to be the only run of the game. After the game, Boudreau refused to second-guess his decision to walk Stanky, although that had forced Feller to eventually face Holmes, a .325 batter. "I passed Stanky to set up the possible double play, and if the same situation came up tomorrow, I'd do the same thing," he said.

Bob Lemon outdueled Warren Spahn in a matchup of future Hall of Famers in Game 2, and the teams traveled to Cleveland for the third game, where the excitement over the Series had reached a level of near-pandemonium. The game was shown in a public plaza downtown on newfangled large-screen televisions. Factory and construction workers across the city were allowed to listen to the games as they worked. More than 70,000 fans packed the Cleveland Stadium stands for each game, including Bud Abbott, Lou Costello, and Indians part-owner Bob Hope. When the Braves' prayers for rain went unanswered, they started righty Vern Bickford against Bearden in Game 3. Bearden pitched for the first time since his pennant-winning victory and threw a five-hit shutout to win 2-0. It took him only 96 minutes to dispatch the Braves on 84 pitches.

The Indians beat Johnny Sain 2-1 behind ex-infielder Steve Gromek the next day, as Gromek pitched a complete game and Cleveland scored its runs on a double by Boudreau and a homer by rookie center fielder Larry Doby. Now the Indians needed just one more victory with Feller scheduled to pitch Game 5 at Cleveland Stadium. Cleveland led the game early, but Boston came back to knock out Feller in the sixth inning. Spahn pitched $5\frac{2}{3}$ innings of masterful relief for the Braves, who prevailed 11-5, sending the Series back to Boston. Cleveland took care of matters in Game 6, as twenty-game winners Lemon and Bearden combined for a 4-3 victory. The Indians returned to Cleveland greeted by traffic jams, ticker tape, and a delirious mob of happy fans. In retrospect, the apocalyptic celebration seems fitting, for the Indians have not won another World Series since.

1948 WORLD SERIES

Braves Field (Boston Braves) ◆ 10.6.48 (Game 1)

	1	2	3	4	5	6	7	8	9	R	H	E
Clev.	0	0	0	0	0	0	0	0	0	0	4	0
Boston	0	0	0	0	0	0	0	1	X	1	2	2

WP–Sain LP–Feller ATT: 40,135

Braves Field ◆ 10.7.48 (Game 2)

	1	2	3	4	5	6	7	8	9	R	H	E
Clev.	0	0	0	2	1	0	0	0	1	4	8	1
Boston	1	0	0	0	0	0	0	0	0	1	8	3

WP–Lemon LP–Spahn ATT: 39,633

Cleveland Stadium (Cleveland Indians) ◆ 10.8.48 (Game 3)

	1	2	3	4	5	6	7	8	9	R	H	E
Boston	0	0	0	0	0	0	0	0	0	0	5	1
Clev.	0	0	1	1	0	0	0	0	X	2	5	0

WP–Bearden LP–Bickford ATT: 70,306

Cleveland Stadium ◆ 10.9.48 (Game 4)

	1	2	3	4	5	6	7	8	9	R	H	E
Boston	0	0	0	0	0	0	1	0	0	1	7	0
Clev.	1	0	1	0	0	0	0	0	X	2	5	0

WP–Gromek LP–Sain HR: BSN–Rickert; CLE–Doby ATT: 81,897

Cleveland Stadium ◆ 10.10.48 (Game 5)

	1	2	3	4	5	6	7	8	9	R	H	E
Boston	3	0	1	0	0	1	6	0	0	11	12	0
Clev.	1	0	0	4	0	0	0	0	0	5	6	2

WP–Spahn LP–Feller HR: BSN–Elliott (2), Salkeld; CLE–Mitchell, Hegan ATT: 86,288

Braves Field ◆ 10.11.48 (Game 6)

	1	2	3	4	5	6	7	8	9	R	H	E
Clev.	0	0	1	0	0	2	0	1	0	4	10	0
Boston	0	0	0	1	0	0	0	2	0	3	9	0

WP–Lemon LP–Voiselle S–Bearden HR: CLE–Gordon ATT: 40,103

1949

New York Yankees (4)
Brooklyn Dodgers (1)

After another embarrassing third-place finish in 1948—the fourth time in five years that they had finished third or worse—the Yankee dynasty appeared to be crumbling, and its star, Joe DiMaggio, was getting old. Ownership decided to change things by bringing in a new manager who at first appeared to be the complete antithesis of everything the Yankees stood for. Casey Stengel was not only a clown, he was also a loser. His teams had lost 162 more games than they won in his nine seasons as a National League manager. But Stengel impressed people by winning the 1948 Pacific Coast League pennant in Oakland with a collection of has-beens called the "Nine Old Men." If Stengel could work such miracles on the Pacific coast, the Yankees figured, why not in New York?

It was a rough year. The Yankees suffered 71 different injuries in 1949, including one to DiMaggio's heel that hampered the 34-year-old slugger for most of the season, but Stengel led them to victory in one of the closest pennant races ever. The Yankees swept the final two games of the season from second-place Boston and would face the Brooklyn Dodgers in the World Series. "Stengel prepared us for the 1949 World Series quite simply," rookie outfielder Gene Woodling remembered. "He said, 'Go get 'em!'"

National League Rookie of the Year Don Newcombe hurled a five-hitter and struck out eleven Yankees in Game 1 at Yankee Stadium. But Allie Reynolds was even better. He struck out nine and threw a two-hitter to beat Newcombe, 1-0. The lone run scored in the bottom of the ninth, when Newcombe gave up a game-ending homer to Tommy Henrich. "I guess that's when Newcombe started to be called a choker," the Dodgers' John "Spider" Jorgensen said. "He wasn't that. He'd won big games all year, including the one that put us up in the pennant race. He was a good pitcher and we had faith in him."

In Game 2 Brooklyn pitcher Elwin "Preacher" Roe baffled Yankee batters with his specialty pitch, the spitball. He cruised to a 1-0 victory over Vic Raschi, who won 21 games in 1949. The Dodgers scored their only run in the second inning, when National League MVP Jackie Robinson doubled and, after driving Raschi crazy with his baserunning antics, was driven home by Gil Hodges. "He was just about the best base runner I've ever seen," Raschi said of Robinson. "I had never seen anything like him before. He did something to me that almost never happened: He broke my concentration and I paid more attention to him than to Hodges. He beat me more than Hodges." It was the first time that two 1-0 games had ever been played in one World Series, perhaps because the "batter's eye," the dark tarpaulin that normally covered a section of the center field bleachers at Yankee Stadium, was filled with paying customers in white shirtsleeves during the Series.

The carnival moved across the East River to Ebbets Field for Game 3. "At Yankee Stadium the spectators maintained, for the most part, an aloof boredom," wrote Ed Comerford in *Newsday*. "But at Ebbets Field,

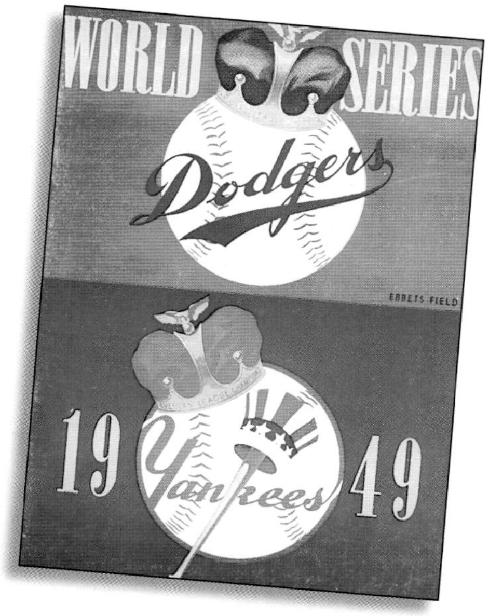

TOP: With this cast of sluggers, the Brooklyn Dodgers won five pennants between 1949 and 1956. Clockwise from top left: Roy Campanella, Gil Hodges, Duke Snider, Pee Wee Reese, Carl Furillo, and Jackie Robinson.

BOTTOM: A victorious Tommy Henrich comes home after hitting a walk-off home run to break a ninth-inning scoreless tie in the opening game of the 1949 Series.

1946–1960

the fans were full of life, howling and shouting." The Series drew such an odd assortment of characters to the Flatbush ballpark that it made one wonder, Comerford wrote, "do crazy people root for the Dodgers, or do people who root for the Dodgers go crazy?" Ralph Branca—who had posted a 13-5 record during the regular season and had gone undefeated at Ebbets Field—pitched a fine Game 3 for Brooklyn, retiring fourteen consecutive batters at one point. But with the game tied 1-1 in the top of the ninth, and Branca just one strike away from ending the inning, all hell broke loose. Two walks and a single loaded the bases for Johnny Mize, who crushed a long single high off the right field wall that scored two runs and knocked Branca out of the game. The Yankees scored three in the inning to take the lead, but the Dodgers weren't done. Luis Olmo and Roy Campanella each homered in the bottom of the ninth to bring Brooklyn within a run, but the Dodgers came up short when pinch hitter Bruce Edwards was called out on strikes to end the game.

Newcombe started Game 4 for Brooklyn on just two days' rest. The decision backfired when the Yankees knocked him out of the game with three runs in the fourth inning. When the Dodgers threatened to come back, Stengel brought in Reynolds, who pitched three-plus innings of hitless relief to nail down a 6-4 Yankee victory. The Yankees had now won two straight on the Dodgers' home turf and led the Series three games to one. New York polished off Brooklyn in the fifth game by pounding six Dodger pitchers for a total of ten runs. Three hits apiece by Gene Woodling and Tulane medical student Bobby Brown led the way. Once again the Yankees were saved by a stellar relief performance when Joe Page came in to stymie the rallying Dodgers in the seventh inning.

Although many believed the Dodgers looked stronger than the Yankees on paper, the New Yorkers had easily dispatched them in the World Series. "Rather than being disappointed that the Yankees won the Series," Brooklyn's Spider Jorgensen said, "I was dumbfounded that they had won it so easily." The Dodgers did not lose because of their pitching. Their starters pitched magnificently in each of the first three games, but the explosive Brooklyn offense, which scored 113 more runs than any other National League team in 1949, fell apart completely in the World Series. Gil Hodges batted just .235, Jackie Robinson .188, Edwin "Duke" Snider .143, and Carl Furillo .125. Still, with such a talented young core of players, Dodger fans expected their Bums to be pennant contenders for years to come. "Just wait 'til next year," they said optimistically.

1949 WORLD SERIES

YANKEE STADIUM I (N.Y. YANKEES) ◆ 10.5.49

	1	2	3	4	5	6	7	8	9	R	H	E
B'klyn	0	0	0	0	0	0	0	0	0	0	2	0
NYY	0	0	0	0	0	0	0	0	1	1	5	1

WP–Reynolds LP–Newcombe HR: NYY–Henrich ATT: 66,224

YANKEE STADIUM I ◆ 10.6.49

	1	2	3	4	5	6	7	8	9	R	H	E
B'klyn	0	1	0	0	0	0	0	0	0	1	7	2
NYY	0	0	0	0	0	0	0	0	0	0	6	1

WP–Roe LP–Raschi ATT: 70,053

EBBETS FIELD (BROOKLYN DODGERS) ◆ 10.7.49

	1	2	3	4	5	6	7	8	9	R	H	E
NYY	0	0	1	0	0	0	0	0	3	4	5	0
B'klyn	0	0	0	1	0	0	0	0	2	3	5	0

WP–Page LP–Branca HR: BKN–Reese, Olmo, Campanella ATT: 32,788

EBBETS FIELD ◆ 10.8.49

	1	2	3	4	5	6	7	8	9	R	H	E
NYY	0	0	0	3	3	0	0	0	0	6	10	0
B'klyn	0	0	0	0	0	4	0	0	0	4	9	1

WP–Lopat LP–Newcombe S–Reynolds ATT: 33,934

EBBETS FIELD ◆ 10.9.49

	1	2	3	4	5	6	7	8	9	R	H	E
NYY	2	0	3	1	1	3	0	0	0	10	11	1
B'klyn	0	0	1	0	0	1	4	0	0	6	11	2

WP–Raschi LP–Barney S–Page HR: NYY–DiMaggio; BKN–Hodges ATT: 33,711

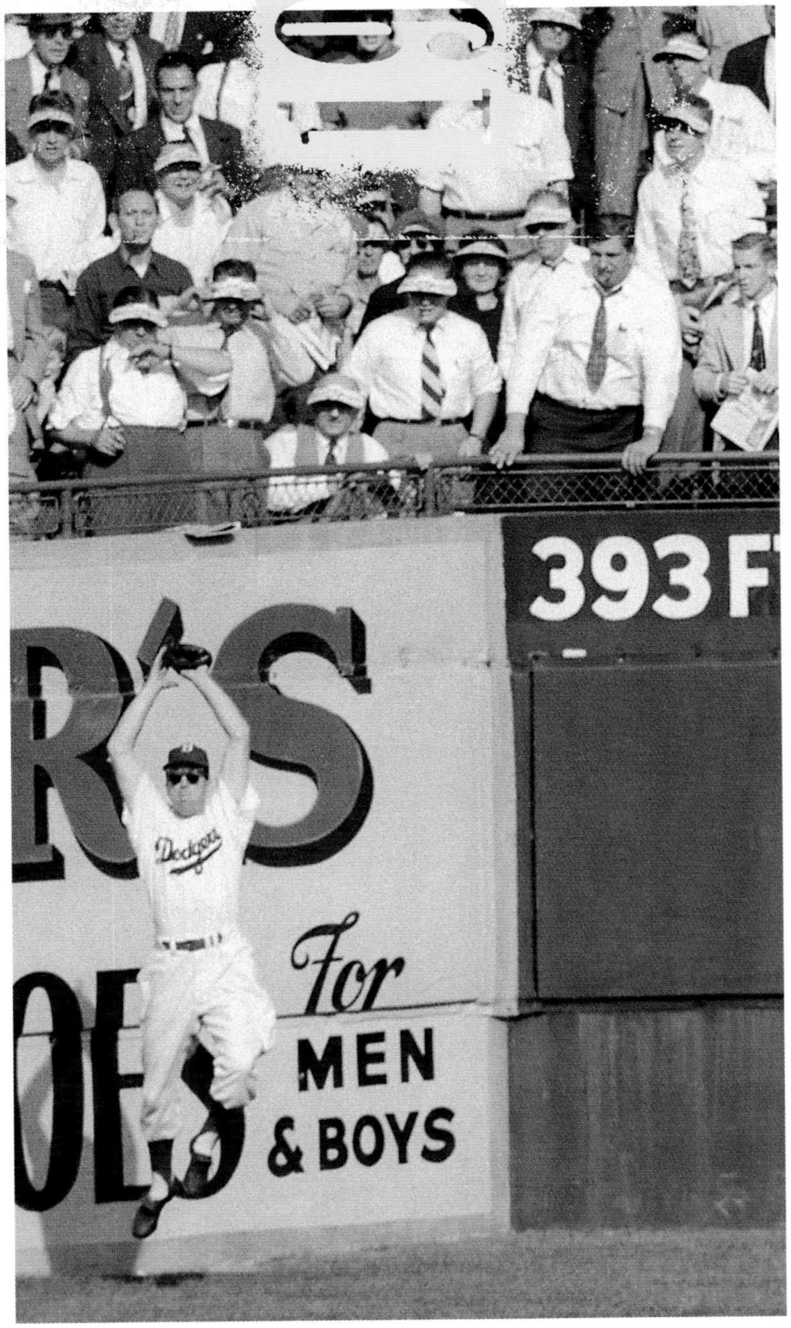

BOTTOM LEFT: Duke Snider leaps to catch Joe DiMaggio's drive in Game 2 of the 1949 World Series at Yankee Stadium.

BOTTOM RIGHT: Joe DiMaggio crosses home after finally getting his first hit of the 1950 World Series, a game-winning homer in Game 5.

1950

New York Yankees (4)
Philadelphia Phillies (0)

A colorful young group of Philadelphia Phillies came of age in 1950. They won the National League pennant and gave baseball fans everywhere hope that the Yankees would soon be dethroned for good. The Phils were youthful, they were brash, and most importantly, they were good. "We had a lot of fun," catcher Andy Seminick remembered. "We would always harmonize in the showers. Mostly country and western songs."

Led by 23-year-old Robin Roberts, 21-year-old Curt Simmons, 25-year-old Del Ennis, and 23-year-old Richie Ashburn, the Phillies were dubbed the "Whiz Kids" by the press. However, their best player wasn't a kid at all, but rather, as Jimmy Powers wrote, a "scholarly, bespectacled man who looks like a Rotarian who had somehow gotten himself into a baseball uniform." Jim Konstanty, a 33-year-old journeyman relief pitcher, was named the National League's MVP after pitching in 74 games, more than any pitcher since 1892. He won 16 of them, saved 22 more, and posted a league-best 2.66 ERA. Although Konstanty, according to sportswriter Joe Williams, had "a fast ball that isn't fast, a curve ball that doesn't curve, and a change of pace which doesn't change," he achieved tremendous success by adopting a new pitch, the palmball.

On the morning of September 23, the Phillies were seven games ahead of second-place Brooklyn with little more than a week left to play—and then the wheels began to come off. The team had lost three of its top six pitchers when Emory "Bubba" Church and Bob Miller were injured and Simmons was inducted into the Army. Seminick was catching with a sore ankle, pinch hitter Bill Nicholson was laid low by diabetes, and third baseman Willie "Puddin' Head" Jones suffered from appendicitis. The Phillies

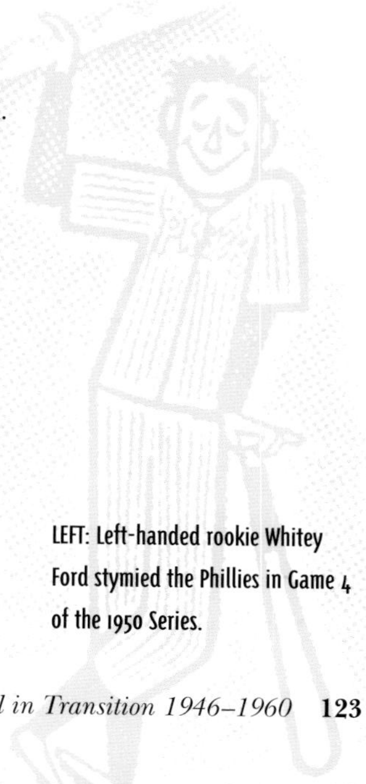

LEFT: Left-handed rookie Whitey Ford stymied the Phillies in Game 4 of the 1950 Series.

found themselves facing the Dodgers on the last day of the season with the pennant on the line. Robin Roberts and Don Newcombe dueled until the tenth inning, when a Dick Sisler homer clinched the pennant for Philadelphia. But the hardest part was yet to come. The decimated Phils still had to face the Yankees in the World Series.

Roberts was exhausted from pitching the pennant-winning game, and Phillies manager Eddie Sawyer surprised everyone by tabbing Konstanty to start the first game of the World Series. It was the big reliever's first start in more than four years, and he pitched admirably, giving up only one run and four hits over eight innings. But Yankee right-hander Vic Raschi was even better, shutting out the Phillies on two hits for a 1-0 victory.

Roberts, making his fourth start in nine days, was ruggedly effective in the second game. He carried a 1-1 tie into the tenth inning, but in the bottom of the tenth, Joe DiMaggio, after failing to get the ball out of the infield in his last ten World Series plate appearances, homered into the left field stands to give New York the margin of victory.

The Series was now effectively over as New York returned home leading two games to none after defeating the Phillies' two best pitchers. Ed Lopat pitched a fine Game 3 for the Yankees, and consecutive ninth-inning singles by Gene Woodling, Phil Rizzuto, and Jerry Coleman won the game for New York. Game 4 was never close, as the Yankees knocked Phillies starter Miller, a rookie, out of the game after only a third of an inning. Meanwhile, the Yankees' own rookie pitcher, lefty Whitey Ford, pitched eight-plus innings and gave up no earned runs. Allie Reynolds entered to get the last out and clinch the world title for New York.

"I think we were somewhat awed by the Yankees," Seminick remembered. "You knew by the way they carried themselves that they were a class act. They looked like champions." The Phils took, as Jimmy Powers wrote, "a quietly efficient, very dignified, and very thorough beating." Konstanty had performed nobly, even drawing comparisons to Hoss Radbourn, the pitcher who had led Providence to the 1884 World Series championship by pitching in almost every game at the end of the season. Konstanty pitched eight innings in Game 1, warmed up intermittently in the bullpen during Game 2, relieved Ken Heintzelman in Game 3, and pitched nearly eight innings of relief in Game 4. But it wasn't nearly enough, as once again, the Yankees seemed to have everything go their way in the World Series. "The Yankees needed pitching and got it," wrote Milton Gross in the *New York Post*. "They needed the big hit and DiMag produced it. When they needed the big defensive play, someone was there to make it."

TOP: The heroes of the Yankees' Game 2 victory: Allie Reynolds (left) pitched a 10-inning complete game, while Joe DiMaggio (center) hit a game-winning homer.

BOTTOM: Jim Konstanty, the 1950 N.L. MVP, pitched in three of the four World Series games that year, posting a 2.40 ERA.

1950 WORLD SERIES

Shibe Park (Philadelphia Phillies) ◆ 10.4.50

	1	2	3	4	5	6	7	8	9	R	H	E
NYY	0	0	0	1	0	0	0	0	0	1	5	0
Phil.	0	0	0	0	0	0	0	0	0	0	2	1

WP–Raschi LP–Konstanty ATT: 30,746

Shibe Park ◆ 10.5.50

	1	2	3	4	5	6	7	8	9	10	R	H	E
NYY	0	1	0	0	0	0	0	0	0	1	2	10	0
Phil.	0	0	0	0	1	0	0	0	0	0	1	7	0

WP–Reynolds LP–Roberts HR: NYY–DiMaggio
ATT: 32,660

Yankee Stadium I (N.Y. Yankees) ◆ 10.6.50

	1	2	3	4	5	6	7	8	9	R	H	E
Phil.	0	0	0	0	0	1	1	0	0	2	10	2
NYY	0	0	1	0	0	0	0	1	1	3	7	0

WP–Ferrick LP–Meyer ATT: 64,505

Yankee Stadium I ◆ 10.7.50

	1	2	3	4	5	6	7	8	9	R	H	E
Phil.	0	0	0	0	0	0	0	0	2	2	7	1
NYY	2	0	0	0	0	3	0	0	X	5	8	2

WP–Ford LP–Miller HR: NYY–Berra ATT: 68,098

1951

NEW YORK YANKEES (4)
NEW YORK GIANTS (2)

THE NEW YORK GIANTS DID NOT WIN THE World Series in 1951, but they must have felt like they had. After being thirteen games behind the Dodgers on August 11, the Giants roared back to force a tie for the pennant on the last day of the season. In the last game of the ensuing three-game playoff, Bobby Thomson hit one of the most famous home runs in baseball history to give the Giants the pennant, and although they had momentum, they were spent. Their top two pitchers, Sal "The Barber" Maglie and Larry Jansen, were exhausted, and their right fielder, Don Mueller, was injured. As a result, "the World Series was anticlamactic," outfielder Monte Irvin later wrote. "We had done the one thing we wanted to do"—beat the Dodgers.

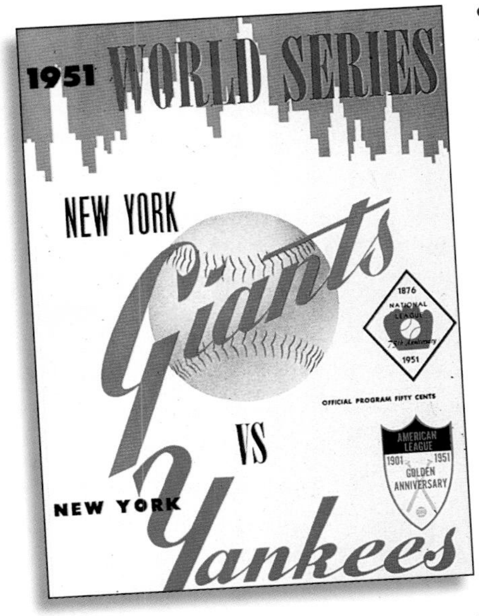

The 1951 World Series was the first to be televised nationwide, and Game 1 featured the first all-black outfield in major league history: Monte Irvin in left, Willie Mays in center, and Hank Thompson in right. The Giants won the first game thanks to Irvin, who collected four hits and started off the Series by stealing home in the top of the first inning—"my greatest thrill in baseball," he later said.

The Yankees threatened in the first inning of Game 2, placing runners on first and second with nobody out and Joe DiMaggio up. Instead of sacrificing, as many believed he should do, Stengel let DiMaggio swing away—and the Yankee Clipper hit into a double play. "I'm batting like a guy who can't see anything at any time," the dejected DiMaggio said afterward. He had hit a home run earlier that day, but it had happened during batting practice, against baseball clown Al Schacht, who had been putting on a pre-game show for the fans. Still, the Yankees managed to score three runs for real, and it was good enough for junkball pitcher Eddie Lopat to prevail, 3-1.

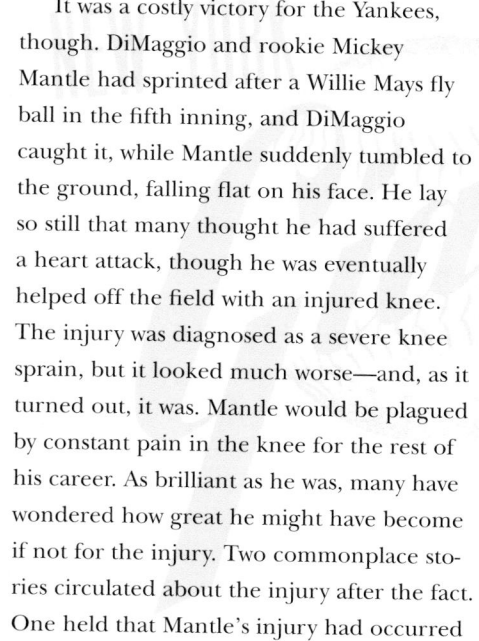

It was a costly victory for the Yankees, though. DiMaggio and rookie Mickey Mantle had sprinted after a Willie Mays fly ball in the fifth inning, and DiMaggio caught it, while Mantle suddenly tumbled to the ground, falling flat on his face. He lay so still that many thought he had suffered a heart attack, though he was eventually helped off the field with an injured knee. The injury was diagnosed as a severe knee sprain, but it looked much worse—and, as it turned out, it was. Mantle would be plagued by constant pain in the knee for the rest of his career. As brilliant as he was, many have wondered how great he might have become if not for the injury. Two commonplace stories circulated about the injury after the fact. One held that Mantle's injury had occurred

BOTTOM LEFT: In Game 3, umpire Joe Paparella changed his call from "out" to "safe" after Yogi Berra dropped the ball. Alvin Dark is the Giants baserunner.

BOTTOM RIGHT: Playing in his first career World Series game, Monte Irvin steals home in the top of the first inning in Game 1.

because he stepped on a drain cover in the outfield while chasing Mays' fly, while the other story said that he had been forced to make an awkward stop because DiMaggio called for the ball at the last minute. Mantle was unsure of how the injury occurred. "I don't know what happened," he told the press after the game. "I didn't try to stop short or anything. I simply was running after the ball and my knee pops. There was no hole in the ground, either."

The Giants won Game 3 at the Polo Grounds, 6-2, in a contest that was marked by an ugly incident between Phil Rizzuto and Eddie Stanky. Stanky was trying to steal second, but the throw from Yogi Berra beat him. So Stanky, in the middle of his slide, kicked at Rizzuto's glove, dislodged the ball, and moved on to third. It was a legal play, but Rizzuto was furious nonetheless. "Since that time I don't think they have spoken and they've had this feud all these years," Irvin wrote in 1996.

The Game 3 victory would be the high point of the Series for the Giants, as the Yankees won the next day thanks in part to the last home run of DiMaggio's career. They won Game 5, too, as Lopat again pitched brilliantly against the Giants, and then closed it out in Game 6. The Giants loaded the bases with nobody out in the bottom of the ninth, but Yankee reliever Bob Kuzava came in and worked out of the jam. The men in pinstripes won the game, 4-3, and the Series, four games to two.

Irvin, playing in the middle of an election campaign—he was a Democratic candidate for Assemblyman in Essex County, New Jersey—was by far the best hitter in the Series, batting a remarkable .458, but it wasn't enough for his team to win. "I just wish that we could have had the same lineup that we had down the stretch and that our pitchers had not been tired. Then, I think we could have probably beaten the Yankees," Irvin wrote. In the end, he said, "the Yankees were good and they were extraordinarily lucky."

One week after the Series ended, *Life* magazine published the scouting reports that the Brooklyn Dodgers, expecting to play in the World Series, had compiled on the Yankee players. "He can't stop quickly and throw hard," the report on DiMaggio said. "You can take the extra base on him. He can't run and won't bunt. His reflexes are very slow, and he can't pull a good fastball at all." The report devastated the 36-year-old DiMaggio, whose biggest fear above all else was public embarrassment. Angry, but painfully aware that the scout's assessments were true, DiMaggio announced his retirement that December.

1951 WORLD SERIES

GAME 1 — YANKEE STADIUM I (N.Y. YANKEES) ◆ 10.4.51

	1	2	3	4	5	6	7	8	9	R	H	E
NYG	2	0	0	0	0	3	0	0	0	5	10	1
NYY	0	1	0	0	0	0	0	0	0	1	7	1

WP–Koslo LP–Reynolds HR: NYG–Dark
ATT: 65,673

GAME 2 — YANKEE STADIUM I ◆ 10.5.51

	1	2	3	4	5	6	7	8	9	R	H	E
NYG	0	0	0	0	0	0	1	0	0	1	5	1
NYY	1	1	0	0	0	0	0	1	X	3	6	0

WP–Lopat LP–Jansen HR: NYY–Collins
ATT: 66,018

GAME 3 — POLO GROUNDS IV (N.Y. GIANTS) ◆ 10.6.51

	1	2	3	4	5	6	7	8	9	R	H	E
NYY	0	0	0	0	0	0	0	1	1	2	5	2
NYG	0	1	0	0	5	0	0	0	X	6	7	2

WP–Hearn LP–Raschi S–Jones HR: NYY–Woodling; NYG–Lockman ATT: 52,035

GAME 4 — POLO GROUNDS IV ◆ 10.8.51

	1	2	3	4	5	6	7	8	9	R	H	E
NYY	0	1	0	1	2	0	2	0	0	6	12	0
NYG	1	0	0	0	0	0	0	0	1	2	8	2

WP–Reynolds LP–Maglie HR: NYY–DiMaggio
ATT: 49,010

GAME 5 — POLO GROUNDS IV ◆ 10.9.51

	1	2	3	4	5	6	7	8	9	R	H	E
NYY	0	0	5	2	0	2	4	0	0	13	12	1
NYG	1	0	0	0	0	0	0	0	0	1	5	3

WP–Lopat LP–Jansen ATT: 47,530

GAME 6 — YANKEE STADIUM I ◆ 10.10.51

	1	2	3	4	5	6	7	8	9	R	H	E
NYG	0	0	0	0	1	0	0	0	2	3	11	1
NYY	1	0	0	0	0	3	0	0	X	4	7	0

WP–Raschi LP–Koslo S–Kuzava ATT: 61,711

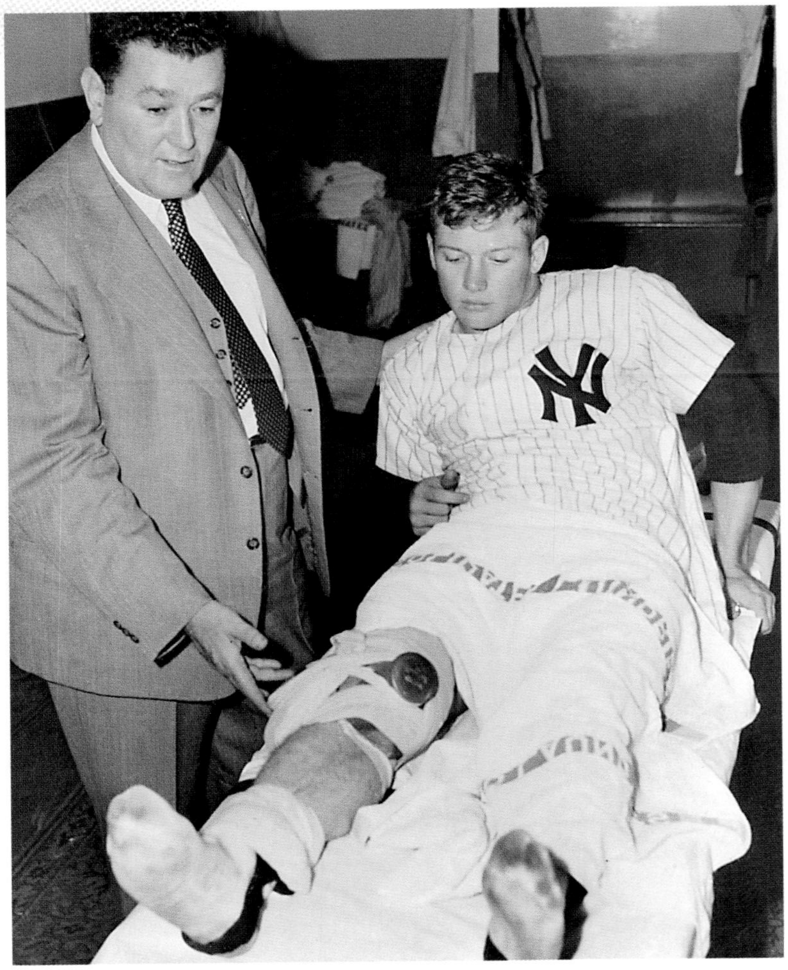

BOTTOM LEFT: The knee injury suffered by Mickey Mantle in Game 2 of the 1951 World Series hampered him the rest of his career. Sidney Gaynor, the Yankees' trainer, is at left.

BOTTOM RIGHT: The Giants' outfield in the 1951 World Series was comprised of ex-Negro League stars (from left) Monte Irvin, Willie Mays, and Hank Thompson.

TOP: For Joe DiMaggio, 1951 was the tenth World Series of his career, tying Babe Ruth's record. Here he grounds out in the third game.

BOTTOM: In the second plate appearance of his World Series career, 20-year-old Willie Mays lines out with the bases loaded in Game 1 of the 1951 Series.

1952

New York Yankees (4)
Brooklyn Dodgers (3)

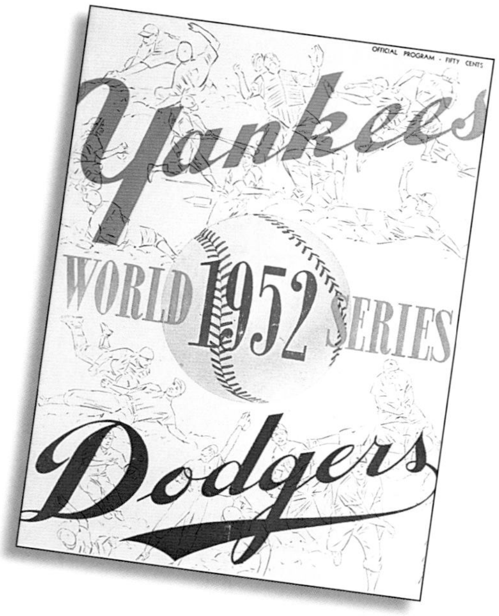

The Brooklyn Dodgers made it back to the Fall Classic in 1952 after losing the pennant in heartbreaking fashion each of the previous two seasons. They were carried to the pennant by the remarkable relief pitching of Joe Black, a 28-year-old veteran of the Negro Leagues who enjoyed one of the best seasons ever by a major league "rookie," going 15-4 with 15 saves and a league-best 2.15 ERA. He was the Dodgers' only outstanding pitcher that year, and manager Charlie Dressen decided to use him as a starter in the World Series, although he had never before started a major league game. Black took the mound to face the New York Yankees in the first game of the World Series after a couple of warm-up starts at the end of the regular season. "I was scared to death," Black admitted after the game. But as Jimmy Powers wrote, Black "carried the team on his broad shoulders all year and gave it a great psychological start in the series," pitching a complete game to beat Allie Reynolds 4-2. Jackie Robinson opened the Series by homering in the top of the second to help Black become the first African-American pitcher to ever win a World Series game.

Brooklyn starter Carl Erskine suffered a mishap before Game 2 at Ebbets Field when he climbed a stepladder in the clubhouse to see if it was raining outside. He fell off the ladder and banged both his knee and forehead on a metal radiator. The Yankees then unloaded on the unfortunate Erskine and reliever Billy Loes, the biggest blow a three-run homer by Billy Martin, en route to a 7-1 Yankees' win. Game 3 at Yankee Stadium was a close affair. The game had been tied until the ninth inning, when Pee Wee Reese and Jackie Robinson pulled off a daring double steal against Yogi Berra. The move paid major dividends when a Tom Gorman pitch later eluded Berra for a passed ball. Berra may have been crossed up, as the ball appeared to carom off his leg, and Reese scored easily from third. As the bewildered Berra looked around for the ball, though, Robinson motored home from second with what turned out to be the winning run. "Legs won for us," said the confident Dressen, whose Dodgers now led the Series two games to one. "We stole the game right out from under them with our baserunning."

Black started again in Game 4 and again he pitched well, allowing one run in seven innings. But Reynolds was even better, allowing the Dodgers only four hits in a complete game shutout. Black blew the Dodgers' best chance on offense when he missed a squeeze bunt with two runners on base in the fifth inning. The next game was the Series masterpiece. The 11-inning affair was "as nerve-wracking a thriller as the World Series has ever seen," Arthur Daley wrote. Carl Erskine, pitching on his fifth wedding anniversary, was pounded for five runs in the fifth inning, including a three-run homer by 39-year-old reserve Johnny Mize, his third home run in as many games. But remarkably, Erskine did not allow a base runner after Mize's home run, retiring the last nineteen consecutive Yankee batters, and Duke Snider had a remarkable day for Brooklyn, homering in the fifth, hitting the game-tying single in the seventh, and driving in the winning run with a double in the top of the eleventh. The Dodgers, one of the greatest defensive teams of all time, saved the game with their remarkable gloves, as George Shuba and Billy Cox both turned in outstanding defensive plays, and outfielders Andy Pafko and Carl Furillo each made leaping catches to rob the Yankees of potential home runs. Furillo's catch came in the bottom of the eleventh inning to preserve Erskine's 6-5 victory.

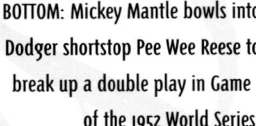

BOTTOM: Mickey Mantle bowls into Dodger shortstop Pee Wee Reese to break up a double play in Game 1 of the 1952 World Series.

The Dodgers now led three games to two and were on the verge of their first world championship. But despite Brooklyn's reputation as, in Arthur Daley's words, "the borough of churches and mass baseball hysteria," only 30,037 fans attended Game 6, well below Ebbets Field's capacity. It was just as well, as pitcher Loes, a cocky, eccentric 22-year-old, gave the Yankees a lead in the seventh when he balked Gene Woodling to second, and then failed to field a hard grounder up the middle, which scored Woodling. ("I lost it in the sun," Loes later said of the grounder, which bounced off his leg.) Snider hit a homer in the top of the seventh to tie the score, but in the bottom of the inning, young Mickey Mantle blasted a homer that turned out to be the game-winner. The Yankees won, 3-2.

Expectations were high for Game 7. "The decision will probably come under floodlights in approximately the 27th inning just before midnight," Daley wrote. "Anything, it would seem, is possible in this unbelievably magnificent World Series." Casey Stengel, who had been forced to use his intended Game 7 starter, Reynolds, to relieve in Game 6, went with the southpaw Lopat. Brooklyn started the exhausted Black, who was pitching on two days' rest for the second consecutive time after pitching in relief all year. Still, things looked good for the Dodgers, who had posted a 19-6 regular season record against lefties, and who had won Game 3 when Lopat started. But both starters tired early, and Reynolds relieved Lopat with the bases loaded and nobody out in the fourth inning and worked out of the jam. The remarkable relief pitching of Reynolds, Vic Raschi, and Bob Kuzava made the difference, as they held Brooklyn to one run over the final six innings. The Dodgers' last threat came in the seventh when they loaded the bases with one out, but Raschi induced Snider to pop out and the next batter, Robinson, also popped up. It should have

TOP: Joe Black started Game 1 of the 1952 World Series after enjoying one of the best rookie seasons in baseball history: a 15-4 record with 15 saves and a 2.15 ERA.

BOTTOM: Center fielder Duke Snider jumps in exuberance after Joe Black strikes out Irv Noren to complete the Dodgers' 4-2 win in Game 1.

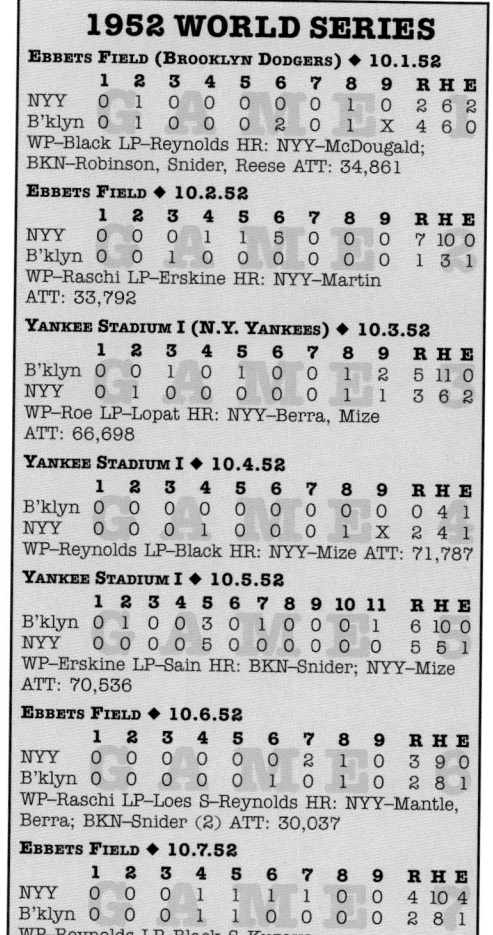

1952 WORLD SERIES

Ebbets Field (Brooklyn Dodgers) ◆ 10.1.52

	1	2	3	4	5	6	7	8	9	R	H	E
NYY	0	1	0	0	0	0	0	1	0	2	6	2
B'klyn	0	1	0	0	0	2	0	1	X	4	6	0

WP–Black LP–Reynolds HR: NYY–McDougald; BKN–Robinson, Snider, Reese ATT: 34,861

Ebbets Field ◆ 10.2.52

	1	2	3	4	5	6	7	8	9	R	H	E
NYY	0	0	0	1	1	5	0	0	0	7	10	0
B'klyn	0	0	1	0	0	0	0	0	0	1	3	1

WP–Raschi LP–Erskine HR: NYY–Martin ATT: 33,792

Yankee Stadium I (N.Y. Yankees) ◆ 10.3.52

	1	2	3	4	5	6	7	8	9	R	H	E
B'klyn	0	0	1	0	1	0	0	1	2	5	11	0
NYY	0	1	0	0	0	0	0	1	1	3	6	2

WP–Roe LP–Lopat HR: NYY–Berra, Mize ATT: 66,698

Yankee Stadium I ◆ 10.4.52

	1	2	3	4	5	6	7	8	9	R	H	E
B'klyn	0	0	0	0	0	0	0	0	0	0	4	1
NYY	0	0	0	1	0	0	0	1	X	2	4	1

WP–Reynolds LP–Black HR: NYY–Mize ATT: 71,787

Yankee Stadium I ◆ 10.5.52

	1	2	3	4	5	6	7	8	9	10	11	R	H	E
B'klyn	0	1	0	0	3	0	1	0	0	0	1	6	10	0
NYY	0	0	0	0	5	0	0	0	0	0	0	5	5	1

WP–Erskine LP–Sain HR: BKN–Snider; NYY–Mize ATT: 70,536

Ebbets Field ◆ 10.6.52

	1	2	3	4	5	6	7	8	9	R	H	E
NYY	0	0	0	0	0	0	2	1	0	3	9	0
B'klyn	0	0	0	0	0	1	0	1	0	2	8	1

WP–Raschi LP–Loes S–Reynolds HR: NYY–Mantle, Berra; BKN–Snider (2) ATT: 30,037

Ebbets Field ◆ 10.7.52

	1	2	3	4	5	6	7	8	9	R	H	E
NYY	0	0	0	1	1	1	1	0	0	4	10	4
B'klyn	0	0	0	1	1	0	0	0	0	2	8	1

WP–Reynolds LP–Black S–Kuzava HR: NYY–Woodling, Mantle ATT: 33,195

been first baseman Joe Collins' ball, but he was blinded by the sun, and at the last minute Billy Martin came rushing in from second base to catch the ball as it was about to hit the ground. The demoralized Dodgers went hitless the rest of the game, and the Yankees had their win.

It had been a remarkably exciting Series, the closest ever played between the two rivals. The Dodgers lost because their offense went south, with four regulars batting under .200 for the Series. Gil Hodges went 0-for-21, becoming the first full-time player to go an entire seven-game Series without a hit. Still, the beloved Hodges received roars of encouraging applause from Brooklyn fans throughout the Series.

With New York beating Brooklyn for the third time in six years, the subway series was becoming something of a tradition. "As a player, you couldn't help but get caught up in the rivalry," Whitey Ford later wrote. "The enthusiasm was unbelievable and it just carried over to the players. We especially loved it because we usually beat the Dodgers and we got a great pleasure out of kicking their ass and shutting up their fans."

1953

New York Yankees (4)
Brooklyn Dodgers (2)

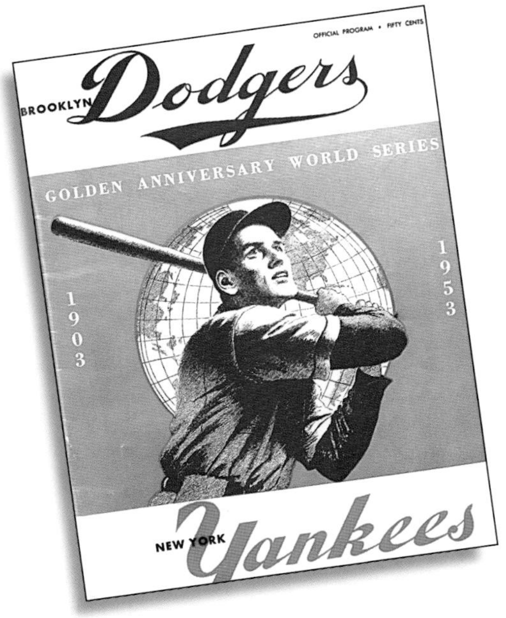

Brooklyn assembled an even more powerful team for their 1953 rematch with the Yankees after taking a wrecking ball to the rest of the league, going 105-49 and winning the pennant by thirteen games. The 1953 Dodgers were widely hailed as the greatest team in Brooklyn history, and were heavily favored to win the World Series despite their loss to the Yankees in 1952. "Statistically, this year, the Dodgers are champions of the world before they ever take the field to play the series," Rud Rennie wrote in the *New York Herald-Tribune.*

The Yankees started the World Series with a bang at Yankee Stadium, scoring four runs and knocking Brooklyn pitcher Carl Erskine out of the game after just one inning. The Dodgers tried to come back in the seventh, scoring a run and seeking more with runners on first and second and nobody out. The Dodgers tried to sacrifice the runners over twice, but both times Yogi Berra threw the lead runner out at third base, effectively ending Brooklyn's chances. They lost the game, 9-5, and even worse, National League MVP Roy Campanella was hit on his right pinky finger by a pitch from

BOTTOM: Yankee catcher Yogi Berra (center) finished second in A.L. MVP balloting in 1953, while his Dodger counterpart, Roy Campanella (right), won the N.L. award.

Allie Reynolds, putting his availability for the rest of the Series in doubt. The Yankees also took Game 2, as Billy Martin hit a game-tying homer in the seventh inning and Mickey Mantle smacked a go-ahead shot in the eighth.

The Series now moved across town to Flatbush, where the teams played, as Roger Kahn wrote in the *New York Herald-Tribune*, "a game that offered one climax after another, each more grinding than the one before, a game that will be remembered with the finest." Ebbets Field was filled with an enthusiastic crowd that included Humphrey Bogart and Lauren Bacall. "You talk about excitement," Yankee Gene Woodling said. "You'd go into Ebbets Field with the small field and colorful billboards, and their little band would be playing in the stands and the crowd would be going crazy. The Ebbets Field fans were wilder than Yankee Stadium fans." With the Dodgers down two games to none, Jackie Robinson and Campanella called a special 10 a.m. batting practice session before Game 3. It must have worked. In the sixth inning Robinson doubled off the wall, went to third on a balk, and scored on a squeeze bunt. Meanwhile, Carl Erskine was pitching a masterpiece, holding the Yankees hitless until the fifth inning, when three infield singles—all of which glanced off the gloves of Dodger infielders—netted a run for New York. Aided by the throng of white shirts in the center field bleachers, which made it hard for batters to pick up the ball, Erskine set a new Series record by striking out fourteen Yankees, including Mantle four times. "He had a beautiful change of pace," Campanella said, "with his best pitch being his overhand curve to those left-handers."

Howard Ehmke, who had set the previous record of thirteen strikeouts in 1929, listened to Erskine's game on his car radio while on a country drive with his wife. The game got so exciting that they couldn't turn it off when they reached their destination. The car battery then died and they were left stranded. "Records are made to be broken, I guess," Ehmke sighed. Meanwhile, Campanella, playing despite the broken finger sustained in Game 1, hit the decisive home run in the seventh inning. After the game, Campy told the press that he'd heard Stengel shout "stick it in his ear" to pitcher Vic Raschi while Campanella was batting, though Stengel denied the charge. "I don't care what the fuck they say," Stengel said. "How can they watch me instead of watching

BOTTOM LEFT: In one of the most controversial plays of the 1953 Series, Billy Martin is forcefully tagged out by Roy Campanella to end Game 4.

BOTTOM RIGHT: Brooklyn center fielder Duke Snider jumps in vain while trying to catch Gene Woodling's leadoff homer in Game 5.

1946–1960

TOP: After getting the hit that won the 1953 World Series for the Yankees, Billy Martin, holding the ball, gets a hug from his double play partner, Phil Rizzuto.

BOTTOM: In Game 1 of the 1953 Series, Gil Hodges is out at third on an attempted sacrifice as Gil McDougald catches Yogi Berra's throw.

the fucking game? I'm interested in our runs, not their opinions."

The Dodgers then won Game 4, as the pitching of Billy Loes and Clem Labine was good enough for a 7-3 victory. "Loes was lucky to get by," Stengel said afterward. "We hit him hard and the balls simply did not fall safe." The Yankees loaded the bases trailing 7-2 in the ninth. A Mantle single then scored Woodling, but Martin, trying to score from second on the play, was tagged out easily by Campanella to end the game. Afterward, Martin fumed that Campanella had used unnecessary force in applying the tag. "There wasn't any chance of scoring, so I just came in standing up, instead of sliding or running into the man full tilt." But Campanella disputed Martin's account. "He tried to run over me, he tried to knock me down," the catcher said. "That boy ought to learn how to slide." Other Dodgers, meanwhile, wondered why Martin was running in the first place. "Four runs behind, two out in the ninth and he tries to come in," said coach Billy Herman. "For two years all I read is how smart that Martin is. Well, what the hell was he thinking about when he tried to score?"

The teams tied a series record with six home runs between them in Game 5, as the Yankees won to take a 3-2 lead in the Series. Woodling was the star for New York, homering to lead off the game and, in the next inning, nailing Gil Hodges at the plate with a stunning throw from left field. The Yankees, confident that they would win at least one of the next two games, ordered a supply of banners proclaiming them "1953 World Champions" before Game 6.

The Yankees took the first lead in Game 6 by scoring three early runs off Erskine, but in the sixth inning, the Dodgers scored on another Robinson special, as he doubled off the wall, stole third base without a throw, and scored on a groundout to bring the Dodgers within two runs. That turned out to be a vital run in the ninth inning when, with the Dodgers just two outs away from losing the Series, Carl Furillo smacked a two-run homer into the right field stands to tie the game for Brooklyn. But the Yankees weren't done. In the bottom of the ninth, Hank Bauer walked and Mantle beat out an infield single. "Then," Bill Voorhees wrote, "up stepped this young upstart, Martin, with all the cockiness he could muster." Martin smashed a single back through the box to drive in Bauer and end the Series. The Yankees had won their fifth consecutive world championship. It's a record that still stands today.

1953 WORLD SERIES

Yankee Stadium I (N.Y. Yankees) ◆ 9.30.53

	1	2	3	4	5	6	7	8	9	R	H	E
B'klyn	0	0	0	0	1	3	1	0	0	5	12	2
NYY	4	0	0	0	1	0	1	3	X	9	12	0

WP–Sain LP–Labine HR: BKN–Gilliam, Hodges, Shuba; NYY–Berra, Collins ATT: 69,374

Yankee Stadium I ◆ 10.1.53

	1	2	3	4	5	6	7	8	9	R	H	E
B'klyn	0	0	0	2	0	0	0	0	0	2	9	1
NYY	1	0	0	0	0	0	1	2	X	4	5	0

WP–Lopat LP–Roe HR: NYY–Martin, Mantle ATT: 66,786

Ebbets Field (Brooklyn Dodgers) ◆ 10.2.53

	1	2	3	4	5	6	7	8	9	R	H	E
NYY	0	0	0	0	1	0	0	1	0	2	6	0
B'klyn	0	0	0	0	1	1	0	1	X	3	9	0

WP–Erskine LP–Raschi HR: BKN–Campanella ATT: 35,270

Ebbets Field ◆ 10.3.53

	1	2	3	4	5	6	7	8	9	R	H	E
NYY	0	0	0	0	2	0	0	0	1	3	9	0
B'klyn	3	0	0	1	0	2	1	0	X	7	12	0

WP–Loes LP–Ford S–Labine HR: NYY–McDougald; BKN–Snider ATT: 36,775

Ebbets Field ◆ 10.4.53

	1	2	3	4	5	6	7	8	9	R	H	E
NYY	1	0	5	0	0	0	3	1	1	11	11	1
B'klyn	0	1	0	0	1	0	0	4	1	7	14	1

WP–McDonald LP–Podres S–Reynolds HR: NYY–Woodling, Mantle, Martin, McDougald; BKN–Cox, Gilliam ATT: 36,775

Yankee Stadium I ◆ 10.5.53

	1	2	3	4	5	6	7	8	9	R	H	E
B'klyn	0	0	0	0	0	1	0	0	2	3	8	3
NYY	2	1	0	0	0	0	0	0	1	4	13	0

WP–Reynolds LP–Labine HR: BKN–Furillo ATT: 62,370

1954

New York Giants (4)
Cleveland Indians (0)

The 1954 Cleveland Indians fielded one of the best teams in American League history, winning a league-record 111 games and beating the still-great Yankees by eight games in the regular season. The Indians had one of the best starting rotations of all time as well, with Bob Lemon, Mike Garcia, and Early Wynn all having superb seasons. Cleveland also had the league batting champion, second baseman Bobby Ávila, and the leader in homers and RBI, Larry Doby. They were widely expected to trounce the New York Giants in the World Series.

As one newspaper headline put it, though, the Indians had everything, but the Giants still had Willie Mays. The young center fielder, just back from military service in Korea, won his first MVP award and impressed the world, *Newsday* said, with "his bubbling laughter, his high-pitched voice, and his infectious good nature." As teammate Monte Irvin later wrote, "When Willie Mays came back, it was like heaven."

BOTTOM: Davey Williams lays down a sacrifice bunt in Game 4 of the 1954 World Series as Cleveland catcher Jim Hegan prepares to pounce on the ball.

With the first game tied 2-2 in the eighth inning, the Indians put two men on base with nobody out and Vic Wertz up. Facing new Giants pitcher Don Liddle, Wertz hit a towering drive to right-center field, the deepest part of the Polo Grounds at 483 feet away. Mays, playing in left-center, ran for what seemed like days. He caught the ball over his head with his back to the infield and, most impressively, quickly whirled and threw to hold the base runner on first. Pitcher Liddle came out of the game after facing only the one batter and stayed on the mound to greet new pitcher Marv Grissom. "Well, I got my man," he told Grissom with a straight face as he walked off the mound. The catch saved the game for the Giants, who ended up winning in the bottom of the tenth when pinch hitter James "Dusty" Rhodes hit a three-run homer that barely reached the stands down the cozy right-field foul line. Clearly, the deciding factor in the game had been the Polo Grounds' unusual dimensions. The 450-foot drive was an out, but the lazy 260-foot fly was a game-winning homer. "Dusty Rhodes had the Midas touch that year," said Irvin, the man Rhodes had pinch hit for. "Everything he touched turned to gold."

Almost immediately, the New York press began comparing Mays' catch to the greatest plays in Series history. But it was no big deal to Mays. "I don't compare 'em—I just catch 'em," he said. "I had a good lead on it all the way. So I just ran until I got it...Anyway, any ball that is hit that high ought to be caught." Bob Feller agreed. "From the time Wertz hit it, we knew Mays had it all the way," he said. "Three things made that catch by Mays one that people still talk about: It was an excellent catch, it was in the World Series, and—never underestimate this reason—it was on national television."

The Giants won again the next day as Johnny Antonelli outdueled Bob Lemon, while Dusty Rhodes, entering the game again as a pinch hitter, singled and homered. The teams traveled to Cleveland for Game 3, and when the Giants loaded the bases in the third inning, Leo Durocher sent up Rhodes to hit for Irvin yet again. Rhodes promptly delivered a two-run single and the Giants won the game to take a 3-0 lead in the Series.

Now with his back against the wall, Cleveland manager Al Lopez faced a decision. Should he give in to sentiment and start the aging Feller, who had never won a Series game, in Game 4? Or should he start Lemon, a much better pitcher, on short rest? Lopez went with Lemon, but it turned out badly for Cleveland, as the Giants lit up both Lemon and his successor, Hal Newhouser, en route to a 7-4 win and a Series sweep. Dusty Rhodes sat on the bench waiting to pinch hit but was never needed.

The Cleveland steamroller had been steamrolled itself, though the Indians did manage to set one World Series record in the four-game sweep: most runners left on base, 37. Wertz, who had played the entire Series with an injured hand that he concealed from everyone, is remembered today only as the victim of baseball's most famous catch. But Wertz batted a remarkable .500 for the Series and was so productive that Durocher had to call a special meeting with his pitchers to discuss how to handle him. Meanwhile, Feller, on the downside of his career at age 35, did not throw a single pitch in the Series. "I've never been quite sure why Lopez didn't use me," he wrote many years later. "I still wonder."

BOTTOM: Giants ace Johnny Antonelli outdueled Early Wynn for a 3-1 win in Game 2.

1954 WORLD SERIES

Polo Grounds IV (New York Giants) ◆ 9.29.54

	1	2	3	4	5	6	7	8	9	10	R	H	E
Clev.	2	0	0	0	0	0	0	0	0	0	2	8	0
NYG	0	0	2	0	0	0	0	0	0	3	5	9	3

WP–Grissom LP–Lemon HR: NYG–Rhodes
ATT: 52,751

Polo Grounds IV ◆ 9.30.54

	1	2	3	4	5	6	7	8	9	R	H	E
Clev.	1	0	0	0	0	0	0	0	0	1	8	0
NYG	0	0	0	0	2	0	1	0	X	3	4	0

WP–Antonelli LP–Wynn HR: CLE–Smith; NYG–Rhodes ATT: 49,099

Cleveland Stadium (Cleveland Indians) ◆ 10.1.54

	1	2	3	4	5	6	7	8	9	R	H	E
NYG	1	0	3	0	1	1	0	0	0	6	10	1
Clev.	0	0	0	0	0	0	1	1	0	2	4	2

WP–Gomez LP–Garcia S–Wilhelm HR: CLE–Wertz
ATT: 71,555

Cleveland Stadium ◆ 10.2.54

	1	2	3	4	5	6	7	8	9	R	H	E
NYG	0	2	1	0	4	0	0	0	0	7	10	3
Clev.	0	0	0	0	3	0	1	0	0	4	6	2

WP–Liddle LP–Lemon S–Antonelli HR: CLE–Majeski
ATT: 78,102

LEFT: The most impressive feature of Willie Mays' famous catch was the sheer amount of ground he had to cover before reaching the ball, as can be seen in the top inset photo. The rest of the sequence shows the remarkable catch and throw. Although Larry Doby tagged up and advanced from second to third on the play, Al Rosen had to hold at first base.

1955

Brooklyn Dodgers (4)
New York Yankees (3)

BOTTOM LEFT: After completing his Game 7 shutout, Johnny Podres is greeted by catcher Roy Campanella and third baseman Don Hoak.

BOTTOM RIGHT: The southpaw Podres won two games in the 1955 Series, the first of four Series wins he would get in his career.

OPPOSITE: Jackie Robinson steals home in Game 1 of the 1955 World Series. Although many believed him to be out, films of the play indicate that Robinson was safe because Yogi Berra applied the tag in the wrong spot. This incredible photograph was taken by Mark Kauffman of *Sports Illustrated*.

The sixth World Series matchup between the Yankees and Dodgers was widely expected to end like the previous five. The Dodgers were the stronger team on paper, as they usually were, but the Yankees always seemed to have luck and fate on their side. This belief was reinforced after New York won Game 1, shellacking Brooklyn's best pitcher, Don Newcombe, by a 6-5 score in a game made close when Jackie Robinson audaciously stole home in the eighth inning. "I knew he was going to steal home," Whitey Ford said. "I almost dared him to by taking a long windup as he danced off the bag. Sure enough, he took off for the plate and I threw the ball to Yogi and got it there in plenty of time. The pitch was low, right where I wanted it, and Yogi just caught it and put his mitt down on the ground in front of the plate and Robinson slid right into the tag. Robinson was out, there was no question about it." But Robinson was called safe, even though Berra argued the call at length. The commonly available World Series film is inconclusive regarding the call, but a more obscure film clip shows a reverse angle which reveals that Robinson was clearly safe. While Berra's glove hovered over the left side (or first base side) of home plate, Robinson's foot touched the right side of the plate unmolested.

The Yankees also won Game 2, as Tommy Byrne became the first left-hander to pitch a complete game victory against the Dodgers all year, beating them 4-2. Although no team had ever come back from a 2-0 deficit to win a best-of-seven World Series, the Dodgers' hopes stayed alive, thanks in part to a pep talk by Jackie Robinson after the game. Brooklyn was down, but not yet out.

Brooklyn finally got a win at Ebbets Field in Game 3. One of the Dodgers' eight runs came after another remarkable baserunning play by Robinson, who overran second base intentionally and, when catcher Elston Howard threw to second, scampered easily to third. Left-hander Johnny Podres, pitching on his 23rd birthday, threw a complete game victory. "It was a masterpiece," said Dodgers vice president Lafeyette "Fresco" Thompson. "I told the kid afterwards that he'd be around for a long time and never would do a more competent job." Thompson would be proved stunningly wrong just four days later.

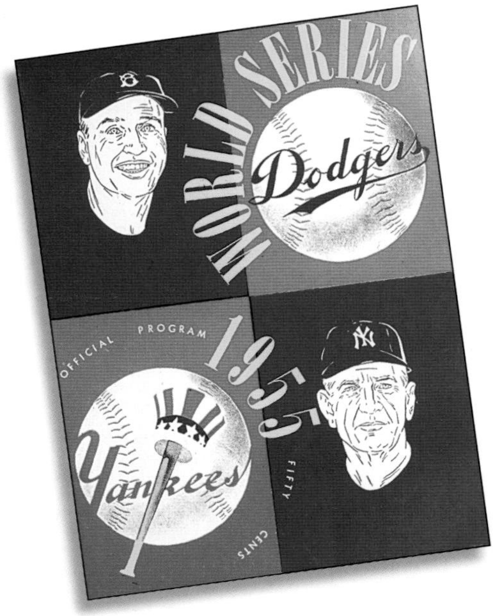

B
Dodgers

TOP: Sandy Amoros, inserted into Game 7 of the 1955 Series as a defensive replacement, makes a tremendous catch in the sixth inning to save the game for Brooklyn.

The Dodgers won Game 4, as Duke Snider, Roy Campanella, and Gil Hodges each homered in an 8-5 victory. Brooklyn then won Game 5 behind the bat of Snider, who hit two home runs off Bob Grim, becoming the first player ever to hit four homers in two different World Series. The homers were the eighth and ninth of Snider's Series career, placing him behind only Babe Ruth and Lou Gehrig on the all-time list. More importantly, the win placed the Dodgers in the driver's seat, as the once-cocky Yankees needed to win two straight games to capture the title. "In all the years I have been with the Dodgers, we have never had a better chance to win the Series than right now," Pee Wee Reese said.

But each team would have to play the deciding games with its best hitter hampered by injury. Mickey Mantle had played games three and four with a bad leg; according to Jimmy Cannon he "was in no shape even to go down to the corner for a beer." He sat out the last three games. Snider, meanwhile, came out of Game 6 after injuring his knee when, he said, he stepped on a sprinkler head while running in the Yankee Stadium outfield. New York won that sixth game with a fine pitching performance from Ford. "I kept watching the Dodgers from the bullpen in those three games at Ebbets Field," Ford said, "and I figured out just how to handle them." The Series was tied at three games apiece and the home team had won every game so far. Game 7 would be played at Yankee Stadium.

The Dodgers, with arguably the most intimidating right-handed lineup in baseball history, usually ate left-handed pitchers for lunch. But Yankee manager Casey Stengel, known for his strict adherence to platoon combinations, abandoned that philosophy in this World Series, throwing lefties in four of the seven games. The Yankees had won the first three, with Ford winning twice and Byrne once. Now Stengel, pushing his luck, decided on Byrne for Game 7. Brooklyn manager Walter Alston went with Podres, who had pitched so effectively in Game 3. "We were getting on to our team bus at Ebbets Field," Snider remembered, and Podres "hopped up the steps, started down the aisle, and told us with all the confidence in the world: 'Just get me one run today. That's all I'll need. Just one.'"

The Dodgers actually got him two runs, both driven in by Hodges. Podres was cruising, leading 2-0 in the sixth inning, when the Yankees put two men on base with Berra at the plate. The Dodger outfield played Berra, a left-handed pull hitter, toward right field, but Berra surprised them by slicing a long drive toward the left field corner that looked like it would surely fall in for a game-tying double. Speedy left fielder Sandy Amoros—who had come into the game that very inning as a defensive replacement—raced over toward the line, stuck out his glove at the last possible moment, caught the ball, and relayed it to Reese for an easy double play. For sheer importance, it was one of the greatest catches in World Series history. The Yankees never threatened again, and Podres completed his 2-0 shutout to give Brooklyn its first and only world championship. "I played the game wrong," Stengel admitted afterward. "I figured [Podres] couldn't last and I had our hitters taking the pitches. But he did last and I was wrong—they should have been up there swinging from the beginning."

Dodger fans went nuts. As one writer put it, "it was the biggest thing that ever happened in Brooklyn, although it happened in the Bronx." Owners of Brooklyn restaurants, candy stores, and butcher shops gave away tons of free product. Confetti showered down from the upper floors of office buildings. People marched through the streets making noise however they could, banging garbage can covers, blowing bicycle horns, and yelling. According to one writer, "Brooklyn last night was a patchwork of neon lights reflected in streets awash from opened fire hydrants." When Johnny Podres arrived at the Dodger victory party at the Hotel Bossert, he was mobbed by more than 3,000 fans waiting outside. "What I remember most about the Series," Dodger pitcher Ed Roebuck said, "was the close relationship between Podres and his father. In the clubhouse after Johnny pitched the shutout to win the final game, they were hugging and crying." So was all of Brooklyn.

1955 WORLD SERIES

Yankee Stadium I (N.Y. Yankees) ◆ 9.28.55

	1	2	3	4	5	6	7	8	9	R	H	E
B'klyn	0	2	1	0	0	0	0	2	0	5	10	0
NYY	0	2	1	1	0	2	0	0	X	6	9	1

WP–Ford LP–Newcombe S–Grim HR: BKN–Furillo, Snider; NYY–Collins (2), Howard ATT: 63,869

Yankee Stadium I ◆ 9.29.55

	1	2	3	4	5	6	7	8	9	R	H	E
B'klyn	0	0	0	1	1	0	0	0	0	2	5	2
NYY	0	0	0	4	0	0	0	0	X	4	8	0

WP–Byrne LP–Loes ATT: 64,707

Ebbets Field (Brooklyn Dodgers) ◆ 9.30.55

	1	2	3	4	5	6	7	8	9	R	H	E
NYY	0	2	0	0	0	0	1	0	0	3	7	0
B'klyn	2	2	0	2	0	0	2	0	X	8	11	1

WP–Podres LP–Turley HR: NYY–Mantle; BKN–Campanella ATT: 34,209

Ebbets Field ◆ 10.1.55

	1	2	3	4	5	6	7	8	9	R	H	E
NYY	1	1	0	1	0	2	0	0	0	5	9	0
B'klyn	0	0	1	3	3	0	1	0	X	8	14	0

WP–Labine LP–Larsen HR: NYY–McDougald; BKN–Campanella, Hodges, Snider ATT: 36,242

Ebbets Field ◆ 10.2.55

	1	2	3	4	5	6	7	8	9	R	H	E
NYY	0	0	0	1	0	0	1	1	0	3	6	0
B'klyn	0	2	1	0	1	0	0	1	X	5	9	2

WP–Craig LP–Grim S–Labine HR: NYY–Cerv, Berra; BKN–Snider (2), Amoros ATT: 36,796

Yankee Stadium I ◆ 10.3.55

	1	2	3	4	5	6	7	8	9	R	H	E
B'klyn	0	0	0	1	0	0	0	0	0	1	4	1
NYY	5	0	0	0	0	0	0	0	X	5	8	0

WP–Ford LP–Spooner HR: NYY–Skowron ATT: 64,022

Yankee Stadium I ◆ 10.4.55

	1	2	3	4	5	6	7	8	9	R	H	E
B'klyn	0	0	0	1	0	1	0	0	0	2	5	0
NYY	0	0	0	0	0	0	0	0	0	0	8	1

WP–Podres LP–Byrne ATT: 62,465

1956

New York Yankees (4)
Brooklyn Dodgers (3)

Pitching for the New York Yankees was no big deal for Don Larsen. As one sportswriter judiciously put it, Larsen had always "shown more concern for good times than for good games." He had tremendous talent, but according to most who knew him, he had no desire to use it. At 27 years old, his two favorite pastimes were drinking beer and reading comic books. "The fact is," Stan Isaacs wrote in *Newsday*, "Larsen doesn't give a damn."

Larsen led the major leagues in losses with 21 in 1954 after the Yankees acquired him in the largest trade in baseball history, an eighteen-player deal with the Orioles. He missed several team trains during the 1956 season and smashed his car into a Florida lamppost after a late-night drinking binge in spring training. But despite his chronic irresponsibility, and despite the fact that the

BOTTOM: The scoreboard at Yankee Stadium is all zeroes for Brooklyn as Don Larsen pitches to Dale Mitchell in the ninth inning of Game 5, 1956.

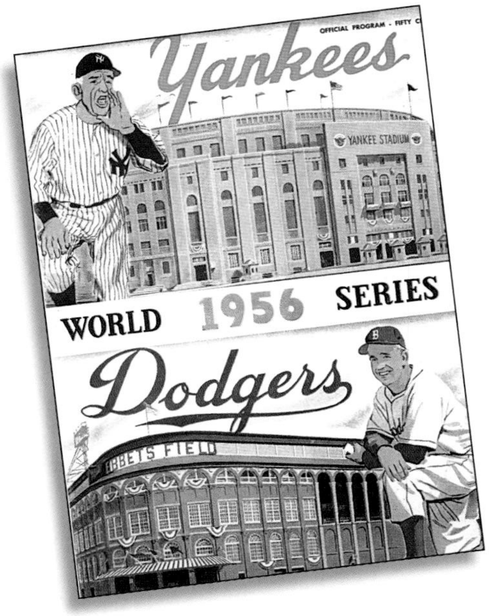

TOP: Roy Campanella catches a Mickey Mantle pop-up in Game 3 of the 1956 World Series as members of the O'Malley family—the owners of the Dodgers—look on from their field-level box.

BOTTOM: In Game 4 of the 1956 World Series, Mickey Mantle backpedals to make a catch in the outfield as the sun warms the monuments at the back of Yankee Stadium. Mantle had his best season ever in 1956, batting .353 with 52 home runs, and continued to have a great postseason. He hit three home runs in the World Series, including one in this game.

Brooklyn Dodgers had pounded him in Game 2 of the 1956 World Series, Larsen found himself on the mound again for Game 5. "Don was a drinker and he went out drinking every night after [Game 2]," teammate Bob Turley told Danny Peary. "On the Yankees, you never knew if you were pitching until you looked in your locker and discovered that our pitching coach, Jim Turner, had put the ball in your shoe. So Larsen didn't know he was pitching until he came to the stadium that day. He'd slept only about half an hour the night before so he went to the training room and took a nap until noon, an hour before the game."

Despite his hangover, Larsen threw a 97-pitch masterpiece that still stands as the greatest pitching performance in World Series history. Twenty-seven men came to the plate for Brooklyn, and all trudged back to the dugout after making outs, including last-ditch pinch hitter Dale Mitchell, who struck out to end the game. It was the first World Series no-hitter ever and the first perfect game in the major leagues in 34 years.

Afterward, Larsen admitted that he hadn't put much thought into his pitch selection. "Phooey on all this deep thinking stuff," he said. "I only shook off a couple of Yogi's signals, but he stuck with them, so I went ahead and pitched what he called." The media made much of the fact that Larsen pitched with an unusual no-windup delivery, something he had adopted during the last two weeks of the regular season, but the Dodgers had pounded the no-windup delivery in Game 2. Jackie Robinson, Gil Hodges, and Duke Snider all said it was Larsen's pitches, not his delivery, that fooled them.

As great as Larsen was, he owes his immortality to two things: luck and good defense. In the second inning, Robinson hit a line drive off third baseman Andy Carey's glove, but shortstop Gil McDougald scooped up the ball and nipped Robinson at first. Hodges sent a long drive to deep left-center in the fifth but Mickey Mantle made a spectacular one-handed catch. The next batter, Sandy Amoros, appeared to hit a long home run down the right field line, but it hooked foul by inches. As the game crept into the late innings, Carey and Joe Collins played unusually close at the corners, so speedsters like Robinson and James "Junior" Gilliam couldn't bunt for hits.

Ironically, on the same day Larsen was making history on the mound, his estranged wife, Vivian, was at the courthouse obtaining an injunction to withhold his World Series check for missed alimony payments. But on the field, the pitcher's performance gave the Yankees a 3-2 edge in the Series after the Dodgers had won each of the first two games. Hodges had put on an impressive hitting display with five hits, two doubles, a homer, and seven RBI, but the Yankees won Game 3 behind Whitey Ford. They also took Game 4 thanks to a Mantle homer that was said to be one of the longest in Series history. "It wouldn't have gone over the fence in Ebbets Field," Roy Campanella said of the low line drive. "Might have gone through it, though."

The day after Larsen's Game 5 masterpiece, Bob Turley pitched a magnificent game for New York—"the best game of my career," he later said—but was beaten by Clem Labine, 1-0. "Enos Slaughter misplayed three balls in left field," Turley remembered. "On Robinson's game-winning hit in the tenth, he lost the ball in the haze and white shirts and charged in, only to have the ball shoot over his head."

Don Newcombe—who had been arrested for punching a parking lot attendant who heckled him after his poor Game 2 performance—took the mound for Brooklyn in the seventh game, facing right-hander Johnny Kucks. The outcome was never in doubt, as Kucks threw a brilliant three-hit shutout and Newcombe was pounded again, giving up two home runs to Berra. "I tried to knock him down with two strikes on him," Newcombe said. "I threw at his head and didn't get it in far enough. He hit the ball over the right field fence." It was yet another in a long line of important games that Newcombe had failed to win. "Don doesn't choke up," Robinson insisted. "He's got plenty of guts, but he's had some bad luck." Just like the rest of the Dodgers.

1956 WORLD SERIES

GAME 1 — Ebbets Field (Brooklyn Dodgers) ◆ 10.3.56

	1	2	3	4	5	6	7	8	9	R	H	E
NYY	2	0	0	1	0	0	0	0	0	3	9	1
B'klyn	0	2	3	1	0	0	0	0	X	6	9	0

WP–Maglie LP–Ford HR: NYY–Mantle, Martin; BKN–Robinson, Hodges ATT: 34,479

GAME 2 — Ebbets Field ◆ 10.5.56

	1	2	3	4	5	6	7	8	9	R	H	E
NYY	1	5	0	1	0	0	0	0	1	8	12	2
B'klyn	0	6	1	2	2	0	0	2	X	13	12	0

WP–Bessent LP–Morgan HR: NYY–Berra; BKN–Snider ATT: 36,217

GAME 3 — Yankee Stadium I (N.Y. Yankees) ◆ 10.6.56

	1	2	3	4	5	6	7	8	9	R	H	E
B'klyn	0	1	0	0	0	1	1	0	0	3	8	1
NYY	0	1	0	0	0	3	0	1	X	5	8	1

WP–Ford LP–Craig HR: NYY–Martin, Slaughter ATT: 73,977

GAME 4 — Yankee Stadium I ◆ 10.7.56

	1	2	3	4	5	6	7	8	9	R	H	E
B'klyn	0	0	0	1	0	0	0	0	1	2	6	0
NYY	1	0	0	2	0	1	2	0	X	6	7	2

WP–Sturdivant LP–Erskine HR: NYY–Mantle, Bauer ATT: 69,705

GAME 5 — Yankee Stadium I ◆ 10.8.56

	1	2	3	4	5	6	7	8	9	R	H	E
B'klyn	0	0	0	0	0	0	0	0	0	0	0	0
NYY	0	0	0	1	0	1	0	0	X	2	5	0

WP–Larsen LP–Maglie HR: NYY–Mantle ATT: 64,519

GAME 6 — Ebbets Field ◆ 10.9.56

	1	2	3	4	5	6	7	8	9	10	R	H	E
NYY	0	0	0	0	0	0	0	0	0	0	0	7	0
B'klyn	0	0	0	0	0	0	0	0	0	1	1	4	0

WP–Labine LP–Turley ATT: 33,224

GAME 7 — Ebbets Field ◆ 10.10.56

	1	2	3	4	5	6	7	8	9	R	H	E
NYY	2	0	2	1	0	0	4	0	0	9	10	0
B'klyn	0	0	0	0	0	0	0	0	0	0	3	1

WP–Kucks LP–Newcombe HR: NYY–Berra (2), Howard, Skowron ATT: 33,782

1957

Milwaukee Braves (4)
New York Yankees (3)

The Braves had played second fiddle in Boston since 1935 and fled Beantown for Milwaukee before the 1953 season. They had been perennial doormats in Boston, but quickly became winners in Wisconsin. By 1957, the Braves had assembled a tremendous team. The starting rotation featured three standout pitchers, Warren Spahn, Lew Burdette, and Bob Buhl, and the lineup was solid from top to bottom, led by 23-year-old Henry Aaron, the National League's MVP and near–Triple Crown winner in 1957. Milwaukee embraced the team with open arms, as a National League record 2.2 million fans came out to see the Braves win 95 games and the National League pennant.

The New York Yankees still owned the American League, further cementing their status as the most hated team in baseball by winning 98 games during the regular season. Baseball fans were so tired of the Yankees winning that even the Yankee Stadium crowd rooted heavily for the Braves throughout the 1957 World Series.

BOTTOM: Lew Burdette, the pitching star of the 1957 World Series, tosses a pitch in the seventh game.

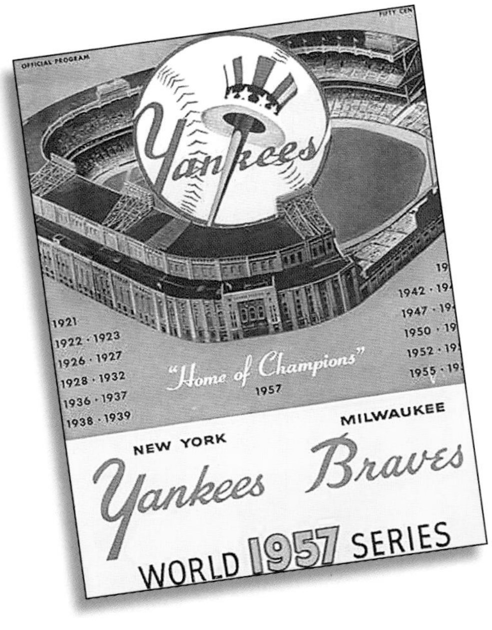

TOP: Milwaukee's Eddie Mathews puts a powerful left-handed swing on a Bob Grim pitch in the tenth inning of Game 4, resulting in a game-winning homer.

BOTTOM: The Yankees successfully execute a suicide squeeze in Game 1 of the 1957 World Series, with Yogi Berra crossing the plate as pitcher Ernie Johnson throws out Jerry Coleman at first. The catcher directing traffic is Del Crandall.

Game 1 in the Bronx was a matchup between two of baseball's all-time great left-handers, as Whitey Ford outdueled Warren Spahn 3-1. The Braves struck back in the second inning of Game 2, though, as Mickey Mantle, playing hurt, misplayed two balls in the outfield that led to a Milwaukee run. In the bottom of that inning, Braves left fielder Wes Covington made an outstanding leaping catch of a likely double, saving his team two runs that turned out to be the difference. New York was stymied by Burdette, an eccentric ex-Yankee farmhand from Nitro, West Virginia, famed for his mastery of crossword puzzles, practical jokes, and spitballs, as Burdette beat the Yankees 4-2 in the first World Series game won by a non–New York team since 1948. "I'm not saying he throws the spitter," Yankee manager Casey Stengel said afterward, "but he goes through all those motions. Maybe he gets some on the ball once in a while."

The Braves were met by 20,000 cheering fans at the airport when they returned to Milwaukee, but they were greeted rudely by the Yankees, who won the third game in a 12-3 romp. Rookie shortstop Tony Kubek, a Milwaukee native playing in his hometown for the first time, crushed two homers for the visitors.

Spahn pitched brilliantly for most of Game 4 and looked as if he had the game all wrapped up, leading 4-1 in the ninth inning and coming within one strike of ending it, but Elston Howard hit the next pitch for a three-run homer to send the game into extra innings. The Yankees wasted no time taking the lead in the tenth, scoring on a triple by Hank Bauer, but the Braves refused to give up. Vernal "Nippy" Jones pinch hit for Spahn in the bottom of the tenth. He was hit on the foot by a pitch, but umpire Augie Donatelli didn't see it and refused to grant him first base. But the clever Jones retrieved the ball, pointed to a black shoe polish stain on it, and was promptly awarded first. Then Johnny Logan ripped a game-tying double, bringing up Ed Mathews, a dangerous left-handed batter who had hit 32 home runs during the regular season, against right-hander Bob Grim. An intentional walk would have set up both a double play and a righty-righty matchup against Aaron. Bucking conventional wisdom, though, Stengel chose to pitch to Mathews, and the strapping third baseman deposited a two-strike pitch over the left-field fence, ending the game, tying the Series, and sending Milwaukee into a frenzy.

The Braves won again at home the next day, as Lew Burdette gained his second victory by blanking the Yankees 1-0 on seven hits. Joe Adcock's opposite-field single scored Mathews with the only run of the game as the New York offense sputtered with Mantle out of the lineup with an injury. The teams traveled back to New York, where Bauer won Game 6 for the Yankees with a homer off the left-field foul pole.

Although Burdette had pitched the full nine innings in Game 5, Braves manager Fred Haney brought him back on two days' rest to start Game 7. Burdette rewarded that decision by tossing a seven-hit shutout against the Yankees for the second game in a row. Indeed, the Yankees were so frustrated by Burdette's breaking pitches that they spent much of the game asking the umpires to check the ball for foreign substances. Nothing was found and Burdette won 5-0, becoming the first pitcher to throw two shutouts in one World Series since Christy Mathewson in 1905. "In the Series, I pitched as I always did," Burdette said. "It was just one of those things. Whenever I needed something I got it."

Although Aaron had a remarkable Series, collecting eleven hits and three home runs, it was Burdette's marvelous pitching that did the Yankees in. "I dare say the result of the 1957 World's Series pleased more people than had the outcome of any classic in the past," Dan Daniel wrote in the *New York World-Telegram*. "The Braves…made the dreams of millions of Yankee Haters come true." Pandemonium reigned in Milwaukee, as an estimated 400,000 Braves fans took to the streets, drinking beer, waving signs, setting off fireworks, and vandalizing anything they could find. "It is," wrote Jimmy Cannon, "as if all the weeping in the world had subsided for this holiday in Milwaukee."

1957 WORLD SERIES

Yankee Stadium I (N.Y. Yankees) ◆ 10.2.57

	1	2	3	4	5	6	7	8	9	R	H	E
Milw.	0	0	0	0	0	0	1	0	0	1	5	0
NYY	0	0	0	0	1	2	0	0	X	3	9	1

WP–Ford LP–Spahn ATT: 69,476

Yankee Stadium I ◆ 10.3.57

	1	2	3	4	5	6	7	8	9	R	H	E
Milw.	0	1	1	2	0	0	0	0	0	4	8	0
NYY	0	1	1	0	0	0	0	0	0	2	7	2

WP–Burdette LP–Shantz HR: MIL–Logan; NYY–Bauer ATT: 65,202

County Stadium (Milwaukee Braves) ◆ 10.5.57

	1	2	3	4	5	6	7	8	9	R	H	E
NYY	3	0	2	2	0	0	5	0	0	12	9	0
Milw.	0	1	0	0	2	0	0	0	0	3	8	1

WP–Larsen LP–Buhl HR: NYY–Kubek (2), Mantle; MIL–Aaron ATT: 45,804

County Stadium ◆ 10.6.57

	1	2	3	4	5	6	7	8	9	10	R	H	E
NYY	1	0	0	0	0	0	0	0	3	1	5	11	0
Milw.	0	0	0	4	0	0	0	0	0	3	7	7	0

WP–Spahn LP–Grim HR: NYY–Howard; MIL–Aaron, Torre, Mathews ATT: 45,804

County Stadium ◆ 10.7.57

	1	2	3	4	5	6	7	8	9	R	H	E
NYY	0	0	0	0	0	0	0	0	0	0	7	0
Milw.	0	0	0	0	0	1	0	0	X	1	6	1

WP–Burdette LP–Ford ATT: 45,811

Yankee Stadium I ◆ 10.9.57

	1	2	3	4	5	6	7	8	9	R	H	E
Milw.	0	0	0	0	1	0	1	0	0	2	4	0
NYY	0	0	2	0	0	0	1	0	X	3	7	0

WP–Turley LP–Johnson HR: MIL–Torre, Aaron; NYY–Berra, Bauer ATT: 61,408

Yankee Stadium I ◆ 10.10.57

	1	2	3	4	5	6	7	8	9	R	H	E
Milw.	0	0	4	0	0	0	0	1	0	5	9	1
NYY	0	0	0	0	0	0	0	0	0	0	7	3

WP–Burdette LP–Larsen HR: MIL–Crandall ATT: 61,207

BOTTOM: In Game 5 of the 1957 World Series, Braves outfielder Wes Covington slams into the outfield fence to rob Gil McDougald of an extra-base hit.

1958

New York Yankees (4)
Milwaukee Braves (3)

As Yogi Berra might have said, 1958 was déjà vu all over again. The World Series again featured a seven-game battle between the Milwaukee Braves and New York Yankees, but this time it was the New Yorkers who overcame long odds to win the Series. As in 1957, Game 1 was a matchup between lefties Whitey Ford and Warren Spahn. Ford had won the first time, but now Spahn evened the score, winning a 10-inning complete game that was decided by Billy Bruton's run-scoring single in the bottom of the tenth. The Braves took Game 2 in more convincing fashion, knocking Yankee 21-game winner Bob Turley out of the game after retiring only one batter. Lew Burdette was on the winning end of that one and provided the biggest hit himself with a three-run homer that was the first World Series longball by a pitcher in eighteen years.

The Yankees took Game 3 at Yankee Stadium, as Don Larsen and Ryne Duren combined on a six-hit shutout to win 4-0. Every Yankee run was driven in by leadoff man Hank Bauer, who had a homer and two singles. The Braves won Game 4 the next day, although it was really the Yankees who beat themselves, since rookie Norm Siebern misplayed three balls in left field that led to three Milwaukee runs. That was more than Spahn needed, as he pitched a two-hit shutout, beating Ford again. Siebern's counterpart in left field, Wes Covington, expressed sympathy after the game. "That's a rough field to play, with the sun and that fog or mist that seems to come in later in the afternoon. Norm just had a couple of tough chances."

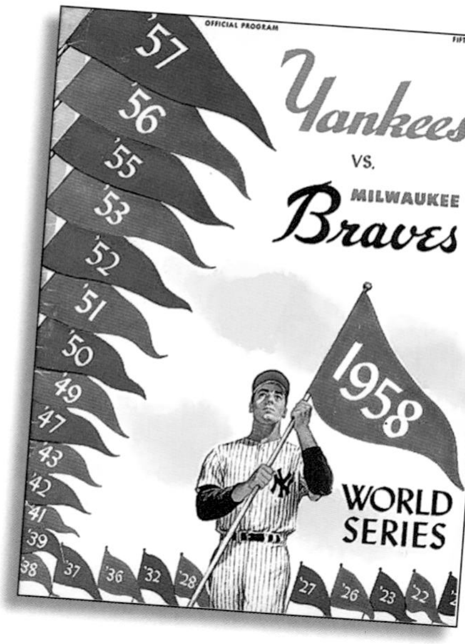

Now the Braves held a commanding three games to one lead, a lead that had been blown only once in history, by the 1925 Washington Senators. Milwaukee also had the 1957 Series hero, Burdette, due to face Turley, who had been able to record only one out in an atrocious Game 2 performance. Everyone assumed the Series was over—everyone, that is, except Turley, who allowed five singles, struck out ten Braves, and won an easy 7-0 shutout over the heavily favored Burdette.

Turley's performance breathed new life into the Yankees, but they still had a daunting task before them. Games 6 and 7 would be on the road against Spahn and Burdette, who had 45 combined victories that year, including three in the World Series. The Braves knocked Whitey Ford out in the second inning of Game 6, but the score was tied 2-2 after nine innings nonetheless. Spahn pitched valiantly, but gave up a

BOTTOM LEFT: Warren Spahn is congratulated by Braves players and owners after pitching a 3-0 shutout in Game 4 of the 1958 Series.

BOTTOM RIGHT: Wes Covington slides home safely in Game 2 with the Braves' fourth run of the first inning. Yogi Berra's jumping barehanded catch of the wild throw from left fielder Elston Howard helped minimize the damage.

tie-breaking homer to Gil McDougald in the top of the tenth. The Braves tried to come back in the bottom of the inning, but with the tying and winning runs on base, the ever-present Turley came in to retire Frank Torre for the last out. "After the game I was interviewed in the locker room for the next morning's *Today* show," winning pitcher Duren said. "I was looking forward to seeing myself but they had to cut the segment because Yogi Berra had been walking around buck naked in the background scratching his rear end."

Burdette started Game 7 on two days' rest, exactly as he had done a year earlier. This time, however, his defense betrayed him, as first baseman Torre's two errors in the second inning led to two unearned runs for the Yankees. The Braves knocked Larsen out of the game early, but for the second day in a row, Turley entered in relief and stymied the Milwaukee hitters, pitching six-plus innings of fabulous relief as Bill Skowron broke the game open with a three-run homer in the eighth inning. The Yankees had won perhaps their unlikeliest world championship after getting obliterated in the first half of the Series. "Being on the mound for the final out in the World Series was the most exciting moment of my career," said Turley, who was named the Series MVP. "I could hardly walk off the mound I was so damn tired."

But few of the Yankees were as excited as Turley. "Most of these Yankees had won so often, they acted as if nothing had happened," the *New York Times* observed. Braves fans, on the other hand, were devastated. The Milwaukee offense had sputtered after gaining a 3-1 Series lead, as the Braves' two top pitchers, Spahn and Burdette, combined for more RBI in the Series than Eddie Mathews and Hank Aaron. During the week of the Series loss, only a handful of beleaguered patrons showed up for the film that was playing at Milwaukee's largest movie theater. The featured title: *Damn Yankees.*

TOP: After beating out an infield hit in Game 6 of the 1958 Series, Hank Aaron heads for second when the throw gets away from first baseman Moose Skowron.

BOTTOM: Managers Fred Haney (left) and Casey Stengel opposed each other in back-to-back World Series, in 1957 and 1958.

1958 WORLD SERIES

County Stadium (Milwaukee Braves) ◆ 10.1.58

	1	2	3	4	5	6	7	8	9	10	R	H	E
NYY	0	0	0	1	2	0	0	0	0	0	3	8	1
Milw.	0	0	0	2	0	0	0	1	0	1	4	10	0

WP–Spahn LP–Duren HR: NYY–Skowron, Bauer ATT: 46,367

County Stadium ◆ 10.2.58

	1	2	3	4	5	6	7	8	9	R	H	E
NYY	1	0	0	1	0	0	0	0	3	5	7	0
Milw.	7	1	0	0	0	0	2	3	X	13	15	1

WP–Burdette LP–Turley HR: NYY–Mantle (2), Bauer; MIL–Bruton, Burdette ATT: 46,367

Yankee Stadium I (N.Y. Yankees) ◆ 10.4.58

	1	2	3	4	5	6	7	8	9	R	H	E
Milw.	0	0	0	0	0	0	0	0	0	0	6	0
NYY	0	0	0	0	2	0	2	0	X	4	4	0

WP–Larsen LP–Rush S–Duren HR: NYY–Bauer ATT: 71,599

Yankee Stadium I ◆ 10.5.58

	1	2	3	4	5	6	7	8	9	R	H	E
Milw.	0	0	0	0	0	1	1	1	0	3	9	0
NYY	0	0	0	0	0	0	0	0	0	0	2	1

WP–Spahn LP–Ford ATT: 71,563

Yankee Stadium I ◆ 10.6.58

	1	2	3	4	5	6	7	8	9	R	H	E
Milw.	0	0	0	0	0	0	0	0	0	0	5	0
NYY	0	0	1	0	0	6	0	0	X	7	10	0

WP–Turley LP–Burdette HR: NYY–McDougald ATT: 65,279

County Stadium ◆ 10.8.58

	1	2	3	4	5	6	7	8	9	10	R	H	E
NYY	1	0	0	0	0	1	0	0	0	2	4	10	1
Milw.	1	1	0	0	0	0	0	0	0	1	3	10	4

WP–Duren LP–Spahn S–Turley HR: NYY–Bauer, McDougald ATT: 46,367

County Stadium ◆ 10.9.58

	1	2	3	4	5	6	7	8	9	R	H	E
NYY	0	2	0	0	0	0	0	4	0	6	8	0
Milw.	1	0	0	0	0	1	0	0	0	2	5	2

WP–Turley LP–Burdette HR: NYY–Skowron; MIL–Crandall ATT: 46,367

AN ALTOGETHER DIFFERENT GAME

THE WORLD SERIES ON THE AIR

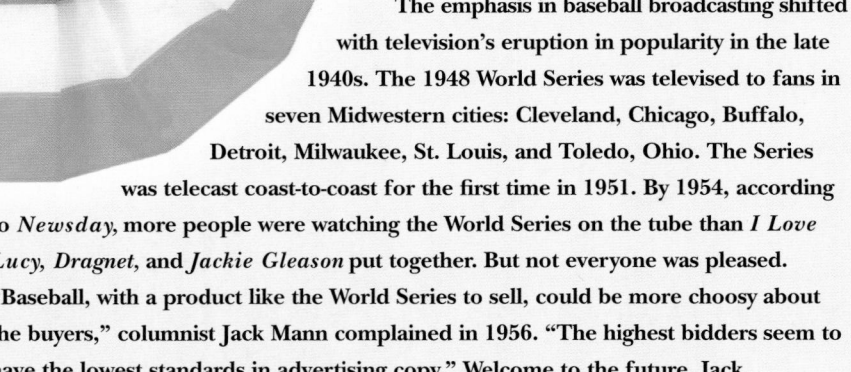

Before radio came along, fans in distant outposts followed the annual World Series action on huge public message boards, often mounted on the front walls of newspaper buildings where operators would move little men from base to base and update the score as telegraph reports arrived. The first radio broadcast of a World Series was performed in 1921 by sports journalism's master of purple prose, Grantland Rice, who sent play-by-play reports over the telephone that were then broadcast over radio stations located in three cities: Pittsburgh, Pennsylvania, Newark, New Jersey, and East Springfield, Massachusetts. "After one inning, it was just as if we had been doing it twenty years," Rice said, "showing how quickly human nature adjusts itself to the ways of science." But it was not Rice's voice going out over the airwaves. His telephoned summaries were re-created in the studio by broadcaster Tommy Cowan.

In 1923 the first true, stadium-originated radio broadcast of World Series games took place. Sportswriter Bill McGeehan did the honors, though he reportedly tired of the chore and quit in the middle of Game 3. Graham McNamee, an ex-concert singer who happened to be there, stepped in. McNamee turned out to be a natural at baseball broadcasting and worked every Series through 1932. World Series radio broadcasters were hired and fired annually at the whim of Commissioner Kenesaw Mountain Landis after that.

The emphasis in baseball broadcasting shifted with television's eruption in popularity in the late 1940s. The 1948 World Series was televised to fans in seven Midwestern cities: Cleveland, Chicago, Buffalo, Detroit, Milwaukee, St. Louis, and Toledo, Ohio. The Series was telecast coast-to-coast for the first time in 1951. By 1954, according to *Newsday*, more people were watching the World Series on the tube than *I Love Lucy*, *Dragnet*, and *Jackie Gleason* put together. But not everyone was pleased. "Baseball, with a product like the World Series to sell, could be more choosy about the buyers," columnist Jack Mann complained in 1956. "The highest bidders seem to have the lowest standards in advertising copy." Welcome to the future, Jack.

The first color telecast of the World Series came in 1955, although few viewers had color televisions yet. Southerners Red Barber and Mel Allen artfully described the action throughout most of that decade, setting a high standard for a number of outstanding broadcasters like Vin Scully to follow. Scully broadcast a record twenty-five World Series on radio and TV through 2001.

Television changed the face of the World Series dramatically. The first Series night game was played in 1971 when Commissioner Bowie Kuhn and NBC executives decided to seek a broader viewership and more advertising dollars. That game went over well and received high ratings, ensuring that all World Series games would eventually be played at night. By the late 1980s day games in October, even on weekends, were but a distant memory. "I suppose it was inevitable," former Pirates pitcher Steve Blass said. "More people could watch at night. Owners got more money. But listening to the World Series during the day was a tradition. Without it something has been lost."

One thing that was lost was the comfort of fans attending the games. It snowed at Cleveland's Jacobs Field in 1997 on the day of Game 4 yet the game went on in the freezing night. Many called the 1976 Series a disaster because the harrowing late-night weather hampered the quality of play. Bowie Kuhn, not wanting the television audience to realize how cold it was, reportedly wore long underwear under his suit so he wouldn't have to put on an overcoat. The hallowed World Series had become, in the words of one *Sporting News* columnist, a "crummy piece of television garbage."

Game times were not the only things that changed over the years. When the World Series first made it to national TV, the only advertisements had been Gillette jingles between innings. The number of ads multiplied exponentially over the next forty years, and players began wearing equipment emblazoned with oversized, television-friendly logos. The networks surreptitiously placed nonexistent, computer-generated billboards in the stadium background. Promotional ads for inane sitcoms were recited by announcers in between pitches. Fans watching the 2001 World Series Game 7 telecast on the Fox network were subjected to a stunning 1,282 advertisements between the first pitch and the last pitch, a rate of one ad every nine seconds. "Not only does it get in the face of consumers, but it interrupts the pace of the game," Bob Costas said. "You can't get into a rhythm because they're flooding stuff in." The television version of the World Series has become an unmitigated disaster to many fans who enjoy watching baseball for its own sake.

TOP: Graham McNamee, an out-of-work concert singer when he started broadcasting baseball in 1923, was a pioneer of early World Series broadcasts. He remained a sportscaster until his death, in 1942. McNamee was given the Ford C. Frick Award in 1984.

BOTTOM: Vin Scully has called a record 25 World Series since his broadcasting career began in 1950.

TOP: A total of 92,394 fans packed the awkwardly shaped Los Angeles Coliseum for Game 3 of the 1959 World Series, which the Dodgers won, 3-1.

1959

Los Angeles Dodgers (4)
Chicago White Sox (2)

ALTHOUGH THEY HAD FOUND A LUCRATIVE new home in Los Angeles, things were looking bleak for the Dodgers in the late 1950s. The Brooklyn dynasty that had won six pennants in ten years was in shambles. Jackie Robinson and Pee Wee Reese, among others, were retired. Roy Campanella was paralyzed in a car accident. Don Newcombe was a Cincinnati Redleg. Carl Furillo was 37 years old and reduced to pinch-hitting duty. Duke Snider and Gil Hodges were part-time players, each enjoying the last productive season of his career. The legends were gone and a new crop of stars was trying to take their place, including catcher Johnny Roseboro, second baseman Charlie Neal, outfielder Wally Moon, and pitcher Don Drysdale.

The Dodgers ended the National League season with 86 victories, a total that in most years would be good for third place. But in 1959 it was enough to tie the Braves for first. The Dodgers swept a best-of-three playoff and were on their way to the World Series. Their .564 winning percentage made them the worst team to reach the Series to that point. Their opponents, the speedy and fundamentally sound Chicago White Sox, were favored to win. The "Go-Go Sox" stole 113 bases that year, 29 more than any other major league team. (In fact, Luis Aparicio's 56 steals were, by themselves, better than the total for ten of the other fifteen teams.) Second baseman Jacob "Nellie" Fox, though he stole only five bases, was named league MVP after batting .306 and playing spectacular defense.

The White Sox won the first game with power, not speed, as aging slugger Ted Kluszewski, who had hit only four homers all season, hit two in the game and tied a World Series record with five RBI. Pitcher Early Wynn was just as good, holding the Dodgers scoreless in an 11-0 thrashing. The Series had started off as expected, but Sox manager Al Lopez knew better than to relax. "They didn't win that pennant over there," he said, "by playing like that."

The second game was much closer, as the White Sox took a 2-1 lead into the seventh inning. But Chuck Essegian, a pinch hitter who had homered just once all year, went deep to tie the game. Then, after a walk, scrawny Charlie Neal, Los Angeles' 156-pound second baseman, hit his second homer of the day to give the Dodgers the lead. Larry Sherry, a rookie who had become the Dodgers' ace reliever over the course of the season, nailed the door shut with help from left fielder Wally Moon and shortstop Maury Wills, who executed a perfect relay to nail a runner at home and end a Chicago rally.

Game 3 took place at the Los Angeles Coliseum, a colossal football stadium where a crowd of 92,394, a World Series record, watched Don Drysdale beat the White Sox 3-1. The Dodgers took Game 4, too, following an eighth-inning Hodges homer that provided the margin of victory.

A new attendance record was set for the third consecutive day in Game 5, as 92,706 fans saw a great pitcher's duel, with Chicago's Bob Shaw outdueling an inconsistent young left-hander named Sandy Koufax. The only run of the game scored on a double play. The teams then returned to Chicago's Comiskey Park. Game 6 was a slugfest, and the Dodgers put the Series

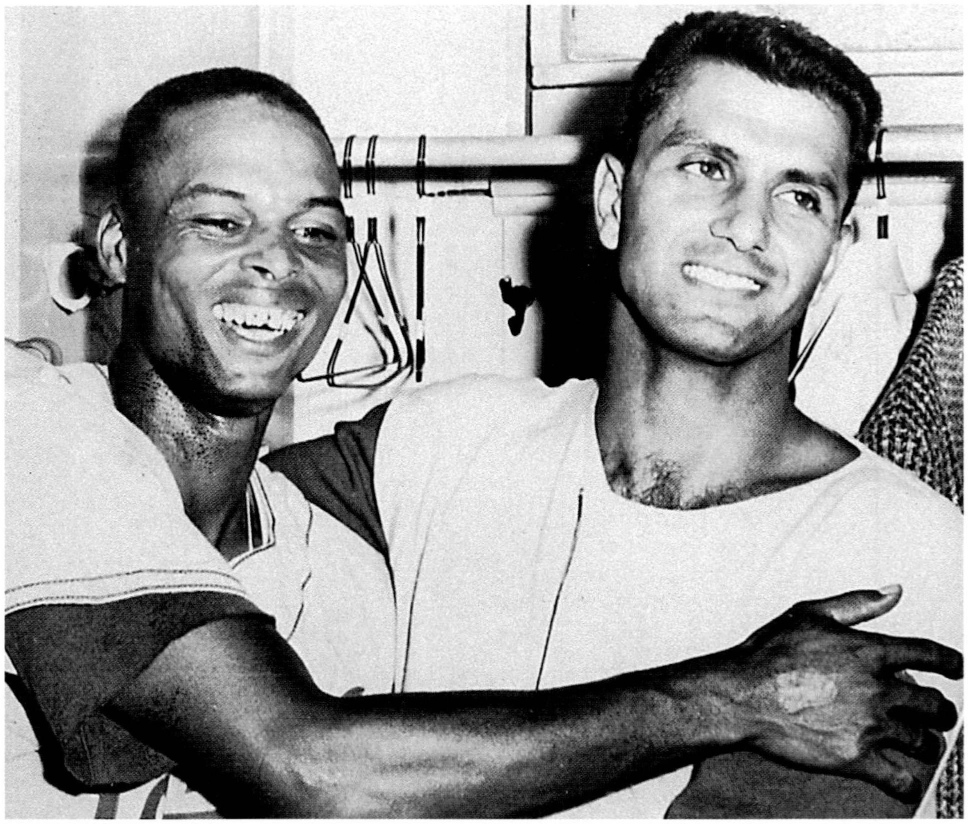

RIGHT: Chuck Essegian (right) homered twice in three at-bats, while Charlie Neal batted .370 with two homers and six RBI. The two combined to be Los Angeles' unlikely hitting stars in the 1959 World Series.

BOTTOM: Gil Hodges is greeted at home plate after hitting a tie-breaking homer in the eighth inning of Game 4. Hodges' hit proved to be the difference in the game, as the Dodgers won 5-4.

away by battering six Chicago pitchers for a total of nine runs. The heroes were the same three men who had won Game 2 for Los Angeles. Essegian hit another pinch homer, Neal collected three hits, and Sherry won the game by pitching 5⅔ innings of magnificent relief.

During the six-game Series the Go-Go Sox were, ironically, outplayed in every speed-related facet of the game. Sox base runners were caught by Roseboro in three of five steal attempts and made two other key outs on the base paths. The Dodgers outstole the White Sox, five to two, and turned seven double plays to Chicago's two. Dodger batters also came through in the clutch, as L.A. scored its first eleven runs of the Series with two outs. "The White Sox built their hopes on slickness and quickness, on poise and determination, on pitching and speed," wrote Roy Terrell in *Sports Illustrated*. "By the time the fourth game was over it was apparent that the Dodgers were better in all of these."

It was Los Angeles native Sherry, a minor leaguer at the beginning of the season, who made the biggest impact, though. He won two of the Dodgers' four victories, saved the other two, and posted a 0.71 ERA in 12-plus innings. "Everything he threw, we hit at somebody," the White Sox' Billy Pierce said. "He did nothing wrong."

1959 WORLD SERIES

Comiskey Park (Chicago White Sox) ◆ 10.1.59

	1	2	3	4	5	6	7	8	9	R	H	E
L.A.	0	0	0	0	0	0	0	0	0	0	8	3
Chi.	2	0	7	2	0	0	0	0	X	11	11	0

WP–Wynn LP–Craig S–Staley
HR: CHW–Kluszewski (2) ATT: 48,013

Comiskey Park ◆ 10.2.59

	1	2	3	4	5	6	7	8	9	R	H	E
L.A.	0	0	0	0	1	0	3	0	0	4	9	1
Chi.	2	0	0	0	0	0	0	1	0	3	8	0

WP–Podres LP–Shaw S–Sherry HR: LA–Neal (2), Essegian ATT: 47,368

L.A. Memorial Coliseum (Dodgers) ◆ 10.4.59

	1	2	3	4	5	6	7	8	9	R	H	E
Chi.	0	0	0	0	0	0	0	1	0	1	12	0
L.A.	0	0	0	0	0	0	2	1	X	3	5	0

WP–Drysdale LP–Donovan S–Sherry ATT: 92,394

L.A. Memorial Coliseum ◆ 10.5.59

	1	2	3	4	5	6	7	8	9	R	H	E
Chi.	0	0	0	0	0	0	4	0	0	4	10	3
L.A.	0	0	4	0	0	0	0	1	X	5	9	0

WP–Sherry LP–Staley HR: CHW–Lollar; LA–Hodges ATT: 92,650

L.A. Memorial Coliseum ◆ 10.6.59

	1	2	3	4	5	6	7	8	9	R	H	E
Chi.	0	0	0	1	0	0	0	0	0	1	5	0
L.A.	0	0	0	0	0	0	0	0	0	0	9	0

WP–Shaw LP–Koufax S–Donovan ATT: 92,706

Comiskey Park ◆ 10.8.59

	1	2	3	4	5	6	7	8	9	R	H	E
L.A.	0	0	2	6	0	0	0	0	1	9	13	0
Chi.	0	0	0	3	0	0	0	0	0	3	6	1

WP–Sherry LP–Wynn HR: LA–Snider, Moon, Essegian; CHW–Kluszewski ATT: 47,653

1960

Pittsburgh Pirates (4)
New York Yankees (3)

The Pittsburgh Pirates won the first game of the 1960 World Series, 6-4, with relief ace Elroy Face fending off the Yankees in the late innings. Game 2 was played on a wet day at Forbes Field, which was appropriate, since it rained all day on the Pirates, too. Everything went smoothly until the fourth inning, when Pittsburgh skipper Danny Murtaugh pulled his pitcher, Bob Friend, for a pinch hitter. The Yankees then proceeded to tee off on five Pirates relievers, scoring sixteen runs and collecting nineteen hits before the game mercifully ended. After a travel day, the Yankees poured it on some more in Game 3 in the Bronx. This is the kind of day it was for the Pirates: light-hitting Yankee Bobby Richardson, after failing in a squeeze bunt attempt, was forced to swing away—and hit a grand slam. The final score was 10-0 Yankees. Whitey Ford pitched a complete game and held Pittsburgh to four hits.

The undaunted Pirates regrouped to win the fourth game, 3-2. Vernon Law, a deacon in the Mormon church, was the winning pitcher, and he also doubled in a run while scoring another. Face, a forkball specialist who had won 28 games in relief over the last two seasons, relieved Law with two men on in the seventh inning. A spectacular leaping catch by center fielder Bill Virdon prevented the tying and winning runs from crossing the plate. The Yankees had outscored the Pirates 32-12 in the first four games, but the World Series was tied nonetheless.

The Pirates took the Series lead in Game 5, as Harvey Haddix and Face combined to subdue the Yankee bats 5-2 in a Pittsburgh victory. Now, remarkably, the Pirates were in the driver's seat. They needed just one more win and they were heading back home, but Game 6 was yet another Yankee blowout, as Ford tossed another shutout in the 12-0 Yankee victory. The Yankees hit no home runs, but they got two triples from Richardson, who drove in his tenth, eleventh, and twelfth runs of the Series, an all-time record.

The Series was now tied at three games apiece. Still, it suffered from an utter lack of tension and excitement. The seventh game changed all that, though. While there had been just one lead change in the first six games combined, Game 7 saw the lead change hands four times. The Pirates led 4-1 until the sixth, when Law was relieved by

BOTTOM: Tony Kubek falls to the ground after being struck in the neck by a bad-hop grounder in Game 7 of the 1960 World Series. With the ball and calling for help is second baseman Bobby Richardson.

Face, who had pitched impressively in relief three times in the Series. This time he failed miserably, giving up a run-scoring single to Mickey Mantle and then a colossal Yogi Berra drive that landed just fair for a three-run homer to give the Yankees the lead. The Yankees scored twice more to increase their lead in the top of the eighth, but the Pirates roared back with five runs in the bottom half, thanks in part to one of the strangest plays in Series history in which a hard but routine grounder by Virdon took a bad hop at the last moment and struck shortstop Tony Kubek viciously in the throat. Kubek dropped to the ground like a stone and began coughing up blood, unable to breathe. (He was rushed to the hospital, but it turned out the injury was not serious.) That freak hit eventually set the stage for Hal Smith, a backup catcher who had entered the game the previous inning. Smith had been one of the Pirates' better hitters that year, and he smashed the ball far over the left field fence for a three-run homer, giving the Pirates a 9-7 lead. But New York rallied for the tying runs in the ninth on hits by Richardson, ex-Pirate Dale Long, and Mantle.

Pittsburgh came up in the bottom of the ninth with the score knotted at nine, but it didn't stay that way for long. The leadoff

TOP LEFT: Bobby Richardson mugs for the cameras after setting a World Series record with six RBI in Game 3 of the 1960 World Series.

TOP RIGHT: Mickey Mantle was not only supremely gifted, but he was a heads-up ballplayer, too. On this play in the eventful ninth inning of Game 7, he saved the Yankees' championship dreams, if only temporarily, by scrambling back to first base on a ball that would ordinarily have been a double play. Pirate first baseman Rocky Nelson (on the ground behind Mantle) attempted the tag, which to the eyes of ump Nestor Chylak was not in time. New York tied the game moments later, little realizing that Bill Mazeroski would untie it in dramatic fashion in the bottom of the inning.

BOTTOM: One of the best relief stoppers of his era, Elroy Face saved 24 games and won ten more for the 1960 Pirates.

1960 WORLD SERIES

Forbes Field (Pittsburgh Pirates) ◆ 10.5.60

	1	2	3	4	5	6	7	8	9	R	H	E
NYY	1	0	0	1	0	0	0	0	2	4	13	2
Pitt.	3	0	0	2	0	1	0	0	X	6	8	0

WP–Law LP–Ditmar S–Face HR: NYY–Maris, Howard; PIT–Mazeroski ATT: 36,676

Forbes Field ◆ 10.6.60

	1	2	3	4	5	6	7	8	9	R	H	E
NYY	0	0	2	1	2	7	3	0	1	16	19	1
Pitt.	0	0	0	1	0	0	0	0	2	3	13	1

WP–Turley LP–Friend HR: NYY–Mantle (2)
ATT: 37,308

Yankee Stadium I (N.Y. Yankees) ◆ 10.8.60

	1	2	3	4	5	6	7	8	9	R	H	E
Pitt.	0	0	0	0	0	0	0	0	0	0	4	0
NYY	6	0	0	4	0	0	0	0	X	10	16	1

WP–Ford LP–Mizell NYY–Richardson, Mantle
ATT: 70,001

Yankee Stadium I ◆ 10.9.60

	1	2	3	4	5	6	7	8	9	R	H	E
Pitt.	0	0	0	0	3	0	0	0	0	3	7	0
NYY	0	0	0	1	0	0	1	0	0	2	8	0

WP–Law LP–Terry S–Face HR: NYY–Skowron
ATT: 67,812

Yankee Stadium I ◆ 10.10.60

	1	2	3	4	5	6	7	8	9	R	H	E
Pitt.	0	3	1	0	0	0	0	0	1	5	10	2
NYY	0	1	1	0	0	0	0	0	0	2	5	2

WP–Haddix LP–Ditmar S–Face HR: NYY–Maris
ATT: 62,753

Forbes Field ◆ 10.12.60

	1	2	3	4	5	6	7	8	9	R	H	E
NYY	0	1	5	0	0	2	2	2	0	12	17	1
Pitt.	0	0	0	0	0	0	0	0	0	0	7	1

WP–Ford LP–Friend ATT: 38,580

Forbes Field ◆ 10.13.60

	1	2	3	4	5	6	7	8	9	R	H	E
NYY	0	0	0	0	1	4	0	2	2	9	13	1
Pitt.	2	2	0	0	0	0	0	5	1	10	11	0

WP–Haddix LP–Terry HR: NYY–Skowron, Berra; PIT–Nelson, Smith, Mazeroski ATT: 36,683

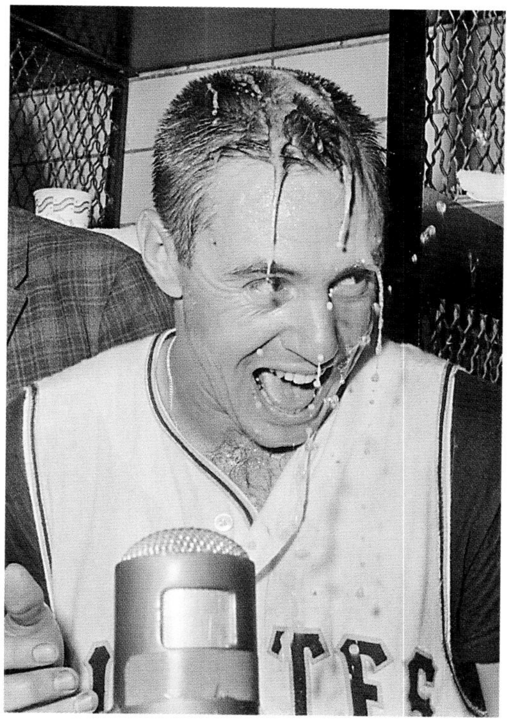

batter, light-hitting second baseman Bill Mazeroski, lifted Ralph Terry's second pitch, a fastball, high into left field. Mazeroski thought the ball might hit the wall for a double as Berra (playing in left field) turned his back and ran after it, but all Berra could do was look up as the ball sailed over the wall. Just like that, the Series was over. Fans, players, and photographers flooded the field. Mazeroski completed his joyous run around the bases while fighting through a jungle of people. Berra would later insist that the ball grazed the ivy on top of the wall as it flew over.

Thus ended one of the most unique World Series ever. Sixty-five new Series records were set, and it was the first World Series ever to end on a home run. The Yankees scored more than twice as many runs as the Pirates, setting new Series team records for most hits, most runs, and highest batting average. "They broke all the records," Pittsburgh's Gino Cimoli said, "But we won the game."

The outcome was bad news for Yankee manager Casey Stengel, who was widely criticized for his decision to bring in reliever Jim Coates in Game 7. Stengel had turned 70 during the season, and the Yankees, who felt he was losing his touch as he aged, unceremoniously fired him after the Series. "I'll never make the mistake of being 70 again," he said.

TOP: A joyful Bill Mazeroski speaks to the press after his Series-winning home run. It was the first time the World Series had ended on a round-tripper.

BOTTOM: Forbes Field erupts in pandemonium as the Pirates win Game 7. Bill Mazeroski, rounding the bases with his victorious home run, can be seen toward the right side of the frame, while Roberto Clemente (#21) waves his arms in joy at home plate.

CHAPTER 4

THE EXPANSION ERA

1961–1975

In 1961, two expansion franchises—the Los Angeles Angels and the Washington Senators—were added to the American League, the first time in the twentieth century that a brand new team was added to either the A.L. or N.L. Six more new teams followed before the decade was out, transforming the face of baseball as never before. In 1957, there were no major league teams on the West Coast. By 1969, a mere dozen years later, there were six.

Of course, the major leagues weren't the only things being expanded in the 1960s and '70s—minds were, too. Appropriately enough, in the signature film of the era—Milos Forman's *One Flew Over the Cuckoo's Nest*, based on the counterculture novel by Ken Kesey—the central conflict revolves around whether patients in a mental hospital will be allowed to watch the 1963 World Series on television. In both book and film, the mental ward serves as a metaphor for oppressive American society, and the rebellious patient Randall P. McMurphy, played by Jack Nicholson, is its liberator. "I'm talking about the *World Series*, Nurse Ratched," McMurphy says. "What's the matter with you, don't you want to watch the World Series?" When his plea fails and the patients are not allowed to watch the game, McMurphy brings a brief moment of joy into their lives when he begins narrating an imaginary game broadcast. "Koufax gets the sign from Roseboro. He kicks once, he pumps, he fires, it's a strike! Koufax's curveball is snapping off like a fucking firecracker!"

As the World Series on television became a staple of American life, the Fall Classic became a stage where a single player could take over a Series and make it his own, in the process cementing his status as a legend of the game. Thanks to their well-timed heroics, World Series stars like Sandy Koufax, Bob Gibson, Brooks Robinson, Roberto Clemente, and Lou Brock all came to enjoy reputations that were somewhat greater than their actual ability as ballplayers.

It made for exciting baseball, too, as the 1961–75 era featured more seven-game World Series—nine—than any other period in baseball history. But even that wasn't enough for baseball executives, who split each league into two divisions in 1969, adding a round of playoffs before the World Series began. It was a transparent attempt to fight off football, which had been encroaching on baseball's popularity for most of the decade. Still, the move was an unqualified success, creating more playoff races and thus more meaningful games in September. The new system also gave hope to fans of mediocre teams like the 1973 New York Mets, who made it to the World Series despite an 82-79 record that was fourth-best in the National League.

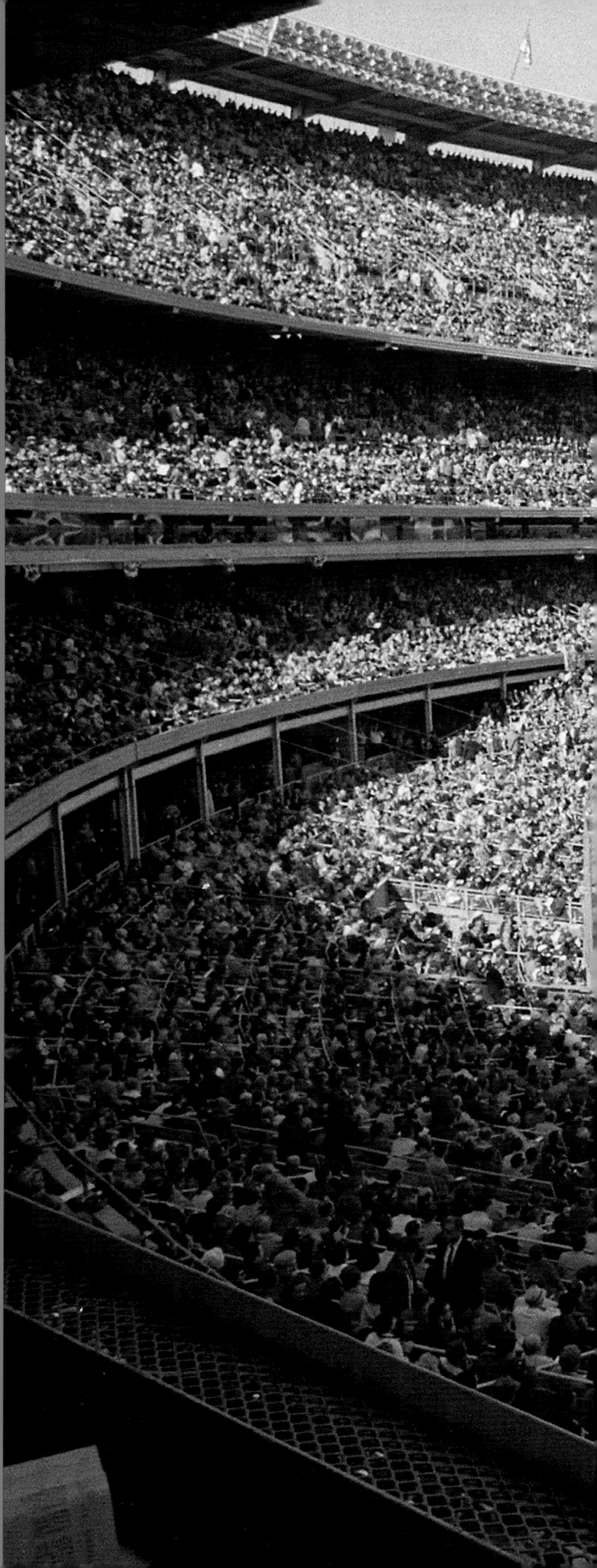

1961

New York Yankees (4)
Cincinnati Reds (1)

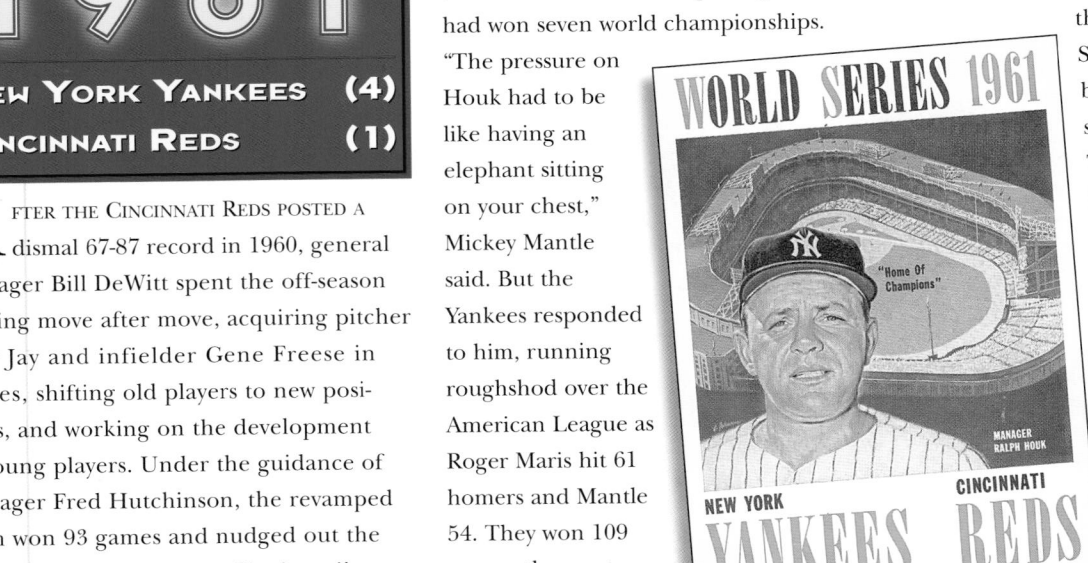

After the Cincinnati Reds posted a dismal 67-87 record in 1960, general manager Bill DeWitt spent the off-season making move after move, acquiring pitcher Joey Jay and infielder Gene Freese in trades, shifting old players to new positions, and working on the development of young players. Under the guidance of manager Fred Hutchinson, the revamped team won 93 games and nudged out the Dodgers for the pennant. Cincinnati's two best players, Frank Robinson and Vada Pinson, each had career years, but the team faced the daunting prospect of playing the New York Yankees in the World Series. "We didn't think we could beat the Yankees, so we just decided to have fun," pitcher Jim Brosnan recalled. "The World Series was a party for us."

PREVIOUS PAGES: Shea Stadium on October 15, 1969, the year of the Miracle Mets. Game 4 of that year's Fall Classic was about to begin; when it was over, the Mets had a commanding 3-1 Series lead over the stunned Baltimore Orioles.

BOTTOM: Elio Chacón scores on Elston Howard's passed ball in Game 2, giving the Reds a 3-2 lead. They eventually won the game 6-2.

Ralph Houk took over Casey Stengel's throne as Yankee manager and, thus, had the unenviable task of replacing a man who had won seven world championships. "The pressure on Houk had to be like having an elephant sitting on your chest," Mickey Mantle said. But the Yankees responded to him, running roughshod over the American League as Roger Maris hit 61 homers and Mantle 54. They won 109 games, the most they'd won since 1927, and the Yankees, as Mantle put it, "went sailing into the World Series like Slim Pickens riding the guided missile in *Dr. Strangelove.*"

The Yanks were prohibitive favorites, but Mickey Mantle was injured for the World Series. He had developed a large abscess on his hip after receiving a bad injection from a quack doctor near the end of the season, and the injury was so bad that he watched most of the Series from the bench with blood from the open wound seeping through his uniform. The Yankees didn't miss him in Game 1 at Yankee Stadium, though, as Whitey Ford tossed a masterful two-hit shutout to beat the Reds, 2-0. But Jay returned the favor the next day, shutting down the Yankees on four hits in a 6-2 Cincinnati victory. The Series was tied 1-1. Many Yankee players emptied out their lockers and apartments as the teams prepared to travel to Cincinnati for the next three games. They had no intention of returning to New York for Games 6 and 7.

Maris homered in the third game, but the Reds managed to keep it close, putting the tying run on second base down 3-2 in the bottom of the ninth. But Yankee reliever Luis Arroyo, who had been dominating all season, nailed the door shut and New York took the Series lead. Game 4 the next day belonged to southpaw Ford, who pitched five shutout innings before leaving with an ankle injury. Those five frames extended his remarkable World Series scoreless streak to thirty-two innings, breaking a 43-year-old record held by Babe Ruth.

By Game 5 the Yankees were weakening physically, even if it didn't show on the field. In addition to Mantle's injury, Yogi Berra sat out with a hurt shoulder, so two part-time players, Johnny Blanchard and Hector Lopez, got the chance to play. Each hit a home run as they collected five hits and seven RBI between them to effectively wrap up the Series for New York. "Two guys had hogged the headlines all year, now some of the others had a chance to shine," Mantle said. The Reds' Jay, who had pitched superbly in Game 2, couldn't even make it out of the first inning of Game 5. "I made more mistakes in one inning than I made at any time all year," he said. The Reds used a record-tying seven relievers to try to stop the Yankee onslaught, but nothing worked, and by the time the game mercifully ended, Cincinnati had been obliterated 13-5. "The

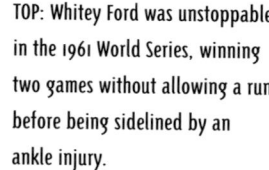

TOP: Whitey Ford was unstoppable in the 1961 World Series, winning two games without allowing a run before being sidelined by an ankle injury.

BOTTOM: Yankee southpaw Luis Arroyo, the best reliever in baseball in 1961, won Game 3 of the World Series behind two innings of shutout relief.

1961 WORLD SERIES

YANKEE STADIUM I (N.Y. YANKEES) ◆ 10.4.61

	1	2	3	4	5	6	7	8	9	R	H	E
Cin.	0	0	0	0	0	0	0	0	0	0	2	0
NYY	0	0	0	1	0	1	0	0	X	2	6	0

WP–Ford LP–O'Toole HR: NYY–Howard, Skowron
ATT: 62,397

YANKEE STADIUM I ◆ 10.5.61

	1	2	3	4	5	6	7	8	9	R	H	E
Cin.	0	0	0	2	1	1	0	2	0	6	9	0
NYY	0	0	0	2	0	0	0	0	0	2	4	3

WP–Jay LP–Terry HR: CIN–Coleman; NYY–Berra
ATT: 63,083

CROSLEY FIELD (CINCINNATI REDS) ◆ 10.7.61

	1	2	3	4	5	6	7	8	9	R	H	E
NYY	0	0	0	0	0	0	1	1	1	3	6	1
Cin.	0	0	1	0	0	0	1	0	0	2	8	0

WP–Arroyo LP–Purkey HR: NYY–Blanchard, Maris
ATT: 32,589

CROSLEY FIELD ◆ 10.8.61

	1	2	3	4	5	6	7	8	9	R	H	E
NYY	0	0	0	1	1	2	3	0	0	7	11	0
Cin.	0	0	0	0	0	0	0	0	0	0	5	1

WP–Ford LP–O'Toole S–Coates ATT: 32,589

CROSLEY FIELD ◆ 10.9.61

	1	2	3	4	5	6	7	8	9	R	H	E
NYY	5	1	0	5	0	2	0	0	0	13	15	1
Cin.	0	0	3	0	2	0	0	0	0	5	11	3

WP–Daley LP–Jay HR: NYY–Blanchard, Lopez; CIN–Robinson, Post ATT: 32,589

Yankees weren't cocky and didn't do anything to show us up," said Reds pitcher Jim O'Toole. "They just went about their business and kicked the shit out of us."

Most of the Yankees declined to return to New York for the victory parade. "There isn't a party in the world that could interest me too much," Maris said. "I have one thing in my mind right now...to be in my own home tonight." Even for Maris, who won his first championship, the one-sided Series failed to generate much excitement. "New York can now yawn and pick up where it left off," wrote Dan Parker in the *New York Mirror*. Score another one for U.S. Steel.

1962

NEW YORK YANKEES (4)
SAN FRANCISCO GIANTS (3)

THE 1962 WORLD SERIES WAS SOMETHING of an anticlimax for the San Francisco Giants. They had endured one of the most hotly contested pennant races in baseball history, playing to a 162-game tie with the Los Angeles Dodgers. Then they won the three-game pennant playoff by coming from behind in the ninth inning of the third game, in the process becoming one of the most unlikely—and exhausted—pennant-winning teams in baseball history. "The way the season ended, and the way the playoffs went, it took away a lot of the excitement of the World Series," pitcher Billy O'Dell said. "You win the pennant, then you have to go out the very next day and play the Yankees," Orlando Cepeda groused.

The Yankees won the first game behind Whitey Ford, but things were not all bad for San Francisco. Willie Mays collected three hits and scored the run that ended Ford's World Series scoreless streak at 33⅔ innings. The next day at Candlestick Park, the Giants' Jack Sanford, pitching with a cold on two days' rest, threw a three-hit shutout, as

BOTTOM: Willie "Stretch" McCovey shows how he got his nickname during Game 5 of the 1962 World Series at Yankee Stadium. Bobby Richardson beat out the play for an infield hit, however, and the Yankees won 5-3.

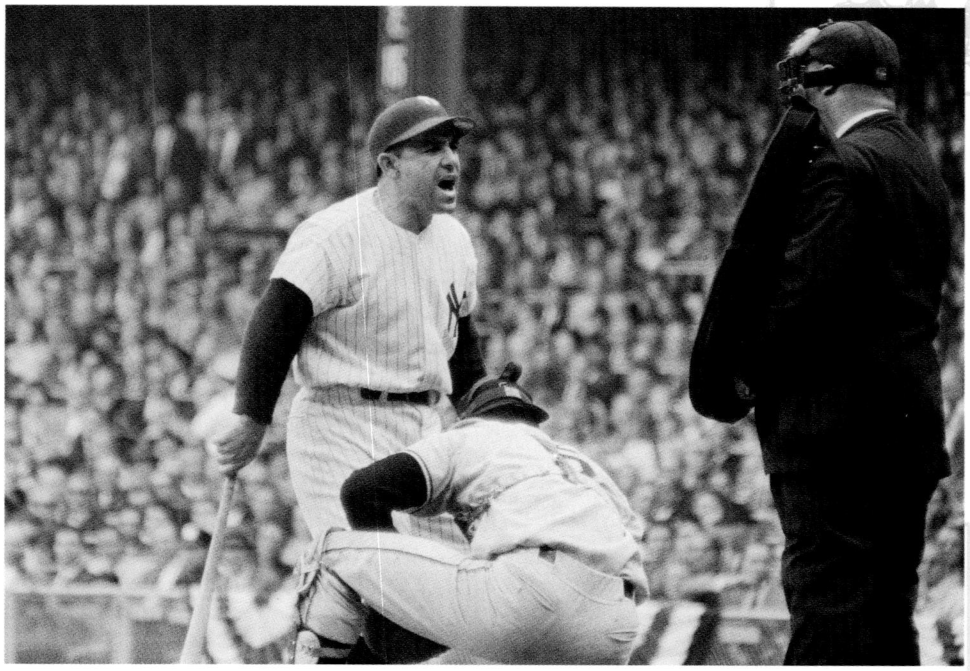

Willie McCovey's titanic homer helped the Giants win 2-0. The Series moved to Yankee Stadium for the third game, where pitching remained the story. Starters Billy Pierce and Bill Stafford dueled to a scoreless tie entering the bottom of the seventh, when the Yankees scored three times in that inning on hits by Mickey Mantle and Roger Maris. The Giants came back with two in the ninth, but Stafford managed to complete the game for a 3-2 Yankee victory.

San Francisco was cruising in Game 4 behind Juan Marichal, who had a 2-0 lead in the fifth inning. But the young pitcher was hit on the hand by a curveball while trying to execute a squeeze bunt and he was sidelined for the rest of the Series. The Yankees scored off two Giants relievers, but San Francisco held out to win 7-3 on a grand slam by Chuck Hiller, the first slam by a National Leaguer in World Series history. The Yankees then won the fifth game on a dramatic eighth-inning homer by Rookie of the Year Tom Tresh.

The teams then returned to San Francisco with New York leading three games to two. But then the weather stepped in. Raging storms on the West Coast killed five people, knocked out power lines, destroyed homes, and delayed the World Series for three days. The postponement favored the Giants, allowing the pitching staff to get some rest after their exhausting pennant race. The field was in deplorable condition when Game 6 was finally played on October 15. It helped the Giants that they had Pierce pitching, as he had a 12-0 lifetime record at Candlestick Park, in part because the groundskeepers heavily watered down the left side of the infield when he pitched, which kept hard-hit grounders from reaching the outfield. With the entire field now soaked, Pierce held the Yankees to three hits, winning 5-2 and handing Ford his first World Series loss since 1958.

Both Ralph Terry and Sanford were brilliant in Game 7, though the Yankees scored a lone run on a double-play grounder. Losing 1-0, the Giants opened the bottom of the ninth with three consecutive bunt attempts. First, Matty Alou bunted for a hit. Then manager Al Dark ordered both Felipe Alou and John Hiller to bunt, but both failed and struck out instead. Mays stepped to the plate with two outs and doubled to right field, and Maris was able to cut off the ball before it reached the wall to hold Alou

TOP: Willie Mays dodges a brushback pitch during the 1962 World Series at Candlestick Park.

CENTER: Yogi Berra argues a called strike two with umpire Jim Honochick during Game 4. Berra eventually walked.

BOTTOM: Ralph Terry is lifted onto the shoulders of his Yankee teammates after pitching a shutout to win Game 7 of the 1962 World Series, 1-0.

at third. Now McCovey, the best left-handed power hitter in the National League, came up to face the right-handed Terry with the Series-winning run on second base. Yankees manager Ralph Houk had the option of either walking McCovey or bringing in a left-hander to face him with first base open. McCovey had homered off Terry earlier in the Series and had tripled off him in his last at bat. But stunningly, Houk allowed Terry—who had given up Bill Mazeroski's series-ending homer two years earlier—to face McCovey. It was one of the worst strategic decisions in World Series history. The Yankees' hearts lurched when McCovey hit a vicious liner that seemed destined to be a Series-ending single. But second baseman Bobby Richardson, playing in exactly the right spot, reached up and flagged it down. The impact nearly caused Richardson to lose his footing, but he held on to the ball, and the World Series was over. "To this day, I won't say he caught the ball," Marichal said. "The ball caught him."

1963

Los Angeles Dodgers (4)
New York Yankees (0)

When Dodger Stadium opened in Los Angeles in 1962, the home team inaugurated it with a style of play perfectly suited to the spacious new park: speed and pitching, and more speed and pitching. Fleet-footed batters like Maury Wills and Willie Davis specialized in "Dodger doubles," hits or walks followed by stolen bases. More often than not they were driven in by Tommy Davis, who won his second straight National League batting title at .326. This kind of one-dimensional offense was good for only a few runs a game, but with the outstanding Dodger pitchers—Sandy Koufax, Don Drysdale, Johnny Podres, and Ron Perranoski—it was usually enough, and they won the pennant by six games.

The New York Yankees, meanwhile, went 104-57, winning the American League pennant with so little effort that Yankee front office personnel even began to hype them as one of the greatest clubs in baseball history. That may have been true during the regular season, but in the four games that counted most, the Yankees played more like the 1963 New York Mets.

The first game was one of the most anticipated pitcher's duels in World Series history. Koufax, with a 25-5 record, and Whitey Ford, at 24-7, were not only the two best left-handers in baseball, but the two best pitchers in baseball, period. Koufax set the tone for the entire Series by striking out the side in the first inning. The Dodgers bashed Ford for four runs in the second inning, including a three-

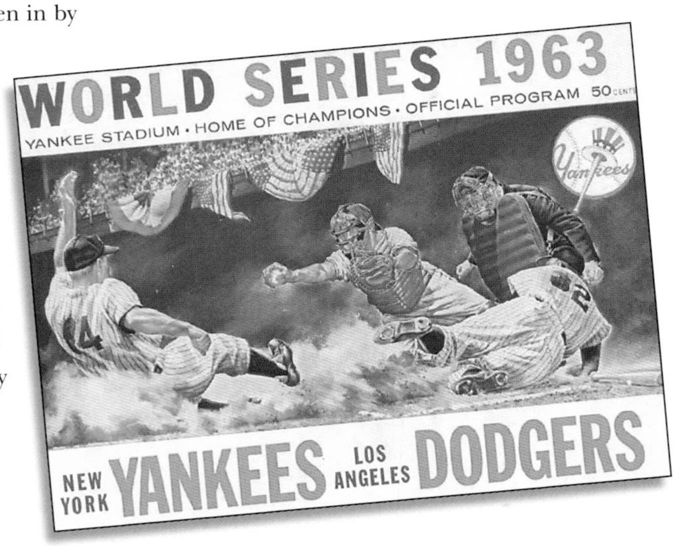
WORLD SERIES 1963
YANKEE STADIUM · HOME OF CHAMPIONS · OFFICIAL PROGRAM 50 CENTS
Yankees
NEW YORK YANKEES
LOS ANGELES DODGERS

BOTTOM: Many students of pitching believe that Sandy Koufax had the perfect pitching motion, as displayed here in Game 4 of the 1963 Series.

1962 WORLD SERIES

Candlestick Park (San Fran. Giants) ◆ 10.4.62

	1	2	3	4	5	6	7	8	9	R	H	E
NYY	2	0	0	0	0	0	1	2	1	6	11	0
S.F.	0	1	1	0	0	0	0	0	0	2	10	0

WP–Ford LP–O'Dell HR: NYY–Boyer ATT: 43,852

Candlestick Park ◆ 10.5.62

	1	2	3	4	5	6	7	8	9	R	H	E
NYY	0	0	0	0	0	0	0	0	0	0	3	1
S.F.	1	0	0	0	0	0	1	0	X	2	6	0

WP–Sanford LP–Terry HR: SFG–McCovey ATT: 32,589

Yankee Stadium I (N.Y. Yankees) ◆ 10.7.62

	1	2	3	4	5	6	7	8	9	R	H	E
S.F.	0	0	0	0	0	0	0	0	2	2	4	3
NYY	0	0	0	0	0	0	3	0	X	3	5	1

WP–Stafford LP–Pierce HR: SFG–Bailey ATT: 71,434

Yankee Stadium I ◆ 10.8.62

	1	2	3	4	5	6	7	8	9	R	H	E
S.F.	0	2	0	0	0	0	4	0	1	7	9	1
NYY	0	0	0	0	0	2	0	0	1	3	9	1

WP–Larsen LP–Coates S–O'Dell HR: SFG–Hiller ATT: 66,607

Yankee Stadium I ◆ 10.10.62

	1	2	3	4	5	6	7	8	9	R	H	E
S.F.	0	0	1	0	1	0	0	0	1	3	8	2
NYY	0	0	0	1	0	1	0	3	X	5	6	0

WP–Terry LP–Sanford HR: SFG–Pagan; NYY–Tresh ATT: 63,165

Candlestick Park ◆ 10.15.62

	1	2	3	4	5	6	7	8	9	R	H	E
NYY	0	0	0	0	1	0	0	1	0	2	3	2
S.F.	0	0	0	3	2	0	0	0	X	5	10	1

WP–Pierce LP–Ford HR: NYY–Maris ATT: 43,948

Candlestick Park ◆ 10.16.62

	1	2	3	4	5	6	7	8	9	R	H	E
NYY	0	0	0	0	1	0	0	0	0	1	7	0
S.F.	0	0	0	0	0	0	0	0	0	0	4	1

WP–Terry LP–Sanford ATT: 43,948

run homer by John Roseboro. After that the only thing in doubt was how many strikeouts Koufax would pile up. In the end Koufax whiffed pinch hitter Harry Bright for his fifteenth K, simultaneously closing out the game and breaking Carl Erskine's ten-year-old World Series strikeout record. Bobby Richardson whiffed three times, more than he had in his twenty-five previous World Series games combined. "I can see how he won twenty-five games," Yogi Berra said of Koufax. "What I don't understand is how he lost five."

Johnny Podres pitched Game 2 at Yankee Stadium, the site of his 1955 series-clinching victory. He retired thirteen consecutive Yankee batters at one point, and Los Angeles scored two runs in the second inning when Roger Maris misplayed a ball in right field. It was academic from that point, as the Dodgers had a 4-1 victory, a two-game head start in the Series, and were now heading home.

Adding injury to insult, the Yankees would be forced to play the rest of the Series without Maris, who had hurt himself running into the outfield wall in Game 2. But it was doubtful that even Maris could have done any damage against Drysdale anyway. Catcher Roseboro said he pitched the best game of his career in Game 3, as Drysdale threw a three-hit shutout, striking out nine. As William Leggett wrote in *Sports Illustrated*, "the Dodgers gave him one cheap, lucky, idio 'c, precious run, and he defended it." That run came in the fourth inning when the Yankees' young pitching star, Jim Bouton, walked Junior Gilliam and wild-pitched him to second. Then Tommy Davis hit a hard grounder that bounced off the pitcher's rubber, ricocheted off second baseman Richardson's shin, and finally landed in the infield dirt as Gilliam scampered across the plate. The Yankees didn't take their whipping silently, complaining frequently to the

TOP: In Game 3, Don Drysdale fires the first World Series pitch ever thrown at Dodger Stadium. It was ball one to Tony Kubek.

BOTTOM: Sandy Koufax exults after the Yankees' Hector López grounds out to end the 1963 World Series. Maury Wills, having just thrown out López at first for the final out, can be seen in the background.

umpire that Drysdale was throwing spitballs. Whatever he was throwing, it worked, and Los Angeles took an insurmountable 3-0 Series lead. Not only that, but it was Koufax's turn to pitch again.

In the fourth game, Ford had, in his estimation, "one of the best games I ever pitched." But it still wasn't good enough to top Koufax, who beat the Yankees 2-1 to complete the Series sweep. The deciding run came in the seventh when third baseman Clete Boyer made a nice leaping stop on a grounder and threw to Joe Pepitone at first, where, as Roger Angell wrote, it "went through the Yankee first baseman as if he had been made of ectoplasm." Pepitone's error put Gilliam on third and he scored on a sacrifice fly. That was all Koufax needed.

The Yankees had not just been beaten; they had been manhandled and embarrassed. They never had a lead in any game of the Series. They batted .171 as a team and scored a total of four runs. Four. In fairness, that was partly due to nagging injuries to Mickey Mantle and Roger Maris, but it was due a good deal more to the excellence of the Dodger pitchers. Things were looking dismal for the Yankee dynasty despite four straight pennants. They had been swept for the first time since 1922. Mantle had batted .167, .120, and .133 in his last three World Series, and Maris had batted .105, .174, and .000 over the same span. Ford, once invincible in the postseason, was now winless in his last four October games. "That's the worst I ever felt after a World Series," Ford later wrote. "The one consolation we had was that if we had to be swept by the Dodgers, at least it happened when they were three thousand miles away."

1963 WORLD SERIES

Yankee Stadium I (N.Y. Yankees) ◆ 10.2.63 (GAME 1)

	1	2	3	4	5	6	7	8	9	R	H	E
L.A.	0	4	1	0	0	0	0	0	0	5	9	0
NYY	0	0	0	0	0	0	0	2	0	2	6	0

WP–Koufax LP–Ford HR: LA–Roseboro; NYY–Tresh (2) ATT: 69,000

Yankee Stadium I ◆ 10.3.63 (GAME 2)

	1	2	3	4	5	6	7	8	9	R	H	E
L.A.	2	0	0	1	0	0	0	1	0	4	10	1
NYY	0	0	0	0	0	0	0	0	1	1	7	0

WP–Podres LP–Downing S–Perranoski HR: LA–Skowron ATT: 66,455

Dodger Stadium (L.A. Dodgers) ◆ 10.5.63 (GAME 3)

	1	2	3	4	5	6	7	8	9	R	H	E
NYY	0	0	0	0	0	0	0	0	0	0	3	0
L.A.	1	0	0	0	0	0	0	0	X	1	4	1

WP–Drysdale LP–Bouton ATT: 55,912

Dodger Stadium ◆ 10.6.63 (GAME 4)

	1	2	3	4	5	6	7	8	9	R	H	E
NYY	0	0	0	0	0	0	1	0	0	1	6	1
L.A.	0	0	0	0	1	0	1	0	X	2	2	1

WP–Koufax LP–Ford HR: NYY–Mantle; LA–F. Howard ATT: 55,912

1964

St. Louis Cardinals (4)
New York Yankees (3)

Meandering along in third place on August 12, 1964, the Yankees called up tall, gangly Mel Stottlemyre from the minor leagues. The 22-year-old rookie proceeded to pitch the Yankees to the pennant, winning an astounding nine games after his recall, as the Yankees outlasted the Chicago White Sox by a single game. Despite their humiliating loss the year before, the Yankees entered the World Series against the St. Louis Cardinals confident that they would bring home the championship. "The Yankees were so blasé, so professional, it was disgusting," reserve infielder Phil Linz said. "There was no display of emotion."

The Series opened in St. Louis with the Cardinals' backup catcher, Bob Uecker, shagging fly balls with a tuba to entertain fans before the game. Whitey Ford, the winningest pitcher in Series history, threw for the Yankees. He was still the team's best pitcher and now its pitching coach, and he made it through five rough innings before leaving in the sixth with what turned out to be a circulatory problem in his arm. "Suddenly I didn't have the strength to grab the ball," Ford later wrote. "My arm lost all of its strength, just like that. I couldn't even throw a warm-up pitch." Ford was done for

BOTTOM: Rookie sensation Mel Stottlemyre throws a pitch in Game 2 of the 1964 World Series, in which he beat the Cardinals 8-3.

TOP: Tim McCarver, the Cardinals' 22-year-old catcher, hits a three-run homer into the right field stands in the tenth inning of Game 5 to give St. Louis the victory.

BOTTOM: St. Louis ace Bob Gibson, an ex-Harlem Globetrotter, pitched two of the Cardinals' four victories in the 1964 World Series.

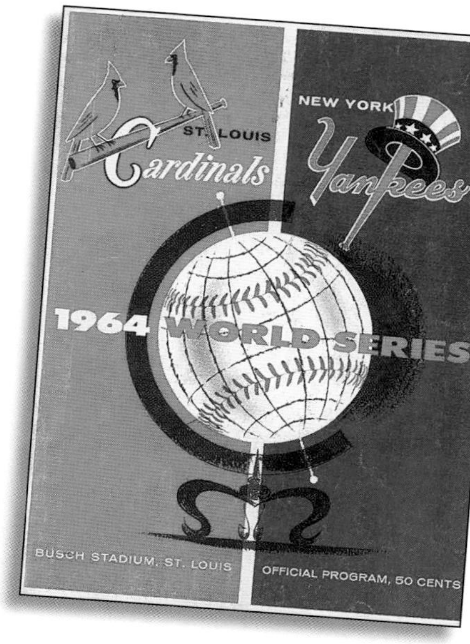

the Series and New York was done for the game, losing 9-5. The second game went to the Yankees, though, as Bob Gibson was outpitched by the rookie Stottlemyre, a lowball specialist who won the game by inducing nineteen ground-ball outs.

The third game was, Elston Howard said, "the most exciting one I've ever seen." For eight innings it was a 1-1 battle between Curt Simmons and the Yankees' Jim Bouton. Bouton's pitching motion was so violent that his cap flew off 38 times according to one writer, 47 times according to another. But Simmons tired in the ninth and was relieved by Barney Schultz, a 38-year-old knuckleballer who had been the Cardinals' top reliever over the last two months of the season. On his first pitch to Mickey Mantle, Schultz threw what he called "a knuckler that didn't knuckle," and Mantle hit it into the third deck to end the game.

BOTTOM: Mickey Mantle was still a formidable hitter in 1964, but his sore legs had made him a defensive liability in the outfield.

The Cardinals won Game 4 on the strength of a Ken Boyer grand slam, which had been set up when New York's Bobby Richardson threw a double-play ball into left field. Game 5 was a rematch between Gibson and Stottlemyre. Gibson, a notoriously quick worker on the mound—"he pitches like he's double-parked," Vin Scully famously said of him—struck out thirteen Yankees and also batted well, starting a two-run Cardinals rally with a single. He led 2-0 and seemed to be in control, but with one out in the bottom of the ninth, Tom Tresh crushed a game-tying homer. St. Louis catcher Tim McCarver untied it in the tenth with a three-run homer and Gibson got the last three outs for a 10-inning victory.

The Yankees roared back in the sixth game. Every starter had at least one hit, and Mantle, Roger Maris, and Joe Pepitone all homered in a one-sided 8-3 decision. That set up a seventh game which would pit Gibson against Stottlemyre for the third time, each pitching on two days' rest. St. Louis struck first with three runs in the fourth inning, one of them coming on a stellar baserunning play. With runners on first and third, Mike Shannon stole second, crashing into Richardson with a take-out slide that enabled McCarver to steal home. Later in the game, both Boyer brothers—the Cardinals' Ken and the Yankees' Clete—homered, as their parents watched from the stands. "When Kenny hit his, he was patted on the back by Clete," Shannon said. "When Clete hit one, Kenny patted him on the back." But the real story of the game turned out to be Gibson, who despite his exhaustion threw a complete game victory, setting a record with 31 total strikeouts in the World Series.

New York had come close to winning, but in the end they could only blame themselves for the loss. The sore-legged Mantle was a defensive liability in center field, and all Series long, the Cardinals took advantage of his limited range and poor throwing by taking extra bases. Richardson, usually a fine defensive second baseman, finished with a Series-record thirteen hits, but his inept defense had helped cost the Yankees the Series. The Cardinals were quick to give credit for winning the Series to Uecker, the backup catcher who had not played in even one game. "If Bob Uecker had not been on the Cardinals, then it's questionable whether we could have beaten the Yankees,"

1964 WORLD SERIES

SPORTSMAN'S PARK IV (ST. LOUIS CARDS) ◆ 10.7.64 (GAME 1)

	1	2	3	4	5	6	7	8	9	R	H	E
NYY	0	3	0	0	1	0	0	1	0	5	12	2
St.L.	1	1	0	0	0	4	0	3	X	9	12	0

WP–Sadecki LP–Ford S–Schultz HR: NYY–Tresh; STL–Shannon ATT: 30,805

SPORTSMAN'S PARK IV ◆ 10.8.64 (GAME 2)

	1	2	3	4	5	6	7	8	9	R	H	E
NYY	0	0	0	1	0	1	2	0	4	8	12	0
St.L.	0	0	1	0	0	0	0	1	1	3	7	0

WP–Stottlemyre LP–Gibson HR: NYY–Linz ATT: 30,805

YANKEE STADIUM I (N.Y. YANKEES) ◆ 10.10.64 (GAME 3)

	1	2	3	4	5	6	7	8	9	R	H	E
St.L.	0	0	0	0	1	0	0	0	0	1	6	0
NYY	0	1	0	0	0	0	0	0	1	2	5	2

WP–Bouton LP–Schultz HR: NYY–Mantle ATT: 67,101

YANKEE STADIUM I ◆ 10.11.64 (GAME 4)

	1	2	3	4	5	6	7	8	9	R	H	E
St.L.	0	0	0	0	0	4	0	0	0	4	6	1
NYY	3	0	0	0	0	0	0	0	1	3	6	1

WP–Craig LP–Downing S–Taylor HR: STL–K. Boyer ATT: 66,312

YANKEE STADIUM I ◆ 10.12.64 (GAME 5)

	1	2	3	4	5	6	7	8	9	10	R	H	E
St.L.	0	0	0	0	2	0	0	0	0	3	5	10	1
NYY	0	0	0	0	0	0	0	0	2	0	2	6	2

WP–Gibson LP–Mikkelsen HR: STL–McCarver; NYY–Tresh ATT: 65,633

SPORTSMAN'S PARK IV ◆ 10.14.64 (GAME 6)

	1	2	3	4	5	6	7	8	9	R	H	E
NYY	0	0	0	0	1	2	0	5	0	8	10	0
St.L.	1	0	0	0	0	0	0	1	1	3	10	1

WP–Bouton LP–Simmons HR: NYY–Maris, Mantle, Pepitone ATT: 30,805

SPORTSMAN'S PARK IV ◆ 10.15.64 (GAME 7)

	1	2	3	4	5	6	7	8	9	R	H	E
NYY	0	0	0	0	0	3	0	0	2	5	9	2
St.L.	0	0	0	3	3	0	1	0	X	7	10	1

WP–Gibson LP–Stottlemyre HR: NYY–Mantle, C. Boyer, Linz; STL–Brock, K. Boyer ATT: 30,346

McCarver said. "He kept everything so funny that we never had the chance to think of what a monumental event we were taking part in."

The biggest surprise of the Series came a few days later when the Yankees fired manager Yogi Berra and replaced him with the manager who had just beaten them, the Cardinals' Johnny Keane. It was the desperate act of a desperate franchise. The Yankees had won five consecutive pennants, but in a league that was a marginal major league. National League teams had accepted integration much sooner than American League ones, and so by 1964, the National League included superstars of color like Willie Mays, Henry Aaron, Frank Robinson, Roberto Clemente, Willie McCovey, Ernie Banks, Juan Marichal, Bob Gibson, Maury Wills, and Tommy Davis—stars of the caliber that were scarcely to be found in the mostly-white American League. With the quality of play far greater in the National League, the early 1960s were hard times for the junior circuit. The Yankees were even being outdrawn at the gate by the New York Mets, the National League's last-place team. As it turned out, Berra would have the last laugh. Keane managed the Yankees straight into last place and the next two New York pennants would be won not by the Yankees, but by the Mets in 1969 and 1973—the latter year under manager Berra.

1965

LOS ANGELES DODGERS (4)
MINNESOTA TWINS (3)

THE LOS ANGELES DODGERS REACHED THE World Series in 1965 thanks to two magnificent pitchers. Don Drysdale went 23-12, while Sandy Koufax had one of the best seasons in baseball history, going 26-8 with 382 strikeouts, a new record. The Los Angeles offense relied on the baserunning skills of Maury Wills, who stole 94 bases despite the physical wear and tear brought on by years of sliding into second base. "His slides tore his skin and beat him up," Johnny Roseboro remembered. "Opposing pitchers threw at his legs, trying to hurt him, scare him, slow him down. They couldn't catch him. They'd soak their infields, but they couldn't stop him. He loved it and lived for it."

The Dodgers' Series opponents were the Minnesota Twins, who were appearing in their first World Series since 1933 when they were known as the Washington Senators. Although they had a history of futility, the Twins were a strong team in 1965. Their power-hitting young shortstop, Zoilo Versalles, won the MVP award, while Tony Oliva won his second consecutive batting title at .321. Although Minnesota was a solid club, the Dodgers were heavily favored to win, and their boastful general manager, Buzzie Bavasi, even went so far as to predict a four-game sweep.

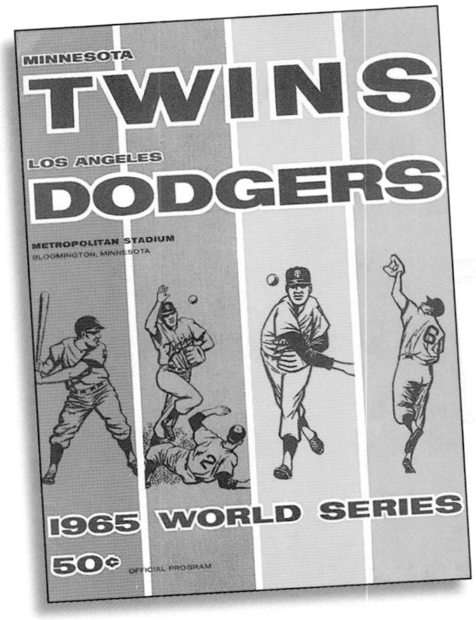

A thirty mph wind blew through Minnesota's Metropolitan Stadium on the opening day of the World Series, which fell on Yom Kippur, the holiest day of the Jewish calendar. Koufax, though he had never been a religious man, declined to pitch so he could observe the holiday. This meant that he could likely pitch only two games in the Series, a potentially fatal blow to the team. Drysdale took the mound instead, opposed by Jim "Mudcat" Grant, a fireballing right-hander who led the American League in wins and shutouts, and who sang in a rock band, The Mudcat and His Kittens, during the off-season. Grant pitched a complete game, and the Twins shocked everyone by pounding Drysdale 8-2. Each team suspected the other's pitcher of throwing spitballs. "I don't know if my guy throws it or not," Twins manager Sam Mele told the press after the game. "But Drysdale was using the spitter. If they can get away with it, what the hell is the difference?"

Game 2 was even worse for the Dodgers, as the Twins beat the previously invincible Koufax by tagging him for two runs in six innings. "I was high with the fastball when I wanted it low," Koufax said after the game. "And when I was trying to get it up, it was down." Twins left-hander Jim Kaat threw a complete game to beat Koufax. "I gained confidence that day," Kaat said, because Koufax "was struggling and seemed human." Things were looking up for Minnesota. Not only had the Twins gained a 2-0 lead, but they had done it against one of the most menacing one-two pitching duos in baseball history.

The unheralded Claude Osteen got the Dodgers back on track when he threw a

TOP: Maury Wills slides home with the Dodgers' first run of Game 5. The lone run was all Sandy Koufax needed, as he pitched a shutout, but the Dodgers scored six more anyway to beat Minnesota 7-0.

BOTTOM: Tony Oliva makes his second outstanding catch of Game 7, running back to snag a fly by the Dodgers' Lou Johnson in the fifth inning.

LA

shutout in Game 3 at Dodger Stadium. And Drysdale bounced back in Game 4 by beating Grant 7-2. Then Koufax came back to the mound for Game 5 and was brilliant. The Dodgers also ran wild on the bases that day, scoring seven runs as Willie Davis stole three sacks to tie a World Series record. "I've never seen a team run like that," said the Twins' flustered catcher, Earl Battey. "The best way to keep them from stealing is to keep them from getting on base in the first place." But the Twins couldn't do that, either, as the Dodgers gathered fourteen hits, including four by Wills and three by Ron Fairly.

The Series returned to the land of many lakes with the Dodgers in the driver's seat. The Twins flooded the infield with sand before Game 6 in an attempt to slow down the Los Angeles running game. It didn't make much of a difference, though, as the fun-loving Grant gave the Dodgers a sound beating, hitting a homer and pitching a complete game to win 5-1.

It was now Drysdale's turn to pitch for the Dodgers, but manager Walter Alston, acting on instinct, picked Koufax to start on two days' rest instead of the well-rested Drysdale. It was a gutsy move, and one that would have drawn much criticism had Koufax lost, but the great left-hander had no intention of losing. The Dodgers scored two runs for Koufax, which was one more than he needed. He pitched a three-hit shutout, striking out ten. The only Twins threat came in the fifth inning, when they placed runners on first and second. Versalles hit a smash down the left field line, but third baseman Jim Gilliam made a diving catch of the ball, turning it into a double play. "I thought we played well," Twins manager Mele said philosophically. "We were beaten by a great pitcher. He's the best I've seen."

1965 WORLD SERIES

Metropolitan Stadium (Minn. Twins) ◆ 10.6.65

	1	2	3	4	5	6	7	8	9	R	H	E
L.A.	0	1	0	0	0	0	0	0	1	2	10	1
Minn.	0	1	6	0	0	1	0	0	X	8	10	0

WP–Grant LP–Drysdale HR: LA–Fairly; MIN–Mincher, Versalles ATT: 47,797

Metropolitan Stadium ◆ 10.7.65

	1	2	3	4	5	6	7	8	9	R	H	E
L.A.	0	0	0	0	0	0	1	0	0	1	7	3
Minn.	0	0	0	0	0	2	1	2	X	5	9	0

WP–Kaat LP–Koufax ATT: 48,700

Dodger Stadium (L.A. Dodgers) ◆ 10.9.65

	1	2	3	4	5	6	7	8	9	R	H	E
Minn.	0	0	0	0	0	0	0	0	0	0	5	0
L.A.	0	0	0	2	1	1	0	0	X	4	10	1

WP–Osteen LP–Pascual ATT: 55,934

Dodger Stadium ◆ 10.10.65

	1	2	3	4	5	6	7	8	9	R	H	E
Minn.	0	0	0	1	0	1	0	0	0	2	5	2
L.A.	1	1	0	1	0	3	0	1	X	7	10	0

WP–Drysdale LP–Grant HR: MIN–Killebrew, Oliva; LA–Parker, Johnson ATT: 55,920

Dodger Stadium ◆ 10.11.65

	1	2	3	4	5	6	7	8	9	R	H	E
Minn.	0	0	0	0	0	0	0	0	0	0	4	1
L.A.	2	0	2	1	0	0	2	0	X	7	14	0

WP–Koufax LP–Kaat ATT: 55,801

Metropolitan Stadium ◆ 10.13.65

	1	2	3	4	5	6	7	8	9	R	H	E
L.A.	0	0	0	0	0	0	1	0	0	1	6	1
Minn.	0	0	0	2	0	3	0	0	X	5	6	1

WP–Grant LP–Osteen HR: LA–Fairly; MIN–Allison, Grant ATT: 38,580

Metropolitan Stadium ◆ 10.14.65

	1	2	3	4	5	6	7	8	9	R	H	E
L.A.	0	0	0	2	0	0	0	0	0	2	7	0
Minn.	0	0	0	0	0	0	0	0	0	0	3	1

WP–Koufax LP–Kaat HR: LA–Johnson ATT: 50,596

1966

Baltimore Orioles (4)
Los Angeles Dodgers (0)

Having just won the American League's triple crown, longtime National Leaguer Frank Robinson was excited to be playing in the World Series with his new team, the Baltimore Orioles. More than anything else, Robinson was looking forward to getting revenge against Don Drysdale, the Dodger pitcher who had been Robinson's biggest nemesis for a decade. Robinson crowded the plate more than any batter in baseball and Drysdale beaned more batters than any other pitcher. With neither man willing to give an inch, many of Drysdale's fastballs ended up plunking Robinson in the ribs, or worse, in the head. "Picking myself up from the dirt—especially those times when I knew he was throwing at me deliberately—really got to me," Robinson said. "It wasn't just that he was knocking me down. It was that he was also getting me out." Before the Series, Robinson, who had spent ten years with the Cincinnati Reds, spent several hours giving his teammates advice on how to hit the Dodger pitchers. Especially Drysdale.

Drysdale pitched the opening game of the World Series because the Dodgers' best pitcher—the unhittable Sandy Koufax—had been forced to pitch the last game of the season as the Dodgers battled for the pennant with the San Francisco Giants. The opener went down the tubes right away for Drysdale, as he gave up back-to-back homers to Frank and Brooks Robinson in the first inning. The real difference in the game, though, was Baltimore's journeyman reliever Moe Drabowsky, who turned in one of the best relief pitching performances in the history of the Fall Classic. Drabowsky walked his first batter after relieving Dave McNally with the bases loaded. That was the last run scored by Los Angeles until spring training 1967. Drabowsky then pitched six-plus innings of scoreless relief, allowing just one hit and striking out eleven as the Orioles won 5-2.

In Game 2 Baltimore's Jim Palmer, a week shy of his 21st birthday, beat the Dodgers 6-0. It was the ninth consecutive game Palmer had won after eating a pregame meal of pancakes, a practice that earned him an endorsement deal with Maryland's Washington Pancakes Company, and he defeated the mighty Koufax, who was pitching his third must-win game in eight days. Koufax pitched a fine game, but he lost for one reason: he had Willie Davis behind him playing center field in the sun. Davis dropped a routine fly ball in the fifth inning when he was blinded by the

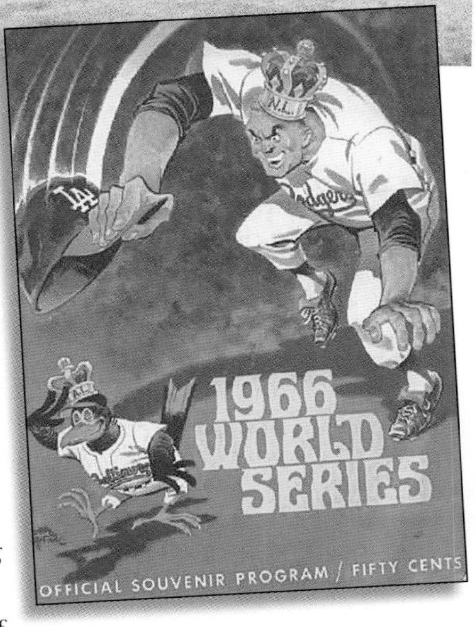

OPPOSITE: L.A. Dodger pitching ace Sandy Koufax turned in dominant postseason performances in 1963 and 1965. In the 1966 Series, Koufax was let down by poor fielding, alas.

TOP: Frank Robinson gained a measure of revenge on his nemesis, Don Drysdale, when he homered in Game 4 of the 1966 Fall Classic, providing the only run in Baltimore's Series-clinching 1-0 victory.

TOP: Moe Drabowsky, the eccentric pitcher who once set Commissioner Bowie Kuhn's shoes on fire, tossed three magnificent innings to win Game 1 of the 1966 World Series for Baltimore.

BOTTOM: Brooks Robinson attempts to set the world high jump record after the Orioles complete their 1966 World Series sweep. Winning pitcher Dave McNally, pictured at center, tossed a four-hit shutout.

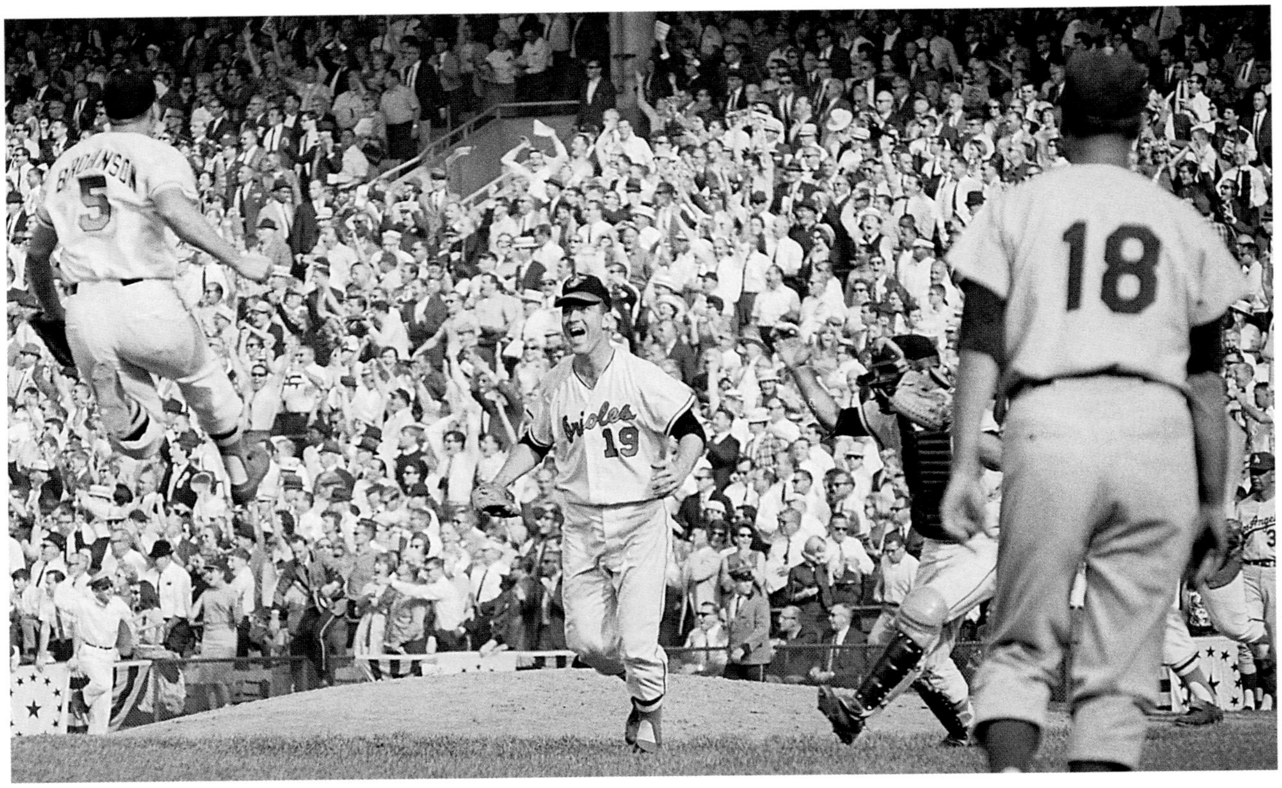

sun. The next batter hit a short fly and Davis jogged in for it. This one, too, dropped at his feet. To make matters worse, Davis threw wildly to third base for his third error of the inning, a new World Series record. "You can't blame a man for the sun, can you?" the usually sure-handed Davis said after the game. "You can't catch what you can't see." Davis' three miscues gave the Orioles their first three runs of the game and they romped to a 6-0 victory thanks to a total of six Dodger errors. Baltimore, it seemed, had won the game by adopting a new take on an old Orioles catch-phrase: "Hit 'em where they are."

Wally Bunker continued the Orioles' domination on the mound in Game 3, shutting out the Dodgers on six hits. After the game, the 21-year-old Bunker sat in front of his desolate locker expecting a horde of reporters who never showed up. "I guess shutting out the Dodgers isn't news anymore," he quipped.

Game 4 presented yet another chance for Frank Robinson to exorcise his personal demons at Drysdale's expense, and the Oriole slugger parked a Drysdale fastball into the left field stands in the fourth inning. That gave Orioles southpaw Dave McNally a 1-0 lead. "Drysdale knew it," Robinson said. "As soon as I connected he dropped his head and kicked the dirt. He didn't even turn around to look at the flight of the ball." Drysdale threw an impressive complete game, using only 78 pitches, but Robinson's homer stood as the only run. Paul Blair preserved McNally's shutout when he robbed Jim Lefebvre of a possible game-tying homer with a fine catch in the eighth inning. Ironically, the outstanding play of the game—indeed, of the entire Series—was made in center field by Davis, who robbed Boog Powell of a home run with a running, leaping catch.

But it was too late for Davis and the Dodgers. Baltimore had swept the World Series in the most convincing manner possible. During the regular season the Orioles had thrown only 23 complete games, four fewer than Koufax threw by himself. But in October they shut out Los Angeles in three straight complete games, a World Series first. No team had ever endured a streak of post-season futility comparable to the Dodgers' thirty-three consecutive scoreless innings. Not even Koufax and Drysdale were good enough to win with that kind of support.

1966 WORLD SERIES

Dodger Stadium (L.A. Dodgers) ◆ 10.5.66 (GAME 1)

	1	2	3	4	5	6	7	8	9	R	H	E
Balt.	3	1	0	1	0	0	0	0	0	5	9	0
L.A.	0	1	1	0	0	0	0	0	0	2	3	0

WP–Drabowsky LP–Drysdale HR: BAL–F. Robinson, B. Robinson; LA–Lefebvre ATT: 55,941

Dodger Stadium ◆ 10.6.66 (GAME 2)

	1	2	3	4	5	6	7	8	9	R	H	E
Balt.	0	0	0	0	3	1	0	2	0	6	8	0
L.A.	0	0	0	0	0	0	0	0	0	0	4	6

WP–Palmer LP–Koufax ATT: 55,947

Memorial Stadium (Balt. Orioles) ◆ 10.8.66 (GAME 3)

	1	2	3	4	5	6	7	8	9	R	H	E
L.A.	0	0	0	0	0	0	0	0	0	0	6	0
Balt.	0	0	0	0	1	0	0	0	X	1	3	0

WP–Bunker LP–Osteen ATT: 54,445

Memorial Stadium ◆ 10.9.66 (GAME 4)

	1	2	3	4	5	6	7	8	9	R	H	E
L.A.	0	0	0	0	0	0	0	0	0	0	4	0
Balt.	0	0	0	1	0	0	0	0	X	1	4	0

WP–McNally LP–Drysdale HR: BAL–F. Robinson ATT: 54,458

1967

St. Louis Cardinals (4)
Boston Red Sox (3)

The Red Sox nosed out Detroit and Minnesota in one of the tightest pennant races in baseball history thanks to the superhuman efforts of a potato farmer's son from Long Island, left fielder Carl Michael Yastrzemski. Yastrzemski batted a sublime .523 (23 for 44) with five homers, fourteen runs scored, and sixteen RBI in Boston's final twelve games. In the last two, must-win games of the season, Yastrzemski went 7-for-8 with five RBI and a three-run homer. The Sox won their first pennant since 1946 by beating the Twins in that final game behind Jim Lonborg, an intellectual but superstitious 22-game winner who always pitched with a paper horseshoe in his pocket. After such a harrowing pennant race, it didn't matter to the Red Sox whether they won or lost the World Series—the impossible dream had already come true. "I don't care about the World Series this year or ten years from now," Yastrzemski said. "There will never be the equal to those last two games with Minnesota."

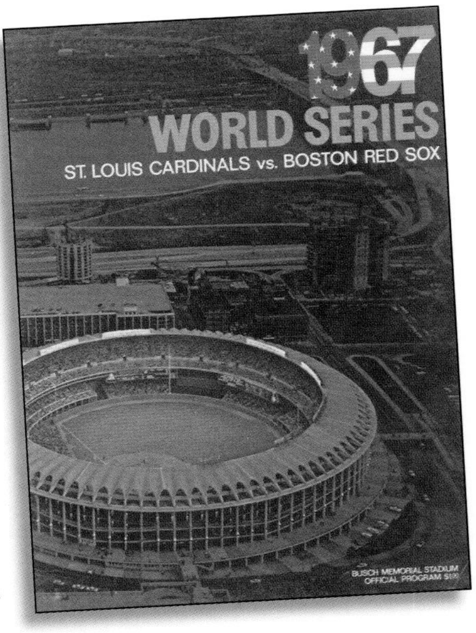

The Red Sox opened the Series against the St. Louis Cardinals at home. The scene at Fenway Park included three hundred policemen and thousands of ticketless fans milling about outside the park. Many wore "Yaz For Governor" buttons and most munched on the corned beef sandwiches and fried clams being hawked by sidewalk vendors. Though riots were predicted, nothing materialized except a group of fans who, unsuccessfully, tried to overpower the security guards and ticket takers to force their way into the game.

One fan who did make it into the game brought a trumpet, playing "Hail to the Chief" whenever Sox manager Dick Williams walked to the pitcher's mound. Bob Gibson was slated to pitch Game 1 for St. Louis. The ace had missed two months late in the season after his leg was broken by a Roberto Clemente line drive, but Gibson, a fierce, confident man, was not intimidated in the least by the unfamiliarity of Fenway Park. "This park is the same as anyplace except for the wall," he said. "You can't change your style of pitching just because of that. You'd be in real trouble."

Yastrzemski contributed two fine defensive plays in the first game, but was held hitless by Gibson, who struck out ten in a 2-1 complete game victory. Lou Brock was the Cardinals' entire offense, collecting a record-tying four hits, stealing two bases, and scoring both runs on grounders by Roger Maris. It was a sign of things to come for Brock, whose baserunning would drive Boston pitchers crazy throughout the Series. "I've never seen a pitcher without

BOTTOM: Carl Yastrzemski, who won the 1967 pennant for Boston nearly single-handedly, tees off in Game 2 of the World Series against the Cardinals.

flaws," he said. "If they know I'm going to run and I know I'm going to run, then I might as well run."

Boston won easily the next day as the two men who had led them to the pennant—Yastrzemski and Lonborg—combined to blow out the Cardinals in Game 2. Yastrzemski hit two homers and drove in four runs, and Lonborg pitched for the first time since his pennant-clinching victory and was magnificent, maintaining a perfect game until the seventh inning and a no-hitter until the eighth. Although immortality escaped him in the end, victory did not, as Lonborg completed the one-hit shutout to send the Series to St. Louis tied at one game apiece.

Lonborg caused a controversy when he admitted afterward that he had purposely thrown at the pesky Brock, and the Cardinals' Nelson Briles plunked Yastrzemski in the first inning of Game 3 in retaliation. The event created a mutual contempt between the two teams that lasted the rest of the Series. Brock, meanwhile, was all over the place. He tripled, got a bunt hit, scored two runs, and ran his team to a 5-2 victory. St. Louis also won Game 4 as Gibson pitched a shutout, but Boston came back in Game 5 when Lonborg outdueled the young Cardinal left-hander, Steve Carlton. The Series returned to Boston with St. Louis needing just one more win to wrap things up.

The Red Sox won the sixth game at Fenway Park, 8-4. Yastrzemski led the way with three hits as eight Cardinals pitchers trudged to the mound. Brock was once again the whole show for St. Louis, as he had two hits, three RBI, and crushed a

TOP: The three Cardinal heroes of Game 7 were (left to right) Lou Brock, Julián Javier, and Bob Gibson.

BOTTOM: Lou Brock set a new World Series record with seven stolen bases in 1967, a feat he repeated a year later.

tremendous home run deep into the center field bleachers. He would end up collecting twelve hits in the Series, including everything from a bunt single to the long home run, and would also steal a Series-record seven bases and score eight runs.

Gibson was the St. Louis starter for Game 7, only the second time all year he had started on three days' rest. The exhausted Gibson kept the Red Sox hitless until the fifth inning, by which time he already led 4-0 thanks in part to his own home run. The nail in Boston's coffin came in the sixth when Julián Javier slammed a Lonborg pitch over the Green Monster to make the score 7-1. It was only a matter of watching Bob Gibson work after that. He finished with a 7-2 victory, a world championship, a record-tying three Series victories, and a new Corvette for being named the World Series MVP. "He's some kind of vicious competitor," catcher Tim McCarver said. "He went the last four innings on guts alone. I know he was tired and I know his elbow was killing him, but I also know that if [manager Red] Schoendienst, or myself, or anybody had tried to take him out, he'd have punched us in the nose."

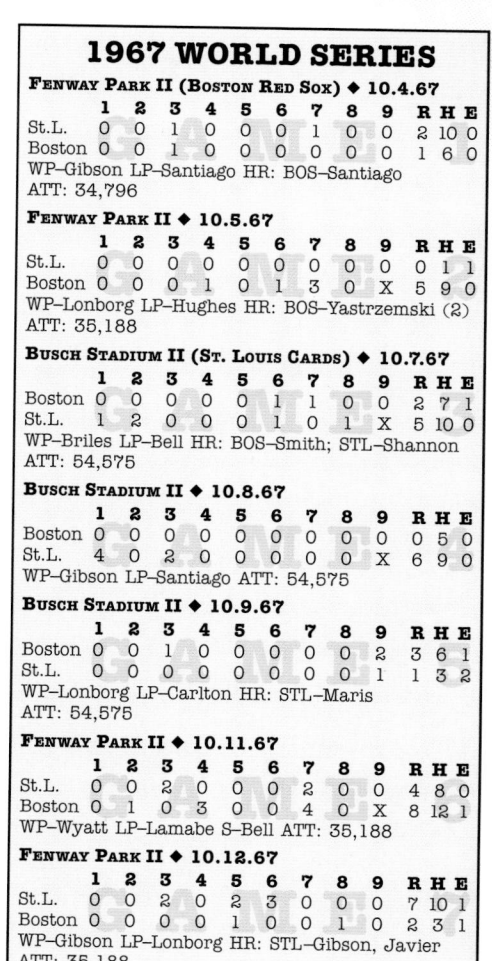

1967 WORLD SERIES

Fenway Park II (Boston Red Sox) ◆ 10.4.67

	1	2	3	4	5	6	7	8	9	R	H	E
St.L.	0	0	1	0	0	0	1	0	0	2	10	0
Boston	0	0	1	0	0	0	0	0	0	1	6	0

WP–Gibson LP–Santiago HR: BOS–Santiago
ATT: 34,796

Fenway Park II ◆ 10.5.67

	1	2	3	4	5	6	7	8	9	R	H	E
St.L.	0	0	0	0	0	0	0	0	0	0	1	1
Boston	0	0	0	1	0	1	3	0	X	5	9	0

WP–Lonborg LP–Hughes HR: BOS–Yastrzemski (2)
ATT: 35,188

Busch Stadium II (St. Louis Cards) ◆ 10.7.67

	1	2	3	4	5	6	7	8	9	R	H	E
Boston	0	0	0	0	0	1	1	0	0	2	7	1
St.L.	1	2	0	0	0	1	0	1	X	5	10	0

WP–Briles LP–Bell HR: BOS–Smith; STL–Shannon
ATT: 54,575

Busch Stadium II ◆ 10.8.67

	1	2	3	4	5	6	7	8	9	R	H	E
Boston	0	0	0	0	0	0	0	0	0	0	5	0
St.L.	4	0	2	0	0	0	0	0	X	6	9	0

WP–Gibson LP–Santiago ATT: 54,575

Busch Stadium II ◆ 10.9.67

	1	2	3	4	5	6	7	8	9	R	H	E
Boston	0	0	1	0	0	0	0	0	2	3	6	1
St.L.	0	0	0	0	0	0	0	0	1	1	3	2

WP–Lonborg LP–Carlton HR: STL–Maris
ATT: 54,575

Fenway Park II ◆ 10.11.67

	1	2	3	4	5	6	7	8	9	R	H	E
St.L.	0	0	2	0	0	0	2	0	0	4	8	0
Boston	0	1	0	3	0	0	4	0	X	8	12	1

WP–Wyatt LP–Lamabe S–Bell ATT: 35,188

Fenway Park II ◆ 10.12.67

	1	2	3	4	5	6	7	8	9	R	H	E
St.L.	0	0	2	0	2	3	0	0	0	7	10	1
Boston	0	0	0	0	1	0	0	1	0	2	3	1

WP–Gibson LP–Lonborg HR: STL–Gibson, Javier
ATT: 35,188

1968

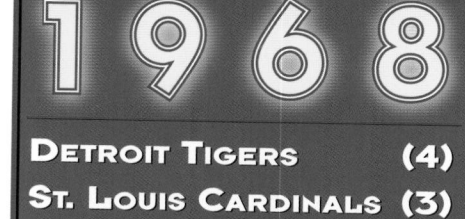

Detroit Tigers (4)
St. Louis Cardinals (3)

Everyone expected the 1968 World Series to feature one of the greatest pitching matchups of all time: Denny McLain against Bob Gibson. With a large strike zone, a tall pitcher's mound, and ever-bigger ballparks, pitchers' dominance reached a fifty-year peak in 1968. American League batters hit .230 collectively, and only one, Carl Yastrzemski, managed to top .300. In this "Year of the Pitcher," Gibson and McLain were baseball's two best pitchers, and each led his team to the pennant. McLain, a free-spirited right-hander who moonlighted as an organ player and amateur pilot, won 31 games for the Detroit Tigers with his outstanding fastball and unhittable curve. Gibson, the militant fireballer, was even better, posting a 1.12 ERA that was the lowest in baseball since 1914 and the fourth-lowest of all time. Although both men performed admirably in the World Series, in the end the spotlight was stolen by a pot-bellied left-hander who looked more at home on a sofa than on a pitcher's mound.

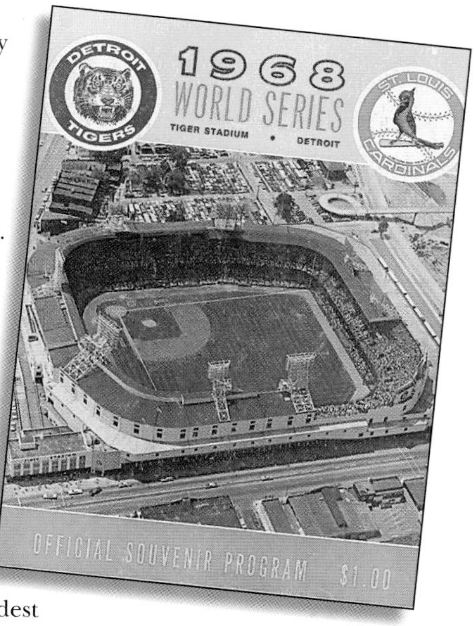

The most important strategic move of the Series came before the first pitch was even thrown. The three Tiger shortstops—Ray Oyler, Tom Matchick, and Dick Tracewski—had hit a combined .165 during the regular season, so manager Mayo Smith enacted probably the boldest World Series experiment since Connie Mack started Howard Ehmke in 1929. Smith moved Mitchell "Mickey" Stanley, his regular center fielder, to shortstop, although Stanley had never played the position before. That allowed him to play Al Kaline, a heavy hitter who would otherwise have sat on the bench, in right field. The move was a stupendous success, as Stanley handled 31 of 33 chances safely, and Kaline batted .379 in the Series and led all players with two homers and eight RBI.

BOTTOM: Mickey Lolich, who played second fiddle to Denny McLain all year, walked away with three wins in the 1968 World Series.

TOP: Tigers pitcher Mickey Lolich yelps as he is doused with champagne following his Game 7 win against the Cardinals. It was his third victory in the 1968 World Series.

BOTTOM: As this scoreboard unequivocally shows, an explosive third inning for the Tigers turned Game 6 into a 12-0 laugher before the game had really begun. When it was over, the Tigers were 13-1 winners.

Gibson lived up to his billing in Game 1, breaking Sandy Koufax's five-year-old Series record by striking out seventeen Tigers as St. Louis won easily, 4-0. The second game belonged to pudgy Detroit southpaw Mickey Lolich, an amateur sailor, scuba diver, archer, target shooter, and National Guard soldier who usually drove one of his five motorcycles to Tiger Stadium. Lolich pitched a complete game 8-1 victory and also hit the first home run of his professional career to tie the Series at one game apiece.

Lou Brock's legs won Game 3. The Cardinal speedster had three hits and stole three bases. Orlando Cepeda contributed a three-run homer as St. Louis won, 7-3. The Cards also captured the next game as Gibson outdueled McLain, striking out ten batters in nine innings.

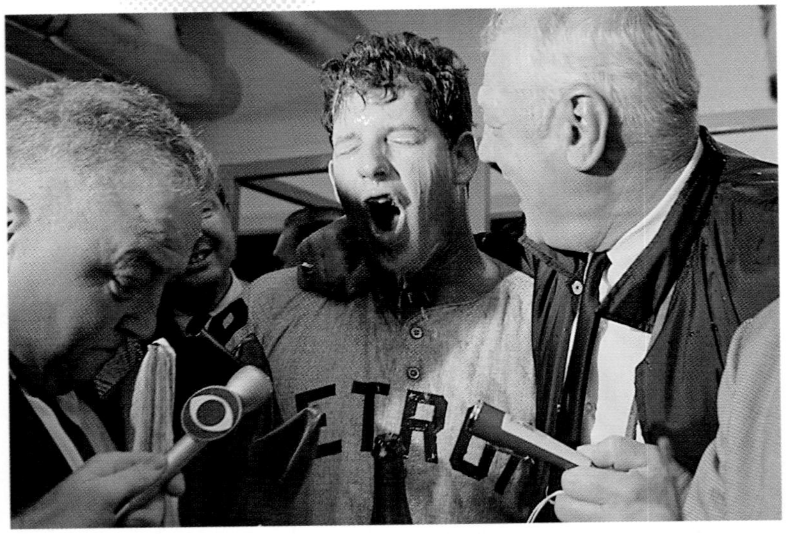

The fifth game in Detroit was preceded by the biggest controversy of the Series, although it had little to do with baseball. At the height of the Vietnam War and the anti-war movement, many fans were disturbed by the version of "The Star-Spangled Banner" sung by blind Puerto Rican folk-rocker José Feliciano. Although Feliciano's version of the anthem was a blues interpretation—the most American of all music styles—thousands of angry television viewers flooded the Tiger Stadium telephone switchboards with complaints about his "anti-American" "desecration" of the song. "I love this country very much," the bewildered Feliciano said. "America is young now, and I thought maybe the anthem could be revived."

On the playing field, the Cardinals were on the verge of a five-game World Series victory. It looked likely to happen as St. Louis led 3-2 in the fifth inning of Game 5, but in that inning, Brock inexplicably tried to score standing up on a single by Julián Javier. He was tagged out by catcher Bill Freehan, but likely would have scored had he chosen to slide. The blunder negated a run that might have forced the Tigers to pinch hit for Mickey Lolich. As it was, the big lefty stayed in, and after a Tiger rally, became the winning pitcher in a 5-3 decision. Detroit won Game 6, too, as Denny McLain pitched a fine game and was spurred to victory by the Tigers' ten-run third inning—an inning highlighted by a grand slam by Jim Northrup.

Bob Gibson started Game 7 for the Cardinals while Detroit pitched Mickey Lolich on two days' rest. The exhausted Lolich matched zeroes with Gibson for six innings. "Usually my fastball sinks three or four inches, not much," Lolich said later. "When I got tired against the Cardinals, the ball sank more than ever, maybe eight inches." He helped his own cause tremendously when, with the game still scoreless in the sixth, he picked off both Brock and Curt Flood, the Cardinals' two best base runners. The game-breaking play came in the next inning, when Detroit's Northrup hit a ball to deep center field. Flood first misjudged it, then slipped on the wet grass as the ball flew over his head for a two-run triple. Lolich and the Tigers were on their way to victory. "I screwed it up," Flood would say after the game. "I don't want to make any alibis about it." The Tigers won 4-1, sweeping the last three games to capture the Series. Gibson's record streak of seven consecutive wins in the World Series was over.

The Cardinals had much to be proud of, though. Brock set or tied records for most hits and stolen bases in a single Series and for most steals in a Series career. Gibson, despite his Game 7 loss, had pitched magnificently. But it was Lolich's Series. The burly southpaw, whose seventeen regular season victories had been overshadowed by McLain, added three more in the World Series to make it an even twenty. He became the new hero of Tigers fans, who went crazy celebrating the franchise's first championship team in a generation. An estimated 35,000 fans packed the Detroit airport to greet the champions returning from St. Louis, forcing the closure of the airport and the cancellation of nineteen flights. About 150,000 more took to the streets, looting stores and throwing ticker tape in the wildest celebration anyone had seen since the end of World War II. Said one policeman, "I hope Detroit never wins another World Series."

1968 WORLD SERIES

Busch Stadium II (St. Louis Cards) ◆ 10.2.68

	1	2	3	4	5	6	7	8	9	R	H	E
Det.	0	0	0	0	0	0	0	0	0	0	5	3
St.L.	0	0	0	3	0	0	1	0	X	4	6	0

WP–Gibson LP–McLain HR: STL–Brock ATT: 54,692

Busch Stadium II ◆ 10.3.68

	1	2	3	4	5	6	7	8	9	R	H	E
Det.	0	1	1	0	0	3	1	0	2	8	13	1
St.L.	0	0	0	0	0	1	0	0	0	1	6	1

WP–Lolich LP–Briles HR: DET–Horton, Lolich, Cash ATT: 54,692

Tiger Stadium (Detroit Tigers) ◆ 10.5.68

	1	2	3	4	5	6	7	8	9	R	H	E
St.L.	0	0	0	0	4	0	3	0	0	7	13	0
Det.	0	0	2	0	1	0	0	0	0	3	4	0

WP–Washburn LP–Wilson S–Hoerner
HR: STL–McCarver, Cepeda; DET–Kaline, McAuliffe
ATT: 53,634

Tiger Stadium ◆ 10.6.68

	1	2	3	4	5	6	7	8	9	R	H	E
St.L.	2	0	2	2	0	0	0	4	0	10	13	0
Det.	0	0	0	1	0	0	0	0	0	1	5	4

WP–Gibson LP–McLain HR: STL–Brock, Gibson; DET–Northrup ATT: 53,634

Tiger Stadium ◆ 10.7.68

	1	2	3	4	5	6	7	8	9	R	H	E
St.L.	3	0	0	0	0	0	0	0	0	3	9	0
Det.	0	0	0	2	0	0	3	0	X	5	9	1

WP–Lolich LP–Hoerner HR: STL–Cepeda
ATT: 54,634

Busch Stadium II ◆ 10.9.68

	1	2	3	4	5	6	7	8	9	R	H	E
Det.	0	2	10	0	1	0	0	0	0	13	12	1
St.L.	0	0	0	0	0	0	0	0	1	1	9	1

WP–McLain LP–Washburn HR: DET–Northrup, Kaline ATT: 54,692

Busch Stadium II ◆ 10.10.68

	1	2	3	4	5	6	7	8	9	R	H	E
Det.	0	0	0	0	0	0	3	0	1	4	8	1
St.L.	0	0	0	0	0	0	0	0	1	1	5	0

WP–Lolich LP–Gibson HR: STL–Shannon
ATT: 54,692

1969

New York Mets (4)
Baltimore Orioles (1)

Men walked on the moon for the first time on July 20, 1969. On October 16, 1969, something even more bizarre happened: The New York Mets won the World Series. The Mets had finished no higher than ninth place since the franchise started in 1962. They came alive in 1969 with outstanding young pitchers like Tom Seaver and Jerry Koosman leading the way. New Yorkers, always supportive of the Mets, flocked to see their team in even greater numbers, bringing with them hundreds of witty banners and signs, the peculiar Shea Stadium art form that later spread to other major league ballparks. The team was beautifully managed by ex-Brooklyn hero Gil Hodges, whose platooning and juggling of the lineup seemed to make the team greater than the sum of its parts. On August 15 the Mets were in third place and ten games out of first. But they went 38-11 after that, beat Atlanta in the first-ever National League Championship Series, and became one of the most unlikely teams ever to reach the World Series. Despite winning 100 games, usually the mark of greatness for a baseball team, the Mets were still heavy underdogs to the Baltimore Orioles, who went 109-53, two wins shy of the American League record.

Don Buford's leadoff homer in Game 1 looked as if it would put Baltimore on the fast track to a Series victory. The Orioles did win the game 4-1 behind the pitching of Mike Cuéllar, but it turned out to be their last win of the decade. After Buford's homer, Orioles leadoff batters reached base in just one of the next 26 innings, stymied by outstanding New York pitching. New York tied the Series in Game 2 as ex-law student Donn Clendenon homered in the fourth inning, and the Mets scored the winning run in the ninth inning on a rally started by third baseman and sometime poet Ed Charles. (The Mets were one of the most intellectual teams in baseball; 22 of their 27 players had been to college.)

With the Series tied 1-1, Game 3 turned the tide in the Mets' favor, as Tommie Agee had what *Sports Illustrated* called "probably the most spectacular World Series game that any centerfielder has ever enjoyed." Agee, who had been benched earlier in the year while struggling at the plate, hit a home run in the game. But it was on defense that he really shone, making a long run and a backhanded catch of an Elrod Hendricks drive with two runners on in the fourth inning. Three innings later, with the bases loaded, he made an even better catch, sprinting and diving to catch Paul Blair's potential triple in the right-center field gap. They were great catches, to be sure, but they were most important for their timing—they saved as many as five runs, and the Mets won the game 5-0. The pitching hero for New York was erratic 22-year-old Nolan Ryan, who entered the game with the bases loaded in the seventh and, after throwing one of his warm-up pitches to the backstop, worked his way out of the jam.

Ron Swoboda tried to repeat Agee's heroics of Game 3 in the fourth game. It was the ninth inning and Seaver was pitching a

BOTTOM LEFT: Jerry Koosman hurls a pitch in the Mets' clinching Game 5 victory.

BOTTOM RIGHT: Tommie Agee batted only .167 in the 1969 World Series, but his spectacular defense helped win the Series for the Mets.

1-0 shutout. The Orioles were threatening with a runner on third. Brooks Robinson then hit a low line drive to right-center field that looked as if it would tie the game, but the normally shaky Swoboda managed to catch the ball. Frank Robinson tagged and scored to tie the game, but Swoboda's catch had prevented Baltimore from taking the lead. "I made a catch like that once before, in high school," Swoboda said later. "A crowd of fifteen people went out of their minds." The Mets scored the winning run in the tenth when Baltimore pitcher Pete Richert fielded J.C. Martin's bunt and hit the base runner with his throw to first. Photographs later showed that Martin had been illegally running inside the baseline, but it was too late. The Mets had captured the game, 2-1.

New York hoped to wrap things up in Game 5 so a return trip to Baltimore would be unnecessary. The Orioles didn't go down easily, though, taking the early lead on homers by Frank Robinson and pitcher Dave McNally. The Mets, appropriately enough, began their winning rally in the sixth inning on the most bizarre play of the Series. New York was trailing 3-0 when a low pitch to Cleon Jones was called a ball. Jones and manager Hodges insisted the ball had hit Jones in the foot. Hodges knew that twelve years earlier the Braves had won a World Series game when Nippy Jones was able to prove he had been hit by pointing to a shoe polish stain on the baseball. So Hodges

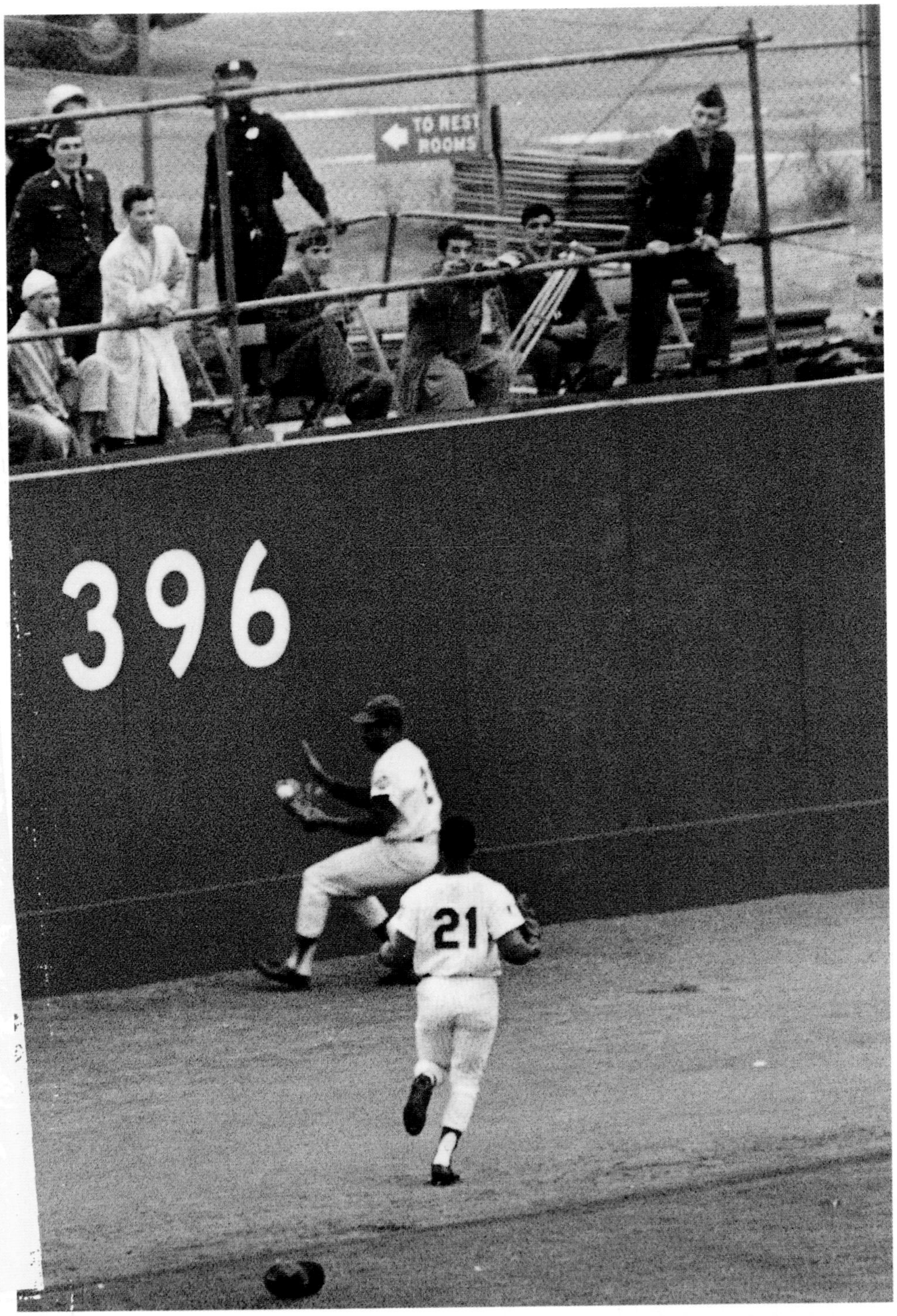

TOP AND BOTTOM: Tommie Agee made two spectacular catches in Game 3 of the 1969 World Series. At top, he snares an Elrod Hendricks drive with two men on base in the fourth inning. Below, the sequence of photographs shows his diving catch of a potential Paul Blair hit with the bases loaded in the seventh.

retrieved the ball, showed it to the umpire, and Cleon Jones trotted to first base. In a fortuitous circumstance that could only happen to the 1969 Mets, the next batter, Clendenon, homered to make the score 3-2. That was still the score when utility infielder Al Weis stepped to the plate in the seventh inning. Weis had never hit a home run in his home ballpark in his eight-year career, but this time he hit one out to tie the game. The Mets took the lead in the next inning on hits by Jones and Swoboda. One of the more improbable World Series contests of all time ended with a 5-3 New York win. As Jones caught a fly ball for the final out, thousands of enthusiastic fans stormed the field, uprooting bases and chunks of sod as souvenirs. Most liquor stores in New York sold out their entire inventories of champagne within ten minutes of the last out.

The Mets' victory gave hope to underdogs everywhere. As William Leggett noted in *Sports Illustrated*, "no world championship will ever be the same again." Although the Mets had been underdogs, they won their title legitimately with superb pitching and defense. The outcomes of previous World Series, especially those of 1912 and 1918, had been determined by defense, but the Mets probably did more to win with their gloves than any championship team ever. In addition to the crucial and spectacular plays by Agee and Swoboda, Jones and shortstop Bud Harrelson turned in top-notch defense throughout the Series.

1969 WORLD SERIES

Memorial Stadium (Balt. Orioles) ◆ 10.11.69

	1	2	3	4	5	6	7	8	9	R	H	E
NYM	0	0	0	0	0	0	1	0	0	1	6	1
Balt.	1	0	0	3	0	0	0	0	X	4	6	0

WP–Cuellar LP–Seaver HR: BAL–Buford
ATT: 50,429

Memorial Stadium ◆ 10.12.69

	1	2	3	4	5	6	7	8	9	R	H	E
NYM	0	0	0	1	0	0	0	0	1	2	6	0
Balt.	0	0	0	0	0	0	1	0	0	1	2	0

WP–Koosman LP–McNally S–Taylor
HR: NYM–Clendenon ATT: 50,850

Shea Stadium (New York Mets) ◆ 10.14.69

	1	2	3	4	5	6	7	8	9	R	H	E
Balt.	0	0	0	0	0	0	0	0	0	0	4	1
NYM	1	2	0	0	0	1	0	1	X	5	6	0

WP–Gentry LP–Palmer S–Ryan HR: NYM–Agee, Kranepool ATT: 56,335

Shea Stadium ◆ 10.5.69

	1	2	3	4	5	6	7	8	9	10	R	H	E
Balt.	0	0	0	0	0	0	0	0	1	0	1	6	1
NYM	0	1	0	0	0	0	0	0	0	1	2	10	1

WP–Seaver LP–Hall HR: NYM–Clendenon
ATT: 57,367

Shea Stadium ◆ 10.16.69

	1	2	3	4	5	6	7	8	9	R	H	E
Balt.	0	0	3	0	0	0	0	0	0	3	5	2
NYM	0	0	0	0	0	2	1	2	X	5	7	0

WP–Koosman LP–Watt HR: BAL–McNally, F. Robinson; NYM–Clendenon, Weis ATT: 57,397

Jerry Koosman summed up the feeling in the clubhouse after Game 5: "God, it's great to be young and a Met." Ted Williams, watching the Series, said the Mets had a good chance to become a National League dynasty. As it turned out, the magic didn't last. The Mets would finish a mere third in their division for the next three years. But for one amazing season, everything went right. "Nothing else will ever be as good as this," Swoboda said. "The only thing left for us to do is to go to the moon."

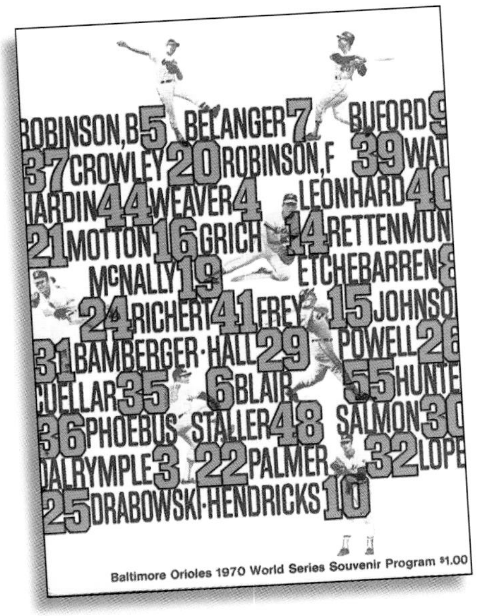

Baltimore Orioles 1970 World Series Souvenir Program $1.00

1970

Baltimore Orioles (4)
Cincinnati Reds (1)

The year 1970 was one of turbulence and change for both the United States and for baseball. The season saw two of the most important off-the-field milestones in the game's history: Jim Bouton published the first serious, uncensored sports book in *Ball Four*, and Curt Flood initiated the downfall of baseball's hated—and illegal—reserve system when he sued baseball after refusing to accept a trade from the Cardinals to the Phillies. Fans looked to the World Series, where two utterly dominant teams prepared to face off, as a way to escape from the harsh world of scandal and litigation.

The Baltimore Orioles outplayed their nearest American League rival by ten games. The Cincinnati Reds had thirteen more wins than the next-best National League team. But the Reds had slumped late in the season, had a weary pitching staff, and as Jim Murray wrote, they came into the Series "like a

BOTTOM: Brooks Robinson made the 1970 World Series his personal showcase, putting on a defensive show that many fans would remember for the rest of their lives.

punched-out fighter." If they weren't already knocked out, Baltimore's Brooks Robinson delivered the final blows. Robinson had perhaps the best World Series ever enjoyed by a position player—a Series so remarkable, so stupendous, that it left the Reds grasping at straws, fans grasping for superlatives, and writers grasping for metaphors. Robinson was the Friendly Ghost, said a *Sports Illustrated* headline writer, because he "made the Reds disappear."

Things started well for the Reds, as they took a 3-0 lead early in the first game, but the Orioles tied it on homers by Boog Powell and Elrod Hendricks. Then Robinson took over the game. He first made an astounding backhanded play on Lee May's leadoff grounder in the sixth inning. This became an important play when the Reds rallied later in the inning. Bernie Carbo tried to score on a chopper in front of the plate, and Carbo, catcher Elrod Hendricks, and umpire Ken Burkhart—who was woefully out of position—all converged on home plate at the same time. As writer Roger Angell noted, replays showed that all three men failed in their mission: Hendricks missed the tag, Carbo missed the plate, and Burkhart missed the call, flashing the out sign after scrambling to get out of the way of the two players. The play turned out to be vital, as Robinson's homer in the next inning proved to be the winning margin in a 4-3 Baltimore victory. The next game was much the same. The Reds took an early lead

TOP: Despite collecting two homers and four RBI during the Series, Frank Robinson was only the second-best player in the 1970 Fall Classic with that last name.

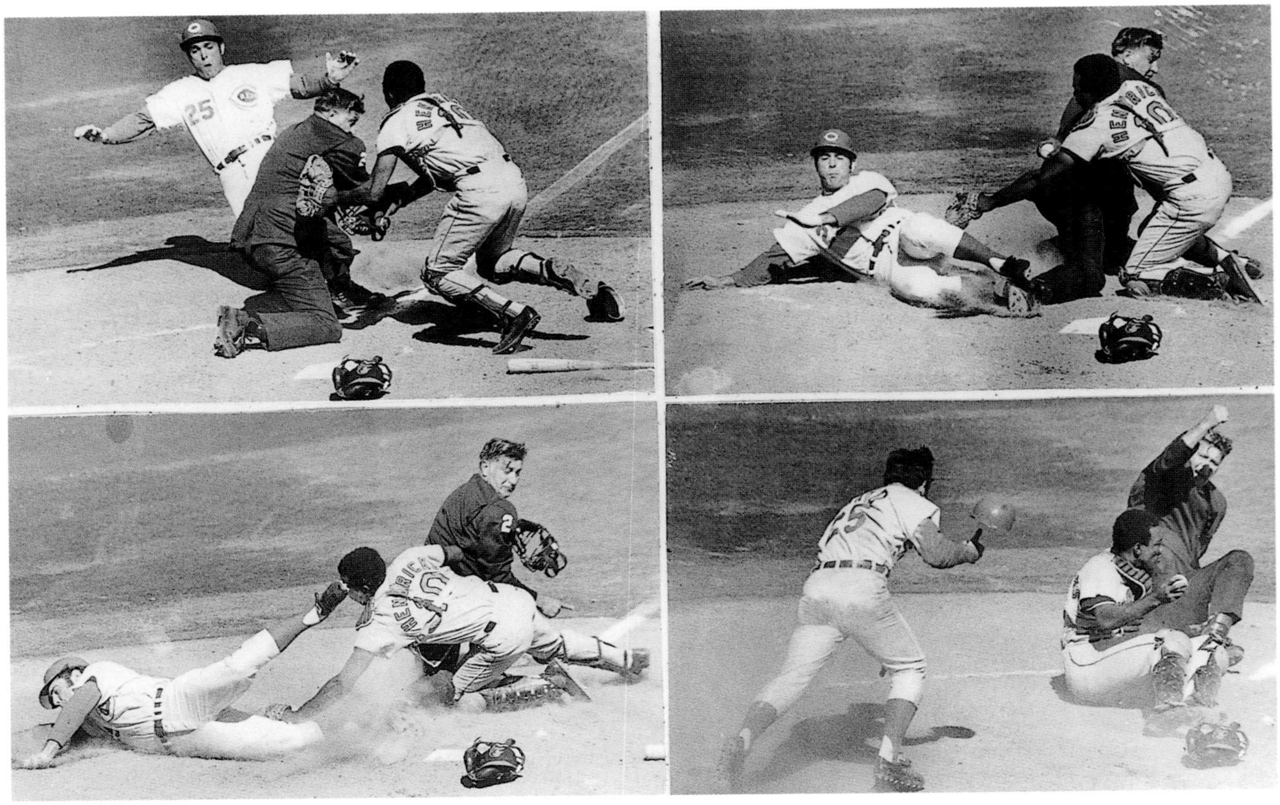

BOTTOM: In this most confusing of plays, Elrod Hendricks tags Bernie Carbo with an empty mitt as umpire Ken Burkhart gets in the way. Hendricks missed the tag, Carbo missed the plate, and Burkhart missed the call, raising his hand with an out signal.

1970 WORLD SERIES

Riverfront Stadium (Cinc. Reds) ◆ 10.10.70 (GAME 1)

	1	2	3	4	5	6	7	8	9	R	H	E
Balt.	0	0	0	2	1	0	1	0	0	4	7	2
Cin.	1	0	2	0	0	0	0	0	0	3	5	0

WP–Palmer LP–Nolan S–Richert HR: BAL–Powell, Hendricks, B. Robinson; CIN–May ATT: 51,531

Riverfront Stadium ◆ 10.11.70 (GAME 2)

	1	2	3	4	5	6	7	8	9	R	H	E
Balt.	0	0	0	1	5	0	0	0	0	6	10	2
Cin.	3	0	1	0	0	1	0	0	0	5	7	0

WP–Phoebus LP–Wilcox S–Hall HR: BAL–Powell; CIN–Tolan, Bench ATT: 51,531

Memorial Stadium (Balt. Orioles) ◆ 10.13.70 (GAME 3)

	1	2	3	4	5	6	7	8	9	R	H	E
Cin.	0	1	0	0	0	0	2	0	0	3	9	0
Balt.	2	0	1	0	1	4	1	0	X	9	10	1

WP–McNally LP–Cloninger HR: BAL–F. Robinson, Buford, McNally ATT: 51,733

Memorial Stadium ◆ 10.14.70 (GAME 4)

	1	2	3	4	5	6	7	8	9	R	H	E
Cin.	0	1	1	0	1	0	0	3	0	6	8	3
Balt.	0	1	3	0	0	1	0	0	0	5	8	0

WP–Carroll LP–Watt HR: CIN–Rose, May BAL–B. Robinson ATT: 53,007

Memorial Stadium ◆ 10.15.70 (GAME 5)

	1	2	3	4	5	6	7	8	9	R	H	E
Cin.	3	0	0	0	0	0	0	0	0	3	6	0
Balt.	2	2	2	0	1	0	0	2	X	9	15	0

WP–Cuellar LP–Merritt HR: BAL–F. Robinson, Rettenmund ATT: 45,341 but Baltimore took it right back on a string of hits by Ruthford "Chico" Salmon, Don Buford, Paul Blair, Boog Powell, Hendricks, and Robinson. Still, the Orioles needed five pitchers to handle the Reds offense, and the game was in doubt until the bottom of the ninth. With the score 6-5, Reds pinch hitter Jimmy Stewart hit a drive to deep center field. It looked like a possible triple, but Paul Blair ran it down to end the game.

The Series became the sole property of Brooks Robinson as the teams moved to Baltimore. He was known as "Hoover," as in the vacuum cleaner, but a more accurate nickname might have been The Mugger, for he single-handedly robbed and beat the Reds in Game 3. In the first inning he turned a nifty double play on Tony Pérez. Then he hit a bases-loaded double in the bottom of the inning. In the second, he threw out Tommy Helms on a slow roller. In the sixth, he dove to his left to backhand a Johnny Bench line drive. Then he hit another double. Robinson had placed the Reds in their coffin, and pitcher Dave McNally nailed it shut when he hit a sixth-inning grand slam. Orioles 9, Reds 3. "I'm beginning to see him in my sleep," Reds manager George "Sparky" Anderson said of Robinson. "If I dropped this paper plate I'm holding now, he'd pick it up on one hop and throw me out." Robinson's defense at third base was so spectacular that he seemed to have special connections in heaven; his teammates jokingly instructed him to make it stop raining.

The Orioles had a three games to none lead and it was just a matter of time before they clinched the Series. Robinson had only one play in the field in Game 4, but showed his versatility by bludgeoning the Reds with his bat. He collected four hits and played a part in all five runs scored by the Orioles, but this time it wasn't enough. The Reds took the lead on a three-run homer by May in the eighth and Clay Carroll closed out the 6-5 Cincinnati victory with three-plus innings of fantastic relief pitching. It was Baltimore's first defeat in the past eighteen games.

The Orioles quickly put the Reds out of their misery in Game 5, pounding six Cincinnati pitchers for nine runs, including homers by Frank Robinson and Merv Rettenmund, a .322 hitter who had been unable to crack Baltimore's strong starting lineup until the fifth game. Brooks Robinson didn't do much at the plate, but he received a standing ovation from the Baltimore crowd when he struck out with two men on in the eighth inning. It was, he said, "the most touching thing that has ever happened to me on a baseball diamond."

"Somebody call the auto club and tell them to come pick up this Big Red Machine," Jim Murray wrote after the Orioles clinched. "It's blocking traffic in all four lanes." The Reds scored first in four of the five games, but the Orioles won four of the five because Cincinnati pitchers couldn't hold the leads. "We came in with a crippled

TOP: Rookie manager Sparky Anderson led the Reds to the World Series in 1970, the first of five pennants he won in a 26-year managerial career.

BOTTOM: Brooks Robinson robs Johnny Bench of a screaming line drive in the fifth inning of Game 3 with a spectacular diving catch. Robinson would do it again to Bench in Game 5.

staff," Clay Carroll said, "and the Orioles crippled what was left of it." Brooks Robinson had done most of the crippling, batting .429 in the Series and leading the Orioles with two home runs and six RBI. After his Series-long defensive performance, he was fined by the Orioles' kangaroo court for "showboating." But the stellar defense was not limited to Robinson alone: According to William Leggett of *Sports Illustrated*, the Orioles as a team robbed the Reds of sixteen hits during the World Series. "You don't usually get a chance to make tough plays so many days in a row like that," Robinson said. "There's gotta be a lot of luck involved because they are all a matter of about three inches one way or another." Pete Rose, however, was unprepared to attribute Robinson's dominance to luck. "Brooks Robinson," he said, "belongs in a higher league."

1971

Pittsburgh Pirates (4)
Baltimore Orioles (3)

Brooks Robinson had grabbed the World Series and made it his own in 1970, dominating the Series so thoroughly that it seemed as if a kind of baseball god had descended to earth for a while to give mere mortals some pointers on how the game should be played. One year later, another long-neglected treasure, Roberto Clemente, did exactly the same thing, shining in the national World Series spotlight as few had ever shone before.

The 1971 Pittsburgh Pirates were among the biggest underdogs in World Series annals, as the defending champion Orioles entered the Series having won fourteen straight games, including a sweep of Oakland in the American League playoffs. The Orioles were the first team in baseball history whose pitching staff featured four twenty-game winners. To make matters worse, the Pirates' veteran star, Clemente, was suffering from food poisoning after eating some bad Baltimore shellfish the night before the first game.

TOP: Jim Palmer was one of four Orioles to win 20 games in 1971, but it wasn't enough for them to win the World Series.

OPPOSITE: Roberto Clemente homers in Game 7 of the 1971 World Series, breaking up a scoreless tie and giving the Pirates a lead they would not relinquish.

The Orioles started the Series off as expected, beating the Pirates 5-3 in the first game and pounding them 11-3 in the second. But not all the news was bad for Pittsburgh. While the Pirates were getting demolished in Game 2, Clemente made a running catch of a fly ball down the right field line, whirled, and fired a bullet, a perfect strike to third base. The runner tagged up and advanced anyway, but Clemente had made what many witnesses would later call the greatest throw they had ever seen, a throw that made an unbelievably close play out of a routine sacrifice fly. The awed Baltimore crowd showed its respect by giving Clemente a standing ovation. Although they were down two games to none, the Pirates, with Clemente on their side, still seemed strangely confident. "Don't worry," Clemente told his teammates after the game. "I will carry the club the rest of the way." He did, with some help from pitcher Steve Blass in Game 3. "I was so nervous the night before,"

Blass said, "that I lay in bed for hours without being able to sleep." Blass then fired a three-hit victory to end Baltimore's sixteen-game winning streak.

The fourth game, played on a Wednesday evening in brand-new Three Rivers Stadium, was the first night game in World Series history. The Orioles led until the third inning, when Clemente launched a drive down the right field line with a runner on base for an

apparent homer. It was called foul despite vociferous protests from the Pirates, and replays later showed that the umpires probably got it right. Clemente shrugged off the controversy and knocked the next pitch for a single that eventually enabled Pittsburgh to score the tying run. The Pirates took the lead for good in the seventh when rookie Milt May delivered a pinch hit RBI single, and sidearmer Bruce Kison pitched six-plus innings of one-hit relief for the victory. The Series was now tied. The Pirates untied it in Game 5 thanks to Nelson Briles, a right-handed pitcher and part-time thespian who spoke half a dozen languages and had once acted in a production of *Damn Yankees*. Briles hurled a two-hit shutout with a pitching motion so violent that it caused him to fall off the mound three times, and the Pirates scored one of their four runs on an RBI single by Clemente.

The sixth game was the first real nail-biter of the Series. The Pirates scored two early runs, one on a Clemente homer, but were mostly quiet after Baltimore's Jim Palmer settled down. The Orioles tied the game in the seventh and it went into extra innings tied at two. Palmer was removed after nine good innings and replaced by 20-game winner Pat Dobson, who got into trouble in the tenth and was relieved by 21-game winner McNally. With the bases loaded in the tenth—the Orioles had walked Clemente intentionally—McNally got Al Oliver to fly out for the third out of the inning. The Orioles won it in the bottom of the tenth on the baserunning of Frank Robinson, who singled, hustled to third on a short single, and tagged up and barely scored on a Brooks Robinson fly to shallow center.

The Orioles had three twenty-game winners ready to pitch in Game 7, but the Pirates had Roberto Clemente, whose solo homer broke up a scoreless game in the fourth inning. The Pirates scored again when Willie Stargell singled leading off the eighth. Jose Pagan then hit a fly ball off the wall and Stargell motored home as outfielder Merv Rettenmund bobbled the rebound. That insurance run turned out to be vital, as Baltimore finally plated a run in the bottom of the eighth, though the Orioles went out meekly in the bottom of the ninth as Blass completed his second superb victory of the Series. The Orioles had been beaten by a

TOP: Roberto Clemente dominated the 1971 World Series offensively and defensively, batting .414 over the seven games.

BOTTOM: Catcher Manny Sanguillen and pitcher Steve Blass celebrate the Pirates' Game 7 victory.

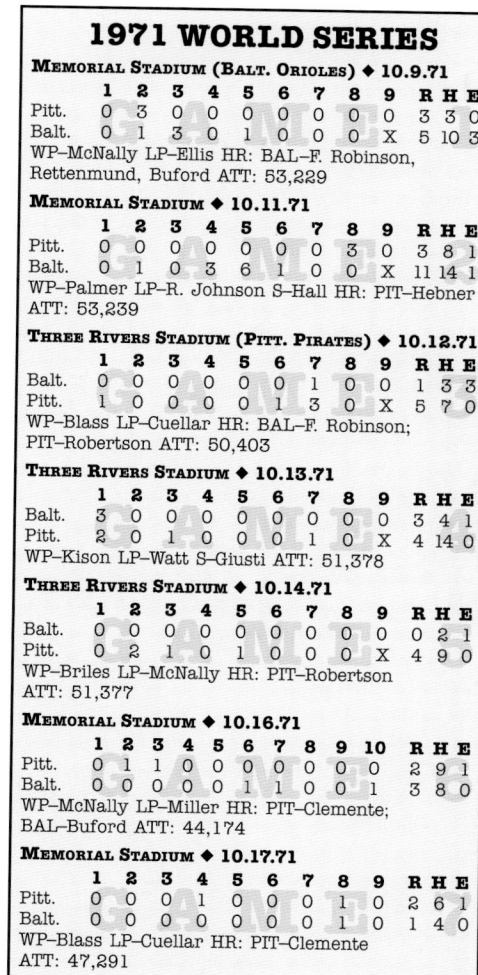

1971 WORLD SERIES

Memorial Stadium (Balt. Orioles) ◆ 10.9.71

	1	2	3	4	5	6	7	8	9	R	H	E
Pitt.	0	3	0	0	0	0	0	0	0	3	3	0
Balt.	0	1	3	0	1	0	0	0	X	5	10	3

WP–McNally LP–Ellis HR: BAL–F. Robinson, Rettenmund, Buford ATT: 53,229

Memorial Stadium ◆ 10.11.71

	1	2	3	4	5	6	7	8	9	R	H	E
Pitt.	0	0	0	0	0	0	0	3	0	3	8	1
Balt.	0	1	0	3	6	1	0	0	X	11	14	1

WP–Palmer LP–R. Johnson S–Hall HR: PIT–Hebner ATT: 53,239

Three Rivers Stadium (Pitt. Pirates) ◆ 10.12.71

	1	2	3	4	5	6	7	8	9	R	H	E
Balt.	0	0	0	0	0	0	1	0	0	1	3	3
Pitt.	1	0	0	0	0	1	3	0	X	5	7	0

WP–Blass LP–Cuellar HR: BAL–F. Robinson; PIT–Robertson ATT: 50,403

Three Rivers Stadium ◆ 10.13.71

	1	2	3	4	5	6	7	8	9	R	H	E
Balt.	3	0	0	0	0	0	0	0	0	3	4	1
Pitt.	2	0	1	0	0	0	1	0	X	4	14	0

WP–Kison LP–Watt S–Giusti ATT: 51,378

Three Rivers Stadium ◆ 10.14.71

	1	2	3	4	5	6	7	8	9	R	H	E
Balt.	0	0	0	0	0	0	0	0	0	0	2	1
Pitt.	0	2	1	0	1	0	0	0	X	4	9	0

WP–Briles LP–McNally HR: PIT–Robertson ATT: 51,377

Memorial Stadium ◆ 10.16.71

	1	2	3	4	5	6	7	8	9	10	R	H	E
Pitt.	0	1	1	0	0	0	0	0	0	0	2	9	1
Balt.	0	0	0	0	0	1	1	0	0	1	3	8	0

WP–McNally LP–Miller HR: PIT–Clemente; BAL–Buford ATT: 44,174

Memorial Stadium ◆ 10.17.71

	1	2	3	4	5	6	7	8	9	R	H	E
Pitt.	0	0	0	1	0	0	0	1	0	2	6	1
Balt.	0	0	0	0	0	0	0	1	0	1	4	0

WP–Blass LP–Cuellar HR: PIT–Clemente ATT: 47,291

team considered to be huge underdogs at the start of the Series for the second time in three years. "When it began you would have thought the Pittsburgh Pirates were nothing more than the invited guests at the St. Valentine's Day massacre," Stargell crowed.

With his all-out baserunning, tremendous defense, and superb batting, Roberto Clemente had turned in one of the great World Series performances in history, and had finally etched his name alongside Willie Mays, Henry Aaron, and Frank Robinson as one of the greatest players of his era. Clemente had hit safely in each of the fourteen World Series games in his career, and in the seven games of 1971 he tormented the Orioles' vaunted pitching staff with twelve hits, a .414 batting average, two home runs, and four RBI. He also played with maximum effort, running and throwing with the exuberance of a much younger player. Asked why he pushed his oft-injured, 37-year-old body to the limit on every play, Clemente replied, "I don't know if I will ever play in another World Series. So I must play hard. I must not think that my body hurts me all the time." As it turned out, of course, Clemente was right. He would never play in another World Series—in fact, he would live for only one more year before dying in a plane crash while on a relief mission to aid earthquake victims in Nicaragua. In baseball's collective memory, Roberto Clemente remains eternally 37 years old, playing baseball with the joy, excellence, and determination of a man on loan from the heavens.

1972

Oakland Athletics (4)
Cincinnati Reds (3)

THEY MAY HAVE BEEN A CHAMPIONSHIP ballclub, but the Oakland Athletics' clubhouse in 1972 resembled nothing so much as a nursery full of whining and fighting four-year-olds. Hairy ones. Nineteen of the 25 Athletics had some type of facial hair, and most of them also had some sort of dislike for someone else on the team. Shortstop Bert Campaneris threw his bat at Tigers pitcher Lerrin LaGrow in the playoffs. Colorful pitchers Vida Blue and Blue Moon Odom brawled in the Oakland clubhouse after the A's polished off the Tigers in five games. Blue was also battling with owner Charlie O. Finley. He accused Finley of "trying to destroy my career" by ordering him into the bullpen for the postseason. Manager Dick Williams and first baseman Mike Epstein got into a drunken shouting match on the team plane after Game 2 of the World Series. There were rumors that Williams was on his way out as manager, and other rumors spread that the A's, whose attendance in Oakland was remarkably poor, were planning a move to New Orleans.

After defeating Pittsburgh in the playoffs, the Cincinnati Reds were favored to win the World Series, too, mostly because they hailed from the National League, considered the superior circuit. Not only that, but Oakland would be playing the Series without the injured Reggie Jackson, who was not yet Mr. October, but was already one of the best power hitters in the American League. The Cincinnati players were confident—so confident that they unwittingly gave Oakland some good bulletin-board material. "The real World Series was between the Reds and the Pirates," Pete Rose scoffed. As it turned out, the real World Series was remarkably well-played and evenly matched, with an unprecedented six one-run games.

Backup catcher Gene Tenace won the first game for Oakland virtually single-handedly, homering in the first two World Series

BOTTOM: Pete Rose grins as he receives an intentional walk from the A's in Game 6 of the 1972 World Series. Three games earlier, Rollie Fingers had tricked Johnny Bench by pretending to walk him intentionally, then firing strike three over the plate.

TOP LEFT: Joe Rudi's spectacular ninth-inning catch saved Game 2 of the 1972 World Series for Oakland.

TOP RIGHT: A's stopper Rollie Fingers pitched magnificently in the 1972 World Series, his first of three consecutive stellar Fall Classics.

BOTTOM: Johnny Bench tags out pinch-running pitcher Blue Moon Odom for the second half of a game-ending double play in Game 5.

1972 WORLD SERIES

Riverfront Stadium (Cinc. Reds) ◆ 10.14.72

	1	2	3	4	5	6	7	8	9	R	H	E
Oak.	0	2	0	0	1	0	0	0	0	3	4	0
Cin.	0	1	0	1	0	0	0	0	0	2	7	0

WP–Holtzman LP–Nolan S–Blue
HR: OAK–Tenace (2) ATT: 52,918

Riverfront Stadium ◆ 10.15.72

	1	2	3	4	5	6	7	8	9	R	H	E
Oak.	0	1	1	0	0	0	0	0	0	2	9	2
Cin.	0	0	0	0	0	0	0	0	1	1	6	0

WP–Hunter LP–Grimsley S–Fingers HR: OAK–Rudi
ATT: 53,224

Oakland Coliseum (Oakl. Athletics) ◆ 10.18.72

	1	2	3	4	5	6	7	8	9	R	H	E
Cin.	0	0	0	0	0	0	1	0	0	1	4	2
Oak.	0	0	0	0	0	0	0	0	0	0	3	2

WP–Billingham LP–Odom S–Carroll ATT: 49,410

Oakland Coliseum ◆ 10.19.72

	1	2	3	4	5	6	7	8	9	R	H	E
Cin.	0	0	0	0	0	0	0	2	0	2	7	1
Oak.	0	0	0	0	1	0	0	0	2	3	10	1

WP–Fingers LP–Carroll HR: OAK–Tenace
ATT: 49,410

Oakland Coliseum ◆ 10.20.72

	1	2	3	4	5	6	7	8	9	R	H	E
Cin.	1	0	0	1	1	0	0	1	1	5	8	0
Oak.	0	3	0	1	0	0	0	0	0	4	7	2

WP–Grimsley LP–Fingers S–Billingham
HR: CIN–Rose, Menke; OAK–Tenace ATT: 49,410

Riverfront Stadium ◆ 10.21.72

	1	2	3	4	5	6	7	8	9	R	H	E
Oak.	0	0	0	0	1	0	0	0	0	1	7	1
Cin.	0	0	0	1	1	1	5	0	X	8	10	0

WP–Grimsley LP–Blue S–Hall HR: CIN–Bench
ATT: 52,737

Riverfront Stadium ◆ 10.22.72

	1	2	3	4	5	6	7	8	9	R	H	E
Oak.	1	0	0	0	0	2	0	0	0	3	6	1
Cin.	0	0	0	0	1	0	0	1	0	2	4	2

WP–Hunter LP–Borbon S–Fingers ATT: 56,040

TOP: Johnny Bench runs after a Bert Campaneris pop-up in Game 6 of the 1972 Series. (He didn't catch it.)

at-bats of his career to give Oakland a 3-2 victory. The A's also won Game 2, as Jim "Catfish" Hunter pitched eight scoreless innings and Joe Rudi made a sensational leaping catch against the left field wall to rob Denis Menke of a ninth-inning double. The catch saved the game, as the Reds scored one run before Rollie Fingers came in to put the lid on a 2-1 Oakland win. Rudi downplayed his vital catch, saying it was a play he had practiced hundreds of times before. "I put my hand out, concentrating on the ball and just feeling where the wall was," he said. "I never would have made that catch without all that practice."

California governor Ronald Reagan threw out the first ball before Game 3 as the Series moved to Oakland. Perhaps foreshadowing his presidential career, the pitch sailed over Tenace's head. Television dictated that the game start at twilight, which made things tough for hitters. Thus, Odom and Jack Billingham combined to strike out seventeen over the first six innings of a scoreless duel. César Gerónimo singled in the seventh for what looked like the first run of the game, but Tony Pérez slipped on the wet grass between third and home and fell flat on his face. Remarkably, he was still able to get up and scamper home safely with what turned out to be the only run in a 1-0 Reds victory. The cleverest play of the game belonged to Oakland, however, and occurred when Cincinnati threatened in the eighth, and Rollie Fingers entered the game. He pretended he was going to intentionally walk Johnny Bench, but instead fired a called strike three past the unsuspecting Bench to stifle the rally.

Tenace hit his third home run of the Series in Game 4, but the Athletics still trailed 2-1 entering the ninth inning. They came back to win it in the bottom of the ninth, 3-2, on three fortuitous pinch hits by Gonzalo Márquez, Don Mincher, and Ángel Mangual, a trio that had only 83 hits between them all season. "Within a week I've learned everything in baseball that you need to know," the now-less-cocky Pete Rose said as his Reds trailed 3-1 in the Series. "One week ago I was the happiest I had ever been...and I never felt so rotten, so low as I did after losing the game last night."

Rose's sorrow didn't last long, though, as he hit Hunter's first pitch of Game 5 over the fence to give the Reds a quick lead. Despite Tenace's fourth home run of the Series—tying a record shared by the likes of Ruth and Gehrig—the Reds scored twice in the late innings when Joe Morgan and Rose each manufactured a run, and won the game 5-4. Oakland threatened to tie it in the ninth, but pitcher Odom, pinch running, ended the game when he was thrown out at the plate trying to score on a short foul fly.

The sixth game was the only blowout of the Series, as the Reds forced a rubber match by clubbing Blue and three relievers, 8-1. Game 7 would be a matchup between Odom and Billingham, who had dueled so magnificently in Game 3. It was tied 1-1 in the sixth inning when Tenace hit a go-ahead double for Oakland. The next batter, Sal Bando, also hit a run-scoring double. That was enough for the win, as Rollie Fingers and his neatly trimmed handlebar moustache nailed the door shut in the last two innings. The Athletics were world champions for the first time since 1930, when they played in Philadelphia. In the clubhouse afterward, the buck naked Vida Blue, with a champagne bottle in his hand, led his hirsute teammates in a stirring rendition of "The Star-Spangled Banner." Connie Mack would have been proud.

1973

Oakland Athletics (4)

New York Mets (3)

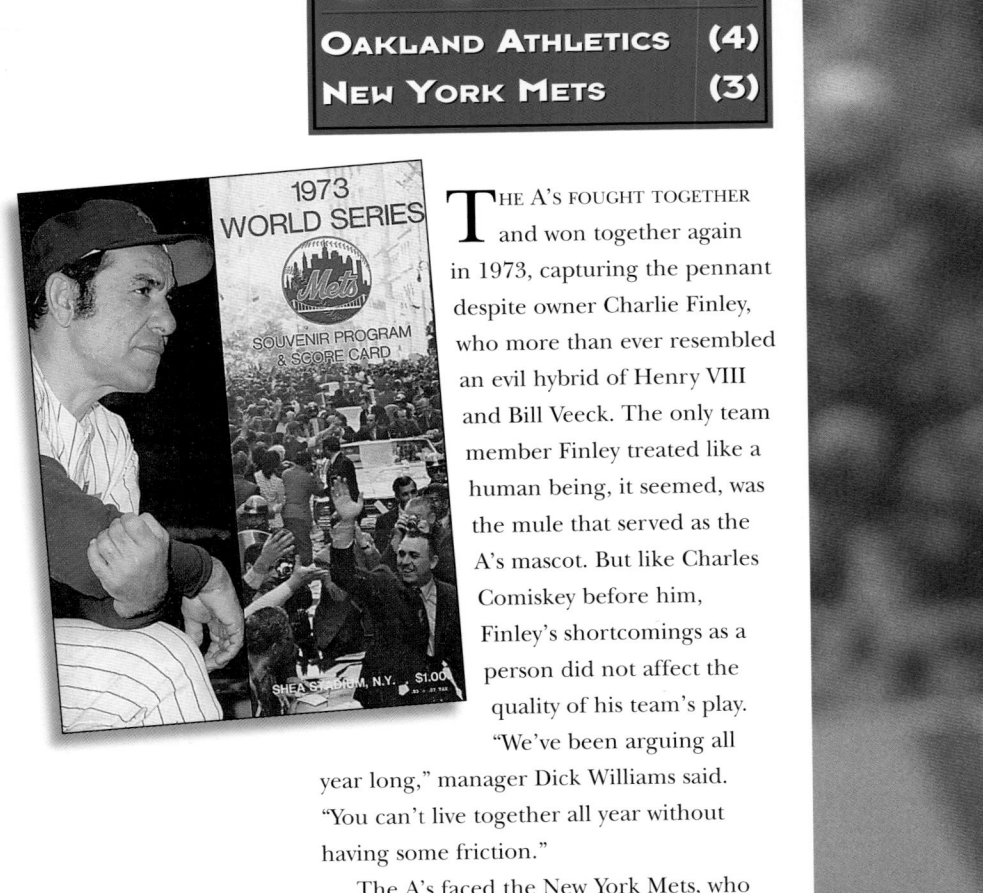

The A's fought together and won together again in 1973, capturing the pennant despite owner Charlie Finley, who more than ever resembled an evil hybrid of Henry VIII and Bill Veeck. The only team member Finley treated like a human being, it seemed, was the mule that served as the A's mascot. But like Charles Comiskey before him, Finley's shortcomings as a person did not affect the quality of his team's play.

"We've been arguing all year long," manager Dick Williams said. "You can't live together all year without having some friction."

The A's faced the New York Mets, who had won the pennant in their second year under manager Yogi Berra, but bore little resemblance to the miracle squad of 1969. The Mets were barely an average team with their 82-79 regular season record, but they were inspired by relief pitcher Tug McGraw's philosophy "You Gotta Believe" and came out on top of the weak National League East. The Mets then beat the Reds in the playoffs and replaced the 1959 Dodgers as the worst team ever to appear in a World Series. It's a title they still hold.

Finley gave the Mets' wives the worst seats in the upper deck of the Oakland Coliseum for the first game, while watching the games from a front-row box himself. His pulse had to be taken by a doctor between innings—ostensibly because he had heart trouble, but really, cynics said, to determine whether he had a heart at all. The game was a pitcher's duel, as the Oakland tandem of Ken Holtzman and Rollie Fingers defeated the equally tough Mets duo of Jon Matlack and Tug McGraw.

The second game was a 12-inning marathon. It must have seemed even longer to 43-year-old Willie Mays, who probably cost

TOP: Free-spirited southpaw Tug McGraw was the emotional leader of the Mets' 1973 pennant-winning team.

BOTTOM: A's owner Charlie Finley, wearing sunglasses, was hated by players and fans alike despite presiding over three consecutive world championships. He is flanked here by actor Rock Hudson and singer Anita Bryant during Game 5 of the 1974 World Series.

OPPOSITE: Though not yet known as Mr. October, Reggie Jackson was already a showboat by 1973, jumping emphatically on home plate after hitting a home run in Game 7.

INN
3
NY
0
OAK
26

TOP: Future Hall of Famers Catfish Hunter (left) and Tom Seaver opposed each other in Games 3 and 6 of the 1973 Series. Both got no-decisions in the first matchup, and Hunter won the second.

the Mets a run when he missed second base in the top of the ninth and also failed to catch a fly ball that went for a double in the bottom of that inning. It was yet another indication that it was time for Mays to retire. "Willie had seen all his splendid triumphs worn away to bare competence," Roger Angell had written two years earlier. "I began—for the first time in my life, and with enormous sadness—not to want him to come up to the plate...Hang them up, Willie, please. Retire." The venerable Mays came to the plate in the top of the twelfth looking to redeem himself with runners on first and third and two outs. "I knew he was going to hit it," teammate Bud Harrelson said. "I could see it in his eyes." Mays did get a hit to drive in the tying run, and the Mets followed with three more runs. Oakland loaded the bases with one out in the bottom of the inning, but the Mets escaped with the win.

Finley was furious at second baseman Mike Andrews after the game. Andrews' two errors in the twelfth inning had contributed to the Oakland loss, so Finley forced Andrews to sign a false affidavit that he was injured so he could replace him on the World Series roster with another player. The Oakland players threatened to boycott the third game if the move went through, but Commissioner Bowie Kuhn didn't fall for Finley's scam and ordered Andrews reinstated. Immediately afterward, Williams resigned as manager, effective at the end of the Series.

Amid all the turmoil, Game 3 at Shea Stadium shaped up as a duel between two top-notch pitchers, Tom Seaver and Catfish Hunter. Seaver struck out five consecutive batters in the early innings, but Hunter and three Oakland relievers held the Mets scoreless for the last ten innings of the game. The A's won it, 3-2, behind shortstop Bert Campaneris, who scored the tying run in the eighth and drove in the winning run in the eleventh. The fourth game ended up a Met blowout, 6-1, thanks to four hits and five RBI by Daniel "Rusty" Staub, though Shea Stadium's loudest applause of the night was reserved for the reinstated Andrews, who came up as a pinch hitter in the eighth inning and grounded out.

Jerry Koosman and Tug McGraw combined on a three-hit shutout in Game 5 to propel the Mets into the Series lead. Now the Athletics were not only facing elimination, but they were also facing Seaver, the best pitcher in baseball, in Game 6. Seaver threw well, but he was outpitched by Hunter, who combined with two relievers on a 3-1 victory. The biggest factor in the win was Reggie Jackson, who had been conspicuously silent as he stranded seventeen runners on base in the first five games. Jackson's three hits were responsible for all three Oakland runs on this night, however, forcing players to prepare for a seventh game showdown.

The A's put the seventh game away in the third inning, scoring four runs capped by a long Jackson homer. It was the first career World Series home run for the future Mr. October, and it sent the A's on their way to a 5-2 victory and a world championship. However, it had been one of the more poorly played Series in memory, in part because of the freezing night games played in New York. The teams combined for a shocking nineteen errors, and the Mets stranded a record 72 runners on base. Oakland had its bullpen to thank for the victory; A's relievers pitched 31 innings in the Series and allowed only three earned runs.

But even the finer moments on the field had been obscured by Finley's egotistical grandstanding, which continued even after the Series was over, when he ordered a set of cheap, diamondless World Series rings for his victorious players. "I wanted to slide and run and hit and get dirty, but the little boy in me was taken out by all the nonsense," Jackson said. "Nobody seemed to care anything about the players, just all that other stuff."

1973 WORLD SERIES

Oakland Coliseum (Oakl. Athletics) ◆ 10.13.73 (GAME 1)

	1	2	3	4	5	6	7	8	9	R	H	E
NYM	0	0	0	1	0	0	0	0	0	1	7	2
Oak.	0	0	2	0	0	0	0	0	X	2	4	0

WP–Holtzman LP–Matlack S–Knowles ATT: 46,021

Oakland Coliseum ◆ 10.14.73 (GAME 2)

	1	2	3	4	5	6	7	8	9	10	11	12	R	H	E
NYM	0	1	1	0	0	4	0	0	0	0	0	4	10	15	1
Oak.	2	1	0	0	0	0	1	0	2	0	0	1	7	13	5

WP–McGraw LP–Fingers S–Stone HR: NYM–Jones, Garrett ATT: 49,151

Shea Stadium (New York Mets) ◆ 10.16.73 (GAME 3)

	1	2	3	4	5	6	7	8	9	10	11	R	H	E
Oak.	0	0	0	0	0	1	0	1	0	0	1	3	10	1
NYM	2	0	0	0	0	0	0	0	0	0	0	2	10	2

WP–Lindblad LP–Parker S–Fingers
HR: NYM–Garrett ATT: 54,817

Shea Stadium ◆ 10.17.73 (GAME 4)

	1	2	3	4	5	6	7	8	9	R	H	E
Oak.	0	0	0	1	0	0	0	0	0	1	5	1
NYM	3	0	0	3	0	0	0	0	X	6	13	1

WP–Matlack LP–Holtzman S–Sadecki
HR: NYM–Staub ATT: 54,817

Shea Stadium ◆ 10.18.73 (GAME 5)

	1	2	3	4	5	6	7	8	9	R	H	E
Oak.	0	0	0	0	0	0	0	0	0	0	3	1
NYM	0	1	0	0	0	1	0	0	X	2	7	1

WP–Koosman LP–Blue S–McGraw ATT: 54,817

Oakland Coliseum ◆ 10.20.73 (GAME 6)

	1	2	3	4	5	6	7	8	9	R	H	E
NYM	0	0	0	0	0	0	0	1	0	1	6	2
Oak.	1	0	1	0	0	0	0	1	X	3	7	0

WP–Hunter LP–Seaver S–Fingers ATT: 49,333

Oakland Coliseum ◆ 10.21.73 (GAME 7)

	1	2	3	4	5	6	7	8	9	R	H	E
NYM	0	0	0	0	0	1	0	0	1	2	8	1
Oak.	0	0	4	0	1	0	0	0	X	5	9	1

WP–Holtzman LP–Matlack S–Knowles
HR: OAK–Campaneris, Jackson ATT: 49,333

1974

Oakland Athletics (4)
Los Angeles Dodgers (1)

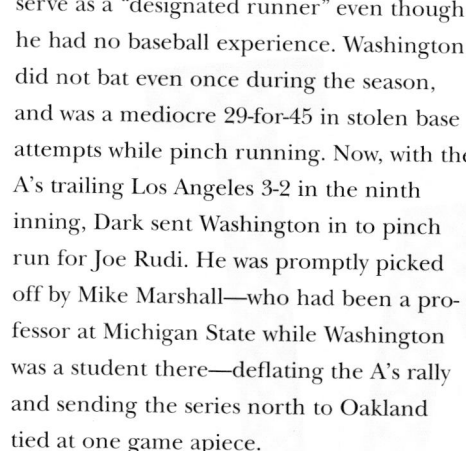

THE RAUCOUS OAKLAND A'S OF 1974 sought to become just the third team ever—and the first team not named the New York Yankees—to win at least three consecutive World Series. It was the first all-California Series, as the Athletics faced the Los Angeles Dodgers, who were appearing in the classic for the first time since the retirement of Sandy Koufax. The Dodgers' strength was still pitching, though—particularly the relief pitching of Mike Marshall, a doctoral candidate in physiology at Michigan State University who in his spare time worked on a dissertation titled *A Comparison of an Estimate of Skeletal Age With Chronological Age When Classifying Adolescent Males for Motor Proficiency Norms.* The intellectual reliever pitched in a record 106 games in 1974, winning 15 of them, saving 22 more, and taking home the Cy Young Award.

It wouldn't have been an A's World Series without a clubhouse fight, and this time the annual affair came the day before the Series started and pitted Blue Moon Odom against Rollie Fingers. The outcome was decidedly against Fingers, who received five stitches in his head. To compound matters, Oakland had a new manager, Alvin Dark, who was tough, devoutly religious, and, many believed, racist. Remarkably, Dark managed to work his way through the minefield of fights, lawsuits, and

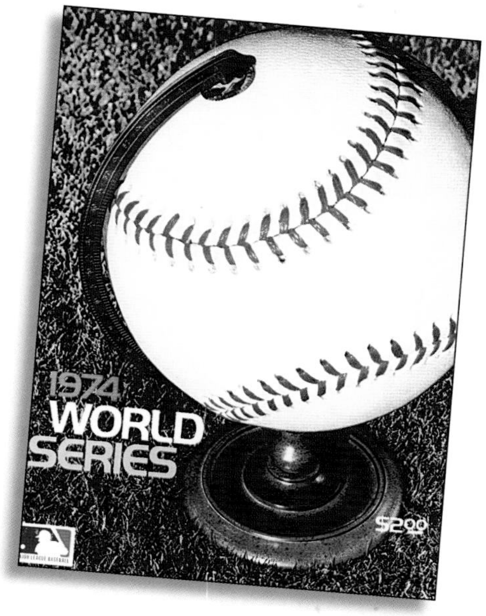

contract disputes that surrounded the team, bringing them home with 90 wins and the American League pennant.

The A's showed the diversity of their offense in Game 1 by scoring their first run on a Reggie Jackson homer, their second on a squeeze bunt by Bert Campaneris, and their third on an error by Ron Cey. It was a story of squandered opportunities for the Dodgers, who lost by one run after stranding twelve runners on base and getting another picked off. Fingers gave up a homer in the bottom of the ninth to Jimmy Wynn that cut the Oakland lead to 3-2, forcing Catfish Hunter to enter in relief for the last out. In a reversal of their usual roles, Hunter struck out Joe Ferguson to save the victory for Fingers.

The Dodgers got their only win in Game 2 thanks to the pitching of Don Sutton and one of the many harebrained schemes of A's owner Charlie Finley. At the start of the season, Finley had hired Herb Washington, a track star from Michigan State University, to serve as a "designated runner" even though he had no baseball experience. Washington did not bat even once during the season, and was a mediocre 29-for-45 in stolen base attempts while pinch running. Now, with the A's trailing Los Angeles 3-2 in the ninth inning, Dark sent Washington in to pinch run for Joe Rudi. He was promptly picked off by Mike Marshall—who had been a professor at Michigan State while Washington was a student there—deflating the A's rally and sending the series north to Oakland tied at one game apiece.

Finley called a mandatory workout for the off-day between games 2 and 3, which served to annoy the A's more than it prepared them. Still, playing at home for the first time in the Series, they won the third game 3-2 after Dodgers catcher Ferguson made two key errors. But the Dodgers were undaunted. "The A's have only a couple of players who could play on our club," Bill Buckner bragged before the fourth game. "I think if we played them 162 times, we could beat them 100." Buckner's popping off may have angered the A's, but pitcher Ken Holtzman

BOTTOM LEFT: In a controversial play in Game 4, Reggie Jackson was called safe although Dodgers catcher Steve Yeager appeared to tag him before he touched the plate.

BOTTOM RIGHT: Vida Blue hurls a pitch in Game 5 of the 1974 Series. Blue and two relievers combined to beat the Dodgers and finish off the Series, four games to one.

had no desire to play for the Dodgers—he just wanted to beat them. Holtzman drove in the first run of Game 4 by homering in his second at-bat of the season and also pitched seven-plus innings in a 5-2 Oakland win. It was the unheralded Holtzman's sixty-fifth victory over the past three years.

The A's sent Vida Blue to the mound to face Sutton in an attempt to wrap up the Series in their final game at home, while Oakland fans became rowdy with the game tied 2-2 in the seventh inning. Remembering Buckner's earlier derogatory comments, the fans in left field at the Oakland Coliseum pelted him with everything from Frisbees to whiskey bottles, forcing a game delay of several minutes. Rudi belted Marshall's first pitch after the break into those same raucous bleachers to give the A's a 3-2 lead. The Dodgers threatened to tie it again when Buckner led off the next inning with a single, but he was thrown out trying to advance to third base on an error. It was smooth sailing the rest of the way for Fingers, who finished off the Dodgers to get both his third save of the Series and the third championship ring of his career. Fingers was named MVP of the Series, although really it could have been a three-year achievement award. In Oakland's three victorious World Series, Fingers had pitched in sixteen of the nineteen games, posting a 1.35 ERA over 33 innings. "Glory be to God," manager Alvin Dark said. Which must have made Finley jealous.

TOP: Reggie Jackson's mighty swing was entertaining even when he missed the pitch.

BOTTOM: Sal Bando (in air) and Ray Fosse (in catcher's gear) join the celebration after defeating the Dodgers 3-2 in the final game of the 1974 World Series.

1974 WORLD SERIES

Dodger Stadium (L.A. Dodgers) ◆ 10.12.74

	1	2	3	4	5	6	7	8	9	R	H	E
Oak.	0	1	0	0	1	0	0	1	0	3	6	2
L.A.	0	0	0	0	1	0	0	0	1	2	11	1

WP–Fingers LP–Messersmith S–Hunter
HR: OAK–Jackson; LA–Wynn ATT: 55,974

Dodger Stadium ◆ 10.13.74

	1	2	3	4	5	6	7	8	9	R	H	E
Oak.	0	0	0	0	0	0	0	0	2	2	6	0
L.A.	0	1	0	0	0	2	0	0	X	3	6	1

WP–Sutton LP–Blue S–Marshall HR: LA–Ferguson
ATT: 55,989

Oakland Coliseum (Oakl. Athletics) ◆ 10.15.74

	1	2	3	4	5	6	7	8	9	R	H	E
L.A.	0	0	0	0	0	0	0	1	1	2	7	2
Oak.	0	0	2	1	0	0	0	0	X	3	5	2

WP–Hunter LP–Downing S–Fingers
HR: LA–Buckner, Crawford ATT: 49,347

Oakland Coliseum ◆ 10.16.74

	1	2	3	4	5	6	7	8	9	R	H	E
L.A.	0	0	0	2	0	0	0	0	0	2	7	1
Oak.	0	0	1	0	0	4	0	0	X	5	7	0

WP–Holtzman LP–Messersmith S–Fingers
HR: OAK–Holtzman ATT: 49,347

Oakland Coliseum ◆ 10.17.74

	1	2	3	4	5	6	7	8	9	R	H	E
L.A.	0	0	0	0	0	2	0	0	0	2	5	1
Oak.	1	1	0	0	0	0	1	0	X	3	6	1

WP–Odom LP–Marshall S–Fingers HR: OAK–Fosse, Rudi ATT: 49,347

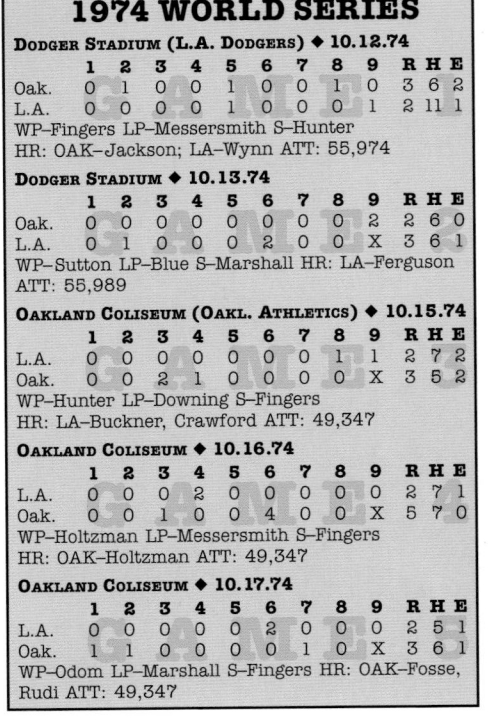

1975

Cincinnati Reds (4)

Boston Red Sox (3)

The 1975 World Series is remembered for Carlton Fisk. But even before Fisk waved his way into history, the Boston Red Sox and Cincinnati Reds had played a Series so tense and exciting that it would have become a classic even without that famous longball. Boston started Luis Tiant in Game 1. The cigar-smoking, fu manchu–wearing hurler seemed to have dozens of different pitching windups, all of them unusual. "He jiggles his glove," said Fisk. "He throws back his head, shakes his leg, twists around and all of a sudden, here comes the ball." Reds manager Sparky Anderson had pointedly wondered in the media before the Series whether Tiant's windup might be a balk, and Anderson's grandstanding paid off as the pitcher was called for a balk in Game 1. It didn't affect the outcome as Tiant pitched the first complete game in the World Series since 1971, baffling the Reds 6-0.

Bill Lee retired the first ten Cincinatti batters in Game 2 with a cold New England rain beating down. Lee, nicknamed "Spaceman," was baseball's most famous free spirit; among other things, he had outraged Bostonians by suggesting that they were bigoted for opposing integration by school busing. His best pitch was a high, arcing blooper pitch that made batters' mouths water but usually got them out. Lee pitched masterfully as he held Cincinnati in check until the ninth inning, but Dick Drago replaced Lee and promptly gave up the tying and winning runs on hits by Dave Concepcion and Ken Griffey. The teams headed for Cincinnati tied at a game apiece.

They played Game 3 to a 5-5 tie after nine innings with each club using five pitchers. César Gerónimo singled to lead off the Reds' tenth inning. Pinch hitter Ed Armbrister tried to bunt him to second, but Armbrister remained in the batter's box after the bunt and Fisk collided with him trying to field the ball. Fisk shoved Armbrister out of the way and then, off balance, threw the ball into center field, sending Gerónimo to third. Despite howls of protest from the Red Sox, home plate umpire Larry Barnett refused to call Armbrister for interference. Joe Morgan singled in the winning run moments later. "It's a damn shame to lose a ball game like that," Fisk said. "One call from an umpire can change the complexion of the whole Series."

Boston evened the Series the next night behind Tiant, the man of many windups. The 34-year-old Cuban appeared to be running out of gas late in the game, but he survived after throwing 163 pitches to polish off the Reds 5-4. Fred Lynn's great catch of a long Griffey drive in the ninth helped preserve the victory. Tony Pérez, hitless in the first four games of the Series, erupted for two home runs and four RBI the next day, propelling Cincinnati to a 6-2 win in Game 5. The Reds led 2-1 going into the bottom of the sixth when Joe Morgan led off with a walk, then drew sixteen pickoff throws from Reggie Cleveland, the perturbed Boston pitcher. In the end Morgan didn't need to steal, as Pérez's second homer, a three-run job, put the game away for the Reds.

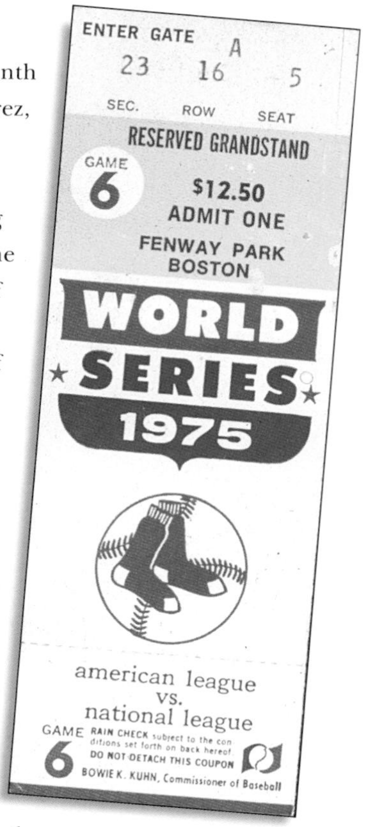

Game Six at Fenway was postponed three times by rain, but it was well worth the wait. After the first ball was thrown out by Duffy Lewis, the 87-year-old hero of Boston's 1915 world championship, Lynn gave the Red Sox a quick lead with a three-run homer. But it was quickly apparent that Tiant was not pitching like his normal self, as the Reds tied it in the fifth on hits by Rose, Bench, and Griffey. The weary Tiant trudged on and stayed in the game until the eighth inning, but he left trailing 6-3. Sportswriters, confident that the Reds would win the game and thus the Series, took a vote and awarded the World Series MVP to Reds rookie reliever Rawly Eastwick, but with two on and two out in the bottom of the eighth, Bernie Carbo, who had been a tremendous hitter for Boston in a part-time

BELOW: In one of the pivotal plays of the 1975 World Series, Denny Doyle is tagged out after trying to score on a short fly ball to left fielder George Foster. Foster's tremendous throw preserved a 6-6 tie in the ninth inning of Game 6.

RED SOX

role, came to the plate to pinch hit against the anointed MVP. He promptly hit one over the center field wall to tie the game.

Two hits that looked like game-winners instead became double plays as the game continued. First, the Red Sox loaded the bases with nobody out in the ninth, but George Foster threw out Denny Doyle, who had tried to tag and score on a short fly ball, to complete a remarkable twin killing. Third base coach Don Zimmer had yelled "No, no, no!" at Doyle, but the runner later said he misheard it as "Go, go, go!" The game went into extra innings. An awed Pete Rose came up to the plate in the tenth and turned around to Fisk. Rose said in wonder, "This is some kind of game, isn't it?" There was more to come. Morgan launched what looked like a go-ahead two-run homer in the eleventh, but Dwight Evans, in a catch reminiscent of Al Gionfriddo's 28 years earlier, stuck out his glove at the last minute and grabbed the ball, then threw to first for an inning-ending—and game-saving—double play.

Fisk led off the bottom of the twelfth against Pat Darcy, the Reds' eighth pitcher of the night. Darcy's second pitch was a sinker, low and inside, and Fisk pounced on it, hitting a towering fly ball down the left field line. It was clearly hit far enough to leave the park. The only question was fair or foul. Fisk, leaping in the air as he left the batter's box, waved his arms instinctively as if to coax the ball fair, and, after hanging in the air for what seemed like hours, the ball smashed into the foul pole, becoming a fair ball and a game-winning home run. New England rejoiced. Every participant, both winners and losers, called it the greatest game they had ever played in. "I don't think I've ever gone through a more emotional game," Fisk said. Wrote Ron Fimrite in *Sports Illustrated*: "For the 35,205 wedged into misshapen Fenway and the millions who watched on television, the sixth game of the 1975 Series will be the standard by which all future thrillers must be measured." Indeed, the sixth game still stands as one of the greatest games in baseball history.

Incidentally, the countless millions who have seen the famous replay of Fisk have a rat to thank for it. As Fisk came to the plate, TV cameraman Lou Gerard, stationed inside the Green Monster's scoreboard, saw "a rat the size of a cat" coming toward him. Not wanting to provoke the rodent, Gerard kept his camera trained on Fisk after the hit, rather than turning it quickly to follow the flight of the ball as he normally would have.

PREVIOUS PAGES: Carlton Fisk's famous home run wave in Game 6 was accidentally shown to television audiences thanks to a large rat inside the Green Monster.

TOP: The infamous Ed Armbrister play in Game 3 on which umpire Larry Barnett refused to call interference. From left to right are Barnett, Carlton Fisk, and Armbrister.

BOTTOM: Boston Red Sox hurler Luis Tiant winds up for a pitch during Game 6 of the 1975 World Series against the Cincinnati Reds. It was a solid outing for Tiant, who went 2-0 in the Series, but the Red Sox once again went down in the stretch. Although painful for Boston fans, it was one of the most exciting, tightly fought Series in history.

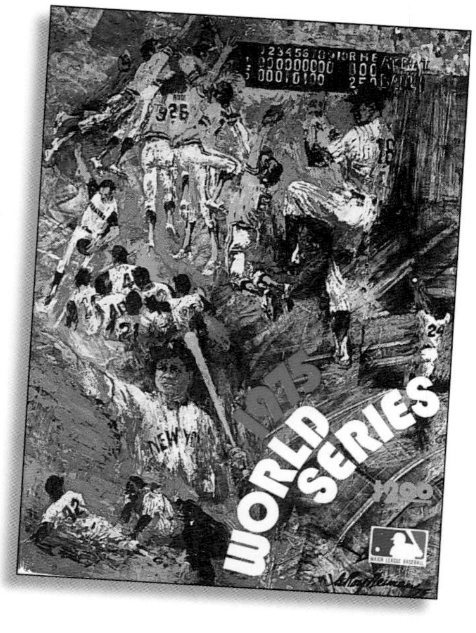

As a result, the memorable image of Fisk waving the ball fair was preserved for posterity. "It was a wonderful aberration that changed television," said John Filippelli, who helped direct the broadcast of the game for NBC. "No one had ever thought of isolating on an individual."

Boston began the seventh game by taking a 3-0 lead as they had done the day before, but Tony Pérez got two of those back when he smashed one of Lee's blooper pitches completely out of Fenway Park. The game went into the ninth inning tied at three, and Joe Morgan blooped a single into center field with two on and two out to give Cincinnati the lead. To the surprise of everyone who had seen the rest of the Series, Boston went quietly in the bottom of the ninth. The Reds had won what would go down in history as one of the most exciting World Series ever played. In addition to the pure excitement, it was also one of the closest Series ever. Boston got 60 hits, Cincinnati 59. Red Sox pitchers had a 3.88 ERA, Reds pitchers, 3.86. The teams played to an utter deadlock until the ninth inning of the seventh game. "We are the best team in baseball," Anderson, the victorious manager, said. "But not by much."

1975 WORLD SERIES

Fenway Park II (Boston Red Sox) ◆ 10.11.75

	1	2	3	4	5	6	7	8	9	R	H	E
Cin.	0	0	0	0	0	0	0	0	0	0	5	0
Boston	0	0	0	0	0	0	6	0	X	6	12	0

WP–Tiant LP–Gullett ATT: 35,205

Fenway Park II ◆ 10.12.75

	1	2	3	4	5	6	7	8	9	R	H	E
Cin.	0	0	0	1	0	0	0	0	2	3	7	1
Boston	1	0	0	0	0	1	0	0	0	2	7	0

WP–Eastwick LP–Drago ATT: 35,205

Riverfront Stadium (Cinc. Reds) ◆ 10.14.75

	1	2	3	4	5	6	7	8	9	10	R	H	E
Boston	0	1	0	0	0	1	1	0	2	0	5	10	2
Cin.	0	0	0	2	3	0	0	0	0	1	6	7	0

WP–Eastwick LP–Willoughby HR: BOS–Fisk, Carbo, Evans; CIN–Bench, Concepcion, Geronimo ATT: 55,392

Riverfront Stadium ◆ 10.15.75

	1	2	3	4	5	6	7	8	9	R	H	E
Boston	0	0	0	5	0	0	0	0	0	5	11	1
Cin.	2	0	0	2	0	0	0	0	0	4	9	1

WP–Tiant LP–Norman ATT: 55,667

Riverfront Stadium ◆ 10.16.75

	1	2	3	4	5	6	7	8	9	R	H	E
Boston	1	0	0	0	0	0	0	0	1	2	5	0
Cin.	0	0	0	1	1	3	0	1	X	6	8	0

WP–Gullett LP–Cleveland S–Eastwick HR: CIN–Perez (2) ATT: 56,393

Fenway Park II ◆ 10.21.75

	1	2	3	4	5	6	7	8	9	10	11	12	R	H	E
Cin.	0	0	0	0	3	0	2	1	0	0	0	0	6	14	0
Boston	3	0	0	0	0	0	0	3	0	0	0	1	7	10	1

WP–Wise LP–Darcy HR: CIN–Geronimo; BOS–Lynn, Carbo, Fisk ATT: 35,205

Fenway Park II ◆ 10.22.75

	1	2	3	4	5	6	7	8	9	R	H	E
Cin.	0	0	0	0	0	2	1	0	1	4	9	0
Boston	0	0	3	0	0	0	0	0	0	3	5	2

WP–Carroll LP–Burton S–McEnaney HR: CIN–Perez ATT: 35,205

TOP: Bernie Carbo's key Game 6 home run came off Rawly Eastwick, the Reds reliever who had just been voted World Series MVP by overanxious sportswriters.

BOTTOM: This Joe Morgan swing resulted in the game-winning hit in the ninth inning of Game 7.

CHAPTER 5
THE FREE AGENT ERA
1976–1994

BEFORE THE 1976 SEASON, PITCHERS ANDY MESSERSMITH AND DAVE MCNALLY were ruled free agents, and the balance of power in baseball began to swing from owners toward players. On the advice of union head Marvin Miller, they had played the 1975 season without contracts in order to test the reserve clause, a bit of standard contract language that kept players committed to teams for life. When arbitrator Peter Seitz ruled in favor of the two pitchers, the Pandora's box that owners had used to artificially depress player salaries was opened. With players now able to choose their own employers after six years in the majors, a new, high-salaried era in baseball began. Contrary to popular belief, the onset of free agency did not appreciably increase player movement from team to team. It did, however, place the power to make those decisions in the hands of the players rather than the owners. (And, as Casey Stengel noted after winning the 1958 Series, "I couldn't have done it without my players.")

Forced to share their wealth, owners now turned to a new cash cow, shaking down the television networks for higher broadcasting rights fees. In return, Commissioner Bowie Kuhn eventually agreed to hold all World Series games late at night, a decision that drew an immense amount of criticism from fans and the press. The 1976 World Series, played in freezing late-night weather in Cincinnati, became a colossal embarrassment. It also made Kuhn something of a national laughingstock, later prompting Red Smith's famous joke about the 1981 strike: "This never would have happened if Bowie Kuhn were alive today." Kuhn, of course, was alive and well, but his lasting legacy as commissioner is that the defining World Series moment of his era, Carlton Fisk's 1975 home run, took place at 12:34 a.m.

Ironically, free agency brought a kind of purity to the World Series, a sense of competing for the sake of the competition itself. In previous decades, the promise of a fat World Series check had always been a player's primary motivation for winning the World Series. For some players, it might double their annual salary, might make the difference on a mortgage. But as free agents started signing million-dollar contracts, the Series dollars became less meaningful. As Don Drysdale reportedly said, "When we played, World Series checks meant something. Now all they do is screw your taxes." By the 1980s, for the first time in baseball history, men were playing their hardest in the World Series for the pure sake of competition.

TCF
Budweiser
Twins

1976

Cincinnati Reds (4)
New York Yankees (0)

PREVIOUS PAGES: Opened in 1982, the Metrodome sits in Minneapolis, looking very much like an overgrown tennis bubble. The roof is made of Teflon-coated fiberglass and requires constant air pressure to keep it aloft. Also known as the Thunderdome because of the noise levels reached within its resonant confines, the stadium set new decibel records during the 1987 playoffs and World Series.

BOTTOM: Johnny Bench blasts one of his two home runs during Game 4 of the 1976 World Series.

At first glance, the 1976 World Series should have been an interesting one, with the defending champion Cincinnati Reds facing a rejuvenated Yankee squad appearing in its first Fall Classic in more than a decade. But after the Reds sent the Yankees packing in four dreary and freezing games, the consensus was that it had been one of the great World Series clunkers of all time—especially when compared to the seven sublime games of a year earlier. Wrote Red Smith in the *New York Times*: "The Yankees looked worse than the Black Sox of 1919, who were trying to lose."

The Yankees had spent two years as tenants in Shea Stadium after George Steinbrenner bought the team. The heir to a shipbuilding fortune was having the House that Ruth Built undergo a $55 million renovation, but the new House that Steinbrenner Built was little more than a gaudy replica of the 1970s cookie-cutter stadiums. The fences were moved in, the hallowed monuments removed from the field of play, and the signature copper frieze torn down and replaced with an inferior plastic version.

And these were not your father's Yankees. They were once the most thoroughly segregated team in baseball. Now they featured a bevy of African-American stars including Roy White, Chris Chambliss, Mickey Rivers, Oscar Gamble, Willie Randolph, and Dock Ellis. All except White were imports from other organizations, a sign that the Yankees were moving away from the policy of grooming their own stars that had produced the likes of Mickey Mantle, Yogi Berra, and Whitey Ford.

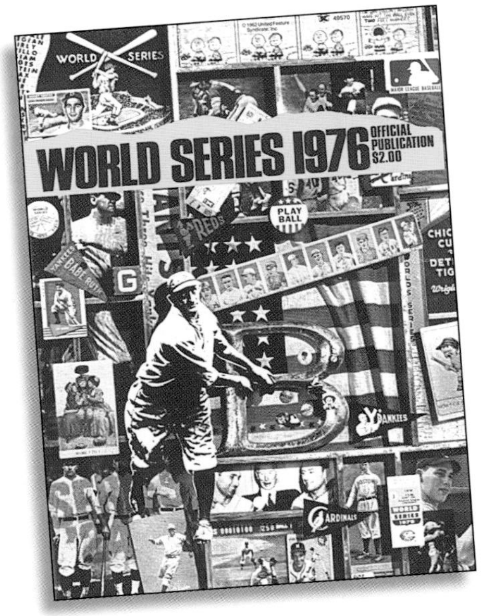

The most interesting subplot of the Series came during Game 1 at Riverfront Stadium. The Reds claimed that Yankee officials were stealing signs off the television broadcast and transmitting them to the dugout via walkie-talkie, though the Yankees denied the charges. The chicanery did little good even if the allegations were true, as Cincinnati won that first game at home, 5-1, on three hits by Tony Pérez. Pérez continued his onslaught the next night by singling in the winning run in the bottom of the ninth. After New York lost again in Game 3, they were finished off in Game 4 by Johnny Bench, who smacked two homers in an easy Cincinnati victory.

The sweep showed the complete dominance and versatility of the Big Red Machine. "We're not a home run hitting club, nor are we a base stealing club," National League MVP Joe Morgan said. "We do whatever is necessary to win. If we have to hit home runs, we can do it. If we must steal a base to win, we'll do that." The Series was epitomized for the Yankees by manager Billy Martin's ejection from Game 4. The only bright spot was catcher Thurman Munson, who hit .529, a record for a player on a losing team. The rest of the Yankees batted .178.

The Series was also notable for the bitter cold that accompanied the late night starting times mandated by television, as the temperature hovered around thirty degrees with a harsh wind chill for the first two games in Cincinatti. Fans in the stands huddled around portable stoves, and several players lost feeling in their fingertips. Yankee coach Yogi Berra complained that an, um, somewhat more sensitive body part had become frozen. Team owners, players, and fans alike excoriated Commissioner Bowie Kuhn's submission to NBC's demands that the games be held in the freezing night. "Baseball has prostituted itself," said Padres owner Ray Kroc. "Pretty soon we'll be starting games at midnight so the people in outer space can watch on television." According to Red Smith, the most memorable image of the Series was "the spectacle of Bowie Kuhn making an utter ass of himself by sitting coatless in the bitter night pretending it was summer."

In contrast to the wild celebration of the year before, the Cincinnati players were surprisingly subdued after wrapping up their second consecutive title. They sat calmly at their lockers, shaking hands, and sipping beer. "I just couldn't get turned on about the World Series this year," Pete Rose said.

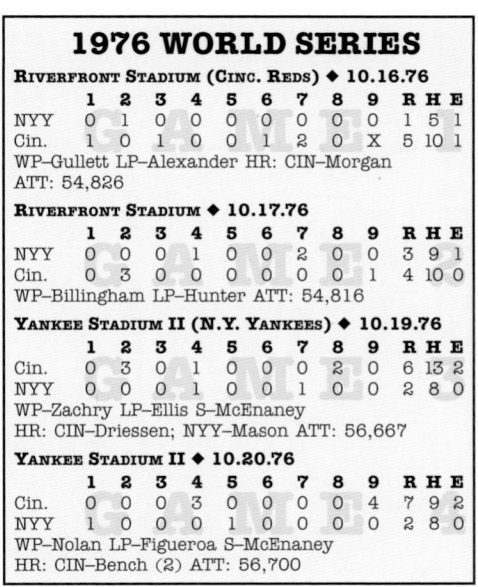

1976 WORLD SERIES

Riverfront Stadium (Cinc. Reds) ◆ 10.16.76

	1	2	3	4	5	6	7	8	9	R	H	E
NYY	0	1	0	0	0	0	0	0	0	1	5	1
Cin.	1	0	1	0	0	1	2	0	X	5	10	1

WP–Gullett LP–Alexander HR: CIN–Morgan
ATT: 54,826

Riverfront Stadium ◆ 10.17.76

	1	2	3	4	5	6	7	8	9	R	H	E
NYY	0	0	0	1	0	0	2	0	0	3	9	1
Cin.	0	3	0	0	0	0	0	0	1	4	10	0

WP–Billingham LP–Hunter ATT: 54,816

Yankee Stadium II (N.Y. Yankees) ◆ 10.19.76

	1	2	3	4	5	6	7	8	9	R	H	E
Cin.	0	3	0	1	0	0	0	2	0	6	13	2
NYY	0	0	0	1	0	0	1	0	0	2	8	0

WP–Zachry LP–Ellis S–McEnaney
HR: CIN–Driessen; NYY–Mason ATT: 56,667

Yankee Stadium II ◆ 10.20.76

	1	2	3	4	5	6	7	8	9	R	H	E
Cin.	0	0	0	3	0	0	0	0	4	7	9	2
NYY	1	0	0	0	1	0	0	0	0	2	8	0

WP–Nolan LP–Figueroa S–McEnaney
HR: CIN–Bench (2) ATT: 56,700

1977

New York Yankees (4)
Los Angeles Dodgers (2)

The long, sweltering summer of 1977 was a particularly eventful time in the life of New York City. As disco fever swept the nation, Studio 54, the now-legendary dance club, opened its doors on West 54th Street. A citywide electrical blackout plunged the city into darkness and panic on July 13, halting subways and trapping people in the upper floors of skyscrapers for more than 24 hours. David Berkowitz, the serial killer known as the "Son of Sam," had the city's residents living in fear until his capture on August 10.

And then there was Reggie Jackson. The obnoxious yet charming slugger was playing his first season in the Bronx after signing a $3.5 million free agent contract and immediately proclaiming himself "the straw that stirs the drink." Jackson backed up his braggadocio with 32 home runs and 110 RBI as the Yankees coasted into the World Series for the second straight year.

But all was not well in the Bronx. In their third season under the profoundly abrasive Billy Martin, the Yankees were as bad off the field as they were good on it. Martin and Jackson nearly came to blows during one nationally televised game. Lou Piniella and Thurman Munson, two of the team's most respected stars, begged George Steinbrenner to fire Martin. Two other vital players, Mickey Rivers and Graig Nettles, demanded to be traded. Every Yankee, it seemed, hated both Martin and Jackson, and Martin and Jackson hated each other.

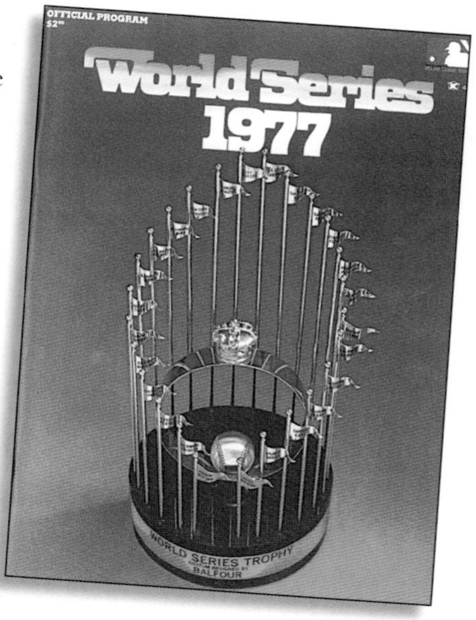

The Los Angeles Dodgers didn't have Reggie Jackson, but they were also led by a loud, self-promoting character: their new manager, Tommy Lasorda. Lasorda was once a mediocre left-handed pitcher. He now claimed to bleed Dodger blue and frequently paid homage to "The Big Dodger in the Sky." He also bucked conventional managerial wisdom by openly fraternizing and making friends with his players, a policy that most believed would undermine team discipline. But the Dodgers got along better than the troubled Yankees, and they also won an impressive 98 games and the National League title.

The teams played Game 1 to a 3-3 tie after nine innings thanks to spectacular

BOTTOM: Steve Garvey is called out after trying to score from first on a single in Game 1 of the 1977 World Series. The Yankee catcher is Thurman Munson.

relief pitching on both sides. In the bottom of the twelfth, Paul Blair—batting in Jackson's spot after he had entered as the slugger's defensive replacement—failed in his attempt to bunt Willie Randolph to third base. Forced to swing away, Blair lined a single to left field to score Randolph with the game-ending run.

The 1977 Dodgers were the first team in baseball history to have four players—Steve Garvey, Reggie Smith, Ron Cey, and Dusty Baker—hit at least thirty home runs in one season. Three of those men, Cey, Smith, and Garvey, went deep in the second game of the Series as the Dodgers pounded the Yankees 6-1. Yankee Stadium degenerated into chaos with the home team losing late in the game. Someone tossed a smoke bomb onto the field in the top of the ninth. Jackson astutely scooped it up with his glove and threw it back into the stands. The Dodgers' Reggie Smith was knocked to his knees after a heavy object thrown from the stands hit him in the head in the bottom of the ninth. Although doctors fitted with him with a cervical collar after the game, he was back in the lineup for Game 3 at friendlier Dodger Stadium.

The Yankees took a commanding 3-1 Series lead in California, as Mike Torrez went the distance in the third game and Ron Guidry did the same in the fourth. Don Sutton won Game 5 for L.A., but New York still had the Series advantage. They headed home to play the last two games at Yankee Stadium.

The sixth game was all the Yankees needed. The show started in batting practice when Reggie Jackson put on a pre-game hitting show that had both players and sportswriters transfixed. "BP was something special," Jackson later wrote. "I cannot ever remember having one like it…the baseball looked like a volleyball to me." That feeling continued into the game. Jackson walked on four straight pitches in the first inning. He sent Burt Hooton's first pitch over the right field fence in the fourth. In the fifth, with Elias Sosa now pitching, Jackson again lined the first pitch over the right field fence. In the eighth, he hit the first pitch from Charlie Hough, a knuckleball, deep into dead center field. Three at-bats against three different pitchers. Three swings. Three home runs. After the third homer, a thundering chant erupted at Yankee Stadium: "REG-gie, REG-gie, REG-gie!" Confetti poured down on him from the stands as he took his position in right field. Going back to Game 5, Jackson had hit four homers on four consecutive swings. He had tied a long-standing World Series record of three home runs in one game and set a new one by hitting five homers in a Series. More importantly, he had brought the world championship back to the Bronx for the first time in fifteen years. "I feel like God was with me as I ran the bases," Jackson said. "I felt so light on my feet, floating on the noise."

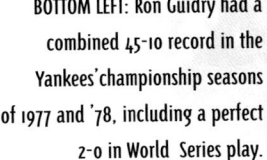

1977 WORLD SERIES

Yankee Stadium II (N.Y. Yankees) ◆ 10.11.77

	1	2	3	4	5	6	7	8	9	10	11	12	R	H	E
L.A.	2	0	0	0	0	0	0	0	1	0	0	0	3	6	0
NYY	1	0	0	0	0	1	0	1	0	0	0	1	4	11	0

WP–Lyle LP–Rhoden HR: NYY–Randolph ATT: 56,668

Yankee Stadium II ◆ 10.12.77

	1	2	3	4	5	6	7	8	9	R	H	E
L.A.	2	1	2	0	0	0	0	0	1	6	9	0
NYY	0	0	0	1	0	0	0	0	0	1	5	0

WP–Hooton LP–Hunter HR: LA–Cey, Yeager, Smith, Garvey ATT: 56,691

Dodger Stadium (L.A. Dodgers) ◆ 10.14.77

	1	2	3	4	5	6	7	8	9	R	H	E
NYY	3	0	0	1	1	0	0	0	0	5	10	0
L.A.	0	0	3	0	0	0	0	0	0	3	7	1

WP–Torrez LP–John HR: LA–Baker ATT: 55,992

Dodger Stadium ◆ 10.15.77

	1	2	3	4	5	6	7	8	9	R	H	E
NYY	0	3	0	0	0	1	0	0	0	4	7	0
L.A.	0	0	2	0	0	0	0	0	0	2	4	0

WP–Guidry LP–Rau HR: NYY–Jackson; LA–Lopes ATT: 55,995

Dodger Stadium ◆ 10.16.77

	1	2	3	4	5	6	7	8	9	R	H	E
NYY	0	0	0	0	0	0	2	2	0	4	9	2
L.A.	1	0	0	4	3	2	0	0	X	10	13	0

WP–Sutton LP–Gullett HR: NYY–Munson, Jackson; LA–Yeager, Smith ATT: 55,955

Yankee Stadium II ◆ 10.18.77

	1	2	3	4	5	6	7	8	9	R	H	E
L.A.	2	0	1	0	0	0	0	0	1	4	9	0
NYY	0	2	0	3	2	0	0	1	X	8	8	1

WP–Torrez LP–Hooton HR: LA–Smith; NYY–Chambliss, Jackson (3) ATT: 56,407

BOTTOM LEFT: Ron Guidry had a combined 45-10 record in the Yankees' championship seasons of 1977 and '78, including a perfect 2-0 in World Series play.

BOTTOM RIGHT: Billy Martin (left) and Tommy Lasorda had much in common: They were both loud and abrasive, and as players each had played a small role in the Yankee-Dodger rivalry of the 1950s. In 1977, they opposed each other as managers in the World Series.

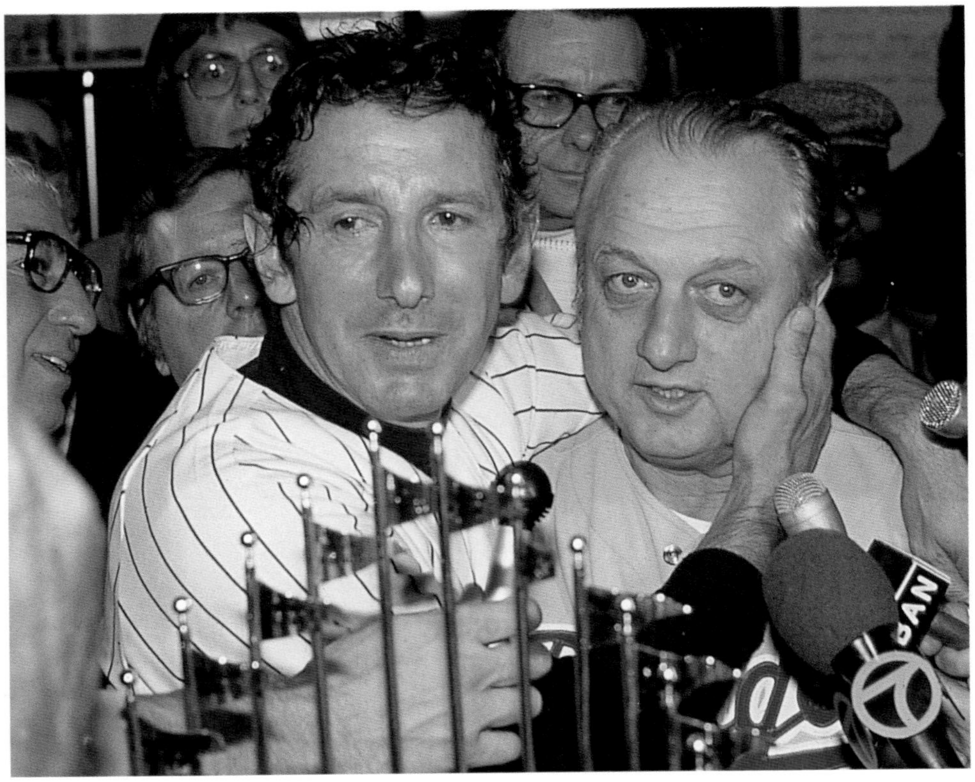

LEFT: In the fourth inning of Game 6 of the 1977 World Series, Reggie Jackson connects for a two-run homer off Dodgers hurler Burt Hooton. It was the beginning of a standout offensive performance for the brash slugger, who ultimately hit three dingers in the game, earning himself the nickname "Mr. October."

1978

New York Yankees (4)
Los Angeles Dodgers (2)

MIDWAY THROUGH THE 1978 SEASON, THE New York Yankees' chances of repeating as world champs seemed smaller than Phil Rizzuto, as manager Billy Martin was fired on July 23 and replaced by Bob Lemon. The Yankees were on a five-game winning streak at the time, but they were ten games behind the front-running Boston Red Sox and tied for third place. Even George Steinbrenner had given up. He told his men that they might have a shot at second place if they played well the rest of the season. The Yankees remained six and a half games behind Boston on September 1, but soon afterward they swept four straight games from the Red Sox. At season's end they

found themselves tied for the division title. Ron Guidry, having one of the best pitching seasons in baseball history, won a memorable one-game playoff on a home run by Bucky Dent, and the Yankees advanced to the World Series.

The Dodgers repeated as National League champions and featured mostly the same cast as the year before, with one shining exception. Bob Welch, a 21-year-old flamethrower from Eastern Michigan University, had been called up in midseason, and he proceeded to pitch the Dodgers to the pennant by posting a dazzling 2.02 ERA in a swingman role. The first game was no contest from the beginning. Bill Russell and Dusty Baker each had three hits and Davey Lopes homered twice to help the Dodgers outslug the Yankees 11-5. The day of Game 2 began on a somber note for the Dodgers, as they spent the morning attending the funeral of Jim Gilliam, their longtime player and coach who had unexpectedly died the day after they clinched the pennant. Lopes chaired a team meeting after the funeral. "After everything we've gone through," he said, "playing this game should be a piece of cake." The Dodgers led 4-3 entering the ninth inning thanks to four RBI by Ron Cey, the squat, comical-looking third baseman who, Jim Murray wrote, "looks as if he should be a ride at Disneyland." The Yankees threatened in the ninth as they put two men on base with one out. Dodger manager Tommy Lasorda summoned Welch from the bullpen and Welch retired Thurman Munson, bringing up Reggie Jackson, Mr. October, with the tying and winning runs on base. Jackson had homered six times in his previous four World Series games and had driven in all three Yankee runs in the game so far. It was as perfect a showdown as one could ask for: two outs in the ninth inning, the cocky slugger facing the young fireballer with a World Series game on the line.

Pitcher and batter played chicken for seven excruciating minutes. Welch threw nothing but smoking fastballs. "I loved every moment of it," Welch told George Vecsey. "I wasn't scared. I was thinking strikeout and he was thinking home run." Jackson worked the count full and fouled off several pitches

BOTTOM LEFT: After being called up from the minors in June 1978, Bob Welch posted a 2.02 ERA in 111 innings for the Dodgers down the stretch. Then, in that year's World Series, after striking out Reggie Jackson to great acclaim six days earlier, Welch gave up a key home run to Jackson in Game 6.

BOTTOM RIGHT: Ron Cey was one of three Dodgers to drive in at least four runs during the 1978 World Series.

to stay alive. Finally, on the ninth pitch of the at-bat, he swung violently and missed, corkscrewing his body around and falling to his knees. Mighty Casey had struck out. He stalked away, cursing and glaring at Welch. Then he threw his bat against the dugout wall. Thanks to Welch, the Dodgers had an imposing two games to none lead in the Series.

The Yankees won Game 3 easily back at Yankee Stadium, as Guidry shut down the Dodgers in a complete-game, one-run performance. Game 4 provided the most controversial play of the Series the next day, which came in the sixth inning with the Dodgers leading 3-1. Lou Piniella hit a soft line drive to shortstop Bill Russell with two men on base, but Russell dropped the liner, perhaps intentionally, and tried for an inning-ending double play. Reggie Jackson, the runner on first base, stuck his hip out and deflected Russell's throw, breaking up the double play and enabling Munson to score from second. Television replays made it clear that Jackson had moved into the path of the ball intentionally, but the umpires, without such replays to aid them, declined to call interference. The run stood and the game went into extra innings despite Tommy Lasorda's vociferous protests. The Dodgers brought in Welch to pitch, but he didn't have his magic on this night. He walked Roy White and gave up singles to Jackson and Munson in the tenth to give the Yankees a 4-3 victory.

The Yankees got their third win in a row in Game 5. This time it was a rout, as rookie Jim Beattie pitched his first major league complete game to beat the Dodgers 12-2. The Bronx Bombers wrapped it up in the sixth game at Dodger Stadium, pounding both Don Sutton and Welch. Welch, in a confrontation not nearly as spine-tingling as that in Game 2, served up a home run to Jackson in the seventh inning, providing the nail in the coffin.

1978 WORLD SERIES

Dodger Stadium (L.A. Dodgers) ◆ 10.10.78 (Game 1)

	1	2	3	4	5	6	7	8	9	R	H	E
NYY	0	0	0	0	0	0	3	2	0	5	9	1
L.A.	0	3	0	3	1	0	3	1	X	11	15	2

WP–John LP–Figueroa HR: NYY–Jackson; LA–Baker, Lopes (2) ATT: 55,997

Dodger Stadium ◆ 10.11.78 (Game 2)

	1	2	3	4	5	6	7	8	9	R	H	E
NYY	0	0	2	0	0	0	1	0	0	3	11	0
L.A.	0	0	0	1	0	3	0	0	X	4	7	0

WP–Hooton LP–Hunter S–Welch HR: LA–Cey ATT: 55,982

Yankee Stadium II (N.Y. Yankees) ◆ 10.13.78 (Game 3)

	1	2	3	4	5	6	7	8	9	R	H	E
L.A.	0	0	1	0	0	0	0	0	0	1	8	0
NYY	1	1	0	0	0	0	3	0	X	5	10	1

WP–Guidry LP–Sutton HR: NYY–White ATT: 56,447

Yankee Stadium II ◆ 10.14.78 (Game 4)

	1	2	3	4	5	6	7	8	9	10	R	H	E
L.A.	0	0	0	0	3	0	0	0	0	0	3	6	1
NYY	0	0	0	0	0	2	0	1	0	1	4	9	0

WP–Gossage LP–Welch HR: LA–Smith ATT: 56,445

Yankee Stadium II ◆ 10.15.78 (Game 5)

	1	2	3	4	5	6	7	8	9	R	H	E
L.A.	1	0	1	0	0	0	0	0	0	2	9	3
NYY	0	0	4	3	0	0	4	1	X	12	18	0

WP–Beattie LP–Hooton ATT: 56,448

Dodger Stadium ◆ 10.17.78 (Game 6)

	1	2	3	4	5	6	7	8	9	R	H	E
NYY	0	3	0	0	0	2	2	0	0	7	11	0
L.A.	1	0	1	0	0	0	0	0	0	2	7	1

WP–Hunter LP–Sutton HR: NYY–Jackson; LA–Lopes ATT: 55,985

Though both teams were filled with veterans, it was rookies who made the difference in the Series. Young Jim Beattie overpowered the Dodgers in the fifth game. Yankee second baseman Brian Doyle had almost as many hits in the World Series (seven) as in his entire previous major league career (ten). And of course there was Welch, who despite posting a 0-1 record and 6.23 ERA for the losing team, became the most memorable image of the 1978 World Series.

1979

Pittsburgh Pirates (4)
Baltimore Orioles (3)

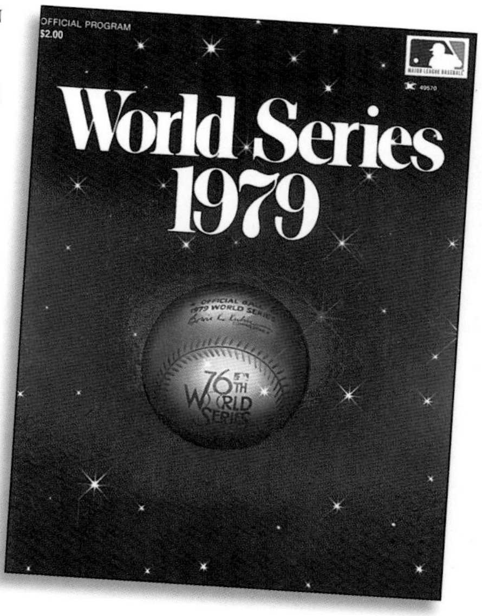

Brooks and Frank Robinson were retired by 1979, but the style of play their teams had espoused—pitching, defense, and three-run homers—was alive and well in Baltimore under Earl Weaver. Only two players, Jim Palmer and Mark Belanger, remained from the Orioles' last pennant-winning team in 1971, but a collection of new stars, including 23-year-old first baseman Eddie Murray, led the Orioles to 102 wins and the American League pennant.

The Pittsburgh Pirates were also appearing in their first World Series since facing the Orioles in 1971. Chuck Tanner was the Pirates' manager in name, but the real leader of the team was unquestionably Willie Stargell, the rotund 38-year-old first baseman who had been the team's top power hitter since the days of Roberto Clemente. Known to his teammates as "Pops," Stargell led the team with 32 home runs. More importantly, he was the central figure in the clubhouse, establishing a system where small gold stars were stitched onto a player's cap for each positive contribution to the team. The team, following Stargell's lead, adopted the Sister Sledge disco anthem "We Are Family" as their theme song. The jolly Pirates led the National League with 98 wins. "When we left spring

BOTTOM: Lou Piniella's tenth-inning single scored Roy White with the winning run of Game 4, ruining two-plus innings of stellar relief pitching by Bob Welch.

TOP LEFT: Jim Bibby's cap displays several of the gold stars that team captain Willie Stargell handed out for special accomplishments during the 1979 season.

TOP RIGHT: If Ken Singleton had scored on this play, Game 3 would have been tied 3-3. He was tagged out by Steve Nicosia, but the Orioles went on to win anyway, 8-4.

BOTTOM: Willie Stargell, 39, was named National League co-MVP in 1979 after batting .281 with 32 homers.

1979 WORLD SERIES

Memorial Stadium (Balt. Orioles) ◆ 10.10.79

	1	2	3	4	5	6	7	8	9	R	H	E
Pitt.	0	0	0	1	0	2	0	1	0	4	11	3
Balt.	5	0	0	0	0	0	0	0	0	5	6	3

WP–Flanagan LP–Kison HR: PIT–Stargell; BAL–DeCinces ATT: 53,735

Memorial Stadium ◆ 10.11.79

	1	2	3	4	5	6	7	8	9	R	H	E
Pitt.	0	2	0	0	0	0	0	0	1	3	11	2
Balt.	0	1	0	0	0	1	0	0	0	2	6	1

WP–D. Robinson LP–Stanhouse S–Tekulve ATT: 53,739

Three Rivers Stadium (Pitts. Pirates) ◆ 10.12.79

	1	2	3	4	5	6	7	8	9	R	H	E
Balt.	0	0	2	5	0	0	1	0	0	8	13	0
Pitt.	1	2	0	0	0	1	0	0	0	4	9	2

WP–McGregor LP–Candelaria HR: BAL–Ayala ATT: 50,848

Three Rivers Stadium ◆ 10.13.79

	1	2	3	4	5	6	7	8	9	R	H	E
Balt.	0	0	3	0	0	0	0	6	0	9	12	0
Pitt.	0	4	0	0	1	1	0	0	0	6	17	1

WP–Stoddard LP–Tekulve HR: PIT–Stargell ATT: 50,883

Three Rivers Stadium ◆ 10.14.79

	1	2	3	4	5	6	7	8	9	R	H	E
Balt.	0	0	0	0	1	0	0	0	0	1	6	2
Pitt.	0	0	0	0	0	2	2	3	X	7	13	1

WP–Blyleven LP–Flanagan ATT: 50,920

Memorial Stadium ◆ 10.16.79

	1	2	3	4	5	6	7	8	9	R	H	E
Pitt.	0	0	0	0	0	0	2	2	0	4	10	0
Balt.	0	0	0	0	0	0	0	0	0	0	7	1

WP–Candelaria LP–Palmer S–Tekulve ATT: 53,739

Memorial Stadium ◆ 10.17.79

	1	2	3	4	5	6	7	8	9	R	H	E
Pitt.	0	0	0	0	0	2	0	0	2	4	10	0
Balt.	0	0	1	0	0	0	0	0	0	1	4	2

WP–Jackson LP–McGregor S–Tekulve HR: PIT–Stargell; BAL–Dauer ATT: 53,733

training this year," Stargell said, "we were not prepared to lose."

It turned out to be a close Series, if not a particularly well-played one. Commissioner Bowie Kuhn was again criticized for ordering the games to start late at night for television purposes, resulting in much of the Series being conducted in a bitter cold that hampered the quality of play, with the teams committing eighteen errors in the seven games. Six of those errors came in the first game, including a vital one by Pittsburgh's Phil Garner that made the difference in the game, as Garner threw an easy double-play ball into left field in the first inning, opening the gates for a five-run Baltimore rally from which the Pirates never recovered. Game 2 was a pitcher's duel between two outstanding curveball artists, Bert Blyleven and Jim Palmer, and the game went undecided until there were two outs in the top of the ninth. At that point, Manny Sanguillen, the once outstanding catcher who at age 35 was now a bench player, delivered a pinch hit single that brought home the winning run for Pittsburgh.

Orioles starter Scott McGregor appeared erratic in the early innings of the third game, but he pulled it together after enduring a 67-minute rain delay to throw a 95-pitch complete game to beat Pittsburgh 8-4. Leadoff hitter Alfonso "Kiki" Garcia provided the offense with four hits including a bases-loaded triple. The Orioles won the fourth game as well, coming from behind when Dave Parker, playing with a bad knee, got a poor jump on a fly ball and watched it land for a single that started a six-run Baltimore rally.

The Series seemed all but over with the Orioles holding a commanding three games to one lead. Much of the credit was due to the remarkable performance of wisecracking catcher Rick Dempsey, who had thoroughly frustrated the Pittsburgh running game. The Pirates, who ranked second in the National League with 180 team steals, were held to a pathetic 0-for-4 on the base paths during the Series. But the Pirates were not ready to give up despite the criticism they had received for their poor play. "We had articles posted all over the clubhouse," Stargell said. "They all said in their own individual ways that we were choking... We felt possessed to win."

And win they did, bouncing back in Game 5 behind the pitching of Jim Rooker and Blyleven to post a 7-1 victory. Pittsburgh also won the sixth game with outstanding pitching, this time by John Candelaria and Kent Tekulve. It was now down to the seventh game.

"Ever since I was five years old, I've dreamed of pitching the seventh game of the World Series," the Orioles' McGregor said, though he probably didn't dream of losing it. The Pirates beat McGregor 4-1 to clinch the championship. Fittingly, the decisive blow was a two-run homer off the bat of Stargell, who also collected three other hits in the game, giving him Series totals of twelve hits, seven RBI, three homers, and a .400 batting average. He was an easy choice for Series MVP. "I wished I could have broken the trophy up into a million little pieces to share with all the fans in Pittsburgh, the radio and television announcers, our wives and kids, the people in the front office, the ushers, the ground crew, the trainer," Stargell said. "We molded together dozens of individuals into one working force...We were products of different races, were raised in different income brackets, believed in different Gods and religions and had varying political beliefs. But in the clubhouse and on the field we were a family."

BOTTOM: Phil Garner displays the gaudy Pirate uniform, which rivaled Oakland, Houston, and the Chicago White Sox as the most outrageous baseball clothing of the 1970s. Remarkably, the Pirates display four different uniforms in the four photographs on these pages, although each photo was taken during the 1979 World Series.

1980

Philadelphia Phillies (4)
Kansas City Royals (2)

The Philadelphia Phillies had firmly established themselves as the single worst franchise in the history of baseball as the 1980s approached. The phutile Phillies had finished over .500 in only 24 of the 78 seasons since the advent of the World Series. They finished last 22 times. They had appeared in the Fall Classic only twice, in 1915 and 1950, getting obliterated both times. Things were so bad in Philadelphia that the two best-known modern challenges to baseball's infamous reserve clause—those by Nap Lajoie in 1901 and Curt Flood in 1970—each happened because the player was seeking the right to *not* play for the Phillies.

But things started to change in 1976, as the Phils captured the first of three straight division titles. They met the Kansas City Royals in the World Series in 1980 in a matchup between two men who were not only the two best players in baseball, but also two of the greatest third basemen in the history of the game. The Phillies' Mike Schmidt led the National League in home runs and RBI while winning his fifth consecutive Gold Glove award. Kansas City's George Brett batted .390, the highest average in the major leagues since Ted Williams' .406 in 1941.

The Phillies got off to a good start by capturing the first game, 7-6. The key was a five-run third inning that included a three-run homer by Arnold "Bake" McBride, just the second World Series home run in Phillies history, after Fred Luderus in 1915. "Fred who?" McBride asked. The next day the Phillies grabbed another game as Steve Carlton labored through eight innings and 159 pitches emerging with a 4-2 win despite not having his best stuff.

The most bizarre subplot of the Series was provided in the second game by Brett, who had been suffering from hemorrhoids for several days and was forced to remove himself in the sixth inning despite borrowing a tube of ointment from Schmidt before the game. "A real pain in the ass," he quipped. "There's nothing you can do about it. The more I move, the more it hurts." With Brett's uncomfortable medical condition widely known, thanks to extensive media coverage, advice poured in from across the country recommending everything from potions to witchcraft as a cure. But the solution ended up being relatively simple: Brett stretched out over three seats on the Royals' team flight to Kansas City, and once there, checked himself into the hospital for a twenty-minute surgery.

Brett was back in the lineup for Game 3 and, remarkably, homered in the first inning to give the Royals an early lead. It was a game of frustration for the Phillies as they stranded fifteen base runners, a World Series record. Still, they managed to send the game into extra innings. In the top of the tenth, Schmidt hit a smashing line drive but it was right at Frank White, who turned it into a double play. In the bottom of the inning Willie Aikens, batting after an intentional walk to Brett, punched a game-winning single for Kansas City. Aikens was even more impressive the next day, clubbing two homers to give the Royals a Series tie.

Schmidt had zero sacrifice bunts during the regular season, but the Phillies won the fifth game of the World Series because of his bunting skills. Schmidt came up in the ninth with Philadelphia down 3-2, and Brett played in close at third base because Schmidt had already bunted twice in the Series. But this time Schmidt swung away, hitting a liner that Brett dove for but couldn't catch. That ignited the Phillies, who rallied for two runs to win the game.

BOTTOM LEFT: In 1980, the World Series was played entirely on AstroTurf for the first time. Phillies reliever Tug McGraw, shown here, was once asked whether he preferred turf or natural grass. His reply: "I don't know. I've never smoked AstroTurf."

BOTTOM RIGHT: During the 1980 World Series, George Brett (right) had quite possibly the world's best-publicized hemorrhoids condition. Here he is teased about it by his third base counterpart on the Phillies, Mike Schmidt.

Steve Carlton had led the National League in wins and strikeouts, and was exhausted after pitching a major league high of 324 innings. Still, Carlton took the mound in Game 6 to try to close out the Phillies' first-ever world championship. He got some offensive support from Schmidt, who had a bases-loaded single, and led 4-0 when he was relieved by Tug McGraw in the eighth inning. McGraw struggled, allowing the Royals to load the bases with one out in the ninth. White represented the winning run but lofted a pop foul near the first base line. Bob Boone had trouble with it, but when it popped out of Boone's mitt, Pete Rose was right there to catch it before it hit the turf. McGraw then struck out Willie Wilson to end the game and give Philadelphia its first-ever Series title. Said McGraw: "Ol' Ben Franklin is somewhere having a couple of Irish whiskies and saying, 'I'm with you, boys, I'm with you.'"

1980 WORLD SERIES

GAME 1 — VETERANS STADIUM (PHIL. PHILLIES) ◆ 10.14.80

	1	2	3	4	5	6	7	8	9	R	H	E
KCR	0	2	2	0	0	0	0	2	0	6	9	1
Phil.	0	0	5	1	1	0	0	0	X	7	11	0

WP–Walk LP–Leonard S–McGraw HR: KC–Otis, Aikens (2); PHI–McBride ATT: 65,791

GAME 2 — VETERANS STADIUM ◆ 10.15.80

	1	2	3	4	5	6	7	8	9	R	H	E
KCR	0	0	0	0	0	1	3	0	0	4	11	0
Phil.	0	0	0	0	2	0	0	4	X	6	8	1

WP–Carlton LP–Quisenberry S–Reed ATT: 65,775

GAME 3 — ROYALS STADIUM (KANS. CITY ROYALS) ◆ 10.17.80

	1	2	3	4	5	6	7	8	9	10	R	H	E
Phil.	0	1	0	0	1	0	0	1	0	0	3	14	0
KCR	1	0	0	1	0	0	1	0	0	1	4	11	0

WP–Quisenberry LP–McGraw HR: PHI–Schmidt; KC–Brett, Otis ATT: 42,380

GAME 4 — ROYALS STADIUM ◆ 10.18.80

	1	2	3	4	5	6	7	8	9	R	H	E
Phil.	0	1	0	0	0	0	1	1	0	3	10	1
KCR	4	1	0	0	0	0	0	0	X	5	10	2

WP–Leonard LP–Christenson S–Quisenberry HR: KC–Aikens (2) ATT: 42,363

GAME 5 — ROYALS STADIUM ◆ 10.19.80

	1	2	3	4	5	6	7	8	9	R	H	E
Phil.	0	0	0	2	0	0	0	0	2	4	7	0
St.L.	0	0	0	0	1	2	0	0	0	3	12	2

WP–McGraw LP–Quisenberry HR: PHI–Schmidt; KC–Otis ATT: 42,369

GAME 6 — VETERANS STADIUM ◆ 10.21.80

	1	2	3	4	5	6	7	8	9	R	H	E
KCR	0	0	0	0	0	0	0	1	0	1	7	2
Phil.	0	0	2	0	1	1	0	0	X	4	9	0

WP–Carlton LP–Gale S–McGraw ATT: 65,838

1981

LOS ANGELES DODGERS (4)
NEW YORK YANKEES (2)

When baseball returned to the field on August 10, 1981, after a two-month strike, all was forgiven as far as Dodger fans were concerned. Los Angeles had been half a game in front of Cincinnati when play stopped. Under the agreement that resolved the labor dispute, that meant the Dodgers were guaranteed a playoff spot as champions of the first half, regardless of what happened the rest of the season.

Dodger fans also were looking forward to seeing Fernando Valenzuela pitch again as he

BOTTOM LEFT: Mike Schmidt, the 1980 National League MVP during the regular season, continued his onslaught during the World Series, batting .381 with two homers and seven RBI.

BOTTOM RIGHT: Fernando Valenzuela enjoyed a magical rookie season in 1981, becoming the first man to win the Rookie of the Year and Cy Young awards in the same season.

had whipped the baseball world into a frenzy ever since shutting out Houston as an emergency starter on Opening Day. By May 14 he was 8-0 with a 0.50 ERA. He made baseball fans of thousands of Mexican-Americans, who had historically been indifferent to the Dodgers because the team had bulldozed a vibrant Hispanic neighborhood, Chávez Ravine, in order to build Dodger Stadium. Valenzuela single-handedly brought them back. "He created more baseball fans than anyone in the game," said Jaime Jarrín, the Dodgers' Spanish-language broadcaster who served as Valenzuela's interpreter throughout the season.

A quiet, pudgy 20-year-old from a tiny village in Mexico, Valenzuela could have been the invention of a pulp novelist's overactive imagination. He turned his eyes to the sky in the middle of his twisting windup as if summoning strength from the heavens. He made no pretense of staying in shape, gleefully guzzling beer in the clubhouse after each victory. His favorite pastime was lassoing his teammates in the clubhouse. "He used to carry this lariat with him," Rick Monday remembered. "He would lasso guys as they walked by. He thought that was hysterical."

TOP: Ron Cey, one of the Dodgers' co-MVPs of the 1981 World Series, makes a diving catch of a Bobby Murcer pop-up in Game 3.

BOTTOM: Graig Nettles made a number of spectacular defensive plays in his World Series career, including this one against the Dodgers in 1981.

The New York Yankees beat the Dodgers in the first game of the World Series thanks to the golden glove of third baseman Graig Nettles. Nettles dove to his right to backhand a screaming liner by Steve Garvey in the eighth inning to rob him of a double that would have put the tying run in scoring position. "I get sick to my stomach seeing him make those plays all the time," Dodger manager Tommy Lasorda said. Lasorda probably felt no better after the second game, as Tommy John, who had left the Dodgers for the Yankees after the 1978 World Series, combined with Richard "Goose" Gossage on a four-hit shutout.

If there was any good news for Los Angeles, it was that Valenzuela would be pitching the third game at Dodger Stadium. He allowed four early runs to the Yankees but, characteristically, grew stronger as the game went on. The Dodgers scored the go-ahead run in the fifth inning on, of all things, a double-play ball. Valenzuela "was in trouble all game," said catcher Steve Yeager, "but Tommy just stayed with him and stayed with him. Finally, he won." Lasorda called Valenzuela's 145-pitch complete game one of the gutsiest performances he had ever seen: "He was like a sharp poker player bluffing his way through some bad hands."

Dodger starter Bob Welch, the fair-haired hero of three years prior, failed to get even a single out in Game 4. But he was hardly alone in his ineptitude, as the two teams used ten pitchers, eight of whom gave up at least one run. That, combined with three errors, several other misplays, and eight walks, made it one of the most chaotic Series games in memory. The Dodgers eventually walked away with an 8-7 victory, the final blow a two-run pinch homer by eternal flake Jay Johnstone, who celebrated by sprinting across the postgame interview room, hurdling a table, and tackling Garvey while he was speaking to the national media. "Don't worry, he has to be back at the home by seven o'clock," Garvey deadpanned.

Game 5 was a much tighter contest between two standout left-handers, as the Dodgers' Jerry Reuss topped Ron Guidry, after Guidry gave up back-to-back homers to Pedro Guerrero and Steve Yeager. In the eighth inning, Ron Cey received a frightful beaning from Gossage, who had relieved Guidry. "I remember falling in slow motion," Cey said. "My wife thought I was dead."

Cey was not dead, but the Yankees almost were. The Dodgers went back to the Bronx needing just one more victory after winning all three games on their home turf. They had Valenzuela poised to pitch the seventh game, but it didn't matter. They romped to an easy 9-2 victory to clinch the world championship in Game 6. Yankee owner George Steinbrenner issued a crass "apology" to Yankee fans for the team's poor play in the World Series just twenty minutes after the last out. Dave Winfield, the free agent whom George Steinbrenner had acquired for $23 million, went a meager 1-for-22 in the Series, prompting the furious owner to dub him "Mr. May."

For the Dodger players, an aging nucleus that had won three pennants and now a World Series, it was a bittersweet victory, as Game 6 marked the last time that Steve Garvey, Davey Lopes, Ron Cey, and Bill Russell—the longest-running infield in baseball history—would play together as a unit. But at least it ended with a victory over the Yankees. "You don't know how sweet it is to beat New York in New York," said Lopes, who made six errors in the Series but also scored six runs. "If somebody has kicked your butt twice, you want the chance to kick his."

1981 WORLD SERIES

Yankee Stadium II (N.Y. Yankees) ◆ 10.20.81

	1	2	3	4	5	6	7	8	9	R	H	E
L.A.	0	0	0	0	1	0	0	2	0	3	5	0
NYY	3	0	1	1	0	0	0	0	X	5	6	0

WP–Guidry LP–Reuss S–Gossage HR: LA–Yeager; NYY–Watson ATT: 56,470

Yankee Stadium II ◆ 10.21.81

	1	2	3	4	5	6	7	8	9	R	H	E
L.A.	0	0	0	0	0	0	0	0	0	0	4	2
NYY	0	0	0	0	1	0	0	2	X	3	6	1

WP–John LP–Hooton S–Gossage ATT: 56,505

Dodger Stadium (L.A. Dodgers) ◆ 10.23.81

	1	2	3	4	5	6	7	8	9	R	H	E
NYY	0	2	2	0	0	0	0	0	0	4	9	0
L.A.	3	0	0	0	2	0	0	0	X	5	11	1

WP–Valenzuela LP–Frazier HR: NYY–Watson, Cerone; LA–Cey ATT: 56,236

Dodger Stadium ◆ 10.24.81

	1	2	3	4	5	6	7	8	9	R	H	E
NYY	2	1	1	0	0	2	0	1	0	7	13	1
L.A.	0	0	2	0	1	3	2	0	X	8	14	2

WP–Howe LP–Frazier HR: NYY–Randolph, Jackson; LA–Johnstone ATT: 56,242

Dodger Stadium ◆ 10.25.81

	1	2	3	4	5	6	7	8	9	R	H	E
NYY	0	1	0	0	0	0	0	0	0	1	5	0
L.A.	0	0	0	0	0	0	2	0	X	2	4	3

WP–Reuss LP–Guidry HR: LA–Guerrero, Yeager ATT: 56,115

Yankee Stadium II ◆ 10.28.81

	1	2	3	4	5	6	7	8	9	R	H	E
L.A.	0	0	0	1	3	4	0	1	0	9	13	1
NYY	0	0	1	0	0	1	0	0	0	2	7	2

WP–Hooton LP–Frazier HR: LA–Guerrero; NYY–Randolph ATT: 56,513

1982

St. Louis Cardinals (4)
Milwaukee Brewers (3)

Many baseball fans found the 1982 World Series refreshing because it featured neither the Yankees nor the Dodgers. Instead, as one writer noted, it was a Midwestern matchup between a man named Bud (Selig, owner of the Milwaukee Brewers) and the man who makes Bud (August Busch, owner of the St. Louis Cardinals).

The Brewers were managed by Harvey Kuenn, a Wisconsin native, and the Cardinals by Dorrel "Whitey" Herzog, a native of the St. Louis area. The two teams presented a clear contrast in styles. The Brewers, dubbed "Harvey's Wallbangers," were a high-powered offensive machine. They featured three of the American League's top five home run hitters in Gorman Thomas, Ben Oglivie, and Cecil Cooper, and as a team they led the majors in runs scored and home runs by comfortable margins. The left side of the Milwaukee infield, Robin Yount and Paul Molitor, combined for 48 home runs, 411 hits, and 265 runs scored. The Cardinals, on the other hand, played a game known as "Whiteyball," emphasizing pitching, defense, and speed. Their pitchers allowed the fewest runs in the National League and their base runners swiped two hundred bases, most in the league.

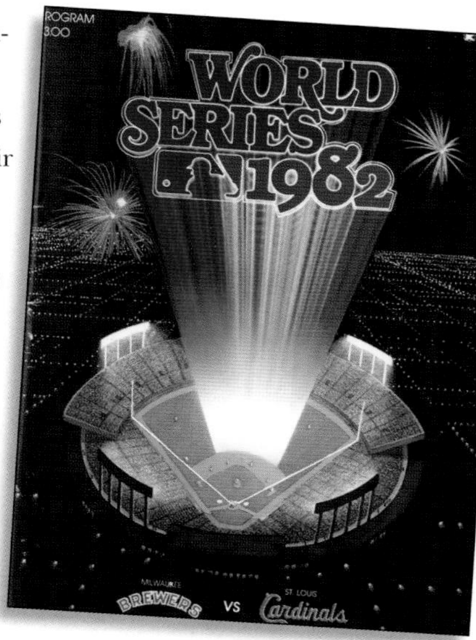

Milwaukee started the Series characteristically, winning 10-0 and pounding the Cardinals for seventeen hits, including five by Molitor and four by Yount. The game also featured a home run by Ted Simmons and a three-hit pitching performance by Mike Caldwell, which was notable because both players had been discarded by the Cardinals a few years earlier. The second game turned into a battle of relief pitching. St. Louis had the best bullpen weapon in the business: forkball specialist Bruce Sutter. Sutter pitched $2\frac{1}{3}$ innings of scoreless ball while his Brewers counterpart, Pete Ladd, walked in the winning run with the bases loaded, granting St. Louis a 5-4 win.

The Cardinals won the third game, too, thanks to the extraordinary performance of Willie McGee, their quiet and unassuming rookie. McGee hit two home runs and made two outstanding catches in center field, one of which robbed Thomas of a probable two-run homer. "Nobody ever

BOTTOM: Willie McGee, the rookie center fielder who had once been discarded by the Yankees, hit two home runs in the 1982 World Series after homering just four times during the regular season.

1976–1994

TOP: Willie McGee makes a game-saving catch of Gorman Thomas' long fly in the ninth inning of Game 3.

played a World Series game better than Willie McGee did tonight," said Herzog, his beaming manager.

The Cardinals appeared to have Game 4 well in hand in the seventh inning with a 5-1 lead. They were on the verge of taking an overwhelming three games to one lead in the Series, so it seemed unimportant when Cardinal pitcher Dave LaPoint dropped a throw from Keith Hernandez as he covered first on a grounder. But five hits and six unearned runs later and the scorching Brewers had a 7-5 lead. They held on to that lead and tied the Series at two wins apiece.

Yount's torrid hitting gave the Brewers a win in Game 5. Yount had his second four-hit game of the Series, a record, as Milwaukee prevailed 6-4. The frustrated Cardinals managed to move only four of their sixteen base runners across the plate, stranding at least one man on base in every inning. "That's the way this game is," St. Louis catcher Darrell Porter philosophized. "This stupid, great game." Brewer fans streamed on to the field as the game ended and celebrated as if they had won the Series. But the Milwaukee players engaged in no such celebrations—they still had one more win to go.

The sixth game looked like easy pickings for Milwaukee, as Don Sutton faced Cardinals rookie John Stuper. As Herzog noted, "Their guy has won 280 games, our guy has won nine." But Stuper pitched a complete game after waiting out a rain delay of more than two hours, and Sutton was knocked out early by the Cardinals in a 13-1 laugher. The rollicking, momentum-shifting Series had come down to a seventh game.

The Brewers led 3-1 going into the second half of the sixth, but the Cardinals grabbed the lead in the bottom of that inning when they scored three runs on timely hits by Ozzie Smith, Lonnie Smith, Hernandez, and George Hendrick. Joaquín Andujar, the self-proclaimed "one tough Dominican" who was the Cardinals' best pitcher, threw seven strong innings before giving way to Sutter. It was lights out for the Brewers, as Sutter retired the last six consecutive Milwaukee batters to clinch the championship.

Both teams played poor defense in the World Series, but the Brewers lost because their glovework—eleven errors and several other misplays—was even worse than the Cardinals' had been. "It was a fan's delight because of the multitude of errors, which shows the players are human too, and because of the way momentum kept swinging back and forth," wrote Bill Veeck, covering the Series for *USA Today*. "But it had to be a complete horror to baseball purists."

1982 WORLD SERIES

Busch Stadium II (St. Louis Cards) ◆ 10.12.82

	1	2	3	4	5	6	7	8	9	R	H	E
Mil.	2	0	0	1	1	2	0	0	4	10	17	0
St.L.	0	0	0	0	0	0	0	0	0	0	3	1

WP–Caldwell LP–Forsch HR: MIL–Simmons
ATT: 53,723

Busch Stadium II ◆ 10.13.82

	1	2	3	4	5	6	7	8	9	R	H	E
Mil.	0	1	2	0	1	0	0	0	0	4	10	1
St.L.	0	0	2	0	0	2	0	1	X	5	8	0

WP–Sutter LP–McClure HR: MIL–Simmons
ATT: 53,723

County Stadium (Milw. Brewers) ◆ 10.15.82

	1	2	3	4	5	6	7	8	9	R	H	E
St.L.	0	0	0	0	3	0	2	0	1	6	6	1
Mil.	0	0	0	0	0	0	0	2	0	2	5	3

WP–Andujar LP–Vuckovich S–Sutter
HR: STL–McGee (2); MIL–Cooper ATT: 56,556

County Stadium ◆ 10.16.82

	1	2	3	4	5	6	7	8	9	R	H	E
St.L.	1	3	0	0	0	1	0	0	0	5	8	1
Mil.	0	0	0	0	1	0	6	0	X	7	10	2

WP–Slaton LP–Bair S–McClure ATT: 56,560

County Stadium ◆ 10.17.82

	1	2	3	4	5	6	7	8	9	R	H	E
St.L.	0	0	1	0	0	0	1	0	2	4	15	2
Mil.	1	0	1	0	1	0	1	2	X	6	11	1

WP–Caldwell LP–Forsch S–McClure HR: MIL–Yount
ATT: 56,562

Busch Stadium II ◆ 10.19.82

	1	2	3	4	5	6	7	8	9	R	H	E
Mil.	0	0	0	0	0	0	0	0	1	1	4	4
St.L.	0	2	0	3	2	6	0	0	X	13	12	1

WP–Stuper LP–Sutton HR: STL–Porter, Hernandez
ATT: 53,723

Busch Stadium II ◆ 10.20.82

	1	2	3	4	5	6	7	8	9	R	H	E
Mil.	0	0	0	0	1	2	0	0	0	3	7	0
St.L.	0	0	0	1	0	3	0	2	X	6	15	1

WP–Andujar LP–McClure S–Sutter HR: MIL–Oglivie
ATT: 53,723

1983

Baltimore Orioles (4)
Philadelphia Phillies (1)

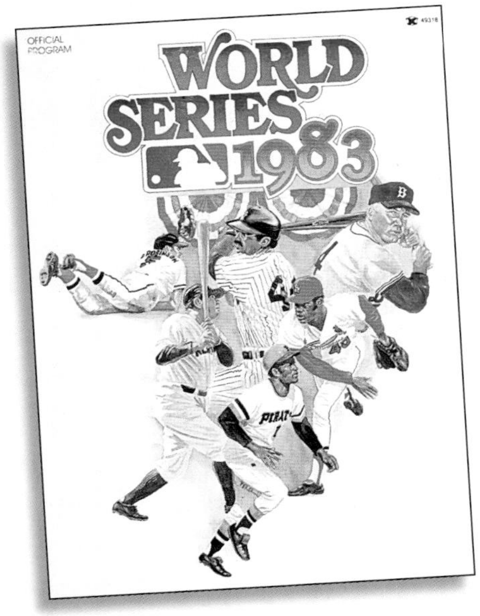

UNTIL THE 1983 WORLD SERIES, RICK Dempsey was best known as the part-time catcher who relieved the boredom of rain delays by sliding on his belly across infield tarps. A .240 lifetime hitter, he specialized in defense—he had to with *that* batting average. Dempsey scoffed when asked whether he thought he might get hot in the upcoming World Series. "I've never been hot at the plate," he said. As it happened, he picked a heck of a time for the first hot streak of his life. In addition to throwing out Joe Morgan twice on the bases, Dempsey batted .385, knocked five extra-base hits, and slugged .923 to give his Orioles the championship over the Philadelphia Phillies.

The Phillies were known as the "Wheeze Kids" because they relied on an aging nucleus of future Hall of Famers. They had won 90 games and defeated the Dodgers in the National League playoffs. Steve Carlton, 38, won fifteen regular season games. Mike Schmidt, 33, led the National League with 40 home runs. To complement that duo, the Phillies had three sputtering remnants of Cincinnati's Big Red Machine: Joe Morgan, 39, who posted a .370 on-base percentage; Tony Pérez, 41, who drove in 43 runs in part-time duty; and Pete Rose, 42, who was the starting first baseman.

The Orioles, meanwhile, posted a winning record for the sixteenth consecutive season, the longest such streak in baseball. They had a strong pitching staff, but their two best players were infielders. Cal Ripken, the sophomore shortstop, batted .318 with 27 home runs, increased his fledgling consecutive games played streak to 280, and won the MVP award. First baseman Eddie Murray was second in the MVP voting after hitting 33 homers and driving in 111 runs.

It wasn't exactly a subway series, but it was close: Charm City and the City of Brotherly Love were only a one hundred–mile train trip apart. The Series started on a rainy night in Baltimore, as Philadelphia's John Denny faced Scott McGregor. Both men pitched a masterful game, but Denny was just a bit stronger, winning 2-1. Mike Boddicker turned in an even more spectacular pitching performance for Baltimore in Game 2, allowing three hits but no walks or earned runs while winning 4-1 to even the Series.

Steve Carlton, the first three hundred–game winner to appear in the World Series since Grover Cleveland Alexander, was beating the Orioles 2-1 in the seventh inning of the third game. But after hits by Dempsey and Benny Ayala and an error by the Phillies, the Orioles were in the lead and Carlton was in the shower. Baltimore won, 3-2. They won the next game, too, scoring five runs as seven different players contributed hits. Diminutive left-hander Felix "Tippy" Martinez, who earlier in the season had picked off three base runners in the same inning, tamed the Phillies with his curveball over the last two innings to save a 5-4 Orioles win.

The Orioles were happy with their three games to one lead, but they remembered

BOTTOM LEFT: Eddie Murray hits one of his two home runs in the Orioles' clinching victory in Game 5 of the 1983 World Series.

BOTTOM RIGHT: Steve Carlton throws a pitch in Game 3, which he lost to Jim Palmer 3-2.

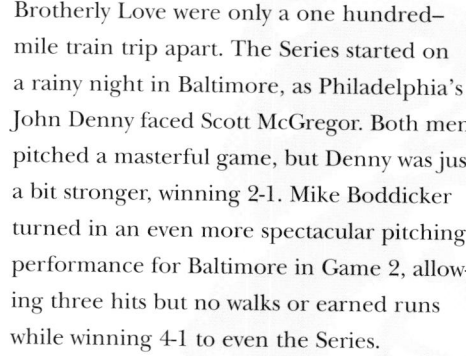

that they had blown an identical lead against Pittsburgh four years earlier and were not prepared to celebrate. The fifth game was never close, though, as Baltimore scored in four of the first five innings and McGregor threw his second gem of the Series, this one a five-hit shutout. Getting shut out was the final mark of futility for the Phillies, whose five Hall of Fame caliber players—Carlton, Morgan, Pérez, Rose, and Schmidt—batted a collective .191 in the Series. Schmidt was 1-for-20 with six strikeouts as he kept chasing high fastballs thrown by the Baltimore pitchers.

Eddie Murray, who had gotten only two hits in his past 37 World Series at-bats dating back to 1979, led the way with two home runs in the clinching game. Fittingly, the last out was a line drive to Ripken, Dempsey's roommate. In one of baseball's ironic twists, the 22-year-old Ripken would play in 2,656 more major league games, but would never again appear in a World Series.

1983 WORLD SERIES

MEMORIAL STADIUM (BALT. ORIOLES) ◆ 10.11.83

	1	2	3	4	5	6	7	8	9	R	H	E
Phil.	0	0	0	0	0	1	0	1	0	2	5	0
Balt.	1	0	0	0	0	0	0	0	0	1	5	1

WP–Denny LP–McGregor S–Holland
HR: PHI–Morgan, Maddox; BAL–Dwyer ATT: 52,204

MEMORIAL STADIUM ◆ 10.12.83

	1	2	3	4	5	6	7	8	9	R	H	E
Phil.	0	0	0	1	0	0	0	0	0	1	3	0
Balt.	0	0	0	0	3	0	1	0	X	4	9	1

WP–Boddicker LP–Hudson HR: BAL–Lowenstein
ATT: 52,132

VETERANS STADIUM (PHIL. PHILLIES) ◆ 10.14.83

	1	2	3	4	5	6	7	8	9	R	H	E
Balt.	0	0	0	0	0	1	2	0	0	3	6	1
Phil.	0	1	1	0	0	0	0	0	0	2	8	2

WP–Palmer LP–Carlton S–T. Martinez
HR: BAL–Ford; PHI–Matthews, Morgan ATT: 65,792

VETERANS STADIUM ◆ 10.15.83

	1	2	3	4	5	6	7	8	9	R	H	E
Balt.	0	0	0	2	0	2	1	0	0	5	10	1
Phil.	0	0	0	1	2	0	0	0	1	4	10	0

WP–Davis LP–Denny S–T. Martinez ATT: 66,947

VETERANS STADIUM ◆ 10.16.83

	1	2	3	4	5	6	7	8	9	R	H	E
Balt.	0	1	1	2	1	0	0	0	0	5	5	0
Phil.	0	0	0	0	0	0	0	0	0	0	5	1

WP–McGregor LP–Hudson HR: BAL–Murray (2), Dempsey ATT: 67,064

1984

DETROIT TIGERS (4)
SAN DIEGO PADRES (1)

BASEBALL PEOPLE ARE FOND OF SAYING THAT the mark of a great team is strength up the middle. The 1984 Detroit Tigers were one of the strongest up-the-middle teams of all time with Lance Parrish at catcher, Lou Whitaker at second base, Alan Trammell at shortstop, and Chet Lemon in center field. They also had right fielder Kirk Gibson, an intense and inspirational ex-football player

TOP: Cal Ripken Jr. is doused in champagne by his teammates after winning the 1983 World Series.

BOTTOM: Alan Trammell collected nine hits in the 1984 Series, including this Game 4 home run.

who, with 27 home runs and 29 stolen bases, was one of the best two-way threats in baseball. The Tigers' best pitcher was their relief ace, Guillermo "Willie" Hernández, a lefty who posted a magnificent 1.90 ERA in 140 innings. That performance won him the American League MVP award. All those pieces fell into place at exactly the right time, and Detroit led the American League East from the first day of the 1984 season through the last, then clobbered Kansas City in the American League playoffs.

The San Diego Padres attempted the unlikely feat of taming the Tigers in the World Series. The Padres had unexpectedly won the National League West—the first time in franchise history that they finished higher than fourth place. Their best player was San Diego State alum Tony Gwynn, who was completing his first full year in the major leagues. Gwynn won the National League batting title with a .351 average, the highest figure in the league in nearly a decade and 67 points better than the next-best Padre.

Oddsmakers considered the Tigers prohibitive favorites, but to the surprise of many Detroit did not flatten San Diego in the first game. The Tigers did win, but by the meager score of 3-2. The key play came when San Diego's Kurt Bevacqua, representing the tying run, opened the seventh inning with a double to right field. He turned on the speed and tried for third but was thrown out by the Tigers, Gibson to Whitaker to Marty Castillo.

The light-hitting Bevacqua—who Tommy Lasorda once said "couldn't hit water if he fell out of a fucking boat"—made up for his baserunning gaffe the next day by launching a three-run homer that provided the margin of victory in a 5-3 Padres win. The Tigers had knocked San Diego starter Ed Whitson out of the game in the first inning, but Andy Hawkins rescued the Padres by throwing five innings of scoreless relief to pick up the victory. San Diego had failed to give in to the anticipated sweep—they played tough in the first game and actually won the second—but that was about to change.

Padres pitchers walked a record-tying eleven batters in Game 3. Those walks led to a 5-2 Detroit win. The Tigers swung their bats plenty the next day, though, knocking out Padres starter Eric Show in the third inning. Trammell did most of the damage by hitting two two-run homers. (Show, subjected to a firestorm of criticism after giving up seven homers in eight postseason innings, died of a drug overdose a decade later.)

With the Tigers up three games to one, the only question that remained was whether they could win Game 5 to clinch

TOP: Jack Morris won a total of 22 games in 1984, including Games 1 and 4 of the World Series.

BOTTOM: A close play at the plate involving Lou Whitaker and Padres catcher Terry Kennedy.

the championship in front of their home fans. Gibson took that as a personal challenge. "When the chips are down," he said, "I want to be the guy they count on." Gibson cranked a two-run homer into Tiger Stadium's upper deck in the first inning, and singled and scored in the fifth to give Detroit a 4-3 lead. Gibson came up again in the eighth with the Tigers still clinging to a one-run lead. He faced Goose Gossage with runners on second and third. The two men had a history: Gossage had struck Gibson out in his first major league at-bat in 1979. Now, with the World Series on the line, it was a situation that called for an intentional walk, but Gossage talked manager Dick Williams into letting him pitch to Gibson. "Strikeout after strikeout, he had tortured me for years, and he wasn't backing away now," Gibson said. While Williams and Gossage discussed things on the mound, Gibson made a bet with his manager, Sparky Anderson, that he would hit a home run off Gossage. Sure enough, the second pitch was a fastball down the middle and Gibson smashed it into the upper deck for a three-run homer that effectively ended the Series. Gibson had also won the ten dollar bet with his manager. The World Series was over three outs later. "First, I thanked God," Anderson said. "Then I thanked Hernández, and Gibson, and Lemon, and Trammell...."

1984 WORLD SERIES

Jack Murphy Stadium (S.D. Padres) ◆ 10.9.84 — GAME 1

	1	2	3	4	5	6	7	8	9	R	H	E
Det.	1	0	0	0	2	0	0	0	0	3	8	0
SDP	2	0	0	0	0	0	0	0	0	2	8	1

WP–Morris LP–Thurmond HR: DET–Herndon
ATT: 57,908

Jack Murphy Stadium ◆ 10.10.84 — GAME 2

	1	2	3	4	5	6	7	8	9	R	H	E
Det.	3	0	0	0	0	0	0	0	0	3	7	3
SDP	1	0	0	1	3	0	0	0	X	5	11	0

WP–Hawkins LP–Petry HR: SD–Bevacqua
ATT: 57,911

Tiger Stadium (Detroit Tigers) ◆ 10.12.84 — GAME 3

	1	2	3	4	5	6	7	8	9	R	H	E
SDP	0	0	1	0	0	0	1	0	0	2	5	0
Det.	0	4	1	0	0	0	0	0	X	5	7	0

WP–Wilcox LP–Lollar S–Hernandez
HR: DET–Castillo ATT: 51,970

Tiger Stadium ◆ 10.13.84 — GAME 4

	1	2	3	4	5	6	7	8	9	R	H	E
SDP	0	1	0	0	0	0	0	0	1	2	10	2
Det.	2	0	2	0	0	0	0	0	X	4	7	0

WP–Morris LP–Show HR: SD–Kennedy;
DET–Trammell (2) ATT: 52,130

Tiger Stadium ◆ 10.14.84 — GAME 5

	1	2	3	4	5	6	7	8	9	R	H	E
SDP	0	0	1	2	0	0	0	1	0	4	10	1
Det.	3	0	0	0	1	0	1	3	X	8	11	1

WP–Lopez LP–Hawkins S–Hernandez
HR: SD–Bevacqua; DET–Gibson (2), Parrish
ATT: 51,901

1985

Kansas City Royals (4)
St. Louis Cardinals (3)

It was an all-Missouri World Series in 1985, as the Kansas City Royals made it to their second Fall Classic and the St. Louis Cardinals appeared in their fourteenth. The Cardinals had taken Whiteyball to its most extreme that year, stealing 314 bases, the most in the National League since 1912, while hitting only 87 home runs. The Cards won 101 games during the regular season and were widely expected to beat the Royals.

St. Louis got the jump in Game 1 as John Tudor, the surly left-hander with a 1.93 ERA, beat Kansas City 3-1. The Royals' Charlie Liebrandt carried a two-hitter into the ninth inning the next day, but St. Louis mounted a furious and improbable comeback. Clutch hits with two outs in the ninth by Jack Clark, Tito Landrum, and Terry Pendleton busted the game open for the Cardinals, who won 4-2.

The third game matched Bret Saberhagen, a 21-year-old whose 20-6 record that year earned him the Cy Young Award, against Joaquín Andujar, the eccentric and unpredictable right-hander who won 21 games for St. Louis. Saberhagen was superb, walking just one batter as the Royals won 6-1. Frank White, the Royals' cleanup hitter throughout the Series despite his .249 batting average, came through with two hits including a two-run homer. Although Saberhagen was brilliant by any standard, Whitey Herzog blamed the outcome of the game on the strike zone of Jim McKean, an American League ump working behind the plate. "Saberhagen's zone that night was about twenty-two by twenty-two inches," Herzog said. "Joaquín's was about six by six." It wouldn't be the last time in the Series that Herzog would complain about the umpiring.

The next night the Cardinals took a three games to one lead after Tudor tamed the Royals, 3-0. Saberhagen was in a joking mood even though the Royals now trailed in the Series three games to one. "They've fallen right into our trap," he said. "We've got them where we want them." The Cardinals arrived at Busch Stadium for Game 5 to find their lockers covered with clear plastic to protect them from the champagne showers that were expected later that night. The Royals fouled

OPPOSITE: Kirk Gibson exults after hitting the three-run homer in Game 5 that wrapped up the 1984 World Series for the Tigers.

BOTTOM: St. Louis slugger Jack Clark is caught in a rundown after hitting an RBI double in the opening game of the 1985 World Series. Clark was out but the Cardinals won anyway, 3-1.

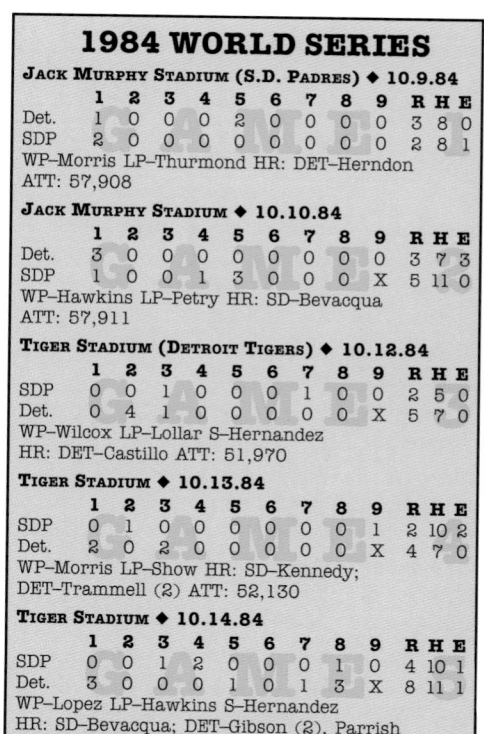

Tantamount Tantrums

WORLD SERIES EJECTIONS

The World Series has always generated its share of controversial calls—calls that during the regular season might enrage a player or manager enough to get him ejected from the game. But during the Fall Classic players seem better able to control their tempers, since a championship—and all the cash that comes with it—is often riding on one game.

In fact an ejection occurs about once every 25 World Series games, a significantly lower rate than during the regular season. There have been 22 bootings in World Series history: one player-manager, seven managers, two coaches, and twelve players. However, only five of those men—volatile pitcher Joaquín Andujar, and Hall of Famers Frank Chance, Ray Schalk, Heinie Manush, and Joe "Ducky" Medwick—were ejected from a game in which they were actually playing. Most players, having finally made it to the World Series, want to stick around until the end.

The first ejection of an active World Series player came on a rainy day in 1910, when special ground rules were enacted to accommodate the overflowing crowd at Chicago's West Side Park. Special bleachers were set up on the playing field in front of the outfield wall, and the managers and umpires agreed that any ball hit into the temporary seats would count as a double. In the third inning of the game, the Athletics' Danny Murphy knocked a ball deep into the right field corner with two men on base. Tommy Connolly, the stern British umpire who was calling plays in the field, ruled the ball a three-run homer, saying that it had bounced off an advertising sign just behind the bleachers. Cubs player-manager Frank Chance—who, as the first baseman, likely had as good a view of the play as anyone—insisted that the ball had landed directly in the bleachers, and should therefore be only a ground-rule double. He argued so vehemently that Connolly booted him from the game. As it turned out, the call made no difference in either the game or the Series. The Cubs lost both comfortably.

Unruliness in the World Series reached a high point in the 1930s, when six men were ejected from World Series games in four separate incidents. In 1933, in the sixth inning of a one-run game, umpire Charlie Moran called the Senators' Heinie Manush out on a close play at first base. Manush immediately began to argue, as did Senators catcher Luke Sewell, second baseman Buddy Myer, and shortstop-manager Joe Cronin. The argument dissipated after several minutes, but Manush started to needle Moran again when he ran out to his position in left field in the next inning. Manush was swiftly ejected. After the highly publicized ejection of the Senators' best hitter, Judge Kenesaw Mountain Landis announced that all future World Series ejections would require the commissioner's prior approval.

Landis' pronouncement came into play the very next year when the Cardinals' Joe Medwick was ejected from the seventh game of the World Series. Medwick, sliding into third on an RBI triple, spiked Detroit third baseman Marv Owen, who got up and began to scuffle with Medwick. The two cooled down soon enough, but the Detroit crowd, upset that their team was getting blown out in the deciding game, did not. When Medwick ran out to his position, he was greeted by an aerial assault of fruit, bottles, garbage, and anything else the fans could get their hands on. After the game was delayed twice by the unruly crowd, Landis was faced with a decision: he could either forfeit the game to St. Louis, or order Medwick banished from the game for his own safety. It might have been a tough decision if the game had been close, but with the Cardinals up 9-0, it was a no-brainer. Medwick, through no fault of his own, was ejected from the game. It remains the only World Series ejection ever ordered by the commissioner rather than the umpires.

BELOW: Billy Martin was ejected from Game 4 of the 1976 World Series. (Perhaps he was commenting on umpire Bruce Froemming's silly hat.)

WORLD SERIES EJECTIONS • Compiled by Doug Pappas

YEAR	PLAYER/MANAGER	OFFICIAL	REASON
1907 Gm 2	Hugh Jennings, Detroit MGR	Hank O'Day	Arguing caught stealing
1909 Gm 4	Wild Bill Donovan, Detroit P	Bill Klem	Refusing to end conference with 3B coach
1910 Gm 3	Frank Chance, Chicago 1B-MGR	Tom Connolly	Arguing homer should've been ground rule double
1910 Gm 4	Tom Needham, Chicago C	Tom Connolly	Arguing safe call at home plate from dugout
1919 Gm 5	Ray Schalk, Chicago C	Cy Rigler	Arguing safe call at home
1919 Gm 5	Jimmy Smith, Cincinnati IF	Cy Rigler	Arguing from 3B coaching line
1933 Gm 4	Heinie Manush, Washington OF	Charlie Moran	Brushing ump in argument
1934 Gm 7	Joe Medwick, St. Louis OF	Kenesaw M. Landis (Commissioner)	Removed for own safety after fans throw objects at him
1935 Gm 3	Charlie Grimm, Chicago MGR	George Moriarty	Bench jockeying
1935 Gm 3	Woody English, Chicago 3B	George Moriarty	Bench jockeying
1935 Gm 3	Tuck Stainback, Chicago OF	George Moriarty	Bench jockeying
1935 Gm 3	Del Baker, Detroit coach	Ernie Quigley	Arguing pickoff play at 3B
1952 Gm 7	Ralph Branca, Brooklyn P	Larry Goetz	Bench jockeying
1959 Gm 6	Charlie Dressen, L.A. coach	Ed Hurley	Arguing balls and strikes
1969 Gm 4	Earl Weaver, Baltimore MGR	Shag Crawford	Arguing balls and strikes
1970 Gm 3	Clay Carroll, Cincinnati P	unknown	Bench jockeying
1976 Gm 4	Billy Martin, New York MGR	Bruce Froemming	Throwing baseball onto field from dugout
1985 Gm 7	Joaquin Andujar, St. Louis P	Don Denkinger	Arguing balls and strikes
1985 Gm 7	Whitey Herzog, St. Louis MGR	Don Denkinger	Arguing balls and strikes
1987 Gm 7	Danny Cox, St. Louis P	Dave Phillips	Arguing balls and strikes
1992 Gm 3	Bobby Cox, Atlanta MGR	Joe West	Arguing check swing
1996 Gm 6	Bobby Cox, Atlanta MGR	Tim Welke	Arguing out call at 2B

up those plans, though, winning 6-1 behind 23-year-old lefty Danny Jackson to send the Series back to Kansas City.

Danny Cox and Charlie Liebrandt both pitched magnificently in Game 6, maintaining a scoreless tie until the eighth inning. The Cardinals scored the first run of the game on a single by little-used catcher Brian Harper, and Herzog sent in rookie stopper Todd Worrell to shut down the Royals and get the final three outs of the Series. Jorge Orta led off the bottom of the ninth for Kansas City and hit a dribbler that first baseman Clark fed to Worrell covering for the first out. It was not a particularly close play, but American League umpire Don Denkinger, who had a clear view of the action, inexplicably called Orta safe. Despite furious arguments by Herzog, Denkinger refused to budge, insisting (incorrectly, as replays clearly showed) that Orta had beaten the throw. The Cardinals felt they had been robbed and promptly imploded. As Herzog remembered, "Guys did things they hadn't done all year. Darrell Porter, my catcher, missed a pitch for a passed ball. Clark misjudged a pop foul. We fell apart." The Royals pounced on the opportunity and scored two runs in the inning to win the game on a Dane Iorg single. St. Louis, which had been 91-0 in games it led after eight innings, picked an inopportune time to lose its first such game of the season. The Orta call had been blown, to be sure, but the Cardinals still managed to record only one out in the ninth inning. The way the inning played out, Kansas City might have scored at least one run even if Orta had been called out. Denkinger may have provided the gun, but it was the Cardinals alone who shot themselves in the foot.

St. Louis was unable to get over the Denkinger call, and they rolled over and played dead in the last ten innings of the Series. "We'd had something taken from us the night before," Herzog admitted, "and we all felt a sense of doom and gloom." Indeed, Game 7 was ugly from the start, as Tudor was knocked out in the third inning. Upon leaving the game he punched an electric fan in the dugout, necessitating a trip to the hospital. His replacements were no more effective. Trailing 8-0 in the fifth, Andujar threw a pitch that Denkinger, calling balls and strikes on this night, ruled a ball. Andujar complained and then, according to Herzog, "Denkinger went apeshit. He jumped out from behind the plate,

BOTTOM LEFT: Twenty-one-year-old Bret Saberhagen was the pitching hero of the 1985 World Series, throwing two complete games while allowing a total of one run.

BOTTOM RIGHT: The 1985 Series featured two of the greatest defensive middle infielders in baseball history, Ozzie Smith (top) and Frank White (bottom).

stormed out there, and started picking an argument." The argument ended with Herzog's ejection. A few moments later, after another disputed pitch, Andujar was ejected, too. St. Louis ended up using five pitchers in that inning alone. Kansas City had an 11-0 lead before the inning was over. Herzog became the first manager to be ejected from a World Series game in nine years and Andujar was the first player to get the heave-ho in fifteen years. "That was the only time I ever had a beer with one of my pitchers before the game was over," Herzog said.

Saberhagen kept his concentration despite the turmoil. Pitching the day after the birth of his first child, he threw a five-hit shutout to put the icing on Kansas City's first-ever championship. Denkinger, whose name became a national joke after the Series, umpired admirably for thirteen more years before retiring in 1998. He continued to receive hate mail from Cardinals fans, getting undeserved blame for denying St. Louis a World Series title. But the fact remained that Kansas City pitching had held the Cards to just thirteen runs in the seven games, something one missed call at first base wasn't going to change.

1985 WORLD SERIES

Royals Stadium (Kans. City Royals) ◆ 10.19.85 — GAME 1

	1	2	3	4	5	6	7	8	9	R	H	E
St.L.	0	0	1	1	0	0	0	0	1	3	7	1
KCR	0	1	0	0	0	0	0	0	0	1	8	0

WP–Tudor LP–Jackson S–Worrell ATT: 41,650

Royals Stadium ◆ 10.20.85 — GAME 2

	1	2	3	4	5	6	7	8	9	R	H	E
St.L.	0	0	0	0	0	0	0	0	4	4	6	0
KCR	0	0	0	2	0	0	0	0	0	2	9	0

WP–Dayley LP–Leibrandt S–Lahti ATT: 41,656

Busch Stadium II (St. Louis Cards) ◆ 10.22.85 — GAME 3

	1	2	3	4	5	6	7	8	9	R	H	E
KCR	0	0	0	2	2	0	2	0	0	6	11	0
St.L.	0	0	0	0	0	1	0	0	0	1	6	0

WP–Saberhagen LP–Andujar HR: KC–White
ATT: 53,634

Busch Stadium II ◆ 10.23.85 — GAME 4

	1	2	3	4	5	6	7	8	9	R	H	E
KCR	0	0	0	0	0	0	0	0	0	0	5	1
St.L.	0	1	1	0	1	0	0	0	X	3	6	0

WP–Tudor LP–Black HR: STL–Landrum, McGee
ATT: 53,634

Busch Stadium II ◆ 10.24.85 — GAME 5

	1	2	3	4	5	6	7	8	9	R	H	E
KCR	1	3	0	0	0	0	0	1	1	6	11	2
St.L.	1	0	0	0	0	0	0	0	0	1	5	1

WP–Jackson LP–Forsch ATT: 53,634

Royals Stadium ◆ 10.26.85 — GAME 6

	1	2	3	4	5	6	7	8	9	R	H	E
St.L.	0	0	0	0	0	0	0	1	0	1	5	0
KCR	0	0	0	0	0	0	0	0	2	2	10	0

WP–Quisenberry LP–Worrell ATT: 41,628

Royals Stadium ◆ 10.27.85 — GAME 7

	1	2	3	4	5	6	7	8	9	R	H	E
St.L.	0	0	0	0	0	0	0	0	0	0	5	0
KCR	0	2	3	0	6	0	0	0	X	11	14	0

WP–Saberhagen LP–Tudor HR: KC–Motley
ATT: 41,658

BOTTOM: Moments after Don Denkinger's famous blown call, the Royals' Jim Sundberg jumps in the air after sliding home with the winning run in the ninth inning of Game 6.

1986

New York Mets (4)
Boston Red Sox (3)

Although the British game of Rounders had not yet evolved into baseball when William Shakespeare wrote *Hamlet* in 1603, the Bard probably would have been fascinated by the 1986 World Series. Like a Shakepearean play, the Series was both drama and tragedy, featuring a bizarre and unlikely plot that involved a ghost, a Knight, a curse, and ultimately, a tragic hero.

The Boston Red Sox had played in only three World Series since selling Babe Ruth to the Yankees. And the Sox had lost each of those series (1946, 1967, and 1975) in seven games. After Dave Henderson's home run heroics propelled Boston to victory over the California Angels in the playoffs, Red Sox fans were cautiously optimistic. It looked as if this might be the year the "Curse of the Bambino" would be broken.

Southpaw Bruce Hurst won the opening game for Boston by beating the New York Mets 1-0, as Met second baseman Tim Teufel let a grounder go through his legs for the only run of the game. Game 2 was one of the most anticipated pitching matchups in baseball history, with Roger Clemens and Dwight Gooden, the two fireballing young right-handers, facing off. The duel never materialized as Boston sent Gooden to the showers early. The Sox pounded out eighteen hits in the 9-3 trouncing.

It was now or never for the Mets after losing the first two games at home. The third game started well for them, as Boston pitcher Dennis Boyd, nicknamed "Oil Can" for his beer drinking proficiency, gave up a leadoff homer to Lenny Dykstra. Gary Carter drove in four more runs with two hits and New York won easily, 7-1. Carter continued to sizzle the next night, hitting two home runs over the Green Monster to give the Mets a 6-2 win and a Series tie. It was Gooden's turn to pitch again in Game 5. Once again the Red Sox tormented the 21-year-old right-hander, knocking him out of the game by scoring four runs in the first five innings. "I'll never forget the look on his young face as Davey Johnson came out to lift him,"

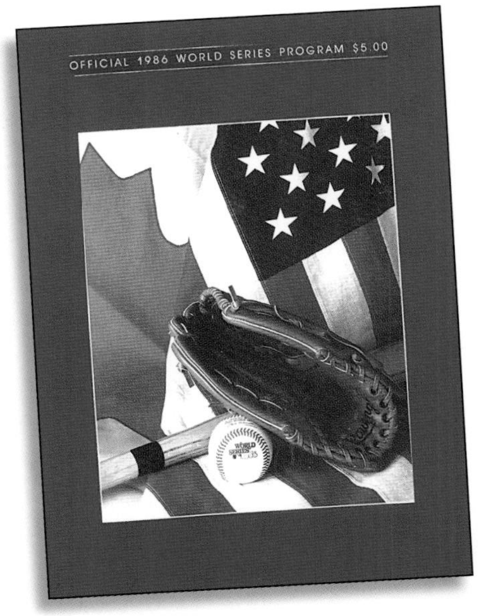

TOP: Twenty-four-game winner Roger Clemens was one of three ex–Texas Longhorns on the 1986 Boston Red Sox. (Spike Owen and Calvin Schiraldi were the others.)

BOTTOM: Mookie Wilson dives out of the way of Bob Stanley's inside pitch in the tenth inning of Game 6. The wild pitch tied the game, setting the stage for the Mets' victory on Bill Buckner's error.

Carter later wrote. "It was a sad, bewildered look, as though he were thinking, 'I can't believe this is happening.'" The four-run lead was plenty for Hurst, who threw a complete game to beat the Mets 4-2.

Now things were looking good for Boston, as they had Clemens ready to pitch Game 6 on five days' rest needing just one more victory. Clemens pitched seven innings and left with a 3-2 lead after popping a blister on his non-pitching hand, but his replacement, Calvin Schiraldi, made a key error that allowed the Mets to tie it in the eighth, and the game went into extra innings. Boston's Dave Henderson untied it with a homer in the top of the tenth, and Wade Boggs and Marty Barrett followed with hits to provide an insurance run. The Red Sox now led 5-3 as they took the field for the bottom of the tenth. Dave Stapleton had entered as a defensive replacement for first baseman Bill Buckner seven times in the playoffs when the Red Sox led in the late innings. Buckner, playing with arthritic ankles and an injured Achilles tendon, had to soak his sore feet in ice for an hour before and after each game just to be able to play. But this time manager John McNamara, perhaps giving in to sentiment, decided he wanted Buckner on the field for the Series-ending celebration.

Schiraldi got two quick outs. The scoreboard operator mistakenly flashed a message reading "Congratulations Red Sox." But there was one more out to go. Carter was the next batter and he singled. Then, rookie Kevin Mitchell—who had to be called out of the clubhouse to pinch hit, having already changed into his street clothes—singled to center field. Ray Knight next poked a single to short center to drive in Carter and make the score 5-4. McNamara had seen enough. He replaced Schiraldi with native New Englander Bob Stanley, the veteran right-hander who had saved 123 games for the Red Sox over the past decade. Stanley worked the count to 2-2 on William "Mookie" Wilson. The Red Sox were one strike away from winning their first World Series since 1918. Stanley's next pitch was far inside—it would have hit Wilson on the kneecap if he hadn't moved out of the way. Catcher Rich Gedman stabbed at the ball, but missed. Mitchell sprinted home from third with the tying run.

Knight was now standing on second base. Stanley made his tenth pitch of the at-bat to Wilson, and Mookie hit a slow roller down the first base line. Buckner stood right in the ball's path, watched it bounce once, twice, and then bent down to get it. Only he didn't bend far enough. The ball rolled under his glove and through his legs while Knight danced home with the winning run. Impossibly, the Mets had won the game. The Red Sox trudged off the field with their heads down as stadium workers hustled to remove all the champagne and television cameras from the Boston clubhouse.

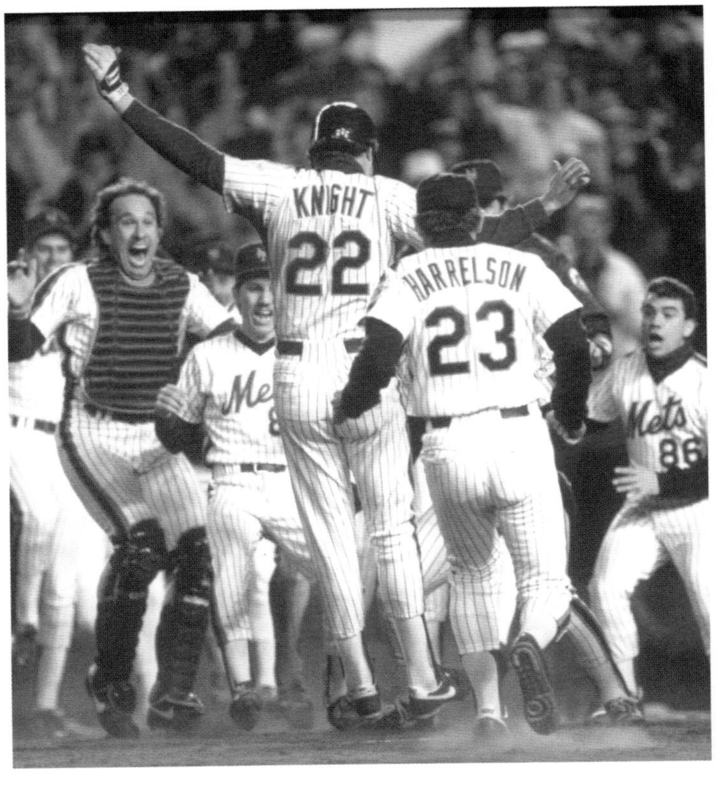

TOP: Proving that baseball is a game of inches, Mookie Wilson's grounder rolls just fair after barely passing under Buckner's glove.

BOTTOM LEFT: Ray Knight emphatically jumps on home plate with the winning run of Game 6, ensuring that the Mets will survive to play a seventh game.

BOTTOM RIGHT: Fans in a Boston bar watch as the Red Sox' best shot at a championship in 68 years rolls through Bill Buckner's legs.

The Shea Stadium crowd gave Buckner a standing ovation when the players were introduced before the seventh game. Boston sent Hurst to the mound for his third start of the Series, but even Hurst couldn't help them this time. The dazed Red Sox lost 8-5, going out one-two-three in the ninth against Jesse Orosco. Orosco threw his glove high into the air as the Mets won their first championship since the miracle year of 1969.

The sixth game of the 1986 World Series lingered in the national imagination long after the last out was made. McNamara was criticized for not replacing Buckner with Dave Stapleton and for removing Clemens from Game 6 too early. The latter move resulted in Schiraldi pitching too long and getting tired. McNamara later claimed that Clemens, who threw 135 pitches, asked to be taken out of the game because of the blister on his hand. Clemens angrily denied that charge. Buckner, meanwhile, was heckled by mean-spirited Boston fans for the rest of his career. Although he successfully fielded 15,252 balls at first base over his 22 years in baseball, he is still remembered for the one he missed. His name became a sort of slang; making an egregious mistake became known as "pulling a Buckner." New England's pain and anger over the play was so intense that Buckner sold his home in Boston and moved his family to Idaho. Although the Boston rock band Slide titled their 1996 album *Forgiving Buckner*, most of New England has never been able to do that.

1986 WORLD SERIES

Shea Stadium (New York Mets) ◆ 10.18.86

	1	2	3	4	5	6	7	8	9	R	H	E
Boston	0	0	0	0	0	0	1	0	0	1	5	0
NYM	0	0	0	0	0	0	0	0	0	0	4	1

WP–Hurst LP–Darling S–Schiraldi ATT: 55,076

Shea Stadium ◆ 10.19.86

	1	2	3	4	5	6	7	8	9	R	H	E
Boston	0	0	3	1	2	0	2	0	1	9	18	0
NYM	0	0	2	0	1	0	0	0	0	3	8	1

WP–Crawford LP–Gooden S–Stanley
HR: BOS–Henderson, Evans ATT: 55,063

Fenway Park II (Boston Red Sox) ◆ 10.21.86

	1	2	3	4	5	6	7	8	9	R	H	E
NYM	4	0	0	0	0	0	2	1	0	7	13	0
Boston	0	0	1	0	0	0	0	0	0	1	5	0

WP–Ojeda LP–Boyd HR: NYM–Dykstra
ATT: 33,595

Fenway Park II ◆ 10.22.86

	1	2	3	4	5	6	7	8	9	R	H	E
NYM	0	0	0	3	0	0	2	1	0	6	12	0
Boston	0	0	0	0	0	0	0	2	0	2	7	1

WP–Darling LP–Nipper S–Orosco
HR: NYM–Carter (2), Dykstra ATT: 33,920

Fenway Park II ◆ 10.23.86

	1	2	3	4	5	6	7	8	9	R	H	E
NYM	0	0	0	0	0	0	0	1	1	2	10	1
Boston	0	1	1	0	2	0	0	0	X	4	12	0

WP–Hurst LP–Gooden HR: NYM–Teufel ATT: 34,010

Shea Stadium ◆ 10.25.86

	1	2	3	4	5	6	7	8	9	10	R	H	E
Boston	1	1	0	0	0	0	1	0	0	2	5	13	3
NYM	0	0	0	0	2	0	0	1	0	3	6	8	2

WP–Aguilera LP–Schiraldi HR: BOS–Henderson
ATT: 55,087

Shea Stadium ◆ 10.27.86

	1	2	3	4	5	6	7	8	9	R	H	E
Boston	0	3	0	0	0	0	0	2	0	5	9	0
NYM	0	0	0	0	0	3	3	2	X	8	10	0

WP–McDowell LP–Schiraldi S–Orosco
HR: BOS–Evans, Gedman; NYM–Knight,
Strawberry ATT: 55,032

1987

Minnesota Twins (4)
St. Louis Cardinals (3)

The Cardinals returned to the World Series in 1987 after their heartbreaking Series loss in 1985. This despite injuries to many of their best players, including Jack Clark, Tommy Herr, John Tudor, and Tony Peña. "It's amazing we got this far with a spring training B team out there," said Jim Lindeman, a rookie who helped fill in for Clark at first base.

The Cardinals' opponents in the Series were the Twins. The Minnesota squad got most of its firepower from Kirby Puckett, the exuberant, roly-poly center fielder who finished third in MVP voting while batting .332. Minnesota's regular season record was a pedestrian 85-77. Fortunately for them, they played in the A.L. West while the four best teams in the American League happened to play in the East. They beat the Detroit Tigers in the playoffs to become the second-worst team ever to grace the World Series. (The 1973 New York Mets, with an 82-79 record, were the worst.)

"Minnesota had the *fifth*-best record in the American League that year," Cardinals manager Whitey Herzog said, "and they proceeded to kick our ass around that lunatic Homerdome, where you can't see a pop fly or hear it come off the bat." Indeed, the plastic-and-concrete hangar known as the Hubert H. Humphrey Metrodome was believed by many to be the Twins' greatest asset. With 55,000 fans screaming and waving their famed Homer Hankies, the building got so loud that many visiting players could neither hear nor think. "The noise level was unbelievable," Puckett said. "Some of the players wore earplugs. It's a good thing our outfield was so used to playing with each other, because communication was impossible once the ball was in the air." Thus, the Twins took the first two games of the Series.

The Cardinals trailed the third game 1-0 until the seventh inning when Vince Coleman ripped a two-run double that proved to be the decisive blow in a 4-1 St. Louis victory. The next day Herzog played a hunch, starting .227 career hitter Tom Lawless at third base in place of the injured Terry Pendleton in Game 4. The veteran utility man had gotten only two hits all year, but he made Herzog look like a genius when he parked a Frank Viola pitch into the seats, instantly doubling his career home run total. Lawless also made a fine play in the field as the Cardinals beat Viola soundly, 7-2. The next day the Cards won their third straight game as they stole five bases, the most in a World Series game since the 1907 Cubs.

The Twins had seen their two games to none lead vanish rapidly in Missouri, but

BOTTOM: Kent Hrbek (#14) is greeted at home plate by Greg Gagne, Kirby Puckett, and Don Baylor, the three runners he drove in with a grand slam in Game 6 of the 1987 World Series.

they were confident that they could win the final two games in their cozy Homerdome. The Cardinals built an early 5-2 lead in Game 6, and were only five innings away from winning the Series. But Kirby Puckett's single—one of four he would get that day—started a fifth-inning rally. The Twins proceeded to unload on Tudor and three Cardinal relievers over the next two innings with Kent Hrbek's grand slam providing the exclamation point. "I wanted to circle the bases twice," the overjoyed Hrbek said. The Twins emerged with a 11-5 win and a ticket for the seventh game.

The Cardinals scored two quick runs off Viola in Game 7. Viola soon noticed that they were hitting his changeup, so he started throwing mostly fastballs, and the Cardinals did not score again. It was a close game thanks mostly to the Twins' overenthusiastic baserunning, as three Minnesota runners were thrown out on the base paths, including two at home plate by jelly-armed left fielder Coleman. (Replays, however, showed that one of the men Coleman threw out—Don Baylor in the second inning—was actually safe.)

The balance started to tilt Minnesota's way in the sixth inning as they took a 3-2 lead and also flustered Cardinal pitcher Danny Cox, who was ejected for arguing with home plate umpire Dave Phillips immediately after being removed from the game. This marked the second time in three years that a Cardinals pitcher was ejected from Game 7 of the World Series. That was the beginning of the end for the Cardinals. The Twins added an insurance run in the eighth, and Jeff Reardon saved the game for Viola. A Minnesota franchise reigned atop the sports world for the first time since George Mikan played for the Minneapolis Lakers.

It was the first World Series in which the winning team had failed to win a road game. Herzog, never one to take defeat with grace, blamed his team's loss on the Twins' ballpark. "I still don't know how you win at the Metrodome, and I'm not sure I want to know," he said. "I do know one week isn't enough for a baseball team to figure it out. The Cardinals could've played there till Easter and never won a game." Viola was named the MVP of the Series. The sweetest

TOP: Known to Twins fans as "Sweet Music," the Bronx-born Frank Viola turned in two harmonious pitching victories in the 1987 World Series.

BOTTOM: Kirby Puckett batted .357 in the 1987 World Series and got at least one hit in six of the seven games.

music to his ears came when the Baseball Hall of Fame asked for the hat he had worn in the seventh game. "One day you're just another player," he said, "and the next someone wants to hang your hat in the Hall of Fame."

1987 WORLD SERIES

Hubert H. Humphery Metrodome (Minnesota Twins) ◆ 10.17.87

	1	2	3	4	5	6	7	8	9	R	H	E
St.L.	0	1	0	0	0	0	0	0	0	1	5	1
Minn.	0	0	0	7	2	0	1	0	X	10	11	0

WP–Viola LP–Magrane HR: MIN–Gladden, Lombardozzi ATT: 55,171

Hubert H. Humphery Metrodome ◆ 10.18.87

	1	2	3	4	5	6	7	8	9	R	H	E
St.L.	0	0	0	0	1	0	1	2	0	4	9	0
Minn.	0	1	0	6	0	1	0	0	X	8	10	0

WP–Blyleven LP–Cox HR: MIN–Gaetti, Laudner ATT: 55,257

Busch Stadium II (St. Louis Cards) ◆ 10.20.87

	1	2	3	4	5	6	7	8	9	R	H	E
Minn.	0	0	0	0	0	1	0	0	0	1	5	1
St.L.	0	0	0	0	0	0	3	0	X	3	9	1

WP–Tudor LP–Berenger S–Worrell ATT: 55,347

Busch Stadium II ◆ 10.21.87

	1	2	3	4	5	6	7	8	9	R	H	E
Minn.	0	0	1	0	1	0	0	0	0	2	7	1
St.L.	0	0	1	6	0	0	0	0	X	7	10	1

WP–Forsch LP–Viola S–Dayley HR: MIN–Gagne; STL–Lawless ATT: 55,347

Busch Stadium II ◆ 10.22.87

	1	2	3	4	5	6	7	8	9	R	H	E
Minn.	0	0	0	0	0	0	0	2	0	2	6	1
St.L.	0	0	0	0	0	3	1	0	X	4	10	0

WP–Cox LP–Blyleven S–Worrell ATT: 55,347

Hubert H. Humphery Metrodome ◆ 10.24.87

	1	2	3	4	5	6	7	8	9	R	H	E
St.L.	1	1	0	2	1	0	0	0	0	5	11	2
Minn.	2	0	0	0	4	4	0	1	X	11	15	0

WP–Schatzeder LP–Tudor HR: STL–Herr; MIN–Baylor, Hrbek ATT: 55,293

Hubert H. Humphery Metrodome ◆ 10.25.87

	1	2	3	4	5	6	7	8	9	R	H	E
St.L.	0	2	0	0	0	0	0	0	0	2	6	1
Minn.	0	1	0	0	1	1	0	1	X	4	10	0

WP–Viola LP–Cox S–Reardon ATT: 55,367

1988

Los Angeles Dodgers (4)
Oakland A's (1)

The 1988 Dodgers should have had a bad year. Fernando Valenzuela, the workhorse of the pitching staff, won just five games before being shelved for the year. Pedro Guerrero, the team's best hitter for a decade, hit only five homers before being traded away. And yet they won. They won on July 6 when, losing 3-0 entering the eighth inning, Franklin Stubbs hit a grand slam. They won on August 13, when pitcher Tim Leary, pinch hitting because no position players were left on the bench, got a game-winning hit in the bottom of the eleventh against the Giants. They won on August 20, when a wild pitch in the bottom of the ninth enabled Kirk Gibson to score the winning run—from second base.

The Dodgers won mostly because of Gibson. He was the team's first big free agent signing in nearly a decade, and his stats were good—he ranked fourth in the league in on-base percentage, seventh in home runs, and stole 31 bases. Still, the statistics didn't tell the whole story. For the most part, Gibson was named National League MVP because of his intense, inspirational leadership. The Dodgers won 94 games following his lead and outlasted the Mets in a marathon National League play-off series. The Dodgers had been expected to lose to the Mets, but they were *really* expected to lose to the Oakland Athletics in the World Series, since the A's won 104 regular season games, a figure not topped in the American League since the 1970 Baltimore Orioles. Their best players were the Bash Brothers, José Canseco and Mark McGwire, both of whom were among the best power hitters in the game. Canseco's 42 homers and 40 steals made him the best all-around player in baseball.

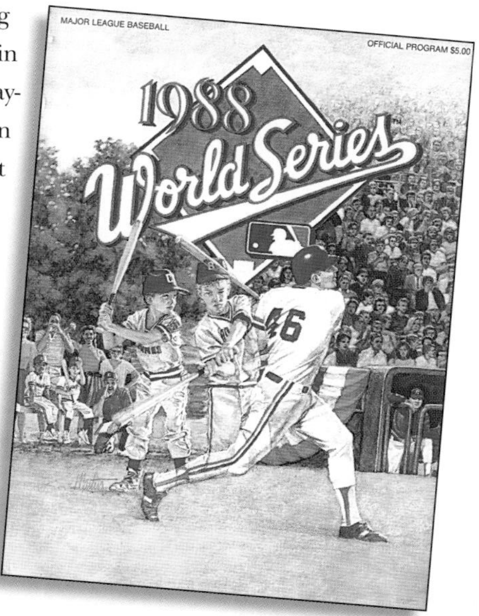

The Dodgers got bad news before the first game. Gibson—who could barely walk after injuring both his right knee and his left hamstring—would not be in the starting line-up. "I tried to do a little jog in my living room today, and it hurt like shit," Gibson said. "It was obvious I couldn't play." Gibson was in the trainer's room getting a cortisone shot while the teams were introduced before the game.

Canseco started the A's off as expected, hitting a grand slam in the second inning. It looked as if the Dodgers were finished as they still trailed 4-3 when Dennis Eckersley entered in the ninth inning to close out the game. Eckersley had been named MVP of

BOTTOM: Mark McGwire got only one hit in the 1988 World Series, but it was a big one: a walk-off homer against the Dodgers' Jay Howell in the ninth inning of Game 3.

1976–1994

TOP: After sitting out most of Game 1 because of a sore left hamstring and swollen right knee, Kirk Gibson came off the bench in the ninth inning to hit perhaps the most dramatic home run in baseball history.

BOTTOM: Gibson said that as he rounded the bases, he was thinking about how "I'd endured a lot, and this made it all worth it."

the American League playoffs after leading the major leagues in saves during the regular season. He was at the beginning of a remarkable five-year run that would see him post a 1.90 ERA over 360 innings to establish himself as one of the greatest relief pitchers in baseball history.

The first sign that something was in the air came when Eckersley, who had walked only eleven batters all year, gave Mike Davis a free pass with two outs. The Dodgers needed a clutch hit with the tying run on first. "The man the Dodgers need is Kirk Gibson," Vin Scully told the television audience, "and he's not even in uniform." Indeed, Gibson was not in uniform. But as the inning started he was underneath the stands taking practice swings off a tee and grunting in pain with every swing. After removing the ice packs from his legs, he sent word to manager Tommy Lasorda: If you need me, I'm ready.

Lasorda sent Gibson to the plate "looking for lightning in a bottle," as Scully put it. Gibson was clearly in pain, as he fouled off fastball after fastball to work the count to 3-2. One more strike and Oakland would win the game. Then Eckersley deviated from his fastball pattern. He tried to sneak a backdoor slider past Gibson. Gibson leaned out on his front foot and put a one-handed swing on the ball. It sailed deep into the right field stands and the Dodgers had won the game. Gibson hobbled around the bases, pumping his arms in joy, and was mobbed by his teammates as he arrived at home plate.

1988 WORLD SERIES

Dodger Stadium (L.A. Dodgers) ◆ 10.15.88

	1	2	3	4	5	6	7	8	9	R	H	E
Oak.	0	4	0	0	0	0	0	0	0	4	7	0
L.A.	2	0	0	0	0	1	0	0	2	5	7	0

WP–Pena LP–Eckersley HR: OAK–Canseco; LA–Hatcher, Gibson ATT: 55,983

Dodger Stadium ◆ 10.16.88

	1	2	3	4	5	6	7	8	9	R	H	E
Oak.	0	0	0	0	0	0	0	0	0	0	3	0
L.A.	0	0	5	1	0	0	0	0	X	6	10	1

WP–Hershiser LP–S. Davis HR: LA–Marshall ATT: 56,051

Oakland Coliseum (Oak. Athletics) ◆ 10.18.88

	1	2	3	4	5	6	7	8	9	R	H	E
L.A.	0	0	0	0	1	0	0	0	0	1	8	1
Oak.	0	0	1	0	0	0	0	0	1	2	5	0

WP–Honeycutt LP–J. Howell HR: OAK–McGwire ATT: 49,316

Oakland Coliseum ◆ 10.19.88

	1	2	3	4	5	6	7	8	9	R	H	E
L.A.	2	0	1	0	0	0	1	0	0	4	8	1
Oak.	1	0	0	0	0	1	1	0	0	3	9	2

WP–Belcher LP–Stewart S–J. Howell ATT: 49,317

Oakland Coliseum ◆ 10.20.88

	1	2	3	4	5	6	7	8	9	R	H	E
L.A.	2	0	0	2	0	1	0	0	0	5	8	0
Oak.	0	0	1	0	0	0	0	1	0	2	4	0

WP–Hershiser LP–S. Davis HR: LA–Hatcher, M. Davis ATT: 49,317

There had never been another homer like it in baseball history. Bobby Thomson's wasn't in the World Series. Carlton Fisk's and Bill Mazeroski's came with their teams tied, not trailing. Not only did Gibson's homer snatch victory from the jaws of defeat, but it came while he was injured, and facing the best relief pitcher in the game. It was the most dramatic, the most unlikely, and one of the most important home runs in baseball history. "Not only did it win the game for us," Lasorda said, "but it also won the Series because they were never able to recover from that home run."

The Dodgers had more ammunition to throw at Oakland in pitcher Orel Hershiser, who was on the hottest hot streak in the history of the game. Hershiser had allowed no runs in his last 59 innings of the season, breaking the Don Drysdale record long thought to be unbreakable. He was named MVP of the National League playoffs. Over his last eleven games, Hershiser was 7-0 with six shutouts, one save, and a 0.51 ERA in 88 innings. The man Lasorda nicknamed "Bulldog" continued his brilliance in Game 2. He pitched a shutout against Oakland, allowing them only three hits while getting three himself. Remarkably, the Dodgers now led Oakland two games to none.

The A's won the third game when McGwire hit a walk-off home run off Dodgers stopper Jay Howell, who was pitching for the first time since being suspended for illegally using pine tar to grip the ball in the National League playoffs. In addition to losing the game, the Dodgers also lost Mike Marshall, their leading RBI man, to injury.

NBC's Bob Costas proclaimed the Dodgers' Game 4 starting lineup without Gibson and Marshall to be probably the weakest ever to appear in a World Series game. The Dodgers watched the pre-game show in their clubhouse and were incensed. "Kill Costas!" Lasorda bellowed. "Kill Costas!" the players shouted in unison. But Costas was right. The Dodgers' number three hitter, Mickey Hatcher, had one home run during the regular season. Cleanup hitter Davis batted .196. First baseman Franklin Stubbs batted .223. Designated hitter Danny Heep had zero home runs and 11 RBI. The nine men in the Dodgers lineup had hit 36 home runs combined, six fewer than José Canseco hit by himself.

But Costas didn't know about the Stuntmen. The Dodgers' collection of bench players were so named because, like Hollywood stuntmen, they did the job when the big stars couldn't. "You do what it takes to win as a team," Rick Dempsey said. "Even if that means just to encourage the guys who are playing ahead of you." The Stuntmen capitalized on the opportunity to shine in Game 4, as Los Angeles took a 4-3 lead into the late innings. Jay Howell, the loser the night before, came in looking for redemption and found it. He retired both Canseco and McGwire with the tying run on base to preserve the Dodger victory.

The A's knew their days were numbered. They were down three games to one and facing Hershiser. What they didn't know was that the crushing blow would be delivered

BOTTOM: Orel Hershiser was both a batting and pitching star in his Game 3 shutout of Oakland, collecting exactly as many hits (three) as he allowed to the A's.

1976–1994

by the wacky Hatcher. He was the spiritual leader of the Stuntmen whose locker contained, among other bizarre items, a Slinky and a pair of swimming goggles, and he delivered his second homer of the Series in the second inning. Unused to home run trots—he had hit only one all year—Hatcher sprinted full-tilt around the bases with his arms raised in triumph. Later, Lasorda allowed Davis to swing away on a 3-0 pitch even though he was struggling, and Davis proceeded to hit a two-run homer deep into the right field stands. That was more than enough for Hershiser, who vanquished the A's with a complete game four-hitter with nine strikeouts.

The humiliation was complete for the vaunted A's. "It wasn't so much that the Dodgers beat us," manager Tony LaRussa said, "but that they beat us when they were all beaten up." Hershiser pitched two complete games and was named World Series MVP. He also got more hits in the Series (three) than Canseco and McGwire combined. But it was his magnificent pitching that people would remember. "As long as we live," Gibson said, "none of us will ever see any pitcher accomplish what Orel has done."

1989

Oakland A's (4)
San Francisco Giants (0)

The Oakland Athletics were not about to stand pat after their inexplicable loss in the 1988 World Series. They took a team that had won 104 games and added the greatest leadoff hitter in baseball history, Rickey Henderson, who joined the A's in mid-season. Henderson's .425 on-base percentage and 72 runs scored in half a season enabled the A's to overcome an injury to José Canseco and still win 99 games. That was six more than the next-best team in baseball. The A's beat the Toronto Blue Jays in the playoffs and entered the World Series heavily favored to beat their rivals from across the bay, the San Francisco Giants. It was the first time since the Dodgers left Brooklyn that two teams from the same metropolitan area had faced each other in the World Series. And with an all–Bay Area

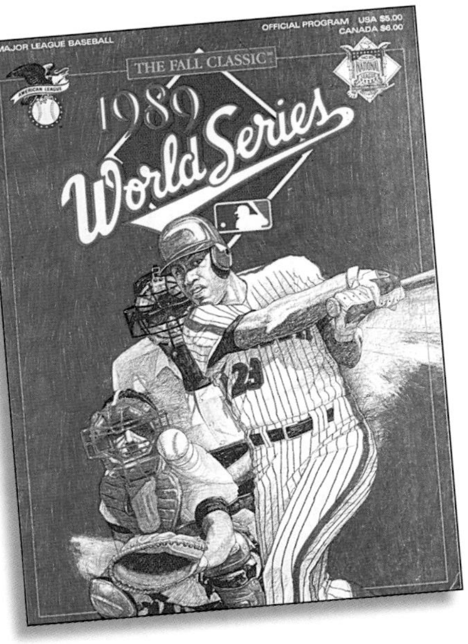

World Series, perhaps it was inevitable that the most Californian of natural disasters—an earthquake—would turn this sweep into one of the longest World Series ever played.

Most fans got to the games on the BART, the Bay Area's ubiquitous subway system, but six brave Giants fans found a more creative mode of transportation. They swam across San Francisco Bay, twelve miles in 55-degree water, to get to the Oakland

BOTTOM: By 1989 Rickey Henderson was widely regarded as the greatest leadoff hitter in baseball history, and he showed it in the World Series against the Giants, getting on base eleven times in the four games.

Coliseum for the opening game. The team they went to see featured some fearsome hitters. San Francisco's Kevin Mitchell was the National League MVP, but Will Clark was the man the Giants counted on most. He had tortured the Cubs with a .650 average in the National League playoffs, enjoying the kind of hot streak that few other players have ever had. But Clark lost the magic as quickly as he had found it, batting a pedestrian .250 with no runs batted in during the World Series.

Dave Stewart was a twenty-game winner for Oakland three consecutive years, and he showed why in the first game as he shut out San Francisco on five hits, 5-0. It was all Oakland in Game 2, too, as Henderson collected three hits, stole a base, and scored the first run in a 5-1 A's win.

The Series moved across the bay to Candlestick Park on October 17, where sixty-two thousand fans were ready for the first World Series game in San Francisco in a quarter of a century. At 5:04 p.m., twenty-one minutes before the scheduled first pitch, players were busy preparing for the game, doing wind sprints and the like, when they felt the ground begin to move beneath them. It was an earthquake measuring 7.1 on the Richter scale. Players who moments earlier were honing their killer instincts suddenly turned into husbands and fathers. Many brought their families out into the middle of the playing field—the safest place in the concrete stadium—and tried to comfort them. The tremors were violent enough to topple buildings in San Francisco's marina district and even destroy a section of the Bay Bridge. The quake killed 67 people, caused $6.8 billion in damage, and delayed Game 3 of the World Series for ten days. Candlestick Park held up remarkably well, suffering only a few serious cracks in the cement in Section 53. An 83-year-old woman who had been in her pregnant mother's womb during the last serious San Francisco earthquake in 1906 was sitting in that section when the quake hit. "If I have to go," she said, "this is the way to do it."

As if the earthquake itself hadn't done enough damage to San Francisco, it also enabled the Athletics to come back after the ten-day layoff with Stewart, who had spent most of the downtime visiting with earthquake victims in Oakland. He threw a solid game while holding the Giants to three runs

TOP: Giants pitcher Kelly Downs carries a frightened fan named Billy Kiehl away from danger after an earthquake struck before Game 3 of the 1989 World Series.

BOTTOM: After the earthquake, Oakland players including Rick Honeycutt (right) and José Canseco (second from right) lead their families onto the middle of the playing field, which at the time was the safest area of Candlestick Park.

SECURITY PACIFIC BANK
5:22
NATIONAL
AMERICAN
Budweiser
KING OF BEERS
PERFORMING
OUR NATIONAL ANTHEM
Winner's Circle
Coca-Cola
SAFEWAY
STEINBACH
36
25
LANSF
HENDERSON
24
LA RUSSA
10
abc

CRAIG
38
BUTLER
2
THOMPSON
6

and five hits over seven innings. The unstoppable Oakland offense, meanwhile, scalded five Giants pitchers for thirteen runs. Veterans Carney Lansford and Dave Henderson combined for six hits, six runs scored, and six RBI to give Oakland a 3-0 lead in the Series.

With the Athletics looking for a sweep, Giants manager Roger Craig decided to start Don Robinson, who had pitched only 1⅔ innings over the previous 32 days. Robinson showed his rust immediately as Rickey Henderson homered to lead off the game. Henderson later added a triple and a single as the A's romped to the championship. It turned out to be one of the most lopsided World Series ever, as Oakland outscored the Giants 32-14. None of the four games were close. But the A's knew their dominance would be remembered by few. The 1989 World Series would always be known as the series interrupted by an earthquake. "I'm happy," Dennis Eckersley said, "but I feel kind of guilty being happy."

1989 WORLD SERIES

Oakland Coliseum (Oak. Athletics) ◆ 10.14.89 (Game 1)

	1	2	3	4	5	6	7	8	9	R	H	E
SFG	0	0	0	0	0	0	0	0	0	0	5	1
Oak.	0	3	1	1	0	0	0	0	X	5	11	1

WP–Stewart LP–Garrelts HR: OAK–Parker, Weiss
ATT: 49,385

Oakland Coliseum ◆ 10.15.89 (Game 2)

	1	2	3	4	5	6	7	8	9	R	H	E
SFG	0	0	1	0	0	0	0	0	0	1	4	0
Oak.	1	0	0	4	0	0	0	0	X	5	7	0

WP–Moore LP–Reuschel HR: OAK–Steinbach
ATT: 49,388

Candlestick Park (S.F. Giants) ◆ 10.27.89 (Game 3)

	1	2	3	4	5	6	7	8	9	R	H	E
Oak.	2	0	0	2	4	1	0	4	0	13	14	0
SFG	0	1	0	2	0	0	0	0	4	7	10	3

WP–Stewart LP–Garrelts
HR: OAK–D. Henderson (2), Phillips, Canseco, Lansford; SFG–Williams, Bathe ATT: 62,038

Candlestick Park ◆ 10.28.89 (Game 4)

	1	2	3	4	5	6	7	8	9	R	H	E
Oak.	1	3	0	0	3	1	0	1	0	9	12	0
SFG	0	0	0	0	0	2	4	0	0	6	9	0

WP–Moore LP–Robinson S–Eckersley
HR: OAK–R. Henderson; SFG–Mitchell, Litton
ATT: 62,032

PREVIOUS PAGES: The Oakland A's and San Francisco Giants—and a packed Candlestick Park—listen reverently as the pregame ritual singing of the national anthem takes place in the center of the ballpark before the start of the long-delayed (due to earthquake) Game 3 of the 1989 World Series.

1990

CINCINNATI REDS (4)
OAKLAND A'S (0)

RICKEY HENDERSON PICKED UP WHERE he had left off in 1989, terrorizing American League pitchers for a .439 on-base percentage, 28 home runs, and 63 stolen bases in one of the greatest multi-dimensional seasons in baseball history. Henderson was the A.L. MVP, but José Canseco and Mark McGwire also contributed to Oakland's dominance. They ranked second and third, respectively, among the league home run leaders. Dave Stewart won twenty games for the fourth year in a row, and seemingly just for kicks, the A's traded for Willie McGee, the National League batting champ, in August. The burning question surrounding the

BOTTOM LEFT: Dave Stewart throws a pitch in the first game of the 1989 World Series, which he won 5-0.

BOTTOM RIGHT: The abrasive reliever Rob Dibble was one of the keys to Cincinnati's 1990 World Series victory, pitching four-plus scoreless innings in the sweep of Oakland.

PRESERVING THE CLASSIC

WORLD SERIES SCRIBES

Though the World Series has never truly been a *world* series, it has attracted worldwide interest from the very beginning. Starting with the first Series game in 1903, countless sportswriters have worked long into the night, banging out pages of type that, usually within 12 hours, make their way into the hands of eager baseball fans in Bangor and Bisbee and Bangladesh. "The entire world is interested in the baseball classic and demands the best and quickest possible information about it," the *Philadelphia Public Ledger* said in 1915. "The first batsman is put out, or makes a hit, or walks, and then every telegraph instrument in the press box begins to play a tune. The instant the last man is out, there is a rush from the press box. The men who represent morning newspapers must get away from the jam and get into the heart of the city quickly, usually in automobiles, where they go to the newspaper offices, hotels or telegraph offices, sit down to typewriters and 'pound out' the special stories which will give fans the 'high spots' and the 'color' for digestion with their eggs and coffee the following morning."

During the Fall Classic's first decade, newspapers vied for the services of ballplayers as "writers," and almost every star player lent his name to a ghostwritten World Series column. But in 1913, two years after a World Series article appearing under Christy Mathewson's byline caused a rift between he and teammate Rube Marquard, the owners banned players from writing during the baseball season. Ostensibly this was to prevent infighting that distracted them from the work at hand, but the real reason was likely that the owners didn't want players reaping even more financial rewards from the World Series.

According to one early account, World Series writers "toil like slaves, and they are weary of mind and body when the day's work is at an end." In 1908 they decided to do something about it. On the morning of the fifth game, the scribes covering the Series—who had been outraged by the shabby seats Cubs owner Charles Murphy gave them for the one-game National League pennant playoff—met at Detroit's Hotel Ponchartrain and formed the Baseball Writers Association of America. This upstart writers' union eventually evolved into the most important electorate body in baseball, whose annual votes now determine MVP, Cy Young, and Rookie of the Year award winners as well as Hall of Fame inductees. By 1915, more than three hundred writers and one hundred photographers were covering each World Series game under the direction of local BBWAA representatives, who helped arrange such things as seating, telephone and telegraph lines, transportation, and accommodations.

By the 1960s, Grantland Rice, Dan Daniel, and other masters of purple prose gave way to a postwar writing style no less emotional but far more intellectual. This was best exemplified by Roger Angell of *The New Yorker*, whose emergence as a baseball writer coincided with an era in which nearly every World Series was dominated by the superhuman performance of one star player: Sandy Koufax in 1963 and 1965, Bob Gibson in 1964 and 1967, Lou Brock in 1968, Brooks Robinson in 1970, and Roberto Clemente in 1971. Angell captured these Hall of Famers at the height of their powers, artfully capturing their fleeting stretches of brilliance for posterity.

In 1963, Angell grew frustrated with the World Series because "a large proportion of the ticket-holders appeared to be well-to-do out-of-towners who came to the games only because they could afford the tickets, who seemed to have only a slipshod knowledge of baseball, and who frequently departed around the sixth or seventh inning." So for a new perspective, instead of going to the ballpark, Angell reported the goings-on of each World Series game from a different New York bar. As Sandy Koufax set a new Series record with 15 strikeouts in one game, Angell wrote, "the young men in O'Leary's burst into sustained applause, like an audience at Lincoln Center." But watching the World Series on a two-dimensional television screen, as most baseball fans do, was a disappointment to Angell. "It is the lack of the third dimension on TV," he wrote, "that makes baseball seem less than half the game it is, that actually deprives it of its essential beauty, clarity, and excitement."

BELOW: Sportswriters covering the 1912 World Series at the Polo Grounds were provided with work tables equipped with telegraph machines.

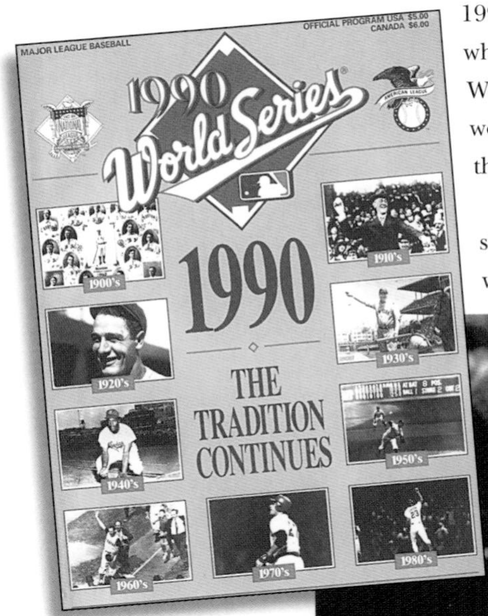

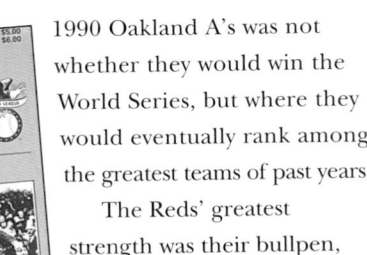

1990 Oakland A's was not whether they would win the World Series, but where they would eventually rank among the greatest teams of past years.

The Reds' greatest strength was their bullpen, which was by led Rob Dibble, Randy Myers, and Norm Charlton, the troika known as the "Nasty Boys" for their demeanor both on and off the field. The trio combined for 24 wins, 44 saves, and a 2.28 ERA during the regular season. The Reds also added Jack Armstrong, the National League's starting pitcher in the All-Star Game, to the bullpen for the World Series.

TOP: Billy Hatcher slides safely into third base during the 1990 World Series, at Riverfront Stadium.

BOTTOM: Chris Sabo batted .563 during the 1990 World Series, the second-best single-Series average in history.

Eric Davis quickly put a stop to the idea of an A's sweep in the first game. Davis hit a two-run homer in the first inning and Cincinnati never trailed after that, winning 7-0 behind seven shutout innings from José Rijo. A voice was heard as the Reds relaxed in the locker room after the game. "Well," said one player, "so much for that '27 Yankees crap."

The A's led the second game 5-4 until the eighth inning, when the Reds' Billy Hatcher lifted a fly ball to right field. A's right fielder Canseco got a bad jump on the ball and it fell for a triple. Hatcher eventually scored the tying run, and the Reds went on to win in the tenth. After the game, infuriated A's manager Tony LaRussa said Canseco did "a horseshit job" trying to field Hatcher's triple. The snafu resulted in Canseco being benched in Game 4 of the Series.

The third game was over quickly. Reds third baseman Chris Sabo homered in the second and third innings, and a McGwire error in the third led to six unearned runs. The Reds won their third consecutive game, 8-3. Now Cincinnati was going for the sweep. They sent Rijo to the mound for Game 4 despite a blister on his pitching hand.

Rijo had been traded away by the A's three years earlier. He was completely dominant in Game 4, allowing only two hits and retiring twenty consecutive Oakland batters at one point. Rijo's best pitch was usually his fastball, but on this night he noticed that the A's couldn't touch his slider, so he started throwing more of those. He outdueled Oakland's best pitcher, Stewart, to clinch the championship for Cincinnati.

1990 WORLD SERIES

Riverfront Stadium (Cinc. Reds) ◆ 10.16.90

	1	2	3	4	5	6	7	8	9	R	H	E
Oak.	0	0	0	0	0	0	0	0	0	0	9	1
Cin.	2	0	2	0	3	0	0	0	X	7	10	0

WP–Rijo LP–Stewart HR: CIN–Davis ATT: 55,830

Riverfront Stadium ◆ 10.17.90

	1	2	3	4	5	6	7	8	9	10	R	H	E
Oak.	1	0	3	0	0	0	0	0	0	0	4	10	2
Cin.	2	0	0	1	0	0	0	1	0	1	5	14	2

WP–Dibble LP–Eckersley HR: OAK–Canseco ATT: 55,832

Oakland Coliseum (Oak. Athletics) ◆ 10.19.90

	1	2	3	4	5	6	7	8	9	R	H	E
Cin.	0	1	7	0	0	0	0	0	0	8	14	1
Oak.	0	2	1	0	0	0	0	0	0	3	7	1

WP–Browning LP–Moore HR: CIN–Sabo (2); OAK–Baines, R. Henderson ATT: 48,269

Oakland Coliseum ◆ 10.20.90

	1	2	3	4	5	6	7	8	9	R	H	E
Cin.	0	0	0	0	0	0	0	2	0	2	7	1
Oak.	1	0	0	0	0	0	0	0	0	1	2	1

WP–Rijo LP–Stewart S–Myers ATT: 48,613

Remarkably, the Reds won the final game with two of their best players in the Oakland hospital. Hatcher was hit in the hand by a pitch and then Davis hurt himself trying to make a diving catch. Davis lacerated his kidney and wound up in the hospital for eleven days. (Tightfisted Reds owner Marge Schott created a controversy by refusing to pay his hospital bill.) Hatcher, meanwhile, had a World Series for the ages. He had seven consecutive hits at one point, and ended up batting .750 to break Babe Ruth's 62-year-old record for highest average in a single Series. Sabo wasn't far behind at .563. The Reds' relievers also lived up to their top billing, as they allowed no runs in thirteen innings. The dismal Oakland offense didn't score a run after the third inning in the entire Series. Stewart had lost two of the four games. He defiantly declared that regardless of the outcome, the A's were still the best team. But the entire world had seen the Reds prove otherwise. "Man, don't make this night end," Rijo said. "This is the greatest."

1991

Minnesota Twins (4)
Atlanta Braves (3)

No team had ever rebounded from a last place finish to appear in the Fall Classic the next year in the 88-year history of the World Series. In 1991, *two* teams did exactly that: the Minnesota Twins and Atlanta Braves. The Braves were a laughingstock, having finished last in four of the previous five seasons. But in their first full year under manager Bobby Cox, they improved by an astounding 29 games, capturing the division title and the pennant. Twenty-one-year-old pitcher Steve Avery went from 3-11 to 18-8. Tom Glavine, a 25-year-old left-hander, improved his ERA by nearly two runs and transformed himself into a Cy Young award winner. Free agent signee Terry Pendleton exploded for a career year en route to the batting title and the MVP award.

The Twins also got much of their improvement from their pitching. Right-hander Scott Erickson blossomed into a star, and free agent Jack Morris, a St. Paul native, won eighteen games. The first game of the World Series was a struggle between two battle-tested veterans, as Morris of the Twins and Charlie Liebrandt of the Braves squared off. Morris prevailed 5-2 on a surprising home run from Greg Gagne, the Twins' shortstop who was known more for his glove than his bat. Minnesota won the second game on another homer by a light-hitting infielder. This time it was Scott Leius, a utility man with six career home runs, who broke an eighth-inning tie and led the Twins to victory over Glavine. The Braves felt the outcome was tainted by a missed call, which occurred when Minnesota tried to pick off Ron Gant rounding first base after he singled in the third inning. Gant made it back, but Kent Hrbek, Minnesota's six-foot-five, 260-pound first baseman, appeared to physically lift Gant off the base as he applied a tag. Umpire Drew Coble called Gant out instead of calling obstruction on Hrbek. It may or may not have affected the outcome, but it was a call that incensed Braves fans would long remember.

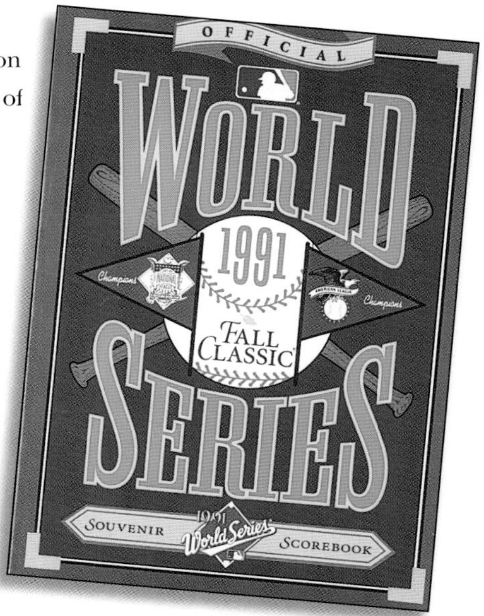

BOTTOM: Lonnie Smith is tagged out at the plate in a Game 3 collision with Brian Harper during the 1991 Series.

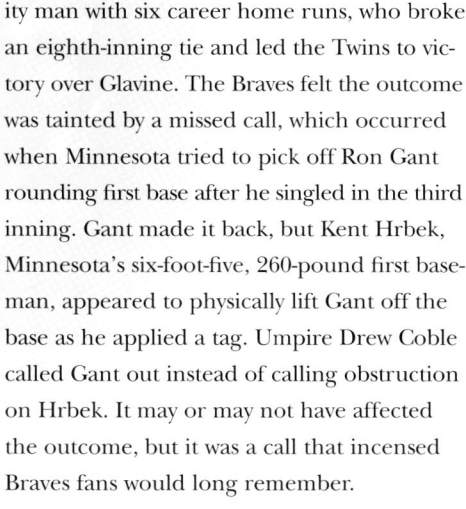

One benefit of having two last-place teams in the World Series was that they were equally hungry. From the very first pitch they fought it out tooth and nail, never giving up on a game. Game 3 in Atlanta looked like a sure Braves victory, but Minnesota's Charles "Chili" Davis—a designated hitter who was riding the pine because the game was in a National League park—hit a two-run pinch hit homer to tie it in the eighth. Each manager went all out to win the game in regulation, but it stretched into extra innings. With a runner on second in the twelfth, Atlanta's Mark Lemke, a .234 hitter, singled. Dan Gladden's throw from the outfield arrived a split-second too late to nail David Justice at the plate, and he scored for a Braves win. A Series record 42 players had been used when the game finally ended at 12:42 a.m. Justice's run was the first allowed by the Minnesota bullpen in its 28 postseason innings.

Morris and John Smoltz faced each other in the fourth game. This game was also tied entering the ninth inning. Atlanta could have put it away early, but in the fifth inning Twins catcher Brian Harper tagged out two runners, Lonnie Smith and Pendleton, at home plate. The exhausted relief pitchers feared another extra-inning battle, but Lemke tripled in the bottom of the ninth. Atlanta then sent third-string catcher Jerry Willard to the plate with one out. Willard did construction work in the off-season to make ends meet, and had driven in only four runs during the regular season. He had also been the only Brave not to see action in the previous night's marathon. Willard flied to shallow right field and Lemke tagged and sprinted home. Remarkably, this game, too, would end on a play at the plate, as Lemke was safe on a close play and the Braves won. Willard retired from baseball three years later. His career World Series stat line read zero at-bats and one all-important RBI.

Game 5 was a stinker compared to its two predecessors. Atlanta pummeled the Twins 14-5 as Smith tied a record by homering for the third consecutive game. Erickson fooled nobody in Game 6, but the Braves seemed to hit all their drives right at fielders or just on the wrong side of the foul line. Erickson

TOP: Although this Game 1 collision knocked Braves catcher Greg Olson head over heels, he was able to hang on to the ball and tag out Dan Gladden.

BOTTOM: Atlanta Brave David Justice (right) and Minnesota Twins catcher Brian Harper look up to see the home plate umpire call Justice "safe." Justice had dashed from second to home just ahead of the throw from outfielder Dan Gladden in the twelfth inning of Game 3 of the 1991 World Series.

struggled mightily but gave up only three runs in six innings. He was fortunate to have Kirby Puckett on his side. Puckett had one of the greatest individual games in Series history: an RBI triple in the first inning, a memorable leaping catch in the third, a go-ahead sacrifice fly in the fifth, a single and stolen base in the eighth, and a game-winning homer in the eleventh.

The homer came off Liebrandt, who had been pounded in the first game. Braves fans, with benefit of hindsight, complained that Cox made the wrong move bringing in Liebrandt to face Puckett. But as Steve Rushin pointed out in *Sports Illustrated*, "It didn't matter whom he put on the mound to face Puckett. The man was going to hit a home run no matter what." It had been a terrific World Series even before this, but Puckett's heroics seemed to lift it into the realm of the magical. "Whatever happens tomorrow, it's been a great Series," Puckett said. "This is a game I'll never forget." Nor would anyone else.

The Twins were fortunate to be playing the seventh game at the raucous Metrodome, where their all-time postseason record was 10-1. Morris acted as if he had been preparing for this his whole life. He had only one thing to say before the game: "In the words of the late, great Marvin Gaye, let's get it on." They did. Morris and Smoltz each pitched remarkably. Neither pitcher allowed the other team to score. Both teams loaded the bases in the eighth inning and both teams got out of the jam by turning a double play. Smoltz exited in that inning, but Morris soldiered on. The game went into extra innings still scoreless and Morris retired the Braves in the top of the tenth.

Gladden, Minnesota's shaggy-haired outfielder, led off the bottom of the tenth with a double, then moved to third on a sacrifice. That brought up Gene Larkin, a journeyman player known mostly for breaking many of Lou Gehrig's hitting records at Columbia University. Larkin lifted Alejandro Peña's pitch over the drawn-in outfield and Gladden pranced home. He jumped on the plate with both feet for the Series-winning run.

The 36-year-old Morris had pitched the game of his life—or of anyone else's. It was every kid pitcher's dream to throw a shutout in the seventh game of the World Series. Seven men had done that before—Babe Adams, Dizzy Dean, Johnny Podres,

TOP: Kirby Puckett's spectacular catch in the third inning of Game 6 robbed Ron Gant of an extra-base hit.

BOTTOM: Jack Morris' 10-inning shutout in Game 7 was his second victory of the Series.

Johnny Kucks, Lew Burdette, Ralph Terry, and Sandy Koufax—but nobody had ever done it in extra innings until Morris. Nobody had ever done it in his hometown until Morris.

The Series was immediately hailed as the greatest ever played by many sportswriters. "The only thing better," Lemke said, "would be if we stopped after nine innings and cut the trophy in half." There were three extra-inning contests. Five of the seven games were decided by one run. Four games were decided on the final play of the game. It was both rewarding and immensely exhausting for the Twins. "I can't smile," Kirby Puckett said. "I'm too tired."

BOTTOM LEFT: Kirby Puckett rounds the bases after hitting the eleventh-inning homer that won Game 6 of the 1991 World Series.

BOTTOM RIGHT: Tom Glavine enjoyed a breakout year in 1991, winning 20 games and the Cy Young award. In 1992, he won 20 games again (and lost 3 fewer than the previous year), though his ERA went from 2.55 to 2.76.

1991 WORLD SERIES

HUBERT H. HUMPHERY METRODOME (MINNESOTA TWINS) ◆ 10.19.91

	1	2	3	4	5	6	7	8	9	R	H	E
Atl.	0	0	0	0	0	1	0	1	0	2	6	1
Minn.	0	0	1	0	3	1	0	0	X	5	9	1

WP–Morris LP–Leibrandt S–Aguilera HR: MIN–Gagne, Hrbek ATT: 55,108

HUBERT H. HUMPHERY METRODOME ◆ 10.20.91

	1	2	3	4	5	6	7	8	9	R	H	E
Atl.	0	1	0	0	1	0	0	0	0	2	8	1
Minn.	2	0	0	0	0	0	0	1	X	3	4	1

WP–Tapani LP–Glavine S–Aguilera HR: MIN–Davis, Leius ATT: 55,145

ATLANTA-FULTON COUNTY STADIUM (ATLANTA BRAVES) ◆ 10.22.91

	1	2	3	4	5	6	7	8	9	10	11	12	R	H	E
Minn.	1	0	0	0	0	0	1	2	0	0	0	0	4	10	1
Atl.	0	1	0	1	2	0	0	0	0	0	0	1	5	8	2

WP–Clancy LP–Aguilera HR: MIN–Puckett, Davis; ATL–Justice, Smith ATT: 50,878

ATLANTA-FULTON COUNTY STADIUM ◆ 10.23.91

	1	2	3	4	5	6	7	8	9	R	H	E
Minn.	0	1	0	0	0	0	1	0	0	2	7	0
Atl.	0	0	1	0	0	0	1	0	1	3	8	0

WP–Stanton LP–Guthrie HR: MIN–Pagliarulo; ATL–Pendleton, Smith ATT: 50,878

ATLANTA-FULTON COUNTY STADIUM ◆ 10.24.91

	1	2	3	4	5	6	7	8	9	R	H	E
Minn.	0	0	0	0	0	3	0	1	1	5	7	1
Atl.	0	0	0	4	1	0	6	3	X	14	17	1

WP–Glavine LP–Tapani HR: ATL–Justice, Smith, Hunter ATT: 50,878

HUBERT H. HUMPHERY METRODOME ◆ 10.26.91

	1	2	3	4	5	6	7	8	9	10	11	R	H	E
Atl.	0	0	0	0	2	0	1	0	0	0	0	3	9	1
Minn.	2	0	0	0	1	0	0	0	0	0	1	4	9	0

WP–Aguilera LP–Leibrandt HR: ATL–Pendleton MIN–Puckett ATT: 55,155

HUBERT H. HUMPHERY METRODOME ◆ 10.27.91

	1	2	3	4	5	6	7	8	9	10	R	H	E
Atl.	0	0	0	0	0	0	0	0	0	0	0	7	0
Minn.	0	0	0	0	0	0	0	0	0	1	1	10	0

WP–Morris LP–Pena ATT: 55,118

1992

TORONTO BLUE JAYS (4)
ATLANTA BRAVES (2)

The young Atlanta Braves fought their way back to the Fall Classic after their heartbreaking loss in the 1991 World Series. Their opponents this time would be the Toronto Blue Jays, who became the fourth expansion franchise to reach the World Series, following in the footsteps of the Royals, Brewers, and Padres. The Blue Jays entered the American League in 1977 and enjoyed their tenth consecutive winning season in 1992, posting 96 wins to capture the American League pennant. They also played in baseball's most state-of-the-art stadium, the three-year-old Skydome. The upscale and groundbreaking park featured a retractable roof, a Hard Rock Cafe in the outfield, and a hotel with windows overlooking the playing field. The park and the winning team attracted Canadians in droves as the Blue Jays became the first team in baseball history to sell 4 million tickets in one season.

Free agent signee Jack Morris, who had so memorably won the last World Series game the year before, started the first game for Toronto. In his own estimation, he made only "one bad pitch," but it was a three-run homer by Damon Berryhill. The blow was enough to give Atlanta a 3-1 win. The second game started with an international controversy, as the bumbling U.S. Marine Corps displayed the Canadian flag upside down during the playing of "O Canada" before the game. The unintentional insult outraged Canadian fans and they called in with thousands of complaints. They were probably appeased, though, when the Jays' Ed Sprague, a backup catcher with 55 hits in his career, came up to face Jeff Reardon in the ninth. Reardon was baseball's career leader in saves at the time, but Sprague hit a two-run pinch hit homer off him to give Toronto a 5-4 victory.

The highlight of the third game was a catch by Toronto's Devon White in center field that ranks among the handful of most spectacular plays in World Series history. Atlanta placed runners on first and second with nobody out in the fourth inning of the scoreless game, when David Justice launched a four-hundred-foot drive deep to center field. White ran back and caught the ball while crashing into the fence. But that was only the beginning. Terry Pendleton, the runner at first, was called out for passing Deion Sanders, the runner on second. That made two outs with Sanders still scrambling to get back to second base. No fielder was at the base, but third baseman Kelly Gruber ran after Sanders, dove at him, and tagged him on the heel. Sanders was ruled safe, although replays later showed otherwise. Umpire Bob Davidson, to his credit, admitted later that he missed the call. If Sanders had been called out it would have been just the second triple play in Series history. As it stood, White's play still ranked among the very best. "That would have been a tough catch for Willie Mays, DiMaggio, or Duke Snider," said Ernie Banks, who attended the game. "I thought he had no chance," Joe Carter said. "But if anybody in baseball can make that catch, it's Devon." The play eventually enabled Toronto to win the game when Candy Maldonado singled in the winning run in the bottom of the ninth.

The Jays won their third straight game the next day, as Jimmy Key's fine pitching beat the Braves, 2-1. Morris would attempt to win the final game of the World Series for the second year in a row with the Blue Jays now leading the Series three games to one. But Morris, still winless in the 1992 postseason, gave up a grand slam to Lonnie Smith as the Braves won Game 5 convincingly, 7-2.

The Blue Jays tried again to close out the Series in Game 6. There were almost as many people watching the game on the Jumbotron in Toronto, 45,551, as attended the real

TOP: This photo shows that the Blue Jays successfully turned a triple play in Game 3 of the 1992 World Series, but Deion Sanders was called safe by umpire Bob Davidson.

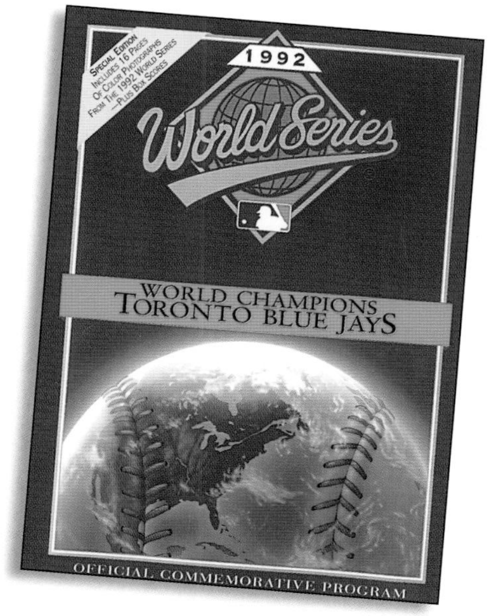

BOTTOM: After faring poorly in his first World Series in 1981, Dave Winfield drove in the Series-winning run for Toronto in 1992.

1992 WORLD SERIES

Atlanta-Fulton County Stadium (Atlanta Braves) ◆ 10.17.92

	1	2	3	4	5	6	7	8	9	R	H	E
Tor.	0	0	0	1	0	0	0	0	0	1	4	0
Atl.	0	0	0	0	0	3	0	0	X	3	4	0

WP–Glavine LP–Morris HR: TOR–Carter; ATL–Berryhill ATT: 51,763

Atlanta-Fulton County Stadium ◆ 10.18.92

	1	2	3	4	5	6	7	8	9	R	H	E
Tor.	0	0	0	0	2	0	0	1	2	5	9	2
Atl.	0	1	0	1	2	0	0	0	0	4	5	1

WP–Ward LP–Reardon S–Henke HR: TOR–Sprague ATT: 51,763

Skydome (Toronto Blue Jays) ◆ 10.20.92

	1	2	3	4	5	6	7	8	9	R	H	E
Atl.	0	0	0	0	0	1	0	1	0	2	9	0
Tor.	0	0	0	1	0	0	0	1	1	3	6	1

WP–Ward LP–Avery HR: TOR–Carter, Gruber ATT: 51,813

Skydome ◆ 10.21.92

	1	2	3	4	5	6	7	8	9	R	H	E
Atl.	0	0	0	0	0	0	0	1	0	1	5	0
Tor.	0	0	1	0	0	0	1	0	X	2	6	0

WP–Key LP–Glavine S–Henke HR: TOR–Borders ATT: 52,090

Skydome ◆ 10.22.92

	1	2	3	4	5	6	7	8	9	R	H	E
Atl.	1	0	0	1	5	0	0	0	0	7	13	0
Tor.	0	1	0	1	0	0	0	0	0	2	6	0

WP–Smoltz LP–Morris S–Stanton HR: ATL–Justice, L. Smith ATT: 52,268

Atlanta-Fulton County Stadium◆ 10.24.92

	1	2	3	4	5	6	7	8	9	10	11	R	H	E
Tor.	1	0	0	1	0	0	0	0	0	0	2	4	14	1
Atl.	0	0	1	0	0	0	0	0	1	0	1	3	8	1

WP–Key LP–Leibrandt S–Timlin HR: TOR–Maldonado ATT: 51,763

thing in Atlanta. The Blue Jays took a 2-1 lead into the bottom of the ninth thanks to the outstanding pitching of David Cone and three relievers. Tom Henke took the mound to close out the game, but the stubborn Braves rallied, scoring the tying run on a two-out single by Otis Nixon, who had missed the previous year's Series after being suspended for cocaine use. It was the first run the Toronto bullpen had allowed in sixteen World Series innings and it sent the game into extra innings. With two Blue Jays on base in the eleventh, 41-year-old Dave Winfield shot a double down the line to score both runners. Toronto was three outs away from winning the Series for the second time in the game, but the pesky Braves again mounted a comeback. One run had scored and pinch runner John Smoltz stood on third with the tying run. Nixon, who had tied the game in the ninth, now batted against Toronto's Mike Timlin. Nixon hoped to surprise Carter at first base with a drag bunt, but both Carter and Timlin were prepared. "You could almost see it in his eyes that he was going to bunt," Carter said. The bunt went to Timlin, who scooped it up and threw to Carter for the final out of the Series.

Toronto Manager Clarence "Cito" Gaston was criticized throughout the season and the Series for his bizarre and seemingly illogical strategies. But he saved his job by winning the world championship, and in the process became the first African-American manager to do so. It was also the first time the championship of America's national game had been won by a team outside the United States. "They turned our flag upside down," one Toronto fan said, "and we turned their world upside down."

BELOW: Paul Molitor's 12 hits in 1993 raised his career World Series batting average to .418, the second-best of all time.

1993

Toronto Blue Jays (4)
Philadelphia Phillies (2)

Not satisfied with just one world championship, the Blue Jays added future Hall of Famers Rickey Henderson and Paul Molitor to their team, transforming an already impressive lineup into a fearsome batting order that drew comparisons to the 1927 Yankees. They faced the Philadelphia Phillies in the 1993 World Series. The Phillies were a hard-drinking, scruffy-looking bunch that had scrapped their way to the National League pennant.

The Phillies had Lenny Dykstra, the leadoff batter who scored 143 runs and chewed so much tobacco that playing center field after he'd been there was "like entering a toxic waste dump," according to one opponent. They had John Kruk, the rotund and shaggy-haired first baseman who batted .314 while extolling the virtues of staying fit by eating Big Macs. They had Darren Daulton, the catcher who drove in 105 runs and was married to a Playboy Playmate. Philadelphia fans were usually so foul-tempered that they once booed Santa Claus at the Thanksgiving Day parade. Naturally, they embraced these Phillies wholeheartedly. "They aren't afraid of getting dirty or working hard," Mayor Ed Rendell said. "That's the way we like to think of Philadelphia."

Each team opened the Series with its ace, but neither man was effective. Toronto's Juan Guzmán labored with control problems, while Philadelphia's Curt Schilling was rocked for seven runs and blew three different leads in the game. The Blue Jays won 8-5, though the Phils evened things the next day, winning 6-4.

The next three games would be played in Philadelphia, where the regal statue of William Penn atop City Hall was newly outfitted with a bright red Phillies cap. The designated hitter rule would be absent for these three games, which created a dilemma for Toronto manager Cito Gaston. His two best players were Molitor and John Olerud, who finished second and third, respectively, in American League MVP voting. Olerud was the regular first baseman and Molitor was the regular DH. His only viable position in the field was first base. It was a no-win situation for Gaston, who played Molitor at first base in Game 3 while Olerud and his league-leading .363 batting average sat out. (Remarkably, it was not the first time a reigning batting champion had been benched in the World Series. Chick Hafey sat out Game 7 for the 1931 Cardinals and Willie McGee started only two of four games for the 1990 Athletics.) Olerud returned to first in the fourth and fifth games. Molitor played third base for the first time in three years in those games, successfully fielding the only two balls hit his way.

Molitor made Gaston look brilliant when he tripled and homered in his first two at-bats in Game 3, as Toronto won easily, 10-3. Game 4 was played the next night in a misty rain. But the rain was nothing compared to the downpour coming from the hitters' bats. The Phillies led 14-9 entering the eighth. Then the Blue Jays mounted a comeback. They led 15-14 after four hits, two walks, and an error. Remarkably, the game's last inning and a half was scoreless. Toronto won to take a three games to one lead. "From a fan's perspective, this was a great game to watch," Dave Stewart said. "From a pitcher's standpoint, it was an ugly, ugly game." The roller-coaster contest had seen five lead changes, while the teams had combined for 32 hits, 14 walks, and 29 runs, a new Series record. Sixteen times in World Series history both teams had combined to score fewer runs than that *in an entire series*. "In the World Series, you don't see games like this," Joe Carter said. "It was like a slow-pitch softball game."

Schilling admitted that he had "overprepared and overanalyzed" before getting shelled in the opening game. He had no such problems in Game 5. The Phillies bullpen was decimated after giving up fifteen runs the night before. Schilling staved off elimination and allowed the relievers to rest by throwing a masterful five-hit shutout to force a sixth game in Toronto.

The Blue Jays jumped out to a 5-1 lead in Game 6, but coughed it back up in the seventh inning as the Phillies erupted for five runs off three Toronto pitchers. Philadelphia entered the ninth with a 6-5 lead, and they turned to Mitch Williams, the erratic closer known—affectionately, until now—as "Wild Thing." Just a day earlier, the *New York Times* had called Williams the "relief pitcher who induces stomach and psychic pain in his followers." That was after Williams had borne the brunt of Toronto's game-winning rally in the crazy fourth game. He had received three death threats after that game, which was his third blown save of the postseason. But despite his previous struggles, Williams said later that he "couldn't have felt better" pitching with the lead in Game 6.

Rickey Henderson walked and Devon White failed to advance the runner when he flied out. But then Molitor singled to bring Joe Carter to the plate with the potential

BOTTOM: Exemplifying the Phillies' hard-nosed style of play, Darren Daulton upends second baseman Roberto Alomar in Game 2 of the 1993 World Series.

1976–1994

tying and winning runs on base. "With Mitch out there, we knew something good was going to happen," Carter said. Williams threw a knee-high slider on a 2-2 count. Although he needed only a single to tie the game, Carter did not try for a single. He swung mightily and hit the ball over the left field fence to end the World Series. Carter jumped around the bases so hysterically that it appeared he had forgotten how to run. "I'm not going to sit here and make excuses," Williams said after the game. "I threw the pitch that cost us the World Series. That's tough to deal with, but I'm going to deal with it...I'm not going to commit suicide." Williams returned to Philadelphia to find that irate fans had broken all the windows in his home.

It was only the second time the World Series had ended on a home run, but unlike Bill Mazeroski's 1960 blast, Carter's had come with his team trailing in the game. "This is what baseball is all about," he said. "I dreamt about this in the back-yard as a kid." After the extra-inning thrillers of 1991 and 1992, it was the third consecutive year that the World Series had ended with a magical flourish. Not since the Series of 1924–26 had three straight Fall Classics concluded on such spine-tingling notes. That streak, however, would end emphatically in 1994.

1993 WORLD SERIES

Skydome (Toronto Blue Jays) ◆ 10.16.93

	1	2	3	4	5	6	7	8	9	R	H	E
Phil.	2	0	1	0	1	0	0	0	1	5	11	1
Tor.	0	2	1	0	1	1	3	0	X	8	10	3

WP–Leiter LP–Schilling S–Ward HR: TOR–White, Olerud ATT: 52,011

Skydome ◆ 10.17.93

	1	2	3	4	5	6	7	8	9	R	H	E
Phil.	0	0	5	0	0	0	1	0	0	6	12	0
Tor.	0	0	0	2	0	1	0	1	0	4	8	0

WP–Mulholland LP–Stewart S–Williams HR: PHI–Dykstra, Eisenreich; TOR–Carter ATT: 52,062

Veterans Stadium (Phil. Phillies) ◆ 10.19.93

	1	2	3	4	5	6	7	8	9	R	H	E
Tor.	3	0	1	0	0	1	3	0	2	10	13	1
Phil.	0	0	0	0	1	0	1	0	1	3	9	0

WP–Hentgen LP–Jackson HR: TOR–Molitor; PHI–Thompson ATT: 62,689

Veterans Stadium ◆ 10.20.93

	1	2	3	4	5	6	7	8	9	R	H	E
Tor.	3	0	4	0	0	2	0	6	0	15	18	0
Phil.	4	2	0	1	5	1	1	0	0	14	14	0

WP–Castillo LP–Williams S–Ward HR: PHI–Dykstra (2), Daulton ATT: 62,731

Veterans Stadium ◆ 10.21.93

	1	2	3	4	5	6	7	8	9	R	H	E
Tor.	0	0	0	0	0	0	0	0	0	0	5	1
Phil.	1	1	0	0	0	0	0	0	X	2	5	1

WP–Schilling LP–Guzman ATT: 62,706

Skydome ◆ 10.23.93

	1	2	3	4	5	6	7	8	9	R	H	E
Phil.	0	0	0	1	0	0	5	0	0	6	7	0
Tor.	3	0	0	1	1	0	0	0	3	8	10	2

WP–Ward LP–Williams HR: PHI–Dykstra; TOR–Molitor, Carter ATT: 52,195

1994

No Series

WITH ATTENDANCE AND PROFITS AT AN all-time high, 1994 should have been a banner year for baseball. Instead it became one of the great black marks in the game's history. Stadium gates were locked for what should have been the most exciting three months of the season. It was a travesty equaled only by the Black Sox scandal. It was the year Commissioner Bud Selig canceled the World Series.

The labor agreement between players and owners had expired on December 31, 1993, and the 1994 season began without a deal in place. The owners had been preparing for an attack on the players' union as far back as September 7, 1992, when they fired the relatively impartial commissioner, Fay Vincent, and replaced him with Milwaukee Brewers owner Selig. Many teams in smaller markets had difficulties both on the field and in the ledger books. Owners felt the only way to ensure competitive balance would be a salary cap placed on each team's payroll. The union refused to consent to the salary cap, though. They believed that it was merely a veiled attempt to funnel a greater proportion of profits to the owners. The owners were the ones who wanted to change things; the players merely wanted to keep the status quo. It appeared both sides were motivated by nothing more than utter greed and neither was prepared to give in.

The players chose August 12 as a strike date because it would rob owners of two of their greatest assets: the pennant races and the playoffs. At that point in the season players had already received most of their salaries. But owners were still counting on the financial windfall the postseason provides. The union was prepared to hold out as long as necessary by relying on a strike relief fund of $175 million.

October came and went without a World Series for the first time in 90 years. President Bill Clinton appointed an experienced labor negotiator, Bill Usery, to mediate the dispute, but Usery failed to make any progress. In December 1994 the owners made a final offer that still included the salary cap. The union refused the offer and the owners officially declared an impasse. This meant that as long as they had negotiated in good faith, they had the legal right to put their final offer into effect whether the players liked it or not. They did exactly that.

However, the owners had clearly failed to negotiate in good faith and the union filed a complaint with the National Labor Relations Board. The NLRB agreed with the union, and on March 26, 1995, it voted to seek a court order that would force the owners to allow the players to play under the old rules until a new agreement could be struck. Federal judge Sonia Sotomayor issued just such an order on March 31, and the owners were forced to allow the players to return to the field.

On April 3, six days before the 1995 season was to start with replacement players, the owners fired the strikebreakers and announced that the season would begin with the real players. Baseball finally returned on April 25, 1995, after 234 days and 921 lost games, as the Dodgers beat the Marlins, 8-7. The strike had cost owners and players an estimated $1 billion. Still, it was an unequivocal victory for the players' union. When the two sides finally did reach an agreement, it did not include a salary cap. The average player salary dropped 5 percent in 1995, but soon skyrocketed to unheard-of levels.

The teams in line for playoff spots when the 1994 season ended had been Atlanta, Cincinnati, Los Angeles, Montreal, Cleveland, Texas, the White Sox, and the Yankees. The biggest losers in the strike were the Montreal Expos, who had owned the best record in baseball, 74-40, when play stopped on August 12. The Expos were led by manager Felipe Alou and had a dynamic young roster that included Pedro Martínez, Larry Walker, Moises Alou (Felipe's son), and John Wetteland. The strike killed the team's bid for a world championship and its last chance for economic survival. The financially strapped Expos were forced to deal away Walker, Wetteland, Marquis Grissom, and Ken Hill by Opening Day 1995. Moises Alou departed for Florida in 1997. Martínez was sent packing to Boston in 1998. "When I talk to my teammates about that 1994 team, we always say 'What if?'" Walker said. "Would I be wearing a World Series ring right now? I think so." Baseball in Montreal has never recovered from the cancellation of the 1994 postseason.

OPPOSITE: A dejected Mitch Williams walks off the mound as Joe Carter, inset, rounds the bases in triumph at the end of the 1993 World Series.

CHAPTER 6
REIGN OF THE SLUGGERS
1995–2002

WELCOME TO MODERN BASEBALL, WHERE SPEED MERCHANTS NEED NOT apply. The game in the late 1990s was marked by unprecedented numbers of walks, strikeouts, and home runs—all of which render speed irrelevant. The spectacular home run totals posted by Mark McGwire, Sammy Sosa, Barry Bonds, and others led many fans to blame a "juiced ball." In fact, though, the phenomenon likely had nothing to do with a juiced ball, but everything to do with juiced players. More than ever before, batters made an effort to increase their power by bulking up in the weight room. Now even wiry middle infielders like Bret Boone fancied themselves power hitters. The bulking-up craze reached a boiling point in 2002, when former MVPs José Canseco and Ken Caminiti revealed that they—and an undetermined number of their colleagues—had used illegal anabolic steroids as workout aids.

If the era of longballs proved anything, though, it is that having a prodigious slugger in your lineup is not necessary to win a championship. Between 1995 and 2000, exactly 200 batters hit more than 30 homers in a season, but none of them played on a World Series–winning team. In Sosa's first eleven years with the Cubs, the team failed to win even a single postseason game. St. Louis won two division titles in McGwire's five seasons there, but failed to advance in the playoffs until 2002, their first year without him. The San Francisco Giants made it to the World Series not in 2001, when Barry Bonds hit 73 homers, but in 2002, when he hit 46.

Players may be paid obscene salaries, but they are also doing more than ever before to earn their money. With two extra rounds of playoffs and the regular season still at an all-time high of 162 games, the baseball season now lasts longer than at any time in the game's history. When the 2001 season lasted a record-breaking 217 days, Earl Weaver's old truism—"this ain't football; we do this every day"—became more relevant than ever before. In 1999 the Braves' Andruw Jones set a new record by playing in 176 games including the postseason. The record was broken again in 2001, when Luis González played in 180 contests: 162 regular season, 17 postseason, and the All-Star Game. Fittingly, in the last game of that never-ending season, González did what only one man (Bill Mazeroski) had ever done before: get a hit in the bottom of the ninth inning to win the seventh game of the World Series.

TOYOTA DEALERS
OF SOUTHERN CALIFORNIA
AT&T Wireless Scoreboard
ups
ANGELS

PREVIOUS PAGES: During opening ceremonies before Game 1 of the 2002 World Series at Edison International Field, the Anaheim fans transform the stands into a sea of red jerseys, jackets, hats, and Thunder Sticks. Opened in 1966 (when it was called Anaheim Stadium), Edison Field is distinguished by the "outfield extravaganza" in left center field: a huge model of the rugged California coastline that comes to life in fireworks and huge jets of water when a particularly spectacular play unfolds on the field.

1995

Atlanta Braves (4)
Cleveland Indians (2)

THE TEAMS WITH THE TWO BEST RECORDS IN baseball faced each other in the 1995 World Series for the first time since 1979. Despite the strike-shortened season, the Cleveland Indians still managed to win 100 of their 144 games for a .694 winning percentage, the best in baseball in 41 years. They played in a luxurious new hitters' park that attracted nightly sellouts, and the Indians batted .291 as a team, the highest in baseball since 1950. Their best hitter was Albert Belle, who became the first player in history to hit fifty doubles and fifty homers in one year despite the short season. The Series was an opportunity for sweet revenge for Belle. He developed a reputation as a hothead in college and the Atlanta Braves' general manager had ordered his employees not to select Belle in the 1987 draft. That general manager was Bobby Cox, who would now face Belle in the World Series as the Braves' manager.

The matchup between the Braves and Indians was a source of ire for Native Americans, who had long urged Cleveland to dump its racist mascot, Chief Wahoo, and who also wanted the Braves to stop encouraging the Tomahawk Chop, a fake war chant, at their games. "We want to stop the chop of the Braves and get rid of that clownish, bucktooth, idiotic mascot called Chief Wahoo," said Vernon Bellecourt, a spokesman for the American Indian Movement. "We wanted both Atlanta and Cleveland to lose in the playoffs, we were all rooting for the Reds and Mariners." AIM went to Federal court to obtain permits to protest outside stadium gates before the Series. "We're not mascots, we're human beings," said one protester, Richard Morales. "People make fun of Native Americans at the games, war-whooping, dancing, getting painted up. It is a total insult."

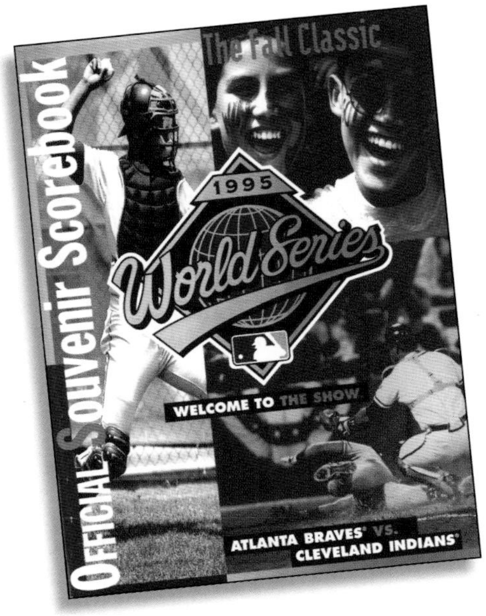

Atlanta had something to prove on the field. They had a pitching staff that historian Bill James called "probably the best in the history of baseball," yet they had failed to win it all in their last three postseason appearances. "They know they can't win a World Series," Cleveland's Omar Vizquel said. "They already lost twice. When you have that on your mind, it's tough to get out."

The first game was a matchup between two cerebral, bespectacled pitching artists who looked more like librarians than ballplayers. Orel Hershiser, hero of the 1988 World Series, faced Greg Maddux, soon to win his fourth consecutive Cy Young Award. Maddux had pinpoint control and managed to throw most of his pitches inside the strike zone yet

still outside a batter's comfort zone. He held the intimidating Cleveland lineup to just two hits in a complete game and won 3-2, with both Cleveland runs scoring on errors. "He just dominated the game," Cleveland manager Mike Hargrove said. "It's as masterful a job of pitching as I've ever seen." Tom Glavine was faced with the task of following Maddux the next day. "If I could pitch half that well, I'd be doing cartwheels," he said. Glavine did pitch about half as well. He made it through six strong innings as Atlanta won again, 4-3.

The third game was marred by an incident involving Belle, who had always been treated with hostility by the media and usually responded in kind. Belle launched into a tirade against NBC television personality Hannah Storm before the game. He felt her presence in the Indians' dugout disrupted his preparations for the game. Though his outburst was understandable, if hardly laudable, Commissioner Bud Selig fined Belle $55,000 and forced him to undergo psychiatric counseling during the off-season. Back on the field the teams battled to a 5-5 tie after nine innings on a freezing Cleveland night. Cleveland won it in the eleventh when Carlos Baerga doubled, Belle got a free pass, and Eddie Murray singled in the winning run.

Cox decided not to start Maddux on short rest in Game 4. He instead picked left-hander Steve Avery, who had struggled all year with a 7-13 record and 4.67 ERA. But on this night Avery pitched well for six innings. "You could set a firecracker off next to him and he wouldn't know it," Glavine said. "That's how focused he was." The game was tied until the seventh. Luis Polonia and David Justice's big hits late in the game sent the Braves to a 5-2 win.

Atlanta needed just one more win as Maddux took the mound to try to polish off the Indians. But Cleveland batters, who had been so helpless against him in the first game, jumped on Maddux for four runs. That was enough for Hershiser, who pitched eight superb innings to win.

Glavine took the mound in Game 6 with his team still looking for that final victory. He pitched eight innings, struck out eight, and allowed only a lone Cleveland hit, a single by Tony Peña, but Atlanta's struggling offense also failed to score until the sixth inning. Cleveland's left-handed relief specialist Jim Poole faced lefty batter David Justice in that inning, and Justice homered for what turned out to be the only run of the game. After the hit, "whatever was left of Atlanta's inferiority complex disappeared over the right field wall," wrote Kevin Sack in the *New York Times*. Cleveland, the offensive juggernaut that led the major leagues in home runs and runs scored, batted only .179 as a team, the lowest for a six-game Series since 1911. Glavine's magnificent pitching had allowed the Braves to throw the World Series monkey off their backs.

1995 WORLD SERIES

ATLANTA-FULTON COUNTY STADIUM (ATLANTA BRAVES) ◆ 10.21.95

	1	2	3	4	5	6	7	8	9	R	H	E
Clev.	1	0	0	0	0	0	0	0	1	2	2	0
Atl.	0	1	0	0	0	0	2	0	X	3	3	2

WP–Maddux LP–Hershiser HR: ATL–McGriff
ATT: 51,876

ATLANTA-FULTON COUNTY STADIUM ◆ 10.22.95

	1	2	3	4	5	6	7	8	9	R	H	E
Clev.	0	2	0	0	0	0	1	0	0	3	6	2
Atl.	0	0	2	0	0	2	0	0	X	4	8	2

WP–Glavine LP–Martinez S–Wohlers HR: CLE–Murray; ATL–Lopez ATT: 51,877

JACOBS FIELD (CLEVELAND INDIANS) ◆ 10.24.95

	1	2	3	4	5	6	7	8	9	10	11	R	H	E
Atl.	1	0	0	0	0	1	1	3	0	0	0	6	12	1
Clev.	2	0	2	0	0	0	1	1	0	0	1	7	12	2

WP–Mesa LP–Pena HR: ATL–McGriff, Klesko
ATT: 43,584

JACOBS FIELD ◆ 10.25.95

	1	2	3	4	5	6	7	8	9	R	H	E
Atl.	0	0	0	0	0	1	3	0	1	5	11	1
Clev.	0	0	0	0	0	1	0	0	1	2	6	0

WP–Avery LP–Hill S–Borbon HR: ATL–Klesko; CLE–Belle, Ramirez ATT: 43,578

JACOBS FIELD ◆ 10.26.95

	1	2	3	4	5	6	7	8	9	R	H	E
Atl.	0	0	0	1	1	0	0	0	2	4	7	0
Clev.	2	0	0	0	0	2	0	1	X	5	8	1

WP–Hershiser LP–Maddux S–Mesa
HR: ATL–Polonia, Klesko; CLE–Belle, Thome
ATT: 43,595

ATLANTA-FULTON COUNTY STADIUM ◆ 10.28.95

	1	2	3	4	5	6	7	8	9	R	H	E
Clev.	0	0	0	0	0	0	0	0	0	0	1	1
Atl.	0	0	0	0	0	1	0	0	X	1	6	0

WP–Glavine LP–Poole S–Wohlers HR: ATL–Justice
ATT: 51,875

OPPOSITE, BOTTOM LEFT: Greg Maddux fires a pitch during Game 1 of the 1995 World Series, in which he outdueled Orel Hershiser 3-2.

OPPOSITE, BOTTOM RIGHT: As Ryan Klesko slides hard into second, Cleveland's Carlos Baerga fires to first to complete a double play in Game 6.

LEFT: David Justice, whose homer won the 1995 World Series for Atlanta, announced his retirement in 2002 after having appeared in the playoffs in ten of his fourteen major league seasons.

1996

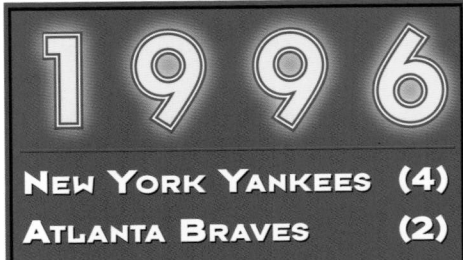

New York Yankees (4)
Atlanta Braves (2)

More than anything else, the 1996 World Series was the tale of two opposites, Joe Torre and Andruw Jones. Torre was the 56-year-old manager of the New York Yankees, who had owned the dubious record of playing and managing longer than anyone in baseball history—4,272 games—without ever making it to the Fall Classic. Meanwhile, the much-hyped Jones, a 19-year-old Braves outfielder, had played all of 31 major league games before his World Series debut. Both Torre and Jones would etch their names in the record books by the time it was over.

Torre was the son of a Brooklyn cop and the only New York native ever to manage the Yankees. He became the man of the hour as he led his team to its first Fall Classic in more than a decade. As one observer noted, "You couldn't watch the local news without seeing a Torre family story." The most poignant such story was

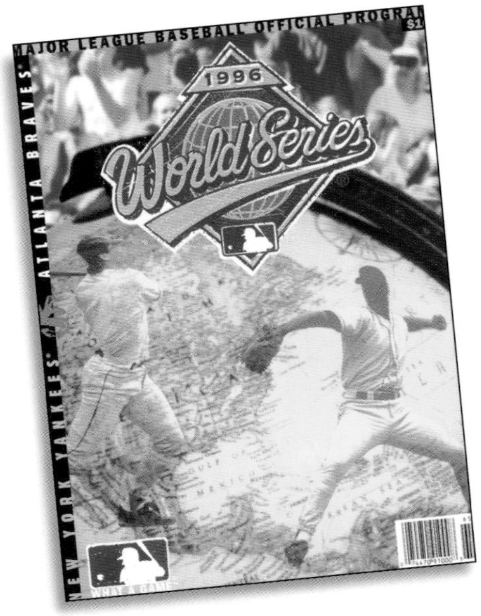

that of Torre's brother Frank, a former Milwaukee Brave who was hospitalized waiting for a heart transplant. (He got that transplant after the Yankees won Game 5.) Other stories talked about Torre's sister Marguerite, a nun, or his brother Rocco, who had died of a heart attack earlier that year. It was like the plot of a schmaltzy TV movie—literally, as *Joe Torre: Curveballs Along the Way* was released the following year.

Torre's calming influence helped the Yankees, who featured little of the sniping and backstabbing that had characterized the franchise's last pennant-winners in the 1976–81 era. They were an amalgam of young standouts (Derek Jeter, Bernie Williams, Mariano Rivera) and aging superstars on the downhill slide (Jimmy Key, Tim Raines, Wade Boggs, Cecil Fielder, Dwight Gooden, Darryl Strawberry, David Cone).

The first game was played at Yankee Stadium. Jones took an Andy Pettitte fastball out of the park in his first World Series at-bat to become the youngest player ever to homer in the World Series. He also became the second youngest a few minutes later when he hit a hanging slider from Brian Boehringer into the seats. Jones' homers helped the Braves whip the Yankees 12-1, the worst World Series loss ever inflicted on the Yankee franchise. They also made Jones a national hero in his native Curaçao, the five-mile-wide Caribbean island with a population of 150,000—fewer people than attended the first three games of the World Series. "This," wrote Ray Ratto in the *San Francisco Examiner*, "is as good as Andruw Jones' life is ever going to get."

It was all Greg Maddux in Game 2. The man who had won the last four Cy Young Awards dominated New York, and he threw just 57 pitches over six innings in a 4-0 Braves win. It seemed that the Yankees were

BOTTOM LEFT: Jim Leyritz, the self-appointed "King" of the Yankee team, rounds the bases after hitting a game-tying homer in the eighth inning of Game 4.

BOTTOM RIGHT: Andruw Jones was out trying to steal second in this play (tagged by Derek Jeter), but he still had a World Series to remember in 1996.

TOP: Andy Pettitte had a terrific regular season in 1996, going 21-8, but split his two appearances in the World Series. After getting shelled by the Braves in Game 1 (he didn't make it out of the third inning), Pettitte pitched a memorable Game 5 for the win: a 4-hit shutout in a duel with Braves ace John Smoltz.

BOTTOM LEFT: Smoltz had had an even better year than Pettitte, going 24-8 for the season, and in fact handily won the first meeting between the hurlers in Game 1. In Game 5, however, even though Smoltz threw a 5-hitter, the Braves lost, 1-0.

BOTTOM RIGHT: After participating in more than 4,000 major league games without making it to the World Series, Joe Torre finally won one in 1996.

down for the count. "That the Braves are going to win this World Series is apparent," wrote Mark Bradley in an Atlanta newspaper. "No longer is this team playing against the overmatched Yankees. The Braves are playing against history."

The "overmatched Yankees" managed to win the third game in Atlanta, but the Braves had a comfortable 6-0 lead after five innings of Game 4. New York scored three in the sixth inning, but some Atlanta fans began to trickle out of the stadium and head for home with the Braves still holding a tidy lead at the start of the eighth. The Yankees, however, were not done, as Atlanta closer Mark Wohlers faced Jim Leyritz with two runners on base. Leyritz was the cocky backup catcher who had given himself the nickname "The King." It turned out to be Leyritz's crowning moment, as he launched a slider over the left-field fence for a three-run blow that eventually sent the game into extra innings. Boggs, a master of the strike zone, drew a bases-loaded walk from Steve Avery in the tenth to drive in the deciding run for New York. "That was the best game I've been involved with, ever," Torre said. "Nothing else comes close."

John Smoltz and Andy Pettitte led their respective leagues in wins in 1996 and faced off in the fifth game. Both pitched brilliantly, but Smoltz was undone when center fielder Marquis Grissom dropped a fly ball for a two-base error. The Yankees won 1-0 and headed back home with the momentum overwhelmingly in their favor. The Yankees needed one more victory and touched Maddux for three runs in the third inning of Game 6, the biggest blow a triple by catcher Joe Girardi. The Braves threatened in the ninth inning, but Yankee closer John Wetteland induced a pop-up that Charlie Hayes caught for the final out of the Series.

Bedlam ensued. Boggs, looking ridiculous and loving every minute of it, mounted a policeman's horse and rode around Yankee Stadium celebrating the first championship of his fifteen-year career. "The next two or three hours," Torre wrote, "were a blur of interviews, hugs, kisses, champagne, showers, and cigar smoke." It was a strange sight for a generation of fans who had grown up watching the imperial and aloof Yankees. These pinstriped men seemed like regular Joes, elated and emotional after a hard-won victory. "The Yankees —who'd thought it—had become lovable," Roger Angell wrote.

1996 WORLD SERIES

Yankee Stadium II (N.Y. Yankees) ◆ 10.20.96

	1	2	3	4	5	6	7	8	9	R	H	E
Atl.	0	2	6	0	1	3	0	0	0	12	13	0
NYY	0	0	0	0	1	0	0	0	0	1	4	1

WP–Smoltz LP–Pettitte HR: ATL–McGriff, A. Jones (2) ATT: 56,365

Yankee Stadium II ◆ 10.21.96

	1	2	3	4	5	6	7	8	9	R	H	E
Atl.	1	0	1	0	1	1	0	0	0	4	10	0
NYY	0	0	0	0	0	0	0	0	0	0	7	1

WP–Maddux LP–Key ATT: 56,340

Atlanta-Fulton County Stadium (Atlanta Braves) ◆ 10.22.96

	1	2	3	4	5	6	7	8	9	R	H	E
NYY	1	0	0	1	0	0	0	3	0	5	8	1
Atl.	0	0	0	0	0	1	0	1	0	2	6	1

WP–Cone LP–Glavine S–Wetteland HR: NYY–Williams ATT: 51,843

Atlanta-Fulton County Stadium ◆ 10.23.96

	1	2	3	4	5	6	7	8	9	10	R	H	E
NYY	0	0	0	0	0	3	0	3	0	2	8	12	0
Atl.	0	4	1	0	1	0	0	0	0	0	6	9	2

WP–Lloyd LP–Avery S–Wetteland HR: NYY–Leyritz; ATL–McGriff ATT: 51,881

Atlanta-Fulton County Stadium ◆ 10.24.96

	1	2	3	4	5	6	7	8	9	R	H	E
NYY	0	0	0	1	0	0	0	0	0	1	4	0
Atl.	0	0	0	0	0	0	0	0	0	0	5	1

WP–Pettitte LP–Smoltz S–Wetteland ATT: 51,881

Yankee Stadium II ◆ 10.26.96

	1	2	3	4	5	6	7	8	9	R	H	E
Atl.	0	0	0	1	0	0	0	0	1	2	8	0
NYY	0	0	3	0	0	0	0	0	X	3	8	1

WP–Key LP–Maddux S–Wetteland ATT: 56,375

1997

Florida Marlins (4)

Cleveland Indians (3)

The Florida Marlins finished under .500 in each of their first four seasons. Their owner, home video mogul H. Wayne Huizenga, decided he wanted a winner, and he authorized the spending of $90 million to sign free agents Moises Alou, Alex Fernández, Bobby Bonilla, and Jim Eisenreich, among others. The moves worked, as the newly revamped team won 92 games to capture the wild card en route to the World Series. The Marlins drew poorly at the gate despite their success on the field, and Huizenga announced that he expected the team to finish the year $34 million in the red, warning the public that he would have to dismantle the team unless taxpayers voted to build him a new stadium.

RIGHT: Liván Hernández did not pitch particularly well in the 1997 World Series, but his 2-0 Series record was enough to earn him the MVP award.

The Marlins were Latin America's team, as they actively sought out Latino players for the purpose of marketing them to the bilingual South Florida crowd. Twelve of the 48 players to appear in the 1997 World Series were Hispanic. That circumstance created unprecedented interest in the games in many Spanish-speaking communities.

Cleveland starter Orel Hershiser, 8-1 with a 1.93 ERA in his postseason career, was blistered for seven runs in four-plus innings in the first game. Liván Hernández, the Cuban defector, media darling, and hero of the Marlins' NLCS victory, pitched $5\frac{2}{3}$ innings for the victory. The media made much of the fact that Hernández's mother was unable to leave Cuba to watch her son pitch. It was unclear whether it was the U.S. or the Cuban government that had denied her permission to travel, but she finally arrived in Miami eight days later in time for the seventh game.

The Indians blasted Marlins ace Kevin Brown for a 6-1 win in Game 2 and the Series headed north to Ohio, where the money-laden Marlins were ironically staying in a run-down hotel in one of Cleveland's bad neighborhoods. One player said it was a place where "if you cross the street, you die." To make matters worse, it was so cold that the Marlins had to take batting practice before Game 3 wearing parkas and mittens while portable heaters sat atop the dugouts to warm each team's bench. Starting pitchers Charles Nagy and Al Leiter were unable to grip the freezing ball properly and struggled with their control. So did the nine relievers who followed them. The main beneficiary was the Marlins' Gary Sheffield, who singled, doubled, homered, and drove in five runs as Florida won a wild game, 14-11.

The next day it snowed, but the game went on. The Indians knocked around Florida's Tony Saunders, a rookie with just four major league wins under his belt, and Cleveland cruised to a 10-3 win. The playing conditions had been so awful and the games so interminable that *Sports Illustrated* dubbed it "The Faux Classic." "It is as if the Marlins and Indians are using this World Series to officially kill baseball," Dan Shaughnessy wrote in the *Boston Globe*. Bud Selig, in his 1,868th day as "interim" baseball commissioner, was furious. "When you have pitchers who can't throw the ball over the plate, and when they do it hits the wall somewhere, you're going to have long games," he said. (Another reason for the long games was the Selig-approved extended advertising time between innings, which he somehow failed to mention.)

Cleveland appeared to have Game 5 in hand, as they led 4-2 behind Hershiser heading into the sixth. But Alou, suffering from the flu and barely able to play, hit a three-run homer that just cleared the center-field fence. Things were close the rest of the way. The game ended with a Marlins victory when Roberto Alomar flew out in the ninth with the tying run on base.

Brown hoped to redeem himself after his embarrassing Game 2 loss by winning the clinching game for the Marlins back in Florida. But he was beaten up by the Indians for the second time in the Series, and the teams looked to an all-important final game, the first seventh game in the World Series in six years.

The players could hardly know that they were about to participate in one of the most thrilling chapters in the game's history. The Marlins were losing 2-1 entering the bottom of the ninth, but they started a rally with singles by Alou and Charles Johnson. The Indians were just two outs away from the championship when Craig Counsell, a utility man with 49 career hits, stepped up with the tying run on third. Counsell lifted a long fly ball to the warning track, deep enough to score Alou with the tying run. Extra innings beckoned, and Nagy, a 15-game winner as a starting pitcher, took the mound in relief for Cleveland. In the bottom of the eleventh with a runner on first, Counsell hit a ball that looked like an inning-ending double play, but the ball skipped off Tony Fernández's glove into the outfield while Bonilla hobbled on injured legs over to third base. There was another grounder to Fernández after an intentional walk that loaded the bases. This time, Fernández threw home for a force out. With two outs and the bases still loaded, 22-year-old Marlins shortstop Edgar Rentería entered the batter's box. The second pitch was a curveball outside.

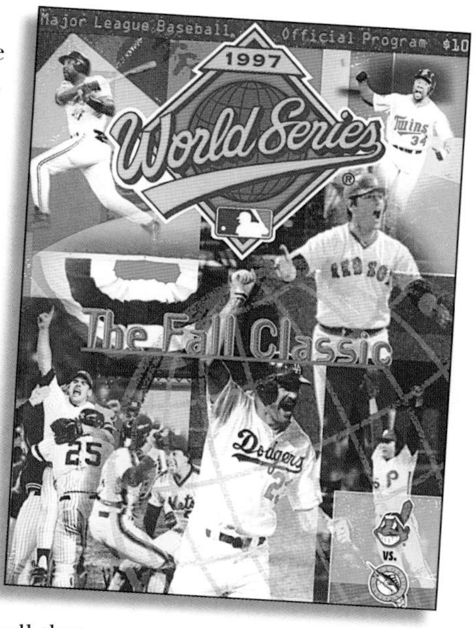

BOTTOM: First-year Marlin Moises Alou was the star of the 1997 Series, batting .321 with three homers and nine RBI.

Rentería hit it off the end of his bat and poked the ball softly into center field. Counsell floated home with the winning run and Rentería jumped in exultation as he crossed first base. The Marlins were world champs in their fifth year of existence.

The champagne quickly turned bitter, though, as Huizenga made good on his threat to disassemble the team by dumping high-salaried players. On October 31, four days after the victory parade in downtown Miami, the team declined to renew the contracts of Jeff Conine and Darren Daulton. On November 11, they traded Alou to Houston. More trades followed: Brown, Leiter, Devon White, Robb Nen, and Dennis Cook were all excised. The Marlins lost 108 games in 1998, the most in the National League since 1969. Their befuddled fans were left to wonder whether the championship had been real or only a strange dream.

TOP AND RIGHT: As Edgar Rentería (top) rounded first base in joy, Craig Counsell scored the Series-winning run on Rentería's hit.

1997 WORLD SERIES

Joe Robbie Stadium (Fla. Marlins) ◆ 10.18.97

	1	2	3	4	5	6	7	8	9	R	H	E
Clev.	1	0	0	0	1	1	0	1	0	4	11	0
Fla.	0	0	1	4	2	0	0	0	X	7	7	1

WP–Hernandez LP–Hershiser S–Nen
HR: CLE–Ramirez, Thome; FLA–Alou, Johnson
ATT: 67,245

Joe Robbie Stadium ◆ 10.19.97

	1	2	3	4	5	6	7	8	9	R	H	E
Clev.	1	0	0	0	3	2	0	0	0	6	14	0
Fla.	1	0	0	0	0	0	0	0	0	1	8	0

WP–Ogea LP–Brown HR: CLE–Alomar
ATT: 67,025

Jacobs Field (Cleveland Indians) ◆ 10.21.97

	1	2	3	4	5	6	7	8	9	R	H	E
Fla.	1	0	1	1	0	2	2	0	7	14	16	3
Clev.	2	0	0	3	2	0	0	0	4	11	10	3

WP–Cook LP–Plunk HR: FLA–Sheffield, Daulton, Eisenreich; CLE–Thome ATT: 44,880

Jacobs Field ◆ 10.22.97

	1	2	3	4	5	6	7	8	9	R	H	E
Fla.	0	0	0	1	0	2	0	0	0	3	6	2
Clev.	3	0	3	0	0	1	1	2	X	10	15	0

WP–Wright LP–Saunders S–Anderson
HR: FLA–Alou; CLE–Ramirez, Williams
ATT: 44,877

Jacobs Field ◆ 10.23.97

	1	2	3	4	5	6	7	8	9	R	H	E
Fla.	0	2	0	0	0	4	0	1	1	8	15	2
Clev.	0	1	3	0	0	0	0	0	3	7	9	0

WP–Hernandez LP–Hershiser S–Nen
HR: FLA–Alou; CLE–Alomar ATT: 44,888

Joe Robbie Stadium ◆ 10.25.97

	1	2	3	4	5	6	7	8	9	R	H	E
Clev.	0	2	1	0	1	0	0	0	0	4	7	0
Fla.	0	0	0	0	1	0	0	0	0	1	8	0

WP–Ogea LP–Brown S–Mesa ATT: 67,498

Joe Robbie Stadium ◆ 10.26.97

	1	2	3	4	5	6	7	8	9	10	11	R	H	E
Clev.	0	0	2	0	0	0	0	0	0	0	0	2	6	2
Fla.	0	0	0	0	0	0	1	0	1	0	1	3	8	0

WP–Powell LP–Nagy HR: FLA–Bonilla ATT: 67,204

1998

New York Yankees (4)
San Diego Padres (0)

The Yankees won the World Series in 1996 by getting some good breaks, by getting hits at the right time, and by moving precariously from win to win. They won it in 1998 by crushing the opposition with a steamroller. Indeed, the 1998 Yankees posted the second-highest win total in the history of baseball.

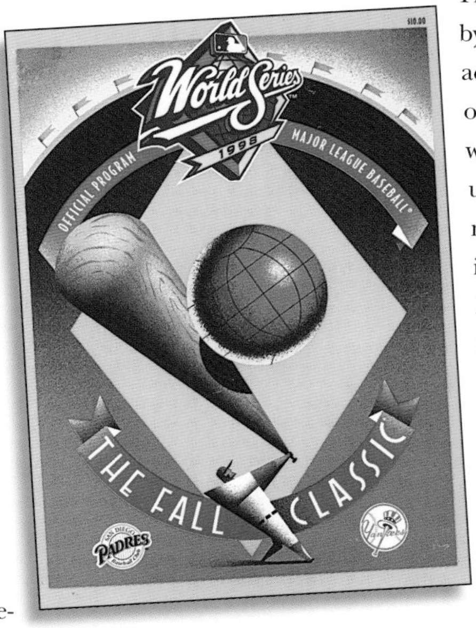

It was one of the most well-balanced teams in baseball history. Many said the Yankees won without superstars, but Bernie Williams was the league batting champ and Derek Jeter turned in a solid season. There were also no egos, no Babe Ruths or Reggie Jacksons who knew the world revolved around them and acted accordingly. Operating with a roster that was an embarrassment of riches, Joe Torre pulled players in and out of his lineup masterfully, much as Gil Hodges had done in 1969. Many of the important players—Jeter, Williams, Jorge Posada, Mariano Rivera, Andy Pettitte, Ramiro Mendoza—were products of the Yankee farm system. They were surrounded by cast-offs and shrewd acquisitions from other organizations, players who seemed to blossom under Torre as they never had before. They included Scott Brosius, David Wells, and Paul O'Neill. The Yankees had nobody with thirty home runs, but they did have ten players with at least ten homers, a major league record. They also got a boost from one of the greatest late-season call-ups in baseball history, nine-year minor leaguer Shane Spencer, who was recalled from Triple A on July 27. Spencer played in 24 games after his recall and batted .410 with 10 homers and 26 RBI, slugging a remarkable 1.000 and joining Ruth, Gehrig, and

TOP AND BOTTOM: Trevor Hoffman (top) was baseball's most dominant reliever in 1998, but in his only World Series appearance he gave up a decisive three-run homer to Scott Brosius (bottom).

DiMaggio on the (short) list of Yankees to hit three grand slams in one season.

The 1998 San Diego Padres were the second club ever to beat two 100-win teams in one postseason (the 1988 Dodgers were the first). They now tried to beat a third when they met the Yankees in the World Series. San Diego entered the first game with a glimmer of hope despite New York's season-long dominance. Kevin Brown, their ace with a 2.38 ERA, had a better lifetime record against the Yankees than any pitcher in baseball history: 12-3 with a 2.50 ERA. The Padres got him an early lead, but Brown was clobbered for the third consecutive time in the World Series, and the Yankee machine pounded its way to a 9-6 win.

The second game belonged to Orlando "El Duque" Hernández, the older half-brother of the previous year's playoff hero, Liván Hernández. The pitcher with the unusual windup had signed with the Yankees after escaping Cuba on a boat in February. He had been banned from playing in his home country one year earlier. Now he was pitching in the World Series for the New York Yankees, scattering six hits and winning easily, 9-3.

San Diego got an early lead in Game 3, but Brosius narrowed the gap with a seventh-inning homer. With the Padres leading 3-2 in the eighth, Trevor Hoffman, San Diego's fearsome closer (who had enjoyed one of the greatest relief pitching seasons of all time), trotted in from the bullpen to the chest-thumping strains of the AC/DC song "Hell's Bells." Hoffman walked off the field as the losing pitcher after a three-run homer by Brosius. It seemed as if the Yankees could not lose.

Spencer was another Yankee hero in the third game, as he contributed a run-scoring double and an outfield assist to help beat his hometown team. He was probably the only player (besides Tony Gwynn) who had also been at the last World Series game in San Diego, having sat in the upper deck as a 12-year-old for Game 2 of the 1984 Series.

The Padres knew it was over as they fell behind three games to none. Andy Pettitte and Kevin Brown matched zeroes for five innings in Game 4, but the Yankees got one in the sixth and two more in the eighth. Although he pitched well this time, Brown failed to win a Series game for the fourth time in two years. He was upset at an earlier

RIGHT: Orlando Hernández said he had always dreamed of playing for the Yankees. He realized that dream in 1998, winning Game 2 of the World Series against San Diego.

call and walked to the showers after offering a sarcastic tip of his cap to the umpire. Rivera entered in the eighth. The Yankees were world champs four outs later.

Although the Padres were swept, 38-year-old Tony Gwynn, playing in his second World Series after a 14-year drought, was stunningly good, batting .500 with a homer and three RBI in the Series. But as in 1984, Gwynn's Padres were simply overwhelmed by a much better team. Yankee owner George Steinbrenner had asked manager Joe Torre before the season whether any team had ever gone 162-0. "He was kidding," Torre said. "I think. I didn't realize how close we would come."

1998 WORLD SERIES

Yankee Stadium II (N.Y. Yankees) ◆ 10.17.98

	1	2	3	4	5	6	7	8	9	R	H	E
SDP	0	0	2	0	3	0	0	1	0	6	8	1
NYY	0	2	0	0	0	0	7	0	X	9	9	1

WP–Wells LP–Wall S–Rivera HR: SD–Vaughn (2), Gwynn; NYY–Knoblauch, Martinez ATT: 56,712

Yankee Stadium II ◆ 10.18.98

	1	2	3	4	5	6	7	8	9	R	H	E
SDP	0	0	0	0	1	0	0	2	0	3	10	1
NYY	3	3	1	0	2	0	0	0	X	9	16	0

WP–Hernandez LP–Ashby HR: NYY–Williams, Posada ATT: 56,692

Qualcomm Stadium (San Diego Padres) ◆ 10.20.98

	1	2	3	4	5	6	7	8	9	R	H	E
NYY	0	0	0	0	0	0	2	3	0	5	9	1
SDP	0	0	0	0	0	3	0	1	0	4	7	1

WP–Mendoza LP–Hoffman S–Rivera HR: NYY–Brosius (2) ATT: 64,667

Qualcomm Stadium ◆ 10.21.98

	1	2	3	4	5	6	7	8	9	R	H	E
NYY	0	0	0	0	0	1	0	2	0	3	9	0
SDP	0	0	0	0	0	0	0	0	0	0	7	0

WP–Pettitte LP–Brown S–Rivera ATT: 65,427

1999

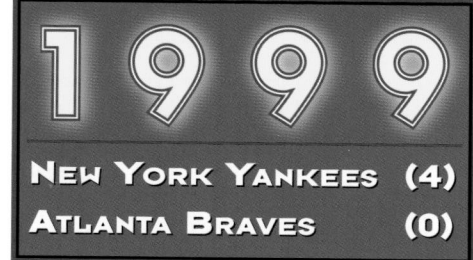

New York Yankees (4)
Atlanta Braves (0)

The Yankees went out and traded for Roger Clemens after flirting with invincibility in 1998. Clemens was the only pitcher ever to win five Cy Young Awards, and though he had a disappointing season, his new team did not. They won 98 games and made it to the World Series for the third time in four years. It had been, as usual, an eventful season in the Bronx. Manager Joe Torre missed the first 36 games of the season while recovering from prostate cancer surgery. Darryl Strawberry fell off the wagon and was readmitted to a rehab clinic. Three Yankee players—Scott Brosius, Luis Sojo, and Paul O'Neill—lost their fathers in the weeks leading up to the World Series. Sojo missed the first two games, while O'Neill played through both the emotional pain and the physical pain that came from his broken right rib.

All the drama mattered little, as the Yankees swatted away the Atlanta Braves in the World Series much as they would a harmless but annoying fly. Torre picked Orlando Hernández, who had been the MVP of the American League championship series, to start the first game in Atlanta. The crafty right-hander mowed the Braves down using a variety of arm angles and off-speed pitches like a latter-day Luis Tiant. El Duque got his twentieth win of the year by outpitching Greg Maddux and holding the Braves to one hit. David Cone did his part the next night by beating the Braves 7-2. It was the tenth consecutive win in the World Series for the Yankees. Now they headed back home to sew up the title, a task that appeared about as challenging as tying their shoes.

Tom Glavine, who had been unable to go in the opening game because of the flu, got the nod for Atlanta in Game 3. It mattered little to New York what pitcher they were facing or what illnesses he had. The Yankees engineered a comeback after falling behind 5-1, as Chad Curtis, Tino Martinez, and Chuck Knoblauch all homered off Glavine to tie the game and send it into extra innings. Curtis came up against lefty Mike

TOP: In the late 1990s Mariano Rivera established himself as the best pitcher in postseason history, with a 14-3 record, 24 saves, and a 0.90 ERA through 2002.

BOTTOM: Two battle-tested veterans, Roger Clemens (left) and David Cone, were anchors of the Yankee starting rotation in 1999.

Remlinger in the tenth and sent another pitch over the fence to give New York a dramatic extra-inning win.

Facing elimination, the Braves thought that John Smoltz, the winningest pitcher in postseason history, might be able to extend their season for one more game. But Smoltz couldn't get the patient Yankees to swing at his tempting pitches out of the strike zone. "These guys won't swing at *anything*," he announced to his teammates after making 75 pitches in the first three innings. Smoltz ended up pitching well, but not as well as Clemens, who made his first World Series start since the excruciating sixth game of 1986. Clemens had been shellacked earlier in the playoffs by his former team, the Red Sox, but he pitched beautifully on this night, allowing just four hits and one run. Mariano Rivera recorded the final four outs and the Yankees, as reliable as the cycles of the moon, won another championship.

Rivera, the shy, doe-eyed reliever from the Panamanian fishing village of Puerto Caimito, was named Series MVP. He was the prime mover behind all three Yankee championships, saving three of the four wins and extending his postseason scoreless streak to 25⅔ innings. "Smoltz, Maddux, and Glavine all threw their A games," Atlanta pitching coach Leo Mazzone said in disbelief, "and we lost every one of 'em. I don't get it. How does that happen?"

It happens when you play the New York Yankees.

BOTTOM: Mariano Rivera was named World Series MVP in 1999.

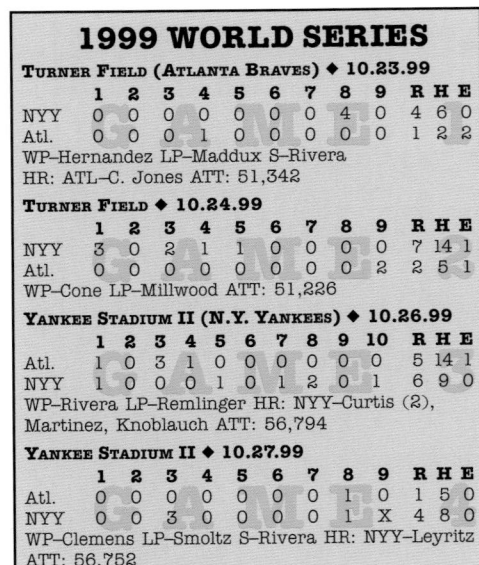

1999 WORLD SERIES

Turner Field (Atlanta Braves) ◆ 10.23.99 (Game 1)

	1	2	3	4	5	6	7	8	9	R	H	E
NYY	0	0	0	0	0	0	0	4	0	4	6	0
Atl.	0	0	0	1	0	0	0	0	0	1	2	2

WP–Hernandez LP–Maddux S–Rivera
HR: ATL–C. Jones ATT: 51,342

Turner Field ◆ 10.24.99 (Game 2)

	1	2	3	4	5	6	7	8	9	R	H	E
NYY	3	0	2	1	1	0	0	0	0	7	14	1
Atl.	0	0	0	0	0	0	0	0	2	2	5	1

WP–Cone LP–Millwood ATT: 51,226

Yankee Stadium II (N.Y. Yankees) ◆ 10.26.99 (Game 3)

	1	2	3	4	5	6	7	8	9	10	R	H	E
Atl.	1	0	3	1	0	0	0	0	0	0	5	14	1
NYY	1	0	0	0	1	0	1	2	0	1	6	9	0

WP–Rivera LP–Remlinger HR: NYY–Curtis (2), Martinez, Knoblauch ATT: 56,794

Yankee Stadium II ◆ 10.27.99 (Game 4)

	1	2	3	4	5	6	7	8	9	R	H	E
Atl.	0	0	0	0	0	0	0	1	0	1	5	0
NYY	0	0	3	0	0	0	0	1	X	4	8	0

WP–Clemens LP–Smoltz S–Rivera HR: NYY–Leyritz ATT: 56,752

2000

New York Yankees (4)
New York Mets (1)

Baseball and the New York subway system had been intertwined ever since Jack Norworth wrote "Take Me Out to the Ball Game" while riding on a subway car in 1908. That was particularly evident in the thirteen subway series matchups involving the Yankees, Dodgers, and Giants. Two Chicago teams had played each other in 1906, two St. Louis teams in 1944, and two Bay Area teams in 1989, but none of those had quite the same mystique as the New York version. Now, for the first time since the Dodgers left Brooklyn, two Big Apple teams prepared to square off again in the World Series.

The Yankees had barely been able to win their division, and they stumbled into the postseason after losing thirteen of their last fifteen games. But they fought their way through the playoffs, as did the Mets, who had sustained a heartbreaking loss to the Atlanta Braves the year before. It was the most-hyped baseball event in New York in decades, but the subway series received little interest from fans around the country and drew the lowest television ratings in recent memory.

The Mets took the early lead in the first game, but they missed the opportunity for an extra run when base runner Timo Pérez didn't run hard, believing Todd Zeile's long fly was a home run. Pérez failed to score when the ball fell for a double, and that blunder came back to haunt the Mets when Armando Benítez, their closer who had a long history of blowing important postseason games, gave up a game-tying sacrifice fly to Chuck Knoblauch in the ninth. The Yankees failed to score after they loaded the bases in the tenth, but they loaded them again in the twelfth. This time José Vizcaino, a utility infielder playing for his sixth major league team, ended the game with a single. It was his fourth hit of the game.

Game 2 will always be remembered for one of the weirdest events in World Series annals. On July 8, 2000, in the first meeting between Mike Piazza and Roger Clemens since Piazza's monstrous grand slam off Clemens in June of 2000, Clemens had hit

Piazza with an horrific fastball to the helmet, rendering the dazed catcher unable to stand for several minutes. "It was definitely intentional," the enraged Piazza had said. The two would now face each other for the first time since. Many experts suggested the three-month-old incident was history. "Like hell it is," the Mets' Todd Zeile responded.

In his first at-bat in the first inning, Piazza fouled off a pitch. The bat broke off at the handle and the barrel flew out toward Clemens. Clemens fielded the bat as if it were a grounder and then flung it with all his might toward Piazza as he ran to first. The bat missed Piazza, but both dugouts emptied as Piazza delivered some choice words to the pitcher. After order was restored, Clemens remarkably escaped without an ejection or suspension. Clemens seemed to draw strength from the incident, as he held the Mets to only two singles in eight innings. The game got interesting when Mariano Rivera entered with the Yankees leading in the ninth. Rivera had a 0.46 ERA in 59 career postseason innings, but the Mets scored three runs after he entered, two of them on a homer by Jay Payton. What had been a blowout for eight innings was now a 6-5 game, though Rivera finally retired Kurt Abbott for the final out.

The game seemed almost secondary, though, as people searched for an explanation for Clemens' attack on Piazza. Some people, mostly Yankee fans, felt it was an instinctual response, that Clemens threw the bat without realizing he was doing it. Some suspected it was a chemical reaction, attributing it to adrenaline or steroids. Still others wondered if Clemens might be mentally ill. He did nothing to dispel that notion in postgame interviews, saying he "thought it was the ball" when he threw the bat at Piazza, as if that would have made it excusable. The normally calm Joe Torre lost his cool during the postgame press conference, as he twisted himself into knots trying to defend his pitcher's indefensible actions. It was just "one of those things that happen sometimes," Torre said, although nothing remotely like it had ever happened in baseball before. "I'm convinced Roger wasn't throwing the bat at him. It was a get-it-off-the-field kind of thing."

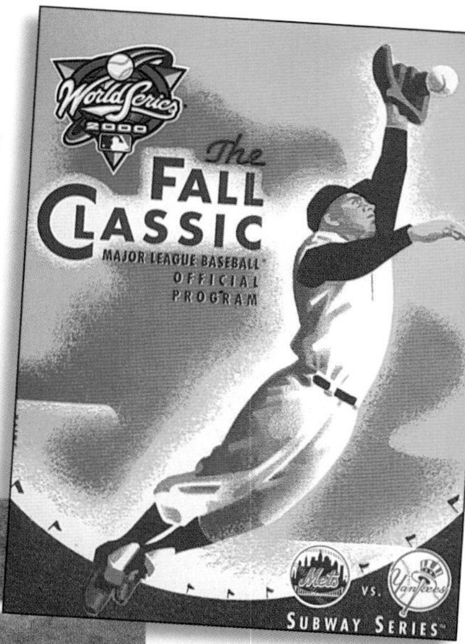

TOP: Timo Pérez is tagged out by Jorge Posada in Game 1 of the 2000 World Series, keeping the game a scoreless tie. (The Yankees eventually won it in 12 innings.)

BOTTOM: The infamous Game 2 bat-throwing incident of 2000 caused bad blood between Roger Clemens (left), Mike Piazza (right), and their respective teams.

Piazza called the incident "bizarre." He said that Clemens "seemed extremely apologetic and unsure and confused and unstable." Mets pitcher John Franco was less diplomatic, saying simply, "He's an asshole."

The incident would mar relations between the teams for the next several years, but for now they both returned to the task at hand: winning the World Series. The Mets took the third game, as Benny Agbayani's eighth-inning double handed Hernández his first career postseason loss, 4-2. The Yankees' 14-game World Series winning streak was over, but they still led this one two games to one. They started off well the next day, as Derek Jeter hit the first pitch of the game for a home run. It remained a close game the whole way, and the Yankee bullpen threw 4⅔ innings of superb relief to preserve a 3-2 win. "This has been a gut-wrenching Series," Paul O'Neill said. "They've been one-run games. When you walk off the field, you know you've been in a battle."

Al Leiter pitched heroically for the Mets in the fifth game, battling through the first eight innings and allowing just two runs. Indeed, he pitched so valiantly that manager Bobby Valentine kept him in even after two runners reached base with the game tied in the ninth. Luis Sojo singled into center field on Leiter's 142nd pitch, and the throw home hit Jorge Posada's thigh as Posada slid in with the go-ahead run. "I know in my heart that I pitched well," Leiter said. "Deep down I felt I could get that third out." Piazza came up in the bottom of the ninth as the tying run, and he lifted a long fly ball to center field for the final out of the Series.

With their 87 regular season wins, the Yankees had joined the 1987 Twins and 1959 Dodgers as one of the worst teams ever to win the World Series. But Torre wasn't buying it. "We can put our record, our dedication, our resolve up against any team that's ever played the game of baseball," he said.

2000 WORLD SERIES

Yankee Stadium II (N.Y. Yankees) ◆ 10.21.00

	1	2	3	4	5	6	7	8	9	10	11	12	R	H	E
NYM	0	0	0	0	0	0	3	0	0	0	0	0	3	10	0
NYY	0	0	0	0	0	2	0	0	1	0	0	1	4	12	0

WP–Stanton LP–Wendell ATT: 55,913

Yankee Stadium II ◆ 10.22.00

	1	2	3	4	5	6	7	8	9	R	H	E
NYM	0	0	0	0	0	0	0	0	5	5	7	3
NYY	2	1	0	0	1	0	1	1	X	6	12	1

WP–Clemens LP–Hampton HR: NYM–Piazza, Payton; NYY–Brosius ATT: 56,059

Shea Stadium (New York Mets) ◆ 10.24.00

	1	2	3	4	5	6	7	8	9	R	H	E
NYY	0	0	1	1	0	0	0	0	0	2	8	0
NYM	0	1	0	0	0	1	0	2	X	4	9	0

WP–Franco LP–Hernandez S–Benitez HR: NYM–Ventura ATT: 55,299

Shea Stadium ◆ 10.25.00

	1	2	3	4	5	6	7	8	9	R	H	E
NYY	1	1	1	0	0	0	0	0	0	3	8	0
NYM	0	0	2	0	0	0	0	0	0	2	6	1

WP–Nelson LP–Bj Jones S–Rivera HR: NYY–Jeter; NYM–Piazza ATT: 55,290

Shea Stadium ◆ 10.26.00

	1	2	3	4	5	6	7	8	9	R	H	E
NYY	0	1	0	0	0	1	0	0	2	4	7	1
NYM	0	2	0	0	0	0	0	0	0	2	8	1

WP–Stanton LP–Leiter S–Rivera HR: NYY–Williams, Jeter ATT: 55,292

BOTTOM LEFT: Little-used infielder Luis Sojo strokes the eventual game-winning hit in Game 5 of the 2000 World Series.

BOTTOM RIGHT: Al Leiter pitched valiantly for the Mets in the final game of the 2000 Series, but lost 4-2 after throwing 142 pitches.

2001

Arizona Diamondbacks (4)
New York Yankees (3)

THE THREE-TIME DEFENDING CHAMPION Yankees were getting older even though they were still one of the most balanced teams in baseball. Anyone was capable of becoming the hero at any given time. They had played in four World Series and five American League Championship Series since 1996. Not only had they won all nine times, but nine different Yankees had been named series MVP. In 2001, they tried to make it four straight titles against the Arizona Diamondbacks, a four-year-old expansion franchise.

The Diamondbacks had invested more money in old players than any team in baseball history. They offered millions to Mark Grace, 37; Jay Bell, 35; Matt Williams, 35; Steve Finley, 36; Luis González, 33; Reggie Sanders, 33; Greg Swindell, 36; Curt Schilling, 34; and Randy Johnson, 37. It should have been a recipe for disaster given the rate at which aging players usually break down. Instead, the remarkable performances of three of those players were enough to lift Arizona to the pennant. The ever-improving González had a season of historic magnitude. He hit 57 home runs with 142 RBI and 419 total bases, the latter figure tying him with Lou Gehrig for tenth on the all-time list. Johnson and Schilling were just as good, becoming arguably the best one-two pitching tandem in baseball history. Counting the National League playoffs, the pair combined for 48 wins, 723 strikeouts, and a 2.60 ERA that was almost two runs better than the league average.

Schilling and Johnson could not be intimidated, not even by the New York Yankees. Schilling was asked about the Yankees' mystique and aura before the first game. He cracked "Mystique and Aura? Those are dancers in a nightclub." He proved it in the opening game by winning 9-1. Johnson shut out the Yankees in Game 2. The third game was tied 1-1 as Roger Clemens and the surprising Brian Anderson pitched to a draw for six innings. Clemens was helped by some fine defensive plays. Anderson had no such luck, and New York scored the go-ahead run in the sixth and won 2-1.

Schilling started Game 4 on three days' rest. He looked tired, but both he and El Duque pitched marvelously for seven innings. Mike Stanton relieved for New York in the eighth, and the Diamondbacks scored two runs to take a 3-1 lead. Arizona manager Bob Brenly then brought in his closer, 22-year-old submariner Byung-Hyun Kim, to try for a two-inning save—something he had done only twice all year. Kim faced Tino Martínez with a runner on and two outs in the ninth, and Martínez hit Kim's first pitch over the center field fence to tie the game. The game went into extra innings. The exhausted Kim was pitching his third inning in the tenth and gave up a fly ball to Derek Jeter that barely reached the right field seats for a game-winning homer.

The Diamondbacks regrouped admirably the next day, taking a 2-0 lead behind Miguel Batista, the poet, novelist, and aspiring law student who doubled as Arizona's fourth starter. Batista pitched seven-plus innings of scoreless baseball. Kim took the mound in the ninth trying to do what he had failed to do the night before: protect a two-run lead. This time Scott Brosius came up with a runner on second and two outs. Like Martínez before him, he hit a two-run homer to tie the game. The shell-shocked Kim fell to his knees as players jumped up and down in the Yankee dugout. Then he wandered around the mound like a young deer that had lost its mother. He was now Ralph Branca times two. That he was done for the Series was obvious; the only question was whether his career would eventually recover.

Arizona loaded the bases in extra innings against the untouchable Mariano Rivera, but a diving catch by rookie Alfonso Soriano helped the Yankees escape unscathed. After saving the game with his glove, Soriano won it with his bat, as he singled in Chuck Knoblauch in the twelfth inning. The Yankees became the first team in Series history to win two straight games in which they trailed after eight innings. "You have to just sit back and chuckle a little bit, because it's so unbelievable," Knoblauch said. Yankee manager Joe Torre was asked if he was surprised at Brosius' homer. "How could I be surprised?" he said. "It happened just the night before." The Series should have been

BOTTOM: Tino Martínez launches a miraculous game-tying home run off Byung-Hyun Kim in the ninth inning of Game 4 in 2001.

over, but after two of the most dramatic comebacks ever, the Yankees led three games to two. One homemade sign at Yankee Stadium was intended as a dig at Schilling and proved prophetic. "MYSTIQUE & AURA," it said, "APPEARING NIGHTLY."

The teams trekked back to the desert and the Diamondbacks—perhaps wary of losing close games—bludgeoned New York 15-2 to set the stage for Game 7. It would be one of the most remarkable games in baseball history. The main players included three 20-game winners with 10 Cy Young Awards between them, a man with 57 home runs, and the best relief pitcher in the history of postseason baseball. It was like an action movie script sent back for rewrite because it was too over-the-top. Clemens and Schilling were the starting pitchers and both pitched well. Clemens departed in the seventh with the game tied at one. The exhausted Schilling was pitching on fumes and gave up an eighth-inning homer to Soriano, who was shaping up as the hero of the Series for New York. Schilling was relieved by Batista and then Johnson, who pitched despite going seven strong innings the night before.

The Yankees appeared to have the Series wrapped up when they brought in Rivera to get the last six outs with a 2-1 lead. The unflappable reliever's career postseason ERA was now 0.70. But Grace, who had led the 1990s in hits, got one to lead off the bottom of the ninth. Then it all unraveled. "It was surreal," Johnson said later, "watching all this develop." Rivera threw wildly on an attempted sacrifice bunt to put the tying run on second and the winning run on first. Tony Womack then shot a double to right to tie the game. Next, a Rivera pitch grazed Craig Counsell's hand to load the bases. With only one out and the winning run at third, the Yankees were forced to play their infield in with the powerful González batting. González poked a soft liner into short center field that Jeter could have caught with the infield playing at normal depth. But with Jeter playing in, the ball flew over his head for a Series-winning hit. It was the first blown save in Rivera's World Series career and it came in the most important game he ever pitched. "That was the one guy we wanted to stay away from the whole Series," González said. "We got him the one time it counted."

Brenly became the first rookie manager to win the World Series since Ralph Houk in 1961, but it seemed clear that Arizona won in spite of Brenly, not because of him. Arizona used four different cleanup hitters during the Series, but Brenly's pitching moves were even more suspect. For example, Brenly allowed Schilling to pitch several meaningless innings in a Game 1 blowout. That robbed his star pitcher of rest that he would need to start the fourth game. As a result, Brenly had to remove Schilling early in that fourth game despite having only a two-run lead. Schilling's replacement, Kim, gave up Martínez's homer. Although Kim threw a career-high 61 pitches in that game, nearly a starter's workload, Brenly invited trouble by pitching Kim the next night also. Not surprisingly, it backfired on him when Kim blew the game again. Brenly wasted Randy Johnson in Game 6 by allowing him to throw 104 pitches in a 15-2 laugher despite knowing that Johnson might have to pitch again the next night. Brenly's work in the World Series was a clinic in how *not* to manage.

But Schilling and Johnson made up for Brenly's apparent mistakes with their remarkable pitching. Johnson was the seventh game's winning pitcher in relief, his third victory of the Series. The pair combined to start five games in the Series, including all four that Arizona won, and posted a 1.40 ERA with 45 strikeouts in 38 innings. Fittingly, they were named co-MVPs, and as they hoisted the trophy over their heads they cemented their place as one of the greatest World Series pitching tandems ever. "Now I know what it takes to win the World Series," Johnson said. "You've got to push the limits."

TOP: Derek Jeter exults after his game-winning homer in the fourth game of the 2001 World Series at Yankee Stadium.

BOTTOM: It's déjà vu all over again for Byung-Hyun Kim, who gave up dramatic ninth-inning homers in Games 4 and 5.

2001 WORLD SERIES

BANK ONE BALLPARK (ARIZONA DIAMONDBACKS) ◆ 10.27.01

	1	2	3	4	5	6	7	8	9	R	H	E
NYY	1	0	0	0	0	0	0	0	0	1	3	2
Ariz.	1	0	4	4	0	0	0	0	X	9	10	0

WP–Schilling LP–Mussina HR: ARI–Counsell, Gonzalez ATT: 49,646

BANK ONE BALLPARK ◆ 10.28.01

	1	2	3	4	5	6	7	8	9	R	H	E
NYY	0	0	0	0	0	0	0	0	0	0	3	0
Ariz.	0	1	0	0	0	0	3	0	X	4	5	0

WP–Johnson LP–Pettitte HR: ARI–M. Williams ATT: 49,646

YANKEE STADIUM II (N.Y. YANKEES) ◆ 10.30.01

	1	2	3	4	5	6	7	8	9	R	H	E
Ariz.	0	0	0	1	0	0	0	0	0	1	3	3
NYY	0	1	0	0	0	1	0	0	X	2	7	1

WP–Clemens LP–Anderson S–Rivera HR: NYY–Posada ATT: 55,820

YANKEE STADIUM II ◆ 10.31.01

	1	2	3	4	5	6	7	8	9	10	R	H	E
Ariz.	0	0	0	1	0	0	0	2	0	0	3	6	0
NYY	0	0	1	0	0	0	0	0	2	1	4	7	0

WP–Rivera LP–Kim HR: ARI–Grace; NYY–Spencer, T. Martinez, Jeter ATT: 55,863

YANKEE STADIUM II ◆ 11.1.01

	1	2	3	4	5	6	7	8	9	10	11	12	R	H	E
Ariz.	0	0	0	0	2	0	0	0	0	0	0	0	2	8	0
NYY	0	0	0	0	0	0	0	0	2	0	0	1	3	9	1

WP–Hitchcock LP–Lopez HR: ARI–Finley, Barajas; NYY–Brosius ATT: 56,018

BANK ONE BALLPARK ◆ 11.3.01

	1	2	3	4	5	6	7	8	9	R	H	E
NYY	0	0	0	0	0	2	0	0	0	2	7	1
Ariz.	1	3	8	3	0	0	0	0	X	15	22	0

WP–Johnson LP–Pettitte ATT: 49,707

BANK ONE BALLPARK ◆ 11.4.01

	1	2	3	4	5	6	7	8	9	R	H	E
NYY	0	0	0	0	0	0	1	1	0	2	6	3
Ariz.	0	0	0	0	0	1	0	0	2	3	11	0

WP–Johnson LP–Rivera HR: NYY–Soriano ATT: 49,589

TOP: N.L. Cy Young winner Randy Johnson set a new record with five postseason wins in 2001.

BOTTOM LEFT: Curt Schilling started Games 4 and 7 of the 2001 World Series on short rest, but pitched well each time.

BOTTOM RIGHT: Luis González rounds first after hitting a Series-winning single off Mariano Rivera in the ninth inning of Game 7.

1995–2002

2002

Anaheim Angels (4)
San Francisco Giants (3)

After enjoying what many hailed as the greatest offensive season ever in 2001, Barry Bonds put together a performance that was almost as good in 2002. His home run total dropped from 73 to 46, but he won the National League batting title with a .370 average, and his .582 on-base percentage smashed the 61-year-old major league record previously held by Ted Williams. Bonds drew a record 198 walks as pitchers realized it was better to put him on base than face his wrath. He was the most terrifying batter in baseball history—more feared than even Babe Ruth had been.

The San Francisco Giants, managed by Dusty Baker, surrounded Bonds with a makeshift lineup that included Jeff Kent and little else. San Francisco's fifth, sixth, and seventh hitters—the men charged with driving in Bonds all those times he reached base—posted a minuscule .406 slugging percentage. Still, the Giants won the wild card and managed to reach the World Series. After compiling a .198 average in his five previous playoff series, 2002 was a perfect opportunity for Bonds to disprove the theory that he was weak in the postseason.

Awaiting the Giants were Mike Scioscia's Anaheim Angels, a team that seemed an afterthought in the playoffs until it crushed the New York Yankees and Minnesota Twins, batting .328 over the first two rounds of the playoffs. In both demeanor and style of play the Angels bore a great resemblance to the 1988 world champion Dodgers, a team on which Scioscia and Anaheim coaches Mickey Hatcher and Alfredo Griffin had played. With a cast of little-known players the Angels mastered the fundamentals of the game, hustling on every play and going from first to third base better than any team in recent memory. "We're not a team that sits back and waits for the three-run home run," third baseman Troy Glaus said. "We try to create situations, put pressure on the defense, and pressure them into making mistakes."

It was power vs. punch-and-judy, a one-man team against an exceptionally balanced one. The only thing the Giants and Angels had in common, it seemed, was a dislike for the Los Angeles Dodgers, the franchise in whose shadow each had toiled for more

than 40 years. Ironically, managers Baker and Scioscia had been teammates on the Dodgers' Series-winning team in 1981.

One notable feature of the 2002 Series was its lack of dominant starting pitching. Only Anaheim's Jarrod Washburn, with 18 victories, was among the major leagues' 20 winningest pitchers, and for the first time since 1993 no World Series hurler ranked among baseball's top ten pitchers in earned run average. Nobody was surprised, then, when the Giants and Angels combined to set new Series records for most runs scored, home runs, and extra-base hits. For the first time ever, no starter managed to last as long as seven innings in a Series game.

Scioscia seemed to be using the starting pitchers to tread water until he could turn to his spectacular bullpen in the fifth and

BOTTOM LEFT: Barry Bonds watches his final home run of the 2002 World Series leave the park in Game 6. Despite Bonds' round-tripper, the Giants lost the game, 6-5.

BOTTOM RIGHT: Bonds receives one of his record seven intentional walks. Bonds swung at only 26 of the 110 pitches he saw during the 2002 Series, a minuscule 24 percent.

sixth innings. Anaheim's six relievers—failed starter Scott Schoeneweis, rookies Scot Shields and Francisco Rodríguez, retreads Ben Weber and Brendan Donnelly, and flamethrowing closer Troy Percival—had each posted a regular season relief ERA better than 3.30. The 20-year-old Rodríguez was especially magnificent. Called up from the minor leagues on September 18 in time to pitch in five late-season games, he racked up five postseason victories—tying Randy Johnson's single-season record—before ever winning a game in the regular season. In almost 19 October innings Rodríguez utterly dominated the opposition, allowing only ten hits while striking out 28. But he wasn't the only one. Outside of a 16-4 drubbing in Game 5, the Angels relief corps posted a 1.90 ERA in more than 23 World Series innings.

Things started off well for San Francisco, which won the first game 4-3 thanks in part to a homer by Bonds in his first career World Series at-bat. Three solid innings of relief preserved the opening win for the Giants, who—presciently—scored all four of their runs on solo homers. The teams mounted a slugfest in the second game, combining for 28 hits and five home runs in a wild 11-10 Anaheim victory. The key blow was a tiebreaking homer in the eighth by Tim Salmon, the longest-serving Angel, who had been with the team since the dark days when they were known as the California Angels and employed such players as Luis Polonia and Hubie Brooks. Bonds, meanwhile, hit another solo homer, but the Angels were unconcerned. "If we can hold Barry to a solo home run every day, we'll be okay," second baseman Adam Kennedy said. Said Percival, the pitcher who gave up Bonds' ninth-inning blast: "I just wanted to see how far he could hit it."

Before the third game the Giants' Liván Hernández, owner of a 6-0 career postseason record, boasted that "I never lose in October." An hour later he was back in the Pac Bell Park clubhouse after getting shelled for six runs in three-plus innings, paving the way for an easy 10-4 Angels win. Even Bonds' third homer of the Series didn't matter, as the Giants now found themselves in a hole, two games to one. They came back in Game 4, however, when the fireballing phenom Rodríguez finally proved vulnerable, giving up a tiebreaking hit to David Bell in the eighth inning and losing the game to San Francisco, 4-3. (On a positive note, the Angels did figure out a way to hold Bonds homerless: by intentionally walking him three times.) The fifth game was nowhere near as close, as the Angels received what Scioscia called "a flat-out whupping." Behind two homers from Jeff Kent and three hits from Bonds, the Giants prevailed, 16-4.

Anaheim now trailed three games to two, but the Angels were heading home to play the last two games at Edison Field, home of the famed Rally Monkey, the jumping primate that appeared on the outfield

TOP: Troy Glaus, shown here batting against Minnesota in the ALCS, hit .344 with seven homers (including three in the World Series) during the 2002 postseason.

BOTTOM: As Angels catcher Bengie Molina prepares for a play at home in Game 5, J.T. Snow pulls Dusty Baker's three-year-old son, Darren, out of harm's way. The incident was one of the most talked-about events in the Series, and the seriousness of it led to a new rule establishing a minimum age for major league batboys.

scoreboard whenever the Angels were in a tight spot. That spot came with one out in the seventh inning of Game 6, with the Giants leading 5-0 and needing only eight more outs for a world championship. As the Rally Monkey energized the crowd, the Angels began to chip away. Troy Glaus singled. Brad Fullmer singled. Scott Spiezio hit a three-run homer. In the next inning, Salmon homered. Darin Erstad singled. Garret Anderson singled. Glaus doubled. By the time it was all over, the Angels had tagged four of the Giants' best pitchers—starter Russ Ortiz and relievers Felix Rodríguez, Tim Worrell, and Robb Nen—for six runs to take a one-run lead. For the seemingly invincible Nen, it was the first blown save in his last 21 attempts, and it was only the fifth time in Series history that any team had overcome a five-run deficit to win. "Everybody's bullpen is a little tired," Dusty Baker said. "That was a heck of a comeback."

Now it came down to a seventh game, and like many seventh games, this one was decided on the strength of the starting pitching. It seemed a mismatch: Liván Hernández, with one World Series MVP award already under his belt, against Anaheim's 24-year-old John Lackey, who had started the season with Triple-A Salt Lake City. But Hernández was knocked around again and Lackey pitched well, enabling Scioscia to hand a 3-1 lead over to his familiar bullpen trio of Donnelly, Rodríguez, and Percival. Although the Giants brought the tying run to the plate in the ninth inning, Baker, with possibly the weakest bench of any Series team ever, was forced to let two inept hitters—Tom Goodwin and Tsuyoshi Shinjo—flail away against Percival. When center fielder Darin Erstad squeezed Kenny Lofton's fly ball, it was all over for the Giants.

As usual, the sportswriters couldn't wait to pounce on Barry Bonds. "One for three with a walk was a good night," the testy slugger told the media after the game. "Am I supposed to go 3-for-3 with three homers? What do you want from me?" When all was said and done, Bonds dominated the World Series as few batters ever had. He reached base in 21 of his 30 plate appearances for a mind-blowing .700 on-base percentage, second-best in Series history. (Lou Gehrig's figure in the four-game 1928 Series was .706.) Bonds' 1.294 Series slugging percentage was the third-best ever, topped only by Gehrig and Ruth. The problem for the Giants was that thirteen of Bonds' times on base came via walks, seven of which were intentional. As teams had done all year, the Angels knew they could walk Bonds with impunity because he was followed in the batting order by the light-hitting Benito Santiago, who batted just .231 in the Series without an extra-base hit. With a slightly better fifth place hitter, the Giants might have been world champions.

The Giants hit 14 home runs, a new Series record, and scored 44 runs, third-most in Series history, but it was small-ball Anaheim that emerged with the championship trophy. The Angels batted .310 in the Series and were no slouches in the power department themselves, hitting seven homers to up their postseason total to a record-setting 24. Glaus, who batted .467 in the Fall Classic while hitting his fifth, sixth, and seventh homers of the postseason, was named Series MVP. "This is why we play," he said after the seventh game. "This is why we put all the time and effort in. You know, this is what all the swings against the garage door when you were a kid, that's what it all builds to, this point here."

BOTTOM: Francisco Rodriguez, a 20-year-old with just five major league games under his belt, was Anaheim's best pitcher in the 2002 playoffs, going 5-1 with a 1.93 ERA.

2002 WORLD SERIES

Edison Int'l Field (Anaheim) ◆ 10.19.02

	1	2	3	4	5	6	7	8	9	R	H	E
Giants	0	2	0	0	0	2	0	0	0	4	6	0
Angels	0	1	0	0	0	2	0	0	3	3	9	0

WP–Schmidt LP–Washburn HR: SF–Bonds, Sanders, Snow; ANA–Glaus (2) ATT: 44,603

Edison Int'l Field ◆ 10.20.02

	1	2	3	4	5	6	7	8	9	R	H	E
Giants	0	4	1	0	4	0	0	0	1	10	12	1
Angels	5	2	0	0	1	1	0	2	X	11	16	1

WP–Francisco Rodriguez S–Percival LP–Felix Rodriguez HR: SF–Sanders, Bell, Kent, Bonds; ANA–Salmon (2) ATT: 44,584

Pacific Bell Park (San Francisco) ◆ 10.22.02

	1	2	3	4	5	6	7	8	9	R	H	E
Angels	0	0	4	4	0	1	0	1	0	10	16	0
Giants	1	0	0	0	3	0	0	0	0	4	6	2

WP–Ortiz LP–Hernández HR: SF–Aurilia, Bonds ATT: 42,707

Pacific Bell Park ◆ 10.23.02

	1	2	3	4	5	6	7	8	9	R	H	E
Angels	0	1	2	0	0	0	0	0	0	3	10	1
Giants	0	0	0	0	3	0	0	1	X	4	12	1

WP–Worrell S–Nen LP–Francisco Rodriguez HR: ANA–Glaus ATT: 42,703

Pacific Bell Park ◆ 10.24.02

	1	2	3	4	5	6	7	8	9	R	H	E
Angels	0	0	0	0	3	1	0	0	0	4	10	2
Giants	3	3	0	0	0	2	4	4	X	16	16	0

WP–Zerbe LP–Washburn HR: SF–Kent (2), Aurilia (2) ATT: 42,713

Edison Int'l Field ◆ 10.26.02

	1	2	3	4	5	6	7	8	9	R	H	E
Giants	0	0	0	0	3	1	1	0	0	5	8	1
Angels	0	0	0	0	0	0	3	3	X	6	10	1

WP–Donnelly LP–Worrell HR: SF–Dunston, Bonds ANA–Spiezio, Erstad ATT: 44,506

Edison Int'l Field ◆ 10.27.02

	1	2	3	4	5	6	7	8	9	R	H	E
Giants	0	1	0	0	0	0	0	0	0	1	6	0
Angels	0	1	3	0	0	0	0	0	X	4	5	0

WP–Lackey LP–Hernández ATT: 44,598

TOP: Tim Salmon electrified the Edison Field crowd with this key go-ahead homer in the eighth inning of Game 2.

BOTTOM: After more than 40 years, the franchise that Gene Autry had started way back in 1961 finally captured its first world championship. Note the red Thunder Sticks with which the Anaheim faithful had created an ever-greater racket at every home game as their team stormed through the playoffs and into the record books.

Appendix I: World Series Composite Statistics

Batting Stats (Career)

GAMES PLAYED

Player	Games
Yogi Berra	75
Mickey Mantle	65
Elston Howard	54
Hank Bauer	53
Gil McDougald	53
Phil Rizzuto	52
Joe DiMaggio	51
Frankie Frisch	50
Pee Wee Reese	44
Roger Maris	41
Babe Ruth	41

AT-BATS

Player	At-Bats
Yogi Berra	259
Mickey Mantle	230
Joe DiMaggio	199
Frankie Frisch	197
Gil McDougald	190
Hank Bauer	188
Phil Rizzuto	183
Elston Howard	171
Pee Wee Reese	169
Roger Maris	152

BATTING AVERAGE (minimum 20 at-bats)

Player	Hits	AB	Avg.
Bobby Brown	18	41	.439
Pepper Martin	23	55	.418
Paul Molitor	23	55	.418
Hal McRae	18	45	.400
Lou Brock	34	87	.391
Marquis Grissom	30	77	.390
George Brett	19	51	.373
Thurman Munson	25	67	.373
Pat Borders	16	43	.372
Hank Aaron	20	55	.364

HITS

Player	Hits	Avg.
Yogi Berra	71	.274
Mickey Mantle	59	.257
Frankie Frisch	58	.294
Joe DiMaggio	54	.271
Hank Bauer	46	.245
PeeWee Reese	46	.272
Gil McDougald	45	.237
Phil Rizzuto	45	.246
Lou Gehrig	43	.361
Eddie Collins	42	.328
Elston Howard	42	.246
Babe Ruth	42	.326

HOME RUNS

Player	HRs	HR%
Mickey Mantle	18	7.8
Babe Ruth	15	11.6
Yogi Berra	12	4.6
Duke Snider	11	8.3
Lou Gehrig	10	8.4
Reggie Jackson	10	10.2
Joe DiMaggio	8	4.0
Frank Robinson	8	8.7
Bill Skowron	8	6.0
Hank Bauer	7	3.7
Goose Goslin	7	5.4
Gil McDougald	7	3.7

RUNS BATTED IN

Player	RBIs	Games
Mickey Mantle	40	65
Yogi Berra	39	75
Lou Gehrig	35	34
Babe Ruth	33	41
Joe DiMaggio	30	51
Bill Skowron	29	39
Duke Snider	26	36
Hank Bauer	24	53
Bill Dickey	24	38
Reggie Jackson	24	27
Gil McDougald	24	53

DOUBLES

Player	Doubles
Frankie Frisch	10
Carl Furillo	9
Jack Barry	9
Pete Fox	9
Lou Gehrig	8
Lonnie Smith	8
Duke Snider	8
Frank Baker	7
Lou Brock	7
Eddie Collins	7
Rick Dempsey	7
Hank Greenberg	7
Chick Hafey	7
Elston Howard	7
Reggie Jackson	7
Marty Marion	7
Pepper Martin	7
Danny Murphy	7
Stan Musial	7
Terry Pendleton	7
Jackie Robinson	7
Devon White	7

TRIPLES

Player	Triples
Billy Johnson	4
Tommy Leach	4
Tris Speaker	4
Hank Bauer	3
Bobby Brown	3
Dave Concepcion	3
Buck Freeman	3
Frankie Frisch	3
Lou Gehrig	3
Dan Gladden	3
Mark Lemke	3
Billy Martin	3
Tim McCarver	3
Bob Meusel	3
Freddie Parent	3
Chick Stahl	3
Devon White	3

RUNS

Player	Runs
Mickey Mantle	42
Yogi Berra	41
Babe Ruth	37
Lou Gehrig	30
Joe DiMaggio	27
Roger Maris	26
Elston Howard	25
Gil McDougald	23
Jackie Robinson	22
Hank Bauer	21
Reggie Jackson	21
Phil Rizzuto	21
Duke Snider	21
Gene Woodling	21

STOLEN BASES

Player	SBs
Lou Brock	14
Eddie Collins	14
Frank Chance	10
Dave Lopes	10
Phil Rizzuto	10
Frank Frisch	9
Honus Wagner	9
Johnny Evers	8
Roberto Alomar	7
Rickey Henderson	7
Pepper Martin	7
Joe Morgan	7
Joe Tinker	7

Pitching Stats (Career)

GAMES PITCHED

Player	Games	ERA
Whitey Ford	22	2.71
Mike Stanton	20	1.54
Mariano Rivera	18	1.67
Rollie Fingers	16	1.35
Allie Reynolds	15	2.79
Bob Turley	15	3.19
Clay Carroll	14	1.33
Clem Labine	13	3.16
Mark Wohlers	13	3.09
Waite Hoyt	12	1.83
Jim (Catifsh) Hunter	12	3.29
Art Nehf	12	2.16

INNINGS PITCHED

Player	Innings	ERA
Whitey Ford	146	2.71
Christy Mathewson	101.2	1.15
Red Ruffing	85.2	2.63
Chief Bender	85	2.44
Waite Hoyt	83.2	1.83
Bob Gibson	81	1.89
Art Nehf	79	2.16
Allie Reynolds	77.1	2.79
Jim Palmer	64.2	3.20
Jim (Catfish) Hunter	63	3.29

WINS

Player	Wins	Games	Record
Whitey Ford	10	22	10-8
Bob Gibson	7	9	7-2
Allie Reynolds	7	15	7-2
Red Ruffing	7	10	7-2
Chief Bender	6	10	6-4
Lefty Gomez	6	7	6-0
Waite Hoyt	6	12	6-4
Three Finger Brown	5	9	5-4
Jack Coombs	5	6	5-0
Jim Hunter	5	12	5-3
Christy Mathewson	5	11	5-5
Herb Pennock	5	10	5-0
Vic Raschi	5	11	5-3

SAVES

Player	Saves
Mariano Rivera	8
Rollie Fingers	6
Johnny Murphy	4
Allie Reynolds	4
John Wetteland	4
Elroy Face	3
Firpo Marberry	3
Will McEnaney	3
Tug McGraw	3
Herb Pennock	3
Kent Tekulve	3
Todd Worrell	3

LOSSES

Player	Losses	Games	Record
Whitey Ford	8	22	10-8
Joe Bush	5	9	2-5
Rube Marquard	5	11	2-5
Christy Mathewson	5	11	5-5
Eddie Plank	5	7	2-5
Schoolboy Rowe	5	8	2-5
Chief Bender	4	10	6-4
Mordecai Brown	4	9	5-4
Paul Derringer	4	11	2-4
Wild Bill Donovan	4	6	1-4
Burleigh Grimes	4	9	3-4
Waite Hoyt	4	12	6-4
Charlie Liebrandt	4	5	0-4
Carl Mays	4	8	3-4
Art Nehf	4	12	4-4
Don Newcombe	4	5	0-4
Bill Sherdel	4	4	0-4
Dave Stewart	4	10	2-4
Ed Summers	4	4	0-4
Ralph Terry	4	9	2-4

COMPLETE GAMES

Player	Complete Games	Starts
Christy Mathewson	10	11
Chief Bender	9	10
Bob Gibson	8	9
Whitey Ford	7	22
Red Ruffing	7	10
George Mullin	6	6
Art Nehf	6	9
Eddie Plank	6	6
Three Finger Brown	5	7
Joe Bush	5	6
Wild Bill Donovan	5	6
George Earnshaw	5	8

SHUTOUTS

Player	Shutouts	Starts
Christy Mathewson	4	11
Three Finger Brown	3	7
Whitey Ford	3	22
Lew Burdette	2	6
Bill Dineen	2	4
Bob Gibson	2	9
Bill Hallahan	2	5
Sandy Koufax	2	7
Art Nehf	2	9
Allie Reynolds	2	9

STRIKEOUTS

Player	Strikeouts	Innings Pitched
Whitey Ford	94	146
Bob Gibson	92	81
Allie Reynolds	62	77.1
Sandy Koufax	61	57
Red Ruffing	61	85.2
Chief Bender	59	85
George Earnshaw	56	62.2
John Smoltz	52	51
Waite Hoyt	49	83.2
Christy Mathewson	48	101.2

ERA (Minimum 25 Innings Pitched)

Player	IP	ER	ERA
Jack Billingham	25.1	1	0.36
Harry Breechen	32.2	3	0.83
Babe Ruth	31.0	3	0.87
Sherry Smith	30.1	3	0.89
Sandy Koufax	57.0	6	0.95
Hippo Vaughn	27.0	3	1.00
Monte Pearson	35.2	4	1.01
Christy Mathewson	101.2	12	1.06
Babe Adams	28.0	4	1.29
Eddie Plank	54.2	8	1.32

MVPs

Year	Player	Position	Team
2002	Troy Glaus	3B	Anaheim (AL)
2001	Randy Johnson*	P	Arizona (NL)
	Curt Schilling*	P	Arizona (NL)
2000	Derek Jeter	SS	New York (AL)
1999	Mariano Rivera	P	New York (AL)
1998	Scott Brosius	3B	New York (AL)
1997	Livian Hernandez	P	Florida (NL)
1996	John Wetteland	P	New York (AL)
1995	Tom Glavine	P	Atlanta (NL)
1994	No World Series		
1993	Paul Molitor	3B/DH	Toronto (NL)
1992	Pat Borders	C	Toronto (AL)
1991	Jack Morris	P	Minnesota (AL)
1990	Jose Rijo	P	Cincinnati (NL)
1989	Dave Stewart	P	Oakland (AL)
1988	Orel Hershiser	P	Los Angeles (NL)
1987	Frank Viola	P	Minnesota (AL)
1986	Ray Knight	3B	New York (NL)
1985	Bret Saberhagen	P	Kansas City (AL)
1984	Alan Trammell	SS	Detroit (AL)
1983	Rick Dempsey	C	Baltimore (AL)
1982	Darrell Porter	C	St. Louis (NL)
1981	Ron Cey*	3B	Los Angeles (NL)
	Pedro Guerrero*	OF	Los Angeles (NL)
	Steve Yeager*	C	Los Angeles (NL)
1980	Mike Schmidt	3B	Philadelphia (NL)
1979	Willie Stargell	1B	Pittsburgh (NL)
1978	Bucky Dent	SS	New York (AL)
1977	Reggie Jackson	OF	New York (AL)
1976	Johnny Bench	C	Cincinnati (NL)
1975	Pete Rose	3B	Cincinnati (NL)
1974	Rollie Fingers	P	Oakland (AL)
1973	Reggie Jackson	OF	Oakland (AL)
1972	Gene Tenace	C	Oakland (AL)
1971	Roberto Clemente	OF	Pittsburgh (NL)
1970	Brooks Robinson	3B	Baltimore (AL)
1969	Donn Clendenon	1B	New York (NL)
1968	Mickey Lolich	P	Detroit (AL)
1967	Bob Gibson	P	St. Louis (NL)
1966	Frank Robinson	OF	Baltimore (AL)
1965	Sandy Koufax	P	Los Angeles (NL)
1964	Bob Gibson	P	St. Louis (NL)
1963	Sandy Koufax	P	Los Angeles (NL)
1962	Ralph Terry	P	New York (AL)
1961	Whitey Ford	P	New York (AL)
1960	Bobby Richardson	2B	New York (AL)
1959	Larry Sherry	P	Los Angeles (NL)
1958	Bob Turley	P	New York (AL)
1957	Lew Burdette	P	Milwaukee (NL)
1956	Don Larsen	P	New York (AL)
1955	Johnny Podres	P	Brooklyn (NL)

* (Co-MVPs)

Appendix II: World Series Box Scores

1903 BOSTON PILGRIMS DEF. PITTSBURG, 5-3

GAME 1 Pittsburg 7 Boston 3
Huntington Avenue Grounds 10/01/03

PITTSBURG	AB	R	H	HR	RBI	BB	AVG
Beaumont cf	5	1	0	0	0	0	.000
Clarke lf	5	0	2	0	0	0	.400
Leach 3b	5	1	4	0	1	0	.800
Wagner ss	3	1	1	0	1	2	.333
Bransfield 1b	5	2	1	0	0	0	.200
Ritchey 2b	4	1	0	0	0	1	.000
Sebring rf	5	1	3	1	4	0	.600
Phelps c	4	0	1	0	0	0	.250
Phillippe p	4	0	0	0	0	0	.000
TOTALS	**40**	**7**	**12**	**1**	**6**	**3**	**.300**

BATTING: 3B: Leach 2 (2, Young), Bransfield (1, Young). **HR:** Sebring (1, 7th off Young 0 on, 1 out). **S:** Leach. **RBI:** Leach 1 (1), Wagner 1 (1), Sebring 4 (4). **2-out RBI:** Wagner 1, Sebring 3. **Runners left in scoring position, 2 out:** Bransfield 2, Phillippe 1. **Team LOB:** 9 **BASERUNNING: SB:** Wagner (1, 2nd base off Young/Criger), Bransfield (1, 2nd base off Young/Criger), Ritchey (1, 2nd base off Young/Criger). **FIELDING: E:** Leach (1), Wagner (1).

BOSTON	AB	R	H	HR	RBI	BB	AVG
Dougherty lf	4	0	0	0	0	0	.000
Collins 3b	4	0	0	0	0	0	.000
Stahl cf	4	0	1	0	0	0	.250
Freeman rf	4	2	2	0	0	0	.500
Parent ss	4	1	2	0	1	0	.500
LaChance 1b	4	0	0	0	2	0	.000
Ferris 2b	3	0	1	0	0	0	.333
Criger c	3	0	0	0	0	0	.000
a-O'Brien ph	1	0	0	0	0	0	.000
Young p	3	0	0	0	0	0	.000
b-Farrell ph	1	0	0	0	0	0	.000
TOTALS	**35**	**3**	**6**	**0**	**3**	**0**	**.171**

a - Batted for Criger in the 9th
b - Batted for Young in the 9th

BATTING: 3B: Freeman (1, Phillippe), Parent (1, Phillippe). **RBI:** Parent 1 (1), LaChance 2 (2). **Runners left in scoring position, 2 out:** LaChance 1, Farrell 1. **Team LOB:** 6 **FIELDING: E:** Ferris 2 (2), Criger 2 (2). **Outfield assists:** Dougherty (1).

PITTSBURG	IP	H	R	ER	BB	SO	HR	ERA
Phillippe (W, 1-0)	9	6	3	2	0	10	0	2.00

BOSTON	IP	H	R	ER	BB	SO	HR	ERA
Young (L, 0-1)	9	12	7	3	3	5	1	3.00

HBP: Ferris (by Phillippe). **Ground balls-fly balls:** Phillippe 9-10, Young 12-11. **Batters faced:** Phillippe 36, Young 43. **UMPIRES:** hp—O'Day, 1b—Connolly **T:** 1:55 **A:** 16,242

GAME 2 Boston 3 Pittsburg 0
Huntington Avenue Grounds 10/02/03

PITTSBURG	AB	R	H	HR	RBI	BB	AVG
Beaumont cf	3	0	0	0	0	1	.000
Clarke lf	3	0	1	0	0	1	.375
Leach 3b	3	0	0	0	0	0	.500
Wagner ss	3	0	0	0	0	0	.167
Bransfield 1b	3	0	0	0	0	0	.125
Ritchey 2b	3	0	1	0	0	0	.143
Sebring rf	3	0	1	0	0	0	.500
Smith c	3	0	0	0	0	0	.000
Leever p	0	0	0	0	0	0	.000
Veil p	2	0	0	0	0	0	.000
a-Phelps ph	1	0	0	0	0	0	.200
TOTALS	**27**	**0**	**3**	**0**	**0**	**2**	**.224**

a - Batted for Veil in the 9th

BATTING: Team LOB: 2 **FIELDING: E:** Veil (1), Smith (1). **DP:** 2 (Ritchey-Wagner-Bransfield, Wagner-Ritchey-Bransfield).

BOSTON	AB	R	H	HR	RBI	BB	AVG
Dougherty lf	4	2	3	2	2	0	.375
Collins 3b	4	0	1	0	0	1	.125
Stahl cf	4	1	1	0	0	0	.250
Freeman rf	4	0	2	0	1	0	.500
Parent ss	3	0	1	0	0	1	.429
LaChance 1b	2	0	0	0	0	1	.000
Ferris 2b	4	0	0	0	0	0	.143
Criger c	3	0	0	0	0	1	.000
Dinneen p	1	0	0	0	0	2	.000
TOTALS	**29**	**3**	**8**	**2**	**3**	**6**	**.219**

BATTING: 2B: Stahl (1, Leever). **HR:** Dougherty 2 (2, 1st off Leever 0 on, 0 out, 6th off Veil 0 on, 1 out). **S:** LaChance, Dinneen. **RBI:** Dougherty 2 (2), Freeman 1 (1). **Runners left in scoring position, 2 out:** Stahl 3, Freeman 1, Ferris 1. **GIDP:** Criger, Collins. **Team LOB:** 11 **BASERUNNING: SB:** Collins 2 (2, 2nd base off Veil/Smith). **FIELDING: Outfield assists:** Dougherty (2). **DP:** 1 (Ferris).

PITTSBURG	IP	H	R	ER	BB	SO	HR	ERA
Leever (L, 0-1)	1	3	2	2	1	0	1	18.00
Veil	7	5	1	1	5	1	1	1.29

BOSTON	IP	H	R	ER	BB	SO	HR	ERA
Dinneen (W, 1-0)	9	3	0	0	2	11	0	0.00

HBP: Dougherty (by Veil). **Ground balls-fly balls:** Leever 1-2, Veil 10-7, Dinneen 6-7. **Batters faced:** Leever 7, Veil 31, Dinneen 29. **UMPIRES:** hp—O'Day, 1b—Connolly **T:** 1:47 **A:** 9,415

GAME 3 Pittsburg 4 Boston 2
Huntington Avenue Grounds 10/03/03

PITTSBURG	AB	R	H	HR	RBI	BB	AVG
Beaumont cf	4	1	0	0	0	1	.000
Clarke lf	4	0	1	0	0	0	.333
Leach 3b	4	1	1	0	1	0	.417
Wagner ss	3	1	1	0	0	0	.222
Bransfield 1b	3	0	0	0	0	0	.091
Ritchey 2b	4	1	2	0	1	0	.273
Sebring rf	3	0	0	0	0	1	.364
Phelps c	4	0	2	0	1	0	.333
Phillippe p	4	0	0	0	0	0	.000
TOTALS	**33**	**4**	**7**	**0**	**3**	**2**	**.220**

BATTING: 2B: Ritchey (1, Hughes), Phelps 2 (2, Hughes, Young), Clarke (1, Hughes), Wagner (1, Young). **S:** Bransfield. **RBI:** Leach 1 (2), Ritchey 1 (1), Phelps 1 (1). **2-out RBI:** Phelps 1. **Runners left in scoring position, 2 out:** Sebring 2, Phillippe 2. **Team LOB:** 6

BOSTON	AB	R	H	HR	RBI	BB	AVG
Dougherty lf	4	0	0	0	0	0	.250
Collins 3b	4	2	2	0	0	0	.250
Stahl cf	3	0	1	0	1	1	.273
Freeman rf	3	0	0	0	0	1	.364
Parent ss	4	0	0	0	1	0	.273
LaChance 1b	3	0	1	0	0	1	.111
Ferris 2b	4	0	0	0	0	0	.091
Criger c	3	0	0	0	0	0	.000
Hughes p	0	0	0	0	0	0	.000
Young p	3	0	0	0	0	0	.000
TOTALS	**31**	**2**	**4**	**0**	**2**	**3**	**.189**

BATTING: 2B: LaChance (1, Phillippe), Collins (1, Phillippe). **RBI:** Stahl 1 (1), Parent 1 (2). **2-out RBI:** Stahl 1. **Runners left in scoring position, 2 out:** Ferris 2. **Team LOB:** 5 **FIELDING: E:** Parent (1), Young (1). **Outfield assists:** Dougherty (3). **DP:** 1 (Dougherty-Collins).

PITTSBURG	IP	H	R	ER	BB	SO	HR	ERA
Phillippe (W, 2-0)	9	4	2	2	3	6	0	2.00

BOSTON	IP	H	R	ER	BB	SO	HR	ERA
Hughes (L, 0-1)	2	4	3	2	2	0	0	9.00
Young	7	3	1	1	0	2	0	2.25

HBP: Wagner (by Young). **Ground balls-fly balls:** Phillippe 15-6, Hughes 6-0, Young 10-8. **Batters faced:** Phillippe 34, Hughes 12, Young 25. **UMPIRES:** hp—O'Day, 1b—Connolly **T:** 1:50 **A:** 18,801

GAME 4 Pittsburg 5 Boston 4
Exposition Park 10/06/03

BOSTON	AB	R	H	HR	RBI	BB	AVG
Dougherty lf	4	0	0	0	0	0	.188
Collins 3b	4	1	1	0	0	0	.250
Stahl cf	4	1	2	0	0	0	.333
Freeman rf	4	0	1	0	1	0	.333
Parent ss	4	1	1	0	1	0	.267
LaChance 1b	4	1	2	0	0	0	.231
Ferris 2b	4	0	1	0	0	0	.133
Criger c	3	0	1	0	1	0	.083
a-Farrell ph	1	0	0	0	1	0	.000
Dinneen p	3	0	0	0	0	0	.000
b-O'Brien ph	1	0	0	0	0	0	.000
TOTALS	**36**	**4**	**9**	**0**	**4**	**0**	**.206**

a - Batted for Criger in the 9th
b - Batted for Dinneen in the 9th

BATTING: RBI: Freeman 1 (2), Parent 1 (3), Criger 1 (1), Farrell 1 (1). **2-out RBI:** Criger 1. **Runners left in scoring position, 2 out:** Dinneen 1, O'Brien 1. **Team LOB:** 5 **FIELDING: E:** Dougherty (1). **Outfield assists:** Stahl (1). **DP:** 1 (Criger-Parent).

PITTSBURG	AB	R	H	HR	RBI	BB	AVG
Beaumont cf	4	2	3	0	0	0	.188
Clarke lf	4	1	1	0	0	0	.313
Leach 3b	4	1	2	0	3	0	.438
Wagner ss	4	0	3	0	1	0	.385
Bransfield 1b	4	0	1	0	1	0	.133
Ritchey 2b	3	0	0	0	0	1	.214
Sebring rf	4	0	0	0	0	0	.267
Phelps c	4	0	1	0	0	0	.308
Phillippe p	3	1	1	0	0	0	.091
TOTALS	**34**	**5**	**12**	**0**	**5**	**1**	**.254**

BATTING: 3B: Beaumont (1, Dinneen), Leach (3, Dinneen). **RBI:** Leach 3 (5), Wagner 1 (2), Bransfield 1 (1). **2-out RBI:** Leach 1, Bransfield 1. **Runners left in scoring position, 2 out:** Bransfield 3. **Team LOB:** 6 **BASERUNNING: SB:** Wagner (2, 2nd base off Dinneen/Criger). **CS:** Wagner (1, 2nd base off Dinneen/Criger). **FIELDING: DP:** 1 (Ritchey-Bransfield).

BOSTON	IP	H	R	ER	BB	SO	HR	ERA
Dinneen (L, 1-1)	8	12	5	5	1	7	0	2.65

PITTSBURG	IP	H	R	ER	BB	SO	HR	ERA
Phillippe (W, 3-0)	9	9	4	4	0	2	0	2.67

Ground balls-fly balls: Dinneen 6-9, Phillippe 13-12. **Batters faced:** Dinneen 35, Phillippe 36. **UMPIRES:** hp—O'Day, 1b—Connolly **T:** 1:30 **A:** 7,600

GAME 5 Boston 11 Pittsburg 2
Exposition Park 10/07/03

BOSTON	AB	R	H	HR	RBI	BB	AVG
Dougherty lf	6	0	3	0	3	0	.273
Collins 3b	6	0	2	0	0	0	.273
Stahl cf	5	2	1	0	0	0	.300
Freeman rf	4	2	2	0	1	1	.368
Parent ss	5	1	2	0	0	0	.300
LaChance 1b	4	2	1	0	1	1	.235
Ferris 2b	5	2	1	0	2	0	.150
Criger c	3	1	0	0	0	1	.067
Young p	5	1	1	0	3	0	.091
TOTALS	**43**	**11**	**13**	**0**	**10**	**3**	**.230**

BATTING: 3B: Collins (1, Kennedy), Young (1, Kennedy), Dougherty 2 (2, Kennedy), Stahl (1, Thompson). **S:** Criger. **RBI:** Dougherty 3 (5), Freeman 1 (3), LaChance 1 (3), Ferris 2 (2), Young 3 (3). **2-out RBI:** Dougherty 2. **Runners left in scoring position, 2 out:** Collins 2, Stahl 1, Freeman 1, LaChance 2. **Team LOB:** 9 **BASERUNNING: SB:** Stahl (1, 2nd base off Kennedy/Phelps), Collins (3, 2nd base off Kennedy/Phelps). **FIELDING: E:** Parent (2).

PITTSBURG	AB	R	H	HR	RBI	BB	AVG
Beaumont cf	4	1	1	0	0	0	.200
Clarke lf	4	1	0	0	0	0	.250
Leach 3b	4	0	2	0	2	0	.450
Wagner ss	4	0	0	0	0	0	.294
Bransfield 1b	4	0	0	0	0	0	.105
Ritchey 2b	4	0	1	0	0	0	.222
Sebring rf	4	0	1	0	0	0	.263
Phelps c	3	0	0	0	0	0	.250
Kennedy p	2	0	1	0	0	0	.500
Thompson p	1	0	0	0	0	0	.000
TOTALS	**34**	**2**	**6**	**0**	**2**	**0**	**.238**

BATTING: 2B: Kennedy (1, Young). **3B:** Leach (4, Young). **S:** Phelps. **RBI:** Leach 2 (7). **2-out RBI:** Leach 2. **Runners left in scoring position, 2 out:** Beaumont 1, Leach 1, Wagner 1, Phelps 1. **Team LOB:** 6 **FIELDING: E:** Leach (2), Clarke (1), Wagner (2).

BOSTON	IP	H	R	ER	BB	SO	HR	ERA
Young (W, 1-1)	9	6	2	0	0	4	0	1.44

PITTSBURG	IP	H	R	ER	BB	SO	HR	ERA
Kennedy (L, 0-1)	7	10	10	4	3	3	0	5.14
Thompson	2	3	1	1	0	1	0	4.50

Ground balls-fly balls: Young 13-11, Kennedy 11-10, Thompson 2-3. **Batters faced:** Young 35, Kennedy 38, Thompson 9. **UMPIRES:** hp—Connolly, 1b—O'Day **T:** 2:00 **A:** 12,322

GAME 6 Boston 6 Pittsburg 3
Exposition Park 10/08/03

BOSTON	AB	R	H	HR	RBI	BB	AVG
Dougherty lf	3	1	1	0	0	2	.280
Collins 3b	5	1	1	0	1	0	.259
Stahl cf	5	1	2	0	1	0	.320
Freeman rf	5	0	0	0	1	0	.292
Parent ss	4	2	1	0	0	0	.292
LaChance 1b	4	0	1	0	1	0	.238
Ferris 2b	4	0	2	0	1	0	.208
Criger c	4	0	1	0	0	0	.105
Dinneen p	4	1	1	0	0	0	.125
TOTALS	**38**	**6**	**10**	**0**	**5**	**2**	**.236**

BATTING: 2B: LaChance (2, Leever). **3B:** Stahl (2, Leever), Parent (2, Leever). **RBI:** Collins 1 (1), Stahl 1 (2), Freeman 1 (4), LaChance 1 (4), Ferris 1 (3). **2-out RBI:** Collins 1, Stahl 1, Ferris 1. **Runners left in scoring position, 2 out:** Collins 2, Parent 1, Criger 2. **GIDP:** LaChance. **Team LOB:** 8 **BASERUNNING: SB:** Stahl (2, 2nd base off Leever/Phelps). **FIELDING: E:** Criger (3). **DP:** 1 (Parent-LaChance).

PITTSBURG	AB	R	H	HR	RBI	BB	AVG
Beaumont cf	5	1	4	0	1	0	.320
Clarke lf	5	0	2	0	2	0	.280
Leach 3b	5	0	0	0	0	0	.360
Wagner ss	3	0	0	0	0	1	.250
Bransfield 1b	3	0	1	0	0	1	.136
Ritchey 2b	3	0	0	0	0	1	.190
Sebring rf	4	1	2	0	0	0	.304
Phelps c	4	1	1	0	0	0	.250
Leever p	4	0	0	0	0	0	.000
TOTALS	**36**	**3**	**10**	**0**	**3**	**3**	**.245**

BATTING: 2B: Clarke (2, Dinneen). **RBI:** Beaumont 1 (1), Clarke 2 (2). **Runners left in scoring position, 2 out:** Leach 2, Wagner 1, Ritchey 2, Phelps 1. **Team LOB:** 9 **BASERUNNING: SB:** Leach (1, 2nd base off Dinneen/Criger), Beaumont 2 (2, 2nd base off Dinneen/Criger), Clarke (1, 3rd base off Dinneen/Criger). **FIELDING: E:** Leach 2 (4), Wagner (3). **DP:** 1 (Ritchey-Wagner-Bransfield).

BOSTON	IP	H	R	ER	BB	SO	HR	ERA
Dinneen (W, 2-1)	9	10	3	3	3	3	0	2.77

PITTSBURG	IP	H	R	ER	BB	SO	HR	ERA
Leever (L, 0-2)	9	10	6	4	2	2	0	5.40

HBP: Parent (by Leever). **Ground balls-fly balls:** Dinneen 12-11, Leever 15-11. **Batters faced:** Dinneen 39, Leever 41. **UMPIRES:** hp—O'Day, 1b—Connolly **T:** 2:02 **A:** 11,556

GAME 7 Boston 7 Pittsburg 3
Exposition Park 10/10/03

BOSTON	AB	R	H	HR	RBI	BB	AVG
Dougherty lf	5	0	1	0	0	0	.267
Collins 3b	5	1	1	0	0	0	.250
Stahl cf	4	1	2	0	1	0	.345
Freeman rf	4	1	1	0	1	0	.286
Parent ss	4	2	2	0	1	0	.321
LaChance 1b	3	1	0	0	0	0	.208
Ferris 2b	3	1	2	0	0	0	.259
Criger c	4	0	2	0	3	0	.174
Young p	4	0	0	0	0	0	.067
TOTALS	**36**	**7**	**11**	**0**	**6**	**0**	**.246**

BATTING: 3B: Collins (2, Phillippe), Stahl (3, Phillippe), Freeman (2, Phillippe), Ferris (1, Phillippe), Parent (3, Phillippe). **S:** LaChance, Ferris. **RBI:** Stahl 1 (3), Freeman 1 (5), Parent 1 (4), Criger 3 (4). **2-out RBI:** Criger 1. **Runners left in scoring position, 2 out:** Freeman 1. **GIDP:** Young. **Team LOB:** 4 **BASERUNNING: CS:** Freeman (1, 2nd base off Phillippe/Phelps), Stahl (1, 2nd base off Phillippe/Phelps). **FIELDING: E:** LaChance 2 (2), Collins (1), Parent (3). **DP:** 1 (Ferris-LaChance).

PITTSBURG	AB	R	H	HR	RBI	BB	AVG
Beaumont cf	5	0	1	0	0	0	.300
Clarke lf	5	1	1	0	0	0	.267
Leach 3b	5	0	0	0	0	0	.300
Wagner ss	3	0	0	0	1	0	.217
Bransfield 1b	4	1	3	0	0	0	.231
Ritchey 2b	4	0	0	0	1	0	.160
Sebring rf	4	1	2	0	0	0	.333
Phelps c	3	0	1	0	0	1	.261
Phillippe p	4	0	2	0	1	0	.200
TOTALS	**37**	**3**	**10**	**0**	**3**	**1**	**.249**

BATTING: 3B: Bransfield (2, Young), Clarke (1, Young). **S:** Wagner. **RBI:** Wagner 1 (3), Ritchey 1 (2), Phillippe 1 (1). **Runners left in scoring position, 2 out:** Leach 2, Wagner 1, Ritchey 1. **GIDP:** Leach. **Team LOB:** 9 **BASERUNNING: CS:** Sebring (1, 2nd base off Young/Criger). **FIELDING: E:** Phillippe (1), Wagner (4). **DP:** 1 (Wagner-Ritchey-Bransfield).

BOSTON	IP	H	R	ER	BB	SO	HR	ERA
Young (W, 2-1)	9	10	3	3	1	6	0	1.85

PITTSBURG	IP	H	R	ER	BB	SO	HR	ERA
Phillippe (L, 3-1)	9	11	7	5	0	2	0	3.25

WP: Phillippe 1. **Ground balls-fly balls:** Young 15-6, Phillippe 16-7. **Batters faced:** Young 39, Phillippe 38. **UMPIRES:** hp—Connolly, 1b—O'Day **T:** 1:45 **A:** 17,038

GAME 8 Boston 3 Pittsburg 0
Huntington Avenue Grounds 10/13/03

PITTSBURG	AB	R	H	HR	RBI	BB	AVG
Beaumont cf	4	0	0	0	0	0	.265
Clarke lf	4	0	1	0	0	0	.265
Leach 3b	3	0	0	0	0	1	.273
Wagner ss	4	0	1	0	0	0	.222
Bransfield 1b	3	0	0	0	0	0	.207
Ritchey 2b	2	0	0	0	0	1	.148
Sebring rf	3	0	1	0	0	0	.333
Phelps c	3	0	0	0	0	0	.231
Phillippe p	3	0	1	0	0	0	.222
TOTALS	**29**	**0**	**4**	**0**	**0**	**2**	**.237**

BATTING: 3B: Sebring (1, Dinneen). **Runners left in scoring position, 2 out:** Phelps 1. **Team LOB:** 4 **BASERUNNING: SB:** Wagner (3, 2nd base off Dinneen/Criger). **FIELDING: E:** Bransfield (1), Phelps (1), Wagner (5). **Outfield assists:** Sebring (1).

BOSTON	AB	R	H	HR	RBI	BB	AVG
Dougherty lf	4	0	0	0	0	0	.235
Collins 3b	4	0	1	0	0	0	.250
Stahl cf	4	0	0	0	0	0	.303
Freeman rf	4	1	1	0	0	0	.281
Parent ss	4	1	0	0	0	0	.281
LaChance 1b	3	1	1	0	0	0	.222
Ferris 2b	4	0	2	0	3	0	.290
Criger c	3	0	2	0	0	0	.231
Dinneen p	3	0	1	0	0	0	.182
TOTALS	**33**	**3**	**8**	**0**	**3**	**0**	**.246**

BATTING: 3B: Freeman (3, Phillippe), LaChance (1, Phillippe). **S:** LaChance. **RBI:** Ferris 3 (6). **2-out RBI:** Ferris 1. **Runners left in scoring position, 2 out:** Dinneen 3. **Team LOB:** 7 **FIELDING: DP:** 1 (Criger-LaChance).

PITTSBURG	IP	H	R	ER	BB	SO	HR	ERA
Phillippe (L, 3-2)	8	8	3	2	0	2	0	3.07

BOSTON	IP	H	R	ER	BB	SO	HR	ERA
Dinneen (W, 3-1)	9	4	0	0	2	7	0	2.06

Ground balls-fly balls: Phillippe 11-12, Dinneen 10-8. **Batters faced:** Phillippe 34, Dinneen 31. **UMPIRES:** hp—O'Day, 1b—Connolly **T:** 1:35 **A:** 7,455

1905 NY GIANTS DEF. PHILADELPHIA A's, 4-1

GAME 1 New York 3 Philadelphia 0
Columbia Park 10/09/05

NY GIANTS	AB	R	H	HR	RBI	BB	AVG
Bresnahan c	3	1	1	0	1	1	.333
Browne rf	5	0	0	0	0	0	.000
Donlin cf	5	1	2	0	1	0	.400
McGann 1b	3	0	1	0	0	1	.333
Mertes lf	4	0	1	0	1	0	.250
Dahlen ss	4	0	0	0	0	0	.000
Devlin 3b	4	0	1	0	0	0	.250
Gilbert 2b	4	1	3	0	0	0	.750
Mathewson p	3	0	1	0	0	0	.333
TOTALS	**35**	**3**	**10**	**0**	**3**	**2**	**.286**

BATTING: 2B: McGann (1, Plank), Mertes (1, Plank). **S:** Mathewson. **RBI:** Bresnahan 1 (1), Donlin 1 (1), Mertes 1 (1). **2-out RBI:** Donlin 1, Mertes 1. **Runners left in scoring position, 2 out:** Browne 2, Donlin 1, McGann 1, Mertes 2, Dahlen 2. **Team LOB:** 9 **BASERUNNING: SB:** Devlin (1, 3rd base off Plank/Schreckengost), Gilbert (1, 3rd base off Plank/Schreckengost), Bresnahan (1, 2nd base off Plank/Schreckengost), Donlin (1, 2nd base off Plank/Schreckengost). **CS:** Gilbert (1, 2nd base off Plank/Schreckengost). **FIELDING: E:** Browne (1). **DP:** 1 (Dahlen-McGann).

PHILADELPHIA	AB	R	H	HR	RBI	BB	AVG
Hartsel lf	4	0	1	0	0	0	.250
Lord cf	4	0	0	0	0	0	.000
Davis 1b	4	0	1	0	0	0	.250
L.Cross 3b	4	0	0	0	0	0	.000
Seybold rf	3	0	0	0	0	0	.000
Murphy 2b	3	0	1	0	0	0	.333
M.Cross ss	3	0	0	0	0	0	.000
Schreckengost c	3	0	1	0	0	0	.333
Plank p	3	0	0	0	0	0	.000
TOTALS	**31**	**0**	**4**	**0**	**0**	**0**	**.129**

BATTING: 2B: Schreckengost (1, Mathewson), Murphy (1, Mathewson), Davis (1, Mathewson). **Runners left in scoring position, 2 out:** L.Cross 1, Plank 1. **GIDP:** Plank. **Team LOB:** 4

NY GIANTS	IP	H	R	ER	BB	SO	HR	ERA
Mathewson (W, 1-0)	9	4	0	0	0	6	0	0.00

PHILADELPHIA	IP	H	R	ER	BB	SO	HR	ERA
Plank (L, 0-1)	9	10	3	3	2	5	0	3.00

IBB: Bresnahan (by Plank). **HBP:** Bresnahan (by Plank). **Ground balls-fly balls:** Mathewson 17-4, Plank 14-6. **Batters faced:** Mathewson 31, Plank 39. **UMPIRES:** hp—Sheridan, 1b—O'Day **T:** 1:46 **A:** 17,955

GAME 2 Philadelphia 3 New York 0
Polo Grounds 10/10/05

PHILADELPHIA	AB	R	H	HR	RBI	BB	AVG
Hartsel lf	4	1	2	0	1	0	.375
Lord cf	4	0	2	0	2	0	.250
Davis 1b	4	0	0	0	0	0	.125
L.Cross 3b	3	0	0	0	0	1	.000
Seybold rf	4	0	0	0	0	0	.000
Murphy 2b	4	0	1	0	0	0	.286
M.Cross ss	4	0	0	0	0	0	.000
Schreckengost c	4	2	1	0	0	0	.286
Bender p	2	0	0	0	0	0	.000
TOTALS	**33**	**3**	**6**	**0**	**3**	**1**	**.156**

BATTING: 2B: Hartsel (1, McGinnity). **S:** Bender. **RBI:** Hartsel 1 (1), Lord 2 (2). **2-out RBI:** Hartsel 1, Lord 2. **Runners left in scoring position, 2 out:** Schreckengost 2. **Team LOB:** 5 **FIELDING: E:** M.Cross (1), Murphy (1).

NY GIANTS	AB	R	H	HR	RBI	BB	AVG
Bresnahan c	4	0	1	0	0	0	.286
Browne rf	4	0	0	0	0	0	.000
Donlin cf	4	0	2	0	0	0	.444
McGann 1b	3	0	0	0	0	1	.167
Mertes lf	4	0	0	0	0	0	.125
Dahlen ss	3	0	0	0	0	1	.000
Devlin 3b	3	0	1	0	0	1	.286
Gilbert 2b	3	0	0	0	0	0	.429
McGinnity p	2	0	0	0	0	0	.000
a-Strang ph	1	0	0	0	0	0	.000
Ames p	0	0	0	0	0	0	.000
TOTALS	**31**	**0**	**4**	**0**	**0**	**3**	**.212**

a - Batted for McGinnity in the 8th

BATTING: 2B: Bresnahan (1, Bender), Donlin (1, Bender). **Runners left in scoring position, 2 out:** Browne 1, McGann 1, Dahlen 1, Devlin 2, Gilbert 1. **Team LOB:** 7 **BASERUNNING: SB:** Dahlen (1, 2nd base off Bender/Schreckengost), Devlin (2, 2nd base off Bender/Schreckengost). **CS:** Donlin (1, 2nd base off Bender/Schreckengost).

PHILADELPHIA	IP	H	R	ER	BB	SO	HR	ERA
Bender (W, 1-0)	9	4	0	0	3	9	0	0.00

NY GIANTS	IP	H	R	ER	BB	SO	HR	ERA
McGinnity (L, 0-1)	8	5	3	0	0	2	0	0.00
Ames	1	1	0	0	1	1	0	0.00

Ground balls-fly balls: Bender 8-10, McGinnity 14-8, Ames 1-1. **Batters faced:** Bender 34, McGinnity 30, Ames 5. **UMPIRES:** hp—O'Day, 1b—Sheridan **T:** 1:55 **A:** 24,992

GAME 3 New York 9 Philadelphia 0
Columbia Park 10/12/05

NY GIANTS	AB	R	H	HR	RBI	BB	AVG
Bresnahan c	3	2	0	0	0	1	.200
Browne rf	5	2	2	0	0	0	.143
Donlin cf	3	3	1	0	0	2	.417
McGann 1b	5	1	3	0	4	0	.364
Mertes lf	3	0	1	0	1	1	.182
Dahlen ss	3	1	0	0	1	1	.000
Devlin 3b	4	0	1	0	1	0	.273
Gilbert 2b	4	0	0	0	0	0	.273
Mathewson p	4	0	1	0	0	0	.286
TOTALS	**34**	**9**	**9**	**0**	**7**	**5**	**.230**

BATTING: 2B: McGann (2, Coakley). **RBI:** McGann 4 (4), Mertes 1 (2), Dahlen 1 (1), Devlin 1 (1). **2-out RBI:** McGann 2, Devlin 1. **Runners left in scoring position, 2 out:** Gilbert 1. **GIDP:** Devlin. **Team LOB:** 4 **BASERUNNING: SB:** Dahlen (2, 2nd base off Coakley/Schreckengost), Devlin (3, 2nd base off Coakley/Schreckengost), Browne 2 (2, 2nd base off Coakley/Powers, 3rd base off Coakley/Powers). **CS:** McGann (1, 2nd base off Coakley/Powers), Mertes (1, 2nd base off Coakley/Powers). **FIELDING: E:** Devlin (1). **DP:** 1 (Bresnahan-Dahlen).

PHILADELPHIA	AB	R	H	HR	RBI	BB	AVG
Hartsel lf	4	0	0	0	0	0	.250
Lord cf	4	0	0	0	0	0	.167
Davis 1b	4	0	1	0	0	0	.167
L.Cross 3b	4	0	1	0	0	0	.091
Seybold rf	3	0	1	0	0	1	.100
Murphy 2b	3	0	0	0	0	0	.200
M.Cross ss	3	0	1	0	0	0	.100
Schreckengost c	2	0	0	0	0	0	.222
Powers c	1	0	0	0	0	0	.000
Coakley p	2	0	0	0	0	0	.000
TOTALS	**30**	**0**	**4**	**0**	**0**	**1**	**.149**

BATTING: Team LOB: 5 **BASERUNNING: SB:** Hartsel (1, 2nd base off Mathewson/Bresnahan). **CS:** Murphy (1, 2nd base off Mathewson/Bresnahan). **FIELDING: E:** Murphy 3 ((3, 4), Hartsel (1). **Outfield assists:** Seybold (1). **DP:** 2 (Coakley-Schreckengost-Davis, Seybold-Davis).

NY GIANTS	IP	H	R	ER	BB	SO	HR	ERA
Mathewson (W, 2-0)	9	4	0	0	1	8	0	0.00

PHILADELPHIA	IP	H	R	ER	BB	SO	HR	ERA
Coakley (L, 0-1)	9	9	9	3	5	2	0	3.00

IBB: Donlin (by Coakley). **HBP:** Bresnahan (by Coakley), Coakley (by Mathewson). **Ground balls-fly balls:** Mathewson 11-7, Coakley 10-13. **Batters faced:** Mathewson 32, Coakley 40. **UMPIRES:** hp—Sheridan, 1b—O'Day **T:** 1:55 **A:** 10,991

GAME 4 New York 1 Philadelphia 0
Polo Grounds 10/13/05

PHILADELPHIA	AB	R	H	HR	RBI	BB	AVG
Hartsel lf	1	0	0	0	0	2	.231
Lord cf	4	0	0	0	0	0	.125
Davis 1b	4	0	1	0	0	0	.188
L.Cross 3b	4	0	1	0	0	0	.133
Seybold rf	3	0	0	0	0	1	.077
Murphy 2b	3	0	1	0	0	0	.231
M.Cross ss	4	0	1	0	0	0	.143
Powers c	3	0	0	0	0	0	.000
a-Hoffman ph	1	0	0	0	0	0	.000
Plank p	3	0	1	0	0	0	.167
TOTALS	**30**	**0**	**5**	**0**	**0**	**3**	**.153**

a - Batted for Powers in the 9th

BATTING: S: Murphy, Hartsel. **Runners left in scoring position, 2 out:** Davis 2, Seybold 1, Powers 2. **Team LOB:** 8 **BASERUNNING: SB:** Hartsel (2, 2nd base off McGinnity/Bresnahan). **FIELDING: E:** M.Cross (2).

NY GIANTS	AB	R	H	HR	RBI	BB	AVG
Bresnahan c	2	0	1	0	0	2	.250
Browne rf	4	0	2	0	0	0	.222
Donlin cf	3	0	0	0	0	0	.333
McGann 1b	3	0	0	0	0	0	.286
Mertes lf	4	1	0	0	0	0	.133
Dahlen ss	3	0	0	0	0	0	.000
Devlin 3b	3	0	1	0	0	0	.286
Gilbert 2b	3	0	1	0	1	0	.286
McGinnity p	3	0	0	0	0	0	.000
TOTALS	**28**	**1**	**5**	**0**	**1**	**2**	**.219**

BATTING: 2B: Devlin (1, Plank). **S:** Donlin, McGann. **RBI:** Gilbert 1 (1). **2-out RBI:** Gilbert 1. **Runners left in scoring position, 2 out:** McGann 2, Mertes 2, Gilbert 1, McGinnity 1. **Team LOB:** 7

PHILADELPHIA	IP	H	R	ER	BB	SO	HR	ERA
Plank (L, 0-2)	8	5	1	0	2	6	0	1.59

NY GIANTS	IP	H	R	ER	BB	SO	HR	ERA
McGinnity (W, 1-1)	9	5	0	0	3	4	0	0.00

WP: Plank 1. **Ground balls-fly balls:** Plank 8-9, McGinnity 8-13. **Batters faced:** Plank 32, McGinnity 35. **UMPIRES:** hp—O'Day, 1b—Sheridan **T:** 1:55 **A:** 13,598

GAME 5 New York 2 Philadelphia 0
Polo Grounds 10/14/05

PHILADELPHIA	AB	R	H	HR	RBI	BB	AVG
Hartsel lf	4	0	1	0	0	0	.235
Lord cf	4	0	0	0	0	0	.100
Davis 1b	4	0	1	0	0	0	.200
L.Cross 3b	4	0	0	0	0	0	.105
Seybold rf	3	0	1	0	0	0	.125
Murphy 2b	3	0	0	0	0	0	.188
M.Cross ss	3	0	1	0	0	0	.176
Powers c	3	0	1	0	0	0	.143
Bender p	3	0	0	0	0	0	.000
TOTALS	**31**	**0**	**5**	**0**	**0**	**0**	**.155**

BATTING: 2B: Powers (1, Mathewson). **Runners left in scoring position, 2 out:** Bender 1. **GIDP:** Murphy. **Team LOB:** 4 **BASERUNNING: CS:** M.Cross (1, 2nd base off Mathewson/Bresnahan). **FIELDING: Outfield assists:** Hartsel (1). **DP:** 1 (Hartsel-Powers-L.Cross).

NY GIANTS	AB	R	H	HR	RBI	BB	AVG
Bresnahan c	4	0	2	0	0	0	.313
Browne rf	4	0	1	0	1	0	.227
Donlin cf	4	0	0	0	0	0	.263
McGann 1b	3	0	0	0	0	0	.235
Mertes lf	2	1	1	0	0	1	.176
Dahlen ss	2	0	0	0	0	1	.000
Devlin 3b	2	0	0	0	0	0	.250
Gilbert 2b	3	0	1	0	1	0	.294
Mathewson p	1	1	0	0	0	1	.250
TOTALS	**25**	**2**	**5**	**0**	**2**	**3**	**.216**

BATTING: 2B: Bresnahan (2, Bender). **S:** Mathewson, Devlin. **RBI:** Browne 1 (1), Gilbert 1 (2). **Runners left in scoring position, 2 out:** Bresnahan 1, Donlin 1, McGann 1. **Team LOB:** 4 **BASERUNNING: CS:** Mertes (2, 2nd base off Bender/Powers). **FIELDING: E:** Mathewson 2 (2). **DP:** 1 (Dahlen-McGann).

PHILADELPHIA	IP	H	R	ER	BB	SO	HR	ERA
Bender (L, 1-1)	8	5	2	2	3	4	0	1.06

NY GIANTS	IP	H	R	ER	BB	SO	HR	ERA
Mathewson (W, 3-0)	9	5	0	0	0	4	0	0.00

Ground balls-fly balls: Bender 8-8, Mathewson 18-4. **Batters faced:** Bender 30, Mathewson 31. **UMPIRES:** hp—Sheridan, 1b—O'Day **T:** 1:35 **A:** 24,187

1906 CHICAGO WHITE SOX DEF. CHICAGO CUBS, 4-2

GAME 1 White Sox 2 Cubs 1
West Side Park 10/09/06

CHICAGO WHITE SOX	AB	R	H	HR	RBI	BB	AVG
Hahn rf	3	0	0	0	0	0	.000
Jones cf	4	1	1	0	0	0	.250
Isbell 2b	4	0	1	0	1	0	.250
Rohe 3b	4	1	1	0	0	0	.250
Donahue 1b	4	0	0	0	0	0	.000
Dougherty lf	3	0	0	0	1	0	.000
Sullivan c	3	0	0	0	0	0	.000
Tannehill ss	3	0	0	0	0	0	.000
Altrock p	2	0	1	0	0	1	.500
TOTALS	**30**	**2**	**4**	**0**	**2**	**1**	**.133**

BATTING: 3B: Rohe (1, Brown). **S:** Hahn. **RBI:** Isbell 1 (1), Dougherty 1 (1). **2-out RBI:** Isbell 1. **Runners left in scoring position, 2 out:** Rohe 1, Tannehill 2. **Team LOB:** 3 **BASERUNNING: SB:** Isbell (1, 2nd base off Brown/Kling), Dougherty (1, 2nd base off Brown/Kling). **CS:** Hahn (1, 2nd base off Brown/Kling).

CHICAGO CUBS	AB	R	H	HR	RBI	BB	AVG
Hofman cf	3	0	0	0	0	0	.000
Sheckard lf	3	0	0	0	0	0	.000
a-Moran ph	1	0	0	0	0	0	.000
Schulte rf	4	0	1	0	0	0	.250
Chance 1b	4	0	1	0	0	0	.250
Steinfeldt 3b	4	0	0	0	0	0	.000
Tinker ss	3	0	0	0	0	0	.000
Evers 2b	3	0	0	0	0	0	.000
Kling c	2	1	1	0	0	1	.500
Brown p	2	0	1	0	0	0	.500
TOTALS	**29**	**1**	**4**	**0**	**0**	**1**	**.138**

a - Batted for Sheckard in the 9th

BATTING: S: Hofman, Brown. **Runners left in scoring position, 2 out:** Hofman 1, Schulte 1, Chance 1. **Team LOB:** 4 **BASERUNNING: CS:** Schulte (1, 2nd base off Altrock/Sullivan).

FIELDING: E: Brown (1). **PB:** Kling, Kling. **Outfield assists:** Hofman (1).

CHICAGO WHITE SOX	IP	H	R	ER	BB	SO	HR	ERA
Altrock (W, 1-0)	9	4	1	1	1	3	0	1.00

CHICAGO CUBS	IP	H	R	ER	BB	SO	HR	ERA
Brown (L, 0-1)	9	4	2	0	1	7	0	0.00

WP: Altrock 1, Brown 1. **Ground balls-fly balls:** Altrock 13-9, Brown 15-4. **Batters faced:** Altrock 32, Brown 32. **UMPIRES:** hp—Johnstone, 1b—O'Loughlin **T:** 1:45 **A:** 12,693

GAME 2 Cubs 7 White Sox 1
South Side Park 10/10/06

CHICAGO CUBS	AB	R	H	HR	RBI	BB	AVG
Hofman cf	4	0	1	0	1	1	.143
Sheckard lf	4	0	0	0	0	0	.000
Schulte rf	4	0	1	0	0	1	.250
Chance 1b	5	2	1	0	0	0	.222
Steinfeldt 3b	3	1	3	0	1	0	.429
Tinker ss	3	3	2	0	1	1	.333
Evers 2b	4	1	1	0	0	0	.143
Kling c	2	0	1	0	0	2	.500
Reulbach p	3	0	0	0	1	0	.000
TOTALS	**32**	**7**	**10**	**0**	**4**	**5**	**.230**

BATTING: 2B: Kling (1, Owen). **S:** Reulbach, Steinfeldt, Sheckard. **RBI:** Hofman 1 (1), Steinfeldt 1 (1), Tinker 1 (1), Reulbach 1 (1). **2-out RBI:** Hofman 1, Steinfeldt 1. **Runners left in scoring position, 2 out:** Hofman 4, Chance 1, Reulbach 2. **Team LOB:** 6 **BASERUNNING: SB:** Chance 2 (2, 2nd base off White/Sullivan, 3rd base off Owen/Sullivan), Tinker 2 (2, 3rd base off Owen/Sullivan, 2nd base off Owen/Sullivan), Evers (1, 3rd base off Owen/Sullivan), Hofman (1, 3rd base off Owen/Sullivan). **CS:** Steinfeldt (1, 2nd base off White/Sullivan), Schulte (2, 2nd base off Owen/Sullivan). **FIELDING: E:** Evers (1), Tinker (1). **Outfield assists:** Sheckard (1). **DP:** 2 (Sheckard-Kling, Evers-Chance).

CHICAGO WHITE SOX	AB	R	H	HR	RBI	BB	AVG
Hahn rf	3	0	0	0	0	1	.000
Jones cf	3	0	0	0	0	1	.143
Isbell 2b	4	0	0	0	0	0	.125
Rohe 3b	2	0	0	0	0	1	.167
Donahue 1b	3	0	1	0	0	1	.143
Dougherty lf	2	1	0	0	0	2	.000
Sullivan c	4	0	0	0	0	0	.000
Tannehill ss	3	0	0	0	0	0	.000
White p	0	0	0	0	0	0	.000
a-Towne ph	1	0	0	0	0	0	.000
Owen p	2	0	0	0	0	0	.000
TOTALS	**27**	**1**	**1**	**0**	**0**	**6**	**.088**

a - Batted for White in the 3th

BATTING: Runners left in scoring position, 2 out: Tannehill 1. **GIDP:** Donahue. **Team LOB:** 6 **BASERUNNING: CS:** Hahn (2, 2nd base off Reulbach/Kling). **FIELDING: E:** Isbell (1), Sullivan 2 (2).

CHICAGO CUBS	IP	H	R	ER	BB	SO	HR	ERA
Reulbach (W, 1-0)	9	1	1	0	6	3	0	0.00

CHICAGO WHITE SOX	IP	H	R	ER	BB	SO	HR	ERA
White (L, 0-1)	3	4	4	0	2	1	0	0.00
Owen	6	6	3	2	3	2	0	3.00

WP: Reulbach 1, Owen 1. **IBB:** Kling (by White). **HBP:** Rohe (by Reulbach). **Ground balls-fly balls:** Reulbach 16-7, White 5-1, Owen 7-6. **Batters faced:** Reulbach 34, White 14, Owen 26. **UMPIRES:** hp—O'Loughlin, 1b—Johnstone **T:** 1:58 **A:** 12,595

GAME 3 White Sox 3 Cubs 0
West Side Park 10/11/06

CHICAGO WHITE SOX	AB	R	H	HR	RBI	BB	AVG
Hahn rf	2	0	0	0	0	0	.000
a-O'Neill pr-rf	1	1	0	0	0	0	.000
Jones cf	4	0	1	0	0	0	.182
Isbell 2b	4	0	0	0	0	0	.083
Rohe 3b	3	0	1	0	3	1	.222
Donahue 1b	3	0	1	0	0	0	.200
Dougherty lf	4	0	0	0	0	0	.000
Sullivan c	3	0	0	0	0	0	.000
Tannehill ss	3	1	1	0	0	0	.111
Walsh p	2	1	0	0	0	1	.000
TOTALS	**29**	**3**	**4**	**0**	**3**	**2**	**.105**

a - Ran for Hahn in the 6th

BATTING: 3B: Donahue (1, Pfiester), Rohe (2, Pfiester). **S:** Sullivan, Donahue. **RBI:** Rohe 3 (3). **2-out RBI:** Rohe 3. **Runners left in scoring position, 2 out:** Donahue 1, Sullivan 1, Walsh 1. **Team LOB:** 4 **BASERUNNING: SB:** Rohe (1, 2nd base off Pfiester/Kling). **CS:** Jones (1, 2nd base off Pfiester/Kling), Donahue (1, 2nd base off Pfiester/Kling). **FIELDING: E:** Isbell (2).

CHICAGO CUBS	AB	R	H	HR	RBI	BB	AVG
Hofman cf	4	0	1	0	0	0	.182
Sheckard lf	4	0	0	0	0	0	.000
Schulte rf	4	0	1	0	0	0	.250
Chance 1b	2	0	0	0	0	1	.182
Steinfeldt 3b	3	0	0	0	0	0	.300
Tinker ss	3	0	0	0	0	0	.222
Evers 2b	3	0	0	0	0	0	.100
Kling c	3	0	0	0	0	0	.286
Pfiester p	2	0	0	0	0	0	.000
a-Gessler ph	1	0	0	0	0	0	.000
TOTALS	**29**	**0**	**2**	**0**	**0**	**1**	**.178**

a - Batted for Pfiester in the 9th

BATTING: 2B: Schulte (1, Walsh). **Runners left in scoring position, 2 out:** Schulte 1, Chance 1. **Team LOB:** 3 **BASERUNNING: CS:** Hofman (1, 2nd base off Walsh/Sullivan). **FIELDING: E:** Pfiester (1), Tinker (2).

CHICAGO WHITE SOX	IP	H	R	ER	BB	SO	HR	ERA
Walsh (W, 1-0)	9	2	0	0	1	12	0	0.00

CHICAGO CUBS	IP	H	R	ER	BB	SO	HR	ERA
Pfiester (L, 0-1)	9	4	3	3	2	9	0	3.00

WP: Walsh 1. **HBP:** Hahn (by Pfiester). **Ground balls-fly balls:** Walsh 13-2, Pfiester 7-9. **Batters faced:** Walsh 30, Pfiester 34. **UMPIRES:** hp—Johnstone, 1b—O'Loughlin **T:** 2:10 **A:** 13,667

GAME 4 Cubs 1 White Sox 0
South Side Park 10/12/06

CHICAGO CUBS	AB	R	H	HR	RBI	BB	AVG
Hofman cf	4	0	2	0	0	0	.267
Sheckard lf	3	0	0	0	0	1	.000
Schulte rf	4	0	0	0	0	0	.188
Chance 1b	4	1	2	0	0	0	.267
Steinfeldt 3b	2	0	1	0	0	0	.333
Tinker ss	1	0	0	0	0	0	.200
Evers 2b	3	0	1	0	1	0	.154
Kling c	3	0	0	0	0	0	.200
Brown p	3	0	1	0	0	0	.400
TOTALS	**27**	**1**	**7**	**0**	**1**	**1**	**.197**

BATTING: 2B: Hofman (1, Altrock). **S:** Tinker, Steinfeldt, Tinker, Steinfeldt, Tinker. **RBI:** Evers 1 (1). **2-out RBI:** Evers 1. **Runners left in scoring position, 2 out:** Schulte 2, Chance 1, Kling 1. **Team LOB:** 5 **BASERUNNING: SB:** Sheckard (1, 2nd base off Altrock/Sullivan). **CS:** Evers (1, 2nd base off Altrock/Sullivan). **FIELDING: E:** Steinfeldt (1). **PB:** Kling. **DP:** 1 (Kling-Evers).

CHICAGO WHITE SOX	AB	R	H	HR	RBI	BB	AVG
Hahn rf	4	0	1	0	0	0	.083
Jones cf	3	0	0	0	0	1	.143
Isbell 2b	4	0	0	0	0	0	.063
Rohe 3b	3	0	0	0	0	0	.167
Donahue 1b	1	0	0	0	0	1	.182
Dougherty lf	3	0	1	0	0	0	.083
Davis ss	3	0	0	0	0	0	.000
Sullivan c	3	0	0	0	0	0	.000
Altrock p	2	0	0	0	0	0	.250
a-McFarland ph	1	0	0	0	0	0	.000
TOTALS	**27**	**0**	**2**	**0**	**0**	**2**	**.097**

a - Batted for Altrock in the 9th

BATTING: S: Donahue. **Runners left in scoring position, 2 out:** Isbell 1, Davis 1. **Team LOB:** 3 **BASERUNNING: CS:** Donahue (2, 2nd base off Brown/Kling), Davis (1, 2nd base off Brown/Kling). **FIELDING: E:** Davis (1). **DP:** 1 (Altrock-Donahue-Sullivan).

CHICAGO CUBS	IP	H	R	ER	BB	SO	HR	ERA
Brown (W, 1-1)	9	2	0	0	2	5	0	0.00

CHICAGO WHITE SOX	IP	H	R	ER	BB	SO	HR	ERA
Altrock (L, 1-1)	9	7	1	1	1	2	0	1.00

Ground balls-fly balls: Brown 13-7, Altrock 11-7. **Batters faced:** Brown 30, Altrock 33. **UMPIRES:** hp—O'Loughlin, 1b—Johnstone **T:** 1:36 **A:** 18,385

GAME 5 White Sox 8 Cubs 6
West Side Park 10/13/06

CHICAGO WHITE SOX	AB	R	H	HR	RBI	BB	AVG
Hahn rf	5	2	1	0	0	0	.118
Jones cf	4	1	1	0	0	0	.167
Isbell 2b	5	3	4	0	2	0	.238
Davis ss	5	2	2	0	3	0	.250
Rohe 3b	4	0	3	0	1	1	.313
Donahue 1b	3	0	1	0	1	1	.214
Dougherty lf	5	0	0	0	0	0	.059
Sullivan c	4	0	0	0	0	0	.000
Walsh p	2	0	0	0	0	2	.000
White p	0	0	0	0	0	0	.000
TOTALS	**37**	**8**	**12**	**0**	**7**	**4**	**.153**

BATTING: 2B: Isbell 4 (4, Reulbach, Pfiester, Overall), Rohe (1, Reulbach), Davis 2 (2, Reulbach, Pfiester), Donahue (1, Overall). **S:** Jones. **RBI:** Isbell 2 (3), Davis 3 (3), Rohe 1 (4), Donahue 1 (1). **2-out RBI:** Rohe 1. **Runners left in scoring position, 2 out:** Donahue 1, Dougherty 3, Sullivan 1. **Team LOB:** 8 **BASERUNNING: SB:** Davis (1, home off Pfiester/Kling), Dougherty (2, home off Pfiester/Kling). **FIELDING: E:** Walsh (1), Davis (2), Rohe 2 (2), Isbell (3).

CHICAGO CUBS	AB	R	H	HR	RBI	BB	AVG
Hofman cf	3	2	1	0	0	2	.278
Sheckard lf	4	0	0	0	0	0	.000
Schulte rf	5	1	3	0	2	0	.286
Chance 1b	4	0	1	0	0	0	.263
Steinfeldt 3b	5	1	1	0	2	0	.294
Tinker ss	4	1	0	0	0	1	.143
Evers 2b	3	0	0	0	0	1	.125
a-Moran ph	1	0	0	0	0	0	.000
Kling c	3	0	0	0	0	1	.154
Reulbach p	0	0	0	0	0	0	.000
Pfiester p	0	0	0	0	0	0	.000
Overall p	2	1	0	0	0	1	.000
TOTALS	**34**	**6**	**6**	**0**	**4**	**6**	**.192**

a - Batted for Evers in the 9th

BATTING: 2B: Chance (1, Walsh), Schulte (2, Walsh), Steinfeldt (1, Walsh). **S:** Sheckard, Reulbach. **RBI:** Schulte 2 (2), Steinfeldt 2 (3). **2-out RBI:** Schulte 2. **Runners left in scoring position, 2 out:** Hofman 1, Sheckard 1, Chance 2, Steinfeldt 1, Tinker 2, Kling 1. **Team LOB:** 10 **BASERUNNING: SB:** Tinker (3, 3rd base off Walsh/Sullivan), Evers (2, 3rd base off Walsh/Sullivan). **FIELDING: Outfield assists:** Schulte (1). **DP:** 1 (Schulte-Evers-Kling).

CHICAGO WHITE SOX	IP	H	R	ER	BB	SO	HR	ERA
Walsh (W, 2-0)	6	5	6	1	5	5	0	0.60
White (S, 1)	3	1	0	0	1	1	0	0.00

CHICAGO CUBS	IP	H	R	ER	BB	SO	HR	ERA
Reulbach	2	5	3	3	2	1	0	2.45
Pfiester (L, 0-2)	1.1	3	4	4	1	2	0	6.10
Overall	5.2	4	1	1	1	5	0	1.59

WP: Walsh 1, Overall 1. **HBP:** Chance (by Walsh), Donahue (by Pfiester). **Ground balls-fly balls:** Walsh 12-2, White 6-2, Reulbach 3-1, Pfiester 2-0, Overall 4-7. **Batters faced:** Walsh 32, White 11, Reulbach 13, Pfiester 9, Overall 21. **UMPIRES:** hp—Johnstone, 1b—O'Loughlin **T:** 2:40 **A:** 23,257

GAME 6 White Sox 8 Cubs 3
South Side Park 10/14/06

CHICAGO CUBS	AB	R	H	HR	RBI	BB	AVG
Hofman cf	5	1	2	0	1	0	.304
Sheckard lf	3	0	0	0	1	1	.000
Schulte rf	5	0	1	0	1	0	.269
Chance 1b	2	0	0	0	0	1	.238
Steinfeldt 3b	3	0	0	0	0	1	.250
Tinker ss	4	0	1	0	0	0	.167
Evers 2b	4	1	1	0	0	0	.150
Kling c	4	1	1	0	0	0	.176
Brown p	1	0	0	0	0	0	.333
Overall p	2	0	1	0	0	0	.250
a-Gessler ph	0	0	0	0	0	1	.000
TOTALS	**33**	**3**	**7**	**0**	**3**	**4**	**.196**

a - Batted for Overall in the 9th

BATTING: 2B: Schulte (3, White), Overall (1, White), Evers (1, White). **S:** Sheckard. **RBI:** Hofman 1 (2), Sheckard 1 (1), Schulte 1 (3). **2-out RBI:** Hofman 1. **Runners left in scoring position, 2 out:** Schulte 3, Steinfeldt 1, Tinker 1. **GIDP:** Kling. **Team LOB:** 9 **BASERUNNING: CS:** Chance (1, 3rd base off White/Sullivan).

CHICAGO WHITE SOX	AB	R	H	HR	RBI	BB	AVG
Hahn rf	5	2	4	0	0	0	.273
Jones cf	3	2	0	0	0	1	.143
Isbell 2b	5	1	3	0	1	0	.308
Davis ss	5	2	2	0	3	0	.308
Rohe 3b	5	1	2	0	0	0	.333
Donahue 1b	4	0	2	0	3	0	.278
Dougherty lf	3	0	1	0	1	1	.100
Sullivan c	4	0	0	0	0	0	.000
White p	3	0	0	0	0	1	.000
TOTALS	**37**	**8**	**14**	**0**	**8**	**3**	**.198**

BATTING: 2B: Davis (3, Brown), Donahue (2, Brown). **S:** Jones. **RBI:** Isbell 1 (4), Davis 3 (6), Donahue 3 (4), Dougherty 1 (2). **2-out RBI:** Davis 2, Donahue 3, Dougherty 1. **Runners left in scoring position, 2 out:** Jones 1, Rohe 1, Dougherty 1, Sullivan 2. **Team LOB:** 9 **BASERUNNING: SB:** Rohe (2, 2nd base off Brown/Kling). **FIELDING: E:** Dougherty (1), Donahue (1), Rohe (3). **DP:** 1 (Davis-Donahue).

CHICAGO CUBS	IP	H	R	ER	BB	SO	HR	ERA
Brown (L, 1-2)	1.2	8	7	7	1	0	0	3.20
Overall	6.1	6	1	1	2	3	0	1.50

CHICAGO WHITE SOX	IP	H	R	ER	BB	SO	HR	ERA
White (W, 1-1)	9	7	3	3	4	2	0	1.80

HBP: Chance (by White). **Ground balls-fly balls:** Brown 5-0, Overall 5-10, White 18-6. **Batters faced:** Brown 14, Overall 27, White 39. **UMPIRES:** hp—O'Loughlin, 1b—Johnstone **T:** 1:55 **A:** 19,249

1907 CHICAGO CUBS DEF. DETROIT, 4-0

GAME 1 Detroit 3 Chicago 3
West Side Park 10/08/07

DETROIT	AB	R	H	HR	RBI	BB	AVG
Jones lf	5	1	3	0	0	1	.600
Schaefer 2b	6	1	1	0	0	0	.167
Crawford cf	5	1	3	0	2	0	.600
Cobb rf	5	0	0	0	0	0	.000
Rossman 1b	4	0	0	0	1	1	.000
Coughlin 3b	5	0	0	0	0	0	.000
Schmidt c	5	0	2	0	0	0	.400
O'Leary ss	4	0	0	0	0	0	.000
Donovan p	5	0	0	0	0	0	.000
TOTALS	**44**	**3**	**9**	**0**	**3**	**2**	**.205**

BATTING: S: O'Leary. **RBI:** Crawford 2 (2), Rossman 1 (1). **Runners left in scoring position, 2 out:** Jones 1, Schaefer 1, Coughlin 1. **Team LOB:** 8 **BASERUNNING: SB:** Jones 2 (2, 2nd base off Overall/Kling). **CS:** Schaefer (1, 2nd base off Overall/Kling). **FIELDING: E:** Schmidt 2 (2), Coughlin (1). **Outfield assists:** Jones (1). **DP:** 1 (Schaefer-Rossman).

CHICAGO CUBS	AB	R	H	HR	RBI	BB	AVG
Slagle cf	6	0	2	0	0	0	.333
Sheckard lf	5	0	1	0	0	0	.200
Chance 1b	4	2	1	0	0	2	.250
Steinfeldt 3b	3	1	1	0	0	0	.333
Kling c	4	0	2	0	1	1	.500
Evers 2b-ss	4	0	2	0	0	0	.500
Schulte rf	5	0	1	0	1	0	.200
Tinker ss	3	0	0	0	0	0	.000
a-Howard ph	1	0	0	0	0	0	.000
Zimmerman 2b	1	0	0	0	0	0	.000
Overall p	3	0	0	0	0	0	.000
b-Moran ph	0	0	0	0	0	0	.000
Reulbach p	2	0	0	0	0	0	.000
TOTALS	**41**	**3**	**10**	**0**	**2**	**3**	**.244**

a - Batted for Tinker in the 9th
b - Batted for Overall in the 9th

BATTING: S: Evers, Steinfeldt, Evers. **RBI:** Kling 1 (1), Schulte 1 (1). **Runners left in scoring position, 2 out:** Steinfeldt 1, Kling 1, Schulte 1, Tinker 1, Reulbach 2. **Team LOB:** 9 **BASERUNNING: SB:** Sheckard (1, 2nd base off Donovan/Schmidt), Evers (1, 2nd base off Donovan/Schmidt), Steinfeldt (1, 2nd base off Donovan/Schmidt), Howard (1, 2nd base off Donovan/Schmidt), Slagle 2 (2, 2nd base off Donovan/Schmidt, 3rd base off Donovan/Schmidt), Chance (1, 3rd base off Donovan/Schmidt). **CS:** Slagle (1, 2nd base off Donovan/Schmidt). **FIELDING: E:** Tinker (1), Kling (1), Evers 2 (2). **DP:** 1 (Evers-Tinker).

DETROIT	IP	H	R	ER	BB	SO	HR	ERA
Donovan	12	10	3	1	3	12	0	0.75

CHICAGO CUBS	IP	H	R	ER	BB	SO	HR	ERA
Overall	9	9	3	1	2	5	0	1.00
Reulbach	3	0	0	0	0	2	0	0.00

HBP: Steinfeldt (by Donovan), Sheckard (by Donovan). **Ground balls-fly balls:** Donovan 10-9, Overall 14-6, Reulbach 4-4. **Batters faced:** Donovan 48, Overall 37, Reulbach 10. **UMPIRES:** hp—O'Day, 1b—Sheridan **T:** 2:40 **A:** 24,377

GAME 2 Chicago 3 Detroit 1
West Side Park 10/09/07

DETROIT	AB	R	H	HR	RBI	BB	AVG
Jones lf	4	0	2	0	0	0	.556
Schaefer 2b	4	0	1	0	0	0	.200
Crawford cf	4	0	0	0	0	0	.333
Cobb rf	3	0	1	0	0	0	.125
Rossman 1b	4	1	3	0	0	0	.500
Coughlin 3b	4	0	0	0	0	0	.000
Payne c	4	0	1	0	1	0	.250
O'Leary ss	2	0	1	0	0	1	.167
Mullin p	3	0	0	0	0	0	.000
TOTALS	**32**	**1**	**9**	**0**	**1**	**1**	**.250**

BATTING: 3B: Rossman (1, Pfiester). **RBI:** Payne 1 (1). **Runners left in scoring position, 2 out:** Payne 1, Mullin 1. **GIDP:** Cobb. **Team LOB:** 6 **BASERUNNING: SB:** Payne (1, 2nd base off Pfiester/Kling). **CS:** Schaefer (2, 2nd base off Pfiester/Kling), O'Leary (1, 2nd base off Pfiester/Kling), Cobb (1, 2nd base off Pfiester/Kling). **FIELDING: E:** Payne (1). **Outfield assists:** Crawford (1). **DP:** 1 (Crawford-Schaefer).

CHICAGO CUBS	AB	R	H	HR	RBI	BB	AVG
Slagle cf	3	1	2	0	1	1	.444
Sheckard lf	3	0	1	0	1	0	.250
Chance 1b	3	0	1	0	0	1	.286
Steinfeldt 3b	3	0	0	0	0	0	.167
Kling c	4	1	1	0	0	0	.375
Evers 2b	4	0	2	0	0	0	.500
Schulte rf	4	0	1	0	0	0	.222
Tinker ss	2	1	1	0	1	1	.200
Pfiester p	2	0	0	0	0	0	.000
TOTALS	**28**	**3**	**9**	**0**	**3**	**3**	**.275**

BATTING: 2B: Sheckard (1, Mullin). **S:** Pfiester, Sheckard. **RBI:** Slagle 1 (1), Sheckard 1 (1), Tinker 1 (1). **Runners left in scoring position, 2 out:** Sheckard 2, Steinfeldt 2, Schulte 2. **Team LOB:** 7 **BASERUNNING: SB:** Slagle 2 (4, 2nd base off Mullin/Payne), Chance (2, 2nd base off Mullin/Payne), Evers (2, 2nd base off Mullin/Payne). **CS:** Sheckard (1, 3rd base off Mullin/Payne). **FIELDING: E:** Tinker (2). **Outfield assists:** Schulte (1). **DP:** 2 (Tinker-Chance 2).

DETROIT	IP	H	R	ER	BB	SO	HR	ERA
Mullin (L, 0-1)	8	9	3	3	3	6	0	3.38

CHICAGO CUBS	IP	H	R	ER	BB	SO	HR	ERA
Pfiester (W, 1-0)	9	9	1	1	1	3	0	1.00

HBP: Steinfeldt (by Mullin), Cobb (by Pfiester). **Ground balls-fly balls:** Mullin 10-3, Pfiester 6-13. **Batters faced:** Mullin 34, Pfiester 34. **UMPIRES:** hp—Sheridan, 1b—O'Day **T:** 2:13 **A:** 21,901

GAME 3 Chicago 5 Detroit 1
West Side Park 10/10/07

DETROIT	AB	R	H	HR	RBI	BB	AVG
Jones lf	3	0	0	0	0	1	.417
Schaefer 2b	4	0	1	0	0	0	.214
Crawford cf	4	0	1	0	1	0	.308
Cobb rf	4	0	1	0	0	0	.167
Rossman 1b	4	0	2	0	0	0	.500
Coughlin 3b	3	0	0	0	0	1	.000
Schmidt c	3	0	0	0	0	1	.250
O'Leary ss	4	0	0	0	0	0	.100
Siever p	1	0	0	0	0	0	.000
Killian p	2	1	1	0	0	0	.500
TOTALS	**32**	**1**	**6**	**0**	**1**	**3**	**.231**

BATTING: RBI: Crawford 1 (3). **2-out RBI:** Crawford 1. **Runners left in scoring position, 2 out:** Jones 1, Cobb 1, Rossman 1. **GIDP:** Schaefer. **Team LOB:** 7 **FIELDING: E:** Jones (1). **Outfield assists:** Crawford (2).

CHICAGO CUBS	AB	R	H	HR	RBI	BB	AVG
Slagle cf	4	0	0	0	0	0	.308
Sheckard lf	4	0	1	0	0	0	.250
Chance 1b	4	1	1	0	0	0	.273
Steinfeldt 3b	3	1	2	0	1	1	.333
Kling c	3	1	1	0	0	0	.364
Evers 2b	4	0	3	0	1	0	.583
Schulte rf	4	1	1	0	1	0	.231
Tinker ss	4	1	0	0	0	0	.111
Reulbach p	3	0	1	0	1	0	.200
TOTALS	**33**	**5**	**10**	**0**	**4**	**1**	**.284**

BATTING: 2B: Steinfeldt (1, Siever), Evers 2 (2, Siever, Killian), Sheckard (2, Siever), Chance (1, Killian). **S:** Kling. **RBI:** Steinfeldt 1 (1), Evers 1 (1), Schulte 1 (2), Reulbach 1 (1). **2-out RBI:** Reulbach 1. **Runners left in scoring position, 2 out:** Chance 1, Schulte 2, Tinker 1. **Team LOB:** 6 **FIELDING: E:** Evers (3). **DP:** 2 (Tinker, Steinfeldt-Evers-Chance).

DETROIT	IP	H	R	ER	BB	SO	HR	ERA
Siever (L, 0-1)	4	7	4	2	0	1	0	4.50
Killian	4	3	1	1	1	1	0	2.25

CHICAGO CUBS	IP	H	R	ER	BB	SO	HR	ERA
Reulbach (W, 1-0)	9	6	1	1	3	2	0	0.75

Ground balls-fly balls: Siever 3-7, Killian 3-8, Reulbach 15-9. **Batters faced:** Siever 19, Killian 16, Reulbach 35. **UMPIRES:** hp—O'Day, 1b—Sheridan **T:** 1:35 **A:** 13,114

GAME 4 Chicago 6 Detroit 1
Bennett Park 10/11/07

CHICAGO CUBS	AB	R	H	HR	RBI	BB	AVG
Slagle cf	5	1	1	0	2	0	.278
Sheckard lf	5	0	2	0	1	0	.294
Chance 1b	3	0	0	0	0	0	.214
Steinfeldt 3b	4	0	2	0	0	0	.385
Kling c	4	0	0	0	0	0	.267
Evers 2b	4	1	0	0	0	0	.438
Schulte rf	3	2	1	0	0	1	.250
Tinker ss	1	2	0	0	0	1	.100
Overall p	2	0	1	0	2	0	.200
TOTALS	**31**	**6**	**7**	**0**	**5**	**2**	**.271**

BATTING: S: Tinker, Tinker, Overall, Overall. **RBI:** Slagle 2 (3), Sheckard 1 (2), Overall 2 (2). **2-out RBI:** Slagle 1. **Runners left in scoring position, 2 out:** Sheckard 1, Steinfeldt 1. **Team LOB:** 5 **BASERUNNING: SB:** Chance (3, 2nd base off Donovan/Schmidt). **CS:** Sheckard (2, 2nd base off Donovan/Schmidt). **FIELDING: E:** Tinker (3), Slagle (1). **Outfield assists:** Schulte (2). **DP:** 1 (Tinker).

DETROIT	AB	R	H	HR	RBI	BB	AVG
Jones lf	2	0	0	0	0	1	.357
Schaefer 2b	3	0	0	0	0	0	.176
Crawford cf	4	0	0	0	0	0	.235
Cobb rf	4	1	1	0	0	0	.188
Rossman 1b	4	0	1	0	1	0	.438
Coughlin 3b	4	0	3	0	0	0	.188
Schmidt c	3	0	0	0	0	1	.182
O'Leary ss	4	0	0	0	0	0	.071
Donovan p	3	0	0	0	0	0	.000
TOTALS	**31**	**1**	**5**	**0**	**1**	**2**	**.216**

BATTING: 3B: Cobb (1, Overall). **S:** Schaefer, Jones. **RBI:** Rossman 1 (2). **2-out RBI:** Rossman 1. **Runners left in scoring position, 2 out:** Crawford 1, Cobb 1, O'Leary 3. **Team LOB:** 7 **FIELDING: E:** O'Leary 2 (2).

CHICAGO CUBS	IP	H	R	ER	BB	SO	HR	ERA
Overall (W, 1-0)	9	5	1	1	2	6	0	1.00

DETROIT	IP	H	R	ER	BB	SO	HR	ERA
Donovan (L, 0-1)	9	7	6	3	2	4	0	1.71

HBP: Chance (by Donovan). **Ground balls-fly balls:** Overall 9-11, Donovan 8-12. **Batters faced:** Overall 35, Donovan 38. **UMPIRES:** hp—Sheridan, 1b—O'Day **T:** 1:45 **A:** 11,306

GAME 5 Chicago 2 Detroit 0
Bennett Park 10/12/07

CHICAGO CUBS	AB	R	H	HR	RBI	BB	AVG
Slagle cf	4	1	1	0	1	1	.273
Sheckard lf	4	0	0	0	0	0	.238
Howard 1b	4	0	1	0	0	0	.200
Steinfeldt 3b	4	0	3	0	1	0	.471
Kling c	4	0	0	0	0	0	.211
Evers 2b	4	1	0	0	0	0	.350
Schulte rf	4	0	1	0	0	0	.250
Tinker ss	3	0	1	0	0	1	.154
Brown p	3	0	0	0	0	1	.000
TOTALS	**34**	**2**	**7**	**0**	**2**	**3**	**.257**

BATTING: 3B: Steinfeldt (1, Mullin). **RBI:** Slagle 1 (4), Steinfeldt 1 (2). **2-out RBI:** Steinfeldt 1. **Runners left in scoring position, 2 out:** Slagle 2, Sheckard 1. **Team LOB:** 8 **BASERUNNING: SB:** Slagle (5, 2nd base off Mullin/Archer), Evers (3, 3rd base off Mullin/Archer), Tinker (1, 3rd base off Mullin/Archer). **CS:** Slagle (2, 2nd base off Mullin/Archer). **FIELDING: E:** Schulte (1).

DETROIT	AB	R	H	HR	RBI	BB	AVG
Jones lf	3	0	1	0	0	1	.353
Schaefer 2b	4	0	0	0	0	0	.143
Crawford cf	4	0	1	0	0	0	.238
Cobb rf	4	0	1	0	0	0	.200
Rossman 1b	4	0	2	0	0	0	.450
a-Payne pr	0	0	0	0	0	0	.250
Coughlin 3b	4	0	2	0	0	0	.250
Archer c	3	0	0	0	0	0	.000
b-Schmidt ph	1	0	0	0	0	0	.167
O'Leary ss	3	0	0	0	0	0	.059
Mullin p	3	0	0	0	0	0	.000
TOTALS	**33**	**0**	**7**	**0**	**0**	**1**	**.215**

a - Ran for Rossman in the 9th
b - Batted for Archer in the 9th

BATTING: 2B: Crawford (1, Brown). **Runners left in scoring position, 2 out:** Schaefer 1, Cobb 1, Archer 2, Mullin 1. **Team LOB:** 7 **BASERUNNING: SB:** Rossman (1, 2nd base off Brown/Kling), Jones (3, 2nd base off Brown/Kling), Coughlin (1, 2nd base off Brown/Kling). **CS:** Cobb (2, 3rd base off Brown/Kling). **FIELDING: E:** Coughlin (2). **Outfield assists:** Jones (2).

CHICAGO CUBS	IP	H	R	ER	BB	SO	HR	ERA
Brown (W, 1-0)	9	7	0	0	1	4	0	0.00

DETROIT	IP	H	R	ER	BB	SO	HR	ERA
Mullin (L, 0-2)	9	7	2	1	3	2	0	2.12

Ground balls-fly balls: Brown 12-10, Mullin 15-10. **Batters faced:** Brown 34, Mullin 37. **UMPIRES:** hp—O'Day, 1b—Sheridan **T:** 1:42 **A:** 7,370

1908 CHICAGO CUBS DEF. DETROIT, 4-1

GAME 1 Chicago 10 Detroit 6
Bennett Park 10/10/08

CHICAGO CUBS	AB	R	H	HR	RBI	BB	AVG
Sheckard lf	6	1	3	0	0	0	.500
Evers 2b	4	1	2	0	0	0	.500
Schulte rf	4	2	2	0	1	0	.500
Chance 1b	4	2	1	0	0	1	.250
Steinfeldt 3b	3	2	2	0	2	1	.667
Hofman cf	4	1	1	0	2	1	.250
Tinker ss	5	1	2	0	2	0	.400
Kling c	3	0	1	0	2	1	.333
Reulbach p	3	0	0	0	0	0	.000
Overall p	1	0	0	0	0	0	.000
Brown p	0	0	0	0	0	0	.000
TOTALS	**37**	**10**	**14**	**0**	**9**	**4**	**.378**

BATTING: 2B: Sheckard 2 (2, Killian). **S:** Evers, Schulte, Kling, Brown. **SF:** Steinfeldt. **RBI:** Schulte 1 (1), Steinfeldt 2 (2), Hofman 2 (2), Tinker 2 (2), Kling 2 (2). **Runners left in scoring position, 2 out:** Sheckard 2, Schulte 1, Steinfeldt 2, Hofman 1. **Team LOB:** 9 **BASERUNNING: SB:** Chance 2 (2, 2nd base off Killian/Schmidt, 2nd base off Summers/Schmidt), Tinker 2 (2, 2nd base off Summers/Schmidt, 3rd base off Summers/Schmidt), Hofman (1, 3rd base off Summers/Schmidt). **CS:** Kling (1, 2nd base off Summers/Schmidt). **FIELDING: E:** Evers (1). **Outfield assists:** Schulte (1).

DETROIT	AB	R	H	HR	RBI	BB	AVG
McIntyre lf	3	1	2	0	0	1	.667
O'Leary ss	4	0	1	0	0	0	.250
b-Thomas ph	1	0	1	0	0	0	1.000
c-Winter pr	0	0	0	0	0	0	.000
Crawford cf	4	1	0	0	0	1	.000
Cobb rf	4	2	2	0	1	0	.500
Rossman 1b	4	1	2	0	2	0	.500
Schaefer 3b	3	0	0	0	0	0	.000
Schmidt c	4	0	0	0	1	0	.000
Downs 2b	4	1	1	0	1	0	.250
Killian p	0	0	0	0	0	0	.000
Summers p	3	0	1	0	1	0	.333
a-Jones ph	1	0	0	0	0	0	.000
TOTALS	**35**	**6**	**10**	**0**	**6**	**2**	**.286**

a - Batted for Summers in the 9th
b - Batted for O'Leary in the 9th
c - Ran for Thomas in the 9th

BATTING: 2B: Downs (1, Reulbach). **S:** Cobb, Schaefer. **RBI:** Cobb 1 (1), Rossman 2 (2), Schmidt 1 (1), Downs 1 (1), Summers 1 (1). **2-out RBI:** Cobb 1, Downs 1, Summers 1. **Runners left in scoring position, 2 out:** O'Leary 1, Crawford 1, Cobb 2, Downs 1. **Team LOB:** 7 **BASERUNNING: SB:** McIntyre (1, 2nd base off Reulbach/Kling). **FIELDING: E:** McIntyre (1), Schaefer (1), Downs (1).

CHICAGO CUBS	IP	H	R	ER	BB	SO	HR	ERA
Reulbach	6.2	8	4	4	0	5	0	5.40
Overall	0.1	0	1	1	1	0	0	27.00
Brown (W, 1-0)	2	2	1	0	1	1	0	0.00

DETROIT	IP	H	R	ER	BB	SO	HR	ERA
Killian	2.1	5	4	3	3	1	0	11.57
Summers (L, 0-1)	6.2	9	6	5	1	2	0	6.75

HBP: McIntyre (by Overall). **Ground balls-fly balls:** Reulbach 9-5, Overall 0-1, Brown 2-2, Killian 4-2, Summers 9-5. **Batters faced:** Reulbach 27, Overall 3, Brown 10, Killian 15, Summers 31. **UMPIRES:** hp—Sheridan, 1b—O'Day **T:** 2:10 **A:** 10,812

GAME 2 Chicago 6 Detroit 1
West Side Park 10/11/08

DETROIT	AB	R	H	HR	RBI	BB	AVG
McIntyre lf	4	0	0	0	0	0	.286
O'Leary ss	3	0	0	0	0	0	.143
a-Jones ph	0	1	0	0	0	1	.000
Crawford cf	4	0	0	0	0	0	.000
Cobb rf	4	0	1	0	1	0	.375
Rossman 1b	4	0	0	0	0	0	.250
Schaefer 3b	3	0	2	0	0	0	.333
Schmidt c	3	0	1	0	0	0	.143
Downs 2b	2	0	0	0	0	1	.167
Donovan p	2	0	0	0	0	0	.000
TOTALS	**29**	**1**	**4**	**0**	**1**	**2**	**.219**

a - Batted for O'Leary in the 9th

BATTING: S: Donovan. **RBI:** Cobb 1 (2). **Runners left in scoring position, 2 out:** McIntyre 1, Schmidt 1, Donovan 1. **GIDP:** Rossman. **Team LOB:** 4 **BASERUNNING: SB:** Schaefer (1, 2nd base off Overall/Kling). **FIELDING: DP:** 1 (Downs-O'Leary-Rossman).

CHICAGO CUBS	AB	R	H	HR	RBI	BB	AVG
Sheckard lf	4	1	1	0	1	0	.400
Evers 2b	4	1	1	0	1	0	.375
Schulte rf	4	1	1	0	1	0	.375
Chance 1b	3	0	0	0	0	1	.143
Steinfeldt 3b	4	0	0	0	0	0	.286
Hofman cf	3	1	1	0	0	0	.286
Tinker ss	3	1	1	1	2	0	.375
Kling c	3	1	1	0	0	0	.333
Overall p	3	0	1	0	0	0	.250
TOTALS	**31**	**6**	**7**	**1**	**5**	**1**	**.309**

BATTING: 2B: Kling (1, Donovan). **3B:** Schulte (1, Donovan). **HR:** Tinker (1, 8th off Donovan 1 on, 1 out). **RBI:** Sheckard 1 (1), Evers 1 (1), Schulte 1 (2), Tinker 2 (4). **2-out RBI:** Sheckard 1, Evers 1, Schulte 1. **Runners left in scoring position, 2 out:** Steinfeldt 1. **GIDP:** Sheckard. **Team LOB:** 2 **BASERUNNING: SB:** Sheckard (1, 2nd base off Donovan/Schmidt), Evers (1, 2nd base off Donovan/Schmidt), Chance (3, 2nd base off Donovan/Schmidt). **FIELDING: DP:** 1 (Tinker-Chance).

DETROIT	IP	H	R	ER	BB	SO	HR	ERA
Donovan (L, 0-1)	8	7	6	6	1	7	1	6.75

CHICAGO CUBS	IP	H	R	ER	BB	SO	HR	ERA
Overall (W, 1-0)	9	4	1	1	2	5	0	1.93

WP: Donovan 1. **Ground balls-fly balls:** Donovan 8-9, Overall 11-9. **Batters faced:** Donovan 32, Overall 32. **UMPIRES:** hp—Klem, 1b—Connolly **T:** 1:30 **A:** 17,760

GAME 3 Detroit 8 Chicago 3
West Side Park 10/12/08

DETROIT	AB	R	H	HR	RBI	BB	AVG
McIntyre lf	4	1	1	0	0	1	.273
O'Leary ss	4	2	1	0	0	0	.182
Crawford cf	5	1	2	0	1	0	.154
Cobb rf	5	1	4	0	2	0	.538
Rossman 1b	4	2	2	0	2	1	.333
Schaefer 2b	4	0	0	0	0	0	.200
Thomas c	3	0	1	0	1	1	.500
Coughlin 3b	3	0	0	0	1	0	.000
Mullin p	3	1	1	0	1	1	.333
TOTALS	**35**	**8**	**12**	**0**	**8**	**4**	**.263**

BATTING: 2B: Thomas (1, Pfiester), Cobb (1, Pfiester). **S:** O'Leary, Cobb. **SF:** Coughlin. **RBI:** Crawford 1 (1), Cobb 2 (4), Rossman 2 (4), Thomas 1 (1), Coughlin 1 (1), Mullin 1 (1). **2-out RBI:** Cobb 1, Thomas 1, Mullin 1. **Runners left in scoring position, 2 out:** McIntyre 1, Crawford 1, Coughlin 1. **Team LOB:** 6 **BASERUNNING: SB:** Cobb 2 (2, 2nd base off Reulbach/Kling, 3rd base off Reulbach/Kling). **FIELDING: E:** Rossman (1), Coughlin (1), O'Leary (1). **DP:** 2 (Schaefer-Rossman, O'Leary-Schaefer-Rossman).

CHICAGO CUBS	AB	R	H	HR	RBI	BB	AVG
Sheckard lf	4	0	0	0	0	0	.286
Evers 2b	3	1	0	0	0	1	.273
Schulte rf	4	0	1	0	0	0	.333
Chance 1b	4	1	2	0	1	0	.273
Steinfeldt 3b	4	1	1	0	1	0	.273
Hofman cf	4	0	2	0	1	0	.364
Tinker ss	3	0	1	0	0	0	.364
Kling c	3	0	0	0	0	0	.222
Pfiester p	2	0	0	0	0	0	.000
a-Howard ph	1	0	0	0	0	0	.000
Reulbach p	0	0	0	0	0	0	.000
TOTALS	**32**	**3**	**7**	**0**	**3**	**1**	**.280**

a - Batted for Pfiester in the 8th

BATTING: 3B: Hofman (1, Mullin). **RBI:** Chance 1 (1), Steinfeldt 1 (3), Hofman 1 (3). **2-out RBI:** Chance 1, Steinfeldt 1, Hofman 1. **Runners left in scoring position, 2 out:** Steinfeldt 1, Hofman 1, Tinker 1. **GIDP:** Sheckard, Kling. **Team LOB:** 3 **BASERUNNING: SB:** Chance 2 (5, 2nd base off Mullin/Thomas), Steinfeldt (1, 2nd base off Mullin/Thomas). **CS:** Schulte (1, 2nd base off Mullin/Thomas), Tinker (1, 2nd base off Mullin/Thomas), Evers (1, 2nd base off Mullin/Thomas). **FIELDING: Outfield assists:** Hofman (1). **DP:** 2 (Evers-Chance, Hofman-Kling).

DETROIT	IP	H	R	ER	BB	SO	HR	ERA
Mullin (W, 1-0)	9	7	3	0	1	8	0	0.00

CHICAGO CUBS	IP	H	R	ER	BB	SO	HR	ERA
Pfiester (L, 0-1)	8	11	8	7	3	1	0	7.87
Reulbach	1	1	0	0	1	0	0	4.70

Ground balls-fly balls: Mullin 11-6, Pfiester 11-9, Reulbach 0-2. **Batters faced:** Mullin 33, Pfiester 37, Reulbach 4. **UMPIRES:** hp—O'Day, 1b—Sheridan **T:** 2:10 **A:** 14,543

GAME 4 Chicago 3 Detroit 0
Bennett Park 10/13/08

CHICAGO CUBS	AB	R	H	HR	RBI	BB	AVG
Sheckard lf	4	0	0	0	0	1	.222
Evers 2b	5	1	1	0	0	0	.250
Schulte rf	3	1	2	0	0	2	.400
Chance 1b	4	1	2	0	0	1	.333
Steinfeldt 3b	3	0	1	0	1	0	.286
Hofman cf	4	0	2	0	1	0	.400
Tinker ss	4	0	0	0	0	0	.267
Kling c	4	0	2	0	0	0	.308
Brown p	4	0	0	0	0	0	.000
TOTALS	**35**	**3**	**10**	**0**	**2**	**4**	**.281**

BATTING: S: Steinfeldt, Schulte. **RBI:** Steinfeldt 1 (4), Hofman 1 (4). **2-out RBI:** Steinfeldt 1, Hofman 1. **Runners left in scoring position, 2 out:** Steinfeldt 2, Tinker 3, Kling 1. **Team LOB:** 10 **BASERUNNING: SB:** Schulte 2 (2, 2nd base off Summers/Schmidt), Hofman (2, 2nd base off Summers/Schmidt), Evers (2, 2nd base off Winter/Schmidt). **CS:** Kling (2, 2nd base off Summers/Schmidt). **FIELDING: PB:** Kling. **DP:** 1 (Brown-Tinker-Chance).

DETROIT	AB	R	H	HR	RBI	BB	AVG
McIntyre lf	4	0	0	0	0	0	.200
O'Leary ss	4	0	2	0	0	0	.267
Crawford cf	4	0	2	0	0	0	.235
Cobb rf	3	0	0	0	0	0	.438
Rossman 1b	3	0	0	0	0	0	.267
Schaefer 2b	3	0	0	0	0	0	.154
Schmidt c	3	0	0	0	0	0	.100
Coughlin 3b	2	0	0	0	0	0	.000
Summers p	2	0	0	0	0	0	.200
a-Jones ph	1	0	0	0	0	0	.000
Winter p	0	0	0	0	0	0	.000
TOTALS	**29**	**0**	**4**	**0**	**0**	**0**	**.234**

a - Batted for Summers in the 8th

BATTING: 2B: Crawford (1, Brown). **Runners left in scoring position, 2 out:** Cobb 1. **GIDP:** Crawford. **Team LOB:** 3 **FIELDING: E:** Cobb (1). **PB:** Schmidt.

CHICAGO CUBS	IP	H	R	ER	BB	SO	HR	ERA
Brown (W, 2-0)	9	4	0	0	0	4	0	0.00

DETROIT	IP	H	R	ER	BB	SO	HR	ERA
Summers (L, 0-2)	8	9	2	2	3	5	0	4.30
Winter	1	1	1	0	1	0	0	0.00

HBP: Coughlin (by Brown). **Ground balls-fly balls:** Brown 18-3, Summers 12-5, Winter 0-3. **Batters faced:** Brown 30, Summers 35, Winter 5. **UMPIRES:** hp—Connolly, 1b—Klem **T:** 1:35 **A:** 12,907

GAME 5 Chicago 2 Detroit 0
Bennett Park 10/14/08

CHICAGO CUBS	AB	R	H	HR	RBI	BB	AVG
Sheckard lf	3	0	1	0	0	1	.238
Evers 2b	4	1	3	0	1	0	.350
Schulte rf	3	0	1	0	0	0	.389
Chance 1b	4	0	3	0	1	0	.421
Steinfeldt 3b	2	0	0	0	0	1	.250
Hofman cf	4	0	0	0	0	0	.316
Tinker ss	4	0	1	0	0	0	.263
Kling c	3	1	0	0	0	1	.250
Overall p	2	0	1	0	0	0	.333
TOTALS	**29**	**2**	**10**	**0**	**2**	**3**	**.293**

BATTING: 2B: Evers (1, Donovan). **S:** Overall, Steinfeldt, Schulte, Steinfeldt, Evers. **RBI:** Evers 1 (2), Chance 1 (2). **2-out RBI:** Evers 1. **Runners left in scoring position, 2 out:** Schulte 2, Hofman 1, Tinker 1. **Team LOB:** 6 **BASERUNNING: CS:** Steinfeldt (1, 2nd base off Donovan/Schmidt).

DETROIT	AB	R	H	HR	RBI	BB	AVG
McIntyre lf	3	0	1	0	0	1	.222
O'Leary ss	4	0	0	0	0	0	.211
Crawford cf	4	0	1	0	0	0	.238
Cobb rf	3	0	0	0	0	1	.368
Rossman 1b	4	0	0	0	0	0	.211
Schaefer 2b	3	0	0	0	0	1	.125
Schmidt c	4	0	0	0	0	0	.071
Coughlin 3b	3	0	1	0	0	0	.125
Donovan p	2	0	0	0	0	1	.000
TOTALS	**30**	**0**	**3**	**0**	**0**	**4**	**.209**

BATTING: 2B: McIntyre (1, Overall). **Runners left in scoring position, 2 out:** McIntyre 1, Crawford 2, Schaefer 2. **Team LOB:** 7 **BASERUNNING: SB:** Donovan (1, 2nd base off Overall/Kling). **CS:** Schaefer (1, 2nd base off Overall/Kling). **FIELDING: DP:** 2 (Schmidt-Schaefer-Schmidt, O'Leary-Rossman-Coughlin).

CHICAGO CUBS	IP	H	R	ER	BB	SO	HR	ERA
Overall (W, 2-0)	9	3	0	0	4	10	0	0.98

DETROIT	IP	H	R	ER	BB	SO	HR	ERA
Donovan (L, 0-2)	9	10	2	2	3	3	0	4.24

WP: Overall 1. **Ground balls-fly balls:** Overall 10-7, Donovan 5-11. **Batters faced:** Overall 34, Donovan 35. **UMPIRES:** hp—Sheridan, 1b—O'Day **T:** 1:25 **A:** 6,210

1909 PITTSBURG DEF. DETROIT, 4-3

GAME 1 Pittsburg 4 Detroit 1
Forbes Field 10/08/09

DETROIT	AB	R	H	HR	RBI	BB	AVG
D.Jones lf	3	0	2	0	0	1	.667
Bush ss	2	0	0	0	0	1	.000
Cobb rf	3	1	0	0	0	1	.000
Crawford cf	4	0	1	0	0	0	.250
Delahanty 2b	4	0	1	0	1	0	.250
Moriarty 3b	4	0	1	0	0	0	.250
T.Jones 1b	3	0	0	0	0	0	.000
a-McIntyre ph	1	0	0	0	0	0	.000
Schmidt c	3	0	0	0	0	1	.000
Mullin p	4	0	1	0	0	0	.250
TOTALS	**31**	**1**	**6**	**0**	**1**	**4**	**.194**

a - Batted for T.Jones in the 9th

BATTING: S: Bush. **RBI:** Delahanty 1 (1). **2-out RBI:** Delahanty 1. **Runners left in scoring position, 2 out:** Cobb 1, Crawford 1, Moriarty 1. **Team LOB:** 8 **BASERUNNING: SB:** Cobb (1, 2nd base off Adams/Gibson). **FIELDING: E:** Delahanty (1), Bush (1), Schmidt (1).

PITTSBURG	AB	R	H	HR	RBI	BB	AVG
Byrne 3b	3	0	0	0	0	0	.000
Leach cf	3	0	0	0	1	0	.000
Clarke lf	4	1	1	1	1	0	.250
Wagner ss	3	1	1	0	0	0	.333
Miller 2b	4	0	1	0	0	0	.250
Abstein 1b	3	1	0	0	1	1	.000
Wilson rf	3	0	1	0	0	0	.333
Gibson c	3	1	1	0	1	0	.333
Adams p	3	0	0	0	0	0	.000
TOTALS	**29**	**4**	**5**	**1**	**4**	**1**	**.172**

BATTING: 2B: Gibson (1, Mullin), Wagner (1, Mullin). **HR:** Clarke (1, 4th off Mullin 0 on, 2 out). **SF:** Leach. **RBI:** Leach 1 (1), Clarke 1 (1), Abstein 1 (1), Gibson 1 (1). **2-out RBI:** Clarke 1. **Runners left in scoring position, 2 out:** Clarke 1, Abstein 1, Gibson 1. **Team LOB:** 5 **BASERUNNING: SB:** Wilson (1, 2nd base off Mullin/Schmidt), Miller (1, 2nd base off Mullin/Schmidt).

DETROIT	IP	H	R	ER	BB	SO	HR	ERA
Mullin (L, 0-1)	8	5	4	1	1	4	1	1.13

PITTSBURG	IP	H	R	ER	BB	SO	HR	ERA
Adams (W, 1-0)	9	6	1	1	4	2	0	1.00

HBP: Wagner (by Mullin), Byrne (by Mullin). **Ground balls-fly balls:** Mullin 10-10, Adams 12-11. **Batters faced:** Mullin 33, Adams 36. **UMPIRES:** hp—Johnstone, 1b—O'Loughlin **T:** 1:55 **A:** 29,264

GAME 2 Detroit 7 Pittsburg 2
Forbes Field 10/09/09

DETROIT	AB	R	H	HR	RBI	BB	AVG
D.Jones lf	5	1	1	0	0	0	.375
Bush ss	3	1	1	0	0	1	.200
Cobb rf	3	1	1	0	0	1	.167
Crawford cf	4	1	1	0	0	0	.250
Delahanty 2b	3	1	1	0	2	1	.286
Moriarty 3b	3	1	1	0	0	1	.286
T.Jones 1b	3	1	1	0	0	1	.167
Schmidt c	4	0	2	0	4	0	.286
Donovan p	4	0	0	0	0	0	.000
TOTALS	**32**	**7**	**9**	**0**	**6**	**5**	**.238**

BATTING: 2B: Schmidt (1, Camnitz), Delahanty (1, Camnitz), Crawford (1, Willis). **S:** Bush. **RBI:** Delahanty 2 (3), Schmidt 4 (4). **2-out RBI:** Schmidt 4. **Runners left in scoring position, 2 out:** Schmidt 3, Donovan 1. **Team LOB:** 4 **BASERUNNING: SB:** Cobb (2, home off Willis/Gibson). **CS:** D.Jones (1, 3rd base off Camnitz/Gibson), Bush (1, 2nd base off Willis/Gibson). **FIELDING: E:** Donovan (1), Delahanty (2). **DP:** 1 (Bush-T.Jones-Moriarty).

PITTSBURG	AB	R	H	HR	RBI	BB	AVG
Byrne 3b	3	1	0	0	0	1	.000
Leach cf	4	1	2	0	1	0	.286
Clarke lf	3	0	0	0	0	0	.143
Wagner ss	4	0	1	0	0	0	.286
Miller 2b	4	0	1	0	1	0	.250
Abstein 1b	4	0	1	0	0	0	.143
Wilson rf	4	0	0	0	0	0	.143
Gibson c	2	0	0	0	0	1	.200
Camnitz p	1	0	0	0	0	0	.000
Willis p	2	0	0	0	0	0	.000
TOTALS	**31**	**2**	**5**	**0**	**2**	**2**	**.167**

BATTING: 2B: Leach 2 (2, Donovan), Miller (1, Donovan). **S:** Clarke. **RBI:** Leach 1 (2), Miller 1 (1). **2-out RBI:** Miller 1. **Runners left in scoring position, 2 out:** Byrne 1, Miller 1, Abstein 1, Wilson 1. **Team LOB:** 5 **BASERUNNING: SB:** Gibson (1, 2nd base off Donovan/Schmidt), Wagner (1, 2nd base off Donovan/Schmidt). **CS:** Wagner (1, 3rd base off Donovan/Schmidt). **FIELDING: Outfield assists:** Leach (1). **DP:** 1 (Miller-Abstein-Byrne).

DETROIT	IP	H	R	ER	BB	SO	HR	ERA
Donovan (W, 1-0)	9	5	2	2	2	7	0	2.00

PITTSBURG	IP	H	R	ER	BB	SO	HR	ERA
Camnitz (L, 0-1)	2.1	6	5	4	1	2	0	15.43
Willis	6.2	3	2	2	4	2	0	2.70

Ground balls-fly balls: Donovan 9-10, Camnitz 3-1, Willis 9-6. **Batters faced:** Donovan 34, Camnitz 14, Willis 24. **UMPIRES:** hp—Evans, 1b—Klem **T:** 1:45 **A:** 30,915

GAME 3 Pittsburg 8 Detroit 6
Bennett Park 10/11/09

PITTSBURG	AB	R	H	HR	RBI	BB	AVG
Byrne 3b	5	1	2	0	0	0	.182
Leach cf	4	3	2	0	0	0	.364
Clarke lf	3	1	0	0	1	0	.100
Wagner ss	5	1	3	0	2	0	.417
Miller 2b	4	1	0	0	0	1	.167
Abstein 1b	4	1	2	0	1	0	.273
Wilson rf	4	0	1	0	1	0	.182
Gibson c	4	0	0	0	0	0	.111
Maddox p	4	0	0	0	0	0	.000
TOTALS	**37**	**8**	**10**	**0**	**5**	**1**	**.206**

BATTING: 2B: Abstein (1, Works), Leach (3, Works). **S:** Leach. **SF:** Clarke. **RBI:** Clarke 1 (2), Wagner 2 (2), Abstein 1 (2), Wilson 1 (1). **2-out RBI:** Wagner 1. **Runners left in scoring position, 2 out:** Miller 2, Wilson 2, Gibson 1, Maddox 1. **Team LOB:** 6 **BASERUNNING: SB:** Wagner 3 (4, 2nd base off Summers/Schmidt, 2nd base off Willett/Schmidt, 2nd base off Works/Schmidt). **CS:** Wagner (2, 2nd base off Willett/Schmidt).

DETROIT	AB	R	H	HR	RBI	BB	AVG
D.Jones lf	5	2	1	0	0	0	.308
Bush ss	5	1	4	0	2	0	.500
Cobb rf	5	0	2	0	2	0	.273
Crawford cf	5	0	0	0	1	0	.154
Delahanty 2b	5	1	3	0	0	0	.417
Moriarty 3b	3	1	0	0	0	1	.200
T.Jones 1b	3	1	1	0	1	1	.222
Schmidt c	4	0	0	0	0	0	.182
Summers p	0	0	0	0	0	0	.000
Willett p	2	0	0	0	0	0	.000
a-McIntyre ph	1	0	0	0	0	0	.000
Works p	0	0	0	0	0	0	.000
b-Mullin ph	1	0	0	0	0	0	.200
TOTALS	**39**	**6**	**11**	**0**	**6**	**2**	**.255**

a - Batted for Willett in the 7th
b - Batted for Works in the 9th

BATTING: 2B: Delahanty 2 (3, Maddox), Cobb (1, Maddox). **RBI:** Bush 2 (2), Cobb 2 (2), Crawford 1 (1), T.Jones 1 (1). **2-out RBI:** Bush 2, Cobb 1. **Runners left in scoring position, 2 out:** Crawford 1, Delahanty 1, Schmidt 1. **Team LOB:** 8 **BASERUNNING: CS:** Moriarty (1, 2nd base off Maddox/Gibson). **FIELDING: E:** Bush 2 (3), Schmidt (2), Crawford (1).

PITTSBURG	IP	H	R	ER	BB	SO	HR	ERA
Maddox (W, 1-0)	9	11	6	1	2	4	0	1.00

DETROIT	IP	H	R	ER	BB	SO	HR	ERA
Summers (L, 0-1)	0.1	3	5	0	1	0	0	0.00
Willett	6.2	3	1	0	0	0	0	0.00
Works	2	4	2	2	0	2	0	9.00

WP: Summers 1. **HBP:** Leach (by Willett), Clarke (by Willett). **Ground balls-fly balls:** Maddox 13-11, Summers 2-0, Willett 9-11, Works 1-2. **Batters faced:** Maddox 41, Summers 6, Willett 25, Works 10. **UMPIRES:** hp—O'Loughlin, 1b—Johnstone, 2b—Evans, 3b—Klem **T:** 1:56 **A:** 18,277

GAME 4 Detroit 5 Pittsburg 0
Bennett Park 10/12/09

PITTSBURG	AB	R	H	HR	RBI	BB	AVG
Byrne 3b	4	0	1	0	0	0	.200
Leach cf	3	0	0	0	0	1	.286
Clarke lf	4	0	0	0	0	0	.071
Wagner ss	3	0	0	0	0	1	.333
Miller 2b	4	0	1	0	0	0	.188
Abstein 1b	4	0	1	0	0	0	.267
Wilson rf	4	0	1	0	0	0	.200
Gibson c	3	0	1	0	0	0	.167
Leifield p	1	0	0	0	0	0	.000
a-O'Connor ph	1	0	0	0	0	0	.000
Phillippe p	1	0	0	0	0	0	.000
TOTALS	**32**	**0**	**5**	**0**	**0**	**2**	**.194**

a - Batted for Leifield in the 5th

BATTING: 2B: Byrne (1, Mullin). **Runners left in scoring position, 2 out:** Wagner 2, Wilson 1, Gibson 1. **Team LOB:** 7 **BASERUNNING: SB:** Byrne (1, 3rd base off Mullin/Stanage), Leach (1, 3rd base off Mullin/Stanage). **FIELDING: E:** Abstein 2 (2), Miller (1), Phillippe (1). **DP:** 1 (Wagner-Abstein).

DETROIT	AB	R	H	HR	RBI	BB	AVG
D.Jones lf	4	1	1	0	0	1	.294
Bush ss	5	1	1	0	1	0	.400
Cobb rf	3	0	1	0	2	0	.286
Crawford cf	4	0	1	0	0	0	.176
Delahanty 2b	3	0	0	0	0	0	.333
Moriarty 3b	4	1	2	0	0	0	.286
T.Jones 1b	3	1	1	0	0	0	.250
Stanage c	3	0	1	0	2	0	.333
Mullin p	3	1	0	0	0	1	.125
TOTALS	**32**	**5**	**8**	**0**	**5**	**2**	**.254**

BATTING: 2B: Bush (1, Leifield), Cobb (2, Leifield). **S:** T.Jones, Stanage. **RBI:** Bush 1 (3), Cobb 2 (4), Stanage 2 (2). **2-out RBI:** Bush 1, Cobb 2. **Runners left in scoring position, 2 out:** D.Jones 1, Bush 2, Crawford 2, Moriarty 1. **GIDP:** Stanage. **Team LOB:** 9 **BASERUNNING: CS:** Cobb (1, 2nd base off Leifield/Gibson), D.Jones (2, 2nd base off Phillippe/Gibson).

PITTSBURG	IP	H	R	ER	BB	SO	HR	ERA
Leifield (L, 0-1)	4	7	5	5	1	0	0	11.25
Phillippe	4	1	0	0	1	1	0	0.00

DETROIT	IP	H	R	ER	BB	SO	HR	ERA
Mullin (W, 1-1)	9	5	0	0	2	10	0	0.53

HBP: Cobb (by Leifield), Delahanty (by Leifield). **Ground balls-fly balls:** Leifield 9-3, Phillippe 8-3, Mullin 12-5. **Batters faced:** Leifield 22, Phillippe 16, Mullin 34. **UMPIRES:** hp—Klem, 1b—Evans, 2b—Johnstone, 3b—O'Loughlin **T:** 1:57 **A:** 17,036

GAME 5 Pittsburg 8 Detroit 4
Forbes Field 10/13/09

DETROIT	AB	R	H	HR	RBI	BB	AVG
D.Jones lf	4	1	1	1	1	0	.286
Bush ss	3	0	0	0	0	1	.333
Cobb rf	4	1	1	0	0	0	.278
Crawford cf	4	2	3	1	2	0	.286
Delahanty 2b	4	0	0	0	0	0	.263
Moriarty 3b	4	0	0	0	0	0	.222
T.Jones 1b	4	0	1	0	0	0	.250
Stanage c	2	0	0	0	0	0	.200
a-McIntyre ph	1	0	0	0	0	0	.000
Schmidt c	1	0	0	0	0	0	.167
Summers p	3	0	0	0	0	0	.000
Willett p	0	0	0	0	0	0	.000
b-Mullin ph	1	0	0	0	0	0	.111
TOTALS	**35**	**4**	**6**	**2**	**3**	**1**	**.237**

a - Batted for Stanage in the 7th
b - Batted for Willett in the 9th

BATTING: 2B: T.Jones (1, Adams), Crawford (2, Adams). **HR:** D.Jones (1, 1st off Adams 0 on, 0 out), Crawford (1, 8th off Adams 0 on, 2 out). **RBI:** D.Jones 1 (1), Crawford 2 (3). **2-out RBI:** Crawford 1. **Runners left in scoring position, 2 out:** D.Jones 1, Moriarty 2, T.Jones 1, Mullin 1. **Team LOB:** 5 **BASERUNNING: SB:** Crawford (1, 2nd base off Adams/Gibson), T.Jones (1, 2nd base off Adams/Gibson). **FIELDING: E:** Schmidt (3).

PITTSBURG	AB	R	H	HR	RBI	BB	AVG
Byrne 3b	5	2	2	0	0	0	.250
Leach cf	4	1	2	0	0	0	.333
Clarke lf	2	2	2	1	3	1	.188
Wagner ss	2	1	1	0	0	1	.353
Miller 2b	4	0	0	0	1	0	.150
Abstein 1b	3	0	0	0	1	1	.222
Wilson rf	4	1	1	0	0	0	.211
Gibson c	4	1	2	0	1	0	.250
Adams p	3	0	0	0	0	0	.000
TOTALS	**31**	**8**	**10**	**1**	**6**	**3**	**.219**

BATTING: 2B: Wilson (1, Summers). **HR:** Clarke (2, 7th off Summers 2 on, 1 out). **S:** Clarke, Adams. **RBI:** Clarke 3 (5), Miller 1 (2), Abstein 1 (3), Gibson 1 (2). **2-out RBI:** Abstein 1. **Runners left in scoring position, 2 out:** Miller 1, Wilson 3. **Team LOB:** 5 **BASERUNNING: SB:** Clarke (1, 2nd base off Summers/Stanage), Wagner 2 (6, 2nd base off Summers/Schmidt, 3rd base off Summers/Schmidt), Gibson (2, 2nd base off Willett/Schmidt). **CS:** Gibson (1, 3rd base off Willett/Schmidt). **FIELDING: E:** Wagner 2 (2).

DETROIT	IP	H	R	ER	BB	SO	HR	ERA
Summers (L, 0-2)	7	10	8	7	3	4	1	8.59
Willett	1	0	0	0	0	1	0	0.00

PITTSBURG	IP	H	R	ER	BB	SO	HR	ERA
Adams (W, 2-0)	9	6	4	3	1	8	2	2.00

WP: Summers 1. **HBP:** Wagner (by Summers). **Ground balls-fly balls:** Summers 9-6, Willett 0-1, Adams 11-10. **Batters faced:** Summers 35, Willett 2, Adams 36. **UMPIRES:** hp—Johnstone, 1b—O'Loughlin, 2b—Klem, 3b—Evans, lf— **T:** 1:46 **A:** 21,706

GAME 6 Detroit 5 Pittsburg 4
Bennett Park 10/14/09

PITTSBURG	AB	R	H	HR	RBI	BB	AVG
Byrne 3b	4	1	1	0	0	0	.250
Leach cf	4	1	1	0	0	0	.318
Clarke lf	3	1	1	0	1	0	.211
Wagner ss	4	0	1	0	2	0	.333
Miller 2b	3	1	2	0	0	1	.217
Abstein 1b	4	0	1	0	0	0	.227
Wilson rf	3	0	0	0	0	0	.182
Gibson c	4	0	1	0	0	0	.250
Willis p	2	0	0	0	0	0	.000
Camnitz p	0	0	0	0	0	0	.000
a-Hyatt ph	1	0	0	0	0	0	.000
Phillippe p	0	0	0	0	0	0	.000
b-Abbaticchio ph	1	0	0	0	0	0	.000
TOTALS	**33**	**4**	**8**	**0**	**3**	**1**	**.223**

a - Batted for Camnitz in the 7th
b - Batted for Phillippe in the 9th

BATTING: 2B: Wagner (2, Mullin). **S:** Clarke, Wilson. **RBI:** Clarke 1 (6), Wagner 2 (4). **Runners left in scoring position, 2 out:** Byrne 1, Abstein 2, Wilson 1. **Team LOB:** 5 **BASERUNNING: SB:** Miller (2, 2nd base off Mullin/Schmidt). **CS:** Wilson (1, 3rd base off Mullin/Schmidt). **FIELDING: E:** Clarke (1). **Outfield assists:** Wilson (1). **DP:** 1 (Byrne-Abstein).

DETROIT	AB	R	H	HR	RBI	BB	AVG
D.Jones lf-cf	5	1	0	0	0	0	.231
Bush ss	2	2	1	0	0	2	.350
Cobb rf	4	0	1	0	1	0	.273
Crawford cf-1b	3	1	1	0	1	1	.292
Delahanty 2b	4	0	2	0	1	0	.304
Moriarty 3b	3	1	1	0	1	1	.238
T.Jones 1b	4	0	1	0	1	0	.250
McIntyre lf	0	0	0	0	0	0	.000
Schmidt c	3	0	1	0	0	1	.200
Mullin p	4	0	2	0	0	0	.231
TOTALS	**32**	**5**	**10**	**0**	**5**	**5**	**.249**

BATTING: 2B: Crawford (3, Willis), Delahanty (4, Willis), Schmidt (2, Camnitz), Cobb (3, Camnitz), Mullin (1, Phillippe). **RBI:** Cobb 1 (5), Crawford 1 (4), Delahanty 1 (4), Moriarty 1 (1), T.Jones 1 (2). **2-out RBI:** Cobb 1, Crawford 1, Delahanty 1. **Runners left in scoring position, 2 out:** D.Jones 1, Bush 1, Cobb 1, Crawford 2, Delahanty 1, T.Jones 1. **Team LOB:** 9 **BASERUNNING: SB:** Bush (1, 2nd base off Willis/Gibson), D.Jones (1, 2nd base off Camnitz/Gibson). **FIELDING: E:** Bush (4), T.Jones (1). **DP:** 2 (Schmidt-Bush, Schmidt-Moriarty).

PITTSBURG	IP	H	R	ER	BB	SO	HR	ERA
Willis (L, 0-1)	5	7	4	4	4	1	0	4.63
Camnitz	1	2	1	1	1	0	0	13.50
Phillippe	2	1	0	0	0	1	0	0.00

DETROIT	IP	H	R	ER	BB	SO	HR	ERA
Mullin (W, 2-1)	9	8	4	3	1	5	0	1.38

HBP: Bush (by Willis). **Ground balls-fly balls:** Willis 4-8, Camnitz 2-1, Phillippe 3-2, Mullin 13-7. **Batters faced:** Willis 25, Camnitz 6, Phillippe 7, Mullin 36. **UMPIRES:** hp—Evans, 1b—Klem, 2b—O'Loughlin, 3b—Johnstone **T:** 2:00 **A:** 10,535

GAME 7 Pittsburg 8 Detroit 0
Bennett Park 10/16/09

PITTSBURG	AB	R	H	HR	RBI	BB	AVG
Byrne 3b	0	0	0	0	0	0	.250
Hyatt cf	3	1	0	0	1	1	.000
Leach cf-3b	3	2	2	0	0	1	.360
Clarke lf	0	2	0	0	1	4	.211
Wagner ss	3	1	1	0	3	2	.333
Miller 2b	5	0	2	0	2	0	.250
Abstein 1b	4	1	1	0	0	1	.231
Wilson rf	4	1	0	0	0	0	.154
Gibson c	5	0	1	0	0	0	.240
Adams p	3	0	0	0	0	1	.000
TOTALS	**30**	**8**	**7**	**0**	**7**	**10**	**.224**

BATTING: 2B: Abstein (2, Donovan), Leach (4, Mullin), Gibson (2, Mullin). **3B:** Wagner (1, Mullin). **S:** Leach, Wilson, Clarke, Adams. **SF:** Hyatt. **RBI:** Hyatt 1 (1), Clarke 1 (7), Wagner 3 (7), Miller 2 (4). **2-out RBI:** Clarke 1, Miller 2. **Runners left in scoring position, 2 out:** Hyatt 2, Wagner 2, Miller 1, Abstein 3. **Team LOB:** 11 **BASERUNNING: SB:** Clarke 2 (3, 2nd base off Donovan/Schmidt, 2nd base off Mullin/Schmidt), Abstein (1, 2nd base off Donovan/Schmidt), Miller (3, 2nd base off Mullin/Schmidt). **CS:** Byrne (1, 3rd base off Donovan/Schmidt).

DETROIT	AB	R	H	HR	RBI	BB	AVG
D.Jones lf	4	0	1	0	0	0	.233
Bush ss	2	0	0	0	0	0	.318
Cobb rf	4	0	0	0	0	0	.231
Crawford cf	4	0	0	0	0	0	.250
Delahanty 2b	3	0	2	0	0	1	.346
Moriarty 3b	1	0	1	0	0	0	.273
a-O'Leary pr-3b	3	0	0	0	0	0	.000
T.Jones 1b	4	0	1	0	0	0	.250
Schmidt c	3	0	1	0	0	0	.222
Donovan p	0	0	0	0	0	0	.000
b-Mullin ph-p	3	0	0	0	0	0	.188
TOTALS	**31**	**0**	**6**	**0**	**0**	**1**	**.241**

a - Ran for Moriarty in the 2nd
b - Batted for Donovan in the 3th

BATTING: 2B: Moriarty (1, Adams), Schmidt (3, Adams), Delahanty (5, Adams). **S:** Bush. **Runners left in scoring position, 2 out:** Cobb 1, T.Jones 1, Schmidt 3, Mullin 1. **Team LOB:** 7 **BASERUNNING: CS:** Bush (2, 2nd base off Adams/Gibson). **FIELDING: E:** D.Jones (1), Crawford (2), Bush (5). **DP:** 1 (Bush-Schmidt-Delahanty).

PITTSBURG	IP	H	R	ER	BB	SO	HR	ERA
Adams (W, 3-0)	9	6	0	0	1	1	0	1.33

DETROIT	IP	H	R	ER	BB	SO	HR	ERA
Donovan (L, 1-1)	3	2	2	2	6	0	0	3.00
Mullin	6	5	6	4	4	1	0	2.25

HBP: Byrne (by Donovan), Bush (by Adams). **Ground balls-fly balls:** Adams 9-15, Donovan 3-2, Mullin 6-11. **Batters faced:** Adams 34, Donovan 17, Mullin 29. **UMPIRES:** hp—O'Loughlin, 1b—Johnstone, 2b—Evans, 3b—Klem **T:** 2:10 **A:** 17,562

1910 PHILADELPHIA A's DEF. CHICAGO CUBS, 4-1

GAME 1 Philadelphia 4 Chicago 1
Shibe Park 10/17/10

CHICAGO CUBS	AB	R	H	HR	RBI	BB	AVG
Sheckard lf	4	0	0	0	0	0	.000
Schulte rf	2	0	1	0	0	2	.500
Hofman cf	4	0	0	0	0	0	.000
Chance 1b	3	0	0	0	0	0	.000
Zimmerman 2b	3	0	0	0	0	0	.000
Steinfeldt 3b	3	0	0	0	0	0	.000
Tinker ss	3	1	1	0	0	0	.333
Kling c	3	0	1	0	1	0	.333
a-Kane pr	0	0	0	0	0	0	.000
Overall p	1	0	0	0	0	0	.000
McIntire p	1	0	0	0	0	0	.000
b-Beaumont ph	1	0	0	0	0	0	.000
TOTALS	**28**	**1**	**3**	**0**	**1**	**2**	**.107**

a - Ran for Kling in the 9th
b - Batted for McIntire in the 9th

BATTING: RBI: Kling 1 (1). **Runners left in scoring position, 2 out:** Hofman 1. **Team LOB:** 2 **BASERUNNING: CS:** Schulte 2 (2, 2nd base off Bender/Thomas). **FIELDING: E:** McIntire (1).

PHILADELPHIA	AB	R	H	HR	RBI	BB	AVG
Strunk cf	3	0	0	0	0	1	.000
Lord lf	4	1	1	0	0	0	.250
Collins 2b	2	1	1	0	0	1	.500
Baker 3b	4	1	3	0	2	0	.750
Davis 1b	3	0	0	0	0	0	.000
Murphy rf	3	1	1	0	1	0	.333
Barry ss	3	0	0	0	0	0	.000
Thomas c	1	0	0	0	0	2	.000
Bender p	3	0	1	0	1	0	.333
TOTALS	**26**	**4**	**7**	**0**	**4**	**4**	**.269**

BATTING: 2B: Baker 2 (2, Overall, McIntire), Lord (1, Overall). **S:** Davis, Collins. **RBI:** Baker 2 (2), Murphy 1 (1), Bender 1 (1). **2-out RBI:** Baker 1, Bender 1. **Runners left in scoring position, 2 out:** Strunk 1, Davis 1. **Team LOB:** 4 **BASERUNNING: SB:** Murphy (1, 2nd base off Overall/Kling). **CS:** Collins (1, 2nd base off Overall/Kling), Baker (1, 2nd base off Overall/Kling), Strunk (1, 2nd base off McIntire/Kling). **FIELDING: E:** Thomas (1), Strunk (1).

CHICAGO CUBS	IP	H	R	ER	BB	SO	HR	ERA
Overall (L, 0-1)	3	6	3	3	1	1	0	9.00
McIntire	5	1	1	0	3	3	0	0.00

PHILADELPHIA	IP	H	R	ER	BB	SO	HR	ERA
Bender (W, 1-0)	9	3	1	0	2	8	0	0.00

Ground balls-fly balls: Overall 2-2, McIntire 9-2, Bender 12-5. **Batters faced:** Overall 14, McIntire 18, Bender 30. **UMPIRES:** hp—Connolly, 1b—O'Day, 2b—Rigler, 3b—Sheridan **T:** 1:54 **A:** 26,891

GAME 2 Philadelphia 9 Chicago 3
Shibe Park 10/18/10

CHICAGO CUBS	AB	R	H	HR	RBI	BB	AVG
Sheckard lf	1	1	1	0	0	3	.200
Schulte rf	3	1	0	0	0	0	.200
Hofman cf	2	1	1	0	0	3	.167
Chance 1b	5	0	2	0	1	0	.250
Zimmerman 2b	3	0	1	0	2	1	.167
Steinfeldt 3b	5	0	1	0	0	0	.125
Tinker ss	4	0	2	0	0	1	.429
Kling c	4	0	0	0	0	1	.143
Brown p	3	0	0	0	0	0	.000
a-Beaumont ph	1	0	0	0	0	0	.000
Richie p	0	0	0	0	0	0	.000
TOTALS	**31**	**3**	**8**	**0**	**3**	**9**	**.186**

a - Batted for Brown in the 8th

BATTING: 2B: Tinker (1, Coombs), Sheckard (1, Coombs), Steinfeldt (1, Coombs), Zimmerman (1, Coombs). **S:** Schulte, Sheckard, Schulte. **SF:** Zimmerman. **RBI:** Chance 1 (1), Zimmerman 2 (2). **2-out RBI:** Chance 1. **Runners left in scoring position, 2 out:** Schulte 2, Zimmerman 2, Steinfeldt 2, Kling 2. **Team LOB:** 14 **BASERUNNING: CS:** Tinker (1, 2nd base off Coombs/Thomas). **FIELDING: E:** Steinfeldt (1), Sheckard (1). **Outfield assists:** Sheckard (1). **DP:** 1 (Tinker-Chance).

PHILADELPHIA	AB	R	H	HR	RBI	BB	AVG
Strunk cf	5	1	2	0	1	0	.250
Lord lf	5	1	1	0	0	0	.222
Collins 2b	4	2	3	0	2	1	.667
Baker 3b	4	1	1	0	0	1	.500
Davis 1b	5	1	2	0	2	0	.250
Murphy rf	4	1	1	0	2	1	.286
Barry ss	3	0	1	0	0	0	.167
Thomas c	3	2	2	0	1	1	.500
Coombs p	4	0	1	0	0	0	.250
TOTALS	**37**	**9**	**14**	**0**	**8**	**4**	**.333**

BATTING: 2B: Collins 2 (2, Brown, Richie), Davis (1, Brown), Murphy (1, Brown), Strunk (1, Brown). **S:** Barry. **RBI:** Strunk 1 (1), Collins 2 (2), Davis 2 (2), Murphy 2 (3), Thomas 1 (1). **2-out RBI:** Strunk 1, Collins 2, Davis 1. **Runners left in scoring position, 2 out:** Lord 1, Baker 2, Murphy 3, Coombs 1. **GIDP:** Barry. **Team LOB:** 9 **BASERUNNING: SB:** Collins 2 (2, 2nd base off Brown/Kling). **CS:** Lord (1, 2nd base off Brown/Kling). **FIELDING: E:** Coombs 2 (2). **Outfield assists:** Murphy (1). **DP:** 3 (Collins-Davis 2, Murphy-Thomas).

CHICAGO CUBS	IP	H	R	ER	BB	SO	HR	ERA
Brown (L, 0-1)	7	13	9	7	4	6	0	9.00
Richie	1	1	0	0	0	0	0	0.00

PHILADELPHIA	IP	H	R	ER	BB	SO	HR	ERA
Coombs (W, 1-0)	9	8	3	3	9	5	0	3.00

Ground balls-fly balls: Brown 10-4, Richie 3-0, Coombs 8-10. **Batters faced:** Brown 38, Richie 4, Coombs 44. **UMPIRES:** hp—Rigler, 1b—Sheridan, 2b—O'Day, 3b—Connolly **T:** 2:25 **A:** 24,597

GAME 3 Philadelphia 12 Chicago 5
West Side Park 10/20/10

PHILADELPHIA	AB	R	H	HR	RBI	BB	AVG
Strunk cf	5	1	1	0	0	1	.231
Lord lf	4	0	1	0	0	0	.231
Collins 2b	5	1	1	0	0	0	.455
Baker 3b	5	2	2	0	2	0	.462
Davis 1b	3	3	3	0	0	1	.455
Murphy rf	5	2	2	1	3	0	.333
Barry ss	5	3	3	0	3	0	.364
Thomas c	4	0	0	0	0	1	.250
Coombs p	5	0	3	0	3	0	.444
TOTALS	**41**	**12**	**16**	**1**	**11**	**3**	**.356**

BATTING: 2B: Barry 2 (2, Reulbach, Pfiester), Coombs (1, Reulbach), Davis (2, Pfiester). **3B:** Baker (1, McIntire). **HR:** Murphy (1, 3th off McIntire 2 on, 1 out). **S:** Lord. **RBI:** Baker 2 (4), Murphy 3 (6), Barry 3 (3), Coombs 3 (3). **2-out RBI:** Baker 1, Barry 2, Coombs 3. **Runners left in scoring position, 2 out:** Strunk 1, Lord 2, Murphy 1. **GIDP:** Coombs. **Team LOB:** 7 **BASERUNNING: CS:** Baker (2, 2nd base off Reulbach/Kling), Collins (2, 2nd base off Pfiester/Kling). **FIELDING: Outfield assists:** Murphy (2). **DP:** 2 (Barry-Collins-Davis, Murphy-Davis).

CHICAGO CUBS	AB	R	H	HR	RBI	BB	AVG
Sheckard lf	1	2	1	0	0	3	.333
Schulte rf	4	0	2	0	2	0	.333
Hofman cf	3	1	1	0	1	0	.222
Chance 1b	1	0	0	0	0	0	.222
Archer 1b	3	0	0	0	0	0	.000
Zimmerman 2b	4	0	0	0	0	0	.100
Steinfeldt 3b	4	0	0	0	0	0	.083
Tinker ss	4	1	3	0	0	0	.545
Kling c	4	0	0	0	0	0	.091
Reulbach p	0	0	0	0	0	0	.000
a-Beaumont ph	0	1	0	0	0	1	.000
McIntire p	0	0	0	0	0	0	.000
Pfiester p	2	0	0	0	0	0	.000
b-Needham ph	1	0	0	0	0	0	.000
TOTALS	**31**	**5**	**7**	**0**	**3**	**4**	**.200**

a - Batted for Reulbach in the 2nd
b - Batted for Pfiester in the 9th

BATTING: 2B: Schulte 2 (2, Coombs), Tinker (2, Coombs). **SF:** Hofman. **RBI:** Schulte 2 (2), Hofman 1 (1). **2-out RBI:** Schulte 2. **Runners left in scoring position, 2 out:** Hofman 2, Zimmerman 1, Needham 1. **GIDP:** Kling. **Team LOB:** 4 **BASERUNNING: SB:** Tinker (1, 2nd base off Coombs/Thomas). **FIELDING: E:** Tinker (1), Steinfeldt (2). **DP:** 1 (Zimmerman-Tinker-Archer).

PHILADELPHIA	IP	H	R	ER	BB	SO	HR	ERA
Coombs (W, 2-0)	9	7	5	5	4	8	0	4.00

CHICAGO CUBS	IP	H	R	ER	BB	SO	HR	ERA
Reulbach	2	3	3	3	2	0	0	13.50
McIntire (L, 0-1)	0.1	3	4	4	0	0	1	6.75
Pfiester	6.2	10	5	0	1	1	0	0.00

WP: Coombs 1. **HBP:** Davis (by McIntire). **Ground balls-fly balls:** Coombs 6-10, Reulbach 2-2, McIntire 0-1, Pfiester 13-6. **Batters faced:** Coombs 36, Reulbach 10, McIntire 5, Pfiester 31. **UMPIRES:** hp—O'Day, 1b—Sheridan, 2b—Rigler, 3b—Connolly **T:** 2:07 **A:** 26,210

GAME 4 Chicago 4 Philadelphia 3
West Side Park 10/22/10

PHILADELPHIA	AB	R	H	HR	RBI	BB	AVG
Strunk cf	5	0	2	0	1	0	.278
Lord lf	5	0	0	0	0	0	.167
Collins 2b	5	1	1	0	0	0	.375
Baker 3b	4	1	3	0	0	1	.529
Davis 1b	3	0	1	0	0	1	.429
Murphy rf	4	0	2	0	2	0	.375
Barry ss	4	0	0	0	0	0	.267
Thomas c	4	0	1	0	0	0	.250
Bender p	3	1	1	0	0	1	.333
TOTALS	**37**	**3**	**11**	**0**	**3**	**3**	**.340**

BATTING: 2B: Baker (3, Cole), Murphy (2, Cole), Davis (3, Brown). **3B:** Strunk (1, Cole). **S:** Davis, Murphy. **RBI:** Strunk 1 (2), Murphy 2 (8). **2-out RBI:** Strunk 1, Murphy 2. **Runners left in scoring position, 2 out:** Collins 1, Barry 1, Bender 2. **GIDP:** Strunk. **Team LOB:** 10 **BASERUNNING: SB:** Baker (3, 2nd base off Cole/Archer). **FIELDING: E:** Davis (1), Baker (1). **DP:** 2 (Baker-Collins-Davis, Bender-Baker-Davis).

CHICAGO CUBS	AB	R	H	HR	RBI	BB	AVG
Sheckard lf	4	1	1	0	1	1	.300
Schulte rf	4	2	3	0	0	0	.462
Hofman cf	3	0	2	0	1	0	.333
Chance 1b	4	0	2	0	2	0	.308
Zimmerman 2b	4	0	1	0	0	0	.143
Steinfeldt 3b	4	0	0	0	0	0	.063
Tinker ss	3	0	0	0	0	1	.429
Archer c	4	1	1	0	0	0	.143
Cole p	2	0	0	0	0	0	.000
a-Kling ph	1	0	0	0	0	0	.083
b-Kane pr	0	0	0	0	0	0	.000
Brown p	1	0	0	0	0	0	.000
TOTALS	**34**	**4**	**10**	**0**	**4**	**2**	**.226**

a - Batted for Cole in the 8th
b - Ran for Kling in the 8th

BATTING: 2B: Schulte (3, Bender), Archer (1, Bender). **3B:** Chance (1, Bender). **S:** Hofman. **RBI:** Sheckard 1 (1), Hofman 1 (2), Chance 2 (3). **2-out RBI:** Sheckard 1. **Runners left in scoring position, 2 out:** Steinfeldt 2. **GIDP:** Zimmerman. **Team LOB:** 4 **BASERUNNING: SB:** Sheckard (1, 2nd base off Bender/Thomas). **CS:** Tinker (2, 2nd base off Bender/Thomas), Schulte (3, 2nd base off Bender/Thomas), Zimmerman (1, 2nd base off Bender/Thomas). **FIELDING: E:** Brown (1). **Outfield assists:** Sheckard (2). **DP:** 1 (Cole-Archer-Chance).

PHILADELPHIA	IP	H	R	ER	BB	SO	HR	ERA
Bender (L, 1-1)	9.2	10	4	4	2	6	0	1.93

CHICAGO CUBS	IP	H	R	ER	BB	SO	HR	ERA
Cole	8	10	3	3	3	5	0	3.38
Brown (W, 1-1)	2	1	0	0	0	1	0	7.00

HBP: Barry (by Cole). **Ground balls-fly balls:** Bender 7-11, Cole 8-6, Brown 4-2. **Batters faced:** Bender 37, Cole 35, Brown 8. **UMPIRES:** hp—Connolly, 1b—Rigler, 2b—Sheridan, 3b—O'Day **T:** 2:14 **A:** 19,150

GAME 5 Philadelphia 7 Chicago 2
West Side Park 10/23/10

PHILADELPHIA	AB	R	H	HR	RBI	BB	AVG
Hartsel lf	5	2	1	0	0	0	.200
Lord cf	4	1	1	0	1	1	.182
Collins 2b	5	0	3	0	2	0	.429
Baker 3b	5	1	0	0	0	0	.409
Davis 1b	3	1	1	0	0	1	.353
Murphy rf	4	2	2	0	2	0	.400
Barry ss	2	0	0	0	0	1	.250
Lapp c	4	0	1	0	1	0	.250
Coombs p	4	0	1	0	0	0	.385
TOTALS	**36**	**7**	**9**	**0**	**6**	**3**	**.322**

BATTING: 2B: Murphy (3, Brown), Lord (2, Brown), Collins 2 (4, Brown). **S:** Barry. **RBI:** Lord 1 (1), Collins 2 (4), Murphy 2 (10), Lapp 1 (1). **2-out RBI:** Murphy 2. **Runners left in scoring position, 2 out:** Hartsel 1, Baker 2, Davis 1, Lapp 1. **Team LOB:** 6 **BASERUNNING: SB:** Hartsel 2 (2, 2nd base off Brown/Archer), Collins 2 (4, 2nd base off Brown/Archer, 3rd base off Brown/Archer). **FIELDING: E:** Baker (2).

CHICAGO CUBS	AB	R	H	HR	RBI	BB	AVG
Sheckard lf	4	1	2	0	0	0	.357
Schulte rf	4	0	1	0	0	0	.412
Hofman cf	3	0	0	0	0	1	.267
Chance 1b	4	1	2	0	1	0	.353
Zimmerman 2b	3	0	2	0	0	0	.235
Steinfeldt 3b	4	0	1	0	1	0	.100
Tinker ss	4	0	0	0	0	0	.333
Archer c	4	0	1	0	0	0	.182
Brown p	3	0	0	0	0	0	.000
a-Kling ph	1	0	0	0	0	0	.077
TOTALS	**34**	**2**	**9**	**0**	**2**	**1**	**.234**

a - Batted for Brown in the 9th

BATTING: 2B: Chance (1, Coombs), Sheckard (2, Coombs). **S:** Zimmerman. **RBI:** Chance 1 (4), Steinfeldt 1 (1). **2-out RBI:** Chance 1. **Runners left in scoring position, 2 out:** Steinfeldt 1, Archer 2. **Team LOB:** 7 **BASERUNNING: SB:** Zimmerman (1, 2nd base off Coombs/Lapp). **CS:** Schulte 2 (5, 2nd base off Coombs/Lapp). **FIELDING: E:** Steinfeldt (3), Zimmerman (1).

PHILADELPHIA	IP	H	R	ER	BB	SO	HR	ERA
Coombs (W, 3-0)	9	9	2	2	1	4	0	3.33

CHICAGO CUBS	IP	H	R	ER	BB	SO	HR	ERA
Brown (L, 1-2)	9	9	7	4	3	7	0	5.50

WP: Brown 1. **Ground balls-fly balls:** Coombs 13-8, Brown 14-6. **Batters faced:** Coombs 36, Brown 40. **UMPIRES:** hp—O'Day, 1b—Sheridan, 2b—Rigler, 3b—Connolly **T:** 2:06 **A:** 27,374

1911 PHILADELPHIA A's DEF. NY GIANTS, 4-2

GAME 1 New York 2 Philadelphia 1
Polo Grounds 10/14/11

PHILADELPHIA	AB	R	H	HR	RBI	BB	AVG
Lord lf	4	0	0	0	0	0	.000
Oldring cf	4	0	2	0	0	0	.500
Collins 2b	3	0	0	0	0	1	.000
Baker 3b	4	1	2	0	0	0	.500
Murphy rf	3	0	0	0	0	0	.000
Davis 1b	4	0	1	0	1	0	.250
Barry ss	3	0	0	0	0	0	.000
Thomas c	3	0	0	0	0	0	.000
Bender p	3	0	1	0	0	0	.333
TOTALS	**31**	**1**	**6**	**0**	**1**	**1**	**.194**

BATTING: 2B: Oldring 2 (2, Mathewson). **S:** Murphy. **RBI:** Davis 1 (1). **Runners left in scoring position, 2 out:** Collins 2, Baker 1, Thomas 1. **Team LOB:** 5 **BASERUNNING: CS:** Baker (1, 2nd base off Mathewson/Meyers). **FIELDING: E:** Collins (1).

NY GIANTS	AB	R	H	HR	RBI	BB	AVG
Devore lf	3	0	1	0	1	1	.333
Doyle 2b	3	0	1	0	0	1	.333
Snodgrass cf	2	1	0	0	0	1	.000
Murray rf	3	0	0	0	0	0	.000
Merkle 1b	4	0	1	0	0	0	.250
Herzog 3b	3	0	0	0	0	1	.000
Fletcher ss	4	0	0	0	0	0	.000
Meyers c	3	1	1	0	0	0	.333
Mathewson p	3	0	1	0	0	0	.333
TOTALS	**28**	**2**	**5**	**0**	**1**	**4**	**.179**

BATTING: 2B: Meyers (1, Bender), Devore (1, Bender). **S:** Murray, Snodgrass. **RBI:** Devore 1 (1). **2-out RBI:** Devore 1. **Runners left in scoring position, 2 out:** Snodgrass 1, Murray 1, Fletcher 1. **Team LOB:** 8 **BASERUNNING: SB:** Doyle (1, 2nd base off Bender/Thomas). **CS:** Snodgrass (1, 3rd base off Bender/Thomas). **FIELDING: PB:** Meyers.

PHILADELPHIA	IP	H	R	ER	BB	SO	HR	ERA
Bender (L, 0-1)	8	5	2	1	4	11	0	1.13

NY GIANTS	IP	H	R	ER	BB	SO	HR	ERA
Mathewson (W, 1-0)	9	6	1	1	1	5	0	1.00

HBP: Snodgrass (by Bender). **Ground balls-fly balls:** Bender 8-4, Mathewson 11-9. **Batters faced:** Bender 34, Mathewson 33. **UMPIRES:** hp—Klem, 1b—Dinneen, 2b—Brennan, 3b—Connolly **T:** 2:12 **A:** 38,281

GAME 2 Philadelphia 3 New York 1
Shibe Park 10/16/11

NY GIANTS	AB	R	H	HR	RBI	BB	AVG
Devore lf	4	0	0	0	0	0	.143
Doyle 2b	4	0	0	0	0	0	.143
Snodgrass cf	3	0	2	0	0	0	.400
Murray rf	4	0	0	0	0	0	.000
Merkle 1b	3	0	1	0	0	0	.286
Herzog 3b	3	1	1	0	0	0	.167
Fletcher ss	3	0	0	0	0	0	.000
Meyers c	3	0	1	0	1	0	.333
Marquard p	2	0	0	0	0	0	.000
a-Crandall ph-p	1	0	0	0	0	0	.000
TOTALS	**30**	**1**	**5**	**0**	**1**	**0**	**.172**

a - Batted for Marquard in the 8th

BATTING: 2B: Herzog (1, Plank). **RBI:** Meyers 1 (1). **2-out RBI:** Meyers 1. **Team LOB:** 3 **FIELDING: E:** Murray (1), Devore (1), Merkle (1).

PHILADELPHIA	AB	R	H	HR	RBI	BB	AVG
Lord lf	4	1	1	0	0	0	.125
Oldring cf	3	0	0	0	0	0	.286
Collins 2b	3	1	2	0	0	0	.333
Baker 3b	3	1	1	1	2	0	.429
Murphy rf	3	0	0	0	0	0	.000
Davis 1b	3	0	0	0	0	0	.143
Barry ss	3	0	0	0	0	0	.000
Thomas c	3	0	0	0	0	0	.000
Plank p	3	0	0	0	0	0	.000
TOTALS	**28**	**3**	**4**	**1**	**2**	**0**	**.169**

BATTING: 2B: Collins (1, Marquard). **HR:** Baker (1, 6th off Marquard 1 on, 2 out). **S:** Oldring. **RBI:** Baker 2 (2). **2-out RBI:** Baker 2. **Runners left in scoring position, 2 out:** Plank 1. **Team LOB:** 2 **Outfield assists:** Lord (1).

NY GIANTS	IP	H	R	ER	BB	SO	HR	ERA
Marquard (L, 0-1)	7	4	3	2	0	4	1	2.57
Crandall	1	0	0	0	0	2	0	0.00

PHILADELPHIA	IP	H	R	ER	BB	SO	HR	ERA
Plank (W, 1-0)	9	5	1	1	0	8	0	1.00

WP: Marquard 1. **HBP:** Snodgrass (by Plank). **Ground balls-fly balls:** Marquard 4-13, Crandall 1-0, Plank 9-8. **Batters faced:** Marquard 26, Crandall 3, Plank 31. **UMPIRES:** hp—Connolly, 1b—Brennan, 2b—Klem, 3b—Dineen **T:** 1:52 **A:** 26,286

GAME 3 Philadelphia 3 New York 2
Polo Grounds 10/17/11

PHILADELPHIA	AB	R	H	HR	RBI	BB	AVG
Lord lf	5	0	0	0	0	0	.077
Oldring cf	5	0	0	0	0	0	.167
Collins 2b	5	1	2	0	0	0	.364
Baker 3b	5	2	2	1	1	0	.417
Murphy rf	5	0	0	0	1	0	.200
Davis 1b	5	0	2	0	0	0	.250
Barry ss	3	0	2	0	0	0	.222
Lapp c	4	0	1	0	0	0	.250
Coombs p	4	0	0	0	0	0	.000
TOTALS	**41**	**3**	**9**	**1**	**3**	**0**	**.190**

BATTING: 2B: Barry (1, Mathewson). **HR:** Baker (2, 9th off Mathewson 0 on, 1 out). **S:** Barry. **RBI:** Baker 1 (3), Murphy 1 (1), Davis 1 (2). **Runners left in scoring position, 2 out:** Oldring 1, Baker 1, Barry 1, Coombs 1. **Team LOB:** 6 **BASERUNNING: SB:** Barry (1, 2nd base off Mathewson/Meyers), Collins (1, 2nd base off Mathewson/Meyers). **CS:** Davis (1, 2nd base off Mathewson/Meyers). **FIELDING: E:** Collins (2).

NY GIANTS	AB	R	H	HR	RBI	BB	AVG
Devore lf	4	0	0	0	1	0	.091
Doyle 2b	4	0	0	0	0	0	.091
Snodgrass cf	3	0	0	0	0	1	.250
Murray rf	2	0	0	0	0	1	.000
Merkle 1b	3	0	0	0	0	1	.200
Herzog 3b	3	1	1	0	0	1	.222
Fletcher ss	4	0	0	0	0	0	.000
Meyers c	4	1	1	0	0	0	.300
Mathewson p	3	0	1	0	0	0	.333
a-Becker ph	1	0	0	0	0	0	.000
TOTALS	**31**	**2**	**3**	**0**	**1**	**4**	**.146**

a - Batted for Mathewson in the 11th

BATTING: 2B: Herzog (2, Coombs). **S:** Murray. **RBI:** Devore 1 (2). **Team LOB:** 1 **BASERUNNING: CS:** Devore (1, 2nd base off Coombs/Lapp), Herzog (1, 2nd base off Coombs/Lapp), Merkle (1, 2nd base off Coombs/Lapp), Fletcher (1, 2nd base off Coombs/Lapp). **FIELDING: E:** Herzog 3 (3), Fletcher (1). **Outfield assists:** Murray (1). **DP:** 1 (Doyle-Fletcher).

PHILADELPHIA	IP	H	R	ER	BB	SO	HR	ERA
Coombs (W, 1-0)	11	3	2	1	4	7	0	0.82

NY GIANTS	IP	H	R	ER	BB	SO	HR	ERA
Mathewson (L, 1-1)	11	9	3	1	0	3	1	0.90

Ground balls-fly balls: Coombs 11-10, Mathewson 17-12. **Batters faced:** Coombs 36, Mathewson 42. **UMPIRES:** hp—Brennan, 1b—Connolly, 2b—Klem, 3b—Dinneen **T:** 2:25 **A:** 37,216

GAME 4 Philadelphia 4 New York 2
Shibe Park 10/24/11

NY GIANTS	AB	R	H	HR	RBI	BB	AVG
Devore lf	4	1	2	0	0	0	.200
Doyle 2b	3	1	1	0	1	1	.143
Snodgrass cf	3	0	0	0	1	0	.182
Murray rf	4	0	0	0	0	0	.000
Merkle 1b	4	0	1	0	0	0	.214
Herzog 3b	4	0	1	0	0	0	.154
Fletcher ss	4	0	2	0	0	0	.133
Meyers c	4	0	1	0	0	0	.286
Mathewson p	1	0	0	0	0	1	.286
a-Becker ph	1	0	0	0	0	0	.000
Wiltse p	0	0	0	0	0	0	.000
TOTALS	**32**	**2**	**7**	**0**	**2**	**2**	**.165**

a - Batted for Mathewson in the 8th

BATTING: 2B: Meyers (2, Bender), Merkle (1, Bender). **3B:** Doyle (1, Bender). **SF:** Snodgrass. **RBI:** Doyle 1 (1), Snodgrass 1 (1). **Runners left in scoring position, 2 out:** Murray 1, Meyers 1. **Team LOB:** 6 **FIELDING: E:** Mathewson (1), Fletcher (2), Murray (2).

PHILADELPHIA	AB	R	H	HR	RBI	BB	AVG
Lord lf	4	0	1	0	0	0	.118
Oldring cf	3	0	0	0	0	0	.133
Collins 2b	3	1	2	0	0	0	.429
Baker 3b	3	1	2	0	1	1	.467
Murphy rf	4	1	2	0	1	0	.133
Davis 1b	4	1	1	0	1	0	.250
Barry ss	4	0	3	0	0	0	.385
Thomas c	3	0	0	0	1	0	.000
Bender p	4	0	0	0	0	0	.143
TOTALS	**32**	**4**	**11**	**0**	**4**	**1**	**.227**

BATTING: 2B: Murphy 2 (2, Mathewson), Baker 2 (2, Mathewson), Davis (1, Mathewson), Barry 2 (3, Mathewson, Wiltse). **S:** Murphy, Oldring, Collins. **SF:** Thomas. **RBI:** Baker 1 (4), Murphy 1 (2), Davis 1 (3), Thomas 1 (1). **2-out RBI:** Baker 1. **Runners left in scoring position, 2 out:** Murphy 2, Bender 2. **Team LOB:** 8 **FIELDING: E:** Baker (1). **DP:** 1 (Baker-Davis).

NY GIANTS	IP	H	R	ER	BB	SO	HR	ERA
Mathewson (L, 1-2)	7	10	4	4	1	5	0	2.00
Wiltse	1	1	0	0	0	1	0	0.00

PHILADELPHIA	IP	H	R	ER	BB	SO	HR	ERA
Bender (W, 1-1)	9	7	2	2	2	4	0	1.59

IBB: Baker (by Mathewson). **Ground balls-fly balls:** Mathewson 12-1, Wiltse 2-0, Bender 11-10. **Batters faced:** Mathewson 32, Wiltse 4, Bender 35. **UMPIRES:** hp—Dinneen, 1b—Klem, 2b—Connolly, 3b—Brennan **T:** 1:49 **A:** 24,355

GAME 5 New York 4 Philadelphia 3
Polo Grounds 10/25/11

PHILADELPHIA	AB	R	H	HR	RBI	BB	AVG
Lord lf	5	0	0	0	0	0	.091
Oldring cf	5	1	2	1	3	0	.200
Collins 2b	3	0	0	0	0	1	.353
Baker 3b	4	0	0	0	0	0	.368
Murphy rf	4	0	1	0	0	0	.158
Davis 1b	4	0	0	0	0	0	.200
Barry ss	4	0	1	0	0	0	.353
Lapp c	4	1	1	0	0	0	.250
Coombs p	4	1	2	0	0	0	.250
a-Strunk pr	0	0	0	0	0	0	.000
Plank p	0	0	0	0	0	0	.000
TOTALS	**37**	**3**	**7**	**1**	**3**	**1**	**.219**

a - Ran for Coombs in the 10th

BATTING: HR: Oldring (1, 3th off Marquard 2 on, 2 out). **RBI:** Oldring 3 (3). **2-out RBI:** Oldring 3. **Runners left in scoring position, 2 out:** Baker 2, Coombs 1. **Team LOB:** 5 **BASERUNNING: SB:** Collins (2, 2nd base off Marquard/Meyers), Barry (2, 2nd base off Ames/Meyers). **CS:** Murphy (2, 2nd base off Marquard/Meyers), Barry (1, 2nd base off Crandall/Meyers). **FIELDING: DP:** 1 (Lapp-Collins).

NY GIANTS	AB	R	H	HR	RBI	BB	AVG
Devore lf	5	0	1	0	1	0	.200
Doyle 2b	5	1	4	0	0	0	.316
Snodgrass cf	4	0	0	0	0	0	.133
Murray rf	5	0	0	0	0	0	.000
Merkle 1b	2	1	0	0	1	1	.188
Herzog 3b	4	0	1	0	0	0	.176
Fletcher ss	4	1	1	0	0	0	.158
Meyers c	3	0	1	0	1	0	.294
Marquard p	0	0	0	0	0	0	.000
a-Becker ph	1	0	0	0	0	0	.000
Ames p	1	0	0	0	0	0	.000
b-Crandall ph-p	1	1	1	0	1	1	.500
TOTALS	**35**	**4**	**9**	**0**	**4**	**2**	**.186**

a - Batted for Marquard in the 3th
b - Batted for Ames in the 7th

BATTING: 2B: Doyle 2 (2, Coombs, Plank), Fletcher (1, Coombs), Crandall (1, Coombs). **S:** Snodgrass. **SF:** Meyers, Merkle. **RBI:** Devore 1 (3), Merkle 1 (1), Meyers 1 (2), Crandall 1 (1). **2-out RBI:** Devore 1, Crandall 1. **Runners left in scoring position, 2 out:** Devore 1, Murray 1, Merkle 1, Herzog 1, Fletcher 1. **Team LOB:** 8 **BASERUNNING: SB:** Herzog (1, 2nd base off Coombs/Lapp), Doyle (2, 2nd base off Coombs/Lapp). **CS:** Meyers (1, 2nd base off Coombs/Lapp), Devore (2, 2nd base off Coombs/Lapp). **FIELDING: E:** Fletcher (3). **DP:** 1 (Meyers-Doyle).

PHILADELPHIA	IP	H	R	ER	BB	SO	HR	ERA
Coombs	9	8	3	2	2	9	0	1.35
Plank (L, 1-1)	0.2	1	1	1	0	0	0	1.86

NY GIANTS	IP	H	R	ER	BB	SO	HR	ERA
Marquard	3	3	3	0	1	2	1	1.80
Ames	4	2	0	0	0	2	0	0.00
Crandall (W, 1-0)	3	2	0	0	0	0	0	0.00

WP: Crandall 1. **HBP:** Merkle (by Coombs). **Ground balls-fly balls:** Coombs 9-6, Plank 1-1, Marquard 4-3, Ames 7-3, Crandall 4-5. **Batters faced:** Coombs 37, Plank 4, Marquard 13, Ames 14, Crandall 11. **UMPIRES:** hp—Klem, 1b—Dinneen, 2b—Connolly, 3b—Brennan **T:** 2:33 **A:** 33,228

GAME 6 Philadelphia 13 New York 2
Shibe Park 10/26/11

NY GIANTS	AB	R	H	HR	RBI	BB	AVG
Devore lf	4	0	0	0	0	0	.167
Doyle 2b	4	1	1	0	0	0	.304
Snodgrass cf	4	0	0	0	0	0	.105
Murray rf	3	0	0	0	0	1	.000
Merkle 1b	4	0	0	0	0	0	.150
Herzog 3b	4	1	1	0	0	0	.190
Fletcher ss	4	0	0	0	1	0	.130
Meyers c	3	0	1	0	0	0	.300
Wilson c	1	0	0	0	0	0	.000
Ames p	1	0	1	0	0	0	.500
a-Crandall ph	0	0	0	0	0	1	.500
Wiltse p	1	0	0	0	0	0	.000
Marquard p	0	0	0	0	0	0	.000
TOTALS	**33**	**2**	**4**	**0**	**1**	**2**	**.175**

a - Batted for Ames in the 5th

BATTING: 2B: Doyle (3, Bender). **RBI:** Fletcher 1 (1). **Runners left in scoring position, 2 out:** Devore 1, Meyers 1. **Team LOB:** 6 **BASERUNNING: SB:** Herzog (2, 3rd base off Bender/Thomas). **CS:** Devore (3, 2nd base off Bender/Thomas). **FIELDING: E:** Ames (1).

PHILADELPHIA	AB	R	H	HR	RBI	BB	AVG
Lord lf	5	1	3	0	1	0	.185
Oldring cf	5	1	1	0	0	0	.200
Collins 2b	4	1	0	0	1	0	.286
Baker 3b	5	2	2	0	1	0	.375
Murphy rf	4	3	4	0	1	0	.304
Davis 1b	4	2	1	0	2	0	.208
McInnis 1b	0	0	0	0	0	0	.000
Barry ss	2	2	1	0	5	0	.368
Thomas c	3	1	1	0	0	1	.083
Bender p	4	0	0	0	0	0	.091
TOTALS	**36**	**13**	**13**	**0**	**11**	**1**	**.244**

BATTING: 2B: Lord 2 (2, Ames, Marquard), Murphy (3, Wiltse), Barry (4, Wiltse). **S:** Barry, Collins. **SF:** Barry. **RBI:** Lord 1 (1), Collins 1 (1), Baker 1 (5), Murphy 1 (3), Davis 2 (5), Barry 5 (5). **Runners left in scoring position, 2 out:** Collins 1, Baker 1, Barry 1. **Team LOB:** 3 **BASERUNNING: CS:** Thomas (1, 2nd base off Marquard/Meyers). **FIELDING: E:** Murphy (1), Barry 3 (3), Oldring (1).

NY GIANTS	IP	H	R	ER	BB	SO	HR	ERA
Ames (L, 0-1)	4	4	5	2	1	4	0	2.25
Wiltse	2.1	7	8	7	0	1	0	18.90
Marquard	1.2	2	0	0	0	2	0	1.54

PHILADELPHIA	IP	H	R	ER	BB	SO	HR	ERA
Bender (W, 2-1)	9	4	2	0	2	5	0	1.04

WP: Marquard 1, Bender 1. **Ground balls-fly balls:** Ames 6-3, Wiltse 3-2, Marquard 1-1, Bender 13-11. **Batters faced:** Ames 19, Wiltse 15, Marquard 6, Bender 35. **UMPIRES:** hp—Connolly, 1b—Brennan, 2b—Klem, 3b—Dinneen **T:** 2:12 **A:** 20,485

1912 BOSTON RED SOX DEF. NY GIANTS, 4-3

GAME 1 Boston 4 New York 3
Polo Grounds 10/08/12

BOSTON	AB	R	H	HR	RBI	BB	AVG
Hooper rf	3	1	1	0	1	1	.333
Yerkes 2b	4	0	1	0	2	0	.250
Speaker cf	3	1	1	0	0	1	.333
Lewis lf	4	0	0	0	1	0	.000
Gardner 3b	4	0	0	0	0	0	.000
Stahl 1b	4	0	0	0	0	0	.000
Wagner ss	3	1	2	0	0	1	.667
Cady c	3	0	1	0	0	0	.333
Wood p	3	1	0	0	0	0	.000
TOTALS	**31**	**4**	**6**	**0**	**4**	**4**	**.194**

BATTING: 2B: Hooper (1, Tesreau), Wagner (1, Crandall). **3B:** Speaker (1, Tesreau). **S:** Hooper, Cady. **RBI:** Hooper 1 (1), Yerkes 2 (2), Lewis 1 (1). **2-out RBI:** Hooper 1, Yerkes 2. **Runners left in scoring position, 2 out:** Hooper 1, Lewis 2. **Team LOB:** 6 **BASERUNNING: CS:** Stahl (1, 2nd base off Tesreau/Meyers). **FIELDING: E:** Wagner (1). **Outfield assists:** Speaker (1). **DP:** 1 (Stahl-Wood).

NY GIANTS	AB	R	H	HR	RBI	BB	AVG
Devore rf	3	1	0	0	0	1	.000
Doyle 2b	4	1	2	0	0	0	.500
Snodgrass cf	4	0	1	0	0	0	.250
Murray lf	3	0	1	0	2	1	.333
Merkle 1b	4	1	1	0	0	0	.250
Herzog 3b	4	0	2	0	0	0	.500
Meyers c	3	0	1	0	1	0	.333
b-Becker pr	0	0	0	0	0	0	.000
Fletcher ss	4	0	0	0	0	0	.000
Tesreau p	2	0	0	0	0	0	.000
a-McCormick ph	1	0	0	0	0	0	.000
Crandall p	1	0	0	0	0	0	.000
TOTALS	**33**	**3**	**8**	**0**	**3**	**2**	**.242**

a - Batted for Tesreau in the 7th
b - Ran for Meyers in the 9th

BATTING: 2B: Doyle (1, Wood). **RBI:** Murray 2 (2), Meyers 1 (1). **2-out RBI:** Murray 2. **Runners left in scoring position, 2 out:** Murray 2, Merkle 1, Fletcher 1, Crandall 2. **Team LOB:** 6 **FIELDING: E:** Fletcher (1).

BOSTON	IP	H	R	ER	BB	SO	HR	ERA
Wood (W, 1-0)	9	8	3	3	2	11	0	3.00

NY GIANTS	IP	H	R	ER	BB	SO	HR	ERA
Tesreau (L, 0-1)	7	5	4	4	4	4	0	5.14
Crandall	2	1	0	0	0	2	0	0.00

HBP: Meyers (by Wood). **Ground balls-fly balls:** Wood 6-8, Tesreau 10-6, Crandall 2-1. **Batters faced:** Wood 36, Tesreau 30, Crandall 7. **UMPIRES:** hp—Klem, 1b—Evans, 2b—Rigler, 3b—O'Loughlin **T:** 2:10 **A:** 35,730

GAME 2 New York 6 Boston 6
Fenway Park 10/09/12

NY GIANTS	AB	R	H	HR	RBI	BB	AVG
Snodgrass lf-rf	4	1	1	0	0	1	.250
Doyle 2b	5	0	1	0	0	1	.333
Becker cf	4	1	0	0	0	2	.000
Murray rf-lf	5	2	3	0	1	0	.500
Merkle 1b	5	1	1	0	0	0	.222
Herzog 3b	4	1	3	0	3	0	.625
Meyers c	4	0	2	0	1	1	.429
a-Shafer pr-ss	0	0	0	0	0	0	.000
Fletcher ss	4	0	0	0	0	0	.000
b-McCormick ph	1	0	0	0	1	0	.000
Wilson c	0	0	0	0	0	0	.000
Mathewson p	5	0	0	0	0	0	.000
TOTALS	**40**	**6**	**11**	**0**	**6**	**5**	**.260**

a - Ran for Meyers in the 10th
b - Batted for Fletcher in the 10th

BATTING: 2B: Snodgrass (1, Collins), Murray (1, Collins), Herzog (1, Hall). **3B:** Herzog (1, Collins), Murray (1, Collins), Merkle (1, Hall). **SF:** Herzog, McCormick. **RBI:** Murray 1 (3), Herzog 3 (3), Meyers 1 (2), McCormick 1 (1). **2-out RBI:** Herzog 2. **Runners left in scoring position, 2 out:** Murray 3, Meyers 1, Mathewson 1. **Team LOB:** 9 **BASERUNNING: SB:** Herzog (1, 2nd base off Collins/Carrigan), Snodgrass (1, 2nd base off Hall/Carrigan). **CS:** Murray (1, 2nd base off Collins/Carrigan), Snodgrass (1, 2nd base off Bedient/Carrigan), Becker (1, 2nd base off Bedient/Carrigan). **FIELDING: E:** Fletcher 3 ((3, 4). **DP:** 1 (Fletcher-Herzog).

BOSTON	AB	R	H	HR	RBI	BB	AVG
Hooper rf	5	1	3	0	0	0	.500
Yerkes 2b	5	1	1	0	1	0	.222
Speaker cf	5	2	2	0	1	0	.375
Lewis lf	5	2	2	0	0	0	.222
Gardner 3b	4	0	0	0	0	0	.000
Stahl 1b	5	0	2	0	2	0	.222
Wagner ss	5	0	0	0	0	0	.250
Carrigan c	5	0	0	0	0	0	.000
Collins p	3	0	0	0	0	0	.000
Hall p	1	0	0	0	0	0	.000
Bedient p	1	0	0	0	0	0	.000
TOTALS	**44**	**6**	**10**	**0**	**5**	**0**	**.213**

BATTING: 2B: Hooper (2, Mathewson), Lewis 2 (2, Mathewson). **3B:** Yerkes (1, Mathewson), Speaker (2, Mathewson). **S:** Gardner. **RBI:** Yerkes 1 (3), Speaker 1 (1), Gardner 1 (1), Stahl 2 (2). **2-out RBI:** Stahl 2. **Runners left in scoring position, 2 out:** Yerkes 1, Stahl 1, Wagner 3. **Team LOB:** 6 **BASERUNNING: SB:** Hooper 2 (2, 2nd base off Mathewson/Meyers), Stahl (1, 2nd base off Mathewson/Meyers). **FIELDING: E:** Lewis (1).

NY GIANTS	IP	H	R	ER	BB	SO	HR	ERA
Mathewson	11	10	6	1	0	4	0	0.82

BOSTON	IP	H	R	ER	BB	SO	HR	ERA
Collins	7.1	9	5	2	0	5	0	2.45
Hall	2.2	2	1	1	4	0	0	3.38
Bedient	1	0	0	0	1	1	0	0.00

IBB: Doyle (by Hall). **HBP:** Snodgrass (by Bedient). **Ground balls-fly balls:** Mathewson 22-8, Collins 7-9, Hall 4-3, Bedient 0-0. **Batters faced:** Mathewson 45, Collins 31, Hall 14, Bedient 3. **UMPIRES:** hp—O'Loughlin, 1b—Rigler, 2b—Klem, 3b—Evans **T:** 2:38 **A:** 30,148

GAME 3 New York 2 Boston 1
Fenway Park 10/10/12

NY GIANTS	AB	R	H	HR	RBI	BB	AVG
Devore rf	4	0	2	0	0	0	.286
Doyle 2b	3	0	0	0	0	1	.250
Snodgrass cf	4	0	1	0	0	0	.250
Murray lf	4	1	1	0	0	0	.417
Merkle 1b	3	0	0	0	0	0	.167
Herzog 3b	2	1	1	0	1	0	.600
Meyers c	4	0	1	0	0	0	.364
Fletcher ss	3	0	1	0	1	1	.091
Marquard p	1	0	0	0	0	1	.000
TOTALS	**28**	**2**	**7**	**0**	**2**	**3**	**.257**

BATTING: 2B: Murray (2, O'Brien), Herzog (2, O'Brien). **S:** Merkle, Marquard. **SF:** Herzog. **RBI:** Herzog 1 (4), Fletcher 1 (1). **Runners left in scoring position, 2 out:** Doyle 1, Snodgrass 2, Merkle 1. **Team LOB:** 6 **BASERUNNING: SB:** Fletcher (1, 2nd base off O'Brien/Carrigan), Devore (1, 2nd base off O'Brien/Carrigan), Herzog (1, 2nd base off O'Brien/Carrigan). **CS:** Devore (1, 2nd base off Bedient/Cady).

BOSTON	AB	R	H	HR	RBI	BB	AVG
Hooper rf	3	0	0	0	0	1	.364
Yerkes 2b	4	0	1	0	0	0	.231
Speaker cf	4	0	1	0	0	0	.333
Lewis lf	4	1	2	0	0	0	.308
Gardner 3b	3	0	1	0	1	0	.091
Stahl 1b	4	0	2	0	0	0	.308
c-Henriksen pr	0	0	0	0	0	0	.000
Wagner ss	4	0	0	0	0	0	.167
Carrigan c	2	0	0	0	0	0	.000
a-Engle ph	1	0	0	0	0	0	.000
Cady c	1	0	0	0	0	0	.000
O'Brien p	2	0	0	0	0	0	.000
b-Ball ph	1	0	0	0	0	0	.000
Bedient p	0	0	0	0	0	0	.000
TOTALS	**33**	**1**	**7**	**0**	**1**	**1**	**.213**

a - Batted for Carrigan in the 8th
b - Batted for O'Brien in the 8th
c - Ran for Stahl in the 9th

BATTING: 2B: Stahl (1, Marquard), Gardner (1, Marquard). **S:** Gardner. **RBI:** Gardner 1 (2). **Runners left in scoring position, 2 out:** Wagner 2, Cady 2. **Team LOB:** 7 **BASERUNNING: SB:** Wagner (1, 2nd base off Marquard/Meyers). **FIELDING: Outfield assists:** Speaker (2). **DP:** 1 (Speaker-Stahl).

NY GIANTS	IP	H	R	ER	BB	SO	HR	ERA
Marquard (W, 1-0)	9	7	1	1	1	6	0	1.00

BOSTON	IP	H	R	ER	BB	SO	HR	ERA
O'Brien (L, 0-1)	8	6	2	2	3	3	0	2.25
Bedient	1	1	0	0	0	0	0	0.00

HBP: Herzog (by Bedient). **Ground balls-fly balls:** Marquard 7-13, O'Brien 10-7, Bedient 0-1. **Batters faced:** Marquard 35, O'Brien 32, Bedient 3. **UMPIRES:** hp—Evans, 1b—Klem, lf—O'Loughlin, rf—Rigler **T:** 2:15 **A:** 34,624

GAME 4 Boston 3 New York 1
Polo Grounds 10/11/12

BOSTON	AB	R	H	HR	RBI	BB	AVG
Hooper rf	4	0	1	0	0	1	.333
Yerkes 2b	3	0	1	0	0	0	.250
Speaker cf	4	0	1	0	0	0	.313
Lewis lf	4	0	0	0	0	0	.235
Gardner 3b	3	2	2	0	0	1	.214
Stahl 1b	3	1	0	0	0	0	.250
Wagner ss	3	0	0	0	0	1	.133
Cady c	4	0	1	0	1	0	.250
Wood p	4	0	2	0	1	0	.286
TOTALS	**32**	**3**	**8**	**0**	**2**	**3**	**.221**

BATTING: 2B: Speaker (1, Ames). **3B:** Gardner (1, Tesreau). **S:** Yerkes, Stahl. **RBI:** Cady 1 (1), Wood 1 (1). **2-out RBI:** Cady 1, Wood 1. **Runners left in scoring position, 2 out:** Hooper 1, Lewis 4. **GIDP:** Speaker. **Team LOB:** 7 **BASERUNNING: SB:** Stahl (2, 2nd base off Tesreau/Meyers). **CS:** Speaker (1, 2nd base off Tesreau/Meyers). **FIELDING: E:** Wagner (2).

NY GIANTS	AB	R	H	HR	RBI	BB	AVG
Devore lf	4	0	1	0	0	0	.273
Doyle 2b	4	0	1	0	0	0	.250
Snodgrass cf	4	0	0	0	0	0	.188
Murray rf	4	0	1	0	0	0	.375
Merkle 1b	4	0	1	0	0	0	.188
Herzog 3b	4	1	2	0	0	0	.571
Meyers c	4	0	0	0	0	0	.267
Fletcher ss	4	0	1	0	1	0	.133
Tesreau p	2	0	1	0	0	0	.250
a-McCormick ph	1	0	1	0	0	0	.500
Ames p	0	0	0	0	0	0	.000
TOTALS	**35**	**1**	**9**	**0**	**1**	**0**	**.257**

a - Batted for Tesreau in the 7th

BATTING: 2B: Fletcher (1, Wood). **RBI:** Fletcher 1 (2). **2-out RBI:** Fletcher 1. **Runners left in scoring position, 2 out:** Murray 1, Merkle 1, Meyers 1, McCormick 1. **Team LOB:** 7 **BASERUNNING: SB:** Merkle (1, 2nd base off Wood/Cady). **FIELDING: E:** Meyers (1). **DP:** 1 (Fletcher-Merkle).

BOSTON	IP	H	R	ER	BB	SO	HR	ERA
Wood (W, 2-0)	9	9	1	1	0	8	0	2.00

NY GIANTS	IP	H	R	ER	BB	SO	HR	ERA
Tesreau (L, 0-2)	7	5	2	2	2	5	0	3.86
Ames	2	3	1	1	1	0	0	4.50

WP: Tesreau 1. **Ground balls-fly balls:** Wood 11-7, Tesreau 8-6, Ames 3-2. **Batters faced:** Wood 35, Tesreau 27, Ames 10. **UMPIRES:** hp—Rigler, 1b—O'Loughlin, 2b—Evans, 3b—Klem **T:** 2:06 **A:** 36,502

GAME 5 Boston 2 New York 1
Fenway Park 10/12/12

NY GIANTS	AB	R	H	HR	RBI	BB	AVG
Devore lf	2	0	0	0	0	2	.231
Doyle 2b	4	0	0	0	0	0	.200
Snodgrass cf	4	0	0	0	0	0	.150
Murray rf	3	0	0	0	0	1	.316
Merkle 1b	4	1	1	0	0	0	.200
Herzog 3b	4	0	0	0	0	0	.444
Meyers c	3	0	1	0	0	0	.278
Fletcher ss	2	0	0	0	0	0	.118
a-McCormick ph	1	0	0	0	0	0	.333
Shafer ss	0	0	0	0	0	0	.000
Mathewson p	3	0	1	0	0	0	.125
TOTALS	**30**	**1**	**3**	**0**	**0**	**3**	**.229**

a - Batted for Fletcher in the 7th

BATTING: 2B: Merkle (1, Bedient). **Runners left in scoring position, 2 out:** Snodgrass 1, Meyers 1. **GIDP:** Snodgrass. **Team LOB:** 5 **FIELDING: E:** Doyle (1).

BOSTON	AB	R	H	HR	RBI	BB	AVG
Hooper rf	4	1	2	0	0	0	.368
Yerkes 2b	4	1	1	0	1	0	.250
Speaker cf	3	0	1	0	1	0	.316
Lewis lf	3	0	0	0	0	0	.200
Gardner 3b	3	0	0	0	0	0	.176
Stahl 1b	3	0	0	0	0	0	.211
Wagner ss	3	0	1	0	0	0	.167
Cady c	3	0	0	0	0	0	.182
Bedient p	3	0	0	0	0	0	.000
TOTALS	**29**	**2**	**5**	**0**	**2**	**0**	**.213**

BATTING: 3B: Hooper (1, Mathewson), Yerkes (2, Mathewson). **RBI:** Yerkes 1 (4), Speaker 1 (2). **Runners left in scoring position, 2 out:** Gardner 1, Bedient 1. **Team LOB:** 3 **FIELDING: E:** Gardner (1). **DP:** 1 (Wagner-Yerkes-Stahl).

NY GIANTS	IP	H	R	ER	BB	SO	HR	ERA
Mathewson (L, 0-1)	8	5	2	2	0	2	0	1.42

BOSTON	IP	H	R	ER	BB	SO	HR	ERA
Bedient (W, 1-0)	9	3	1	0	3	4	0	0.00

Ground balls-fly balls: Mathewson 16-6, Bedient 7-16. **Batters faced:** Mathewson 29, Bedient 33. **UMPIRES:** hp—O'Loughlin, 1b—Rigler, 2b—Klem, 3b—Evans **T:** 1:43 **A:** 34,683

GAME 6 New York 5 Boston 2
Polo Grounds 10/14/12

BOSTON	AB	R	H	HR	RBI	BB	AVG
Hooper rf	4	0	1	0	0	0	.348
Yerkes 2b	4	0	2	0	0	0	.292
Speaker cf	3	0	0	0	0	1	.273
Lewis lf	4	0	0	0	0	0	.167
Gardner 3b	4	1	0	0	0	0	.143
Stahl 1b	4	1	2	0	0	0	.261
Wagner ss	4	0	0	0	0	0	.136
Cady c	3	0	1	0	0	0	.214
O'Brien p	0	0	0	0	0	0	.000
a-Engle ph	1	0	1	0	2	0	.500
Collins p	2	0	0	0	0	0	.000
TOTALS	**33**	**2**	**7**	**0**	**2**	**1**	**.213**

a - Batted for O'Brien in the 2nd

BATTING: 2B: Engle (1, Marquard). **RBI:** Engle 2 (2). **2-out RBI:** Engle 2. **Runners left in scoring position, 2 out:** Hooper 1, Lewis 1. **GIDP:** Collins. **Team LOB:** 5 **BASERUNNING: SB:** Speaker (1, 2nd base off Marquard/Meyers). **FIELDING: E:** Yerkes (1), Cady (1). **Outfield assists:** Hooper 2 (2). **DP:** 1 (Hooper-Stahl).

NY GIANTS	AB	R	H	HR	RBI	BB	AVG
Devore lf	4	0	1	0	0	0	.235
Doyle 2b	4	1	1	0	0	0	.208
Snodgrass cf	4	0	1	0	0	0	.167
Murray rf	3	1	2	0	0	0	.364
Merkle 1b	3	1	2	0	1	0	.261
Herzog 3b	3	1	1	0	1	0	.429
Meyers c	3	1	2	0	0	0	.333
Fletcher ss	3	0	1	0	1	0	.150
Marquard p	3	0	0	0	0	0	.000
TOTALS	**30**	**5**	**11**	**0**	**3**	**0**	**.250**

BATTING: 2B: Merkle (2, O'Brien), Herzog (3, O'Brien). **3B:** Meyers (1, Collins). **RBI:** Merkle 1 (1), Herzog 1 (5), Fletcher 1 (3). **2-out RBI:** Merkle 1, Herzog 1, Fletcher 1. **Runners left in scoring position, 2 out:** Marquard 1. **Team LOB:** 1 **BASERUNNING: SB:** Doyle (1, 2nd base off O'Brien/Cady), Herzog (2, home off O'Brien/Cady), Meyers (1, home off O'Brien/Cady). **CS:** Merkle (1, 2nd base off Collins/Cady), Snodgrass (2, 2nd base off Collins/Cady). **FIELDING: E:** Marquard (1). **DP:** 1 (Fletcher-Doyle-Merkle).

BOSTON	IP	H	R	ER	BB	SO	HR	ERA
O'Brien (L, 0-2)	1	6	5	3	0	1	0	5.00
Collins	7	5	0	0	0	1	0	1.26

NY GIANTS	IP	H	R	ER	BB	SO	HR	ERA
Marquard (W, 2-0)	9	7	2	0	1	3	0	0.50

BK: O'Brien 1. **Ground balls-fly balls:** O'Brien 1-0, Collins 3-13, Marquard 4-19. **Batters faced:** O'Brien 8, Collins 22, Marquard 34. **UMPIRES:** hp—Klem , 1b—Evans, 2b—O'Loughlin, 3b—Rigler **T:** 1:58 **A:** 30,622

GAME 7 New York 11 Boston 4
Fenway Park 10/15/12

NY GIANTS	AB	R	H	HR	RBI	BB	AVG
Devore rf	4	2	1	0	0	2	.238
Doyle 2b	4	3	3	1	2	1	.286
Snodgrass cf	5	1	2	0	2	0	.207
Murray lf	4	0	0	0	0	0	.308
Merkle 1b	5	1	2	0	1	0	.286
Herzog 3b	4	2	1	0	0	1	.400
Meyers c	4	1	3	0	1	0	.400
Wilson c	1	0	1	0	1	0	1.000
Fletcher ss	5	1	1	0	0	0	.160
Tesreau p	4	0	2	0	2	1	.375
TOTALS	**40**	**11**	**16**	**1**	**9**	**5**	**.275**

BATTING: 2B: Snodgrass (2, Wood). **HR:** Doyle (1, 6th off Hall 1 on, 1 out). **S:** Murray. **RBI:** Doyle 2 (2), Snodgrass 2 (2), Merkle 1 (2), Meyers 1 (3), Wilson 1 (1), Tesreau 2 (2). **2-out RBI:** Meyers 1, Tesreau 2. **Runners left in scoring position, 2 out:** Devore 3, Merkle 2. **Team LOB:** 8 **BASERUNNING: SB:** Devore 2 (3, 3rd base off Wood/Cady, 2nd base off Hall/Cady), Doyle (2, 3rd base off Wood/Cady). **CS:** Tesreau (1, 2nd base off Wood/Cady). **FIELDING: E:** Merkle (1), Doyle 2 (3), Devore (1). **Outfield assists:** Devore (1). **DP:** 1 (Devore-Meyers).

BOSTON	AB	R	H	HR	RBI	BB	AVG
Hooper rf	3	0	1	0	1	1	.346
Yerkes 2b	4	0	0	0	0	1	.250
Speaker cf	4	1	1	0	0	1	.269
Lewis lf	4	1	1	0	0	1	.179
Gardner 3b	4	1	1	1	2	0	.160
Stahl 1b	5	0	1	0	0	0	.250
Wagner ss	5	0	1	0	0	0	.148
Cady c	4	1	0	0	0	0	.167
Wood p	0	0	0	0	0	0	.286
Hall p	3	0	3	0	0	1	.750
TOTALS	**36**	**4**	**9**	**1**	**3**	**5**	**.218**

BATTING: 2B: Hall (1, Tesreau), Lewis (3, Tesreau). **HR:** Gardner (1, 2nd off Tesreau 0 on, 0 out). **SF:** Hooper. **RBI:** Hooper 1 (2), Gardner 2 (4). **Runners left in scoring position, 2 out:** Hooper 1, Speaker 1, Gardner 2, Cady 1. **Team LOB:** 12 **FIELDING: E:** Hall (1), Speaker (1). **Outfield assists:** Hooper (3). **DP:** 1 (Speaker).

NY GIANTS	IP	H	R	ER	BB	SO	HR	ERA
Tesreau (W, 1-2)	9	9	4	2	5	6	1	3.13

BOSTON	IP	H	R	ER	BB	SO	HR	ERA
Wood (L, 2-1)	1	7	6	4	0	0	0	3.79
Hall	8	9	5	3	5	1	1	3.38

WP: Tesreau 2. **HBP:** Gardner (by Tesreau). **Ground balls-fly balls:** Tesreau 14-7, Wood 1-0, Hall 13-9. **Batters faced:** Tesreau 43, Wood 9, Hall 37. **UMPIRES:** hp—Evans, 1b—Klem, 2b—O'Loughlin, 3b—Rigler **T:** 2:21 **A:** 32,694

GAME 8 Boston 3 New York 2
Fenway Park 10/16/12

NY GIANTS	AB	R	H	HR	RBI	BB	AVG
Devore rf	3	1	1	0	0	2	.250
Doyle 2b	5	0	0	0	0	0	.242
Snodgrass cf	4	0	1	0	0	1	.212
Murray lf	5	1	2	0	1	0	.323
Merkle 1b	5	0	1	0	1	0	.273
Herzog 3b	5	0	2	0	0	0	.400
Meyers c	3	0	0	0	0	1	.357
Fletcher ss	3	0	1	0	0	0	.179
a-McCormick ph	1	0	0	0	0	0	.250
Shafer ss	0	0	0	0	0	0	.000
Mathewson p	4	0	1	0	0	0	.167
TOTALS	**38**	**2**	**9**	**0**	**2**	**4**	**.270**

a - Batted for Fletcher in the 9th

BATTING: 2B: Murray 2 (4, Bedient, Wood), Herzog (4, Bedient). **S:** Meyers. **RBI:** Murray 1 (4), Merkle 1 (3). **2-out RBI:** Murray 1. **Runners left in scoring position, 2 out:** Snodgrass 1, Murray 1, Merkle 1, Meyers 1, Mathewson 3. **Team LOB:** 11 **BASERUNNING: SB:** Devore (4, 2nd base off Bedient/Cady). **CS:** Snodgrass (3, 2nd base off Bedient/Cady), Meyers (1, 3rd base off Bedient/Cady), Devore (2, 2nd base off Bedient/Cady). **FIELDING: E:** Snodgrass (1). **Outfield assists:** Devore (2), Snodgrass (1).

BOSTON	AB	R	H	HR	RBI	BB	AVG
Hooper rf	5	0	0	0	0	0	.290
Yerkes 2b	4	1	1	0	0	1	.250
Speaker cf	4	0	2	0	1	1	.300
Lewis lf	4	0	0	0	0	1	.156
Gardner 3b	3	0	1	0	1	1	.179
Stahl 1b	4	1	2	0	0	0	.281
Wagner ss	3	0	1	0	0	1	.167
Cady c	4	0	0	0	0	0	.136
Bedient p	2	0	0	0	0	0	.000
a-Henriksen ph	1	0	1	0	1	0	1.000
Wood p	0	0	0	0	0	0	.286
b-Engle ph	1	1	0	0	0	0	.333
TOTALS	**35**	**3**	**8**	**0**	**3**	**5**	**.220**

a - Batted for Bedient in the 7th
b - Batted for Wood in the 10th

BATTING: 2B: Gardner (2, Mathewson), Henriksen (1, Mathewson), Stahl (2, Mathewson). **SF:** Gardner. **RBI:** Speaker 1 (3), Gardner 1 (5), Henriksen 1 (1). **2-out RBI:** Henriksen 1. **Runners left in scoring position, 2 out:** Hooper 2, Lewis 1, Stahl 1, Cady 1, Bedient 1. **Team LOB:** 9 **FIELDING: E:** Gardner (2), Speaker (2).

NY GIANTS	IP	H	R	ER	BB	SO	HR	ERA
Mathewson (L, 0-2)	9.2	8	3	1	5	4	0	1.26

BOSTON	IP	H	R	ER	BB	SO	HR	ERA
Bedient	7	6	1	1	3	2	0	0.50
Wood (W, 3-1)	3	3	1	1	1	2	0	3.68

IBB: Lewis (by Mathewson). **Ground balls-fly balls:** Mathewson 8-15, Bedient 10-8, Wood 6-1. **Batters faced:** Mathewson 41, Bedient 30, Wood 13. **UMPIRES:** hp—O'Loughlin, 1b—Rigler, 2b—Klem, 3b—Evans **T:** 2:37 **A:** 17,034

1913 PHILADELPHIA A's DEF. NY GIANTS, 4-1

GAME 1 Philadelphia 6 New York 3
Polo Grounds 10/07/13

PHILADELPHIA	AB	R	H	HR	RBI	BB	AVG
Murphy rf	4	0	1	0	0	1	.250
Oldring lf	4	0	1	0	0	0	.250
Collins 2b	3	3	3	0	0	1	1.000
Baker 3b	4	1	3	1	3	0	.750
McInnis 1b	3	0	1	0	1	0	.333
Strunk cf	4	1	0	0	0	0	.000
Barry ss	4	1	1	0	0	0	.250
Schang c	4	0	1	0	2	0	.250
Bender p	4	0	0	0	0	0	.000
TOTALS	**34**	**6**	**11**	**1**	**6**	**2**	**.324**

BATTING: 2B: Barry (1, Marquard), McInnis (1, Crandall). **3B:** Collins (1, Marquard), Schang (1, Marquard). **HR:** Baker (1, 5th off Marquard 1 on, 2 out). **S:** McInnis. **RBI:** Baker 3 (3), McInnis 1 (1), Schang 2 (2). **2-out RBI:** Baker 2, Schang 2. **Runners left in scoring position, 2 out:** Barry 1, Bender 1. **Team LOB:** 4 **BASERUNNING: SB:** Collins (1, 2nd base off Marquard/Meyers). **CS:** Murphy (1, 2nd base off Tesreau/Meyers). **FIELDING: E:** Barry (1). **DP:** 1 (Barry-Collins-McInnis).

NY GIANTS	AB	R	H	HR	RBI	BB	AVG
Shafer cf	5	0	1	0	0	0	.200
Doyle 2b	4	0	2	0	2	0	.500
Fletcher ss	4	0	2	0	1	0	.500
Burns lf	4	0	1	0	0	0	.250
Herzog 3b	4	0	0	0	0	0	.000
Murray rf	4	0	2	0	0	0	.500
Meyers c	4	0	0	0	0	0	.000
Merkle 1b	4	2	2	0	0	0	.500
Marquard p	0	0	0	0	0	0	.000
a-McCormick ph	1	1	1	0	0	0	1.000
Crandall p	1	0	0	0	0	0	.000
Tesreau p	0	0	0	0	0	0	.000
b-McLean ph	1	0	0	0	0	0	.000
TOTALS	**36**	**3**	**11**	**0**	**3**	**0**	**.306**

a - Batted for Marquard in the 5th
b - Batted for Tesreau in the 9th

BATTING: 2B: Burns (1, Bender). **S:** Marquard. **RBI:** Doyle 2 (2), Fletcher 1 (1). **2-out RBI:** Doyle 1. **Runners left in scoring position, 2 out:** Herzog 1. **GIDP:** Fletcher. **Team LOB:** 7 **BASERUNNING: CS:** Fletcher (1, 2nd base off Bender/Schang).

PHILADELPHIA	IP	H	R	ER	BB	SO	HR	ERA
Bender (W, 1-0)	9	11	3	3	0	4	0	3.00

NY GIANTS	IP	H	R	ER	BB	SO	HR	ERA
Marquard (L, 0-1)	5	8	5	5	1	1	1	9.00
Crandall	2	3	1	1	0	1	0	4.50
Tesreau	2	0	0	0	1	1	0	0.00

Ground balls-fly balls: Bender 12-9, Marquard 8-4, Crandall 1-4, Tesreau 2-1. **Batters faced:** Bender 37, Marquard 23, Crandall 9, Tesreau 5. **UMPIRES:** hp—Klem, 1b—Egan, 2b—Rigler, 3b—Connolly **T:** 2:06 **A:** 36,291

GAME 2 New York 3 Philadelphia 0
Shibe Park 10/08/13

NY GIANTS	AB	R	H	HR	RBI	BB	AVG
Herzog 3b	5	1	0	0	0	0	.000
Doyle 2b	4	0	0	0	0	0	.250
Fletcher ss	5	0	2	0	2	0	.444
Burns lf	4	0	0	0	0	1	.125
Shafer cf	5	0	0	0	0	0	.100
Murray rf	4	0	0	0	0	0	.250
McLean c	4	0	2	0	0	0	.400
b-Grant pr	0	1	0	0	0	0	.000
Wilson c	0	0	0	0	0	0	.000
Snodgrass 1b	1	0	1	0	0	0	1.000
a-Wiltse pr-1b	2	0	0	0	0	0	.000
Mathewson p	3	1	2	0	1	1	.667
TOTALS	**37**	**3**	**7**	**0**	**3**	**2**	**.247**

a - Ran for Snodgrass in the 3th
b - Ran for McLean in the 10th

BATTING: S: Wiltse. **RBI:** Fletcher 2 (3), Mathewson 1 (1). **Runners left in scoring position, 2 out:** Herzog 1, Doyle 2, Shafer 1, Murray 1. **Team LOB:** 8 **BASERUNNING: CS:** Shafer (1, 2nd base off Plank/Lapp). **FIELDING: E:** Doyle 2 (2).

PHILADELPHIA	AB	R	H	HR	RBI	BB	AVG
Murphy rf	5	0	0	0	0	0	.111
Oldring lf	5	0	1	0	0	0	.222
Collins 2b	4	0	1	0	0	0	.571
Baker 3b	5	0	2	0	0	0	.556
McInnis 1b	4	0	0	0	0	0	.143
Strunk cf	3	0	1	0	0	1	.143
Barry ss	4	0	1	0	0	0	.250
Lapp c	4	0	1	0	0	0	.250
Plank p	4	0	1	0	0	0	.250
TOTALS	**38**	**0**	**8**	**0**	**0**	**1**	**.264**

BATTING: S: Collins. **Runners left in scoring position, 2 out:** Murphy 2, McInnis 3, Barry 1. **Team LOB:** 10 **FIELDING: E:** Baker (1), Collins (1).

NY GIANTS	IP	H	R	ER	BB	SO	HR	ERA
Mathewson (W, 1-0)	10	8	0	0	1	5	0	0.00

PHILADELPHIA	IP	H	R	ER	BB	SO	HR	ERA
Plank (L, 0-1)	10	7	3	2	2	6	0	1.80

IBB: Strunk (by Mathewson). **HBP:** Doyle (by Plank). **Ground balls-fly balls:** Mathewson 19-6, Plank 7-17. **Batters faced:** Mathewson 40, Plank 41. **UMPIRES:** hp—Connolly, 1b—Rigler, 2b—Klem, 3b—Egan **T:** 2:22 **A:** 20,563

GAME 3 Philadelphia 8 New York 2
Polo Grounds 10/09/13

PHILADELPHIA	AB	R	H	HR	RBI	BB	AVG
Murphy rf	5	1	2	0	0	0	.214
Oldring lf	5	3	2	0	0	0	.286
Collins 2b	5	2	3	0	3	0	.583
Baker 3b	4	1	2	0	2	0	.538
McInnis 1b	4	0	0	0	0	0	.091
Strunk cf	4	0	0	0	0	0	.091
Barry ss	4	0	1	0	0	0	.250
Schang c	4	1	1	1	1	0	.250
Bush p	4	0	1	0	0	0	.250
TOTALS	**39**	**8**	**12**	**1**	**6**	**0**	**.279**

BATTING: 3B: Collins (2, Tesreau). **HR:** Schang (1, 8th off Crandall 0 on, 2 out). **RBI:** Collins 3 (3), Baker 2 (5), Schang 1 (3). **2-out RBI:** Collins 2, Schang 1. **Runners left in scoring position, 2 out:** Barry 1. **Team LOB:** 4 **BASERUNNING: SB:** Collins (2, 3rd base off Tesreau/McLean), Baker (1, 3rd base off Tesreau/McLean), Oldring (1, 2nd base off Tesreau/McLean). **FIELDING: E:** Schang (1). **DP:** 3 (Collins-Barry, Bush-Barry-McInnis, Schang-Collins).

NY GIANTS	AB	R	H	HR	RBI	BB	AVG
Herzog 3b	4	0	0	0	0	0	.000
Doyle 2b	4	0	1	0	0	0	.250
Fletcher ss	2	0	1	0	0	1	.455
Burns lf	4	0	0	0	0	0	.083
Shafer cf	3	1	1	0	0	1	.154
Murray rf	3	1	1	0	1	1	.273
McLean c	2	0	1	0	1	0	.429
a-Cooper pr	0	0	0	0	0	0	.000
Wilson c	2	0	0	0	0	0	.000
Merkle 1b	2	0	0	0	0	1	.333
b-Wiltse pr-1b	0	0	0	0	0	0	.000
Tesreau p	2	0	0	0	0	0	.000
Crandall p	1	0	0	0	0	0	.000
TOTALS	**29**	**2**	**5**	**0**	**2**	**4**	**.225**

a - Ran for McLean in the 5th
b - Ran for Merkle in the 7th

BATTING: 2B: Shafer (1, Bush). **RBI:** Murray 1 (1), McLean 1 (1). **Runners left in scoring position, 2 out:** Herzog 1, Shafer 1. **GIDP:** Burns. **Team LOB:** 5 **BASERUNNING: SB:** Fletcher (1, 2nd base off Bush/Schang), Murray (1, 2nd base off Bush/Schang), Cooper (1, 2nd base off Bush/Schang). **CS:** Murray (1, 2nd base off Bush/Schang). **FIELDING: E:** Fletcher (1). **DP:** 1 (Doyle).

PHILADELPHIA	IP	H	R	ER	BB	SO	HR	ERA
Bush (W, 1-0)	9	5	2	1	4	3	0	1.00

NY GIANTS	IP	H	R	ER	BB	SO	HR	ERA
Tesreau (L, 0-1)	6.1	11	7	5	0	3	0	5.40
Crandall	2.2	1	1	1	0	1	1	3.86

HBP: Fletcher (by Bush). **Ground balls-fly balls:** Bush 9-12, Tesreau 5-12, Crandall 2-4. **Batters faced:** Bush 34, Tesreau 31, Crandall 8. **UMPIRES:** hp—Rigler, 1b—Connolly, 2b—Klem, 3b—Egan **T:** 2:11 **A:** 36,896

GAME 4 Philadelphia 6 New York 5
Shibe Park 10/10/13

NY GIANTS	AB	R	H	HR	RBI	BB	AVG
Snodgrass cf	2	0	0	0	0	0	.333
Herzog 3b	2	0	1	0	0	0	.067
Doyle 2b	4	0	0	0	0	0	.188
Fletcher ss	4	1	0	0	0	0	.333
Burns lf	4	2	2	0	1	0	.188
Shafer 3b-cf	4	0	1	0	1	0	.176
Murray rf	2	1	1	0	0	1	.308
McLean c	2	0	2	0	0	0	.556
a-Cooper pr	0	0	0	0	0	0	.000
Wilson c	1	0	0	0	0	0	.000
c-Crandall ph	1	0	0	0	0	0	.000
Merkle 1b	4	1	1	1	3	0	.300
Demaree p	1	0	0	0	0	0	.000
b-McCormick ph	1	0	0	0	0	0	.500
Marquard p	1	0	0	0	0	0	.000
d-Grant ph	1	0	0	0	0	0	.000
TOTALS	**34**	**5**	**8**	**1**	**5**	**1**	**.228**

a - Ran for McLean in the 5th
b - Batted for Demaree in the 5th
c - Batted for Wilson in the 9th
d - Batted for Marquard in the 9th

BATTING: 2B: Burns (2, Bender). **3B:** Shafer (1, Bender). **HR:** Merkle (1, 7th off Bender 2 on, 2 out). **RBI:** Burns 1 (1), Shafer 1 (1), Merkle 3 (3). **2-out RBI:** Burns 1, Shafer 1, Merkle 3. **Runners left in scoring position, 2 out:** Murray 1, Merkle 1. **Team LOB:** 4 **BASERUNNING: SB:** Burns (1, 3rd base off Bender/Schang), Murray (2, 3rd base off Bender/Schang). **CS:** Cooper (1, 2nd base off Bender/Schang). **FIELDING: E:** Merkle 2 (2). **PB:** McLean.

PHILADELPHIA	AB	R	H	HR	RBI	BB	AVG
Murphy rf	5	0	0	0	0	0	.158
Oldring lf	4	0	2	0	0	0	.333
Collins 2b	4	0	0	0	0	0	.438
Baker 3b	4	0	0	0	0	0	.412
McInnis 1b	4	1	1	0	0	0	.133
Strunk cf	2	2	1	0	0	1	.154
Barry ss	4	2	3	0	1	0	.375
Schang c	2	1	2	0	4	2	.400
Bender p	4	0	0	0	1	0	.000
TOTALS	**33**	**6**	**9**	**0**	**6**	**3**	**.278**

BATTING: 2B: Barry 2 (3, Demaree, Marquard). **3B:** Oldring (1, Demaree). **S:** Strunk. **RBI:** Barry 1 (1), Schang 4 (7), Bender 1 (1). **2-out RBI:** Schang 2. **Runners left in scoring position, 2 out:** Murphy 1, Collins 1, Baker 1. **Team LOB:** 7 **BASERUNNING: SB:** Collins (3, 2nd base off Demaree/McLean).

NY GIANTS	IP	H	R	ER	BB	SO	HR	ERA
Demaree (L, 0-1)	4	7	4	2	1	0	0	4.50
Marquard	4	2	2	2	2	2	0	7.00

PHILADELPHIA	IP	H	R	ER	BB	SO	HR	ERA
Bender (W, 2-0)	9	8	5	5	1	5	1	4.00

HBP: Murray (by Bender). **Ground balls-fly balls:** Demaree 5-7, Marquard 5-5, Bender 8-13. **Batters faced:** Demaree 21, Marquard 16, Bender 36. **UMPIRES:** hp—Egan, 1b—Klem, 2b—Connolly, 3b—Rigler **T:** 2:09 **A:** 20,568

GAME 5 Philadelphia 3 New York 1
Polo Grounds 10/11/13

PHILADELPHIA	AB	R	H	HR	RBI	BB	AVG
Murphy rf	3	1	2	0	0	1	.227
Oldring lf	4	2	0	0	0	0	.273
Collins 2b	3	0	1	0	0	0	.421
Baker 3b	3	0	2	0	2	0	.450
McInnis 1b	2	0	0	0	1	0	.118
Strunk cf	4	0	0	0	0	0	.118
Barry ss	4	0	0	0	0	0	.300
Schang c	4	0	1	0	0	0	.357
Plank p	3	0	0	0	0	0	.143
TOTALS	**30**	**3**	**6**	**0**	**3**	**1**	**.264**

BATTING: S: Collins, McInnis. **SF:** Baker, McInnis. **RBI:** Baker 2 (7), McInnis 1 (2). **Runners left in scoring position, 2 out:** McInnis 1, Barry 1. **Team LOB:** 5 **FIELDING: E:** Plank (1). **DP:** 2 (Collins-Barry-McInnis, Barry-Collins-McInnis).

NY GIANTS	AB	R	H	HR	RBI	BB	AVG
Herzog 3b	4	0	0	0	0	0	.053
Doyle 2b	4	0	0	0	0	0	.150
Fletcher ss	3	0	0	0	0	0	.278
Burns lf	3	0	0	0	0	0	.158
Shafer cf	2	1	0	0	0	1	.158
Murray rf	3	0	0	0	0	0	.250
McLean c	3	0	1	0	1	0	.500
Merkle 1b	3	0	0	0	0	0	.231
Mathewson p	2	0	1	0	0	0	.600
a-Crandall ph	1	0	0	0	0	0	.000
TOTALS	**28**	**1**	**2**	**0**	**1**	**1**	**.201**

a - Batted for Mathewson in the 9th

BATTING: RBI: McLean 1 (2). **GIDP:** Merkle, Herzog. **Team LOB:** 1 **FIELDING: E:** Doyle (3).

PHILADELPHIA	IP	H	R	ER	BB	SO	HR	ERA
Plank (W, 1-1)	9	2	1	0	1	1	0	0.95

NY GIANTS	IP	H	R	ER	BB	SO	HR	ERA
Mathewson (L, 1-1)	9	6	3	2	1	2	0	0.95

Ground balls-fly balls: Plank 12-13, Mathewson 15-7. **Batters faced:** Plank 29, Mathewson 35. **UMPIRES:** hp—Klem, 1b—Egan, 2b—Rigler, 3b—Connolly **T:** 1:39 **A:** 36,632

1914 BOSTON BRAVES DEF. PHILADELPHIA A's, 4-0

GAME 1 Boston 7 Philadelphia 1
Shibe Park 10/09/14

BOSTON	AB	R	H	HR	RBI	BB	AVG
Moran rf	5	0	0	0	0	0	.000
Evers 2b	4	1	1	0	0	0	.250
Connolly lf	3	1	1	0	0	1	.333
Whitted cf	3	2	1	0	2	1	.333
Schmidt 1b	4	1	2	0	1	0	.500
Gowdy c	3	2	3	0	1	1	1.000
Maranville ss	4	0	2	0	2	0	.500
Deal 3b	4	0	0	0	0	0	.000
Rudolph p	4	0	1	0	0	0	.250
TOTALS	**34**	**7**	**11**	**0**	**6**	**3**	**.324**

BATTING: 2B: Gowdy (1, Bender). **3B:** Gowdy (1, Bender), Whitted (1, Bender). **RBI:** Whitted 2 (2), Schmidt 1 (1), Gowdy 1 (1), Maranville 2 (2). **Runners left in scoring position, 2 out:** Connolly 1. **GIDP:** Deal, Whitted, Deal. **Team LOB:** 3 **BASERUNNING: SB:** Moran (1, 2nd base off Wyckoff/Lapp), Schmidt (1, home off Wyckoff/Lapp), Gowdy (1, home off Wyckoff/Lapp). **FIELDING: E:** Moran (1), Evers (1). **Outfield assists:** Connolly (1). **DP:** 1 (Schmidt-Deal).

PHILADELPHIA	AB	R	H	HR	RBI	BB	AVG
Murphy rf	4	0	1	0	0	0	.250
Oldring lf	3	0	0	0	0	0	.000
Collins 2b	3	0	0	0	0	1	.000
Baker 3b	4	0	1	0	0	0	.250
McInnis 1b	2	1	0	0	0	2	.000
Strunk cf	4	0	2	0	1	0	.500
Barry ss	4	0	0	0	0	0	.000
Schang c	2	0	0	0	0	0	.000
Lapp c	1	0	0	0	0	0	.000
Bender p	2	0	0	0	0	0	.000
Wyckoff p	1	0	1	0	0	0	1.000
TOTALS	**30**	**1**	**5**	**0**	**1**	**3**	**.167**

BATTING: 2B: Wyckoff (1, Rudolph), Baker (1, Rudolph). **S:** Oldring. **RBI:** Strunk 1 (1). **Runners left in scoring position, 2 out:** Collins 1, Barry 1, Lapp 2. **Team LOB:** 6 **FIELDING: DP:** 5 (Barry-Collins-McInnis, Bender-Barry-McInnis, Bender-McInnis, Baker-McInnis, Lapp-Baker).

BOSTON	IP	H	R	ER	BB	SO	HR	ERA
Rudolph (W, 1-0)	9	5	1	0	3	8	0	0.00

PHILADELPHIA	IP	H	R	ER	BB	SO	HR	ERA
Bender (L, 0-1)	5.1	8	6	6	2	3	0	10.13
Wyckoff	3.2	3	1	1	1	2	0	2.45

Ground balls-fly balls: Rudolph 12-5, Bender 4-6, Wyckoff 7-1. **Batters faced:** Rudolph 34, Bender 23, Wyckoff 14. **UMPIRES:** hp—Dinneen, 1b—Klem, 2b—Byron, 3b—Hildebrand **T:** 1:58 **A:** 20,562

GAME 2 Boston 1 Philadelphia 0
Shibe Park 10/10/14

BOSTON	AB	R	H	HR	RBI	BB	AVG
Mann rf	5	0	2	0	1	0	.400
Evers 2b	4	0	2	0	0	1	.375
Cather lf	5	0	0	0	0	0	.000
Whitted cf	3	0	0	0	0	1	.167
Schmidt 1b	4	0	1	0	0	0	.375
Gowdy c	2	0	0	0	0	2	.600
Maranville ss	2	0	1	0	0	0	.500
Deal 3b	4	1	1	0	0	0	.125
James p	4	0	0	0	0	0	.000
TOTALS	**33**	**1**	**7**	**0**	**1**	**4**	**.269**

BATTING: 2B: Deal (1, Plank). **S:** Maranville. **RBI:** Mann 1 (1). **2-out RBI:** Mann 1. **Runners left in scoring position, 2 out:** Cather 1, Schmidt 1, Deal 2, James 1. **Team LOB:** 11 **BASERUNNING: SB:** Deal 2 (2, 2nd base off Plank/Schang, 3rd base off Plank/Schang). **CS:** Evers (1, 2nd base off Plank/Schang). **FIELDING: E:** Maranville (1). **DP:** 1 (Maranville-Schmidt).

PHILADELPHIA	AB	R	H	HR	RBI	BB	AVG
Murphy rf	3	0	0	0	0	1	.143
Oldring lf	3	0	0	0	0	0	.000
Collins 2b	3	0	1	0	0	0	.167
Baker 3b	3	0	0	0	0	0	.143
McInnis 1b	3	0	0	0	0	0	.000
Strunk cf	3	0	0	0	0	0	.286
Barry ss	2	0	0	0	0	1	.000
Schang c	3	0	1	0	0	0	.200
Plank p	2	0	0	0	0	0	.000
a-Walsh ph	0	0	0	0	0	1	.000
TOTALS	**25**	**0**	**2**	**0**	**0**	**3**	**.127**

a - Batted for Plank in the 9th

BATTING: 2B: Schang (1, James). **GIDP:** Murphy. **Team LOB:** 1 **BASERUNNING: SB:** Barry (1, 2nd base off James/Gowdy). **FIELDING: E:** Barry (1). **PB:** Schang.

BOSTON	IP	H	R	ER	BB	SO	HR	ERA
James (W, 1-0)	9	2	0	0	3	8	0	0.00

PHILADELPHIA	IP	H	R	ER	BB	SO	HR	ERA
Plank (L, 0-1)	9	7	1	1	4	6	0	1.00

HBP: Maranville (by Plank). **Ground balls-fly balls:** James 10-5, Plank 12-8. **Batters faced:** James 28, Plank 39. **UMPIRES:** hp—Hildebrand, 1b—Byron, 2b—Klem, 3b—Dinneen **T:** 1:56 **A:** 20,562

GAME 3 Boston 5 Philadelphia 4
Fenway Park 10/12/14

PHILADELPHIA	AB	R	H	HR	RBI	BB	AVG
Murphy rf	5	2	2	0	0	1	.250
Oldring lf	5	0	0	0	0	0	.000
Collins 2b	4	0	1	0	1	1	.200
Baker 3b	5	0	2	0	2	1	.250
McInnis 1b	5	1	1	0	0	1	.100
Walsh cf	4	0	1	0	1	1	.250
Barry ss	5	0	0	0	0	0	.000
Schang c	4	1	1	0	0	1	.222
Bush p	5	0	0	0	0	0	.000
TOTALS	**42**	**4**	**8**	**0**	**4**	**6**	**.155**

BATTING: 2B: Murphy 2 (2, Tyler), McInnis (1, Tyler), Baker (2, Tyler). **S:** Oldring. **SF:** Collins. **RBI:** Collins 1 (1), Baker 2 (2), Walsh 1 (1). **2-out RBI:** Baker 2, Walsh 1. **Runners left in scoring position, 2 out:** Oldring 1, McInnis 2, Barry 1. **GIDP:** Baker. **Team LOB:** 10 **BASERUNNING: SB:** Collins (1, 2nd base off Tyler/Gowdy). **FIELDING: E:** Schang (1), Bush (1).

BOSTON	AB	R	H	HR	RBI	BB	AVG
Moran rf	4	1	0	0	0	1	.000
Evers 2b	5	0	3	0	0	0	.462
Connolly lf	4	0	0	0	1	0	.143
Whitted cf	5	0	0	0	0	0	.091
Schmidt 1b	5	1	1	0	0	0	.308
Deal 3b	5	0	1	0	0	0	.154
Maranville ss	4	1	1	0	1	1	.400
Gowdy c	4	1	3	1	2	1	.667
b-Mann pr	0	1	0	0	0	0	.400
Tyler p	3	0	0	0	0	0	.000
a-Devore ph	1	0	0	0	0	0	.000
James p	0	0	0	0	0	0	.000
c-Gilbert ph	0	0	0	0	0	1	.000
TOTALS	**40**	**5**	**9**	**1**	**4**	**4**	**.252**

a - Batted for Tyler in the 10th
b - Ran for Gowdy in the 12th
c - Batted for James in the 12th

BATTING: 2B: Gowdy 2 (3, Bush), Deal (2, Bush). **HR:** Gowdy (1, 10th off Bush 0 on, 0 out). **S:** Maranville, Moran. **SF:** Connolly. **RBI:** Connolly 1 (1), Maranville 1 (3), Gowdy 2 (3). **2-out RBI:** Maranville 1, Gowdy 1. **Runners left in scoring position, 2 out:** Whitted 1, Maranville 1, Tyler 1. **Team LOB:** 8 **BASERUNNING: SB:** Evers (1, 2nd base off Bush/Schang), Maranville 2 (2, 2nd base off Bush/Schang). **FIELDING: E:** Connolly (1). **DP:** 1 (Evers-Maranville-Schmidt).

PHILADELPHIA	IP	H	R	ER	BB	SO	HR	ERA
Bush (L, 0-1)	11	9	5	4	4	4	1	3.27

BOSTON	IP	H	R	ER	BB	SO	HR	ERA
Tyler	10	8	4	4	3	4	0	3.60
James (W, 2-0)	2	0	0	0	3	1	0	0.00

IBB: Walsh (by Tyler), Baker (by James), Gilbert (by Bush). **Ground balls-fly balls:** Bush 18-9, Tyler 13-11, James 4-1. **Batters faced:** Bush 46, Tyler 41, James 9. **UMPIRES:** hp—Klem, 1b—Dinneen, 2b—Byron, 3b—Hildebrand **T:** 3:06 **A:** 35,520

GAME 4 Boston 3 Philadelphia 1
Fenway Park 10/13/14

PHILADELPHIA	AB	R	H	HR	RBI	BB	AVG
Murphy rf	4	0	0	0	0	0	.188
Oldring lf	4	0	1	0	0	0	.067
Collins 2b	4	0	1	0	0	0	.214
Baker 3b	4	0	1	0	0	0	.250
McInnis 1b	4	0	1	0	0	0	.143
Walsh cf	2	0	1	0	0	1	.333
Barry ss	3	1	1	0	0	0	.071
Schang c	3	0	0	0	0	0	.167
Shawkey p	2	0	1	0	1	0	.500
Pennock p	1	0	0	0	0	0	.000
TOTALS	**31**	**1**	**7**	**0**	**1**	**1**	**.172**

BATTING: 2B: Walsh (1, Rudolph), Shawkey (1, Rudolph). **RBI:** Shawkey 1 (1). **Runners left in scoring position, 2 out:** Oldring 1, Walsh 1, Schang 2. **Team LOB:** 4 **BASERUNNING: CS:** Oldring (1, 2nd base off Rudolph/Gowdy). **FIELDING: PB:** Schang.

BOSTON	AB	R	H	HR	RBI	BB	AVG
Moran rf	4	1	1	0	0	0	.077
Evers 2b	3	1	1	0	2	1	.438
Connolly lf	2	0	0	0	0	0	.111
a-Mann ph-lf	2	0	0	0	0	0	.286
Whitted cf	3	0	2	0	0	1	.214
Schmidt 1b	4	0	1	0	1	0	.294
Gowdy c	2	0	0	0	0	1	.545
Maranville ss	3	0	0	0	0	0	.308
Deal 3b	3	0	0	0	0	0	.125
Rudolph p	2	1	1	0	0	1	.333
TOTALS	**28**	**3**	**6**	**0**	**3**	**4**	**.244**

a - Batted for Connolly in the 6th

BATTING: 2B: Moran (1, Shawkey). **RBI:** Evers 2 (2), Schmidt 1 (2). **2-out RBI:** Evers 2. **Runners left in scoring position, 2 out:** Schmidt 1, Gowdy 1. **Team LOB:** 5 **BASERUNNING: SB:** Whitted (1, 2nd base off Pennock/Schang). **CS:** Schmidt (1, 2nd base off Pennock/Schang). **FIELDING: Outfield assists:** Connolly (2). **DP:** 1 (Gowdy-Evers).

PHILADELPHIA	IP	H	R	ER	BB	SO	HR	ERA
Shawkey (L, 0-1)	5	4	3	2	2	0	0	3.60
Pennock	3	2	0	0	2	3	0	0.00

BOSTON	IP	H	R	ER	BB	SO	HR	ERA
Rudolph (W, 2-0)	9	7	1	1	1	7	0	0.50

WP: Rudolph 1. **Ground balls-fly balls:** Shawkey 11-3, Pennock 3-2, Rudolph 12-5. **Batters faced:** Shawkey 20, Pennock 12, Rudolph 32. **UMPIRES:** hp—Byron, 1b—Hildebrand, 2b—Klem, 3b—Dinneen **T:** 1:49 **A:** 34,365

1915 BOSTON RED SOX DEF. PHILADELPHIA PHILLIES, 4-1

GAME 1 Philadelphia 3 Boston 1
Baker Bowl 10/08/15

BOSTON	AB	R	H	HR	RBI	BB	AVG
Hooper rf	5	0	1	0	0	0	.200
Scott ss	3	0	1	0	0	0	.333
Speaker cf	2	1	0	0	0	2	.000
Hoblitzel 1b	4	0	1	0	0	0	.250
Lewis lf	4	0	2	0	1	0	.500
Gardner 3b	3	0	1	0	0	0	.333
Barry 2b	4	0	1	0	0	0	.250
Cady c	2	0	0	0	0	0	.000
a-Henriksen ph	1	0	0	0	0	0	.000
Shore p	3	0	1	0	0	0	.333
b-Ruth ph	1	0	0	0	0	0	.000
TOTALS	**32**	**1**	**8**	**0**	**1**	**2**	**.250**

a - Batted for Cady in the 9th
b - Batted for Shore in the 9th

BATTING: S: Scott, Gardner, Cady. **RBI:** Lewis 1 (1). **2-out RBI:** Lewis 1. **Runners left in scoring position, 2 out:** Hooper 2,

Gardner 2, Cady 1. **Team LOB:** 9 **BASERUNNING: SB:** Hoblitzel (1, 2nd base off Alexander/Burns). **FIELDING: E:** Shore (1).

PHILADELPHIA	AB	R	H	HR	RBI	BB	AVG
Stock 3b	3	1	0	0	0	1	.000
Bancroft ss	4	1	1	0	0	0	.250
Paskert cf	3	1	1	0	0	1	.333
Cravath rf	2	0	0	0	1	1	.000
Luderus 1b	4	0	1	0	1	0	.250
Whitted lf	2	0	1	0	1	1	.500
Niehoff 2b	3	0	0	0	0	0	.000
Burns c	3	0	0	0	0	0	.000
Alexander p	3	0	1	0	0	0	.333
TOTALS	**27**	**3**	**5**	**0**	**3**	**4**	**.185**

BATTING: S: Cravath. **RBI:** Cravath 1 (1), Luderus 1 (1), Whitted 1 (1). **2-out RBI:** Luderus 1, Whitted 1. **Runners left in scoring position, 2 out:** Niehoff 1. **Team LOB:** 5 **BASERUNNING: SB:** Whitted (1, 2nd base off Shore/Cady). **CS:** Luderus 2 (2, 2nd base off Shore/Cady). **FIELDING: E:** Luderus (1).

BOSTON	IP	H	R	ER	BB	SO	HR	ERA
Shore (L, 0-1)	8	5	3	3	4	2	0	3.38
PHILADELPHIA	**IP**	**H**	**R**	**ER**	**BB**	**SO**	**HR**	**ERA**
Alexander (W, 1-0)	9	8	1	1	2	6	0	1.00

Ground balls-fly balls: Shore 12-8, Alexander 9-9. **Batters faced:** Shore 32, Alexander 37. **UMPIRES:** hp—Klem, 1b—O'Loughlin, 2b—Evans, 3b—Rigler **T:** 1:58 **A:** 19,343

GAME 2 Boston 2 Philadelphia 1
Baker Bowl 10/09/15

BOSTON	AB	R	H	HR	RBI	BB	AVG
Hooper rf	3	1	1	0	0	2	.250
Scott ss	3	0	0	0	0	0	.167
a-Henriksen ph	1	0	0	0	0	0	.000
Cady c	0	0	0	0	0	0	.000
Speaker cf	4	0	1	0	0	0	.167
Hoblitzel 1b	4	0	1	0	0	0	.250
Lewis lf	4	0	1	0	0	0	.375
Gardner 3b	4	1	2	0	0	0	.429
Barry 2b	4	0	1	0	0	0	.250
Thomas c	3	0	0	0	0	0	.000
Janvrin ss	1	0	0	0	0	0	.000
Foster p	4	0	3	0	1	0	.750
TOTALS	**35**	**2**	**10**	**0**	**1**	**2**	**.269**

a - Batted for Scott in the 7th

BATTING: 2B: Foster (1, Mayer). **S:** Speaker. **RBI:** Foster 1 (1). **2-out RBI:** Foster 1. **Runners left in scoring position, 2 out:** Hooper 1, Scott 1, Henriksen 2. **Team LOB:** 9 **BASERUNNING: CS:** Hoblitzel (1, 2nd base off Mayer/Burns).

PHILADELPHIA	AB	R	H	HR	RBI	BB	AVG
Stock 3b	4	0	0	0	0	0	.000
Bancroft ss	4	0	1	0	0	0	.250
Paskert cf	4	0	0	0	0	0	.143
Cravath rf	3	1	1	0	0	0	.200
Luderus 1b	3	0	1	0	1	0	.286
Whitted lf	3	0	0	0	0	0	.200
Niehoff 2b	3	0	0	0	0	0	.000
Burns c	3	0	0	0	0	0	.000
Mayer p	3	0	0	0	0	0	.000
TOTALS	**30**	**1**	**3**	**0**	**1**	**0**	**.140**

BATTING: 2B: Cravath (1, Foster), Luderus (1, Foster). **RBI:** Luderus 1 (2). **Runners left in scoring position, 2 out:** Burns 1. **Team LOB:** 2

BOSTON	IP	H	R	ER	BB	SO	HR	ERA
Foster (W, 1-0)	9	3	1	1	0	8	0	1.00
PHILADELPHIA	**IP**	**H**	**R**	**ER**	**BB**	**SO**	**HR**	**ERA**
Mayer (L, 0-1)	9	10	2	1	2	7	0	1.00

Ground balls-fly balls: Foster 9-10, Mayer 8-10. **Batters faced:** Foster 30, Mayer 37. **UMPIRES:** hp—Rigler, 1b—Evans, 2b—O'Loughlin, 3b—Klem **T:** 2:05 **A:** 20,306

GAME 3 Boston 2 Philadelphia 1
Braves Field 10/11/15

PHILADELPHIA	AB	R	H	HR	RBI	BB	AVG
Stock 3b	3	0	1	0	0	0	.100
Bancroft ss	3	0	1	0	1	0	.273
Paskert cf	4	0	0	0	0	0	.091
Cravath rf	4	0	0	0	0	0	.111
Luderus 1b	3	0	0	0	0	0	.200
Whitted lf	3	0	0	0	0	0	.125
Niehoff 2b	3	0	0	0	0	0	.000
Burns c	3	1	1	0	0	0	.111
Alexander p	2	0	0	0	0	0	.200
TOTALS	**28**	**1**	**3**	**0**	**1**	**0**	**.129**

BATTING: 2B: Stock (1, Leonard). **S:** Bancroft, Alexander, Stock. **RBI:** Bancroft 1 (1). **Runners left in scoring position, 2 out:** Cravath 3. **Team LOB:** 3 **FIELDING: DP:** 1 (Burns-Bancroft-Luderus).

BOSTON	AB	R	H	HR	RBI	BB	AVG
Hooper rf	4	1	1	0	0	0	.250
Scott ss	3	0	0	0	0	0	.111
Speaker cf	3	1	2	0	0	1	.333
Hoblitzel 1b	3	0	0	0	1	0	.182
Lewis lf	4	0	3	0	1	0	.500
Gardner 3b	3	0	0	0	0	0	.300
Barry 2b	3	0	0	0	0	0	.182
Carrigan c	2	0	0	0	0	1	.000
Leonard p	3	0	0	0	0	0	.000
TOTALS	**28**	**2**	**6**	**0**	**2**	**2**	**.253**

BATTING: 3B: Speaker (1, Alexander). **S:** Scott. **SF:** Hoblitzel. **RBI:** Hoblitzel 1 (1), Lewis 1 (2). **2-out RBI:** Lewis 1. **GIDP:** Hoblitzel. **Team LOB:** 4 **BASERUNNING: CS:** Lewis (1, 2nd base off Alexander/Burns).

PHILADELPHIA	IP	H	R	ER	BB	SO	HR	ERA
Alexander (L, 1-1)	8.2	6	2	2	2	4	0	1.53
BOSTON	**IP**	**H**	**R**	**ER**	**BB**	**SO**	**HR**	**ERA**
Leonard (W, 1-0)	9	3	1	1	0	6	0	1.00

IBB: Speaker (by Alexander). **Ground balls-fly balls:** Alexander 4-14, Leonard 7-12. **Batters faced:** Alexander 32, Leonard 31. **UMPIRES:** hp—O'Loughlin, 1b—Klem, 2b—Rigler, 3b—Evans **T:** 1:48 **A:** 42,300

GAME 4 Boston 2 Philadelphia 1
Braves Field 10/12/15

PHILADELPHIA	AB	R	H	HR	RBI	BB	AVG
Stock 3b	4	0	1	0	0	0	.143
Bancroft ss	2	0	0	0	0	2	.231
Paskert cf	4	0	0	0	0	0	.067
Cravath rf	4	1	1	0	0	0	.154
Luderus 1b	4	0	3	0	1	0	.357
a-Dugey pr	0	0	0	0	0	0	.000
Becker lf	0	0	0	0	0	0	.000
Whitted lf-1b	3	0	0	0	0	0	.091
Niehoff 2b	3	0	0	0	0	1	.000
Burns c	3	0	1	0	0	1	.167
Chalmers p	3	0	1	0	0	0	.333
b-Byrne ph	1	0	0	0	0	0	.000
TOTALS	**31**	**1**	**7**	**0**	**1**	**4**	**.155**

a - Ran for Luderus in the 8th
b - Batted for Chalmers in the 9th

BATTING: 3B: Cravath (1, Shore). **S:** Whitted. **RBI:** Luderus 1 (3). **2-out RBI:** Luderus 1. **Runners left in scoring position, 2 out:** Cravath 1, Whitted 1, Chalmers 2. **Team LOB:** 8 **BASERUNNING: SB:** Dugey (1, 2nd base off Shore/Cady). **CS:** Bancroft (1, 2nd base off Shore/Cady). **FIELDING: DP:** 1 (Chalmers-Burns-Whitted).

BOSTON	AB	R	H	HR	RBI	BB	AVG
Hooper rf	4	0	1	0	1	0	.250
Scott ss	4	0	0	0	0	0	.077
Speaker cf	3	0	1	0	0	1	.333
Hoblitzel 1b	4	1	3	0	0	0	.333
Lewis lf	2	0	1	0	1	1	.500
Gardner 3b	4	0	0	0	0	0	.214
Barry 2b	2	1	0	0	0	1	.154
Cady c	3	0	2	0	0	0	.400
Shore p	2	0	0	0	0	0	.200
TOTALS	**28**	**2**	**8**	**0**	**2**	**3**	**.260**

BATTING: 2B: Lewis (1, Chalmers). **S:** Shore, Lewis. **RBI:** Hooper 1 (1), Lewis 1 (3). **Runners left in scoring position, 2 out:** Speaker 1, Barry 2. **GIDP:** Gardner. **Team LOB:** 7 **BASERUNNING: CS:** Speaker (2, 2nd base off Chalmers/Burns). **FIELDING: Outfield assists:** Lewis (1). **DP:** 1 (Scott-Barry-Hoblitzel-Barry).

PHILADELPHIA	IP	H	R	ER	BB	SO	HR	ERA
Chalmers (L, 0-1)	8	8	2	2	3	6	0	2.25
BOSTON	**IP**	**H**	**R**	**ER**	**BB**	**SO**	**HR**	**ERA**
Shore (W, 1-1)	9	7	1	1	4	4	0	2.12

Ground balls-fly balls: Chalmers 7-7, Shore 7-13. **Batters faced:** Chalmers 33, Shore 36. **UMPIRES:** hp—Evans, 1b—Rigler, 2b—O'Loughlin, 3b—Klem **T:** 2:05 **A:** 41,096

GAME 5 Boston 5 Philadelphia 4
Baker Bowl 10/13/15

BOSTON	AB	R	H	HR	RBI	BB	AVG
Hooper rf	4	2	3	2	2	0	.350
Scott ss	5	0	0	0	0	0	.056
Speaker cf	5	0	1	0	0	0	.294
Hoblitzel 1b	1	0	0	0	0	0	.313
a-Gainer ph-1b	3	1	1	0	0	0	.333
Lewis lf	4	1	1	1	2	0	.444
Gardner 3b	3	1	1	0	0	1	.235
Barry 2b	4	0	1	0	1	0	.176
Thomas c	2	0	1	0	0	0	.200
b-Cady ph-c	1	0	0	0	0	1	.333
Foster p	4	0	1	0	0	0	.500
TOTALS	**36**	**5**	**10**	**3**	**5**	**2**	**.264**

a - Batted for Hoblitzel in the 3th
b - Batted for Thomas in the 6th

BATTING: 3B: Gardner (1, Mayer). **HR:** Hooper 2 (2, 3th off Mayer 0 on, 0 out, 9th off Rixey 0 on, 1 out), Lewis (1, 8th off Rixey 1 on, 0 out). **RBI:** Hooper 2 (3), Lewis 2 (5), Barry 1 (1). **2-out RBI:** Barry 1. **Runners left in scoring position, 2 out:** Gainer 2, Foster 2. **GIDP:** Gainer. **Team LOB:** 7 **BASERUNNING: CS:** Speaker (3, 2nd base off Mayer/Burns). **FIELDING: E:** Hooper (1). **DP:** 1 (Foster-Thomas-Hoblitzel).

PHILADELPHIA	AB	R	H	HR	RBI	BB	AVG
Stock 3b	3	0	0	0	0	0	.118
Bancroft ss	4	1	2	0	0	0	.294
Paskert cf	4	1	2	0	0	0	.158
Cravath rf	3	0	0	0	0	1	.125
a-Dugey pr	0	0	0	0	0	0	.000
Becker rf	0	0	0	0	0	0	.000
Luderus 1b	2	1	2	1	3	1	.438
Whitted lf	4	0	0	0	0	0	.067
Niehoff 2b	4	1	1	0	0	0	.063
Burns c	4	0	1	0	1	0	.188
Mayer p	1	0	0	0	0	0	.000
Rixey p	2	0	1	0	0	0	.500
b-Killefer ph	1	0	0	0	0	0	.000
TOTALS	**32**	**4**	**9**	**1**	**4**	**2**	**.182**

a - Ran for Cravath in the 8th
b - Batted for Rixey in the 9th

BATTING: 2B: Luderus (2, Foster). **HR:** Luderus (1, 4th off Foster 0 on, 1 out). **RBI:** Luderus 3 (6), Burns 1 (1). **2-out RBI:** Luderus 2, Burns 1. **Runners left in scoring position, 2 out:** Whitted 2. **GIDP:** Cravath. **Team LOB:** 5 **BASERUNNING: CS:** Paskert (1, 2nd base off Foster/Thomas), Bancroft (2, 2nd base off Foster/Thomas), Luderus (3, 2nd base off Foster/Cady). **FIELDING: E:** Bancroft (1). **DP:** 1 (Bancroft-Luderus).

BOSTON	IP	H	R	ER	BB	SO	HR	ERA
Foster (W, 2-0)	9	9	4	3	2	5	1	2.00
PHILADELPHIA	**IP**	**H**	**R**	**ER**	**BB**	**SO**	**HR**	**ERA**
Mayer	2.1	6	2	2	0	0	1	2.38
Rixey (L, 0-1)	6.2	4	3	3	2	2	2	4.05

HBP: Stock (by Foster), Hooper (by Rixey), Luderus (by Foster). **Ground balls-fly balls:** Foster 9-9, Mayer 3-3, Rixey 10-8. **Batters faced:** Foster 36, Mayer 12, Rixey 27. **UMPIRES:** hp—Klem, 1b—O'Loughlin, 2b—Evans, 3b—Rigler **T:** 2:15 **A:** 20,306

1916 BOSTON RED SOX DEF. BROOKLYN, 4-1

GAME 1 Boston 6 Brooklyn 5
Braves Field 10/07/16

BROOKLYN	AB	R	H	HR	RBI	BB	AVG
Myers cf	5	0	2	0	1	0	.400
Daubert 1b	4	0	0	0	0	1	.000
Stengel rf	4	2	2	0	0	0	.500
Wheat lf	4	1	2	0	1	0	.500
Cutshaw 2b	3	1	0	0	0	0	.000
Mowrey 3b	3	1	1	0	1	1	.333
Olson ss	4	0	1	0	0	0	.250
Meyers c	4	0	1	0	0	0	.250
Marquard p	2	0	0	0	0	0	.000
a-Johnston ph	1	0	1	0	0	0	1.000
Pfeffer p	0	0	0	0	0	0	.000
b-Merkle ph	0	0	0	0	1	1	.000
TOTALS	**34**	**5**	**10**	**0**	**4**	**3**	**.294**

a - Batted for Marquard in the 8th
b - Batted for Pfeffer in the 9th

BATTING: 3B: Wheat (1, Shore), Meyers (1, Shore). **RBI:** Myers 1 (1), Wheat 1 (1), Mowrey 1 (1), Merkle 1 (1). **2-out RBI:** Myers 1, Merkle 1. **Runners left in scoring position, 2 out:** Myers 1, Daubert 2. **GIDP:** Cutshaw, Olson, Myers. **Team LOB:** 6 **FIELDING: E:** Olson 2 (2), Cutshaw (1), Stengel (1). **PB:** Meyers.

BOSTON	AB	R	H	HR	RBI	BB	AVG
Hooper rf	4	2	1	0	0	1	.250
Janvrin 2b	4	1	2	0	1	0	.500
Walker cf	4	1	2	0	1	1	.500
Hoblitzel 1b	5	2	1	0	1	0	.200
Lewis lf	3	0	1	0	1	1	.333
Gardner 3b	4	0	1	0	1	0	.250
Scott ss	2	0	0	0	1	0	.000
Cady c	1	0	0	0	0	3	.000
Thomas c	0	0	0	0	0	0	.000
Shore p	4	0	0	0	0	0	.000
Mays p	0	0	0	0	0	0	.000
TOTALS	**31**	**6**	**8**	**0**	**6**	**6**	**.258**

BATTING: 2B: Lewis (1, Marquard), Hooper (1, Marquard), Janvrin (1, Marquard). **3B:** Walker (1, Marquard), Hoblitzel (1, Marquard). **S:** Scott, Janvrin, Lewis. **SF:** Scott. **RBI:** Janvrin 1 (1), Walker 1 (1), Hoblitzel 1 (1), Lewis 1 (1), Gardner 1 (1), Scott 1 (1). **2-out RBI:** Lewis 1. **Runners left in scoring position, 2 out:** Hooper 3, Hoblitzel 1, Lewis 2. **Team LOB:** 11 **FIELDING: E:** Janvrin (1). **Outfield assists:** Hooper (1). **DP:** 4 (Janvrin-Scott-Hoblitzel, Hooper-Cady, Gardner-Janvrin-Hoblitzel, Shore-Scott-Janvrin-Hoblitzel).

BROOKLYN	IP	H	R	ER	BB	SO	HR	ERA
Marquard (L, 0-1)	7	7	5	3	4	6	0	3.86
Pfeffer	1	1	1	0	2	0	0	0.00
BOSTON	**IP**	**H**	**R**	**ER**	**BB**	**SO**	**HR**	**ERA**
Shore (W, 1-0)	8.2	9	5	3	3	5	0	3.12
Mays (S, 1)	0.1	1	0	0	0	0	0	0.00

HBP: Cutshaw (by Shore). **Ground balls-fly balls:** Marquard 9-5, Pfeffer 1-2, Shore 14-4, Mays 1-0. **Batters faced:** Marquard 35, Pfeffer 6, Shore 36, Mays 2. **UMPIRES:** hp—Connolly, 1b—O'Day, 2b—Quigley, 3b—Dineen **T:** 2:16 **A:** 36,117

GAME 2 Boston 2 Brooklyn 1
Braves Field 10/09/16

BROOKLYN	AB	R	H	HR	RBI	BB	AVG
Johnston rf	5	0	1	0	0	1	.333
Daubert 1b	5	0	0	0	0	1	.000
Myers cf	6	1	1	1	1	0	.273
Wheat lf	5	0	0	0	0	0	.222
Cutshaw 2b	5	0	0	0	0	0	.000
Mowrey 3b	5	0	1	0	0	0	.250
Olson ss	2	0	1	0	0	1	.333
Miller c	5	0	1	0	0	0	.200
Smith p	5	0	1	0	0	0	.200
TOTALS	**43**	**1**	**6**	**1**	**1**	**3**	**.208**

BATTING: 2B: Smith (1, Ruth). **HR:** Myers (1, 1st off Ruth 0 on, 2 out). **S:** Olson, Olson. **RBI:** Myers 1 (2). **2-out RBI:** Myers 1. **Runners left in scoring position, 2 out:** Johnston 2, Smith 1. **GIDP:** Myers. **Team LOB:** 5 **BASERUNNING: CS:** Johnston 2 (2, 2nd base off Ruth/Thomas). **FIELDING: E:** Cutshaw (2). **Outfield assists:** Myers (1). **DP:** 2 (Mowrey-Cutshaw-Daubert, Myers-Miller).

BOSTON	AB	R	H	HR	RBI	BB	AVG
Hooper rf	6	0	1	0	0	0	.200
Janvrin 2b	6	0	1	0	0	0	.300
Walker cf	3	0	0	0	0	0	.286
a-Walsh ph-cf	3	0	0	0	0	0	.000
Hoblitzel 1b	2	0	0	0	0	4	.143
b-McNally pr	0	1	0	0	0	0	.000
Lewis lf	3	0	1	0	0	1	.333
Gardner 3b	5	0	0	0	0	0	.111
c-Gainer ph	1	0	1	0	1	0	1.000
Scott ss	4	1	2	0	0	1	.333
Thomas c	4	0	1	0	0	0	.250
Ruth p	5	0	0	0	1	0	.000
TOTALS	**42**	**2**	**7**	**0**	**2**	**6**	**.205**

a - Batted for Walker in the 9th
b - Ran for Hoblitzel in the 14th
c - Batted for Gardner in the 14th

BATTING: 2B: Janvrin (2, Smith). **3B:** Scott (1, Smith), Thomas (1, Smith). **S:** Lewis, Thomas, Lewis. **RBI:** Gainer 1 (1), Ruth 1 (1). **Runners left in scoring position, 2 out:** Hooper 1, Gardner 1, Scott 1, Ruth 1. **GIDP:** Lewis. **Team LOB:** 9 **FIELDING: E:** Gardner (1). **Outfield assists:** Hooper (2). **DP:** 1 (Scott-Janvrin-Hoblitzel).

BROOKLYN	IP	H	R	ER	BB	SO	HR	ERA
Smith (L, 0-1)	13.1	7	2	2	6	2	0	1.35
BOSTON	**IP**	**H**	**R**	**ER**	**BB**	**SO**	**HR**	**ERA**
Ruth (W, 1-0)	14	6	1	1	3	4	1	0.64

IBB: Lewis (by Smith). **Ground balls-fly balls:** Smith 19-14, Ruth 22-11. **Batters faced:** Smith 51, Ruth 48. **UMPIRES:** hp—Dinneen, 1b—Quigley, 2b—Connolly, 3b—O'Day **T:** 2:32 **A:** 47,373

GAME 3 Brooklyn 4 Boston 3
Ebbets Field 10/10/16

BOSTON	AB	R	H	HR	RBI	BB	AVG
Hooper rf	4	1	2	0	1	0	.286
Janvrin 2b	4	0	0	0	0	0	.214
Shorten cf	4	0	3	0	1	0	.750
Hoblitzel 1b	4	0	1	0	0	0	.182
Lewis lf	4	0	0	0	0	0	.200
Gardner 3b	3	1	1	1	1	0	.167
Scott ss	3	0	0	0	0	0	.222
Thomas c	3	0	0	0	0	0	.143
Mays p	1	0	0	0	0	0	.000
a-Henriksen ph	0	1	0	0	0	1	.000
Foster p	1	0	0	0	0	0	.000
TOTALS	**31**	**3**	**7**	**1**	**3**	**1**	**.212**

a - Batted for Mays in the 6th

BATTING: 3B: Hooper (1, Coombs). **HR:** Gardner (1, 7th off Coombs 0 on, 1 out). **RBI:** Hooper 1 (1), Shorten 1 (1), Gardner 1 (2). **2-out RBI:** Shorten 1. **Team LOB:** 2 **BASERUNNING: CS:** Hooper (1, 2nd base off Coombs/Miller), Shorten (1, 2nd base off Coombs/Miller). **FIELDING: E:** Gardner (2). **Outfield assists:** Lewis (1).

BROOKLYN	AB	R	H	HR	RBI	BB	AVG
Myers cf	3	0	0	0	0	0	.214
Daubert 1b	4	1	3	0	0	0	.231
Stengel rf	3	0	1	0	0	0	.429
Wheat lf	2	1	1	0	0	2	.273
Cutshaw 2b	4	0	1	0	1	0	.083
Mowrey 3b	3	1	0	0	0	1	.182
Olson ss	4	1	2	0	2	0	.400
Miller c	3	0	0	0	0	0	.125
Coombs p	3	0	1	0	1	0	.333
Pfeffer p	1	0	1	0	0	0	1.000
TOTALS	**30**	**4**	**10**	**0**	**4**	**3**	**.243**

BATTING: 3B: Olson (1, Mays), Daubert (1, Foster). **S:** Stengel, Miller, Myers. **RBI:** Cutshaw 1 (1), Olson 2 (2), Coombs 1 (1). **2-out RBI:** Cutshaw 1, Olson 2. **Runners left in scoring position, 2 out:** Daubert 1, Mowrey 5, Miller 1. **Team LOB:** 9 **BASERUNNING: SB:** Wheat (1, 2nd base off Foster/Thomas). **Outfield assists:** Stengel (1).

BOSTON	IP	H	R	ER	BB	SO	HR	ERA
Mays (L, 0-1)	5	7	4	3	3	2	0	5.06
Foster	3	3	0	0	0	1	0	0.00
BROOKLYN	**IP**	**H**	**R**	**ER**	**BB**	**SO**	**HR**	**ERA**
Coombs (W, 1-0)	6.1	7	3	3	1	1	1	4.26
Pfeffer (S, 1)	2.2	0	0	0	0	3	0	0.00

IBB: Wheat (by Mays). **HBP:** Myers (by Mays). **Ground balls-fly balls:** Mays 8-2, Foster 3-4, Coombs 5-10, Pfeffer 2-3. **Batters faced:** Mays 26, Foster 11, Coombs 24, Pfeffer 8. **UMPIRES:** hp—O'Day, 1b—Connolly, 2b—Quigley, 3b—Dineen **T:** 2:01 **A:** 21,087

GAME 4 Boston 6 Brooklyn 2
Ebbets Field 10/11/16

BOSTON	AB	R	H	HR	RBI	BB	AVG
Hooper rf	4	1	2	0	0	1	.333
Janvrin 2b	5	1	0	0	0	0	.158
Walker cf	4	0	1	0	0	0	.273
Hoblitzel 1b	3	1	2	0	2	1	.286
Lewis lf	4	2	2	0	0	0	.286
Gardner 3b	3	1	1	1	3	0	.200
Scott ss	4	0	0	0	0	0	.154
Carrigan c	3	0	2	0	1	0	.667
Leonard p	3	0	0	0	0	1	.000
TOTALS	**33**	**6**	**10**	**1**	**6**	**3**	**.234**

BATTING: 2B: Lewis (2, Marquard), Hoblitzel (1, Cheney). **HR:** Gardner (2, 2nd off Marquard 2 on, 0 out). **S:** Carrigan, Gardner. **RBI:** Hoblitzel 2 (3), Gardner 3 (5), Carrigan 1 (1). **2-out RBI:** Hoblitzel 2, Carrigan 1. **Runners left in scoring position, 2 out:** Hooper 1, Lewis 1. **Team LOB:** 5 **BASERUNNING: SB:** Hooper (1, 2nd base off Cheney/Meyers). **CS:** Walker (1, 2nd base off Marquard/Meyers), Hooper (2, 3rd base off Rucker/Meyers). **FIELDING: E:** Janvrin (2).

BROOKLYN	AB	R	H	HR	RBI	BB	AVG
Johnston rf	4	1	1	0	0	0	.300
Myers cf	4	1	1	0	1	0	.222
Merkle 1b	3	0	1	0	0	1	.333
Wheat lf	4	0	1	0	0	0	.267
Cutshaw 2b	4	0	1	0	1	0	.125
Mowrey 3b	3	0	0	0	0	1	.143
Olson ss	3	0	0	0	0	1	.308
Meyers c	3	0	0	0	0	1	.143
c-Stengel pr	0	0	0	0	0	0	.429
Marquard p	1	0	0	0	0	0	.000
a-Pfeffer ph	1	0	0	0	0	0	.500
Cheney p	0	0	0	0	0	0	.000
b-O'Mara ph	1	0	0	0	0	0	.000
Rucker p	0	0	0	0	0	0	.000
d-Getz ph	1	0	0	0	0	0	.000
TOTALS	**32**	**2**	**5**	**0**	**2**	**4**	**.223**

a - Batted for Marquard in the 4th
b - Batted for Cheney in the 7th
c - Ran for Meyers in the 9th
d - Batted for Rucker in the 9th

BATTING: 2B: Cutshaw (1, Leonard). **3B:** Johnston (1, Leonard). **S:** Wheat. **RBI:** Myers 1 (3), Cutshaw 1 (2). **Runners left in scoring position, 2 out:** Johnston 1, Cutshaw 1, Mowrey 1, Pfeffer 1. **Team LOB:** 7 **FIELDING: E:** Wheat (1), Cheney (1), Merkle (1), Johnston (1). **PB:** Meyers.

BOSTON	IP	H	R	ER	BB	SO	HR	ERA
Leonard (W, 1-0)	9	5	2	1	4	3	0	1.00
BROOKLYN	**IP**	**H**	**R**	**ER**	**BB**	**SO**	**HR**	**ERA**
Marquard (L, 0-2)	4	5	4	4	2	3	1	5.73
Cheney	3	4	2	1	1	5	0	3.00
Rucker	2	1	0	0	0	3	0	0.00

WP: Leonard 1. **Ground balls-fly balls:** Leonard 8-16, Marquard 4-2, Cheney 3-1, Rucker 2-0. **Batters faced:** Leonard 36, Marquard 18, Cheney 14, Rucker 6. **UMPIRES:** hp—Quigley, 1b—Dinneen, 2b—O'Day, 3b—Connolly **T:** 2:30 **A:** 21,662

GAME 5 Boston 4 Brooklyn 1
Braves Field 10/12/16

BROOKLYN	AB	R	H	HR	RBI	BB	AVG
Myers cf	4	0	0	0	0	0	.182
Daubert 1b	4	0	0	0	0	0	.176
Stengel rf	4	0	1	0	0	0	.364
Wheat lf	4	0	0	0	0	0	.211
Cutshaw 2b	3	1	0	0	0	1	.105
Mowrey 3b	3	0	1	0	0	0	.176
Olson ss	3	0	0	0	0	0	.250
Meyers c	3	0	1	0	0	0	.200
Pfeffer p	2	0	0	0	0	0	.250
a-Merkle ph	1	0	0	0	0	0	.250
Dell p	0	0	0	0	0	0	.000
TOTALS	**31**	**1**	**3**	**0**	**0**	**1**	**.200**

a - Batted for Pfeffer in the 8th

BATTING: S: Mowrey. **Runners left in scoring position, 2 out:** Mowrey 1, Meyers 2. **Team LOB:** 5 **FIELDING: E:** Mowrey (1), Olson (3).

BOSTON	AB	R	H	HR	RBI	BB	AVG
Hooper rf	3	2	1	0	0	1	.333
Janvrin 2b	4	0	2	0	2	0	.217
Shorten cf	3	0	1	0	1	0	.571
Hoblitzel 1b	3	0	0	0	0	1	.235
Lewis lf	3	1	2	0	0	0	.353
Gardner 3b	2	0	0	0	1	0	.176
Scott ss	3	0	0	0	0	0	.125
Cady c	3	1	1	0	0	0	.250
Shore p	3	0	0	0	0	0	.000
TOTALS	**27**	**4**	**7**	**0**	**4**	**2**	**.238**

BATTING: 2B: Janvrin (3, Pfeffer). **3B:** Lewis (1, Pfeffer). **S:** Lewis, Shorten. **SF:** Gardner. **RBI:** Janvrin 2 (3), Shorten 1 (2), Gardner 1 (6). **2-out RBI:** Janvrin 1, Shorten 1. **Runners left in scoring position, 2 out:** Shorten 1, Lewis 1, Scott 2. **Team LOB:** 4 **BASERUNNING: CS:** Janvrin (1, 2nd base off Pfeffer/Meyers), Shorten (2, 2nd base off Pfeffer/Meyers). **FIELDING: E:** Scott 2 (2). **PB:** Cady.

BROOKLYN	IP	H	R	ER	BB	SO	HR	ERA
Pfeffer (L, 0-1)	7	6	4	2	2	2	0	1.69
Dell	1	1	0	0	0	0	0	0.00
BOSTON	**IP**	**H**	**R**	**ER**	**BB**	**SO**	**HR**	**ERA**
Shore (W, 2-0)	9	3	1	0	1	4	0	1.53

WP: Pfeffer 2. **Ground balls-fly balls:** Pfeffer 11-5, Dell 0-2, Shore 14-10. **Batters faced:** Pfeffer 28, Dell 4, Shore 33. **UMPIRES:** hp—Connolly, 1b—O'Day, 2b—Dinneen, 3b—Quigley **T:** 1:43 **A:** 43,620

1917 CHICAGO WHITE SOX DEF. NY GIANTS, 4-2

GAME 1 Chicago 2 New York 1
Comiskey Park 10/06/17

NY GIANTS	AB	R	H	HR	RBI	BB	AVG
Burns lf	3	0	1	0	0	1	.333
Herzog 2b	4	0	1	0	0	0	.250
Kauff cf	4	0	0	0	0	0	.000
Zimmerman 3b	4	0	0	0	0	0	.000
Fletcher ss	4	0	0	0	0	0	.000
Robertson rf	4	0	1	0	0	0	.250
Holke 1b	3	0	2	0	0	0	.667
McCarty c	3	1	1	0	0	0	.333
Sallee p	3	0	1	0	1	0	.333
TOTALS	**32**	**1**	**7**	**0**	**1**	**1**	**.219**

BATTING: 2B: Robertson (1, Cicotte). **3B:** McCarty (1, Cicotte). **RBI:** Sallee 1 (1). **Runners left in scoring position, 2 out:** Kauff 1, Zimmerman 1, Holke 1. **GIDP:** Burns. **Team LOB:** 5 **BASERUNNING: SB:** Burns (1, 2nd base off Cicotte/Schalk). **FIELDING: E:** McCarty (1). **Outfield assists:** Robertson (1).

CHICAGO WHITE SOX	AB	R	H	HR	RBI	BB	AVG
S.Collins rf	4	1	3	0	0	0	.750
McMullin 3b	3	0	1	0	1	0	.333
E.Collins 2b	3	0	0	0	0	0	.000
Jackson lf	3	0	0	0	0	0	.000
Felsch cf	3	1	1	1	1	0	.333
Gandil 1b	3	0	1	0	0	0	.333
Weaver ss	3	0	0	0	0	0	.000
Schalk c	3	0	0	0	0	0	.000
Cicotte p	3	0	1	0	0	0	.333
TOTALS	**28**	**2**	**7**	**1**	**2**	**0**	**.250**

BATTING: 2B: McMullin (1, Sallee), S.Collins (1, Sallee). **HR:** Felsch (1, 4th off Sallee 0 on, 1 out). **S:** McMullin. **RBI:** McMullin 1 (1), Felsch 1 (1). **2-out RBI:** McMullin 1. **Runners left in scoring position, 2 out:** E.Collins 1, Jackson 1, Schalk 1. **Team LOB:** 3 **BASERUNNING: SB:** Gandil (1, 2nd base off Sallee/McCarty). **CS:** McMullin (1, 2nd base off Sallee/McCarty). **FIELDING: E:** Weaver (1). **DP:** 1 (Weaver-E.Collins-Gandil).

NY GIANTS	IP	H	R	ER	BB	SO	HR	ERA
Sallee (L, 0-1)	8	7	2	2	0	2	1	2.25
CHICAGO WHITE SOX	**IP**	**H**	**R**	**ER**	**BB**	**SO**	**HR**	**ERA**
Cicotte (W, 1-0)	9	7	1	1	1	2	0	1.00

Ground balls-fly balls: Sallee 14-5, Cicotte 7-16. **Batters faced:** Sallee 29, Cicotte 33. **UMPIRES:** hp—O'Loughlin, 1b—Klem, 2b—Rigler, 3b—Evans **T:** 1:48 **A:** 32,000

GAME 2 Chicago 7 New York 2
Comiskey Park 10/07/17

NY GIANTS	AB	R	H	HR	RBI	BB	AVG
Burns lf	3	0	1	0	0	1	.333
Herzog 2b	4	0	0	0	0	0	.125
Kauff cf	4	0	0	0	0	0	.000
Zimmerman 3b	4	0	0	0	0	0	.000
Fletcher ss	4	0	1	0	0	0	.125
Robertson rf	3	1	2	0	0	0	.429
Holke 1b	3	1	1	0	0	0	.500
McCarty c	1	0	1	0	2	0	.500
Rariden c	2	0	1	0	0	0	.500
Schupp p	1	0	0	0	0	0	.000
Anderson p	0	0	0	0	0	0	.000
Perritt p	1	0	1	0	0	0	1.000
a-Wilhoit ph	1	0	0	0	0	0	.000
Tesreau p	0	0	0	0	0	0	.000
TOTALS	**31**	**2**	**8**	**0**	**2**	**1**	**.238**

a - Batted for Perritt in the 8th

BATTING: RBI: McCarty 2 (2). **Runners left in scoring position, 2 out:** Burns 1. **GIDP:** Burns. **Team LOB:** 3 **BASERUNNING: CS:** Holke (1, 2nd base off Faber/Schalk). **FIELDING: E:** Fletcher (1). **DP:** 1 (Herzog).

CHICAGO WHITE SOX	AB	R	H	HR	RBI	BB	AVG
S.Collins rf	1	0	0	0	0	0	.600
a-Leibold ph-rf	3	1	1	0	1	1	.333
McMullin 3b	5	1	1	0	1	0	.250
E.Collins 2b	4	1	2	0	1	0	.286
Jackson lf	3	1	3	0	2	1	.500
Felsch cf	4	1	1	0	0	0	.286
Gandil 1b	4	0	1	0	1	0	.286
Weaver ss	4	1	3	0	1	0	.429
Schalk c	4	1	1	0	0	0	.143
Faber p	3	0	1	0	0	1	.333
TOTALS	**35**	**7**	**14**	**0**	**7**	**3**	**.333**

a - Batted for S.Collins in the 2nd

BATTING: RBI: Leibold 1 (1), McMullin 1 (2), E.Collins 1 (1), Jackson 2 (2), Gandil 1 (1), Weaver 1 (1). **Runners left in scoring position, 2 out:** McMullin 2, Felsch 1, Gandil 1, Faber 1. **Team LOB:** 7 **BASERUNNING: SB:** Jackson (1, 2nd base off Anderson/McCarty), E.Collins 2 (2, 2nd base off Perritt/Rariden, 3rd base off Perritt/Rariden). **CS:** Weaver (1, 2nd base off Perritt/Rariden), Leibold (1, 2nd base off Tesreau/Rariden). **FIELDING: Outfield assists:** S.Collins (1), Jackson (1), Felsch (1). **DP:** 3 (Faber-Weaver-Gandil, Felsch-E.Collins-Weaver, Weaver-Gandil).

NY GIANTS	IP	H	R	ER	BB	SO	HR	ERA
Schupp	1.1	4	2	2	1	2	0	13.50
Anderson (L, 0-1)	2	5	4	4	0	3	0	18.00
Perritt	3.2	5	1	1	1	0	0	2.45
Tesreau	1	0	0	0	1	1	0	0.00
CHICAGO WHITE SOX	**IP**	**H**	**R**	**ER**	**BB**	**SO**	**HR**	**ERA**
Faber (W, 1-0)	9	8	2	2	1	1	0	2.00

Ground balls-fly balls: Schupp 1-1, Anderson 2-1, Perritt 5-4, Tesreau 0-1, Faber 15-7. **Batters faced:** Schupp 9, Anderson 11, Perritt 15, Tesreau 3, Faber 32. **UMPIRES:** hp—Evans, 1b—Rigler, 2b—Klem, 3b—O'Loughlin **T:** 2:13 **A:** 32,000

GAME 3 New York 2 Chicago 0
Polo Grounds 10/10/17

CHICAGO WHITE SOX	AB	R	H	HR	RBI	BB	AVG
S.Collins rf	4	0	0	0	0	0	.333
McMullin 3b	4	0	0	0	0	0	.167
E.Collins 2b	4	0	2	0	0	0	.364
Jackson lf	4	0	0	0	0	0	.300
Felsch cf	3	0	1	0	0	0	.300
Gandil 1b	3	0	0	0	0	0	.200
Weaver ss	3	0	2	0	0	0	.500
Schalk c	3	0	0	0	0	0	.100
Cicotte p	3	0	0	0	0	0	.167
TOTALS	**31**	**0**	**5**	**0**	**0**	**0**	**.277**

BATTING: 2B: Weaver (1, Benton). **Runners left in scoring position, 2 out:** Schalk 1. **Team LOB:** 4 **BASERUNNING: CS:** Weaver (2, 2nd base off Benton/Rariden), Schalk (1, 2nd base off Benton/Rariden). **FIELDING: E:** S.Collins 2 (2), Cicotte (1).

NY GIANTS	AB	R	H	HR	RBI	BB	AVG
Burns lf	4	0	1	0	1	0	.300
Herzog 2b	4	0	1	0	0	0	.167
Kauff cf	4	0	0	0	0	0	.000
Zimmerman 3b	4	0	1	0	0	0	.083
Fletcher ss	4	0	0	0	0	0	.083
Robertson rf	4	1	3	0	0	0	.545
Holke 1b	4	1	1	0	1	0	.400
Rariden c	2	0	1	0	0	0	.500
Benton p	3	0	0	0	0	0	.000
TOTALS	**33**	**2**	**8**	**0**	**2**	**0**	**.240**

BATTING: 2B: Holke (1, Cicotte). **3B:** Robertson (1, Cicotte). **S:** Rariden. **RBI:** Burns 1 (1), Holke 1 (1). **2-out RBI:** Burns 1. **Runners left in scoring position, 2 out:** Burns 2, Herzog 1, Fletcher 2, Holke 1. **Team LOB:** 8 **BASERUNNING: SB:** Robertson (1, 2nd base off Cicotte/Schalk). **FIELDING: E:** Holke (1). **DP:** 1 (Rariden-Herzog).

CHICAGO WHITE SOX	IP	H	R	ER	BB	SO	HR	ERA
Cicotte (L, 1-1)	8	8	2	2	0	8	0	1.59
NY GIANTS	**IP**	**H**	**R**	**ER**	**BB**	**SO**	**HR**	**ERA**
Benton (W, 1-0)	9	5	0	0	0	5	0	0.00

Ground balls-fly balls: Cicotte 6-11, Benton 12-9. **Batters faced:** Cicotte 34, Benton 31. **UMPIRES:** hp—Klem, 1b—O'Loughlin, 2b—Evans, 3b—Rigler **T:** 1:55 **A:** 33,616

GAME 4 New York 5 Chicago 0
Polo Grounds 10/11/17

CHICAGO WHITE SOX	AB	R	H	HR	RBI	BB	AVG
S.Collins rf	4	0	2	0	0	0	.385
McMullin 3b	4	0	1	0	0	0	.188
E.Collins 2b	3	0	1	0	0	1	.357
Jackson lf	4	0	0	0	0	0	.214
Felsch cf	4	0	0	0	0	0	.214
Gandil 1b	4	0	1	0	0	0	.214
Weaver ss	3	0	0	0	0	0	.385
Schalk c	3	0	2	0	0	0	.231
Faber p	2	0	0	0	0	0	.200
a-Risberg ph	1	0	0	0	0	0	.000
Danforth p	0	0	0	0	0	0	.000
TOTALS	**32**	**0**	**7**	**0**	**0**	**1**	**.262**

a - Batted for Faber in the 8th

BATTING: 2B: E.Collins (1, Schupp). **Runners left in scoring position, 2 out:** Jackson 1, Gandil 1. **GIDP:** Weaver. **Team LOB:** 6 **BASERUNNING: SB:** E.Collins (3, 3rd base off Schupp/Rariden). **CS:** S.Collins (1, 2nd base off Schupp/Rariden). **FIELDING: Outfield assists:** Felsch (2). **DP:** 1 (Faber-Schalk-Gandil).

NY GIANTS	AB	R	H	HR	RBI	BB	AVG
Burns lf	4	0	1	0	0	0	.286
Herzog 2b	3	1	1	0	0	0	.200
Kauff cf	4	2	2	2	3	0	.125
Zimmerman 3b	4	0	1	0	0	0	.125
Fletcher ss	4	1	2	0	0	0	.188
Robertson rf	3	1	1	0	0	0	.500
Holke 1b	2	0	1	0	0	0	.417
Rariden c	3	0	0	0	1	0	.286
Schupp p	3	0	1	0	1	0	.250
TOTALS	**30**	**5**	**10**	**2**	**5**	**0**	**.262**

BATTING: 3B: Zimmerman (1, Danforth). **HR:** Kauff 2 (2, 4th off Faber 0 on, 2 out, 8th off Danforth 1 on, 1 out). **S:** Herzog, Zimmerman. **RBI:** Kauff 3 (3), Rariden 1 (1), Schupp 1 (1). **2-out RBI:** Kauff 1, Schupp 1. **Runners left in scoring position, 2 out:** Zimmerman 1, Schupp 3. **GIDP:** Rariden. **Team LOB:** 3 **FIELDING: DP:** 1 (Herzog-Fletcher-Holke).

CHICAGO WHITE SOX	IP	H	R	ER	BB	SO	HR	ERA
Faber (L, 1-1)	7	7	3	3	0	3	1	2.81
Danforth	1	3	2	2	0	2	1	18.00

NY GIANTS	IP	H	R	ER	BB	SO	HR	ERA
Schupp (W, 1-0)	9	7	0	0	1	7	0	1.74

WP: Faber 1. **HBP:** Holke (by Faber). **Ground balls-fly balls:** Faber 12-3, Danforth 0-0, Schupp 9-9. **Batters faced:** Faber 27, Danforth 5, Schupp 33. **UMPIRES:** hp—Rigler, 1b—Evans, 2b—O'Loughlin, 3b—Klem **T:** 2:09 **A:** 27,746

GAME 5 Chicago 8 New York 5
Comiskey Park 10/13/17

NY GIANTS	AB	R	H	HR	RBI	BB	AVG
Burns lf	4	2	1	0	1	1	.278
Herzog 2b	5	0	1	0	0	0	.200
Kauff cf	5	0	2	0	2	0	.190
Zimmerman 3b	5	1	1	0	0	0	.143
Fletcher ss	5	1	1	0	0	0	.190
Thorpe rf	0	0	0	0	0	0	.000
a-Robertson ph-rf	5	0	3	0	1	0	.526
Holke 1b	5	0	0	0	0	0	.294
Rariden c	3	1	3	0	1	1	.500
Sallee p	3	0	0	0	0	0	.167
Perritt p	0	0	0	0	0	0	1.000
TOTALS	**40**	**5**	**12**	**0**	**5**	**2**	**.271**

a - Batted for Thorpe in the 1st

BATTING: 2B: Kauff (1, Russell), Fletcher (1, Williams). **S:** Sallee. **RBI:** Burns 1 (2), Kauff 2 (5), Robertson 1 (1), Rariden 1 (2). **2-out RBI:** Robertson 1. **Runners left in scoring position, 2 out:** Burns 1, Kauff 1, Zimmerman 1, Holke 2, Sallee 1. **GIDP:** Zimmerman. **Team LOB:** 11 **BASERUNNING: SB:** Robertson (2, 2nd base off Cicotte/Schalk), Kauff (1, 2nd base off Cicotte/Schalk). **FIELDING: E:** Fletcher (2), Herzog (1), Zimmerman (1).

CHICAGO WHITE SOX	AB	R	H	HR	RBI	BB	AVG
S.Collins rf	5	1	1	0	0	0	.333
McMullin 3b	3	0	0	0	0	1	.158
E.Collins 2b	4	2	3	0	1	1	.444
Jackson lf	5	2	3	0	1	0	.316
Felsch cf	5	1	3	0	2	0	.316
Gandil 1b	5	1	1	0	2	0	.211
Weaver ss	4	1	1	0	0	0	.353
Schalk c	3	0	1	0	0	1	.250
Russell p	0	0	0	0	0	0	.000
Cicotte p	1	0	0	0	0	1	.143
a-Risberg ph	1	0	1	0	1	0	.500
Williams p	0	0	0	0	0	0	.000
b-Lynn ph	1	0	0	0	0	0	.000
Faber p	0	0	0	0	0	0	.200
TOTALS	**37**	**8**	**14**	**0**	**7**	**4**	**.288**

a - Batted for Cicotte in the 6th
b - Batted for Williams in the 7th

BATTING: 2B: Felsch (1, Sallee), Gandil (1, Sallee). **S:** McMullin. **RBI:** E.Collins 1 (2), Jackson 1 (3), Felsch 2 (3), Gandil 2 (3), Risberg 1 (1). **2-out RBI:** Felsch 1. **Runners left in scoring position, 2 out:** McMullin 2, Felsch 1, Gandil 3, Lynn 1. **Team LOB:** 10 **BASERUNNING: SB:** Schalk (1, 2nd base off Sallee/Rariden). **CS:** Felsch (1, 2nd base off Perritt/Rariden). **FIELDING: E:** Weaver 2 (3), S.Collins (3), Gandil (1), Williams (1). **DP:** 2 (McMullin-Gandil, McMullin-E.Collins-Gandil).

NY GIANTS	IP	H	R	ER	BB	SO	HR	ERA
Sallee (L, 0-2)	7.1	13	8	7	4	2	0	5.28
Perritt	0.2	1	0	0	0	0	0	2.08

CHICAGO WHITE SOX	IP	H	R	ER	BB	SO	HR	ERA
Russell	0	2	2	2	1	0	0	0.00
Cicotte	6	8	2	1	1	3	0	1.57
Williams	1	2	1	1	0	3	0	9.00
Faber (W, 2-1)	2	0	0	0	0	1	0	2.50

IBB: Rariden (by Cicotte). **Ground balls-fly balls:** Sallee 10-10, Perritt 0-1, Russell 0-0, Cicotte 11-4, Williams 1-0, Faber 3-2. **Batters faced:** Sallee 40, Perritt 2, Russell 3, Cicotte 28, Williams 6, Faber 6. **UMPIRES:** hp—O'Loughlin, 1b—Klem, 2b—Rigler, 3b—Evans **T:** 2:37 **A:** 27,323

GAME 6 Chicago 4 New York 2
Polo Grounds 10/15/17

CHICAGO WHITE SOX	AB	R	H	HR	RBI	BB	AVG
S.Collins rf	3	0	0	0	0	0	.286
a-Leibold ph-rf	2	0	1	0	0	0	.400
McMullin 3b	5	0	0	0	0	0	.125
E.Collins 2b	4	1	1	0	0	0	.409
Jackson lf	4	1	1	0	0	0	.304
Felsch cf	3	1	0	0	0	1	.273
Gandil 1b	4	0	2	0	2	0	.261
Weaver ss	4	1	1	0	0	0	.333
Schalk c	3	0	1	0	0	1	.263
Faber p	2	0	0	0	0	1	.143
TOTALS	**34**	**4**	**7**	**0**	**2**	**3**	**.274**

a - Batted for S.Collins in the 7th

BATTING: S: Faber. **RBI:** Gandil 2 (5). **Runners left in scoring position, 2 out:** S.Collins 1, McMullin 1, Schalk 1. **Team LOB:** 7 **BASERUNNING: CS:** Felsch (2, 2nd base off Perritt/Rariden). **FIELDING: E:** Schalk (1). **PB:** Schalk.

NY GIANTS	AB	R	H	HR	RBI	BB	AVG
Burns lf	4	1	0	0	0	0	.227
Herzog 2b	4	0	2	0	2	0	.250
Kauff cf	4	0	0	0	0	0	.160
Zimmerman 3b	4	0	0	0	0	0	.120
Fletcher ss	4	0	1	0	0	0	.200
Robertson rf	3	0	1	0	0	0	.500
Holke 1b	4	0	1	0	0	0	.286
Rariden c	3	1	0	0	0	1	.385
Benton p	1	0	0	0	0	0	.000
a-Wilhoit ph	0	0	0	0	0	1	.000
Perritt p	1	0	1	0	0	0	1.000
b-McCarty ph	1	0	0	0	0	0	.400
TOTALS	**33**	**2**	**6**	**0**	**2**	**2**	**.256**

a - Batted for Benton in the 5th
b - Batted for Perritt in the 9th

BATTING: 2B: Holke (2, Faber). **3B:** Herzog (1, Faber). **RBI:** Herzog 2 (2). **2-out RBI:** Herzog 2. **Runners left in scoring position, 2 out:** Herzog 1, Kauff 1, Rariden 1, McCarty 1. **Team LOB:** 7 **FIELDING: E:** Zimmerman (2), Robertson (1), Kauff (1). **Outfield assists:** Robertson (2).

CHICAGO WHITE SOX	IP	H	R	ER	BB	SO	HR	ERA
Faber (W, 3-1)	9	6	2	2	2	4	0	2.33

NY GIANTS	IP	H	R	ER	BB	SO	HR	ERA
Benton (L, 1-1)	5	4	3	0	1	3	0	0.00
Perritt	4	3	1	0	2	3	0	1.08

HBP: Robertson (by Faber). **Ground balls-fly balls:** Faber 12-11, Benton 8-6, Perritt 4-3. **Batters faced:** Faber 36, Benton 22, Perritt 16. **UMPIRES:** hp—Klem, 1b—O'Loughlin, 2b—Evans, 3b—Rigler **T:** 2:18 **A:** 33,969

1918 BOSTON RED SOX DEF. CHICAGO CUBS, 4-2

GAME 1 Boston 1 Chicago 0
Wrigley Field 09/05/18

BOSTON	AB	R	H	HR	RBI	BB	AVG
Hooper rf	4	0	1	0	0	0	.250
Shean 2b	2	1	1	0	0	2	.500
Strunk cf	3	0	0	0	0	0	.000
Whiteman lf	4	0	2	0	0	0	.500
McInnis 1b	2	0	1	0	1	1	.500
Scott ss	4	0	0	0	0	0	.000
Thomas 3b	3	0	0	0	0	0	.000
Agnew c	3	0	0	0	0	0	.000
Ruth p	3	0	0	0	0	0	.000
TOTALS	**28**	**1**	**5**	**0**	**1**	**3**	**.179**

BATTING: S: McInnis, Strunk. **RBI:** McInnis 1 (1). **Runners left in scoring position, 2 out:** Scott 1, Thomas 2. **Team LOB:** 5 **BASERUNNING: CS:** Hooper (1, 2nd base off Vaughn/Killefer).

CHICAGO CUBS	AB	R	H	HR	RBI	BB	AVG
Flack rf	3	0	1	0	0	0	.333
Hollocher ss	3	0	0	0	0	0	.000
Mann lf	4	0	1	0	0	0	.250
Paskert cf	4	0	2	0	0	0	.500
Merkle 1b	3	0	1	0	0	1	.333
Pick 2b	3	0	0	0	0	0	.000
a-O'Farrell ph	1	0	0	0	0	0	.000
Deal 3b	4	0	1	0	0	0	.250
b-McCabe pr	0	0	0	0	0	0	.000
Killefer c	4	0	0	0	0	0	.000
Vaughn p	3	0	0	0	0	0	.000
TOTALS	**32**	**0**	**6**	**0**	**0**	**1**	**.188**

a - Batted for Pick in the 9th
b - Ran for Deal in the 9th

BATTING: S: Hollocher. **Runners left in scoring position, 2 out:** Paskert 1, Pick 2, Deal 2. **Team LOB:** 8

BOSTON	IP	H	R	ER	BB	SO	HR	ERA
Ruth (W, 1-0)	9	6	0	0	1	4	0	0.00

CHICAGO CUBS	IP	H	R	ER	BB	SO	HR	ERA
Vaughn (L, 0-1)	9	5	1	1	3	6	0	1.00

IBB: McInnis (by Vaughn). **HBP:** Flack (by Ruth). **Ground balls-fly balls:** Ruth 9-13, Vaughn 10-7. **Batters faced:** Ruth 35, Vaughn 33. **UMPIRES:** hp—O'Day, 1b—Hildebrand, 2b—Klem, 3b—Owens **T:** 1:50 **A:** 19,274

GAME 2 Chicago 3 Boston 1
Wrigley Field 09/06/18

BOSTON	AB	R	H	HR	RBI	BB	AVG
Hooper rf	3	0	1	0	0	1	.286
Shean 2b	4	0	1	0	0	0	.333
Strunk cf	4	1	1	0	0	0	.143
Whiteman lf	3	0	1	0	1	1	.429
McInnis 1b	4	0	1	0	0	0	.333
Scott ss	2	0	0	0	0	1	.000
Thomas 3b	3	0	0	0	0	0	.000
b-Dubuc ph	1	0	0	0	0	0	.000
Agnew c	2	0	0	0	0	0	.000
a-Schang ph-c	2	0	1	0	0	0	.500
Bush p	2	0	0	0	0	1	.000
TOTALS	**30**	**1**	**6**	**0**	**1**	**4**	**.190**

a - Batted for Agnew in the 8th
b - Batted for Thomas in the 9th

BATTING: 3B: Strunk (1, Tyler), Whiteman (1, Tyler). **S:** Scott. **RBI:** Whiteman 1 (1). **Runners left in scoring position, 2 out:** Agnew 1, Schang 1. **GIDP:** Whiteman. **Team LOB:** 7 **BASERUNNING: CS:** Hooper (2, 2nd base off Tyler/Killefer). **FIELDING: E:** Whiteman (1). **Outfield assists:** Strunk 2 (2).

CHICAGO CUBS	AB	R	H	HR	RBI	BB	AVG
Flack rf	4	0	2	0	0	0	.429
Hollocher ss	4	0	1	0	0	0	.143
Mann lf	4	0	0	0	0	0	.125
Paskert cf	4	0	0	0	0	0	.250
Merkle 1b	2	1	1	0	0	1	.400
Pick 2b	2	1	1	0	0	1	.200
Deal 3b	2	0	0	0	0	0	.167
Killefer c	2	1	1	0	1	1	.167
Tyler p	3	0	1	0	2	0	.333
TOTALS	**27**	**3**	**7**	**0**	**3**	**3**	**.220**

BATTING: 2B: Killefer (1, Bush). **3B:** Hollocher (1, Bush). **S:** Deal. **RBI:** Killefer 1 (1), Tyler 2 (2). **Runners left in scoring position, 2 out:** Flack 1. **Team LOB:** 4 **BASERUNNING: CS:** Flack (1, 2nd base off Bush/Agnew), Pick (1, 2nd base off Bush/Agnew), Merkle (1, 2nd base off Bush/Agnew). **FIELDING: E:** Deal (1). **Outfield assists:** Flack (1). **DP:** 2 (Killefer-Hollocher, Hollocher-Pick-Merkle).

BOSTON	IP	H	R	ER	BB	SO	HR	ERA
Bush (L, 0-1)	8	7	3	3	3	0	0	3.38

CHICAGO CUBS	IP	H	R	ER	BB	SO	HR	ERA
Tyler (W, 1-0)	9	6	1	1	4	2	0	1.00

Ground balls-fly balls: Bush 8-12, Tyler 12-10. **Batters faced:** Bush 31, Tyler 35. **UMPIRES:** hp—Hildebrand, 1b—Klem, 2b—Owens, 3b—O'Day **T:** 1:58 **A:** 20,040

GAME 3 Boston 2 Chicago 1
Wrigley Field 09/07/18

BOSTON	AB	R	H	HR	RBI	BB	AVG
Hooper rf	3	0	1	0	0	1	.300
Shean 2b	4	0	0	0	0	0	.200
Strunk cf	4	0	0	0	0	0	.091
Whiteman lf	3	1	1	0	0	0	.400
McInnis 1b	4	1	1	0	0	0	.300
Schang c	4	0	2	0	1	0	.500
Scott ss	4	0	1	0	1	0	.100
Thomas 3b	3	0	1	0	0	0	.111
Mays p	3	0	0	0	0	0	.000
TOTALS	**32**	**2**	**7**	**0**	**2**	**1**	**.200**

BATTING: RBI: Schang 1 (1), Scott 1 (1). **Runners left in scoring position, 2 out:** Scott 1, Thomas 1, Mays 2. **Team LOB:** 5 **BASERUNNING: SB:** Whiteman (1, 2nd base off Vaughn/Killefer), Schang (1, 2nd base off Vaughn/Killefer). **FIELDING: PB:** Schang.

CHICAGO CUBS	AB	R	H	HR	RBI	BB	AVG
Flack rf	3	0	0	0	0	1	.300
Hollocher ss	3	0	0	0	0	0	.100
Mann lf	4	0	2	0	0	0	.250
Paskert cf	4	0	1	0	0	0	.250
Merkle 1b	4	0	0	0	0	0	.222
Pick 2b	4	1	2	0	0	0	.333
Deal 3b	3	0	1	0	0	0	.222
a-Barber ph	0	0	0	0	0	0	.000
Killefer c	3	0	1	0	1	0	.222
Vaughn p	3	0	0	0	0	0	.000
TOTALS	**31**	**1**	**7**	**0**	**1**	**1**	**.222**

a - Batted for Deal in the 9th

BATTING: 2B: Mann (1, Mays), Pick (1, Mays). **S:** Hollocher. **RBI:** Killefer 1 (2). **Runners left in scoring position, 2 out:** Paskert 1, Merkle 2, Vaughn 1. **Team LOB:** 5 **BASERUNNING: SB:** Pick (1, 2nd base off Mays/Schang). **CS:** Killefer (1, 2nd base off Mays/Schang). **FIELDING: E:** Hollocher (1). **Outfield assists:** Flack (2). **DP:** 2 (Hollocher-Merkle, Vaughn-Merkle).

BOSTON	IP	H	R	ER	BB	SO	HR	ERA
Mays (W, 1-0)	9	7	1	1	1	4	0	1.00

CHICAGO CUBS	IP	H	R	ER	BB	SO	HR	ERA
Vaughn (L, 0-2)	9	7	2	2	1	7	0	1.50

HBP: Whiteman (by Vaughn). **Ground balls-fly balls:** Mays 11-9, Vaughn 8-10. **Batters faced:** Mays 33, Vaughn 34. **UMPIRES:** hp—Klem, 1b—Owens, 2b—O'Day, 3b—Hildebrand **T:** 1:57 **A:** 27,054

GAME 4 Boston 3 Chicago 2
Fenway Park 09/09/18

CHICAGO CUBS	AB	R	H	HR	RBI	BB	AVG
Flack rf	4	0	1	0	0	0	.286
Hollocher ss	4	0	0	0	1	0	.071
Mann lf	4	0	1	0	1	0	.250
Paskert cf	4	0	0	0	0	0	.188
Merkle 1b	3	0	1	0	0	1	.250
Pick 2b	2	0	2	0	0	0	.455
a-Zeider ph-3b	0	0	0	0	0	2	.000
Deal 3b	2	0	1	0	0	0	.273
b-O'Farrell ph	1	0	0	0	0	0	.000
Wortman 2b	1	0	0	0	0	0	.000
Killefer c	2	1	0	0	0	1	.182
e-Barber ph	1	0	0	0	0	0	.000
Tyler p	0	0	0	0	0	2	.333
c-Hendrix ph	1	0	1	0	0	0	1.000
d-McCabe pr	0	1	0	0	0	0	.000
Douglas p	0	0	0	0	0	0	.000
TOTALS	**29**	**2**	**7**	**0**	**2**	**6**	**.227**

a - Batted for Pick in the 7th
b - Batted for Deal in the 7th
c - Batted for Tyler in the 8th
d - Ran for Hendrix in the 8th e - Batted for Killefer in the 9th

BATTING: RBI: Hollocher 1 (1), Mann 1 (1). **2-out RBI:** Mann 1. **Runners left in scoring position, 2 out:** Mann 1, Killefer 1. **GIDP:** Killefer, O'Farrell, Barber. **Team LOB:** 6 **FIELDING: E:** Douglas (1). **PB:** Killefer.

BOSTON	AB	R	H	HR	RBI	BB	AVG
Hooper rf	3	0	0	0	0	0	.231
Shean 2b	3	0	1	0	0	1	.231
Strunk cf	4	0	0	0	0	0	.067
Whiteman lf	3	1	0	0	0	1	.308
Bush p	0	0	0	0	0	0	.000
McInnis 1b	3	1	1	0	0	0	.308
Ruth p-lf	2	0	1	0	2	0	.200
Scott ss	3	0	0	0	0	0	.077
Thomas 3b	3	0	0	0	0	0	.083
Agnew c	2	0	0	0	0	0	.000
a-Schang ph-c	1	1	1	0	0	0	.571
TOTALS	**27**	**3**	**4**	**0**	**2**	**2**	**.188**

a - Batted for Agnew in the 8th

BATTING: 2B: Shean (1, Tyler). **3B:** Ruth (1, Tyler). **S:** Ruth, Hooper. **RBI:** Ruth 2 (2). **2-out RBI:** Ruth 2. **Runners left in scoring position, 2 out:** Whiteman 2, Scott 1. **Team LOB:** 4 **BASERUNNING: SB:** Shean (1, 2nd base off Tyler/Killefer). **FIELDING: DP:** 3 (Ruth-Scott-McInnis, Scott-Shean-McInnis 2).

CHICAGO CUBS	IP	H	R	ER	BB	SO	HR	ERA
Tyler	7	3	2	2	2	1	0	1.69
Douglas (L, 0-1)	1	1	1	0	0	0	0	0.00

BOSTON	IP	H	R	ER	BB	SO	HR	ERA
Ruth (W, 2-0)	8	7	2	2	6	0	0	1.06
Bush (S, 1)	1	0	0	0	0	0	0	3.00

WP: Ruth 1. **Ground balls-fly balls:** Tyler 10-9, Douglas 1-2, Ruth 16-4, Bush 2-0. **Batters faced:** Tyler 26, Douglas 5, Ruth 33, Bush 2. **UMPIRES:** hp—Owens, 1b—O'Day, 2b—Hildebrand, 3b—Klem **T:** 1:50 **A:** 22,183

GAME 5 Chicago 3 Boston 0
Fenway Park 09/10/18

CHICAGO CUBS	AB	R	H	HR	RBI	BB	AVG
Flack rf	2	1	0	0	0	2	.250
Hollocher ss	3	2	3	0	0	1	.235
Mann lf	3	0	1	0	1	0	.263
Paskert cf	3	0	1	0	2	1	.211
Merkle 1b	3	0	1	0	0	1	.267
Pick 2b	4	0	1	0	0	0	.400
Deal 3b	4	0	0	0	0	0	.200
Killefer c	4	0	0	0	0	0	.133
Vaughn p	4	0	0	0	0	0	.000
TOTALS	**30**	**3**	**7**	**0**	**3**	**5**	**.228**

BATTING: 2B: Mann (2, Jones), Paskert (1, Jones). **S:** Mann. **RBI:** Mann 1 (2), Paskert 2 (2). **2-out RBI:** Mann 1. **Runners left in scoring position, 2 out:** Paskert 1, Pick 3, Killefer 1. **Team LOB:** 6 **BASERUNNING: SB:** Hollocher (1, 2nd base off Jones/Agnew). **FIELDING: DP:** 3 (Merkle-Hollocher, Hollocher-Pick-Merkle 2).

BOSTON	AB	R	H	HR	RBI	BB	AVG
Hooper rf	4	0	1	0	0	0	.235
Shean 2b	3	0	1	0	0	0	.250
Strunk cf	4	0	1	0	0	0	.105
Whiteman lf	3	0	1	0	0	0	.313
McInnis 1b	3	0	0	0	0	0	.250
Scott ss	3	0	0	0	0	0	.063
Thomas 3b	3	0	1	0	0	0	.133
Agnew c	2	0	0	0	0	0	.000
a-Schang ph-c	1	0	0	0	0	0	.500
Jones p	1	0	0	0	0	1	.000
b-Miller ph	1	0	0	0	0	0	.000
TOTALS	**28**	**0**	**5**	**0**	**0**	**1**	**.186**

a - Batted for Agnew in the 8th
b - Batted for Jones in the 9th

BATTING: 2B: Strunk (1, Vaughn). **S:** Shean. **Runners left in scoring position, 2 out:** Whiteman 1. **GIDP:** Agnew, McInnis. **Team LOB:** 3 **FIELDING: Outfield assists:** Whiteman 2 (2). **DP:** 1 (Whiteman-Shean).

CHICAGO CUBS	IP	H	R	ER	BB	SO	HR	ERA
Vaughn (W, 1-2)	9	5	0	0	1	4	0	1.00

BOSTON	IP	H	R	ER	BB	SO	HR	ERA
Jones (L, 0-1)	9	7	3	3	5	5	0	3.00

Ground balls-fly balls: Vaughn 8-11, Jones 8-10. **Batters faced:** Vaughn 30, Jones 36. **UMPIRES:** hp—O'Day, 1b—Hildebrand, 2b—Klem, 3b—Owens **T:** 1:42 **A:** 24,694

GAME 6 Boston 2 Chicago 1
Fenway Park 09/11/18

CHICAGO CUBS	AB	R	H	HR	RBI	BB	AVG
Flack rf	3	1	1	0	0	1	.263
Hollocher ss	4	0	0	0	0	0	.190
Mann lf	3	0	0	0	0	0	.227
Paskert cf	2	0	0	0	0	1	.190
Merkle 1b	3	0	1	0	1	0	.278
Pick 2b	3	0	1	0	0	0	.389
Deal 3b	2	0	0	0	0	0	.176
a-Barber ph	1	0	0	0	0	0	.000
Zeider 3b	0	0	0	0	0	0	.000
Killefer c	2	0	0	0	0	0	.118
b-O'Farrell ph-c	1	0	0	0	0	0	.000
Tyler p	2	0	0	0	0	0	.200
c-McCabe ph	1	0	0	0	0	0	.000
Hendrix p	0	0	0	0	0	0	1.000
TOTALS	**27**	**1**	**3**	**0**	**1**	**2**	**.210**

a - Batted for Deal in the 8th
b - Batted for Killefer in the 8th
c - Batted for Tyler in the 8th

BATTING: RBI: Merkle 1 (1). **2-out RBI:** Merkle 1. **Runners left in scoring position, 2 out:** Pick 1. **Team LOB:** 2 **BASERUNNING: SB:** Flack (1, 3rd base off Mays/Schang). **CS:** Mann (1, 2nd base off Mays/Schang). **FIELDING: E:** Flack (1), Tyler (1).

BOSTON	AB	R	H	HR	RBI	BB	AVG
Hooper rf	3	0	0	0	0	0	.200
Shean 2b	3	1	0	0	0	1	.211
Strunk cf	4	0	2	0	0	0	.174
Whiteman lf	4	0	0	0	0	0	.250
Ruth lf	0	0	0	0	0	0	.200
McInnis 1b	4	0	1	0	0	0	.250
Scott ss	4	0	1	0	0	0	.100
Thomas 3b	2	0	0	0	0	1	.118
Schang c	1	0	0	0	0	2	.444
Mays p	2	1	1	0	0	1	.200
TOTALS	**27**	**2**	**5**	**0**	**0**	**5**	**.186**

BATTING: S: Hooper, Thomas. **Runners left in scoring position, 2 out:** Shean 2. **Team LOB:** 8 **BASERUNNING: CS:** Schang (1, 2nd base off Tyler/Killefer).

CHICAGO CUBS	IP	H	R	ER	BB	SO	HR	ERA
Tyler (L, 1-1)	7	5	2	0	5	1	0	1.17
Hendrix	1	0	0	0	0	0	0	0.00

BOSTON	IP	H	R	ER	BB	SO	HR	ERA
Mays (W, 2-0)	9	3	1	1	2	1	0	1.00

HBP: Mann (by Mays). **Ground balls-fly balls:** Tyler 11-7, Hendrix 0-3, Mays 16-7. **Batters faced:** Tyler 31, Hendrix 3, Mays 30. **UMPIRES:** hp—Hildebrand, 1b—Klem, 2b—Owens, 3b—O'Day **T:** 1:46 **A:** 15,238

1919 CINCINNATI DEF. CHICAGO WHITE SOX, 5-3

GAME 1 Cincinnati 9 Chicago 1
Redland Field 10/01/19

CHICAGO WHITE SOX	AB	R	H	HR	RBI	BB	AVG
S.Collins rf	4	0	1	0	0	0	.250
E.Collins 2b	4	0	1	0	0	0	.250
Weaver 3b	4	0	1	0	0	0	.250
Jackson lf	4	1	0	0	0	0	.000
Felsch cf	3	0	0	0	0	0	.000
Gandil 1b	4	0	2	0	1	0	.500
Risberg ss	2	0	0	0	0	1	.000
Schalk c	3	0	0	0	0	0	.000
Cicotte p	1	0	0	0	0	0	.000
Wilkinson p	1	0	0	0	0	0	.000
a-McMullin ph	1	0	1	0	0	0	1.000
Lowdermilk p	0	0	0	0	0	0	.000
TOTALS	**31**	**1**	**6**	**0**	**1**	**1**	**.194**

a - Batted for Wilkinson in the 8th

BATTING: S: Felsch. **RBI:** Gandil 1 (1). **Runners left in scoring position, 2 out:** Felsch 2. **Team LOB:** 5 **BASERUNNING: CS:** E.Collins (1, 2nd base off Ruether/Wingo), Gandil (1, 2nd base off Ruether/Wingo). **FIELDING: DP:** 2 (Risberg-E.Collins, Risberg-E.Collins-Gandil).

CINCINNATI	AB	R	H	HR	RBI	BB	AVG
Rath 2b	3	2	1	0	1	0	.333
Daubert 1b	4	1	3	0	1	0	.750
Groh 3b	3	1	1	0	2	1	.333
Roush cf	3	0	0	0	0	1	.000
Duncan lf	4	0	2	0	1	0	.500
Kopf ss	4	1	0	0	0	0	.000
Neale rf	4	2	3	0	0	0	.750
Wingo c	3	1	1	0	1	0	.333
Ruether p	3	1	3	0	3	1	1.000
TOTALS	**31**	**9**	**14**	**0**	**9**	**3**	**.452**

BATTING: 2B: Rath (1, Cicotte). **3B:** Ruether 2 (2, Cicotte, Lowdermilk), Daubert (1, Wilkinson). **S:** Rath, Roush, Wingo. **SF:** Groh. **RBI:** Rath 1 (1), Daubert 1 (1), Groh 2 (2), Duncan 1 (1), Wingo 1 (1), Ruether 3 (3). **2-out RBI:** Rath 1, Daubert 1, Wingo 1, Ruether 2. **Runners left in scoring position, 2 out:** Groh 2, Roush 2, Duncan 1. **GIDP:** Kopf. **Team LOB:** 7 **BASERUNNING: SB:** Roush (1, 2nd base off Cicotte/Schalk). **CS:** Daubert (1, 2nd base off Cicotte/Schalk), Duncan (1, 2nd base off Wilkinson/Schalk). **FIELDING: E:** Kopf (1).

CHICAGO WHITE SOX	IP	H	R	ER	BB	SO	HR	ERA
Cicotte (L, 0-1)	3.2	7	6	6	2	1	0	14.73
Wilkinson	3.1	5	2	1	0	1	0	2.70
Lowdermilk	1	2	1	1	1	0	0	9.00

CINCINNATI	IP	H	R	ER	BB	SO	HR	ERA
Ruether (W, 1-0)	9	6	1	0	1	1	0	0.00

HBP: Rath (by Cicotte), Daubert (by Lowdermilk). **Ground balls-fly balls:** Cicotte 3-4, Wilkinson 3-3, Lowdermilk 2-0, Ruether 12-12. **Batters faced:** Cicotte 20, Wilkinson 13, Lowdermilk 7, Ruether 33. **UMPIRES:** hp—Rigler, 1b—Evans, 2b—Nallin, 3b—Quigley **T:** 1:42 **A:** 30,511

GAME 2 Cincinnati 4 Chicago 2
Redland Field 10/02/19

CHICAGO WHITE SOX	AB	R	H	HR	RBI	BB	AVG
S.Collins rf	4	0	0	0	0	0	.125
E.Collins 2b	3	0	0	0	0	1	.143
Weaver 3b	4	0	2	0	0	0	.375
Jackson lf	4	0	3	0	0	0	.375
Felsch cf	2	0	0	0	0	0	.000
Gandil 1b	4	0	1	0	0	0	.375
Risberg ss	4	1	1	0	0	0	.167
Schalk c	4	1	2	0	2	0	.286
Williams p	3	0	1	0	0	0	.333
a-McMullin ph	1	0	0	0	0	0	.500
TOTALS	**33**	**2**	**10**	**0**	**2**	**1**	**.250**

a - Batted for Williams in the 9th

BATTING: 2B: Jackson (1, Sallee), Weaver (1, Sallee). **S:** Felsch, Felsch. **RBI:** Schalk 2 (2). **Runners left in scoring position, 2 out:** Felsch 2, Risberg 3. **GIDP:** Risberg. **Team LOB:** 7 **BASERUNNING: SB:** Gandil (1, 2nd base off Sallee/Rariden). **FIELDING: E:** Risberg (1). **Outfield assists:** Felsch (1). **DP:** 2 (E.Collins-Gandil, Felsch-Gandil).

CINCINNATI	AB	R	H	HR	RBI	BB	AVG
Rath 2b	3	1	0	0	0	1	.167
Daubert 1b	3	0	0	0	0	0	.429
Groh 3b	2	1	0	0	0	2	.200
Roush cf	2	1	1	0	1	2	.200
Duncan lf	1	1	0	0	0	1	.400
Kopf ss	3	0	1	0	2	0	.143
Neale rf	3	0	1	0	1	0	.571
Rariden c	3	0	1	0	0	0	.333
Sallee p	3	0	0	0	0	0	.000
TOTALS	**23**	**4**	**4**	**0**	**4**	**6**	**.333**

BATTING: 3B: Kopf (1, Williams). **S:** Daubert, Duncan. **RBI:** Roush 1 (1), Kopf 2 (2), Neale 1 (1). **2-out RBI:** Kopf 2, Neale 1. **Runners left in scoring position, 2 out:** Groh 1, Neale 1. **Team LOB:** 3 **BASERUNNING: CS:** Roush (1, 2nd base off Williams/Schalk), Neale (1, 2nd base off Williams/Schalk). **FIELDING: E:** Neale (1), Daubert (1). **DP:** 2 (Kopf-Daubert, Rath-Kopf-Daubert).

CHICAGO WHITE SOX	IP	H	R	ER	BB	SO	HR	ERA
Williams (L, 0-1)	8	4	4	4	6	1	0	4.50

CINCINNATI	IP	H	R	ER	BB	SO	HR	ERA
Sallee (W, 1-0)	9	10	2	0	1	2	0	0.00

BK: Sallee 1. **Ground balls-fly balls:** Williams 3-15, Sallee 11-10. **Batters faced:** Williams 31, Sallee 36. **UMPIRES:** hp—Evans, 1b—Quigley, 2b—Nallin, 3b—Rigler **T:** 1:42 **A:** 29,698

GAME 3 Chicago 3 Cincinnati 0
Comiskey Park 10/03/19

CINCINNATI	AB	R	H	HR	RBI	BB	AVG
Rath 2b	4	0	0	0	0	0	.100
Daubert 1b	4	0	0	0	0	0	.273
Groh 3b	3	0	0	0	0	1	.125
Roush cf	3	0	0	0	0	0	.125
Duncan lf	3	0	1	0	0	0	.375
Kopf ss	3	0	1	0	0	0	.200
Neale rf	3	0	0	0	0	0	.400
Rariden c	3	0	0	0	0	0	.167
Fisher p	2	0	1	0	0	0	.500
a-Magee ph	1	0	0	0	0	0	.000
Luque p	0	0	0	0	0	0	.000
TOTALS	**29**	**0**	**3**	**0**	**0**	**1**	**.253**

a - Batted for Fisher in the 8th

BATTING: Runners left in scoring position, 2 out: Neale 1, Fisher 1. **Team LOB:** 3 **FIELDING: E:** Fisher (1). **DP:** 1 (Groh-Rath-Daubert).

CHICAGO WHITE SOX	AB	R	H	HR	RBI	BB	AVG
Leibold rf	4	0	0	0	0	0	.000
E.Collins 2b	4	0	1	0	0	0	.182
Weaver 3b	4	0	1	0	0	0	.333
Jackson lf	3	1	2	0	0	0	.455
Felsch cf	2	1	0	0	0	1	.000
Gandil 1b	3	0	1	0	2	0	.364
Risberg ss	2	1	1	0	0	1	.250
Schalk c	3	0	1	0	1	0	.300
Kerr p	3	0	0	0	0	0	.000
TOTALS	**28**	**3**	**7**	**0**	**3**	**2**	**.250**

BATTING: 3B: Risberg (1, Fisher). **RBI:** Gandil 2 (3), Schalk 1 (3). **Runners left in scoring position, 2 out:** Leibold 1. **GIDP:** Felsch. **Team LOB:** 3 **BASERUNNING: CS:** Schalk (1, 2nd base off Fisher/Rariden), Jackson (1, 2nd base off Fisher/Rariden), Felsch (1, 2nd base off Fisher/Rariden). **FIELDING: DP:** 1 (Risberg-E.Collins).

CINCINNATI	IP	H	R	ER	BB	SO	HR	ERA
Fisher (L, 0-1)	7	7	3	2	2	1	0	2.57
Luque	1	0	0	0	0	1	0	0.00

CHICAGO WHITE SOX	IP	H	R	ER	BB	SO	HR	ERA
Kerr (W, 1-0)	9	3	0	0	1	4	0	0.00

Ground balls-fly balls: Fisher 14-3, Luque 2-0, Kerr 15-7. **Batters faced:** Fisher 27, Luque 3, Kerr 30. **UMPIRES:** hp—Quigley, 1b—Nallin, 2b—Rigler, 3b—Evans **T:** 1:30 **A:** 29,126

GAME 4 Cincinnati 2 Chicago 0
Comiskey Park 10/04/19

CINCINNATI	AB	R	H	HR	RBI	BB	AVG
Rath 2b	4	0	1	0	0	0	.143
Daubert 1b	4	0	0	0	0	0	.200
Groh 3b	4	0	0	0	0	0	.083
Roush cf	3	0	0	0	0	0	.091
Duncan lf	3	1	0	0	0	0	.273
Kopf ss	3	1	1	0	0	0	.231
Neale rf	3	0	1	0	1	0	.385
Wingo c	3	0	2	0	0	0	.500
Ring p	3	0	0	0	0	0	.000
TOTALS	**30**	**2**	**5**	**0**	**1**	**0**	**.230**

BATTING: 2B: Neale (1, Cicotte). **RBI:** Neale 1 (2). **Runners left in scoring position, 2 out:** Ring 1. **GIDP:** Daubert, Ring. **Team LOB:** 1 **BASERUNNING: CS:** Wingo (1, 2nd base off Cicotte/Schalk). **FIELDING: E:** Rath (1), Groh (1).

CHICAGO WHITE SOX	AB	R	H	HR	RBI	BB	AVG
Leibold rf	5	0	0	0	0	0	.000
E.Collins 2b	3	0	0	0	0	0	.143
Weaver 3b	4	0	0	0	0	0	.250
Jackson lf	4	0	1	0	0	0	.400
Felsch cf	3	0	1	0	0	0	.100
Gandil 1b	4	0	1	0	0	0	.333
Risberg ss	3	0	0	0	0	1	.182
Schalk c	1	0	0	0	0	2	.273
Cicotte p	3	0	0	0	0	0	.000
a-Murphy ph	1	0	0	0	0	0	.000
TOTALS	**31**	**0**	**3**	**0**	**0**	**3**	**.211**

a - Batted for Cicotte in the 9th

BATTING: 2B: Jackson (2, Ring). **S:** Felsch. **Runners left in scoring position, 2 out:** Felsch 1, Cicotte 2. **Team LOB:** 10 **BASERUNNING: SB:** Risberg (1, 2nd base off Ring/Wingo). **FIELDING: E:** Cicotte 2 (2). **DP:** 2 (E.Collins-Risberg-Gandil, Cicotte-Risberg-Gandil).

CINCINNATI	IP	H	R	ER	BB	SO	HR	ERA
Ring (W, 1-0)	9	3	0	0	3	2	0	0.00

CHICAGO WHITE SOX	IP	H	R	ER	BB	SO	HR	ERA
Cicotte (L, 0-2)	9	5	2	0	0	2	0	4.26

HBP: E.Collins (by Ring), Schalk (by Ring). **Ground balls-fly balls:** Ring 11-15, Cicotte 14-9. **Batters faced:** Ring 37, Cicotte 30. **UMPIRES:** hp—Nallin, 1b—Rigler, 2b—Evans, 3b—Quigley **T:** 1:37 **A:** 34,363

GAME 5 Cincinnati 5 Chicago 0
Comiskey Park 10/06/19

CINCINNATI	AB	R	H	HR	RBI	BB	AVG
Rath 2b	3	1	1	0	1	1	.176
Daubert 1b	2	0	0	0	0	0	.176
Groh 3b	3	1	0	0	0	1	.067
Roush cf	4	2	1	0	2	0	.133
Duncan lf	2	0	0	0	1	1	.231
Kopf ss	3	0	1	0	0	0	.250
Neale rf	4	0	0	0	1	0	.294
Rariden c	4	0	0	0	0	0	.100
Eller p	3	1	1	0	0	0	.333
TOTALS	**28**	**5**	**4**	**0**	**5**	**3**	**.213**

BATTING: 2B: Eller (1, Williams). **3B:** Roush (1, Williams). **S:** Daubert, Daubert, Kopf. **SF:** Duncan. **RBI:** Rath 1 (2), Roush 2 (3), Duncan 1 (2), Neale 1 (3). **Runners left in scoring position, 2 out:** Roush 1, Duncan 1, Rariden 1. **Team LOB:** 3
BASERUNNING: SB: Roush (2, 2nd base off Williams/Schalk). **CS:** Neale (2, 2nd base off Williams/Schalk).

CHICAGO WHITE SOX	AB	R	H	HR	RBI	BB	AVG
Leibold rf	3	0	0	0	0	1	.000
E.Collins 2b	4	0	0	0	0	0	.111
Weaver 3b	4	0	2	0	0	0	.300
Jackson lf	4	0	0	0	0	0	.316
Felsch cf	3	0	0	0	0	0	.077
Gandil 1b	3	0	0	0	0	0	.278
Risberg ss	3	0	0	0	0	0	.143
Schalk c	2	0	1	0	0	0	.308
Lynn c	1	0	0	0	0	0	.000
Williams p	2	0	0	0	0	0	.200
a-Murphy ph	1	0	0	0	0	0	.000
Mayer p	0	0	0	0	0	0	.000
TOTALS	**30**	**0**	**3**	**0**	**0**	**1**	**.190**

a - Batted for Williams in the 8th

BATTING: 3B: Weaver (1, Eller). **Runners left in scoring position, 2 out:** Jackson 1, Felsch 1. **Team LOB:** 4 **FIELDING: E:** Risberg (2), Felsch (1), E.Collins (1).

CINCINNATI	IP	H	R	ER	BB	SO	HR	ERA
Eller (W, 1-0)	9	3	0	0	1	9	0	0.00

CHICAGO WHITE SOX	IP	H	R	ER	BB	SO	HR	ERA
Williams (L, 0-2)	8	4	4	4	2	3	0	4.50
Mayer	1	0	1	0	1	0	0	0.00

Ground balls-fly balls: Eller 11-7, Williams 5-13, Mayer 3-0. **Batters faced:** Eller 31, Williams 30, Mayer 5. **UMPIRES:** hp—Rigler, 1b—Evans, 2b—Quigley, 3b—Nallin **T:** 1:45 **A:** 34,379

GAME 6 Chicago 5 Cincinnati 4
Redland Field 10/07/19

CHICAGO WHITE SOX	AB	R	H	HR	RBI	BB	AVG
S.Collins rf	3	0	0	0	0	0	.091
a-Leibold ph-rf	1	0	0	0	0	1	.000
E.Collins 2b	4	0	0	0	1	0	.091
Weaver 3b	5	2	3	0	0	0	.360
Jackson lf	4	1	2	0	1	1	.348
Felsch cf	5	1	2	0	1	0	.167
Gandil 1b	4	0	1	0	1	1	.273
Risberg ss	4	1	0	0	0	1	.111
Schalk c	2	0	1	0	1	2	.333
Kerr p	3	0	1	0	0	0	.167
TOTALS	**35**	**5**	**10**	**0**	**5**	**6**	**.207**

a - Batted for S.Collins in the 7th

BATTING: 2B: Weaver 2 (3, Ruether, Ring), Felsch (1, Ruether). **S:** Kerr. **SF:** E.Collins. **RBI:** E.Collins 1 (1), Jackson 1 (1), Felsch 1 (1), Gandil 1 (4), Schalk 1 (4). **2-out RBI:** Schalk 1. **Runners left in scoring position, 2 out:** E.Collins 2, Kerr 1. **Team LOB:** 8 **BASERUNNING: SB:** Schalk (1, 2nd base off Ring/Rariden), Leibold (1, 2nd base off Ring/Rariden). **FIELDING: E:** Risberg 2 (4), Felsch (2). **Outfield assists:** Jackson (1). **DP:** 2 (Jackson-Schalk, Risberg-E.Collins-Gandil).

CINCINNATI	AB	R	H	HR	RBI	BB	AVG
Rath 2b	5	0	1	0	0	0	.182
Daubert 1b	4	1	2	0	0	0	.238
Groh 3b	4	0	1	0	0	1	.105
Roush cf	4	1	1	0	0	0	.158
Duncan lf	5	0	1	0	2	0	.222
Kopf ss	4	0	0	0	0	1	.200
Neale rf	4	1	3	0	0	0	.381
Rariden c	4	0	1	0	0	0	.143
Ruether p	2	1	1	0	1	0	.800
Ring p	2	0	0	0	0	0	.000
TOTALS	**38**	**4**	**11**	**0**	**3**	**2**	**.229**

BATTING: 2B: Groh (1, Kerr), Duncan (1, Kerr), Ruether (1, Kerr). **3B:** Neale (1, Kerr). **S:** Daubert. **RBI:** Duncan 2 (4), Ruether 1 (4). **2-out RBI:** Duncan 2. **Runners left in scoring position, 2 out:** Roush 1, Kopf 2, Ruether 1, Ring 1. **GIDP:** Roush. **Team LOB:** 8 **BASERUNNING: SB:** Daubert (1, 2nd base off Kerr/Schalk), Rath (1, 3rd base off Kerr/Schalk). **CS:** Neale (3, 2nd base off Kerr/Schalk), Groh (1, 2nd base off Kerr/Schalk). **FIELDING: Outfield assists:** Roush 2 (2). **DP:** 3 (Roush-Groh, Roush-Rath, Kopf-Rath).

CHICAGO WHITE SOX	IP	H	R	ER	BB	SO	HR	ERA
Kerr (W, 2-0)	10	11	4	3	2	2	0	1.42

CINCINNATI	IP	H	R	ER	BB	SO	HR	ERA
Ruether	5	6	4	4	3	0	0	2.57
Ring (L, 1-1)	5	4	1	1	3	2	0	0.64

HBP: Roush (by Kerr). **Ground balls-fly balls:** Kerr 15-10, Ruether 2-10, Ring 5-6. **Batters faced:** Kerr 42, Ruether 23, Ring 20. **UMPIRES:** hp—Evans, 1b—Quigley, 2b—Nallin, 3b—Rigler **T:** 2:06 **A:** 32,006

GAME 7 Chicago 4 Cincinnati 1
Redland Field 10/08/19

CHICAGO WHITE SOX	AB	R	H	HR	RBI	BB	AVG
S.Collins cf	5	2	3	0	0	0	.250
E.Collins 2b	4	1	2	0	0	0	.154
Weaver 3b	4	1	0	0	0	0	.310
Jackson lf	4	0	2	0	2	0	.370
Felsch rf	4	0	2	0	2	0	.227
Gandil 1b	4	0	0	0	0	0	.231
Risberg ss	4	0	0	0	0	0	.091
Schalk c	4	0	1	0	0	0	.316
Cicotte p	4	0	0	0	0	0	.000
TOTALS	**37**	**4**	**10**	**0**	**4**	**0**	**.218**

BATTING: 2B: S.Collins (1, Luque). **S:** E.Collins. **RBI:** Jackson 2 (3), Felsch 2 (3). **2-out RBI:** Jackson 2. **Runners left in scoring position, 2 out:** E.Collins 1, Gandil 1, Risberg 2. **Team LOB:** 7 **FIELDING: E:** E.Collins (2).

CINCINNATI	AB	R	H	HR	RBI	BB	AVG
Rath 2b	5	0	1	0	0	0	.185
Daubert 1b	4	0	0	0	0	0	.200
Groh 3b	4	1	1	0	0	0	.130
Roush cf	4	0	0	0	0	0	.130
Duncan lf	4	0	1	0	1	0	.227
Kopf ss	4	0	1	0	0	0	.208
Neale rf	4	0	1	0	0	0	.360
Wingo c	1	0	1	0	0	3	.571
Sallee p	1	0	0	0	0	0	.000
Fisher p	0	0	0	0	0	0	.500
a-Ruether ph	1	0	0	0	0	0	.667
Luque p	1	0	0	0	0	0	.000
b-Magee ph	1	0	1	0	0	0	.500
c-Smith pr	0	0	0	0	0	0	.000
TOTALS	**34**	**1**	**7**	**0**	**1**	**3**	**.225**

a - Batted for Fisher in the 5th
b - Batted for Luque in the 9th
c - Ran for Magee in the 9th

BATTING: 2B: Groh (2, Cicotte). **RBI:** Duncan 1 (5). **2-out RBI:** Duncan 1. **Runners left in scoring position, 2 out:** Rath 2, Daubert 1. **Team LOB:** 9 **BASERUNNING: CS:** Kopf (1, 2nd base off Cicotte/Schalk). **FIELDING: E:** Groh (2), Rath (2), Roush (1). **DP:** 1 (Kopf-Daubert).

CHICAGO WHITE SOX	IP	H	R	ER	BB	SO	HR	ERA
Cicotte (W, 1-2)	9	7	1	1	3	4	0	2.91

CINCINNATI	IP	H	R	ER	BB	SO	HR	ERA
Sallee (L, 1-1)	4.1	9	4	2	0	0	0	1.35
Fisher	0.2	0	0	0	0	1	0	2.35
Luque	4	1	0	0	0	5	0	0.00

Ground balls-fly balls: Cicotte 13-10, Sallee 6-7, Fisher 1-0, Luque 3-4. **Batters faced:** Cicotte 37, Sallee 23, Fisher 2, Luque 13. **UMPIRES:** hp—Quigley, 1b—Nallin, 2b—Rigler, 3b—Evans **T:** 1:47 **A:** 13,923

GAME 8 Cincinnati 10 Chicago 5
Comiskey Park 10/09/19

CINCINNATI	AB	R	H	HR	RBI	BB	AVG
Rath 2b	4	1	2	0	0	2	.226
Daubert 1b	4	2	2	0	0	1	.241
Groh 3b	6	2	2	0	0	0	.172
Roush cf	5	2	3	0	4	0	.214
Duncan lf	4	1	2	0	3	0	.269
Kopf ss	3	1	1	0	0	2	.222
Neale rf	3	0	1	0	1	2	.357
Rariden c	5	0	2	0	2	0	.211
Eller p	4	1	1	0	0	0	.286
TOTALS	**38**	**10**	**16**	**0**	**10**	**7**	**.255**

BATTING: 2B: Roush 2 (2, Williams, James), Duncan (2, Williams). **3B:** Kopf (2, James). **S:** Duncan, Daubert. **RBI:** Roush 4 (7), Duncan 3 (8), Neale 1 (4), Rariden 2 (2). **2-out RBI:** Roush 1, Neale 1, Rariden 2. **Runners left in scoring position, 2 out:** Groh 3, Roush 1, Rariden 1, Eller 4. **Team LOB:** 12 **BASERUNNING: SB:** Rariden (1, 2nd base off James/Schalk), Neale (1, 2nd base off James/Schalk), Rath (2, 2nd base off Wilkinson/Schalk). **CS:** Neale (4, 2nd base off James/Schalk). **FIELDING: E:** Rariden (1), Roush (2).

CHICAGO WHITE SOX	AB	R	H	HR	RBI	BB	AVG
Leibold cf	5	0	1	0	0	0	.056
E.Collins 2b	5	1	3	0	0	0	.226
Weaver 3b	5	1	2	0	0	0	.324
Jackson lf	5	2	2	1	3	0	.375
Felsch rf	4	0	0	0	0	0	.192
Gandil 1b	4	1	1	0	1	0	.233
Risberg ss	3	0	0	0	0	1	.080
Schalk c	4	0	1	0	0	0	.304
Williams p	0	0	0	0	0	0	.200
James p	2	0	0	0	0	0	.000
Wilkinson p	1	0	0	0	0	0	.000
a-Murphy ph	0	0	0	0	0	0	.000
TOTALS	**38**	**5**	**10**	**1**	**4**	**1**	**.224**

a - Batted for Wilkinson in the 9th

BATTING: 2B: E.Collins (1, Eller), Weaver (4, Eller), Jackson (3, Eller). **3B:** Gandil (1, Eller). **HR:** Jackson (1, 3th off Eller 0 on, 2 out). **RBI:** Jackson 3 (6), Gandil 1 (5). **2-out RBI:** Jackson 1, Gandil 1. **Runners left in scoring position, 2 out:** Leibold 1, Jackson 2, Felsch 2. **Team LOB:** 8 **BASERUNNING: SB:** E.Collins (1, 2nd base off Eller/Rariden). **FIELDING: E:** Schalk (1). **Outfield assists:** Leibold 2 (2).

CINCINNATI	IP	H	R	ER	BB	SO	HR	ERA
Eller (W, 2-0)	9	10	5	4	1	6	1	2.00

CHICAGO WHITE SOX	IP	H	R	ER	BB	SO	HR	ERA
Williams (L, 0-3)	0.1	4	4	4	0	0	0	6.61
James	4.2	8	4	4	3	2	0	7.71
Wilkinson	4	4	2	1	4	2	0	2.45

HBP: Eller (by James), Roush (by Wilkinson), Murphy (by Eller). **Ground balls-fly balls:** Eller 6-16, Williams 0-1, James 4-5, Wilkinson 4-4. **Batters faced:** Eller 40, Williams 5, James 23, Wilkinson 21. **UMPIRES:** hp—Nallin, 1b—Rigler, 2b—Evans, 3b—Quigley **T:** 2:27 **A:** 32,930

1920 CLEVELAND DEF. BROOKLYN, 5-2

GAME 1 Cleveland 3 Brooklyn 1
Ebbets Field 10/05/20

CLEVELAND	AB	R	H	HR	RBI	BB	AVG
Evans lf	2	0	0	0	0	1	.000
a-Jamieson ph-lf	1	0	0	0	0	0	.000
Wambsganss 2b	3	0	0	0	0	0	.000
Speaker cf	4	0	0	0	0	0	.000
Burns 1b	3	1	1	0	1	0	.333
b-E.Smith ph-rf	1	0	0	0	0	0	.000
Gardner 3b	4	0	0	0	0	0	.000
Wood rf	2	2	1	0	0	1	.500
c-D.Johnston ph-1b	1	0	0	0	0	0	.000
Sewell ss	3	0	1	0	0	0	.333
O'Neill c	3	0	2	0	2	0	.667
Coveleski p	3	0	0	0	0	0	.000
TOTALS	**30**	**3**	**5**	**0**	**3**	**2**	**.167**

a - Batted for Evans in the 8th
b - Batted for Burns in the 9th
c - Batted for Wood in the 9th

BATTING: 2B: O'Neill 2 (2, Marquard), Wood (1, Marquard). **S:** Wambsganss. **RBI:** Burns 1 (1), O'Neill 2 (2). **2-out RBI:** O'Neill 1. **Runners left in scoring position, 2 out:** Burns 1, Coveleski 1. **Team LOB:** 3

BROOKLYN	AB	R	H	HR	RBI	BB	AVG
Olson ss	3	0	2	0	0	1	.667
J.Johnston 3b	3	0	0	0	0	0	.000
Griffith rf	4	0	1	0	0	0	.250
Wheat lf	4	1	1	0	0	0	.250
Myers cf	4	0	0	0	0	0	.000
Konetchy 1b	4	0	0	0	1	0	.000
Kilduff 2b	3	0	0	0	0	0	.000
Krueger c	3	0	0	0	0	0	.000
Marquard p	1	0	0	0	0	0	.000
a-Lamar ph	1	0	0	0	0	0	.000
Mamaux p	0	0	0	0	0	0	.000
b-Mitchell ph	1	0	1	0	0	0	1.000
c-Neis pr	0	0	0	0	0	0	.000
Cadore p	0	0	0	0	0	0	.000
TOTALS	**31**	**1**	**5**	**0**	**1**	**1**	**.161**

a - Batted for Marquard in the 6th
b - Batted for Mamaux in the 8th
c - Ran for Mitchell in the 8th

BATTING: 2B: Wheat (1, Coveleski). **S:** J.Johnston. **RBI:** Konetchy 1 (1). **Runners left in scoring position, 2 out:** Griffith 2, Myers 1. **Team LOB:** 5 **FIELDING: E:** Konetchy (1). **DP:** 1 (Konetchy-Krueger-J.Johnston).

CLEVELAND	IP	H	R	ER	BB	SO	HR	ERA
Coveleski (W, 1-0)	9	5	1	1	1	3	0	1.00

BROOKLYN	IP	H	R	ER	BB	SO	HR	ERA
Marquard (L, 0-1)	6	5	3	3	2	4	0	4.50
Mamaux	2	0	0	0	0	3	0	0.00
Cadore	1	0	0	0	0	0	0	0.00

Ground balls-fly balls: Coveleski 12-11, Marquard 6-6, Mamaux 3-0, Cadore 3-0. **Batters faced:** Coveleski 33, Marquard 24, Mamaux 6, Cadore 3. **UMPIRES:** hp—Klem, 1b—Connolly, 2b—O'Day, 3b—Dinneen **T:** 1:41 **A:** 23,573

GAME 2 Brooklyn 3 Cleveland 0
Ebbets Field 10/06/20

CLEVELAND	AB	R	H	HR	RBI	BB	AVG
Jamieson lf	4	0	1	0	0	1	.200
Wambsganss 2b	3	0	0	0	0	0	.000
b-Burns ph	0	0	0	0	0	1	.333
Lunte 2b	0	0	0	0	0	0	.000
Speaker cf	3	0	2	0	0	1	.286
E.Smith rf	4	0	0	0	0	0	.000
Gardner 3b	3	0	2	0	0	1	.286
D.Johnston 1b	4	0	0	0	0	0	.000
Sewell ss	4	0	0	0	0	0	.143
O'Neill c	4	0	1	0	0	0	.429
Bagby p	2	0	0	0	0	0	.000
a-Graney ph	1	0	0	0	0	0	.000
Uhle p	0	0	0	0	0	0	.000
c-Nunamaker ph	1	0	1	0	0	0	1.000
TOTALS	**33**	**0**	**7**	**0**	**0**	**4**	**.190**

a - Batted for Bagby in the 7th
b - Batted for Wambsganss in the 8th
c - Batted for Uhle in the 9th

BATTING: 2B: Gardner (1, Grimes), Speaker (1, Grimes). **Runners left in scoring position, 2 out:** E.Smith 1, D.Johnston 3, Graney 1. **Team LOB:** 10 **BASERUNNING: CS:** D.Johnston (1, 2nd base off Grimes/Miller). **FIELDING: E:** Bagby (1). **DP:** 1 (Gardner-O'Neill-D.Johnston-O'Neill).

BROOKLYN	AB	R	H	HR	RBI	BB	AVG
Olson ss	4	1	1	0	0	0	.429
J.Johnston 3b	4	1	1	0	0	0	.143
Griffith rf	4	0	2	0	2	0	.375
Wheat lf	3	0	1	0	1	1	.286
Myers cf	3	0	1	0	0	0	.143
Konetchy 1b	3	0	0	0	0	0	.000
Kilduff 2b	3	0	0	0	0	0	.000
Miller c	3	0	0	0	0	0	.000
Grimes p	3	1	1	0	0	0	.333
TOTALS	**30**	**3**	**7**	**0**	**3**	**1**	**.197**

BATTING: 2B: Wheat (2, Bagby), Griffith (1, Bagby). **RBI:** Griffith 2 (2), Wheat 1 (1). **2-out RBI:** Griffith 1, Wheat 1. **Runners left in scoring position, 2 out:** Myers 1. **Team LOB:** 4 **BASERUNNING: SB:** J.Johnston (1, 2nd base off Bagby/O'Neill). **CS:** Griffith (1, 2nd base off Bagby/O'Neill).

CLEVELAND	IP	H	R	ER	BB	SO	HR	ERA
Bagby (L, 0-1)	6	7	3	2	1	0	0	3.00
Uhle	2	0	0	0	0	3	0	0.00

BROOKLYN	IP	H	R	ER	BB	SO	HR	ERA
Grimes (W, 1-0)	9	7	0	0	4	2	0	0.00

IBB: Wheat (by Bagby). **Ground balls-fly balls:** Bagby 7-10, Uhle 0-3, Grimes 14-10. **Batters faced:** Bagby 25, Uhle 6, Grimes 37. **UMPIRES:** hp—Connolly, 1b—O'Day, 2b—Dinneen, 3b—Klem **T:** 1:55 **A:** 22,559

GAME 3 Brooklyn 2 Cleveland 1
Ebbets Field 10/07/20

CLEVELAND	AB	R	H	HR	RBI	BB	AVG
Evans lf	4	0	0	0	0	0	.000
Wambsganss 2b	3	0	0	0	0	1	.000
Speaker cf	4	1	1	0	0	0	.273
Burns 1b	3	0	0	0	0	0	.167
Gardner 3b	3	0	0	0	0	0	.200
Wood rf	3	0	0	0	0	0	.200
Sewell ss	2	0	0	0	0	1	.111
O'Neill c	3	0	2	0	0	0	.500
a-Jamieson pr	0	0	0	0	0	0	.200
Uhle p	0	0	0	0	0	0	.000
Caldwell p	0	0	0	0	0	0	.000
Mails p	2	0	0	0	0	0	.000
b-Nunamaker ph-c	1	0	0	0	0	0	.500
TOTALS	**28**	**1**	**3**	**0**	**0**	**2**	**.165**

a - Ran for O'Neill in the 8th
b - Batted for Mails in the 8th

BATTING: 2B: Speaker (2, S.Smith). **Runners left in scoring position, 2 out:** Burns 1. **GIDP:** Mails, Nunamaker. **Team LOB:** 2 **FIELDING: E:** Sewell (1). **DP:** 2 (Mails-Burns, Wambsganss-Sewell-Burns).

BROOKLYN	AB	R	H	HR	RBI	BB	AVG
Olson ss	2	1	1	0	0	2	.444
J.Johnston 3b	3	0	0	0	0	0	.100
Griffith rf	1	1	0	0	0	0	.333
a-Neis ph-rf	3	0	0	0	0	0	.000
Wheat lf	4	0	3	0	1	0	.455
Myers cf	4	0	2	0	1	0	.273
Konetchy 1b	3	0	0	0	0	1	.000
Kilduff 2b	1	0	0	0	0	1	.000
Miller c	1	0	0	0	0	1	.000
S.Smith p	3	0	0	0	0	0	.000
TOTALS	**25**	**2**	**6**	**0**	**2**	**5**	**.209**

a - Batted for Griffith in the 3th

BATTING: S: J.Johnston, Kilduff, Miller. **RBI:** Wheat 1 (2), Myers 1 (1). **Runners left in scoring position, 2 out:** J.Johnston 1, Konetchy 1, Kilduff 1, S.Smith 1. **GIDP:** Konetchy. **Team LOB:** 7 **BASERUNNING: CS:** Olson (1, 2nd base off Mails/O'Neill). **FIELDING: E:** Wheat (1). **DP:** 2 (Olson-Kilduff-Konetchy, J.Johnston-Kilduff-Konetchy).

CLEVELAND	IP	H	R	ER	BB	SO	HR	ERA
Caldwell (L, 0-1)	0.1	2	2	1	1	0	0	27.00
Mails	6.2	3	0	0	4	2	0	0.00
Uhle	1	1	0	0	0	0	0	0.00

BROOKLYN	IP	H	R	ER	BB	SO	HR	ERA
S.Smith (W, 1-0)	9	3	1	0	2	2	0	0.00

Ground balls-fly balls: Caldwell 1-0, Mails 5-8, Uhle 1-2, S.Smith 17-6. **Batters faced:** Caldwell 5, Mails 24, Uhle 4, S.Smith 30. **UMPIRES:** hp—O'Day, 1b—Dinneen, 2b—Klem, 3b—Connolly **T:** 1:47 **A:** 25,088

GAME 4 Cleveland 5 Brooklyn 1
League Park 10/09/20

BROOKLYN	AB	R	H	HR	RBI	BB	AVG
Olson ss	4	0	1	0	0	0	.385
J.Johnston 3b	4	1	2	0	0	0	.214
b-Neis pr	0	0	0	0	0	0	.000
Griffith rf	4	0	1	0	1	0	.308
Wheat lf	4	0	0	0	0	0	.333
Myers cf	3	0	0	0	0	0	.214
Konetchy 1b	2	0	0	0	0	1	.000
Kilduff 2b	3	0	1	0	0	0	.100
Miller c	3	0	0	0	0	0	.000
Cadore p	0	0	0	0	0	0	.000
Mamaux p	1	0	0	0	0	0	.000
Marquard p	0	0	0	0	0	0	.000
a-Lamar ph	1	0	0	0	0	0	.000
Pfeffer p	1	0	0	0	0	0	.000
TOTALS	**30**	**1**	**5**	**0**	**1**	**1**	**.198**

a - Batted for Marquard in the 6th
b - Ran for J.Johnston in the 9th

BATTING: 2B: Griffith (2, Coveleski). **RBI:** Griffith 1 (3). **Runners left in scoring position, 2 out:** Myers 1. **GIDP:** Miller, Miller. **Team LOB:** 3 **FIELDING: E:** Wheat (2). **PB:** Miller. **Outfield assists:** Myers (1). **DP:** 1 (Myers-Olson-Kilduff).

CLEVELAND	AB	R	H	HR	RBI	BB	AVG
Jamieson lf	2	0	0	0	0	0	.143
c-Evans ph-lf	3	0	1	0	0	0	.111
Wambsganss 2b	4	2	2	0	1	1	.154
Speaker cf	5	2	2	0	0	0	.313
E.Smith rf	1	0	1	0	1	0	.167
a-Burns ph-1b	2	0	1	0	2	1	.250
Gardner 3b	3	0	1	0	1	0	.231
D.Johnston 1b	1	0	0	0	0	0	.000
b-Wood ph-rf	2	0	0	0	0	0	.143
d-Graney ph-rf	1	0	0	0	0	0	.000
Sewell ss	4	0	2	0	0	0	.231
O'Neill c	2	0	1	0	0	2	.500
Coveleski p	4	1	1	0	0	0	.143
TOTALS	**34**	**5**	**12**	**0**	**5**	**4**	**.216**

a - Batted for E.Smith in the 3th
b - Batted for D.Johnston in the 3th
c - Batted for Jamieson in the 4th
d - Batted for Wood in the 7th

BATTING: SF: Gardner. **RBI:** Wambsganss 1 (1), E.Smith 1 (1), Burns 2 (3), Gardner 1 (1). **2-out RBI:** Wambsganss 1. **Runners left in scoring position, 2 out:** Speaker 1, D.Johnston 1, Coveleski 4. **Team LOB:** 10 **FIELDING: DP:** 2 (Sewell-Wambsganss-Burns, Gardner-Wambsganss-Burns).

BROOKLYN	IP	H	R	ER	BB	SO	HR	ERA
Cadore (L, 0-1)	1	4	2	2	1	1	0	9.00
Mamaux	1	2	2	2	0	1	0	6.00
Marquard	3	2	0	0	1	2	0	3.00
Pfeffer	3	4	1	1	2	1	0	3.00

CLEVELAND	IP	H	R	ER	BB	SO	HR	ERA
Coveleski (W, 2-0)	9	5	1	1	1	4	0	1.00

WP: Pfeffer 1. **IBB:** O'Neill 2 (by Marquard, by Pfeffer). **Ground balls-fly balls:** Cadore 0-1, Mamaux 0-1, Marquard 4-3, Pfeffer 3-5, Coveleski 15-6. **Batters faced:** Cadore 8, Mamaux 4, Marquard 12, Pfeffer 15, Coveleski 31. **UMPIRES:** hp—Dinneen, 1b—Klem, 2b—Connolly, 3b—O'Day **T:** 1:54 **A:** 25,734

GAME 5 Cleveland 8 Brooklyn 1
League Park 10/10/20

BROOKLYN	AB	R	H	HR	RBI	BB	AVG
Olson ss	4	0	2	0	0	0	.412
Sheehan 3b	3	0	1	0	0	0	.333
Griffith rf	4	0	0	0	0	0	.235
Wheat lf	4	1	2	0	0	0	.368
Myers cf	4	0	2	0	0	0	.278
Konetchy 1b	4	0	2	0	1	0	.125
Kilduff 2b	4	0	1	0	0	0	.143
Miller c	2	0	2	0	0	0	.222
Krueger c	2	0	1	0	0	0	.200
Grimes p	1	0	0	0	0	0	.250
Mitchell p	2	0	0	0	0	0	.333
TOTALS	**34**	**1**	**13**	**0**	**1**	**0**	**.240**

BATTING: 3B: Konetchy (1, Bagby). **S:** Sheehan. **RBI:** Konetchy 1 (2). **Runners left in scoring position, 2 out:** Griffith 1, Wheat 1, Kilduff 1, Krueger 2. **GIDP:** Grimes, Mitchell. **Team LOB:** 7 **BASERUNNING: CS:** Myers 2 (2, 3rd base off Bagby/O'Neill, 2nd base off Bagby/O'Neill). **FIELDING: E:** Sheehan (1). **PB:** Miller. **DP:** 1 (Olson-Kilduff-Konetchy).

CLEVELAND	AB	R	H	HR	RBI	BB	AVG
Jamieson lf	4	1	2	0	0	0	.273
a-Graney ph-lf	1	0	0	0	0	0	.000
Wambsganss 2b	5	1	1	0	0	0	.167
Speaker cf	3	2	1	0	0	1	.316
E.Smith rf	4	1	3	1	4	0	.400
Gardner 3b	4	0	1	0	1	0	.235
D.Johnston 1b	3	1	2	0	0	0	.222
Sewell ss	3	0	0	0	0	1	.188
O'Neill c	2	1	0	0	0	2	.429
Thomas c	0	0	0	0	0	0	.000
Bagby p	4	1	2	1	3	0	.333
TOTALS	**33**	**8**	**12**	**2**	**8**	**4**	**.247**

a - Batted for Jamieson in the 8th

BATTING: 3B: E.Smith (1, Grimes). **HR:** E.Smith (1, 1st off Grimes 3 on, 0 out), Bagby (1, 4th off Grimes 2 on, 1 out). **S:** D.Johnston. **RBI:** E.Smith 4 (5), Gardner 1 (2), Bagby 3 (3). **Runners left in scoring position, 2 out:** Gardner 1, Bagby 2. **GIDP:** Sewell. **Team LOB:** 6 **BASERUNNING: CS:** Jamieson (1, 2nd base off Mitchell/Miller), Sewell (1, 2nd base off Mitchell/Krueger). **FIELDING: E:** Gardner (1). **Outfield assists:** Jamieson (1). **DP:** 3 (Jamieson-O'Neill, Gardner-Wambsganss-D.Johnston, D.Johnston-Sewell-D.Johnston). **TP:** 8 (Wambsganss).

BROOKLYN	IP	H	R	ER	BB	SO	HR	ERA
Grimes (L, 1-1)	3.1	9	7	7	1	0	2	5.11
Mitchell	4.2	3	1	0	3	1	0	0.00

CLEVELAND	IP	H	R	ER	BB	SO	HR	ERA
Bagby (W, 1-1)	9	13	1	1	0	3	0	1.80

WP: Bagby 1. **IBB:** O'Neill (by Grimes). **Ground balls-fly balls:** Grimes 7-2, Mitchell 7-4, Bagby 11-7. **Batters faced:** Grimes 19, Mitchell 19, Bagby 35. **UMPIRES:** hp—Klem, 1b—Connolly, 2b—O'Day, 3b—Dinneen **T:** 1:49 **A:** 26,884

GAME 6 Cleveland 1 Brooklyn 0
League Park 10/11/20

BROOKLYN	AB	R	H	HR	RBI	BB	AVG
Olson ss	4	0	1	0	0	0	.381
Sheehan 3b	4	0	0	0	0	0	.143
Neis rf	2	0	0	0	0	1	.000
a-Krueger ph	1	0	0	0	0	0	.167
Griffith rf	0	0	0	0	0	0	.235
Wheat lf	4	0	0	0	0	0	.304
Myers cf	4	0	1	0	0	0	.273
Konetchy 1b	3	0	1	0	0	1	.158
b-McCabe pr	0	0	0	0	0	0	.000
Kilduff 2b	4	0	0	0	0	0	.111
Miller c	3	0	0	0	0	0	.167
S.Smith p	3	0	0	0	0	0	.000
TOTALS	**32**	**0**	**3**	**0**	**0**	**2**	**.214**

a - Batted for Neis in the 8th
b - Ran for Konetchy in the 9th

BATTING: 2B: Olson (1, Mails). **Runners left in scoring position, 2 out:** Krueger 1, Miller 1, S.Smith 2. **Team LOB:** 7

CLEVELAND	AB	R	H	HR	RBI	BB	AVG
Evans lf	4	0	3	0	0	0	.308
Wambsganss 2b	4	0	0	0	0	0	.136
Speaker cf	3	1	1	0	0	0	.318
Burns 1b	2	0	1	0	1	1	.300
Gardner 3b	3	0	0	0	0	0	.200
Wood rf	3	0	1	0	0	0	.200
Sewell ss	3	0	1	0	0	0	.211
O'Neill c	3	0	0	0	0	0	.353
Mails p	3	0	0	0	0	0	.000
TOTALS	**28**	**1**	**7**	**0**	**1**	**1**	**.247**

BATTING: 2B: Burns (1, S.Smith). **RBI:** Burns 1 (4). **2-out RBI:** Burns 1. **Runners left in scoring position, 2 out:** Gardner 1, O'Neill 1. **Team LOB:** 4 **BASERUNNING: CS:** Evans (1, 2nd base off S.Smith/Miller), Sewell (2, 2nd base off S.Smith/Miller). **FIELDING: E:** Sewell 2 (3), Gardner (2).

BROOKLYN	IP	H	R	ER	BB	SO	HR	ERA
S.Smith (L, 1-1)	8	7	1	1	1	1	0	0.53

CLEVELAND	IP	H	R	ER	BB	SO	HR	ERA
Mails (W, 1-0)	9	3	0	0	2	4	0	0.00

Ground balls-fly balls: S.Smith 11-9, Mails 12-13. **Batters faced:** S.Smith 29, Mails 34. **UMPIRES:** hp—Connolly, 1b—O'Day, 2b—Dinneen, 3b—Klem **T:** 1:34 **A:** 27,194

GAME 7 Cleveland 3 Brooklyn 0
League Park 10/12/20

BROOKLYN	AB	R	H	HR	RBI	BB	AVG
Olson ss	4	0	0	0	0	0	.320
Sheehan 3b	4	0	1	0	0	0	.182
Griffith rf	4	0	0	0	0	0	.190
Wheat lf	4	0	2	0	0	0	.333
Myers cf	4	0	0	0	0	0	.231
Konetchy 1b	4	0	1	0	0	0	.174
Kilduff 2b	3	0	0	0	0	0	.095
Miller c	2	0	0	0	0	0	.143
a-Lamar ph	1	0	0	0	0	0	.000
Krueger c	0	0	0	0	0	0	.167
Grimes p	2	0	1	0	0	0	.333
b-Schmandt ph	1	0	0	0	0	0	.000
Mamaux p	0	0	0	0	0	0	.000
TOTALS	**33**	**0**	**5**	**0**	**0**	**0**	**.205**

a - Batted for Miller in the 7th
b - Batted for Grimes in the 8th

BATTING: Runners left in scoring position, 2 out: Griffith 1, Lamar 1. **Team LOB:** 6 **FIELDING: E:** Sheehan (2), Grimes (1).

CLEVELAND	AB	R	H	HR	RBI	BB	AVG
Jamieson lf	4	1	2	0	1	0	.333
Wambsganss 2b	4	0	1	0	0	0	.154
Speaker cf	3	0	1	0	1	1	.320
E.Smith rf	3	0	0	0	0	1	.308
Gardner 3b	4	1	1	0	0	0	.208
D.Johnston 1b	2	0	1	0	0	2	.273
Sewell ss	4	0	0	0	0	0	.174
O'Neill c	4	0	1	0	0	0	.333
Coveleski p	3	1	0	0	0	0	.100
TOTALS	**31**	**3**	**7**	**0**	**2**	**4**	**.244**

BATTING: 2B: O'Neill (3, Grimes), Jamieson (1, Grimes). **3B:** Speaker (1, Grimes). **RBI:** Jamieson 1 (1), Speaker 1 (1). **2-out RBI:** Speaker 1. **Runners left in scoring position, 2 out:** E.Smith 1, Gardner 2, O'Neill 2. **Team LOB:** 8 **BASERUNNING: SB:** D.Johnston (1, 2nd base off Grimes/Miller), Jamieson (1, 2nd base off Grimes/Miller). **CS:** D.Johnston (2, 2nd base off Grimes/Miller). **FIELDING: E:** Sewell 2 (5). **Outfield assists:** E.Smith (1).

BROOKLYN	IP	H	R	ER	BB	SO	HR	ERA
Grimes (L, 1-2)	7	7	3	2	4	2	0	4.19
Mamaux	1	0	0	0	0	1	0	4.50

CLEVELAND	IP	H	R	ER	BB	SO	HR	ERA
Coveleski (W, 3-0)	9	5	0	0	0	1	0	0.67

Ground balls-fly balls: Grimes 10-9, Mamaux 0-2, Coveleski 16-11. **Batters faced:** Grimes 32, Mamaux 3, Coveleski 33. **UMPIRES:** hp—O'Day, 1b—Dinneen, 2b—Klem, 3b—Connolly **T:** 1:55 **A:** 27,525

1921 NY GIANTS DEF. NY YANKEES, 5-3

GAME 1 Yankees 3 Giants 0
Polo Grounds 10/05/21

NY YANKEES	AB	R	H	HR	RBI	BB	AVG
Miller cf	4	1	1	0	0	0	.250
Peckinpaugh ss	3	1	1	0	0	0	.333
Ruth lf	3	0	1	0	1	1	.333
B.Meusel rf	4	0	0	0	1	0	.000
Pipp 1b	2	0	0	0	0	1	.000
Ward 2b	3	0	1	0	0	1	.333
McNally 3b	4	1	2	0	0	0	.500
Schang c	2	0	0	0	0	1	.000
Mays p	3	0	1	0	0	0	.333
TOTALS	**28**	**3**	**7**	**0**	**2**	**4**	**.250**

BATTING: 2B: McNally (1, Douglas). **S:** Peckinpaugh, Pipp, Schang. **RBI:** Ruth 1 (1), B.Meusel 1 (1). **Runners left in scoring position, 2 out:** Ward 1, Schang 3. **GIDP:** B.Meusel. **Team LOB:** 5 **BASERUNNING: SB:** McNally 2 (2, home off Douglas/Snyder, 2nd base off Barnes/Snyder). **CS:** Pipp (1, 2nd base off Douglas/Snyder). **FIELDING: DP:** 1 (Peckinpaugh-Ward-Pipp).

NY GIANTS	AB	R	H	HR	RBI	BB	AVG
Burns cf	4	0	0	0	0	0	.000
Bancroft ss	4	0	0	0	0	0	.000
Frisch 3b	4	0	4	0	0	0	1.000
Youngs rf	3	0	0	0	0	0	.000
Kelly 1b	4	0	0	0	0	0	.000
I.Meusel lf	3	0	0	0	0	0	.000
Rawlings 2b	2	0	1	0	0	0	.500
Snyder c	3	0	0	0	0	0	.000
Douglas p	2	0	0	0	0	0	.000
a-Smith ph	1	0	0	0	0	0	.000
Barnes p	0	0	0	0	0	0	.000
TOTALS	**30**	**0**	**5**	**0**	**0**	**0**	**.167**

a - Batted for Douglas in the 8th

BATTING: 3B: Frisch (1, Mays). **S:** Youngs. **Runners left in scoring position, 2 out:** Youngs 1, I.Meusel 1. **GIDP:** Kelly. **Team LOB:** 5 **BASERUNNING: SB:** Frisch (1, 2nd base off Mays/Schang). **FIELDING: PB:** Snyder. **Outfield assists:** I.Meusel (1). **DP:** 1 (Frisch-Rawlings-Kelly).

NY YANKEES	IP	H	R	ER	BB	SO	HR	ERA
Mays (W, 1-0)	9	5	0	0	0	1	0	0.00

NY GIANTS	IP	H	R	ER	BB	SO	HR	ERA
Douglas (L, 0-1)	8	5	3	3	4	6	0	3.38
Barnes	1	2	0	0	0	1	0	0.00

HBP: Rawlings (by Mays). **Ground balls-fly balls:** Mays 18-6, Douglas 9-3, Barnes 1-1. **Batters faced:** Mays 32, Douglas 30, Barnes 5. **UMPIRES:** hp—Rigler, 1b—Moriarty, 2b—Quigley, 3b—Chill **T:** 1:38 **A:** 30,203

GAME 2 Yankees 3 Giants 0
Polo Grounds 10/06/21

NY GIANTS	AB	R	H	HR	RBI	BB	AVG
Burns cf	3	0	0	0	0	1	.000
Bancroft ss	4	0	0	0	0	0	.000
Frisch 3b	4	0	1	0	0	0	.625
Youngs rf	2	0	0	0	0	2	.000
Kelly 1b	4	0	0	0	0	0	.000
I.Meusel lf	2	0	0	0	0	1	.000
Rawlings 2b	3	0	1	0	0	0	.400
Smith c	3	0	0	0	0	0	.000
Nehf p	2	0	0	0	0	1	.000
TOTALS	**27**	**0**	**2**	**0**	**0**	**5**	**.123**

BATTING: Runners left in scoring position, 2 out: Frisch 1. **GIDP:** Kelly. **Team LOB:** 5 **BASERUNNING: CS:** Burns (1, 2nd base off Hoyt/Schang). **FIELDING: E:** Nehf (1), Frisch (1). **DP:** 2 (Frisch-Rawlings, Rawlings-Kelly-Smith).

NY YANKEES	AB	R	H	HR	RBI	BB	AVG
Miller cf	3	0	0	0	0	1	.143
Peckinpaugh ss	3	0	0	0	0	1	.167
Ruth lf	1	1	0	0	0	3	.250
B.Meusel rf	4	1	1	0	0	0	.125
Pipp 1b	3	0	0	0	1	1	.000
Ward 2b	4	1	1	0	0	0	.286
McNally 3b	3	0	0	0	0	0	.286
Schang c	2	0	0	0	0	1	.000
Hoyt p	3	0	1	0	1	0	.333
TOTALS	**26**	**3**	**3**	**0**	**2**	**7**	**.185**

BATTING: RBI: Pipp 1 (1), Hoyt 1 (1). **Runners left in scoring position, 2 out:** B.Meusel 3. **Team LOB:** 6 **BASERUNNING: SB:** Ruth 2 (2, 2nd base off Nehf/Smith, 3rd base off Nehf/Smith), B.Meusel (1, home off Nehf/Smith). **CS:** McNally (1, 2nd base off Nehf/Smith). **FIELDING: DP:** 1 (McNally-Ward-Pipp).

NY GIANTS	IP	H	R	ER	BB	SO	HR	ERA
Nehf (L, 0-1)	8	3	3	1	7	0	0	1.13

NY YANKEES	IP	H	R	ER	BB	SO	HR	ERA
Hoyt (W, 1-0)	9	2	0	0	5	5	0	0.00

Ground balls-fly balls: Nehf 13-10, Hoyt 16-4. **Batters faced:** Nehf 33, Hoyt 32. **UMPIRES:** hp—Moriarty, 1b—Quigley, 2b—Chill, 3b—Rigler **T:** 1:55 **A:** 34,939

GAME 3 Giants 13 Yankees 5
Polo Grounds 10/07/21

NY YANKEES	AB	R	H	HR	RBI	BB	AVG
Miller cf	5	1	1	0	1	0	.167
Peckinpaugh ss	3	1	0	0	0	1	.111
Ruth lf	3	0	1	0	2	1	.286
a-Fewster pr-lf	0	1	0	0	0	0	.000
B.Meusel rf	3	0	2	0	0	1	.273
Pipp 1b	3	0	0	0	1	0	.000
Ward 2b	4	0	2	0	1	0	.364
McNally 3b	3	0	0	0	0	0	.200
Schang c	2	1	1	0	0	1	.167
DeVormer c	1	0	0	0	0	0	.000
Shawkey p	1	1	1	0	0	0	1.000
Quinn p	2	0	0	0	0	0	.000
Collins p	0	0	0	0	0	0	.000
Rogers p	0	0	0	0	0	0	.000
b-Baker ph	1	0	0	0	0	0	.000
TOTALS	**31**	**5**	**8**	**0**	**5**	**4**	**.212**

a - Ran for Ruth in the 8th
b - Batted for Rogers in the 9th

BATTING: 2B: B.Meusel (1, Toney). **S:** Pipp. **RBI:** Miller 1 (1), Ruth 2 (3), Pipp 1 (2), Ward 1 (1). **2-out RBI:** Ward 1. **Runners left in scoring position, 2 out:** Miller 1, Ward 1. **Team LOB:** 5 **BASERUNNING: CS:** Ruth (1, 2nd base off Barnes/Snyder), B.Meusel (1, 2nd base off Barnes/Snyder). **FIELDING: DP:** 2 (Ward-Pipp, Quinn-Peckinpaugh-Pipp).

NY GIANTS	AB	R	H	HR	RBI	BB	AVG
Burns cf	6	1	4	0	0	0	.308
Bancroft ss	5	1	1	0	1	0	.077
Frisch 3b	2	3	2	0	0	3	.700
Youngs rf	3	2	2	0	4	2	.250
Kelly 1b	3	1	0	0	1	2	.000
I.Meusel lf	5	2	3	0	3	0	.300
Rawlings 2b	5	0	2	0	3	0	.400
Snyder c	5	1	4	0	1	0	.500
Toney p	0	0	0	0	0	0	.000
Barnes p	5	2	2	0	0	0	.400
TOTALS	**39**	**13**	**20**	**0**	**13**	**7**	**.281**

BATTING: 2B: Youngs (1, Quinn), I.Meusel (1, Quinn), Burns (1, Rogers). **3B:** Burns (1, Quinn), Youngs (1, Collins). **SF:** Bancroft. **RBI:** Bancroft 1 (1), Youngs 4 (4), Kelly 1 (1), I.Meusel 3 (3), Rawlings 3 (3), Snyder 1 (1). **2-out RBI:** Youngs 3, Rawlings 1. **Runners left in scoring position, 2 out:** Bancroft 3, Youngs 2, Kelly 2, Snyder 1. **GIDP:** Barnes. **Team LOB:** 10 **BASERUNNING: SB:** Frisch (2, 2nd base off Quinn/Schang), Burns (1, 2nd base off Quinn/Schang), I.Meusel (1, 2nd base off Rogers/DeVormer). **CS:** Snyder (1, 2nd base off Shawkey/Schang), Rawlings (1, 2nd base off Collins/Schang). **Outfield assists:** Youngs (1).

NY YANKEES	IP	H	R	ER	BB	SO	HR	ERA
Shawkey	2.1	5	4	4	4	0	0	15.43
Quinn (L, 0-1)	3.2	8	4	4	2	2	0	9.82
Collins	0.2	4	4	4	1	0	0	54.00
Rogers	1.1	3	1	1	0	1	0	6.75

NY GIANTS	IP	H	R	ER	BB	SO	HR	ERA
Toney	2	4	4	4	2	1	0	18.00
Barnes (W, 1-0)	7	4	1	1	2	7	0	1.13

WP: Barnes 1. **HBP:** McNally (by Barnes). **Ground balls-fly balls:** Shawkey 2-3, Quinn 6-2, Collins 0-0, Rogers 2-1, Toney 3-1, Barnes 7-4. **Batters faced:** Shawkey 14, Quinn 20, Collins 6, Rogers 7, Toney 12, Barnes 25. **UMPIRES:** hp—Quigley, 1b—Chill, 2b—Rigler, 3b—Moriarty **T:** 2:40 **A:** 36,509

GAME 4 Giants 4 Yankees 2
Polo Grounds 10/09/21

NY GIANTS	AB	R	H	HR	RBI	BB	AVG
Burns cf	4	0	2	0	2	0	.353
Bancroft ss	4	0	0	0	0	0	.059
Frisch 3b	4	0	0	0	0	0	.500
Youngs rf	4	0	1	0	0	0	.250
Kelly 1b	4	1	1	0	0	0	.067
I.Meusel lf	4	1	2	0	1	0	.357
Rawlings 2b	4	1	2	0	1	0	.429
Snyder c	4	1	1	0	0	0	.417
Douglas p	2	0	0	0	0	0	.000
TOTALS	**34**	**4**	**9**	**0**	**4**	**0**	**.277**

BATTING: 2B: Burns (2, Mays), Kelly (1, Mays). **3B:** I.Meusel (1, Mays). **S:** Douglas. **RBI:** Burns 2 (2), I.Meusel 1 (4), Rawlings 1 (4). **Runners left in scoring position, 2 out:** Burns 1, Frisch 1. **GIDP:** Kelly. **Team LOB:** 4 **BASERUNNING: CS:** I.Meusel (1, 2nd base off Mays/Schang).

NY YANKEES	AB	R	H	HR	RBI	BB	AVG
Miller cf	4	0	0	0	0	0	.125
Peckinpaugh ss	4	0	1	0	0	0	.154
Ruth lf	4	1	2	1	1	0	.364
B.Meusel rf	4	0	0	0	0	0	.200
Pipp 1b	4	0	1	0	0	0	.083
Ward 2b	2	0	0	0	0	0	.308
McNally 3b	3	1	1	0	0	0	.231
Schang c	3	0	2	0	1	0	.333
Mays p	3	0	0	0	0	0	.167
TOTALS	**31**	**2**	**7**	**1**	**2**	**0**	**.216**

BATTING: 3B: Schang (1, Douglas). **HR:** Ruth (1, 9th off Douglas 0 on, 1 out). **S:** Ward. **RBI:** Ruth 1 (4), Schang 1 (1). **2-out RBI:** Schang 1. **Runners left in scoring position, 2 out:** Miller 1, Mays 1. **Team LOB:** 3 **BASERUNNING: CS:** McNally (2, 2nd base off Douglas/Snyder), Peckinpaugh (1, 2nd base off Douglas/Snyder). **FIELDING: E:** McNally (1). **DP:** 1 (Ward-Peckinpaugh-Pipp).

NY GIANTS	IP	H	R	ER	BB	SO	HR	ERA
Douglas (W, 1-1)	9	7	2	2	0	8	1	2.65

NY YANKEES	IP	H	R	ER	BB	SO	HR	ERA
Mays (L, 1-1)	9	9	4	4	0	1	0	2.00

Ground balls-fly balls: Douglas 11-5, Mays 17-7. **Batters faced:** Douglas 32, Mays 35. **UMPIRES:** hp—Chill, 1b—Rigler, 2b—Moriarty, 3b—Quigley **T:** 1:38 **A:** 36,372

GAME 5 Yankees 3 Giants 1
Polo Grounds 10/10/21

NY YANKEES	AB	R	H	HR	RBI	BB	AVG
Miller cf	3	0	1	0	1	0	.158
Peckinpaugh ss	4	0	1	0	0	0	.176
Ruth lf	4	1	1	0	0	0	.333
B.Meusel rf	4	1	2	0	1	0	.263
Pipp 1b	3	0	0	0	0	0	.067
Ward 2b	3	0	0	0	1	0	.250
McNally 3b	2	1	0	0	0	1	.200
Schang c	3	0	1	0	0	0	.333
Hoyt p	3	0	0	0	0	0	.167
TOTALS	**29**	**3**	**6**	**0**	**3**	**1**	**.214**

BATTING: 2B: Schang (1, Nehf), B.Meusel (2, Nehf), Miller (1, Nehf). **S:** Pipp. **SF:** Miller, Ward. **RBI:** Miller 1 (2), B.Meusel 1 (2), Ward 1 (2). **Runners left in scoring position, 2 out:** Peckinpaugh 2. **Team LOB:** 3 **BASERUNNING: CS:** B.Meusel (2, 3rd base off Nehf/Smith). **FIELDING: E:** McNally (2). **Outfield assists:** B.Meusel 2 (2).

NY GIANTS	AB	R	H	HR	RBI	BB	AVG
Burns cf	5	0	1	0	0	0	.318
Bancroft ss	4	1	1	0	0	0	.095
Frisch 3b	4	0	2	0	0	0	.500
Youngs rf	3	0	1	0	0	1	.267
Kelly 1b	4	0	3	0	1	0	.211
I.Meusel lf	4	0	1	0	0	0	.333
Rawlings 2b	4	0	1	0	0	0	.389
Smith c	3	0	0	0	0	1	.000
Nehf p	3	0	0	0	0	0	.000
a-Snyder ph	1	0	0	0	0	0	.385
TOTALS	**35**	**1**	**10**	**0**	**1**	**2**	**.279**

a - Batted for Nehf in the 9th

BATTING: 2B: I.Meusel (2, Hoyt), Rawlings (1, Hoyt). **RBI:** Kelly 1 (2). **Runners left in scoring position, 2 out:** Burns 1, I.Meusel 1, Rawlings 4. **Team LOB:** 9 **BASERUNNING: CS:** Smith (1, 2nd base off Hoyt/Schang).

NY YANKEES	IP	H	R	ER	BB	SO	HR	ERA
Hoyt (W, 2-0)	9	10	1	0	2	6	0	0.00

NY GIANTS	IP	H	R	ER	BB	SO	HR	ERA
Nehf (L, 0-2)	9	6	3	3	1	5	0	2.12

Ground balls-fly balls: Hoyt 9-10, Nehf 10-8. **Batters faced:** Hoyt 37, Nehf 33. **UMPIRES:** hp—Rigler, 1b—Moriarty, 2b—Quigley, 3b—Chill **T:** 1:52 **A:** 35,758

GAME 6 Giants 8 Yankees 5
Polo Grounds 10/11/21

NY GIANTS	AB	R	H	HR	RBI	BB	AVG
Burns cf	3	1	1	0	0	1	.320
Bancroft ss	5	0	2	0	2	0	.154
Frisch 3b	4	2	0	0	1	1	.409
Youngs rf	5	0	1	0	0	0	.250
Kelly 1b	4	1	3	0	2	1	.304
I.Meusel lf	4	1	2	1	2	1	.364
Rawlings 2b	5	0	0	0	0	0	.304
Snyder c	4	2	2	1	1	0	.412
Toney p	0	0	0	0	0	0	.000
Barnes p	4	1	2	0	0	0	.444
TOTALS	**38**	**8**	**13**	**2**	**8**	**4**	**.291**

BATTING: HR: I.Meusel (1, 2nd off Harper 1 on, 0 out), Snyder (1, 2nd off Harper 0 on, 1 out). **S:** Burns. **RBI:** Bancroft 2 (3), Frisch 1 (1), Kelly 2 (4), I.Meusel 2 (6), Snyder 1 (2). **2-out RBI:** Kelly 2. **Runners left in scoring position, 2 out:** Burns 1, Frisch 1. **Team LOB:** 8 **BASERUNNING: SB:** Frisch (3, 2nd base off Shawkey/Schang). **CS:** Kelly (1, 2nd base off Shawkey/Schang), Bancroft (1, 3rd base off Shawkey/Schang), Youngs (1, 2nd base off Piercy/Schang).

NY YANKEES	AB	R	H	HR	RBI	BB	AVG
Fewster lf	3	2	1	1	2	2	.333
Peckinpaugh ss	5	0	0	0	0	0	.136
Miller cf	5	1	1	0	0	0	.167
B.Meusel rf	3	1	1	0	1	1	.273
Pipp 1b	4	0	1	0	0	0	.105
Ward 2b	4	0	1	0	2	0	.250
McNally 3b	4	0	0	0	0	0	.158
Schang c	2	0	1	0	0	2	.357
Harper p	0	0	0	0	0	0	.000
Shawkey p	3	1	1	0	0	0	.500
a-Baker ph	1	0	0	0	0	0	.000
Piercy p	0	0	0	0	0	0	.000
TOTALS	**34**	**5**	**7**	**1**	**5**	**5**	**.212**

a - Batted for Shawkey in the 8th

BATTING: HR: Fewster (1, 2nd off Barnes 1 on, 1 out). **RBI:** Fewster 2 (2), B.Meusel 1 (3), Ward 2 (4). **2-out RBI:** Ward 2. **Runners left in scoring position, 2 out:** Miller 1, McNally 1. **Team LOB:** 7 **BASERUNNING: SB:** Pipp (1, 2nd base off Barnes/Snyder). **FIELDING: E:** McNally (3), Ward (1). **DP:** 2 (Schang-McNally, Schang-Peckinpaugh).

NY GIANTS	IP	H	R	ER	BB	SO	HR	ERA
Toney	0.2	3	3	3	1	0	0	23.63
Barnes (W, 2-0)	8.1	4	2	2	4	10	1	1.65

NY YANKEES	IP	H	R	ER	BB	SO	HR	ERA
Harper	1.1	3	3	3	2	1	2	20.25
Shawkey (L, 0-1)	6.2	8	5	3	2	5	0	7.00
Piercy	1	2	0	0	0	2	0	0.00

Ground balls-fly balls: Toney 0-2, Barnes 7-8, Harper 0-3, Shawkey 5-9, Piercy 0-0. **Batters faced:** Toney 6, Barnes 33, Harper 9, Shawkey 30, Piercy 4. **UMPIRES:** hp—Moriarty, 1b—Quigley, 2b—Chill, 3b—Rigler **T:** 2:31 **A:** 34,283

GAME 7 Giants 2 Yankees 1
Polo Grounds 10/12/21

NY YANKEES	AB	R	H	HR	RBI	BB	AVG
Fewster lf	4	0	1	0	0	0	.286
Peckinpaugh ss	4	0	2	0	0	0	.192
Miller cf	3	0	0	0	0	1	.148
B.Meusel rf	4	0	0	0	0	0	.231
Pipp 1b	4	1	1	0	0	0	.130
Ward 2b	3	0	0	0	0	0	.217
McNally 3b	1	0	1	0	1	0	.200
Baker 3b	3	0	2	0	0	0	.400
a-DeVormer pr	0	0	0	0	0	0	.000
Schang c	4	0	1	0	0	0	.333
Mays p	3	0	0	0	0	0	.111
TOTALS	**33**	**1**	**8**	**0**	**1**	**1**	**.217**

a - Ran for Baker in the 9th

BATTING: 2B: Peckinpaugh (1, Douglas), Pipp (1, Douglas). **S:** Ward. **RBI:** McNally 1 (1). **Runners left in scoring position, 2 out:** B.Meusel 1, Mays 2. **Team LOB:** 7 **FIELDING: E:** Ward (2). **Outfield assists:** Miller (1).

NY GIANTS	AB	R	H	HR	RBI	BB	AVG
Burns cf	4	0	2	0	0	0	.345
Bancroft ss	4	0	1	0	0	0	.167
Frisch 3b	4	0	0	0	0	0	.346
Youngs rf	3	1	1	0	0	0	.261
Kelly 1b	3	0	0	0	0	0	.269
I.Meusel lf	3	0	1	0	1	0	.360
Rawlings 2b	3	1	0	0	0	0	.269
Snyder c	3	0	1	0	1	0	.400
Douglas p	3	0	0	0	0	0	.000
TOTALS	**30**	**2**	**6**	**0**	**2**	**0**	**.279**

BATTING: 2B: Bancroft (1, Mays), Burns 2 (4, Mays), Snyder (1, Mays). **RBI:** I.Meusel 1 (7), Snyder 1 (3). **2-out RBI:** I.Meusel 1, Snyder 1. **Runners left in scoring position, 2 out:** Bancroft 1, Youngs 1, Douglas 1. **Team LOB:** 4 **BASERUNNING: SB:** Youngs (1, 2nd base off Mays/Schang). **Outfield assists:** I.Meusel (2).

NY YANKEES	IP	H	R	ER	BB	SO	HR	ERA
Mays (L, 1-2)	8	6	2	1	0	7	0	1.73

NY GIANTS	IP	H	R	ER	BB	SO	HR	ERA
Douglas (W, 2-1)	9	8	1	1	1	3	0	2.08

WP: Douglas 1. **Ground balls-fly balls:** Mays 14-3, Douglas 13-9. **Batters faced:** Mays 30, Douglas 35. **UMPIRES:** hp—Quigley, 1b—Chill, 2b—Rigler, 3b—Moriarty **T:** 1:40 **A:** 36,503

GAME 8 Giants 1 Yankees 0
Polo Grounds 10/13/21

NY GIANTS	AB	R	H	HR	RBI	BB	AVG
Burns cf	4	0	1	0	0	1	.333
Bancroft ss	3	1	0	0	0	1	.152
Frisch 3b	4	0	0	0	0	0	.300
Youngs rf	2	0	1	0	0	2	.280
Kelly 1b	4	0	0	0	0	0	.233
I.Meusel lf	4	0	1	0	0	0	.345
Rawlings 2b	4	0	3	0	0	0	.333
Snyder c	2	0	0	0	0	0	.364
Nehf p	4	0	0	0	0	0	.000
TOTALS	**31**	**1**	**6**	**0**	**0**	**4**	**.269**

BATTING: 2B: Rawlings 2 (3, Hoyt). **S:** Snyder, Snyder. **Runners left in scoring position, 2 out:** Burns 1, Bancroft 1, I.Meusel 2. **Team LOB:** 9 **BASERUNNING: SB:** Youngs (2, 2nd base off Hoyt/Schang). **CS:** I.Meusel (2, 2nd base off Hoyt/Schang). **FIELDING: DP:** 2 (Bancroft-Rawlings-Kelly, Rawlings-Kelly-Frisch).

NY YANKEES	AB	R	H	HR	RBI	BB	AVG
Fewster lf	3	0	0	0	0	1	.200
Peckinpaugh ss	2	0	0	0	0	2	.179
Miller cf	4	0	1	0	0	0	.161
B.Meusel rf	4	0	0	0	0	0	.200
Pipp 1b	3	0	1	0	0	0	.154
a-Ruth ph	1	0	0	0	0	0	.313
Ward 2b	3	0	1	0	0	1	.231
Baker 3b	3	0	0	0	0	1	.250
Schang c	3	0	0	0	0	0	.286
Hoyt p	3	0	1	0	0	0	.222
TOTALS	**29**	**0**	**4**	**0**	**0**	**5**	**.207**

a - Batted for Pipp in the 9th

BATTING: Runners left in scoring position, 2 out: Pipp 2, Schang 2. **GIDP:** Peckinpaugh. **Team LOB:** 7 **FIELDING: E:** Peckinpaugh (1).

NY GIANTS	IP	H	R	ER	BB	SO	HR	ERA
Nehf (W, 1-2)	9	4	0	0	5	3	0	1.38

NY YANKEES	IP	H	R	ER	BB	SO	HR	ERA
Hoyt (L, 2-1)	9	6	1	0	4	7	0	0.00

WP: Nehf 1. **Ground balls-fly balls:** Nehf 12-10, Hoyt 10-8. **Batters faced:** Nehf 34, Hoyt 37. **UMPIRES:** hp—Chill, 1b—Rigler, 2b—Moriarty, 3b—Quigley **T:** 1:57 **A:** 25,410

1922 NY GIANTS DEF. NY YANKEES, 4-0

GAME 1 Giants 3 Yankees 2
Polo Grounds 10/04/22

NY YANKEES	AB	R	H	HR	RBI	BB	AVG
Witt cf	4	0	1	0	0	0	.250
Dugan 3b	4	1	1	0	0	0	.250
Ruth rf	4	0	1	0	1	0	.250
Pipp 1b	4	0	1	0	0	0	.250
B.Meusel lf	4	1	2	0	0	0	.500
Schang c	2	0	1	0	0	0	.500
Ward 2b	1	0	0	0	1	1	.000
E.Scott ss	3	0	0	0	0	0	.000
Bush p	3	0	0	0	0	0	.000
Hoyt p	0	0	0	0	0	0	.000
TOTALS	**29**	**2**	**7**	**0**	**2**	**1**	**.241**

BATTING: 3B: Witt (1, Nehf). **S:** Schang, Schang. **SF:** Ward. **RBI:** Ruth 1 (1), Ward 1 (1). **2-out RBI:** Ruth 1. **Runners left in scoring position, 2 out:** Pipp 1, Bush 1. **Team LOB:** 4 **BASERUNNING: CS:** Ruth (1, 2nd base off Nehf/Snyder). **FIELDING: PB:** Schang. **DP:** 1 (E.Scott-Ward-Pipp).

NY GIANTS	AB	R	H	HR	RBI	BB	AVG
Bancroft ss	4	1	1	0	0	0	.250
Groh 3b	3	1	3	0	0	1	1.000
Frisch 2b	4	1	2	0	0	0	.500
I.Meusel lf	4	0	1	0	2	0	.250
Youngs rf	3	0	0	0	1	0	.000
Kelly 1b	4	0	2	0	0	0	.500
Stengel cf	4	0	1	0	0	0	.250
Snyder c	3	0	1	0	0	0	.333
Nehf p	2	0	0	0	0	0	.000
a-Ea.Smith ph	1	0	0	0	0	0	.000
Ryan p	0	0	0	0	0	0	.000
TOTALS	**32**	**3**	**11**	**0**	**3**	**1**	**.344**

a - Batted for Nehf in the 7th

BATTING: 3B: Groh (1, Bush). **SF:** Youngs. **RBI:** I.Meusel 2 (2), Youngs 1 (1). **Runners left in scoring position, 2 out:** Frisch 1, Youngs 2. **GIDP:** Ea.Smith. **Team LOB:** 7 **BASERUNNING: CS:** Groh (1, 2nd base off Bush/Schang). **FIELDING: E:** Youngs (1), Nehf (1). **Outfield assists:** Youngs (1). **DP:** 3 (Snyder-Bancroft, Youngs-Frisch, Frisch-Kelly).

NY YANKEES	IP	H	R	ER	BB	SO	HR	ERA
Bush (L, 0-1)	7	11	3	3	1	3	0	3.86
Hoyt	1	0	0	0	0	2	0	0.00

NY GIANTS	IP	H	R	ER	BB	SO	HR	ERA
Nehf	7	6	2	1	1	3	0	1.29
Ryan (W, 1-0)	2	1	0	0	0	2	0	0.00

Ground balls-fly balls: Bush 9-7, Hoyt 0-0, Nehf 9-5, Ryan 1-2. **Batters faced:** Bush 31, Hoyt 3, Nehf 27, Ryan 6. **UMPIRES:** hp—Klem, 1b—Hildebrand, 2b—McCormick, 3b—Owens **T:** 2:08 **A:** 36,514

GAME 2 Giants 3 Yankees 3
Polo Grounds 10/05/22

NY GIANTS	AB	R	H	HR	RBI	BB	AVG
Bancroft ss	5	0	1	0	0	0	.222
Groh 3b	4	1	1	0	0	1	.571
Frisch 2b	4	1	2	0	0	0	.500
I.Meusel lf	4	1	1	1	3	0	.250
Youngs rf	3	0	1	0	0	1	.167
Kelly 1b	4	0	0	0	0	0	.250
Stengel cf	1	0	1	0	0	0	.400
a-Cunningham pr-cf	2	0	0	0	0	0	.000
b-Ea.Smith ph	1	0	0	0	0	0	.000
King cf	0	0	0	0	0	0	.000
Snyder c	4	0	1	0	0	0	.286
Barnes p	4	0	0	0	0	0	.000
TOTALS	**36**	**3**	**8**	**1**	**3**	**2**	**.279**

a - Ran for Stengel in the 2nd
b - Batted for Cunningham in the 9th

BATTING: HR: I.Meusel (1, 1st off Shawkey 2 on, 1 out). **RBI:** I.Meusel 3 (5). **Runners left in scoring position, 2 out:** Bancroft 1, I.Meusel 1, Kelly 1. **GIDP:** Barnes. **Team LOB:** 5 **BASERUNNING: SB:** Frisch (1, 2nd base off Shawkey/Schang). **FIELDING: E:** Bancroft (1).

NY YANKEES	AB	R	H	HR	RBI	BB	AVG
Witt cf	5	0	1	0	0	0	.222
Dugan 3b	5	1	2	0	0	0	.333
Ruth rf	4	1	1	0	0	1	.250
Pipp 1b	5	0	1	0	1	0	.222
B.Meusel lf	4	0	1	0	1	1	.375
Schang c	4	0	0	0	0	0	.167
Ward 2b	4	1	1	1	1	0	.200
E.Scott ss	4	0	1	0	0	0	.143
Shawkey p	4	0	0	0	0	0	.000
TOTALS	**39**	**3**	**8**	**1**	**3**	**2**	**.221**

BATTING: 2B: Dugan (1, Barnes), Ruth (1, Barnes), B.Meusel (1, Barnes). **HR:** Ward (1, 4th off Barnes 0 on, 2 out). **RBI:** Pipp 1 (1), B.Meusel 1 (1), Ward 1 (2). **2-out RBI:** Pipp 1, B.Meusel 1, Ward 1. **Runners left in scoring position, 2 out:** Dugan 1, Pipp 1, Schang 1, Ward 1. **Team LOB:** 8 **FIELDING: Outfield assists:** Witt (1). **DP:** 1 (E.Scott-Ward-Pipp).

NY GIANTS	IP	H	R	ER	BB	SO	HR	ERA
Barnes	10	8	3	2	2	6	1	1.80

NY YANKEES	IP	H	R	ER	BB	SO	HR	ERA
Shawkey	10	8	3	3	2	4	1	2.70

WP: Shawkey 1. **Ground balls-fly balls:** Barnes 16-9, Shawkey 10-14. **Batters faced:** Barnes 41, Shawkey 38. **UMPIRES:** hp—Hildebrand, 1b—McCormick, 2b—Owens, 3b—Klem **T:** 2:40 **A:** 37,020

GAME 3 Giants 3 Yankees 0
Polo Grounds 10/06/22

NY YANKEES	AB	R	H	HR	RBI	BB	AVG
Witt cf	3	0	0	0	0	1	.167
Dugan 3b	4	0	0	0	0	0	.231
Ruth rf	3	0	0	0	0	0	.182
Pipp 1b	4	0	1	0	0	0	.231
B.Meusel lf	4	0	1	0	0	0	.333
Schang c	3	0	1	0	0	0	.222
Ward 2b	2	0	0	0	0	0	.143
a-El.Smith ph	1	0	0	0	0	0	.000
McNally 2b	0	0	0	0	0	0	.000
E.Scott ss	3	0	0	0	0	0	.100
Hoyt p	2	0	1	0	0	0	.500
b-Baker ph	1	0	0	0	0	0	.000
Jones p	0	0	0	0	0	0	.000
TOTALS	**30**	**0**	**4**	**0**	**0**	**1**	**.194**

a - Batted for Ward in the 7th
b - Batted for Hoyt in the 8th

BATTING: 2B: Schang (1, J.Scott). **Runners left in scoring position, 2 out:** Ward 1, E.Scott 2. **Team LOB:** 5 **BASERUNNING: SB:** Pipp (1, 2nd base off J.Scott/Ea.Smith). **FIELDING: E:** Ward (1). **Outfield assists:** B.Meusel (1). **DP:** 1 (Ward-Pipp).

NY GIANTS	AB	R	H	HR	RBI	BB	AVG
Bancroft ss	3	2	0	0	0	1	.167
Groh 3b	4	1	2	0	0	0	.545
Frisch 2b	2	0	2	0	2	1	.600
I.Meusel lf	4	0	1	0	1	0	.250
Youngs rf	4	0	3	0	0	0	.400
Kelly 1b	3	0	1	0	0	0	.273
Cunningham cf	3	0	1	0	0	1	.200
Ea.Smith c	4	0	1	0	0	0	.167
J.Scott p	4	0	1	0	0	0	.250
TOTALS	**31**	**3**	**12**	**0**	**3**	**3**	**.313**

BATTING: S: Kelly. **SF:** Frisch. **RBI:** Frisch 2 (2), I.Meusel 1 (6). **2-out RBI:** Frisch 1, I.Meusel 1. **Runners left in scoring position, 2 out:** I.Meusel 1, J.Scott 1. **Team LOB:** 9 **BASERUNNING: CS:** Kelly (1, 2nd base off Hoyt/Schang), Frisch (1, 2nd base off Hoyt/Schang). **FIELDING: E:** Frisch (1).

NY YANKEES	IP	H	R	ER	BB	SO	HR	ERA
Hoyt (L, 0-1)	7	11	3	1	2	2	0	1.13
Jones	1	1	0	0	1	0	0	0.00

NY GIANTS	IP	H	R	ER	BB	SO	HR	ERA
J.Scott (W, 1-0)	9	4	0	0	1	2	0	0.00

HBP: Ruth (by J.Scott). **Ground balls-fly balls:** Hoyt 12-3, Jones 0-2, J.Scott 16-8. **Batters faced:** Hoyt 31, Jones 5, J.Scott 32. **UMPIRES:** hp—McCormick, 1b—Owens, 2b—Klem, 3b—Hildebrand **T:** 1:48 **A:** 37,630

GAME 4 Giants 4 Yankees 3
Polo Grounds 10/07/22

NY GIANTS	AB	R	H	HR	RBI	BB	AVG
Bancroft ss	3	1	2	0	2	1	.267
Groh 3b	4	1	1	0	0	0	.467
Frisch 2b	3	0	0	0	0	0	.462
I.Meusel lf	4	0	1	0	1	0	.250
Youngs rf	4	0	2	0	1	0	.429
Kelly 1b	4	0	0	0	0	0	.200
Cunningham cf	3	0	0	0	0	1	.125
Snyder c	4	1	2	0	0	0	.364
McQuillan p	4	1	1	0	0	0	.250
TOTALS	**33**	**4**	**9**	**0**	**4**	**2**	**.303**

BATTING: 2B: McQuillan (1, Mays). **S:** Frisch. **RBI:** Bancroft 2 (2), I.Meusel 1 (7), Youngs 1 (2). **2-out RBI:** Youngs 1. **Runners left in scoring position, 2 out:** I.Meusel 1. **GIDP:** Kelly. **Team LOB:** 5 **FIELDING: E:** Snyder (1). **Outfield assists:** Cunningham 2 (2). **DP:** 1 (Frisch-Bancroft-Kelly).

NY YANKEES	AB	R	H	HR	RBI	BB	AVG
Witt cf	4	1	2	0	0	0	.250
Dugan 3b	4	1	1	0	0	0	.235
Ruth rf	3	0	0	0	0	1	.143
Pipp 1b	4	0	2	0	1	0	.294
B.Meusel lf	4	0	1	0	1	0	.313
Schang c	4	0	1	0	0	0	.231
Ward 2b	4	1	1	1	1	0	.182
E.Scott ss	2	0	0	0	0	1	.083
Mays p	2	0	0	0	0	0	.000
a-El.Smith ph	1	0	0	0	0	0	.000
Jones p	0	0	0	0	0	0	.000
TOTALS	**32**	**3**	**8**	**1**	**3**	**2**	**.208**

a - Batted for Mays in the 8th

BATTING: 2B: Witt (1, McQuillan), Pipp (1, McQuillan). **HR:** Ward (2, 7th off McQuillan 0 on, 2 out). **RBI:** Pipp 1 (2), B.Meusel 1 (2), Ward 1 (3). **2-out RBI:** B.Meusel 1, Ward 1. **Runners left in scoring position, 2 out:** Ruth 1, Schang 1, Ward 1. **GIDP:** Witt. **Team LOB:** 4 **BASERUNNING: SB:** B.Meusel (1, 2nd base off McQuillan/Snyder). **FIELDING: DP:** 1 (Pipp-E.Scott).

NY GIANTS	IP	H	R	ER	BB	SO	HR	ERA
McQuillan (W, 1-0)	9	8	3	3	2	4	1	3.00

NY YANKEES	IP	H	R	ER	BB	SO	HR	ERA
Mays (L, 0-1)	8	9	4	4	2	1	0	4.50
Jones	1	0	0	0	0	0	0	0.00

Ground balls-fly balls: McQuillan 8-12, Mays 10-10, Jones 0-3. **Batters faced:** McQuillan 34, Mays 33, Jones 3. **UMPIRES:** hp—Owens, 1b—Klem, 2b—Hildebrand, 3b—McCormick **T:** 1:41 **A:** 36,242

GAME 5 Giants 5 Yankees 3
Polo Grounds 10/08/22

NY YANKEES	AB	R	H	HR	RBI	BB	AVG
Witt cf	2	0	0	0	0	0	.222
a-McMillan ph-cf	2	0	0	0	0	0	.000
Dugan 3b	3	1	1	0	0	0	.250
Ruth rf	3	0	0	0	0	0	.118
Pipp 1b	4	0	1	0	1	0	.286
B.Meusel lf	4	1	1	0	0	0	.300
Schang c	3	0	0	0	0	0	.188
Ward 2b	2	1	0	0	0	2	.154
E.Scott ss	2	0	1	0	1	0	.143
Bush p	3	0	1	0	1	0	.167
TOTALS	**28**	**3**	**5**	**0**	**3**	**2**	**.203**

a - Batted for Witt in the 5th

BATTING: S: Ruth, Schang. **SF:** E.Scott. **RBI:** Pipp 1 (3), E.Scott 1 (1), Bush 1 (1). **2-out RBI:** Pipp 1. **Runners left in scoring position, 2 out:** McMillan 1, Pipp 1, Bush 1. **Team LOB:** 4 **FIELDING: DP:** 3 (Bush-E.Scott-Pipp 2, Ward-E.Scott-Pipp).

NY GIANTS	AB	R	H	HR	RBI	BB	AVG
Bancroft ss	4	0	0	0	0	0	.211
Groh 3b	4	0	2	0	0	0	.474
Frisch 2b	4	1	2	0	0	0	.471
I.Meusel lf	4	2	1	0	0	0	.250
Youngs rf	2	2	0	0	0	2	.375
Kelly 1b	3	0	2	0	2	0	.278
Cunningham cf	2	0	1	0	2	0	.200
a-Ea.Smith ph	1	0	0	0	0	0	.143
King cf	1	0	1	0	1	0	1.000
Snyder c	4	0	1	0	0	0	.333
Nehf p	1	0	0	0	0	2	.000
TOTALS	**30**	**5**	**10**	**0**	**5**	**4**	**.309**

a - Batted for Cunningham in the 7th

BATTING: 2B: Frisch (1, Bush). **S:** Kelly. **RBI:** Kelly 2 (2), Cunningham 2 (2), King 1 (1). **2-out RBI:** Kelly 2, King 1. **Runners left in scoring position, 2 out:** Groh 2, Snyder 1. **GIDP:** Frisch, Cunningham, Bancroft. **Team LOB:** 6 **Outfield assists:** Youngs (2).

NY YANKEES	IP	H	R	ER	BB	SO	HR	ERA
Bush (L, 0-2)	8	10	5	5	4	3	0	4.80

NY GIANTS	IP	H	R	ER	BB	SO	HR	ERA
Nehf (W, 1-0)	9	5	3	3	2	3	0	2.25

WP: Nehf 1. **IBB:** Ward (by Nehf), Youngs (by Bush). **HBP:** Dugan (by Nehf). **Ground balls-fly balls:** Bush 10-7, Nehf 13-7. **Batters faced:** Bush 35, Nehf 34. **UMPIRES:** hp—Klem, 1b—Hildebrand, 2b—McCormick, 3b—Owens **T:** 2:00 **A:** 38,551

1923 NY YANKEES DEF. NY GIANTS, 4-2

GAME 1 Giants 5 Yankees 4
Yankee Stadium 10/10/23

NY GIANTS	AB	R	H	HR	RBI	BB	AVG
Bancroft ss	4	1	1	0	1	0	.250
Groh 3b	4	1	2	0	2	0	.500
Frisch 2b	4	0	1	0	1	0	.250
Youngs rf	3	0	0	0	0	1	.000
I.Meusel lf	4	0	0	0	0	0	.000
Stengel cf	3	1	2	1	1	1	.667
Cunningham cf	0	0	0	0	0	0	.000
Kelly 1b	4	1	1	0	0	0	.250
Gowdy c	0	0	0	0	0	1	.000
a-Maguire pr	0	1	0	0	0	0	.000
Snyder c	2	0	0	0	0	0	.000
Watson p	0	0	0	0	0	0	.000
b-Bentley ph	1	0	1	0	0	0	1.000
c-Gearin pr	0	0	0	0	0	0	.000
Ryan p	2	0	0	0	0	0	.000
TOTALS	**31**	**5**	**8**	**1**	**5**	**3**	**.258**

a - Ran for Gowdy in the 3th
b - Batted for Watson in the 3th
c - Ran for Bentley in the 3th

BATTING: 3B: Groh (1, Hoyt). **HR:** Stengel (1, 9th off Bush 0 on, 2 out). **RBI:** Bancroft 1 (1), Groh 2 (2), Frisch 1 (1), Stengel 1 (1). **2-out RBI:** Stengel 1. **Runners left in scoring position, 2 out:** Frisch 1, I.Meusel 1. **GIDP:** Kelly, Kelly. **Team LOB:** 2 **BASERUNNING: SB:** Bancroft (1, 2nd base off Hoyt/Schang). **CS:** Frisch (1, 2nd base off Hoyt/Schang). **FIELDING: DP:** 2 (Ryan-Groh-Frisch, Frisch-Snyder).

NY YANKEES	AB	R	H	HR	RBI	BB	AVG
Witt cf	5	0	1	0	2	0	.200
Dugan 3b	4	0	1	0	1	1	.250
Ruth rf	4	1	1	0	0	0	.250
B.Meusel lf	4	0	1	0	1	0	.250
Pipp 1b	4	0	2	0	0	0	.500
Ward 2b	4	1	2	0	0	0	.500
Schang c	3	1	2	0	0	1	.667
E.Scott ss	2	0	0	0	0	0	.000
a-Hendrick ph	1	0	0	0	0	0	.000
Johnson ss	0	0	0	0	0	0	.000
Hoyt p	1	0	0	0	0	0	.000
Bush p	3	1	2	0	0	0	.667
TOTALS	**35**	**4**	**12**	**0**	**4**	**2**	**.343**

a - Batted for E.Scott in the 8th

BATTING: 2B: B.Meusel (1, Watson), Bush (1, Ryan), Schang (1, Ryan). **3B:** Ruth (1, Ryan), Dugan (1, Ryan). **S:** E.Scott. **RBI:** Witt 2 (2), Dugan 1 (1), B.Meusel 1 (1). **2-out RBI:** Witt 2, B.Meusel 1. **Runners left in scoring position, 2 out:** Pipp 1, E.Scott 1, Hendrick 1. **Team LOB:** 7 **FIELDING: E:** Schang (1). **DP:** 2 (E.Scott-Ward-Pipp 2).

NY GIANTS	IP	H	R	ER	BB	SO	HR	ERA
Watson	2	4	3	3	1	1	0	13.50
Ryan (W, 1-0)	7	8	1	1	1	2	0	1.29

NY YANKEES	IP	H	R	ER	BB	SO	HR	ERA
Hoyt	2.1	4	4	4	1	0	0	15.43
Bush (L, 0-1)	6.2	4	1	1	2	2	1	1.35

WP: Ryan 1. **Ground balls-fly balls:** Watson 2-2, Ryan 6-10, Hoyt 3-3, Bush 9-6. **Batters faced:** Watson 11, Ryan 27, Hoyt 11, Bush 23. **UMPIRES:** hp—Evans, 1b—O'Day, 2b—Nallin, 3b—Hart **T:** 2:05 **A:** 55,307

GAME 2 Yankees 4 Giants 2
Polo Grounds 10/11/23

NY YANKEES	AB	R	H	HR	RBI	BB	AVG
Witt cf	5	0	0	0	0	0	.100
Dugan 3b	4	0	1	0	0	1	.250
Ruth rf	3	2	2	2	2	2	.429
B.Meusel lf	4	0	1	0	0	0	.250
Pipp 1b	3	1	1	0	0	1	.429
Ward 2b	4	1	2	1	1	0	.500
Schang c	4	0	1	0	0	0	.429
E.Scott ss	4	0	2	0	1	0	.333
Pennock p	3	0	0	0	0	0	.000
TOTALS	**34**	**4**	**10**	**3**	**4**	**4**	**.319**

BATTING: 2B: Dugan (1, Bentley). **HR:** Ward (1, 2nd off McQuillan 0 on, 1 out), Ruth 2 (2, 4th off McQuillan 0 on, 0 out, 5th off Bentley 0 on, 1 out). **RBI:** Ruth 2 (2), Ward 1 (1), E.Scott 1 (1). **2-out RBI:** E.Scott 1. **Runners left in scoring position, 2 out:** Witt 2, Ruth 1, Ward 1, E.Scott 1. **GIDP:** B.Meusel, Pennock. **Team LOB:** 8 **FIELDING: DP:** 1 (E.Scott-Ward-Pipp).

NY GIANTS	AB	R	H	HR	RBI	BB	AVG
Bancroft ss	4	0	0	0	0	0	.125
Groh 3b	3	1	1	0	0	1	.429
Frisch 2b	4	0	2	0	0	0	.375
Youngs rf	4	0	2	0	1	0	.286
I.Meusel lf	4	1	2	1	1	0	.250
Cunningham cf	3	0	0	0	0	0	.000
a-Gowdy ph	1	0	0	0	0	0	.000
Stengel cf	0	0	0	0	0	0	.667
Kelly 1b	4	0	1	0	0	0	.250
Snyder c	4	0	0	0	0	0	.000
McQuillan p	1	0	0	0	0	0	.000
Bentley p	2	0	1	0	0	0	.667
b-Jackson ph	1	0	0	0	0	0	.000
TOTALS	**35**	**2**	**9**	**1**	**2**	**1**	**.258**

a - Batted for Cunningham in the 8th
b - Batted for Bentley in the 9th

BATTING: 2B: Bentley (1, Pennock). **HR:** I.Meusel (1, 2nd off Pennock 0 on, 1 out). **RBI:** Youngs 1 (1), I.Meusel 1 (1). **Runners left in scoring position, 2 out:** Bancroft 1, Youngs 1, Gowdy 1. **GIDP:** Cunningham. **Team LOB:** 7 **FIELDING: E:** Youngs 2 (2). **DP:** 2 (Bancroft-Frisch-Kelly 2).

NY YANKEES	IP	H	R	ER	BB	SO	HR	ERA
Pennock (W, 1-0)	9	9	2	2	1	1	1	2.00

NY GIANTS	IP	H	R	ER	BB	SO	HR	ERA
McQuillan (L, 0-1)	3.2	5	3	3	2	1	2	7.36
Bentley	5.1	5	1	1	2	0	1	1.69

HBP: Pennock (by Bentley). **Ground balls-fly balls:** Pennock 13-12, McQuillan 5-4, Bentley 8-6. **Batters faced:** Pennock 36, McQuillan 17, Bentley 22. **UMPIRES:** hp—O'Day, 1b—Nallin, 2b—Hart, 3b—Evans **T:** 2:08 **A:** 40,402

GAME 3 Giants 1 Yankees 0
Yankee Stadium 10/12/23

NY GIANTS	AB	R	H	HR	RBI	BB	AVG
Bancroft ss	3	0	0	0	0	1	.091
Groh 3b	4	0	0	0	0	0	.273
Frisch 2b	4	0	2	0	0	0	.417
Youngs rf	4	0	0	0	0	0	.182
I.Meusel lf	4	0	0	0	0	0	.167
Stengel cf	3	1	1	1	1	1	.500
Kelly 1b	3	0	0	0	0	0	.182
Snyder c	3	0	0	0	0	0	.000
Nehf p	3	0	1	0	0	0	.333
TOTALS	**31**	**1**	**4**	**1**	**1**	**2**	**.216**

BATTING: HR: Stengel (2, 7th off Jones 0 on, 1 out). **RBI:** Stengel 1 (2). **Runners left in scoring position, 2 out:** Youngs 1. **GIDP:** Kelly. **Team LOB:** 5 **FIELDING: DP:** 2 (Bancroft-Frisch-Kelly, Frisch-Bancroft-Kelly).

NY YANKEES	AB	R	H	HR	RBI	BB	AVG
Witt cf	4	0	1	0	0	0	.143
Dugan 3b	4	0	1	0	0	0	.250
Ruth rf-1b	2	0	1	0	0	2	.444
B.Meusel lf	4	0	0	0	0	0	.167
Pipp 1b	2	0	0	0	0	1	.333
Haines rf	1	0	0	0	0	0	.000
Ward 2b	4	0	1	0	0	0	.417
Schang c	4	0	1	0	0	0	.364
E.Scott ss	3	0	1	0	0	0	.333
Jones p	2	0	0	0	0	0	.000
a-Hofmann ph	1	0	0	0	0	0	.000
Bush p	0	0	0	0	0	0	.667
TOTALS	**31**	**0**	**6**	**0**	**0**	**3**	**.280**

a - Batted for Jones in the 8th

BATTING: 2B: Dugan (2, Nehf). **Runners left in scoring position, 2 out:** B.Meusel 1, Pipp 1, E.Scott 1. **GIDP:** B.Meusel, Jones. **Team LOB:** 7 **FIELDING: E:** E.Scott (1). **DP:** 1 (Jones-E.Scott-Pipp).

NY GIANTS	IP	H	R	ER	BB	SO	HR	ERA
Nehf (W, 1-0)	9	6	0	0	3	4	0	0.00

NY YANKEES	IP	H	R	ER	BB	SO	HR	ERA
Jones (L, 0-1)	8	4	1	1	2	3	1	1.13
Bush	1	0	0	0	0	0	0	1.17

Ground balls-fly balls: Nehf 13-8, Jones 10-11, Bush 1-2. **Batters faced:** Nehf 34, Jones 30, Bush 3. **UMPIRES:** hp—Nallin, 1b—Hart, 2b—Evans, 3b—O'Day **T:** 2:05 **A:** 62,430

GAME 4 Yankees 8 Giants 4
Polo Grounds 10/13/23

NY YANKEES	AB	R	H	HR	RBI	BB	AVG
Witt cf	4	0	3	0	2	0	.278
Dugan 3b	5	1	0	0	0	0	.176
Ruth rf	3	2	1	0	0	2	.417
B.Meusel lf	5	0	1	0	2	0	.176
Pipp 1b	4	1	2	0	0	1	.385
Ward 2b	4	2	2	0	1	1	.438
Schang c	3	1	1	0	0	0	.357
E.Scott ss	5	1	2	0	2	0	.357
Shawkey p	3	0	1	0	1	0	.333
Pennock p	1	0	0	0	0	0	.000
TOTALS	**37**	**8**	**13**	**0**	**8**	**4**	**.299**

BATTING: 2B: Witt 2 (2, Ryan, McQuillan), Ruth (1, Jonnard). **3B:** B.Meusel (1, Ryan). **S:** Schang, Schang, Witt. **SF:** Shawkey. **RBI:** Witt 2 (4), B.Meusel 2 (3), Ward 1 (2), E.Scott 2 (3), Shawkey 1 (1). **2-out RBI:** Witt 1, B.Meusel 2. **Runners left in scoring position, 2 out:** Witt 1, Dugan 2, Ruth 1, Pipp 1, Ward 1, E.Scott 1. **Team LOB:** 10 **FIELDING: E:** Ruth (1). **DP:** 2 (Shawkey-Dugan-Pipp, Dugan-Pipp).

NY GIANTS	AB	R	H	HR	RBI	BB	AVG
Bancroft ss	5	0	1	0	0	0	.125
Groh 3b	3	0	0	0	0	2	.214
Frisch 2b	5	0	2	0	0	0	.412
Youngs rf	5	2	4	1	1	0	.375
I.Meusel lf	5	1	1	0	0	0	.176
Stengel cf	2	1	2	0	1	2	.625
d-Cunningham ph	1	0	0	0	0	0	.000
Kelly 1b	5	0	2	0	1	0	.250
Snyder c	4	0	0	0	1	0	.000
J.Scott p	0	0	0	0	0	0	.000
Ryan p	0	0	0	0	0	0	.000
McQuillan p	2	0	0	0	0	0	.000
a-Bentley ph	1	0	1	0	0	0	.750
b-Maguire pr	0	0	0	0	0	0	.000
Jonnard p	0	0	0	0	0	0	.000
c-O'Connell ph	0	0	0	0	0	0	.000
Barnes p	0	0	0	0	0	0	.000
TOTALS	**38**	**4**	**13**	**1**	**4**	**4**	**.252**

a - Batted for McQuillan in the 7th
b - Ran for Bentley in the 7th
c - Batted for Jonnard in the 8th
d - Batted for Stengel in the 9th

BATTING: HR: Youngs (1, 9th off Pennock 0 on, 0 out). **RBI:** Youngs 1 (2), Stengel 1 (3), Kelly 1 (1), Snyder 1 (1). **Runners left in scoring position, 2 out:** Bancroft 2, Frisch 2, I.Meusel 1, Snyder 1, McQuillan 1. **GIDP:** Snyder. **Team LOB:** 12 **FIELDING: E:** J.Scott (1).

NY YANKEES	IP	H	R	ER	BB	SO	HR	ERA
Shawkey (W, 1-0)	7.2	12	3	3	4	2	0	3.52
Pennock (S, 1)	1.1	1	1	1	0	1	1	2.61

NY GIANTS	IP	H	R	ER	BB	SO	HR	ERA
J.Scott (L, 0-1)	1	4	4	3	0	1	0	27.00
Ryan	0.2	2	2	0	1	0	0	1.17
McQuillan	5.1	6	2	2	2	2	0	5.00
Jonnard	1	1	0	0	1	0	0	0.00
Barnes	1	0	0	0	0	2	0	0.00

HBP: O'Connell (by Shawkey). **Ground balls-fly balls:** Shawkey 9-10, Pennock 1-2, J.Scott 1-1, Ryan 1-0, McQuillan 2-10, Jonnard 2-1, Barnes 1-0. **Batters faced:** Shawkey 38, Pennock 5, J.Scott 8, Ryan 5, McQuillan 24, Jonnard 5, Barnes 3. **UMPIRES:** hp—Hart, 1b—Evans, 2b—O'Day, 3b—Nallin **T:** 2:32 **A:** 46,302

GAME 5 Yankees 8 Giants 1
Yankee Stadium 10/14/23

NY GIANTS	AB	R	H	HR	RBI	BB	AVG
Bancroft ss	4	0	0	0	0	0	.100
Groh 3b	4	0	0	0	0	0	.167
Frisch 2b	4	0	0	0	0	0	.333
Youngs rf	3	0	0	0	0	1	.316
I.Meusel lf	4	1	3	0	0	0	.286
Stengel cf	3	0	0	0	1	0	.455
Kelly 1b	2	0	0	0	0	1	.222
Gowdy c	3	0	0	0	0	0	.000
Bentley p	0	0	0	0	0	0	.750
J.Scott p	1	0	0	0	0	0	.000
Barnes p	1	0	0	0	0	0	.000
a-O'Connell ph	1	0	0	0	0	0	.000
Jonnard p	0	0	0	0	0	0	.000
TOTALS	**30**	**1**	**3**	**0**	**1**	**2**	**.224**

a - Batted for Barnes in the 8th

BATTING: 2B: I.Meusel (1, Bush). **3B:** I.Meusel (1, Bush). **RBI:** Stengel 1 (4). **Runners left in scoring position, 2 out:** Stengel 2, Gowdy 1. **Team LOB:** 4 **FIELDING: E:** Kelly (1), Frisch (1). **Outfield assists:** Youngs (1). **DP:** 1 (Bancroft-Frisch).

NY YANKEES	AB	R	H	HR	RBI	BB	AVG
Witt cf	4	1	1	0	0	1	.273
Dugan 3b	5	3	4	1	3	0	.318
Ruth rf	4	2	1	0	0	1	.375
B.Meusel lf	5	1	3	0	3	0	.273
Pipp 1b	3	0	0	0	2	1	.313
Ward 2b	4	0	2	0	0	0	.450
Schang c	4	0	1	0	0	0	.333
E.Scott ss	4	0	1	0	0	0	.333
Bush p	4	1	1	0	0	0	.429
TOTALS	**37**	**8**	**14**	**1**	**8**	**3**	**.316**

BATTING: 3B: B.Meusel (2, Bentley). **HR:** Dugan (1, 2nd off Bentley 2 on, 1 out). **SF:** Pipp. **RBI:** Dugan 3 (4), B.Meusel 3 (6), Pipp 2 (2). **Runners left in scoring position, 2 out:** Ruth 1, Schang 2, E.Scott 1. **Team LOB:** 9 **BASERUNNING: SB:** Ward (1, 2nd base off Bentley/Gowdy).

NY GIANTS	IP	H	R	ER	BB	SO	HR	ERA
Bentley (L, 0-1)	1.1	5	7	6	2	1	1	9.45
J.Scott	2	5	1	1	1	1	0	12.00
Barnes	3.2	4	0	0	0	2	0	0.00
Jonnard	1	0	0	0	0	1	0	0.00

NY YANKEES	IP	H	R	ER	BB	SO	HR	ERA
Bush (W, 1-1)	9	3	1	1	2	3	0	1.08

Ground balls-fly balls: Bentley 1-2, J.Scott 2-2, Barnes 7-2, Jonnard 1-1, Bush 13-11. **Batters faced:** Bentley 12, J.Scott 11, Barnes 15, Jonnard 3, Bush 32. **UMPIRES:** hp—Evans, 1b—O'Day, 2b—Nallin, 3b—Hart **T:** 1:55 **A:** 62,817

GAME 6 Yankees 6 Giants 4
Polo Grounds 10/15/23

NY YANKEES	AB	R	H	HR	RBI	BB	AVG
Witt cf	3	0	0	0	0	0	.240
c-Bush ph	0	0	0	0	1	1	.429
d-Johnson pr	0	1	0	0	0	0	.000
Jones p	0	0	0	0	0	0	.000
Dugan 3b	3	1	0	0	1	1	.280
Ruth rf	3	1	1	1	1	1	.368
B.Meusel lf	4	0	1	0	3	0	.269
Pipp 1b	4	0	0	0	0	0	.250
Ward 2b	4	0	1	0	0	0	.417
Schang c	4	1	1	0	0	0	.318
E.Scott ss	4	1	1	0	0	0	.318
Pennock p	2	0	0	0	0	0	.000
a-Hofmann ph	0	0	0	0	0	1	.000
b-Haines pr-cf	0	1	0	0	0	0	.000
TOTALS	**31**	**6**	**5**	**1**	**6**	**4**	**.293**

a - Batted for Pennock in the 8th
b - Ran for Hofmann in the 8th
c - Batted for Witt in the 8th
d - Ran for Bush in the 8th

BATTING: HR: Ruth (3, 1st off Nehf 0 on, 2 out). **RBI:** Bush 1 (1), Dugan 1 (5), Ruth 1 (3), B.Meusel 3 (9). **2-out RBI:** Ruth 1, B.Meusel 3. **Runners left in scoring position, 2 out:** Pipp 2. **GIDP:** Schang. **Team LOB:** 2 **Outfield assists:** Witt (1).

NY GIANTS	AB	R	H	HR	RBI	BB	AVG
Bancroft ss	4	0	0	0	0	0	.083
Groh 3b	4	1	1	0	0	0	.182
Frisch 2b	4	2	3	0	0	0	.400
Youngs rf	4	0	2	0	1	0	.348
I.Meusel lf	4	0	1	0	1	0	.280
Cunningham cf	3	0	1	0	1	0	.143
a-Stengel ph-cf	1	0	0	0	0	0	.417
Kelly 1b	4	0	0	0	0	0	.182
Snyder c	4	1	2	1	1	0	.118
Nehf p	3	0	0	0	0	0	.167
Ryan p	0	0	0	0	0	0	.000
b-Bentley ph	1	0	0	0	0	0	.600
TOTALS	**36**	**4**	**10**	**1**	**4**	**0**	**.234**

a - Batted for Cunningham in the 8th
b - Batted for Ryan in the 9th

BATTING: 3B: Frisch (1, Pennock). **HR:** Snyder (1, 5th off Pennock 0 on, 0 out). **RBI:** Youngs 1 (3), I.Meusel 1 (2), Cunningham 1 (1), Snyder 1 (2). **2-out RBI:** Cunningham 1. **Runners left in scoring position, 2 out:** Groh 1, Kelly 1. **Team LOB:** 5 **FIELDING: E:** Cunningham (1). **DP:** 1 (Nehf-Bancroft-Kelly).

NY YANKEES	IP	H	R	ER	BB	SO	HR	ERA
Pennock (W, 2-0)	7	9	4	4	0	6	1	3.63
Jones (S, 1)	2	1	0	0	0	0	0	0.90

NY GIANTS	IP	H	R	ER	BB	SO	HR	ERA
Nehf (L, 1-1)	7.1	4	5	5	3	3	1	2.76
Ryan	1.2	1	1	0	1	1	0	0.96

Ground balls-fly balls: Pennock 8-6, Jones 4-2, Nehf 14-4, Ryan 4-0. **Batters faced:** Pennock 29, Jones 7, Nehf 28, Ryan 7. **UMPIRES:** hp—O'Day, 1b—Nallin, 2b—Hart, 3b—Evans **T:** 2:05 **A:** 0,000

1924 WASHINGTON DEF. NY GIANTS, 4-3

GAME 1 New York 4 Washington 3
Griffith Stadium 10/04/24

NY GIANTS	AB	R	H	HR	RBI	BB	AVG
Lindstrom 3b	5	0	0	0	0	0	.000
a-Bentley ph	0	0	0	0	0	1	.000
b-Southworth pr-cf	0	1	0	0	0	0	.000
Frisch 2b-3b	5	0	2	0	0	1	.400
Youngs rf	6	0	2	0	1	0	.333
Kelly cf-2b	5	1	1	1	2	0	.200
Terry 1b	5	1	3	1	1	1	.600
Wilson lf	6	0	2	0	0	0	.333
Jackson ss	3	0	0	0	0	1	.000
Gowdy c	3	0	1	0	0	2	.333
Nehf p	5	1	3	0	0	0	.600
TOTALS	**43**	**4**	**14**	**2**	**4**	**6**	**.326**

a - Batted for Lindstrom in the 12th
b - Ran for Bentley in the 12th

BATTING: 2B: Frisch (1, Johnson), Youngs (1, Johnson). **HR:** Kelly (1, 2nd off Johnson 0 on, 0 out), Terry (1, 4th off Johnson 0 on, 2 out). **S:** Youngs, Jackson. **SF:** Kelly. **RBI:** Youngs 1 (1), Kelly 2 (2), Terry 1 (1). **2-out RBI:** Terry 1. **Runners left in scoring position, 2 out:** Lindstrom 2, Kelly 1, Wilson 2, Nehf 1. **GIDP:** Jackson. **Team LOB:** 11 **BASERUNNING: SB:** Frisch (1, 2nd base off Johnson/Ruel). **FIELDING: E:** Jackson (1). **Outfield assists:** Southworth (1). **DP:** 1 (Jackson-Frisch-Terry).

WASHINGTON	AB	R	H	HR	RBI	BB	AVG
McNeely cf	5	1	1	0	0	1	.200
Harris 2b	6	0	2	0	1	0	.333
Rice rf	5	0	2	0	1	1	.400
Goslin lf	6	0	1	0	0	0	.167
Judge 1b	4	0	1	0	0	1	.250
Bluege 3b	5	1	1	0	0	0	.200
Peckinpaugh ss	5	0	2	0	1	0	.400
Ruel c	3	0	0	0	0	2	.000
Johnson p	4	0	0	0	0	0	.000
a-Shirley ph	1	1	0	0	0	0	.000
TOTALS	**44**	**3**	**10**	**0**	**3**	**5**	**.227**

a - Batted for Johnson in the 12th

BATTING: 2B: McNeely (1, Nehf), Peckinpaugh (1, Nehf). **RBI:** Harris 1 (1), Rice 1 (1), Peckinpaugh 1 (1). **Runners left in scoring position, 2 out:** Goslin 2, Judge 1, Johnson 2. **GIDP:** Johnson. **Team LOB:** 10 **BASERUNNING: SB:** Peckinpaugh (1, 2nd base off Nehf/Gowdy), Rice (1, 2nd base off Nehf/Gowdy). **CS:** Goslin (1, 2nd base off Nehf/Gowdy). **FIELDING: E:** McNeely (1). **Outfield assists:** Rice (1). **DP:** 2 (Peckinpaugh-Harris, Bluege-Harris-Judge).

NY GIANTS	IP	H	R	ER	BB	SO	HR	ERA
Nehf (W, 1-0)	12	10	3	2	5	3	0	1.50

WASHINGTON	IP	H	R	ER	BB	SO	HR	ERA
Johnson (L, 0-1)	12	14	4	3	6	12	2	2.25

WP: Johnson 1. **IBB:** Terry (by Johnson). **Ground balls-fly balls:** Nehf 15-16, Johnson 7-10. **Batters faced:** Nehf 49, Johnson 51. **UMPIRES:** hp—Connolly, 1b—Klem, 2b—Dinneen, 3b—Quigley **T:** 3:07 **A:** 35,760

GAME 2 Washington 4 New York 3
Griffith Stadium 10/05/24

NY GIANTS	AB	R	H	HR	RBI	BB	AVG
Lindstrom 3b	3	0	1	0	0	1	.125
Frisch 2b	3	1	1	0	0	1	.375
Youngs rf	4	0	1	0	0	0	.300
Kelly 1b	3	2	1	0	1	1	.250
Meusel lf	4	0	1	0	0	0	.250
Wilson cf	4	0	1	0	1	0	.300
Jackson ss	4	0	0	0	0	0	.000
Gowdy c	3	0	0	0	0	0	.167
Bentley p	3	0	0	0	0	0	.000
TOTALS	**31**	**3**	**6**	**0**	**2**	**3**	**.270**

BATTING: RBI: Kelly 1 (3), Wilson 1 (1). **2-out RBI:** Wilson 1. **Runners left in scoring position, 2 out:** Jackson 1. **GIDP:** Meusel, Kelly, Wilson. **Team LOB:** 4

WASHINGTON	AB	R	H	HR	RBI	BB	AVG
McNeely cf	4	0	0	0	0	0	.111
Harris 2b	3	1	1	1	1	1	.333
Rice rf	3	1	2	0	0	0	.500
Goslin lf	4	1	1	1	2	0	.200
Judge 1b	2	1	1	0	0	2	.333
Bluege 3b	3	0	0	0	0	0	.125
Peckinpaugh ss	4	0	1	0	1	0	.333
Ruel c	3	0	0	0	0	0	.000
Zachary p	2	0	0	0	0	1	.000
Marberry p	0	0	0	0	0	0	.000
TOTALS	**28**	**4**	**6**	**2**	**4**	**4**	**.222**

BATTING: 2B: Peckinpaugh (2, Bentley). **HR:** Goslin (1, 1st off Bentley 1 on, 2 out), Harris (1, 5th off Bentley 0 on, 2 out). **S:** Rice, Bluege. **RBI:** Harris 1 (2), Goslin 2 (2), Peckinpaugh 1 (2). **2-out RBI:** Harris 1, Goslin 2. **Team LOB:** 5 **BASERUNNING: SB:** Rice (2, 2nd base off Bentley/Gowdy). **FIELDING: E:** Harris (1). **DP:** 3 (Bluege-Harris-Judge 2, Harris-Peckinpaugh-Judge).

NY GIANTS	IP	H	R	ER	BB	SO	HR	ERA
Bentley (L, 0-1)	8.1	6	4	4	4	6	2	4.32

WASHINGTON	IP	H	R	ER	BB	SO	HR	ERA
Zachary (W, 1-0)	8.2	6	3	3	3	0	0	3.12
Marberry (S, 1)	0.1	0	0	0	0	1	0	0.00

Ground balls-fly balls: Bentley 12-4, Zachary 16-8, Marberry 0-0. **Batters faced:** Bentley 34, Zachary 33, Marberry 1. **UMPIRES:** hp—Klem, 1b—Dinneen, 2b—Quigley, 3b—Connolly **T:** 1:58 **A:** 35,922

GAME 3 New York 6 Washington 4
Polo Grounds 10/06/24

WASHINGTON	AB	R	H	HR	RBI	BB	AVG
Leibold cf	4	0	0	0	0	1	.000
Harris 2b	5	1	1	0	0	0	.286
Rice rf	3	1	1	0	0	2	.455
Goslin lf	5	0	1	0	0	0	.200
Judge 1b	5	1	3	0	0	0	.455
Bluege 3b-ss	3	1	1	0	1	2	.182
Peckinpaugh ss	1	0	0	0	0	0	.300
Miller 3b	2	0	1	0	1	1	.500
Ruel c	3	0	0	0	0	2	.000
Marberry p	1	0	0	0	0	0	.000
a-Tate ph	0	0	0	0	1	1	.000
Russell p	0	0	0	0	0	0	.000
b-McNeely ph	1	0	0	0	0	0	.100
Martina p	0	0	0	0	0	0	.000
c-Shirley ph	1	0	1	0	1	0	.500
Speece p	0	0	0	0	0	0	.000
TOTALS	**34**	**4**	**9**	**0**	**4**	**9**	**.236**

a - Batted for Marberry in the 4th
b - Batted for Russell in the 7th
c - Batted for Martina in the 8th

BATTING: 2B: Judge (1, McQuillan). **SF:** Miller. **RBI:** Bluege 1 (1), Miller 1 (1), Tate 1 (1), Shirley 1 (1). **2-out RBI:** Tate 1, Shirley 1. **Runners left in scoring position, 2 out:** Leibold 3, Goslin 1, Ruel 2. **GIDP:** Bluege. **Team LOB:** 13 **FIELDING: E:** Miller (1). **Outfield assists:** Goslin (1). **DP:** 1 (Marberry-Bluege-Harris-Judge).

NY GIANTS	AB	R	H	HR	RBI	BB	AVG
Lindstrom 3b	4	0	1	0	1	1	.167
Frisch 2b	4	0	2	0	0	0	.417
Youngs rf	4	0	1	0	0	0	.286
Kelly cf	4	1	2	0	0	0	.333
Southworth cf	0	0	0	0	0	0	.000
Terry 1b	4	1	2	0	0	0	.556
Wilson lf	4	0	0	0	0	0	.214
Jackson ss	4	2	1	0	0	0	.091
Gowdy c	4	1	2	0	1	0	.300
McQuillan p	0	0	0	0	0	1	.000
Ryan p	2	1	1	1	2	0	.500
Jonnard p	0	0	0	0	0	0	.000
Watson p	0	0	0	0	0	0	.000
TOTALS	**34**	**6**	**12**	**1**	**4**	**2**	**.296**

BATTING: 2B: Lindstrom (1, Russell). **HR:** Ryan (1, 4th off Russell 0 on, 1 out). **S:** Ryan. **RBI:** Lindstrom 1 (1), Gowdy 1 (1), Ryan 2 (2). **Runners left in scoring position, 2 out:** Frisch 1, Youngs 3. **GIDP:** Wilson. **Team LOB:** 8 **BASERUNNING: SB:** Jackson (1, 2nd base off Speece/Ruel). **FIELDING: DP:** 1 (McQuillan-Frisch-Terry).

WASHINGTON	IP	H	R	ER	BB	SO	HR	ERA
Marberry (L, 0-1)	3	5	3	1	2	4	0	2.70
Russell	3	4	2	1	0	0	1	3.00
Martina	1	0	0	0	0	1	0	0.00
Speece	1	3	1	1	0	0	0	9.00

NY GIANTS	IP	H	R	ER	BB	SO	HR	ERA
McQuillan (W, 1-0)	3.2	2	2	2	5	0	0	4.91
Ryan	4.2	7	2	2	3	2	0	3.86
Jonnard	0	0	0	0	1	0	0	0.00
Watson (S, 1)	0.2	0	0	0	0	0	0	0.00

WP: Marberry 1. **HBP:** Frisch (by Marberry). **Ground balls-fly balls:** Marberry 3-1, Russell 3-6, Martina 0-2, Speece 1-1, McQuillan 5-4, Ryan 5-7, Jonnard 0-0, Watson 1-1. **Batters faced:** Marberry 16, Russell 14, Martina 3, Speece 5, McQuillan 17, Ryan 24, Jonnard 1, Watson 2. **UMPIRES:** hp—Dinneen, 1b—Quigley, 2b—Connolly, 3b—Klem **T:** 2:25 **A:** 47,608

GAME 4 Washington 7 New York 4
Polo Grounds 10/07/24

WASHINGTON	AB	R	H	HR	RBI	BB	AVG
McNeely cf	5	2	3	0	0	0	.267
Harris 2b	5	2	2	0	0	0	.316
Rice rf	5	0	0	0	0	0	.313
Goslin lf	4	2	4	1	4	0	.368
Judge 1b	4	1	1	0	0	0	.400
Bluege ss	4	0	3	0	2	0	.333
Ruel c	3	0	0	0	0	0	.000
Miller 3b	4	0	0	0	0	0	.167
Mogridge p	4	0	0	0	0	0	.000
Marberry p	0	0	0	0	0	0	.000
TOTALS	**38**	**7**	**13**	**1**	**6**	**0**	**.264**

BATTING: 2B: McNeely (2, Baldwin). **HR:** Goslin (2, 3th off Barnes 2 on, 2 out). **S:** Ruel. **RBI:** Goslin 4 (6), Bluege 2 (3). **2-out RBI:** Goslin 3. **Runners left in scoring position, 2 out:** Rice 1, Miller 2, Mogridge 2. **Team LOB:** 5 **BASERUNNING: CS:** Goslin (2, 2nd base off Barnes/Gowdy). **FIELDING: E:** Bluege (1), Miller (2), Rice (1). **Outfield assists:** Rice (2).

NY GIANTS	AB	R	H	HR	RBI	BB	AVG
Lindstrom 3b	4	1	3	0	1	1	.313
Frisch 2b	4	0	0	0	0	1	.313
Youngs rf	4	1	0	0	0	1	.222
Kelly 1b	5	1	1	0	0	0	.294
Meusel lf	2	0	0	0	0	2	.167
Wilson cf	4	0	1	0	2	0	.222
Jackson ss	4	0	0	0	0	0	.067
Gowdy c	4	1	1	0	0	0	.286
Barnes p	0	0	0	0	0	1	.000
a-Terry ph	1	0	0	0	0	0	.500
Baldwin p	0	0	0	0	0	0	.000
b-Southworth ph	1	0	0	0	0	0	.000
Dean p	0	0	0	0	0	0	.000
c-Bentley ph	1	0	0	0	0	0	.000
TOTALS	**34**	**4**	**6**	**0**	**3**	**6**	**.268**

a - Batted for Barnes in the 5th
b - Batted for Baldwin in the 7th
c - Batted for Dean in the 9th

BATTING: 2B: Kelly (1, Mogridge), Wilson (1, Marberry). **RBI:** Lindstrom 1 (2), Wilson 2 (3). **Runners left in scoring position, 2 out:** Frisch 1, Kelly 1, Wilson 1, Jackson 1. **Team LOB:** 9 **FIELDING: E:** Meusel (1).

WASHINGTON	IP	H	R	ER	BB	SO	HR	ERA
Mogridge (W, 1-0)	7.1	3	3	2	5	2	0	2.45
Marberry (S, 2)	1.2	3	1	0	1	2	0	1.80

NY GIANTS	IP	H	R	ER	BB	SO	HR	ERA
Barnes (L, 0-1)	5	9	5	5	0	3	1	9.00
Baldwin	2	1	0	0	0	1	0	0.00
Dean	2	3	2	1	0	2	0	4.50

WP: Barnes 1. **Ground balls-fly balls:** Mogridge 14-8, Marberry 2-0, Barnes 6-4, Baldwin 1-4, Dean 2-2. **Batters faced:** Mogridge 32, Marberry 8, Barnes 23, Baldwin 7, Dean 9. **UMPIRES:** hp—Quigley, 1b—Connolly, 2b—Klem, 3b—Dinneen **T:** 2:10 **A:** 49,243

GAME 5 New York 6 Washington 2
Polo Grounds 10/08/24

WASHINGTON	AB	R	H	HR	RBI	BB	AVG
McNeely cf	4	0	1	0	0	1	.263
Harris 2b	5	0	1	0	0	0	.292
Rice rf	4	0	0	0	0	0	.250
Goslin lf	4	1	2	1	1	0	.391
Judge 1b	4	1	3	0	0	0	.474
Bluege ss	3	0	0	0	0	0	.278
Ruel c	2	0	0	0	0	2	.000
Miller 3b	3	0	1	0	1	0	.222
a-Leibold ph	1	0	0	0	0	0	.000
Johnson p	3	0	1	0	0	0	.143
b-Tate ph	0	0	0	0	0	1	.000
c-Taylor pr	0	0	0	0	0	0	.000
TOTALS	**33**	**2**	**9**	**1**	**2**	**4**	**.266**

a - Batted for Miller in the 9th
b - Batted for Johnson in the 9th
c - Ran for Tate in the 9th

BATTING: HR: Goslin (3, 8th off Bentley 0 on, 1 out). **S:** Bluege. **RBI:** Goslin 1 (7), Miller 1 (2). **2-out RBI:** Miller 1. **Runners left in scoring position, 2 out:** Harris 2, Goslin 1, Ruel 1, Miller 2. **Team LOB:** 9 **FIELDING: E:** Johnson (1). **Outfield assists:** Rice 2 (4). **DP:** 2 (Rice-Johnson-Ruel, Bluege-Harris-Judge).

NY GIANTS	AB	R	H	HR	RBI	BB	AVG
Lindstrom 3b	5	0	4	0	2	0	.429
Frisch 2b	5	0	1	0	0	0	.286
Youngs rf	3	0	1	0	0	0	.238
Kelly cf	4	1	1	0	0	0	.286
Terry 1b	2	1	1	0	0	2	.500
Wilson lf	3	0	0	0	0	0	.190
Jackson ss	3	1	1	0	1	0	.111
Gowdy c	4	2	1	0	0	0	.278
Bentley p	3	1	2	1	2	0	.286
McQuillan p	1	0	1	0	1	0	1.000
TOTALS	**33**	**6**	**13**	**1**	**6**	**2**	**.291**

BATTING: 2B: Frisch (2, Johnson). **3B:** Terry (1, Johnson). **HR:** Bentley (1, 5th off Johnson 1 on, 0 out). **S:** Lindstrom, Wilson. **SF:** Jackson. **RBI:** Lindstrom 2 (4), Jackson 1 (1), Bentley 2 (2), McQuillan 1 (1). **2-out RBI:** Lindstrom 1, McQuillan 1. **Runners left in scoring position, 2 out:** Frisch 1, Jackson 1. **GIDP:** Kelly. **Team LOB:** 8 **BASERUNNING: CS:** Lindstrom (1, 2nd base off Johnson/Ruel). **Outfield assists:** Wilson (1), Youngs (1).

WASHINGTON	IP	H	R	ER	BB	SO	HR	ERA
Johnson (L, 0-2)	8	13	6	3	2	3	1	2.70

NY GIANTS	IP	H	R	ER	BB	SO	HR	ERA
Bentley (W, 1-1)	7.1	9	2	2	3	4	1	3.45
McQuillan (S, 1)	1.2	0	0	0	1	1	0	3.38

HBP: Youngs (by Johnson). **Ground balls-fly balls:** Johnson 8-9, Bentley 7-8, McQuillan 2-2. **Batters faced:** Johnson 38, Bentley 32, McQuillan 6. **UMPIRES:** hp—Connolly, 1b—Klem, 2b—Dinneen, 3b—Quigley **T:** 2:30 **A:** 49,271

GAME 6 Washington 2 New York 1
Griffith Stadium 10/09/24

NY GIANTS	AB	R	H	HR	RBI	BB	AVG
Lindstrom 3b	4	0	0	0	0	0	.360
Frisch 2b	4	0	2	0	0	0	.320
Youngs rf	4	1	0	0	0	0	.200
Kelly 1b	4	0	2	0	1	0	.320
b-Southworth pr	0	0	0	0	0	0	.000
Meusel lf	4	0	0	0	0	0	.100
Wilson cf	4	0	2	0	0	0	.240
Jackson ss	3	0	0	0	0	0	.095
Gowdy c	3	0	1	0	0	0	.286
Nehf p	2	0	0	0	0	0	.429
a-Snyder ph	1	0	0	0	0	0	.000
Ryan p	0	0	0	0	0	0	.500
TOTALS	**33**	**1**	**7**	**0**	**1**	**0**	**.279**

a - Batted for Nehf in the 8th
b - Ran for Kelly in the 9th

BATTING: 2B: Frisch 2 (4, Zachary). **RBI:** Kelly 1 (4). **2-out RBI:** Kelly 1. **Runners left in scoring position, 2 out:** Kelly 1. **GIDP:** Jackson. **Team LOB:** 5 **FIELDING: E:** Kelly (1).

WASHINGTON	AB	R	H	HR	RBI	BB	AVG
McNeely cf	2	1	0	0	0	2	.238
Harris 2b	4	0	1	0	2	0	.286
Rice rf	4	0	1	0	0	0	.250
Goslin lf	4	0	0	0	0	0	.333
Judge 1b	3	0	0	0	0	1	.409
Bluege 3b-ss	3	0	0	0	0	1	.238
Peckinpaugh ss	2	1	2	0	0	1	.417
Taylor 3b	0	0	0	0	0	0	.000
Ruel c	2	0	0	0	0	0	.000
Zachary p	3	0	0	0	0	0	.000
TOTALS	**27**	**2**	**4**	**0**	**2**	**5**	**.250**

BATTING: S: Ruel. **RBI:** Harris 2 (4). **2-out RBI:** Harris 2. **Runners left in scoring position, 2 out:** Rice 1, Judge 1, Ruel 1. **Team LOB:** 7 **BASERUNNING: SB:** McNeely (1, 2nd base off Nehf/Gowdy), Bluege (1, 2nd base off Nehf/Gowdy). **FIELDING: DP:** 1 (Harris-Peckinpaugh-Judge).

NY GIANTS	IP	H	R	ER	BB	SO	HR	ERA
Nehf (L, 1-1)	7	4	2	2	4	4	0	1.89
Ryan	1	0	0	0	1	1	0	3.18

WASHINGTON	IP	H	R	ER	BB	SO	HR	ERA
Zachary (W, 2-0)	9	7	1	1	0	3	0	2.04

Ground balls-fly balls: Nehf 8-8, Ryan 2-0, Zachary 12-11. **Batters faced:** Nehf 29, Ryan 4, Zachary 33. **UMPIRES:** hp—Klem, 1b—Dinneen, 2b—Quigley, 3b—Connolly **T:** 1:57 **A:** 34,254

GAME 7 Washington 4 New York 3
Griffith Stadium 10/10/24

NY GIANTS	AB	R	H	HR	RBI	BB	AVG
Lindstrom 3b	5	0	1	0	0	0	.333
Frisch 2b	5	0	2	0	0	1	.333
Youngs rf-lf-rf	2	1	0	0	0	4	.185
Kelly cf-1b	6	1	1	0	0	0	.290
Terry 1b	2	0	0	0	0	0	.429
a-Meusel ph-lf-rf-lf	3	0	1	0	1	0	.154
Wilson lf-cf	5	1	1	0	0	1	.233
Jackson ss	6	0	0	0	0	0	.074
Gowdy c	6	0	1	0	0	0	.259
Barnes p	4	0	0	0	0	0	.000
Nehf p	0	0	0	0	0	0	.429
McQuillan p	0	0	0	0	0	0	1.000
b-Groh ph	1	0	1	0	0	0	1.000
c-Southworth pr	0	0	0	0	0	0	.000
Bentley p	0	0	0	0	0	0	.286
TOTALS	**45**	**3**	**8**	**0**	**1**	**6**	**.261**

a - Batted for Terry in the 6th
b - Batted for McQuillan in the 11th
c - Ran for Groh in the 11th

BATTING: 2B: Lindstrom (2, Mogridge). **3B:** Frisch (1, Johnson). **S:** Lindstrom. **SF:** Meusel. **RBI:** Meusel 1 (1). **Runners left in scoring position, 2 out:** Lindstrom 1, Frisch 1, Kelly 1, Meusel 3, Barnes 1. **GIDP:** Gowdy. **Team LOB:** 14 **BASERUNNING: SB:** Youngs (1, 2nd base off Johnson/Ruel). **FIELDING: E:** Gowdy (1), Jackson (2). **DP:** 2 (Kelly-Jackson, Jackson-Frisch-Kelly).

WASHINGTON	AB	R	H	HR	RBI	BB	AVG
McNeely cf	6	0	1	0	1	0	.222
Harris 2b	5	1	3	1	3	0	.333
Rice rf	5	0	0	0	0	0	.207
Goslin lf	5	0	2	0	0	0	.344
Judge 1b	4	0	1	0	0	1	.385
Bluege ss	5	0	0	0	0	0	.192
Taylor 3b	2	0	0	0	0	0	.000
a-Leibold ph	1	1	1	0	0	0	.167
Miller 3b	2	0	0	0	0	0	.182
Ruel c	5	2	2	0	0	0	.095
Ogden p	0	0	0	0	0	0	.000
Mogridge p	1	0	0	0	0	0	.000
Marberry p	1	0	0	0	0	0	.000
b-Tate ph	0	0	0	0	0	1	.000
c-Shirley pr	0	0	0	0	0	0	.500
Johnson p	2	0	0	0	0	0	.111
TOTALS	**44**	**4**	**10**	**1**	**4**	**2**	**.246**

a - Batted for Taylor in the 8th
b - Batted for Marberry in the 8th
c - Ran for Tate in the 8th

BATTING: 2B: Leibold (1, Barnes), Goslin (1, Bentley), Ruel (1, Bentley), McNeely (3, Bentley). **HR:** Harris (2, 4th off Barnes 0 on, 1 out). **RBI:** McNeely 1 (1), Harris 3 (7). **2-out RBI:** Harris 2. **Runners left in scoring position, 2 out:** Rice 1, Bluege 1. **GIDP:** Rice, Miller. **Team LOB:** 8 **FIELDING: E:** Taylor (1), Judge (1), Bluege 2 (3). **DP:** 1 (Johnson-Bluege-Judge).

NY GIANTS	IP	H	R	ER	BB	SO	HR	ERA
Barnes	7.2	6	3	3	1	6	1	5.68
Nehf	0.2	1	0	0	0	0	0	1.83
McQuillan	1.2	0	0	0	0	1	0	2.57
Bentley (L, 1-2)	1.1	3	1	0	1	0	0	3.18

WASHINGTON	IP	H	R	ER	BB	SO	HR	ERA
Ogden	0.1	0	0	0	1	1	0	0.00
Mogridge	4.2	4	2	1	1	3	0	2.25
Marberry	3	1	1	0	1	3	0	1.13
Johnson (W, 1-2)	4	3	0	0	3	5	0	2.25

IBB: Youngs 2 (by Johnson), Judge (by Bentley). **Ground balls-fly balls:** Barnes 10-6, Nehf 3-0, McQuillan 2-1, Bentley 3-2, Ogden 0-0, Mogridge 9-3, Marberry 5-3, Johnson 3-2. **Batters faced:** Barnes 29, Nehf 4, McQuillan 4, Bentley 9, Ogden 2, Mogridge 20, Marberry 14, Johnson 17. **UMPIRES:** hp—Dinneen, 1b—Quigley, 2b—Connolly, 3b—Klem **T:** 3:00 **A:** 31,667

1925 PITTSBURGH DEF. WASHINGTON, 4-3

GAME 1 Washington 4 Pittsburgh 1
Forbes Field 10/07/25

WASHINGTON	AB	R	H	HR	RBI	BB	AVG
Rice cf-rf	4	0	2	0	2	0	.500
B.Harris 2b	3	0	0	0	0	0	.000
Goslin lf	4	1	1	0	0	0	.250
Judge 1b	3	0	0	0	0	0	.000
J.Harris rf	4	2	2	1	1	0	.500
McNeely cf	0	0	0	0	0	0	.000
Bluege 3b	4	1	2	0	1	0	.500
Peckinpaugh ss	4	0	1	0	0	0	.250
Ruel c	3	0	0	0	0	0	.000
Johnson p	3	0	0	0	0	0	.000
TOTALS	**32**	**4**	**8**	**1**	**4**	**0**	**.250**

BATTING: HR: J.Harris (1, 2nd off Meadows 0 on, 1 out). **S:** Judge. **RBI:** Rice 2 (2), J.Harris 1 (1), Bluege 1 (1). **2-out RBI:** Rice 2, Bluege 1. **Runners left in scoring position, 2 out:** B.Harris 1. **Team LOB:** 3 **FIELDING: E:** Peckinpaugh (1). **DP:** 1 (Peckinpaugh-Judge).

PITTSBURGH	AB	R	H	HR	RBI	BB	AVG
Moore 2b	4	0	0	0	0	0	.000
Carey cf	2	0	0	0	0	0	.000
Cuyler rf	4	0	1	0	0	0	.250
Barnhart lf	4	0	1	0	0	0	.250
Traynor 3b	4	1	2	1	1	0	.500
Wright ss	4	0	0	0	0	0	.000
Grantham 1b	3	0	0	0	0	0	.000
Smith c	3	0	1	0	0	0	.333
a-Bigbee pr	0	0	0	0	0	0	.000
Gooch c	0	0	0	0	0	0	.000
Meadows p	1	0	0	0	0	1	.000
b-McInnis ph	1	0	0	0	0	0	.000
Morrison p	0	0	0	0	0	0	.000
TOTALS	**30**	**1**	**5**	**1**	**1**	**1**	**.167**

a - Ran for Smith in the 8th
b - Batted for Meadows in the 8th

BATTING: HR: Traynor (1, 5th off Johnson 0 on, 0 out). **RBI:** Traynor 1 (1). **Runners left in scoring position, 2 out:** Moore 1, Wright 1, Meadows 1. **GIDP:** Moore. **Team LOB:** 5 **BASERUNNING: SB:** Grantham (1, 2nd base off Johnson/Ruel), Bigbee (1, 2nd base off Johnson/Ruel). **CS:** Carey (1, 2nd base off Johnson/Ruel). **FIELDING: DP:** 1 (Grantham).

WASHINGTON	IP	H	R	ER	BB	SO	HR	ERA
Johnson (W, 1-0)	9	5	1	1	1	10	1	1.00

PITTSBURGH	IP	H	R	ER	BB	SO	HR	ERA
Meadows (L, 0-1)	8	6	3	3	0	4	1	3.38
Morrison	1	2	1	1	0	1	0	9.00

HBP: Carey 2 (by Johnson), B.Harris (by Meadows). **Ground balls-fly balls:** Johnson 6-9, Meadows 11-7, Morrison 1-0. **Batters faced:** Johnson 33, Meadows 29, Morrison 5. **UMPIRES:** hp—Rigler, 1b—Owens, 2b—McCormick, 3b—Moriarty **T:** 1:57 **A:** 41,723

GAME 2 Pittsburgh 3 Washington 2
Forbes Field 10/08/25

WASHINGTON	AB	R	H	HR	RBI	BB	AVG
Rice cf	5	0	2	0	0	0	.444
B.Harris 2b	3	0	0	0	0	0	.000
Goslin lf	4	0	0	0	0	0	.125
Judge 1b	4	1	1	1	1	0	.143
J.Harris rf	3	0	2	0	0	1	.571
b-McNeely pr	0	1	0	0	0	0	.000
Bluege 3b	2	0	0	0	0	0	.333
a-Myer pr-3b	1	0	1	0	0	0	1.000
Peckinpaugh ss	3	0	1	0	0	1	.286
Ruel c	3	0	1	0	0	0	.167
c-Veach ph	0	0	0	0	1	0	.000
Coveleski p	2	0	0	0	0	0	.000
d-Ruether ph	1	0	0	0	0	0	.000
TOTALS	**31**	**2**	**8**	**1**	**2**	**2**	**.254**

a - Ran for Bluege in the 6th
b - Ran for J.Harris in the 9th
c - Batted for Ruel in the 9th
d - Batted for Coveleski in the 9th

BATTING: HR: Judge (1, 2nd off Aldridge 0 on, 0 out). **S:** Coveleski, B.Harris. **SF:** Veach. **RBI:** Judge 1 (1), Veach 1 (1). **Runners left in scoring position, 2 out:** Rice 1, B.Harris 1, Goslin 2, Judge 1. **Team LOB:** 8 **BASERUNNING: CS:** J.Harris (1, 2nd base off Aldridge/Smith), Myer (1, 2nd base off Aldridge/Smith). **FIELDING: E:** Peckinpaugh 2 (3). **PB:** Ruel.

PITTSBURGH	AB	R	H	HR	RBI	BB	AVG
Moore 2b	4	1	0	0	0	0	.000
Carey cf	4	0	2	0	0	0	.333
Cuyler rf	3	1	1	1	2	0	.286
Barnhart lf	4	0	1	0	0	0	.250
Traynor 3b	3	0	0	0	0	1	.286
Wright ss	4	1	2	1	1	0	.250
Grantham 1b	4	0	0	0	0	0	.000
Smith c	3	0	1	0	0	0	.333
Aldridge p	3	0	0	0	0	0	.000
TOTALS	**32**	**3**	**7**	**2**	**3**	**1**	**.194**

BATTING: HR: Wright (1, 4th off Coveleski 0 on, 2 out), Cuyler (1, 8th off Coveleski 1 on, 1 out). **S:** Cuyler. **RBI:** Cuyler 2 (2), Wright 1 (1). **2-out RBI:** Wright 1. **Runners left in scoring position, 2 out:** Cuyler 1, Wright 1, Grantham 2. **Team LOB:** 7

WASHINGTON	IP	H	R	ER	BB	SO	HR	ERA
Coveleski (L, 0-1)	8	7	3	2	1	3	2	2.25

PITTSBURGH	IP	H	R	ER	BB	SO	HR	ERA
Aldridge (W, 1-0)	9	8	2	2	2	4	1	2.00

BK: Aldridge 1. **HBP:** Bluege (by Aldridge). **Ground balls-fly balls:** Coveleski 16-6, Aldridge 11-8. **Batters faced:** Coveleski 34, Aldridge 37. **UMPIRES:** hp—Owens, 1b—McCormick, 2b—Moriarty, 3b—Rigler **T:** 2:04 **A:** 43,364

GAME 3 Washington 4 Pittsburgh 3
Griffith Stadium 10/10/25

PITTSBURGH	AB	R	H	HR	RBI	BB	AVG
Moore 2b	3	0	1	0	0	2	.091
Carey cf	4	0	2	0	0	0	.400
Cuyler rf	4	1	1	0	0	0	.273
Barnhart lf	5	0	1	0	1	0	.231
Traynor 3b	4	1	1	0	0	1	.273
Wright ss	3	1	0	0	1	0	.182
Grantham 1b	4	0	0	0	0	0	.000
Smith c	3	0	1	0	0	1	.333
Kremer p	3	0	1	0	1	0	.333
a-Bigbee ph	1	0	0	0	0	0	.000
TOTALS	**34**	**3**	**8**	**0**	**3**	**4**	**.208**

a - Batted for Kremer in the 9th

BATTING: 2B: Cuyler (1, Ferguson), Carey (1, Ferguson). **3B:** Traynor (1, Ferguson). **SF:** Wright. **RBI:** Barnhart 1 (1), Wright 1 (2), Kremer 1 (1). **2-out RBI:** Kremer 1. **Runners left in scoring position, 2 out:** Carey 2, Barnhart 1, Traynor 2, Kremer 2. **GIDP:** Barnhart. **Team LOB:** 11 **FIELDING: E:** Carey (1), Wright (1). **PB:** Smith. **DP:** 1 (Moore-Grantham).

WASHINGTON	AB	R	H	HR	RBI	BB	AVG
Rice cf-rf	5	1	2	0	0	0	.429
B.Harris 2b	3	1	1	0	0	0	.111
Goslin lf	4	1	2	1	1	0	.250
Judge 1b	3	0	1	0	2	0	.200
J.Harris rf	4	0	2	0	1	0	.545
Marberry p	0	0	0	0	0	0	.000
Myer 3b	3	0	0	0	0	1	.250
Peckinpaugh ss	4	0	1	0	0	0	.273
Ruel c	3	0	1	0	0	1	.222
Ferguson p	2	0	0	0	0	0	.000
a-Leibold ph	0	0	0	0	0	1	.000
b-McNeely pr-cf	0	1	0	0	0	0	.000
TOTALS	**31**	**4**	**10**	**1**	**4**	**3**	**.277**

a - Batted for Ferguson in the 7th
b - Ran for Leibold in the 7th

BATTING: 2B: Judge (1, Kremer). **HR:** Goslin (1, 6th off Kremer 0 on, 0 out). **S:** B.Harris, Marberry. **SF:** Judge. **RBI:** Goslin 1 (1), Judge 2 (3), J.Harris 1 (2). **2-out RBI:** Judge 1, J.Harris 1. **Runners left in scoring position, 2 out:** Rice 1, J.Harris 1, Myer 1, Ruel 1, Ferguson 1. **Team LOB:** 9 **BASERUNNING: CS:** Peckinpaugh (1, 2nd base off Kremer/Smith). **FIELDING: E:** Peckinpaugh (4). **DP:** 1 (Peckinpaugh-B.Harris-Judge).

PITTSBURGH	IP	H	R	ER	BB	SO	HR	ERA
Kremer (L, 0-1)	8	10	4	4	3	5	1	4.50

WASHINGTON	IP	H	R	ER	BB	SO	HR	ERA
Ferguson (W, 1-0)	7	6	3	2	4	5	0	2.57
Marberry (S, 1)	2	2	0	0	0	2	0	0.00

IBB: Smith (by Ferguson). **HBP:** Carey (by Ferguson), Cuyler (by Marberry). **Ground balls-fly balls:** Kremer 7-9, Ferguson 5-10, Marberry 0-4. **Batters faced:** Kremer 37, Ferguson 32, Marberry 9. **UMPIRES:** hp—McCormick, 1b—Moriarty, 2b—Rigler, 3b—Owens **T:** 2:10 **A:** 36,495

GAME 4 Washington 4 Pittsburgh 0
Griffith Stadium 10/11/25

PITTSBURGH	AB	R	H	HR	RBI	BB	AVG
Moore 2b	4	0	1	0	0	0	.133
Carey cf	3	0	1	0	0	1	.385
Cuyler rf	4	0	0	0	0	0	.200
Barnhart lf	3	0	0	0	0	1	.188
Traynor 3b	4	0	2	0	0	0	.333
Wright ss	4	0	0	0	0	0	.133
Grantham 1b	3	0	2	0	0	0	.143
Gooch c	3	0	0	0	0	0	.000
Yde p	1	0	0	0	0	0	.000
Morrison p	1	0	0	0	0	0	.000
a-Bigbee ph	1	0	0	0	0	0	.000
B.Adams p	0	0	0	0	0	0	.000
TOTALS	**31**	**0**	**6**	**0**	**0**	**2**	**.205**

a - Batted for Morrison in the 8th

BATTING: Runners left in scoring position, 2 out: Barnhart 2, Yde 2. **GIDP:** Traynor. **Team LOB:** 6 **BASERUNNING: SB:** Carey (1, 2nd base off Johnson/Ruel). **FIELDING: Outfield assists:** Barnhart (1). **DP:** 1 (Traynor-Moore-Grantham).

WASHINGTON	AB	R	H	HR	RBI	BB	AVG
Rice cf	5	1	2	0	0	0	.421
B.Harris 2b	3	1	1	0	0	1	.167
Goslin lf	3	1	2	1	3	1	.333
J.Harris rf	4	1	1	1	1	0	.467
Judge 1b	3	0	0	0	0	1	.154
Peckinpaugh ss	4	0	1	0	0	0	.267
Ruel c	3	0	3	0	0	1	.417
Myer 3b	4	0	1	0	0	0	.250
Johnson p	4	0	1	0	0	0	.143
TOTALS	**33**	**4**	**12**	**2**	**4**	**4**	**.299**

BATTING: 2B: Ruel (1, B.Adams). **HR:** Goslin (2, 3th off Yde 2 on, 1 out), J.Harris (2, 3th off Yde 0 on, 1 out). **RBI:** Goslin 3 (4), J.Harris 1 (3). **Runners left in scoring position, 2 out:** Rice 2, Myer 1. **GIDP:** J.Harris. **Team LOB:** 9 **BASERUNNING: SB:** Peckinpaugh (1, 2nd base off Morrison/Gooch). **CS:** Judge (1, 2nd base off Morrison/Gooch). **FIELDING: DP:** 2 (B.Harris-Judge 2).

PITTSBURGH	IP	H	R	ER	BB	SO	HR	ERA
Yde (L, 0-1)	2.1	5	4	3	3	1	2	11.57
Morrison	4.2	5	0	0	1	4	0	1.59
B.Adams	1	2	0	0	0	0	0	0.00

WASHINGTON	IP	H	R	ER	BB	SO	HR	ERA
Johnson (W, 2-0)	9	6	0	0	2	2	0	0.50

Ground balls-fly balls: Yde 4-1, Morrison 5-3, B.Adams 3-0, Johnson 9-14. **Batters faced:** Yde 14, Morrison 18, B.Adams 5, Johnson 33. **UMPIRES:** hp—Moriarty, 1b—Rigler, 2b—Owens, 3b—McCormick **T:** 2:00 **A:** 38,701

GAME 5 Pittsburgh 6 Washington 3
Griffith Stadium 10/12/25

PITTSBURGH	AB	R	H	HR	RBI	BB	AVG
Moore 2b	4	1	1	0	0	1	.158
Carey cf	4	2	2	0	0	1	.412
Cuyler rf	4	1	2	0	1	1	.263
Barnhart lf	4	1	2	0	2	1	.250
Traynor 3b	3	0	1	0	1	1	.333
Wright ss	5	1	2	0	1	0	.200
McInnis 1b	5	0	1	0	1	0	.167
Smith c	3	0	2	0	0	0	.417
Aldridge p	4	0	0	0	0	0	.000
TOTALS	**36**	**6**	**13**	**0**	**6**	**5**	**.239**

BATTING: 2B: Wright (1, Zachary). **S:** Smith. **SF:** Traynor. **RBI:** Cuyler 1 (3), Barnhart 2 (3), Traynor 1 (2), Wright 1 (3), McInnis 1 (1). **2-out RBI:** Wright 1. **Runners left in scoring position, 2 out:** Carey 1, Wright 3, McInnis 1. **GIDP:** Aldridge, Smith. **Team LOB:** 10 **BASERUNNING: SB:** Carey (2, 2nd base off Coveleski/Ruel), Barnhart (1, 2nd base off Coveleski/Ruel). **FIELDING: DP:** 1 (Smith-Traynor).

WASHINGTON	AB	R	H	HR	RBI	BB	AVG
Rice cf	5	1	2	0	1	0	.417
B.Harris 2b	3	0	0	0	0	0	.133
Goslin lf	4	0	1	0	1	0	.316
Judge 1b	3	0	0	0	0	1	.125
J.Harris rf	3	1	2	1	1	1	.500
Peckinpaugh ss	3	0	0	0	0	0	.222
Ruel c	3	0	1	0	0	1	.400
Bluege 3b	4	0	1	0	0	0	.300
Coveleski p	1	0	0	0	0	1	.000
Ballou p	0	0	0	0	0	0	.000
a-Leibold ph	1	1	1	0	0	0	1.000
Zachary p	0	0	0	0	0	0	.000
Marberry p	0	0	0	0	0	0	.000
b-S.Adams ph	1	0	0	0	0	0	.000
TOTALS	**31**	**3**	**8**	**1**	**3**	**4**	**.291**

a - Batted for Ballou in the 7th
b - Batted for Marberry in the 9th

BATTING: 2B: Goslin (1, Aldridge), Bluege (1, Aldridge), Leibold (1, Aldridge). **HR:** J.Harris (3, 4th off Aldridge 0 on, 0 out). **S:** B.Harris, Peckinpaugh, B.Harris. **RBI:** Rice 1 (3), Goslin 1 (5), J.Harris 1 (4). **Runners left in scoring position, 2 out:** Rice 2, J.Harris 1, Peckinpaugh 1. **Team LOB:** 8 **BASERUNNING: CS:** J.Harris (2, 3rd base off Aldridge/Smith). **FIELDING: E:** Peckinpaugh (5). **DP:** 2 (Bluege-B.Harris-Judge, Coveleski-Peckinpaugh-Judge).

PITTSBURGH	IP	H	R	ER	BB	SO	HR	ERA
Aldridge (W, 2-0)	9	8	3	3	4	5	1	2.50

WASHINGTON	IP	H	R	ER	BB	SO	HR	ERA
Coveleski (L, 0-2)	6.1	9	4	4	4	0	0	3.77
Ballou	0.2	0	0	0	0	1	0	0.00
Zachary	1.2	3	2	2	1	0	0	10.80
Marberry	0.1	1	0	0	0	0	0	0.00

Ground balls-fly balls: Aldridge 10-8, Coveleski 9-8, Ballou 0-0, Zachary 3-1, Marberry 0-1. **Batters faced:** Aldridge 38, Coveleski 31, Ballou 1, Zachary 9, Marberry 2. **UMPIRES:** hp—Rigler, 1b—Owens, 2b—McCormick, 3b—Moriarty **T:** 2:26 **A:** 35,899

GAME 6 Pittsburgh 3 Washington 2
Forbes Field 10/13/25

WASHINGTON	AB	R	H	HR	RBI	BB	AVG
Rice cf	4	0	0	0	0	0	.357
B.Harris 2b	3	0	0	0	0	0	.111
c-Veach ph	1	0	0	0	0	0	.000
Ballou p	0	0	0	0	0	0	.000
Goslin lf	3	1	1	1	1	1	.318
J.Harris rf	4	0	1	0	0	0	.455
Judge 1b	4	0	1	0	0	0	.150
Bluege 3b	4	1	1	0	0	0	.286
Peckinpaugh ss	3	0	1	0	1	0	.238
Severeid c	3	0	1	0	0	0	.333
a-McNeely pr	0	0	0	0	0	0	.000
S.Adams 2b	0	0	0	0	0	0	.000
Ferguson p	2	0	0	0	0	0	.000
b-Leibold ph	1	0	0	0	0	0	.500
Ruel c	0	0	0	0	0	0	.400
TOTALS	**32**	**2**	**6**	**1**	**2**	**1**	**.274**

a - Ran for Severeid in the 8th
b - Batted for Ferguson in the 8th
c - Batted for B.Harris in the 8th

BATTING: 2B: Peckinpaugh (1, Kremer), J.Harris (1, Kremer). **HR:** Goslin (3, 1st off Kremer 0 on, 2 out). **RBI:** Goslin 1 (6), Peckinpaugh 1 (1). **2-out RBI:** Goslin 1. **Runners left in scoring position, 2 out:** Veach 1, Bluege 1, Ferguson 1. **Team LOB:** 4 **BASERUNNING: SB:** McNeely (1, 2nd base off Kremer/Smith). **FIELDING: E:** Severeid (1), Peckinpaugh (6). **DP:** 1 (Judge).

PITTSBURGH	AB	R	H	HR	RBI	BB	AVG
Moore 2b	3	2	2	1	1	1	.227
Carey cf	2	1	0	0	0	0	.368
Cuyler rf	3	0	0	0	0	0	.227
Barnhart lf	3	0	1	0	1	1	.261
Traynor 3b	4	0	2	0	1	0	.364
Wright ss	3	0	0	0	0	1	.174
McInnis 1b	4	0	1	0	0	0	.200
Smith c	4	0	1	0	0	0	.375
Kremer p	3	0	0	0	0	0	.167
TOTALS	**29**	**3**	**7**	**1**	**3**	**3**	**.240**

BATTING: 2B: Barnhart (1, Ferguson). **HR:** Moore (1, 5th off Ferguson 0 on, 0 out). **S:** Carey, Cuyler, Carey. **RBI:** Moore 1 (1), Barnhart 1 (4), Traynor 1 (3). **2-out RBI:** Traynor 1. **Runners left in scoring position, 2 out:** Barnhart 1, Traynor 2, Wright 1, Kremer 1. **Team LOB:** 8 **BASERUNNING: SB:** Traynor (1, 2nd base off Ferguson/Severeid). **FIELDING: E:** Kremer (1).

WASHINGTON	IP	H	R	ER	BB	SO	HR	ERA
Ferguson (L, 1-1)	7	7	3	3	2	6	1	3.21
Ballou	1	0	0	0	1	0	0	0.00

PITTSBURGH	IP	H	R	ER	BB	SO	HR	ERA
Kremer (W, 1-1)	9	6	2	2	1	3	1	3.18

Ground balls-fly balls: Ferguson 8-6, Ballou 1-1, Kremer 12-11. **Batters faced:** Ferguson 32, Ballou 3, Kremer 33. **UMPIRES:** hp—Owens, 1b—McCormick, 2b—Moriarty, 3b—Rigler **T:** 1:57 **A:** 43,810

GAME 7 Pittsburgh 9 Washington 7
Forbes Field 10/15/25

WASHINGTON	AB	R	H	HR	RBI	BB	AVG
Rice cf	5	2	2	0	0	0	.364
B.Harris 2b	5	0	0	0	0	0	.087
Goslin lf	4	2	1	0	0	1	.308
J.Harris rf	3	1	1	0	2	1	.440
Judge 1b	3	1	1	0	1	1	.174
Bluege 3b	4	0	1	0	1	0	.278
Peckinpaugh ss	3	1	1	1	2	0	.250
Ruel c	4	0	0	0	1	0	.316
Johnson p	4	0	0	0	0	0	.091
TOTALS	**35**	**7**	**7**	**1**	**7**	**3**	**.262**

BATTING: 2B: J.Harris (2, Morrison). **HR:** Peckinpaugh (1, 8th off Kremer 0 on, 1 out). **RBI:** J.Harris 2 (6), Judge 1 (4), Bluege 1 (2), Peckinpaugh 2 (3), Ruel 1 (1). **2-out RBI:** J.Harris 2. **Runners left in scoring position, 2 out:** Rice 2, Judge 1, Ruel 1. **Team LOB:** 5 **FIELDING: E:** Peckinpaugh 2 (8). **Outfield assists:** J.Harris (1). **DP:** 1 (B.Harris-Judge).

PITTSBURGH	AB	R	H	HR	RBI	BB	AVG
Moore 2b	4	3	1	0	1	1	.231
Carey cf	5	3	4	0	2	0	.458
Cuyler rf	4	0	2	0	3	0	.269
Barnhart lf	5	0	1	0	1	0	.250
Oldham p	0	0	0	0	0	0	.000
Traynor 3b	4	0	1	0	1	0	.346
Wright ss	4	0	1	0	0	0	.185
McInnis 1b	4	0	2	0	0	0	.286
Smith c	4	0	1	0	0	0	.350
b-Yde pr	0	1	0	0	0	0	.000
Gooch c	0	0	0	0	0	0	.000
Aldridge p	0	0	0	0	0	0	.000
Morrison p	1	1	1	0	0	0	.500
a-Grantham ph	1	0	0	0	0	0	.133
Kremer p	1	0	0	0	0	0	.143
c-Bigbee ph-lf	1	1	1	0	1	0	.333
TOTALS	**38**	**9**	**15**	**0**	**9**	**1**	**.265**

a - Batted for Morrison in the 4th
b - Ran for Smith in the 8th
c - Batted for Kremer in the 8th

BATTING: 2B: Carey 3 (4, Johnson), Moore (1, Johnson), Cuyler 2 (3, Johnson), Smith (1, Johnson), Bigbee (1, Johnson). **3B:** Traynor (2, Johnson). **S:** Cuyler. **RBI:** Moore 1 (2), Carey 2 (2), Cuyler 3 (6), Barnhart 1 (5), Traynor 1 (4), Bigbee 1 (1). **2-out RBI:** Cuyler 2, Traynor 1, Bigbee 1. **Runners left in scoring position, 2 out:** Barnhart 3, Traynor 1, Wright 1. **GIDP:** Smith. **Team LOB:** 7 **BASERUNNING: SB:** Carey (3, 3rd base off Johnson/Ruel). **FIELDING: E:** Smith (1), Moore (1).

WASHINGTON	IP	H	R	ER	BB	SO	HR	ERA
Johnson (L, 2-1)	8	15	9	5	1	3	0	2.08

PITTSBURGH	IP	H	R	ER	BB	SO	HR	ERA
Aldridge	0.1	2	4	4	3	0	0	4.42
Morrison	3.2	4	2	2	0	2	0	2.89
Kremer (W, 2-1)	4	1	1	1	0	1	1	3.00
Oldham (S, 1)	1	0	0	0	0	2	0	0.00

WP: Aldridge 2. **Ground balls-fly balls:** Johnson 7-13, Aldridge 0-1, Morrison 2-8, Kremer 6-5, Oldham 0-1. **Batters faced:** Johnson 40, Aldridge 6, Morrison 17, Kremer 13, Oldham 3. **UMPIRES:** hp—McCormick, 1b—Moriarty, 2b—Rigler, 3b—Owens **T:** 2:31 **A:** 42,856

1926 ST.LOUIS CARDINALS DEF. NY YANKEES, 4-3

GAME 1 New York 2 St. Louis 1
Yankee Stadium 10/02/26

ST.LOUIS	AB	R	H	HR	RBI	BB	AVG
Douthit cf	3	1	1	0	0	1	.333
Southworth rf	3	0	0	0	0	0	.000
b-Holm ph-rf	1	0	0	0	0	0	.000
Hornsby 2b	4	0	0	0	0	0	.000
Bottomley 1b	4	0	2	0	1	0	.500
L.Bell 3b	3	0	0	0	0	1	.000
Hafey lf	4	0	0	0	0	0	.000
O'Farrell c	2	0	0	0	0	1	.000
Thevenow ss	2	0	0	0	0	0	.000
Sherdel p	2	0	0	0	0	0	.000
a-Flowers ph	1	0	0	0	0	0	.000
Haines p	0	0	0	0	0	0	.000
TOTALS	**29**	**1**	**3**	**0**	**1**	**3**	**.103**

a - Batted for Sherdel in the 8th
b - Batted for Southworth in the 8th

BATTING: 2B: Douthit (1, Pennock). **S:** Thevenow. **RBI:** Bottomley 1 (1). **2-out RBI:** Bottomley 1. **Runners left in scoring position, 2 out:** Holm 1. **Team LOB:** 5 **FIELDING: E:** L.Bell (1). **Outfield assists:** Hafey (1). **DP:** 1 (Thevenow-Hornsby-Bottomley).

NY YANKEES	AB	R	H	HR	RBI	BB	AVG
Combs cf	3	1	1	0	0	1	.333
Koenig ss	4	0	1	0	0	0	.250
Ruth rf	3	1	1	0	0	1	.333
Meusel lf	1	0	0	0	0	2	.000
Gehrig 1b	4	0	1	0	2	0	.250
Lazzeri 2b	4	0	1	0	0	0	.250
Dugan 3b	3	0	1	0	0	0	.333
Severeid c	3	0	0	0	0	0	.000
Pennock p	2	0	0	0	0	0	.000
TOTALS	**27**	**2**	**6**	**0**	**2**	**4**	**.222**

BATTING: S: Pennock, Meusel. **RBI:** Gehrig 2 (2). **Runners left in scoring position, 2 out:** Combs 1, Gehrig 1, Lazzeri 1, Severeid 1. **GIDP:** Koenig. **Team LOB:** 7

ST.LOUIS	IP	H	R	ER	BB	SO	HR	ERA
Sherdel (L, 0-1)	7	6	2	2	3	1	0	2.57
Haines	1	0	0	0	1	0	0	0.00

NY YANKEES	IP	H	R	ER	BB	SO	HR	ERA
Pennock (W, 1-0)	9	3	1	1	3	4	0	1.00

Ground balls-fly balls: Sherdel 11-6, Haines 2-1, Pennock 13-9. **Batters faced:** Sherdel 29, Haines 4, Pennock 33. **UMPIRES:** hp—Dinneen, 1b—O'Day, 2b—Hildebrand, 3b—Klem **T:** 1:48 **A:** 61,658

GAME 2 St. Louis 6 New York 2
Yankee Stadium 10/03/26

ST.LOUIS	AB	R	H	HR	RBI	BB	AVG
Douthit cf	4	1	1	0	0	1	.286
Southworth rf	5	2	3	1	3	0	.375
Hornsby 2b	3	0	1	0	0	1	.143
Bottomley 1b	5	0	2	0	2	0	.444
L.Bell 3b	4	0	0	0	0	0	.000
Hafey lf	4	0	0	0	0	0	.000
O'Farrell c	4	1	2	0	0	0	.333
Thevenow ss	4	2	3	1	1	0	.500
Alexander p	4	0	0	0	0	0	.000
TOTALS	**37**	**6**	**12**	**2**	**6**	**2**	**.227**

BATTING: 2B: Hornsby (1, Shocker), O'Farrell (1, Shocker). **HR:** Southworth (1, 7th off Shocker 2 on, 2 out), Thevenow (1, 9th off Jones 0 on, 1 out). **S:** Hornsby. **RBI:** Southworth 3 (3), Bottomley 2 (3), Thevenow 1 (1). **2-out RBI:** Southworth 3. **Runners left in scoring position, 2 out:** Bottomley 3, Alexander 1. **Team LOB:** 7 **BASERUNNING: CS:** Bottomley (1, 2nd base off Shawkey/Severeid). **FIELDING: DP:** 1 (Alexander-Thevenow-Hornsby-Bottomley).

NY YANKEES	AB	R	H	HR	RBI	BB	AVG
Combs cf	3	0	1	0	0	1	.333
Koenig ss	4	0	0	0	0	0	.125
Ruth rf	4	0	0	0	0	0	.143
Meusel lf	4	1	1	0	0	0	.200
Gehrig 1b	3	0	0	0	0	0	.143
Lazzeri 2b	3	1	1	0	1	0	.286
Dugan 3b	3	0	1	0	0	0	.333
Severeid c	2	0	0	0	0	0	.000
a-Paschal ph	1	0	0	0	0	0	.000
Collins c	0	0	0	0	0	0	.000
Shocker p	2	0	0	0	0	0	.000
Shawkey p	0	0	0	0	0	0	.000
b-Ruether ph	1	0	0	0	0	0	.000
Jones p	0	0	0	0	0	0	.000
TOTALS	**30**	**2**	**4**	**0**	**1**	**1**	**.175**

a - Batted for Severeid in the 8th
b - Batted for Shawkey in the 8th

BATTING: S: Lazzeri. **RBI:** Lazzeri 1 (1). **Runners left in scoring position, 2 out:** Shocker 1. **GIDP:** Koenig. **Team LOB:** 2

ST.LOUIS	IP	H	R	ER	BB	SO	HR	ERA
Alexander (W, 1-0)	9	4	2	1	1	10	0	1.00

NY YANKEES	IP	H	R	ER	BB	SO	HR	ERA
Shocker (L, 0-1)	7	10	5	5	0	2	1	6.43
Shawkey	1	0	0	0	0	2	0	0.00
Jones	1	2	1	1	2	1	1	9.00

Ground balls-fly balls: Alexander 13-3, Shocker 7-11, Shawkey 0-0, Jones 1-1. **Batters faced:** Alexander 31, Shocker 31, Shawkey 2, Jones 7. **UMPIRES:** hp—O'Day, 1b—Hildebrand, 2b—Klem, 3b—Dinneen **T:** 1:57 **A:** 63,600

GAME 3 St. Louis 4 New York 0
Sportsman's Park 10/05/26

NY YANKEES	AB	R	H	HR	RBI	BB	AVG
Combs cf	3	0	1	0	0	1	.333
Koenig ss	4	0	0	0	0	0	.083
Ruth rf	3	0	1	0	0	1	.200
Meusel lf	4	0	0	0	0	0	.111
Gehrig 1b	4	0	2	0	0	0	.273
Lazzeri 2b	4	0	0	0	0	0	.182
Dugan 3b	3	0	1	0	0	0	.333
Severeid c	2	0	0	0	0	0	.000
Ruether p	2	0	0	0	0	0	.000
Shawkey p	0	0	0	0	0	0	.000
a-Paschal ph	0	0	0	0	0	1	.000
Thomas p	0	0	0	0	0	0	.000
TOTALS	**29**	**0**	**5**	**0**	**0**	**3**	**.174**

a - Batted for Shawkey in the 8th

BATTING: S: Severeid. **Runners left in scoring position, 2 out:** Koenig 1, Ruth 1, Lazzeri 1, Severeid 1. **GIDP:** Koenig, Lazzeri. **Team LOB:** 6 **FIELDING: DP:** 1 (Koenig-Lazzeri-Gehrig).

ST.LOUIS	AB	R	H	HR	RBI	BB	AVG
Douthit cf	3	0	0	0	0	1	.200
Southworth rf	3	1	2	0	0	0	.455
Hornsby 2b	4	0	1	0	0	0	.182
Bottomley 1b	4	0	1	0	1	0	.385
L.Bell 3b	4	1	1	0	0	0	.091
Hafey lf	3	0	1	0	0	0	.091
O'Farrell c	2	0	0	0	0	1	.250
Thevenow ss	3	1	0	0	0	0	.333
Haines p	3	1	2	1	2	0	.667
TOTALS	**29**	**4**	**8**	**1**	**3**	**2**	**.242**

BATTING: 2B: Hafey (1, Ruether). **HR:** Haines (1, 4th off Ruether 1 on, 2 out). **S:** Southworth, Hafey. **RBI:** Bottomley 1 (4), Haines 2 (2). **2-out RBI:** Haines 2. **Runners left in scoring position, 2 out:** Bottomley 2, Hafey 1, Thevenow 1. **GIDP:** L.Bell. **Team LOB:** 5 **FIELDING: DP:** 2 (Hornsby-Thevenow-Bottomley, Thevenow-Hornsby-Bottomley).

NY YANKEES	IP	H	R	ER	BB	SO	HR	ERA
Ruether (L, 0-1)	4.1	7	4	2	2	1	1	4.15
Shawkey	2.2	0	0	0	0	1	0	0.00
Thomas	1	1	0	0	0	0	0	0.00

ST.LOUIS	IP	H	R	ER	BB	SO	HR	ERA
Haines (W, 1-0)	9	5	0	0	3	3	0	0.00

Ground balls-fly balls: Ruether 4-6, Shawkey 4-3, Thomas 2-0, Haines 12-9. **Batters faced:** Ruether 22, Shawkey 8, Thomas 3, Haines 33. **UMPIRES:** hp—Hildebrand, 1b—Klem, 2b—Dinneen, 3b—O'Day **T:** 1:41 **A:** 37,708

GAME 4 New York 10 St. Louis 5
Sportsman's Park 10/06/26

NY YANKEES	AB	R	H	HR	RBI	BB	AVG
Combs cf	5	2	2	0	1	1	.357
Koenig ss	6	1	1	0	1	0	.111
Ruth lf	3	4	3	3	4	2	.385
Meusel rf	2	1	1	0	0	3	.182
Gehrig 1b	3	0	2	0	1	1	.357
Lazzeri 2b	3	1	1	0	1	1	.214
Dugan 3b	4	0	1	0	2	1	.308
Severeid c	4	1	3	0	0	1	.273
Hoyt p	4	0	0	0	0	0	.000
TOTALS	**34**	**10**	**14**	**3**	**10**	**10**	**.242**

BATTING: 2B: Lazzeri (1, Rhem), Dugan (1, Rhem), Koenig (1, Reinhart), Gehrig (1, H.Bell), Combs (1, Hallahan). **HR:** Ruth 3 (3, 1st off Rhem 0 on, 2 out, 3th off Rhem 0 on, 2 out, 6th off H.Bell 1 on, 1 out). **S:** Hoyt, Gehrig. **SF:** Lazzeri. **RBI:** Combs 1 (1), Koenig 1 (1), Ruth 4 (4), Gehrig 1 (3), Lazzeri 1 (2), Dugan 2 (2). **2-out RBI:** Combs 1, Ruth 2. **Runners left in scoring position, 2 out:** Koenig 1, Lazzeri 1, Severeid 2, Hoyt 2. **Team LOB:** 10 **FIELDING: E:** Koenig (1). **Outfield assists:** Ruth (1).

ST.LOUIS	AB	R	H	HR	RBI	BB	AVG
Douthit cf	5	1	2	0	1	0	.267
Southworth rf	5	0	3	0	0	0	.500
Hornsby 2b	5	1	2	0	1	0	.250
Bottomley 1b	4	0	1	0	0	1	.353
L.Bell 3b	4	0	1	0	1	0	.133
Hafey lf	5	1	1	0	0	0	.125
O'Farrell c	4	1	2	0	0	0	.333
Thevenow ss	4	1	2	0	1	0	.385
Rhem p	1	0	0	0	0	0	.000
a-Toporcer ph	0	0	0	0	1	0	.000
Reinhart p	0	0	0	0	0	0	.000
H.Bell p	0	0	0	0	0	0	.000
b-Flowers ph	1	0	0	0	0	0	.000
Hallahan p	0	0	0	0	0	0	.000
c-Holm ph	1	0	0	0	0	0	.000
Keen p	0	0	0	0	0	0	.000
TOTALS	**39**	**5**	**14**	**0**	**5**	**1**	**.276**

a - Batted for Rhem in the 4th
b - Batted for H.Bell in the 6th
c - Batted for Hallahan in the 8th

BATTING: 2B: Thevenow (1, Hoyt), Douthit (2, Hoyt). **SF:** L.Bell, Toporcer. **RBI:** Douthit 1 (1), Hornsby 1 (1), L.Bell 1 (1), Thevenow 1 (2), Toporcer 1 (1). **2-out RBI:** Douthit 1, L.Bell 1. **Runners left in scoring position, 2 out:** Southworth 2, Hafey 3. **Team LOB:** 10 **BASERUNNING: SB:** Hornsby (1, 2nd base off Hoyt/Severeid). **Outfield assists:** Southworth 2 (2), Douthit 2 (2).

NY YANKEES	IP	H	R	ER	BB	SO	HR	ERA
Hoyt (W, 1-0)	9	14	5	2	1	8	0	2.00

ST.LOUIS	IP	H	R	ER	BB	SO	HR	ERA
Rhem	4	7	3	3	2	4	2	6.75
Reinhart (L, 0-1)	0	1	4	4	4	0	0	0.00
H.Bell	2	4	2	2	1	1	1	9.00
Hallahan	2	2	1	1	3	1	0	4.50
Keen	1	0	0	0	0	0	0	0.00

BK: H.Bell 1. **Ground balls-fly balls:** Hoyt 9-8, Rhem 2-3, Reinhart 0-0, H.Bell 1-2, Hallahan 2-1, Keen 2-1. **Batters faced:** Hoyt 42, Rhem 18, Reinhart 5, H.Bell 10, Hallahan 11, Keen 3. **UMPIRES:** hp—Klem, 1b—Dinneen, 2b—O'Day, 3b—Hildebrand **T:** 2:38 **A:** 38,825

GAME 5 New York 3 St. Louis 2
Sportsman's Park 10/07/26

NY YANKEES	AB	R	H	HR	RBI	BB	AVG
Combs cf	4	0	1	0	0	1	.333
Koenig ss	5	1	2	0	1	0	.174
Ruth lf	3	0	0	0	0	2	.313
Meusel rf	3	0	0	0	0	0	.143
Gehrig 1b	3	1	2	0	0	2	.412
Lazzeri 2b	4	0	2	0	1	0	.278
Dugan 3b	3	0	0	0	0	0	.250
a-Paschal ph	1	0	1	0	1	0	.500
Gazella 3b	0	0	0	0	0	0	.000
Severeid c	5	0	0	0	0	0	.188
Pennock p	4	1	1	0	0	0	.167
TOTALS	**35**	**3**	**9**	**0**	**3**	**5**	**.245**

a - Batted for Dugan in the 9th

BATTING: 2B: Pennock (1, Sherdel), Gehrig (2, Sherdel). **S:** Meusel. **SF:** Meusel, Lazzeri. **RBI:** Koenig 1 (2), Lazzeri 1 (3), Paschal 1 (1). **Runners left in scoring position, 2 out:** Combs 1, Lazzeri 2, Severeid 2. **GIDP:** Dugan. **Team LOB:** 11 **FIELDING: E:** Koenig (2). **PB:** Severeid. **DP:** 1 (Lazzeri-Koenig-Gehrig).

ST.LOUIS	AB	R	H	HR	RBI	BB	AVG
Holm cf	4	0	0	0	0	1	.000
Southworth rf	4	0	0	0	0	0	.400
Hornsby 2b	4	0	0	0	0	0	.200
Bottomley 1b	4	1	1	0	0	0	.333
L.Bell 3b	4	1	2	0	1	0	.211
Hafey lf	4	0	0	0	0	0	.100
O'Farrell c	4	0	3	0	1	0	.438
Thevenow ss	4	0	1	0	0	0	.353
Sherdel p	3	0	0	0	0	0	.000
a-Flowers ph	1	0	0	0	0	0	.000
TOTALS	**36**	**2**	**7**	**0**	**2**	**1**	**.259**

a - Batted for Sherdel in the 10th

BATTING: 2B: Bottomley (1, Pennock), L.Bell (1, Pennock). **RBI:** L.Bell 1 (2), O'Farrell 1 (1). **Runners left in scoring position, 2 out:** Holm 1, Bottomley 1. **GIDP:** Hornsby. **Team LOB:** 5 **BASERUNNING: SB:** Southworth (1, 2nd base off Pennock/Severeid). **CS:** L.Bell (1, 2nd base off Pennock/Severeid). **FIELDING: DP:** 1 (Hornsby-Bottomley).

NY YANKEES	IP	H	R	ER	BB	SO	HR	ERA
Pennock (W, 2-0)	10	7	2	2	1	4	0	1.42

ST.LOUIS	IP	H	R	ER	BB	SO	HR	ERA
Sherdel (L, 0-2)	10	9	3	2	5	2	0	2.12

WP: Sherdel 1. **IBB:** Gehrig (by Sherdel). **HBP:** Gazella (by Sherdel). **Ground balls-fly balls:** Pennock 15-10, Sherdel 12-12. **Batters faced:** Pennock 37, Sherdel 44. **UMPIRES:** hp—Dinneen, 1b—O'Day, 2b—Hildebrand, 3b—Klem **T:** 2:28 **A:** 39,552

GAME 6 St. Louis 10 New York 2
Yankee Stadium 10/09/26

ST.LOUIS	AB	R	H	HR	RBI	BB	AVG
Holm cf	5	1	2	0	1	0	.182
Southworth rf	5	3	2	0	1	0	.400
Hornsby 2b	4	1	1	0	3	1	.208
Bottomley 1b	5	2	2	0	1	0	.346
L.Bell 3b	4	1	3	1	4	1	.304
Hafey lf	3	0	1	0	0	0	.130
O'Farrell c	4	0	0	0	0	0	.350
Thevenow ss	3	1	2	0	0	0	.400
Alexander p	2	1	0	0	0	0	.000
TOTALS	**35**	**10**	**13**	**1**	**10**	**2**	**.278**

BATTING: 2B: Bottomley 2 (3, Shawkey), Southworth (1, Shawkey), Hafey (2, Shocker). **3B:** Southworth (1, Thomas). **HR:** L.Bell (1, 7th off Shocker 1 on, 2 out). **S:** Hafey, Alexander, Alexander. **RBI:** Holm 1 (1), Southworth 1 (4), Hornsby 3 (4), Bottomley 1 (5), L.Bell 4 (6). **2-out RBI:** L.Bell 2. **Runners left in scoring position, 2 out:** Hornsby 1, O'Farrell 2. **GIDP:** Holm. **Team LOB:** 4 **BASERUNNING: CS:** L.Bell (2, 3rd base off Shawkey/Severeid). **FIELDING: E:** Thevenow (1), L.Bell (2). **Outfield assists:** Southworth (3). **DP:** 1 (Southworth-Thevenow).

NY YANKEES	AB	R	H	HR	RBI	BB	AVG
Combs cf	5	0	2	0	1	0	.348
Koenig ss	5	0	0	0	0	0	.143
Ruth rf	3	0	0	0	0	1	.263
Meusel lf	3	1	2	0	0	1	.235
Gehrig 1b	4	0	1	0	1	0	.381
Lazzeri 2b	4	0	0	0	0	0	.227
Dugan 3b	4	1	2	0	0	0	.300
Severeid c	3	0	1	0	0	0	.211
a-Adams pr	0	0	0	0	0	0	.000
Collins c	1	0	0	0	0	0	.000
Shawkey p	2	0	0	0	0	0	.000
Shocker p	0	0	0	0	0	0	.000
b-Paschal ph	1	0	0	0	0	0	.333
Thomas p	0	0	0	0	0	0	.000
c-Ruether ph	1	0	0	0	0	0	.000
TOTALS	**36**	**2**	**8**	**0**	**2**	**2**	**.241**

a - Ran for Severeid in the 7th
b - Batted for Shocker in the 7th
c - Batted for Thomas in the 9th

BATTING: 2B: Meusel (1, Alexander), Combs (2, Alexander). **3B:** Meusel (1, Alexander). **RBI:** Combs 1 (2), Gehrig 1 (4). **Runners left in scoring position, 2 out:** Koenig 1, Ruth 3, Lazzeri 1, Dugan 1. **Team LOB:** 9 **BASERUNNING: SB:** Ruth (1, 2nd base off Alexander/O'Farrell). **FIELDING: Outfield assists:** Ruth (2). **DP:** 1 (Gehrig-Koenig).

ST.LOUIS	IP	H	R	ER	BB	SO	HR	ERA
Alexander (W, 2-0)	9	8	2	2	2	6	0	1.50

NY YANKEES	IP	H	R	ER	BB	SO	HR	ERA
Shawkey (L, 0-1)	6.1	8	7	6	2	4	0	5.40
Shocker	0.2	3	2	0	0	1	1	5.87
Thomas	2	2	1	1	0	0	0	3.00

HBP: Thevenow (by Thomas). **Ground balls-fly balls:** Alexander 14-8, Shawkey 5-7, Shocker 1-0, Thomas 3-1. **Batters faced:** Alexander 38, Shawkey 29, Shocker 5, Thomas 7. **UMPIRES:** hp—O'Day, 1b—Hildebrand, 2b—Klem, 3b—Dinneen **T:** 2:05 **A:** 48,615

GAME 7 St. Louis 3 New York 2
Yankee Stadium 10/10/26

ST.LOUIS	AB	R	H	HR	RBI	BB	AVG
Holm cf	5	0	0	0	0	0	.125
Southworth rf	4	0	0	0	0	0	.345
Hornsby 2b	4	0	2	0	0	0	.250
Bottomley 1b	3	1	1	0	0	0	.345
L.Bell 3b	4	1	0	0	0	0	.259
Hafey lf	4	1	2	0	0	0	.185
O'Farrell c	3	0	0	0	1	0	.304
Thevenow ss	4	0	2	0	2	0	.417
Haines p	2	0	1	0	0	0	.600
Alexander p	1	0	0	0	0	0	.000
TOTALS	**34**	**3**	**8**	**0**	**3**	**0**	**.272**

BATTING: S: Haines, Bottomley. **SF:** O'Farrell. **RBI:** O'Farrell 1 (2), Thevenow 2 (4). **Runners left in scoring position, 2 out:** Holm 1, Southworth 1, O'Farrell 1. **Team LOB:** 7 **BASERUNNING: CS:** Hafey (1, 2nd base off Hoyt/Severeid).

NY YANKEES	AB	R	H	HR	RBI	BB	AVG
Combs cf	5	0	2	0	0	0	.357
Koenig ss	4	0	0	0	0	0	.125
Ruth rf	1	1	1	1	1	4	.300
Meusel lf	4	0	1	0	0	0	.238
Gehrig 1b	2	0	0	0	0	2	.348
Lazzeri 2b	4	0	0	0	0	0	.192
Dugan 3b	4	1	2	0	0	0	.333
Severeid c	3	0	2	0	1	0	.273
a-Adams pr	0	0	0	0	0	0	.000
Collins c	1	0	0	0	0	0	.000
Hoyt p	2	0	0	0	0	0	.000
b-Paschal ph	1	0	0	0	0	0	.250
Pennock p	1	0	0	0	0	0	.143
TOTALS	**32**	**2**	**8**	**1**	**2**	**6**	**.242**

a - Ran for Severeid in the 6th
b - Batted for Hoyt in the 6th

BATTING: 2B: Severeid (1, Haines). **HR:** Ruth (4, 3th off Haines 0 on, 2 out). **S:** Koenig. **RBI:** Ruth 1 (5), Severeid 1 (1). **2-out RBI:** Ruth 1, Severeid 1. **Runners left in scoring position, 2 out:** Meusel 1, Gehrig 1, Lazzeri 2, Severeid 1, Paschal 1. **Team LOB:** 10 **BASERUNNING: CS:** Dugan (1, 2nd base off Haines/O'Farrell), Ruth (1, 2nd base off Alexander/O'Farrell). **FIELDING: E:** Koenig (3), Meusel (1), Dugan (1).

ST.LOUIS	IP	H	R	ER	BB	SO	HR	ERA
Haines (W, 2-0)	6.2	8	2	2	5	2	1	1.08
Alexander (S, 1)	2.1	0	0	0	1	1	0	1.33

NY YANKEES	IP	H	R	ER	BB	SO	HR	ERA
Hoyt (L, 1-1)	6	5	3	0	0	2	0	1.20
Pennock	3	3	0	0	0	0	0	1.23

IBB: Ruth (by Haines). **Ground balls-fly balls:** Haines 10-6, Alexander 3-2, Hoyt 6-10, Pennock 6-2. **Batters faced:** Haines 32, Alexander 7, Hoyt 25, Pennock 12. **UMPIRES:** hp—Hildebrand, 1b—Klem, 2b—Dinneen, 3b—O'Day **T:** 2:15 **A:** 38,093

1927 NY YANKEES DEF. PITTSBURGH, 4-0

GAME 1 New York 5 Pittsburgh 4
Forbes Field 10/05/27

NY YANKEES	AB	R	H	HR	RBI	BB	AVG
Combs cf	4	0	0	0	0	0	.000
Koenig ss	4	2	1	0	0	0	.250
Ruth rf	4	2	3	0	0	0	.750
Gehrig 1b	2	1	1	0	2	1	.500
Meusel lf	3	0	0	0	1	1	.000
Lazzeri 2b	4	0	1	0	1	0	.250
Dugan 3b	3	0	0	0	0	0	.000
Collins c	2	0	0	0	0	2	.000
Hoyt p	3	0	0	0	0	0	.000
Moore p	1	0	0	0	0	0	.000
TOTALS	**30**	**5**	**6**	**0**	**4**	**4**	**.200**

BATTING: 2B: Koenig (1, Kremer), Lazzeri (1, Kremer). **3B:** Gehrig (1, Kremer). **S:** Dugan. **SF:** Gehrig. **RBI:** Gehrig 2 (2), Meusel 1 (1), Lazzeri 1 (1). **2-out RBI:** Gehrig 1. **Runners left in scoring position, 2 out:** Meusel 1, Dugan 1. **GIDP:** Hoyt. **Team LOB:** 4 **FIELDING: E:** Meusel (1). **DP:** 1 (Lazzeri-Gehrig).

PITTSBURGH	AB	R	H	HR	RBI	BB	AVG
L.Waner cf	4	2	1	0	0	0	.250
Barnhart lf	5	0	1	0	1	0	.200
P.Waner rf	4	0	3	0	1	0	.750
Wright ss	2	1	1	0	1	0	.500
Traynor 3b	4	0	1	0	0	0	.250
Grantham 2b	3	0	0	0	0	1	.000
Harris 1b	4	0	1	0	1	0	.250
Smith c	4	0	0	0	0	0	.000
Kremer p	2	1	1	0	0	0	.500
Miljus p	1	0	0	0	0	0	.000
a-Brickell ph	1	0	0	0	0	0	.000
TOTALS	**34**	**4**	**9**	**0**	**4**	**1**	**.265**

a - Batted for Miljus in the 9th

BATTING: 2B: P.Waner (1, Hoyt), Kremer (1, Hoyt), L.Waner (1, Hoyt). **SF:** Wright, Wright. **RBI:** Barnhart 1 (1), P.Waner 1 (1), Wright 1 (1), Harris 1 (1). **2-out RBI:** Harris 1. **Runners left in scoring position, 2 out:** Traynor 3, Smith 1. **GIDP:** Harris. **Team LOB:** 7 **FIELDING: E:** Grantham (1). **DP:** 1 (Wright-Grantham-Harris).

NY YANKEES	IP	H	R	ER	BB	SO	HR	ERA
Hoyt (W, 1-0)	7.1	8	4	4	1	2	0	4.91
Moore (S, 1)	1.2	1	0	0	0	0	0	0.00

PITTSBURGH	IP	H	R	ER	BB	SO	HR	ERA
Kremer (L, 0-1)	5	5	5	2	3	1	0	3.60
Miljus	4	1	0	0	1	3	0	0.00

HBP: L.Waner (by Hoyt). **Ground balls-fly balls:** Hoyt 8-10, Moore 4-1, Kremer 5-9, Miljus 6-0. **Batters faced:** Hoyt 32, Moore 6, Kremer 24, Miljus 12. **UMPIRES:** hp—Quigley, 1b—Nallin, 2b—Moran, 3b—Ormsby **T:** 2:04 **A:** 41,467

GAME 2 New York 6 Pittsburgh 2
Forbes Field 10/06/27

NY YANKEES	AB	R	H	HR	RBI	BB	AVG
Combs cf	4	1	1	0	1	0	.125
Koenig ss	5	1	3	0	2	0	.444
Ruth rf	3	0	0	0	1	1	.429
Gehrig 1b	3	1	1	0	0	1	.400
Meusel lf	5	1	2	0	0	0	.250
Lazzeri 2b	4	0	2	0	1	0	.375
Dugan 3b	5	1	1	0	0	0	.125
Bengough c	3	1	0	0	0	1	.000
Pipgras p	3	0	1	0	0	1	.333
TOTALS	**35**	**6**	**11**	**0**	**5**	**4**	**.262**

BATTING: 2B: Gehrig (1, Aldridge). **SF:** Ruth, Lazzeri, Gehrig. **RBI:** Combs 1 (1), Koenig 2 (2), Ruth 1 (1), Lazzeri 1 (2). **Runners left in scoring position, 2 out:** Combs 1, Gehrig 2, Meusel 2, Dugan 1. **Team LOB:** 10 **BASERUNNING: SB:** Meusel (1, 2nd base off Dawson/Gooch). **FIELDING: DP:** 1 (Lazzeri-Koenig).

PITTSBURGH	AB	R	H	HR	RBI	BB	AVG
L.Waner cf	3	2	1	0	0	1	.286
Barnhart lf	3	0	2	0	1	0	.375
P.Waner rf	3	0	1	0	1	0	.571
Wright ss	4	0	0	0	0	0	.167
Traynor 3b	4	0	1	0	0	0	.250
Grantham 2b	4	0	2	0	0	0	.286
Harris 1b	4	0	0	0	0	0	.125
Gooch c	3	0	0	0	0	0	.000
Aldridge p	2	0	0	0	0	0	.000
Cvengros p	0	0	0	0	0	0	.000
a-Smith ph	1	0	0	0	0	0	.000
Dawson p	0	0	0	0	0	0	.000
TOTALS	**31**	**2**	**7**	**0**	**2**	**1**	**.246**

a - Batted for Cvengros in the 8th

BATTING: 2B: Traynor (1, Pipgras), Grantham (1, Pipgras). **3B:** L.Waner (1, Pipgras). **SF:** Barnhart, P.Waner. **RBI:** Barnhart 1 (2), P.Waner 1 (2). **Runners left in scoring position, 2 out:** Harris 1, Gooch 1. **Team LOB:** 5 **FIELDING: E:** L.Waner (1), Wright (1).

NY YANKEES	IP	H	R	ER	BB	SO	HR	ERA
Pipgras (W, 1-0)	9	7	2	2	1	2	0	2.00

PITTSBURGH	IP	H	R	ER	BB	SO	HR	ERA
Aldridge (L, 0-1)	7.1	10	6	6	4	4	0	7.36
Cvengros	0.2	1	0	0	0	0	0	0.00
Dawson	1	0	0	0	0	0	0	0.00

WP: Aldridge 1. **HBP:** Combs (by Cvengros). **Ground balls-fly balls:** Pipgras 9-13, Aldridge 4-11, Cvengros 2-0, Dawson 1-2. **Batters faced:** Pipgras 34, Aldridge 36, Cvengros 4, Dawson 3. **UMPIRES:** hp—Nallin, 1b—Moran, 2b—Ormsby, 3b—Quigley **T:** 2:20 **A:** 41,634

GAME 3 New York 8 Pittsburgh 1
Yankee Stadium 10/07/27

PITTSBURGH	AB	R	H	HR	RBI	BB	AVG
L.Waner cf	4	0	1	0	0	0	.273
Rhyne 2b	4	0	0	0	0	0	.000
P.Waner rf	4	0	0	0	0	0	.364
Wright ss	3	0	0	0	0	0	.111
Traynor 3b	3	1	1	0	0	0	.273
Barnhart lf	3	0	1	0	1	0	.364
Harris 1b	3	0	0	0	0	0	.091
Gooch c	2	0	0	0	0	0	.000
a-Spencer ph-c	1	0	0	0	0	0	.000
Meadows p	2	0	0	0	0	0	.000
Cvengros p	0	0	0	0	0	0	.000
b-Groh ph	1	0	0	0	0	0	.000
TOTALS	**30**	**1**	**3**	**0**	**1**	**0**	**.200**

a - Batted for Gooch in the 8th
b - Batted for Cvengros in the 9th

BATTING: 2B: Barnhart (1, Pennock). **RBI:** Barnhart 1 (3). **Runners left in scoring position, 2 out:** P.Waner 1, Spencer 1. **Team LOB:** 2 **FIELDING: E:** Traynor (1). **Outfield assists:** L.Waner (1).

NY YANKEES	AB	R	H	HR	RBI	BB	AVG
Combs cf	4	2	2	0	1	0	.250
Koenig ss	4	2	2	0	1	0	.462
Ruth rf	4	1	1	1	3	0	.364
Gehrig 1b	3	0	2	0	2	1	.500
Meusel lf	4	0	0	0	0	0	.167
Lazzeri 2b	4	1	1	0	0	0	.333
Dugan 3b	3	1	1	0	0	0	.182
Grabowski c	2	0	0	0	0	0	.000
a-Durst ph	1	0	0	0	0	0	.000
Bengough c	1	0	0	0	0	0	.000
Pennock p	4	1	0	0	1	0	.000
TOTALS	**34**	**8**	**9**	**1**	**8**	**1**	**.263**

a - Batted for Grabowski in the 7th

BATTING: 2B: Gehrig (2, Meadows), Koenig (2, Meadows). **3B:** Gehrig (2, Meadows). **HR:** Ruth (1, 7th off Cvengros 2 on, 1 out). **S:** Dugan. **RBI:** Combs 1 (2), Koenig 1 (3), Ruth 3 (4), Gehrig 2 (4), Pennock 1 (1). **Runners left in scoring position, 2 out:** Meusel 2, Dugan 2, Pennock 1. **Team LOB:** 4

PITTSBURGH	IP	H	R	ER	BB	SO	HR	ERA
Meadows (L, 0-1)	6.1	7	7	7	1	6	0	9.95
Cvengros	1.2	2	1	1	0	2	1	3.86

NY YANKEES	IP	H	R	ER	BB	SO	HR	ERA
Pennock (W, 1-0)	9	3	1	1	0	1	0	1.00

Ground balls-fly balls: Meadows 10-4, Cvengros 3-0, Pennock 12-14. **Batters faced:** Meadows 29, Cvengros 7, Pennock 30. **UMPIRES:** hp—Moran, 1b—Ormsby, 2b—Quigley, 3b—Nallin **T:** 2:04 **A:** 60,695

GAME 4 New York 4 Pittsburgh 3
Yankee Stadium 10/08/27

PITTSBURGH	AB	R	H	HR	RBI	BB	AVG
L.Waner cf	4	1	3	0	0	0	.400
Barnhart lf	5	0	1	0	1	0	.313
P.Waner rf	4	0	1	0	1	0	.333
Wright ss	4	0	1	0	1	0	.154
Traynor 3b	4	0	0	0	0	0	.200
Grantham 2b	4	0	2	0	0	0	.364
Harris 1b	4	0	2	0	0	0	.200
Smith c	3	0	0	0	0	0	.000
a-Yde pr	0	1	0	0	0	0	.000
Gooch c	0	0	0	0	0	1	.000
Hill p	1	0	0	0	0	1	.000
b-Brickell ph	1	1	0	0	0	0	.000
Miljus p	1	0	0	0	0	0	.000
TOTALS	**35**	**3**	**10**	**0**	**3**	**2**	**.223**

a - Ran for Smith in the 7th
b - Batted for Hill in the 7th

BATTING: S: L.Waner. **SF:** P.Waner. **RBI:** Barnhart 1 (4), P.Waner 1 (3), Wright 1 (2). **2-out RBI:** Wright 1. **Runners left in scoring position, 2 out:** Barnhart 2, Traynor 1, Miljus 1. **GIDP:** Wright, Barnhart. **Team LOB:** 9 **FIELDING: E:** L.Waner (2). **DP:** 1 (Traynor-Wright-Harris).

NY YANKEES	AB	R	H	HR	RBI	BB	AVG
Combs cf	4	3	2	0	0	1	.313
Koenig ss	5	0	3	0	0	0	.500
Ruth rf	4	1	2	1	3	1	.400
Gehrig 1b	5	0	0	0	0	0	.308
Meusel lf	5	0	0	0	0	0	.118
Lazzeri 2b	3	0	0	0	0	1	.267
Dugan 3b	4	0	1	0	0	0	.200
Collins c	3	0	3	0	0	1	.600
Moore p	4	0	1	0	0	0	.200
TOTALS	**37**	**4**	**12**	**1**	**3**	**4**	**.279**

BATTING: 2B: Collins (1, Hill). **HR:** Ruth (2, 5th off Hill 1 on, 1 out). **RBI:** Ruth 3 (7). **Runners left in scoring position, 2 out:** Combs 2, Lazzeri 2, Moore 2. **GIDP:** Ruth. **Team LOB:** 11 **BASERUNNING: SB:** Ruth (1, 2nd base off Hill/Smith). **FIELDING: E:** Lazzeri (1). **DP:** 2 (Lazzeri-Gehrig, Dugan-Lazzeri-Gehrig).

PITTSBURGH	IP	H	R	ER	BB	SO	HR	ERA
Hill	6	9	3	3	1	6	1	4.50
Miljus (L, 0-1)	2.2	3	1	1	3	3	0	1.35

NY YANKEES	IP	H	R	ER	BB	SO	HR	ERA
Moore (W, 1-0)	9	10	3	1	2	2	0	0.84

WP: Miljus 2. **IBB:** Gooch (by Moore), Ruth (by Miljus). **Ground balls-fly balls:** Hill 10-2, Miljus 2-2, Moore 18-5. **Batters faced:** Hill 28, Miljus 13, Moore 39. **UMPIRES:** hp—Ormsby, 1b—Quigley, 2b—Nallin, 3b—Moran **T:** 2:15 **A:** 57,909

1928 NY YANKEES DEF. ST.LOUIS CARDINALS, 4-0

GAME 1 New York 4 St. Louis 1
Yankee Stadium 10/04/28

ST.LOUIS	AB	R	H	HR	RBI	BB	AVG
Douthit cf	3	0	0	0	0	1	.000
High 3b	4	0	0	0	0	0	.000
Frisch 2b	4	0	0	0	0	0	.000
Bottomley 1b	3	1	2	1	1	1	.667
Hafey lf	4	0	0	0	0	0	.000
Harper rf	3	0	1	0	0	0	.333
Wilson c	3	0	0	0	0	0	.000
Maranville ss	2	0	0	0	0	0	.000
a-Orsatti ph	0	0	0	0	0	1	.000
Thevenow ss	0	0	0	0	0	0	.000
Sherdel p	2	0	0	0	0	0	.000
b-Holm ph	1	0	0	0	0	0	.000
Johnson p	0	0	0	0	0	0	.000
TOTALS	**29**	**1**	**3**	**1**	**1**	**3**	**.103**

a - Batted for Maranville in the 8th
b - Batted for Sherdel in the 8th

BATTING: HR: Bottomley (1, 7th off Hoyt 0 on, 1 out). **RBI:** Bottomley 1 (1). **Team LOB:** 4 **BASERUNNING: CS:** Wilson (1, 2nd base off Hoyt/Bengough). **FIELDING: E:** Maranville (1).

NY YANKEES	AB	R	H	HR	RBI	BB	AVG
Paschal cf	4	0	0	0	0	0	.000
Durst cf	0	0	0	0	0	0	.000
Koenig ss	4	1	1	0	0	0	.250
Ruth rf	4	2	3	0	0	0	.750
Gehrig 1b	4	0	2	0	2	0	.500
Meusel lf	4	1	1	1	2	0	.250
Lazzeri 2b	2	0	0	0	0	0	.000
Durocher 2b	1	0	0	0	0	0	.000
Dugan 3b	3	0	0	0	0	0	.000
Bengough c	3	0	0	0	0	0	.000
Hoyt p	3	0	0	0	0	0	.000
TOTALS	**32**	**4**	**7**	**1**	**4**	**0**	**.219**

BATTING: 2B: Ruth 2 (2, Sherdel), Gehrig (1, Sherdel). **HR:** Meusel (1, 4th off Sherdel 1 on, 1 out). **SF:** Hoyt. **RBI:** Gehrig 2 (2), Meusel 2 (2). **2-out RBI:** Gehrig 2. **Runners left in scoring position, 2 out:** Meusel 2. **Team LOB:** 4

ST.LOUIS	IP	H	R	ER	BB	SO	HR	ERA
Sherdel (L, 0-1)	7	4	3	3	0	2	1	3.86
Johnson	1	3	1	1	0	0	0	9.00

NY YANKEES	IP	H	R	ER	BB	SO	HR	ERA
Hoyt (W, 1-0)	9	3	1	1	3	6	1	1.00

Ground balls-fly balls: Sherdel 10-10, Johnson 1-2, Hoyt 7-13. **Batters faced:** Sherdel 26, Johnson 6, Hoyt 32. **UMPIRES:** hp—Owens, 1b—Rigler, 2b—McGowan, 3b—Pfirman **T:** 1:49 **A:** 61,425

GAME 2 New York 9 St. Louis 3
Yankee Stadium 10/05/28

ST.LOUIS	AB	R	H	HR	RBI	BB	AVG
Douthit cf	4	0	0	0	1	0	.000
High 3b	3	0	0	0	0	1	.000
Frisch 2b	3	0	2	0	0	1	.286
Bottomley 1b	4	0	0	0	0	0	.286
Hafey lf	4	0	0	0	0	0	.000
Harper rf	3	1	0	0	0	1	.167
Wilson c	4	1	1	0	1	0	.143
Maranville ss	3	1	1	0	0	1	.200
Alexander p	1	0	0	0	1	0	.000
Mitchell p	2	0	0	0	0	0	.000
a-Orsatti ph	1	0	0	0	0	0	.000
TOTALS	**32**	**3**	**4**	**0**	**3**	**4**	**.115**

a - Batted for Mitchell in the 9th

BATTING: 2B: Wilson (1, Pipgras). **RBI:** Douthit 1 (1), Wilson 1 (1), Alexander 1 (1). **Runners left in scoring position, 2 out:** Hafey 2, Harper 1. **GIDP:** Douthit. **Team LOB:** 6 **BASERUNNING: SB:** Frisch 2 (2, 2nd base off Pipgras/Bengough). **FIELDING: E:** Mitchell (1). **Outfield assists:** Douthit (1). **DP:** 1 (Frisch-Maranville-Bottomley).

NY YANKEES	AB	R	H	HR	RBI	BB	AVG
Durst cf	2	1	2	0	1	0	1.000
a-Paschal ph-cf	2	0	1	0	1	1	.167
Koenig ss	5	0	0	0	0	0	.111
Ruth rf	3	2	2	0	0	1	.714
Gehrig 1b	3	2	1	1	3	1	.429
Meusel lf	3	2	1	0	1	1	.286
Lazzeri 2b	3	0	0	0	0	0	.000
Durocher 2b	0	0	0	0	0	0	.000
Robertson 3b	2	1	0	0	0	1	.000
b-Dugan ph-3b	0	0	0	0	1	0	.000
Bengough c	3	1	1	0	1	1	.167
Pipgras p	2	0	0	0	1	0	.000
TOTALS	**28**	**9**	**8**	**1**	**9**	**6**	**.250**

a - Batted for Durst in the 3th
b - Batted for Robertson in the 7th

BATTING: 2B: Meusel (1, Alexander), Ruth (3, Mitchell). **HR:** Gehrig (1, 1st off Alexander 2 on, 1 out). **S:** Pipgras, Lazzeri. **SF:** Dugan. **RBI:** Durst 1 (1), Paschal 1 (1), Gehrig 3 (5), Meusel 1 (3), Dugan 1 (1), Bengough 1 (1), Pipgras 1 (1). **2-out RBI:** Durst 1. **Runners left in scoring position, 2 out:** Koenig 1, Lazzeri 1. **GIDP:** Bengough. **Team LOB:** 5 **BASERUNNING: SB:** Meusel (1, 2nd base off Mitchell/Wilson). **FIELDING: E:** Lazzeri (1), Koenig (1). **DP:** 1 (Koenig-Lazzeri-Gehrig).

ST.LOUIS	IP	H	R	ER	BB	SO	HR	ERA
Alexander (L, 0-1)	2.1	6	8	8	4	1	1	30.86
Mitchell	5.2	2	1	1	2	3	0	1.59

NY YANKEES	IP	H	R	ER	BB	SO	HR	ERA
Pipgras (W, 1-0)	9	4	3	2	4	8	0	2.00

HBP: Pipgras (by Mitchell). **Ground balls-fly balls:** Alexander 3-2, Mitchell 3-8, Pipgras 9-11. **Batters faced:** Alexander 17, Mitchell 21, Pipgras 36. **UMPIRES:** hp—Rigler, 1b—McGowan, 2b—Pfirman, 3b—Owens **T:** 2:04 **A:** 60,714

GAME 3 New York 7 St. Louis 3
Sportsman's Park 10/07/28

NY YANKEES	AB	R	H	HR	RBI	BB	AVG
Durst cf	5	1	0	0	0	0	.286
Koenig ss	5	0	1	0	0	0	.143
Ruth lf	4	2	2	0	1	0	.636
Gehrig 1b	2	2	2	2	3	2	.556
Meusel rf	3	1	0	0	1	1	.200
Lazzeri 2b	3	1	0	0	0	1	.000
Durocher 2b	0	0	0	0	0	0	.000
Robertson 3b	4	0	1	0	1	0	.167
Bengough c	4	0	1	0	0	0	.200
Zachary p	4	0	0	0	0	0	.000
TOTALS	**34**	**7**	**7**	**2**	**6**	**4**	**.234**

BATTING: HR: Gehrig 2 (3, 2nd off Haines 0 on, 0 out, 4th off Haines 1 on, 1 out). **RBI:** Ruth 1 (1), Gehrig 3 (8), Meusel 1 (4), Robertson 1 (1). **2-out RBI:** Ruth 1, Robertson 1. **Runners left in scoring position, 2 out:** Meusel 1. **GIDP:** Lazzeri. **Team LOB:** 4 **BASERUNNING: SB:** Meusel (2, home off Haines/Wilson), Lazzeri (1, home off Haines/Wilson). **FIELDING: E:** Robertson (1), Lazzeri (2). **Outfield assists:** Ruth (1). **DP:** 1 (Koenig-Durocher-Gehrig).

ST.LOUIS	AB	R	H	HR	RBI	BB	AVG
Douthit cf	4	1	1	0	0	0	.091
High 3b	5	1	2	0	1	0	.167
Frisch 2b	2	1	1	0	0	1	.333
Bottomley 1b	4	0	1	0	2	0	.273
Hafey lf	4	0	2	0	0	0	.167
Holm rf	4	0	1	0	0	0	.200
Wilson c	4	0	0	0	0	0	.091
Maranville ss	4	0	1	0	0	0	.222
Haines p	2	0	0	0	0	0	.000
Johnson p	0	0	0	0	0	0	.000
a-Blades ph	1	0	0	0	0	0	.000
Rhem p	0	0	0	0	0	0	.000
b-Orsatti ph	1	0	0	0	0	0	.000
TOTALS	**35**	**3**	**9**	**0**	**3**	**1**	**.167**

a - Batted for Johnson in the 7th
b - Batted for Rhem in the 9th

BATTING: 2B: High (1, Zachary). **3B:** Bottomley (1, Zachary). **S:** Frisch. **RBI:** High 1 (1), Bottomley 2 (3). **Runners left in scoring position, 2 out:** High 1, Bottomley 1, Hafey 1, Holm 1, Maranville 1. **GIDP:** Wilson. **Team LOB:** 8 **FIELDING: E:** Hafey (1). **DP:** 1 (High-Frisch-Bottomley).

NY YANKEES	IP	H	R	ER	BB	SO	HR	ERA
Zachary (W, 1-0)	9	9	3	3	1	7	0	3.00

ST.LOUIS	IP	H	R	ER	BB	SO	HR	ERA
Haines (L, 0-1)	6	6	6	3	3	3	2	4.50
Johnson	1	1	1	0	1	1	0	4.50
Rhem	2	0	0	0	0	1	0	0.00

HBP: Douthit (by Zachary). **Ground balls-fly balls:** Zachary 11-8, Haines 7-7, Johnson 0-3, Rhem 2-3. **Batters faced:** Zachary 38, Haines 26, Johnson 6, Rhem 6. **UMPIRES:** hp—McGowan, 1b—Pfirman, 2b—Owens, 3b—Rigler **T:** 2:00 **A:** 39,602

GAME 4 New York 7 St. Louis 3
Sportsman's Park 10/09/28

NY YANKEES	AB	R	H	HR	RBI	BB	AVG
Paschal cf	4	0	1	0	0	0	.200
Durst cf	1	1	1	1	1	0	.375
Koenig ss	5	0	1	0	0	0	.158
Ruth lf	5	3	3	3	3	0	.625
Gehrig 1b	2	1	1	1	1	3	.545
Meusel rf	5	1	1	0	0	0	.200
Lazzeri 2b	4	1	3	0	0	0	.250
Durocher 2b	1	0	0	0	0	0	.000
Dugan 3b	3	0	1	0	0	0	.167
Robertson 3b	2	0	0	0	1	0	.125
Bengough c	3	0	1	0	0	0	.231
a-Combs ph	0	0	0	0	1	0	.000
Collins c	1	0	1	0	0	0	1.000
Hoyt p	4	0	1	0	0	0	.143
TOTALS	**40**	**7**	**15**	**5**	**7**	**3**	**.276**

a - Batted for Bengough in the 7th

BATTING: 2B: Lazzeri (1, Alexander), Collins (1, Alexander). **HR:** Ruth 3 (3, 4th off Sherdel 0 on, 0 out, 7th off Sherdel 0 on, 1 out, 8th off Alexander 0 on, 1 out), Gehrig (4, 7th off Sherdel 0 on, 1 out), Durst (1, 8th off Alexander 0 on, 0 out). **S:** Hoyt. **SF:** Combs. **RBI:** Durst 1 (2), Ruth 3 (4), Gehrig 1 (9), Robertson 1 (2), Combs 1 (1). **Runners left in scoring position, 2 out:** Paschal 1, Koenig 1, Meusel 2, Bengough 1, Hoyt 1. **GIDP:** Ruth. **Team LOB:** 11 **BASERUNNING: SB:** Lazzeri (2, 3rd base off Sherdel/Smith). **FIELDING: E:** Hoyt (1). **DP:** 1 (Koenig-Gehrig).

ST.LOUIS	AB	R	H	HR	RBI	BB	AVG
Orsatti cf	5	1	2	0	0	0	.286
High 3b	5	0	3	0	0	0	.294
Frisch 2b	4	0	0	0	1	0	.231
Bottomley 1b	3	0	0	0	0	1	.214
Hafey lf	3	0	1	0	0	1	.200
Harper rf	3	0	0	0	0	1	.111
Smith c	4	0	3	0	0	0	.750
a-Martin pr	0	1	0	0	0	0	.000
Maranville ss	4	1	2	0	0	0	.308
Sherdel p	3	0	0	0	0	0	.000
Alexander p	0	0	0	0	0	0	.000
b-Holm ph	1	0	0	0	1	0	.167
TOTALS	**35**	**3**	**11**	**0**	**2**	**3**	**.206**

a - Ran for Smith in the 9th
b - Batted for Alexander in the 9th

BATTING: 2B: High (2, Hoyt), Maranville (1, Hoyt), Orsatti (1, Hoyt). **SF:** Frisch. **RBI:** Frisch 1 (1), Holm 1 (1). **Runners left in scoring position, 2 out:** Frisch 1, Hafey 1, Harper 1, Sherdel 3. **GIDP:** Harper. **Team LOB:** 9 **BASERUNNING: SB:** Maranville (1, 2nd base off Hoyt/Bengough). **CS:** Smith (1, 2nd base off Hoyt/Bengough). **FIELDING: DP:** 1 (Bottomley-Maranville).

NY YANKEES	IP	H	R	ER	BB	SO	HR	ERA
Hoyt (W, 2-0)	9	11	3	2	3	8	0	1.50

ST.LOUIS	IP	H	R	ER	BB	SO	HR	ERA
Sherdel (L, 0-2)	6.1	11	4	4	3	1	3	4.72
Alexander	2.2	4	3	3	0	1	2	19.80

Ground balls-fly balls: Hoyt 7-9, Sherdel 5-11, Alexander 5-2. **Batters faced:** Hoyt 39, Sherdel 32, Alexander 13. **UMPIRES:** hp—Pfirman, 1b—Owens, 2b—Rigler, 3b—McGowan **T:** 2:25 **A:** 37,331

1929 PHILADELPHIA A's DEF. CHICAGO CUBS, 4-1

GAME 1 Philadelphia 3 Chicago 1
Wrigley Field 10/08/29

PHILADELPHIA	AB	R	H	HR	RBI	BB	AVG
Bishop 2b	4	0	0	0	0	0	.000
Haas cf	3	0	0	0	0	1	.000
Cochrane c	3	1	1	0	0	1	.333
Simmons lf	4	1	0	0	0	0	.000
Foxx 1b	4	1	2	1	1	0	.500
Miller rf	4	0	1	0	2	0	.250
Dykes 3b	4	0	1	0	0	0	.250
Boley ss	4	0	0	0	0	0	.000
Ehmke p	4	0	1	0	0	0	.250
TOTALS	**34**	**3**	**6**	**1**	**3**	**2**	**.176**

BATTING: HR: Foxx (1, 7th off Root 0 on, 1 out). **RBI:** Foxx 1 (1), Miller 2 (2). **Runners left in scoring position, 2 out:** Ehmke 1. **GIDP:** Boley. **Team LOB:** 6 **FIELDING: E:** Dykes (1).

CHICAGO CUBS	AB	R	H	HR	RBI	BB	AVG
McMillan 3b	4	0	1	0	0	0	.250
English ss	4	0	2	0	0	0	.500
Hornsby 2b	4	0	0	0	0	0	.000
Wilson cf	4	0	0	0	0	0	.000
Cuyler rf	4	1	1	0	0	0	.250
Stephenson lf	4	0	2	0	1	0	.500
Grimm 1b	2	0	2	0	0	1	1.000
Taylor c	2	0	0	0	0	0	.000
a-Heathcote ph	1	0	0	0	0	0	.000
Gonzalez c	0	0	0	0	0	0	.000
c-Blair ph	1	0	0	0	0	0	.000
Root p	2	0	0	0	0	0	.000
b-Hartnett ph	1	0	0	0	0	0	.000
Bush p	0	0	0	0	0	0	.000
d-Tolson ph	1	0	0	0	0	0	.000
TOTALS	**34**	**1**	**8**	**0**	**1**	**1**	**.235**

a - Batted for Taylor in the 7th
b - Batted for Root in the 7th
c - Batted for Gonzalez in the 9th
d - Batted for Bush in the 9th

BATTING: 2B: English (1, Ehmke). **S:** Grimm. **RBI:** Stephenson 1 (1). **Runners left in scoring position, 2 out:** Wilson 2, Hartnett 2, Tolson 1. **Team LOB:** 8 **BASERUNNING: CS:** Grimm (1, 2nd base off Ehmke/Cochrane). **FIELDING: E:** English 2 (2). **DP:** 1 (English-Hornsby-Grimm).

PHILADELPHIA	IP	H	R	ER	BB	SO	HR	ERA
Ehmke (W, 1-0)	9	8	1	0	1	13	0	0.00

CHICAGO CUBS	IP	H	R	ER	BB	SO	HR	ERA
Root (L, 0-1)	7	3	1	1	2	5	1	1.29
Bush	2	3	2	0	0	0	0	0.00

Ground balls-fly balls: Ehmke 4-9, Root 6-9, Bush 6-2. **Batters faced:** Ehmke 36, Root 25, Bush 11. **UMPIRES:** hp—Klem, 1b—Dinneen, 2b—Moran, 3b—Van Graflan **T:** 2:03 **A:** 50,740

GAME 2 Philadelphia 9 Chicago 3
Wrigley Field 10/09/29

PHILADELPHIA	AB	R	H	HR	RBI	BB	AVG
Bishop 2b	4	0	0	0	0	1	.000
Haas cf	5	1	1	0	1	0	.125
Cochrane c	2	2	1	0	0	3	.400
Simmons lf	4	2	2	1	4	1	.250
Foxx 1b	5	2	3	1	3	0	.556
Miller rf	4	0	1	0	0	0	.250
Dykes 3b	4	1	3	0	1	1	.500
Boley ss	3	0	1	0	0	0	.143
Earnshaw p	3	1	0	0	0	0	.000
Grove p	2	0	0	0	0	0	.000
TOTALS	**36**	**9**	**12**	**2**	**9**	**6**	**.257**

BATTING: 2B: Foxx (1, Carlson). **HR:** Foxx (2, 3th off Malone 2 on, 2 out), Simmons (1, 8th off Carlson 1 on, 2 out). **S:** Boley, Boley, Miller. **RBI:** Haas 1 (1), Simmons 4 (4), Foxx 3 (4), Dykes 1 (1). **2-out RBI:** Simmons 4, Foxx 3. **Runners left in scoring position, 2 out:** Bishop 2, Foxx 1, Miller 1, Earnshaw 1. **GIDP:** Cochrane. **Team LOB:** 9 **FIELDING: DP:** 1 (Bishop-Boley-Foxx).

CHICAGO CUBS	AB	R	H	HR	RBI	BB	AVG
McMillan 3b	4	0	0	0	0	1	.125
English ss	5	0	1	0	0	0	.333
Hornsby 2b	4	1	1	0	0	1	.125
Wilson cf	3	1	3	0	0	2	.429
Cuyler rf	4	0	0	0	0	1	.125
Stephenson lf	5	1	1	0	1	0	.333
Grimm 1b	4	0	2	0	1	0	.667
Taylor c	4	0	2	0	1	0	.333
Malone p	1	0	0	0	0	0	.000
Blake p	1	0	1	0	0	0	1.000
a-Heathcote ph	0	0	0	0	0	0	.000
b-Hartnett ph	1	0	0	0	0	0	.000
Carlson p	0	0	0	0	0	0	.000
c-Gonzalez ph	1	0	0	0	0	0	.000
Nehf p	0	0	0	0	0	0	.000
TOTALS	**37**	**3**	**11**	**0**	**3**	**5**	**.268**

a - Batted for Blake in the 5th
b - Batted for Heathcote in the 5th
c - Batted for Carlson in the 8th

BATTING: 2B: English (2, Earnshaw). **RBI:** Stephenson 1 (2), Grimm 1 (1), Taylor 1 (1). **2-out RBI:** Stephenson 1, Grimm 1, Taylor 1. **Runners left in scoring position, 2 out:** Cuyler 1, Stephenson 3, Hartnett 1. **GIDP:** Stephenson. **Team LOB:** 12 **FIELDING: E:** English (3). **DP:** 1 (English-Hornsby-Grimm).

PHILADELPHIA	IP	H	R	ER	BB	SO	HR	ERA
Earnshaw (W, 1-0)	4.2	8	3	3	4	7	0	5.79
Grove (S, 1)	4.1	3	0	0	1	6	0	0.00

CHICAGO CUBS	IP	H	R	ER	BB	SO	HR	ERA
Malone (L, 0-1)	3.2	5	6	3	5	5	1	7.36
Blake	1.1	2	0	0	0	1	0	0.00
Carlson	3	5	3	3	1	2	1	9.00
Nehf	1	0	0	0	0	0	0	0.00

Ground balls-fly balls: Earnshaw 3-4, Grove 5-1, Malone 3-3, Blake 0-2, Carlson 2-3, Nehf 1-2. **Batters faced:** Earnshaw 26, Grove 16, Malone 22, Blake 6, Carlson 14, Nehf 3. **UMPIRES:** hp—Dinneen, 1b—Moran, 2b—Van Graflan, 3b—Klem **T:** 2:29 **A:** 49,987

GAME 3 Chicago 3 Philadelphia 1
Shibe Park 10/11/29

CHICAGO CUBS	AB	R	H	HR	RBI	BB	AVG
McMillan 3b	4	0	0	0	0	0	.083
English ss	4	1	0	0	0	0	.231
Hornsby 2b	4	1	2	0	1	0	.250
Wilson cf	3	0	2	0	0	1	.500
Cuyler rf	4	0	1	0	2	0	.167
Stephenson lf	4	0	1	0	0	0	.308
Grimm 1b	4	0	0	0	0	0	.400
Taylor c	4	0	0	0	0	0	.200
Bush p	3	1	0	0	0	1	.000
TOTALS	**34**	**3**	**6**	**0**	**3**	**2**	**.238**

BATTING: 2B: Hornsby (1, Earnshaw), Stephenson (1, Earnshaw). **3B:** Wilson (1, Earnshaw). **RBI:** Hornsby 1 (1), Cuyler 2 (2). **2-out RBI:** Cuyler 2. **Runners left in scoring position, 2 out:** Cuyler 1, Bush 1. **Team LOB:** 6 **FIELDING: E:** English (4).

PHILADELPHIA	AB	R	H	HR	RBI	BB	AVG
Bishop 2b	4	0	1	0	0	1	.083
Haas cf	5	0	2	0	0	0	.231
Cochrane c	3	1	2	0	0	1	.500
Simmons lf	3	0	0	0	0	0	.182
Foxx 1b	4	0	0	0	0	0	.385
Miller rf	4	0	1	0	1	0	.250
Dykes 3b	4	0	1	0	0	0	.417
Boley ss	4	0	2	0	0	0	.273
Earnshaw p	2	0	0	0	0	0	.000
a-Summa ph	1	0	0	0	0	0	.000
TOTALS	**34**	**1**	**9**	**0**	**1**	**2**	**.260**

a - Batted for Earnshaw in the 9th

BATTING: S: Earnshaw. **SF:** Simmons. **RBI:** Miller 1 (3). **2-out RBI:** Miller 1. **Runners left in scoring position, 2 out:** Haas 1, Foxx 2, Miller 2, Earnshaw 2. **Team LOB:** 10 **BASERUNNING: CS:** Miller (1, 2nd base off Bush/Taylor). **FIELDING: E:** Dykes (2).

CHICAGO CUBS	IP	H	R	ER	BB	SO	HR	ERA
Bush (W, 1-0)	9	9	1	1	2	4	0	0.82

PHILADELPHIA	IP	H	R	ER	BB	SO	HR	ERA
Earnshaw (L, 1-1)	9	6	3	1	2	10	0	2.63

WP: Bush 1. **Ground balls-fly balls:** Bush 7-14, Earnshaw 9-9. **Batters faced:** Bush 38, Earnshaw 36. **UMPIRES:** hp—Moran, 1b—Van Graflan, 2b—Klem, 3b—Dinneen **T:** 2:09 **A:** 29,921

GAME 4 Philadelphia 10 Chicago 8
Shibe Park 10/12/29

CHICAGO CUBS	AB	R	H	HR	RBI	BB	AVG
McMillan 3b	4	0	0	0	0	1	.063
English ss	4	0	0	0	0	1	.176
Hornsby 2b	5	2	2	0	0	0	.294
Wilson cf	3	1	2	0	0	1	.538
Cuyler rf	4	2	3	0	2	0	.313
Stephenson lf	4	1	1	0	1	0	.294
Grimm 1b	4	2	2	1	2	0	.429
Taylor c	3	0	0	0	1	0	.154
Root p	3	0	0	0	0	0	.000
Nehf p	0	0	0	0	0	0	.000
Blake p	0	0	0	0	0	0	1.000
Malone p	0	0	0	0	0	0	.000
a-Hartnett ph	1	0	0	0	0	0	.000
Carlson p	0	0	0	0	0	0	.000
TOTALS	**35**	**8**	**10**	**1**	**6**	**3**	**.250**

a - Batted for Malone in the 8th

BATTING: 3B: Hornsby (1, Rommel). **HR:** Grimm (1, 4th off Quinn 1 on, 2 out). **SF:** Taylor. **RBI:** Cuyler 2 (4), Stephenson 1 (3), Grimm 2 (3), Taylor 1 (2). **2-out RBI:** Grimm 2. **Runners left in scoring position, 2 out:** Cuyler 1. **GIDP:** Stephenson. **Team LOB:** 4 **FIELDING: E:** Cuyler (1), Wilson (1). **Outfield assists:** Stephenson (1).

PHILADELPHIA	AB	R	H	HR	RBI	BB	AVG
Bishop 2b	5	1	2	0	1	0	.176
Haas cf	4	1	1	1	3	0	.235
Cochrane c	4	1	2	0	0	1	.500
Simmons lf	5	2	2	1	1	0	.250
Foxx 1b	4	2	2	0	1	0	.412
Miller rf	3	1	2	0	0	0	.333
Dykes 3b	4	1	3	0	3	0	.500
Boley ss	3	1	1	0	1	0	.286
Quinn p	2	0	0	0	0	0	.000
Walberg p	0	0	0	0	0	0	.000
Rommel p	0	0	0	0	0	0	.000
a-Burns ph	2	0	0	0	0	0	.000
Grove p	0	0	0	0	0	0	.000
TOTALS	**36**	**10**	**15**	**2**	**10**	**1**	**.300**

a - Batted for Rommel in the 7th

BATTING: 2B: Cochrane (1, Root), Dykes (1, Malone). **HR:** Simmons (2, 7th off Root 0 on, 0 out), Haas (1, 7th off Nehf 2 on, 1 out). **S:** Boley, Haas. **RBI:** Bishop 1 (1), Haas 3 (4), Simmons 1 (5), Foxx 1 (5), Dykes 3 (4), Boley 1 (1). **Runners left in scoring position, 2 out:** Bishop 1, Simmons 1, Burns 2. **Team LOB:** 6 **BASERUNNING: CS:** Miller (2, 3rd base off Root/Taylor). **FIELDING: E:** Miller (1), Walberg (1). **DP:** 1 (Dykes-Bishop-Foxx).

CHICAGO CUBS	IP	H	R	ER	BB	SO	HR	ERA
Root	6.1	9	6	6	0	3	1	4.72
Nehf	0	1	2	2	1	0	1	18.00
Blake (L, 0-1)	0	2	2	2	0	0	0	13.50
Malone	0.2	1	0	0	0	2	0	6.23
Carlson	1	2	0	0	0	1	0	6.75

PHILADELPHIA	IP	H	R	ER	BB	SO	HR	ERA
Quinn	5	7	6	5	2	2	1	9.00
Walberg	1	1	1	0	0	2	0	0.00
Rommel (W, 1-0)	1	2	1	1	1	0	0	9.00
Grove (S, 2)	2	0	0	0	0	4	0	0.00

HBP: Miller (by Malone). **Ground balls-fly balls:** Root 6-9, Nehf 0-0, Blake 0-0, Malone 0-0, Carlson 0-0, Quinn 7-6, Walberg 0-0, Rommel 1-1, Grove 1-1. **Batters faced:** Root 28, Nehf 2, Blake 2, Malone 4, Carlson 4, Quinn 24, Walberg 4, Rommel 5, Grove 6. **UMPIRES:** hp—Van Graflan, 1b—Klem, 2b—Dinneen, 3b—Moran **T:** 2:12 **A:** 29,921

GAME 5 Philadelphia 3 Chicago 2
Shibe Park 10/14/29

CHICAGO CUBS	AB	R	H	HR	RBI	BB	AVG
McMillan 3b	4	0	1	0	0	0	.100
English ss	4	0	1	0	0	0	.190
Hornsby 2b	4	0	0	0	0	0	.238
Wilson cf	4	0	1	0	0	0	.471
Cuyler rf	4	1	1	0	0	0	.300
Stephenson lf	2	1	1	0	0	2	.316
Grimm 1b	4	0	1	0	1	0	.389
Taylor c	4	0	1	0	1	0	.176
Malone p	3	0	1	0	0	0	.250
TOTALS	**33**	**2**	**8**	**0**	**2**	**2**	**.249**

BATTING: 2B: Malone (1, Ehmke), Cuyler (1, Ehmke). **RBI:** Grimm 1 (4), Taylor 1 (3). **2-out RBI:** Grimm 1, Taylor 1. **Runners left in scoring position, 2 out:** English 1, Wilson 1, Malone 1. **Team LOB:** 6 **BASERUNNING: SB:** McMillan (1, 2nd base off Walberg/Cochrane). **CS:** English (1, 2nd base off Ehmke/Cochrane). **FIELDING: E:** Hornsby (1). **DP:** 2 (Hornsby-Grimm, English-Hornsby-Grimm).

PHILADELPHIA	AB	R	H	HR	RBI	BB	AVG
Bishop 2b	4	1	1	0	0	0	.190
Haas cf	4	1	1	1	2	0	.238
Cochrane c	3	0	0	0	0	1	.400
Simmons lf	4	1	2	0	0	0	.300
Foxx 1b	3	0	0	0	0	1	.350
Miller rf	4	0	2	0	1	0	.368
Dykes 3b	3	0	0	0	0	0	.421
Boley ss	3	0	0	0	0	0	.235
Ehmke p	1	0	0	0	0	0	.200
Walberg p	1	0	0	0	0	0	.000
a-French ph	1	0	0	0	0	0	.000
TOTALS	**31**	**3**	**6**	**1**	**3**	**2**	**.281**

a - Batted for Walberg in the 9th

BATTING: 2B: Simmons (1, Malone), Miller (1, Malone). **HR:** Haas (2, 9th off Malone 1 on, 1 out). **RBI:** Haas 2 (6), Miller 1 (4). **2-out RBI:** Miller 1. **Runners left in scoring position, 2 out:** Boley 1. **GIDP:** Foxx. **Team LOB:** 4

CHICAGO CUBS	IP	H	R	ER	BB	SO	HR	ERA
Malone (L, 0-2)	8.2	6	3	3	2	4	1	4.15

PHILADELPHIA	IP	H	R	ER	BB	SO	HR	ERA
Ehmke	3.2	6	2	2	2	0	0	1.42
Walberg (W, 1-0)	5.1	2	0	0	0	6	0	0.00

IBB: Foxx (by Malone). **Ground balls-fly balls:** Malone 10-11, Ehmke 6-3, Walberg 2-8. **Batters faced:** Malone 33, Ehmke 17, Walberg 18. **UMPIRES:** hp—Klem, 1b—Dinneen, 2b—Moran, 3b—Van Graflan **T:** 1:42 **A:** 29,921

1930 PHILADELPHIA A's DEF. ST.LOUIS, 4-2

GAME 1 Philadelphia 5 St. Louis 2
Shibe Park 10/01/30

ST.LOUIS	AB	R	H	HR	RBI	BB	AVG
Douthit cf	4	0	0	0	1	0	.000
Adams 3b	3	0	1	0	1	0	.333
Frisch 2b	4	0	2	0	0	0	.500
Bottomley 1b	4	0	0	0	0	0	.000
Hafey lf	4	0	1	0	0	0	.250
Blades rf	3	0	0	0	0	1	.000
Mancuso c	4	1	1	0	0	0	.250
Gelbert ss	4	1	2	0	0	0	.500
Grimes p	3	0	2	0	0	0	.667
a-Puccinelli ph	1	0	0	0	0	0	.000
TOTALS	**34**	**2**	**9**	**0**	**2**	**1**	**.265**

a - Batted for Grimes in the 9th

BATTING: 2B: Frisch (1, Grove), Hafey (1, Grove). **SF:** Douthit, Adams. **RBI:** Douthit 1 (1), Adams 1 (1). **Runners left in scoring position, 2 out:** Frisch 1, Bottomley 2, Mancuso 1, Grimes 1. **Team LOB:** 8

PHILADELPHIA	AB	R	H	HR	RBI	BB	AVG
Bishop 2b	3	1	0	0	0	1	.000
Dykes 3b	4	0	1	0	1	0	.250
Cochrane c	3	1	1	1	1	1	.333
Simmons lf	3	1	1	1	1	1	.333
Foxx 1b	3	1	1	0	0	0	.333
Miller rf	2	0	0	0	1	0	.000
Haas cf	3	1	1	0	0	0	.333
Boley ss	2	0	0	0	1	0	.000
Grove p	3	0	0	0	0	0	.000
TOTALS	**26**	**5**	**5**	**2**	**5**	**3**	**.192**

BATTING: 2B: Dykes (1, Grimes). **3B:** Foxx (1, Grimes), Haas (1, Grimes). **HR:** Simmons (1, 4th off Grimes 0 on, 2 out), Cochrane (1, 8th off Grimes 0 on, 2 out). **S:** Boley. **SF:** Miller. **RBI:** Dykes 1 (1), Cochrane 1 (1), Simmons 1 (1), Miller 1 (1), Boley 1 (1). **2-out RBI:** Cochrane 1, Simmons 1. **Runners left in scoring position, 2 out:** Foxx 1. **Team LOB:** 2 **BASERUNNING: CS:** Cochrane (1, 2nd base off Grimes/Mancuso).

ST.LOUIS	IP	H	R	ER	BB	SO	HR	ERA
Grimes (L, 0-1)	8	5	5	5	3	6	2	5.63

PHILADELPHIA	IP	H	R	ER	BB	SO	HR	ERA
Grove (W, 1-0)	9	9	2	2	1	5	0	2.00

IBB: Simmons (by Grimes). **Ground balls-fly balls:** Grimes 11-4, Grove 8-12. **Batters faced:** Grimes 31, Grove 37. **UMPIRES:** hp—Moriarty, 1b—Rigler, 2b—Geisel, 3b—Reardon **T:** 1:48 **A:** 32,295

GAME 2 Philadelphia 6 St. Louis 1
Shibe Park 10/02/30

ST.LOUIS	AB	R	H	HR	RBI	BB	AVG
Douthit cf	4	0	0	0	0	0	.000
Adams 3b	4	0	1	0	0	0	.286
Frisch 2b	4	0	1	0	0	0	.375
Bottomley 1b	4	0	0	0	0	0	.000
Hafey lf	4	0	0	0	0	0	.125
Watkins rf	4	1	1	1	1	0	.250
Mancuso c	3	0	1	0	0	1	.286
Gelbert ss	3	0	1	0	0	0	.429
Rhem p	1	0	0	0	0	0	.000
Lindsey p	1	0	1	0	0	0	1.000
a-Fisher ph	1	0	0	0	0	0	.000
Johnson p	0	0	0	0	0	0	.000
TOTALS	**33**	**1**	**6**	**1**	**1**	**1**	**.224**

a - Batted for Lindsey in the 7th

BATTING: 2B: Frisch (2, Earnshaw). **HR:** Watkins (1, 2nd off Earnshaw 0 on, 1 out). **RBI:** Watkins 1 (1). **Runners left in scoring position, 2 out:** Douthit 1, Bottomley 1, Hafey 1. **Team LOB:** 6 **BASERUNNING: SB:** Frisch (1, 2nd base off Earnshaw/Cochrane). **FIELDING: E:** Frisch (1), Rhem (1). **DP:** 1 (Gelbert).

PHILADELPHIA	AB	R	H	HR	RBI	BB	AVG
Bishop 2b	2	1	0	0	0	2	.000
Dykes 3b	3	0	1	0	2	0	.286
Cochrane c	3	2	1	1	1	1	.333
Simmons lf	4	2	2	0	1	0	.429
Foxx 1b	3	0	1	0	1	1	.333
Miller rf	4	0	1	0	1	0	.167
Haas cf	4	0	0	0	0	0	.143
Boley ss	4	1	1	0	0	0	.167
Earnshaw p	3	0	0	0	0	0	.000
TOTALS	**30**	**6**	**7**	**1**	**6**	**4**	**.214**

BATTING: 2B: Foxx (1, Rhem), Simmons (1, Rhem), Dykes (2, Rhem). **HR:** Cochrane (2, 1st off Rhem 0 on, 2 out). **S:** Dykes. **RBI:** Dykes 2 (3), Cochrane 1 (2), Simmons 1 (2), Foxx 1 (1), Miller 1 (2). **2-out RBI:** Cochrane 1, Simmons 1, Foxx 1, Miller 1. **Runners left in scoring position, 2 out:** Foxx 2, Miller 1, Haas 2. **Team LOB:** 5 **FIELDING: E:** Boley (1), Cochrane (1). **DP:** 1 (Dykes-Foxx).

ST.LOUIS	IP	H	R	ER	BB	SO	HR	ERA
Rhem (L, 0-1)	3.1	7	6	4	2	3	1	10.80
Lindsey	2.2	0	0	0	0	2	0	0.00
Johnson	2	0	0	0	2	2	0	0.00

PHILADELPHIA	IP	H	R	ER	BB	SO	HR	ERA
Earnshaw (W, 1-0)	9	6	1	1	1	8	1	1.00

IBB: Foxx (by Rhem). **Ground balls-fly balls:** Rhem 4-4, Lindsey 1-4, Johnson 1-2, Earnshaw 5-14. **Batters faced:** Rhem 20, Lindsey 7, Johnson 8, Earnshaw 34. **UMPIRES:** hp—Rigler, 1b—Geisel, 2b—Reardon, 3b—Moriarty **T:** 1:47 **A:** 32,295

GAME 3 St. Louis 5 Philadelphia 0
Sportsman's Park 10/04/30

PHILADELPHIA	AB	R	H	HR	RBI	BB	AVG
Bishop 2b	4	0	3	0	0	1	.333
Dykes 3b	4	0	0	0	0	1	.182
Cochrane c	2	0	0	0	0	2	.250
Simmons lf	4	0	2	0	0	0	.455
Foxx 1b	4	0	1	0	0	0	.300
Miller rf	4	0	0	0	0	0	.100
Haas cf	3	0	0	0	0	0	.100
a-Moore ph	1	0	1	0	0	0	1.000
Boley ss	4	0	0	0	0	0	.100
Walberg p	2	0	0	0	0	0	.000
Shores p	0	0	0	0	0	1	.000
Quinn p	0	0	0	0	0	0	.000
b-McNair ph	1	0	0	0	0	0	.000
TOTALS	**33**	**0**	**7**	**0**	**0**	**5**	**.213**

a - Batted for Haas in the 9th
b - Batted for Quinn in the 9th

BATTING: 2B: Simmons (2, Hallahan). **Runners left in scoring position, 2 out:** Dykes 2, Miller 4. **GIDP:** Simmons. **Team LOB:** 11 **Outfield assists:** Simmons (1).

Douthit cf	4	1	2	1	1	0	.167
Adams 3b	4	0	0	0	0	0	.182
Frisch 2b	4	0	0	0	0	0	.250
Bottomley 1b	4	1	1	0	0	0	.083
Hafey lf	4	1	2	0	1	0	.250
Blades rf	2	1	1	0	0	0	.200
Watkins rf	2	1	1	0	0	0	.333
Wilson c	4	0	2	0	2	0	.500
Gelbert ss	3	0	1	0	1	0	.400
Hallahan p	2	0	0	0	0	1	.000
TOTALS	**33**	**5**	**10**	**1**	**5**	**1**	**.250**

BATTING: 2B: Bottomley (1, Quinn), Hafey (2, Quinn). **HR:** Douthit (1, 4th off Walberg 0 on, 0 out). **RBI:** Douthit 1 (2), Hafey 1 (1), Wilson 2 (2), Gelbert 1 (1). **Runners left in scoring position, 2 out:** Douthit 1, Adams 1, Wilson 1. **Team LOB:** 5 **FIELDING: DP:** 1 (Gelbert-Frisch-Bottomley).

PHILADELPHIA	IP	H	R	ER	BB	SO	HR	ERA
Walberg (L, 0-1)	4.2	4	2	2	1	3	1	3.86
Shores	1.1	3	2	2	0	0	0	13.50
Quinn	2	3	1	1	0	1	0	4.50

ST.LOUIS	IP	H	R	ER	BB	SO	HR	ERA
Hallahan (W, 1-0)	9	7	0	0	5	6	0	0.00

Ground balls-fly balls: Walberg 3-7, Shores 3-1, Quinn 4-1, Hallahan 13-7. **Batters faced:** Walberg 18, Shores 7, Quinn 9, Hallahan 38. **UMPIRES:** hp—Geisel, 1b—Reardon, 2b—Moriarty, 3b—Rigler **T:** 1:55 **A:** 36,944

GAME 4 St. Louis 3 Philadelphia 1
Sportsman's Park 10/05/30

PHILADELPHIA	AB	R	H	HR	RBI	BB	AVG
Bishop 2b	3	1	1	0	0	1	.333
Dykes 3b	2	0	0	0	0	1	.154
Cochrane c	4	0	0	0	0	0	.167
Simmons lf	3	0	2	0	1	1	.500
Foxx 1b	4	0	1	0	0	0	.286
Miller rf	4	0	0	0	0	0	.071
Haas cf	3	0	0	0	0	1	.077
Boley ss	4	0	0	0	0	0	.071
Grove p	3	0	0	0	0	0	.000
TOTALS	**30**	**1**	**4**	**0**	**1**	**4**	**.193**

BATTING: S: Dykes. **RBI:** Simmons 1 (3). **2-out RBI:** Simmons 1. **Runners left in scoring position, 2 out:** Dykes 1, Foxx 1, Miller 2. **GIDP:** Foxx. **Team LOB:** 7 **FIELDING: E:** Dykes (1).

ST.LOUIS	AB	R	H	HR	RBI	BB	AVG
Douthit cf	4	0	0	0	0	0	.125
Adams 3b	4	0	0	0	0	0	.133
Frisch 2b	4	0	0	0	0	0	.188
Bottomley 1b	4	0	0	0	0	0	.063
Hafey lf	3	1	1	0	0	0	.267
Blades rf	3	1	0	0	0	0	.125
Wilson c	3	0	1	0	0	0	.429
Gelbert ss	2	1	2	0	1	1	.500
Haines p	2	0	1	0	1	0	.500
TOTALS	**29**	**3**	**5**	**0**	**2**	**1**	**.233**

BATTING: 2B: Hafey (3, Grove). **3B:** Gelbert (1, Grove). **S:** Haines. **RBI:** Gelbert 1 (2), Haines 1 (1). **2-out RBI:** Gelbert 1. **Runners left in scoring position, 2 out:** Douthit 1, Haines 1. **Team LOB:** 4 **FIELDING: E:** Frisch (2). **DP:** 1 (Gelbert-Frisch-Bottomley).

PHILADELPHIA	IP	H	R	ER	BB	SO	HR	ERA
Grove (L, 1-1)	8	5	3	1	1	3	0	1.59

ST.LOUIS	IP	H	R	ER	BB	SO	HR	ERA
Haines (W, 1-0)	9	4	1	1	4	2	0	1.00

WP: Haines 1. **Ground balls-fly balls:** Grove 4-17, Haines 10-14. **Batters faced:** Grove 31, Haines 35. **UMPIRES:** hp—Reardon, 1b—Moriarty, 2b—Rigler, 3b—Geisel **T:** 1:41 **A:** 39,946

GAME 5 Philadelphia 2 St. Louis 0
Sportsman's Park 10/06/30

PHILADELPHIA	AB	R	H	HR	RBI	BB	AVG
Bishop 2b	4	0	0	0	0	0	.250
Dykes 3b	3	0	0	0	0	1	.125
Cochrane c	3	1	1	0	0	1	.200
Simmons lf	4	0	0	0	0	0	.389
Foxx 1b	4	1	2	1	2	0	.333
Miller rf	4	0	0	0	0	0	.056
Haas cf	4	0	1	0	0	0	.118
Boley ss	3	0	1	0	0	0	.118
Earnshaw p	2	0	0	0	0	0	.000
a-Moore ph	0	0	0	0	0	1	1.000
Grove p	0	0	0	0	0	0	.000
TOTALS	**31**	**2**	**5**	**1**	**2**	**3**	**.187**

a - Batted for Earnshaw in the 8th

BATTING: HR: Foxx (1, 9th off Grimes 1 on, 1 out). **RBI:** Foxx 2 (3). **Runners left in scoring position, 2 out:** Dykes 2. **GIDP:** Haas. **Team LOB:** 5 **BASERUNNING: CS:** Haas (1, 2nd base off Grimes/Wilson).

Douthit cf	4	0	0	0	0	0	.100
Adams 3b	4	0	1	0	0	0	.158
Frisch 2b	4	0	1	0	0	0	.200
Bottomley 1b	4	0	0	0	0	0	.050
Hafey lf	3	0	0	0	0	1	.222
Watkins rf	3	0	0	0	0	0	.222
a-Blades ph	0	0	0	0	0	1	.125
Wilson c	4	0	1	0	0	0	.364
Gelbert ss	2	0	0	0	0	2	.429
Grimes p	2	0	0	0	0	0	.400
TOTALS	**30**	**0**	**3**	**0**	**0**	**4**	**.208**

a - Batted for Watkins in the 9th

BATTING: 2B: Wilson (1, Earnshaw). **S:** Grimes. **Runners left in scoring position, 2 out:** Frisch 1, Gelbert 1, Grimes 1. **Team LOB:** 8 **FIELDING: DP:** 1 (Adams-Frisch-Bottomley).

PHILADELPHIA	IP	H	R	ER	BB	SO	HR	ERA
Earnshaw	7	2	0	0	3	5	0	0.56
Grove (W, 2-1)	2	1	0	0	1	2	0	1.42

ST.LOUIS	IP	H	R	ER	BB	SO	HR	ERA
Grimes (L, 0-2)	9	5	2	2	3	7	1	3.71

IBB: Gelbert (by Earnshaw). **Ground balls-fly balls:** Earnshaw 7-9, Grove 2-2, Grimes 12-7. **Batters faced:** Earnshaw 27, Grove 8, Grimes 34. **UMPIRES:** hp—Moriarty, 1b—Rigler, 2b—Geisel, 3b—Reardon **T:** 1:58 **A:** 38,844

GAME 6 Philadelphia 7 St. Louis 1
Shibe Park 10/08/30

ST.LOUIS	AB	R	H	HR	RBI	BB	AVG
Douthit cf	4	0	0	0	0	0	.083
Adams 3b	2	0	0	0	0	0	.143
c-High ph-3b	2	1	1	0	0	0	.500
Watkins rf	3	0	0	0	0	1	.167
Frisch 2b	4	0	1	0	0	0	.208
Hafey lf	4	0	2	0	1	0	.273
Bottomley 1b	2	0	0	0	0	2	.045
Wilson c	4	0	0	0	0	0	.267
Gelbert ss	3	0	0	0	0	0	.353
Hallahan p	0	0	0	0	0	0	.000
a-Fisher ph	1	0	1	0	0	0	.500
Johnson p	0	0	0	0	0	0	.000
b-Blades ph	1	0	0	0	0	0	.111
Lindsey p	0	0	0	0	0	0	1.000
d-Orsatti ph	1	0	0	0	0	0	.000
Bell p	0	0	0	0	0	0	.000
TOTALS	**31**	**1**	**5**	**0**	**1**	**3**	**.200**

a - Batted for Hallahan in the 3th
b - Batted for Johnson in the 6th
c - Batted for Adams in the 6th
d - Batted for Lindsey in the 8th

BATTING: 2B: Fisher (1, Earnshaw), Hafey 2 (5, Earnshaw). **RBI:** Hafey 1 (2). **2-out RBI:** Hafey 1. **Runners left in scoring position, 2 out:** Douthit 1, Wilson 2. **Team LOB:** 6 **FIELDING: E:** Watkins (1). **PB:** Wilson.

PHILADELPHIA	AB	R	H	HR	RBI	BB	AVG
Bishop 2b	2	2	0	0	0	2	.222
Dykes 3b	2	2	2	1	2	2	.222
Cochrane c	3	1	1	0	2	0	.222
Simmons cf-lf	4	1	1	1	1	0	.364
Foxx 1b	3	1	1	0	0	1	.333
Miller rf	3	0	2	0	1	0	.143
Moore lf	2	0	0	0	0	0	.333
Haas cf	1	0	0	0	1	0	.111
Boley ss	4	0	0	0	0	0	.095
Earnshaw p	4	0	0	0	0	0	.000
TOTALS	**28**	**7**	**7**	**2**	**7**	**5**	**.197**

BATTING: 2B: Cochrane (1, Hallahan), Miller 2 (2, Hallahan, Johnson), Foxx (2, Johnson), Dykes (3, Lindsey). **HR:** Simmons (2, 3th off Johnson 0 on, 0 out), Dykes (1, 4th off Johnson 1 on, 1 out). **S:** Miller. **SF:** Haas, Cochrane. **RBI:** Dykes 2 (5), Cochrane 2 (4), Simmons 1 (4), Miller 1 (3), Haas 1 (1). **2-out RBI:** Miller 1. **Runners left in scoring position, 2 out:** Cochrane 1, Simmons 1, Moore 2, Boley 1. **Team LOB:** 6 **FIELDING: DP:** 1 (Foxx).

ST.LOUIS	IP	H	R	ER	BB	SO	HR	ERA
Hallahan (L, 1-1)	2	2	2	2	3	2	0	1.64
Johnson	3	4	4	4	1	2	2	7.20
Lindsey	2	1	1	1	1	0	0	1.93
Bell	1	0	0	0	0	0	0	0.00

PHILADELPHIA	IP	H	R	ER	BB	SO	HR	ERA
Earnshaw (W, 2-0)	9	5	1	1	3	6	0	0.72

HBP: Bishop (by Hallahan). **Ground balls-fly balls:** Hallahan 1-3, Johnson 2-3, Lindsey 1-4, Bell 2-1, Earnshaw 9-11. **Batters faced:** Hallahan 12, Johnson 14, Lindsey 8, Bell 3, Earnshaw 34. **UMPIRES:** hp—Rigler, 1b—Geisel, 2b—Reardon, 3b—Moriarty **T:** 1:46 **A:** 32,295

1931 ST.LOUIS CARDINALS DEF. PHILADELPHIA A's, 4-3

GAME 1 Philadelphia 6 St. Louis 2
Sportsman's Park 10/01/31

PHILADELPHIA	AB	R	H	HR	RBI	BB	AVG
Bishop 2b	5	1	1	0	0	0	.200
Haas cf	5	1	1	0	1	0	.200
Cochrane c	4	2	2	0	0	1	.500
Simmons lf	4	1	1	1	3	1	.250
Foxx 1b	4	0	2	0	2	0	.500
Miller rf	4	0	0	0	0	0	.000
Dykes 3b	3	0	2	0	0	1	.667
Williams ss	4	1	2	0	0	0	.500
Grove p	4	0	0	0	0	0	.000
TOTALS	**37**	**6**	**11**	**1**	**6**	**3**	**.297**

BATTING: 2B: Haas (1, Derringer). **HR:** Simmons (1, 7th off Derringer 1 on, 1 out). **RBI:** Haas 1 (1), Simmons 3 (3), Foxx 2 (2). **2-out RBI:** Haas 1, Simmons 1, Foxx 2. **Runners left in scoring position, 2 out:** Haas 1, Miller 1. **Team LOB:** 7 **FIELDING: DP:** 1 (Bishop-Williams-Foxx).

ST.LOUIS	AB	R	H	HR	RBI	BB	AVG
High 3b	4	0	1	0	0	0	.250
c-Mancuso ph	1	0	0	0	0	0	.000
Roettger rf	5	1	2	0	0	0	.400
Frisch 2b	4	1	2	0	0	0	.500
Bottomley 1b	4	0	1	0	1	0	.250
Hafey lf	4	0	1	0	0	0	.250
Martin cf	4	0	3	0	1	0	.750
Wilson c	4	0	0	0	0	0	.000
Gelbert ss	4	0	2	0	0	0	.500
Derringer p	2	0	0	0	0	0	.000
a-Flowers ph	1	0	0	0	0	0	.000
Johnson p	0	0	0	0	0	0	.000
b-Blades ph	1	0	0	0	0	0	.000
TOTALS	**38**	**2**	**12**	**0**	**2**	**0**	**.316**

a - Batted for Derringer in the 7th
b - Batted for Johnson in the 9th
c - Batted for High in the 9th

BATTING: 2B: Martin (1, Grove), Gelbert (1, Grove). **RBI:** Bottomley 1 (1), Martin 1 (1). **2-out RBI:** Martin 1. **Runners left in scoring position, 2 out:** Roettger 1, Bottomley 1, Wilson 2, Gelbert 2. **GIDP:** Wilson. **Team LOB:** 9 **BASERUNNING: SB:** Hafey (1, 3rd base off Grove/Cochrane), Martin (1, 3rd base off Grove/Cochrane). **FIELDING: DP:** 1 (Bottomley).

PHILADELPHIA	IP	H	R	ER	BB	SO	HR	ERA
Grove (W, 1-0)	9	12	2	2	0	7	0	2.00

ST.LOUIS	IP	H	R	ER	BB	SO	HR	ERA
Derringer (L, 0-1)	7	11	6	6	3	9	1	7.71
Johnson	2	0	0	0	0	2	0	0.00

Ground balls-fly balls: Grove 8-11, Derringer 7-4, Johnson 0-4. **Batters faced:** Grove 38, Derringer 34, Johnson 6. **UMPIRES:** hp—Klem, 1b—Nallin, 2b—Stark, 3b—McGowan **T:** 1:55 **A:** 38,529

GAME 2 St. Louis 2 Philadelphia 0
Sportsman's Park 10/02/31

PHILADELPHIA	AB	R	H	HR	RBI	BB	AVG
Bishop 2b	5	0	0	0	0	0	.100
Haas cf	4	0	1	0	0	0	.222
Cochrane c	2	0	0	0	0	2	.333
Simmons lf	4	0	0	0	0	0	.125
Foxx 1b	2	0	1	0	0	2	.500
Miller rf	4	0	1	0	0	0	.125
Dykes 3b	2	0	0	0	0	1	.400
Williams ss	2	0	0	0	0	2	.333
Earnshaw p	3	0	0	0	0	0	.000
a-Moore ph	1	0	0	0	0	0	.000
TOTALS	**29**	**0**	**3**	**0**	**0**	**7**	**.212**

a - Batted for Earnshaw in the 9th

BATTING: S: Dykes. **Runners left in scoring position, 2 out:** Bishop 2, Earnshaw 1. **GIDP:** Earnshaw. **Team LOB:** 10

Flowers 3b	4	0	0	0	0	0	.000
Watkins rf	4	0	2	0	0	0	.500
Frisch 2b	4	0	1	0	0	0	.375
Bottomley 1b	3	0	0	0	0	1	.143
Hafey lf	4	0	0	0	0	0	.125
Martin cf	3	2	2	0	0	0	.714
Wilson c	3	0	0	0	1	0	.000
Gelbert ss	2	0	1	0	1	0	.500
Hallahan p	2	0	0	0	0	0	.000
TOTALS	**29**	**2**	**6**	**0**	**2**	**1**	**.269**

BATTING: 2B: Watkins (1, Earnshaw), Martin (2, Earnshaw), Frisch (1, Earnshaw). **S:** Gelbert, Hallahan. **RBI:** Wilson 1 (1), Gelbert 1 (1). **Runners left in scoring position, 2 out:** Flowers 1, Bottomley 1, Hafey 1. **Team LOB:** 6 **BASERUNNING: SB:** Martin 2 (3, 3rd base off Earnshaw/Cochrane, 2nd base off Earnshaw/Cochrane). **FIELDING: E:** Wilson (1). **DP:** 1 (Frisch-Gelbert-Bottomley).

PHILADELPHIA	IP	H	R	ER	BB	SO	HR	ERA
Earnshaw (L, 0-1)	8	6	2	2	1	5	0	2.25

ST.LOUIS	IP	H	R	ER	BB	SO	HR	ERA
Hallahan (W, 1-0)	9	3	0	0	7	8	0	0.00

WP: Hallahan 1. **IBB:** Williams (by Hallahan). **Ground balls-fly balls:** Earnshaw 10-8, Hallahan 7-11. **Batters faced:** Earnshaw 32, Hallahan 37. **UMPIRES:** hp—Nallin, 1b—Stark, 2b—McGowan, 3b—Klem **T:** 1:49 **A:** 35,947

GAME 3 St. Louis 5 Philadelphia 2
Shibe Park 10/05/31

ST.LOUIS	AB	R	H	HR	RBI	BB	AVG
Adams 3b	3	0	0	0	0	0	.000
Flowers 3b	1	0	0	0	0	1	.000
Roettger rf	5	0	1	0	0	0	.300
a-Watkins pr-rf	0	1	0	0	0	0	.500
Frisch 2b	5	0	1	0	0	0	.308
Bottomley 1b	4	1	1	0	1	1	.182
Hafey lf	5	1	1	0	0	0	.154
Martin cf	4	2	2	0	0	0	.636
Wilson c	4	0	3	0	1	0	.273
Gelbert ss	4	0	1	0	1	0	.400
Grimes p	4	0	2	0	2	0	.500
TOTALS	**39**	**5**	**12**	**0**	**5**	**2**	**.283**

a - Ran for Roettger in the 9th

BATTING: 2B: Martin (3, Grove), Roettger (1, Grove), Bottomley (1, Mahaffey). **RBI:** Bottomley 1 (2), Wilson 1 (2), Gelbert 1 (2), Grimes 2 (2). **2-out RBI:** Bottomley 1, Grimes 2. **Runners left in scoring position, 2 out:** Adams 1, Bottomley 1, Hafey 1, Grimes 1. **Team LOB:** 9 **FIELDING: DP:** 1 (Gelbert-Frisch-Bottomley).

PHILADELPHIA	AB	R	H	HR	RBI	BB	AVG
Bishop 2b	3	0	0	0	0	1	.077
Haas cf	4	0	0	0	0	0	.154
Cochrane c	3	0	0	0	0	1	.222
b-McNair pr	0	1	0	0	0	0	.000
Simmons lf	4	1	1	1	2	0	.167
Foxx 1b	2	0	0	0	0	2	.375
Miller rf	3	0	1	0	0	0	.182
Dykes 3b	3	0	0	0	0	0	.250
Williams ss	3	0	0	0	0	0	.222
Grove p	2	0	0	0	0	0	.000
a-Cramer ph	1	0	0	0	0	0	.000
Mahaffey p	0	0	0	0	0	0	.000
TOTALS	**28**	**2**	**2**	**1**	**2**	**4**	**.170**

a - Batted for Grove in the 8th
b - Ran for Cochrane in the 9th

BATTING: HR: Simmons (2, 9th off Grimes 1 on, 2 out). **RBI:** Simmons 2 (5). **2-out RBI:** Simmons 2. **Runners left in scoring position, 2 out:** Cramer 1. **GIDP:** Dykes. **Team LOB:** 3

ST.LOUIS	IP	H	R	ER	BB	SO	HR	ERA
Grimes (W, 1-0)	9	2	2	2	4	5	1	2.00

PHILADELPHIA	IP	H	R	ER	BB	SO	HR	ERA
Grove (L, 1-1)	8	11	4	4	1	2	0	3.18
Mahaffey	1	1	1	1	1	0	0	9.00

Ground balls-fly balls: Grimes 12-9, Grove 13-9, Mahaffey 2-1. **Batters faced:** Grimes 32, Grove 36, Mahaffey 5. **UMPIRES:** hp—Stark, 1b—McGowan, 2b—Klem, 3b—Nallin **T:** 2:10 **A:** 32,295

GAME 4 Philadelphia 3 St. Louis 0
Shibe Park 10/06/31

ST.LOUIS	AB	R	H	HR	RBI	BB	AVG
Flowers 3b	1	0	0	0	0	0	.000
High 3b	3	0	0	0	0	0	.143
Watkins rf	4	0	0	0	0	0	.250
Frisch 2b	3	0	0	0	0	1	.250
Bottomley 1b	3	0	0	0	0	0	.143
Hafey lf	3	0	0	0	0	0	.125
Martin cf	3	0	2	0	0	0	.643
Wilson c	3	0	0	0	0	0	.214
Gelbert ss	3	0	0	0	0	0	.308
Johnson p	2	0	0	0	0	0	.000
Lindsey p	0	0	0	0	0	0	.000
a-Collins ph	1	0	0	0	0	0	.000
Derringer p	0	0	0	0	0	0	.000
TOTALS	**29**	**0**	**2**	**0**	**0**	**1**	**.237**

a - Batted for Lindsey in the 8th

BATTING: 2B: Martin (4, Earnshaw). **Runners left in scoring position, 2 out:** Bottomley 1, Gelbert 1, Collins 1. **Team LOB:** 3 **BASERUNNING: SB:** Frisch (1, 2nd base off Earnshaw/Cochrane), Martin (4, 2nd base off Earnshaw/Cochrane). **FIELDING: DP:** 1 (Frisch-Gelbert-Bottomley).

PHILADELPHIA	AB	R	H	HR	RBI	BB	AVG
Bishop 2b	4	1	2	0	0	0	.176
Haas cf	3	0	1	0	0	0	.188
Cochrane c	3	0	0	0	0	1	.167
Simmons lf	4	0	2	0	1	0	.250
Foxx 1b	3	1	1	1	1	1	.364
Miller rf	4	1	1	0	0	0	.200
Dykes 3b	4	0	2	0	1	0	.333
Williams ss	4	0	1	0	0	0	.231
Earnshaw p	3	0	0	0	0	0	.000
TOTALS	**32**	**3**	**10**	**1**	**3**	**2**	**.206**

BATTING: 2B: Simmons (1, Johnson), Miller (1, Johnson). **HR:** Foxx (1, 6th off Johnson 0 on, 2 out). **S:** Haas. **RBI:** Simmons 1 (6), Foxx 1 (3), Dykes 1 (1). **2-out RBI:** Simmons 1, Foxx 1, Dykes 1. **Runners left in scoring position, 2 out:** Bishop 1, Foxx 2, Miller 1, Earnshaw 1. **GIDP:** Simmons. **Team LOB:** 8

ST.LOUIS	IP	H	R	ER	BB	SO	HR	ERA
Johnson (L, 0-1)	5.2	9	3	3	1	2	1	3.52
Lindsey	1.1	1	0	0	1	2	0	0.00
Derringer	1	0	0	0	0	1	0	6.75

PHILADELPHIA	IP	H	R	ER	BB	SO	HR	ERA
Earnshaw (W, 1-1)	9	2	0	0	1	8	0	1.06

Ground balls-fly balls: Johnson 7-6, Lindsey 0-2, Derringer 1-1, Earnshaw 6-13. **Batters faced:** Johnson 26, Lindsey 6, Derringer 3, Earnshaw 30. **UMPIRES:** hp—McGowan, 1b—Klem, 2b—Nallin, 3b—Stark **T:** 1:58 **A:** 32,295

GAME 5 St. Louis 5 Philadelphia 1
Shibe Park 10/07/31

ST.LOUIS	AB	R	H	HR	RBI	BB	AVG
Adams 3b	1	0	1	0	0	0	.250
a-High pr-3b	4	1	0	0	0	0	.091
Watkins rf	3	1	0	0	0	1	.182
Frisch 2b	4	1	2	0	0	0	.300
Martin cf	4	1	3	1	4	0	.667
Hafey lf	4	0	1	0	0	0	.150
Bottomley 1b	4	1	2	0	0	0	.222
Wilson c	4	0	2	0	0	0	.278
Gelbert ss	4	0	1	0	1	0	.294
Hallahan p	4	0	0	0	0	0	.000
TOTALS	**36**	**5**	**12**	**1**	**5**	**1**	**.257**

a - Ran for Adams in the 1st

BATTING: 2B: Frisch (2, Hoyt). **HR:** Martin (1, 6th off Hoyt 1 on, 1 out). **RBI:** Martin 4 (5), Gelbert 1 (3). **2-out RBI:** Martin 1. **Runners left in scoring position, 2 out:** High 1, Hafey 1. **Team LOB:** 5 **BASERUNNING: SB:** Watkins (1, 2nd base off Walberg/Cochrane). **CS:** Wilson (1, 2nd base off Walberg/Cochrane), Martin (1, 2nd base off Walberg/Cochrane). **FIELDING: DP:** 1 (Gelbert-Bottomley-Wilson).

PHILADELPHIA	AB	R	H	HR	RBI	BB	AVG
Bishop 2b	2	0	0	0	0	0	.158
a-McNair ph-2b	2	0	0	0	0	0	.000
Haas cf	2	0	0	0	0	0	.167
b-Moore ph-lf	2	0	1	0	0	0	.333
Cochrane c	4	0	1	0	0	0	.188
Simmons lf-cf	4	1	3	0	0	0	.350
Foxx 1b	3	0	2	0	0	1	.429
Miller rf	4	0	0	0	1	0	.158
Dykes 3b	4	0	1	0	0	0	.313
Williams ss	4	0	1	0	0	0	.235
Hoyt p	2	0	0	0	0	0	.000
Walberg p	0	0	0	0	0	0	.000
c-Heving ph	1	0	0	0	0	0	.000
Rommel p	0	0	0	0	0	0	.000
d-Boley ph	1	0	0	0	0	0	.000
TOTALS	**35**	**1**	**9**	**0**	**1**	**1**	**.217**

a - Batted for Bishop in the 6th
b - Batted for Haas in the 6th
c - Batted for Walberg in the 8th
d - Batted for Rommel in the 9th

BATTING: 2B: Simmons (2, Hallahan). **RBI:** Miller 1 (1). **Runners left in scoring position, 2 out:** Simmons 1, Williams 2, Boley 1. **Team LOB:** 8 **FIELDING: DP:** 1 (Bishop-Foxx).

ST.LOUIS	IP	H	R	ER	BB	SO	HR	ERA
Hallahan (W, 2-0)	9	9	1	1	1	4	0	0.50
PHILADELPHIA	**IP**	**H**	**R**	**ER**	**BB**	**SO**	**HR**	**ERA**
Hoyt (L, 0-1)	6	7	3	3	0	1	1	4.50
Walberg	2	2	1	1	1	2	0	4.50
Rommel	1	3	1	1	0	0	0	9.00

Ground balls-fly balls: Hallahan 8-14, Hoyt 6-10, Walberg 1-1, Rommel 2-1. **Batters faced:** Hallahan 36, Hoyt 24, Walberg 7, Rommel 6. **UMPIRES:** hp—Klem, 1b—Nallin, 2b—Stark, 3b—McGowan **T:** 1:56 **A:** 32,295

GAME 6 Philadelphia 8 St. Louis 1
Sportsman's Park 10/09/31

PHILADELPHIA	AB	R	H	HR	RBI	BB	AVG
Bishop 2b	4	2	1	0	0	1	.174
Haas cf	2	0	0	0	1	2	.150
Cochrane c	5	0	1	0	1	0	.190
Simmons lf	4	1	1	0	2	1	.333
Foxx 1b	5	2	2	0	0	0	.421
Miller rf	3	1	1	0	0	0	.182
Dykes 3b	3	1	0	0	1	2	.263
Williams ss	4	1	2	0	1	0	.286
Grove p	4	0	0	0	0	0	.000
TOTALS	**34**	**8**	**8**	**0**	**6**	**6**	**.221**

BATTING: 2B: Williams (1, Johnson). **S:** Miller, Haas. **RBI:** Haas 1 (2), Cochrane 1 (1), Simmons 2 (8), Dykes 1 (2), Williams 1 (1). **2-out RBI:** Haas 1, Cochrane 1, Simmons 2, Dykes 1. **Runners left in scoring position, 2 out:** Foxx 2, Dykes 1, Grove 2. **GIDP:** Cochrane. **Team LOB:** 8 **FIELDING: E:** Cochrane (1). **DP:** 1 (Bishop-Williams-Foxx).

ST.LOUIS	AB	R	H	HR	RBI	BB	AVG
Flowers 3b	4	1	1	0	0	0	.091
Roettger rf	4	0	1	0	0	0	.286
Frisch 2b	4	0	1	0	1	0	.292
Martin cf	3	0	0	0	0	1	.571
Hafey lf	4	0	1	0	0	0	.167
Bottomley 1b	4	0	0	0	0	0	.182
Wilson c	3	0	0	0	0	0	.238
Mancuso c	0	0	0	0	0	0	.000
Gelbert ss	3	0	1	0	0	0	.300
Derringer p	0	0	0	0	0	0	.000
Johnson p	0	0	0	0	0	0	.000
a-Blades ph	1	0	0	0	0	0	.000
Lindsey p	0	0	0	0	0	0	.000
b-Collins ph	1	0	0	0	0	0	.000
Rhem p	0	0	0	0	0	0	.000
TOTALS	**31**	**1**	**5**	**0**	**1**	**1**	**.243**

a - Batted for Johnson in the 6th
b - Batted for Lindsey in the 8th

BATTING: 2B: Flowers (1, Grove). **S:** Derringer. **RBI:** Frisch 1 (1). **2-out RBI:** Frisch 1. **Runners left in scoring position, 2 out:** Flowers 1, Bottomley 1. **GIDP:** Frisch. **Team LOB:** 5 **FIELDING: E:** Flowers (1), Hafey (1). **DP:** 1 (Frisch-Gelbert-Bottomley).

PHILADELPHIA	IP	H	R	ER	BB	SO	HR	ERA
Grove (W, 2-1)	9	5	1	1	1	7	0	2.42
ST.LOUIS	**IP**	**H**	**R**	**ER**	**BB**	**SO**	**HR**	**ERA**
Derringer (L, 0-2)	4.2	3	4	0	4	4	0	4.26
Johnson	1.1	1	0	0	0	2	0	3.00
Lindsey	2	3	4	2	2	0	0	5.40
Rhem	1	1	0	0	0	1	0	0.00

WP: Derringer 1. **HBP:** Miller (by Lindsey). **Ground balls-fly balls:** Grove 5-14, Derringer 7-3, Johnson 0-2, Lindsey 3-2, Rhem 0-2. **Batters faced:** Grove 33, Derringer 22, Johnson 5, Lindsey 12, Rhem 4. **UMPIRES:** hp—Nallin, 1b—Stark, 2b—McGowan, 3b—Klem **T:** 1:57 **A:** 39,401

GAME 7 St. Louis 4 Philadelphia 2
Sportsman's Park 10/10/31

PHILADELPHIA	AB	R	H	HR	RBI	BB	AVG
Bishop 2b	4	0	0	0	0	1	.148
Haas cf	3	0	0	0	0	1	.130
Cochrane c	4	0	0	0	0	0	.160
Simmons lf	3	0	1	0	0	1	.333
Foxx 1b	4	0	0	0	0	0	.348
Miller rf	4	1	3	0	0	0	.269
Dykes 3b	3	1	0	0	0	1	.227
Williams ss	4	0	2	0	0	0	.320
Earnshaw p	2	0	0	0	0	0	.000
a-Todt ph	0	0	0	0	0	1	.000
Walberg p	0	0	0	0	0	0	.000
b-Cramer ph	1	0	1	0	2	0	.500
TOTALS	**32**	**2**	**7**	**0**	**2**	**5**	**.220**

a - Batted for Earnshaw in the 8th
b - Batted for Walberg in the 9th

BATTING: RBI: Cramer 2 (2). **2-out RBI:** Cramer 2. **Runners left in scoring position, 2 out:** Bishop 1, Cochrane 1, Williams 1. **GIDP:** Earnshaw. **Team LOB:** 8 **FIELDING: DP:** 1 (Dykes-Bishop-Foxx).

ST.LOUIS	AB	R	H	HR	RBI	BB	AVG
High 3b	4	2	3	0	0	0	.267
Watkins rf	3	2	2	1	2	1	.286
Frisch 2b	3	0	0	0	0	0	.259
Martin cf	3	0	0	0	0	1	.500
Orsatti lf	3	0	0	0	0	0	.000
Bottomley 1b	3	0	0	0	0	0	.160
Wilson c	2	0	0	0	0	1	.217
Gelbert ss	3	0	0	0	0	0	.261
Grimes p	3	0	0	0	0	0	.286
Hallahan p	0	0	0	0	0	0	.000
TOTALS	**27**	**4**	**5**	**1**	**2**	**3**	**.236**

BATTING: HR: Watkins (1, 3th off Earnshaw 1 on, 0 out). **S:** Frisch. **RBI:** Watkins 2 (2). **Runners left in scoring position, 2 out:** Martin 1, Bottomley 1. **GIDP:** Gelbert. **Team LOB:** 3 **BASERUNNING: SB:** Martin (5, 2nd base off Earnshaw/Cochrane). **FIELDING: DP:** 1 (Frisch-Gelbert-Bottomley).

PHILADELPHIA	IP	H	R	ER	BB	SO	HR	ERA
Earnshaw (L, 1-2)	7	4	4	3	2	7	1	1.88
Walberg	1	1	0	0	1	2	0	3.00
ST.LOUIS	**IP**	**H**	**R**	**ER**	**BB**	**SO**	**HR**	**ERA**
Grimes (W, 2-0)	8.2	7	2	2	5	6	0	2.04
Hallahan (S, 1)	0.1	0	0	0	0	0	0	0.49

WP: Earnshaw 1. **Ground balls-fly balls:** Earnshaw 7-5, Walberg 0-1, Grimes 13-5, Hallahan 0-1. **Batters faced:** Earnshaw 26, Walberg 5, Grimes 36, Hallahan 1. **UMPIRES:** hp—Stark, 1b—McGowan, 2b—Klem, 3b—Nallin **T:** 1:57 **A:** 20,805

1932 NY YANKEES DEF. CHICAGO CUBS, 4-0

GAME 1 New York 12 Chicago 6
Yankee Stadium 09/28/32

CHICAGO CUBS	AB	R	H	HR	RBI	BB	AVG
Herman 2b	5	2	2	0	1	0	.400
English 3b	4	1	1	0	1	1	.250
Cuyler rf	5	1	1	0	0	0	.200
Stephenson lf	5	0	3	0	3	0	.600
J.Moore cf	4	0	0	0	0	1	.000
Grimm 1b	3	0	0	0	0	2	.000
Hartnett c	5	1	2	0	0	0	.400
Koenig ss	4	1	1	0	1	1	.250
Bush p	1	0	0	0	0	1	.000
Grimes p	1	0	0	0	0	0	.000
a-Gudat ph	1	0	0	0	0	0	.000
Smith p	0	0	0	0	0	0	.000
TOTALS	**38**	**6**	**10**	**0**	**6**	**6**	**.263**

a - Batted for Grimes in the 8th

BATTING: 2B: Hartnett 2 (2, Ruffing). **3B:** Koenig (1, Ruffing). **RBI:** Herman 1 (1), English 1 (1), Stephenson 3 (3), Koenig 1 (1). **2-out RBI:** Stephenson 2. **Runners left in scoring position, 2 out:** Herman 2, Stephenson 1, Grimm 1, Koenig 1. **Team LOB:** 11 **BASERUNNING: SB:** Cuyler (1, 2nd base off Ruffing/Dickey). **FIELDING: E:** English (1). **DP:** 1 (Herman-Koenig-Grimm).

NY YANKEES	AB	R	H	HR	RBI	BB	AVG
Combs cf	4	2	2	0	2	1	.500
Sewell 3b	4	1	1	0	1	1	.250
Ruth rf	3	3	1	0	1	2	.333
Gehrig 1b	4	3	2	1	2	1	.500
Lazzeri 2b	4	1	1	0	1	0	.250
Dickey c	3	0	1	0	2	0	.333
Chapman lf	4	1	0	0	2	0	.000
Crosetti ss	2	1	0	0	0	1	.000
Ruffing p	4	0	0	0	0	0	.000
TOTALS	**32**	**12**	**8**	**1**	**11**	**6**	**.250**

BATTING: 2B: Combs (1, Smith). **HR:** Gehrig (1, 4th off Bush 1 on, 1 out). **S:** Crosetti. **RBI:** Combs 2 (2), Sewell 1 (1), Ruth 1 (1), Gehrig 2 (2), Lazzeri 1 (1), Dickey 2 (2), Chapman 2 (2). **2-out RBI:** Combs 2. **Runners left in scoring position, 2 out:** Sewell 1. **GIDP:** Combs. **Team LOB:** 4 **FIELDING: E:** Ruth (1), Crosetti (1).

CHICAGO CUBS	IP	H	R	ER	BB	SO	HR	ERA
Bush (L, 0-1)	5.1	3	8	8	5	2	1	13.50
Grimes	1.2	3	3	3	1	0	0	16.20
Smith	1	2	1	1	0	1	0	9.00
NY YANKEES	**IP**	**H**	**R**	**ER**	**BB**	**SO**	**HR**	**ERA**
Ruffing (W, 1-0)	9	10	6	3	6	10	0	3.00

WP: Grimes 1. **IBB:** Koenig (by Ruffing). **HBP:** Dickey (by Grimes). **Ground balls-fly balls:** Bush 10-5, Grimes 3-1, Smith 0-2, Ruffing 9-9. **Batters faced:** Bush 26, Grimes 9, Smith 5, Ruffing 44. **UMPIRES:** hp—Dinneen, 1b—Klem, 2b—Van Graflan, 3b—Magerkurth **T:** 2:31 **A:** 41,459

GAME 2 New York 5 Chicago 2
Yankee Stadium 09/29/32

CHICAGO CUBS	AB	R	H	HR	RBI	BB	AVG
Herman 2b	4	1	1	0	0	0	.333
English 3b	4	0	1	0	0	0	.250
Cuyler rf	4	0	1	0	0	0	.222
Stephenson lf	4	1	2	0	1	0	.556
Demaree cf	4	0	1	0	1	0	.250
Grimm 1b	4	0	2	0	0	0	.286
Hartnett c	3	0	1	0	0	1	.375
Jurges ss	3	0	0	0	0	0	.000
Warneke p	3	0	0	0	0	0	.000
a-Hemsley ph	1	0	0	0	0	0	.000
TOTALS	**34**	**2**	**9**	**0**	**2**	**1**	**.264**

a - Batted for Warneke in the 9th

BATTING: 2B: Herman (1, Gomez), Stephenson (1, Gomez). **3B:** Cuyler (1, Gomez). **S:** Jurges. **RBI:** Stephenson 1 (4), Demaree 1 (1). **2-out RBI:** Demaree 1. **Runners left in scoring position, 2 out:** Herman 2, Stephenson 1, Grimm 1. **Team LOB:** 7 **FIELDING: DP:** 4 (Warneke-Hartnett-Jurges, Hartnett-Herman, Herman-Jurges-Grimm 2).

NY YANKEES	AB	R	H	HR	RBI	BB	AVG
Combs cf	3	1	1	0	0	1	.429
Sewell 3b	3	1	1	0	0	1	.286
Ruth rf	3	1	1	0	0	1	.333
Gehrig 1b	4	2	3	0	1	0	.625
Lazzeri 2b	4	0	1	0	0	0	.250
Dickey c	3	0	2	0	2	1	.500
Chapman lf	4	0	1	0	2	0	.125
Crosetti ss	3	0	0	0	0	0	.000
Gomez p	3	0	0	0	0	0	.000
TOTALS	**30**	**5**	**10**	**0**	**5**	**4**	**.290**

BATTING: SF: Lazzeri. **RBI:** Gehrig 1 (3), Dickey 2 (4), Chapman 2 (4). **2-out RBI:** Dickey 1, Chapman 2. **Runners left in scoring position, 2 out:** Chapman 1, Crosetti 1. **GIDP:** Gehrig, Dickey. **Team LOB:** 5 **BASERUNNING: CS:** Dickey (1, 2nd base off Warneke/Hartnett). **FIELDING: E:** Crosetti (2). **Outfield assists:** Chapman (1).

CHICAGO CUBS	IP	H	R	ER	BB	SO	HR	ERA
Warneke (L, 0-1)	8	10	5	5	4	7	0	5.63
NY YANKEES	**IP**	**H**	**R**	**ER**	**BB**	**SO**	**HR**	**ERA**
Gomez (W, 1-0)	9	9	2	1	1	8	0	1.00

IBB: Dickey (by Warneke). **Ground balls-fly balls:** Warneke 9-4, Gomez 8-9. **Batters faced:** Warneke 34, Gomez 36. **UMPIRES:** hp—Klem, 1b—Van Graflan, 2b—Magerkurth, 3b—Dinneen **T:** 1:46 **A:** 50,709

GAME 3 New York 7 Chicago 5
Wrigley Field 10/01/32

NY YANKEES	AB	R	H	HR	RBI	BB	AVG
Combs cf	5	1	0	0	0	0	.250
Sewell 3b	2	1	0	0	0	2	.222
Ruth lf	4	2	2	2	4	1	.400
Gehrig 1b	5	2	2	2	2	0	.538
Lazzeri 2b	4	1	0	0	0	1	.167
Dickey c	4	0	1	0	0	1	.400
Chapman rf	4	0	2	0	1	1	.250
Crosetti ss	4	0	1	0	0	1	.111
Pipgras p	5	0	0	0	0	0	.000
Pennock p	0	0	0	0	0	0	.000
TOTALS	**37**	**7**	**8**	**4**	**7**	**7**	**.263**

BATTING: 2B: Chapman (1, May). **HR:** Ruth 2 (2, 1st off Root 2 on, 0 out, 5th off Root 0 on, 1 out), Gehrig 2 (3, 3th off Root 0 on, 0 out, 5th off Root 0 on, 1 out). **RBI:** Ruth 4 (5), Gehrig 2 (5), Chapman 1 (5). **Runners left in scoring position, 2 out:** Crosetti 1, Pipgras 5. **GIDP:** Ruth. **Team LOB:** 11 **BASERUNNING: CS:** Chapman (1, 2nd base off Root/Hartnett). **FIELDING: E:** Lazzeri (1). **DP:** 1 (Sewell-Lazzeri-Gehrig).

CHICAGO CUBS	AB	R	H	HR	RBI	BB	AVG
Herman 2b	4	1	0	0	0	1	.231
English 3b	4	0	0	0	0	1	.167
Cuyler rf	4	1	3	1	2	0	.385
Stephenson lf	4	0	1	0	0	0	.462
J.Moore cf	3	1	0	0	0	1	.000
Grimm 1b	4	0	1	0	1	0	.273
Hartnett c	4	1	1	1	1	0	.333
Jurges ss	4	1	3	0	0	0	.429
Root p	2	0	0	0	0	0	.000
Malone p	0	0	0	0	0	0	.000
a-Gudat ph	1	0	0	0	0	0	.000
May p	0	0	0	0	0	0	.000
Tinning p	0	0	0	0	0	0	.000
b-Koenig ph	0	0	0	0	0	0	.250
c-Hemsley ph	1	0	0	0	0	0	.000
TOTALS	**35**	**5**	**9**	**2**	**4**	**3**	**.262**

a - Batted for Malone in the 7th
b - Batted for Tinning in the 9th
c - Batted for Koenig in the 9th

BATTING: 2B: Cuyler (1, Pipgras), Grimm (1, Pipgras), Jurges (1, Pipgras). **HR:** Cuyler (1, 3th off Pipgras 0 on, 1 out), Hartnett (1, 9th off Pipgras 0 on, 0 out). **RBI:** Cuyler 2 (2), Grimm 1 (1), Hartnett 1 (1). **2-out RBI:** Grimm 1. **Runners left in scoring position, 2 out:** Herman 1, English 1, Grimm 1, Hartnett 1. **GIDP:** Stephenson. **Team LOB:** 6 **BASERUNNING: SB:** Jurges 2 (2, 2nd base off Pipgras/Dickey, 3rd base off Pennock/Dickey). **CS:** English (1, 2nd base off Pipgras/Dickey). **FIELDING: E:** Jurges 2 (2), Hartnett (1), Herman (1). **DP:** 1 (Herman-Jurges-Grimm).

NY YANKEES	IP	H	R	ER	BB	SO	HR	ERA
Pipgras (W, 1-0)	8	9	5	4	3	1	2	4.50
Pennock (S, 1)	1	0	0	0	0	1	0	0.00
CHICAGO CUBS	**IP**	**H**	**R**	**ER**	**BB**	**SO**	**HR**	**ERA**
Root (L, 0-1)	4.1	6	6	5	3	4	4	10.38
Malone	2.2	1	0	0	4	4	0	0.00
May	1.1	1	1	0	0	1	0	0.00
Tinning	0.2	0	0	0	0	1	0	0.00

IBB: Crosetti (by Malone). **HBP:** Sewell (by May). **Ground balls-fly balls:** Pipgras 14-8, Pennock 2-0, Root 5-4, Malone 3-2, May 1-3, Tinning 0-1. **Batters faced:** Pipgras 35, Pennock 3, Root 22, Malone 14, May 7, Tinning 2. **UMPIRES:** hp—Van Graflan, 1b—Magerkurth, 2b—Dinneen, 3b—Klem **T:** 2:11 **A:** 49,986

GAME 4 New York 13 Chicago 6
Wrigley Field 10/02/32

NY YANKEES	AB	R	H	HR	RBI	BB	AVG
Combs cf	4	4	3	1	2	2	.375
Sewell 3b	6	1	3	0	2	0	.333
Ruth lf	5	0	1	0	1	0	.333
Byrd lf	0	0	0	0	0	0	.000
Gehrig 1b	4	2	2	0	3	1	.529
Lazzeri 2b	5	2	3	2	4	1	.294
Dickey c	6	2	3	0	0	0	.438
Chapman rf	5	0	2	0	1	1	.294
Crosetti ss	6	1	1	0	0	0	.133
Allen p	0	0	0	0	0	0	.000
W.Moore p	3	0	1	0	0	0	.333
a-Ruffing ph	0	0	0	0	0	1	.000
b-Hoag pr	0	1	0	0	0	0	.000
Pennock p	1	0	0	0	0	0	.000
TOTALS	**45**	**13**	**19**	**3**	**13**	**6**	**.313**

a - Batted for W.Moore in the 7th
b - Ran for Ruffing in the 7th

BATTING: 2B: Gehrig (1, Warneke), Sewell (1, May), Crosetti (1, May), Chapman (2, Grimes). **HR:** Lazzeri 2 (2, 3th off Warneke 1 on, 2 out, 9th off Grimes 1 on, 2 out), Combs (1, 9th off Grimes 0 on, 0 out). **RBI:** Combs 2 (4), Sewell 2 (3), Ruth 1 (6), Gehrig 3 (8), Lazzeri 4 (5), Chapman 1 (6). **2-out RBI:** Gehrig 2, Lazzeri 4, Chapman 1. **Runners left in scoring position, 2 out:** Gehrig 1, Dickey 2, Chapman 2, Crosetti 2. **GIDP:** Crosetti. **Team LOB:** 13 **FIELDING: E:** Crosetti (3), Gehrig (1), Sewell (1).

CHICAGO CUBS	AB	R	H	HR	RBI	BB	AVG
Herman 2b	5	1	1	0	0	0	.222
English 3b	5	1	1	0	1	0	.176
Cuyler rf	5	0	0	0	0	0	.278
Stephenson lf	5	1	2	0	0	0	.444
Demaree cf	3	1	1	1	3	1	.286
Grimm 1b	4	2	2	0	0	0	.333
Hartnett c	4	0	1	0	0	0	.313
a-Hack pr	0	0	0	0	0	0	.000
Grimes p	0	0	0	0	0	0	.000
Jurges ss	4	0	1	0	1	0	.364
Bush p	0	0	0	0	0	0	.000
Warneke p	1	0	0	0	0	0	.000
May p	2	0	0	0	0	0	.000
Tinning p	0	0	0	0	0	0	.000
b-Hemsley ph-c	1	0	0	0	0	0	.000
TOTALS	**39**	**6**	**9**	**1**	**5**	**1**	**.253**

a - Ran for Hartnett in the 8th
b - Batted for Tinning in the 8th

BATTING: 2B: Grimm (2, W.Moore). **HR:** Demaree (1, 1st off Allen 2 on, 2 out). **RBI:** English 1 (2), Demaree 3 (4), Jurges 1 (1). **2-out RBI:** Demaree 3, Jurges 1. **Runners left in scoring position, 2 out:** Hartnett 1, Warneke 1, May 1, Hemsley 2. **Team LOB:** 7 **FIELDING: E:** Demaree (1). **DP:** 1 (Herman-Jurges-Grimm).

NY YANKEES	IP	H	R	ER	BB	SO	HR	ERA
Allen	0.2	5	4	3	0	0	1	40.50
W.Moore (W, 1-0)	5.1	2	1	0	0	1	0	0.00
Pennock (S, 2)	3	2	1	1	1	3	0	2.25
CHICAGO CUBS	**IP**	**H**	**R**	**ER**	**BB**	**SO**	**HR**	**ERA**
Bush	0.1	2	1	1	1	0	0	14.29
Warneke	2.2	5	2	2	1	1	1	5.91
May (L, 0-1)	3.1	8	6	6	3	3	0	11.57
Tinning	1.2	0	0	0	0	2	0	0.00
Grimes	1	4	4	4	1	0	2	23.63

IBB: Ruffing (by May). **HBP:** Ruth (by Bush), Gehrig (by May). **Ground balls-fly balls:** Allen 1-2, W.Moore 10-6, Pennock 4-3, Bush 0-1, Warneke 4-3, May 2-4, Tinning 1-2, Grimes 2-1. **Batters faced:** Allen 8, W.Moore 19, Pennock 13, Bush 5, Warneke 14, May 21, Tinning 5, Grimes 8. **UMPIRES:** hp—Magerkurth, 1b—Dinneen, 2b—Klem, 3b—Van Graflan **T:** 2:27 **A:** 49,844

1933 NY GIANTS DEF. WASHINGTON, 4-1

GAME 1 New York 4 Washington 2
Polo Grounds 10/03/33

WASHINGTON	AB	R	H	HR	RBI	BB	AVG
Myer 2b	4	1	1	0	0	0	.250
Goslin rf	4	0	0	0	0	0	.000
Manush lf	4	1	0	0	0	0	.000
Cronin ss	4	0	2	0	1	0	.500
Schulte cf	4	0	2	0	0	0	.500
Kuhel 1b	4	0	0	0	1	0	.000
Bluege 3b	4	0	0	0	0	0	.000
Sewell c	3	0	0	0	0	1	.000
Stewart p	1	0	0	0	0	0	.000
Russell p	1	0	0	0	0	0	.000
a-Harris ph	0	0	0	0	0	1	.000
Thomas p	0	0	0	0	0	0	.000
TOTALS	**33**	**2**	**5**	**0**	**2**	**2**	**.152**

a - Batted for Russell in the 8th

BATTING: RBI: Cronin 1 (1), Kuhel 1 (1). **Runners left in scoring position, 2 out:** Goslin 1, Kuhel 1, Sewell 2. **Team LOB:** 6 **BASERUNNING: CS:** Schulte (1, 2nd base off Hubbell/Mancuso). **FIELDING: E:** Myer 2 (2).

NY GIANTS	AB	R	H	HR	RBI	BB	AVG
Moore lf	4	1	0	0	0	0	.000
Critz 2b	4	1	1	0	0	0	.250
Terry 1b	4	1	1	0	0	0	.250
Ott rf	4	1	4	1	3	0	1.000
Davis cf	4	0	2	0	0	0	.500
Jackson 3b	4	0	0	0	1	0	.000
Mancuso c	4	0	0	0	0	0	.000
Ryan ss	4	0	1	0	0	0	.250
Hubbell p	3	0	1	0	0	0	.333
TOTALS	**35**	**4**	**10**	**1**	**4**	**0**	**.286**

BATTING: HR: Ott (1, 1st off Stewart 1 on, 2 out). **RBI:** Ott 3 (3), Jackson 1 (1). **2-out RBI:** Ott 2. **Runners left in scoring position, 2 out:** Moore 1, Davis 1, Jackson 1, Mancuso 1. **Team LOB:** 7 **BASERUNNING: CS:** Ott (1, 2nd base off Russell/Sewell). **FIELDING: E:** Critz (1), Ryan (1). **DP:** 1 (Mancuso-Ryan).

WASHINGTON	IP	H	R	ER	BB	SO	HR	ERA
Stewart (L, 0-1)	2	6	4	2	0	0	1	9.00
Russell	5	4	0	0	0	3	0	0.00
Thomas	1	0	0	0	0	2	0	0.00
NY GIANTS	**IP**	**H**	**R**	**ER**	**BB**	**SO**	**HR**	**ERA**
Hubbell (W, 1-0)	9	5	2	0	2	10	0	0.00

Ground balls-fly balls: Stewart 2-5, Russell 7-5, Thomas 0-1, Hubbell 13-5. **Batters faced:** Stewart 13, Russell 19, Thomas 3, Hubbell 35. **UMPIRES:** hp—Moran, 1b—Moriarty, 2b—Pfirman, 3b—Ormsby **T:** 2:07 **A:** 46,672

GAME 2 New York 6 Washington 1
Polo Grounds 10/04/33

WASHINGTON	AB	R	H	HR	RBI	BB	AVG
Myer 2b	3	0	0	0	0	1	.143
Goslin rf	4	1	2	1	1	0	.250
Manush lf	3	0	1	0	0	1	.143
Cronin ss	4	0	0	0	0	0	.250
Schulte cf	4	0	0	0	0	0	.250
Kuhel 1b	3	0	0	0	0	1	.000
Bluege 3b	2	0	0	0	0	1	.000
b-Harris ph	1	0	0	0	0	0	.000
Sewell c	3	0	0	0	0	0	.000
c-Bolton ph	1	0	0	0	0	0	.000
Crowder p	2	0	1	0	0	0	.500
Thomas p	0	0	0	0	0	0	.000
a-Rice ph	1	0	1	0	0	0	1.000
McColl p	0	0	0	0	0	0	.000
TOTALS	**31**	**1**	**5**	**1**	**1**	**4**	**.156**

a - Batted for Thomas in the 7th
b - Batted for Bluege in the 9th
c - Batted for Sewell in the 9th

BATTING: HR: Goslin (1, 3th off Schumacher 0 on, 2 out). **RBI:** Goslin 1 (1). **2-out RBI:** Goslin 1. **Runners left in scoring position, 2 out:** Cronin 1, Bluege 2. **GIDP:** Cronin. **Team LOB:** 7 **FIELDING: DP:** 1 (Cronin-Myer-Kuhel).

NY GIANTS	AB	R	H	HR	RBI	BB	AVG
Moore lf	4	0	2	0	1	0	.250
Critz 2b	3	1	1	0	0	1	.286
Terry 1b	4	1	1	0	0	0	.250
Ott rf	2	1	0	0	0	2	.667
Davis cf	2	0	1	0	0	0	.500
a-O'Doul ph	1	1	1	0	2	0	1.000
Peel cf	1	0	0	0	0	0	.000
Jackson 3b	3	1	1	0	1	0	.143
Mancuso c	4	1	1	0	1	0	.125
Ryan ss	4	0	1	0	0	0	.250
Schumacher p	4	0	1	0	1	0	.250
TOTALS	**32**	**6**	**10**	**0**	**6**	**3**	**.299**

a - Batted for Davis in the 6th

BATTING: 2B: Terry (1, Crowder). **S:** Jackson. **RBI:** Moore 1 (1), O'Doul 2 (2), Jackson 1 (2), Mancuso 1 (1), Schumacher 1 (1). **2-out RBI:** Moore 1, Schumacher 1. **Runners left in scoring position, 2 out:** Terry 2, Ryan 2. **GIDP:** Schumacher. **Team LOB:** 6 **FIELDING: DP:** 1 (Jackson-Critz-Terry).

WASHINGTON	IP	H	R	ER	BB	SO	HR	ERA
Crowder (L, 0-1)	5.2	9	6	6	3	3	0	9.53
Thomas	0.1	1	0	0	0	0	0	0.00
McColl	2	0	0	0	0	0	0	0.00
NY GIANTS	**IP**	**H**	**R**	**ER**	**BB**	**SO**	**HR**	**ERA**
Schumacher (W, 1-0)	9	5	1	1	4	2	1	1.00

WP: Schumacher 1. **IBB:** Ott (by Crowder). **Ground balls-fly balls:** Crowder 8-4, Thomas 1-0, McColl 5-1, Schumacher 12-12. **Batters faced:** Crowder 28, Thomas 2, McColl 6, Schumacher 35. **UMPIRES:** hp—Moriarty, 1b—Pfirman, 2b—Ormsby, 3b—Moran **T:** 2:09 **A:** 35,461

GAME 3 Washington 4 New York 0
Griffith Stadium 10/05/33

NY GIANTS	AB	R	H	HR	RBI	BB	AVG
Moore lf	4	0	0	0	0	0	.167
Critz 2b	4	0	1	0	0	0	.273
Terry 1b	4	0	0	0	0	0	.167
Ott rf	3	0	0	0	0	1	.444
Davis cf	4	0	1	0	0	0	.400
Jackson 3b	3	0	1	0	0	1	.200
Mancuso c	4	0	0	0	0	0	.083
Ryan ss	3	0	0	0	0	0	.182
Fitzsimmons p	2	0	1	0	0	0	.500
a-Peel ph	1	0	1	0	0	0	.500
Bell p	0	0	0	0	0	0	.000
TOTALS	**32**	**0**	**5**	**0**	**0**	**2**	**.253**

a - Batted for Fitzsimmons in the 8th

BATTING: 2B: Jackson (1, Whitehill). **Runners left in scoring position, 2 out:** Terry 3, Mancuso 2. **GIDP:** Mancuso. **Team LOB:** 7 **FIELDING: Outfield assists:** Moore (1). **DP:** 1 (Moore-Mancuso).

WASHINGTON	AB	R	H	HR	RBI	BB	AVG
Myer 2b	4	1	3	0	2	0	.364
Goslin rf	4	1	1	0	0	0	.250
Manush lf	4	0	0	0	0	0	.091
Cronin ss	4	0	1	0	1	0	.250
Schulte cf	4	0	2	0	1	0	.333
Kuhel 1b	3	0	0	0	0	0	.000
Bluege 3b	3	1	1	0	0	0	.111
Sewell c	3	1	1	0	0	0	.111
Whitehill p	3	0	0	0	0	0	.000
TOTALS	**32**	**4**	**9**	**0**	**4**	**0**	**.198**

BATTING: 2B: Goslin (1, Fitzsimmons), Schulte (1, Fitzsimmons), Bluege (1, Fitzsimmons), Myer (1, Fitzsimmons). **RBI:** Myer 2 (2), Cronin 1 (2), Schulte 1 (1). **2-out RBI:** Myer 1, Schulte 1. **Runners left in scoring position, 2 out:** Kuhel 1. **Team LOB:** 4 **BASERUNNING: SB:** Sewell (1, 2nd base off Fitzsimmons/Mancuso). **CS:** Kuhel (1, 2nd base off Fitzsimmons/Mancuso). **FIELDING: E:** Cronin (1). **DP:** 1 (Cronin-Myer-Kuhel).

NY GIANTS	IP	H	R	ER	BB	SO	HR	ERA
Fitzsimmons (L, 0-1)	7	9	4	4	0	2	0	5.14
Bell	1	0	0	0	0	0	0	0.00
WASHINGTON	**IP**	**H**	**R**	**ER**	**BB**	**SO**	**HR**	**ERA**
Whitehill (W, 1-0)	9	5	0	0	2	2	0	0.00

WP: Whitehill 1. **Ground balls-fly balls:** Fitzsimmons 10-8, Bell 1-2, Whitehill 17-8. **Batters faced:** Fitzsimmons 29, Bell 3, Whitehill 34. **UMPIRES:** hp—Pfirman, 1b—Ormsby, 2b—Moran, 3b—Moriarty **T:** 1:55 **A:** 25,727

GAME 4 New York 2 Washington 1
Griffith Stadium 10/06/33

NY GIANTS	AB	R	H	HR	RBI	BB	AVG
Moore lf	5	0	2	0	0	1	.235
Critz 2b	6	0	0	0	0	0	.176
Terry 1b	5	1	2	1	1	0	.235
Ott rf	4	0	2	0	0	1	.462
Davis cf	4	0	1	0	0	0	.357
Jackson 3b	5	1	1	0	0	0	.200
Mancuso c	2	0	0	0	0	2	.071
Ryan ss	5	0	2	0	1	0	.250
Hubbell p	4	0	1	0	0	0	.286
TOTALS	**40**	**2**	**11**	**1**	**2**	**4**	**.259**

BATTING: 2B: Moore (1, Weaver). **HR:** Terry (1, 4th off Weaver 0 on, 1 out). **S:** Davis, Hubbell, Mancuso. **RBI:** Terry 1 (1), Ryan 1 (1). **Runners left in scoring position, 2 out:** Critz 2, Terry 1, Mancuso 1, Ryan 3. **Team LOB:** 12 **FIELDING: E:** Hubbell (1). **DP:** 1 (Ryan-Critz-Terry).

WASHINGTON	AB	R	H	HR	RBI	BB	AVG
Myer 2b	4	0	2	0	0	1	.400
Goslin rf-lf	4	0	1	0	0	0	.250
Manush lf	2	0	0	0	0	1	.077
Harris rf	1	0	0	0	0	1	.000
Cronin ss	5	0	1	0	0	0	.235
Schulte cf	5	0	1	0	0	0	.294
Kuhel 1b	5	1	1	0	0	0	.067
Bluege 3b	3	0	0	0	0	0	.083
Sewell c	4	0	2	0	1	1	.231
Weaver p	4	0	0	0	0	0	.000
Russell p	0	0	0	0	0	0	.000
a-Bolton ph	1	0	0	0	0	0	.000
TOTALS	**38**	**1**	**8**	**0**	**1**	**4**	**.201**

a - Batted for Russell in the 11th

BATTING: S: Goslin, Bluege, Bluege. **RBI:** Sewell 1 (1). **2-out RBI:** Sewell 1. **Runners left in scoring position, 2 out:** Cronin 2, Schulte 2. **GIDP:** Bolton. **Team LOB:** 11 **FIELDING: DP:** 1 (Myer-Kuhel).

NY GIANTS	IP	H	R	ER	BB	SO	HR	ERA
Hubbell (W, 2-0)	11	8	1	0	4	5	0	0.00
WASHINGTON	**IP**	**H**	**R**	**ER**	**BB**	**SO**	**HR**	**ERA**
Weaver (L, 0-1)	10.1	11	2	2	4	3	1	1.74
Russell	0.2	0	0	0	0	1	0	0.00

IBB: Mancuso (by Weaver), Sewell (by Hubbell). **Ground balls-fly balls:** Hubbell 11-14, Weaver 12-12, Russell 0-1. **Batters faced:** Hubbell 45, Weaver 45, Russell 2. **UMPIRES:** hp—Ormsby, 1b—Moran, 2b—Moriarty, 3b—Pfirman **T:** 2:59 **A:** 26,762

GAME 5 New York 4 Washington 3
Griffith Stadium 10/07/33

NY GIANTS	AB	R	H	HR	RBI	BB	AVG
Moore lf	5	0	1	0	0	0	.227
Critz 2b	5	0	0	0	0	0	.136
Terry 1b	5	0	2	0	0	0	.273
Ott rf	5	1	1	1	1	0	.389
Davis cf	5	1	2	0	0	0	.368
Jackson 3b	3	1	1	0	0	0	.222
Mancuso c	3	1	1	0	1	1	.118
Ryan ss	2	0	1	0	0	1	.278
Schumacher p	3	0	1	0	2	0	.286
Luque p	1	0	1	0	0	0	1.000
TOTALS	**37**	**4**	**11**	**1**	**4**	**2**	**.267**

BATTING: 2B: Davis (1, Crowder), Mancuso (1, Crowder). **HR:** Ott (2, 10th off Russell 0 on, 2 out). **S:** Ryan, Jackson. **RBI:** Ott 1 (4), Mancuso 1 (2), Schumacher 2 (3). **2-out RBI:** Ott 1. **Runners left in scoring position, 2 out:** Moore 1, Davis 1, Schumacher 1. **GIDP:** Jackson. **Team LOB:** 7 **FIELDING: E:** Jackson (1). **DP:** 1 (Jackson-Terry).

WASHINGTON	AB	R	H	HR	RBI	BB	AVG
Myer 2b	5	0	0	0	0	0	.300
Goslin rf	4	0	1	0	0	1	.250
Manush lf	5	1	1	0	0	0	.111
Cronin ss	5	1	3	0	0	0	.318
Schulte cf	4	1	2	1	3	1	.333
a-Kerr pr	0	0	0	0	0	0	.000
Kuhel 1b	5	0	2	0	0	0	.150
Bluege 3b	4	0	1	0	0	0	.125
Sewell c	4	0	0	0	0	0	.176
Crowder p	2	0	0	0	0	0	.250
Russell p	1	0	0	0	0	1	.000
TOTALS	**39**	**3**	**10**	**1**	**3**	**3**	**.214**

a - Ran for Schulte in the 10th

BATTING: HR: Schulte (1, 6th off Schumacher 2 on, 2 out). **RBI:** Schulte 3 (4). **2-out RBI:** Schulte 3. **Runners left in scoring position, 2 out:** Kuhel 1, Sewell 1, Crowder 1. **Team LOB:** 9 **FIELDING: Outfield assists:** Goslin (1). **DP:** 1 (Cronin-Kuhel).

NY GIANTS	IP	H	R	ER	BB	SO	HR	ERA
Schumacher	5.2	8	3	3	1	1	1	2.45
Luque (W, 1-0)	4.1	2	0	0	2	5	0	0.00
WASHINGTON	**IP**	**H**	**R**	**ER**	**BB**	**SO**	**HR**	**ERA**
Crowder	5.1	7	3	3	2	4	0	7.36
Russell (L, 0-1)	4.2	4	1	1	0	3	1	0.87

WP: Schumacher 1, Crowder 1. **Ground balls-fly balls:** Schumacher 7-8, Luque 6-2, Crowder 2-8, Russell 5-4. **Batters faced:** Schumacher 25, Luque 17, Crowder 25, Russell 16. **UMPIRES:** hp—Moran, 1b—Moriarty, 2b—Pfirman, 3b—Ormsby **T:** 2:38 **A:** 28,454

1934 ST.LOUIS DEF. DETROIT, 4-3

GAME 1 St. Louis 8 Detroit 3
Navin Field 10/03/34

ST.LOUIS	AB	R	H	HR	RBI	BB	AVG
Martin 3b	5	1	1	0	1	0	.200
Rothrock rf	4	0	2	0	2	0	.500
Frisch 2b	4	0	0	0	0	0	.000
Medwick lf	5	2	4	1	2	0	.800
Collins 1b	4	2	1	0	0	1	.250
DeLancey c	5	0	1	0	2	0	.200
Orsatti cf	4	1	2	0	0	0	.500
Fullis cf	1	0	1	0	0	0	1.000
Durocher ss	5	0	0	0	0	0	.000
D.Dean p	5	2	1	0	0	0	.200
TOTALS	**42**	**8**	**13**	**1**	**7**	**1**	**.310**

BATTING: 2B: D.Dean (1, Marberry), DeLancey (1, Hogsett). **HR:** Medwick (1, 5th off Crowder 0 on, 1 out). **S:** Rothrock, Frisch. **RBI:** Martin 1 (1), Rothrock 2 (2), Medwick 2 (2), DeLancey 2 (2). **2-out RBI:** Rothrock 2, Medwick 1, DeLancey 2. **Runners left in scoring position, 2 out:** Frisch 1, Collins 2, Orsatti 1, Durocher 1. **Team LOB:** 10 **FIELDING: E:** Orsatti 2 (2). **DP:** 1 (DeLancey-Frisch).

DETROIT	AB	R	H	HR	RBI	BB	AVG
White cf	2	1	0	0	0	2	.000
Cochrane c	4	0	1	0	0	0	.250
Gehringer 2b	4	0	2	0	1	0	.500
Greenberg 1b	4	2	2	1	1	0	.500
Goslin lf	4	0	2	0	1	0	.500
Rogell ss	4	0	1	0	0	0	.250
Owen 3b	4	0	0	0	0	0	.000
Fox rf	4	0	0	0	0	0	.000
Crowder p	1	0	0	0	0	0	.000
a-Doljack ph	1	0	0	0	0	0	.000
Marberry p	0	0	0	0	0	0	.000
Hogsett p	1	0	0	0	0	0	.000
b-G.Walker ph	1	0	0	0	0	0	.000
TOTALS	**34**	**3**	**8**	**1**	**3**	**2**	**.235**

a - Batted for Crowder in the 5th
b - Batted for Hogsett in the 9th

BATTING: HR: Greenberg (1, 8th off D.Dean 0 on, 2 out). **RBI:** Gehringer 1 (1), Greenberg 1 (1), Goslin 1 (1). **2-out RBI:** Gehringer 1, Greenberg 1. **Runners left in scoring position, 2 out:** Greenberg 2, Owen 1. **Team LOB:** 6 **BASERUNNING: CS:** Goslin (1, 2nd base off D.Dean/DeLancey). **FIELDING: E:** Owen 2 (2), Gehringer (1), Greenberg (1).

ST.LOUIS	IP	H	R	ER	BB	SO	HR	ERA
D.Dean (W, 1-0)	9	8	3	3	2	6	1	3.00

DETROIT	IP	H	R	ER	BB	SO	HR	ERA
Crowder (L, 0-1)	5	6	4	1	1	1	1	1.80
Marberry	0.2	4	4	4	0	0	0	54.00
Hogsett	3.1	3	0	0	0	1	0	0.00

Ground balls-fly balls: D.Dean 13-7, Crowder 7-11, Marberry 0-1, Hogsett 6-2. **Batters faced:** D.Dean 36, Crowder 26, Marberry 6, Hogsett 13. **UMPIRES:** hp—Owens, 1b—Klem, 2b—Geisel, 3b—Reardon **T:** 2:13 **A:** 42,505

GAME 2 Detroit 3 St. Louis 2
Navin Field 10/04/34

ST.LOUIS	AB	R	H	HR	RBI	BB	AVG
Martin 3b	5	1	2	0	0	0	.300
Rothrock rf	4	0	0	0	0	0	.250
Frisch 2b	5	0	1	0	0	0	.111
Medwick lf	5	0	1	0	1	0	.500
Collins 1b	5	0	1	0	0	0	.222
DeLancey c	5	1	1	0	0	0	.200
Orsatti cf	4	0	1	0	1	0	.375
Durocher ss	4	0	0	0	0	0	.000
Hallahan p	3	0	0	0	0	0	.000
B.Walker p	1	0	0	0	0	0	.000
TOTALS	**41**	**2**	**7**	**0**	**2**	**0**	**.241**

BATTING: 2B: Martin (1, Rowe). **3B:** Orsatti (1, Rowe). **S:** Rothrock. **RBI:** Medwick 1 (3), Orsatti 1 (1). **2-out RBI:** Medwick 1. **Runners left in scoring position, 2 out:** Frisch 1, Collins 1, Hallahan 1. **Team LOB:** 4 **FIELDING: E:** Martin (1), Frisch (1).

DETROIT	AB	R	H	HR	RBI	BB	AVG
White cf	4	0	0	0	0	0	.000
a-G.Walker ph	1	0	1	0	1	0	.500
Doljack cf	1	0	0	0	0	0	.000
Cochrane c	4	0	0	0	0	2	.125
Gehringer 2b	4	1	1	0	0	2	.375
Greenberg 1b	4	0	0	0	0	2	.250
Goslin lf	6	0	2	0	1	0	.400
Rogell ss	4	1	1	0	0	1	.250
Owen 3b	5	0	0	0	0	0	.000
Fox rf	5	1	2	0	1	0	.222
Rowe p	4	0	0	0	0	0	.000
TOTALS	**42**	**3**	**7**	**0**	**3**	**7**	**.197**

a - Batted for White in the 9th

BATTING: 2B: Rogell (1, Hallahan), Fox (1, Hallahan). **S:** Rowe. **RBI:** G.Walker 1 (1), Goslin 1 (2), Fox 1 (1). **2-out RBI:** Fox 1. **Runners left in scoring position, 2 out:** Greenberg 1, Goslin 1, Owen 1, Rowe 1. **Team LOB:** 13 **BASERUNNING: SB:** Gehringer (1, 2nd base off B.Walker/DeLancey). **Outfield assists:** Goslin (1).

ST.LOUIS	IP	H	R	ER	BB	SO	HR	ERA
Hallahan	8.1	6	2	2	4	6	0	2.16
B.Walker (L, 0-1)	3	1	1	1	3	2	0	3.00

DETROIT	IP	H	R	ER	BB	SO	HR	ERA
Rowe (W, 1-0)	12	7	2	2	0	7	0	1.50

Ground balls-fly balls: Hallahan 12-8, B.Walker 2-5, Rowe 11-16. **Batters faced:** Hallahan 37, B.Walker 13, Rowe 42. **UMPIRES:** hp—Klem, 1b—Geisel, 2b—Reardon, 3b—Owens **T:** 2:49 **A:** 43,451

GAME 3 St. Louis 4 Detroit 1
Sportsman's Park 10/05/34

DETROIT	AB	R	H	HR	RBI	BB	AVG
White cf	5	1	2	0	0	0	.182
Cochrane c	3	0	0	0	0	2	.091
Gehringer 2b	5	0	2	0	0	0	.385
Greenberg 1b	4	0	1	0	1	1	.250
Goslin lf	4	0	1	0	0	1	.357
Rogell ss	4	0	1	0	0	0	.250
Owen 3b	3	0	0	0	0	0	.000
Fox rf	4	0	1	0	0	0	.231
Bridges p	1	0	0	0	0	1	.000
Hogsett p	2	0	0	0	0	0	.000
TOTALS	**35**	**1**	**8**	**0**	**1**	**5**	**.207**

BATTING: 2B: Gehringer (1, P.Dean). **3B:** Greenberg (1, P.Dean). **RBI:** Greenberg 1 (2). **2-out RBI:** Greenberg 1. **Runners left in scoring position, 2 out:** Gehringer 2, Goslin 1, Rogell 2, Fox 1, Bridges 1. **Team LOB:** 13 **FIELDING: E:** Rogell (1). **DP:** 2 (Cochrane-Gehringer, Rogell-Gehringer-Greenberg).

ST.LOUIS	AB	R	H	HR	RBI	BB	AVG
Martin 3b	3	2	2	0	0	1	.385
Rothrock rf	4	1	1	0	2	0	.250
Frisch 2b	4	0	2	0	1	0	.231
Medwick lf	4	0	1	0	0	0	.429
Collins 1b	4	1	2	0	0	0	.308
DeLancey c	4	0	1	0	0	0	.214
Orsatti cf	2	0	0	0	0	1	.300
Durocher ss	3	0	0	0	0	0	.000
P.Dean p	3	0	0	0	1	0	.000
TOTALS	**31**	**4**	**9**	**0**	**4**	**2**	**.254**

BATTING: 2B: DeLancey (2, Bridges), Martin (2, Bridges). **3B:** Martin (1, Bridges), Rothrock (1, Bridges). **RBI:** Rothrock 2 (4), Frisch 1 (1), P.Dean 1 (1). **Runners left in scoring position, 2 out:** Martin 1, Frisch 1, Orsatti 1. **GIDP:** Medwick. **Team LOB:** 6 **BASERUNNING: CS:** Frisch (1, 2nd base off Bridges/Cochrane), Collins (1, 2nd base off Hogsett/Cochrane), Martin (1, 3rd base off Hogsett/Cochrane). **FIELDING: E:** Rothrock (1).

DETROIT	IP	H	R	ER	BB	SO	HR	ERA
Bridges (L, 0-1)	4	8	4	4	1	3	0	9.00
Hogsett	4	1	0	0	1	2	0	0.00

ST.LOUIS	IP	H	R	ER	BB	SO	HR	ERA
P.Dean (W, 1-0)	9	8	1	1	5	7	0	1.00

IBB: Goslin (by P.Dean). **HBP:** Owen (by P.Dean), Orsatti (by Bridges). **Ground balls-fly balls:** Bridges 0-8, Hogsett 6-3, P.Dean 3-17. **Batters faced:** Bridges 21, Hogsett 13, P.Dean 41. **UMPIRES:** hp—Geisel, 1b—Reardon, 2b—Owens, 3b—Klem **T:** 2:07 **A:** 34,073

GAME 4 Detroit 10 St. Louis 4
Sportsman's Park 10/06/34

DETROIT	AB	R	H	HR	RBI	BB	AVG
White cf	4	2	1	0	0	2	.200
Cochrane c	5	2	1	0	0	0	.125
Gehringer 2b	4	2	2	0	0	1	.412
Goslin lf	3	2	0	0	0	2	.294
Rogell ss	5	1	2	0	4	0	.294
Greenberg 1b	5	1	4	0	3	0	.412
Owen 3b	5	0	2	0	1	0	.118
Fox rf	4	0	1	0	0	1	.235
Auker p	4	0	0	0	0	0	.000
TOTALS	**39**	**10**	**13**	**0**	**8**	**6**	**.240**

BATTING: 2B: Cochrane (1, Carleton), Fox (2, B.Walker), Greenberg 2 (2, B.Walker). **S:** Auker, Goslin, Gehringer, Cochrane. **RBI:** Rogell 4 (4), Greenberg 3 (5), Owen 1 (1). **2-out RBI:** Rogell 2, Greenberg 1. **Runners left in scoring position, 2 out:** Cochrane 1, Goslin 1, Fox 2, Auker 3. **Team LOB:** 12 **BASERUNNING: SB:** White (1, 2nd base off Vance/DeLancey), Owen (1, 2nd base off Haines/DeLancey), Greenberg (1, 2nd base off Haines/DeLancey). **FIELDING: DP:** 3 (Auker-Rogell-Greenberg, Greenberg-Rogell, Rogell-Greenberg).

ST.LOUIS	AB	R	H	HR	RBI	BB	AVG
Martin 3b	4	0	1	0	1	1	.353
Rothrock rf	5	0	0	0	0	0	.176
Frisch 2b	5	1	1	0	0	0	.222
Medwick lf	3	1	2	0	0	1	.471
Collins 1b	4	0	2	0	1	0	.353
DeLancey c	2	0	0	0	0	2	.188
Orsatti cf	4	1	2	0	1	0	.357
Durocher ss	4	1	1	0	0	0	.063
Carleton p	1	0	0	0	0	0	.000
Vance p	0	0	0	0	0	0	.000
a-Davis ph	1	0	1	0	1	0	1.000
b-D.Dean pr	0	0	0	0	0	0	.200
B.Walker p	1	0	0	0	0	0	.000
Haines p	0	0	0	0	0	0	.000
c-Crawford ph	1	0	0	0	0	0	.000
Mooney p	0	0	0	0	0	0	.000
TOTALS	**35**	**4**	**10**	**0**	**4**	**4**	**.262**

a - Batted for Vance in the 4th
b - Ran for Davis in the 4th
c - Batted for Haines in the 8th

BATTING: 2B: Collins (1, Auker). **RBI:** Martin 1 (2), Collins 1 (1), Orsatti 1 (2), Davis 1 (1). **2-out RBI:** Collins 1. **Runners left in scoring position, 2 out:** DeLancey 1, Carleton 1. **GIDP:** Rothrock, Frisch. **Team LOB:** 8 **FIELDING: E:** Martin (2), B.Walker (1). **Outfield assists:** Orsatti (1).

DETROIT	IP	H	R	ER	BB	SO	HR	ERA
Auker (W, 1-0)	9	10	4	3	4	1	0	3.00

ST.LOUIS	IP	H	R	ER	BB	SO	HR	ERA
Carleton	2.2	4	3	3	2	2	0	10.13
Vance	1.1	2	1	0	1	3	0	0.00
B.Walker (L, 0-2)	3.1	5	6	4	3	0	0	7.11
Haines	0.2	1	0	0	0	2	0	0.00
Mooney	1	1	0	0	0	0	0	0.00

WP: Vance 1. **IBB:** Fox (by B.Walker), Goslin (by B.Walker). **Ground balls-fly balls:** Auker 14-10, Carleton 1-5, Vance 1-0, B.Walker 6-4, Haines 0-0, Mooney 1-1. **Batters faced:** Auker 39, Carleton 14, Vance 7, B.Walker 21, Haines 3, Mooney 4. **UMPIRES:** hp—Reardon, 1b—Owens, 2b—Klem, 3b—Geisel **T:** 2:43 **A:** 37,492

GAME 5 Detroit 3 St. Louis 1
Sportsman's Park 10/07/34

DETROIT	AB	R	H	HR	RBI	BB	AVG
White cf	2	0	0	0	0	2	.176
Cochrane c	4	0	1	0	0	0	.150
Gehringer 2b	4	1	1	1	1	0	.381
Goslin lf	4	0	1	0	0	0	.286
Rogell ss	4	1	2	0	0	0	.333
Greenberg 1b	3	1	0	0	1	1	.350
Owen 3b	4	0	0	0	0	0	.095
Fox rf	4	0	1	0	1	0	.238
Bridges p	4	0	1	0	0	0	.200
TOTALS	**33**	**3**	**7**	**1**	**3**	**3**	**.235**

BATTING: 2B: Fox (3, D.Dean), Goslin (1, D.Dean). **HR:** Gehringer (1, 6th off D.Dean 0 on, 0 out). **RBI:** Gehringer 1 (2), Greenberg 1 (6), Fox 1 (2). **2-out RBI:** Fox 1. **Runners left in scoring position, 2 out:** Gehringer 1, Fox 2, Bridges 1. **GIDP:** Cochrane. **Team LOB:** 7 **BASERUNNING: SB:** Rogell (1, 2nd base off D.Dean/DeLancey).

Martin 3b	4	0	2	0	0	0	.381
Rothrock rf	4	0	0	0	0	0	.143
Frisch 2b	4	0	1	0	0	0	.227
Medwick lf	4	0	0	0	0	0	.381
Collins 1b	4	0	1	0	0	0	.333
DeLancey c	4	1	1	1	1	0	.200
Fullis cf	3	0	0	0	0	0	.250
d-Orsatti ph	1	0	0	0	0	0	.333
Durocher ss	2	0	1	0	0	0	.111
a-Davis ph	1	0	1	0	0	0	1.000
b-Whitehead pr-ss	0	0	0	0	0	0	.000
D.Dean p	2	0	0	0	0	0	.143
c-Crawford ph	1	0	0	0	0	0	.000
Carleton p	0	0	0	0	0	0	.000
TOTALS	**34**	**1**	**7**	**1**	**1**	**0**	**.251**

a - Batted for Durocher in the 8th
b - Ran for Davis in the 8th
c - Batted for D.Dean in the 8th
d - Batted for Fullis in the 9th

BATTING: 2B: Martin (3, Bridges). **HR:** DeLancey (1, 7th off Bridges 0 on, 2 out). **RBI:** DeLancey 1 (3). **2-out RBI:** DeLancey 1. **Runners left in scoring position, 2 out:** Frisch 1, Medwick 1, Orsatti 1. **Team LOB:** 6 **FIELDING: E:** Fullis (1). **DP:** 1 (Collins-Durocher-Collins).

DETROIT	IP	H	R	ER	BB	SO	HR	ERA
Bridges (W, 1-1)	9	7	1	1	0	7	1	3.46

ST.LOUIS	IP	H	R	ER	BB	SO	HR	ERA
D.Dean (L, 1-1)	8	6	3	2	3	6	1	2.65
Carleton	1	1	0	0	0	0	0	7.36

WP: Bridges 1. **HBP:** White (by D.Dean). **Ground balls-fly balls:** Bridges 7-13, D.Dean 4-13, Carleton 2-1. **Batters faced:** Bridges 34, D.Dean 33, Carleton 4. **UMPIRES:** hp—Owens, 1b—Klem, 2b—Geisel, 3b—Reardon **T:** 1:58 **A:** 38,536

GAME 6 St. Louis 4 Detroit 3
Navin Field 10/08/34

ST.LOUIS	AB	R	H	HR	RBI	BB	AVG
Martin 3b	5	1	1	0	1	0	.346
Rothrock rf	4	1	2	0	1	0	.200
Frisch 2b	4	0	0	0	0	0	.192
Medwick lf	4	0	2	0	1	0	.400
Collins 1b	4	0	0	0	0	0	.280
DeLancey c	4	0	0	0	0	0	.167
Orsatti cf	4	0	1	0	0	0	.316
Durocher ss	4	2	3	0	0	0	.227
P.Dean p	3	0	1	0	1	0	.167
TOTALS	**36**	**4**	**10**	**0**	**4**	**0**	**.256**

BATTING: 2B: Rothrock (1, Rowe), Durocher (1, Rowe). **S:** P.Dean. **RBI:** Martin 1 (3), Rothrock 1 (5), Medwick 1 (4), P.Dean 1 (2). **2-out RBI:** Medwick 1. **Runners left in scoring position, 2 out:** Martin 1, Collins 1. **Team LOB:** 6 **FIELDING: E:** P.Dean (1).

DETROIT	AB	R	H	HR	RBI	BB	AVG
White cf	2	2	0	0	0	2	.158
Cochrane c	4	0	3	0	1	0	.250
Gehringer 2b	4	1	1	0	0	0	.360
Goslin lf	4	0	1	0	0	0	.280
Rogell ss	4	0	0	0	0	0	.280
Greenberg 1b	4	0	1	0	1	0	.333
Owen 3b	4	0	0	0	0	0	.080
Fox rf	4	0	1	0	0	0	.240
Rowe p	3	0	0	0	0	0	.000
TOTALS	**33**	**3**	**7**	**0**	**2**	**2**	**.231**

BATTING: 2B: Fox (4, P.Dean). **S:** Rowe. **RBI:** Cochrane 1 (1), Greenberg 1 (7). **2-out RBI:** Cochrane 1, Greenberg 1. **Runners left in scoring position, 2 out:** Goslin 1, Greenberg 1, Owen 1. **Team LOB:** 6 **BASERUNNING: CS:** White 2 (2, 2nd base off P.Dean/DeLancey). **FIELDING: E:** Goslin (1).

ST.LOUIS	IP	H	R	ER	BB	SO	HR	ERA
P.Dean (W, 2-0)	9	7	3	1	2	4	0	1.00

DETROIT	IP	H	R	ER	BB	SO	HR	ERA
Rowe (L, 1-1)	9	10	4	3	0	5	0	2.14

Ground balls-fly balls: P.Dean 9-13, Rowe 11-10. **Batters faced:** P.Dean 36, Rowe 37. **UMPIRES:** hp—Klem, 1b—Geisel, 2b—Reardon, 3b—Owens **T:** 1:58 **A:** 44,551

GAME 7 St. Louis 11 Detroit 0
Navin Field 10/09/34

ST.LOUIS	AB	R	H	HR	RBI	BB	AVG
Martin 3b	5	3	2	0	1	1	.355
Rothrock rf	5	1	2	0	1	1	.233
Frisch 2b	5	1	1	0	3	0	.194
Medwick lf	4	1	1	0	1	0	.379
Fullis lf	1	0	1	0	0	0	.400
Collins 1b	5	1	4	0	2	0	.367
DeLancey c	5	1	1	0	1	0	.172
Orsatti cf	3	1	1	0	0	2	.318
Durocher ss	5	1	2	0	0	0	.259
D.Dean p	5	1	2	0	1	0	.250
TOTALS	**43**	**11**	**17**	**0**	**10**	**4**	**.279**

BATTING: 2B: Rothrock 2 (3, Auker, Bridges), D.Dean (2, Auker), Frisch (1, Auker), DeLancey (3, Rowe). **3B:** Medwick (1, Bridges), Durocher (1, Bridges). **RBI:** Martin 1 (4), Rothrock 1 (6), Frisch 3 (4), Medwick 1 (5), Collins 2 (3), DeLancey 1 (4), D.Dean 1 (1). **2-out RBI:** Martin 1, Rothrock 1, Medwick 1, Collins 2, DeLancey 1, D.Dean 1. **Runners left in scoring position, 2 out:** Rothrock 2, Frisch 1, Medwick 1, DeLancey 1, Durocher 1. **GIDP:** DeLancey. **Team LOB:** 9 **BASERUNNING: SB:** Martin 2 (2, 2nd base off Auker/Cochrane, 2nd base off Bridges/Cochrane). **CS:** Orsatti (1, 2nd base off Auker/Cochrane).

White cf	4	0	0	0	0	0	.130
Cochrane c	4	0	0	0	0	0	.214
Hayworth c	0	0	0	0	0	0	.000
Gehringer 2b	4	0	2	0	0	0	.379
Goslin lf	4	0	0	0	0	0	.241
Rogell ss	4	0	1	0	0	0	.276
Greenberg 1b	4	0	1	0	0	0	.321
Owen 3b	4	0	0	0	0	0	.069
Fox rf	3	0	2	0	0	0	.286
Auker p	0	0	0	0	0	0	.000
Rowe p	0	0	0	0	0	0	.000
Hogsett p	0	0	0	0	0	0	.000
Bridges p	2	0	0	0	0	0	.143
Marberry p	0	0	0	0	0	0	.000
a-G.Walker ph	1	0	0	0	0	0	.333
Crowder p	0	0	0	0	0	0	.000
TOTALS	**34**	**0**	**6**	**0**	**0**	**0**	**.224**

a - Batted for Marberry in the 8th

BATTING: 2B: Fox 2 (6, D.Dean). **Runners left in scoring position, 2 out:** White 2, Cochrane 1, Owen 1. **Team LOB:** 7 **FIELDING: E:** Goslin (2), White (1), Gehringer (2). **DP:** 1 (Owen-Gehringer-Greenberg).

ST.LOUIS	IP	H	R	ER	BB	SO	HR	ERA
D.Dean (W, 2-1)	9	6	0	0	0	5	0	1.73

DETROIT	IP	H	R	ER	BB	SO	HR	ERA
Auker (L, 1-1)	2.1	6	4	4	1	1	0	5.56
Rowe	0.1	2	2	2	0	0	0	2.95
Hogsett	0	2	1	1	2	0	0	1.23
Bridges	4.1	6	4	2	0	2	0	3.63
Marberry	1	1	0	0	1	0	0	21.60
Crowder	1	0	0	0	0	1	0	1.50

Ground balls-fly balls: D.Dean 12-11, Auker 1-3, Rowe 1-0, Hogsett 0-0, Bridges 5-7, Marberry 2-1, Crowder 0-2. **Batters faced:** D.Dean 34, Auker 12, Rowe 3, Hogsett 4, Bridges 20, Marberry 5, Crowder 3. **UMPIRES:** hp—Geisel, 1b—Reardon, 2b—Owens, 3b—Klem **T:** 2:19 **A:** 40,902

1935 DETROIT DEF. CHICAGO CUBS, 4-2

GAME 1 Chicago 3 Detroit 0
Navin Field 10/02/35

CHICAGO CUBS	AB	R	H	HR	RBI	BB	AVG
Galan lf	4	1	1	0	0	0	.250
Herman 2b	3	1	0	0	0	0	.000
Lindstrom cf	3	0	1	0	0	0	.333
Hartnett c	4	0	2	0	1	0	.500
Demaree rf	4	1	2	1	1	0	.500
Cavarretta 1b	3	0	0	0	0	0	.000
Hack 3b	4	0	0	0	0	0	.000
Jurges ss	4	0	1	0	0	0	.250
Warneke p	3	0	0	0	0	0	.000
TOTALS	**32**	**3**	**7**	**1**	**2**	**0**	**.219**

BATTING: 2B: Galan (1, Rowe). **HR:** Demaree (1, 9th off Rowe 0 on, 0 out). **S:** Lindstrom, Cavarretta, Herman. **RBI:** Hartnett 1 (1), Demaree 1 (1). **Runners left in scoring position, 2 out:** Galan 1, Hartnett 1, Jurges 1. **Team LOB:** 5 **BASERUNNING: CS:** Lindstrom (1, 2nd base off Rowe/Cochrane).

White cf	4	0	1	0	0	0	.250
Cochrane c	4	0	0	0	0	0	.000
Gehringer 2b	3	0	0	0	0	1	.000
Greenberg 1b	3	0	0	0	0	1	.000
Goslin lf	3	0	0	0	0	1	.000
Fox rf	4	0	2	0	0	0	.500
Rogell ss	4	0	0	0	0	0	.000
Owen 3b	3	0	0	0	0	1	.000
Rowe p	3	0	1	0	0	0	.333
TOTALS	**31**	**0**	**4**	**0**	**0**	**4**	**.129**

BATTING: 2B: Fox (1, Warneke), Rowe (1, Warneke). **Runners left in scoring position, 2 out:** Cochrane 1, Rogell 3, Owen 1. **Team LOB:** 8 **FIELDING: E:** Rowe (1), Goslin (1), Greenberg (1). **PB:** Cochrane. **DP:** 1 (Cochrane-Gehringer).

CHICAGO CUBS	IP	H	R	ER	BB	SO	HR	ERA
Warneke (W, 1-0)	9	4	0	0	4	1	0	0.00

DETROIT	IP	H	R	ER	BB	SO	HR	ERA
Rowe (L, 0-1)	9	7	3	2	0	8	1	2.00

Ground balls-fly balls: Warneke 18-8, Rowe 8-9. **Batters faced:** Warneke 35, Rowe 35. **UMPIRES:** hp—Moriarty, 1b—Quigley, 2b—McGowan, 3b—Stark **T:** 1:51 **A:** 47,391

GAME 2 Detroit 8 Chicago 3
Navin Field 10/03/35

CHICAGO CUBS	AB	R	H	HR	RBI	BB	AVG
Galan lf	4	0	0	0	0	1	.125
Herman 2b	4	0	1	0	2	0	.143
Lindstrom cf	3	0	0	0	0	1	.167
Hartnett c	4	0	1	0	0	0	.375
Demaree rf	4	0	1	0	0	0	.375
Cavarretta 1b	4	1	0	0	0	0	.000
Hack 3b	3	0	1	0	0	1	.143
Jurges ss	3	1	1	0	1	1	.286
Root p	0	0	0	0	0	0	.000
Henshaw p	1	0	0	0	0	0	.000
Kowalik p	2	1	1	0	0	0	.500
a-Klein ph	1	0	0	0	0	0	.000
TOTALS	**33**	**3**	**6**	**0**	**3**	**4**	**.200**

a - Batted for Kowalik in the 9th

BATTING: 2B: Demaree (1, Bridges). **RBI:** Herman 2 (2), Jurges 1 (1). **2-out RBI:** Herman 2. **Runners left in scoring position, 2 out:** Herman 1, Lindstrom 1, Cavarretta 1. **GIDP:** Herman, Hartnett. **Team LOB:** 7 **FIELDING: E:** Kowalik (1). **Outfield assists:** Galan (1), Demaree (1). **DP:** 2 (Herman-Cavarretta, Jurges-Herman-Cavarretta).

DETROIT	AB	R	H	HR	RBI	BB	AVG
White cf	3	2	1	0	0	2	.286
Cochrane c	2	1	1	0	1	2	.167
Gehringer 2b	3	2	2	0	3	1	.333
Greenberg 1b	3	1	1	1	2	0	.167
Goslin lf	3	0	0	0	0	1	.000
Fox rf	4	0	1	0	1	0	.375
Rogell ss	4	0	2	0	0	0	.250
Owen 3b	2	1	0	0	0	0	.000
Bridges p	4	1	1	0	0	0	.250
TOTALS	**28**	**8**	**9**	**1**	**7**	**6**	**.220**

BATTING: 2B: Cochrane (1, Root), Rogell (1, Kowalik). **HR:** Greenberg (1, 1st off Root 1 on, 0 out). **S:** Owen. **RBI:** Cochrane 1 (1), Gehringer 3 (3), Greenberg 2 (2), Fox 1 (1). **2-out RBI:** Gehringer 2, Fox 1. **Runners left in scoring position, 2 out:** White 1, Greenberg 1, Fox 1. **GIDP:** Greenberg. **Team LOB:** 5 **FIELDING: E:** Greenberg (2). **DP:** 2 (Bridges-Rogell-Greenberg, Rogell-Gehringer-Greenberg).

CHICAGO CUBS	IP	H	R	ER	BB	SO	HR	ERA
Root (L, 0-1)	0	4	4	4	0	0	1	0.00
Henshaw	3.2	2	3	3	5	2	0	7.36
Kowalik	4.1	3	1	1	1	1	0	2.08

DETROIT	IP	H	R	ER	BB	SO	HR	ERA
Bridges (W, 1-0)	9	6	3	2	4	2	0	2.00

WP: Henshaw 1. **HBP:** Owen (by Henshaw), Greenberg (by Kowalik). **Ground balls-fly balls:** Root 0-0, Henshaw 3-4, Kowalik 5-4, Bridges 11-14. **Batters faced:** Root 4, Henshaw 17, Kowalik 16, Bridges 37. **UMPIRES:** hp—Quigley, 1b—McGowan, 2b—Stark, 3b—Moriarty **T:** 1:59 **A:** 46,742

GAME 3 Detroit 6 Chicago 5
Wrigley Field 10/04/35

DETROIT	AB	R	H	HR	RBI	BB	AVG
White cf	5	1	2	0	1	1	.333
Cochrane c	5	0	0	0	0	1	.091
Gehringer 2b	5	1	2	0	0	0	.364
Goslin lf	5	2	3	0	2	0	.273
Fox rf	5	1	2	0	1	0	.385
Rogell ss	5	0	3	0	1	0	.385
Owen 1b	5	1	0	0	0	0	.000
Clifton 3b	4	0	0	0	0	1	.000
Auker p	2	0	0	0	0	0	.000
a-Walker ph	1	0	0	0	0	0	.000
Hogsett p	0	0	0	0	0	0	.000
Rowe p	2	0	0	0	0	0	.200
TOTALS	**44**	**6**	**12**	**0**	**5**	**3**	**.243**

a - Batted for Auker in the 7th

BATTING: 2B: Gehringer (1, Lee), Goslin (1, French). **3B:** Fox (1, Lee). **RBI:** White 1 (1), Goslin 2 (2), Fox 1 (2), Rogell 1 (1). **2-out RBI:** White 1. **Runners left in scoring position, 2 out:** Cochrane 2, Goslin 2, Fox 1, Clifton 1. **GIDP:** Walker. **Team LOB:** 8 **BASERUNNING: CS:** Rogell (1, 2nd base off Warneke/Hartnett). **FIELDING: E:** Clifton (1), Cochrane (1). **DP:** 2 (Rogell-Gehringer-Owen, Gehringer-Rogell-Owen).

CHICAGO CUBS	AB	R	H	HR	RBI	BB	AVG
Galan lf	4	0	2	0	2	1	.250
Herman 2b	5	0	1	0	0	0	.167
Lindstrom cf-3b	5	0	2	0	0	0	.273
Hartnett c	4	0	0	0	0	0	.250
Demaree rf-cf	4	1	1	1	1	1	.333
Cavarretta 1b	5	0	0	0	0	0	.000
Hack 3b-ss	5	2	2	0	0	0	.250
Jurges ss	1	1	0	0	0	1	.250
a-Klein ph-rf	2	1	1	0	0	0	.333
Lee p	1	0	0	0	1	0	.000
Warneke p	0	0	0	0	0	0	.000
b-O'Dea ph	1	0	1	0	1	0	1.000
French p	0	0	0	0	0	0	.000
c-Stephenson ph	1	0	0	0	0	0	.000
TOTALS	**38**	**5**	**10**	**1**	**5**	**3**	**.223**

a - Batted for Jurges in the 9th
b - Batted for Warneke in the 9th
c - Batted for French in the 11th

BATTING: 2B: Lindstrom (1, Rowe). **HR:** Demaree (2, 2nd off Auker 0 on, 0 out). **S:** Lee, Lee, Hartnett. **RBI:** Galan 2 (2), Demaree 1 (2), Lee 1 (1), O'Dea 1 (1). **Runners left in scoring position, 2 out:** Galan 1, Herman 1, Cavarretta 1. **GIDP:** Hartnett, Lindstrom. **Team LOB:** 7 **BASERUNNING: SB:** Hack (1, 2nd base off Auker/Cochrane). **CS:** Cavarretta (1, 2nd base off Auker/Cochrane). **FIELDING: E:** Herman (1), Cavarretta (1), Lindstrom (1). **DP:** 1 (Jurges-Herman-Cavarretta).

DETROIT	IP	H	R	ER	BB	SO	HR	ERA
Auker	6	6	3	2	2	1	1	3.00
Hogsett	1	0	0	0	1	0	0	0.00
Rowe (W, 1-1)	4	4	2	2	0	3	0	2.77

CHICAGO CUBS	IP	H	R	ER	BB	SO	HR	ERA
Lee	7.1	7	4	4	3	3	0	4.91
Warneke	1.2	2	1	1	0	2	0	0.84
French (L, 0-1)	2	3	1	0	0	1	0	0.00

HBP: Jurges (by Hogsett). **Ground balls-fly balls:** Auker 11-3, Hogsett 2-0, Rowe 4-4, Lee 7-11, Warneke 1-1, French 2-4. **Batters faced:** Auker 24, Hogsett 5, Rowe 16, Lee 31, Warneke 6, French 10. **UMPIRES:** hp—McGowan, 1b—Stark, 2b—Moriarty, 3b—Quigley **T:** 2:27 **A:** 45,532

GAME 4 Detroit 2 Chicago 1
Wrigley Field 10/05/35

DETROIT	AB	R	H	HR	RBI	BB	AVG
White cf	3	0	1	0	0	2	.333
Cochrane c	4	0	1	0	0	1	.133
Gehringer 2b	4	0	2	0	1	0	.400
Goslin lf	3	0	1	0	0	2	.286
Fox rf	5	0	1	0	0	0	.333
Rogell ss	3	0	0	0	0	2	.313
Owen 1b	4	0	0	0	0	0	.000
Clifton 3b	4	1	0	0	0	0	.000
Crowder p	3	1	1	0	0	1	.333
TOTALS	**33**	**2**	**7**	**0**	**1**	**8**	**.235**

BATTING: 2B: Fox (2, Carleton), Gehringer (2, Carleton). **S:** Gehringer. **RBI:** Gehringer 1 (4). **Runners left in scoring position, 2 out:** Cochrane 2, Rogell 3, Owen 1. **Team LOB:** 13 **BASERUNNING: SB:** Gehringer (1, 2nd base off Carleton/Hartnett). **FIELDING: DP:** 1 (Rogell-Gehringer-Owen).

CHICAGO CUBS	AB	R	H	HR	RBI	BB	AVG
Galan lf	4	0	0	0	0	0	.188
Herman 2b	4	0	1	0	0	0	.188
Lindstrom cf	4	0	0	0	0	0	.200
Hartnett c	4	1	1	1	1	0	.250
Demaree rf	4	0	1	0	0	0	.313
Cavarretta 1b	4	0	2	0	0	0	.125
Hack 3b	4	0	0	0	0	0	.188
Jurges ss	1	0	0	0	0	2	.222
Carleton p	1	0	0	0	0	1	.000
a-Klein ph	1	0	0	0	0	0	.250
Root p	0	0	0	0	0	0	.000
TOTALS	**31**	**1**	**5**	**1**	**1**	**3**	**.209**

a - Batted for Carleton in the 7th

BATTING: 2B: Herman (1, Crowder). **HR:** Hartnett (1, 2nd off Crowder 0 on, 0 out). **RBI:** Hartnett 1 (2). **Runners left in scoring position, 2 out:** Galan 1, Demaree 1. **GIDP:** Hack. **Team LOB:** 6 **FIELDING: E:** Galan (1), Jurges (1). **Outfield assists:** Demaree (2). **DP:** 1 (Jurges-Herman).

DETROIT	IP	H	R	ER	BB	SO	HR	ERA
Crowder (W, 1-0)	9	5	1	1	3	5	1	1.00

CHICAGO CUBS	IP	H	R	ER	BB	SO	HR	ERA
Carleton (L, 0-1)	7	6	2	1	7	4	0	1.29
Root	2	1	0	0	1	2	0	18.00

BK: Carleton 1. **IBB:** Goslin 2 (by Carleton, by Root). **Ground balls-fly balls:** Crowder 12-9, Carleton 5-12, Root 0-3. **Batters faced:** Crowder 34, Carleton 34, Root 8. **UMPIRES:** hp—Stark, 1b—Moriarty, 2b—Quigley, 3b—McGowan **T:** 2:28 **A:** 49,350

GAME 5 Chicago 3 Detroit 1
Wrigley Field 10/06/35

DETROIT	AB	R	H	HR	RBI	BB	AVG
White cf	4	0	0	0	0	0	.263
Cochrane c	4	0	2	0	0	0	.211
Gehringer 2b	4	1	1	0	0	0	.368
Goslin lf	3	0	1	0	0	1	.294
Fox rf	4	0	2	0	1	0	.364
Rogell ss	4	0	0	0	0	0	.250
Owen 1b	3	0	0	0	0	0	.000
a-Walker ph	1	0	0	0	0	0	.000
Clifton 3b	3	0	0	0	0	1	.000
Rowe p	3	0	1	0	0	0	.250
TOTALS	**33**	**1**	**7**	**0**	**1**	**2**	**.231**

a - Batted for Owen in the 9th

BATTING: RBI: Fox 1 (3). **Runners left in scoring position, 2 out:** Cochrane 1, Goslin 1, Rogell 1, Clifton 2. **GIDP:** Rogell. **Team LOB:** 7 **FIELDING: E:** Owen (1).

CHICAGO CUBS	AB	R	H	HR	RBI	BB	AVG
Galan lf	4	1	0	0	0	0	.150
Herman 2b	4	1	2	0	1	0	.250
Klein cf	4	1	2	1	2	0	.375
Hartnett c	4	0	1	0	0	0	.250
Demaree rf	4	0	1	0	0	0	.300
Cavarretta 1b	4	0	0	0	0	0	.100
Hack 3b	2	0	0	0	0	1	.167
Jurges ss	3	0	1	0	0	0	.250
Warneke p	2	0	1	0	0	0	.200
Lee p	0	0	0	0	0	0	.000
TOTALS	**31**	**3**	**8**	**1**	**3**	**1**	**.218**

BATTING: 2B: Herman (2, Rowe). **3B:** Herman (1, Rowe). **HR:** Klein (1, 3th off Rowe 1 on, 0 out). **S:** Lee. **RBI:** Herman 1 (3), Klein 2 (2). **2-out RBI:** Herman 1. **Runners left in scoring position, 2 out:** Galan 1, Klein 1, Demaree 1. **Team LOB:** 6 **FIELDING: DP:** 1 (Jurges-Cavarretta).

DETROIT	IP	H	R	ER	BB	SO	HR	ERA
Rowe (L, 1-2)	8	8	3	2	1	3	1	2.57

CHICAGO CUBS	IP	H	R	ER	BB	SO	HR	ERA
Warneke (W, 2-0)	6	3	0	0	0	2	0	0.54
Lee (S, 1)	3	4	1	1	2	2	0	4.35

Ground balls-fly balls: Rowe 8-12, Warneke 9-7, Lee 3-3. **Batters faced:** Rowe 33, Warneke 21, Lee 14. **UMPIRES:** hp—Moriarty, 1b—Quigley, 2b—McGowan, 3b—Stark **T:** 1:49 **A:** 49,237

GAME 6 Detroit 4 Chicago 3
Navin Field 10/07/35

CHICAGO CUBS	AB	R	H	HR	RBI	BB	AVG
Galan lf	5	0	1	0	0	0	.160
Herman 2b	4	1	3	1	3	0	.333
Klein rf	4	0	1	0	0	0	.333
Hartnett c	4	0	2	0	0	0	.292
Demaree cf	4	0	0	0	0	0	.250
Cavarretta 1b	4	0	1	0	0	0	.125
Hack 3b	4	0	2	0	0	0	.227
Jurges ss	4	1	1	0	0	0	.250
French p	4	1	1	0	0	0	.250
TOTALS	**37**	**3**	**12**	**1**	**3**	**0**	**.238**

BATTING: 2B: Hack (1, Bridges). **3B:** Hack (1, Bridges). **HR:** Herman (1, 5th off Bridges 1 on, 2 out). **RBI:** Herman 3 (6). **2-out RBI:** Herman 2. **Runners left in scoring position, 2 out:** Galan 1, Hack 1, Jurges 1. **GIDP:** Demaree. **Team LOB:** 7

Clifton 3b	5	0	0	0	0	0	.000
Cochrane c	5	2	3	0	0	0	.292
Gehringer 2b	5	0	2	0	0	0	.375
Goslin lf	5	0	1	0	1	0	.273
Fox rf	4	0	2	0	1	0	.385
Walker cf	2	1	1	0	0	1	.250
Rogell ss	4	1	2	0	0	0	.292
Owen 1b	3	0	1	0	1	1	.050
Bridges p	4	0	0	0	1	0	.125
TOTALS	**37**	**4**	**12**	**0**	**4**	**2**	**.248**

BATTING: 2B: Fox (3, French), Gehringer (3, French), Rogell (2, French). **S:** Walker. **RBI:** Goslin 1 (3), Fox 1 (4), Owen 1 (1), Bridges 1 (1). **2-out RBI:** Goslin 1, Fox 1, Owen 1. **Runners left in scoring position, 2 out:** Fox 1, Rogell 2, Bridges 1. **Team LOB:** 10 **FIELDING: E:** Fox (1). **Outfield assists:** Fox (1). **DP:** 1 (Gehringer-Rogell-Owen).

CHICAGO CUBS	IP	H	R	ER	BB	SO	HR	ERA
French (L, 0-2)	8.2	12	4	4	2	7	0	3.38

DETROIT	IP	H	R	ER	BB	SO	HR	ERA
Bridges (W, 2-0)	9	12	3	3	0	7	1	2.50

IBB: Walker (by French), Owen (by French). **Ground balls-fly balls:** French 11-7, Bridges 11-7. **Batters faced:** French 40, Bridges 37. **UMPIRES:** hp—Quigley, 1b—McGowan, 2b—Stark, 3b—Moriarty **T:** 1:57 **A:** 48,420

1936 NY YANKEES DEF. NY GIANTS, 4-2

GAME 1 Giants 6 Yankees 1
Polo Grounds 09/30/36

NY YANKEES	AB	R	H	HR	RBI	BB	AVG
Crosetti ss	4	0	1	0	0	0	.250
Rolfe 3b	3	0	1	0	0	0	.333
DiMaggio cf	4	0	1	0	0	0	.250
Gehrig 1b	3	0	0	0	0	0	.000
Dickey c	4	0	0	0	0	0	.000
Powell lf	4	0	3	0	0	0	.750
Lazzeri 2b	3	0	0	0	0	1	.000
Selkirk rf	4	1	1	1	1	0	.250
Ruffing p	3	0	0	0	0	0	.000
TOTALS	**32**	**1**	**7**	**1**	**1**	**1**	**.219**

BATTING: 2B: Powell (1, Hubbell), Crosetti (1, Hubbell). **HR:** Selkirk (1, 3th off Hubbell 0 on, 0 out). **S:** Rolfe. **RBI:** Selkirk 1 (1). **Runners left in scoring position, 2 out:** Gehrig 1, Dickey 1, Selkirk 1. **Team LOB:** 7 **BASERUNNING: CS:** Powell (1, 3rd base off Hubbell/Mancuso). **FIELDING: E:** Crosetti (1).

NY GIANTS	AB	R	H	HR	RBI	BB	AVG
Moore lf	5	0	0	0	0	0	.000
Bartell ss	4	1	2	1	1	0	.500
Terry 1b	4	1	2	0	0	0	.500
Ott rf	2	2	2	0	0	2	1.000
Ripple cf	2	0	0	0	0	0	.000
Mancuso c	3	1	1	0	1	1	.333
Whitehead 2b	3	1	0	0	1	1	.000
Jackson 3b	4	0	0	0	1	0	.000
Hubbell p	4	0	2	0	2	0	.500
TOTALS	**31**	**6**	**9**	**1**	**6**	**4**	**.290**

BATTING: 2B: Ott (1, Ruffing). **HR:** Bartell (1, 5th off Ruffing 0 on, 2 out). **S:** Ripple, Ripple. **RBI:** Bartell 1 (1), Mancuso 1 (1), Whitehead 1 (1), Jackson 1 (1), Hubbell 2 (2). **2-out RBI:** Bartell 1, Hubbell 2. **Runners left in scoring position, 2 out:** Moore 1, Ripple 3. **Team LOB:** 7 **FIELDING: E:** Hubbell (1). **DP:** 1 (Whitehead-Terry).

NY YANKEES	IP	H	R	ER	BB	SO	HR	ERA
Ruffing (L, 0-1)	8	9	6	4	4	5	1	4.50

NY GIANTS	IP	H	R	ER	BB	SO	HR	ERA
Hubbell (W, 1-0)	9	7	1	1	1	8	1	1.00

IBB: Mancuso (by Ruffing). **HBP:** Gehrig (by Hubbell). **Ground balls-fly balls:** Ruffing 5-12, Hubbell 13-4. **Batters faced:** Ruffing 37, Hubbell 35. **UMPIRES:** hp—Pfirman, 1b—Geisel, 2b—Magerkurth, 3b—Summers **T:** 2:40 **A:** 39,419

GAME 2 Yankees 18 Giants 4
Polo Grounds 10/02/36

NY YANKEES	AB	R	H	HR	RBI	BB	AVG
Crosetti ss	5	4	3	0	0	1	.444
Rolfe 3b	4	3	2	0	1	2	.429
DiMaggio cf	5	2	3	0	2	0	.444
Gehrig 1b	5	1	2	0	3	1	.250
Dickey c	5	3	2	1	5	1	.222
Selkirk rf	5	1	1	0	0	1	.222
Powell lf	3	2	2	0	0	2	.714
Lazzeri 2b	4	1	1	1	5	1	.143
Gomez p	5	1	1	0	2	0	.200
TOTALS	**41**	**18**	**17**	**2**	**18**	**9**	**.329**

BATTING: 2B: DiMaggio (1, Gabler). **HR:** Lazzeri (1, 3th off Coffman 3 on, 1 out), Dickey (1, 9th off Gumbert 2 on, 2 out). **S:** DiMaggio. **RBI:** Rolfe 1 (1), DiMaggio 2 (2), Gehrig 3 (3), Dickey 5 (5), Lazzeri 5 (5), Gomez 2 (2). **2-out RBI:** Dickey 3. **Runners left in scoring position, 2 out:** Crosetti 1, Selkirk 1. **Team LOB:** 6 **BASERUNNING: SB:** Powell (1, 2nd base off Gumbert/Mancuso). **CS:** Selkirk (1, 2nd base off Schumacher/Mancuso), Gehrig (1, 2nd base off Coffman/Mancuso).

GIANTS	AB	R	H	HR	RBI	BB	AVG
Moore lf	5	0	0	0	0	0	.000
Bartell ss	3	0	1	0	1	2	.429
Terry 1b	5	0	2	0	2	0	.444
Leiber cf	4	0	0	0	0	1	.000
Ott rf	4	0	0	0	0	0	.333
Mancuso c	2	2	1	0	0	2	.400
Whitehead 2b	4	0	0	0	0	0	.000
Jackson 3b	4	1	1	0	0	0	.125
Schumacher p	0	0	0	0	0	1	.000
Smith p	0	0	0	0	0	0	.000
Coffman p	0	0	0	0	0	0	.000
a-Davis ph	1	1	1	0	0	0	1.000
Gabler p	0	0	0	0	0	1	.000
b-Danning ph	1	0	0	0	0	0	.000
Gumbert p	0	0	0	0	0	0	.000
TOTALS	**33**	**4**	**6**	**0**	**3**	**7**	**.234**

a - Batted for Coffman in the 4th
b - Batted for Gabler in the 8th

BATTING: 2B: Mancuso (1, Gomez), Bartell (1, Gomez). **RBI:** Bartell 1 (2), Terry 2 (2). **2-out RBI:** Bartell 1, Terry 2. **Runners left in scoring position, 2 out:** Moore 1, Leiber 2, Ott 1, Danning 1. **Team LOB:** 9 **FIELDING: E:** Jackson (1). **Outfield assists:** Leiber (1). **DP:** 1 (Leiber-Jackson-Bartell).

NY YANKEES	IP	H	R	ER	BB	SO	HR	ERA
Gomez (W, 1-0)	9	6	4	4	7	8	0	4.00

NY GIANTS	IP	H	R	ER	BB	SO	HR	ERA
Schumacher (L, 0-1)	2	3	5	4	4	1	0	18.00
Smith	0.1	2	3	3	1	0	0	81.00
Coffman	1.2	2	1	1	0	1	1	5.40
Gabler	4	5	3	3	3	0	0	6.75
Gumbert	1	5	6	6	1	1	1	54.00

WP: Gomez 1, Schumacher 1. **Ground balls-fly balls:** Gomez 4-15, Schumacher 0-3, Smith 0-1, Coffman 2-1, Gabler 4-8, Gumbert 1-1. **Batters faced:** Gomez 40, Schumacher 12, Smith 4, Coffman 6, Gabler 20, Gumbert 9. **UMPIRES:** hp—Geisel, 1b—Magerkurth, 2b—Summers, 3b—Pfirman **T:** 2:49 **A:** 43,543

GAME 3 Yankees 2 Giants 1
Yankee Stadium 10/03/36

NY GIANTS	AB	R	H	HR	RBI	BB	AVG
Moore lf	5	0	1	0	0	0	.067
Bartell ss	3	0	1	0	0	0	.400
Terry 1b	4	0	1	0	0	0	.385
Ott rf	4	0	2	0	0	0	.400
Ripple cf	4	1	1	1	1	0	.167
Mancuso c	4	0	1	0	0	0	.333
Whitehead 2b	4	0	0	0	0	0	.000
Jackson 3b	2	0	1	0	0	1	.200
a-Koenig ph	1	0	0	0	0	0	.000
Fitzsimmons p	3	0	2	0	0	0	.667
b-Leslie ph	1	0	1	0	0	0	1.000
c-Davis pr	0	0	0	0	0	0	1.000
TOTALS	**35**	**1**	**11**	**1**	**1**	**1**	**.263**

a - Batted for Jackson in the 9th
b - Batted for Fitzsimmons in the 9th
c - Ran for Leslie in the 9th

BATTING: HR: Ripple (1, 5th off Hadley 0 on, 0 out). **S:** Bartell. **RBI:** Ripple 1 (1). **Runners left in scoring position, 2 out:** Moore 2, Mancuso 2. **GIDP:** Ott. **Team LOB:** 9 **BASERUNNING: CS:** Whitehead (1, 2nd base off Hadley/Dickey). **FIELDING: DP:** 1 (Bartell-Whitehead-Terry).

NY YANKEES	AB	R	H	HR	RBI	BB	AVG
Crosetti ss	4	0	1	0	1	0	.385
Rolfe 3b	4	0	0	0	0	0	.273
DiMaggio cf	3	0	1	0	0	0	.417
Gehrig 1b	3	1	1	1	1	0	.273
Dickey c	2	0	0	0	0	1	.182
Selkirk rf	3	0	1	0	0	0	.250
Powell lf	2	1	0	0	0	1	.556
Lazzeri 2b	2	0	0	0	0	0	.111
Hadley p	2	0	0	0	0	0	.000
a-Ruffing ph	1	0	0	0	0	0	.000
b-Johnson pr	0	0	0	0	0	0	.000
Malone p	0	0	0	0	0	0	.000
TOTALS	**26**	**2**	**4**	**1**	**2**	**2**	**.283**

a - Batted for Hadley in the 8th
b - Ran for Ruffing in the 8th

BATTING: 2B: DiMaggio (2, Fitzsimmons). **HR:** Gehrig (1, 2nd off Fitzsimmons 0 on, 0 out). **S:** Lazzeri. **RBI:** Crosetti 1 (1), Gehrig 1 (4). **2-out RBI:** Crosetti 1. **Runners left in scoring position, 2 out:** Rolfe 1, Dickey 1. **GIDP:** Powell. **Team LOB:** 3 **FIELDING: DP:** 1 (Crosetti-Gehrig).

NY GIANTS	IP	H	R	ER	BB	SO	HR	ERA
Fitzsimmons (L, 0-1)	8	4	2	2	2	5	1	2.25

NY YANKEES	IP	H	R	ER	BB	SO	HR	ERA
Hadley (W, 1-0)	8	10	1	1	1	2	1	1.13
Malone (S, 1)	1	1	0	0	0	1	0	0.00

Ground balls-fly balls: Fitzsimmons 7-10, Hadley 9-10, Malone 2-0. **Batters faced:** Fitzsimmons 29, Hadley 33, Malone 4. **UMPIRES:** hp—Magerkurth, 1b—Summers, 2b—Pfirman, 3b—Geisel **T:** 2:01 **A:** 64,842

GAME 4 Yankees 5 Giants 2
Yankee Stadium 10/04/36

NY GIANTS	AB	R	H	HR	RBI	BB	AVG
Moore lf	3	0	1	0	0	1	.111
Bartell ss	4	1	1	0	0	0	.357
Terry 1b	3	0	0	0	1	1	.313
Ott rf	4	0	0	0	0	0	.286
Ripple cf	4	0	2	0	1	0	.300
Mancuso c	4	0	0	0	0	0	.231
Whitehead 2b	3	0	0	0	0	0	.000
c-Koenig ph	1	0	1	0	0	0	.500
Jackson 3b	4	0	1	0	0	0	.214
Hubbell p	2	0	0	0	0	0	.333
a-Leslie ph	1	0	1	0	0	0	1.000
b-Davis pr	0	1	0	0	0	0	1.000
Gabler p	0	0	0	0	0	0	.000
TOTALS	**33**	**2**	**7**	**0**	**2**	**2**	**.250**

a - Batted for Hubbell in the 8th
b - Ran for Leslie in the 8th
c - Batted for Whitehead in the 9th

BATTING: RBI: Terry 1 (3), Ripple 1 (2). **Runners left in scoring position, 2 out:** Moore 1, Ott 1, Whitehead 1. **Team LOB:** 6 **BASERUNNING: CS:** Moore (1, 2nd base off Pearson/Dickey), Ripple (1, 2nd base off Pearson/Dickey). **FIELDING: E:** Jackson (2). **DP:** 1 (Bartell-Whitehead-Terry).

NY YANKEES	AB	R	H	HR	RBI	BB	AVG
Crosetti ss	4	1	2	0	0	0	.412
Rolfe 3b	3	1	2	0	1	1	.357
DiMaggio cf	4	0	0	0	0	0	.313
Gehrig 1b	4	2	2	1	2	0	.333
Dickey c	4	0	0	0	0	0	.133
Powell lf	4	1	1	0	1	0	.462
Lazzeri 2b	4	0	0	0	0	0	.077
Selkirk rf	3	0	1	0	1	1	.267
Pearson p	4	0	2	0	0	0	.500
TOTALS	**34**	**5**	**10**	**1**	**5**	**2**	**.286**

BATTING: 2B: Crosetti (2, Hubbell), Pearson (1, Hubbell), Gehrig (1, Gabler). **HR:** Gehrig (2, 3th off Hubbell 1 on, 1 out). **RBI:** Rolfe 1 (2), Gehrig 2 (6), Powell 1 (1), Selkirk 1 (2). **2-out RBI:** Selkirk 1. **Runners left in scoring position, 2 out:** Pearson 1. **GIDP:** DiMaggio. **Team LOB:** 7 **FIELDING: E:** Selkirk (1).

NY GIANTS	IP	H	R	ER	BB	SO	HR	ERA
Hubbell (L, 1-1)	7	8	4	3	1	2	1	2.25
Gabler	1	2	1	1	1	0	0	7.20

NY YANKEES	IP	H	R	ER	BB	SO	HR	ERA
Pearson (W, 1-0)	9	7	2	2	2	7	0	2.00

WP: Hubbell 1. **Ground balls-fly balls:** Hubbell 11-8, Gabler 3-0, Pearson 8-11. **Batters faced:** Hubbell 30, Gabler 6, Pearson 35. **UMPIRES:** hp—Summers, 1b—Pfirman, 2b—Geisel, 3b—Magerkurth **T:** 2:12 **A:** 66,669

GAME 5 Giants 5 Yankees 4
Yankee Stadium 10/05/36

NY GIANTS	AB	R	H	HR	RBI	BB	AVG
Moore lf	5	2	2	0	0	0	.174
Bartell ss	4	1	1	0	1	0	.333
Terry 1b	5	0	0	0	1	0	.238
Ott rf	5	1	1	0	0	0	.263
Ripple cf	2	1	1	0	1	2	.333
Mancuso c	3	0	2	0	0	0	.313
Whitehead 2b	4	0	1	0	1	0	.056
Jackson 3b	4	0	0	0	0	0	.167
Schumacher p	4	0	0	0	0	0	.000
TOTALS	**36**	**5**	**8**	**0**	**4**	**2**	**.244**

BATTING: 2B: Moore 2 (2, Ruffing, Malone), Bartell (2, Ruffing), Mancuso (2, Ruffing). **S:** Mancuso, Bartell. **RBI:** Bartell 1 (3), Terry 1 (4), Ripple 1 (3), Whitehead 1 (2). **2-out RBI:** Ripple 1, Whitehead 1. **Runners left in scoring position, 2 out:** Jackson 1, Schumacher 1. **GIDP:** Mancuso. **Team LOB:** 5 **FIELDING: E:** Ott (1), Bartell (1), Jackson (3). **DP:** 3 (Schumacher-Terry-Mancuso, Bartell-Whitehead-Terry, Mancuso-Whitehead).

NY YANKEES	AB	R	H	HR	RBI	BB	AVG
Crosetti ss	5	0	0	0	1	0	.318
Rolfe 3b	5	0	2	0	0	0	.368
DiMaggio cf	4	0	1	0	0	1	.300
Gehrig 1b	4	0	1	0	0	1	.316
Dickey c	5	0	1	0	0	0	.150
b-Seeds pr	0	0	0	0	0	0	.000
Selkirk rf	4	2	2	1	1	1	.316
Powell lf	4	1	1	0	0	1	.412
Lazzeri 2b	3	1	1	0	1	1	.125
Ruffing p	1	0	0	0	0	1	.000
a-Johnson ph	1	0	0	0	0	0	.000
Malone p	1	0	1	0	0	0	1.000
TOTALS	**37**	**4**	**10**	**1**	**3**	**6**	**.282**

a - Batted for Ruffing in the 6th
b - Ran for Dickey in the 10th

BATTING: 2B: DiMaggio (3, Schumacher). **HR:** Selkirk (2, 2nd off Schumacher 0 on, 2 out). **RBI:** Crosetti 1 (2), Selkirk 1 (3), Lazzeri 1 (6). **2-out RBI:** Selkirk 1, Lazzeri 1. **Runners left in scoring position, 2 out:** Gehrig 1, Dickey 3. **GIDP:** Ruffing. **Team LOB:** 9 **BASERUNNING: CS:** Rolfe (1, 2nd base off Schumacher/Mancuso), Seeds (1, 2nd base off Schumacher/Mancuso). **FIELDING: E:** Crosetti (2). **DP:** 1 (Crosetti-Lazzeri-Gehrig).

NY GIANTS	IP	H	R	ER	BB	SO	HR	ERA
Schumacher (W, 1-1)	10	10	4	3	6	10	1	5.25

NY YANKEES	IP	H	R	ER	BB	SO	HR	ERA
Ruffing	6	7	4	4	1	7	0	5.14
Malone (L, 0-1)	4	1	1	1	1	1	0	1.80

WP: Schumacher 1. **Ground balls-fly balls:** Schumacher 10-7, Ruffing 5-6, Malone 3-6. **Batters faced:** Schumacher 43, Ruffing 27, Malone 13. **UMPIRES:** hp—Pfirman, 1b—Geisel, 2b—Magerkurth, 3b—Summers **T:** 2:45 **A:** 50,024

GAME 6 Yankees 13 Giants 5
Polo Grounds 10/06/36

NY YANKEES	AB	R	H	HR	RBI	BB	AVG
Crosetti ss	4	0	0	0	1	2	.269
Rolfe 3b	6	1	3	0	2	0	.400
DiMaggio cf	6	1	3	0	1	0	.346
Gehrig 1b	5	1	1	0	1	1	.292
Dickey c	5	2	0	0	0	1	.120
Selkirk rf	5	2	2	0	0	1	.333
Powell lf	5	3	3	1	4	0	.455
Lazzeri 2b	4	2	3	0	1	1	.250
Gomez p	3	0	1	0	1	0	.250
Murphy p	2	1	1	0	1	0	.500
TOTALS	**45**	**13**	**17**	**1**	**12**	**6**	**.302**

BATTING: 3B: Selkirk (1, Fitzsimmons). **HR:** Powell (1, 2nd off Fitzsimmons 1 on, 2 out). **RBI:** Crosetti 1 (3), Rolfe 2 (4), DiMaggio 1 (3), Gehrig 1 (7), Powell 4 (5), Lazzeri 1 (7), Gomez 1 (3), Murphy 1 (1). **2-out RBI:** Rolfe 1, Powell 2. **Runners left in scoring position, 2 out:** Rolfe 2, DiMaggio 1, Selkirk 2. **Team LOB:** 11 **FIELDING: E:** Rolfe (1), DiMaggio (1).

NY GIANTS	AB	R	H	HR	RBI	BB	AVG
Moore lf	5	2	2	1	1	0	.214
Bartell ss	3	2	2	0	0	2	.381
Terry 1b	4	0	1	0	1	0	.240
Leiber cf	2	0	0	0	0	1	.000
Mayo 3b	1	0	0	0	0	0	.000
Ott rf	4	1	2	1	3	1	.304
Mancuso c	3	0	0	0	0	0	.263
a-Leslie ph	1	0	0	0	0	0	.667
Danning c	1	0	0	0	0	0	.000
Whitehead 2b	3	0	0	0	0	0	.048
b-Ripple ph-cf	0	0	0	0	0	1	.333
Jackson 3b	3	0	1	0	0	0	.190
c-Koenig ph-2b	1	0	0	0	0	0	.333
Fitzsimmons p	1	0	0	0	0	0	.500
Castleman p	2	0	1	0	0	0	.500
d-Davis ph	1	0	0	0	0	0	.500
Coffman p	0	0	0	0	0	0	.000
Gumbert p	0	0	0	0	0	0	.000
TOTALS	**35**	**5**	**9**	**2**	**5**	**5**	**.246**

a - Batted for Mancuso in the 7th
b - Batted for Whitehead in the 7th
c - Batted for Jackson in the 7th
d - Batted for Castleman in the 8th

BATTING: 2B: Ott (2, Gomez), Bartell (3, Gomez). **HR:** Ott (1, 5th off Gomez 0 on, 1 out), Moore (1, 8th off Murphy 0 on, 1 out). **S:** Terry, Leiber. **RBI:** Moore 1 (1), Terry 1 (5), Ott 3 (3). **Runners left in scoring position, 2 out:** Terry 2, Whitehead 2, Koenig 2. **Team LOB:** 10 **FIELDING: E:** Danning (1).

NY YANKEES	IP	H	R	ER	BB	SO	HR	ERA
Gomez (W, 2-0)	6.1	8	4	4	4	1	1	4.70
Murphy (S, 1)	2.2	1	1	1	1	1	1	3.38

NY GIANTS	IP	H	R	ER	BB	SO	HR	ERA
Fitzsimmons (L, 0-2)	3.2	9	5	5	0	1	1	5.40
Castleman	4.1	3	1	1	2	5	0	2.08
Coffman	0	3	5	5	1	0	0	32.40
Gumbert	1	2	2	2	3	1	0	36.00

IBB: Selkirk (by Coffman). **Ground balls-fly balls:** Gomez 8-9, Murphy 2-5, Fitzsimmons 1-9, Castleman 4-4, Coffman 1-0, Gumbert 1-1. **Batters faced:** Gomez 32, Murphy 10, Fitzsimmons 20, Castleman 18, Coffman 5, Gumbert 8. **UMPIRES:** hp—Geisel, 1b—Magerkurth, 2b—Summers, 3b—Pfirman **T:** 2:50 **A:** 38,427

1937 NY YANKEES DEF. NY GIANTS, 4-1

GAME 1 Yankees 8 Giants 1
Yankee Stadium 10/06/37

NY GIANTS	AB	R	H	HR	RBI	BB	AVG
Moore lf	4	0	2	0	0	0	.500
Bartell ss	4	0	1	0	0	0	.250
Ott 3b	4	0	0	0	0	0	.000
Leiber cf	4	0	0	0	0	0	.000
Ripple rf	3	1	1	0	0	1	.333
McCarthy 1b	4	0	1	0	0	0	.250
Mancuso c	3	0	0	0	1	0	.000
Whitehead 2b	3	0	1	0	0	0	.333
Hubbell p	2	0	0	0	0	0	.000
Gumbert p	0	0	0	0	0	0	.000
Coffman p	0	0	0	0	0	0	.000
a-Berger ph	1	0	0	0	0	0	.000
Smith p	0	0	0	0	0	0	.000
TOTALS	**32**	**1**	**6**	**0**	**1**	**1**	**.188**

a - Batted for Coffman in the 8th

BATTING: 2B: Whitehead (1, Gomez). **RBI:** Mancuso 1 (1). **Runners left in scoring position, 2 out:** Hubbell 1. **GIDP:** Mancuso. **Team LOB:** 5 **FIELDING: E:** Whitehead (1). **DP:** 1 (Ott-Whitehead-McCarthy).

NY YANKEES	AB	R	H	HR	RBI	BB	AVG
Crosetti ss	4	1	1	0	0	1	.250
Rolfe 3b	4	1	1	0	1	1	.250
DiMaggio cf	4	0	2	0	2	0	.500
Gehrig 1b	2	1	0	0	0	2	.000
Dickey c	3	1	1	0	1	1	.333
Hoag lf	4	1	0	0	0	0	.000
Selkirk rf	4	1	1	0	2	0	.250
Lazzeri 2b	4	1	1	1	1	0	.250
Gomez p	2	1	0	0	0	2	.000
TOTALS	**31**	**8**	**7**	**1**	**7**	**7**	**.226**

BATTING: HR: Lazzeri (1, 8th off Smith 0 on, 0 out). **RBI:** Rolfe 1 (1), DiMaggio 2 (2), Dickey 1 (1), Selkirk 2 (2), Lazzeri 1 (1). **2-out RBI:** Rolfe 1. **Runners left in scoring position, 2 out:** DiMaggio 2, Dickey 1, Selkirk 1. **GIDP:** Hoag. **Team LOB:** 6 **FIELDING: DP:** 1 (Crosetti-Lazzeri-Gehrig).

NY GIANTS	IP	H	R	ER	BB	SO	HR	ERA
Hubbell (L, 0-1)	5.1	6	7	4	3	3	0	6.75
Gumbert	0	0	0	0	0	0	0	0.00
Coffman	1.2	0	0	0	4	0	0	0.00
Smith	1	1	1	1	0	0	1	9.00

NY YANKEES	IP	H	R	ER	BB	SO	HR	ERA
Gomez (W, 1-0)	9	6	1	1	1	2	0	1.00

IBB: Gehrig (by Hubbell). **Ground balls-fly balls:** Hubbell 7-6, Gumbert 1-0, Coffman 2-2, Smith 0-3, Gomez 8-16. **Batters faced:** Hubbell 25, Gumbert 1, Coffman 8, Smith 4, Gomez 33. **UMPIRES:** hp—Ormsby, 1b—Barr, 2b—Basil, 3b—Stewart **T:** 2:20 **A:** 60,573

GAME 2 Yankees 8 Giants 1
Yankee Stadium 10/07/37

NY GIANTS	AB	R	H	HR	RBI	BB	AVG
Moore lf	5	0	2	0	0	0	.444
Bartell ss	4	1	2	0	0	0	.375
Ott 3b	4	0	1	0	1	0	.125
Ripple rf	4	0	0	0	0	0	.143
McCarthy 1b	4	0	0	0	0	0	.125
Chiozza cf	4	0	1	0	0	0	.250
Mancuso c	4	0	0	0	0	0	.000
Whitehead 2b	3	0	1	0	0	1	.333
Melton p	1	0	0	0	0	1	.000
Gumbert p	0	0	0	0	0	0	.000
Coffman p	1	0	0	0	0	0	.000
a-Leslie ph	0	0	0	0	0	1	.000
TOTALS	**34**	**1**	**7**	**0**	**1**	**3**	**.197**

a - Batted for Coffman in the 9th

BATTING: 2B: Bartell (1, Ruffing), Moore (1, Ruffing). **RBI:** Ott 1 (1). **Runners left in scoring position, 2 out:** Moore 2, Bartell 1, Ripple 1, McCarthy 1. **Team LOB:** 9 **FIELDING: DP:** 1 (Bartell-Whitehead-McCarthy).

NY YANKEES	AB	R	H	HR	RBI	BB	AVG
Crosetti ss	5	0	0	0	0	0	.111
Rolfe 3b	5	0	0	0	0	0	.111
DiMaggio cf	4	1	2	0	0	0	.500
Gehrig 1b	2	1	1	0	0	2	.250
Dickey c	4	1	2	0	1	0	.429
Hoag lf	4	2	1	0	1	0	.125
Selkirk rf	4	2	2	0	3	0	.375
Lazzeri 2b	3	1	2	0	0	1	.429
Ruffing p	4	0	2	0	3	0	.500
TOTALS	**35**	**8**	**12**	**0**	**8**	**3**	**.288**

BATTING: 2B: Hoag (1, Melton), Selkirk (1, Gumbert), Ruffing (1, Gumbert). **RBI:** Dickey 1 (2), Hoag 1 (1), Selkirk 3 (5), Ruffing 3 (3). **Runners left in scoring position, 2 out:** Rolfe 1, DiMaggio 1, Dickey 1. **GIDP:** Ruffing. **Team LOB:** 6

NY GIANTS	IP	H	R	ER	BB	SO	HR	ERA
Melton (L, 0-1)	4	6	2	2	1	2	0	4.50
Gumbert	1.1	4	4	4	1	1	0	27.00
Coffman	2.2	2	2	2	1	1	0	4.15

NY YANKEES	IP	H	R	ER	BB	SO	HR	ERA
Ruffing (W, 1-0)	9	7	1	1	3	8	0	1.00

IBB: Lazzeri (by Gumbert). **Ground balls-fly balls:** Melton 5-4, Gumbert 2-1, Coffman 4-3, Ruffing 11-8. **Batters faced:** Melton 18, Gumbert 9, Coffman 11, Ruffing 37. **UMPIRES:** hp—Barr, 1b—Basil, 2b—Stewart, 3b—Ormsby **T:** 2:11 **A:** 57,675

GAME 3 Yankees 5 Giants 1
Polo Grounds 10/08/37

NY YANKEES	AB	R	H	HR	RBI	BB	AVG
Crosetti ss	4	0	0	0	0	1	.077
Rolfe 3b	4	1	2	0	0	1	.231
DiMaggio cf	5	0	1	0	0	0	.385
Gehrig 1b	5	1	1	0	1	0	.222
Dickey c	5	1	1	0	1	0	.333
Selkirk rf	4	2	1	0	1	1	.333
Hoag lf	4	0	2	0	1	0	.250
Lazzeri 2b	2	0	1	0	1	2	.444
Pearson p	3	0	0	0	0	1	.000
Murphy p	0	0	0	0	0	0	.000
TOTALS	**36**	**5**	**9**	**0**	**5**	**6**	**.275**

BATTING: 2B: Rolfe 2 (2, Schumacher). **3B:** Dickey (1, Schumacher). **S:** Hoag. **RBI:** Gehrig 1 (1), Dickey 1 (3), Selkirk 1 (6), Hoag 1 (2), Lazzeri 1 (2). **Runners left in scoring position, 2 out:** Crosetti 1, Rolfe 2, Gehrig 1, Dickey 1, Pearson 1. **GIDP:** Pearson. **Team LOB:** 11

NY GIANTS	AB	R	H	HR	RBI	BB	AVG
Moore lf	4	0	1	0	0	0	.385
Bartell ss	4	0	0	0	0	0	.250
Ott 3b	4	0	1	0	0	0	.167
Ripple rf	4	1	1	0	0	0	.182
McCarthy 1b	3	0	1	0	1	1	.182
Chiozza cf	3	0	1	0	0	1	.286
Danning c	4	0	0	0	0	0	.000
Whitehead 2b	3	0	0	0	0	0	.222
Schumacher p	1	0	0	0	0	0	.000
a-Berger ph	1	0	0	0	0	0	.000
Melton p	0	0	0	0	0	0	.000
b-Leslie ph	1	0	0	0	0	0	.000
Brennan p	0	0	0	0	0	0	.000
TOTALS	**32**	**1**	**5**	**0**	**1**	**2**	**.184**

a - Batted for Schumacher in the 6th
b - Batted for Melton in the 8th

BATTING: 2B: McCarthy (1, Pearson). **RBI:** McCarthy 1 (1). **Runners left in scoring position, 2 out:** Danning 3. **Team LOB:** 6 **FIELDING: E:** McCarthy (1), Chiozza (1), Melton (1). **DP:** 1 (Whitehead-Bartell-McCarthy).

NY YANKEES	IP	H	R	ER	BB	SO	HR	ERA
Pearson (W, 1-0)	8.2	5	1	1	2	4	0	1.04
Murphy (S, 1)	0.1	0	0	0	0	0	0	0.00

NY GIANTS	IP	H	R	ER	BB	SO	HR	ERA
Schumacher (L, 0-1)	6	9	5	4	4	3	0	6.00
Melton	2	0	0	0	2	0	0	3.00
Brennan	1	0	0	0	0	0	0	0.00

WP: Schumacher 1. **IBB:** Lazzeri 2 (by Schumacher, by Melton). **Ground balls-fly balls:** Pearson 13-9, Murphy 0-1, Schumacher 8-7, Melton 2-4, Brennan 0-3. **Batters faced:** Pearson 33, Murphy 1, Schumacher 32, Melton 8, Brennan 3. **UMPIRES:** hp—Basil, 1b—Stewart, 2b—Ormsby, 3b—Barr **T:** 2:07 **A:** 37,385

GAME 4 Giants 7 Yankees 3
Polo Grounds 10/09/37

NY YANKEES	AB	R	H	HR	RBI	BB	AVG
Crosetti ss	4	1	0	0	0	0	.059
Rolfe 3b	4	1	2	0	0	0	.294
DiMaggio cf	4	0	0	0	1	0	.294
Gehrig 1b	4	1	1	1	1	0	.231
Dickey c	4	0	0	0	0	0	.250
Hoag lf	4	0	2	0	0	0	.313
Selkirk rf	3	0	0	0	0	1	.267
Lazzeri 2b	3	0	1	0	0	0	.417
Hadley p	0	0	0	0	0	0	.000
Andrews p	2	0	0	0	0	0	.000
a-Powell ph	1	0	0	0	0	0	.000
Wicker p	0	0	0	0	0	0	.000
TOTALS	**33**	**3**	**6**	**1**	**2**	**1**	**.252**

a - Batted for Andrews in the 8th

BATTING: 3B: Rolfe (1, Hubbell). **HR:** Gehrig (1, 9th off Hubbell 0 on, 1 out). **RBI:** DiMaggio 1 (3), Gehrig 1 (2). **Runners left in scoring position, 2 out:** Gehrig 1. **GIDP:** Crosetti. **Team LOB:** 4

NY GIANTS	AB	R	H	HR	RBI	BB	AVG
Moore lf	5	1	1	0	1	0	.333
Bartell ss	5	1	1	0	1	0	.235
Ott 3b	5	0	1	0	0	0	.176
Ripple rf	2	0	1	0	0	2	.231
Leiber cf	3	2	2	0	2	1	.286
McCarthy 1b	4	1	2	0	0	0	.267
Danning c	4	0	3	0	2	0	.375
Whitehead 2b	3	1	1	0	0	1	.250
Hubbell p	4	1	0	0	1	0	.000
TOTALS	**35**	**7**	**12**	**0**	**7**	**4**	**.226**

BATTING: 2B: Danning (1, Andrews). **RBI:** Moore 1 (1), Bartell 1 (1), Leiber 2 (2), Danning 2 (2), Hubbell 1 (1). **2-out RBI:** Leiber 2, Danning 1. **Runners left in scoring position, 2 out:** Moore 1, McCarthy 1, Hubbell 2. **Team LOB:** 8 **BASERUNNING: SB:** Whitehead (1, 2nd base off Andrews/Dickey). **CS:** Ripple (1, 2nd base off Andrews/Dickey). **FIELDING: E:** Bartell (1), Ott (1). **DP:** 2 (Whitehead-Bartell, Hubbell-Whitehead-McCarthy).

NY YANKEES	IP	H	R	ER	BB	SO	HR	ERA
Hadley (L, 0-1)	1.1	6	5	5	0	0	0	33.75
Andrews	5.2	6	2	2	4	1	0	3.18
Wicker	1	0	0	0	0	0	0	0.00

NY GIANTS	IP	H	R	ER	BB	SO	HR	ERA
Hubbell (W, 1-1)	9	6	3	2	1	4	1	3.77

IBB: Whitehead (by Andrews). **Ground balls-fly balls:** Hadley 2-2, Andrews 9-6, Wicker 1-2, Hubbell 11-12. **Batters faced:** Hadley 10, Andrews 26, Wicker 3, Hubbell 34. **UMPIRES:** hp—Stewart, 1b—Ormsby, 2b—Barr, 3b—Basil **T:** 1:57 **A:** 44,293

GAME 5 Yankees 4 Giants 2
Polo Grounds 10/10/37

NY YANKEES	AB	R	H	HR	RBI	BB	AVG
Crosetti ss	4	0	0	0	0	1	.048
Rolfe 3b	3	0	1	0	0	1	.300
DiMaggio cf	5	1	1	1	1	0	.273
Gehrig 1b	4	0	2	0	1	1	.294
Dickey c	3	0	0	0	0	1	.211
Hoag lf	4	1	1	1	1	0	.300
Selkirk rf	4	0	1	0	0	0	.263
Lazzeri 2b	3	1	1	0	0	0	.400
Gomez p	4	1	1	0	1	0	.167
TOTALS	**34**	**4**	**8**	**2**	**4**	**4**	**.249**

BATTING: 2B: Gehrig (1, Melton). **3B:** Lazzeri (1, Melton), Gehrig (1, Smith). **HR:** Hoag (1, 2nd off Melton 0 on, 0 out), DiMaggio (1, 3th off Melton 0 on, 2 out). **S:** Rolfe. **RBI:** DiMaggio 1 (4), Gehrig 1 (3), Hoag 1 (3), Gomez 1 (1). **2-out RBI:** DiMaggio 1, Gehrig 1. **Runners left in scoring position, 2 out:** Gehrig 1, Dickey 2, Hoag 2. **Team LOB:** 9 **FIELDING: DP:** 1 (Gehrig).

NY GIANTS	AB	R	H	HR	RBI	BB	AVG
Moore lf	5	0	3	0	0	0	.391
Bartell ss	4	1	1	0	0	0	.238
Ott 3b	3	1	1	1	2	1	.200
Ripple rf	4	0	2	0	0	0	.294
Leiber cf	4	0	2	0	0	0	.364
McCarthy 1b	4	0	0	0	0	0	.211
Danning c	4	0	0	0	0	0	.250
Whitehead 2b	4	0	1	0	0	0	.250
Melton p	1	0	0	0	0	0	.000
a-Ryan ph	1	0	0	0	0	0	.000
Smith p	0	0	0	0	0	0	.000
b-Mancuso ph	1	0	0	0	0	0	.000
Brennan p	0	0	0	0	0	0	.000
c-Berger ph	1	0	0	0	0	0	.000
TOTALS	**36**	**2**	**10**	**1**	**2**	**1**	**.237**

a - Batted for Melton in the 5th
b - Batted for Smith in the 7th
c - Batted for Brennan in the 9th

BATTING: 2B: Whitehead (2, Gomez). **HR:** Ott (1, 3th off Gomez 1 on, 1 out). **RBI:** Ott 2 (3). **Runners left in scoring position, 2 out:** Ripple 1, Leiber 1, Whitehead 1, Melton 1. **Team LOB:** 8

NY YANKEES	IP	H	R	ER	BB	SO	HR	ERA
Gomez (W, 2-0)	9	10	2	2	1	6	1	1.50

NY GIANTS	IP	H	R	ER	BB	SO	HR	ERA
Melton (L, 0-2)	5	6	4	4	3	5	2	4.91
Smith	2	1	0	0	0	1	0	3.00
Brennan	2	1	0	0	1	1	0	0.00

WP: Melton 1. **HBP:** Lazzeri (by Smith). **Ground balls-fly balls:** Gomez 8-12, Melton 2-8, Smith 4-1, Brennan 0-4. **Batters faced:** Gomez 37, Melton 24, Smith 8, Brennan 8. **UMPIRES:** hp—Ormsby, 1b—Barr, 2b—Basil, 3b—Stewart **T:** 2:06 **A:** 38,216

1938 NY YANKEES DEF. CHICAGO CUBS, 4-0

GAME 1 New York 3 Chicago 1
Wrigley Field 10/05/38

NY YANKEES	AB	R	H	HR	RBI	BB	AVG
Crosetti ss	4	0	1	0	0	0	.250
Rolfe 3b	5	0	1	0	0	0	.200
Henrich rf	4	1	2	0	0	0	.500
DiMaggio cf	4	0	0	0	0	0	.000
Gehrig 1b	3	1	1	0	0	1	.333
Dickey c	4	1	4	0	1	0	1.000
Selkirk lf	4	0	1	0	1	0	.250
Gordon 2b	4	0	2	0	1	0	.500
Ruffing p	3	0	0	0	0	0	.000
TOTALS	**35**	**3**	**12**	**0**	**3**	**1**	**.343**

BATTING: 2B: Gordon (1, Lee), Henrich (1, Lee), Crosetti (1, Russell). **S:** Ruffing. **RBI:** Dickey 1 (1), Selkirk 1 (1), Gordon 1 (1). **2-out RBI:** Dickey 1. **Runners left in scoring position, 2 out:** Rolfe 2, Selkirk 1, Gordon 1. **GIDP:** Ruffing. **Team LOB:** 8 **BASERUNNING: SB:** Dickey (1, 2nd base off Lee/Hartnett). **CS:** Henrich (1, 2nd base off Lee/Hartnett). **FIELDING: E:** Henrich (1). **DP:** 2 (Crosetti-Gehrig, Gordon-Crosetti-Gehrig).

CHICAGO CUBS	AB	R	H	HR	RBI	BB	AVG
Hack 3b	4	0	3	0	1	0	.750
Herman 2b	4	0	1	0	0	0	.250
Demaree lf	4	0	0	0	0	0	.000
Cavarretta rf	4	0	2	0	0	0	.500
Reynolds cf	4	0	0	0	0	0	.000
Hartnett c	3	0	1	0	0	0	.333
Collins 1b	3	1	1	0	0	0	.333
Jurges ss	3	0	1	0	0	0	.333
Lee p	2	0	0	0	0	0	.000
a-O'Dea ph	1	0	0	0	0	0	.000
Russell p	0	0	0	0	0	0	.000
TOTALS	**32**	**1**	**9**	**0**	**1**	**0**	**.281**

a - Batted for Lee in the 8th

BATTING: 3B: Hartnett (1, Ruffing). **RBI:** Hack 1 (1). **2-out RBI:** Hack 1. **Runners left in scoring position, 2 out:** Herman 1, Reynolds 1, Collins 1. **GIDP:** Reynolds, Hack. **Team LOB:** 4 **BASERUNNING: CS:** Hack (1, 2nd base off Ruffing/Dickey). **FIELDING: E:** Herman (1). **Outfield assists:** Cavarretta (1). **DP:** 2 (Jurges-Herman-Collins, Collins).

NY YANKEES	IP	H	R	ER	BB	SO	HR	ERA
Ruffing (W, 1-0)	9	9	1	1	0	5	0	1.00

CHICAGO CUBS	IP	H	R	ER	BB	SO	HR	ERA
Lee (L, 0-1)	8	11	3	3	1	6	0	3.38
Russell	1	1	0	0	0	0	0	0.00

HBP: Crosetti (by Lee). **Ground balls-fly balls:** Ruffing 10-8, Lee 7-7, Russell 2-1. **Batters faced:** Ruffing 32, Lee 34, Russell 4. **UMPIRES:** hp—Moran, 1b—Kolls, 2b—Sears, 3b—Hubbard **T:** 1:53 **A:** 43,642

GAME 2 New York 6 Chicago 3
Wrigley Field 10/06/38

NY YANKEES	AB	R	H	HR	RBI	BB	AVG
Crosetti ss	4	1	1	1	2	0	.250
Rolfe 3b	4	0	0	0	0	0	.111
Henrich rf	4	1	1	0	0	0	.375
DiMaggio cf	4	2	2	1	2	0	.250
Gehrig 1b	3	1	1	0	0	1	.333
Dickey c	4	0	0	0	0	0	.500
Selkirk lf	3	0	1	0	0	1	.286
Powell lf	0	0	0	0	0	0	.000
Gordon 2b	4	0	1	0	2	0	.375
Gomez p	2	0	0	0	0	0	.000
a-Hoag ph	1	1	0	0	0	0	.000
Murphy p	0	0	0	0	0	0	.000
TOTALS	**33**	**6**	**7**	**2**	**6**	**2**	**.279**

a - Batted for Gomez in the 8th

BATTING: 2B: Gordon (2, Dean). **HR:** Crosetti (1, 8th off Dean 1 on, 2 out), DiMaggio (1, 9th off Dean 1 on, 0 out). **RBI:** Crosetti 2 (2), DiMaggio 2 (2), Gordon 2 (3). **2-out RBI:** Crosetti 2, Gordon 2. **Runners left in scoring position, 2 out:** Gomez 1. **GIDP:** Dickey. **Team LOB:** 2 **FIELDING: E:** Rolfe 2 (2). **DP:** 2 (Crosetti-Gordon-Gehrig, Gordon-Crosetti-Gehrig).

CHICAGO CUBS	AB	R	H	HR	RBI	BB	AVG
Hack 3b	5	2	2	0	0	0	.556
Herman 2b	4	1	1	0	0	0	.250
Demaree rf	3	0	1	0	0	0	.143
Marty cf	4	0	3	0	3	0	.750
Reynolds lf	3	0	0	0	0	1	.000
Hartnett c	4	0	0	0	0	0	.143
Collins 1b	4	0	1	0	0	0	.286
Jurges ss	3	0	0	0	0	1	.167
Dean p	3	0	2	0	0	0	.667
French p	0	0	0	0	0	0	.000
a-Cavarretta ph	1	0	1	0	0	0	.600
TOTALS	**34**	**3**	**11**	**0**	**3**	**2**	**.303**

a - Batted for French in the 9th

BATTING: 2B: Marty (1, Gomez). **S:** Demaree. **RBI:** Marty 3 (3). **Runners left in scoring position, 2 out:** Hack 1, Reynolds 1, Collins 1. **GIDP:** Hack, Reynolds. **Team LOB:** 7 **BASERUNNING: CS:** Marty (1, 2nd base off Gomez/Dickey). **FIELDING: DP:** 1 (Herman-Jurges-Collins).

NY YANKEES	IP	H	R	ER	BB	SO	HR	ERA
Gomez (W, 1-0)	7	9	3	3	1	5	0	3.86
Murphy (S, 1)	2	2	0	0	1	1	0	0.00

CHICAGO CUBS	IP	H	R	ER	BB	SO	HR	ERA
Dean (L, 0-1)	8	7	6	6	1	2	2	6.75
French	1	0	0	0	1	2	0	0.00

Ground balls-fly balls: Gomez 6-7, Murphy 2-2, Dean 10-11, French 1-0. **Batters faced:** Gomez 29, Murphy 8, Dean 31, French 4. **UMPIRES:** hp—Kolls, 1b—Sears, 2b—Hubbard, 3b—Moran **T:** 1:53 **A:** 42,108

GAME 3 New York 5 Chicago 2
Yankee Stadium 10/08/38

CHICAGO CUBS	AB	R	H	HR	RBI	BB	AVG
Hack 3b	3	1	1	0	0	1	.500
Herman 2b	3	0	0	0	0	1	.182
Cavarretta rf	4	0	1	0	0	0	.444
Marty cf	4	1	3	1	2	0	.750
Reynolds lf	4	0	0	0	0	0	.000
Hartnett c	4	0	0	0	0	0	.091
Collins 1b	4	0	0	0	0	0	.182
Jurges ss	3	0	0	0	0	0	.111
b-Lazzeri ph	1	0	0	0	0	0	.000
Bryant p	2	0	0	0	0	0	.000
Russell p	0	0	0	0	0	0	.000
a-Galan ph	1	0	0	0	0	0	.000
French p	0	0	0	0	0	0	.000
c-O'Dea ph	1	0	0	0	0	0	.000
TOTALS	**34**	**2**	**5**	**1**	**2**	**2**	**.250**

a - Batted for Russell in the 7th
b - Batted for Jurges in the 9th
c - Batted for French in the 9th

BATTING: 2B: Hack (1, Pearson). **HR:** Marty (1, 8th off Pearson 0 on, 1 out). **RBI:** Marty 2 (5). **Runners left in scoring position, 2 out:** Hack 1, Hartnett 3. **Team LOB:** 7 **FIELDING: E:** Herman (2).

NY YANKEES	AB	R	H	HR	RBI	BB	AVG
Crosetti ss	3	0	0	0	0	2	.182
Rolfe 3b	4	0	1	0	1	0	.154
Henrich rf	4	0	0	0	0	0	.250
DiMaggio cf	3	1	1	0	0	1	.273
Gehrig 1b	4	1	1	0	0	0	.300
Dickey c	3	1	1	1	1	1	.455
Selkirk lf	3	0	0	0	0	1	.200
Gordon 2b	4	1	2	1	3	0	.417
Pearson p	3	1	1	0	0	1	.333
TOTALS	**31**	**5**	**7**	**2**	**5**	**6**	**.263**

BATTING: HR: Gordon (1, 5th off Bryant 0 on, 2 out), Dickey (1, 8th off French 0 on, 0 out). **RBI:** Rolfe 1 (1), Dickey 1 (2), Gordon 3 (6). **2-out RBI:** Rolfe 1, Gordon 1. **Runners left in scoring position, 2 out:** Rolfe 2, Henrich 1, Gordon 1. **Team LOB:** 8 **BASERUNNING: CS:** Crosetti (1, 2nd base off Bryant/Hartnett). **FIELDING: E:** Crosetti (1), Gordon (1).

CHICAGO CUBS	IP	H	R	ER	BB	SO	HR	ERA
Bryant (L, 0-1)	5.1	6	4	4	5	3	1	6.75
Russell	0.2	0	0	0	1	0	0	0.00
French	2	1	1	1	0	0	1	3.00

NY YANKEES	IP	H	R	ER	BB	SO	HR	ERA
Pearson (W, 1-0)	9	5	2	1	2	9	1	1.00

Ground balls-fly balls: Bryant 5-7, Russell 0-2, French 5-2, Pearson 8-12. **Batters faced:** Bryant 26, Russell 3, French 8, Pearson 36. **UMPIRES:** hp—Sears, 1b—Hubbard, 2b—Moran, 3b—Kolls **T:** 1:57 **A:** 55,236

GAME 4 New York 8 Chicago 3
Yankee Stadium 10/09/38

CHICAGO CUBS	AB	R	H	HR	RBI	BB	AVG
Hack 3b	5	0	2	0	0	0	.471
Herman 2b	5	0	1	0	0	0	.188
Cavarretta rf	4	1	2	0	0	0	.462
Marty cf	4	0	0	0	0	0	.500
Demaree lf	3	1	0	0	0	1	.100
O'Dea c	3	1	1	1	2	1	.200
Collins 1b	4	0	0	0	0	0	.133
Jurges ss	4	0	2	0	0	0	.231
Lee p	1	0	0	0	0	0	.000
a-Galan ph	1	0	0	0	0	0	.000
Root p	0	0	0	0	0	0	.000
b-Lazzeri ph	1	0	0	0	0	0	.000
Page p	0	0	0	0	0	0	.000
French p	0	0	0	0	0	0	.000
Carleton p	0	0	0	0	0	0	.000
Dean p	0	0	0	0	0	0	.667
c-Reynolds ph	1	0	0	0	0	0	.000
TOTALS	**36**	**3**	**8**	**1**	**2**	**2**	**.243**

a - Batted for Lee in the 4th
b - Batted for Root in the 7th
c - Batted for Dean in the 9th

BATTING: 2B: Jurges (1, Ruffing), Cavarretta (1, Ruffing). **HR:** O'Dea (1, 8th off Ruffing 1 on, 2 out). **RBI:** O'Dea 2 (2). **2-out RBI:** O'Dea 2. **Runners left in scoring position, 2 out:** Herman 1, Cavarretta 1, Galan 1. **Team LOB:** 8 **FIELDING: E:** Jurges (1).

NY YANKEES	AB	R	H	HR	RBI	BB	AVG
Crosetti ss	5	0	2	0	4	0	.250
Rolfe 3b	5	0	1	0	0	0	.167
Henrich rf	4	1	1	1	1	0	.250
DiMaggio cf	4	1	1	0	0	0	.267
Gehrig 1b	4	1	1	0	0	0	.286
Dickey c	4	0	1	0	0	0	.400
Hoag lf	4	2	2	0	1	0	.400
Gordon 2b	3	2	1	0	0	1	.400
Ruffing p	3	1	1	0	1	1	.167
TOTALS	**36**	**8**	**11**	**1**	**7**	**2**	**.274**

BATTING: 2B: Hoag (1, Carleton), Crosetti (2, Dean). **3B:** Crosetti (1, Lee). **HR:** Henrich (1, 6th off Root 0 on, 0 out). **RBI:** Crosetti 4 (6), Henrich 1 (1), Hoag 1 (1), Ruffing 1 (1). **2-out RBI:** Crosetti 4, Hoag 1, Ruffing 1. **Runners left in scoring position, 2 out:** Rolfe 3, DiMaggio 1, Gordon 1. **Team LOB:** 6 **BASERUNNING: SB:** Rolfe (1, 2nd base off Lee/O'Dea), Gordon (1, 2nd base off Carleton/O'Dea).

CHICAGO CUBS	IP	H	R	ER	BB	SO	HR	ERA
Lee (L, 0-2)	3	4	3	0	0	2	0	2.45
Root	3	3	1	1	0	1	1	3.00
Page	1.1	2	2	2	0	0	0	13.50
French	0.1	0	0	0	0	0	0	2.70
Carleton	0	1	2	2	2	0	0	0.00
Dean	0.1	1	0	0	0	0	0	6.48

NY YANKEES	IP	H	R	ER	BB	SO	HR	ERA
Ruffing (W, 2-0)	9	8	3	2	2	6	1	1.50

WP: Carleton 2. **IBB:** Gordon (by Carleton). **Ground balls-fly balls:** Lee 6-2, Root 0-8, Page 3-1, French 0-1, Carleton 0-0, Dean 0-1, Ruffing 10-12. **Batters faced:** Lee 14, Root 12, Page 6, French 1, Carleton 3, Dean 2, Ruffing 38. **UMPIRES:** hp—Hubbard, 1b—Moran, 2b—Kolls, 3b—Sears **T:** 2:11 **A:** 59,847

1939 NY YANKEES DEF. CINCINNATI, 4-0

GAME 1 New York 2 Cincinnati 1
Yankee Stadium 10/04/39

CINCINNATI	AB	R	H	HR	RBI	BB	AVG
Werber 3b	4	0	0	0	0	0	.000
Frey 2b	4	0	0	0	0	0	.000
Goodman rf	2	1	0	0	0	1	.000
McCormick 1b	3	0	2	0	1	0	.667
Lombardi c	3	0	0	0	0	0	.000
Craft cf	3	0	1	0	0	0	.333
Berger lf	3	0	0	0	0	0	.000
Myers ss	3	0	1	0	0	0	.333
Derringer p	3	0	0	0	0	0	.000
TOTALS	**28**	**1**	**4**	**0**	**1**	**1**	**.143**

BATTING: RBI: McCormick 1 (1). **2-out RBI:** McCormick 1. **GIDP:** Lombardi, Derringer, Myers. **Team LOB:** 1 **BASERUNNING: SB:** Goodman (1, 2nd base off Ruffing/Dickey).

NY YANKEES	AB	R	H	HR	RBI	BB	AVG
Crosetti ss	4	0	0	0	0	0	.000
Rolfe 3b	4	0	0	0	0	0	.000
Keller rf	4	1	1	0	0	0	.250
DiMaggio cf	3	0	1	0	0	1	.333
Dickey c	4	0	1	0	1	0	.250
Selkirk lf	3	0	0	0	0	0	.000
Gordon 2b	3	1	1	0	0	0	.333
Dahlgren 1b	3	0	1	0	1	0	.333
Ruffing p	3	0	1	0	0	0	.333
TOTALS	**31**	**2**	**6**	**0**	**2**	**1**	**.194**

BATTING: 2B: Dahlgren (1, Derringer). **3B:** Keller (1, Derringer). **RBI:** Dickey 1 (1), Dahlgren 1 (1). **Runners left in scoring position, 2 out:** Crosetti 1. **Team LOB:** 5 **FIELDING: DP:** 3 (Rolfe-Gordon-Dahlgren, Ruffing-Crosetti-Gordon-Dahlgren, Gordon-Crosetti-Dahlgren).

CINCINNATI	IP	H	R	ER	BB	SO	HR	ERA
Derringer (L, 0-1)	8.1	6	2	2	1	7	0	2.16

NY YANKEES	IP	H	R	ER	BB	SO	HR	ERA
Ruffing (W, 1-0)	9	4	1	1	1	4	0	1.00

IBB: DiMaggio (by Derringer). **Ground balls-fly balls:** Derringer 8-10, Ruffing 12-8. **Batters faced:** Derringer 32, Ruffing 29. **UMPIRES:** hp—McGowan, 1b—Reardon, 2b—Summers, 3b—Pinelli **T:** 1:33 **A:** 58,541

GAME 2 New York 4 Cincinnati 0
Yankee Stadium 10/05/39

CINCINNATI	AB	R	H	HR	RBI	BB	AVG
Werber 3b	3	0	1	0	0	1	.143
Frey 2b	4	0	0	0	0	0	.000
Goodman rf	3	0	0	0	0	0	.000
McCormick 1b	3	0	0	0	0	0	.333
Lombardi c	3	0	1	0	0	0	.167
a-Bordagaray pr	0	0	0	0	0	0	.000
Hershberger c	0	0	0	0	0	0	.000
Craft cf	3	0	0	0	0	0	.167
Berger lf	3	0	0	0	0	0	.000
Myers ss	3	0	0	0	0	0	.167
Walters p	2	0	0	0	0	0	.000
b-Gamble ph	1	0	0	0	0	0	.000
TOTALS	**28**	**0**	**2**	**0**	**0**	**1**	**.107**

a - Ran for Lombardi in the 8th
b - Batted for Walters in the 9th

BATTING: Team LOB: 2 **BASERUNNING: CS:** Werber (1, 2nd base off Pearson/Dickey). **FIELDING: Outfield assists:** Craft (1). **DP:** 1 (Walters-Myers-McCormick).

NY YANKEES	AB	R	H	HR	RBI	BB	AVG
Crosetti ss	4	0	1	0	1	0	.125
Rolfe 3b	4	1	1	0	0	0	.125
Keller rf	4	1	2	0	1	0	.375
DiMaggio cf	4	0	1	0	0	0	.286
Dickey c	3	0	1	0	1	0	.286
Selkirk lf	3	0	1	0	0	0	.167
Gordon 2b	3	0	0	0	0	0	.167
Dahlgren 1b	3	2	2	1	1	0	.500
Pearson p	2	0	0	0	0	0	.000
TOTALS	**30**	**4**	**9**	**1**	**4**	**0**	**.246**

BATTING: 2B: Dahlgren (2, Walters), Keller (1, Walters). **HR:** Dahlgren (1, 4th off Walters 0 on, 1 out). **S:** Pearson. **RBI:** Crosetti 1 (1), Keller 1 (1), Dickey 1 (2), Dahlgren 1 (2). **2-out RBI:** Keller 1, Dickey 1. **Runners left in scoring position, 2 out:** Selkirk 1. **GIDP:** DiMaggio. **Team LOB:** 3 **FIELDING: DP:** 1 (Dickey-Crosetti).

CINCINNATI	IP	H	R	ER	BB	SO	HR	ERA
Walters (L, 0-1)	8	9	4	4	0	5	1	4.50

NY YANKEES	IP	H	R	ER	BB	SO	HR	ERA
Pearson (W, 1-0)	9	2	0	0	1	8	0	0.00

Ground balls-fly balls: Walters 9-7, Pearson 8-10. **Batters faced:** Walters 31, Pearson 29. **UMPIRES:** hp—Reardon, 1b—Summers, 2b—Pinelli, 3b—McGowan **T:** 1:27 **A:** 59,791

GAME 3 New York 7 Cincinnati 3
Crosley Field 10/07/39

NY YANKEES	AB	R	H	HR	RBI	BB	AVG
Crosetti ss	4	1	0	0	0	1	.083
Rolfe 3b	4	1	1	0	0	0	.167
Keller rf	3	3	2	2	4	1	.455
DiMaggio cf	4	1	1	1	2	0	.273
Dickey c	3	1	1	1	1	1	.300
Selkirk lf	2	0	0	0	0	2	.125
Gordon 2b	4	0	0	0	0	0	.100
Dahlgren 1b	4	0	0	0	0	0	.300
Gomez p	1	0	0	0	0	0	.000
Hadley p	3	0	0	0	0	0	.000
TOTALS	**32**	**7**	**5**	**4**	**7**	**5**	**.215**

BATTING: HR: Keller 2 (2, 1st off Thompson 1 on, 1 out, 5th off Thompson 1 on, 1 out), DiMaggio (1, 3th off Thompson 1 on, 2 out), Dickey (1, 5th off Thompson 0 on, 2 out). **RBI:** Keller 4 (5), DiMaggio 2 (2), Dickey 1 (3). **2-out RBI:** DiMaggio 2, Dickey 1. **Runners left in scoring position, 2 out:** Selkirk 1. **Team LOB:** 3 **FIELDING: E:** Hadley (1). **DP:** 1 (Rolfe-Gordon-Dahlgren).

CINCINNATI	AB	R	H	HR	RBI	BB	AVG
Werber 3b	4	1	1	0	1	1	.182
Frey 2b	4	0	0	0	0	1	.000
Goodman rf	5	1	3	0	1	0	.300
McCormick 1b	5	0	2	0	0	0	.364
Lombardi c	3	0	1	0	1	0	.222
b-Bordagaray pr	0	0	0	0	0	0	.000
Hershberger c	1	0	0	0	0	0	.000
Craft cf	4	0	0	0	0	0	.100
Berger lf	4	0	0	0	0	0	.000
Myers ss	3	1	2	0	0	1	.333
Thompson p	1	0	1	0	0	0	1.000
Grissom p	0	0	0	0	0	0	.000
a-Bongiovanni ph	1	0	0	0	0	0	.000
Moore p	1	0	0	0	0	0	.000
TOTALS	**36**	**3**	**10**	**0**	**3**	**3**	**.174**

a - Batted for Grissom in the 6th
b - Ran for Lombardi in the 7th

BATTING: S: Thompson. **RBI:** Werber 1 (1), Goodman 1 (1), Lombardi 1 (1). **2-out RBI:** Goodman 1, Lombardi 1. **Runners left in scoring position, 2 out:** Frey 2, McCormick 1, Hershberger 1, Craft 1. **GIDP:** Craft. **Team LOB:** 11

NY YANKEES	IP	H	R	ER	BB	SO	HR	ERA
Gomez	1	3	1	1	0	1	0	9.00
Hadley (W, 1-0)	8	7	2	2	3	2	0	2.25

CINCINNATI	IP	H	R	ER	BB	SO	HR	ERA
Thompson (L, 0-1)	4.2	5	7	7	4	3	4	13.50
Grissom	1.1	0	0	0	1	0	0	0.00
Moore	3	0	0	0	0	2	0	0.00

WP: Thompson 1. **HBP:** Lombardi (by Hadley). **Ground balls-fly balls:** Gomez 1-1, Hadley 11-10, Thompson 6-5, Grissom 2-2, Moore 3-4. **Batters faced:** Gomez 6, Hadley 35, Thompson 23, Grissom 5, Moore 9. **UMPIRES:** hp—Summers, 1b—Pinelli, 2b—McGowan, 3b—Reardon **T:** 2:01 **A:** 32,723

GAME 4 New York 7 Cincinnati 4
Crosley Field 10/08/39

NY YANKEES	AB	R	H	HR	RBI	BB	AVG
Crosetti ss	4	1	0	0	0	1	.063
Rolfe 3b	4	0	0	0	0	0	.125
Keller rf	5	3	2	1	1	0	.438
DiMaggio cf	5	2	2	0	3	0	.313
Dickey c	5	1	1	1	2	0	.267
Selkirk lf	4	0	1	0	0	1	.167
Gordon 2b	4	0	1	0	1	0	.143
Dahlgren 1b	4	0	0	0	0	0	.214
Hildebrand p	1	0	0	0	0	0	.000
Sundra p	0	0	0	0	0	1	.000
Murphy p	2	0	0	0	0	0	.000
TOTALS	**38**	**7**	**7**	**2**	**7**	**3**	**.206**

BATTING: 2B: Selkirk (1, Derringer). **HR:** Keller (3, 7th off Derringer 0 on, 0 out), Dickey (2, 7th off Derringer 0 on, 1 out). **S:** Rolfe. **RBI:** Keller 1 (6), DiMaggio 3 (5), Dickey 2 (5), Gordon 1 (1). **Runners left in scoring position, 2 out:** Gordon 1, Murphy 1. **Team LOB:** 5 **FIELDING: E:** Rolfe (1).

CINCINNATI	AB	R	H	HR	RBI	BB	AVG
Werber 3b	5	0	2	0	1	0	.250
Frey 2b	5	0	0	0	0	0	.000
Goodman rf	5	1	2	0	0	0	.333
McCormick 1b	4	1	2	0	0	0	.400
Lombardi c	5	0	1	0	1	0	.214
Craft cf	1	0	0	0	0	0	.091
Simmons lf	4	1	1	0	0	0	.250
Berger lf-cf	5	0	0	0	1	0	.000
Myers ss	3	1	1	0	0	1	.333
Derringer p	2	0	1	0	0	0	.200
a-Hershberger ph	1	0	1	0	1	0	.500
Walters p	1	0	0	0	0	0	.000
TOTALS	**41**	**4**	**11**	**0**	**4**	**1**	**.203**

a - Batted for Derringer in the 7th

BATTING: 2B: McCormick (1, Hildebrand), Simmons (1, Sundra), Goodman (1, Murphy). **3B:** Myers (1, Sundra). **S:** McCormick. **RBI:** Werber 1 (2), Lombardi 1 (2), Berger 1 (1), Hershberger 1 (1). **2-out RBI:** Werber 1, Hershberger 1. **Runners left in scoring position, 2 out:** Frey 1, Berger 2, Derringer 1. **Team LOB:** 9 **FIELDING: E:** Myers (1), Goodman (1). **Outfield assists:** Goodman (1).

NY YANKEES	IP	H	R	ER	BB	SO	HR	ERA
Hildebrand	4	2	0	0	0	3	0	0.00
Sundra	2.2	4	3	0	1	2	0	0.00
Murphy (W, 1-0)	3.1	5	1	1	0	2	0	2.70

CINCINNATI	IP	H	R	ER	BB	SO	HR	ERA
Derringer	7	3	2	2	2	2	2	2.35
Walters (L, 0-2)	3	4	5	2	1	1	0	4.91

Ground balls-fly balls: Hildebrand 6-3, Sundra 4-3, Murphy 2-5, Derringer 8-11, Walters 2-7. **Batters faced:** Hildebrand 14, Sundra 14, Murphy 15, Derringer 26, Walters 16. **UMPIRES:** hp—Pinelli, 1b—McGowan, 2b—Reardon, 3b—Summers **T:** 2:04 **A:** 32,794

1940 CINCINNATI DEF. DETROIT, 4-3

GAME 1 Detroit 7 Cincinnati 2
Crosley Field 10/02/40

DETROIT	AB	R	H	HR	RBI	BB	AVG
Bartell ss	4	0	2	0	2	1	.500
McCosky cf	5	0	2	0	1	0	.400
Gehringer 2b	4	0	0	0	0	1	.000
Greenberg lf	5	1	1	0	0	0	.200
York 1b	4	2	2	0	0	1	.500
Campbell rf	3	1	2	1	2	1	.667
Higgins 3b	4	1	1	0	2	0	.250
Sullivan c	3	1	0	0	0	1	.000
Newsom p	4	1	0	0	0	0	.000
TOTALS	**36**	**7**	**10**	**1**	**7**	**5**	**.278**

BATTING: 3B: York (1, Moore). **HR:** Campbell (1, 5th off Moore 1 on, 1 out). **S:** Campbell. **RBI:** Bartell 2 (2), McCosky 1 (1), Campbell 2 (2), Higgins 2 (2). **Runners left in scoring position, 2 out:** Gehringer 2, Greenberg 1, Sullivan 2. **Team LOB:** 8 **BASERUNNING: CS:** Campbell (1, 2nd base off Moore/Wilson), Bartell (1, 2nd base off Moore/Baker). **FIELDING: DP:** 1 (Higgins-Gehringer-York).

CINCINNATI	AB	R	H	HR	RBI	BB	AVG
Werber 3b	4	1	1	0	0	0	.250
M.McCormick cf	4	0	1	0	0	0	.250
Goodman rf	4	1	2	0	1	0	.500
F.McCormick 1b	3	0	0	0	0	1	.000
Ripple lf	4	0	1	0	1	0	.250
Wilson c	2	0	0	0	0	0	.000
a-Riggs ph	1	0	0	0	0	0	.000
Baker c	1	0	1	0	0	0	1.000
Joost 2b	4	0	2	0	0	0	.500
Myers ss	4	0	0	0	0	0	.000
Derringer p	0	0	0	0	0	0	.000
Moore p	2	0	0	0	0	0	.000
b-Craft ph	1	0	0	0	0	0	.000
Riddle p	0	0	0	0	0	0	.000
TOTALS	**34**	**2**	**8**	**0**	**2**	**1**	**.235**

a - Batted for Wilson in the 7th
b - Batted for Moore in the 8th

BATTING: 2B: M.McCormick (1, Newsom), Goodman (1, Newsom), Werber (1, Newsom). **RBI:** Goodman 1 (1), Ripple 1 (1). **2-out RBI:** Goodman 1. **Runners left in scoring position, 2 out:** Werber 1, F.McCormick 1. **GIDP:** Wilson. **Team LOB:** 6 **BASERUNNING: CS:** Joost (1, 2nd base off Newsom/Sullivan). **FIELDING: E:** Werber (1), Baker (1). **DP:** 1 (Wilson-Joost).

DETROIT	IP	H	R	ER	BB	SO	HR	ERA
Newsom (W, 1-0)	9	8	2	2	1	4	0	2.00

CINCINNATI	IP	H	R	ER	BB	SO	HR	ERA
Derringer (L, 0-1)	1.1	5	5	4	1	1	0	27.00
Moore	6.2	5	2	2	4	7	1	2.70
Riddle	1	0	0	0	0	2	0	0.00

Ground balls-fly balls: Newsom 9-13, Derringer 2-1, Moore 4-8, Riddle 0-1. **Batters faced:** Newsom 35, Derringer 11, Moore 28, Riddle 3. **UMPIRES:** hp—Klem, 1b—Ormsby, 2b—Ballanfant, 3b—Basil **T:** 2:09 **A:** 31,793

GAME 2 Cincinnati 5 Detroit 3
Crosley Field 10/03/40

DETROIT	AB	R	H	HR	RBI	BB	AVG
Bartell ss	3	1	0	0	0	1	.286
McCosky cf	2	1	0	0	0	2	.286
Gehringer 2b	4	1	1	0	1	0	.125
Greenberg lf	3	0	1	0	2	1	.250
York 1b	4	0	0	0	0	0	.250
Campbell rf	4	0	0	0	0	0	.286
Higgins 3b	3	0	1	0	0	0	.286
Tebbetts c	3	0	0	0	0	0	.000
Rowe p	1	0	0	0	0	0	.000
Gorsica p	2	0	0	0	0	0	.000
TOTALS	**29**	**3**	**3**	**0**	**3**	**4**	**.200**

BATTING: 2B: Higgins (1, Walters), Greenberg (1, Walters). **RBI:** Gehringer 1 (1), Greenberg 2 (2). **Runners left in scoring position, 2 out:** Bartell 1, Campbell 1. **GIDP:** Greenberg. **Team LOB:** 3 **FIELDING: E:** Tebbetts (1).

CINCINNATI	AB	R	H	HR	RBI	BB	AVG
Werber 3b	3	0	1	0	1	1	.286
M.McCormick cf	4	0	0	0	0	0	.125
Goodman rf	4	1	1	0	0	0	.375
F.McCormick 1b	4	1	1	0	0	0	.143
Ripple lf	4	1	1	1	2	0	.250
Wilson c	4	1	2	0	0	0	.333
Joost 2b	4	0	1	0	1	0	.375
Myers ss	3	0	1	0	1	0	.143
Walters p	3	1	1	0	0	0	.333
TOTALS	**33**	**5**	**9**	**1**	**5**	**1**	**.254**

BATTING: 2B: Walters (1, Rowe), Werber (2, Rowe). **HR:** Ripple (1, 3th off Rowe 1 on, 1 out). **RBI:** Werber 1 (1), Ripple 2 (3), Joost 1 (1), Myers 1 (1). **Runners left in scoring position, 2 out:** M.McCormick 2. **Team LOB:** 5 **FIELDING: DP:** 1 (Werber-Joost-F.McCormick).

DETROIT	IP	H	R	ER	BB	SO	HR	ERA
Rowe (L, 0-1)	3.1	8	5	5	1	1	1	13.50
Gorsica	4.2	1	0	0	0	1	0	0.00

CINCINNATI	IP	H	R	ER	BB	SO	HR	ERA
Walters (W, 1-0)	9	3	3	3	4	4	0	3.00

Ground balls-fly balls: Rowe 2-7, Gorsica 9-4, Walters 10-12. **Batters faced:** Rowe 19, Gorsica 15, Walters 33. **UMPIRES:** hp—Ormsby, 1b—Ballanfant, 2b—Basil, 3b—Klem **T:** 1:54 **A:** 30,640

GAME 3 Detroit 7 Cincinnati 4
Briggs Stadium 10/04/40

CINCINNATI	AB	R	H	HR	RBI	BB	AVG
Werber 3b	4	1	3	0	1	1	.455
M.McCormick cf	5	0	2	0	1	0	.231
Goodman rf	4	0	1	0	1	0	.333
F.McCormick 1b	4	0	0	0	0	0	.091
Ripple lf	4	1	1	0	0	0	.250
Lombardi c	3	0	1	0	0	0	.333
Baker c	1	1	0	0	0	0	.500
Joost 2b	4	0	1	0	1	0	.333
Myers ss	4	0	1	0	0	0	.182
Turner p	2	0	0	0	0	0	.000
Moore p	0	0	0	0	0	0	.000
a-Riggs ph	1	1	0	0	0	0	.000
Beggs p	0	0	0	0	0	0	.000
b-Frey ph	1	0	0	0	0	0	.000
TOTALS	**37**	**4**	**10**	**0**	**4**	**1**	**.260**

a - Batted for Moore in the 8th
b - Batted for Beggs in the 9th

BATTING: 2B: Werber (3, Bridges), Lombardi (1, Bridges). **RBI:** Werber 1 (2), M.McCormick 1 (1), Goodman 1 (2), Joost 1 (2). **2-out RBI:** Werber 1. **Runners left in scoring position, 2 out:** M.McCormick 1, F.McCormick 1, Turner 1. **Team LOB:** 7 **BASERUNNING: CS:** Werber (1, 2nd base off Bridges/Tebbetts). **FIELDING: E:** M.McCormick (1). **DP:** 2 (Werber-F.McCormick-Joost, Myers-F.McCormick-Baker).

DETROIT	AB	R	H	HR	RBI	BB	AVG
Bartell ss	4	0	1	0	0	0	.273
McCosky cf	4	1	2	0	0	0	.364
Gehringer 2b	4	0	1	0	0	0	.167
Greenberg lf	4	2	2	0	1	0	.333
York 1b	4	1	2	1	2	0	.333
Campbell rf	4	2	3	0	1	0	.455
Higgins 3b	4	1	2	1	3	0	.364
Tebbetts c	4	0	0	0	0	0	.000
Bridges p	3	0	0	0	0	0	.000
TOTALS	**35**	**7**	**13**	**2**	**7**	**0**	**.260**

BATTING: 2B: Campbell (1, Turner), McCosky (1, Moore), Higgins (2, Beggs). **3B:** Greenberg (1, Beggs). **HR:** York (1, 7th off Turner 1 on, 0 out), Higgins (1, 7th off Turner 1 on, 0 out). **RBI:** Greenberg 1 (3), York 2 (2), Campbell 1 (3), Higgins 3 (5). **Runners left in scoring position, 2 out:** Gehringer 2, Higgins 1. **GIDP:** Greenberg. **Team LOB:** 4 **FIELDING: E:** Higgins (1).

CINCINNATI	IP	H	R	ER	BB	SO	HR	ERA
Turner (L, 0-1)	6	8	5	5	0	4	2	7.50
Moore	1	2	0	0	0	0	0	2.35
Beggs	1	3	2	1	0	1	0	9.00

DETROIT	IP	H	R	ER	BB	SO	HR	ERA
Bridges (W, 1-0)	9	10	4	3	1	5	0	3.00

Ground balls-fly balls: Turner 7-6, Moore 1-2, Beggs 1-0, Bridges 12-10. **Batters faced:** Turner 25, Moore 5, Beggs 5, Bridges 38. **UMPIRES:** hp—Ballanfant, 1b—Basil, 2b—Klem, 3b—Ormsby **T:** 2:08 **A:** 52,877

GAME 4 Cincinnati 5 Detroit 2
Briggs Stadium 10/05/40

CINCINNATI	AB	R	H	HR	RBI	BB	AVG
Werber 3b	3	2	2	0	0	2	.500
M.McCormick cf	5	1	2	0	1	0	.278
Goodman rf	5	2	2	0	2	0	.353
F.McCormick 1b	5	0	2	0	0	0	.188
Ripple lf	2	0	1	0	1	1	.286
a-Arnovich ph-lf	1	0	0	0	0	0	.000
Wilson c	5	0	1	0	0	0	.273
Joost 2b	5	0	1	0	0	0	.294
Myers ss	3	0	0	0	0	1	.143
Derringer p	4	0	0	0	0	0	.000
TOTALS	**38**	**5**	**11**	**0**	**4**	**4**	**.268**

a - Batted for Ripple in the 7th

BATTING: 2B: Goodman (2, Trout), Ripple (1, Trout), M.McCormick (2, Smith). **S:** Arnovich. **RBI:** M.McCormick 1 (2), Goodman 2 (4), Ripple 1 (4). **2-out RBI:** M.McCormick 1. **Runners left in scoring position, 2 out:** M.McCormick 1, Wilson 1, Joost 1, Derringer 2. **Team LOB:** 11 **FIELDING: E:** Myers (1). **DP:** 2 (Joost-Myers-F.McCormick, Derringer-Myers-F.McCormick).

DETROIT	AB	R	H	HR	RBI	BB	AVG
Bartell ss	4	0	0	0	0	0	.200
c-Fox ph	1	0	0	0	0	0	.000
McCosky cf	2	1	1	0	0	2	.385
Gehringer 2b	4	0	0	0	0	0	.125
Greenberg lf	4	0	1	0	1	0	.313
York 1b	2	0	0	0	0	2	.286
Campbell rf	4	1	1	0	0	0	.400
Higgins 3b	4	0	2	0	1	0	.400
Sullivan c	2	0	0	0	0	2	.000
Trout p	1	0	0	0	0	0	.000
Smith p	1	0	0	0	0	0	.000
a-Averill ph	1	0	0	0	0	0	.000
McKain p	0	0	0	0	0	0	.000
b-Tebbetts ph	1	0	0	0	0	0	.000
TOTALS	**31**	**2**	**5**	**0**	**2**	**6**	**.237**

a - Batted for Smith in the 6th
b - Batted for McKain in the 9th
c - Batted for Bartell in the 9th

BATTING: 2B: Greenberg (2, Derringer). **3B:** Higgins (1, Derringer). **RBI:** Greenberg 1 (4), Higgins 1 (6). **2-out RBI:** Greenberg 1, Higgins 1. **Runners left in scoring position, 2 out:** Campbell 1, Trout 2, Averill 1. **GIDP:** Gehringer, Gehringer. **Team LOB:** 8 **FIELDING: E:** Higgins (2).

CINCINNATI	IP	H	R	ER	BB	SO	HR	ERA
Derringer (W, 1-1)	9	5	2	2	6	4	0	5.23

DETROIT	IP	H	R	ER	BB	SO	HR	ERA
Trout (L, 0-1)	2	6	3	2	1	1	0	9.00
Smith	4	1	1	1	3	1	0	2.25
McKain	3	4	1	1	0	0	0	3.00

WP: McKain 1. **IBB:** Sullivan (by Derringer), Myers (by Smith), Ripple (by Smith). **Ground balls-fly balls:** Derringer 10-12, Trout 5-1, Smith 7-4, McKain 5-3. **Batters faced:** Derringer 37, Trout 14, Smith 16, McKain 13. **UMPIRES:** hp—Basil, 1b—Klem, 2b—Ormsby, 3b—Ballanfant **T:** 2:06 **A:** 54,093

GAME 5 Detroit 8 Cincinnati 0
Briggs Stadium 10/06/40

CINCINNATI	AB	R	H	HR	RBI	BB	AVG
Werber 3b	4	0	1	0	0	0	.444
M.McCormick cf	4	0	1	0	0	0	.273
Goodman rf	4	0	0	0	0	0	.286
F.McCormick 1b	4	0	1	0	0	0	.200
Ripple lf	2	0	0	0	0	1	.250
Wilson c	1	0	0	0	0	0	.250
a-Baker ph-c	2	0	0	0	0	0	.250
Joost 2b	3	0	0	0	0	0	.250
Myers ss	2	0	0	0	0	1	.125
Thompson p	1	0	0	0	0	0	.000
Moore p	0	0	0	0	0	0	.000
b-Frey ph	1	0	0	0	0	0	.000
Vander Meer p	0	0	0	0	0	0	.000
c-Riggs ph	1	0	0	0	0	0	.000
Hutchings p	0	0	0	0	0	0	.000
TOTALS	**29**	**0**	**3**	**0**	**0**	**2**	**.240**

a - Batted for Wilson in the 5th
b - Batted for Moore in the 5th
c - Batted for Vander Meer in the 8th

BATTING: Runners left in scoring position, 2 out: Ripple 1. **GIDP:** M.McCormick. **Team LOB:** 4 **FIELDING: PB:** Wilson. **Outfield assists:** M.McCormick (1).

DETROIT	AB	R	H	HR	RBI	BB	AVG
Bartell ss	4	1	2	0	1	1	.263
McCosky cf	3	2	2	0	0	2	.438
Gehringer 2b	4	2	2	0	0	1	.200
Greenberg lf	5	2	3	1	4	0	.381
York 1b	4	0	0	0	0	1	.222
Campbell rf	4	0	3	0	2	1	.474
Higgins 3b	2	0	0	0	0	3	.353
Sullivan c	4	1	1	0	0	1	.111
Newsom p	4	0	0	0	0	0	.000
TOTALS	**34**	**8**	**13**	**1**	**7**	**10**	**.267**

BATTING: 2B: Bartell (1, Thompson). **HR:** Greenberg (1, 3th off Thompson 2 on, 0 out). **S:** Newsom. **RBI:** Bartell 1 (3), Greenberg 4 (8), Campbell 2 (5). **2-out RBI:** Campbell 2. **Runners left in scoring position, 2 out:** Bartell 1, Gehringer 1, York 1, Higgins 1, Sullivan 1, Newsom 1. **Team LOB:** 13 **BASERUNNING: CS:** Campbell (2, 2nd base off Thompson/Wilson). **FIELDING: DP:** 1 (Bartell-Gehringer-York).

CINCINNATI	IP	H	R	ER	BB	SO	HR	ERA
Thompson (L, 0-1)	3.1	8	6	6	4	2	1	16.20
Moore	0.2	1	1	1	2	0	0	3.24
Vander Meer	3	2	0	0	3	2	0	0.00
Hutchings	1	2	1	1	1	0	0	9.00

DETROIT	IP	H	R	ER	BB	SO	HR	ERA
Newsom (W, 2-0)	9	3	0	0	2	7	0	1.00

WP: Hutchings 1. **Ground balls-fly balls:** Thompson 1-4, Moore 1-1, Vander Meer 1-6, Hutchings 1-2, Newsom 7-12. **Batters faced:** Thompson 20, Moore 5, Vander Meer 14, Hutchings 6, Newsom 31. **UMPIRES:** hp—Klem, 1b—Ormsby, 2b—Ballanfant, 3b—Basil **T:** 2:26 **A:** 55,189

GAME 6 Cincinnati 4 Detroit 0
Crosley Field 10/07/40

DETROIT	AB	R	H	HR	RBI	BB	AVG
Bartell ss	3	0	2	0	0	0	.318
b-Sullivan ph	1	0	0	0	0	0	.100
Croucher ss	0	0	0	0	0	0	.000
McCosky cf	4	0	0	0	0	0	.350
Gehringer 2b	4	0	0	0	0	0	.167
Greenberg lf	3	0	0	0	0	1	.333
York 1b	4	0	2	0	0	0	.273
Campbell rf	3	0	0	0	0	1	.409
Higgins 3b	3	0	1	0	0	0	.350
Tebbetts c	3	0	0	0	0	0	.000
Rowe p	0	0	0	0	0	0	.000
Gorsica p	2	0	0	0	0	0	.000
a-Averill ph	1	0	0	0	0	0	.000
Hutchinson p	0	0	0	0	0	0	.000
TOTALS	**31**	**0**	**5**	**0**	**0**	**2**	**.250**

a - Batted for Gorsica in the 8th
b - Batted for Bartell in the 8th

BATTING: 2B: Bartell (2, Walters). **Runners left in scoring position, 2 out:** Gehringer 1, Campbell 1, Higgins 1, Tebbetts 1. **GIDP:** Campbell, Gehringer, York. **Team LOB:** 6 **FIELDING: DP:** 1 (Gorsica-Tebbetts-York).

CINCINNATI	AB	R	H	HR	RBI	BB	AVG
Werber 3b	5	1	2	0	0	0	.435
M.McCormick cf	3	0	1	0	0	1	.280
Goodman rf	4	1	2	0	1	0	.320
F.McCormick 1b	4	0	1	0	0	0	.208
Ripple lf	2	0	2	0	1	2	.333
Wilson c	3	1	1	0	0	1	.267
Joost 2b	3	0	0	0	0	1	.217
Myers ss	4	0	0	0	0	0	.100
Walters p	4	1	1	1	2	0	.286
TOTALS	**32**	**4**	**10**	**1**	**4**	**5**	**.251**

BATTING: 2B: Werber (4, Rowe). **HR:** Walters (1, 8th off Hutchinson 0 on, 1 out). **S:** M.McCormick, Goodman. **RBI:** Goodman 1 (5), Ripple 1 (5), Walters 2 (2). **Runners left in scoring position, 2 out:** Joost 3. **GIDP:** Werber. **Team LOB:** 11 **FIELDING: E:** F.McCormick (1), Myers (2). **DP:** 3 (Joost-Myers-F.McCormick, F.McCormick-Myers-F.McCormick, Werber-Joost-F.McCormick).

DETROIT	IP	H	R	ER	BB	SO	HR	ERA
Rowe (L, 0-2)	0.1	4	2	2	0	0	0	17.18
Gorsica	6.2	5	1	1	4	3	0	0.79
Hutchinson	1	1	1	1	1	1	1	9.00

CINCINNATI	IP	H	R	ER	BB	SO	HR	ERA
Walters (W, 2-0)	9	5	0	0	2	2	0	1.50

IBB: Ripple (by Gorsica). **Ground balls-fly balls:** Rowe 0-0, Gorsica 11-5, Hutchinson 0-2, Walters 13-11. **Batters faced:** Rowe 5, Gorsica 29, Hutchinson 5, Walters 33. **UMPIRES:** hp—Ormsby, 1b—Ballanfant, 2b—Basil, 3b—Klem **T:** 2:01 **A:** 30,481

GAME 7 Cincinnati 2 Detroit 1
Crosley Field 10/08/40

DETROIT	AB	R	H	HR	RBI	BB	AVG
Bartell ss	4	0	0	0	0	0	.269
McCosky cf	3	0	0	0	0	1	.304
Gehringer 2b	4	0	2	0	1	0	.214
Greenberg lf	4	0	2	0	0	0	.357
York 1b	4	0	0	0	0	0	.231
Campbell rf	3	0	0	0	0	1	.360
Higgins 3b	4	0	1	0	0	0	.333
Sullivan c	3	1	1	0	0	1	.154
Newsom p	2	0	1	0	0	0	.100
a-Averill ph	1	0	0	0	0	0	.000
TOTALS	**32**	**1**	**7**	**0**	**1**	**3**	**.246**

a - Batted for Newsom in the 9th

BATTING: 2B: Higgins (3, Derringer). **S:** Newsom. **RBI:** Gehringer 1 (2). **2-out RBI:** Gehringer 1. **Runners left in scoring position, 2 out:** Greenberg 1, Higgins 1, Sullivan 1, Newsom 1. **Team LOB:** 8 **FIELDING: DP:** 1 (Gehringer-Bartell-York).

CINCINNATI	AB	R	H	HR	RBI	BB	AVG
Werber 3b	4	0	0	0	0	0	.370
M.McCormick cf	4	0	2	0	0	0	.310
Goodman rf	4	0	0	0	0	0	.276
F.McCormick 1b	4	1	1	0	0	0	.214
Ripple lf	3	1	1	0	1	0	.333
Wilson c	2	0	2	0	0	0	.353
Joost 2b	2	0	0	0	0	0	.200
a-Lombardi ph	0	0	0	0	0	1	.333
b-Frey pr-2b	0	0	0	0	0	0	.000
Myers ss	3	0	1	0	1	0	.130
Derringer p	3	0	0	0	0	0	.000
TOTALS	**29**	**2**	**7**	**0**	**2**	**1**	**.250**

a - Batted for Joost in the 7th
b - Ran for Lombardi in the 7th

BATTING: 2B: M.McCormick (3, Newsom), F.McCormick (1, Newsom), Ripple (2, Newsom). **S:** Wilson. **RBI:** Ripple 1 (6), Myers 1 (2). **Runners left in scoring position, 2 out:** Goodman 1, Joost 1. **GIDP:** Joost. **Team LOB:** 5 **BASERUNNING: SB:** Wilson (1, 2nd base off Newsom/Sullivan). **FIELDING: E:** Werber (2).

DETROIT	IP	H	R	ER	BB	SO	HR	ERA
Newsom (L, 2-1)	8	7	2	2	1	6	0	1.38

CINCINNATI	IP	H	R	ER	BB	SO	HR	ERA
Derringer (W, 2-1)	9	7	1	0	3	1	0	2.79

IBB: Sullivan (by Derringer), Lombardi (by Newsom). **Ground balls-fly balls:** Newsom 7-9, Derringer 8-16. **Batters faced:** Newsom 31, Derringer 36. **UMPIRES:** hp—Ballanfant, 1b—Basil, 2b—Klem, 3b—Ormsby **T:** 1:47 **A:** 26,854

1941 NY YANKEES DEF. BROOKLYN, 4-1

GAME 1 New York 3 Brooklyn 2
Yankee Stadium 10/01/41

BROOKLYN	AB	R	H	HR	RBI	BB	AVG
Walker rf	3	0	0	0	0	1	.000
Herman 2b	3	0	0	0	0	1	.000
Reiser cf	3	0	0	0	0	1	.000
Camilli 1b	4	0	0	0	0	0	.000
Medwick lf	4	0	1	0	0	0	.250
Lavagetto 3b	4	1	0	0	0	0	.000
Reese ss	4	1	3	0	0	0	.750
Owen c	2	0	1	0	1	0	.500
a-Riggs ph	1	0	1	0	1	0	1.000
Franks c	1	0	0	0	0	0	.000
Davis p	2	0	0	0	0	0	.000
Casey p	0	0	0	0	0	0	.000
b-Wasdell ph	1	0	0	0	0	0	.000
Allen p	0	0	0	0	0	0	.000
TOTALS	**32**	**2**	**6**	**0**	**2**	**3**	**.188**

a - Batted for Owen in the 7th
b - Batted for Casey in the 7th

BATTING: 3B: Owen (1, Ruffing). **RBI:** Owen 1 (1), Riggs 1 (1). **2-out RBI:** Owen 1. **Runners left in scoring position, 2 out:** Camilli 1, Medwick 1, Davis 1. **GIDP:** Franks. **Team LOB:** 6

NY YANKEES	AB	R	H	HR	RBI	BB	AVG
Sturm 1b	3	0	1	0	0	0	.333
Rolfe 3b	3	0	1	0	0	1	.333
Henrich rf	4	0	0	0	0	0	.000
DiMaggio cf	4	0	0	0	0	0	.000
Keller lf	2	2	0	0	0	2	.000
Dickey c	4	0	2	0	1	0	.500
Gordon 2b	2	1	2	1	2	2	1.000
Rizzuto ss	4	0	0	0	0	0	.000
Ruffing p	3	0	0	0	0	0	.000
TOTALS	**29**	**3**	**6**	**1**	**3**	**5**	**.207**

BATTING: 2B: Dickey (1, Davis). **HR:** Gordon (1, 2nd off Davis 0 on, 2 out). **RBI:** Dickey 1 (1), Gordon 2 (2). **2-out RBI:** Dickey 1, Gordon 1. **Runners left in scoring position, 2 out:** Rizzuto 1, Ruffing 1. **Team LOB:** 8 **BASERUNNING: CS:** Sturm (1, 2nd base off Allen/Franks). **FIELDING: E:** Rizzuto (1). **DP:** 2 (Rolfe-Rizzuto, Gordon-Rizzuto-Sturm).

BROOKLYN	IP	H	R	ER	BB	SO	HR	ERA
Davis (L, 0-1)	5.1	6	3	3	3	1	1	5.06
Casey	0.2	0	0	0	0	0	0	0.00
Allen	2	0	0	0	2	0	0	0.00

NY YANKEES	IP	H	R	ER	BB	SO	HR	ERA
Ruffing (W, 1-0)	9	6	2	1	3	5	0	1.00

IBB: Gordon (by Davis). **HBP:** Sturm (by Allen). **Ground balls-fly balls:** Davis 8-7, Casey 0-2, Allen 2-3, Ruffing 9-12. **Batters faced:** Davis 25, Casey 2, Allen 8, Ruffing 35. **UMPIRES:** hp—McGowan, 1b—Pinelli, 2b—Grieve, 3b—Goetz **T:** 2:08 **A:** 68,540

GAME 2 Brooklyn 3 New York 2
Yankee Stadium 10/02/41

BROOKLYN	AB	R	H	HR	RBI	BB	AVG
Walker rf	4	1	0	0	0	0	.000
Herman 2b	4	0	1	0	0	0	.143
Reiser cf	4	0	0	0	0	0	.000
Camilli 1b	3	1	1	0	1	1	.143
Medwick lf	4	1	2	0	0	0	.375
Lavagetto 3b	3	0	1	0	0	1	.143
Reese ss	4	0	0	0	1	0	.375
Owen c	2	0	1	0	1	1	.500
Wyatt p	3	0	0	0	0	0	.000
TOTALS	**31**	**3**	**6**	**0**	**3**	**3**	**.190**

BATTING: 2B: Medwick (1, Chandler). **RBI:** Camilli 1 (1), Reese 1 (1), Owen 1 (2). **Runners left in scoring position, 2 out:** Lavagetto 1. **GIDP:** Lavagetto, Wyatt. **Team LOB:** 4 **BASERUNNING: CS:** Owen (1, 2nd base off Murphy/Dickey). **FIELDING: E:** Reese (1). **Outfield assists:** Reiser (1). **DP:** 1 (Reese-Herman-Camilli).

NY YANKEES	AB	R	H	HR	RBI	BB	AVG
Sturm 1b	5	0	1	0	0	0	.250
Rolfe 3b	5	0	1	0	0	0	.250
Henrich rf	4	1	1	0	0	1	.125
DiMaggio cf	3	0	0	0	0	1	.000
Keller lf	4	1	2	0	1	0	.333
Dickey c	4	0	0	0	0	0	.250
a-Bordagaray pr	0	0	0	0	0	0	.000
Rosar c	0	0	0	0	0	0	.000
Gordon 2b	1	0	1	0	0	3	1.000
Rizzuto ss	4	0	1	0	0	0	.125
Chandler p	2	0	1	0	1	0	.500
Murphy p	1	0	0	0	0	0	.000
b-Selkirk ph	1	0	1	0	0	0	1.000
TOTALS	**34**	**2**	**9**	**0**	**2**	**5**	**.238**

a - Ran for Dickey in the 8th
b - Batted for Murphy in the 9th

BATTING: 2B: Henrich (1, Wyatt). **RBI:** Keller 1 (1), Chandler 1 (1). **2-out RBI:** Keller 1, Chandler 1. **Runners left in scoring position, 2 out:** Dickey 1, Rizzuto 1, Chandler 2, Murphy 1. **GIDP:** DiMaggio. **Team LOB:** 10 **FIELDING: E:** Gordon (1). **DP:** 3 (Gordon-Rizzuto-Sturm 2, Dickey-Gordon).

BROOKLYN	IP	H	R	ER	BB	SO	HR	ERA
Wyatt (W, 1-0)	9	9	2	2	5	5	0	2.00

NY YANKEES	IP	H	R	ER	BB	SO	HR	ERA
Chandler (L, 0-1)	5	4	3	2	2	2	0	3.60
Murphy	4	2	0	0	1	2	0	0.00

IBB: Gordon (by Wyatt). **Ground balls-fly balls:** Wyatt 12-8, Chandler 10-2, Murphy 3-6. **Batters faced:** Wyatt 39, Chandler 20, Murphy 14. **UMPIRES:** hp—Pinelli, 1b—Grieve, 2b—Goetz, 3b—McGowan **T:** 2:31 **A:** 66,248

GAME 3 New York 2 Brooklyn 1
Ebbets Field 10/04/41

NY YANKEES	AB	R	H	HR	RBI	BB	AVG
Sturm 1b	4	0	1	0	0	0	.250
Rolfe 3b	4	1	2	0	0	0	.333
Henrich rf	3	1	1	0	0	1	.182
DiMaggio cf	4	0	2	0	1	0	.182
Keller lf	4	0	1	0	1	0	.300
Dickey c	4	0	0	0	0	0	.167
Gordon 2b	3	0	1	0	0	1	.667
Rizzuto ss	3	0	0	0	0	1	.091
Russo p	4	0	0	0	0	0	.000
TOTALS	**33**	**2**	**8**	**0**	**2**	**3**	**.240**

BATTING: 3B: Gordon (1, Fitzsimmons). **RBI:** DiMaggio 1 (1), Keller 1 (2). **Runners left in scoring position, 2 out:** Keller 1, Gordon 1, Russo 3. **GIDP:** Dickey. **Team LOB:** 7 **BASERUNNING: SB:** Rizzuto (1, 2nd base off Fitzsimmons/Owen), Sturm (1, 2nd base off Fitzsimmons/Owen). **FIELDING: DP:** 1 (Rizzuto-Sturm).

BROOKLYN	AB	R	H	HR	RBI	BB	AVG
Reese ss	4	0	1	0	1	0	.333
Herman 2b	1	0	0	0	0	1	.125
Coscarart 2b	2	0	0	0	0	0	.000
Reiser cf	4	0	1	0	0	0	.091
Medwick lf	4	0	1	0	0	0	.333
Lavagetto 3b	3	0	0	0	0	1	.100
Camilli 1b	3	0	0	0	0	0	.100
Walker rf	3	1	1	0	0	0	.100
Owen c	3	0	0	0	0	0	.286
Fitzsimmons p	2	0	0	0	0	0	.000
Casey p	0	0	0	0	0	0	.000
French p	0	0	0	0	0	0	.000
a-Galan ph	1	0	0	0	0	0	.000
Allen p	0	0	0	0	0	0	.000
TOTALS	**30**	**1**	**4**	**0**	**1**	**2**	**.172**

a - Batted for French in the 8th

BATTING: 2B: Reiser (1, Russo), Walker (1, Russo). **RBI:** Reese 1 (2). **2-out RBI:** Reese 1. **Runners left in scoring position, 2 out:** Camilli 1. **GIDP:** Camilli. **Team LOB:** 4 **FIELDING: DP:** 1 (Reese-Camilli).

NY YANKEES	IP	H	R	ER	BB	SO	HR	ERA
Russo (W, 1-0)	9	4	1	1	2	5	0	1.00

BROOKLYN	IP	H	R	ER	BB	SO	HR	ERA
Fitzsimmons	7	4	0	0	3	1	0	0.00
Casey (L, 0-1)	0.1	4	2	2	0	0	0	18.00
French	0.2	0	0	0	0	0	0	0.00
Allen	1	0	0	0	0	0	0	0.00

IBB: Rizzuto (by Fitzsimmons). **Ground balls-fly balls:** Russo 11-10, Fitzsimmons 9-10, Casey 0-1, French 1-0, Allen 0-3. **Batters faced:** Russo 32, Fitzsimmons 27, Casey 5, French 1, Allen 3. **UMPIRES:** hp—Grieve, 1b—Goetz, 2b—McGowan, 3b—Pinelli **T:** 2:22 **A:** 33,100

GAME 4 New York 7 Brooklyn 4
Ebbets Field 10/05/41

NY YANKEES	AB	R	H	HR	RBI	BB	AVG
Sturm 1b	5	0	2	0	2	0	.294
Rolfe 3b	5	1	2	0	0	0	.353
Henrich rf	4	1	0	0	0	0	.133
DiMaggio cf	4	1	2	0	0	1	.267
Keller lf	5	1	4	0	3	0	.467
Dickey c	2	2	0	0	0	3	.143
Gordon 2b	5	1	2	0	2	0	.545
Rizzuto ss	4	0	0	0	0	1	.067
Donald p	2	0	0	0	0	0	.000
Breuer p	1	0	0	0	0	0	.000
a-Selkirk ph	1	0	0	0	0	0	.500
Murphy p	1	0	0	0	0	0	.000
TOTALS	**39**	**7**	**12**	**0**	**7**	**5**	**.259**

a - Batted for Breuer in the 8th

BATTING: 2B: Keller 2 (2, Higbe, Casey), Gordon (1, Casey). **RBI:** Sturm 2 (2), Keller 3 (5), Gordon 2 (4). **2-out RBI:** Sturm 2, Keller 3, Gordon 2. **Runners left in scoring position, 2 out:** Dickey 1, Gordon 2, Murphy 1. **Team LOB:** 11 **FIELDING: DP:** 1 (Gordon-Rizzuto-Sturm).

BROOKLYN	AB	R	H	HR	RBI	BB	AVG
Reese ss	5	0	0	0	0	0	.235
Walker rf	5	1	2	0	0	0	.200
Reiser cf	5	1	2	1	2	0	.188
Camilli 1b	4	0	2	0	0	0	.214
Riggs 3b	3	0	0	0	0	1	.250
Medwick lf	2	0	0	0	0	0	.286
Allen p	0	0	0	0	0	0	.000
Casey p	2	0	1	0	0	0	.500
Owen c	2	1	0	0	0	2	.222
Coscarart 2b	3	1	0	0	0	1	.000
Higbe p	1	0	1	0	0	0	1.000
French p	0	0	0	0	0	0	.000
a-Wasdell ph-lf	3	0	1	0	2	0	.250
TOTALS	**35**	**4**	**9**	**1**	**4**	**4**	**.195**

a - Batted for French in the 4th

BATTING: 2B: Camilli (1, Donald), Wasdell (1, Donald), Walker (2, Donald). **HR:** Reiser (1, 5th off Donald 1 on, 0 out). **RBI:** Reiser 2 (2), Wasdell 2 (2). **2-out RBI:** Wasdell 2. **Runners left in scoring position, 2 out:** Reese 1, Camilli 1, Casey 1, Coscarart 1. **GIDP:** Reiser. **Team LOB:** 8 **FIELDING: E:** Owen (1).

NY YANKEES	IP	H	R	ER	BB	SO	HR	ERA
Donald	4	6	4	4	3	2	1	9.00
Breuer	3	3	0	0	1	2	0	0.00
Murphy (W, 1-0)	2	0	0	0	0	1	0	0.00

BROOKLYN	IP	H	R	ER	BB	SO	HR	ERA
Higbe	3.2	6	3	3	2	1	0	7.36
French	0.1	0	0	0	0	0	0	0.00
Allen	0.2	1	0	0	1	0	0	0.00
Casey (L, 0-2)	4.1	5	4	0	2	1	0	3.38

HBP: Henrich (by Allen). **Ground balls-fly balls:** Donald 5-5, Breuer 3-3, Murphy 3-2, Higbe 5-5, French 0-0, Allen 0-2, Casey 6-7. **Batters faced:** Donald 21, Breuer 12, Murphy 6, Higbe 19, French 0, Allen 5, Casey 21. **UMPIRES:** hp—Goetz, 1b—McGowan, 2b—Pinelli, 3b—Grieve **T:** 2:54 **A:** 33,813

GAME 5 New York 3 Brooklyn 1
Ebbets Field 10/06/41

NY YANKEES	AB	R	H	HR	RBI	BB	AVG
Sturm 1b	4	0	1	0	0	0	.286
Rolfe 3b	3	0	0	0	0	1	.300
Henrich rf	3	1	1	1	1	1	.167
DiMaggio cf	4	0	1	0	0	0	.263
Keller lf	3	1	0	0	0	1	.389
Dickey c	4	1	1	0	0	0	.167
Gordon 2b	3	0	1	0	1	1	.500
Rizzuto ss	3	0	1	0	0	1	.111
Bonham p	4	0	0	0	0	0	.000
TOTALS	**31**	**3**	**6**	**1**	**2**	**5**	**.247**

BATTING: HR: Henrich (1, 5th off Wyatt 0 on, 1 out). **RBI:** Henrich 1 (1), Gordon 1 (5). **Runners left in scoring position, 2 out:** Sturm 1. **GIDP:** Gordon, Keller. **Team LOB:** 6 **BASERUNNING: CS:** Rolfe (1, 3rd base off Wyatt/Owen).

BROOKLYN	AB	R	H	HR	RBI	BB	AVG
Walker rf	3	0	1	0	0	1	.222
Riggs 3b	4	0	1	0	0	0	.250
Reiser cf	4	0	1	0	1	0	.200
Camilli 1b	4	0	0	0	0	0	.167
Medwick lf	3	0	0	0	0	1	.235
Reese ss	3	0	0	0	0	0	.200
b-Wasdell ph	1	0	0	0	0	0	.200
Owen c	3	0	0	0	0	0	.167
Coscarart 2b	2	0	0	0	0	0	.000
a-Galan ph	1	0	0	0	0	0	.000
Herman 2b	0	0	0	0	0	0	.125
Wyatt p	3	1	1	0	0	0	.167
TOTALS	**31**	**1**	**4**	**0**	**1**	**2**	**.182**

a - Batted for Coscarart in the 7th
b - Batted for Reese in the 9th

BATTING: 2B: Wyatt (1, Bonham). **3B:** Reiser (1, Bonham). **RBI:** Reiser 1 (3). **Runners left in scoring position, 2 out:** Camilli 1. **Team LOB:** 5 **FIELDING: E:** Reese (2). **DP:** 3 (Owen-Riggs, Reese-Coscarart-Camilli, Herman-Reese-Camilli).

NY YANKEES	IP	H	R	ER	BB	SO	HR	ERA
Bonham (W, 1-0)	9	4	1	1	2	2	0	1.00

BROOKLYN	IP	H	R	ER	BB	SO	HR	ERA
Wyatt (L, 1-1)	9	6	3	3	5	9	1	2.50

WP: Wyatt 1. **Ground balls-fly balls:** Bonham 6-19, Wyatt 13-3. **Batters faced:** Bonham 33, Wyatt 36. **UMPIRES:** hp—McGowan, 1b—Pinelli, 2b—Grieve, 3b—Goetz **T:** 2:13 **A:** 34,072

1942 ST. LOUIS CARDINALS DEF. NY YANKEES, 4-1

GAME 1 New York 7 St. Louis 4
Sportsman's Park 09/30/42

NY YANKEES	AB	R	H	HR	RBI	BB	AVG
Rizzuto ss	4	0	0	0	0	1	.000
Rolfe 3b	5	2	2	0	0	0	.400
Cullenbine rf	3	1	1	0	0	1	.333
DiMaggio cf	5	2	3	0	1	0	.600
Keller lf	4	0	0	0	0	1	.000
Gordon 2b	5	0	0	0	0	0	.000
Dickey c	4	1	2	0	0	1	.500
Hassett 1b	4	1	2	0	2	0	.500
Ruffing p	4	0	1	0	0	0	.250
Chandler p	0	0	0	0	0	0	.000
TOTALS	**38**	**7**	**11**	**0**	**3**	**4**	**.289**

BATTING: 2B: Hassett (1, M.Cooper), Cullenbine (1, M.Cooper). **S:** Cullenbine. **RBI:** DiMaggio 1 (1), Hassett 2 (2). **2-out RBI:** Hassett 2. **Runners left in scoring position, 2 out:** Rizzuto 1, Keller 1, Ruffing 2. **Team LOB:** 9

ST.LOUIS	AB	R	H	HR	RBI	BB	AVG
Brown 2b	4	0	1	0	0	1	.250
Moore cf	4	0	2	0	1	1	.500
Slaughter rf	3	0	1	0	0	2	.333
Musial lf	4	0	0	0	0	1	.000
W.Cooper c	4	1	1	0	0	0	.250
Hopp 1b	4	0	0	0	0	0	.000
Kurowski 3b	3	0	0	0	0	0	.000
b-Sanders ph	0	1	0	0	0	1	.000
Marion ss	4	1	1	0	2	0	.250
M.Cooper p	2	0	0	0	0	0	.000
Gumbert p	0	0	0	0	0	0	.000
a-Walker ph	1	0	0	0	0	0	.000
Lanier p	0	0	0	0	0	0	.000
c-O'Dea ph	1	0	1	0	1	0	1.000
d-Crespi pr	0	1	0	0	0	0	.000
TOTALS	**34**	**4**	**7**	**0**	**4**	**6**	**.206**

a - Batted for Gumbert in the 8th
b - Batted for Kurowski in the 9th
c - Batted for Lanier in the 9th
d - Ran for O'Dea in the 9th

BATTING: 3B: Marion (1, Ruffing). **RBI:** Moore 1 (1), Marion 2 (2), O'Dea 1 (1). **2-out RBI:** Moore 1, Marion 2, O'Dea 1. **Runners left in scoring position, 2 out:** Musial 2, W.Cooper 2. **Team LOB:** 9 **FIELDING: E:** Brown (1), Slaughter (1), Lanier 2 (2).

NY YANKEES	IP	H	R	ER	BB	SO	HR	ERA
Ruffing (W, 1-0)	8.2	5	4	4	6	8	0	4.15
Chandler (S, 1)	0.1	2	0	0	0	0	0	0.00

ST.LOUIS	IP	H	R	ER	BB	SO	HR	ERA
M.Cooper (L, 0-1)	7.2	10	5	3	3	7	0	3.52
Gumbert	0.1	0	0	0	0	0	0	0.00
Lanier	1	1	2	0	1	1	0	0.00

Ground balls-fly balls: Ruffing 4-14, Chandler 1-0, M.Cooper 8-8, Gumbert 1-0, Lanier 2-0. **Batters faced:** Ruffing 37, Chandler 3, M.Cooper 36, Gumbert 1, Lanier 6. **UMPIRES:** hp—Magerkurth, 1b—Summers, 2b—Barr, 3b—Hubbard **T:** 2:35 **A:** 34,769

GAME 2 St. Louis 4 New York 3
Sportsman's Park 10/01/42

NY YANKEES	AB	R	H	HR	RBI	BB	AVG
Rizzuto ss	4	0	1	0	0	1	.125
Rolfe 3b	4	0	1	0	0	0	.333
Cullenbine rf	4	1	1	0	0	0	.286
DiMaggio cf	4	1	1	0	1	0	.444
Keller lf	4	1	2	1	2	0	.250
Gordon 2b	4	0	1	0	0	0	.111
Dickey c	4	0	2	0	0	0	.500
a-Stainback pr	0	0	0	0	0	0	.000
Hassett 1b	4	0	1	0	0	0	.375
Bonham p	2	0	0	0	0	1	.000
b-Ruffing ph	1	0	0	0	0	0	.200
TOTALS	**35**	**3**	**10**	**1**	**3**	**2**	**.288**

a - Ran for Dickey in the 9th
b - Batted for Bonham in the 9th

BATTING: 2B: Gordon (1, Beazley), Rolfe (1, Beazley). **HR:** Keller (1, 8th off Beazley 1 on, 2 out). **RBI:** DiMaggio 1 (2), Keller 2 (2). **2-out RBI:** DiMaggio 1, Keller 2. **Runners left in scoring position, 2 out:** Cullenbine 2, DiMaggio 1, Hassett 2. **GIDP:** Rolfe. **Team LOB:** 7 **BASERUNNING: SB:** Rizzuto (1, 2nd base off Beazley/W.Cooper), Cullenbine (1, 2nd base off Beazley/W.Cooper). **FIELDING: E:** Hassett (1), Rizzuto (1).

ST.LOUIS	AB	R	H	HR	RBI	BB	AVG
Brown 2b	3	1	0	0	0	1	.143
Moore cf	3	1	0	0	0	0	.286
Slaughter rf	4	1	1	0	0	0	.286
Musial lf	4	0	1	0	1	0	.125
W.Cooper c	4	0	1	0	2	0	.250
Hopp 1b	3	1	2	0	0	0	.286
Kurowski 3b	3	0	1	0	1	0	.167
Marion ss	3	0	0	0	0	0	.143
Beazley p	3	0	0	0	0	0	.000
TOTALS	**30**	**4**	**6**	**0**	**4**	**1**	**.203**

BATTING: 2B: W.Cooper (1, Bonham), Slaughter (1, Bonham). **3B:** Kurowski (1, Bonham). **S:** Moore. **RBI:** Musial 1 (1), W.Cooper 2 (2), Kurowski 1 (1). **2-out RBI:** Musial 1, W.Cooper 2. **Runners left in scoring position, 2 out:** Hopp 1, Kurowski 1, Beazley 1. **Team LOB:** 4 **FIELDING: Outfield assists:** Slaughter (1). **DP:** 1 (Brown-Marion-Hopp).

NY YANKEES	IP	H	R	ER	BB	SO	HR	ERA
Bonham (L, 0-1)	8	6	4	4	1	3	0	4.50

ST.LOUIS	IP	H	R	ER	BB	SO	HR	ERA
Beazley (W, 1-0)	9	10	3	3	2	4	1	3.00

Ground balls-fly balls: Bonham 8-13, Beazley 9-12. **Batters faced:** Bonham 32, Beazley 37. **UMPIRES:** hp—Summers, 1b—Barr, 2b—Hubbard, 3b—Magerkurth **T:** 1:57 **A:** 34,255

GAME 3 St. Louis 2 New York 0
Yankee Stadium 10/03/42

ST.LOUIS	AB	R	H	HR	RBI	BB	AVG
Brown 2b	4	1	1	0	1	0	.182
Moore cf	4	0	0	0	0	0	.182
Slaughter rf	4	0	1	0	1	0	.273
Musial lf	3	0	1	0	0	1	.182
W.Cooper c	4	0	0	0	0	0	.167
Hopp 1b	4	0	0	0	0	0	.182
Kurowski 3b	2	1	1	0	0	1	.250
Marion ss	3	0	1	0	0	0	.200
White p	2	0	0	0	0	0	.000
TOTALS	**30**	**2**	**5**	**0**	**2**	**2**	**.191**

BATTING: S: White. **RBI:** Brown 1 (1), Slaughter 1 (1). **Runners left in scoring position, 2 out:** Moore 1. **Team LOB:** 4 **BASERUNNING: CS:** Musial (1, 2nd base off Chandler/Dickey). **FIELDING: E:** W.Cooper (1).

NY YANKEES	AB	R	H	HR	RBI	BB	AVG
Rizzuto ss	4	0	2	0	0	0	.250
Hassett 1b	1	0	0	0	0	0	.333
Crosetti 3b	3	0	0	0	0	0	.000
Cullenbine rf	4	0	1	0	0	0	.273
DiMaggio cf	4	0	2	0	0	0	.462
Gordon 2b	4	0	0	0	0	0	.077
Keller lf	4	0	0	0	0	0	.167
Dickey c	3	0	1	0	0	0	.455
Priddy 3b-1b	3	0	0	0	0	0	.000
Chandler p	2	0	0	0	0	0	.000
a-Ruffing ph	1	0	0	0	0	0	.167
Breuer p	0	0	0	0	0	0	.000
Turner p	0	0	0	0	0	0	.000
TOTALS	**33**	**0**	**6**	**0**	**0**	**0**	**.255**

a - Batted for Chandler in the 8th

BATTING: Runners left in scoring position, 2 out: DiMaggio 1. **Team LOB:** 6 **BASERUNNING: SB:** Rizzuto (2, 2nd base off White/W.Cooper). **FIELDING: E:** Breuer (1). **Outfield assists:** Keller (1). **DP:** 1 (Keller-Dickey).

ST.LOUIS	IP	H	R	ER	BB	SO	HR	ERA
White (W, 1-0)	9	6	0	0	0	6	0	0.00

NY YANKEES	IP	H	R	ER	BB	SO	HR	ERA
Chandler (L, 0-1)	8	3	1	1	1	3	0	1.08
Breuer	0	2	1	0	0	0	0	0.00
Turner	1	0	0	0	1	0	0	0.00

IBB: Musial (by Turner). **Ground balls-fly balls:** White 6-15, Chandler 13-6, Breuer 1-0, Turner 0-2. **Batters faced:** White 33, Chandler 27, Breuer 3, Turner 3. **UMPIRES:** hp—Barr, 1b—Hubbard, 2b—Magerkurth, 3b—Summers **T:** 2:30 **A:** 69,123

GAME 4 St. Louis 9 New York 6
Yankee Stadium 10/04/42

ST.LOUIS	AB	R	H	HR	RBI	BB	AVG
Brown 2b	6	0	2	0	0	0	.235
Moore cf	3	0	2	0	1	1	.286
Slaughter rf	4	1	0	0	0	1	.200
Musial lf	3	2	2	0	1	2	.286
W.Cooper c	5	1	2	0	1	0	.235
Hopp 1b	3	2	1	0	0	1	.214
Kurowski 3b	3	1	1	0	2	1	.273
Marion ss	4	1	0	0	1	1	.143
M.Cooper p	3	1	1	0	2	0	.200
Gumbert p	0	0	0	0	0	0	.000
Pollet p	0	0	0	0	0	0	.000
a-Sanders ph	1	0	0	0	0	0	.000
Lanier p	1	0	1	0	1	0	1.000
TOTALS	**36**	**9**	**12**	**0**	**9**	**7**	**.231**

a - Batted for Pollet in the 7th

BATTING: 2B: Moore (1, Borowy), Musial (1, Donald). **S:** Hopp, Moore, Kurowski. **RBI:** Moore 1 (2), Musial 1 (2), W.Cooper 1 (3), Kurowski 2 (3), Marion 1 (3), M.Cooper 2 (2), Lanier 1 (1). **2-out RBI:** Musial 1, Lanier 1. **Runners left in scoring position, 2 out:** Slaughter 1, Musial 1, W.Cooper 3, Sanders 2. **Team LOB:** 10 **FIELDING: E:** Kurowski (1). **DP:** 1 (Marion-Brown).

NY YANKEES	AB	R	H	HR	RBI	BB	AVG
Rizzuto ss	5	1	3	0	0	0	.353
Rolfe 3b	4	2	2	0	0	1	.385
Cullenbine rf	4	1	2	0	2	0	.333
DiMaggio cf	4	0	0	0	0	0	.353
Keller lf	4	1	1	1	3	0	.188
Gordon 2b	4	1	0	0	0	0	.059
Dickey c	4	0	0	0	0	0	.333
Priddy 1b	4	0	1	0	1	0	.143
Borowy p	1	0	0	0	0	0	.000
Donald p	2	0	0	0	0	0	.000
Bonham p	0	0	0	0	0	0	.000
a-Rosar ph	1	0	1	0	0	0	1.000
TOTALS	**37**	**6**	**10**	**1**	**6**	**1**	**.259**

a - Batted for Bonham in the 9th

BATTING: 2B: Rolfe (2, M.Cooper), Priddy (1, Gumbert). **HR:** Keller (2, 6th off M.Cooper 2 on, 1 out). **RBI:** Cullenbine 2 (2), Keller 3 (5), Priddy 1 (1). **2-out RBI:** Priddy 1. **Runners left in scoring position, 2 out:** Donald 1. **Team LOB:** 5 **FIELDING: E:** Dickey (1).

ST.LOUIS	IP	H	R	ER	BB	SO	HR	ERA
M.Cooper	5.1	7	5	5	1	2	1	5.54
Gumbert	0.1	1	1	0	0	0	0	0.00
Pollet	0.1	0	0	0	0	0	0	0.00
Lanier (W, 1-0)	3	2	0	0	0	0	0	0.00

NY YANKEES	IP	H	R	ER	BB	SO	HR	ERA
Borowy	3	6	6	6	3	1	0	18.00
Donald (L, 0-1)	3	3	2	2	2	1	0	6.00
Bonham	3	3	1	1	2	0	0	4.09

IBB: Kurowski (by Bonham), Musial (by Bonham). **Ground balls-fly balls:** M.Cooper 2-11, Gumbert 2-0, Pollet 1-0, Lanier 4-5, Borowy 3-5, Donald 3-5, Bonham 3-3. **Batters faced:** M.Cooper 23, Gumbert 3, Pollet 1, Lanier 11, Borowy 18, Donald 14, Bonham 14. **UMPIRES:** hp—Hubbard, 1b—Magerkurth, 2b—Summers, 3b—Barr **T:** 2:28 **A:** 69,902

GAME 5 St. Louis 4 New York 2
Yankee Stadium 10/05/42

ST.LOUIS	AB	R	H	HR	RBI	BB	AVG
Brown 2b	3	0	2	0	0	1	.300
Moore cf	3	1	1	0	0	0	.294
Slaughter rf	4	1	2	1	1	0	.263
Musial lf	4	0	0	0	0	0	.222
W.Cooper c	4	1	2	0	1	0	.286
Hopp 1b	3	0	0	0	0	0	.176
Kurowski 3b	4	1	1	1	2	0	.267
Marion ss	4	0	0	0	0	0	.111
Beazley p	4	0	1	0	0	0	.143
TOTALS	**33**	**4**	**9**	**2**	**4**	**1**	**.239**

BATTING: HR: Slaughter (1, 4th off Ruffing 0 on, 0 out), Kurowski (1, 9th off Ruffing 1 on, 1 out). **S:** Moore, Hopp. **RBI:** Slaughter 1 (2), W.Cooper 1 (4), Kurowski 2 (5). **Runners left in scoring position, 2 out:** Musial 1, Hopp 1. **GIDP:** Slaughter. **Team LOB:** 5 **FIELDING: E:** Beazley (1), Hopp (1), Brown 2 (3). **DP:** 1 (Hopp-Marion-Brown).

NY YANKEES	AB	R	H	HR	RBI	BB	AVG
Rizzuto ss	4	1	2	1	1	0	.381
Rolfe 3b	4	1	1	0	0	0	.353
Cullenbine rf	4	0	0	0	0	0	.263
DiMaggio cf	4	0	1	0	1	0	.333
Keller lf	4	0	1	0	0	0	.200
Gordon 2b	4	0	1	0	0	0	.095
Dickey c	4	0	0	0	0	0	.263
a-Stainback pr	0	0	0	0	0	0	.000
Priddy 1b	3	0	0	0	0	1	.100
Ruffing p	3	0	1	0	0	0	.222
b-Selkirk ph	1	0	0	0	0	0	.000
TOTALS	**35**	**2**	**7**	**1**	**2**	**1**	**.247**

a - Ran for Dickey in the 9th
b - Batted for Ruffing in the 9th

BATTING: HR: Rizzuto (1, 1st off Beazley 0 on, 0 out). **RBI:** Rizzuto 1 (1), DiMaggio 1 (3). **Runners left in scoring position, 2 out:** DiMaggio 2, Dickey 1. **GIDP:** Ruffing. **Team LOB:** 7 **FIELDING: DP:** 1 (Gordon-Rizzuto-Priddy).

ST.LOUIS	IP	H	R	ER	BB	SO	HR	ERA
Beazley (W, 2-0)	9	7	2	2	1	2	1	2.50

NY YANKEES	IP	H	R	ER	BB	SO	HR	ERA
Ruffing (L, 1-1)	9	9	4	4	1	3	2	4.08

Ground balls-fly balls: Beazley 17-9, Ruffing 5-16. **Batters faced:** Beazley 36, Ruffing 36. **UMPIRES:** hp—Magerkurth, 1b—Summers, 2b—Barr, 3b—Hubbard **T:** 1:58 **A:** 69,052

1943 NY YANKEES DEF. ST.LOUIS CARDINALS, 4-1

GAME 1 New York 4 St. Louis 2
Yankee Stadium 10/05/43

ST.LOUIS	AB	R	H	HR	RBI	BB	AVG
Klein 2b	4	0	1	0	0	0	.250
Walker cf	4	0	0	0	0	0	.000
Musial rf	4	0	1	0	0	0	.250
W.Cooper c	4	1	1	0	0	0	.250
Kurowski 3b	3	0	0	0	0	0	.000
Sanders 1b	4	1	2	0	0	0	.500
Litwhiler lf	3	0	0	0	0	1	.000
Marion ss	3	0	1	0	1	0	.333
Lanier p	2	0	1	0	1	0	.500
a-Garms ph	1	0	0	0	0	0	.000
Brecheen p	0	0	0	0	0	0	.000
TOTALS	**32**	**2**	**7**	**0**	**2**	**1**	**.219**

a - Batted for Lanier in the 8th

BATTING: 2B: Marion (1, Chandler). **S:** Kurowski. **RBI:** Marion 1 (1), Lanier 1 (1). **2-out RBI:** Marion 1, Lanier 1. **Runners left in scoring position, 2 out:** W.Cooper 1, Marion 1. **GIDP:** Marion. **Team LOB:** 5 **FIELDING: E:** Klein (1). **DP:** 1 (Klein-Marion-Sanders).

NY YANKEES	AB	R	H	HR	RBI	BB	AVG
Stainback rf	4	0	1	0	0	0	.250
Crosetti ss	4	2	1	0	0	0	.250
Johnson 3b	4	1	2	0	0	0	.500
Keller lf	4	0	1	0	1	0	.250
Gordon 2b	3	1	1	1	1	1	.333
Dickey c	4	0	1	0	1	0	.250
Etten 1b	4	0	0	0	0	0	.000
Lindell cf	3	0	0	0	0	0	.000
Chandler p	3	0	1	0	0	0	.333
TOTALS	**33**	**4**	**8**	**1**	**3**	**1**	**.242**

BATTING: HR: Gordon (1, 4th off Lanier 0 on, 2 out). **RBI:** Keller 1 (1), Gordon 1 (1), Dickey 1 (1). **2-out RBI:** Gordon 1, Dickey 1. **Runners left in scoring position, 2 out:** Etten 1. **GIDP:** Keller. **Team LOB:** 6 **BASERUNNING: SB:** Crosetti (1, 2nd base off Lanier/W.Cooper). **FIELDING: E:** Etten (1), Crosetti (1). **Outfield assists:** Stainback (1). **DP:** 1 (Gordon-Crosetti-Etten).

ST.LOUIS	IP	H	R	ER	BB	SO	HR	ERA
Lanier (L, 0-1)	7	7	4	2	0	7	1	2.57
Brecheen	1	1	0	0	1	1	0	0.00

NY YANKEES	IP	H	R	ER	BB	SO	HR	ERA
Chandler (W, 1-0)	9	7	2	1	1	3	0	1.00

WP: Lanier 1. **Ground balls-fly balls:** Lanier 7-8, Brecheen 1-1, Chandler 15-7. **Batters faced:** Lanier 29, Brecheen 5, Chandler 34. **UMPIRES:** hp—Rommel, 1b—Reardon, 2b—Rue, 3b—Stewart **T:** 2:07 **A:** 68,676

GAME 2 St. Louis 4 New York 3
Yankee Stadium 10/06/43

ST.LOUIS	AB	R	H	HR	RBI	BB	AVG
Klein 2b	4	0	1	0	0	1	.250
Walker cf	5	0	1	0	0	0	.111
Musial rf	4	1	1	0	0	0	.250
W.Cooper c	3	0	1	0	0	0	.286
Kurowski 3b	4	1	1	0	1	0	.143
Sanders 1b	3	1	1	1	2	1	.429
Litwhiler lf	3	0	0	0	0	1	.000
Marion ss	3	1	1	1	1	1	.333
M.Cooper p	3	0	0	0	0	0	.000
TOTALS	**32**	**4**	**7**	**2**	**4**	**4**	**.219**

BATTING: HR: Marion (1, 3th off Bonham 0 on, 0 out), Sanders (1, 4th off Bonham 1 on, 1 out). **S:** W.Cooper, M.Cooper. **RBI:** Kurowski 1 (1), Sanders 2 (2), Marion 1 (2). **Runners left in scoring position, 2 out:** Walker 2, W.Cooper 1. **Team LOB:** 7 **BASERUNNING: SB:** Marion (1, 2nd base off Bonham/Dickey). **FIELDING: E:** Walker (1), W.Cooper (1). **DP:** 1 (Marion-Klein-Sanders).

NY YANKEES	AB	R	H	HR	RBI	BB	AVG
Crosetti ss	4	1	2	0	0	0	.375
Metheny rf	3	0	0	0	0	0	.000
Johnson 3b	4	1	2	0	0	0	.500
Keller lf	4	1	1	0	2	0	.250
Dickey c	3	0	0	0	0	1	.143
Etten 1b	4	0	0	0	1	0	.000
Gordon 2b	4	0	1	0	0	0	.286
Stainback cf	3	0	0	0	0	0	.143
Bonham p	2	0	0	0	0	0	.000
a-Weatherly ph	1	0	0	0	0	0	.000
Murphy p	0	0	0	0	0	0	.000
TOTALS	**32**	**3**	**6**	**0**	**3**	**1**	**.215**

a - Batted for Bonham in the 8th

BATTING: 2B: Johnson (1, M.Cooper). **3B:** Keller (1, M.Cooper). **RBI:** Keller 2 (3), Etten 1 (1). **Runners left in scoring position, 2 out:** Keller 1, Bonham 1. **GIDP:** Johnson. **Team LOB:** 4

ST.LOUIS	IP	H	R	ER	BB	SO	HR	ERA
M.Cooper (W, 1-0)	9	6	3	3	1	4	0	3.00

NY YANKEES	IP	H	R	ER	BB	SO	HR	ERA
Bonham (L, 0-1)	8	6	4	4	3	9	2	4.50
Murphy	1	1	0	0	1	0	0	0.00

Ground balls-fly balls: M.Cooper 7-15, Bonham 3-11, Murphy 1-1. **Batters faced:** M.Cooper 34, Bonham 33, Murphy 5. **UMPIRES:** hp—Reardon, 1b—Rue, 2b—Stewart, 3b—Rommel **T:** 2:08 **A:** 68,578

GAME 3 New York 6 St. Louis 2
Yankee Stadium 10/07/43

ST.LOUIS	AB	R	H	HR	RBI	BB	AVG
Klein 2b	4	0	0	0	0	0	.167
Walker cf	4	0	1	0	0	0	.154
Musial rf	3	1	1	0	0	1	.273
W.Cooper c	4	0	1	0	0	0	.273
Kurowski 3b	3	1	1	0	0	0	.200
a-O'Dea ph	1	0	0	0	0	0	.000
Sanders 1b	3	0	0	0	0	1	.300
Litwhiler lf	4	0	2	0	2	0	.200
Marion ss	2	0	0	0	0	1	.250
Brazle p	3	0	0	0	0	0	.000
Krist p	0	0	0	0	0	0	.000
Brecheen p	0	0	0	0	0	0	.000
TOTALS	**31**	**2**	**6**	**0**	**2**	**3**	**.211**

a - Batted for Kurowski in the 9th

BATTING: 2B: Walker (1, Borowy), Kurowski (1, Borowy). **RBI:** Litwhiler 2 (2). **Runners left in scoring position, 2 out:** Klein 2. **GIDP:** W.Cooper. **Team LOB:** 5 **BASERUNNING: CS:** W.Cooper (1, 2nd base off Borowy/Dickey). **FIELDING: E:** Marion (1), Kurowski (1), Walker (2). **Outfield assists:** Musial (1). **DP:** 1 (Marion-Klein-Sanders).

NY YANKEES	AB	R	H	HR	RBI	BB	AVG
Stainback cf	4	0	1	0	0	0	.182
Crosetti ss	2	1	0	0	0	1	.300
Johnson 3b	4	1	1	0	3	0	.417
Keller lf	3	1	0	0	0	1	.182
Gordon 2b	4	0	1	0	1	0	.273
Dickey c	4	0	2	0	0	0	.273
Etten 1b	4	0	1	0	1	0	.083
Lindell rf	3	1	1	0	0	0	.167
Borowy p	2	1	1	0	0	0	.500
a-Stirnweiss ph	1	1	0	0	0	0	.000
Murphy p	0	0	0	0	0	0	.000
TOTALS	**31**	**6**	**8**	**0**	**5**	**2**	**.229**

a - Batted for Borowy in the 8th

BATTING: 2B: Borowy (1, Brazle). **3B:** Johnson (1, Brazle). **S:** Crosetti. **RBI:** Johnson 3 (3), Gordon 1 (2), Etten 1 (2). **2-out RBI:** Etten 1. **Runners left in scoring position, 2 out:** Etten 1. **GIDP:** Johnson. **Team LOB:** 4 **FIELDING: DP:** 1 (Crosetti-Gordon-Etten).

ST.LOUIS	IP	H	R	ER	BB	SO	HR	ERA
Brazle (L, 0-1)	7.1	5	6	3	2	4	0	3.68
Krist	0	1	0	0	0	0	0	0.00
Brecheen	0.2	2	0	0	0	0	0	0.00

NY YANKEES	IP	H	R	ER	BB	SO	HR	ERA
Borowy (W, 1-0)	8	6	2	2	3	4	0	2.25
Murphy (S, 1)	1	0	0	0	0	1	0	0.00

IBB: Sanders (by Borowy), Marion (by Borowy), Crosetti (by Brazle). **Ground balls-fly balls:** Brazle 13-6, Krist 0-0, Brecheen 0-0, Borowy 7-11, Murphy 0-2. **Batters faced:** Brazle 31, Krist 1, Brecheen 2, Borowy 31, Murphy 3. **UMPIRES:** hp—Rue, 1b—Stewart, 2b—Rommel, 3b—Reardon **T:** 2:10 **A:** 69,990

GAME 4 New York 2 St. Louis 1
Sportsman's Park 10/10/43

NY YANKEES	AB	R	H	HR	RBI	BB	AVG
Stainback cf	3	0	0	0	0	0	.143
Crosetti ss	4	0	1	0	1	0	.286
Johnson 3b	4	0	0	0	0	0	.313
Keller lf	4	0	1	0	0	0	.200
Gordon 2b	4	1	1	0	0	0	.267
Dickey c	3	0	1	0	1	1	.286
Etten 1b	4	0	0	0	0	0	.063
Lindell rf	3	0	0	0	0	1	.111
Russo p	3	1	2	0	0	1	.667
TOTALS	**32**	**2**	**6**	**0**	**2**	**3**	**.219**

BATTING: 2B: Gordon (1, Lanier), Russo 2 (2, Lanier, Brecheen). **S:** Stainback. **RBI:** Crosetti 1 (1), Dickey 1 (2). **2-out RBI:** Dickey 1. **Runners left in scoring position, 2 out:** Crosetti 2, Russo 2. **Team LOB:** 7 **BASERUNNING: SB:** Keller (1, 2nd base off Brecheen/W.Cooper). **FIELDING: E:** Crosetti (2), Johnson (1).

ST.LOUIS	AB	R	H	HR	RBI	BB	AVG
Klein 2b	5	0	0	0	0	0	.118
Walker cf	4	0	0	0	0	0	.118
Musial rf	4	0	2	0	0	0	.333
W.Cooper c	4	0	1	0	0	0	.267
Kurowski 3b	4	0	0	0	0	0	.143
Sanders 1b	4	1	1	0	0	0	.286
Litwhiler lf	4	0	1	0	0	0	.214
Marion ss	3	0	2	0	0	1	.364
Lanier p	2	0	0	0	0	0	.250
a-Demaree ph	1	0	0	0	0	0	.000
b-White pr	0	0	0	0	0	0	.000
Brecheen p	0	0	0	0	0	0	.000
c-Narron ph	1	0	0	0	0	0	.000
TOTALS	**36**	**1**	**7**	**0**	**0**	**1**	**.206**

a - Batted for Lanier in the 7th
b - Ran for Demaree in the 7th
c - Batted for Brecheen in the 9th

BATTING: 2B: Litwhiler (1, Russo), Marion (2, Russo). **Runners left in scoring position, 2 out:** Klein 3, Sanders 1. **Team LOB:** 9 **FIELDING: E:** Klein (2). **Outfield assists:** Musial (2).

NY YANKEES	IP	H	R	ER	BB	SO	HR	ERA
Russo (W, 1-0)	9	7	1	0	1	2	0	0.00

ST.LOUIS	IP	H	R	ER	BB	SO	HR	ERA
Lanier	7	4	1	1	1	5	0	1.93
Brecheen (L, 0-1)	2	2	1	1	2	2	0	2.45

IBB: Marion (by Russo), Dickey (by Brecheen), Lindell (by Brecheen). **Ground balls-fly balls:** Russo 14-13, Lanier 7-9, Brecheen 2-1. **Batters faced:** Russo 37, Lanier 26, Brecheen 10. **UMPIRES:** hp—Stewart, 1b—Rommel, 2b—Reardon, 3b—Rue **T:** 2:06 **A:** 36,196

GAME 5 New York 2 St. Louis 0
Sportsman's Park 10/11/43

NY YANKEES	AB	R	H	HR	RBI	BB	AVG
Crosetti ss	4	0	1	0	0	1	.278
Metheny rf	5	0	1	0	0	0	.125
Lindell rf	0	0	0	0	0	0	.111
Johnson 3b	4	0	1	0	0	0	.300
Keller lf	3	1	1	0	0	1	.222
Dickey c	4	1	1	1	2	0	.278
Etten 1b	3	0	1	0	0	1	.105
Gordon 2b	2	0	0	0	0	2	.235
Stainback cf	3	0	1	0	0	0	.176
Chandler p	3	0	0	0	0	0	.167
TOTALS	**31**	**2**	**7**	**1**	**2**	**5**	**.220**

BATTING: HR: Dickey (1, 6th off M.Cooper 1 on, 2 out). **S:** Chandler, Stainback. **RBI:** Dickey 2 (4). **2-out RBI:** Dickey 2. **Runners left in scoring position, 2 out:** Crosetti 2, Metheny 2, Johnson 1, Gordon 1. **GIDP:** Dickey. **Team LOB:** 9 **FIELDING: Outfield assists:** Keller (1). **DP:** 1 (Crosetti-Gordon-Etten).

ST.LOUIS	AB	R	H	HR	RBI	BB	AVG
Klein 2b	5	0	1	0	0	0	.136
Garms lf	4	0	0	0	0	0	.000
Musial rf	3	0	0	0	0	1	.278
W.Cooper c	2	0	1	0	0	0	.294
O'Dea c	2	0	2	0	0	0	.667
Kurowski 3b	4	0	2	0	0	0	.222
Sanders 1b	3	0	1	0	0	1	.294
Hopp cf	4	0	0	0	0	0	.000
Marion ss	3	0	1	0	0	0	.357
M.Cooper p	2	0	0	0	0	0	.000
a-Walker ph	1	0	1	0	0	0	.167
Lanier p	0	0	0	0	0	0	.250
Dickson p	0	0	0	0	0	0	.000
b-Litwhiler ph	1	0	1	0	0	0	.267
TOTALS	**34**	**0**	**10**	**0**	**0**	**2**	**.224**

a - Batted for M.Cooper in the 7th
b - Batted for Dickson in the 9th

BATTING: S: Garms, Marion. **Runners left in scoring position, 2 out:** Klein 2, Garms 1, Kurowski 1, Sanders 1, M.Cooper 1. **GIDP:** Kurowski. **Team LOB:** 11 **FIELDING: E:** W.Cooper (2). **DP:** 1 (Klein-Marion-Sanders).

NY YANKEES	IP	H	R	ER	BB	SO	HR	ERA
Chandler (W, 2-0)	9	10	0	0	2	7	0	0.50

ST.LOUIS	IP	H	R	ER	BB	SO	HR	ERA
M.Cooper (L, 1-1)	7	5	2	2	2	6	1	2.81
Lanier	1.1	2	0	0	2	1	0	1.76
Dickson	0.2	0	0	0	1	0	0	0.00

WP: M.Cooper 1. **Ground balls-fly balls:** Chandler 14-3, M.Cooper 6-7, Lanier 2-0, Dickson 1-1. **Batters faced:** Chandler 38, M.Cooper 28, Lanier 7, Dickson 3. **UMPIRES:** hp—Rommel, 1b—Reardon, 2b—Rue, 3b—Stewart **T:** 2:24 **A:** 33,872

1944 STL CARDINALS DEF. STL BROWNS, 4-2

GAME 1 Browns 2 Cardinals 1
Sportsman's Park 10/04/44

STL BROWNS	AB	R	H	HR	RBI	BB	AVG
Gutteridge 2b	4	0	0	0	0	0	.000
Kreevich cf	4	0	0	0	0	0	.000
Laabs lf	4	0	0	0	0	0	.000
Stephens ss	3	0	0	0	0	1	.000
Moore rf	3	1	1	0	0	1	.333
McQuinn 1b	3	1	1	1	2	0	.333
Christman 3b	3	0	0	0	0	0	.000
Hayworth c	3	0	0	0	0	0	.000
Galehouse p	2	0	0	0	0	1	.000
TOTALS	**29**	**2**	**2**	**1**	**2**	**3**	**.069**

BATTING: HR: McQuinn (1, 4th off M.Cooper 1 on, 2 out). **RBI:** McQuinn 2 (2). **2-out RBI:** McQuinn 2. **Team LOB:** 3 **FIELDING: DP:** 1 (Gutteridge-Stephens-McQuinn).

STL CARDINALS	AB	R	H	HR	RBI	BB	AVG
Hopp cf	5	0	1	0	0	0	.200
Sanders 1b	3	0	1	0	0	1	.333
Musial rf	3	0	1	0	0	0	.333
W.Cooper c	3	0	0	0	0	1	.000
Kurowski 3b	4	0	1	0	0	0	.250
Litwhiler lf	2	0	0	0	0	1	.000
Fallon 2b	1	0	0	0	0	0	.000
Marion ss	4	1	2	0	0	0	.500
Verban 2b	2	0	1	0	0	0	.500
a-Bergamo ph-lf	1	0	0	0	0	1	.000
M.Cooper p	2	0	0	0	0	0	.000
b-Garms ph	1	0	0	0	0	0	.000
Donnelly p	0	0	0	0	0	0	.000
c-O'Dea ph	1	0	0	0	1	0	.000
TOTALS	**32**	**1**	**7**	**0**	**1**	**4**	**.219**

a - Batted for Verban in the 7th
b - Batted for M.Cooper in the 7th
c - Batted for Donnelly in the 9th

BATTING: 2B: Marion 2 (2, Galehouse). **S:** Musial. **RBI:** O'Dea 1 (1). **Runners left in scoring position, 2 out:** Sanders 1, Litwhiler 2, M.Cooper 1. **GIDP:** Musial. **Team LOB:** 9

STL BROWNS	IP	H	R	ER	BB	SO	HR	ERA
Galehouse (W, 1-0)	9	7	1	1	4	5	0	1.00

STL CARDINALS	IP	H	R	ER	BB	SO	HR	ERA
M.Cooper (L, 0-1)	7	2	2	2	3	4	1	2.57
Donnelly	2	0	0	0	0	2	0	0.00

IBB: W.Cooper (by Galehouse). **Ground balls-fly balls:** Galehouse 9-11, M.Cooper 9-8, Donnelly 3-1. **Batters faced:** Galehouse 37, M.Cooper 26, Donnelly 6. **UMPIRES:** hp—Sears, 1b—McGowan, 2b—Dunn, 3b—Pipgras **T:** 2:05 **A:** 33,242

GAME 2 Cardinals 3 Browns 2
Sportsman's Park 10/05/44

STL BROWNS	AB	R	H	HR	RBI	BB	AVG
Gutteridge 2b	4	0	0	0	0	1	.000
Kreevich cf	5	0	2	0	0	0	.222
Laabs lf	4	0	0	0	0	0	.000
c-Zarilla ph-lf	1	0	0	0	0	0	.000
Stephens ss	5	0	0	0	0	0	.000
McQuinn 1b	2	0	1	0	0	3	.400
Christman 3b	5	0	0	0	0	0	.000
Moore rf	5	1	2	0	0	0	.375
Hayworth c	5	1	1	0	1	0	.125
Potter p	2	0	0	0	0	0	.000
a-Mancuso ph	1	0	1	0	1	0	1.000
b-Shirley pr	0	0	0	0	0	0	.000
Muncrief p	1	0	0	0	0	0	.000
TOTALS	**40**	**2**	**7**	**0**	**2**	**4**	**.130**

a - Batted for Potter in the 7th
b - Ran for Mancuso in the 7th
c - Batted for Laabs in the 10th

BATTING: 2B: Hayworth (1, Lanier), Kreevich (1, Lanier), McQuinn (1, Donnelly). **RBI:** Hayworth 1 (1), Mancuso 1 (1). **2-out RBI:** Hayworth 1, Mancuso 1. **Runners left in scoring position, 2 out:** Gutteridge 1, Christman 1. **Team LOB:** 9 **FIELDING: E:** Potter (1), Christman (1), Gutteridge (1). **DP:** 2 (Stephens-Gutteridge, Stephens-Gutteridge-McQuinn).

STL CARDINALS	AB	R	H	HR	RBI	BB	AVG
Bergamo lf	5	0	0	0	1	0	.000
Hopp cf	5	0	0	0	0	0	.100
Musial rf	5	0	1	0	0	0	.250
W.Cooper c	4	0	1	0	0	0	.143
Sanders 1b	3	2	1	0	0	2	.333
Kurowski 3b	4	0	2	0	0	0	.375
Marion ss	3	0	0	0	0	2	.286
Verban 2b	3	1	1	0	1	1	.400
a-O'Dea ph	1	0	1	0	1	0	.500
Lanier p	2	0	0	0	0	0	.000
Donnelly p	1	0	0	0	0	0	.000
TOTALS	**36**	**3**	**7**	**0**	**3**	**5**	**.206**

a - Batted for Verban in the 11th

BATTING: 2B: W.Cooper (1, Potter), Kurowski (1, Potter). **S:** Lanier, W.Cooper, Kurowski. **RBI:** Bergamo 1 (1), Verban 1 (1), O'Dea 1 (2). **Runners left in scoring position, 2 out:** Musial 1, Marion 1, Verban 1, Lanier 2. **GIDP:** W.Cooper. **Team LOB:** 10

STL BROWNS	IP	H	R	ER	BB	SO	HR	ERA
Potter	6	4	2	0	2	3	0	0.00
Muncrief (L, 0-1)	4.1	3	1	1	3	4	0	2.08

STL CARDINALS	IP	H	R	ER	BB	SO	HR	ERA
Lanier	7	5	2	2	3	6	0	2.57
Donnelly (W, 1-0)	4	2	0	0	1	7	0	0.00

IBB: Marion 2 (by Potter, by Muncrief), McQuinn (by Donnelly), Sanders (by Muncrief). **Ground balls-fly balls:** Potter 9-7, Muncrief 4-2, Lanier 10-5, Donnelly 3-2. **Batters faced:** Potter 26, Muncrief 18, Lanier 29, Donnelly 15. **UMPIRES:** hp—McGowan, 1b—Dunn, 2b—Pipgras, 3b—Sears **T:** 2:32 **A:** 35,076

GAME 3 Browns 6 Cardinals 2
Sportsman's Park 10/06/44

STL CARDINALS	AB	R	H	HR	RBI	BB	AVG
Litwhiler lf	5	0	0	0	0	0	.000
Hopp cf	4	1	1	0	0	0	.143
Musial rf	4	0	1	0	0	0	.250
W.Cooper c	4	0	2	0	1	0	.273
Sanders 1b	3	0	1	0	0	1	.333
Kurowski 3b	4	1	0	0	0	0	.250
Marion ss	4	0	2	0	1	0	.364
Verban 2b	2	0	0	0	0	0	.286
a-Garms ph	1	0	0	0	0	0	.000
Fallon 2b	1	0	0	0	0	0	.000
Wilks p	1	0	0	0	0	0	.000
Schmidt p	1	0	0	0	0	0	.000
b-Bergamo ph	0	0	0	0	0	1	.000
Jurisich p	0	0	0	0	0	0	.000
Byerly p	0	0	0	0	0	0	.000
c-O'Dea ph	1	0	0	0	0	0	.333
TOTALS	**35**	**2**	**7**	**0**	**2**	**2**	**.204**

a - Batted for Verban in the 7th
b - Batted for Schmidt in the 7th
c - Batted for Byerly in the 9th

BATTING: 2B: W.Cooper (2, Kramer). **RBI:** W.Cooper 1 (1), Marion 1 (1). **2-out RBI:** W.Cooper 1. **Runners left in scoring position, 2 out:** Litwhiler 2, Kurowski 3. **Team LOB:** 8 **FIELDING: PB:** W.Cooper. **DP:** 1 (Marion-Sanders).

STL BROWNS	AB	R	H	HR	RBI	BB	AVG
Gutteridge 2b	4	1	1	0	0	0	.083
Kreevich cf	4	0	0	0	0	0	.154
Moore rf	4	1	1	0	0	0	.333
Stephens ss	2	2	1	0	0	2	.100
McQuinn 1b	3	1	3	0	2	1	.625
Zarilla lf	4	1	1	0	1	0	.200
Christman 3b	4	0	1	0	1	0	.083
Hayworth c	2	0	0	0	0	2	.100
Kramer p	4	0	0	0	0	0	.000
TOTALS	**31**	**6**	**8**	**0**	**4**	**5**	**.170**

BATTING: 2B: Gutteridge (1, Jurisich), McQuinn (2, Jurisich). **RBI:** McQuinn 2 (4), Zarilla 1 (1), Christman 1 (1). **2-out RBI:** McQuinn 2, Zarilla 1, Christman 1. **Runners left in scoring position, 2 out:** Zarilla 1, Kramer 4. **GIDP:** Zarilla. **Team LOB:** 6 **FIELDING: E:** Stephens (1).

STL CARDINALS	IP	H	R	ER	BB	SO	HR	ERA
Wilks (L, 0-1)	2.2	5	4	4	3	3	0	13.50
Schmidt	3.1	1	0	0	1	1	0	0.00
Jurisich	0.2	2	2	2	1	0	0	27.00
Byerly	1.1	0	0	0	0	1	0	0.00

STL BROWNS	IP	H	R	ER	BB	SO	HR	ERA
Kramer (W, 1-0)	9	7	2	0	2	10	0	0.00

WP: Schmidt 1. **IBB:** Hayworth (by Schmidt). **Ground balls-fly balls:** Wilks 2-3, Schmidt 5-3, Jurisich 1-1, Byerly 3-0, Kramer 7-11. **Batters faced:** Wilks 16, Schmidt 11, Jurisich 5, Byerly 4, Kramer 37. **UMPIRES:** hp—Dunn, 1b—Pipgras, 2b—Sears, 3b—McGowan **T:** 2:19 **A:** 34,737

GAME 4 Cardinals 5 Browns 1
Sportsman's Park 10/07/44

STL CARDINALS	AB	R	H	HR	RBI	BB	AVG
Litwhiler lf	4	1	2	0	0	1	.182
Hopp cf	5	1	2	0	0	0	.211
Musial rf	4	2	3	1	2	1	.375
W.Cooper c	4	0	2	0	1	1	.333
Sanders 1b	5	1	1	0	0	0	.286
Kurowski 3b	4	0	0	0	0	0	.188
Marion ss	4	0	1	0	1	0	.333
Verban 2b	4	0	1	0	0	0	.273
Brecheen p	4	0	0	0	0	0	.000
TOTALS	**38**	**5**	**12**	**1**	**4**	**3**	**.234**

BATTING: 2B: Marion (3, Hollingsworth), Musial (1, Hollingsworth). **3B:** W.Cooper (1, Shirley). **HR:** Musial (1, 1st off Jakucki 1 on, 1 out). **RBI:** Musial 2 (2), W.Cooper 1 (2), Marion 1 (2). **2-out RBI:** W.Cooper 1. **Runners left in scoring position, 2 out:** Hopp 1, Sanders 1, Kurowski 3, Brecheen 1. **Team LOB:** 9 **FIELDING: DP:** 2 (Kurowski-Verban-Sanders, Marion-Verban-Sanders).

STL BROWNS	AB	R	H	HR	RBI	BB	AVG
Gutteridge 2b	4	0	2	0	0	1	.188
Kreevich cf	5	0	1	0	0	0	.167
Moore rf	3	1	0	0	0	1	.267
Stephens ss	4	0	1	0	0	0	.143
Laabs lf	4	0	2	0	1	0	.167
McQuinn 1b	3	0	1	0	0	1	.545
Christman 3b	4	0	1	0	0	0	.125
Hayworth c	2	0	0	0	0	0	.083
Mancuso c	2	0	1	0	0	0	.667
Jakucki p	0	0	0	0	0	0	.000
a-Clary ph	1	0	0	0	0	0	.000
Hollingsworth p	1	0	0	0	0	0	.000
b-Byrnes ph	0	0	0	0	0	1	.000
Shirley p	0	0	0	0	0	0	.000
c-Turner ph	1	0	0	0	0	0	.000
TOTALS	**34**	**1**	**9**	**0**	**1**	**4**	**.194**

a - Batted for Jakucki in the 3th
b - Batted for Hollingsworth in the 7th
c - Batted for Shirley in the 9th

BATTING: 2B: Laabs (1, Brecheen). **RBI:** Laabs 1 (1). **Runners left in scoring position, 2 out:** Kreevich 1, Christman 2. **GIDP:** Hayworth, Laabs. **Team LOB:** 10 **FIELDING: E:** Gutteridge (2). **Outfield assists:** Kreevich 2 (2).

STL CARDINALS	IP	H	R	ER	BB	SO	HR	ERA
Brecheen (W, 1-0)	9	9	1	1	4	4	0	1.00

STL BROWNS	IP	H	R	ER	BB	SO	HR	ERA
Jakucki (L, 0-1)	3	5	4	3	0	4	1	9.00
Hollingsworth	4	5	1	1	2	1	0	2.25
Shirley	2	2	0	0	1	1	0	0.00

IBB: W.Cooper (by Hollingsworth). **Ground balls-fly balls:** Brecheen 11-10, Jakucki 5-1, Hollingsworth 5-5, Shirley 2-2. **Batters faced:** Brecheen 38, Jakucki 15, Hollingsworth 18, Shirley 8. **UMPIRES:** hp—Pipgras, 1b—Sears, 2b—McGowan, 3b—Dunn **T:** 2:22 **A:** 35,455

GAME 5 Cardinals 2 Browns 0
Sportsman's Park 10/08/44

STL CARDINALS	AB	R	H	HR	RBI	BB	AVG
Litwhiler lf	4	1	2	1	1	0	.267
Hopp cf	4	0	0	0	0	0	.174
Musial rf	3	0	1	0	0	1	.368
W.Cooper c	4	0	0	0	0	0	.263
Sanders 1b	4	1	1	1	1	0	.278
Kurowski 3b	4	0	1	0	0	0	.200
Marion ss	4	0	0	0	0	0	.263
Verban 2b	3	0	1	0	0	0	.286
M.Cooper p	2	0	0	0	0	0	.000
TOTALS	**32**	**2**	**6**	**2**	**2**	**1**	**.225**

BATTING: 2B: Litwhiler (1, Galehouse), Musial (2, Galehouse). **HR:** Sanders (1, 6th off Galehouse 0 on, 2 out), Litwhiler (1, 8th off Galehouse 0 on, 0 out). **S:** M.Cooper. **RBI:** Litwhiler 1 (1), Sanders 1 (1). **2-out RBI:** Sanders 1. **Runners left in scoring position, 2 out:** Hopp 1, W.Cooper 1, Sanders 1. **GIDP:** M.Cooper. **Team LOB:** 5 **FIELDING: E:** Musial (1).

STL BROWNS	AB	R	H	HR	RBI	BB	AVG
Gutteridge 2b	2	0	0	0	0	1	.167
a-Baker ph-2b	1	0	0	0	0	0	.000
Kreevich cf	4	0	2	0	0	0	.227
Moore rf	4	0	0	0	0	0	.211
Stephens ss	4	0	3	0	0	0	.278
McQuinn 1b	3	0	0	0	0	1	.429
Zarilla lf	4	0	0	0	0	0	.111
Christman 3b	3	0	0	0	0	0	.105
b-Byrnes ph	1	0	0	0	0	0	.000
Hayworth c	3	0	1	0	0	0	.133
c-Laabs ph	1	0	0	0	0	0	.154
Galehouse p	3	0	1	0	0	0	.200
d-Chartak ph	1	0	0	0	0	0	.000
TOTALS	**34**	**0**	**7**	**0**	**0**	**2**	**.196**

a - Batted for Gutteridge in the 7th
b - Batted for Christman in the 9th
c - Batted for Hayworth in the 9th
d - Batted for Galehouse in the 9th

BATTING: 2B: Kreevich (2, M.Cooper), Stephens (1, M.Cooper). **Runners left in scoring position, 2 out:** Gutteridge 1, Moore 1, McQuinn 1, Zarilla 1, Christman 2. **Team LOB:** 9 **FIELDING: E:** Stephens (2). **DP:** 1 (Stephens-McQuinn).

STL CARDINALS	IP	H	R	ER	BB	SO	HR	ERA
M.Cooper (W, 1-1)	9	7	0	0	2	12	0	1.13

STL BROWNS	IP	H	R	ER	BB	SO	HR	ERA
Galehouse (L, 1-1)	9	6	2	2	1	10	2	1.50

Ground balls-fly balls: M.Cooper 5-10, Galehouse 6-10. **Batters faced:** M.Cooper 36, Galehouse 34. **UMPIRES:** hp—Sears, 1b—Pipgras, 2b—Dunn, 3b—McGowan **T:** 2:04 **A:** 36,568

GAME 6 Cardinals 3 Browns 1
Sportsman's Park 10/09/44

STL BROWNS	AB	R	H	HR	RBI	BB	AVG
Gutteridge 2b	3	0	0	0	0	0	.143
b-Baker ph-2b	1	0	0	0	0	0	.000
Kreevich cf	4	0	1	0	0	0	.231
Moore rf	3	0	0	0	0	1	.182
Stephens ss	4	0	0	0	0	0	.227
Laabs lf	2	1	1	0	0	2	.200
McQuinn 1b	2	0	1	0	1	1	.438
Christman 3b	3	0	0	0	0	0	.091
c-Byrnes ph	1	0	0	0	0	0	.000
Hayworth c	2	0	0	0	0	1	.118
d-Chartak ph	1	0	0	0	0	0	.000
Potter p	2	0	0	0	0	0	.000
Muncrief p	0	0	0	0	0	0	.000
a-Zarilla ph	1	0	0	0	0	0	.100
Kramer p	0	0	0	0	0	0	.000
TOTALS	**29**	**1**	**3**	**0**	**1**	**5**	**.183**

a - Batted for Muncrief in the 7th
b - Batted for Gutteridge in the 7th
c - Batted for Christman in the 9th
d - Batted for Hayworth in the 9th

BATTING: 2B: Kreevich (3, Lanier). **3B:** Laabs (1, Lanier). **S:** McQuinn. **RBI:** McQuinn 1 (5). **Runners left in scoring position, 2 out:** Stephens 1, Hayworth 1, Potter 1. **Team LOB:** 7 **FIELDING: E:** Stephens (3), Hayworth (1). **Outfield assists:** Laabs (1).

STL CARDINALS	AB	R	H	HR	RBI	BB	AVG
Litwhiler lf	5	0	0	0	0	0	.200
Hopp cf	4	0	1	0	0	0	.185
Musial rf	4	0	0	0	0	0	.304
W.Cooper c	3	1	2	0	0	1	.318
Sanders 1b	3	1	1	0	0	1	.286
Kurowski 3b	3	1	1	0	1	1	.217
Marion ss	3	0	0	0	0	0	.227
Verban 2b	3	0	3	0	1	1	.412
Lanier p	2	0	2	0	1	0	.500
Wilks p	1	0	0	0	0	0	.000
TOTALS	**31**	**3**	**10**	**0**	**3**	**4**	**.240**

BATTING: S: Wilks, Marion. **RBI:** Kurowski 1 (1), Verban 1 (2), Lanier 1 (1). **2-out RBI:** Verban 1, Lanier 1. **Runners left in scoring position, 2 out:** Litwhiler 4, Hopp 1, Kurowski 1. **Team LOB:** 10

STL BROWNS	IP	H	R	ER	BB	SO	HR	ERA
Potter (L, 0-1)	3.2	6	3	1	1	3	0	0.93
Muncrief	2.1	2	0	0	1	0	0	1.35
Kramer	2	2	0	0	2	2	0	0.00

STL CARDINALS	IP	H	R	ER	BB	SO	HR	ERA
Lanier (W, 1-0)	5.1	3	1	1	5	5	0	2.19
Wilks (S, 1)	3.2	0	0	0	0	4	0	5.68

WP: Lanier 1. **IBB:** Hayworth (by Lanier), Verban (by Kramer). **Ground balls-fly balls:** Potter 3-5, Muncrief 1-5, Kramer 1-1, Lanier 5-5, Wilks 2-5. **Batters faced:** Potter 18, Muncrief 10, Kramer 9, Lanier 24, Wilks 11. **UMPIRES:** hp—McGowan, 1b—Dunn, 2b—Pipgras, 3b—Sears **T:** 2:06 **A:** 31,630

1945 DETROIT DEF. CHICAGO CUBS, 4-3

GAME 1 Chicago 9 Detroit 0
Briggs Stadium 10/03/45

CHICAGO CUBS	AB	R	H	HR	RBI	BB	AVG
Hack 3b	5	0	1	0	0	0	.200
Johnson 2b	5	2	2	0	0	0	.400
Lowrey lf	4	0	0	0	0	0	.000
Cavarretta 1b	4	3	3	1	2	1	.750
Pafko cf	4	3	3	0	1	1	.750
Nicholson rf	4	1	2	0	3	0	.500
Livingston c	4	0	2	0	2	0	.500
Hughes ss	3	0	0	0	0	1	.000
Borowy p	3	0	0	0	0	0	.000
TOTALS	**36**	**9**	**13**	**1**	**8**	**3**	**.361**

BATTING: 2B: Johnson (1, Newhouser), Pafko (1, Newhouser). **3B:** Nicholson (1, Newhouser). **HR:** Cavarretta (1, 7th off Tobin 0 on, 2 out). **S:** Lowrey, Borowy. **RBI:** Cavarretta 2 (2), Pafko 1 (1), Nicholson 3 (3), Livingston 2 (2). **2-out RBI:** Cavarretta 1, Nicholson 3, Livingston 2. **Runners left in scoring position, 2 out:** Hack 1. **Team LOB:** 5 **BASERUNNING: SB:** Johnson (1, 2nd base off Newhouser/Richards), Pafko (1, 2nd base off Tobin/Richards). **CS:** Livingston 2 (2, 2nd base off Newhouser/Richards, 2nd base off Benton/Richards). **FIELDING: Outfield assists:** Pafko (1). **DP:** 2 (Hughes-Johnson-Cavarretta, Johnson-Hughes-Cavarretta).

DETROIT	AB	R	H	HR	RBI	BB	AVG
Webb ss	4	0	1	0	0	0	.250
d-McHale ph	1	0	0	0	0	0	.000
Mayo 2b	4	0	2	0	0	0	.500
Cramer cf	3	0	0	0	0	1	.000
Greenberg lf	2	0	1	0	0	1	.500
Cullenbine rf	3	0	0	0	0	1	.000
York 1b	3	0	1	0	0	1	.333
Outlaw 3b	4	0	1	0	0	0	.250
Richards c	2	0	0	0	0	1	.000
b-Hostetler ph	1	0	0	0	0	0	.000
Newhouser p	1	0	0	0	0	0	.000
Benton p	0	0	0	0	0	0	.000
a-Eaton ph	1	0	0	0	0	0	.000
Tobin p	1	0	0	0	0	0	.000
Mueller p	0	0	0	0	0	0	.000
c-Borom ph	1	0	0	0	0	0	.000
TOTALS	**31**	**0**	**6**	**0**	**0**	**5**	**.194**

a - Batted for Benton in the 4th
b - Batted for Richards in the 9th
c - Batted for Mueller in the 9th
d - Batted for Webb in the 9th

BATTING: Runners left in scoring position, 2 out: Webb 2, Cullenbine 1, York 2. **GIDP:** Cramer, Newhouser. **Team LOB:** 10 **FIELDING: PB:** Richards, Richards.

CHICAGO CUBS	IP	H	R	ER	BB	SO	HR	ERA
Borowy (W, 1-0)	9	6	0	0	5	4	0	0.00

DETROIT	IP	H	R	ER	BB	SO	HR	ERA
Newhouser (L, 0-1)	2.2	8	7	7	1	3	0	23.63
Benton	1.1	1	0	0	0	1	0	0.00
Tobin	3	4	2	2	1	0	1	6.00
Mueller	2	0	0	0	1	1	0	0.00

IBB: Pafko (by Newhouser). **HBP:** Greenberg (by Borowy). **Ground balls-fly balls:** Borowy 8-13, Newhouser 1-2, Benton 1-1, Tobin 4-4, Mueller 1-4. **Batters faced:** Borowy 37, Newhouser 16, Benton 4, Tobin 14, Mueller 7. **UMPIRES:** hp—Summers, 1b—Jorda, 2b—Passarella, 3b—Conlan **T:** 2:10 **A:** 54,637

GAME 2 Detroit 4 Chicago 1
Briggs Stadium 10/04/45

CHICAGO CUBS	AB	R	H	HR	RBI	BB	AVG
Hack 3b	3	0	3	0	0	1	.500
Johnson 2b	3	0	0	0	0	0	.250
Lowrey lf	4	0	2	0	0	0	.250
Cavarretta 1b	4	1	1	0	0	0	.500
Pafko cf	4	0	0	0	0	0	.375
Nicholson rf	3	0	1	0	1	1	.429
Gillespie c	4	0	0	0	0	0	.000
Hughes ss	3	0	0	0	0	1	.000
Wyse p	2	0	0	0	0	0	.000
a-Secory ph	1	0	0	0	0	0	.000
Erickson p	0	0	0	0	0	0	.000
b-Becker ph	1	0	0	0	0	0	.000
TOTALS	**32**	**1**	**7**	**0**	**1**	**3**	**.294**

a - Batted for Wyse in the 7th
b - Batted for Erickson in the 9th

BATTING: 2B: Cavarretta (1, Trucks), Hack (1, Trucks). **S:** Johnson. **RBI:** Nicholson 1 (4). **2-out RBI:** Nicholson 1. **Runners left in scoring position, 2 out:** Johnson 1, Cavarretta 1, Pafko 2, Becker 1. **Team LOB:** 8

DETROIT	AB	R	H	HR	RBI	BB	AVG
Webb ss	4	1	2	0	0	0	.375
Mayo 2b	3	1	0	0	0	1	.286
Cramer cf	4	1	3	0	1	0	.429
Greenberg lf	3	1	1	1	3	1	.400
Cullenbine rf	2	0	0	0	0	2	.000
York 1b	4	0	0	0	0	0	.143
Outlaw 3b	4	0	1	0	0	0	.250
Richards c	4	0	0	0	0	0	.000
Trucks p	3	0	0	0	0	0	.000
TOTALS	**31**	**4**	**7**	**1**	**4**	**4**	**.210**

BATTING: HR: Greenberg (1, 5th off Wyse 2 on, 2 out). **RBI:** Cramer 1 (1), Greenberg 3 (3). **2-out RBI:** Cramer 1, Greenberg 3. **Runners left in scoring position, 2 out:** Cullenbine 2, outlaw 1, Richards 1. **Team LOB:** 7 **Outfield assists:** Greenberg (1).

CHICAGO CUBS	IP	H	R	ER	BB	SO	HR	ERA
Wyse (L, 0-1)	6	5	4	4	3	1	1	6.00
Erickson	2	2	0	0	1	1	0	0.00

DETROIT	IP	H	R	ER	BB	SO	HR	ERA
Trucks (W, 1-0)	9	7	1	1	3	4	0	1.00

Ground balls-fly balls: Wyse 8-9, Erickson 1-4, Trucks 11-10. **Batters faced:** Wyse 26, Erickson 9, Trucks 36. **UMPIRES:** hp—Jorda, 1b—Passarella, 2b—Conlan, 3b—Summers **T:** 1:47 **A:** 53,636

GAME 3 Chicago 3 Detroit 0
Briggs Stadium 10/05/45

CHICAGO CUBS	AB	R	H	HR	RBI	BB	AVG
Hack 3b	5	0	2	0	0	0	.462
Johnson 2b	5	0	0	0	0	0	.154
Lowrey lf	4	1	2	0	0	0	.333
Cavarretta 1b	2	0	1	0	0	1	.500
Pafko cf	2	1	0	0	0	1	.300
Nicholson rf	4	0	1	0	1	0	.364
Livingston c	4	1	1	0	0	0	.375
Hughes ss	3	0	1	0	1	0	.111
Passeau p	4	0	0	0	1	0	.000
TOTALS	**33**	**3**	**8**	**0**	**3**	**2**	**.277**

BATTING: 2B: Lowrey (1, Overmire), Livingston (1, Benton), Hack (2, Benton). **S:** Cavarretta, Hughes, Pafko. **RBI:** Nicholson 1 (5), Hughes 1 (1), Passeau 1 (1). **2-out RBI:** Hughes 1. **Runners left in scoring position, 2 out:** Johnson 1, Lowrey 1, Pafko 1, Livingston 1, Passeau 1. **Team LOB:** 8 **BASERUNNING: CS:** Hack (1, 2nd base off Benton/Richards). **FIELDING: DP:** 1 (Johnson-Cavarretta).

DETROIT	AB	R	H	HR	RBI	BB	AVG
Webb ss	3	0	0	0	0	0	.273
d-McHale ph	1	0	0	0	0	0	.000
Mayo 2b	3	0	0	0	0	0	.200
Cramer cf	3	0	0	0	0	0	.300
Greenberg lf	3	0	0	0	0	0	.250
Cullenbine rf	3	0	0	0	0	0	.000
York 1b	3	0	1	0	0	0	.200
Outlaw 3b	3	0	0	0	0	0	.182
Swift c	1	0	0	0	0	1	.000
a-Borom pr	0	0	0	0	0	0	.000
Richards c	1	0	0	0	0	0	.000
Overmire p	1	0	0	0	0	0	.000
b-Walker ph	1	0	0	0	0	0	.000
Benton p	0	0	0	0	0	0	.000
c-Hostetler ph	1	0	0	0	0	0	.000
TOTALS	**27**	**0**	**1**	**0**	**0**	**1**	**.157**

a - Ran for Swift in the 6th
b - Batted for Overmire in the 6th
c - Batted for Benton in the 9th
d - Batted for Webb in the 9th

BATTING: GIDP: Walker. **Team LOB:** 1 **FIELDING: E:** Mayo (1).

CHICAGO CUBS	IP	H	R	ER	BB	SO	HR	ERA
Passeau (W, 1-0)	9	1	0	0	1	1	0	0.00

DETROIT	IP	H	R	ER	BB	SO	HR	ERA
Overmire (L, 0-1)	6	4	2	2	2	2	0	3.00
Benton	3	4	1	1	0	3	0	2.08

Ground balls-fly balls: Passeau 10-15, Overmire 8-7, Benton 3-2. **Batters faced:** Passeau 28, Overmire 24, Benton 14. **UMPIRES:** hp—Passarella, 1b—Conlan, 2b—Summers, 3b—Jorda **T:** 1:55 **A:** 55,500

GAME 4 Detroit 4 Chicago 1
Wrigley Field 10/06/45

DETROIT	AB	R	H	HR	RBI	BB	AVG
Webb ss	5	0	0	0	0	0	.188
Mayo 2b	3	1	0	0	0	1	.154
Cramer cf	4	1	2	0	0	0	.357
Greenberg lf	3	1	1	0	1	1	.273
Cullenbine rf	3	1	1	0	1	1	.091
York 1b	3	0	0	0	0	1	.154
Outlaw 3b	4	0	1	0	1	0	.200
Richards c	4	0	1	0	1	0	.091
Trout p	4	0	1	0	0	0	.250
TOTALS	**33**	**4**	**7**	**0**	**4**	**4**	**.172**

BATTING: 2B: Cullenbine (1, Prim). **RBI:** Greenberg 1 (4), Cullenbine 1 (1), outlaw 1 (1), Richards 1 (1). **2-out RBI:** Richards 1. **Runners left in scoring position, 2 out:** Cullenbine 1, Trout 1. **Team LOB:** 6

CHICAGO CUBS	AB	R	H	HR	RBI	BB	AVG
Hack 3b	4	0	0	0	0	0	.353
Johnson 2b	4	1	2	0	0	0	.235
Lowrey lf	4	0	1	0	1	0	.313
Cavarretta 1b	4	0	0	0	0	0	.357
Pafko cf	4	0	0	0	0	0	.214
Nicholson rf	4	0	0	0	0	0	.267
Livingston c	3	0	1	0	0	0	.364
Hughes ss	1	0	0	0	0	1	.100
b-Becker ph	1	0	1	0	0	0	.500
c-Merullo pr-ss	0	0	0	0	0	0	.000
Prim p	0	0	0	0	0	0	.000
Derringer p	0	0	0	0	0	0	.000
a-Secory ph	1	0	0	0	0	0	.000
Vandenberg p	0	0	0	0	0	0	.000
d-Gillespie ph	1	0	0	0	0	0	.000
Erickson p	0	0	0	0	0	0	.000
TOTALS	**31**	**1**	**5**	**0**	**1**	**1**	**.250**

a - Batted for Derringer in the 5th
b - Batted for Hughes in the 7th
c - Ran for Becker in the 7th
d - Batted for Vandenberg in the 7th

BATTING: 3B: Johnson (1, Trout). **S:** Prim. **RBI:** Lowrey 1 (1). **Runners left in scoring position, 2 out:** Hack 1, Nicholson 2. **Team LOB:** 5 **FIELDING: E:** Nicholson (1). **PB:** Livingston.

DETROIT	IP	H	R	ER	BB	SO	HR	ERA
Trout (W, 1-0)	9	5	1	0	1	6	0	0.00

CHICAGO CUBS	IP	H	R	ER	BB	SO	HR	ERA
Prim (L, 0-1)	3.1	3	4	4	1	1	0	10.80
Derringer	1.2	2	0	0	2	1	0	0.00
Vandenberg	2	0	0	0	0	0	0	0.00
Erickson	2	2	0	0	1	2	0	0.00

IBB: York (by Derringer). **Ground balls-fly balls:** Trout 13-7, Prim 5-4, Derringer 3-1, Vandenberg 2-4, Erickson 1-2. **Batters faced:** Trout 33, Prim 14, Derringer 9, Vandenberg 6, Erickson 8. **UMPIRES:** hp—Conlan, 1b—Summers, 2b—Jorda, 3b—Passarella **T:** 2:00 **A:** 42,923

GAME 5 Detroit 8 Chicago 4
Wrigley Field 10/07/45

DETROIT	AB	R	H	HR	RBI	BB	AVG
Webb ss	4	1	1	0	1	1	.200
Mayo 2b	4	0	2	0	0	1	.235
Cramer cf	4	2	1	0	1	0	.333
Greenberg lf	5	3	3	0	1	0	.375
Cullenbine rf	4	1	2	0	2	0	.200
York 1b	5	1	1	0	1	0	.167
Outlaw 3b	4	0	0	0	1	0	.158
Richards c	4	0	1	0	0	1	.133
Newhouser p	3	0	0	0	1	1	.000
TOTALS	**37**	**8**	**11**	**0**	**8**	**4**	**.201**

BATTING: 2B: Greenberg 3 (3, Borowy, Derringer, Erickson), Cullenbine (2, Erickson). **S:** outlaw, Cullenbine. **RBI:** Webb 1 (1), Cramer 1 (2), Greenberg 1 (5), Cullenbine 2 (3), York 1 (1), outlaw 1 (2), Newhouser 1 (1). **Runners left in scoring position, 2 out:** Cramer 2, Cullenbine 1, Richards 1. **GIDP:** Newhouser. **Team LOB:** 9 **FIELDING: DP:** 1 (Mayo-York-Webb-Mayo).

CHICAGO CUBS	AB	R	H	HR	RBI	BB	AVG
Hack 3b	3	0	1	0	1	1	.350
Johnson 2b	3	0	0	0	0	0	.200
Lowrey lf	4	1	1	0	0	0	.300
Cavarretta 1b	3	1	1	0	0	1	.353
Pafko cf	4	1	0	0	0	0	.167
Nicholson rf	4	0	1	0	2	0	.263
Livingston c	4	0	1	0	1	0	.333
Merullo ss	2	0	0	0	0	0	.000
b-Williams ph	1	0	0	0	0	0	.000
Schuster ss	1	0	0	0	0	0	.000
Borowy p	1	1	1	0	0	0	.250
Vandenberg p	0	0	0	0	0	0	.000
Chipman p	0	0	0	0	0	0	.000
a-Sauer ph	1	0	0	0	0	0	.000
Derringer p	0	0	0	0	0	0	.000
c-Secory ph	1	0	1	0	0	0	.333
Erickson p	0	0	0	0	0	0	.000
TOTALS	**32**	**4**	**7**	**0**	**4**	**2**	**.244**

a - Batted for Chipman in the 6th
b - Batted for Merullo in the 7th
c - Batted for Derringer in the 8th

BATTING: 2B: Borowy (1, Newhouser), Livingston (2, Newhouser), Cavarretta (2, Newhouser). **S:** Johnson. **RBI:** Hack 1 (1), Nicholson 2 (7), Livingston 1 (3). **2-out RBI:** Hack 1, Nicholson 1, Livingston 1. **Runners left in scoring position, 2 out:** Lowrey 1, Williams 2. **GIDP:** Lowrey. **Team LOB:** 4 **FIELDING: E:** Hack (1), Pafko (1). **DP:** 1 (Johnson-Merullo-Cavarretta).

DETROIT	IP	H	R	ER	BB	SO	HR	ERA
Newhouser (W, 1-1)	9	7	4	4	2	9	0	8.49

CHICAGO CUBS	IP	H	R	ER	BB	SO	HR	ERA
Borowy (L, 1-1)	5	8	5	5	1	4	0	3.21
Vandenberg	0.2	0	0	0	2	0	0	0.00
Chipman	0.1	0	0	0	1	0	0	0.00
Derringer	2	1	1	1	0	0	0	2.45
Erickson	1	2	2	2	0	0	0	3.60

IBB: Richards (by Vandenberg). **HBP:** Cramer (by Erickson). **Ground balls-fly balls:** Newhouser 11-5, Borowy 5-6, Vandenberg 1-0, Chipman 1-0, Derringer 2-4, Erickson 2-1. **Batters faced:** Newhouser 35, Borowy 24, Vandenberg 4, Chipman 2, Derringer 8, Erickson 6. **UMPIRES:** hp—Summers, 1b—Jorda, 2b—Passarella, 3b—Conlan **T:** 2:18 **A:** 43,463

GAME 6 Chicago 8 Detroit 7
Wrigley Field 10/08/45

DETROIT	AB	R	H	HR	RBI	BB	AVG
Webb ss	3	0	0	0	0	0	.174
c-Hostetler ph	1	0	0	0	0	0	.000
Hoover ss	3	1	1	0	1	0	.333
Mayo 2b	6	0	1	0	1	0	.217
Cramer cf	6	1	2	0	1	0	.333
Greenberg lf	5	2	1	1	1	1	.333
Cullenbine rf	5	1	2	0	1	1	.250
York 1b	6	0	2	0	1	0	.208
Outlaw 3b	5	0	1	0	0	1	.167
Richards c	0	0	0	0	1	2	.133
a-Maier ph	1	0	1	0	0	0	1.000
Swift c	2	1	1	0	0	1	.333
Trucks p	1	0	0	0	0	1	.000
Caster p	0	0	0	0	0	0	.000
b-McHale ph	1	0	0	0	0	0	.000
Bridges p	0	0	0	0	0	0	.000
Benton p	0	0	0	0	0	0	.000
d-Walker ph	1	1	1	0	0	0	.500
Trout p	2	0	0	0	0	0	.167
TOTALS	**48**	**7**	**13**	**1**	**7**	**7**	**.217**

a - Batted for Richards in the 6th
b - Batted for Caster in the 6th
c - Batted for Webb in the 7th
d - Batted for Benton in the 8th

BATTING: 2B: York (1, Passeau), Walker (1, Wyse). **HR:** Greenberg (2, 8th off Prim 0 on, 2 out). **RBI:** Hoover 1 (1), Mayo 1 (1), Cramer 1 (3), Greenberg 1 (6), Cullenbine 1 (4), York 1 (2), Richards 1 (2). **2-out RBI:** Greenberg 1, Cullenbine 1, York 1. **Runners left in scoring position, 2 out:** Webb 4, Hoover 1, outlaw 1, McHale 1. **GIDP:** Greenberg. **Team LOB:** 12 **BASERUNNING: SB:** Cullenbine (1, 2nd base off Passeau/Livingston). **CS:** Hoover (1, 2nd base off Borowy/Williams). **FIELDING: E:** Richards (1). **DP:** 2 (Mayo-Webb-Richards-Webb, Mayo-Hoover-York).

CHICAGO CUBS	AB	R	H	HR	RBI	BB	AVG
Hack 3b	5	1	4	0	3	2	.440
Johnson 2b	4	0	0	0	0	0	.167
Lowrey lf	5	1	1	0	0	1	.280
Cavarretta 1b	5	1	2	0	2	1	.364
Pafko cf	6	0	2	0	0	0	.208
Nicholson rf	5	0	0	0	0	1	.208
Livingston c	3	2	2	0	1	1	.389
a-Gillespie ph	1	0	0	0	0	0	.000
Williams c	1	0	0	0	0	0	.000
Hughes ss	4	1	3	0	2	0	.286
b-Becker ph	0	0	0	0	0	1	.500
c-Block pr	0	0	0	0	0	0	.000
Merullo ss	0	0	0	0	0	0	.000
d-Secory ph	1	0	1	0	0	0	.500
e-Schuster pr	0	1	0	0	0	0	.000
Passeau p	3	1	0	0	0	0	.000
Wyse p	1	0	0	0	0	0	.000
Prim p	0	0	0	0	0	0	.000
Borowy p	2	0	0	0	0	0	.167
TOTALS	**46**	**8**	**15**	**0**	**8**	**7**	**.262**

a - Batted for Livingston in the 9th
b - Batted for Hughes in the 9th
c - Ran for Becker in the 9th
d - Batted for Merullo in the 12th e - Ran for Secory in the 12th

BATTING: 2B: Livingston (3, Bridges), Hughes (1, Bridges), Pafko (2, Trout), Hack (3, Trout). **S:** Johnson, Johnson. **RBI:** Hack 3 (4), Cavarretta 2 (4), Livingston 1 (4), Hughes 2 (3). **2-out RBI:** Hack 1, Livingston 1, Hughes 1. **Runners left in scoring position, 2 out:** Cavarretta 2, Nicholson 1, Wyse 2, Borowy 1. **GIDP:** Lowrey. **Team LOB:** 12 **FIELDING: E:** Johnson (1), Hack 2 (3). **Outfield assists:** Lowrey (1), Pafko (2). **DP:** 1 (Merullo-Johnson-Cavarretta).

DETROIT	IP	H	R	ER	BB	SO	HR	ERA
Trucks	4.1	7	4	4	2	3	0	3.38
Caster	0.2	0	0	0	0	1	0	0.00
Bridges	1.2	3	3	3	3	1	0	16.20
Benton	0.1	1	0	0	0	1	0	1.93
Trout (L, 1-1)	4.2	4	1	1	2	3	0	0.66

CHICAGO CUBS	IP	H	R	ER	BB	SO	HR	ERA
Passeau	6.2	5	3	3	6	2	0	1.72
Wyse	0.2	3	3	2	1	0	0	8.10
Prim	0.2	1	1	0	0	0	1	9.00
Borowy (W, 2-1)	4	4	0	0	0	0	0	2.50

IBB: outlaw (by Passeau), Richards (by Passeau), Becker (by Trout). **Ground balls-fly balls:** Trucks 4-5, Caster 0-1, Bridges 1-2, Benton 0-0, Trout 5-4, Passeau 11-8, Wyse 2-0, Prim 1-1, Borowy 4-6. **Batters faced:** Trucks 22, Caster 2, Bridges 10, Benton 2, Trout 19, Passeau 32, Wyse 6, Prim 3, Borowy 14. **UMPIRES:** hp—Jorda, 1b—Passarella, 2b—Conlan, 3b—Summers **T:** 3:28 **A:** 41,708

GAME 7 Detroit 9 Chicago 3
Wrigley Field 10/10/45

DETROIT	AB	R	H	HR	RBI	BB	AVG
Webb ss	4	2	1	0	0	1	.185
Mayo 2b	5	2	2	0	1	0	.250
Cramer cf	5	2	3	0	1	0	.379
Greenberg lf	2	0	0	0	1	2	.304
Mierkowicz lf	0	0	0	0	0	0	.000
Cullenbine rf	2	2	0	0	0	3	.227
York 1b	4	0	0	0	1	1	.179
Outlaw 3b	4	1	1	0	1	1	.179
Richards c	4	0	2	0	4	0	.211
Swift c	1	0	0	0	0	0	.250
Newhouser p	4	0	0	0	0	0	.000
TOTALS	**35**	**9**	**9**	**0**	**9**	**8**	**.223**

BATTING: 2B: Richards 2 (2, Derringer, Erickson), Mayo (1, Passeau). **S:** Greenberg. **RBI:** Mayo 1 (2), Cramer 1 (4), Greenberg 1 (7), York 1 (3), outlaw 1 (3), Richards 4 (6). **2-out RBI:** York 1, outlaw 1, Richards 4. **Runners left in scoring position, 2 out:** Greenberg 1, outlaw 2, Newhouser 3. **Team LOB:** 8 **BASERUNNING: SB:** outlaw (1, 2nd base off Vandenberg/Livingston), Cramer (1, 2nd base off Erickson/Livingston). **FIELDING: E:** Newhouser (1). **DP:** 1 (Webb-Mayo-York).

CHICAGO CUBS	AB	R	H	HR	RBI	BB	AVG
Hack 3b	5	0	0	0	0	0	.367
Johnson 2b	5	1	1	0	0	0	.172
Lowrey lf	4	1	2	0	0	0	.310
Cavarretta 1b	4	1	3	0	1	0	.423
Pafko cf	4	0	1	0	1	0	.214
Nicholson rf	4	0	1	0	1	0	.214
Livingston c	4	0	1	0	0	0	.364
Hughes ss	3	0	1	0	0	1	.294
Borowy p	0	0	0	0	0	0	.167
Derringer p	0	0	0	0	0	0	.000
Vandenberg p	1	0	0	0	0	0	.000
a-Sauer ph	1	0	0	0	0	0	.000
Erickson p	0	0	0	0	0	0	.000
b-Secory ph	1	0	0	0	0	0	.400
Passeau p	0	0	0	0	0	0	.000
Wyse p	0	0	0	0	0	0	.000
c-McCullough ph	1	0	0	0	0	0	.000
TOTALS	**37**	**3**	**10**	**0**	**3**	**1**	**.263**

a - Batted for Vandenberg in the 5th
b - Batted for Erickson in the 7th
c - Batted for Wyse in the 9th

BATTING: 2B: Johnson (2, Newhouser), Nicholson (1, Newhouser). **3B:** Pafko (1, Newhouser). **RBI:** Cavarretta 1 (5), Pafko 1 (2), Nicholson 1 (8). **2-out RBI:** Nicholson 1. **Runners left in scoring position, 2 out:** Hack 1, Livingston 3. **GIDP:** Pafko. **Team LOB:** 8

DETROIT	IP	H	R	ER	BB	SO	HR	ERA
Newhouser (W, 2-1)	9	10	3	3	1	10	0	6.10

CHICAGO CUBS	IP	H	R	ER	BB	SO	HR	ERA
Borowy (L, 2-2)	0	3	3	3	0	0	0	4.00
Derringer	1.2	2	3	3	5	0	0	6.75
Vandenberg	3.1	1	0	0	1	3	0	0.00
Erickson	2	2	1	1	1	2	0	3.86
Passeau	1	1	2	2	1	0	0	2.70
Wyse	1	0	0	0	0	0	0	7.04

WP: Newhouser 1. **IBB:** Cullenbine (by Derringer). **Ground balls-fly balls:** Newhouser 12-5, Borowy 0-0, Derringer 1-3, Vandenberg 5-2, Erickson 0-4, Passeau 1-2, Wyse 1-2. **Batters faced:** Newhouser 38, Borowy 3, Derringer 12, Vandenberg 12, Erickson 9, Passeau 5, Wyse 3. **UMPIRES:** hp—Passarella, 1b—Conlan, 2b—Summers, 3b—Jorda **T:** 2:31 **A:** 41,590

1946 ST.LOUIS DEF. BOSTON RED SOX, 4-3

GAME 1 Boston 3 St. Louis 2
Sportsman's Park 10/06/46

BOSTON	AB	R	H	HR	RBI	BB	AVG
McBride rf	5	0	1	0	1	0	.200
Moses rf	0	0	0	0	0	0	.000
Pesky ss	5	0	0	0	0	0	.000
DiMaggio cf	5	0	2	0	0	0	.400
Williams lf	3	0	1	0	0	2	.333
York 1b	4	2	1	1	1	0	.250
Doerr 2b	4	0	1	0	0	1	.250
Higgins 3b	4	0	2	0	1	0	.500
a-Gutteridge pr	0	1	0	0	0	0	.000
Johnson p	1	0	0	0	0	0	.000
Wagner c	3	0	0	0	0	0	.000
b-Russell ph-3b	1	0	1	0	0	0	1.000
Hughson p	2	0	0	0	0	1	.000
c-Partee ph-c	1	0	0	0	0	0	.000
TOTALS	**38**	**3**	**9**	**1**	**3**	**4**	**.237**

a - Ran for Higgins in the 9th
b - Batted for Wagner in the 9th
c - Batted for Hughson in the 9th

BATTING: HR: York (1, 10th off Pollet 0 on, 2 out). **RBI:** McBride 1 (1), York 1 (1), Higgins 1 (1). **2-out RBI:** McBride 1, York 1. **Runners left in scoring position, 2 out:** Pesky 1, York 1, Hughson 1. **Team LOB:** 10 **FIELDING: E:** McBride (1), Pesky (1). **Outfield assists:** DiMaggio (1).

ST.LOUIS	AB	R	H	HR	RBI	BB	AVG
Schoendienst 2b	5	1	2	0	0	0	.400
Moore cf	4	0	0	0	0	0	.000
Musial 1b	5	0	1	0	1	0	.200
Slaughter rf	4	0	1	0	0	1	.250
Kurowski 3b	3	1	1	0	0	0	.333
Garagiola c	4	0	1	0	1	0	.250
Walker lf	2	0	1	0	0	1	.500
a-Dusak ph-lf	1	0	0	0	0	0	.000
Marion ss	3	0	0	0	0	0	.000
Pollet p	4	0	0	0	0	0	.000
TOTALS	**35**	**2**	**7**	**0**	**2**	**2**	**.200**

a - Batted for Walker in the 9th

BATTING: 2B: Musial (1, Hughson), Garagiola (1, Hughson). **3B:** Slaughter (1, Hughson). **S:** Marion, Moore. **RBI:** Musial 1 (1), Garagiola 1 (1). **2-out RBI:** Musial 1, Garagiola 1. **Runners left in scoring position, 2 out:** Schoendienst 1, Moore 2, Slaughter 1, Kurowski 1, Garagiola 2. **Team LOB:** 8 **BASERUNNING: SB:** Schoendienst (1, 2nd base off Hughson/Wagner). **Outfield assists:** Moore (1).

BOSTON	IP	H	R	ER	BB	SO	HR	ERA
Hughson	8	7	2	2	2	5	0	2.25
Johnson (W, 1-0)	2	0	0	0	0	1	0	0.00

ST.LOUIS	IP	H	R	ER	BB	SO	HR	ERA
Pollet (L, 0-1)	10	9	3	3	4	3	1	2.70

IBB: Slaughter (by Hughson). **HBP:** York (by Pollet), Kurowski (by Hughson). **Ground balls-fly balls:** Hughson 8-9, Johnson 3-2, Pollet 12-14. **Batters faced:** Hughson 33, Johnson 7, Pollet 43. **UMPIRES:** hp—Ballanfant, 1b—Hubbard, 2b—Barlick, 3b—Berry **T:** 2:39 **A:** 36,218

GAME 2 St. Louis 3 Boston 0
Sportsman's Park 10/07/46

BOSTON	AB	R	H	HR	RBI	BB	AVG
McBride rf	4	0	1	0	0	0	.222
Pesky ss	4	0	0	0	0	0	.000
DiMaggio cf	4	0	1	0	0	0	.333
Williams lf	4	0	0	0	0	0	.143
York 1b	2	0	0	0	0	2	.167
Doerr 2b	4	0	1	0	0	0	.250
Higgins 3b	2	0	0	0	0	1	.333
Partee c	2	0	0	0	0	0	.000
Wagner c	1	0	0	0	0	0	.000
Harris p	2	0	1	0	0	0	.500
a-Culberson ph	1	0	0	0	0	0	.000
Dobson p	0	0	0	0	0	0	.000
TOTALS	**30**	**0**	**4**	**0**	**0**	**3**	**.191**

a - Batted for Harris in the 8th

BATTING: Runners left in scoring position, 2 out: Higgins 1, Partee 1. **GIDP:** DiMaggio. **Team LOB:** 6 **FIELDING: E:** Higgins (1).

ST.LOUIS	AB	R	H	HR	RBI	BB	AVG
Schoendienst 2b	3	0	0	0	0	0	.250
Moore cf	3	0	1	0	1	1	.143
Musial 1b	4	0	0	0	1	0	.111
Kurowski 3b	4	0	1	0	0	0	.286
Slaughter rf	4	0	0	0	0	0	.125
Dusak lf	2	0	1	0	0	1	.333
a-Sisler ph	1	0	0	0	0	0	.000
Walker lf	0	0	0	0	0	0	.500
Marion ss	4	0	0	0	0	0	.000
Rice c	2	2	2	0	0	1	1.000
Brecheen p	3	1	1	0	1	0	.333
TOTALS	**30**	**3**	**6**	**0**	**3**	**3**	**.200**

a - Batted for Dusak in the 8th

BATTING: 2B: Rice (1, Harris), Dusak (1, Harris). **S:** Schoendienst. **RBI:** Moore 1 (1), Musial 1 (2), Brecheen 1 (1). **Runners left in scoring position, 2 out:** Musial 1, Brecheen 1. **Team LOB:** 7 **FIELDING: DP:** 1 (Marion-Musial).

BOSTON	IP	H	R	ER	BB	SO	HR	ERA
Harris (L, 0-1)	7	6	3	1	3	3	0	1.29
Dobson	1	0	0	0	0	0	0	0.00

ST.LOUIS	IP	H	R	ER	BB	SO	HR	ERA
Brecheen (W, 1-0)	9	4	0	0	3	4	0	0.00

IBB: Higgins (by Brecheen), Rice (by Harris). **Ground balls-fly balls:** Harris 9-9, Dobson 2-1, Brecheen 12-10. **Batters faced:** Harris 31, Dobson 3, Brecheen 33. **UMPIRES:** hp—Hubbard, 1b—Barlick, 2b—Berry, 3b—Ballanfant **T:** 1:56 **A:** 35,815

GAME 3 Boston 4 St. Louis 0
Fenway Park 10/09/46

ST.LOUIS	AB	R	H	HR	RBI	BB	AVG
Schoendienst 2b	4	0	0	0	0	0	.167
Moore cf	4	0	0	0	0	0	.091
Musial 1b	3	0	1	0	0	1	.167
Slaughter rf	4	0	1	0	0	0	.167
Kurowski 3b	3	0	0	0	0	0	.200
Garagiola c	3	0	1	0	0	0	.286
Walker lf	3	0	1	0	0	0	.400
Marion ss	3	0	1	0	0	0	.100
Dickson p	2	0	1	0	0	0	.500
a-Sisler ph	1	0	0	0	0	0	.000
Wilks p	0	0	0	0	0	0	.000
TOTALS	**30**	**0**	**6**	**0**	**0**	**1**	**.200**

a - Batted for Dickson in the 8th

BATTING: 2B: Dickson (1, Ferriss). **3B:** Musial (1, Ferriss). **Runners left in scoring position, 2 out:** Slaughter 1. **GIDP:** Kurowski. **Team LOB:** 4 **BASERUNNING: SB:** Musial (1, 2nd base off Ferriss/Wagner). **FIELDING: E:** Schoendienst (1). **PB:** Garagiola.

BOSTON	AB	R	H	HR	RBI	BB	AVG
Moses rf	3	0	0	0	0	1	.000
Pesky ss	4	1	2	0	0	0	.154
DiMaggio cf	4	0	1	0	0	0	.308
Williams lf	3	1	1	0	0	1	.200
York 1b	4	2	2	1	3	0	.300
Doerr 2b	4	0	2	0	0	0	.333
Higgins 3b	3	0	0	0	0	1	.222
Wagner c	3	0	0	0	0	0	.000
Ferriss p	4	0	0	0	0	0	.000
TOTALS	**32**	**4**	**8**	**1**	**3**	**3**	**.210**

BATTING: 2B: DiMaggio (1, Dickson), Doerr (1, Wilks). **HR:** York (2, 1st off Dickson 2 on, 2 out). **S:** Wagner. **RBI:** York 3 (4). **2-out RBI:** York 3. **Runners left in scoring position, 2 out:** Moses 1, DiMaggio 1, Williams 1, Ferriss 2. **Team LOB:** 8 **FIELDING: Outfield assists:** DiMaggio (2). **DP:** 2 (DiMaggio-Pesky, Pesky-Doerr-York).

ST.LOUIS	IP	H	R	ER	BB	SO	HR	ERA
Dickson (L, 0-1)	7	6	3	3	3	4	1	3.86
Wilks	1	2	1	0	0	0	0	0.00

BOSTON	IP	H	R	ER	BB	SO	HR	ERA
Ferriss (W, 1-0)	9	6	0	0	1	2	0	0.00

IBB: Williams (by Dickson). **Ground balls-fly balls:** Dickson 7-9, Wilks 3-1, Ferriss 13-9. **Batters faced:** Dickson 30, Wilks 6, Ferriss 31. **UMPIRES:** hp—Barlick, 1b—Berry, 2b—Ballanfant, 3b—Hubbard **T:** 1:54 **A:** 34,500

GAME 4 St. Louis 12 Boston 3
Fenway Park 10/10/46

ST.LOUIS	AB	R	H	HR	RBI	BB	AVG
Schoendienst 2b	6	1	1	0	0	0	.167
Moore cf	4	1	1	0	0	1	.133
Musial 1b	5	1	1	0	2	1	.176
Slaughter rf	6	4	4	1	1	0	.333
Kurowski 3b	5	2	4	0	1	0	.400
Garagiola c	5	1	4	0	3	0	.500
Walker lf	2	1	1	0	1	2	.429
Marion ss	4	1	3	0	3	0	.286
Munger p	4	0	1	0	0	0	.250
TOTALS	**41**	**12**	**20**	**1**	**11**	**4**	**.287**

BATTING: 2B: Kurowski 2 (2, Hughson, Bagby), Musial (2, Hughson), Slaughter (1, Bagby), Garagiola (2, Zuber), Marion (1, Ryba). **HR:** Slaughter (1, 2nd off Hughson 0 on, 0 out). **S:** Marion, Moore, Munger, Walker. **RBI:** Musial 2 (4), Slaughter 1 (1), Kurowski 1 (1), Garagiola 3 (4), Walker 1 (1), Marion 3 (3). **2-out RBI:** Garagiola 1. **Runners left in scoring position, 2 out:** Moore 1, Slaughter 2, Marion 1. **GIDP:** Marion. **Team LOB:** 10 **BASERUNNING: CS:** Walker (1, 2nd base off Hughson/Wagner). **FIELDING: E:** Marion (1). **Outfield assists:** Slaughter (1). **DP:** 2 (Slaughter-Garagiola, Schoendienst-Musial).

BOSTON	AB	R	H	HR	RBI	BB	AVG
Moses rf	5	0	4	0	0	0	.500
Pesky ss	5	0	0	0	0	0	.111
DiMaggio cf	4	1	0	0	0	0	.235
Williams lf	3	1	1	0	0	1	.231
York 1b	3	0	1	0	1	1	.308
Doerr 2b	3	1	2	1	2	1	.400
Gutteridge 2b	0	0	0	0	0	0	.000
Higgins 3b	4	0	1	0	0	0	.231
Wagner c	4	0	0	0	0	0	.000
Hughson p	0	0	0	0	0	0	.000
Bagby p	1	0	0	0	0	0	.000
a-Metkovich ph	1	0	0	0	0	0	.000
Zuber p	0	0	0	0	0	0	.000
b-McBride ph	1	0	0	0	0	0	.200
Brown p	0	0	0	0	0	0	.000
Ryba p	0	0	0	0	0	0	.000
Dreisewerd p	0	0	0	0	0	0	.000
c-Culberson ph	1	0	0	0	0	0	.000
TOTALS	**35**	**3**	**9**	**1**	**3**	**3**	**.222**

a - Batted for Bagby in the 5th
b - Batted for Zuber in the 7th
c - Batted for Dreisewerd in the 9th

BATTING: 2B: York (1, Munger). **HR:** Doerr (1, 8th off Munger 1 on, 2 out). **RBI:** York 1 (5), Doerr 2 (2). **2-out RBI:** Doerr 2. **Runners left in scoring position, 2 out:** Wagner 1. **Team LOB:** 8 **FIELDING: E:** Pesky (2), Hughson (1), Higgins (2). **Outfield assists:** DiMaggio (3), Williams (1). **DP:** 2 (Doerr-Pesky-York, Pesky-Doerr).

ST.LOUIS	IP	H	R	ER	BB	SO	HR	ERA
Munger (W, 1-0)	9	9	3	1	3	2	1	1.00

BOSTON	IP	H	R	ER	BB	SO	HR	ERA
Hughson (L, 0-1)	2	5	6	3	0	1	1	4.50
Bagby	3	6	1	1	1	1	0	3.00
Zuber	2	3	1	1	1	1	0	4.50
Brown	1	4	3	3	1	0	0	27.00
Ryba	0.2	2	1	1	1	0	0	13.50
Dreisewerd	0.1	0	0	0	0	0	0	0.00

IBB: Walker 2 (by Bagby, by Zuber). **Ground balls-fly balls:** Munger 7-17, Hughson 2-2, Bagby 1-4, Zuber 2-2, Brown 1-1, Ryba 2-0, Dreisewerd 0-1. **Batters faced:** Munger 38, Hughson 12, Bagby 14, Zuber 9, Brown 7, Ryba 6, Dreisewerd 1. **UMPIRES:** hp—Berry, 1b—Ballanfant, 2b—Hubbard, 3b—Barlick **T:** 2:31 **A:** 35,645

GAME 5 Boston 6 St. Louis 3
Fenway Park 10/11/46

ST.LOUIS	AB	R	H	HR	RBI	BB	AVG
Schoendienst 2b	4	0	1	0	0	0	.182
Moore cf	4	0	0	0	0	0	.105
Musial 1b	3	1	1	0	0	1	.200
Slaughter rf	2	0	0	0	0	0	.300
Dusak lf	1	0	0	0	0	0	.250
Kurowski 3b	4	1	0	0	0	0	.316
Garagiola c	4	1	0	0	0	0	.375
Walker lf-rf	4	0	2	0	3	0	.455
Marion ss	4	0	0	0	0	0	.222
Pollet p	0	0	0	0	0	0	.000
Brazle p	2	0	0	0	0	0	.000
a-Jones ph	1	0	0	0	0	0	.000
Beazley p	0	0	0	0	0	0	.000
TOTALS	**33**	**3**	**4**	**0**	**3**	**1**	**.254**

a - Batted for Brazle in the 8th

BATTING: 2B: Walker (1, Dobson), Musial (3, Dobson). **RBI:** Walker 3 (4). **2-out RBI:** Walker 3. **Runners left in scoring position, 2 out:** Slaughter 1, Garagiola 1, Marion 1. **Team LOB:** 5 **BASERUNNING: SB:** Slaughter (1, 2nd base off Dobson/Partee). **CS:** Schoendienst (1, 2nd base off Dobson/Partee). **FIELDING: E:** Marion (2). **DP:** 1 (Marion-Schoendienst-Musial).

BOSTON	AB	R	H	HR	RBI	BB	AVG
Gutteridge 2b	5	0	2	0	1	0	.400
Pesky ss	5	1	3	0	0	0	.217
DiMaggio cf	3	1	1	0	0	1	.250
Williams lf	5	0	1	0	1	0	.222
York 1b	2	1	0	0	0	3	.267
Higgins 3b	4	1	1	0	1	0	.235
Culberson rf	3	1	2	1	1	1	.400
Partee c	3	1	1	0	1	1	.167
Dobson p	3	0	0	0	0	0	.000
TOTALS	**33**	**6**	**11**	**1**	**5**	**6**	**.244**

BATTING: 2B: DiMaggio (2, Brazle), Higgins (1, Brazle). **HR:** Culberson (1, 6th off Brazle 0 on, 0 out). **S:** Dobson, DiMaggio. **RBI:** Gutteridge 1 (1), Williams 1 (1), Higgins 1 (2), Culberson 1 (1), Partee 1 (1). **Runners left in scoring position, 2 out:**

Gutteridge 3, York 1, Higgins 1, Culberson 2. **GIDP:** DiMaggio. **Team LOB:** 11 **BASERUNNING: SB:** Culberson (1, 2nd base off Brazle/Garagiola), Pesky (1, 2nd base off Brazle/Garagiola). **CS:** Pesky (1, 3rd base off Brazle/Garagiola). **FIELDING: E:** Pesky 2 (4). **DP:** 1 (Partee-Pesky).

ST.LOUIS	IP	H	R	ER	BB	SO	HR	ERA
Pollet	0.1	3	1	1	0	0	0	3.48
Brazle (L, 0-1)	6.2	7	5	4	6	4	1	5.40
Beazley	1	1	0	0	0	1	0	0.00

BOSTON	IP	H	R	ER	BB	SO	HR	ERA
Dobson (W, 1-0)	9	4	3	0	1	8	0	0.00

WP: Beazley 1. **IBB:** York 3 ((by Brazle, by Brazle), Culberson (by Brazle). **HBP:** Slaughter (by Dobson). **Ground balls-fly balls:** Pollet 1-0, Brazle 10-5, Beazley 0-1, Dobson 10-11. **Batters faced:** Pollet 4, Brazle 33, Beazley 4, Dobson 35. **UMPIRES:** hp—Ballanfant, 1b—Hubbard, 2b—Barlick, 3b—Berry **T:** 2:23 **A:** 35,982

GAME 6 St. Louis 4 Boston 1
Sportsman's Park 10/13/46

BOSTON	AB	R	H	HR	RBI	BB	AVG
Culberson rf	4	0	0	0	0	0	.222
Pesky ss	3	0	1	0	0	1	.231
DiMaggio cf	4	0	1	0	0	0	.250
Williams lf	3	0	1	0	0	1	.238
York 1b	4	1	1	0	0	0	.263
Doerr 2b	3	0	1	0	1	0	.389
Higgins 3b	3	0	1	0	0	0	.250
Partee c	3	0	0	0	0	0	.111
Harris p	1	0	0	0	0	0	.333
Hughson p	1	0	1	0	0	0	.333
a-McBride ph	1	0	0	0	0	0	.182
Johnson p	0	0	0	0	0	0	.000
TOTALS	**30**	**1**	**7**	**0**	**1**	**2**	**.242**

a - Batted for Hughson in the 8th

BATTING: 3B: York (1, Brecheen). **RBI:** Doerr 1 (3). **GIDP:** York, DiMaggio, York. **Team LOB:** 4

ST.LOUIS	AB	R	H	HR	RBI	BB	AVG
Schoendienst 2b	4	1	1	0	0	0	.192
Moore cf	4	0	1	0	1	0	.130
Musial 1b	4	1	1	0	0	0	.208
Kurowski 3b	4	0	1	0	1	0	.304
Slaughter rf	2	0	1	0	1	2	.318
Dusak lf	0	0	0	0	0	1	.250
a-Walker ph-lf	3	1	0	0	0	0	.357
Marion ss	4	0	2	0	1	0	.273
Rice c	3	0	1	0	0	1	.600
Brecheen p	4	1	0	0	0	0	.143
TOTALS	**32**	**4**	**8**	**0**	**4**	**4**	**.254**

a - Batted for Dusak in the 3th

BATTING: 2B: Schoendienst (1, Harris), Marion (2, Johnson). **RBI:** Moore 1 (2), Kurowski 1 (2), Slaughter 1 (2), Marion 1 (4). **2-out RBI:** Kurowski 1, Slaughter 1, Marion 1. **Runners left in scoring position, 2 out:** Walker 1, Rice 1, Brecheen 1. **Team LOB:** 8 **FIELDING: Outfield assists:** Dusak (1). **DP:** 3 (Kurowski-Schoendienst-Musial 2, Brecheen-Schoendienst-Marion-Musial).

BOSTON	IP	H	R	ER	BB	SO	HR	ERA
Harris (L, 0-2)	2.2	5	3	3	1	2	0	3.72
Hughson	4.1	2	0	0	1	2	0	3.14
Johnson	1	1	1	1	2	0	0	3.00

ST.LOUIS	IP	H	R	ER	BB	SO	HR	ERA
Brecheen (W, 2-0)	9	7	1	1	2	6	0	0.50

IBB: Rice (by Johnson). **Ground balls-fly balls:** Harris 2-4, Hughson 2-9, Johnson 2-1, Brecheen 4-13. **Batters faced:** Harris 14, Hughson 16, Johnson 6, Brecheen 32. **UMPIRES:** hp—Hubbard, 1b—Barlick, 2b—Berry, 3b—Ballanfant **T:** 1:56 **A:** 35,768

GAME 7 St. Louis 4 Boston 3
Sportsman's Park 10/15/46

BOSTON	AB	R	H	HR	RBI	BB	AVG
Moses rf	4	1	1	0	0	0	.417
Pesky ss	4	0	1	0	0	0	.233
DiMaggio cf	3	0	1	0	3	1	.259
c-Culberson pr-cf	0	0	0	0	0	0	.222
Williams lf	4	0	0	0	0	0	.200
York 1b	4	0	1	0	0	0	.261
d-Campbell pr	0	0	0	0	0	0	.000
Doerr 2b	4	0	2	0	0	0	.409
Higgins 3b	4	0	0	0	0	0	.208
Wagner c	2	0	0	0	0	0	.000
a-Russell ph	1	1	1	0	0	0	1.000
Partee c	1	0	0	0	0	0	.100
Ferriss p	2	0	0	0	0	0	.000
Dobson p	0	0	0	0	0	0	.000
b-Metkovich ph	1	1	1	0	0	0	.500
Klinger p	0	0	0	0	0	0	.000
Johnson p	0	0	0	0	0	0	.000
e-McBride ph	1	0	0	0	0	0	.167
TOTALS	**35**	**3**	**8**	**0**	**3**	**1**	**.240**

a - Batted for Wagner in the 8th
b - Batted for Dobson in the 8th
c - Ran for DiMaggio in the 8th
d - Ran for York in the 9th e - Batted for Johnson in the 9th

BATTING: 2B: Metkovich (1, Dickson), DiMaggio (3, Brecheen). **RBI:** DiMaggio 3 (3). **2-out RBI:** DiMaggio 2. **Runners left in scoring position, 2 out:** Williams 1, Ferriss 1, McBride 1. **Team LOB:** 6 **Outfield assists:** Williams (2).

ST.LOUIS	AB	R	H	HR	RBI	BB	AVG
Schoendienst 2b	4	0	2	0	1	0	.233
Moore cf	4	0	1	0	0	0	.148
Musial 1b	3	0	1	0	0	1	.222
Slaughter rf	3	1	1	0	0	1	.320
Kurowski 3b	4	1	1	0	0	0	.296
Garagiola c	3	0	0	0	0	0	.316
Rice c	1	0	0	0	0	0	.500
Walker lf	3	1	2	0	2	1	.412
Marion ss	2	0	0	0	0	1	.250
Dickson p	3	1	1	0	1	0	.400
Brecheen p	1	0	0	0	0	0	.125
TOTALS	**31**	**4**	**9**	**0**	**4**	**4**	**.259**

BATTING: 2B: Musial (4, Ferriss), Kurowski (3, Ferriss), Dickson (2, Ferriss), Walker (2, Klinger). **S:** Marion. **RBI:** Schoendienst 1 (1), Walker 2 (6), Dickson 1 (1). **2-out RBI:** Walker 1. **Runners left in scoring position, 2 out:** Slaughter 1, Kurowski 2, Dickson 1, Brecheen 1. **Team LOB:** 8 **FIELDING: E:** Kurowski (1).

BOSTON	IP	H	R	ER	BB	SO	HR	ERA
Ferriss	4.1	7	3	3	1	2	0	2.03
Dobson	2.2	0	0	0	2	2	0	0.00
Klinger (L, 0-1)	0.2	2	1	1	1	0	0	13.50
Johnson	0.1	0	0	0	0	0	0	2.70

ST.LOUIS	IP	H	R	ER	BB	SO	HR	ERA
Dickson	7	5	3	3	1	3	0	3.86
Brecheen (W, 3-0)	2	3	0	0	0	1	0	0.45

IBB: Slaughter (by Dobson), Marion (by Klinger). **Ground balls-fly balls:** Ferriss 4-5, Dobson 5-1, Klinger 0-2, Johnson 1-0, Dickson 5-13, Brecheen 2-3. **Batters faced:** Ferriss 20, Dobson 10, Klinger 5, Johnson 1, Dickson 27, Brecheen 9. **UMPIRES:** hp—Barlick, 1b—Berry, 2b—Ballanfant, 3b—Hubbard **T:** 2:17 **A:** 36,143

1947 NY YANKEES DEF. BROOKLYN, 4-3

GAME 1 New York 5 Brooklyn 3
Yankee Stadium 09/30/47

BROOKLYN	AB	R	H	HR	RBI	BB	AVG
Stanky 2b	4	0	1	0	0	0	.250
J.Robinson 1b	2	1	0	0	0	2	.000
Reiser cf-lf	4	1	1	0	0	0	.250
Walker rf	4	0	2	0	1	0	.500
Hermanski lf	2	0	0	0	0	0	.000
a-Furillo ph-cf	1	0	1	0	1	1	1.000
Edwards c	4	0	0	0	0	0	.000
Jorgensen 3b	2	0	0	0	0	0	.000
b-Lavagetto ph-3b	2	0	0	0	0	0	.000
Reese ss	4	1	1	0	0	0	.250
Branca p	2	0	0	0	0	0	.000
Behrman p	0	0	0	0	0	0	.000
c-Miksis ph	1	0	0	0	0	0	.000
Casey p	0	0	0	0	0	0	.000
TOTALS	**32**	**3**	**6**	**0**	**2**	**3**	**.188**

a - Batted for Hermanski in the 6th
b - Batted for Jorgensen in the 7th
c - Batted for Behrman in the 7th

BATTING: RBI: Walker 1 (1), Furillo 1 (1). **2-out RBI:** Walker 1, Furillo 1. **Runners left in scoring position, 2 out:** Reiser 1, Edwards 1. **Team LOB:** 5 **BASERUNNING: SB:** J.Robinson (1, 2nd base off Shea/Berra), Reese (1, 2nd base off Page/Berra).

NY YANKEES	AB	R	H	HR	RBI	BB	AVG
Stirnweiss 2b	4	0	0	0	0	0	.000
Henrich rf	4	0	1	0	2	0	.250
Berra c	4	0	0	0	0	0	.000
DiMaggio cf	4	1	1	0	0	0	.250
McQuinn 1b	3	1	0	0	0	1	.000
Johnson 3b	2	1	0	0	0	0	.000
Lindell lf	3	0	1	0	2	0	.333
Rizzuto ss	2	1	1	0	0	1	.500
Shea p	1	0	0	0	0	0	.000
a-Brown ph	0	1	0	0	1	1	.000
Page p	1	0	0	0	0	0	.000
TOTALS	**28**	**5**	**4**	**0**	**5**	**3**	**.143**

a - Batted for Shea in the 5th

BATTING: 2B: Lindell (1, Branca). **RBI:** Henrich 2 (2), Lindell 2 (2), Brown 1 (1). **Runners left in scoring position, 2 out:** Henrich 1, DiMaggio 1. **Team LOB:** 3 **FIELDING: DP:** 1 (Johnson-McQuinn).

BROOKLYN	IP	H	R	ER	BB	SO	HR	ERA
Branca (L, 0-1)	4	2	5	5	3	5	0	11.25
Behrman	2	1	0	0	0	0	0	0.00
Casey	2	1	0	0	0	1	0	0.00

NY YANKEES	IP	H	R	ER	BB	SO	HR	ERA
Shea (W, 1-0)	5	2	1	1	2	3	0	1.80
Page (S, 1)	4	4	2	2	1	2	0	4.50

WP: Page 1. **BK:** Shea 1. **HBP:** Johnson (by Branca). **Ground balls-fly balls:** Branca 4-3, Behrman 2-4, Casey 3-2, Shea 5-6, Page 6-4. **Batters faced:** Branca 18, Behrman 7, Casey 7, Shea 18, Page 17. **UMPIRES:** hp—McGowan, 1b—Pinelli, 2b—Rommel, 3b—Goetz, lf—Magerkurth, rf—Boyer **T:** 2:20 **A:** 73,365

GAME 2 New York 10 Brooklyn 3
Yankee Stadium 10/01/47

BROOKLYN	AB	R	H	HR	RBI	BB	AVG
Stanky 2b	4	0	1	0	0	0	.250
J.Robinson 1b	4	0	2	0	1	0	.333
Reiser cf	4	0	1	0	0	0	.250
Walker rf	4	1	1	1	1	0	.375
Hermanski lf	3	1	0	0	0	1	.000
Edwards c	4	0	1	0	0	0	.125
Reese ss	3	1	2	0	0	1	.429
Jorgensen 3b	4	0	1	0	1	0	.167
Lombardi p	2	0	0	0	0	0	.000
Gregg p	0	0	0	0	0	0	.000
a-Vaughan ph	1	0	0	0	0	0	.000
Behrman p	0	0	0	0	0	0	.000
Barney p	0	0	0	0	0	0	.000
b-Gionfriddo ph	1	0	0	0	0	0	.000
TOTALS	**34**	**3**	**9**	**1**	**3**	**2**	**.227**

a - Batted for Gregg in the 7th
b - Batted for Barney in the 9th

BATTING: 2B: J.Robinson (1, Reynolds). **HR:** Walker (1, 4th off Reynolds 0 on, 0 out). **RBI:** J.Robinson 1 (1), Walker 1 (2), Jorgensen 1 (1). **2-out RBI:** J.Robinson 1. **Runners left in scoring position, 2 out:** Reiser 1, Walker 1, Vaughan 1. **GIDP:** Walker. **Team LOB:** 6 **BASERUNNING: SB:** Reese (2, 2nd base off Reynolds/Berra). **CS:** Reese (1, 2nd base off Reynolds/Berra). **FIELDING: E:** Reiser (1). **DP:** 1 (Jorgensen-Stanky-J.Robinson).

NY YANKEES	AB	R	H	HR	RBI	BB	AVG
Stirnweiss 2b	4	2	3	0	1	1	.375
Henrich rf	4	1	2	1	1	0	.375
Lindell lf	4	1	2	0	3	1	.429
DiMaggio cf	4	0	1	0	0	1	.250
McQuinn 1b	5	1	2	0	1	0	.250
Johnson 3b	5	2	2	0	1	0	.286
Rizzuto ss	5	0	1	0	1	0	.286
Berra c	3	1	0	0	0	1	.000
Reynolds p	4	2	2	0	1	0	.500
TOTALS	**38**	**10**	**15**	**1**	**9**	**4**	**.288**

BATTING: 2B: Rizzuto (1, Lombardi), Lindell (2, Lombardi). **3B:** Stirnweiss (1, Lombardi), Lindell (1, Lombardi), Johnson (1, Lombardi). **HR:** Henrich (1, 5th off Lombardi 0 on, 0 out). **S:** Henrich. **RBI:** Stirnweiss 1 (1), Henrich 1 (3), Lindell 3 (5), McQuinn 1 (1), Johnson 1 (1), Rizzuto 1 (1), Reynolds 1 (1). **2-out RBI:** Lindell 1. **Runners left in scoring position, 2 out:** Stirnweiss 1, DiMaggio 2, McQuinn 1, Berra 1. **GIDP:** Lindell. **Team LOB:** 9 **FIELDING: E:** Berra (1). **DP:** 1 (Stirnweiss-Rizzuto-McQuinn).

BROOKLYN	IP	H	R	ER	BB	SO	HR	ERA
Lombardi (L, 0-1)	4	9	5	5	1	3	1	11.25
Gregg	2	2	1	1	1	2	0	4.50
Behrman	0.1	3	4	4	1	0	0	15.43
Barney	1.2	1	0	0	1	0	0	0.00

NY YANKEES	IP	H	R	ER	BB	SO	HR	ERA
Reynolds (W, 1-0)	9	9	3	3	2	6	1	3.00

WP: Behrman 1, Barney 1. **IBB:** DiMaggio (by Lombardi), Berra (by Behrman). **Ground balls-fly balls:** Lombardi 5-3, Gregg 2-2, Behrman 0-1, Barney 1-4, Reynolds 8-11. **Batters faced:** Lombardi 21, Gregg 10, Behrman 5, Barney 7, Reynolds 36. **UMPIRES:** hp—Pinelli, 1b—Rommel, 2b—Goetz, 3b—McGowan, lf—Boyer, rf—Magerkurth **T:** 2:36 **A:** 69,865

GAME 3 Brooklyn 9 New York 8
Ebbets Field 10/02/47

NY YANKEES	AB	R	H	HR	RBI	BB	AVG
Stirnweiss 2b	5	0	2	0	1	0	.385
Henrich rf	4	0	1	0	1	1	.333
Lindell lf	4	1	2	0	1	1	.455
DiMaggio cf	4	1	2	1	3	1	.333
McQuinn 1b	4	0	0	0	0	1	.167
Johnson 3b	4	1	1	0	0	1	.273
Rizzuto ss	5	0	1	0	0	0	.250
Lollar c	3	2	2	0	1	0	.667
d-Berra ph-c	2	1	1	1	1	0	.111
Newsom p	0	0	0	0	0	0	.000
Raschi p	0	0	0	0	0	0	.000
a-Clark ph	0	1	0	0	0	1	.000
Drews p	0	0	0	0	0	0	.000
b-Phillips ph	1	0	0	0	0	0	.000
Chandler p	0	0	0	0	0	0	.000
c-Brown ph	1	1	1	0	0	0	1.000
Page p	1	0	0	0	0	0	.000
TOTALS	**38**	**8**	**13**	**2**	**8**	**6**	**.308**

a - Batted for Raschi in the 3th
b - Batted for Drews in the 4th
c - Batted for Chandler in the 6th
d - Batted for Lollar in the 7th

BATTING: 2B: Lollar (1, Hatten), Brown (1, Branca), Henrich (1, Branca). **HR:** DiMaggio (1, 5th off Hatten 1 on, 0 out), Berra (1, 7th off Branca 0 on, 1 out). **RBI:** Stirnweiss 1 (2), Henrich 1 (4), Lindell 1 (6), DiMaggio 3 (3), Lollar 1 (1), Berra 1 (1). **2-out RBI:** Stirnweiss 1, Lindell 1, DiMaggio 1. **Runners left in scoring position, 2 out:** Henrich 1, McQuinn 2, Johnson 2. **GIDP:** Henrich, DiMaggio. **Team LOB:** 9 **FIELDING: PB:** Lollar.

BROOKLYN	AB	R	H	HR	RBI	BB	AVG
Stanky 2b	4	2	1	0	2	1	.250
J.Robinson 1b	4	1	2	0	0	0	.400
Reiser cf	0	0	0	0	0	1	.250
a-Furillo ph-cf	3	1	2	0	2	1	.750
Walker rf	5	0	2	0	1	0	.385
Hermanski lf	3	2	1	0	1	1	.125
Edwards c	4	1	1	0	1	1	.167
Reese ss	3	1	1	0	1	1	.400
Jorgensen 3b	4	0	2	0	1	0	.300
Hatten p	2	1	1	0	0	0	.500
Branca p	1	0	0	0	0	0	.000
Casey p	1	0	0	0	0	0	.000
TOTALS	**34**	**9**	**13**	**0**	**9**	**6**	**.280**

a - Batted for Reiser in the 2nd

BATTING: 2B: Edwards (1, Newsom), Stanky (1, Newsom), Furillo (1, Raschi), Jorgensen (1, Page). **S:** J.Robinson. **RBI:** Stanky 2 (2), Furillo 2 (3), Walker 1 (3), Hermanski 1 (1), Edwards 1 (1), Reese 1 (1), Jorgensen 1 (2). **2-out RBI:** Stanky 2, Furillo 2, Jorgensen 1. **Runners left in scoring position, 2 out:** J.Robinson 1, Walker 1, Edwards 1, Reese 1, Jorgensen 2. **Team LOB:** 9 **BASERUNNING: SB:** J.Robinson (2, 2nd base off Newsom/Lollar), Walker (1, 2nd base off Page/Lollar). **CS:** Reiser (1, 2nd base off Newsom/Lollar). **FIELDING: E:** Furillo (1). **DP:** 2 (Reese-Stanky-J.Robinson, Stanky-J.Robinson).

NY YANKEES	IP	H	R	ER	BB	SO	HR	ERA
Newsom (L, 0-1)	1.2	5	5	5	2	0	0	27.00
Raschi	0.1	2	1	1	0	0	0	27.00
Drews	1	1	1	1	0	0	0	9.00
Chandler	2	2	2	2	3	1	0	9.00
Page	3	3	0	0	1	3	0	2.57

BROOKLYN	IP	H	R	ER	BB	SO	HR	ERA
Hatten	4.1	8	6	6	3	3	1	12.46
Branca	2	4	2	2	2	1	1	10.50
Casey (W, 1-0)	2.2	1	0	0	1	1	0	0.00

WP: Drews 1, Page 1. **HBP:** Hermanski (by Drews). **Ground balls-fly balls:** Newsom 2-1, Raschi 1-0, Drews 3-0, Chandler 1-3, Page 2-4, Hatten 5-4, Branca 2-3, Casey 5-1. **Batters faced:** Newsom 10, Raschi 3, Drews 5, Chandler 11, Page 13, Hatten 23, Branca 12, Casey 9. **UMPIRES:** hp—Rommel, 1b—Goetz, 2b—McGowan, 3b—Pinelli, lf—Magerkurth, rf—Boyer **T:** 3:05 **A:** 33,098

GAME 4 Brooklyn 3 New York 2
Ebbets Field 10/03/47

NY YANKEES	AB	R	H	HR	RBI	BB	AVG
Stirnweiss 2b	4	1	2	0	0	1	.412
Henrich rf	5	0	1	0	0	0	.294
Berra c	4	0	0	0	0	0	.077
DiMaggio cf	2	0	0	0	1	2	.286
McQuinn 1b	4	0	1	0	0	0	.188
Johnson 3b	4	1	1	0	0	0	.267
Lindell lf	3	0	2	0	1	1	.500
Rizzuto ss	4	0	1	0	0	0	.250
Bevens p	3	0	0	0	0	0	.000
TOTALS	**33**	**2**	**8**	**0**	**2**	**4**	**.292**

BATTING: 2B: Lindell (3, Gregg). **3B:** Johnson (2, Gregg). **S:** Bevens. **RBI:** DiMaggio 1 (4), Lindell 1 (7). **Runners left in scoring position, 2 out:** Stirnweiss 2. **GIDP:** Johnson, Henrich, Henrich. **Team LOB:** 9 **BASERUNNING: SB:** Rizzuto (1, 2nd base off Gregg/Edwards). **FIELDING: E:** Berra (2).

BROOKLYN	AB	R	H	HR	RBI	BB	AVG
Stanky 2b	1	0	0	0	0	2	.231
e-Lavagetto ph	1	0	1	0	2	0	.333
Reese ss	4	0	0	0	1	0	.286
J.Robinson 1b	4	0	0	0	0	0	.286
Walker rf	2	0	0	0	0	2	.333
Hermanski lf	4	0	0	0	0	0	.083
Edwards c	4	0	0	0	0	0	.125
Furillo cf	3	0	0	0	0	1	.429
b-Gionfriddo pr	0	1	0	0	0	0	.000
Jorgensen 3b	2	1	0	0	0	2	.250
Taylor p	0	0	0	0	0	0	.000
Gregg p	1	0	0	0	0	1	.000
a-Vaughan ph	0	0	0	0	0	1	.000
Behrman p	0	0	0	0	0	0	.000
Casey p	0	0	0	0	0	0	.000
c-Reiser ph	0	0	0	0	0	1	.250
d-Miksis pr	0	1	0	0	0	0	.000
TOTALS	**26**	**3**	**1**	**0**	**3**	**10**	**.230**

a - Batted for Gregg in the 7th
b - Ran for Furillo in the 9th
c - Batted for Casey in the 9th
d - Ran for Reiser in the 9th e - Batted for Stanky in the 9th

BATTING: 2B: Lavagetto (1, Bevens). **S:** Stanky. **RBI:** Lavagetto 2 (2), Reese 1 (2). **2-out RBI:** Lavagetto 2. **Runners left in scoring position, 2 out:** J.Robinson 1, Walker 1, Hermanski 1. **Team LOB:** 8 **BASERUNNING: SB:** Reese (3, 2nd base off Bevens/Berra), Gionfriddo (1, 2nd base off Bevens/Berra). **FIELDING: E:** Edwards (1), Jorgensen (1). **DP:** 3 (Reese-Stanky-J.Robinson, Gregg-Reese-J.Robinson, Casey-Edwards-J.Robinson).

NY YANKEES	IP	H	R	ER	BB	SO	HR	ERA
Bevens (L, 0-1)	8.2	1	3	3	10	5	0	3.12

BROOKLYN	IP	H	R	ER	BB	SO	HR	ERA
Taylor	0	2	1	0	1	0	0	0.00
Gregg	7	4	1	1	3	5	0	2.00
Behrman	1.1	2	0	0	0	0	0	9.82
Casey (W, 2-0)	0.2	0	0	0	0	0	0	0.00

WP: Bevens 1. **IBB:** Reiser (by Bevens). **Ground balls-fly balls:** Bevens 7-13, Taylor 1-0, Gregg 8-5, Behrman 4-1, Casey 1-0. **Batters faced:** Bevens 37, Taylor 4, Gregg 25, Behrman 8, Casey 1. **UMPIRES:** hp—Goetz, 1b—McGowan, 2b—Pinelli, 3b—Rommel, lf—Boyer, rf—Magerkurth **T:** 2:20 **A:** 33,443

GAME 5 New York 2 Brooklyn 1
Ebbets Field 10/04/47

NY YANKEES	AB	R	H	HR	RBI	BB	AVG
Stirnweiss 2b	3	0	0	0	0	2	.350
Henrich rf	4	0	2	0	0	1	.333
Lindell lf	2	0	0	0	0	2	.438
DiMaggio cf	4	1	1	1	1	1	.278
McQuinn 1b	4	0	0	0	0	0	.150
Johnson 3b	3	0	0	0	0	1	.222
A.Robinson c	3	1	0	0	0	1	.000
Rizzuto ss	2	0	0	0	0	2	.222
Shea p	4	0	2	0	1	0	.400
TOTALS	**29**	**2**	**5**	**1**	**2**	**10**	**.271**

BATTING: 2B: Henrich (2, Barney), Shea (1, Casey). **HR:** DiMaggio (2, 5th off Barney 0 on, 1 out). **RBI:** DiMaggio 1 (5), Shea 1 (1). **2-out RBI:** Shea 1. **Runners left in scoring position, 2 out:** Stirnweiss 1, Henrich 2, Johnson 4. **GIDP:** DiMaggio, DiMaggio. **Team LOB:** 11 **BASERUNNING: CS:** Rizzuto (1, 3rd base off Barney/Edwards).

BROOKLYN	AB	R	H	HR	RBI	BB	AVG
Stanky 2b	3	0	0	0	0	0	.188
c-Reiser ph	0	0	0	0	0	1	.250
d-Miksis pr-2b	0	0	0	0	0	0	.000
Reese ss	2	0	0	0	0	2	.250
J.Robinson 1b	4	0	1	0	1	0	.278
Walker rf	4	0	0	0	0	0	.263
Hermanski lf	4	0	1	0	0	0	.125
Edwards c	3	0	1	0	0	1	.158
e-Lombardi pr	0	0	0	0	0	0	.000
Furillo cf	3	0	0	0	0	0	.300
Jorgensen 3b	4	0	0	0	0	0	.188
Barney p	1	0	0	0	0	0	.000
Hatten p	0	0	0	0	0	0	.500
a-Gionfriddo ph	0	1	0	0	0	1	.000
Behrman p	0	0	0	0	0	0	.000
b-Vaughan ph	1	0	1	0	0	0	.500
Casey p	0	0	0	0	0	0	.000
f-Lavagetto ph	1	0	0	0	0	0	.250
TOTALS	**30**	**1**	**4**	**0**	**1**	**5**	**.212**

a - Batted for Hatten in the 6th
b - Batted for Behrman in the 7th
c - Batted for Stanky in the 7th
d - Ran for Reiser in the 7th e - Ran for Edwards in the 9th f - Batted for Casey in the 9th

BATTING: 2B: Vaughan (1, Shea). **S:** Furillo. **RBI:** J.Robinson 1 (2). **Runners left in scoring position, 2 out:** Reese 2, Hermanski 2, Lavagetto 1. **Team LOB:** 8 **FIELDING: E:** Miksis (1). **PB:** Edwards, Edwards. **DP:** 2 (Reese-Stanky-J.Robinson, Reese-Miksis-J.Robinson).

NY YANKEES	IP	H	R	ER	BB	SO	HR	ERA
Shea (W, 2-0)	9	4	1	1	5	7	0	1.29

BROOKLYN	IP	H	R	ER	BB	SO	HR	ERA
Barney (L, 0-1)	4.2	3	2	2	9	3	1	2.84
Hatten	1.1	0	0	0	0	1	0	9.53
Behrman	1	1	0	0	1	2	0	7.71
Casey	2	1	0	0	0	1	0	0.00

WP: Barney 1. **IBB:** Reiser (by Shea). **HBP:** Lindell (by Casey). **Ground balls-fly balls:** Shea 6-13, Barney 4-5, Hatten 0-3, Behrman 1-0, Casey 2-2. **Batters faced:** Shea 36, Barney 24, Hatten 4, Behrman 5, Casey 7. **UMPIRES:** hp—McGowan, 1b—Pinelli, 2b—Rommel, 3b—Goetz, lf—Magerkurth, rf—Boyer **T:** 2:46 **A:** 34,379

GAME 6 Brooklyn 8 New York 6
Yankee Stadium 10/05/47

BROOKLYN	AB	R	H	HR	RBI	BB	AVG
Stanky 2b	5	2	2	0	0	0	.238
Reese ss	4	2	3	0	2	1	.350
J.Robinson 1b	5	1	2	0	1	0	.304
Walker rf	5	0	1	0	2	0	.250
Hermanski lf	1	0	0	0	0	1	.118
a-Miksis ph-lf	1	0	0	0	0	0	.000
Gionfriddo lf	2	0	0	0	0	0	.000
Edwards c	4	1	1	0	0	0	.174
Furillo cf	4	1	2	0	0	0	.357
Jorgensen 3b	2	0	0	0	0	0	.167
b-Lavagetto ph-3b	2	0	0	0	1	0	.167
Lombardi p	1	0	0	0	0	0	.000
Branca p	1	0	0	0	0	0	.000
c-Bragan ph	1	0	1	0	1	0	1.000
d-Bankhead pr	0	1	0	0	0	0	.000
Hatten p	1	0	0	0	0	0	.333
Casey p	0	0	0	0	0	0	.000
TOTALS	**39**	**8**	**12**	**0**	**7**	**2**	**.231**

a - Batted for Hermanski in the 5th
b - Batted for Jorgensen in the 6th
c - Batted for Branca in the 6th
d - Ran for Bragan in the 6th

BATTING: 2B: Reese (1, Reynolds), J.Robinson (2, Reynolds), Walker (1, Reynolds), Furillo (2, Page), Bragan (1, Page). **RBI:** Reese 2 (4), J.Robinson 1 (3), Walker 2 (5), Lavagetto 1 (3), Bragan 1 (1). **Runners left in scoring position, 2 out:** Edwards 1. **GIDP:** Walker. **Team LOB:** 6 **FIELDING: E:** Jorgensen (2). **Outfield assists:** Furillo (1).

NY YANKEES	AB	R	H	HR	RBI	BB	AVG
Stirnweiss 2b	5	0	0	0	1	1	.280
Henrich rf-lf	5	1	2	0	0	0	.346
Lindell lf	2	1	2	0	1	0	.500
Berra rf	3	0	2	0	1	0	.188
DiMaggio cf	5	1	1	0	0	0	.261
Johnson 3b	5	1	2	0	1	0	.261
Phillips 1b	1	0	0	0	0	0	.000
a-Brown ph	1	0	1	0	1	0	1.000
McQuinn 1b	1	0	0	0	0	2	.143
Rizzuto ss	4	0	1	0	0	1	.227
Lollar c	1	1	1	0	0	0	.750
A.Robinson c	4	1	2	0	0	0	.286
Reynolds p	0	0	0	0	0	0	.500
Drews p	2	0	0	0	0	0	.000
Page p	0	0	0	0	0	0	.000
Newsom p	0	0	0	0	0	0	.000
b-Clark ph	1	0	0	0	0	0	.000
Raschi p	0	0	0	0	0	0	.000
c-Houk ph	1	0	1	0	0	0	1.000
Wensloff p	0	0	0	0	0	0	.000
d-Frey ph	1	0	0	0	1	0	.000
TOTALS	**42**	**6**	**15**	**0**	**6**	**4**	**.288**

a - Batted for Phillips in the 3th
b - Batted for Newsom in the 6th
c - Batted for Raschi in the 7th
d - Batted for Wensloff in the 9th

BATTING: 2B: Lollar (2, Lombardi). **RBI:** Stirnweiss 1 (3), Lindell 1 (8), Berra 1 (2), Johnson 1 (2), Brown 1 (2), Frey 1 (1). **2-out RBI:** Lindell 1, Berra 1, Johnson 1, Brown 1. **Runners left in scoring position, 2 out:** Stirnweiss 3, DiMaggio 2, Rizzuto 1. **Team LOB:** 13 **FIELDING: E:** A.Robinson (1), McQuinn (1). **PB:** Lollar. **DP:** 1 (Rizzuto-Phillips).

BROOKLYN	IP	H	R	ER	BB	SO	HR	ERA
Lombardi	2.2	5	4	4	0	2	0	12.15
Branca (W, 1-1)	2.1	6	1	1	0	2	0	8.64
Hatten	3	3	1	1	4	0	0	7.27
Casey (S, 1)	1	1	0	0	0	0	0	0.00

NY YANKEES	IP	H	R	ER	BB	SO	HR	ERA
Reynolds	2.1	6	4	3	1	0	0	4.76
Drews	2	1	0	0	1	0	0	3.00
Page (L, 0-1)	1	4	4	4	0	1	0	6.75
Newsom	0.2	1	0	0	0	0	0	19.29
Raschi	1	0	0	0	0	1	0	6.75
Wensloff	2	0	0	0	0	0	0	0.00

WP: Lombardi 1. **Ground balls-fly balls:** Lombardi 4-2, Branca 3-2, Hatten 1-8, Casey 2-1, Reynolds 3-3, Drews 5-1, Page 0-2, Newsom 0-2, Raschi 2-0, Wensloff 5-2. **Batters faced:** Lombardi 13, Branca 13, Hatten 16, Casey 4, Reynolds 13, Drews 8, Page 7, Newsom 3, Raschi 3, Wensloff 7. **UMPIRES:** hp—Pinelli, 1b—Rommel, 2b—Goetz, 3b—McGowan, lf—Boyer, rf—Magerkurth **T:** 3:19 **A:** 74,065

GAME 7 New York 5 Brooklyn 2
Yankee Stadium 10/06/47

BROOKLYN	AB	R	H	HR	RBI	BB	AVG
Stanky 2b	4	0	1	0	0	0	.240
Reese ss	3	0	0	0	0	1	.304
J.Robinson 1b	4	0	0	0	0	0	.259
Walker rf	3	0	0	0	0	1	.222
Hermanski lf	2	1	1	0	0	0	.158
a-Miksis ph-lf	2	0	1	0	0	0	.250
Edwards c	4	1	2	0	1	0	.222
Furillo cf	3	0	1	0	0	0	.353
Jorgensen 3b	2	0	1	0	1	0	.200
b-Lavagetto ph-3b	1	0	0	0	0	0	.143
Gregg p	2	0	0	0	0	0	.000
Behrman p	0	0	0	0	0	0	.000
Hatten p	0	0	0	0	0	0	.333
Barney p	0	0	0	0	0	0	.000
c-Hodges ph	1	0	0	0	0	0	.000
Casey p	0	0	0	0	0	0	.000
TOTALS	**31**	**2**	**7**	**0**	**2**	**2**	**.230**

a - Batted for Hermanski in the 6th
b - Batted for Jorgensen in the 7th
c - Batted for Barney in the 7th

BATTING: 2B: Jorgensen (2, Bevens). **3B:** Hermanski (1, Shea). **RBI:** Edwards 1 (2), Jorgensen 1 (3). **Runners left in scoring position, 2 out:** Stanky 1. **GIDP:** Edwards. **Team LOB:** 4 **BASERUNNING: CS:** Stanky (1, 2nd base off Shea/A.Robinson), Reese (2, 2nd base off Shea/A.Robinson).

NY YANKEES	AB	R	H	HR	RBI	BB	AVG
Stirnweiss 2b	2	0	0	0	0	3	.259
Henrich lf	5	0	1	0	1	0	.323
Berra rf	3	0	0	0	0	0	.158
b-Clark ph-rf	1	0	1	0	1	0	.500
DiMaggio cf	3	0	0	0	0	1	.231
McQuinn 1b	2	1	0	0	0	1	.130
Johnson 3b	3	2	1	0	0	1	.269
A.Robinson c	3	0	0	0	1	1	.200
Rizzuto ss	4	2	3	0	1	0	.308
Shea p	0	0	0	0	0	0	.400
Bevens p	1	0	0	0	0	0	.000
a-Brown ph	1	0	1	0	1	0	1.000
Page p	2	0	0	0	0	0	.000
TOTALS	**30**	**5**	**7**	**0**	**5**	**7**	**.282**

a - Batted for Bevens in the 4th
b - Batted for Berra in the 6th

BATTING: 2B: Brown (2, Gregg). **3B:** Johnson (3, Casey). **S:** McQuinn. **RBI:** Henrich 1 (5), Clark 1 (1), A.Robinson 1 (1), Rizzuto 1 (2), Brown 1 (3). **2-out RBI:** Henrich 1, Clark 1, Rizzuto 1, Brown 1. **Runners left in scoring position, 2 out:** Berra 2, DiMaggio 1, A.Robinson 1, Bevens 1. **Team LOB:** 9 **BASERUNNING: SB:** Rizzuto (2, 2nd base off Behrman/Edwards). **FIELDING: DP:** 1 (Rizzuto-Stirnweiss-McQuinn).

BROOKLYN	IP	H	R	ER	BB	SO	HR	ERA
Gregg (L, 0-1)	3.2	3	3	3	4	3	0	3.55
Behrman	1.2	2	1	1	3	1	0	7.11
Hatten	0.1	1	0	0	0	1	0	7.00
Barney	0.1	0	0	0	0	0	0	2.70
Casey	2	1	1	1	0	0	0	0.87

NY YANKEES	IP	H	R	ER	BB	SO	HR	ERA
Shea	1.1	4	2	2	1	0	0	2.35
Bevens	2.2	2	0	0	1	2	0	2.38
Page (W, 1-1)	5	1	0	0	0	1	0	4.15

Ground balls-fly balls: Gregg 1-7, Behrman 2-1, Hatten 0-0, Barney 0-1, Casey 2-4, Shea 0-2, Bevens 2-4, Page 4-9. **Batters faced:** Gregg 18, Behrman 10, Hatten 2, Barney 1, Casey 7, Shea 7, Bevens 11, Page 15. **UMPIRES:** hp—Rommel, 1b—Goetz, 2b—McGowan, 3b—Pinelli, lf—Magerkurth, rf—Boyer **T:** 2:19 **A:** 71,548

1948 CLEVELAND DEF. BOSTON BRAVES, 4-2

GAME 1 Boston 1 Cleveland 0
Braves Field 10/06/48

CLEVELAND	AB	R	H	HR	RBI	BB	AVG
Mitchell lf	4	0	0	0	0	0	.000
Doby cf	4	0	1	0	0	0	.250
Boudreau ss	4	0	0	0	0	0	.000
Gordon 2b	4	0	1	0	0	0	.250
Keltner 3b	4	0	1	0	0	0	.250
Judnich rf	4	0	0	0	0	0	.000
Robinson 1b	3	0	0	0	0	0	.000
Hegan c	3	0	1	0	0	0	.333
Feller p	2	0	0	0	0	0	.000
TOTALS	**32**	**0**	**4**	**0**	**0**	**0**	**.125**

BATTING: S: Feller. **Runners left in scoring position, 2 out:** Mitchell 1, Doby 1, Keltner 1, Judnich 2. **Team LOB:** 6 **BASERUNNING: SB:** Hegan (1, 2nd base off Sain/Salkeld), Gordon (1, 2nd base off Sain/Salkeld).

BOSTON	AB	R	H	HR	RBI	BB	AVG
Holmes rf	4	0	1	0	1	0	.250
Dark ss	4	0	0	0	0	0	.000
Torgeson 1b	2	0	0	0	0	1	.000
Elliott 3b	3	0	0	0	0	0	.000
Rickert lf	3	0	1	0	0	0	.333
Salkeld c	1	0	0	0	0	1	.000
a-Masi pr-c	0	1	0	0	0	0	.000
M.McCormick cf	2	0	0	0	0	0	.000
Stanky 2b	2	0	0	0	0	1	.000
b-Sisti pr-2b	0	0	0	0	0	0	.000
Sain p	3	0	0	0	0	0	.000
TOTALS	**24**	**1**	**2**	**0**	**1**	**3**	**.083**

a - Ran for Salkeld in the 8th
b - Ran for Stanky in the 8th

BATTING: S: Salkeld, M.McCormick. **RBI:** Holmes 1 (1). **2-out RBI:** Holmes 1. **Runners left in scoring position, 2 out:** Dark 2, Elliott 1, Stanky 1. **Team LOB:** 4 **BASERUNNING: SB:** Torgeson (1, 2nd base off Feller/Hegan). **FIELDING: E:** Elliott 2 (2).

CLEVELAND	IP	H	R	ER	BB	SO	HR	ERA
Feller (L, 0-1)	8	2	1	1	3	2	0	1.13

BOSTON	IP	H	R	ER	BB	SO	HR	ERA
Sain (W, 1-0)	9	4	0	0	0	6	0	0.00

IBB: Stanky (by Feller). **Ground balls-fly balls:** Feller 8-12, Sain 5-17. **Batters faced:** Feller 29, Sain 33. **UMPIRES:** hp—Barr, 1b—Summers, 2b—Stewart, 3b—Grieve, lf—Paparella, rf—Pinelli **T:** 1:42 **A:** 40,135

GAME 2 Cleveland 4 Boston 1
Braves Field 10/07/48

CLEVELAND	AB	R	H	HR	RBI	BB	AVG
Mitchell lf	5	1	1	0	0	0	.111
Clark rf	3	0	0	0	0	0	.000
Kennedy rf	1	0	1	0	1	0	1.000
Boudreau ss	5	1	2	0	1	0	.222
Gordon 2b	4	1	1	0	1	0	.250
Keltner 3b	4	0	0	0	0	0	.125
Doby cf	4	0	2	0	1	0	.375
Robinson 1b	3	0	1	0	0	1	.167
Hegan c	3	1	0	0	0	1	.167
Lemon p	4	0	0	0	0	0	.000
TOTALS	**36**	**4**	**8**	**0**	**4**	**2**	**.176**

BATTING: 2B: Doby (1, Spahn), Boudreau (1, Spahn). **S:** Clark. **RBI:** Kennedy 1 (1), Boudreau 1 (1), Gordon 1 (1), Doby 1 (1). **2-out RBI:** Kennedy 1. **Runners left in scoring position, 2 out:** Gordon 1, Keltner 1, Hegan 1, Lemon 1. **Team LOB:** 8 **FIELDING: E:** Gordon (1). **DP:** 2 (Boudreau-Gordon-Robinson, Gordon-Boudreau-Robinson).

BOSTON	AB	R	H	HR	RBI	BB	AVG
Holmes rf	4	0	0	0	0	0	.125
Dark ss	4	1	1	0	0	0	.125
Torgeson 1b	4	0	2	0	0	0	.333
Elliott 3b	4	0	1	0	1	0	.143
Rickert lf	4	0	0	0	0	0	.143
Salkeld c	1	0	1	0	0	2	.500
Masi c	1	0	0	0	0	0	.000
M.McCormick cf	4	0	2	0	0	0	.333
Stanky 2b	2	0	1	0	0	1	.250
Spahn p	2	0	0	0	0	0	.000
Barrett p	0	0	0	0	0	0	.000
a-F.McCormick ph	1	0	0	0	0	0	.000
Potter p	0	0	0	0	0	0	.000
b-Sanders ph	1	0	0	0	0	0	.000
TOTALS	**32**	**1**	**8**	**0**	**1**	**3**	**.179**

a - Batted for Barrett in the 7th
b - Batted for Potter in the 9th

BATTING: 2B: Stanky (1, Lemon). **S:** Stanky. **RBI:** Elliott 1 (1). **Runners left in scoring position, 2 out:** Holmes 4, Sanders 1. **GIDP:** Stanky, Elliott. **Team LOB:** 8 **FIELDING: E:** Dark 2 (2), Elliott (3). **Outfield assists:** Holmes (1). **DP:** 1 (Holmes-Torgeson).

CLEVELAND	IP	H	R	ER	BB	SO	HR	ERA
Lemon (W, 1-0)	9	8	1	0	3	5	0	0.00

BOSTON	IP	H	R	ER	BB	SO	HR	ERA
Spahn (L, 0-1)	4.1	6	3	3	2	1	0	6.23
Barrett	2.2	1	0	0	0	1	0	0.00
Potter	2	1	1	0	0	1	0	0.00

IBB: Hegan (by Spahn). **Ground balls-fly balls:** Lemon 11-8, Spahn 4-7, Barrett 6-2, Potter 6-0. **Batters faced:** Lemon 36, Spahn 21, Barrett 10, Potter 8. **UMPIRES:** hp—Stewart, 1b—Grieve, 2b—Barr, 3b—Summers, lf—Paparella, rf—Pinelli **T:** 2:14 **A:** 39,633

GAME 3 Cleveland 2 Boston 0
Municipal Stadium 10/08/48

BOSTON	AB	R	H	HR	RBI	BB	AVG
Holmes rf	4	0	0	0	0	0	.083
Dark ss	4	0	1	0	0	0	.167
M.McCormick lf	4	0	1	0	0	0	.300
Elliott 3b	3	0	1	0	0	0	.200
F.McCormick 1b	3	0	1	0	0	0	.250
Conatser cf	3	0	0	0	0	0	.000
Masi c	3	0	0	0	0	0	.000
Stanky 2b	3	0	1	0	0	0	.286
Bickford p	0	0	0	0	0	0	.000
Voiselle p	1	0	0	0	0	0	.000
a-Ryan ph	1	0	0	0	0	0	.000
Barrett p	0	0	0	0	0	0	.000
TOTALS	**29**	**0**	**5**	**0**	**0**	**0**	**.176**

a - Batted for Voiselle in the 8th

BATTING: 2B: Dark (1, Bearden). **S:** Bickford. **Runners left in scoring position, 2 out:** Dark 1, M.McCormick 1, Masi 1. **GIDP:** F.McCormick, Conatser. **Team LOB:** 3 **FIELDING: DP:** 1 (Dark-Stanky-F.McCormick).

CLEVELAND	AB	R	H	HR	RBI	BB	AVG
Mitchell lf	3	0	0	0	0	1	.083
Doby cf	3	0	1	0	1	1	.364
Boudreau ss	3	0	0	0	0	1	.167
Gordon 2b	4	0	0	0	0	0	.167
Keltner 3b	3	1	0	0	0	1	.091
Judnich rf	3	0	0	0	0	1	.000
Robinson 1b	3	0	1	0	0	0	.222
Hegan c	3	0	1	0	1	0	.222
Bearden p	3	1	2	0	0	0	.667
TOTALS	**28**	**2**	**5**	**0**	**2**	**5**	**.177**

BATTING: 2B: Bearden (1, Bickford). **RBI:** Doby 1 (2), Hegan 1 (1). **Runners left in scoring position, 2 out:** Doby 2, Gordon 1. **GIDP:** Boudreau. **Team LOB:** 7 **FIELDING: DP:** 2 (Bearden-Gordon-Robinson, Keltner-Gordon-Robinson).

BOSTON	IP	H	R	ER	BB	SO	HR	ERA
Bickford (L, 0-1)	3.1	4	2	1	5	1	0	2.70
Voiselle	3.2	1	0	0	0	0	0	0.00
Barrett	1	0	0	0	0	0	0	0.00

CLEVELAND	IP	H	R	ER	BB	SO	HR	ERA
Bearden (W, 1-0)	9	5	0	0	0	4	0	0.00

Ground balls-fly balls: Bickford 3-5, Voiselle 3-8, Barrett 1-2, Bearden 14-6. **Batters faced:** Bickford 18, Voiselle 12, Barrett 3, Bearden 30. **UMPIRES:** hp—Stewart, 1b—Grieve, 2b—Barr, 3b—Summers, lf—Pinelli, rf—Paparella **T:** 1:36 **A:** 70,306

GAME 4 Cleveland 2 Boston 1
Municipal Stadium 10/09/48

BOSTON	AB	R	H	HR	RBI	BB	AVG
Holmes rf	4	0	0	0	0	0	.063
Dark ss	4	0	0	0	0	0	.125
Torgeson 1b	3	0	2	0	0	1	.444
Elliott 3b	4	0	0	0	0	0	.143
Rickert lf	4	1	2	1	1	0	.273
M.McCormick cf	4	0	1	0	0	0	.286
Masi c	3	0	0	0	0	0	.000
a-Salkeld ph	1	0	0	0	0	0	.333
Stanky 2b	3	0	1	0	0	0	.300
Sain p	2	0	1	0	0	0	.200
TOTALS	**32**	**1**	**7**	**1**	**1**	**1**	**.188**

a - Batted for Masi in the 9th

BATTING: 2B: Torgeson 2 (2, Gromek). **HR:** Rickert (1, 7th off Gromek 0 on, 0 out). **S:** Sain. **RBI:** Rickert 1 (1). **Runners left in scoring position, 2 out:** Dark 1, Elliott 2. **GIDP:** Elliott. **Team LOB:** 6 **Outfield assists:** Holmes (2).

CLEVELAND	AB	R	H	HR	RBI	BB	AVG
Mitchell lf	4	1	1	0	0	0	.125
Doby cf	3	1	1	1	1	0	.357
Boudreau ss	3	0	1	0	1	0	.200
Gordon 2b	3	0	0	0	0	0	.133
Keltner 3b	3	0	0	0	0	0	.071
Judnich rf	3	0	0	0	0	0	.000
Kennedy rf	0	0	0	0	0	0	1.000
Robinson 1b	3	0	2	0	0	0	.333
Hegan c	2	0	0	0	0	0	.182
Gromek p	3	0	0	0	0	0	.000
TOTALS	**27**	**2**	**5**	**1**	**2**	**0**	**.179**

BATTING: 2B: Boudreau (2, Sain). **HR:** Doby (1, 3th off Sain 0 on, 2 out). **S:** Hegan. **RBI:** Doby 1 (3), Boudreau 1 (2). **2-out RBI:** Doby 1. **Runners left in scoring position, 2 out:** Mitchell 1, Gordon 1. **Team LOB:** 2 **FIELDING: DP:** 1 (Boudreau-Gordon-Robinson).

BOSTON	IP	H	R	ER	BB	SO	HR	ERA
Sain (L, 1-1)	8	5	2	2	0	3	1	1.06

CLEVELAND	IP	H	R	ER	BB	SO	HR	ERA
Gromek (W, 1-0)	9	7	1	1	1	2	1	1.00

Ground balls-fly balls: Sain 11-8, Gromek 8-15. **Batters faced:** Sain 28, Gromek 34. **UMPIRES:** hp—Grieve, 1b—Barr, 2b—Summers, 3b—Stewart, lf—Pinelli, rf—Paparella **T:** 1:31 **A:** 81,897

GAME 5 Boston 11 Cleveland 5
Municipal Stadium 10/10/48

BOSTON	AB	R	H	HR	RBI	BB	AVG
Holmes rf	5	2	2	0	0	0	.143
Dark ss	4	1	1	0	0	0	.150
Torgeson 1b	5	1	2	0	1	0	.429
Elliott 3b	4	3	2	2	4	1	.222
Rickert lf	5	1	1	0	2	0	.250
Salkeld c	4	2	1	1	1	1	.286
M.McCormick cf	5	1	1	0	1	0	.263
Stanky 2b	3	0	1	0	1	2	.308
Potter p	2	0	1	0	0	0	.500
Spahn p	2	0	0	0	1	0	.000
TOTALS	**39**	**11**	**12**	**3**	**11**	**4**	**.218**

BATTING: HR: Elliott 2 (2, 1st off Feller 2 on, 1 out, 3th off Feller 0 on, 2 out), Salkeld (1, 6th off Feller 0 on, 1 out). **S:** Dark. **RBI:** Torgeson 1 (1), Elliott 4 (5), Rickert 2 (3), Salkeld 1 (1), M.McCormick 1 (1), Stanky 1 (1), Spahn 1 (1). **2-out RBI:** Elliott 1. **Runners left in scoring position, 2 out:** Holmes 2. **Team LOB:** 6

CLEVELAND	AB	R	H	HR	RBI	BB	AVG
Mitchell lf	3	1	1	1	1	1	.158
Doby cf	4	0	0	0	0	0	.278
Boudreau ss	4	0	2	0	0	0	.263
Gordon 2b	3	1	1	0	0	1	.167
Keltner 3b	3	1	0	0	0	1	.059
Judnich rf	3	1	1	0	1	0	.077
b-Boone ph	1	0	0	0	0	0	.000
Peck rf	0	0	0	0	0	0	.000
Robinson 1b	4	0	0	0	0	0	.250
Hegan c	4	1	1	1	3	0	.200
Feller p	2	0	0	0	0	0	.000
Klieman p	0	0	0	0	0	0	.000
Christopher p	0	0	0	0	0	0	.000
Paige p	0	0	0	0	0	0	.000
a-Rosen ph	1	0	0	0	0	0	.000
Muncrief p	0	0	0	0	0	0	.000
c-Tipton ph	1	0	0	0	0	0	.000
TOTALS	**33**	**5**	**6**	**2**	**5**	**3**	**.179**

a - Batted for Paige in the 7th
b - Batted for Judnich in the 8th
c - Batted for Muncrief in the 9th

BATTING: 2B: Boudreau (3, Spahn). **HR:** Mitchell (1, 1st off Potter 0 on, 0 out), Hegan (1, 4th off Potter 2 on, 1 out). **RBI:** Mitchell 1 (1), Judnich 1 (1), Hegan 3 (4). **Runners left in scoring position, 2 out:** Judnich 1, Boone 1. **Team LOB:** 4 **FIELDING: E:** Keltner (1), Doby (1).

BOSTON	IP	H	R	ER	BB	SO	HR	ERA
Potter	3.1	5	5	5	2	0	2	8.44
Spahn (W, 1-1)	5.2	1	0	0	1	7	0	2.70

CLEVELAND	IP	H	R	ER	BB	SO	HR	ERA
Feller (L, 0-2)	6.1	8	7	7	2	5	3	5.02
Klieman	0	1	3	3	2	0	0	0.00
Christopher	0	2	1	1	0	0	0	0.00
Paige	0.2	0	0	0	0	0	0	0.00
Muncrief	2	1	0	0	0	0	0	0.00

BK: Paige 1. **Ground balls-fly balls:** Potter 6-4, Spahn 3-7, Feller 6-8, Klieman 0-0, Christopher 0-0, Paige 1-1, Muncrief 2-4. **Batters faced:** Potter 17, Spahn 19, Feller 30, Klieman 3, Christopher 2, Paige 2, Muncrief 7. **UMPIRES:** hp—Barr, 1b—Summers, 2b—Stewart, 3b—Grieve, lf—Paparella, rf—Pinelli **T:** 2:39 **A:** 86,288

GAME 6 Cleveland 4 Boston 3
Braves Field 10/11/48

CLEVELAND	AB	R	H	HR	RBI	BB	AVG
Mitchell lf	4	1	1	0	0	0	.174
Kennedy lf	1	0	0	0	0	0	.500
Doby rf	4	0	2	0	0	1	.318
Boudreau ss	3	0	1	0	1	0	.273
Gordon 2b	4	1	1	1	1	0	.182
Keltner 3b	4	1	1	0	0	0	.095
Tucker cf	3	1	1	0	0	1	.333
Robinson 1b	4	0	2	0	1	0	.300
Hegan c	4	0	1	0	1	0	.211
Lemon p	3	0	0	0	0	0	.000
Bearden p	1	0	0	0	0	0	.500
TOTALS	**35**	**4**	**10**	**1**	**4**	**2**	**.199**

BATTING: 2B: Mitchell (1, Voiselle), Boudreau (4, Voiselle). **HR:** Gordon (1, 6th off Voiselle 0 on, 0 out). **RBI:** Boudreau 1 (3), Gordon 1 (2), Robinson 1 (1), Hegan 1 (5). **Runners left in scoring position, 2 out:** Keltner 2. **GIDP:** Boudreau. **Team LOB:** 7 **FIELDING: Outfield assists:** Tucker (1). **DP:** 4 (Tucker-Robinson, Lemon-Boudreau-Robinson, Gordon-Boudreau-Robinson, Hegan-Gordon).

BOSTON	AB	R	H	HR	RBI	BB	AVG
Holmes rf	5	1	2	0	0	0	.192
Dark ss	4	0	1	0	0	0	.167
Torgeson 1b	4	1	1	0	0	0	.389
Elliott 3b	3	1	3	0	0	1	.333
Rickert lf	3	0	0	0	0	0	.211
b-Conatser ph-cf	1	0	0	0	1	0	.000
Salkeld c	2	0	0	0	0	1	.222
c-Masi ph-c	1	0	1	0	1	0	.125
M.McCormick cf-lf	4	0	1	0	1	0	.261
Stanky 2b	1	0	0	0	0	3	.286
d-Ryan pr	0	0	0	0	0	0	.000
Voiselle p	1	0	0	0	0	0	.000
a-F.McCormick ph	1	0	0	0	0	0	.200
Spahn p	0	0	0	0	0	0	.000
e-Sisti ph	1	0	0	0	0	0	.000
TOTALS	**31**	**3**	**9**	**0**	**3**	**5**	**.230**

a - Batted for Voiselle in the 7th
b - Batted for Rickert in the 8th
c - Batted for Salkeld in the 8th
d - Ran for Stanky in the 9th e - Batted for Spahn in the 9th

BATTING: 2B: Torgeson (3, Lemon), Masi (1, Bearden). **S:** Voiselle. **RBI:** Conatser 1 (1), Masi 1 (1), M.McCormick 1 (2). **2-out RBI:** Masi 1, M.McCormick 1. **Runners left in scoring position, 2 out:** M.McCormick 3, Voiselle 2. **GIDP:** Dark, Rickert. **Team LOB:** 7 **FIELDING: DP:** 1 (Elliott-Stanky-Torgeson).

CLEVELAND	IP	H	R	ER	BB	SO	HR	ERA
Lemon (W, 2-0)	7.1	8	3	3	4	1	0	1.65
Bearden (S, 1)	1.2	1	0	0	1	0	0	0.00

BOSTON	IP	H	R	ER	BB	SO	HR	ERA
Voiselle (L, 0-1)	7	7	3	3	2	2	1	2.53
Spahn	2	3	1	1	0	4	0	3.00

BK: Lemon 1. **HBP:** Boudreau (by Voiselle). **Ground balls-fly balls:** Lemon 9-8, Bearden 1-3, Voiselle 5-13, Spahn 0-1. **Batters faced:** Lemon 31, Bearden 6, Voiselle 30, Spahn 8. **UMPIRES:** hp—Summers, 1b—Stewart, 2b—Grieve, 3b—Barr, lf—Pinelli, rf—Paparella **T:** 2:16 **A:** 40,103

1949 NY YANKEES DEF. BROOKLYN, 4-1

GAME 1 New York 1 Brooklyn 0
Yankee Stadium 10/05/49

BROOKLYN	AB	R	H	HR	RBI	BB	AVG
Reese ss	4	0	1	0	0	0	.250
Jorgensen 3b	3	0	1	0	0	1	.333
Snider cf	4	0	0	0	0	0	.000
Robinson 2b	4	0	0	0	0	0	.000
Hermanski lf	3	0	0	0	0	1	.000
Furillo rf	3	0	0	0	0	1	.000
Hodges 1b	2	0	0	0	0	0	.000
Campanella c	2	0	0	0	0	1	.000
Newcombe p	3	0	0	0	0	0	.000
TOTALS	**28**	**0**	**2**	**0**	**0**	**4**	**.071**

BATTING: 2B: Jorgensen (1, Reynolds). **S:** Hodges. **Runners left in scoring position, 2 out:** Reese 1, Snider 1, Robinson 1, Campanella 1. **GIDP:** Hodges. **Team LOB:** 6 **BASERUNNING: SB:** Reese (1, 2nd base off Reynolds/Berra).

NY YANKEES	AB	R	H	HR	RBI	BB	AVG
Rizzuto ss	4	0	0	0	0	0	.000
Henrich 1b	4	1	1	1	1	0	.250
Berra c	3	0	0	0	0	0	.000
DiMaggio cf	3	0	0	0	0	0	.000
Lindell lf	3	0	1	0	0	0	.333
Johnson 3b	3	0	0	0	0	0	.000
Mapes rf	3	0	0	0	0	0	.000
Coleman 2b	3	0	1	0	0	0	.333
Reynolds p	3	0	2	0	0	0	.667
TOTALS	**29**	**1**	**5**	**1**	**1**	**0**	**.172**

BATTING: 2B: Reynolds (1, Newcombe), Coleman (1, Newcombe). **HR:** Henrich (1, 9th off Newcombe 0 on, 0 out). **RBI:** Henrich 1 (1). **Runners left in scoring position, 2 out:** Rizzuto 1, Henrich 1. **Team LOB:** 4 **FIELDING: E:** Coleman (1). **DP:** 1 (Reynolds-Coleman-Henrich).

BROOKLYN	IP	H	R	ER	BB	SO	HR	ERA
Newcombe (L, 0-1)	8	5	1	1	0	11	1	1.13

NY YANKEES	IP	H	R	ER	BB	SO	HR	ERA
Reynolds (W, 1-0)	9	2	0	0	4	9	0	0.00

Ground balls-fly balls: Newcombe 4-9, Reynolds 9-8. **Batters faced:** Newcombe 29, Reynolds 33. **UMPIRES:** hp—Hubbard, 1b—Reardon, 2b—Passarella, 3b—Jorda, lf—Hurley, rf—Barr **T:** 2:24 **A:** 66,224

GAME 2 Brooklyn 1 New York 0
Yankee Stadium 10/06/49

BROOKLYN	AB	R	H	HR	RBI	BB	AVG
Reese ss	4	0	0	0	0	0	.125
Jorgensen 3b	4	0	1	0	0	0	.286
Snider cf	4	0	1	0	0	0	.125
Robinson 2b	3	1	1	0	0	0	.143
Hermanski rf	3	0	1	0	0	0	.167
a-Furillo ph	1	0	0	0	0	0	.000
McCormick rf	0	0	0	0	0	0	.000
Rackley lf	2	0	0	0	0	0	.000
Olmo lf	2	0	1	0	0	0	.500
Hodges 1b	3	0	1	0	1	0	.200
Campanella c	2	0	1	0	0	1	.250
Roe p	3	0	0	0	0	0	.000
TOTALS	**31**	**1**	**7**	**0**	**1**	**1**	**.153**

a - Batted for Hermanski in the 9th

BATTING: 2B: Robinson (1, Raschi), Jorgensen (2, Raschi). **3B:** Hermanski (1, Raschi). **S:** Robinson. **RBI:** Hodges 1 (1). **2-out RBI:** Hodges 1. **Runners left in scoring position, 2 out:** Hermanski 1, Olmo 1, Roe 1. **GIDP:** Hodges. **Team LOB:** 5 **FIELDING: E:** Reese (1), Roe (1). **Outfield assists:** Snider (1).

NY YANKEES	AB	R	H	HR	RBI	BB	AVG
Rizzuto ss	3	0	1	0	0	0	.143
Henrich 1b	4	0	0	0	0	0	.125
Bauer rf	4	0	1	0	0	0	.250
DiMaggio cf	4	0	1	0	0	0	.143
Lindell lf	4	0	0	0	0	0	.143
Johnson 3b	4	0	1	0	0	0	.143
Coleman 2b	4	0	1	0	0	0	.286
Silvera c	2	0	0	0	0	0	.000
a-Mize ph	1	0	1	0	0	0	1.000
b-Stirnweiss pr	0	0	0	0	0	0	.000
Niarhos c	0	0	0	0	0	0	.000
Raschi p	2	0	0	0	0	0	.000
c-B.Brown ph	1	0	0	0	0	0	.000
Page p	0	0	0	0	0	0	.000
TOTALS	**33**	**0**	**6**	**0**	**0**	**0**	**.177**

a - Batted for Silvera in the 8th
b - Ran for Mize in the 8th
c - Batted for Raschi in the 8th

BATTING: 2B: Coleman (2, Roe). **S:** Rizzuto. **Runners left in scoring position, 2 out:** Henrich 1, Bauer 1, Coleman 1, Raschi 1. **Team LOB:** 7 **BASERUNNING: SB:** Rizzuto (1, 2nd base off Roe/Campanella), Johnson (1, 2nd base off Roe/Campanella). **FIELDING: E:** Lindell (1). **Outfield assists:** Lindell (1). **DP:** 1 (Rizzuto-Coleman-Henrich).

BROOKLYN	IP	H	R	ER	BB	SO	HR	ERA
Roe (W, 1-0)	9	6	0	0	0	3	0	0.00

NY YANKEES	IP	H	R	ER	BB	SO	HR	ERA
Raschi (L, 0-1)	8	6	1	1	1	4	0	1.13
Page	1	1	0	0	0	0	0	0.00

IBB: Campanella (by Raschi). **Ground balls-fly balls:** Roe 12-12, Raschi 11-7, Page 1-1. **Batters faced:** Roe 34, Raschi 29, Page 4. **UMPIRES:** hp—Reardon, 1b—Passarella, 2b—Jorda, 3b—Hubbard, lf—Hurley, rf—Barr **T:** 2:30 **A:** 70,053

GAME 3 New York 4 Brooklyn 3
Ebbets Field 10/07/49

NY YANKEES	AB	R	H	HR	RBI	BB	AVG
Rizzuto ss	4	0	0	0	1	0	.091
Henrich 1b	3	0	0	0	0	1	.091
Berra c	3	1	0	0	0	1	.000
DiMaggio cf	4	0	0	0	0	0	.091
B.Brown 3b	4	1	1	0	0	0	.200
Woodling lf	3	1	1	0	0	1	.333
Mapes rf	2	1	0	0	0	1	.000
a-Mize ph	1	0	1	0	2	0	1.000
b-Bauer pr-rf	0	0	0	0	0	0	.250
Coleman 2b	4	0	1	0	1	0	.273
Byrne p	1	0	1	0	0	0	1.000
Page p	3	0	0	0	0	0	.000
TOTALS	**32**	**4**	**5**	**0**	**4**	**4**	**.170**

a - Batted for Mapes in the 9th
b - Ran for Mize in the 9th

BATTING: 2B: Woodling (1, Branca). **RBI:** Rizzuto 1 (1), Mize 2 (2), Coleman 1 (1). **2-out RBI:** Mize 2, Coleman 1. **Runners left in scoring position, 2 out:** Berra 1, Mapes 1, Page 1. **Team LOB:** 5 **FIELDING: DP:** 1 (Berra-Coleman).

BROOKLYN	AB	R	H	HR	RBI	BB	AVG
Reese ss	2	1	1	1	1	1	.200
Miksis 3b	4	0	1	0	0	0	.250
Furillo rf	4	0	1	0	0	0	.125
Robinson 2b	2	0	0	0	0	2	.111
Hodges 1b	3	0	0	0	0	1	.125
Olmo lf	4	1	1	1	1	0	.333
Snider cf	4	0	0	0	0	0	.083
Campanella c	4	1	1	1	1	0	.250
Branca p	3	0	0	0	0	0	.000
Banta p	0	0	0	0	0	0	.000
a-Edwards ph	1	0	0	0	0	0	.000
TOTALS	**31**	**3**	**5**	**3**	**3**	**4**	**.156**

a - Batted for Banta in the 9th

BATTING: HR: Reese (1, 4th off Byrne 0 on, 0 out), Olmo (1, 9th off Page 0 on, 1 out), Campanella (1, 9th off Page 0 on, 2 out). **RBI:** Reese 1 (1), Olmo 1 (1), Campanella 1 (1). **2-out RBI:** Campanella 1. **Runners left in scoring position, 2 out:** Robinson 1, Snider 2. **Team LOB:** 6

NY YANKEES	IP	H	R	ER	BB	SO	HR	ERA
Byrne	3.1	2	1	1	2	1	1	2.70
Page (W, 1-0)	5.2	3	2	2	2	4	2	2.70

BROOKLYN	IP	H	R	ER	BB	SO	HR	ERA
Branca (L, 0-1)	8.2	4	4	4	4	6	0	4.15
Banta	0.1	1	0	0	0	1	0	0.00

HBP: Reese (by Byrne). **Ground balls-fly balls:** Byrne 2-6, Page 6-7, Branca 7-13, Banta 0-0. **Batters faced:** Byrne 14, Page 22, Branca 34, Banta 2. **UMPIRES:** hp—Passarella, 1b—Jorda, 2b—Hubbard, 3b—Reardon, lf—Barr, rf—Hurley **T:** 2:30 **A:** 32,788

GAME 4 New York 6 Brooklyn 4
Ebbets Field 10/08/49

NY YANKEES	AB	R	H	HR	RBI	BB	AVG
Rizzuto ss	4	0	2	0	0	1	.200
Henrich 1b	4	1	3	0	0	1	.267
Berra c	5	1	1	0	0	0	.091
DiMaggio cf	3	1	0	0	0	2	.071
B.Brown 3b	3	1	2	0	3	1	.375
Woodling lf	3	1	0	0	0	1	.167
Mapes rf	2	1	1	0	2	0	.143
a-Bauer ph-rf	2	0	0	0	0	0	.167
Coleman 2b	4	0	0	0	0	0	.200
Lopat p	3	0	1	0	1	0	.333
Reynolds p	1	0	0	0	0	0	.500
TOTALS	**34**	**6**	**10**	**0**	**6**	**6**	**.203**

a - Batted for Mapes in the 5th

BATTING: 2B: B.Brown (1, Newcombe), Mapes (1, Newcombe), Lopat (1, Newcombe). **3B:** B.Brown (1, Hatten). **RBI:** B.Brown 3 (3), Mapes 2 (2), Lopat 1 (1). **2-out RBI:** Lopat 1. **Runners left in scoring position, 2 out:** Rizzuto 1, Woodling 2, Coleman 1. **Team LOB:** 7 **FIELDING: DP:** 1 (Rizzuto-Henrich).

BROOKLYN	AB	R	H	HR	RBI	BB	AVG
Reese ss	4	1	2	0	0	0	.286
Miksis 3b	2	0	0	0	0	0	.167
b-Cox ph-3b	2	0	1	0	0	0	.500
Snider cf	4	0	0	0	0	0	.063
Robinson 2b	3	1	1	0	1	1	.167
Hodges 1b	4	1	1	0	0	0	.167
Olmo lf	4	1	1	0	1	0	.300
Campanella c	4	0	1	0	1	0	.250
Hermanski rf	4	0	2	0	1	0	.300
Newcombe p	1	0	0	0	0	0	.000
Hatten p	0	0	0	0	0	0	.000
a-T.Brown ph	1	0	0	0	0	0	.000
Erskine p	0	0	0	0	0	0	.000
c-Jorgensen ph	1	0	0	0	0	0	.250
Banta p	0	0	0	0	0	0	.000
d-Whitman ph	1	0	0	0	0	0	.000
TOTALS	**35**	**4**	**9**	**0**	**4**	**1**	**.184**

a - Batted for Hatten in the 5th
b - Batted for Miksis in the 6th
c - Batted for Erskine in the 6th
d - Batted for Banta in the 9th

BATTING: 2B: Reese (1, Lopat). **RBI:** Robinson 1 (1), Olmo 1 (2), Campanella 1 (2), Hermanski 1 (1). **2-out RBI:** Robinson 1, Olmo 1, Campanella 1, Hermanski 1. **Runners left in scoring position, 2 out:** Robinson 1, Jorgensen 1. **GIDP:** Snider. **Team LOB:** 5 **FIELDING: E:** Miksis (1). **Outfield assists:** Olmo (1). **DP:** 1 (Miksis-Campanella-Robinson).

NY YANKEES	IP	H	R	ER	BB	SO	HR	ERA
Lopat (W, 1-0)	5.2	9	4	4	1	4	0	6.35
Reynolds (S, 1)	3.1	0	0	0	0	5	0	0.00

BROOKLYN	IP	H	R	ER	BB	SO	HR	ERA
Newcombe (L, 0-2)	3.2	5	3	3	3	0	0	3.09
Hatten	1.1	3	3	3	2	0	0	20.25
Erskine	1	1	0	0	0	0	0	0.00
Banta	3	1	0	0	1	1	0	0.00

IBB: DiMaggio (by Hatten). **Ground balls-fly balls:** Lopat 5-7, Reynolds 3-2, Newcombe 4-6, Hatten 1-2, Erskine 0-3, Banta 4-3. **Batters faced:** Lopat 26, Reynolds 10, Newcombe 18, Hatten 8, Erskine 4, Banta 10. **UMPIRES:** hp—Jorda, 1b—Hubbard, 2b—Reardon, 3b—Passarella, lf—Hurley, rf—Barr **T:** 2:42 **A:** 33,934

GAME 5 New York 10 Brooklyn 6
Ebbets Field 10/09/49

NY YANKEES	AB	R	H	HR	RBI	BB	AVG
Rizzuto ss	3	2	0	0	0	2	.167
Henrich 1b	4	2	1	0	0	1	.263
Berra c	5	0	0	0	1	0	.063
DiMaggio cf	4	1	1	1	2	1	.111
B.Brown 3b	4	2	3	0	3	1	.500
Woodling lf	4	2	3	0	0	1	.400
Mapes rf	3	1	0	0	0	1	.100
Coleman 2b	5	0	2	0	3	0	.250
Raschi p	3	0	1	0	1	1	.200
Page p	1	0	0	0	0	0	.000
TOTALS	**36**	**10**	**11**	**1**	**10**	**8**	**.226**

BATTING: 2B: Woodling 2 (3, Banta, Hatten), Coleman (3, Minner). **3B:** B.Brown (2, Erskine). **HR:** DiMaggio (1, 4th off Banta 0 on, 2 out). **S:** Rizzuto, Mapes. **RBI:** Berra 1 (1), DiMaggio 2 (2), B.Brown 3 (6), Coleman 3 (4), Raschi 1 (1). **2-out RBI:** DiMaggio 1, B.Brown 3, Coleman 2, Raschi 1. **Runners left in scoring position, 2 out:** Rizzuto 2, Henrich 1, Woodling 1, Mapes 2. **Team LOB:** 9 **FIELDING: E:** Mapes (1). **DP:** 1 (Page-Rizzuto-Henrich).

BROOKLYN	AB	R	H	HR	RBI	BB	AVG
Reese ss	5	0	2	0	1	0	.316
Jorgensen 3b	3	1	0	0	0	1	.182
e-Miksis ph	1	0	1	0	0	0	.286
Snider cf	5	2	2	0	0	0	.143
Robinson 2b	4	0	1	0	1	1	.188
Hermanski rf	3	1	1	0	1	2	.308
Hodges 1b	5	1	2	1	3	0	.235
Rackley lf	3	0	0	0	0	0	.000
c-Olmo ph-lf	1	0	0	0	0	0	.273
Campanella c	3	1	1	0	0	1	.267
Barney p	0	0	0	0	0	0	.000
Banta p	1	0	0	0	0	0	.000
a-T.Brown ph	1	0	0	0	0	0	.000
Erskine p	0	0	0	0	0	0	.000
Hatten p	0	0	0	0	0	0	.000
b-Cox ph	1	0	0	0	0	0	.333
Palica p	0	0	0	0	0	0	.000
d-Edwards ph	1	0	1	0	0	0	.500
Minner p	0	0	0	0	0	0	.000
TOTALS	**37**	**6**	**11**	**1**	**6**	**5**	**.210**

a - Batted for Banta in the 5th
b - Batted for Hatten in the 6th
c - Batted for Rackley in the 7th
d - Batted for Palica in the 8th e - Batted for Jorgensen in the 9th

BATTING: 2B: Campanella (1, Raschi), Snider (1, Raschi), Miksis (1, Page). **HR:** Hodges (1, 7th off Raschi 2 on, 2 out). **RBI:** Reese 1 (2), Robinson 1 (2), Hermanski 1 (2), Hodges 3 (4). **2-out RBI:** Reese 1, Hodges 3. **Runners left in scoring position, 2 out:** Hodges 1, Rackley 1, Cox 2. **GIDP:** Reese. **Team LOB:** 9 **FIELDING: E:** Barney (1), Robinson (1).

NY YANKEES	IP	H	R	ER	BB	SO	HR	ERA
Raschi (W, 1-1)	6.2	9	6	6	4	7	1	4.30
Page (S, 1)	2.1	2	0	0	1	4	0	2.00

BROOKLYN	IP	H	R	ER	BB	SO	HR	ERA
Barney (L, 0-1)	2.2	3	5	5	6	2	0	16.88
Banta	2.1	3	2	2	0	2	1	3.18
Erskine	0.2	2	3	3	1	0	0	16.20
Hatten	0.1	1	0	0	0	0	0	16.20
Palica	2	1	0	0	1	1	0	0.00
Minner	1	1	0	0	0	0	0	0.00

Ground balls-fly balls: Raschi 6-7, Page 1-1, Barney 2-3, Banta 2-2, Erskine 0-2, Hatten 0-1, Palica 2-3, Minner 1-2. **Batters faced:** Raschi 33, Page 9, Barney 17, Banta 10, Erskine 5, Hatten 2, Palica 8, Minner 4. **UMPIRES:** hp—Hubbard, 1b—Reardon, 2b—Passarella, 3b—Jorda, lf—Barr, rf—Hurley **T:** 3:04 **A:** 33,711

1950 NY YANKEES DEF. PHILADELPHIA PHILLIES, 4-0

GAME 1 New York 1 Philadelphia 0
Shibe Park 10/04/50

NY YANKEES	AB	R	H	HR	RBI	BB	AVG
Woodling lf	3	0	1	0	0	2	.333
Rizzuto ss	3	0	1	0	0	0	.333
Berra c	4	0	0	0	0	0	.000
DiMaggio cf	2	0	0	0	0	2	.000
Mize 1b	4	0	0	0	0	0	.000
Hopp 1b	0	0	0	0	0	0	.000
Brown 3b	4	1	1	0	0	0	.250
B.Johnson 3b	0	0	0	0	0	0	.000
Bauer rf	4	0	1	0	0	0	.250
Coleman 2b	4	0	0	0	1	0	.000
Raschi p	3	0	1	0	0	0	.333
TOTALS	**31**	**1**	**5**	**0**	**1**	**4**	**.161**

BATTING: 2B: Brown (1, Konstanty). **S:** Rizzuto, Raschi. **RBI:** Coleman 1 (1). **Runners left in scoring position, 2 out:** Woodling 1, Berra 1, Mize 3. **Team LOB:** 9

PHILADELPHIA	AB	R	H	HR	RBI	BB	AVG
Waitkus 1b	3	0	0	0	0	1	.000
Ashburn cf	4	0	0	0	0	0	.000
Sisler lf	4	0	0	0	0	0	.000
Ennis rf	3	0	0	0	0	0	.000
Jones 3b	3	0	1	0	0	0	.333
Hamner ss	3	0	0	0	0	0	.000
Seminick c	3	0	1	0	0	0	.333
Goliat 2b	3	0	0	0	0	0	.000
Konstanty p	2	0	0	0	0	0	.000
a-Whitman ph	1	0	0	0	0	0	.000
Meyer p	0	0	0	0	0	0	.000
TOTALS	**29**	**0**	**2**	**0**	**0**	**1**	**.069**

a - Batted for Konstanty in the 8th

BATTING: Runners left in scoring position, 2 out: Goliat 1. **Team LOB:** 3 **FIELDING: E:** Jones (1).

NY YANKEES	IP	H	R	ER	BB	SO	HR	ERA
Raschi (W, 1-0)	9	2	0	0	1	5	0	0.00

PHILADELPHIA	IP	H	R	ER	BB	SO	HR	ERA
Konstanty (L, 0-1)	8	4	1	1	4	0	0	1.13
Meyer	1	1	0	0	0	0	0	0.00

IBB: DiMaggio (by Konstanty). **Ground balls-fly balls:** Raschi 8-14, Konstanty 9-15, Meyer 0-2. **Batters faced:** Raschi 30, Konstanty 33, Meyer 4. **UMPIRES:** hp—Conlan, 1b—McGowan, 2b—Boggess, 3b—Berry, lf—Barlick, rf—McKinley **T:** 2:17 **A:** 30,746

GAME 2 New York 2 Philadelphia 1
Shibe Park 10/05/50

NY YANKEES	AB	R	H	HR	RBI	BB	AVG
Woodling lf	5	0	2	0	1	0	.375
Rizzuto ss	4	0	0	0	0	1	.143
Berra c	5	0	1	0	0	0	.111
DiMaggio cf	5	1	1	1	1	0	.143
Mize 1b	4	0	1	0	0	0	.125
B.Johnson 3b	1	0	0	0	0	0	.000
Brown 3b	4	0	2	0	0	0	.375
a-Hopp pr-1b	1	0	0	0	0	0	.000
Bauer rf	5	0	1	0	0	0	.222
Coleman 2b	3	1	1	0	0	1	.143
Reynolds p	3	0	1	0	0	1	.333
TOTALS	**40**	**2**	**10**	**1**	**2**	**3**	**.211**

a - Ran for Brown in the 8th

BATTING: 2B: Coleman (1, Roberts). **HR:** DiMaggio (1, 10th off Roberts 0 on, 0 out). **RBI:** Woodling 1 (1), DiMaggio 1 (1). **2-out RBI:** Woodling 1. **Runners left in scoring position, 2 out:** Rizzuto 2, Mize 1, Reynolds 2. **Team LOB:** 11 **FIELDING: DP:** 2 (B.Johnson-Coleman-Hopp, Rizzuto-Coleman-Hopp).

PHILADELPHIA	AB	R	H	HR	RBI	BB	AVG
Waitkus 1b	4	0	2	0	0	0	.286
Ashburn cf	5	0	2	0	1	0	.222
Sisler lf	5	0	0	0	0	0	.000
Ennis rf	4	0	0	0	0	0	.000
Jones 3b	4	0	0	0	0	0	.143
Hamner ss	3	0	2	0	0	1	.333
Seminick c	2	0	0	0	0	1	.200
a-Caballero pr	0	0	0	0	0	0	.000
Silvestri c	0	0	0	0	0	0	.000
b-Whitman ph	0	0	0	0	0	1	.000
Lopata c	0	0	0	0	0	0	.000
Goliat 2b	4	1	1	0	0	0	.143
Roberts p	2	0	0	0	0	0	.000
c-Mayo ph	0	0	0	0	0	1	.000
TOTALS	**33**	**1**	**7**	**0**	**1**	**4**	**.145**

a - Ran for Seminick in the 7th
b - Batted for Silvestri in the 9th
c - Batted for Roberts in the 10th

BATTING: 2B: Ashburn (1, Reynolds), Waitkus (1, Reynolds), Hamner (1, Reynolds). **3B:** Hamner (1, Reynolds). **S:** Roberts, Waitkus. **RBI:** Ashburn 1 (1). **Runners left in scoring position, 2 out:** Waitkus 1, Sisler 2, Ennis 1, Seminick 1, Goliat 1. **GIDP:** Ennis, Goliat. **Team LOB:** 8 **BASERUNNING: SB:** Hamner (1, 2nd base off Reynolds/Berra).

NY YANKEES	IP	H	R	ER	BB	SO	HR	ERA
Reynolds (W, 1-0)	10	7	1	1	4	6	0	0.90

PHILADELPHIA	IP	H	R	ER	BB	SO	HR	ERA
Roberts (L, 0-1)	10	10	2	2	3	5	1	1.80

IBB: Whitman (by Reynolds). **Ground balls-fly balls:** Reynolds 7-13, Roberts 4-21. **Batters faced:** Reynolds 39, Roberts 43. **UMPIRES:** hp—McGowan, 1b—Boggess, 2b—Berry, 3b—Conlan, lf—McKinley, rf—Barlick **T:** 3:06 **A:** 32,660

GAME 3 New York 3 Philadelphia 2
Yankee Stadium 10/06/50

PHILADELPHIA	AB	R	H	HR	RBI	BB	AVG
Waitkus 1b	5	0	1	0	0	0	.250
Ashburn cf	4	0	1	0	0	0	.231
Jones 3b	3	0	1	0	0	0	.200
Ennis rf	4	1	1	0	0	0	.091
Sisler lf	4	0	1	0	1	0	.077
Mayo lf	0	0	0	0	0	0	.000
Hamner ss	4	1	3	0	0	0	.500
Seminick c	2	0	1	0	0	0	.286
Goliat 2b	3	0	1	0	1	1	.200
b-Caballero pr	0	0	0	0	0	0	.000
Bloodworth 2b	0	0	0	0	0	0	.000
Heintzelman p	2	0	0	0	0	0	.000
Konstanty p	0	0	0	0	0	0	.000
a-Whitman ph	1	0	0	0	0	0	.000
Meyer p	0	0	0	0	0	0	.000
TOTALS	**32**	**2**	**10**	**0**	**2**	**1**	**.202**

a - Batted for Konstanty in the 9th
b - Ran for Goliat in the 9th

BATTING: 2B: Ennis (1, Lopat), Hamner (2, Ferrick). **S:** Seminick, Heintzelman, Jones, Seminick. **RBI:** Sisler 1 (1), Goliat 1 (1). **2-out RBI:** Sisler 1. **Runners left in scoring position, 2 out:** Waitkus 2, Ennis 1, Sisler 1, Heintzelman 2. **Team LOB:** 8 **FIELDING: E:** Seminick (1), Hamner (1). **Outfield assists:** Sisler (1). **DP:** 1 (Hamner-Waitkus).

NY YANKEES	AB	R	H	HR	RBI	BB	AVG
Rizzuto ss	3	1	1	0	0	2	.200
Coleman 2b	4	1	3	0	2	1	.364
Berra c	2	0	0	0	0	2	.091
DiMaggio cf	3	0	1	0	0	1	.200
Bauer lf	3	0	0	0	0	0	.167
b-Brown ph	1	0	0	0	0	0	.333
c-Jensen pr	0	0	0	0	0	0	.000
Ferrick p	0	0	0	0	0	0	.000
Mize 1b	4	0	0	0	0	0	.083
Collins 1b	0	0	0	0	0	0	.000
B.Johnson 3b	4	0	0	0	0	0	.000
Mapes rf	4	0	0	0	0	0	.000
Lopat p	2	0	1	0	0	0	.500
a-Woodling ph-lf	2	1	1	0	0	0	.400
TOTALS	**32**	**3**	**7**	**0**	**2**	**6**	**.214**

a - Batted for Lopat in the 8th
b - Batted for Bauer in the 8th
c - Ran for Brown in the 8th

BATTING: RBI: Coleman 2 (3). **2-out RBI:** Coleman 2. **Runners left in scoring position, 2 out:** Coleman 1, Mize 2. **Team LOB:** 9 **BASERUNNING: SB:** Rizzuto (1, 2nd base off Heintzelman/Seminick).

PHILADELPHIA	IP	H	R	ER	BB	SO	HR	ERA
Heintzelman	7.2	4	2	1	6	3	0	1.17
Konstanty	0.1	0	0	0	0	0	0	1.08
Meyer (L, 0-1)	0.2	3	1	1	0	1	0	5.40

NY YANKEES	IP	H	R	ER	BB	SO	HR	ERA
Lopat	8	9	2	2	0	5	0	2.25
Ferrick (W, 1-0)	1	1	0	0	1	0	0	0.00

IBB: Goliat (by Ferrick). **Ground balls-fly balls:** Heintzelman 6-12, Konstanty 1-1, Meyer 0-1, Lopat 8-7, Ferrick 1-1. **Batters faced:** Heintzelman 31, Konstanty 2, Meyer 5, Lopat 32, Ferrick 5. **UMPIRES:** hp—Boggess, 1b—Berry, 2b—Conlan, 3b—McGowan, lf—Barlick, rf—McKinley **T:** 2:35 **A:** 64,505

GAME 4 New York 5 Philadelphia 2
Yankee Stadium 10/07/50

PHILADELPHIA	AB	R	H	HR	RBI	BB	AVG
Waitkus 1b	3	0	1	0	0	1	.267
Ashburn cf	4	0	0	0	0	0	.176
Jones 3b	4	1	2	0	0	0	.286
Ennis rf	3	0	1	0	0	0	.143
Sisler lf	4	0	0	0	0	0	.059
b-K.Johnson pr	0	1	0	0	0	0	.000
Hamner ss	4	0	1	0	0	0	.429
Seminick c	4	0	0	0	0	0	.182
c-Mayo pr	0	0	0	0	0	0	.000
Goliat 2b	4	0	1	0	0	0	.214
Miller p	2	0	0	0	0	0	.000
Konstanty p	2	0	1	0	0	0	.250
a-Caballero ph	1	0	0	0	0	0	.000
Roberts p	0	0	0	0	0	0	.000
d-Lopata ph	1	0	0	0	0	0	.000
TOTALS	**34**	**2**	**7**	**0**	**0**	**1**	**.203**

a - Batted for Konstanty in the 8th
b - Ran for Sisler in the 9th
c - Ran for Seminick in the 9th
d - Batted for Roberts in the 9th

BATTING: 2B: Jones (1, Ford). **Runners left in scoring position, 2 out:** Sisler 1, Lopata 1. **GIDP:** Sisler. **Team LOB:** 7 **FIELDING: E:** Goliat (1).

NY YANKEES	AB	R	H	HR	RBI	BB	AVG
Woodling lf	4	1	2	0	0	0	.429
Rizzuto ss	4	0	0	0	0	0	.143
Berra c	4	2	2	1	2	0	.200
DiMaggio cf	3	1	2	0	1	0	.308
Mize 1b	3	0	1	0	0	0	.133
Hopp 1b	1	0	0	0	0	0	.000
Brown 3b	3	1	1	0	1	0	.333
B.Johnson 3b	1	0	0	0	0	0	.000
Bauer rf	3	0	0	0	1	0	.133
Coleman 2b	3	0	0	0	0	0	.286
Ford p	3	0	0	0	0	0	.000
Reynolds p	0	0	0	0	0	0	.333
TOTALS	**32**	**5**	**8**	**1**	**5**	**0**	**.222**

BATTING: 2B: DiMaggio (1, Miller). **3B:** Brown (1, Konstanty). **HR:** Berra (1, 6th off Konstanty 0 on, 0 out). **RBI:** Berra 2 (2), DiMaggio 1 (2), Brown 1 (1), Bauer 1 (1). **Runners left in scoring position, 2 out:** Brown 1. **Team LOB:** 4 **BASERUNNING: CS:** Woodling (1, 2nd base off Konstanty/Seminick). **FIELDING: E:** Brown (1), Woodling (1). **DP:** 2 (Mize-Berra, Coleman-Rizzuto-Mize).

PHILADELPHIA	IP	H	R	ER	BB	SO	HR	ERA
Miller (L, 0-1)	0.1	2	2	1	0	0	0	27.00
Konstanty	6.2	5	3	3	0	3	1	2.40
Roberts	1	1	0	0	0	0	0	1.64

NY YANKEES	IP	H	R	ER	BB	SO	HR	ERA
Ford (W, 1-0)	8.2	7	2	0	1	7	0	0.00
Reynolds (S, 1)	0.1	0	0	0	0	1	0	0.87

WP: Miller 1. **HBP:** DiMaggio (by Konstanty), Ennis (by Ford). **Ground balls-fly balls:** Miller 2-0, Konstanty 8-8, Roberts 2-1, Ford 10-9, Reynolds 0-0. **Batters faced:** Miller 4, Konstanty 25, Roberts 4, Ford 35, Reynolds 1. **UMPIRES:** hp—Berry, 1b—Conlan, 2b—McGowan, 3b—Boggess, lf—McKinley, rf—Barlick **T:** 2:05 **A:** 68,098

1951 NY YANKEES DEF. NY GIANTS, 4-2

GAME 1 Giants 5 Yankees 1
Yankee Stadium 10/04/51

NY GIANTS	AB	R	H	HR	RBI	BB	AVG
Stanky 2b	4	1	0	0	0	1	.000
Dark ss	5	1	2	1	3	0	.400
Thompson rf	3	1	0	0	0	2	.000
Irvin lf	5	1	4	0	0	0	.800
Lockman 1b	4	0	1	0	1	1	.250
Thomson 3b	3	0	1	0	0	2	.333
Mays cf	5	0	0	0	0	0	.000
Westrum c	3	1	2	0	0	2	.667
Koslo p	3	0	0	0	0	0	.000
TOTALS	**35**	**5**	**10**	**1**	**4**	**8**	**.286**

BATTING: 2B: Lockman (1, Reynolds). **3B:** Irvin (1, Reynolds). **HR:** Dark (1, 6th off Reynolds 2 on, 2 out). **S:** Koslo, Koslo. **RBI:** Dark 3 (3), Lockman 1 (1). **2-out RBI:** Dark 3, Lockman 1. **Runners left in scoring position, 2 out:** Dark 1, Irvin 1, Lockman 1, Thomson 1, Mays 3, Koslo 1. **GIDP:** Stanky. **Team LOB:** 13 **BASERUNNING: SB:** Irvin (1, home off Reynolds/Berra). **FIELDING: E:** Thompson (1).

NY YANKEES	AB	R	H	HR	RBI	BB	AVG
Mantle rf	3	0	0	0	0	2	.000
Rizzuto ss	4	0	2	0	0	0	.500
Bauer lf	4	0	0	0	0	0	.000
DiMaggio cf	4	0	0	0	0	0	.000
Berra c	4	0	1	0	0	0	.250
McDougald 3b	4	1	1	0	0	0	.250
Coleman 2b	3	0	1	0	1	1	.333
Collins 1b	3	0	1	0	0	0	.333
b-Mize ph	1	0	0	0	0	0	.000
Reynolds p	2	0	1	0	0	0	.500
Hogue p	0	0	0	0	0	0	.000
a-Brown ph	1	0	0	0	0	0	.000
Morgan p	0	0	0	0	0	0	.000
c-Woodling ph	1	0	0	0	0	0	.000
TOTALS	**34**	**1**	**7**	**0**	**1**	**3**	**.206**

a - Batted for Hogue in the 7th
b - Batted for Collins in the 9th
c - Batted for Morgan in the 9th

BATTING: 2B: McDougald (1, Koslo). **RBI:** Coleman 1 (1). **Runners left in scoring position, 2 out:** Rizzuto 2, McDougald 1. **Team LOB:** 9 **FIELDING: E:** McDougald (1). **DP:** 1 (McDougald-Coleman-Collins).

NY GIANTS	IP	H	R	ER	BB	SO	HR	ERA
Koslo (W, 1-0)	9	7	1	1	3	3	0	1.00

NY YANKEES	IP	H	R	ER	BB	SO	HR	ERA
Reynolds (L, 0-1)	6	8	5	5	7	1	1	7.50
Hogue	1	0	0	0	0	0	0	0.00
Morgan	2	2	0	0	1	3	0	0.00

Ground balls-fly balls: Koslo 7-17, Reynolds 8-6, Hogue 1-2, Morgan 2-2. **Batters faced:** Koslo 37, Reynolds 32, Hogue 3, Morgan 10. **UMPIRES:** hp—Summers, 1b—Ballanfant, 2b—Paparella, 3b—Barlick, lf—Stevens, rf—Gore **T:** 2:58 **A:** 65,673

GAME 2 Yankees 3 Giants 1
Yankee Stadium 10/05/51

NY GIANTS	AB	R	H	HR	RBI	BB	AVG
Stanky 2b	3	0	0	0	0	1	.000
Dark ss	4	0	1	0	0	0	.333
Thomson 3b	4	0	0	0	0	0	.143
Irvin lf	4	1	3	0	0	0	.778
Lockman 1b	4	0	1	0	0	0	.250
Mays cf	4	0	0	0	0	0	.000
Westrum c	2	0	0	0	0	1	.400
a-Schenz pr	0	0	0	0	0	0	.000
Hartung rf	1	0	0	0	0	0	.000
Thompson rf	2	0	0	0	0	0	.000
b-Rigney ph	1	0	0	0	1	0	.000
Spencer p	0	0	0	0	0	0	.000
Jansen p	2	0	0	0	0	0	.000
c-Noble ph-c	1	0	0	0	0	0	.000
TOTALS	**32**	**1**	**5**	**0**	**1**	**2**	**.224**

a - Ran for Westrum in the 7th
b - Batted for Thompson in the 7th
c - Batted for Jansen in the 7th

BATTING: RBI: Rigney 1 (1). **Runners left in scoring position, 2 out:** Westrum 1, Noble 1. **Team LOB:** 6 **BASERUNNING: SB:** Irvin (2, 2nd base off Lopat/Berra). **FIELDING: E:** Lockman (1). **DP:** 1 (Dark-Stanky-Lockman).

NY YANKEES	AB	R	H	HR	RBI	BB	AVG
Mantle rf	2	1	1	0	0	0	.200
Bauer rf	2	0	0	0	0	0	.000
Rizzuto ss	4	0	1	0	0	0	.375
McDougald 2b-3b	3	0	1	0	1	0	.286
DiMaggio cf	3	0	0	0	0	0	.000
Berra c	3	0	0	0	0	0	.143
Woodling lf	3	0	0	0	0	0	.000
Brown 3b	3	0	1	0	0	0	.250
a-Martin pr	0	1	0	0	0	0	.000
Coleman 2b	0	0	0	0	0	0	.333
Collins 1b	3	1	1	1	1	0	.333
Lopat p	3	0	1	0	1	0	.333
TOTALS	**29**	**3**	**6**	**1**	**3**	**0**	**.206**

a - Ran for Brown in the 8th

BATTING: HR: Collins (1, 2nd off Jansen 0 on, 2 out). **RBI:** McDougald 1 (1), Collins 1 (1), Lopat 1 (1). **2-out RBI:** Collins 1. **Runners left in scoring position, 2 out:** Berra 1. **GIDP:** DiMaggio. **Team LOB:** 2

NY GIANTS	IP	H	R	ER	BB	SO	HR	ERA
Jansen (L, 0-1)	6	4	2	2	0	5	1	3.00
Spencer	2	2	1	1	0	0	0	4.50

NY YANKEES	IP	H	R	ER	BB	SO	HR	ERA
Lopat (W, 1-0)	9	5	1	1	2	1	0	1.00

Ground balls-fly balls: Jansen 7-5, Spencer 4-2, Lopat 13-13. **Batters faced:** Jansen 21, Spencer 8, Lopat 34. **UMPIRES:** hp—Ballanfant, 1b—Paparella, 2b—Barlick, 3b—Summers, lf—Gore, rf—Stevens **T:** 2:05 **A:** 66,018

GAME 3 Giants 6 Yankees 2
Polo Grounds 10/06/51

NY YANKEES	AB	R	H	HR	RBI	BB	AVG
Woodling lf	4	1	1	1	1	1	.125
Rizzuto ss	4	1	1	0	0	0	.333
McDougald 2b	3	0	2	0	0	2	.400
DiMaggio cf	4	0	0	0	0	0	.000
Berra c	3	0	1	0	0	1	.200
Brown 3b	3	0	0	0	0	1	.143
Collins 1b	3	0	0	0	1	1	.222
Bauer rf	4	0	0	0	0	0	.000
Raschi p	1	0	0	0	0	1	.000
Hogue p	0	0	0	0	0	0	.000
a-Hopp ph	0	0	0	0	0	1	.000
Ostrowski p	0	0	0	0	0	0	.000
b-Mize ph	1	0	0	0	0	0	.000
TOTALS	**30**	**2**	**5**	**1**	**2**	**8**	**.194**

a - Batted for Hogue in the 7th
b - Batted for Ostrowski in the 9th

BATTING: HR: Woodling (1, 9th off Jones 0 on, 1 out). **RBI:** Woodling 1 (1), Collins 1 (2). **2-out RBI:** Collins 1. **Runners left in scoring position, 2 out:** Brown 1, Bauer 2. **GIDP:** Collins. **Team LOB:** 10 **BASERUNNING: CS:** Rizzuto (1, 2nd base off Hearn/Westrum). **FIELDING: DP:** 1 (Rizzuto-McDougald-Collins).

NY GIANTS	AB	R	H	HR	RBI	BB	AVG
Stanky 2b	2	1	1	0	0	1	.111
Dark ss	4	1	1	0	1	0	.308
Thompson rf	3	1	1	0	0	1	.125
Irvin lf	3	1	0	0	1	1	.583
Lockman 1b	4	1	1	1	3	0	.250
Thomson 3b	4	1	1	0	0	0	.182
Mays cf	4	0	2	0	1	0	.154
Westrum c	4	0	0	0	0	0	.222
Hearn p	3	0	0	0	0	0	.000
Jones p	0	0	0	0	0	0	.000
TOTALS	**31**	**6**	**7**	**1**	**6**	**3**	**.224**

BATTING: 2B: Thomson (1, Raschi). **HR:** Lockman (1, 5th off Raschi 2 on, 1 out). **RBI:** Dark 1 (4), Irvin 1 (1), Lockman 3 (4), Mays 1 (1). **Runners left in scoring position, 2 out:** Lockman 1. **GIDP:** Westrum. **Team LOB:** 5 **BASERUNNING: CS:** Stanky (1, 2nd base off Raschi/Berra). **FIELDING: E:** Westrum (1). **DP:** 2 (Stanky-Dark-Lockman, Hearn-Dark-Lockman-Dark).

NY YANKEES	IP	H	R	ER	BB	SO	HR	ERA
Raschi (L, 0-1)	4.1	5	6	1	3	3	1	2.08
Hogue	1.2	1	0	0	0	0	0	0.00
Ostrowski	2	1	0	0	0	1	0	0.00

NY GIANTS	IP	H	R	ER	BB	SO	HR	ERA
Hearn (W, 1-0)	7.2	4	1	1	8	1	0	1.17
Jones (S, 1)	1.1	1	1	1	0	0	1	6.75

HBP: Stanky (by Raschi), Rizzuto (by Hearn). **Ground balls-fly balls:** Raschi 3-8, Hogue 0-5, Ostrowski 3-1, Hearn 12-8, Jones 1-3. **Batters faced:** Raschi 23, Hogue 6, Ostrowski 6, Hearn 34, Jones 5. **UMPIRES:** hp—Paparella, 1b—Barlick, 2b—Summers, 3b—Ballanfant, lf—Stevens, rf—Gore **T:** 2:42 **A:** 52,035

GAME 4 Yankees 6 Giants 2
Polo Grounds 10/08/51

NY YANKEES	AB	R	H	HR	RBI	BB	AVG
Bauer rf	4	0	2	0	0	1	.143
Rizzuto ss	5	1	1	0	0	0	.294
Berra c	5	1	1	0	0	0	.200
DiMaggio cf	5	1	2	1	2	0	.125
Woodling lf	4	2	1	0	0	1	.167
McDougald 2b-3b	4	0	1	0	1	0	.357
Brown 3b	4	1	2	0	0	0	.273
Coleman 2b	0	0	0	0	0	0	.333
Collins 1b	3	0	1	0	1	1	.250
Reynolds p	4	0	1	0	1	0	.333
TOTALS	**38**	**6**	**12**	**1**	**5**	**3**	**.229**

BATTING: 2B: Woodling (1, Maglie), Brown (1, Jones). **HR:** DiMaggio (1, 5th off Maglie 1 on, 1 out). **RBI:** DiMaggio 2 (2), McDougald 1 (2), Collins 1 (3), Reynolds 1 (1). **2-out RBI:** McDougald 1. **Runners left in scoring position, 2 out:** Bauer 3, Brown 1. **Team LOB:** 8 **FIELDING: DP:** 4 (Rizzuto-McDougald-Collins, Reynolds-Rizzuto-Collins 2, Rizzuto-Coleman-Collins).

NY GIANTS	AB	R	H	HR	RBI	BB	AVG
Stanky 2b	4	0	1	0	0	0	.154
Dark ss	4	1	3	0	0	0	.412
Thompson rf	3	1	0	0	0	1	.091
Irvin lf	4	0	2	0	1	0	.563
Lockman 1b	4	0	0	0	0	0	.188
Thomson 3b	2	0	2	0	1	2	.308
Mays cf	4	0	0	0	0	0	.118
Westrum c	2	0	0	0	0	1	.182
Maglie p	1	0	0	0	0	0	.000
a-Lohrke ph	1	0	0	0	0	0	.000
Jones p	0	0	0	0	0	0	.000
b-Rigney ph	1	0	0	0	0	0	.000
Kennedy p	0	0	0	0	0	0	.000
TOTALS	**30**	**2**	**8**	**0**	**2**	**4**	**.234**

a - Batted for Maglie in the 5th
b - Batted for Jones in the 8th

BATTING: 2B: Dark 3 (3, Reynolds). **RBI:** Irvin 1 (2), Thomson 1 (1). **2-out RBI:** Irvin 1. **Runners left in scoring position, 2 out:** Irvin 1, Lockman 1. **GIDP:** Mays, Mays, Dark, Mays. **Team LOB:** 5 **BASERUNNING: CS:** Irvin (1, 2nd base off Reynolds/Berra). **FIELDING: E:** Thomson (1). **Outfield assists:** Mays (1).

NY YANKEES	IP	H	R	ER	BB	SO	HR	ERA
Reynolds (W, 1-1)	9	8	2	2	4	7	0	4.20

NY GIANTS	IP	H	R	ER	BB	SO	HR	ERA
Maglie (L, 0-1)	5	8	4	4	2	3	1	7.20
Jones	3	4	2	0	1	2	0	2.08
Kennedy	1	0	0	0	0	2	0	0.00

Ground balls-fly balls: Reynolds 6-9, Maglie 3-8, Jones 1-6, Kennedy 0-1. **Batters faced:** Reynolds 34, Maglie 24, Jones 14, Kennedy 3. **UMPIRES:** hp—Barlick, 1b—Summers, 2b—Ballanfant, 3b—Paparella, lf—Gore, rf—Stevens **T:** 2:57 **A:** 49,010

GAME 5 Yankees 13 Giants 1
Polo Grounds 10/09/51

NY YANKEES	AB	R	H	HR	RBI	BB	AVG
Woodling lf	3	3	1	0	0	3	.200
Rizzuto ss	4	3	2	1	3	2	.333
Berra c	4	2	1	0	1	1	.211
DiMaggio cf	5	1	3	0	3	0	.238
Mize 1b	3	1	1	0	1	1	.200
Bauer rf	1	0	0	0	0	0	.133
McDougald 2b-3b	5	1	1	1	4	0	.316
Brown 3b	3	0	2	0	0	1	.357
a-Coleman pr-2b	1	1	0	0	0	0	.250
Collins rf-1b	5	1	1	0	0	0	.235
Lopat p	5	0	0	0	0	0	.125
TOTALS	**39**	**13**	**12**	**2**	**12**	**8**	**.247**

a - Ran for Brown in the 7th

BATTING: 2B: Mize (1, Spencer), DiMaggio (1, Corwin). **3B:** Woodling (1, Konikowski). **HR:** McDougald (1, 3th off Jansen 3 on, 2 out), Rizzuto (1, 4th off Kennedy 1 on, 1 out). **RBI:** Rizzuto 3 (3), Berra 1 (1), DiMaggio 3 (5), Mize 1 (1), McDougald 4 (6). **2-out RBI:** DiMaggio 3, Mize 1, McDougald 4. **Runners left in scoring position, 2 out:** Rizzuto 1, Bauer 1, McDougald 1, Collins 1. **Team LOB:** 7 **FIELDING: E:** Woodling (1). **DP:** 1 (Lopat-McDougald-Mize).

NY GIANTS	AB	R	H	HR	RBI	BB	AVG
Stanky 2b	4	0	0	0	0	0	.118
Dark ss	4	1	2	0	0	0	.429
Thomson 3b	4	0	0	0	0	0	.235
Irvin lf	4	0	2	0	1	0	.550
Lockman 1b	4	0	0	0	0	0	.150
Mays cf	2	0	0	0	0	1	.105
Hartung rf	3	0	0	0	0	0	.000
Westrum c	3	0	1	0	0	0	.214
Jansen p	0	0	0	0	0	0	.000
a-Lohrke ph	1	0	0	0	0	0	.000
Kennedy p	0	0	0	0	0	0	.000
b-Rigney ph	1	0	0	0	0	0	.000
Spencer p	0	0	0	0	0	0	.000
Corwin p	0	0	0	0	0	0	.000
c-Williams ph	1	0	0	0	0	0	.000
Konikowski p	0	0	0	0	0	0	.000
TOTALS	**31**	**1**	**5**	**0**	**1**	**1**	**.220**

a - Batted for Jansen in the 3th
b - Batted for Kennedy in the 5th
c - Batted for Corwin in the 8th

BATTING: 2B: Westrum (1, Lopat). **RBI:** Irvin 1 (3). **2-out RBI:** Irvin 1. **Runners left in scoring position, 2 out:** Stanky 1, Lockman 1. **GIDP:** Hartung. **Team LOB:** 4 **FIELDING: E:** Thomson (2), Irvin (1), Hartung (1). **Outfield assists:** Hartung (1).

NY YANKEES	IP	H	R	ER	BB	SO	HR	ERA
Lopat (W, 2-0)	9	5	1	0	1	3	0	0.50

NY GIANTS	IP	H	R	ER	BB	SO	HR	ERA
Jansen (L, 0-2)	3	3	5	5	4	1	1	7.00
Kennedy	2	3	2	2	1	2	1	6.00
Spencer	1.1	4	6	6	3	0	0	18.90
Corwin	1.2	1	0	0	0	1	0	0.00
Konikowski	1	1	0	0	0	0	0	0.00

WP: Corwin 1. **IBB:** Mize (by Jansen). **Ground balls-fly balls:** Lopat 13-10, Jansen 6-3, Kennedy 2-2, Spencer 3-1, Corwin 3-1, Konikowski 1-1. **Batters faced:** Lopat 32, Jansen 17, Kennedy 10, Spencer 11, Corwin 6, Konikowski 3. **UMPIRES:** hp—Summers, 1b—Ballanfant, 2b—Paparella, 3b—Barlick, lf—Stevens, rf—Gore **T:** 2:31 **A:** 47,530

GAME 6 Yankees 4 Giants 3
Yankee Stadium 10/10/51

NY GIANTS	AB	R	H	HR	RBI	BB	AVG
Stanky 2b	5	1	1	0	1	0	.136
Dark ss	3	1	1	0	0	2	.417
Lockman 1b	5	0	3	0	0	0	.240
Irvin lf	4	0	0	0	1	1	.458
Thomson 3b	4	0	1	0	1	1	.238
Thompson rf	3	0	1	0	0	1	.143
d-Yvars ph	1	0	0	0	0	0	.000
Westrum c	3	0	1	0	0	1	.235
b-Williams pr	0	0	0	0	0	0	.000
Jansen p	0	0	0	0	0	0	.000
Mays cf	3	1	2	0	0	1	.182
Koslo p	2	0	0	0	0	0	.000
a-Rigney ph	1	0	1	0	0	0	.250
Hearn p	0	0	0	0	0	0	.000
c-Noble ph-c	1	0	0	0	0	0	.000
TOTALS	**35**	**3**	**11**	**0**	**3**	**7**	**.237**

a - Batted for Koslo in the 7th
b - Ran for Westrum in the 8th
c - Batted for Hearn in the 8th
d - Batted for Thompson in the 9th

BATTING: 2B: Lockman (2, Raschi). **RBI:** Stanky 1 (1), Irvin 1 (4), Thomson 1 (2). **Runners left in scoring position, 2 out:** Lockman 1, Irvin 2, Yvars 1, Koslo 1, Noble 2. **GIDP:** Lockman, Westrum, Thompson. **Team LOB:** 12 **FIELDING: E:** Thompson (2). **DP:** 1 (Dark-Stanky-Lockman).

NY YANKEES	AB	R	H	HR	RBI	BB	AVG
Rizzuto ss	4	0	1	0	0	0	.320
Coleman 2b	4	1	1	0	0	0	.250
Berra c	4	1	2	0	0	0	.261
DiMaggio cf	2	1	1	0	0	2	.261
McDougald 3b	4	0	0	0	1	0	.261
Mize 1b	2	1	1	0	0	1	.286
Collins 1b	1	0	0	0	0	0	.222
Bauer rf	3	0	1	0	3	0	.167
Woodling lf	3	0	0	0	0	0	.167
Raschi p	1	0	0	0	0	1	.000
Sain p	1	0	0	0	0	0	.000
Kuzava p	0	0	0	0	0	0	.000
TOTALS	**29**	**4**	**7**	**0**	**4**	**4**	**.246**

BATTING: 2B: Berra (1, Koslo), DiMaggio (2, Jansen). **3B:** Bauer (1, Koslo). **RBI:** McDougald 1 (7), Bauer 3 (3). **2-out RBI:** Bauer 3. **Runners left in scoring position, 2 out:** Mize 1, Woodling 1. **GIDP:** Rizzuto. **Team LOB:** 5 **BASERUNNING: CS:** McDougald (1, 2nd base off Jansen/Noble). **FIELDING: PB:** Berra. **DP:** 3 (Rizzuto-Mize 2, Rizzuto-Coleman-Mize).

NY GIANTS	IP	H	R	ER	BB	SO	HR	ERA
Koslo (L, 1-1)	6	5	4	4	4	3	0	3.00
Hearn	1	1	0	0	0	0	0	1.04
Jansen	1	1	0	0	0	0	0	6.30

NY YANKEES	IP	H	R	ER	BB	SO	HR	ERA
Raschi (W, 1-1)	6	7	1	0	5	1	0	0.87
Sain	2	4	2	2	2	2	0	9.00
Kuzava (S, 1)	1	0	0	0	0	0	0	0.00

WP: Koslo 1. **IBB:** DiMaggio 2 (by Koslo). **Ground balls-fly balls:** Koslo 4-10, Hearn 2-1, Jansen 1-1, Raschi 7-7, Sain 0-4, Kuzava 0-3. **Batters faced:** Koslo 26, Hearn 4, Jansen 3, Raschi 27, Sain 12, Kuzava 3. **UMPIRES:** hp—Ballanfant, 1b—Paparella, 2b—Barlick, 3b—Summers, lf—Gore, rf—Stewart **T:** 2:59 **A:** 61,711

1952 NY YANKEES DEF. BROOKLYN, 4-3

GAME 1 Brooklyn 4 New York 2
Ebbets Field 10/01/52

NY YANKEES	AB	R	H	HR	RBI	BB	AVG
Bauer rf	4	0	0	0	1	0	.000
Rizzuto ss	4	0	1	0	0	0	.250
Mantle cf	4	0	2	0	0	0	.500
Berra c	4	0	0	0	0	0	.000
Collins 1b	4	0	0	0	0	0	.000
Noren lf	3	0	0	0	0	1	.000
McDougald 3b	2	1	1	1	1	1	.500
Martin 2b	3	0	1	0	0	0	.333
Reynolds p	2	0	0	0	0	0	.000
a-Woodling ph	1	1	1	0	0	0	1.000
Scarborough p	0	0	0	0	0	0	.000
TOTALS	**31**	**2**	**6**	**1**	**2**	**2**	**.194**

a - Batted for Reynolds in the 8th

BATTING: 3B: Woodling (1, Black). **HR:** McDougald (1, 3th off Black 0 on, 0 out). **RBI:** Bauer 1 (1), McDougald 1 (1). **Runners left in scoring position, 2 out:** Bauer 1, Noren 1. **GIDP:** McDougald. **Team LOB:** 4 **FIELDING: E:** McDougald (1), Reynolds (1). **DP:** 1 (Martin-Collins).

BROOKLYN	AB	R	H	HR	RBI	BB	AVG
Cox 3b	3	0	0	0	0	1	.000
Reese ss	4	2	2	1	1	0	.500
Snider cf	4	1	2	1	2	0	.500
Robinson 2b	2	1	1	1	1	1	.500
Campanella c	3	0	1	0	0	0	.333
Pafko lf	3	0	0	0	0	0	.000
Hodges 1b	3	0	0	0	0	0	.000
Furillo rf	3	0	0	0	0	0	.000
Black p	3	0	0	0	0	0	.000
TOTALS	**28**	**4**	**6**	**3**	**4**	**2**	**.214**

BATTING: 2B: Snider (1, Reynolds). **HR:** Robinson (1, 2nd off Reynolds 0 on, 0 out), Snider (1, 6th off Reynolds 1 on, 2 out), Reese (1, 8th off Scarborough 0 on, 2 out). **RBI:** Reese 1 (1), Snider 2 (2), Robinson 1 (1). **2-out RBI:** Reese 1, Snider 2. **Runners left in scoring position, 2 out:** Campanella 1. **GIDP:** Campanella. **Team LOB:** 2 **BASERUNNING: CS:** Campanella (1, 2nd base off Reynolds/Berra), Cox (1, 2nd base off Reynolds/Berra). **FIELDING: Outfield assists:** Pafko (1). **DP:** 1 (Cox-Robinson-Hodges).

NY YANKEES	IP	H	R	ER	BB	SO	HR	ERA
Reynolds (L, 0-1)	7	5	3	3	2	4	2	3.86
Scarborough	1	1	1	1	0	1	1	9.00

BROOKLYN	IP	H	R	ER	BB	SO	HR	ERA
Black (W, 1-0)	9	6	2	2	2	6	1	2.00

WP: Reynolds 1. **Ground balls-fly balls:** Reynolds 7-8, Scarborough 2-0, Black 8-11. **Batters faced:** Reynolds 26, Scarborough 4, Black 33. **UMPIRES:** hp—Pinelli, 1b—Passarella, 2b—Goetz, 3b—McKinley, lf—Boggess, rf—Honochick **T:** 2:21 **A:** 34,861

GAME 2 New York 7 Brooklyn 1
Ebbets Field 10/02/52

NY YANKEES	AB	R	H	HR	RBI	BB	AVG
Bauer rf	4	0	1	0	0	1	.125
Rizzuto ss	4	0	0	0	0	1	.125
Mantle cf	5	2	3	0	0	0	.556
Woodling lf	4	1	1	0	0	1	.400
Berra c	3	0	2	0	1	1	.286
Collins 1b	3	1	0	0	0	1	.000
McDougald 3b	3	2	1	0	1	1	.400
Martin 2b	4	1	2	1	4	0	.429
Raschi p	3	0	0	0	0	1	.000
TOTALS	**33**	**7**	**10**	**1**	**6**	**7**	**.250**

BATTING: 2B: Mantle (1, Erskine). **HR:** Martin (1, 6th off Loes 2 on, 1 out). **RBI:** Berra 1 (1), McDougald 1 (2), Martin 4 (4). **Runners left in scoring position, 2 out:** Rizzuto 1, Martin 1, Raschi 1. **GIDP:** Bauer. **Team LOB:** 6 **BASERUNNING: SB:** McDougald (1, 2nd base off Erskine/Campanella). **CS:** Bauer (1, 2nd base off Erskine/Campanella), Rizzuto (1, 2nd base off Erskine/Campanella).

BROOKLYN	AB	R	H	HR	RBI	BB	AVG
Cox 3b	4	0	0	0	0	0	.000
Reese ss	3	1	1	0	0	1	.429
Snider cf	4	0	1	0	0	0	.375
Robinson 2b	3	0	0	0	0	1	.200
Campanella c	4	0	1	0	1	0	.286
Pafko lf	4	0	0	0	0	0	.000
Hodges 1b	3	0	0	0	0	1	.000
Furillo rf	3	0	0	0	0	1	.000
Erskine p	2	0	0	0	0	0	.000
Loes p	0	0	0	0	0	0	.000
a-Nelson ph	0	0	0	0	0	1	.000
Lehman p	0	0	0	0	0	0	.000
TOTALS	**30**	**1**	**3**	**0**	**1**	**5**	**.155**

a - Batted for Loes in the 7th

BATTING: RBI: Campanella 1 (1). **2-out RBI:** Campanella 1. **Runners left in scoring position, 2 out:** Pafko 1, Erskine 2. **Team LOB:** 7 **FIELDING: DP:** 1 (Reese-Robinson-Hodges).

NY YANKEES	IP	H	R	ER	BB	SO	HR	ERA
Raschi (W, 1-0)	9	3	1	1	5	9	0	1.00

BROOKLYN	IP	H	R	ER	BB	SO	HR	ERA
Erskine (L, 0-1)	5	6	5	4	6	4	0	7.20
Loes	2	2	2	2	0	2	1	9.00
Lehman	2	2	0	0	1	0	0	0.00

WP: Erskine 1. **Ground balls-fly balls:** Raschi 7-11, Erskine 6-1, Loes 2-2, Lehman 2-4. **Batters faced:** Raschi 35, Erskine 23, Loes 8, Lehman 9. **UMPIRES:** hp—Passarella, 1b—Goetz, 2b—McKinley, 3b—Pinelli, lf—Honochick, rf—Boggess **T:** 2:47 **A:** 33,792

GAME 3 Brooklyn 5 New York 3
Yankee Stadium 10/03/52

BROOKLYN	AB	R	H	HR	RBI	BB	AVG
Furillo rf	5	1	1	0	0	0	.091
Reese ss	5	1	3	0	1	0	.500
Robinson 2b	4	2	2	0	1	1	.333
Campanella c	5	0	1	0	0	0	.250
Pafko lf	5	0	2	0	1	0	.167
Snider cf	5	0	1	0	0	0	.308
Hodges 1b	3	0	0	0	0	1	.000
Cox 3b	2	1	1	0	0	2	.111
Roe p	2	0	0	0	0	0	.000
TOTALS	**36**	**5**	**11**	**0**	**3**	**4**	**.213**

BATTING: 2B: Furillo (1, Lopat). **S:** Roe, Roe. **RBI:** Reese 1 (2), Robinson 1 (2), Pafko 1 (1). **2-out RBI:** Reese 1. **Runners left in scoring position, 2 out:** Reese 1, Roe 3. **Team LOB:** 10 **BASERUNNING: SB:** Snider (1, 2nd base off Lopat/Berra), Reese (1, 3rd base off Gorman/Berra), Robinson (1, 3rd base off Gorman/Berra).

NY YANKEES	AB	R	H	HR	RBI	BB	AVG
Rizzuto ss	4	0	0	0	0	1	.083
Collins 1b	4	0	0	0	0	0	.000
b-Sain ph	1	0	0	0	0	0	.000
Mantle cf	4	0	0	0	0	0	.385
Woodling lf	4	0	1	0	0	0	.333
Berra c	4	1	3	1	1	0	.455
Bauer rf	2	1	0	0	0	1	.100
McDougald 3b	4	0	0	0	0	0	.222
Martin 2b	1	0	0	0	0	2	.375
Lopat p	2	0	1	0	1	1	.500
Gorman p	0	0	0	0	0	0	.000
a-Mize ph	1	1	1	1	1	0	1.000
TOTALS	**31**	**3**	**6**	**2**	**3**	**5**	**.232**

a - Batted for Gorman in the 9th
b - Batted for Collins in the 9th

BATTING: 2B: Berra (1, Roe). **HR:** Berra (1, 8th off Roe 0 on, 1 out), Mize (1, 9th off Roe 0 on, 1 out). **S:** Bauer. **RBI:** Berra 1 (2), Lopat 1 (1), Mize 1 (1). **2-out RBI:** Lopat 1. **Runners left in scoring position, 2 out:** Rizzuto 3, Bauer 1. **Team LOB:** 8 **BASERUNNING: CS:** Martin (1, 2nd base off Roe/Campanella). **FIELDING: E:** McDougald (2), Berra (1). **PB:** Berra. **DP:** 2 (Rizzuto-Martin, McDougald-Collins).

BROOKLYN	IP	H	R	ER	BB	SO	HR	ERA
Roe (W, 1-0)	9	6	3	3	5	5	2	3.00
NY YANKEES	**IP**	**H**	**R**	**ER**	**BB**	**SO**	**HR**	**ERA**
Lopat (L, 0-1)	8.1	10	5	5	4	0	0	5.40
Gorman	0.2	1	0	0	0	0	0	0.00

IBB: Cox 2 (by Lopat), Martin (by Roe), Hodges (by Lopat). **HBP:** Martin (by Roe). **Ground balls-fly balls:** Roe 11-9, Lopat 8-15, Gorman 0-2. **Batters faced:** Roe 38, Lopat 39, Gorman 3. **UMPIRES:** hp—Goetz, 1b—McKinley, 2b—Pinelli, 3b—Passarella, lf—Boggess, rf—Honochick **T:** 2:56 **A:** 66,698

GAME 4 New York 2 Brooklyn 0
Yankee Stadium 10/04/52

BROOKLYN	AB	R	H	HR	RBI	BB	AVG
Cox 3b	3	0	0	0	0	0	.083
b-Nelson ph	1	0	0	0	0	0	.000
Morgan 3b	0	0	0	0	0	0	.000
Reese ss	4	0	2	0	0	0	.500
Snider cf	4	0	0	0	0	0	.235
Robinson 2b	4	0	0	0	0	0	.231
Campanella c	3	0	0	0	0	1	.200
Pafko lf	3	0	1	0	0	0	.200
Hodges 1b	2	0	0	0	0	1	.000
Furillo rf	2	0	1	0	0	0	.154
Black p	1	0	0	0	0	1	.000
a-Shuba ph	1	0	0	0	0	0	.000
Rutherford p	0	0	0	0	0	0	.000
TOTALS	**28**	**0**	**4**	**0**	**0**	**3**	**.197**

a - Batted for Black in the 8th
b - Batted for Cox in the 8th

BATTING: S: Furillo, Pafko. **Runners left in scoring position, 2 out:** Cox 1, Campanella 1. **GIDP:** Hodges. **Team LOB:** 5 **BASERUNNING: CS:** Reese (1, 2nd base off Reynolds/Berra). **FIELDING: E:** Reese (1).

NY YANKEES	AB	R	H	HR	RBI	BB	AVG
McDougald 3b	3	0	0	0	0	1	.167
Rizzuto ss	2	0	0	0	0	2	.071
Mantle cf	3	1	1	0	1	1	.375
Mize 1b	3	1	2	1	1	1	.750
a-Collins pr-1b	0	0	0	0	0	0	.000
Berra c	4	0	0	0	0	0	.333
Woodling lf	3	0	1	0	0	1	.333
Bauer rf	4	0	0	0	0	0	.071
Martin 2b	3	0	0	0	0	0	.273
Reynolds p	3	0	0	0	0	0	.000
TOTALS	**28**	**2**	**4**	**1**	**2**	**6**	**.211**

a - Ran for Mize in the 8th

BATTING: 2B: Woodling (1, Black), Mize (1, Black). **3B:** Mantle (1, Rutherford). **HR:** Mize (2, 4th off Black 0 on, 0 out). **RBI:** Mantle 1 (1), Mize 1 (2). **Runners left in scoring position, 2 out:** Mantle 1, Bauer 1, Martin 2. **Team LOB:** 8 **FIELDING: E:** Martin (1). **DP:** 1 (Rizzuto-Martin-Mize).

BROOKLYN	IP	H	R	ER	BB	SO	HR	ERA
Black (L, 1-1)	7	3	1	1	5	2	1	1.69
Rutherford	1	1	1	1	1	1	0	9.00
NY YANKEES	**IP**	**H**	**R**	**ER**	**BB**	**SO**	**HR**	**ERA**
Reynolds (W, 1-1)	9	4	0	0	3	10	0	1.69

IBB: Woodling (by Black). **Ground balls-fly balls:** Black 10-9, Rutherford 1-1, Reynolds 7-7. **Batters faced:** Black 29, Rutherford 5, Reynolds 32. **UMPIRES:** hp—McKinley, 1b—Pinelli, 2b—Passarella, 3b—Goetz, lf—Honochick, rf—Boggess **T:** 2:33 **A:** 71,787

GAME 5 Brooklyn 6 New York 5
Yankee Stadium 10/05/52

BROOKLYN	AB	R	H	HR	RBI	BB	AVG
Cox 3b	5	2	3	0	0	0	.235
Reese ss	5	0	1	0	1	0	.429
Snider cf	5	1	3	1	4	0	.318
Robinson 2b	2	1	0	0	0	4	.200
Shuba lf	2	0	1	0	0	0	.333
Furillo rf	4	0	1	0	0	0	.176
Campanella c	5	0	0	0	0	0	.150
Pafko rf-lf	4	0	1	0	1	0	.211
Holmes lf	1	0	0	0	0	0	.000
Hodges 1b	3	1	0	0	0	2	.000
Erskine p	4	1	0	0	0	0	.000
TOTALS	**40**	**6**	**10**	**1**	**6**	**6**	**.210**

BATTING: 2B: Furillo (2, Sain), Snider (2, Sain). **HR:** Snider (2, 5th off Blackwell 1 on, 2 out). **S:** Erskine, Cox, Reese. **RBI:** Reese 1 (3), Snider 4 (6), Pafko 1 (2). **2-out RBI:** Snider 3. **Runners left in scoring position, 2 out:** Cox 2, Furillo 2, Hodges 1. **GIDP:** Snider, Furillo. **Team LOB:** 11 **BASERUNNING: SB:** Robinson (2, 3rd base off Blackwell/Berra).

NY YANKEES	AB	R	H	HR	RBI	BB	AVG
McDougald 3b	4	1	0	0	1	1	.125
Rizzuto ss	5	1	1	0	0	0	.105
Mantle cf	5	0	1	0	0	0	.333
Mize 1b	5	1	1	1	3	0	.444
Berra c	4	0	0	0	0	1	.263
Woodling lf	4	0	0	0	0	0	.250
Bauer rf	3	1	0	0	0	1	.059
Martin 2b	4	1	1	0	0	0	.267
Blackwell p	1	0	0	0	0	0	.000
a-Noren ph	1	0	1	0	1	0	.250
Sain p	2	0	0	0	0	0	.000
TOTALS	**38**	**5**	**5**	**1**	**5**	**3**	**.193**

a - Batted for Blackwell in the 5th

BATTING: HR: Mize (3, 5th off Erskine 2 on, 2 out). **RBI:** McDougald 1 (3), Mize 3 (5), Noren 1 (1). **2-out RBI:** Mize 3. **Team LOB:** 3 **FIELDING: E:** Rizzuto (1). **DP:** 2 (Martin-Rizzuto-Mize, McDougald-Berra-Mize).

BROOKLYN	IP	H	R	ER	BB	SO	HR	ERA
Erskine (W, 1-1)	11	5	5	5	3	6	1	5.06
NY YANKEES	**IP**	**H**	**R**	**ER**	**BB**	**SO**	**HR**	**ERA**
Blackwell	5	4	4	4	3	4	1	7.20
Sain (L, 0-1)	6	6	2	2	3	3	0	3.00

IBB: Robinson 2 (by Sain). **HBP:** Snider (by Sain). **Ground balls-fly balls:** Erskine 6-21, Blackwell 3-6, Sain 8-6. **Batters faced:** Erskine 41, Blackwell 22, Sain 28. **UMPIRES:** hp—Pinelli, 1b—Passarella, 2b—Goetz, 3b—McKinley, lf—Boggess, rf—Honochick **T:** 3:00 **A:** 70,536

GAME 6 New York 3 Brooklyn 2
Ebbets Field 10/06/52

NY YANKEES	AB	R	H	HR	RBI	BB	AVG
McDougald 3b	4	0	1	0	0	1	.150
Rizzuto ss	4	0	1	0	0	1	.130
Mantle cf	3	1	1	1	1	2	.333
Mize 1b	3	0	0	0	0	1	.333
Collins 1b	1	0	0	0	0	0	.000
Berra c	5	1	1	1	1	0	.250
Woodling lf	3	1	2	0	0	1	.316
Noren rf	4	0	2	0	0	0	.375
Bauer rf	0	0	0	0	0	0	.059
Martin 2b	4	0	0	0	0	0	.211
Raschi p	3	0	1	0	1	0	.167
Reynolds p	1	0	0	0	0	0	.000
TOTALS	**35**	**3**	**9**	**2**	**3**	**6**	**.204**

BATTING: HR: Berra (2, 7th off Loes 0 on, 0 out), Mantle (1, 8th off Loes 0 on, 0 out). **RBI:** Mantle 1 (2), Berra 1 (3), Raschi 1 (1). **2-out RBI:** Raschi 1. **Runners left in scoring position, 2 out:** Rizzuto 1, Berra 2, Woodling 1, Martin 1. **GIDP:** Raschi. **Team LOB:** 11

BROOKLYN	AB	R	H	HR	RBI	BB	AVG
Cox 3b	5	0	2	0	0	0	.273
Reese ss	4	0	0	0	0	0	.360
Snider cf	3	2	2	2	2	1	.360
Robinson 2b	4	0	0	0	0	0	.158
Shuba lf	4	0	1	0	0	0	.286
a-Amoros pr	0	0	0	0	0	0	.000
Holmes lf	0	0	0	0	0	0	.000
Campanella c	4	0	1	0	0	0	.167
Hodges 1b	3	0	0	0	0	0	.000
b-Nelson ph	1	0	0	0	0	0	.000
Furillo rf	3	0	1	0	0	1	.200
Loes p	3	0	1	0	0	0	.333
Roe p	0	0	0	0	0	0	.000
c-Pafko ph	1	0	0	0	0	0	.200
TOTALS	**35**	**2**	**8**	**2**	**2**	**2**	**.213**

a - Ran for Shuba in the 8th
b - Batted for Hodges in the 9th
c - Batted for Roe in the 9th

BATTING: 2B: Cox (1, Raschi), Shuba (1, Raschi). **HR:** Snider 2 (4, 6th off Raschi 0 on, 0 out, 8th off Raschi 0 on, 1 out). **RBI:** Snider 2 (8). **Runners left in scoring position, 2 out:** Cox 1, Shuba 1, Campanella 1. **Team LOB:** 8 **BASERUNNING: SB:** Loes (1, 2nd base off Raschi/Berra). **FIELDING: DP:** 1 (Hodges-Reese-Robinson).

NY YANKEES	IP	H	R	ER	BB	SO	HR	ERA
Raschi (W, 2-0)	7.2	8	2	2	1	9	2	1.62
Reynolds (S, 1)	1.1	0	0	0	1	2	0	1.56
BROOKLYN	**IP**	**H**	**R**	**ER**	**BB**	**SO**	**HR**	**ERA**
Loes (L, 0-1)	8.1	9	3	3	5	3	2	4.35
Roe	0.2	0	0	0	1	1	0	2.79

BK: Loes 1. **Ground balls-fly balls:** Raschi 10-4, Reynolds 1-1, Loes 8-13, Roe 0-1. **Batters faced:** Raschi 32, Reynolds 5, Loes 38, Roe 3. **UMPIRES:** hp—Passarella, 1b—Goetz, 2b—McKinley, 3b—Pinelli, lf—Honochick, rf—Boggess **T:** 2:56 **A:** 30,037

GAME 7 New York 4 Brooklyn 2
Ebbets Field 10/07/52

NY YANKEES	AB	R	H	HR	RBI	BB	AVG
McDougald 3b	5	1	2	0	0	0	.200
Rizzuto ss	4	1	1	0	0	0	.148
Mantle cf	5	1	2	1	2	0	.345
Mize 1b	3	0	2	0	1	1	.400
Collins 1b	0	0	0	0	0	0	.000
Berra c	4	0	0	0	0	0	.214
Woodling lf	4	1	2	1	1	0	.348
Noren rf	2	0	0	0	0	0	.300
a-Bauer ph-rf	1	0	0	0	0	1	.056
Martin 2b	4	0	1	0	0	0	.217
Lopat p	1	0	0	0	0	0	.333
Reynolds p	1	0	0	0	0	0	.000
b-Houk ph	1	0	0	0	0	0	.000
Raschi p	0	0	0	0	0	0	.167
Kuzava p	1	0	0	0	0	0	.000
TOTALS	**36**	**4**	**10**	**2**	**4**	**2**	**.216**

a - Batted for Noren in the 6th
b - Batted for Reynolds in the 7th

BATTING: 2B: Rizzuto (1, Black). **HR:** Woodling (1, 5th off Black 0 on, 0 out), Mantle (2, 6th off Black 0 on, 1 out). **S:** Rizzuto. **RBI:** Mantle 2 (4), Mize 1 (6), Woodling 1 (1). **2-out RBI:** Mantle 1. **Runners left in scoring position, 2 out:** McDougald 1, Martin 2. **GIDP:** Berra. **Team LOB:** 8 **FIELDING: E:** McDougald 2 (4), Woodling (1). **DP:** 1 (Rizzuto-Martin-Mize).

BROOKLYN	AB	R	H	HR	RBI	BB	AVG
Cox 3b	5	1	2	0	0	0	.296
Reese ss	4	0	1	0	1	1	.345
Snider cf	4	1	1	0	0	0	.345
Robinson 2b	4	0	1	0	0	0	.174
Campanella c	4	0	2	0	0	0	.214
Hodges 1b	4	0	0	0	1	0	.000
Shuba lf	3	0	1	0	0	0	.300
b-Pafko ph	1	0	0	0	0	0	.190
Holmes lf	0	0	0	0	0	0	.000
Furillo rf	3	0	0	0	0	1	.174
Black p	2	0	0	0	0	0	.000
Roe p	0	0	0	0	0	0	.000
a-Nelson ph	1	0	0	0	0	0	.000
Erskine p	0	0	0	0	0	0	.000
c-Morgan ph	1	0	0	0	0	0	.000
TOTALS	**36**	**2**	**8**	**0**	**2**	**2**	**.215**

a - Batted for Roe in the 7th
b - Batted for Shuba in the 8th
c - Batted for Erskine in the 9th

BATTING: 2B: Cox (2, Reynolds). **RBI:** Reese 1 (4), Hodges 1 (1). **Runners left in scoring position, 2 out:** Robinson 3, Furillo 1. **GIDP:** Hodges. **Team LOB:** 9 **FIELDING: E:** Cox (1). **DP:** 1 (Robinson-Reese-Hodges).

NY YANKEES	IP	H	R	ER	BB	SO	HR	ERA
Lopat	3	4	1	1	0	3	0	4.76
Reynolds (W, 2-1)	3	3	1	1	0	2	0	1.77
Raschi	0.1	1	0	0	2	0	0	1.59
Kuzava (S, 1)	2.2	0	0	0	0	2	0	0.00
BROOKLYN	**IP**	**H**	**R**	**ER**	**BB**	**SO**	**HR**	**ERA**
Black (L, 1-2)	5.1	6	3	3	1	1	2	2.53
Roe	1.2	3	1	1	0	1	0	3.18
Erskine	2	1	0	0	1	0	0	4.50

Ground balls-fly balls: Lopat 4-3, Reynolds 3-3, Raschi 0-1, Kuzava 2-5, Black 7-7, Roe 2-2, Erskine 2-4. **Batters faced:** Lopat 14, Reynolds 11, Raschi 4, Kuzava 9, Black 22, Roe 9, Erskine 8. **UMPIRES:** hp—Goetz, 1b—McKinley, 2b—Pinelli, 3b—Passarella, lf—Boggess, rf—Honochick **T:** 2:54 **A:** 33,195

1953 NY YANKEES DEF. BROOKLYN, 4-2

GAME 1 New York 9 Brooklyn 5
Yankee Stadium 09/30/53

BROOKLYN	AB	R	H	HR	RBI	BB	AVG
Gilliam 2b	5	1	2	1	1	0	.400
Reese ss	3	0	0	0	0	2	.000
Snider cf	5	0	2	0	0	0	.400
Robinson lf	4	0	0	0	0	1	.000
Campanella c	4	1	1	0	0	0	.250
Hodges 1b	5	1	3	1	1	0	.600
Furillo rf	4	0	1	0	1	1	.250
Cox 3b	5	1	2	0	0	0	.400
Erskine p	0	0	0	0	0	0	.000
a-Belardi ph	1	0	0	0	0	0	.000
Hughes p	1	0	0	0	0	0	.000
b-Shuba ph	1	1	1	1	2	0	1.000
Labine p	1	0	0	0	0	0	.000
Wade p	0	0	0	0	0	0	.000
TOTALS	**39**	**5**	**12**	**3**	**5**	**4**	**.308**

a - Batted for Erskine in the 2nd
b - Batted for Hughes in the 6th

BATTING: 2B: Cox (1, Reynolds), Snider (1, Reynolds). **HR:** Gilliam (1, 5th off Reynolds 0 on, 1 out), Hodges (1, 6th off Reynolds 0 on, 0 out), Shuba (1, 6th off Reynolds 1 on, 1 out). **RBI:** Gilliam 1 (1), Hodges 1 (1), Furillo 1 (1), Shuba 2 (2). **Runners left in scoring position, 2 out:** Gilliam 1, Robinson 2, Campanella 1, Belardi 2. **Team LOB:** 12 **FIELDING: E:** Hughes (1).

NY YANKEES	AB	R	H	HR	RBI	BB	AVG
McDougald 3b	5	0	0	0	0	0	.000
Collins 1b	4	2	2	1	2	1	.500
Bauer rf	5	1	2	0	1	0	.400
Berra c	4	1	2	1	1	0	.500
Mantle cf	3	1	1	0	0	1	.333
Woodling lf	3	1	1	0	0	1	.333
Martin 2b	4	1	3	0	3	0	.750
Rizzuto ss	3	1	0	0	0	1	.000
Reynolds p	1	0	0	0	0	1	.000
Sain p	2	1	1	0	2	0	.500
TOTALS	**34**	**9**	**12**	**2**	**9**	**5**	**.353**

BATTING: 2B: Sain (1, Wade). **3B:** Bauer (1, Erskine), Martin (1, Erskine). **HR:** Berra (1, 5th off Hughes 0 on, 2 out), Collins (1, 7th off Labine 0 on, 2 out). **RBI:** Collins 2 (2), Bauer 1 (1), Berra 1 (1), Martin 3 (3), Sain 2 (2). **2-out RBI:** Collins 2, Berra 1, Martin 3. **Runners left in scoring position, 2 out:** McDougald 1, Mantle 1, Rizzuto 1. **Team LOB:** 6 **BASERUNNING: SB:** Martin (1, 2nd base off Wade/Campanella). **CS:** Mantle (1, 2nd base off Hughes/Campanella), Martin (1, 2nd base off Labine/Campanella).

BROOKLYN	IP	H	R	ER	BB	SO	HR	ERA
Erskine	1	2	4	4	3	1	0	36.00
Hughes	4	3	1	1	1	3	1	2.25
Labine (L, 0-1)	1.2	4	1	1	0	1	1	5.40
Wade	1.1	3	3	3	1	2	0	20.25
NY YANKEES	**IP**	**H**	**R**	**ER**	**BB**	**SO**	**HR**	**ERA**
Reynolds	5.1	7	4	4	3	6	3	6.75
Sain (W, 1-0)	3.2	5	1	1	1	0	0	2.45

HBP: Campanella (by Reynolds). **Ground balls-fly balls:** Erskine 1-1, Hughes 4-4, Labine 2-1, Wade 1-1, Reynolds 2-8, Sain 6-5. **Batters faced:** Erskine 8, Hughes 15, Labine 8, Wade 8, Reynolds 27, Sain 17. **UMPIRES:** hp—Grieve, 1b—Stewart, 2b—Hurley, 3b—Gore, lf—Soar, rf—Dascoli **T:** 3:10 **A:** 69,734

GAME 2 New York 4 Brooklyn 2
Yankee Stadium 10/01/53

BROOKLYN	AB	R	H	HR	RBI	BB	AVG
Gilliam 2b	5	0	0	0	0	0	.200
Reese ss	3	0	2	0	0	2	.333
Snider cf	5	0	0	0	0	0	.200
Robinson lf	4	0	1	0	0	0	.125
Campanella c	4	0	0	0	0	0	.125
Hodges 1b	3	1	2	0	0	1	.625
Furillo rf	4	1	2	0	0	0	.375
Cox 3b	3	0	1	0	2	1	.375
Roe p	3	0	0	0	0	0	.000
a-Williams ph	1	0	1	0	0	0	1.000
TOTALS	**35**	**2**	**9**	**0**	**2**	**4**	**.284**

a - Batted for Roe in the 9th

BATTING: 2B: Cox (2, Lopat), Furillo (1, Lopat). **3B:** Reese (1, Lopat). **RBI:** Cox 2 (2). **2-out RBI:** Cox 2. **Runners left in scoring position, 2 out:** Snider 1, Robinson 2, Campanella 1, Roe 3. **GIDP:** Furillo. **Team LOB:** 10 **BASERUNNING: SB:** Hodges (1, 3rd base off Lopat/Berra). **FIELDING: E:** Furillo (1).

NY YANKEES	AB	R	H	HR	RBI	BB	AVG
Woodling lf	3	1	0	0	0	1	.167
Collins 1b	3	0	0	0	0	1	.286
Bauer rf	4	1	1	0	0	0	.333
Berra c	3	0	0	0	1	1	.286
Mantle cf	3	1	1	1	2	1	.333
McDougald 3b	3	0	0	0	0	0	.000
Martin 2b	3	1	2	1	1	0	.714
Rizzuto ss	2	0	1	0	0	0	.200
Lopat p	3	0	0	0	0	0	.000
TOTALS	**27**	**4**	**5**	**2**	**4**	**4**	**.279**

BATTING: 2B: Rizzuto (1, Roe). **HR:** Martin (1, 7th off Roe 0 on, 0 out), Mantle (1, 8th off Roe 1 on, 2 out). **S:** Rizzuto. **RBI:** Berra 1 (2), Mantle 2 (2), Martin 1 (4). **2-out RBI:** Mantle 2. **Runners left in scoring position, 2 out:** Martin 2, Lopat 1. **Team LOB:** 5 **BASERUNNING: CS:** Berra (1, 2nd base off Roe/Campanella). **FIELDING: DP:** 1 (Martin-Rizzuto-Collins).

BROOKLYN	IP	H	R	ER	BB	SO	HR	ERA
Roe (L, 0-1)	8	5	4	4	4	4	2	4.50
NY YANKEES	**IP**	**H**	**R**	**ER**	**BB**	**SO**	**HR**	**ERA**
Lopat (W, 1-0)	9	9	2	2	4	3	0	2.00

IBB: Cox (by Lopat). **HBP:** McDougald (by Roe). **Ground balls-fly balls:** Roe 8-10, Lopat 14-9. **Batters faced:** Roe 33, Lopat 39. **UMPIRES:** hp—Stewart, 1b—Hurley, 2b—Gore, 3b—Grieve, lf—Dascoli, rf—Soar **T:** 2:42 **A:** 66,786

GAME 3 Brooklyn 3 New York 2
Ebbets Field 10/02/53

NY YANKEES	AB	R	H	HR	RBI	BB	AVG
McDougald 3b	4	0	1	0	1	0	.083
c-Noren ph	0	0	0	0	0	1	.000
Collins 1b	5	0	0	0	0	0	.167
Bauer rf	4	1	1	0	0	0	.308
Berra c	1	0	1	0	0	1	.375
Mantle cf	4	0	0	0	0	0	.200
Woodling lf	4	0	1	0	1	0	.200
Martin 2b	3	1	1	0	0	1	.600
Rizzuto ss	3	0	1	0	0	0	.250
a-Bollweg ph	1	0	0	0	0	0	.000
Raschi p	2	0	0	0	0	0	.000
b-Mize ph	1	0	0	0	0	0	.000
TOTALS	**32**	**2**	**6**	**0**	**2**	**3**	**.247**

a - Batted for Rizzuto in the 9th
b - Batted for Raschi in the 9th
c - Batted for McDougald in the 9th

BATTING: S: Raschi. **RBI:** McDougald 1 (1), Woodling 1 (1). **2-out RBI:** Woodling 1. **Runners left in scoring position, 2 out:** Bauer 1, Martin 1, Rizzuto 1. **Team LOB:** 9 **FIELDING: DP:** 1 (Rizzuto-Martin-Collins).

BROOKLYN	AB	R	H	HR	RBI	BB	AVG
Gilliam 2b	4	0	1	0	0	0	.214
Reese ss	4	0	1	0	0	0	.300
Snider cf	3	1	1	0	0	1	.231
Hodges 1b	2	0	1	0	0	2	.600
Campanella c	4	1	1	1	1	0	.167
Furillo rf	4	0	0	0	0	0	.250
Robinson lf	4	1	3	0	1	0	.333
Thompson lf	0	0	0	0	0	0	.000
Cox 3b	3	0	0	0	1	0	.273
Erskine p	3	0	1	0	0	0	.333
TOTALS	**31**	**3**	**9**	**1**	**3**	**3**	**.286**

BATTING: 2B: Robinson (1, Raschi). **HR:** Campanella (1, 8th off Raschi 0 on, 1 out). **S:** Cox. **RBI:** Campanella 1 (1), Robinson 1 (1), Cox 1 (3). **2-out RBI:** Robinson 1. **Runners left in scoring position, 2 out:** Reese 1, Campanella 1, Cox 1. **GIDP:** Furillo. **Team LOB:** 8 **BASERUNNING: CS:** Gilliam (1, 2nd base off Raschi/Berra).

NY YANKEES	IP	H	R	ER	BB	SO	HR	ERA
Raschi (L, 0-1)	8	9	3	3	3	4	1	3.38
BROOKLYN	**IP**	**H**	**R**	**ER**	**BB**	**SO**	**HR**	**ERA**
Erskine (W, 1-0)	9	6	2	2	3	14	0	5.40

WP: Erskine 1. **BK:** Raschi 1. **HBP:** Berra 2 (by Erskine). **Ground balls-fly balls:** Raschi 9-9, Erskine 9-3. **Batters faced:** Raschi 35, Erskine 38. **UMPIRES:** hp—Hurley, 1b—Gore, 2b—Grieve, 3b—Stewart, lf—Soar, rf—Dascoli **T:** 3:00 **A:** 35,270

GAME 4 Brooklyn 7 New York 3
Ebbets Field 10/03/53

NY YANKEES	AB	R	H	HR	RBI	BB	AVG
Mantle cf	5	0	1	0	1	0	.200
Collins 1b	4	0	0	0	0	0	.125
Bauer rf	4	0	1	0	0	0	.294
Berra c	4	0	2	0	0	0	.417
Woodling lf	3	1	1	0	0	1	.231
Martin 2b	4	1	2	0	0	0	.571
McDougald 3b	3	1	1	1	2	1	.133
Rizzuto ss	4	0	1	0	0	0	.250
Ford p	0	0	0	0	0	0	.000
Gorman p	1	0	0	0	0	0	.000
a-Bollweg ph	1	0	0	0	0	0	.000
Sain p	0	0	0	0	0	0	.500
b-Noren ph	1	0	0	0	0	0	.000
Schallock p	0	0	0	0	0	0	.000
c-Mize ph	1	0	0	0	0	0	.000
TOTALS	**35**	**3**	**9**	**1**	**3**	**2**	**.250**

a - Batted for Gorman in the 5th
b - Batted for Sain in the 7th
c - Batted for Schallock in the 9th

BATTING: 3B: Martin (2, Loes). **HR:** McDougald (1, 5th off Loes 1 on, 0 out). **RBI:** Mantle 1 (3), McDougald 2 (3). **2-out RBI:** Mantle 1. **Runners left in scoring position, 2 out:** Mantle 2. **Team LOB:** 7

BROOKLYN	AB	R	H	HR	RBI	BB	AVG
Gilliam 2b	5	1	3	0	2	0	.316
Reese ss	5	0	0	0	0	0	.200
Robinson lf	4	0	1	0	1	0	.313
Thompson lf	0	0	0	0	0	0	.000
Hodges 1b	4	1	0	0	0	0	.429
Campanella c	2	2	0	0	0	2	.143
Snider cf	4	1	3	1	4	0	.353
Furillo rf	4	1	1	0	0	0	.250
Cox 3b	4	1	2	0	0	0	.333
Loes p	3	0	2	0	0	0	.667
Labine p	0	0	0	0	0	0	.000
TOTALS	**35**	**7**	**12**	**1**	**7**	**2**	**.300**

BATTING: 2B: Gilliam 3 (3, Ford, Gorman, Gorman), Snider 2 (3, Ford, Schallock), Cox (3, Sain). **HR:** Snider (1, 6th off Sain 0 on, 0 out). **S:** Loes. **RBI:** Gilliam 2 (3), Robinson 1 (2), Snider 4 (4). **2-out RBI:** Gilliam 1, Snider 3. **Runners left in scoring position, 2 out:** Reese 5, Furillo 2. **Team LOB:** 7 **Outfield assists:** Thompson (1).

NY YANKEES	IP	H	R	ER	BB	SO	HR	ERA
Ford (L, 0-1)	1	3	3	3	1	0	0	27.00
Gorman	3	4	1	1	0	1	0	3.00
Sain	2	3	2	2	0	1	1	4.76
Schallock	2	2	1	1	1	1	0	4.50
BROOKLYN	**IP**	**H**	**R**	**ER**	**BB**	**SO**	**HR**	**ERA**
Loes (W, 1-0)	8	8	3	3	2	8	1	3.38
Labine (S, 1)	1	1	0	0	0	1	0	3.38

WP: Ford 1. **IBB:** Campanella (by Ford). **Ground balls-fly balls:** Ford 2-1, Gorman 4-4, Sain 4-1, Schallock 1-3, Loes 6-10, Labine 0-1. **Batters faced:** Ford 7, Gorman 13, Sain 9, Schallock 9, Loes 34, Labine 3. **UMPIRES:** hp—Gore, 1b—Grieve, 2b—Stewart, 3b—Hurley, lf—Dascoli, rf—Soar **T:** 2:46 **A:** 36,775

GAME 5 New York 11 Brooklyn 7
Ebbets Field 10/04/53

NY YANKEES	AB	R	H	HR	RBI	BB	AVG
Woodling lf	3	1	1	1	1	2	.250
Collins 1b	5	2	1	0	0	0	.143
Bauer rf	3	1	0	0	0	0	.250
Berra c	4	2	2	0	1	1	.438
Mantle cf	5	1	1	1	4	0	.200
Martin 2b	5	1	2	1	2	0	.526
McDougald 3b	5	1	2	1	1	0	.200
Rizzuto ss	3	2	1	0	0	2	.267
McDonald p	2	0	1	0	1	1	.500
Kuzava p	1	0	0	0	0	0	.000
Reynolds p	0	0	0	0	0	0	.000
TOTALS	**36**	**11**	**11**	**4**	**10**	**6**	**.262**

BATTING: 2B: McDonald (1, Meyer), Collins (1, Wade). **3B:** McDougald (1, Meyer). **HR:** Woodling (1, 1st off Podres 0 on, 0 out), Mantle (2, 3th off Meyer 3 on, 2 out), Martin (2, 7th off Meyer 1 on, 1 out), McDougald (2, 9th off Black 0 on, 1 out). **S:** McDonald, Bauer. **RBI:** Woodling 1 (2), Berra 1 (3), Mantle 4 (7), Martin 2 (6), McDougald 1 (4), McDonald 1 (1). **2-out RBI:** Mantle 4, McDonald 1. **Runners left in scoring position, 2 out:** Woodling 1, Collins 1, Bauer 2. **Team LOB:** 7 **BASERUNNING: SB:** Rizzuto (1, 2nd base off Meyer/Campanella). **CS:** Martin (2, 2nd base off Meyer/Campanella). **FIELDING: E:** Rizzuto (1). **Outfield assists:** Woodling (1). **DP:** 3 (Woodling-Berra, Rizzuto-Collins, Martin-Rizzuto-Collins).

BROOKLYN	AB	R	H	HR	RBI	BB	AVG
Gilliam 2b	4	2	2	1	1	0	.348
Reese ss	5	0	1	0	0	0	.200
Snider cf	5	0	2	0	1	0	.364
Robinson lf	5	1	1	0	0	0	.286
Campanella c	4	2	3	0	0	0	.278
Hodges 1b	4	0	2	0	0	0	.444
Furillo rf	4	1	1	0	1	0	.250
Cox 3b	4	1	1	1	3	0	.316
Podres p	1	0	1	0	0	0	1.000
Meyer p	1	0	0	0	0	0	.000
a-Belardi ph	1	0	0	0	0	0	.000
Wade p	0	0	0	0	0	0	.000
b-Shuba ph	0	0	0	0	0	0	1.000
c-Williams ph	1	0	0	0	0	0	.500
Black p	0	0	0	0	0	0	.000
TOTALS	**39**	**7**	**14**	**2**	**6**	**0**	**.313**

a - Batted for Meyer in the 7th
b - Batted for Wade in the 8th
c - Batted for Shuba in the 8th

BATTING: HR: Cox (1, 8th off McDonald 2 on, 2 out), Gilliam (2, 9th off Kuzava 0 on, 0 out). **RBI:** Gilliam 1 (4), Snider 1 (5), Furillo 1 (2), Cox 3 (6). **2-out RBI:** Furillo 1, Cox 3. **Runners left in scoring position, 2 out:** Gilliam 1, Campanella 1, Cox 1. **GIDP:** Furillo, Robinson. **Team LOB:** 6 **FIELDING: E:** Hodges (1).

NY YANKEES	IP	H	R	ER	BB	SO	HR	ERA
McDonald (W, 1-0)	7.2	12	6	5	0	3	1	5.87
Kuzava	0.2	2	1	1	0	1	1	13.50
Reynolds (S, 1)	0.2	0	0	0	0	0	0	6.00
BROOKLYN	**IP**	**H**	**R**	**ER**	**BB**	**SO**	**HR**	**ERA**
Podres (L, 0-1)	2.2	1	5	1	2	0	1	3.38
Meyer	4.1	8	4	3	4	5	2	6.23
Wade	1	1	1	1	0	0	0	15.43
Black	1	1	1	1	0	2	1	9.00

IBB: Woodling (by Meyer). **HBP:** Bauer (by Podres), Gilliam (by McDonald). **Ground balls-fly balls:** McDonald 11-8, Kuzava 0-1, Reynolds 1-0, Podres 5-3, Meyer 7-0, Wade 1-1, Black 0-1. **Batters faced:** McDonald 35, Kuzava 4, Reynolds 1, Podres 13, Meyer 24, Wade 4, Black 4. **UMPIRES:** hp—Grieve, 1b—Stewart, 2b—Hurley, 3b—Gore, lf—Soar, rf—Dascoli **T:** 3:02 **A:** 36,775

GAME 6 New York 4 Brooklyn 3
Yankee Stadium 10/05/53

BROOKLYN	AB	R	H	HR	RBI	BB	AVG
Gilliam 2b	4	0	0	0	0	0	.296
Reese ss	4	0	1	0	0	0	.208
Robinson lf	4	1	2	0	0	0	.320
Campanella c	4	0	1	0	1	0	.273
Hodges 1b	4	0	0	0	0	0	.364
Snider cf	3	1	0	0	0	1	.320
Furillo rf	4	1	3	1	2	0	.333
Cox 3b	4	0	1	0	0	0	.304
Erskine p	1	0	0	0	0	0	.250
a-Williams ph	0	0	0	0	0	1	.500
Milliken p	0	0	0	0	0	0	.000
b-Morgan ph	1	0	0	0	0	0	.000
Labine p	1	0	0	0	0	0	.000
TOTALS	**34**	**3**	**8**	**1**	**3**	**2**	**.300**

a - Batted for Erskine in the 5th
b - Batted for Milliken in the 7th

BATTING: 2B: Furillo (2, Ford), Robinson (2, Ford). **HR:** Furillo (1, 9th off Reynolds 1 on, 1 out). **RBI:** Campanella 1 (2), Furillo 2 (4). **Runners left in scoring position, 2 out:** Gilliam 1, Hodges 1. **Team LOB:** 6 **BASERUNNING: SB:** Robinson (1, 3rd base off Ford/Berra). **FIELDING: E:** Gilliam (1), Erskine (1), Cox (1). **Outfield assists:** Snider (1). **DP:** 3 (Cox-Gilliam-Hodges, Snider-Gilliam-Campanella, Labine-Gilliam-Hodges).

NY YANKEES	AB	R	H	HR	RBI	BB	AVG
Woodling lf	4	1	2	0	1	1	.300
Collins 1b	3	0	1	0	0	1	.167
a-Mize ph	1	0	0	0	0	0	.000
Bollweg 1b	0	0	0	0	0	0	.000
Bauer rf	3	2	1	0	0	2	.261
Berra c	5	0	2	0	1	0	.429
Mantle cf	4	0	1	0	0	1	.208
Martin 2b	5	0	2	0	2	0	.500
McDougald 3b	4	0	0	0	0	0	.167
Rizzuto ss	4	1	2	0	0	0	.316
Ford p	3	0	1	0	0	0	.333
Reynolds p	1	0	1	0	0	0	.500
TOTALS	**37**	**4**	**13**	**0**	**4**	**5**	**.279**

a - Batted for Collins in the 8th

BATTING: 2B: Berra (1, Erskine), Martin (1, Milliken). **RBI:** Woodling 1 (3), Berra 1 (4), Martin 2 (8). **Runners left in scoring position, 2 out:** Mize 1, Bauer 1, McDougald 1. **GIDP:** McDougald, Martin. **Team LOB:** 13

BROOKLYN	IP	H	R	ER	BB	SO	HR	ERA
Erskine	4	6	3	3	3	1	0	5.79
Milliken	2	2	0	0	1	0	0	0.00
Labine (L, 0-2)	2.1	5	1	1	1	1	0	3.60
NY YANKEES	**IP**	**H**	**R**	**ER**	**BB**	**SO**	**HR**	**ERA**
Ford	7	6	1	1	1	7	0	4.50
Reynolds (W, 1-0)	2	2	2	2	1	3	1	6.75

IBB: Mantle (by Erskine). **Ground balls-fly balls:** Erskine 5-6, Milliken 2-4, Labine 3-2, Ford 5-8, Reynolds 0-3. **Batters faced:** Erskine 21, Milliken 9, Labine 12, Ford 27, Reynolds 9. **UMPIRES:** hp—Stewart, 1b—Hurley, 2b—Gore, 3b—Grieve, lf—Dascoli, rf—Soar **T:** 2:55 **A:** 62,370

1954 NY GIANTS DEF. CLEVELAND, 4-0

GAME 1 New York 5 Cleveland 2
Polo Grounds 09/29/54

CLEVELAND	AB	R	H	HR	RBI	BB	AVG
Smith lf	4	1	1	0	0	0	.250
Avila 2b	5	1	1	0	0	0	.200
Doby cf	3	0	1	0	0	2	.333
Rosen 3b	5	0	1	0	0	0	.200
Wertz 1b	5	0	4	0	2	0	.800
d-Regalado pr	0	0	0	0	0	0	.000
Grasso c	0	0	0	0	0	0	.000
Philley rf	3	0	0	0	0	0	.000
a-Majeski ph	0	0	0	0	0	0	.000
b-Mitchell ph	0	0	0	0	0	1	.000
Dente ss	0	0	0	0	0	0	.000
Strickland ss	3	0	0	0	0	0	.000
c-Pope ph-rf	1	0	0	0	0	1	.000
Hegan c	4	0	0	0	0	0	.000
e-Glynn ph-1b	1	0	0	0	0	0	.000
Lemon p	4	0	0	0	0	1	.000
TOTALS	**38**	**2**	**8**	**0**	**2**	**5**	**.211**

a - Batted for Philley in the 8th
b - Batted for Majeski in the 8th
c - Batted for Strickland in the 8th
d - Ran for Wertz in the 10th e - Batted for Hegan in the 10th

BATTING: 2B: Wertz (1, Grissom). **3B:** Wertz (1, Maglie). **S:** Dente. **RBI:** Wertz 2 (2). **2-out RBI:** Wertz 2. **Runners left in scoring position, 2 out:** Rosen 2, Philley 1, Hegan 4, Lemon 1. **Team LOB:** 13

NY GIANTS	AB	R	H	HR	RBI	BB	AVG
Lockman 1b	5	1	1	0	0	0	.200
Dark ss	4	0	2	0	0	1	.500
Mueller rf	5	1	2	0	1	0	.400
Mays cf	3	1	0	0	0	2	.000
Thompson 3b	3	1	1	0	1	2	.333
Irvin lf	3	0	0	0	0	0	.000
a-Rhodes ph	1	1	1	1	3	0	1.000
Williams 2b	4	0	0	0	0	0	.000
Westrum c	4	0	2	0	0	0	.500
Maglie p	3	0	0	0	0	0	.000
Liddle p	0	0	0	0	0	0	.000
Grissom p	1	0	0	0	0	0	.000
TOTALS	**36**	**5**	**9**	**1**	**5**	**5**	**.250**

a - Batted for Irvin in the 10th

BATTING: HR: Rhodes (1, 10th off Lemon 2 on, 1 out). **S:** Irvin. **RBI:** Mueller 1 (1), Thompson 1 (1), Rhodes 3 (3). **Runners left in scoring position, 2 out:** Mueller 1, Thompson 1, Williams 1, Westrum 1. **Team LOB:** 9 **BASERUNNING: SB:** Mays (1, 2nd base off Lemon/Grasso). **FIELDING: E:** Mueller 2 (2), Irvin (1).

CLEVELAND	IP	H	R	ER	BB	SO	HR	ERA
Lemon (L, 0-1)	9.1	9	5	5	5	6	1	4.82

NY GIANTS	IP	H	R	ER	BB	SO	HR	ERA
Maglie	7	7	2	2	2	2	0	2.57
Liddle	0.1	0	0	0	0	0	0	0.00
Grissom (W, 1-0)	2.2	1	0	0	3	2	0	0.00

WP: Lemon 1. **IBB:** Doby (by Grissom), Pope (by Grissom), Thompson (by Lemon). **HBP:** Smith (by Maglie). **Ground balls-fly balls:** Lemon 14-7, Maglie 7-12, Liddle 0-1, Grissom 0-6. **Batters faced:** Lemon 42, Maglie 31, Liddle 1, Grissom 13. **UMPIRES:** hp—Barlick, 1b—Berry, 2b—Conlan, 3b—Stevens, lf—Warneke, rf—Napp **T:** 3:11 **A:** 52,751

GAME 2 New York 3 Cleveland 1
Polo Grounds 09/30/54

CLEVELAND	AB	R	H	HR	RBI	BB	AVG
Smith lf	4	1	2	1	1	1	.375
Avila 2b	4	0	1	0	0	1	.222
Doby cf	5	0	0	0	0	0	.125
Rosen 3b	3	0	1	0	0	1	.250
a-Regalado pr-3b	1	0	0	0	0	0	.000
Wertz 1b	3	0	1	0	0	2	.625
Westlake rf	3	0	1	0	0	1	.333
Strickland ss	3	0	0	0	0	0	.000
b-Philley ph	1	0	0	0	0	0	.000
Dente ss	0	0	0	0	0	0	.000
Hegan c	4	0	1	0	0	0	.125
Wynn p	2	0	1	0	0	0	.500
c-Majeski ph	1	0	0	0	0	0	.000
Mossi p	0	0	0	0	0	0	.000
TOTALS	**34**	**1**	**8**	**1**	**1**	**6**	**.222**

a - Ran for Rosen in the 7th
b - Batted for Strickland in the 8th
c - Batted for Wynn in the 8th

BATTING: 2B: Hegan (1, Antonelli), Wynn (1, Antonelli). **HR:** Smith (1, 1st off Antonelli 0 on, 0 out). **S:** Wynn. **RBI:** Smith 1 (1). **Runners left in scoring position, 2 out:** Smith 1, Avila 1, Wertz 1, Westlake 1, Strickland 3. **Team LOB:** 13

NY GIANTS	AB	R	H	HR	RBI	BB	AVG
Lockman 1b	4	0	0	0	0	0	.111
Dark ss	4	0	1	0	0	0	.375
Mueller rf	4	0	0	0	0	0	.222
Mays cf	2	1	0	0	0	1	.000
Thompson 3b	3	1	1	0	0	0	.333
Irvin lf	1	0	0	0	0	0	.000
a-Rhodes ph-lf	2	1	2	1	2	0	1.000
Williams 2b	3	0	0	0	0	0	.000
Westrum c	2	0	0	0	0	1	.333
Antonelli p	3	0	0	0	1	0	.000
TOTALS	**28**	**3**	**4**	**1**	**3**	**2**	**.203**

a - Batted for Irvin in the 5th

BATTING: HR: Rhodes (2, 7th off Wynn 0 on, 0 out). **RBI:** Rhodes 2 (5), Antonelli 1 (1). **Runners left in scoring position, 2 out:** Lockman 1, Thompson 1. **Team LOB:** 3

CLEVELAND	IP	H	R	ER	BB	SO	HR	ERA
Wynn (L, 0-1)	7	4	3	3	2	5	1	3.86
Mossi	1	0	0	0	0	0	0	0.00

NY GIANTS	IP	H	R	ER	BB	SO	HR	ERA
Antonelli (W, 1-0)	9	8	1	1	6	9	1	1.00

WP: Wynn 1. **Ground balls-fly balls:** Wynn 5-11, Mossi 1-2, Antonelli 9-8. **Batters faced:** Wynn 27, Mossi 3, Antonelli 41. **UMPIRES:** hp—Berry, 1b—Conlan, 2b—Stevens, 3b—Barlick, lf—Warneke, rf—Napp **T:** 2:50 **A:** 49,099

GAME 3 New York 6 Cleveland 2
Municipal Stadium 10/01/54

NY GIANTS	AB	R	H	HR	RBI	BB	AVG
Lockman 1b	4	1	1	0	0	1	.154
Dark ss	4	0	1	0	0	0	.333
Mueller rf	5	2	2	0	0	0	.286
Mays cf	5	1	3	0	2	0	.300
Thompson 3b	3	2	1	0	0	2	.333
Irvin lf	1	0	0	0	0	0	.000
a-Rhodes ph-lf	3	0	1	0	2	1	.667
Williams 2b	2	0	0	0	1	1	.000
Westrum c	4	0	1	0	1	0	.300
Gomez p	4	0	0	0	0	0	.000
Wilhelm p	0	0	0	0	0	0	.000
TOTALS	**35**	**6**	**10**	**0**	**6**	**5**	**.232**

a - Batted for Irvin in the 3th

BATTING: 2B: Thompson (1, Houtteman). **S:** Williams, Dark. **RBI:** Mays 2 (2), Rhodes 2 (7), Williams 1 (1), Westrum 1 (1). **2-out RBI:** Mays 2, Westrum 1. **Runners left in scoring position, 2 out:** Lockman 1, Irvin 1, Rhodes 1, Gomez 3. **Team LOB:** 9 **FIELDING: E:** Dark (1). **DP:** 1 (Dark-Williams-Lockman).

CLEVELAND	AB	R	H	HR	RBI	BB	AVG
Smith lf	3	0	0	0	1	1	.273
Avila 2b	2	0	0	0	0	1	.182
Doby cf	4	0	1	0	0	0	.167
Wertz 1b	4	1	1	1	1	0	.500
Majeski 3b	4	0	0	0	0	0	.000
Philley rf	3	0	1	0	0	1	.143
Strickland ss	3	0	0	0	0	0	.000
e-Pope ph	1	0	0	0	0	0	.000
Hegan c	2	0	0	0	0	0	.100
c-Glynn ph	1	1	1	0	0	0	.500
Naragon c	0	0	0	0	0	0	.000
Garcia p	0	0	0	0	0	0	.000
a-Lemon ph	1	0	0	0	0	0	.000
Houtteman p	0	0	0	0	0	0	.000
b-Regalado ph	1	0	0	0	0	0	.000
Narleski p	0	0	0	0	0	0	.000
d-Mitchell ph	1	0	0	0	0	0	.000
Mossi p	0	0	0	0	0	0	.000
TOTALS	**30**	**2**	**4**	**1**	**2**	**3**	**.196**

a - Batted for Garcia in the 3th
b - Batted for Houtteman in the 5th
c - Batted for Hegan in the 8th
d - Batted for Narleski in the 8th e - Batted for Strickland in the 9th

BATTING: 2B: Glynn (1, Gomez). **HR:** Wertz (1, 7th off Gomez 0 on, 0 out). **S:** Avila. **RBI:** Smith 1 (2), Wertz 1 (3). **Runners left in scoring position, 2 out:** Wertz 3. **GIDP:** Majeski. **Team LOB:** 5 **FIELDING: E:** Garcia (1). **DP:** 1 (Strickland-Wertz).

NY GIANTS	IP	H	R	ER	BB	SO	HR	ERA
Gomez (W, 1-0)	7.1	4	2	2	3	2	1	2.45
Wilhelm (S, 1)	1.2	0	0	0	0	2	0	0.00

CLEVELAND	IP	H	R	ER	BB	SO	HR	ERA
Garcia (L, 0-1)	3	5	4	3	3	3	0	9.00
Houtteman	2	2	1	1	1	1	0	4.50
Narleski	3	1	1	1	1	2	0	3.00
Mossi	1	2	0	0	0	1	0	0.00

WP: Garcia 1. **IBB:** Thompson (by Garcia), Rhodes (by Houtteman). **Ground balls-fly balls:** Gomez 10-9, Wilhelm 3-0, Garcia 3-3, Houtteman 2-3, Narleski 3-3, Mossi 0-1. **Batters faced:** Gomez 29, Wilhelm 5, Garcia 18, Houtteman 9, Narleski 11, Mossi 4. **UMPIRES:** hp—Conlan, 1b—Stevens, 2b—Barlick, 3b—Berry, lf—Napp, rf—Warneke **T:** 2:28 **A:** 71,555

GAME 4 New York 7 Cleveland 4
Municipal Stadium 10/02/54

NY GIANTS	AB	R	H	HR	RBI	BB	AVG
Lockman 1b	5	0	0	0	0	0	.111
Dark ss	5	2	3	0	0	0	.412
Mueller rf	4	1	3	0	0	0	.389
Mays cf	4	1	1	0	1	1	.286
Thompson 3b	2	2	1	0	1	3	.364
Irvin lf	4	1	2	0	2	0	.222
Williams 2b	2	0	0	0	0	1	.000
Westrum c	1	0	0	0	2	0	.273
Liddle p	3	0	0	0	0	0	.000
Wilhelm p	1	0	0	0	0	0	.000
Antonelli p	0	0	0	0	0	0	.000
TOTALS	**31**	**7**	**10**	**0**	**6**	**5**	**.254**

BATTING: 2B: Irvin (1, Lemon), Mays (1, Lemon). **S:** Williams, Westrum, Mueller. **SF:** Westrum, Westrum. **RBI:** Mays 1 (3), Thompson 1 (2), Irvin 2 (2), Westrum 2 (3). **Runners left in scoring position, 2 out:** Lockman 1, Thompson 1, Williams 2, Liddle 1. **GIDP:** Irvin. **Team LOB:** 7 **BASERUNNING: CS:** Westrum (1, 2nd base off Lemon/Hegan). **FIELDING: E:** Williams (1), Wilhelm (1). **DP:** 1 (Thompson-Williams-Lockman).

CLEVELAND	AB	R	H	HR	RBI	BB	AVG
Smith lf	3	0	0	0	0	0	.214
c-Pope ph-lf	1	0	0	0	0	0	.000
e-Mitchell ph	1	0	0	0	0	0	.000
Avila 2b	4	0	0	0	0	0	.133
Doby cf	4	0	0	0	0	0	.125
Rosen 3b	4	0	1	0	0	0	.250
Wertz 1b	4	1	2	0	0	0	.500
Westlake rf	4	0	0	0	0	0	.143
Dente ss	3	1	0	0	0	1	.000
Hegan c	3	1	1	0	0	1	.154
Lemon p	1	0	0	0	0	0	.000
Newhouser p	0	0	0	0	0	0	.000
Narleski p	0	0	0	0	0	0	.000
a-Majeski ph	1	1	1	1	3	0	.167
Mossi p	0	0	0	0	0	0	.000
b-Regalado ph	1	0	1	0	1	0	.333
Garcia p	0	0	0	0	0	0	.000
d-Philley ph	1	0	0	0	0	0	.125
TOTALS	**35**	**4**	**6**	**1**	**4**	**2**	**.190**

a - Batted for Narleski in the 5th
b - Batted for Mossi in the 7th
c - Batted for Smith in the 7th
d - Batted for Garcia in the 9th e - Batted for Pope in the 9th

BATTING: 2B: Wertz (2, Liddle). **HR:** Majeski (1, 5th off Liddle 2 on, 2 out). **RBI:** Majeski 3 (3), Regalado 1 (1). **2-out RBI:** Majeski 3, Regalado 1. **Runners left in scoring position, 2 out:** Pope 1, Westlake 1, Dente 1. **GIDP:** Smith. **Team LOB:** 6 **FIELDING: E:** Westlake (1). **DP:** 1 (Dente-Avila-Wertz).

NY GIANTS	IP	H	R	ER	BB	SO	HR	ERA
Liddle (W, 1-0)	6.2	5	4	1	1	2	1	1.29
Wilhelm	0.2	1	0	0	0	1	0	0.00
Antonelli (S, 1)	1.2	0	0	0	1	3	0	0.84

CLEVELAND	IP	H	R	ER	BB	SO	HR	ERA
Lemon (L, 0-2)	4	7	6	5	3	5	0	6.75
Newhouser	0	1	1	1	1	0	0	0.00
Narleski	1	0	0	0	0	0	0	2.25
Mossi	2	1	0	0	0	0	0	0.00
Garcia	2	1	0	0	1	1	0	5.40

WP: Liddle 1. **IBB:** Thompson (by Lemon). **Ground balls-fly balls:** Liddle 9-10, Wilhelm 1-1, Antonelli 0-2, Lemon 3-3, Newhouser 0-0, Narleski 1-0, Mossi 4-1, Garcia 2-1. **Batters faced:** Liddle 27, Wilhelm 4, Antonelli 6, Lemon 22, Newhouser 2, Narleski 3, Mossi 6, Garcia 8. **UMPIRES:** hp—Stevens, 1b—Barlick, 2b—Berry, 3b—Conlan, lf—Warneke, rf—Napp **T:** 2:52 **A:** 78,102

1955 BROOKLYN DEF. NY YANKEES, 4-3

GAME 1 New York 6 Brooklyn 5
Yankee Stadium 09/28/55

BROOKLYN	AB	R	H	HR	RBI	BB	AVG
Gilliam lf	3	0	0	0	0	2	.000
Reese ss	5	0	1	0	0	0	.200
Snider cf	5	1	2	1	1	0	.400
Campanella c	5	0	0	0	0	0	.000
Furillo rf	4	2	3	1	1	1	.750
Hodges 1b	4	0	1	0	0	0	.250
J.Robinson 3b	4	2	1	0	0	0	.250
Zimmer 2b	2	0	1	0	2	1	.500
Newcombe p	3	0	0	0	0	0	.000
Bessent p	0	0	0	0	0	0	.000
a-Kellert ph	1	0	1	0	0	0	1.000
b-Hoak pr	0	0	0	0	0	0	.000
Labine p	0	0	0	0	0	0	.000
TOTALS	**36**	**5**	**10**	**2**	**4**	**4**	**.278**

a - Batted for Bessent in the 8th
b - Ran for Kellert in the 8th

BATTING: 3B: J.Robinson (1, Ford). **HR:** Furillo (1, 2nd off Ford 0 on, 0 out), Snider (1, 3th off Ford 0 on, 0 out). **SF:** Zimmer. **RBI:** Snider 1 (1), Furillo 1 (1), Zimmer 2 (2). **Runners left in scoring position, 2 out:** Reese 1, J.Robinson 1. **GIDP:** Reese. **Team LOB:** 9 **BASERUNNING: SB:** J.Robinson (1, home off Ford/Berra). **FIELDING: DP:** 2 (Zimmer-Hodges, Hodges-Reese-Hodges).

NY YANKEES	AB	R	H	HR	RBI	BB	AVG
Bauer rf	4	0	2	0	0	0	.500
McDougald 3b	4	0	1	0	0	0	.250
Noren cf	4	0	0	0	1	0	.000
Berra c	3	1	1	0	0	1	.333
Collins 1b	3	3	2	2	3	1	.667
Howard lf	3	1	1	1	2	0	.333
Martin 2b	3	0	2	0	0	0	.667
Rizzuto ss	2	0	0	0	0	0	.000
a-E.Robinson ph	0	0	0	0	0	0	.000
J.Coleman ss	1	0	0	0	0	0	.000
Ford p	2	1	0	0	0	1	.000
Grim p	0	0	0	0	0	0	.000
TOTALS	**29**	**6**	**9**	**3**	**6**	**3**	**.310**

a - Batted for Rizzuto in the 6th

BATTING: 3B: Martin (1, Newcombe). **HR:** Howard (1, 2nd off Newcombe 1 on, 1 out), Collins 2 (2, 4th off Newcombe 0 on, 0 out, 6th off Newcombe 1 on, 1 out). **S:** Martin. **RBI:** Noren 1 (1), Collins 3 (3), Howard 2 (2). **Runners left in scoring position, 2 out:** Berra 1. **GIDP:** Noren, Noren. **Team LOB:** 2 **BASERUNNING: CS:** Martin (1, 2nd base off Newcombe/Campanella). **FIELDING: E:** McDougald (1). **DP:** 1 (Martin-Rizzuto-Collins).

BROOKLYN	IP	H	R	ER	BB	SO	HR	ERA
Newcombe (L, 0-1)	5.2	8	6	6	2	4	3	9.53
Bessent	1.1	0	0	0	0	0	0	0.00
Labine	1	1	0	0	1	0	0	0.00

NY YANKEES	IP	H	R	ER	BB	SO	HR	ERA
Ford (W, 1-0)	8	9	5	3	4	2	2	3.38
Grim (S, 1)	1	1	0	0	0	2	0	0.00

Ground balls-fly balls: Newcombe 9-2, Bessent 2-1, Labine 1-1, Ford 10-11, Grim 0-1. **Batters faced:** Newcombe 25, Bessent 3, Labine 4, Ford 37, Grim 4. **UMPIRES:** hp—Summers, 1b—Ballanfant, 2b—Honochick, 3b—Dascoli, lf—Flaherty, rf—Donatelli **T:** 2:31 **A:** 63,869

GAME 2 New York 4 Brooklyn 2
Yankee Stadium 09/29/55

BROOKLYN	AB	R	H	HR	RBI	BB	AVG
Gilliam lf	4	0	1	0	1	0	.143
Reese ss	4	1	2	0	0	0	.333
Snider cf	4	0	1	0	1	0	.333
Campanella c	3	0	0	0	0	1	.000
Furillo rf	3	0	0	0	0	1	.429
Hodges 1b	3	0	0	0	0	1	.143
J.Robinson 3b	2	1	0	0	0	1	.167
Zimmer 2b	3	0	1	0	0	0	.400
Loes p	1	0	0	0	0	0	.000
Bessent p	0	0	0	0	0	0	.000
a-Kellert ph	1	0	0	0	0	0	.500
Spooner p	0	0	0	0	0	0	.000
b-Hoak ph	0	0	0	0	0	1	.000
Labine p	0	0	0	0	0	0	.000
TOTALS	**28**	**2**	**5**	**0**	**2**	**5**	**.234**

a - Batted for Bessent in the 5th
b - Batted for Spooner in the 8th

BATTING: 2B: Reese (1, Byrne). **RBI:** Gilliam 1 (1), Snider 1 (2). **2-out RBI:** Gilliam 1. **GIDP:** Kellert, Gilliam. **Team LOB:** 4 **BASERUNNING: CS:** Hodges (1, 2nd base off Byrne/Berra). **FIELDING: E:** Zimmer (1). **Outfield assists:** Gilliam (1). **DP:** 3 (Campanella-Zimmer, Zimmer-Reese-Hodges, Hodges-Reese).

NY YANKEES	AB	R	H	HR	RBI	BB	AVG
Bauer rf	1	0	1	0	0	0	.600
Cerv cf	3	0	0	0	0	0	.000
McDougald 3b	4	0	1	0	0	0	.250
Noren cf-lf	3	0	0	0	0	1	.000
Berra c	3	1	2	0	0	0	.500
Collins 1b	3	1	0	0	0	1	.333
Howard lf-rf	4	1	1	0	1	0	.286
Martin 2b	3	1	1	0	1	0	.500
Rizzuto ss	1	0	1	0	0	0	.333
a-E.Robinson ph	0	0	0	0	0	0	.000
b-J.Coleman pr-ss	1	0	0	0	0	0	.000
Byrne p	3	0	1	0	2	0	.333
TOTALS	**29**	**4**	**8**	**0**	**4**	**2**	**.293**

a - Batted for Rizzuto in the 4th
b - Ran for E.Robinson in the 4th

BATTING: RBI: Howard 1 (3), Martin 1 (1), Byrne 2 (2). **2-out RBI:** Howard 1, Martin 1, Byrne 2. **Runners left in scoring position, 2 out:** Cerv 1, Martin 1. **GIDP:** Byrne, Noren. **Team LOB:** 5 **BASERUNNING: CS:** Bauer (1, 2nd base off Loes/Campanella), Berra (1, 2nd base off Loes/Campanella). **FIELDING: Outfield assists:** Howard (1). **DP:** 3 (J.Coleman-Martin-Collins, Berra-Martin, Martin-J.Coleman-Collins).

BROOKLYN	IP	H	R	ER	BB	SO	HR	ERA
Loes (L, 0-1)	3.2	7	4	4	1	5	0	9.82
Bessent	0.1	0	0	0	0	0	0	0.00
Spooner	3	1	0	0	1	5	0	0.00
Labine	1	0	0	0	0	1	0	0.00

NY YANKEES	IP	H	R	ER	BB	SO	HR	ERA
Byrne (W, 1-0)	9	5	2	2	5	6	0	2.00

HBP: Berra (by Loes), E.Robinson (by Loes). **Ground balls-fly balls:** Loes 2-1, Bessent 1-0, Spooner 3-0, Labine 1-2, Byrne 4-13. **Batters faced:** Loes 18, Bessent 1, Spooner 10, Labine 4, Byrne 33. **UMPIRES:** hp—Ballanfant, 1b—Honochick, 2b—Dascoli, 3b—Summers, lf—Flaherty, rf—Donatelli **T:** 2:28 **A:** 64,707

GAME 3 Brooklyn 8 New York 3
Ebbets Field 09/30/55

NY YANKEES	AB	R	H	HR	RBI	BB	AVG
Cerv lf-cf	4	0	0	0	0	0	.000
McDougald 3b	4	0	1	0	0	0	.250
Berra c	4	0	1	0	0	0	.400
Mantle cf-rf	4	1	1	1	1	0	.250
Skowron 1b	4	1	2	0	0	0	.500
Howard rf-lf	4	0	0	0	0	0	.182
Martin 2b	4	0	0	0	0	0	.300
Rizzuto ss	2	1	1	0	1	2	.400
Turley p	1	0	0	0	0	0	.000
Morgan p	0	0	0	0	0	0	.000
a-Bauer ph	1	0	0	0	0	0	.500
Kucks p	0	0	0	0	0	0	.000
b-Carey ph	1	0	1	0	1	0	1.000
Sturdivant p	0	0	0	0	0	0	.000
TOTALS	**33**	**3**	**7**	**1**	**3**	**2**	**.264**

a - Batted for Morgan in the 5th
b - Batted for Kucks in the 7th

BATTING: 2B: Skowron (1, Podres). **3B:** Carey (1, Podres). **HR:** Mantle (1, 2nd off Podres 0 on, 0 out). **RBI:** Mantle 1 (1), Rizzuto 1 (1), Carey 1 (1). **2-out RBI:** Rizzuto 1, Carey 1. **Runners left in scoring position, 2 out:** Cerv 1, Skowron 1, Turley 1. **GIDP:** Mantle. **Team LOB:** 5

BROOKLYN	AB	R	H	HR	RBI	BB	AVG
Gilliam 2b	3	1	1	0	1	2	.200
Reese ss	3	1	1	0	2	2	.333
Snider cf	4	1	1	0	0	1	.308
Campanella c	5	1	3	1	3	0	.231
Furillo rf	5	0	1	0	1	0	.333
Hodges 1b	5	0	0	0	0	0	.083
J.Robinson 3b	5	2	2	0	0	0	.273
Amoros lf	1	1	1	0	1	2	1.000
Podres p	3	1	1	0	0	0	.333
TOTALS	**34**	**8**	**11**	**1**	**8**	**7**	**.265**

BATTING: 2B: Furillo (1, Morgan), J.Robinson (1, Sturdivant), Campanella (1, Sturdivant). **HR:** Campanella (1, 1st off Turley 1 on, 2 out). **S:** Podres. **RBI:** Gilliam 1 (2), Reese 2 (2), Campanella 3 (3), Furillo 1 (2), Amoros 1 (1). **2-out RBI:** Reese 1, Campanella 2. **Runners left in scoring position, 2 out:** Gilliam 1, Snider 1, Campanella 2, Hodges 1, J.Robinson 1, Podres 1. **Team LOB:** 11 **FIELDING: Outfield assists:** Amoros (1). **DP:** 1 (Reese-Gilliam-Hodges).

NY YANKEES	IP	H	R	ER	BB	SO	HR	ERA
Turley (L, 0-1)	1.1	3	4	4	2	1	1	27.00
Morgan	2.2	3	2	2	3	1	0	6.75
Kucks	2	1	0	0	1	0	0	0.00
Sturdivant	2	4	2	2	1	0	0	9.00

BROOKLYN	IP	H	R	ER	BB	SO	HR	ERA
Podres (W, 1-0)	9	7	3	2	2	6	1	2.00

IBB: Amoros (by Morgan). **HBP:** Amoros (by Turley). **Ground balls-fly balls:** Turley 0-3, Morgan 3-4, Kucks 2-3, Sturdivant 1-5, Podres 12-8. **Batters faced:** Turley 10, Morgan 14, Kucks 8, Sturdivant 11, Podres 35. **UMPIRES:** hp—Honochick, 1b—Dascoli, 2b—Summers, 3b—Ballanfant, lf—Donatelli, rf—Flaherty **T:** 2:20 **A:** 34,209

GAME 4 Brooklyn 8 New York 5
Ebbets Field 10/01/55

NY YANKEES	AB	R	H	HR	RBI	BB	AVG
Noren cf	5	0	1	0	0	0	.083
McDougald 3b	5	1	1	1	1	0	.235
Mantle rf	5	0	1	0	0	0	.222
Berra c	3	0	1	0	0	1	.385
Collins 1b	2	2	0	0	0	2	.250
Howard lf	3	1	1	0	0	0	.214
Martin 2b	4	1	2	0	2	0	.357
Rizzuto ss	3	0	1	0	1	1	.375
Larsen p	2	0	0	0	0	0	.000
Kucks p	0	0	0	0	0	0	.000
a-E.Robinson ph	1	0	1	0	1	0	1.000
b-Carroll pr	0	0	0	0	0	0	.000
R.Coleman p	0	0	0	0	0	0	.000
Morgan p	0	0	0	0	0	0	.000
c-Skowron ph	1	0	0	0	0	0	.400
Sturdivant p	0	0	0	0	0	0	.000
TOTALS	**34**	**5**	**9**	**1**	**5**	**4**	**.264**

a - Batted for Kucks in the 6th
b - Ran for E.Robinson in the 6th
c - Batted for Morgan in the 8th

BATTING: 2B: Martin (1, Labine). **HR:** McDougald (1, 1st off Erskine 0 on, 1 out). **S:** Howard. **RBI:** McDougald 1 (1), Martin 2 (3), Rizzuto 1 (2), E.Robinson 1 (1). **2-out RBI:** Rizzuto 1. **Runners left in scoring position, 2 out:** Collins 2, Larsen 1. **GIDP:** Rizzuto. **Team LOB:** 7 **BASERUNNING: SB:** Rizzuto (1, 2nd base off Erskine/Campanella), Collins (1, 3rd base off Bessent/Campanella).

BROOKLYN	AB	R	H	HR	RBI	BB	AVG
Gilliam 2b	4	1	2	0	1	1	.286
Reese ss	4	1	2	0	0	0	.375
Snider cf	4	1	1	1	3	1	.294
Campanella c	5	2	3	1	1	0	.333
Furillo rf	5	1	2	0	0	0	.353
Hodges 1b	4	1	3	1	3	0	.250
J.Robinson 3b	4	0	0	0	0	0	.200
Amoros lf	3	1	1	0	0	1	.500
Erskine p	1	0	0	0	0	0	.000
Bessent p	1	0	0	0	0	0	.000
Labine p	2	0	0	0	0	0	.000
TOTALS	**37**	**8**	**14**	**3**	**8**	**3**	**.296**

BATTING: 2B: Gilliam (1, Larsen), Campanella (2, Kucks). **HR:** Campanella (2, 4th off Larsen 0 on, 0 out), Hodges (1, 4th off Larsen 1 on, 0 out), Snider (2, 5th off Kucks 2 on, 0 out). **S:** Reese. **RBI:** Gilliam 1 (3), Snider 3 (5), Campanella 1 (4), Hodges 3 (3). **Runners left in scoring position, 2 out:** Snider 2, Furillo 1, J.Robinson 1, Labine 2. **Team LOB:** 9 **BASERUNNING: SB:** Gilliam (1, 2nd base off Larsen/Berra). **FIELDING: DP:** 1 (J.Robinson-Gilliam-Hodges).

NY YANKEES	IP	H	R	ER	BB	SO	HR	ERA
Larsen (L, 0-1)	4	5	5	5	2	2	2	11.25
Kucks	1	3	2	2	0	1	1	6.00
R.Coleman	1	5	1	1	0	1	0	9.00
Morgan	1	0	0	0	0	0	0	4.91
Sturdivant	1	1	0	0	1	0	0	6.00

BROOKLYN	IP	H	R	ER	BB	SO	HR	ERA
Erskine	3	3	3	3	2	3	1	9.00
Bessent	1.2	3	0	0	1	1	0	0.00
Labine (W, 1-0)	4.1	3	2	2	1	0	0	2.84

IBB: Snider (by Sturdivant). **Ground balls-fly balls:** Larsen 5-5, Kucks 1-1, R.Coleman 2-0, Morgan 2-1, Sturdivant 0-2, Erskine 2-3, Bessent 3-0, Labine 5-8. **Batters faced:** Larsen 19, Kucks 6, R.Coleman 8, Morgan 3, Sturdivant 5, Erskine 14, Bessent 8, Labine 17. **UMPIRES:** hp—Dascoli, 1b—Summers, 2b—Ballanfant, 3b—Honochick, lf—Donatelli, rf—Flaherty **T:** 2:57 **A:** 36,242

GAME 5 Brooklyn 5 New York 3
Ebbets Field 10/02/55

NY YANKEES	AB	R	H	HR	RBI	BB	AVG
Howard lf	4	0	1	0	0	1	.222
Noren cf	4	0	0	0	0	0	.063
McDougald 3b	3	0	0	0	0	1	.200
Berra c	4	2	2	1	1	0	.412
Collins rf-1b	3	0	0	0	0	1	.182
E.Robinson 1b	2	0	1	0	0	2	.667
c-Carroll pr	0	0	0	0	0	0	.000
Bauer rf	0	0	0	0	0	0	.500
Martin 2b	4	0	1	0	1	0	.333
Rizzuto ss	1	0	0	0	0	0	.333
a-Skowron ph	1	0	0	0	0	0	.333
J.Coleman ss	1	0	0	0	0	0	.000
d-Carey ph	1	0	0	0	0	0	.500
Grim p	2	0	0	0	0	0	.000
b-Cerv ph	1	1	1	1	1	0	.125
Turley p	0	0	0	0	0	0	.000
e-Byrne ph	1	0	0	0	0	0	.250
TOTALS	**32**	**3**	**6**	**2**	**3**	**5**	**.248**

a - Batted for Rizzuto in the 4th
b - Batted for Grim in the 7th
c - Ran for E.Robinson in the 8th
d - Batted for J.Coleman in the 9th e - Batted for Turley in the 9th

BATTING: HR: Cerv (1, 7th off Craig 0 on, 0 out), Berra (1, 8th off Labine 0 on, 0 out). **RBI:** Berra 1 (1), Martin 1 (4), Cerv 1 (1). **Runners left in scoring position, 2 out:** Grim 3. **GIDP:** Noren, Noren, Martin. **Team LOB:** 7 **FIELDING: DP:** 2 (Martin-E.Robinson, J.Coleman-Martin-E.Robinson).

BROOKLYN	AB	R	H	HR	RBI	BB	AVG
Gilliam 2b	3	0	1	0	0	1	.294
Reese ss	3	0	0	0	0	1	.316
Snider cf	4	2	3	2	2	0	.381
Campanella c	3	0	0	0	0	1	.286
Furillo rf	4	1	1	0	0	0	.333
Hodges 1b	3	1	2	0	0	0	.316
J.Robinson 3b	3	0	1	0	1	1	.222
Amoros lf	4	1	1	1	2	0	.375
Craig p	0	0	0	0	0	1	.000
Labine p	2	0	0	0	0	0	.000
TOTALS	**29**	**5**	**9**	**3**	**5**	**5**	**.299**

BATTING: 2B: Snider (1, Turley). **HR:** Amoros (1, 2nd off Grim 1 on, 2 out), Snider 2 (4, 3th off Grim 0 on, 0 out, 5th off Grim 0 on, 1 out). **S:** Craig, Hodges. **RBI:** Snider 2 (7), J.Robinson 1 (1), Amoros 2 (3). **2-out RBI:** Amoros 2. **Runners left in scoring position, 2 out:** Gilliam 1, Reese 1, Campanella 2. **GIDP:** Furillo, J.Robinson. **Team LOB:** 7 **FIELDING: E:** Reese (1), J.Robinson (1). **DP:** 3 (Gilliam-Reese-Hodges, Hodges-Reese-Hodges, J.Robinson-Gilliam-Hodges).

NY YANKEES	IP	H	R	ER	BB	SO	HR	ERA
Grim (L, 0-1)	6	6	4	4	4	5	3	5.14
Turley	2	3	1	1	1	5	0	13.50

BROOKLYN	IP	H	R	ER	BB	SO	HR	ERA
Craig (W, 1-0)	6	4	2	2	5	4	1	3.00
Labine (S, 1)	3	2	1	1	0	1	1	2.89

Ground balls-fly balls: Grim 6-4, Turley 0-0, Craig 9-6, Labine 6-0. **Batters faced:** Grim 26, Turley 10, Craig 28, Labine 9. **UMPIRES:** hp—Summers, 1b—Ballanfant, 2b—Honochick, 3b—Dascoli, lf—Donatelli, rf—Flaherty **T:** 2:40 **A:** 36,796

GAME 6 New York 5 Brooklyn 1
Yankee Stadium 10/03/55

BROOKLYN	AB	R	H	HR	RBI	BB	AVG
Gilliam 2b-lf	3	0	1	0	0	1	.300
Reese ss	4	1	1	0	0	0	.304
Snider cf	1	0	0	0	0	0	.364
a-Zimmer ph-2b	2	0	0	0	0	1	.286
Campanella c	3	0	0	0	0	1	.250
Furillo rf	3	0	1	0	1	0	.333
Hodges 1b	3	0	0	0	0	1	.273
J.Robinson 3b	4	0	0	0	0	0	.182
Amoros lf-cf	4	0	1	0	0	0	.333
Spooner p	0	0	0	0	0	0	.000
Meyer p	2	0	0	0	0	0	.000
b-Kellert ph	1	0	0	0	0	0	.333
Roebuck p	0	0	0	0	0	0	.000
TOTALS	**30**	**1**	**4**	**0**	**1**	**4**	**.273**

a - Batted for Snider in the 4th
b - Batted for Meyer in the 7th

BATTING: RBI: Furillo 1 (3). **Runners left in scoring position, 2 out:** Reese 1, Hodges 1, J.Robinson 1. **GIDP:** J.Robinson. **Team LOB:** 7 **FIELDING: E:** J.Robinson (2). **DP:** 1 (J.Robinson-Hodges).

NY YANKEES	AB	R	H	HR	RBI	BB	AVG
Rizzuto ss	3	1	0	0	0	1	.250
Martin 2b	4	0	1	0	0	0	.318
McDougald 3b	3	1	0	0	0	1	.174
Berra c	3	1	2	0	1	1	.450
Bauer rf	4	1	3	0	1	0	.600
Skowron 1b	2	1	1	1	3	0	.375
a-Collins ph-1b	1	0	0	0	0	1	.167
Cerv cf	4	0	1	0	0	0	.167
Howard lf	4	0	0	0	0	0	.182
Noren lf	0	0	0	0	0	0	.063
Ford p	4	0	0	0	0	0	.000
TOTALS	**32**	**5**	**8**	**1**	**5**	**4**	**.249**

a - Batted for Skowron in the 5th

BATTING: HR: Skowron (1, 1st off Spooner 2 on, 1 out). **RBI:** Berra 1 (2), Bauer 1 (1), Skowron 3 (3). **Runners left in scoring position, 2 out:** Collins 1, Cerv 2. **GIDP:** Cerv. **Team LOB:** 7 **BASERUNNING: SB:** Rizzuto (2, 2nd base off Spooner/Campanella). **FIELDING: DP:** 1 (McDougald-Martin-Skowron).

BROOKLYN	IP	H	R	ER	BB	SO	HR	ERA
Spooner (L, 0-1)	0.1	3	5	5	2	1	1	13.50
Meyer	5.2	4	0	0	2	4	0	0.00
Roebuck	2	1	0	0	0	0	0	0.00

NY YANKEES	IP	H	R	ER	BB	SO	HR	ERA
Ford (W, 2-0)	9	4	1	1	4	8	0	2.12

WP: Ford 1. **HBP:** Furillo (by Ford). **Ground balls-fly balls:** Spooner 0-0, Meyer 6-6, Roebuck 4-3, Ford 14-4. **Batters faced:** Spooner 6, Meyer 22, Roebuck 8, Ford 35. **UMPIRES:** hp—Ballanfant, 1b—Honochick, 2b—Dascoli, 3b—Summers, lf—Flaherty, rf—Donatelli **T:** 2:34 **A:** 64,022

GAME 7 Brooklyn 2 New York 0
Yankee Stadium 10/04/55

BROOKLYN	AB	R	H	HR	RBI	BB	AVG
Gilliam lf-2b	4	0	1	0	0	1	.292
Reese ss	4	1	1	0	0	0	.296
Snider cf	3	0	0	0	0	0	.320
Campanella c	3	1	1	0	0	0	.259
Furillo rf	3	0	0	0	0	1	.296
Hodges 1b	2	0	1	0	2	1	.292
Hoak 3b	3	0	1	0	0	1	.333
Zimmer 2b	2	0	0	0	0	0	.222
a-Shuba ph	1	0	0	0	0	0	.000
Amoros lf	0	0	0	0	0	1	.333
Podres p	4	0	0	0	0	0	.143
TOTALS	**29**	**2**	**5**	**0**	**2**	**5**	**.260**

a - Batted for Zimmer in the 6th

BATTING: 2B: Campanella (3, Byrne). **S:** Snider, Campanella. **SF:** Hodges. **RBI:** Hodges 2 (5). **2-out RBI:** Hodges 1. **Runners left in scoring position, 2 out:** Gilliam 1, Shuba 2. **Team LOB:** 8 **BASERUNNING: CS:** Gilliam (1, 2nd base off Grim/Berra). **FIELDING: Outfield assists:** Amoros (2). **DP:** 1 (Amoros-Reese-Hodges).

NY YANKEES	AB	R	H	HR	RBI	BB	AVG
Rizzuto ss	3	0	1	0	0	1	.267
Martin 2b	3	0	1	0	0	1	.320
McDougald 3b	4	0	3	0	0	0	.259
Berra c	4	0	1	0	0	0	.417
Bauer rf	4	0	0	0	0	0	.429
Skowron 1b	4	0	1	0	0	0	.333
Cerv cf	4	0	0	0	0	0	.125
Howard lf	4	0	1	0	0	0	.192
Byrne p	2	0	0	0	0	0	.167
Grim p	0	0	0	0	0	0	.000
a-Mantle ph	1	0	0	0	0	0	.200
Turley p	0	0	0	0	0	0	.000
TOTALS	**33**	**0**	**8**	**0**	**0**	**2**	**.248**

a - Batted for Grim in the 7th

BATTING: 2B: Skowron (2, Podres), Berra (1, Podres). **Runners left in scoring position, 2 out:** McDougald 1, Bauer 2, Cerv 2. **Team LOB:** 8

BROOKLYN	IP	H	R	ER	BB	SO	HR	ERA
Podres (W, 2-0)	9	8	0	0	2	4	0	1.00

NY YANKEES	IP	H	R	ER	BB	SO	HR	ERA
Byrne (L, 1-1)	5.1	3	2	1	3	2	0	1.88
Grim	1.2	1	0	0	1	1	0	4.15
Turley	2	1	0	0	1	1	0	8.44

WP: Grim 1. **IBB:** Furillo (by Byrne). **Ground balls-fly balls:** Podres 9-12, Byrne 9-4, Grim 2-0, Turley 0-5. **Batters faced:** Podres 35, Byrne 23, Grim 6, Turley 8. **UMPIRES:** hp—Honochick, 1b—Dascoli, 2b—Summers, 3b—Ballanfant, lf—Flaherty, rf—Donatelli **T:** 2:44 **A:** 62,465

1956 NY YANKEES DEF. BROOKLYN, 4-3

GAME 1 Brooklyn 6 New York 3
Ebbets Field 10/03/56

NY YANKEES	AB	R	H	HR	RBI	BB	AVG
Bauer rf	5	0	2	0	0	0	.400
Slaughter lf	5	1	3	0	0	0	.600
Mantle cf	3	1	1	1	2	2	.333
Berra c	3	0	0	0	0	1	.000
Skowron 1b	4	0	0	0	0	0	.000
McDougald ss	4	0	0	0	0	0	.000
Martin 2b-3b	3	1	1	1	1	1	.333
Carey 3b	3	0	1	0	0	0	.333
c-Collins ph	1	0	0	0	0	0	.000
Turley p	0	0	0	0	0	0	.000
Ford p	1	0	0	0	0	0	.000
a-Wilson ph	1	0	0	0	0	0	.000
Kucks p	0	0	0	0	0	0	.000
b-Cerv ph	1	0	1	0	0	0	1.000
Morgan p	0	0	0	0	0	0	.000
d-Byrne ph	1	0	0	0	0	0	.000
Coleman 2b	0	0	0	0	0	0	.000
TOTALS	**35**	**3**	**9**	**2**	**3**	**4**	**.257**

a - Batted for Ford in the 4th
b - Batted for Kucks in the 6th
c - Batted for Carey in the 8th
d - Batted for Morgan in the 8th

BATTING: HR: Mantle (1, 1st off Maglie 1 on, 1 out), Martin (1, 4th off Maglie 0 on, 1 out). **RBI:** Mantle 2 (2), Martin 1 (1). **Runners left in scoring position, 2 out:** Bauer 1, Skowron 2. **GIDP:** Mantle. **Team LOB:** 9 **FIELDING: E:** Skowron (1). **Outfield assists:** Mantle (1). **DP:** 1 (Skowron-McDougald-Martin).

BROOKLYN	AB	R	H	HR	RBI	BB	AVG
Gilliam 2b	3	0	0	0	0	1	.000
Reese ss	4	1	2	0	0	0	.500
Snider cf	3	1	1	0	0	1	.333
Robinson 3b	4	1	1	1	1	0	.250
Hodges 1b	4	2	2	1	3	0	.500
Furillo rf	4	0	1	0	1	0	.250
Campanella c	4	1	1	0	0	0	.250
Amoros lf	3	0	1	0	1	0	.333
Maglie p	3	0	0	0	0	0	.000
TOTALS	**32**	**6**	**9**	**2**	**6**	**2**	**.281**

BATTING: 2B: Furillo (1, Ford), Campanella (1, Kucks). **HR:** Robinson (1, 2nd off Ford 0 on, 0 out), Hodges (1, 3th off Ford 2 on, 2 out). **RBI:** Robinson 1 (1), Hodges 3 (3), Furillo 1 (1), Amoros 1 (1). **2-out RBI:** Hodges 3. **Runners left in scoring position, 2 out:** Reese 1, Robinson 1, Maglie 1. **GIDP:** Maglie. **Team LOB:** 4 **BASERUNNING: SB:** Gilliam (1, 2nd base off Kucks/Berra). **FIELDING: DP:** 1 (Gilliam-Reese-Hodges).

NY YANKEES	IP	H	R	ER	BB	SO	HR	ERA
Ford (L, 0-1)	3	6	5	5	0	1	2	15.00
Kucks	2	2	1	1	0	1	0	4.50
Morgan	2	1	0	0	2	0	0	0.00
Turley	1	0	0	0	0	2	0	0.00

BROOKLYN	IP	H	R	ER	BB	SO	HR	ERA
Maglie (W, 1-0)	9	9	3	3	4	10	2	3.00

IBB: Snider (by Morgan). **Ground balls-fly balls:** Ford 2-6, Kucks 3-2, Morgan 2-3, Turley 1-0, Maglie 3-13. **Batters faced:** Ford 15, Kucks 8, Morgan 8, Turley 3, Maglie 39. **UMPIRES:** hp—Pinelli, 1b—Soar, 2b—Boggess, 3b—Napp, lf—Gorman, rf—Runge **T:** 2:32 **A:** 34,479

GAME 2 Brooklyn 13 New York 8
Ebbets Field 10/05/56

NY YANKEES	AB	R	H	HR	RBI	BB	AVG
McDougald ss	3	0	1	0	0	1	.143
Slaughter lf	4	3	2	0	1	0	.556
Mantle cf	4	1	1	0	0	1	.286
Berra c	4	1	2	1	4	1	.286
Collins 1b	4	0	1	0	2	1	.200
Bauer rf	5	0	1	0	0	0	.300
Martin 3b-2b	4	1	1	0	0	0	.286
Coleman 2b	2	0	0	0	0	0	.000
b-Skowron ph	1	0	0	0	0	0	.000
Carey 3b	0	0	0	0	0	0	.333
Larsen p	1	1	1	0	1	0	1.000
Kucks p	0	0	0	0	0	0	.000
Byrne p	0	0	0	0	0	0	.000
Sturdivant p	0	0	0	0	0	0	.000
Morgan p	1	1	1	0	0	0	1.000
Turley p	0	0	0	0	0	0	.000
a-Siebern ph	1	0	0	0	0	0	.000
McDermott p	1	0	1	0	0	0	1.000
TOTALS	**35**	**8**	**12**	**1**	**8**	**4**	**.300**

a - Batted for Turley in the 6th
b - Batted for Coleman in the 8th

BATTING: HR: Berra (1, 2nd off Newcombe 3 on, 2 out). **S:** Coleman, McDougald. **SF:** Slaughter. **RBI:** Slaughter 1 (1), Berra 4 (4), Collins 2 (2), Larsen 1 (1). **2-out RBI:** Berra 4, Collins 1. **Runners left in scoring position, 2 out:** Bauer 1. **GIDP:** Martin. **Team LOB:** 7 **FIELDING: E:** Collins (1), Bauer (1). **DP:** 1 (Martin-Collins).

BROOKLYN	AB	R	H	HR	RBI	BB	AVG
Gilliam 2b	3	1	1	0	2	3	.167
Reese ss	6	1	1	0	2	0	.300
Snider cf	4	3	2	1	3	2	.429
Robinson 3b	4	2	2	0	0	1	.375
Hodges 1b	3	2	3	0	4	2	.714
Amoros lf	4	1	0	0	0	0	.143
b-Jackson ph	1	0	0	0	0	0	.000
Cimoli lf	0	0	0	0	0	0	.000
Furillo rf	4	2	2	0	0	1	.375
Campanella c	3	1	0	0	1	1	.143
Newcombe p	0	0	0	0	0	0	.000
Roebuck p	0	0	0	0	0	0	.000
a-Mitchell ph	1	0	0	0	0	0	.000
Bessent p	2	0	1	0	1	1	.500
TOTALS	**35**	**13**	**12**	**1**	**13**	**11**	**.313**

a - Batted for Roebuck in the 2nd
b - Batted for Amoros in the 7th

BATTING: 2B: Hodges 2 (2, Morgan). **HR:** Snider (1, 2nd off Byrne 2 on, 2 out). **S:** Bessent. **SF:** Campanella. **RBI:** Gilliam 2 (2), Reese 2 (2), Snider 3 (3), Hodges 4 (7), Campanella 1 (1), Bessent 1 (1). **2-out RBI:** Reese 2, Snider 3, Hodges 2, Bessent 1. **Runners left in scoring position, 2 out:** Reese 2, Amoros 1, Jackson 1, Bessent 1. **GIDP:** Robinson. **Team LOB:** 11 **FIELDING: DP:** 1 (Reese-Gilliam-Hodges).

NY YANKEES	IP	H	R	ER	BB	SO	HR	ERA
Larsen	1.2	1	4	0	4	0	0	0.00
Kucks	0	1	1	0	0	0	0	4.50
Byrne	0.1	1	1	0	0	1	1	0.00
Sturdivant	0.2	2	1	1	2	2	0	13.50
Morgan (L, 0-1)	2	5	4	4	2	3	0	9.00
Turley	0.1	0	0	0	0	1	0	0.00
McDermott	3	2	2	1	3	3	0	3.00

BROOKLYN	IP	H	R	ER	BB	SO	HR	ERA
Newcombe	1.2	6	6	6	2	0	1	32.40
Roebuck	0.1	0	0	0	0	0	0	0.00
Bessent (W, 1-0)	7	6	2	2	2	4	0	2.57

WP: Bessent 1. **IBB:** Campanella (by Morgan). **Ground balls-fly balls:** Larsen 2-2, Kucks 0-0, Byrne 0-0, Sturdivant 0-0, Morgan 1-2, Turley 0-0, McDermott 2-4, Newcombe 2-2, Roebuck 1-0, Bessent 6-8. **Batters faced:** Larsen 10, Kucks 1, Byrne 2, Sturdivant 6, Morgan 13, Turley 1, McDermott 15, Newcombe 13, Roebuck 1, Bessent 28. **UMPIRES:** hp—Soar, 1b—Boggess, 2b—Napp, 3b—Pinelli, lf—Runge, rf—Gorman **T:** 3:26 **A:** 36,217

GAME 3 New York 5 Brooklyn 3
Yankee Stadium 10/06/56

BROOKLYN	AB	R	H	HR	RBI	BB	AVG
Gilliam lf	4	0	0	0	0	0	.100
Reese ss	4	1	2	0	0	0	.357
Snider cf	3	0	0	0	1	0	.300
Robinson 3b	3	1	1	0	0	1	.364
Hodges 1b	3	1	1	0	0	1	.600
Furillo rf	4	0	2	0	0	0	.417
Campanella c	3	0	1	0	1	0	.200
Neal 2b	4	0	0	0	0	0	.000
Craig p	2	0	1	0	0	0	.500
a-Jackson ph	1	0	0	0	0	0	.000
Labine p	0	0	0	0	0	0	.000
TOTALS	**31**	**3**	**8**	**0**	**2**	**2**	**.296**

a - Batted for Craig in the 7th

BATTING: 2B: Furillo (2, Ford). **3B:** Reese (1, Ford). **SF:** Campanella, Snider. **RBI:** Snider 1 (4), Campanella 1 (2). **Runners left in scoring position, 2 out:** Gilliam 1, Neal 1. **GIDP:** Gilliam. **Team LOB:** 5 **BASERUNNING: CS:** Campanella (1, 2nd base off Ford/Berra). **FIELDING: E:** Neal (1). **DP:** 2 (Craig-Reese-Hodges, Neal-Reese-Hodges).

NY YANKEES	AB	R	H	HR	RBI	BB	AVG
Bauer rf	4	1	1	0	0	0	.286
Collins 1b	4	1	0	0	0	0	.111
Mantle cf	4	0	1	0	0	0	.273
Berra c	4	1	2	0	1	0	.364
Slaughter lf	3	1	2	1	3	1	.583
Martin 2b	4	1	1	1	1	0	.273
McDougald ss	2	0	1	0	0	1	.222
Carey 3b	3	0	0	0	0	0	.167
Ford p	3	0	0	0	0	0	.000
TOTALS	**31**	**5**	**8**	**2**	**5**	**2**	**.287**

BATTING: 2B: Berra (1, Labine). **HR:** Martin (2, 2nd off Craig 0 on, 1 out), Slaughter (1, 6th off Craig 2 on, 2 out). **RBI:** Berra 1 (5), Slaughter 3 (4), Martin 1 (2). **2-out RBI:** Berra 1, Slaughter 3. **Runners left in scoring position, 2 out:** Martin 1. **GIDP:** Martin, Ford. **Team LOB:** 4 **FIELDING: E:** McDougald (1). **Outfield assists:** Bauer (1). **DP:** 1 (Martin-McDougald-Collins).

BROOKLYN	IP	H	R	ER	BB	SO	HR	ERA
Craig (L, 0-1)	6	7	4	4	1	4	2	6.00
Labine	2	1	1	0	1	2	0	0.00

NY YANKEES	IP	H	R	ER	BB	SO	HR	ERA
Ford (W, 1-1)	9	8	3	2	2	7	0	5.25

IBB: Slaughter (by Labine). **Ground balls-fly balls:** Craig 4-8, Labine 2-3, Ford 10-6. **Batters faced:** Craig 24, Labine 9, Ford 35. **UMPIRES:** hp—Boggess, 1b—Napp, 2b—Pinelli, 3b—Soar, lf—Gorman, rf—Runge **T:** 2:17 **A:** 73,977

GAME 4 New York 6 Brooklyn 2
Yankee Stadium 10/07/56

BROOKLYN	AB	R	H	HR	RBI	BB	AVG
Gilliam 2b	4	0	0	0	0	1	.071
Reese ss	4	0	1	0	0	0	.333
Snider cf	4	1	1	0	0	0	.286
Robinson 3b	3	1	1	0	0	1	.357
Hodges 1b	4	0	1	0	1	0	.500
Amoros lf	3	0	0	0	0	1	.100
Furillo rf	3	0	0	0	0	1	.333
Campanella c	2	0	2	0	1	2	.333
Erskine p	1	0	0	0	0	0	.000
a-Walker ph	1	0	0	0	0	0	.000
Roebuck p	0	0	0	0	0	0	.000
b-Mitchell ph	1	0	0	0	0	0	.000
Drysdale p	0	0	0	0	0	0	.000
c-Jackson ph	1	0	0	0	0	0	.000
TOTALS	**31**	**2**	**6**	**0**	**2**	**6**	**.271**

a - Batted for Erskine in the 5th
b - Batted for Roebuck in the 7th
c - Batted for Drysdale in the 9th

BATTING: 2B: Snider (1, Sturdivant), Robinson (1, Sturdivant). **RBI:** Hodges 1 (8), Campanella 1 (3). **Runners left in scoring position, 2 out:** Gilliam 3, Hodges 1. **GIDP:** Walker. **Team LOB:** 8 **BASERUNNING: CS:** Gilliam (1, 2nd base off Sturdivant/Berra). **FIELDING: DP:** 1 (Gilliam-Reese-Hodges).

NY YANKEES	AB	R	H	HR	RBI	BB	AVG
Bauer rf	4	1	1	1	2	0	.278
Collins 1b	3	1	1	0	0	1	.167
Mantle cf	3	2	1	1	1	1	.286
Berra c	4	0	1	0	1	0	.333
Slaughter lf	3	1	0	0	0	1	.467
Martin 2b	4	0	1	0	1	0	.267
McDougald ss	2	0	0	0	1	0	.182
Carey 3b	3	1	1	0	0	0	.222
Sturdivant p	3	0	1	0	0	0	.333
TOTALS	**29**	**6**	**7**	**2**	**6**	**3**	**.277**

BATTING: 2B: Collins (1, Erskine). **HR:** Mantle (2, 6th off Roebuck 0 on, 0 out), Bauer (1, 7th off Drysdale 1 on, 2 out). **SF:** McDougald. **RBI:** Bauer 2 (2), Mantle 1 (3), Berra 1 (6), Martin 1 (3), McDougald 1 (1). **2-out RBI:** Bauer 2, Berra 1. **GIDP:** Collins. **Team LOB:** 3 **BASERUNNING: SB:** Mantle (1, 2nd base off Erskine/Campanella). **FIELDING: E:** Carey (1). **DP:** 2 (Collins, Martin-McDougald-Collins).

BROOKLYN	IP	H	R	ER	BB	SO	HR	ERA
Erskine (L, 0-1)	4	4	3	3	2	2	0	6.75
Roebuck	2	1	1	1	0	2	1	3.86
Drysdale	2	2	2	2	1	1	1	9.00

NY YANKEES	IP	H	R	ER	BB	SO	HR	ERA
Sturdivant (W, 1-0)	9	6	2	2	6	7	0	2.79

IBB: Slaughter (by Erskine). **Ground balls-fly balls:** Erskine 5-3, Roebuck 1-3, Drysdale 5-0, Sturdivant 8-10. **Batters faced:** Erskine 17, Roebuck 7, Drysdale 9, Sturdivant 37. **UMPIRES:** hp—Napp, 1b—Pinelli, 2b—Soar, 3b—Boggess, lf—Runge, rf—Gorman **T:** 2:43 **A:** 69,705

GAME 5 New York 2 Brooklyn 0
Yankee Stadium 10/08/56

BROOKLYN	AB	R	H	HR	RBI	BB	AVG
Gilliam 2b	3	0	0	0	0	0	.059
Reese ss	3	0	0	0	0	0	.286
Snider cf	3	0	0	0	0	0	.235
Robinson 3b	3	0	0	0	0	0	.294
Hodges 1b	3	0	0	0	0	0	.412
Amoros lf	3	0	0	0	0	0	.077
Furillo rf	3	0	0	0	0	0	.278
Campanella c	3	0	0	0	0	0	.267
Maglie p	2	0	0	0	0	0	.000
a-Mitchell ph	1	0	0	0	0	0	.000
TOTALS	**27**	**0**	**0**	**0**	**0**	**0**	**.224**

a - Batted for Maglie in the 9th

BATTING: Team LOB: 0 **FIELDING: DP:** 2 (Reese-Hodges, Hodges-Campanella-Robinson-Campanella-Robinson).

NY YANKEES	AB	R	H	HR	RBI	BB	AVG
Bauer rf	4	0	1	0	1	0	.273
Collins 1b	4	0	1	0	0	0	.188
Mantle cf	3	1	1	1	1	0	.294
Berra c	3	0	0	0	0	0	.278
Slaughter lf	2	0	0	0	0	1	.412
Martin 2b	3	0	1	0	0	0	.278
McDougald ss	2	0	0	0	0	1	.154
Carey 3b	3	1	1	0	0	0	.250
Larsen p	2	0	0	0	0	0	.333
TOTALS	**26**	**2**	**5**	**1**	**2**	**2**	**.263**

BATTING: HR: Mantle (3, 4th off Maglie 0 on, 2 out). **S:** Larsen. **RBI:** Bauer 1 (3), Mantle 1 (4). **2-out RBI:** Mantle 1. **Runners left in scoring position, 2 out:** Carey 1. **Team LOB:** 3

BROOKLYN	IP	H	R	ER	BB	SO	HR	ERA
Maglie (L, 1-1)	8	5	2	2	2	5	1	2.65

NY YANKEES	IP	H	R	ER	BB	SO	HR	ERA
Larsen (W, 1-0)	9	0	0	0	0	7	0	0.00

Ground balls-fly balls: Maglie 6-10, Larsen 6-14. **Batters faced:** Maglie 29, Larsen 27. **UMPIRES:** hp—Pinelli, 1b—Soar, 2b—Boggess, 3b—Napp, lf—Gorman, rf—Runge **T:** 2:06 **A:** 64,519

GAME 6 Brooklyn 1 New York 0
Ebbets Field 10/09/56

NY YANKEES	AB	R	H	HR	RBI	BB	AVG
Bauer rf	5	0	2	0	0	0	.296
Collins 1b	5	0	2	0	0	0	.238
Mantle cf	3	0	0	0	0	1	.250
Berra c	4	0	2	0	0	0	.318
Slaughter lf	3	0	0	0	0	1	.350
Martin 2b	4	0	1	0	0	0	.273
McDougald ss	4	0	0	0	0	0	.118
Carey 3b	4	0	0	0	0	0	.188
Turley p	4	0	0	0	0	0	.000
TOTALS	**36**	**0**	**7**	**0**	**0**	**2**	**.250**

BATTING: 2B: Berra (2, Labine), Collins (2, Labine). **Runners left in scoring position, 2 out:** Mantle 1, Slaughter 1, Martin 1. **GIDP:** Collins. **Team LOB:** 8 **Outfield assists:** Slaughter (1).

BROOKLYN	AB	R	H	HR	RBI	BB	AVG
Gilliam 2b	3	1	1	0	0	2	.100
Reese ss	4	0	0	0	0	0	.240
Snider cf	2	0	1	0	0	3	.263
Robinson 3b	4	0	1	0	1	1	.286
Hodges 1b	3	0	0	0	0	1	.350
Amoros lf	3	0	0	0	0	1	.063
Furillo rf	4	0	0	0	0	0	.227
Campanella c	4	0	0	0	0	0	.211
Labine p	4	0	1	0	0	0	.250
TOTALS	**31**	**1**	**4**	**0**	**1**	**8**	**.209**

BATTING: 2B: Labine (1, Turley). **S:** Reese. **RBI:** Robinson 1 (2). **2-out RBI:** Robinson 1. **Runners left in scoring position, 2 out:** Robinson 1, Hodges 1. **Team LOB:** 10 **FIELDING: DP:** 1 (Gilliam-Reese-Hodges).

NY YANKEES	IP	H	R	ER	BB	SO	HR	ERA
Turley (L, 0-1)	9.2	4	1	1	8	11	0	0.82

BROOKLYN	IP	H	R	ER	BB	SO	HR	ERA
Labine (W, 1-0)	10	7	0	0	2	5	0	0.00

IBB: Mantle (by Labine), Snider 2 (by Turley). **Ground balls-fly balls:** Turley 3-13, Labine 14-10. **Batters faced:** Turley 40, Labine 38. **UMPIRES:** hp—Soar, 1b—Boggess, 2b—Napp, 3b—Pinelli, lf—Runge, rf—Gorman **T:** 2:37 **A:** 33,224

GAME 7 New York 9 Brooklyn 0
Ebbets Field 10/10/56

NY YANKEES	AB	R	H	HR	RBI	BB	AVG
Bauer rf	5	1	1	0	0	0	.281
Martin 2b	5	2	2	0	0	0	.296
Mantle cf	4	1	1	0	0	1	.250
Berra c	3	3	2	2	4	2	.360
Skowron 1b	5	1	1	1	4	0	.100
Howard lf	5	1	2	1	1	0	.400
McDougald ss	4	0	1	0	0	0	.143
Carey 3b	3	0	0	0	0	1	.158
Kucks p	3	0	0	0	0	0	.000
TOTALS	**37**	**9**	**10**	**4**	**9**	**4**	**.253**

BATTING: 2B: Mantle (1, Bessent), Howard (1, Craig). **HR:** Berra 2 (3, 1st off Newcombe 1 on, 2 out, 3th off Newcombe 1 on, 2 out), Howard (1, 4th off Newcombe 0 on, 0 out), Skowron (1, 7th off Craig 3 on, 0 out). **S:** Kucks. **RBI:** Berra 4 (10), Skowron 4 (4), Howard 1 (1). **2-out RBI:** Berra 4. **Runners left in scoring position, 2 out:** Bauer 2, Howard 1, Kucks 1. **Team LOB:** 6 **BASERUNNING: SB:** Bauer (1, 2nd base off Newcombe/Campanella). **FIELDING: DP:** 2 (Kucks-Martin-Skowron, McDougald-Skowron).

BROOKLYN	AB	R	H	HR	RBI	BB	AVG
Gilliam 2b	4	0	0	0	0	0	.083
Reese ss	2	0	0	0	0	2	.222
Snider cf	4	0	2	0	0	0	.304
Robinson 3b	3	0	0	0	0	1	.250
Hodges 1b	3	0	0	0	0	0	.304
Amoros lf	3	0	0	0	0	0	.053
Furillo rf	3	0	1	0	0	0	.240
Campanella c	3	0	0	0	0	0	.182
Newcombe p	1	0	0	0	0	0	.000
Bessent p	0	0	0	0	0	0	.500
a-Mitchell ph	1	0	0	0	0	0	.000
Craig p	0	0	0	0	0	0	.500
Roebuck p	0	0	0	0	0	0	.000
b-Walker ph	1	0	0	0	0	0	.000
Erskine p	0	0	0	0	0	0	.000
TOTALS	**28**	**0**	**3**	**0**	**0**	**3**	**.195**

a - Batted for Bessent in the 6th
b - Batted for Roebuck in the 8th

BATTING: GIDP: Robinson. **Team LOB:** 4 **FIELDING: E:** Reese (1).

NY YANKEES	IP	H	R	ER	BB	SO	HR	ERA
Kucks (W, 1-0)	9	3	0	0	3	1	0	0.82

BROOKLYN	IP	H	R	ER	BB	SO	HR	ERA
Newcombe (L, 0-1)	3	5	5	5	1	4	3	21.21
Bessent	3	2	0	0	1	1	0	1.80
Craig	0	3	4	4	2	0	1	12.00
Roebuck	2	0	0	0	0	3	0	2.08
Erskine	1	0	0	0	0	0	0	5.40

WP: Craig 1. **IBB:** Berra 2 (by Bessent, by Craig). **Ground balls-fly balls:** Kucks 15-9, Newcombe 3-2, Bessent 5-3, Craig 0-0, Roebuck 1-2, Erskine 2-1. **Batters faced:** Kucks 31, Newcombe 15, Bessent 13, Craig 5, Roebuck 6, Erskine 3. **UMPIRES:** hp—Boggess, 1b—Napp, 2b—Pinelli, 3b—Soar, lf—Gorman, rf—Runge **T:** 2:19 **A:** 33,782

1957 MILWAUKEE DEF. NY YANKEES, 4-3

GAME 1 New York 3 Milwaukee 1
Yankee Stadium 10/02/57

MILWAUKEE	AB	R	H	HR	RBI	BB	AVG
Schoendienst 2b	4	0	1	0	1	0	.250
Logan ss	3	0	0	0	0	1	.000
Mathews 3b	2	0	0	0	0	2	.000
Aaron cf	4	0	1	0	0	0	.250
Adcock 1b	4	0	0	0	0	0	.000
Torre 1b	0	0	0	0	0	0	.000
Pafko rf	4	0	0	0	0	0	.000
Covington lf	4	1	2	0	0	0	.500
Crandall c	4	0	1	0	0	0	.250
Spahn p	1	0	0	0	0	1	.000
Johnson p	0	0	0	0	0	0	.000
a-Jones ph	1	0	0	0	0	0	.000
McMahon p	0	0	0	0	0	0	.000
TOTALS	**31**	**1**	**5**	**0**	**1**	**4**	**.161**

a - Batted for Johnson in the 7th

BATTING: 2B: Covington (1, Ford). **RBI:** Schoendienst 1 (1). **2-out RBI:** Schoendienst 1. **Runners left in scoring position, 2 out:** Schoendienst 1, Pafko 2. **GIDP:** Adcock. **Team LOB:** 7 **FIELDING: DP:** 1 (Crandall-Logan).

NY YANKEES	AB	R	H	HR	RBI	BB	AVG
Bauer rf	4	0	1	0	1	0	.250
McDougald ss	4	0	1	0	0	0	.250
Mantle cf	4	0	2	0	0	0	.500
Skowron 1b	1	0	0	0	0	0	.000
Howard 1b	2	1	1	0	0	0	.500
Collins 1b	1	0	0	0	0	0	.000
Berra c	3	1	1	0	0	1	.333
Carey 3b	3	0	1	0	1	1	.333
Coleman 2b	3	1	2	0	1	0	.667
Kubek lf	3	0	0	0	0	0	.000
Ford p	3	0	0	0	0	0	.000
TOTALS	**31**	**3**	**9**	**0**	**3**	**2**	**.290**

BATTING: 2B: Coleman (1, Spahn), Bauer (1, Spahn). **S:** Coleman. **RBI:** Bauer 1 (1), Carey 1 (1), Coleman 1 (1). **2-out RBI:** Bauer 1. **Runners left in scoring position, 2 out:** McDougald 1, Berra 1, Coleman 1, Kubek 1, Ford 1. **Team LOB:** 7 **BASERUNNING: CS:** Mantle (1, 2nd base off McMahon/Crandall). **FIELDING: DP:** 1 (McDougald-Coleman-Howard).

MILWAUKEE	IP	H	R	ER	BB	SO	HR	ERA
Spahn (L, 0-1)	5.1	7	3	3	1	0	0	5.06
Johnson	0.2	0	0	0	0	1	0	0.00
McMahon	2	2	0	0	1	3	0	0.00

NY YANKEES	IP	H	R	ER	BB	SO	HR	ERA
Ford (W, 1-0)	9	5	1	1	4	5	0	1.00

Ground balls-fly balls: Spahn 6-10, Johnson 0-0, McMahon 2-0, Ford 13-8. **Batters faced:** Spahn 24, Johnson 2, McMahon 8, Ford 35. **UMPIRES:** hp—Paparella, 1b—Conlan, 2b—McKinley, 3b—Donatelli, lf—Secory, rf—Chylak **T:** 2:10 **A:** 69,476

GAME 2 Milwaukee 4 New York 2
Yankee Stadium 10/03/57

MILWAUKEE	AB	R	H	HR	RBI	BB	AVG
Schoendienst 2b	4	0	0	0	0	0	.125
Logan ss	3	1	1	1	1	0	.167
Mathews 3b	4	0	0	0	0	0	.000
Aaron cf	4	1	1	0	0	0	.250
Adcock 1b	4	1	2	0	1	0	.250
Torre 1b	0	0	0	0	0	0	.000
Pafko rf	4	1	1	0	0	0	.125
Covington lf	4	0	2	0	2	0	.500
Crandall c	3	0	1	0	0	1	.286
Burdette p	3	0	0	0	0	0	.000
TOTALS	**33**	**4**	**8**	**1**	**4**	**1**	**.203**

BATTING: 3B: Aaron (1, Shantz). **HR:** Logan (1, 3th off Shantz 0 on, 1 out). **S:** Burdette. **RBI:** Logan 1 (1), Adcock 1 (1), Covington 2 (2). **Runners left in scoring position, 2 out:** Schoendienst 1, Logan 1, Burdette 2. **GIDP:** Mathews. **Team LOB:** 5

NY YANKEES	AB	R	H	HR	RBI	BB	AVG
Bauer rf	5	1	1	1	1	0	.222
McDougald ss	4	0	0	0	0	0	.125
Mantle cf	3	0	0	0	0	1	.286
Berra c	4	0	0	0	0	0	.143
Slaughter lf	3	1	1	0	0	1	.333
Simpson 1b	4	0	0	0	0	0	.000
Kubek 3b	4	0	2	0	0	0	.286
Coleman 2b	2	0	1	0	1	1	.600
b-Collins ph	1	0	0	0	0	0	.000
Shantz p	1	0	0	0	0	0	.000
Ditmar p	1	0	0	0	0	0	.000
a-Lumpe ph	1	0	1	0	0	0	1.000
Grim p	0	0	0	0	0	0	.000
c-Howard ph	1	0	1	0	0	0	.667
d-Richardson pr	0	0	0	0	0	0	.000
TOTALS	**34**	**2**	**7**	**1**	**2**	**3**	**.246**

a - Batted for Ditmar in the 7th
b - Batted for Coleman in the 9th
c - Batted for Grim in the 9th
d - Ran for Howard in the 9th

BATTING: 2B: Slaughter (1, Burdette). **HR:** Bauer (1, 3th off Burdette 0 on, 0 out). **RBI:** Bauer 1 (2), Coleman 1 (2). **2-out RBI:** Coleman 1. **Runners left in scoring position, 2 out:** Bauer 1, McDougald 1, Kubek 2, Shantz 1. **Team LOB:** 8 **FIELDING: E:** Mantle (1), Kubek (1). **DP:** 1 (McDougald-Simpson).

MILWAUKEE	IP	H	R	ER	BB	SO	HR	ERA
Burdette (W, 1-0)	9	7	2	2	3	5	1	2.00

NY YANKEES	IP	H	R	ER	BB	SO	HR	ERA
Shantz (L, 0-1)	3	6	4	3	1	3	1	9.00
Ditmar	4	1	0	0	0	1	0	0.00
Grim	2	1	0	0	0	2	0	0.00

HBP: Logan (by Ditmar). **Ground balls-fly balls:** Burdette 12-10, Shantz 1-5, Ditmar 3-6, Grim 2-2. **Batters faced:** Burdette 37, Shantz 16, Ditmar 13, Grim 7. **UMPIRES:** hp—Conlan, 1b—McKinley, 2b—Donatelli, 3b—Paparella, lf—Secory, rf—Chylak **T:** 2:26 **A:** 65,202

GAME 3 New York 12 Milwaukee 3
County Stadium 10/05/57

NY YANKEES	AB	R	H	HR	RBI	BB	AVG
Bauer rf	5	1	1	0	2	1	.214
Kubek lf	5	3	3	2	4	0	.417
Mantle cf	3	2	2	1	2	2	.400
Berra c	4	2	1	0	0	1	.182
McDougald ss	1	2	0	0	1	3	.111
Simpson 1b	1	0	1	0	1	0	.200
a-Howard ph-1b	2	0	0	0	0	1	.400
Collins 1b	1	0	0	0	0	0	.000
Lumpe 3b	5	0	1	0	2	0	.333
Coleman 2b	4	1	0	0	0	1	.333
Turley p	1	0	0	0	0	0	.000
Larsen p	2	1	0	0	0	2	.000
TOTALS	**34**	**12**	**9**	**3**	**12**	**11**	**.253**

a - Batted for Simpson in the 3th

BATTING: HR: Kubek 2 (2, 1st off Buhl 0 on, 1 out, 7th off Trowbridge 2 on, 2 out), Mantle (1, 4th off Conley 1 on, 1 out). **SF:** McDougald. **RBI:** Bauer 2 (4), Kubek 4 (4), Mantle 2 (2), McDougald 1 (1), Simpson 1 (1), Lumpe 2 (2). **2-out RBI:** Bauer 2, Kubek 3, Simpson 1. **Runners left in scoring position, 2 out:** Lumpe 1, Larsen 1. **GIDP:** Bauer. **Team LOB:** 7 **BASERUNNING: SB:** McDougald (1, 2nd base off Trowbridge/Rice).

MILWAUKEE	AB	R	H	HR	RBI	BB	AVG
Schoendienst 2b	5	0	3	0	1	0	.308
Logan ss	4	1	2	0	0	1	.300
Mathews 3b	2	0	0	0	0	3	.000
Aaron cf	5	1	2	1	2	0	.308
Covington lf	3	0	0	0	0	2	.364
Adcock 1b	3	0	0	0	0	0	.182
Trowbridge p	0	0	0	0	0	0	.000
c-Jones ph	1	0	0	0	0	0	.000
McMahon p	0	0	0	0	0	0	.000
e-Pafko ph	0	0	0	0	0	0	.125
Hazle rf	4	1	0	0	0	1	.000
Rice c	3	0	1	0	0	1	.333
d-DeMerit pr	0	0	0	0	0	0	.000
Crandall c	1	0	0	0	0	0	.250
Buhl p	0	0	0	0	0	0	.000
Pizarro p	1	0	0	0	0	0	.000
Conley p	0	0	0	0	0	0	.000
a-Sawatski ph	1	0	0	0	0	0	.000
Johnson p	0	0	0	0	0	0	.000
b-Torre ph-1b	2	0	0	0	0	0	.000
TOTALS	**35**	**3**	**8**	**1**	**3**	**8**	**.212**

a - Batted for Conley in the 4th
b - Batted for Johnson in the 6th
c - Batted for Trowbridge in the 7th
d - Ran for Rice in the 8th e - Batted for McMahon in the 9th

BATTING: HR: Aaron (1, 5th off Larsen 1 on, 1 out). **RBI:** Schoendienst 1 (2), Aaron 2 (2). **Runners left in scoring position, 2 out:** Aaron 4, Adcock 2, Crandall 2. **Team LOB:** 14 **FIELDING: E:** Buhl (1). **PB:** Rice. **DP:** 1 (Schoendienst-Torre).

NY YANKEES	IP	H	R	ER	BB	SO	HR	ERA
Turley	1.2	3	1	1	4	2	0	5.40
Larsen (W, 1-0)	7.1	5	2	2	4	4	1	2.45

MILWAUKEE	IP	H	R	ER	BB	SO	HR	ERA
Buhl (L, 0-1)	0.2	2	3	2	2	0	1	27.00
Pizarro	1.2	3	2	2	2	1	0	10.80
Conley	1.2	2	2	2	1	0	1	10.80
Johnson	2	0	0	0	1	2	0	0.00
Trowbridge	1	2	5	5	3	1	1	45.00
McMahon	2	0	0	0	2	2	0	0.00

WP: Turley 1. **HBP:** Pafko (by Larsen). **Ground balls-fly balls:** Turley 0-3, Larsen 7-11, Buhl 1-0, Pizarro 2-2, Conley 4-1, Johnson 4-0, Trowbridge 0-2, McMahon 2-1. **Batters faced:** Turley 12, Larsen 32, Buhl 6, Pizarro 10, Conley 8, Johnson 7, Trowbridge 8, McMahon 7. **UMPIRES:** hp—McKinley, 1b—Donatelli, 2b—Paparella, 3b—Conlan, lf—Chylak, rf—Secory **T:** 3:18 **A:** 45,804

GAME 4 Milwaukee 7 New York 5
County Stadium 10/06/57

NY YANKEES	AB	R	H	HR	RBI	BB	AVG
Kubek lf-cf	5	1	2	0	0	0	.412
Bauer rf	5	0	1	0	1	0	.211
Mantle cf	5	1	0	0	0	0	.267
Slaughter lf	0	0	0	0	0	0	.333
Berra c	3	1	2	0	0	1	.286
McDougald ss	4	1	2	0	1	0	.231
Howard 1b	4	1	1	1	3	0	.333
Collins 1b	0	0	0	0	0	0	.000
Carey 3b	4	0	1	0	0	0	.286
Coleman 2b	4	0	1	0	0	0	.308
Sturdivant p	1	0	0	0	0	0	.000
a-Simpson ph	1	0	0	0	0	0	.167
Shantz p	0	0	0	0	0	0	.000
b-Lumpe ph	1	0	1	0	0	0	.429
Kucks p	0	0	0	0	0	0	.000
Byrne p	1	0	0	0	0	0	.000
Grim p	0	0	0	0	0	0	.000
TOTALS	**38**	**5**	**11**	**1**	**5**	**1**	**.263**

a - Batted for Sturdivant in the 5th
b - Batted for Shantz in the 8th

BATTING: 2B: Carey (1, Spahn). **3B:** Bauer (1, Spahn). **HR:** Howard (1, 9th off Spahn 2 on, 2 out). **RBI:** Bauer 1 (5), McDougald 1 (2), Howard 3 (3). **2-out RBI:** Bauer 1, McDougald 1, Howard 3. **Runners left in scoring position, 2 out:** Mantle 1, Howard 1. **GIDP:** Simpson, Howard, Kubek. **Team LOB:** 4

MILWAUKEE	AB	R	H	HR	RBI	BB	AVG
Schoendienst 2b	4	0	1	0	0	0	.294
Logan ss	4	2	1	0	1	1	.286
Mathews 3b	4	2	2	1	2	1	.167
Aaron cf	3	1	2	1	3	1	.375
Covington lf	4	0	0	0	0	0	.267
Torre 1b	3	1	1	1	1	0	.200
a-Adcock ph-1b	1	0	0	0	0	0	.167
Hazle rf	2	0	0	0	0	0	.000
Pafko rf	2	0	0	0	0	0	.100
Crandall c	4	0	0	0	0	0	.167
Spahn p	3	0	0	0	0	0	.000
b-Jones ph	0	0	0	0	0	0	.000
c-Mantilla pr	0	1	0	0	0	0	.000
TOTALS	**34**	**7**	**7**	**3**	**7**	**3**	**.211**

a - Batted for Torre in the 9th
b - Batted for Spahn in the 10th
c - Ran for Jones in the 10th

BATTING: 2B: Mathews (1, Sturdivant), Schoendienst (1, Kucks), Logan (1, Grim). **HR:** Aaron (2, 4th off Sturdivant 2 on, 0 out), Torre (1, 4th off Sturdivant 0 on, 1 out), Mathews (1, 10th off Grim 1 on, 1 out). **S:** Schoendienst. **RBI:** Logan 1 (2), Mathews 2 (2), Aaron 3 (5), Torre 1 (1). **Runners left in scoring position, 2 out:** Covington 1, Hazle 1. **Team LOB:** 4 **BASERUNNING: SB:** Covington (1, 2nd base off Sturdivant/Berra). **FIELDING: DP:** 3 (Schoendienst-Torre, Logan-Schoendienst-Torre 2).

NY YANKEES	IP	H	R	ER	BB	SO	HR	ERA
Sturdivant	4	4	4	4	1	1	2	9.00
Shantz	3	0	0	0	1	4	0	4.50
Kucks	0.2	1	0	0	1	1	0	0.00
Byrne	1.1	0	1	1	0	1	0	6.75
Grim (L, 0-1)	0.1	2	2	2	0	0	1	7.71

MILWAUKEE	IP	H	R	ER	BB	SO	HR	ERA
Spahn (W, 1-1)	10	11	5	5	1	2	1	4.70

HBP: Jones (by Byrne). **Ground balls-fly balls:** Sturdivant 8-3, Shantz 2-3, Kucks 0-1, Byrne 2-1, Grim 0-0, Spahn 19-6. **Batters faced:** Sturdivant 17, Shantz 10, Kucks 4, Byrne 5, Grim 3, Spahn 39. **UMPIRES:** hp—Donatelli, 1b—Paparella, 2b—Conlan, 3b—McKinley, lf—Chylak, rf—Secory **T:** 2:31 **A:** 45,804

GAME 5 Milwaukee 1 New York 0
County Stadium 10/07/57

NY YANKEES	AB	R	H	HR	RBI	BB	AVG
Bauer rf	4	0	2	0	0	0	.261
Kubek cf	3	0	0	0	0	0	.350
McDougald ss	4	0	1	0	0	0	.235
Berra c	4	0	1	0	0	0	.278
Slaughter lf	3	0	2	0	0	0	.500
Simpson 1b	3	0	0	0	0	0	.111
Lumpe 3b	3	0	0	0	0	0	.300
Coleman 2b	3	0	1	0	0	0	.313
a-Mantle pr	0	0	0	0	0	0	.267
Turley p	0	0	0	0	0	0	.000
Ford p	2	0	0	0	0	0	.000
b-Howard ph	1	0	0	0	0	0	.300
Richardson 2b	0	0	0	0	0	0	.000
TOTALS	**30**	**0**	**7**	**0**	**0**	**0**	**.257**

a - Ran for Coleman in the 8th
b - Batted for Ford in the 8th

BATTING: S: Kubek. **Runners left in scoring position, 2 out:** Berra 1. **GIDP:** Simpson, Slaughter. **Team LOB:** 4 **BASERUNNING: CS:** Slaughter (1, 2nd base off Burdette/Crandall), Mantle (2, 2nd base off Burdette/Crandall). **FIELDING: DP:** 1 (McDougald-Coleman-Simpson).

MILWAUKEE	AB	R	H	HR	RBI	BB	AVG
Schoendienst 2b	1	0	0	0	0	0	.278
Mantilla 2b	3	0	0	0	0	0	.000
Logan ss	4	0	0	0	0	0	.222
Mathews 3b	3	1	1	0	0	1	.200
Aaron cf	3	0	2	0	0	0	.421
Adcock 1b	3	0	1	0	1	0	.200
Torre 1b	0	0	0	0	0	0	.200
Pafko rf	3	0	2	0	0	0	.231
Covington lf	2	0	0	0	0	0	.235
Crandall c	3	0	0	0	0	0	.133
Burdette p	3	0	0	0	0	0	.000
TOTALS	**28**	**1**	**6**	**0**	**1**	**1**	**.211**

BATTING: S: Covington. **RBI:** Adcock 1 (2). **2-out RBI:** Adcock 1. **Runners left in scoring position, 2 out:** Pafko 1, Burdette 1. **GIDP:** Adcock. **Team LOB:** 5 **FIELDING: E:** Adcock (1). **DP:** 3 (Crandall-Logan, Mathews-Mantilla-Adcock, Logan-Adcock).

NY YANKEES	IP	H	R	ER	BB	SO	HR	ERA
Ford (L, 1-1)	7	6	1	1	1	2	0	1.13
Turley	1	0	0	0	0	2	0	3.38

MILWAUKEE	IP	H	R	ER	BB	SO	HR	ERA
Burdette (W, 2-0)	9	7	0	0	0	5	0	1.00

Ground balls-fly balls: Ford 9-8, Turley 0-1, Burdette 14-4. **Batters faced:** Ford 27, Turley 3, Burdette 31. **UMPIRES:** hp—Paparella, 1b—Conlan, 2b—McKinley, 3b—Donatelli, lf—Chylak, rf—Secory **T:** 2:00 **A:** 45,811

GAME 6 New York 3 Milwaukee 2
Yankee Stadium 10/09/57

MILWAUKEE	AB	R	H	HR	RBI	BB	AVG
Mantilla 2b	3	0	0	0	0	1	.000
Logan ss	4	0	0	0	0	0	.182
Mathews 3b	3	0	1	0	0	1	.222
Aaron cf	4	1	1	1	1	0	.391
Covington lf	4	0	0	0	0	0	.190
Torre 1b	3	1	2	1	1	0	.375
Hazle rf	3	0	0	0	0	0	.000
Rice c	3	0	0	0	0	0	.167
Buhl p	1	0	0	0	0	0	.000
Johnson p	1	0	0	0	0	0	.000
a-Sawatski ph	1	0	0	0	0	0	.000
McMahon p	0	0	0	0	0	0	.000
TOTALS	**30**	**2**	**4**	**2**	**2**	**2**	**.199**

a - Batted for Johnson in the 8th

BATTING: 2B: Mathews (2, Turley). **HR:** Torre (2, 5th off Turley 0 on, 0 out), Aaron (3, 7th off Turley 0 on, 0 out). **RBI:** Aaron 1 (6), Torre 1 (2). **Runners left in scoring position, 2 out:** Covington 1. **GIDP:** Covington. **Team LOB:** 3 **FIELDING: Outfield assists:** Covington (1). **DP:** 2 (Rice-Logan, Covington-Rice).

NY YANKEES	AB	R	H	HR	RBI	BB	AVG
Bauer rf	4	1	1	1	1	0	.259
Kubek cf	4	0	0	0	0	0	.292
Slaughter lf	2	1	0	0	0	2	.375
Berra c	4	1	3	1	2	0	.364
McDougald ss	3	0	1	0	0	0	.250
Lumpe 3b	3	0	1	0	0	1	.308
Simpson 1b	3	0	0	0	0	0	.083
Collins 1b	0	0	0	0	0	0	.000
Coleman 2b	2	0	1	0	0	1	.333
Turley p	3	0	0	0	0	0	.000
TOTALS	**28**	**3**	**7**	**2**	**3**	**4**	**.256**

BATTING: 2B: Coleman (2, Johnson), Berra (1, McMahon). **HR:** Berra (1, 3th off Buhl 1 on, 2 out), Bauer (2, 7th off Johnson 0 on, 1 out). **S:** McDougald. **RBI:** Bauer 1 (6), Berra 2 (2). **2-out RBI:** Berra 2. **Runners left in scoring position, 2 out:** Kubek 1, McDougald 2, Simpson 1. **Team LOB:** 6 **BASERUNNING: CS:** Lumpe (1, 2nd base off Buhl/Rice). **FIELDING: DP:** 1 (Turley-McDougald-Collins).

MILWAUKEE	IP	H	R	ER	BB	SO	HR	ERA
Buhl	2.2	4	2	2	4	4	1	10.80
Johnson (L, 0-1)	4.1	2	1	1	0	5	1	1.29
McMahon	1	1	0	0	0	0	0	0.00

NY YANKEES	IP	H	R	ER	BB	SO	HR	ERA
Turley (W, 1-0)	9	4	2	2	2	8	2	2.31

WP: Buhl 1. **Ground balls-fly balls:** Buhl 2-1, Johnson 6-2, McMahon 0-1, Turley 8-10. **Batters faced:** Buhl 15, Johnson 15, McMahon 3, Turley 32. **UMPIRES:** hp—Conlan, 1b—McKinley, 2b—Donatelli, 3b—Paparella, lf—Secory, rf—Chylak **T:** 2:09 **A:** 61,408

GAME 7 Milwaukee 5 New York 0
Yankee Stadium 10/10/57

MILWAUKEE	AB	R	H	HR	RBI	BB	AVG
Hazle rf	4	1	2	0	0	0	.154
a-Pafko ph-rf	1	0	0	0	0	0	.214
Logan ss	5	1	1	0	0	0	.185
Mathews 3b	4	1	1	0	2	0	.227
Aaron cf	5	1	2	0	1	0	.393
Covington lf	3	0	1	0	0	0	.208
Torre 1b	2	0	0	0	1	2	.300
Mantilla 2b	4	0	0	0	0	0	.000
Crandall c	4	1	2	1	1	0	.211
Burdette p	2	0	0	0	0	1	.000
TOTALS	**34**	**5**	**9**	**1**	**5**	**3**	**.209**

a - Batted for Hazle in the 8th

BATTING: 2B: Mathews (3, Larsen). **HR:** Crandall (1, 8th off Byrne 0 on, 2 out). **S:** Covington, Burdette, Mathews. **RBI:** Mathews 2 (4), Aaron 1 (7), Torre 1 (3), Crandall 1 (1). **2-out RBI:** Crandall 1. **Runners left in scoring position, 2 out:** Mathews 1, Covington 1, Mantilla 1, Crandall 1. **GIDP:** Mantilla. **Team LOB:** 8 **BASERUNNING: CS:** Crandall (1, 3rd base off Sturdivant/Berra). **FIELDING: E:** Mathews (1).

NY YANKEES	AB	R	H	HR	RBI	BB	AVG
Bauer rf	4	0	1	0	0	0	.258
Slaughter lf	4	0	0	0	0	0	.250
Mantle cf	4	0	1	0	0	0	.263
Berra c	3	0	0	0	0	1	.320
McDougald ss	4	0	1	0	0	0	.250
Kubek 3b	4	0	1	0	0	0	.286
Coleman 2b	4	0	2	0	0	0	.364
Collins 1b	2	0	0	0	0	0	.000
Sturdivant p	0	0	0	0	0	0	.000
c-Howard ph	1	0	0	0	0	0	.273
Byrne p	1	0	1	0	0	0	.500
Larsen p	0	0	0	0	0	0	.000
Shantz p	0	0	0	0	0	0	.000
a-Lumpe ph	1	0	0	0	0	0	.286
Ditmar p	0	0	0	0	0	0	.000
b-Skowron ph-1b	3	0	0	0	0	0	.000
TOTALS	**35**	**0**	**7**	**0**	**0**	**1**	**.248**

a - Batted for Shantz in the 3th
b - Batted for Ditmar in the 5th
c - Batted for Sturdivant in the 7th

BATTING: 2B: Bauer (2, Burdette). **Runners left in scoring position, 2 out:** McDougald 2, Skowron 3. **Team LOB:** 9 **FIELDING: E:** Kubek (2), McDougald (1), Berra (1). **DP:** 1 (McDougald-Coleman-Skowron).

MILWAUKEE	IP	H	R	ER	BB	SO	HR	ERA
Burdette (W, 3-0)	9	7	0	0	1	3	0	0.67

NY YANKEES	IP	H	R	ER	BB	SO	HR	ERA
Larsen (L, 1-1)	2.1	3	3	2	1	2	0	3.72
Shantz	0.2	2	1	0	0	0	0	4.05
Ditmar	2	1	0	0	0	1	0	0.00
Sturdivant	2	2	0	0	0	1	0	6.00
Byrne	2	1	1	1	2	0	1	5.40

IBB: Berra (by Burdette). **Ground balls-fly balls:** Burdette 13-12, Larsen 3-2, Shantz 1-1, Ditmar 5-2, Sturdivant 0-2, Byrne 2-3. **Batters faced:** Burdette 36, Larsen 12, Shantz 4, Ditmar 9, Sturdivant 7, Byrne 8. **UMPIRES:** hp—McKinley, 1b—Donatelli, 2b—Paparella, 3b—Conlan, lf—Chylak, rf—Secory **T:** 2:34 **A:** 61,207

1958 NY YANKEES DEF. MILWAUKEE, 4-3

GAME 1 Milwaukee 4 New York 3
County Stadium 10/01/58

NY YANKEES	AB	R	H	HR	RBI	BB	AVG
Bauer rf	5	1	2	1	2	0	.400
McDougald 2b	4	0	2	0	0	1	.500
Mantle cf	3	0	0	0	0	2	.000
Howard lf	5	0	0	0	0	0	.000
Berra c	4	0	2	0	0	0	.500
Skowron 1b	4	1	2	1	1	0	.500
Carey 3b	4	0	0	0	0	0	.000
Kubek ss	4	0	0	0	0	0	.000
Ford p	2	1	0	0	0	1	.000
Duren p	1	0	0	0	0	0	.000
TOTALS	**36**	**3**	**8**	**2**	**3**	**4**	**.222**

BATTING: 2B: Berra (1, Spahn). **HR:** Skowron (1, 4th off Spahn 0 on, 2 out), Bauer (1, 5th off Spahn 1 on, 1 out). **RBI:** Bauer 2 (2), Skowron 1 (1). **2-out RBI:** Skowron 1. **Runners left in scoring position, 2 out:** Howard 2, Kubek 2. **Team LOB:** 7 **FIELDING: E:** Kubek (1). **PB:** Berra.

MILWAUKEE	AB	R	H	HR	RBI	BB	AVG
Schoendienst 2b	4	0	0	0	0	1	.000
Logan ss	4	0	1	0	0	0	.250
b-Torre ph	1	0	0	0	0	0	.000
Mantilla ss	0	0	0	0	0	0	.000
Mathews 3b	3	1	0	0	0	2	.000
Aaron rf	4	1	1	0	0	1	.250
Adcock 1b	5	1	2	0	0	0	.400
Covington lf	4	0	0	0	1	0	.000
Crandall c	5	1	2	0	1	0	.400
Pafko cf	3	0	1	0	0	0	.333
a-Bruton ph-cf	2	0	1	0	1	0	.500
Spahn p	4	0	2	0	1	0	.500
TOTALS	**39**	**4**	**10**	**0**	**4**	**4**	**.256**

a - Batted for Pafko in the 9th
b - Batted for Logan in the 9th

BATTING: 2B: Logan (1, Ford), Aaron (1, Ford). **SF:** Covington. **RBI:** Covington 1 (1), Crandall 1 (1), Bruton 1 (1), Spahn 1 (1). **2-out RBI:** Crandall 1, Bruton 1, Spahn 1. **Runners left in scoring position, 2 out:** Schoendienst 1, Mathews 1, Aaron 1, Crandall 1, Spahn 1. **Team LOB:** 11 **Outfield assists:** Covington (1).

NY YANKEES	IP	H	R	ER	BB	SO	HR	ERA
Ford	7	6	3	3	3	8	0	3.86
Duren (L, 0-1)	2.2	4	1	1	1	5	0	3.38

MILWAUKEE	IP	H	R	ER	BB	SO	HR	ERA
Spahn (W, 1-0)	10	8	3	3	4	6	2	2.70

WP: Ford 1, Spahn 1. **Ground balls-fly balls:** Ford 7-7, Duren 0-2, Spahn 10-12. **Batters faced:** Ford 31, Duren 13, Spahn 40. **UMPIRES:** hp—Barlick, 1b—Berry, 2b—Gorman, 3b—Flaherty, lf—Jackowski, rf—Umont **T:** 3:09 **A:** 46,367

GAME 2 Milwaukee 13 New York 5
County Stadium 10/02/58

NY YANKEES	AB	R	H	HR	RBI	BB	AVG
Bauer rf	4	2	2	1	1	0	.444
McDougald 2b	4	1	1	0	0	0	.375
Mantle cf	3	2	2	2	3	1	.333
Howard lf	1	0	0	0	1	0	.000
Siebern lf	3	0	1	0	0	0	.333
Berra c	4	0	0	0	0	0	.250
Skowron 1b	4	0	0	0	0	0	.250
Carey 3b	2	0	0	0	0	0	.000
b-Slaughter ph	1	0	0	0	0	0	.000
Richardson 3b	1	0	0	0	0	0	.000
Kubek ss	3	0	0	0	0	0	.000
Turley p	0	0	0	0	0	0	.000
Maas p	0	0	0	0	0	0	.000
Kucks p	1	0	1	0	0	0	1.000
a-Lumpe ph	1	0	0	0	0	0	.000
Dickson p	0	0	0	0	0	0	.000
c-Throneberry ph	1	0	0	0	0	0	.000
Monroe p	0	0	0	0	0	0	.000
TOTALS	**33**	**5**	**7**	**3**	**5**	**1**	**.217**

a - Batted for Kucks in the 5th
b - Batted for Carey in the 8th
c - Batted for Dickson in the 8th

BATTING: HR: Mantle 2 (2, 4th off Burdette 0 on, 0 out, 9th off Burdette 1 on, 0 out), Bauer (2, 9th off Burdette 0 on, 0 out). **RBI:** Bauer 1 (3), Mantle 3 (3), Howard 1 (1). **GIDP:** Berra, Bauer. **Team LOB:** 2

MILWAUKEE	AB	R	H	HR	RBI	BB	AVG
Bruton cf	4	2	3	1	1	1	.667
Schoendienst 2b	5	2	2	0	0	0	.222
Mathews 3b	5	2	2	0	2	0	.250
Aaron rf	4	2	2	0	0	1	.375
Covington lf	4	1	3	0	2	0	.375
a-Mantilla pr	0	1	0	0	0	0	.000
Pafko lf	0	0	0	0	1	0	.333
Torre 1b	5	0	1	0	1	0	.167
Crandall c	2	1	0	0	1	1	.286
Logan ss	4	1	1	0	2	0	.250
Burdette p	4	1	1	1	3	0	.250
TOTALS	**37**	**13**	**15**	**2**	**13**	**3**	**.329**

a - Ran for Covington in the 7th

BATTING: 2B: Schoendienst 2 (2, Turley, Monroe), Mathews (1, Kucks). **HR:** Bruton (1, 1st off Turley 0 on, 0 out), Burdette (1, 1st off Maas 2 on, 2 out). **SF:** Crandall, Pafko. **RBI:** Bruton 1 (2), Mathews 2 (2), Covington 2 (3), Pafko 1 (1), Torre 1 (1), Crandall 1 (2), Logan 2 (2), Burdette 3 (3). **2-out RBI:** Covington 1, Logan 2, Burdette 3. **Runners left in scoring position, 2 out:** Aaron 1. **Team LOB:** 5 **BASERUNNING: SB:** Mathews (1, 2nd base off Kucks/Berra). **FIELDING: E:** Mathews (1). **DP:** 2 (Schoendienst-Logan-Torre, Logan-Schoendienst-Torre).

NY YANKEES	IP	H	R	ER	BB	SO	HR	ERA
Turley (L, 0-1)	0.1	3	4	4	1	1	1	108.00
Maas	0.1	2	3	3	1	0	1	81.00
Kucks	3.1	3	1	1	0	0	0	2.70
Dickson	3	4	2	2	0	1	0	6.00
Monroe	1	3	3	3	1	1	0	27.00

MILWAUKEE	IP	H	R	ER	BB	SO	HR	ERA
Burdette (W, 1-0)	9	7	5	4	1	5	3	4.00

IBB: Mantle (by Burdette). **Ground balls-fly balls:** Turley 0-0, Maas 0-1, Kucks 7-3, Dickson 2-5, Monroe 1-0, Burdette 11-10. **Batters faced:** Turley 5, Maas 4, Kucks 13, Dickson 13, Monroe 7, Burdette 34. **UMPIRES:** hp—Berry, 1b—Gorman, 2b—Flaherty, 3b—Barlick, lf—Umont, rf—Jackowski **T:** 2:43 **A:** 46,367

GAME 3 New York 4 Milwaukee 0
Yankee Stadium 10/04/58

MILWAUKEE	AB	R	H	HR	RBI	BB	AVG
Bruton cf	3	0	0	0	0	2	.444
Schoendienst 2b	4	0	2	0	0	0	.308
Mathews 3b	3	0	0	0	0	1	.182
Aaron rf	3	0	0	0	0	1	.273
Covington lf	3	0	1	0	0	1	.364
Torre 1b	4	0	2	0	0	0	.300
Crandall c	4	0	1	0	0	0	.273
Logan ss	3	0	0	0	0	1	.182
Rush p	2	0	0	0	0	0	.000
a-Hanebrink ph	1	0	0	0	0	0	.000
McMahon p	0	0	0	0	0	0	.000
b-Wise ph	1	0	0	0	0	0	.000
TOTALS	**31**	**0**	**6**	**0**	**0**	**6**	**.290**

a - Batted for Rush in the 7th
b - Batted for McMahon in the 9th

BATTING: Runners left in scoring position, 2 out: Schoendienst 1, Mathews 1, Torre 1, Crandall 2. **GIDP:** Bruton. **Team LOB:** 10 **FIELDING: DP:** 1 (Crandall-Torre).

NY YANKEES	AB	R	H	HR	RBI	BB	AVG
Bauer rf	4	1	3	1	4	0	.538
Kubek ss	4	0	0	0	0	0	.000
Mantle cf	2	0	0	0	0	2	.250
Berra c	4	0	0	0	0	0	.167
Siebern lf	2	1	0	0	0	2	.200
Lumpe 3b	3	0	1	0	0	0	.250
Richardson 3b	1	0	0	0	0	0	.000
Skowron 1b	4	0	0	0	0	0	.167
McDougald 2b	2	1	0	0	0	1	.300
Larsen p	1	0	0	0	0	1	.000
a-Slaughter ph	0	1	0	0	0	1	.000
Duren p	0	0	0	0	0	0	.000
TOTALS	**27**	**4**	**4**	**1**	**4**	**7**	**.198**

a - Batted for Larsen in the 7th

BATTING: HR: Bauer (3, 7th off McMahon 1 on, 1 out). **RBI:** Bauer 4 (7). **2-out RBI:** Bauer 2. **Runners left in scoring position, 2 out:** Kubek 1, Skowron 1. **Team LOB:** 6 **FIELDING: DP:** 1 (Duren-Kubek-Skowron).

MILWAUKEE	IP	H	R	ER	BB	SO	HR	ERA
Rush (L, 0-1)	6	3	2	2	5	2	0	3.00
McMahon	2	1	2	2	2	2	1	9.00

NY YANKEES	IP	H	R	ER	BB	SO	HR	ERA
Larsen (W, 1-0)	7	6	0	0	3	8	0	0.00
Duren (S, 1)	2	0	0	0	3	1	0	1.93

WP: Duren 1. **IBB:** McDougald (by Rush). **Ground balls-fly balls:** Rush 5-10, McMahon 3-1, Larsen 1-11, Duren 2-2. **Batters faced:** Rush 25, McMahon 9, Larsen 29, Duren 8. **UMPIRES:** hp—Gorman, 1b—Flaherty, 2b—Barlick, 3b—Berry, lf—Jackowski, rf—Umont **T:** 2:42 **A:** 71,599

GAME 4 Milwaukee 3 New York 0
Yankee Stadium 10/05/58

MILWAUKEE	AB	R	H	HR	RBI	BB	AVG
Schoendienst 2b	5	1	1	0	0	0	.278
Logan ss	5	1	1	0	0	0	.188
Mathews 3b	4	0	1	0	1	0	.200
Aaron cf-rf	4	0	2	0	0	0	.333
Adcock 1b	3	0	0	0	0	0	.250
a-Torre ph-1b	1	0	0	0	0	0	.273
Crandall c	3	1	2	0	0	1	.357
Covington lf	3	0	0	0	0	1	.286
b-Bruton pr-cf	0	0	0	0	0	0	.444
Pafko rf-lf	4	0	1	0	0	0	.286
Spahn p	4	0	1	0	1	0	.375
TOTALS	**36**	**3**	**9**	**0**	**2**	**2**	**.280**

a - Batted for Adcock in the 8th
b - Ran for Covington in the 8th

BATTING: 2B: Aaron (2, Ford), Pafko (1, Ford), Logan (2, Ford), Mathews (2, Ford). **3B:** Schoendienst (1, Ford). **RBI:** Mathews 1 (3), Spahn 1 (2). **Runners left in scoring position, 2 out:** Adcock 1, Pafko 2. **GIDP:** Schoendienst. **Team LOB:** 8

NY YANKEES	AB	R	H	HR	RBI	BB	AVG
Siebern lf	3	0	0	0	0	1	.125
McDougald 2b	4	0	0	0	0	0	.214
Bauer rf	4	0	0	0	0	0	.412
Mantle cf	4	0	1	0	0	0	.250
Skowron 1b	3	0	1	0	0	0	.200
Berra c	3	0	0	0	0	0	.133
Richardson 3b	2	0	0	0	0	0	.000
a-Howard ph	1	0	0	0	0	0	.000
Carey 3b	0	0	0	0	0	0	.000
Kubek ss	2	0	0	0	0	0	.000
b-Slaughter ph	1	0	0	0	0	0	.000
Dickson p	0	0	0	0	0	0	.000
Ford p	1	0	0	0	0	1	.000
Kucks p	0	0	0	0	0	0	1.000
c-Lumpe ph-ss	1	0	0	0	0	0	.200
TOTALS	**29**	**0**	**2**	**0**	**0**	**2**	**.168**

a - Batted for Richardson in the 7th
b - Batted for Kubek in the 8th
c - Batted for Kucks in the 8th

BATTING: 3B: Mantle (1, Spahn). **Runners left in scoring position, 2 out:** Berra 1. **Team LOB:** 4 **FIELDING: E:** Kubek (2). **DP:** 1 (McDougald-Kubek-Skowron).

MILWAUKEE	IP	H	R	ER	BB	SO	HR	ERA
Spahn (W, 2-0)	9	2	0	0	2	7	0	1.42

NY YANKEES	IP	H	R	ER	BB	SO	HR	ERA
Ford (L, 0-1)	7	8	3	2	1	6	0	3.21
Kucks	1	1	0	0	1	0	0	2.08
Dickson	1	0	0	0	0	0	0	4.50

WP: Ford 1. **Ground balls-fly balls:** Spahn 11-9, Ford 10-5, Kucks 1-2, Dickson 1-2. **Batters faced:** Spahn 31, Ford 30, Kucks 5, Dickson 3. **UMPIRES:** hp—Flaherty, 1b—Barlick, 2b—Berry, 3b—Gorman, lf—Umont, rf—Jackowski **T:** 2:17 **A:** 71,563

GAME 5 New York 7 Milwaukee 0
Yankee Stadium 10/06/58

MILWAUKEE	AB	R	H	HR	RBI	BB	AVG
Bruton cf	3	0	2	0	0	1	.500
Schoendienst 2b	3	0	1	0	0	0	.286
Mathews 3b	4	0	1	0	0	0	.211
Aaron rf	4	0	0	0	0	0	.263
Covington lf	4	0	1	0	0	0	.278
b-Wise pr	0	0	0	0	0	0	.000
Torre 1b	3	0	0	0	0	1	.214
Crandall c	3	0	0	0	0	1	.294
Logan ss	3	0	0	0	0	0	.158
Burdette p	2	0	0	0	0	0	.167
Pizarro p	0	0	0	0	0	0	.000
a-Hanebrink ph	1	0	0	0	0	0	.000
Willey p	0	0	0	0	0	0	.000
TOTALS	**30**	**0**	**5**	**0**	**0**	**3**	**.260**

a - Batted for Pizarro in the 8th
b - Ran for Covington in the 9th

BATTING: S: Schoendienst. **Runners left in scoring position, 2 out:** Aaron 1. **Team LOB:** 7 **FIELDING: DP:** 1 (Mathews-Torre).

NY YANKEES	AB	R	H	HR	RBI	BB	AVG
Bauer rf	4	1	1	0	0	0	.381
Lumpe 3b	3	0	1	0	0	0	.250
Richardson 3b	1	0	0	0	0	0	.000
Mantle cf	3	1	2	0	0	1	.333
Berra c	4	1	1	0	1	0	.158
Howard lf	3	1	0	0	0	1	.000
Skowron 1b	4	1	1	0	1	0	.211
McDougald 2b	4	2	2	1	3	0	.278
Kubek ss	4	0	1	0	0	0	.059
Turley p	3	0	1	0	2	0	.333
TOTALS	**33**	**7**	**10**	**1**	**7**	**2**	**.196**

BATTING: 2B: Berra (2, Burdette), McDougald (1, Pizarro). **HR:** McDougald (1, 3th off Burdette 0 on, 0 out). **RBI:** Berra 1 (1), Skowron 1 (2), McDougald 3 (3), Turley 2 (2). **2-out RBI:** Turley 2. **Runners left in scoring position, 2 out:** Bauer 1, Howard 2. **GIDP:** Berra. **Team LOB:** 4 **FIELDING: Outfield assists:** Howard (1). **DP:** 1 (Howard-McDougald-Skowron).

MILWAUKEE	IP	H	R	ER	BB	SO	HR	ERA
Burdette (L, 1-1)	5.1	8	6	6	1	4	1	6.28
Pizarro	1.2	2	1	1	1	3	0	5.40
Willey	1	0	0	0	0	2	0	0.00

NY YANKEES	IP	H	R	ER	BB	SO	HR	ERA
Turley (W, 1-1)	9	5	0	0	3	10	0	3.86

WP: Pizarro 1. **IBB:** Howard (by Burdette). **Ground balls-fly balls:** Burdette 7-4, Pizarro 2-0, Willey 0-1, Turley 5-10. **Batters faced:** Burdette 24, Pizarro 8, Willey 3, Turley 34. **UMPIRES:** hp—Barlick, 1b—Berry, 2b—Gorman, 3b—Flaherty, lf—Jackowski, rf—Umont **T:** 2:19 **A:** 65,279

GAME 6 New York 4 Milwaukee 3
County Stadium 10/08/58

NY YANKEES	AB	R	H	HR	RBI	BB	AVG
Carey 3b	5	0	0	0	0	0	.000
McDougald 2b	5	1	2	1	1	0	.304
Bauer rf	5	1	2	1	1	0	.385
Mantle cf	5	1	1	0	0	0	.300
Howard lf	5	1	2	0	0	0	.133
Berra c	4	0	2	0	1	0	.217
Skowron 1b	4	0	1	0	1	1	.217
Kubek ss	2	0	0	0	0	0	.053
a-Slaughter ph	1	0	0	0	0	0	.000
Duren p	2	0	0	0	0	0	.000
Turley p	0	0	0	0	0	0	.333
Ford p	1	0	0	0	0	0	.000
Ditmar p	1	0	0	0	0	0	.000
b-Lumpe ph-ss	1	0	0	0	0	1	.222
TOTALS	**41**	**4**	**10**	**2**	**4**	**2**	**.206**

a - Batted for Kubek in the 6th
b - Batted for Ditmar in the 6th

BATTING: HR: Bauer (4, 1st off Spahn 0 on, 2 out), McDougald (2, 10th off Spahn 0 on, 0 out). **SF:** Berra. **RBI:** McDougald 1 (4), Bauer 1 (8), Berra 1 (2), Skowron 1 (3). **2-out RBI:** Bauer 1, Skowron 1. **Runners left in scoring position, 2 out:** Duren 1, Lumpe 2. **Team LOB:** 10 **BASERUNNING: CS:** Lumpe (1, 2nd base off Spahn/Crandall). **FIELDING: E:** Ditmar (1). **Outfield assists:** Howard (2). **DP:** 1 (Howard-Berra).

MILWAUKEE	AB	R	H	HR	RBI	BB	AVG
Schoendienst 2b	4	1	2	0	0	1	.320
Logan ss	2	1	0	0	0	1	.143
Mathews 3b	5	0	0	0	0	0	.167
Aaron rf	5	0	3	0	2	0	.333
Adcock 1b	4	0	1	0	0	1	.250
a-Mantilla pr	0	0	0	0	0	0	.000
Crandall c	4	0	0	0	0	0	.238
b-Torre ph	1	0	0	0	0	0	.200
Covington lf	4	1	2	0	0	0	.318
Pafko cf	2	0	1	0	0	0	.333
Bruton cf	2	0	0	0	0	0	.429
Spahn p	4	0	1	0	1	0	.333
McMahon p	0	0	0	0	0	0	.000
TOTALS	**37**	**3**	**10**	**0**	**3**	**3**	**.262**

a - Ran for Adcock in the 10th
b - Batted for Crandall in the 10th

BATTING: 2B: Schoendienst (3, Ditmar). **S:** Logan, Logan. **RBI:** Aaron 2 (2), Spahn 1 (3). **2-out RBI:** Aaron 2. **Runners left in scoring position, 2 out:** Aaron 1, Crandall 1, Torre 1. **Team LOB:** 9 **FIELDING: E:** Schoendienst (1), Logan 2 (2), Bruton (1). **DP:** 1 (Crandall-Schoendienst).

NY YANKEES	IP	H	R	ER	BB	SO	HR	ERA
Ford	1.1	5	2	2	1	2	0	4.11
Ditmar	3.2	2	0	0	0	2	0	0.00
Duren (W, 1-1)	4.2	3	1	1	2	8	0	1.93
Turley (S, 1)	0.1	0	0	0	0	0	0	3.72

MILWAUKEE	IP	H	R	ER	BB	SO	HR	ERA
Spahn (L, 2-1)	9.2	9	4	4	2	5	2	2.20
McMahon	0.1	1	0	0	0	1	0	7.71

Ground balls-fly balls: Ford 1-0, Ditmar 4-3, Duren 3-3, Turley 0-1, Spahn 13-12, McMahon 0-0. **Batters faced:** Ford 10, Ditmar 12, Duren 19, Turley 1, Spahn 42, McMahon 2. **UMPIRES:** hp—Berry, 1b—Gorman, 2b—Flaherty, 3b—Barlick, lf—Umont, rf—Jackowski **T:** 3:07 **A:** 46,367

GAME 7 New York 6 Milwaukee 2
County Stadium 10/09/58

NY YANKEES	AB	R	H	HR	RBI	BB	AVG
Bauer rf	5	0	0	0	0	0	.323
McDougald 2b	5	0	2	0	0	0	.321
Mantle cf	4	0	0	0	0	1	.250
Berra c	4	2	1	0	0	1	.222
Howard lf	3	2	2	0	1	0	.222
Lumpe 3b	3	0	0	0	0	0	.167
Carey 3b	1	1	1	0	0	0	.083
Skowron 1b	4	1	2	1	4	0	.259
Kubek ss	2	0	0	0	1	1	.048
Larsen p	1	0	0	0	0	0	.000
Turley p	2	0	0	0	0	0	.200
TOTALS	**34**	**6**	**8**	**1**	**6**	**3**	**.210**

BATTING: 2B: McDougald (2, Burdette), Berra (3, Burdette). **HR:** Skowron (2, 8th off Burdette 2 on, 2 out). **S:** Howard, Turley. **SF:** Kubek. **RBI:** Howard 1 (2), Skowron 4 (7), Kubek 1 (1). **2-out RBI:** Howard 1, Skowron 3. **Runners left in scoring position, 2 out:** Bauer 1, Berra 2, Turley 1. **Team LOB:** 7 **BASERUNNING: SB:** Howard (1, 2nd base off Burdette/Crandall). **FIELDING: DP:** 1 (McDougald-Skowron).

MILWAUKEE	AB	R	H	HR	RBI	BB	AVG
Schoendienst 2b	5	1	1	0	0	0	.300
Bruton cf	3	0	1	0	0	1	.412
Torre 1b	2	0	0	0	0	1	.176
Aaron rf	3	0	1	0	0	1	.333
Covington lf	4	0	0	0	1	0	.269
Mathews 3b	1	0	0	0	0	3	.160
Crandall c	4	1	1	1	1	0	.240
Logan ss	4	0	0	0	0	0	.120
Burdette p	3	0	0	0	0	0	.111
McMahon p	0	0	0	0	0	0	.000
a-Adcock ph	1	0	1	0	0	0	.308
b-Mantilla pr	0	0	0	0	0	0	.000
TOTALS	**30**	**2**	**5**	**1**	**2**	**6**	**.250**

a - Batted for McMahon in the 9th
b - Ran for Adcock in the 9th

BATTING: HR: Crandall (1, 6th off Turley 0 on, 2 out). **S:** Torre. **RBI:** Covington 1 (4), Crandall 1 (3). **2-out RBI:** Crandall 1. **Runners left in scoring position, 2 out:** Schoendienst 1, Crandall 4. **GIDP:** Aaron. **Team LOB:** 8 **FIELDING: E:** Torre 2 (2).

NY YANKEES	IP	H	R	ER	BB	SO	HR	ERA
Larsen	2.1	3	1	1	3	1	0	0.96
Turley (W, 2-1)	6.2	2	1	1	3	2	1	2.76

MILWAUKEE	IP	H	R	ER	BB	SO	HR	ERA
Burdette (L, 1-2)	8	7	6	4	2	3	1	5.64
McMahon	1	1	0	0	1	2	0	5.40

IBB: Mathews 2 (by Larsen, by Turley), Kubek (by Burdette). **Ground balls-fly balls:** Larsen 3-2, Turley 7-10, Burdette 12-8, McMahon 1-0. **Batters faced:** Larsen 13, Turley 24, Burdette 35, McMahon 5. **UMPIRES:** hp—Gorman, 1b—Flaherty, 2b—Barlick, 3b—Berry, lf—Jackowski, rf—Umont **T:** 2:31 **A:** 46,367

1959 LOS ANGELES DEF. CHICAGO WHITE SOX, 4-2

GAME 1 Chicago 11 Los Angeles 0
Comiskey Park 10/01/59

LOS ANGELES	AB	R	H	HR	RBI	BB	AVG
Gilliam 3b	4	0	1	0	0	0	.250
Neal 2b	4	0	2	0	0	0	.500
Moon lf	4	0	1	0	0	0	.250
Snider cf	2	0	0	0	0	1	.000
Demeter cf	1	0	0	0	0	0	.000
Larker rf	4	0	1	0	0	0	.250
Hodges 1b	4	0	2	0	0	0	.500
Roseboro c	4	0	0	0	0	0	.000
Wills ss	3	0	1	0	0	0	.333
c-Furillo ph	1	0	0	0	0	0	.000
Craig p	1	0	0	0	0	0	.000
Churn p	0	0	0	0	0	0	.000
Labine p	0	0	0	0	0	0	.000
a-Essegian ph	1	0	0	0	0	0	.000
Koufax p	0	0	0	0	0	0	.000
b-Fairly ph	1	0	0	0	0	0	.000
Klippstein p	0	0	0	0	0	0	.000
TOTALS	**34**	**0**	**8**	**0**	**0**	**1**	**.235**

a - Batted for Labine in the 5th
b - Batted for Koufax in the 7th
c - Batted for Wills in the 9th

BATTING: Runners left in scoring position, 2 out: Larker 2, Roseboro 1, Furillo 1. **GIDP:** Neal. **Team LOB:** 8 **BASERUNNING: SB:** Neal (1, 2nd base off Wynn/Lollar). **FIELDING: E:** Snider 2 (2), Neal (1).

CHICAGO WHITE SOX	AB	R	H	HR	RBI	BB	AVG
Aparicio ss	5	0	0	0	0	0	.000
Fox 2b	4	2	1	0	0	1	.250
Landis cf	4	3	3	0	1	0	.750
Kluszewski 1b	4	2	3	2	5	0	.750
Lollar c	3	1	0	0	1	0	.000
Goodman 3b	2	1	1	0	1	0	.500
Esposito 3b	2	0	0	0	0	0	.000
Smith lf	4	1	2	0	1	0	.500
Rivera rf	4	1	0	0	1	0	.000
Wynn p	3	0	1	0	1	0	.333
Staley p	1	0	0	0	0	0	.000
TOTALS	**36**	**11**	**11**	**2**	**11**	**1**	**.306**

BATTING: 2B: Fox (1, Craig), Smith 2 (2, Churn, Klippstein), Wynn (1, Churn). **HR:** Kluszewski 2 (2, 3th off Craig 1 on, 1 out, 4th off Churn 1 on, 0 out). **SF:** Lollar. **RBI:** Landis 1 (1), Kluszewski 5 (5), Lollar 1 (1), Goodman 1 (1), Smith 1 (1), Rivera 1 (1), Wynn 1 (1). **Runners left in scoring position, 2 out:** Fox 1, Rivera 1. **Team LOB:** 3 **FIELDING: DP:** 1 (Aparicio-Fox-Kluszewski).

LOS ANGELES	IP	H	R	ER	BB	SO	HR	ERA
Craig (L, 0-1)	2.1	5	5	5	1	1	1	19.29
Churn	0.2	5	6	2	0	0	1	27.00
Labine	1	0	0	0	0	1	0	0.00
Koufax	2	0	0	0	0	1	0	0.00
Klippstein	2	1	0	0	0	2	0	0.00

CHICAGO WHITE SOX	IP	H	R	ER	BB	SO	HR	ERA
Wynn (W, 1-0)	7	6	0	0	1	6	0	0.00
Staley (S, 1)	2	2	0	0	0	1	0	0.00

Ground balls-fly balls: Craig 1-4, Churn 3-1, Labine 0-2, Koufax 2-3, Klippstein 4-0, Wynn 6-9, Staley 3-1. **Batters faced:** Craig 13, Churn 9, Labine 3, Koufax 6, Klippstein 7, Wynn 28, Staley 7. **UMPIRES:** hp—Summers, 1b—Dascoli, 2b—Hurley, 3b—Secory, lf—Rice, rf—Dixon **T:** 2:35 **A:** 48,013

GAME 2 Los Angeles 4 Chicago 3
Comiskey Park 10/02/59

LOS ANGELES	AB	R	H	HR	RBI	BB	AVG
Gilliam 3b	4	1	1	0	0	1	.250
Neal 2b	5	2	2	2	3	0	.444
Moon lf	3	0	1	0	0	1	.286
Snider cf	4	0	1	0	0	0	.167
Demeter cf	0	0	0	0	0	0	.000
Larker rf	3	0	0	0	0	0	.143
Sherry p	1	0	0	0	0	0	.000
Hodges 1b	4	0	0	0	0	0	.250
Roseboro c	4	0	1	0	0	0	.125
Wills ss	4	0	1	0	0	0	.286
Podres p	2	0	1	0	0	0	.500
a-Essegian ph	1	1	1	1	1	0	.500
Fairly rf	1	0	0	0	0	0	.000
TOTALS	**36**	**4**	**9**	**3**	**4**	**2**	**.243**

a - Batted for Podres in the 7th

BATTING: HR: Neal 2 (2, 5th off Shaw 0 on, 2 out, 7th off Shaw 1 on, 2 out), Essegian (1, 7th off Shaw 0 on, 2 out). **RBI:** Neal 3 (3), Essegian 1 (1). **2-out RBI:** Neal 3, Essegian 1. **Runners left in scoring position, 2 out:** Gilliam 1, Neal 1, Larker 1. **Team LOB:** 7 **BASERUNNING: SB:** Moon (1, 2nd base off Shaw/Lollar), Gilliam (1, 2nd base off Lown/Lollar). **FIELDING: E:** Wills (1). **Outfield assists:** Moon (1).

CHICAGO WHITE SOX	AB	R	H	HR	RBI	BB	AVG
Aparicio ss	5	1	2	0	0	0	.200
Fox 2b	4	0	0	0	0	1	.125
Landis cf	3	1	0	0	0	1	.429
Kluszewski 1b	4	0	1	0	1	0	.500
a-Torgeson pr-1b	0	1	0	0	0	0	.000
Lollar c	4	0	2	0	1	0	.286
Smith lf	3	0	1	0	1	1	.429
Phillips 3b	3	0	1	0	0	0	.333
b-Goodman ph-3b	1	0	0	0	0	0	.333
McAnany rf	3	0	0	0	0	0	.000
Rivera rf	1	0	0	0	0	0	.000
Shaw p	3	0	1	0	0	0	.333
Lown p	0	0	0	0	0	0	.000
c-Cash ph	1	0	0	0	0	0	.000
TOTALS	**35**	**3**	**8**	**0**	**3**	**3**	**.268**

a - Ran for Kluszewski in the 8th
b - Batted for Phillips in the 8th
c - Batted for Lown in the 9th

BATTING: 2B: Aparicio (1, Podres), Phillips (1, Podres), Smith (3, Sherry). **RBI:** Kluszewski 1 (6), Lollar 1 (2), Smith 1 (2). **2-out RBI:** Lollar 1. **Runners left in scoring position, 2 out:** Landis 1, Phillips 1, Rivera 1, Shaw 1. **Team LOB:** 8

LOS ANGELES	IP	H	R	ER	BB	SO	HR	ERA
Podres (W, 1-0)	6	5	2	2	3	3	0	3.00
Sherry (S, 1)	3	3	1	1	0	1	0	3.00

CHICAGO WHITE SOX	IP	H	R	ER	BB	SO	HR	ERA
Shaw (L, 0-1)	6.2	8	4	4	1	1	3	5.40
Lown	2.1	1	0	0	1	3	0	0.00

Ground balls-fly balls: Podres 10-6, Sherry 5-2, Shaw 8-11, Lown 0-4. **Batters faced:** Podres 27, Sherry 11, Shaw 29, Lown 9. **UMPIRES:** hp—Dascoli, 1b—Hurley, 2b—Secory, 3b—Summers, lf—Rice, rf—Dixon **T:** 2:21 **A:** 47,368

GAME 3 Los Angeles 3 Chicago 1
Memorial Coluseum 10/04/59

CHICAGO WHITE SOX	AB	R	H	HR	RBI	BB	AVG
Aparicio ss	4	0	2	0	0	1	.286
Fox 2b	4	0	3	0	0	1	.333
Landis cf	5	0	1	0	0	0	.333
Kluszewski 1b	3	1	1	0	0	1	.455
Lollar c	4	0	2	0	0	0	.364
Goodman 3b	3	0	2	0	0	0	.500
a-Esposito pr-3b	0	0	0	0	0	0	.000
Smith lf	4	0	0	0	1	0	.273
Rivera rf	3	0	0	0	0	1	.000
Donovan p	3	0	1	0	0	0	.333
Staley p	0	0	0	0	0	0	.000
b-Cash ph	1	0	0	0	0	0	.000
TOTALS	**34**	**1**	**12**	**0**	**1**	**4**	**.295**

a - Ran for Goodman in the 8th
b - Batted for Staley in the 9th

BATTING: RBI: Smith 1 (3). **Runners left in scoring position, 2 out:** Fox 1, Landis 1, Goodman 2, Smith 1, Rivera 1. **GIDP:** Smith, Smith. **Team LOB:** 11 **BASERUNNING: SB:** Landis (1, 2nd base off Drysdale/Roseboro). **CS:** Rivera (1, 2nd base off Drysdale/Roseboro), Aparicio (1, 2nd base off Drysdale/Roseboro), Fox (1, 2nd base off Drysdale/Roseboro). **FIELDING: DP:** 1 (Aparicio-Fox-Kluszewski).

LOS ANGELES	AB	R	H	HR	RBI	BB	AVG
Gilliam 3b	4	0	0	0	0	0	.167
Neal 2b	4	1	2	0	1	0	.462
Moon rf	4	0	0	0	0	0	.182
Larker lf	2	1	0	0	0	1	.111
Hodges 1b	2	0	1	0	0	1	.300
Demeter cf	2	0	0	0	0	0	.000
a-Furillo ph	1	0	1	0	2	0	.500
b-Fairly pr-cf	0	0	0	0	0	0	.000
Roseboro c	3	0	0	0	0	0	.091
Wills ss	3	1	1	0	0	0	.300
Drysdale p	2	0	0	0	0	0	.000
Sherry p	0	0	0	0	0	0	.000
TOTALS	**27**	**3**	**5**	**0**	**3**	**2**	**.227**

a - Batted for Demeter in the 7th
b - Ran for Furillo in the 7th

BATTING: 2B: Neal (1, Staley). **S:** Sherry. **RBI:** Neal 1 (4), Furillo 2 (2). **2-out RBI:** Neal 1, Furillo 2. **Runners left in scoring position, 2 out:** Moon 1, Roseboro 1. **GIDP:** Demeter. **Team LOB:** 3 **FIELDING: DP:** 3 (Roseboro-Neal, Gilliam-Neal-Hodges, Wills-Neal-Hodges).

CHICAGO WHITE SOX	IP	H	R	ER	BB	SO	HR	ERA
Donovan (L, 0-1)	6.2	2	2	2	2	5	0	2.70
Staley	1.1	3	1	1	0	0	0	2.70

LOS ANGELES	IP	H	R	ER	BB	SO	HR	ERA
Drysdale (W, 1-0)	7	11	1	1	4	5	0	1.29
Sherry (S, 2)	2	1	0	0	0	3	0	1.80

IBB: Kluszewski (by Drysdale). **HBP:** Goodman (by Sherry). **Ground balls-fly balls:** Donovan 9-5, Staley 2-1, Drysdale 6-6, Sherry 1-1. **Batters faced:** Donovan 23, Staley 7, Drysdale 32, Sherry 7. **UMPIRES:** hp—Hurley, 1b—Secory, 2b—Summers, 3b—Dascoli, lf—Dixon, rf—Rice **T:** 2:33 **A:** 92,394

GAME 4 Los Angeles 5 Chicago 4
Memorial Coluseum 10/05/59

CHICAGO WHITE SOX	AB	R	H	HR	RBI	BB	AVG
Landis cf	5	1	1	0	0	0	.294
Aparicio ss	3	0	1	0	0	1	.294
Fox 2b	5	1	3	0	0	0	.412
Kluszewski 1b	4	1	2	0	1	1	.467
Lollar c	4	1	1	1	3	0	.333
Goodman 3b	4	0	0	0	0	0	.300
Smith lf	3	0	2	0	0	1	.357
Rivera rf	3	0	0	0	0	1	.000
Wynn p	1	0	0	0	0	0	.250
Lown p	0	0	0	0	0	0	.000
a-Cash ph	1	0	0	0	0	0	.000
Pierce p	0	0	0	0	0	0	.000
b-Torgeson ph	1	0	0	0	0	0	.000
Staley p	0	0	0	0	0	1	.000
TOTALS	**34**	**4**	**10**	**1**	**4**	**5**	**.295**

a - Batted for Lown in the 4th
b - Batted for Pierce in the 7th

BATTING: 2B: Fox (2, Craig). **HR:** Lollar (1, 7th off Craig 2 on, 2 out). **S:** Aparicio. **RBI:** Kluszewski 1 (7), Lollar 3 (5). **2-out RBI:** Kluszewski 1, Lollar 3. **Runners left in scoring position, 2 out:** Rivera 1, Cash 1. **GIDP:** Lollar, Kluszewski. **Team LOB:** 9 **BASERUNNING: SB:** Aparicio (1, 2nd base off Craig/Roseboro). **FIELDING: E:** Landis (1), Pierce (1). **PB:** Lollar. **Outfield assists:** Rivera (1).

LOS ANGELES	AB	R	H	HR	RBI	BB	AVG
Gilliam 3b	4	0	0	0	0	0	.125
Neal 2b	4	0	0	0	0	0	.353
Moon rf-lf	4	1	2	0	0	0	.267
Larker lf	2	1	1	0	1	0	.182
a-Furillo ph-rf	1	0	0	0	0	0	.333
Fairly rf	1	0	0	0	0	0	.000
Hodges 1b	4	2	2	1	2	0	.357
Demeter cf	3	1	2	0	0	1	.333
Roseboro c	3	0	1	0	1	0	.143
Wills ss	4	0	1	0	0	0	.286
Craig p	2	0	0	0	0	0	.000
Sherry p	0	0	0	0	0	0	.000
TOTALS	**32**	**5**	**9**	**1**	**4**	**1**	**.240**

a - Batted for Larker in the 5th

BATTING: HR: Hodges (1, 8th off Staley 0 on, 0 out). **S:** Roseboro, Craig. **RBI:** Larker 1 (1), Hodges 2 (2), Roseboro 1 (1). **2-out RBI:** Larker 1, Hodges 1, Roseboro 1. **Runners left in scoring position, 2 out:** Gilliam 2, Wills 1, Craig 2. **Team LOB:** 6 **BASERUNNING: SB:** Wills (1, 2nd base off Wynn/Lollar). **FIELDING: DP:** 2 (Wills-Neal-Hodges, Neal-Wills-Hodges).

CHICAGO WHITE SOX	IP	H	R	ER	BB	SO	HR	ERA
Wynn	2.2	8	4	3	0	2	0	2.79
Lown	0.1	0	0	0	0	0	0	0.00
Pierce	3	0	0	0	1	2	0	0.00
Staley (L, 0-1)	2	1	1	1	0	2	1	3.38

LOS ANGELES	IP	H	R	ER	BB	SO	HR	ERA
Craig	7	10	4	4	4	7	1	8.68
Sherry (W, 1-0)	2	0	0	0	1	0	0	1.29

IBB: Kluszewski (by Craig). **Ground balls-fly balls:** Wynn 1-5, Lown 1-0, Pierce 2-4, Staley 3-1, Craig 4-7, Sherry 5-1. **Batters faced:** Wynn 16, Lown 1, Pierce 11, Staley 7, Craig 33, Sherry 7. **UMPIRES:** hp—Secory, 1b—Summers, 2b—Dascoli, 3b—Hurley, lf—Dixon, rf—Rice **T:** 2:30 **A:** 92,650

GAME 5 Chicago 1 Los Angeles 0
Memorial Coluseum 10/06/59

CHICAGO WHITE SOX	AB	R	H	HR	RBI	BB	AVG
Aparicio ss	4	0	2	0	0	0	.333
Fox 2b	3	1	1	0	0	1	.400
Landis cf	4	0	1	0	0	0	.286
Lollar c	4	0	0	0	1	0	.263
Kluszewski 1b	4	0	0	0	0	0	.368
Smith rf-lf	4	0	0	0	0	0	.278
Phillips 3b	3	0	1	0	0	0	.333
McAnany lf	1	0	0	0	0	1	.000
Rivera rf	0	0	0	0	0	1	.000
Shaw p	1	0	0	0	0	0	.250
Pierce p	0	0	0	0	0	0	.000
Donovan p	0	0	0	0	0	0	.333
TOTALS	**28**	**1**	**5**	**0**	**1**	**3**	**.275**

BATTING: S: Shaw, Shaw. **RBI:** Lollar 1 (6). **Runners left in scoring position, 2 out:** Aparicio 1, Landis 1. **GIDP:** Lollar. **Team LOB:** 5

LOS ANGELES	AB	R	H	HR	RBI	BB	AVG
Gilliam 3b	5	0	4	0	0	0	.286
Neal 2b	5	0	1	0	0	0	.318
Moon rf-cf	4	0	1	0	0	0	.263
Larker lf	4	0	0	0	0	0	.133
Hodges 1b	4	0	3	0	0	0	.444
Demeter cf	3	0	0	0	0	0	.222
e-Fairly ph	0	0	0	0	0	0	.000
f-Repulski ph-rf	0	0	0	0	0	1	.000
Roseboro c	3	0	0	0	0	0	.118
g-Furillo ph	1	0	0	0	0	0	.250
Pignatano c	0	0	0	0	0	0	.000
Wills ss	2	0	0	0	0	0	.250
a-Essegian ph	0	0	0	0	0	1	.500
b-Zimmer pr-ss	1	0	0	0	0	0	.000
Koufax p	2	0	0	0	0	0	.000
c-Snider ph	1	0	0	0	0	0	.143
d-Podres pr	0	0	0	0	0	0	.500
Williams p	0	0	0	0	0	0	.000
h-Sherry ph	1	0	0	0	0	0	.000
TOTALS	**36**	**0**	**9**	**0**	**0**	**2**	**.242**

a - Batted for Wills in the 7th
b - Ran for Essegian in the 7th
c - Batted for Koufax in the 7th
d - Ran for Snider in the 7th e - Batted for Demeter in the 8th f - Batted for Fairly in the 8th g - Batted for Roseboro in the 8th h - Batted for Williams in the 9th

BATTING: 3B: Hodges (1, Shaw). **Runners left in scoring position, 2 out:** Neal 3, Moon 1, Larker 1, Roseboro 1, Zimmer 2. **Team LOB:** 11 **BASERUNNING: SB:** Gilliam (2, 2nd base off Shaw/Lollar). **FIELDING: Outfield assists:** Larker (1). **DP:** 1 (Neal-Hodges).

CHICAGO WHITE SOX	IP	H	R	ER	BB	SO	HR	ERA
Shaw (W, 1-1)	7.1	9	0	0	1	1	0	2.57
Pierce	0	0	0	0	1	0	0	0.00
Donovan (S, 1)	1.2	0	0	0	0	0	0	2.16

LOS ANGELES	IP	H	R	ER	BB	SO	HR	ERA
Koufax (L, 0-1)	7	5	1	1	1	6	0	1.00
Williams	2	0	0	0	2	1	0	0.00

WP: Shaw 1. **IBB:** Repulski (by Pierce). **Ground balls-fly balls:** Shaw 12-9, Pierce 0-0, Donovan 3-2, Koufax 4-8, Williams 3-1. **Batters faced:** Shaw 32, Pierce 1, Donovan 5, Koufax 25, Williams 8. **UMPIRES:** hp—Summers, 1b—Dascoli, 2b—Hurley, 3b—Secory, lf—Dixon, rf—Rice **T:** 2:28 **A:** 92,706

GAME 6 Los Angeles 9 Chicago 3
Comiskey Park 10/08/59

LOS ANGELES	AB	R	H	HR	RBI	BB	AVG
Gilliam 3b	4	1	0	0	0	1	.240
Neal 2b	5	1	3	0	2	0	.370
Moon lf	4	2	1	1	2	1	.261
Snider cf-rf	3	1	1	1	2	1	.200
b-Essegian ph	1	1	1	1	1	0	.667
Fairly rf	0	0	0	0	0	0	.000
Hodges 1b	5	0	1	0	0	0	.391
Larker rf	1	0	1	0	0	1	.188
a-Demeter pr-cf	3	1	1	0	0	0	.250
Roseboro c	4	0	0	0	0	0	.095
Wills ss	4	1	1	0	1	0	.250
Podres p	2	1	1	0	1	0	.500
Sherry p	2	0	2	0	0	0	.500
TOTALS	**38**	**9**	**13**	**3**	**9**	**4**	**.261**

a - Ran for Larker in the 4th
b - Batted for Snider in the 9th

BATTING: 2B: Podres (1, Wynn), Neal (2, Donovan). **HR:** Snider (1, 3th off Wynn 1 on, 2 out), Moon (1, 4th off Donovan 1 on, 1 out), Essegian (2, 9th off Moore 0 on, 0 out). **S:** Roseboro. **RBI:** Neal 2 (6), Moon 2 (2), Snider 2 (2), Essegian 1 (2), Wills 1 (1), Podres 1 (1). **2-out RBI:** Snider 2. **Runners left in scoring position, 2 out:** Moon 1, Hodges 1, Demeter 1, Podres 1. **Team LOB:** 7 **BASERUNNING: CS:** Demeter (1, 2nd base off Staley/Lollar). **FIELDING: DP:** 1 (Podres-Neal-Hodges).

CHICAGO WHITE SOX	AB	R	H	HR	RBI	BB	AVG
Aparicio ss	5	0	1	0	0	0	.308
Fox 2b	4	0	1	0	0	0	.375
Landis cf	3	1	1	0	0	0	.292
Lollar c	3	1	0	0	0	1	.227
Kluszewski 1b	4	1	2	1	3	0	.391
Smith lf	2	0	0	0	0	2	.250
Phillips 3b-rf	4	0	1	0	0	0	.300
McAnany rf	1	0	0	0	0	0	.000
a-Goodman ph-3b	3	0	0	0	0	0	.231
Wynn p	1	0	0	0	0	0	.200
Donovan p	0	0	0	0	0	0	.333
Lown p	0	0	0	0	0	0	.000
b-Torgeson ph	0	0	0	0	0	1	.000
Staley p	0	0	0	0	0	0	.000
c-Romano ph	1	0	0	0	0	0	.000
Pierce p	0	0	0	0	0	0	.000
Moore p	0	0	0	0	0	0	.000
d-Cash ph	1	0	0	0	0	0	.000
TOTALS	**32**	**3**	**6**	**1**	**3**	**4**	**.261**

a - Batted for McAnany in the 4th
b - Batted for Lown in the 4th
c - Batted for Staley in the 7th
d - Batted for Moore in the 9th

BATTING: 2B: Fox (3, Sherry), Kluszewski (1, Sherry). **HR:** Kluszewski (3, 4th off Podres 2 on, 1 out). **RBI:** Kluszewski 3 (10). **Runners left in scoring position, 2 out:** Aparicio 2, Kluszewski 1, Phillips 1. **GIDP:** Phillips. **Team LOB:** 7 **FIELDING: E:** Aparicio (1).

LOS ANGELES	IP	H	R	ER	BB	SO	HR	ERA
Podres	3.1	2	3	3	3	1	1	4.82
Sherry (W, 2-0)	5.2	4	0	0	1	1	0	0.71

CHICAGO WHITE SOX	IP	H	R	ER	BB	SO	HR	ERA
Wynn (L, 1-1)	3.1	5	5	5	3	2	1	5.54
Donovan	0	2	3	3	1	0	1	5.40
Lown	0.2	1	0	0	0	0	0	0.00
Staley	3	2	0	0	0	0	0	2.16
Pierce	1	2	0	0	0	1	0	0.00
Moore	1	1	1	1	0	1	1	9.00

HBP: Landis (by Podres). **Ground balls-fly balls:** Podres 5-3, Sherry 7-9, Wynn 2-5, Donovan 0-0, Lown 2-0, Staley 2-6, Pierce 1-1, Moore 1-1. **Batters faced:** Podres 15, Sherry 22, Wynn 18, Donovan 3, Lown 3, Staley 10, Pierce 5, Moore 4. **UMPIRES:** hp—Dascoli, 1b—Hurley, 2b—Secory, 3b—Summers, lf—Rice, rf—Dixon **T:** 2:33 **A:** 47,653

1960 PITTSBURGH DEF. NY YANKEES, 4-3

GAME 1 Pittsburgh 6 New York 4
Forbes Field 10/05/60

NY YANKEES	AB	R	H	HR	RBI	BB	AVG
Kubek ss	5	0	3	0	0	0	.600
Lopez lf	5	0	1	0	0	0	.200
Maris rf	4	2	3	1	1	0	.750
Mantle cf	3	0	0	0	0	1	.000
Berra c	4	0	1	0	0	0	.250
Skowron 1b	4	0	2	0	1	0	.500
Boyer 3b	0	0	0	0	0	0	.000
a-Long ph	1	0	0	0	0	0	.000
McDougald 3b	3	0	1	0	0	0	.333
Richardson 2b	4	1	0	0	0	0	.000
Ditmar p	0	0	0	0	0	0	.000
Coates p	1	0	0	0	0	0	.000
b-Blanchard ph	1	0	0	0	0	0	.000
Maas p	0	0	0	0	0	0	.000
c-Cerv ph	1	0	1	0	0	0	1.000
Duren p	0	0	0	0	0	0	.000
d-Howard ph	1	1	1	1	2	0	1.000
TOTALS	**37**	**4**	**13**	**2**	**4**	**1**	**.351**

a - Batted for Boyer in the 2nd
b - Batted for Coates in the 5th
c - Batted for Maas in the 7th
d - Batted for Duren in the 9th

BATTING: HR: Maris (1, 1st off Law 0 on, 2 out), Howard (1, 9th off Face 1 on, 1 out). **RBI:** Maris 1 (1), Skowron 1 (1), Howard 2 (2). **2-out RBI:** Maris 1. **Runners left in scoring position, 2 out:** Kubek 1, Skowron 1, Richardson 1. **GIDP:** Lopez, Lopez. **Team LOB:** 7 **FIELDING: E:** Kubek (1), Richardson (1). **Outfield assists:** Lopez (1).

PITTSBURGH	AB	R	H	HR	RBI	BB	AVG
Virdon cf	3	1	1	0	1	1	.333
Groat ss	4	1	2	0	1	0	.500
Skinner lf	3	1	1	0	1	0	.333
Cimoli lf	0	0	0	0	0	0	.000
Stuart 1b	4	0	1	0	0	0	.250
Clemente rf	4	0	1	0	1	0	.250
Burgess c	4	0	0	0	0	0	.000
Hoak 3b	2	1	0	0	0	2	.000
Mazeroski 2b	4	2	2	1	2	0	.500
Law p	1	0	0	0	0	0	.000
Face p	1	0	0	0	0	0	.000
TOTALS	**30**	**6**	**8**	**1**	**6**	**3**	**.267**

BATTING: 2B: Groat (1, Ditmar), Virdon (1, Maas). **HR:** Mazeroski (1, 4th off Coates 1 on, 1 out). **S:** Law. **RBI:** Virdon 1 (1), Groat 1 (1), Skinner 1 (1), Clemente 1 (1), Mazeroski 2 (2). **2-out RBI:** Virdon 1. **Runners left in scoring position, 2 out:** Groat 1, Clemente 1. **Team LOB:** 6 **BASERUNNING: SB:** Virdon (1, 2nd base off Ditmar/Berra), Skinner (1, 2nd base off Ditmar/Berra). **CS:** Hoak (1, 2nd base off Duren/Berra). **FIELDING: Outfield assists:** Skinner (1). **DP:** 3 (Mazeroski-Stuart, Skinner-Mazeroski, Mazeroski-Groat-Stuart).

NY YANKEES	IP	H	R	ER	BB	SO	HR	ERA
Ditmar (L, 0-1)	0.1	3	3	3	1	0	0	81.00
Coates	3.2	3	2	2	1	2	1	4.91
Maas	2	2	1	1	0	1	0	4.50
Duren	2	0	0	0	1	1	0	0.00

PITTSBURGH	IP	H	R	ER	BB	SO	HR	ERA
Law (W, 1-0)	7	10	2	2	1	3	1	2.57
Face (S, 1)	2	3	2	2	0	2	1	9.00

WP: Law 1. **HBP:** Law (by Coates), Skinner (by Duren). **Ground balls-fly balls:** Ditmar 0-1, Coates 3-5, Maas 4-1, Duren 2-2, Law 6-10, Face 2-1. **Batters faced:** Ditmar 5, Coates 15, Maas 9, Duren 7, Law 30, Face 8. **UMPIRES:** hp—Boggess, 1b—Stevens, 2b—Jackowski, 3b—Chylak, lf—Landes, rf—Honochick **T:** 2:29 **A:** 36,676

GAME 2 New York 16 Pittsburgh 3
Forbes Field 10/06/60

NY YANKEES	AB	R	H	HR	RBI	BB	AVG
Kubek ss-lf	6	3	3	0	1	0	.545
McDougald 3b	3	1	2	0	2	1	.500
DeMaestri ss	2	1	1	0	0	0	.500
Maris rf	5	2	1	0	0	1	.444
Mantle cf	4	3	2	2	5	2	.286
Berra lf	4	1	1	0	2	0	.250
Boyer 3b	2	0	1	0	0	0	.500
Skowron 1b	6	1	2	0	1	0	.400
Howard c	5	1	2	0	1	0	.500
Richardson 2b	4	3	3	0	2	1	.375
Turley p	4	0	1	0	1	0	.250
Shantz p	0	0	0	0	0	0	.000
TOTALS	**45**	**16**	**19**	**2**	**15**	**5**	**.390**

BATTING: 2B: McDougald (1, Friend), Richardson (1, Green), Boyer (1, Cheney). **3B:** Howard (1, Green). **HR:** Mantle 2 (2, 5th off Green 1 on, 1 out, 7th off Gibbon 2 on, 1 out). **S:** Turley. **RBI:** Kubek 1 (1), McDougald 2 (2), Mantle 5 (5), Berra 2 (2), Skowron 1 (2), Howard 1 (3), Richardson 2 (2), Turley 1 (1). **2-out RBI:** Berra 2, Skowron 1, Howard 1, Richardson 1, Turley 1. **Runners left in scoring position, 2 out:** Berra 1, Skowron 1, Turley 1. **Team LOB:** 8 **BASERUNNING: CS:** Kubek (1, 2nd base off Friend/Burgess). **FIELDING: E:** Richardson (2). **DP:** 1 (Shantz-Richardson-Skowron).

PITTSBURGH	AB	R	H	HR	RBI	BB	AVG
Virdon cf	5	0	0	0	0	0	.125
Groat ss	4	0	1	0	0	0	.375
Gibbon p	0	0	0	0	0	0	.000
Cheney p	0	0	0	0	0	0	.000
c-Christopher ph	0	1	0	0	0	0	.000
Clemente rf	5	0	2	0	0	0	.333
Nelson 1b	5	1	2	0	0	0	.400
Cimoli lf	4	1	2	0	1	1	.500
Burgess c	4	0	2	0	1	1	.250
Hoak 3b	5	0	2	0	1	0	.286
Mazeroski 2b	4	0	1	0	0	0	.375
Friend p	1	0	0	0	0	0	.000
a-Baker ph	1	0	0	0	0	0	.000
Green p	0	0	0	0	0	0	.000
Labine p	0	0	0	0	0	0	.000
Witt p	0	0	0	0	0	0	.000
b-Schofield ph-ss	1	0	1	0	0	1	1.000
TOTALS	**39**	**3**	**13**	**0**	**3**	**3**	**.304**

a - Batted for Friend in the 4th
b - Batted for Witt in the 6th
c - Batted for Cheney in the 9th

BATTING: 2B: Mazeroski (1, Turley), Hoak 2 (2, Turley). **RBI:** Cimoli 1 (1), Burgess 1 (1), Hoak 1 (1). **Runners left in scoring position, 2 out:** Virdon 3, Groat 1, Burgess 1, Friend 2. **GIDP:** Hoak. **Team LOB:** 13 **FIELDING: E:** Groat (1). **PB:** Burgess, Burgess.

NY YANKEES	IP	H	R	ER	BB	SO	HR	ERA
Turley (W, 1-0)	8.1	13	3	2	3	0	0	2.16
Shantz (S, 1)	0.2	0	0	0	0	0	0	0.00

PITTSBURGH	IP	H	R	ER	BB	SO	HR	ERA
Friend (L, 0-1)	4	6	3	2	2	6	0	4.50
Green	1	3	4	4	1	0	1	36.00
Labine	0.2	3	5	0	1	1	0	0.00
Witt	0.1	2	0	0	0	0	0	0.00
Gibbon	2	4	3	3	0	2	1	13.50
Cheney	1	1	1	1	1	2	0	9.00

WP: Cheney 1. **HBP:** Christopher (by Turley). **Ground balls-fly balls:** Turley 9-16, Shantz 1-0, Friend 2-2, Green 2-1, Labine 2-0, Witt 0-1, Gibbon 2-2, Cheney 1-0. **Batters faced:** Turley 42, Shantz 1, Friend 19, Green 7, Labine 7, Witt 3, Gibbon 10, Cheney 5. **UMPIRES:** hp—Stevens, 1b—Jackowski, 2b—Chylak, 3b—Boggess, lf—Landes, rf—Honochick **T:** 3:14 **A:** 37,308

GAME 3 New York 10 Pittsburgh 0
Yankee Stadium 10/08/60

PITTSBURGH	AB	R	H	HR	RBI	BB	AVG
Virdon cf	4	0	1	0	0	0	.167
Groat ss	4	0	0	0	0	0	.250
Clemente rf	4	0	1	0	0	0	.308
Stuart 1b	4	0	1	0	0	0	.250
Cimoli lf	3	0	0	0	0	1	.286
Smith c	3	0	0	0	0	0	.000
Hoak 3b	3	0	0	0	0	0	.200
Mazeroski 2b	3	0	1	0	0	0	.364
Mizell p	0	0	0	0	0	0	.000
Labine p	0	0	0	0	0	0	.000
Green p	1	0	0	0	0	0	.000
Witt p	0	0	0	0	0	0	.000
a-Baker ph	1	0	0	0	0	0	.000
Cheney p	0	0	0	0	0	0	.000
b-Schofield ph	1	0	0	0	0	0	.500
Gibbon p	0	0	0	0	0	0	.000
TOTALS	**31**	**0**	**4**	**0**	**0**	**1**	**.250**

a - Batted for Witt in the 6th
b - Batted for Cheney in the 8th

BATTING: 2B: Virdon (2, Ford). **Runners left in scoring position, 2 out:** Groat 1, Stuart 1, Cimoli 1. **GIDP:** Smith. **Team LOB:** 5

NY YANKEES	AB	R	H	HR	RBI	BB	AVG
Cerv lf	5	1	2	0	0	0	.500
Maris rf	3	0	0	0	0	1	.333
Berra rf	1	0	1	0	0	0	.333
Mantle cf	5	2	4	1	2	0	.500
Skowron 1b	5	2	2	0	1	0	.400
McDougald 3b	4	2	1	0	0	1	.400
Howard c	4	1	2	0	1	1	.500
Richardson 2b	5	1	2	1	6	0	.385
Kubek ss	3	0	1	0	0	1	.500
Ford p	4	1	1	0	0	0	.250
TOTALS	**39**	**10**	**16**	**2**	**10**	**4**	**.397**

BATTING: 2B: Mantle (1, Witt). **HR:** Richardson (1, 1st off Labine 3 on, 1 out), Mantle (3, 4th off Green 1 on, 2 out). **RBI:** Mantle 2 (7), Skowron 1 (3), Howard 1 (4), Richardson 6 (8). **2-out RBI:** Mantle 2, Richardson 2. **Runners left in scoring position, 2 out:** Maris 1, McDougald 2, Ford 2. **Team LOB:** 9 **BASERUNNING: CS:** Mantle (1, 3rd base off Green/Smith). **FIELDING: E:** Kubek (2). **DP:** 1 (Ford-Richardson-Skowron).

PITTSBURGH	IP	H	R	ER	BB	SO	HR	ERA
Mizell (L, 0-1)	0.1	3	4	4	1	0	0	108.00
Labine	0.1	4	2	2	0	0	1	18.00
Green	3	5	4	4	0	3	1	18.00
Witt	1.1	3	0	0	2	1	0	0.00
Cheney	2	1	0	0	0	3	0	3.00
Gibbon	1	0	0	0	1	0	0	9.00

NY YANKEES	IP	H	R	ER	BB	SO	HR	ERA
Ford (W, 1-0)	9	4	0	0	1	3	0	0.00

WP: Green 1, Witt 1. **IBB:** Kubek (by Witt). **Ground balls-fly balls:** Mizell 0-1, Labine 1-0, Green 3-2, Witt 3-0, Cheney 0-3, Gibbon 1-2, Ford 15-9. **Batters faced:** Mizell 5, Labine 5, Green 13, Witt 9, Cheney 7, Gibbon 4, Ford 32. **UMPIRES:** hp—Jackowski, 1b—Chylak, 2b—Boggess, 3b—Stevens, lf—Honochick, rf—Landes **T:** 2:41 **A:** 70,001

GAME 4 Pittsburgh 3 New York 2
Yankee Stadium 10/09/60

PITTSBURGH	AB	R	H	HR	RBI	BB	AVG
Virdon cf	4	0	1	0	2	0	.188
Groat ss	4	0	0	0	0	0	.188
Clemente rf	4	0	1	0	0	0	.294
Stuart 1b	4	0	0	0	0	0	.167
Cimoli lf	4	1	1	0	0	0	.273
Burgess c	3	1	0	0	0	1	.182
Oldis c	0	0	0	0	0	0	.000
Hoak 3b	4	0	1	0	0	0	.214
Mazeroski 2b	3	0	1	0	0	0	.357
Law p	3	1	2	0	1	0	.500
Face p	1	0	0	0	0	0	.000
TOTALS	**34**	**3**	**7**	**0**	**3**	**1**	**.239**

BATTING: 2B: Law (1, Terry). **S:** Mazeroski. **RBI:** Virdon 2 (3), Law 1 (1). **2-out RBI:** Virdon 2, Law 1. **Runners left in scoring position, 2 out:** Groat 2, Burgess 1. **Team LOB:** 6 **FIELDING: DP:** 1 (Hoak-Stuart).

NY YANKEES	AB	R	H	HR	RBI	BB	AVG
Cerv lf	4	0	1	0	0	0	.400
Kubek ss	4	0	1	0	0	0	.444
Maris rf	4	0	0	0	0	0	.250
Mantle cf	3	0	0	0	0	1	.400
Berra c	4	0	0	0	0	0	.231
Skowron 1b	4	2	2	1	1	0	.421
McDougald 3b	4	0	1	0	0	0	.357
Richardson 2b	3	0	2	0	1	0	.438
c-Long ph	1	0	0	0	0	0	.000
Terry p	2	0	0	0	0	0	.000
Shantz p	0	0	0	0	0	0	.000
a-Blanchard ph	1	0	1	0	0	0	.500
b-DeMaestri pr	0	0	0	0	0	0	.500
Coates p	0	0	0	0	0	0	.000
TOTALS	**34**	**2**	**8**	**1**	**2**	**1**	**.361**

a - Batted for Shantz in the 7th
b - Ran for Blanchard in the 7th
c - Batted for Richardson in the 9th

BATTING: 2B: Kubek (1, Law), Richardson (2, Law), Skowron (1, Law). **HR:** Skowron (1, 4th off Law 0 on, 2 out). **RBI:** Skowron 1 (4), Richardson 1 (9). **2-out RBI:** Skowron 1. **Runners left in scoring position, 2 out:** Kubek 1, Terry 1. **GIDP:** Berra. **Team LOB:** 6

PITTSBURGH	IP	H	R	ER	BB	SO	HR	ERA
Law (W, 2-0)	6.1	8	2	2	1	5	1	2.70
Face (S, 2)	2.2	0	0	0	0	1	0	3.86

NY YANKEES	IP	H	R	ER	BB	SO	HR	ERA
Terry (L, 0-1)	6.1	6	3	3	1	5	0	4.26
Shantz	0.2	0	0	0	0	1	0	0.00
Coates	2	1	0	0	0	1	0	3.18

IBB: Mantle (by Law). **Ground balls-fly balls:** Law 9-4, Face 3-4, Terry 6-8, Shantz 1-0, Coates 3-2. **Batters faced:** Law 27, Face 8, Terry 27, Shantz 2, Coates 7. **UMPIRES:** hp—Chylak, 1b—Boggess, 2b—Stevens, 3b—Jackowski, lf—Landes, rf—Honochick **T:** 2:29 **A:** 67,812

GAME 5 Pittsburgh 5 New York 2
Yankee Stadium 10/10/60

PITTSBURGH	AB	R	H	HR	RBI	BB	AVG
Virdon cf	5	0	1	0	0	0	.190
Groat ss	4	1	1	0	0	0	.200
Clemente rf	4	0	1	0	1	0	.286
Stuart 1b	4	0	1	0	0	0	.188
Nelson 1b	0	0	0	0	0	0	.400
Cimoli lf	4	1	0	0	0	0	.200
Burgess c	4	1	2	0	0	0	.267
a-Christopher pr	0	1	0	0	0	0	.000
Oldis c	0	0	0	0	0	0	.000
Hoak 3b	4	1	2	0	2	0	.278
Mazeroski 2b	4	0	1	0	2	0	.333
Haddix p	3	0	1	0	0	0	.333
Face p	1	0	0	0	0	0	.000
TOTALS	**37**	**5**	**10**	**0**	**5**	**0**	**.246**

a - Ran for Burgess in the 9th

BATTING: 2B: Burgess (1, Ditmar), Mazeroski (2, Ditmar), Groat (2, Arroyo), Virdon (3, Stafford). **RBI:** Clemente 1 (2), Hoak 2 (3), Mazeroski 2 (4). **Runners left in scoring position, 2 out:** Virdon 1, Groat 2. **GIDP:** Haddix. **Team LOB:** 5 **FIELDING: E:** Hoak (1), Groat (2). **PB:** Burgess. **DP:** 1 (Mazeroski-Stuart).

NY YANKEES	AB	R	H	HR	RBI	BB	AVG
McDougald 3b	4	0	0	0	0	0	.278
Maris rf	4	1	1	1	1	0	.250
Cerv lf	4	0	1	0	0	0	.357
Mantle cf	1	0	0	0	0	3	.375
Skowron 1b	4	0	0	0	0	0	.348
Howard c	3	1	1	0	0	0	.462
b-Berra ph-c	1	0	0	0	0	0	.214
Richardson 2b	4	0	0	0	0	0	.350
Kubek ss	4	0	1	0	1	0	.409
Ditmar p	0	0	0	0	0	0	.000
Arroyo p	1	0	0	0	0	0	.000
Stafford p	1	0	0	0	0	0	.000
a-Lopez ph	1	0	1	0	0	0	.333
Duren p	0	0	0	0	0	0	.000
c-Blanchard ph	1	0	0	0	0	0	.333
TOTALS	**33**	**2**	**5**	**1**	**2**	**3**	**.324**

a - Batted for Stafford in the 7th
b - Batted for Howard in the 8th
c - Batted for Duren in the 9th

BATTING: 2B: Howard (1, Haddix). **HR:** Maris (2, 3th off Haddix 0 on, 1 out). **RBI:** Maris 1 (2), Kubek 1 (2). **Runners left in scoring position, 2 out:** Maris 1, Skowron 1. **Team LOB:** 7 **FIELDING: E:** Cerv (1). **DP:** 1 (Stafford-Kubek-Skowron).

PITTSBURGH	IP	H	R	ER	BB	SO	HR	ERA
Haddix (W, 1-0)	6.1	5	2	2	2	6	1	2.84
Face (S, 3)	2.2	0	0	0	1	1	0	2.45

NY YANKEES	IP	H	R	ER	BB	SO	HR	ERA
Ditmar (L, 0-2)	1.1	3	3	1	0	0	0	21.60
Arroyo	0.2	2	1	1	0	1	0	13.50
Stafford	5	3	0	0	0	2	0	0.00
Duren	2	2	1	1	0	4	0	2.25

WP: Duren 1. **IBB:** Mantle (by Haddix). **Ground balls-fly balls:** Haddix 8-6, Face 3-4, Ditmar 3-2, Arroyo 0-1, Stafford 7-5, Duren 1-1. **Batters faced:** Haddix 27, Face 9, Ditmar 8, Arroyo 4, Stafford 17, Duren 8. **UMPIRES:** hp—Boggess, 1b—Stevens, 2b—Jackowski, 3b—Chylak, lf—Landes, rf—Honochick **T:** 2:32 **A:** 62,753

GAME 6 New York 12 Pittsburgh 0
Forbes Field 10/12/60

NY YANKEES	AB	R	H	HR	RBI	BB	AVG
Boyer 3b	6	1	1	0	0	0	.250
Kubek ss-lf	5	2	1	0	1	0	.370
Maris rf	5	1	3	0	0	0	.320
Mantle cf	4	2	1	0	2	1	.350
Berra lf	4	3	3	0	2	1	.333
DeMaestri ss	0	0	0	0	0	0	.500
Skowron 1b	4	0	2	0	1	0	.370
Howard c	0	0	0	0	0	0	.462
a-Grba pr	0	0	0	0	0	0	.000
Blanchard c	4	2	3	0	1	0	.571
Richardson 2b	5	1	2	0	3	0	.360
Ford p	4	0	1	0	2	0	.250
TOTALS	**41**	**12**	**17**	**0**	**12**	**2**	**.341**

a - Ran for Howard in the 2nd

BATTING: 2B: Maris (1, Friend), Skowron (2, Mizell), Blanchard 2 (2, Labine). **3B:** Richardson 2 (2, Cheney, Labine), Boyer (1, Green). **S:** Ford. **SF:** Skowron. **RBI:** Kubek 1 (3), Mantle 2 (9), Berra 2 (4), Skowron 1 (5), Blanchard 1 (1), Richardson 3 (12), Ford 2 (2). **2-out RBI:** Blanchard 1, Ford 1. **Runners left in scoring position, 2 out:** Boyer 3, Richardson 1, Ford 1. **GIDP:** Skowron, Boyer. **Team LOB:** 8 **FIELDING: E:** Kubek (3). **DP:** 3 (Richardson-Kubek-Skowron, Boyer-Richardson-Skowron 2).

PITTSBURGH	AB	R	H	HR	RBI	BB	AVG
Virdon cf	4	0	1	0	0	0	.200
Groat ss	4	0	1	0	0	0	.208
Witt p	0	0	0	0	0	0	.000
Clemente rf	4	0	2	0	0	0	.320
Stuart 1b	4	0	0	0	0	0	.150
Cimoli lf	4	0	1	0	0	0	.211
Smith c	4	0	2	0	0	0	.286
Hoak 3b	2	0	0	0	0	1	.250
Mazeroski 2b	3	0	0	0	0	0	.286
Friend p	0	0	0	0	0	0	.000
Cheney p	0	0	0	0	0	0	.000
a-Baker ph	1	0	0	0	0	0	.000
Mizell p	0	0	0	0	0	0	.000
b-Nelson ph	1	0	0	0	0	0	.333
Green p	0	0	0	0	0	0	.000
Labine p	0	0	0	0	0	0	.000
c-Schofield ph-ss	1	0	0	0	0	0	.333
TOTALS	**32**	**0**	**7**	**0**	**0**	**1**	**.241**

a - Batted for Cheney in the 3th
b - Batted for Mizell in the 5th
c - Batted for Labine in the 8th

BATTING: Runners left in scoring position, 2 out: Nelson 1. **GIDP:** Groat, Mazeroski, Smith. **Team LOB:** 6 **FIELDING: E:** Virdon (1). **DP:** 2 (Groat-Mazeroski-Stuart, Hoak-Mazeroski-Stuart).

NY YANKEES	IP	H	R	ER	BB	SO	HR	ERA
Ford (W, 2-0)	9	7	0	0	1	5	0	0.00

PITTSBURGH	IP	H	R	ER	BB	SO	HR	ERA
Friend (L, 0-2)	2	5	5	5	1	1	0	10.50
Cheney	1	2	1	1	0	1	0	4.50
Mizell	2	1	0	0	1	1	0	15.43
Green	0	3	2	2	0	0	0	22.50
Labine	3	6	4	4	0	1	0	13.50
Witt	1	0	0	0	0	0	0	0.00

WP: Labine 1. **HBP:** Howard (by Friend), Kubek (by Friend). **Ground balls-fly balls:** Ford 17-3, Friend 3-2, Cheney 0-1, Mizell 2-3, Green 0-0, Labine 4-2, Witt 2-1. **Batters faced:** Ford 33, Friend 14, Cheney 5, Mizell 8, Green 3, Labine 14, Witt 3. **UMPIRES:** hp—Stevens, 1b—Jackowski, 2b—Chylak, 3b—Boggess, lf—Landes, rf—Honochick **T:** 2:38 **A:** 38,580

GAME 7 Pittsburgh 10 New York 9
Forbes Field 10/13/60

NY YANKEES	AB	R	H	HR	RBI	BB	AVG
Richardson 2b	5	2	2	0	0	0	.367
Kubek ss	3	1	0	0	0	1	.333
DeMaestri ss	0	0	0	0	0	0	.500
b-Long ph	1	0	1	0	0	0	.333
c-McDougald pr-3b	0	1	0	0	0	0	.278
Maris rf	5	0	0	0	0	0	.267
Mantle cf	5	1	3	0	2	0	.400
Berra lf	4	2	1	1	4	1	.318
Skowron 1b	5	2	2	1	1	0	.375
Blanchard c	4	0	1	0	1	0	.455
Boyer 3b-ss	4	0	1	0	1	0	.250
Turley p	0	0	0	0	0	0	.250
Stafford p	0	0	0	0	0	0	.000
a-Lopez ph	1	0	1	0	0	0	.429
Shantz p	3	0	1	0	0	0	.333
Coates p	0	0	0	0	0	0	.000
Terry p	0	0	0	0	0	0	.000
TOTALS	**40**	**9**	**13**	**2**	**9**	**2**	**.338**

a - Batted for Stafford in the 3th
b - Batted for DeMaestri in the 9th
c - Ran for Long in the 9th

BATTING: 2B: Boyer (2, Face). **HR:** Skowron (2, 5th off Law 0 on, 0 out), Berra (1, 6th off Face 2 on, 1 out). **RBI:** Mantle 2 (11), Berra 4 (8), Skowron 1 (6), Blanchard 1 (2), Boyer 1 (1). **2-out RBI:** Blanchard 1, Boyer 1. **Runners left in scoring position, 2 out:** Shantz 2. **Team LOB:** 6 **FIELDING: E:** Maris (1). **DP:** 3 (Stafford-Blanchard-Skowron, Richardson-Kubek-Skowron, Kubek-Richardson-Skowron).

PITTSBURGH	AB	R	H	HR	RBI	BB	AVG
Virdon cf	4	1	2	0	2	0	.241
Groat ss	4	1	1	0	1	0	.214
Skinner lf	2	1	0	0	0	1	.200
Nelson 1b	3	1	1	1	2	1	.333
Clemente rf	4	1	1	0	1	0	.310
Burgess c	3	0	2	0	0	0	.333
a-Christopher pr	0	0	0	0	0	0	.000
Smith c	1	1	1	1	3	0	.375
Hoak 3b	3	1	0	0	0	1	.217
Mazeroski 2b	4	2	2	1	1	0	.320
Law p	2	0	0	0	0	0	.333
Face p	0	0	0	0	0	0	.000
b-Cimoli ph	1	1	1	0	0	0	.250
Friend p	0	0	0	0	0	0	.000
Haddix p	0	0	0	0	0	0	.333
TOTALS	**31**	**10**	**11**	**3**	**10**	**3**	**.256**

a - Ran for Burgess in the 7th
b - Batted for Face in the 8th

BATTING: HR: Nelson (1, 1st off Turley 1 on, 2 out), Smith (1, 8th off Coates 2 on, 2 out), Mazeroski (2, 9th off Terry 0 on, 0 out). **S:** Skinner. **RBI:** Virdon 2 (5), Groat 1 (2), Nelson 2 (2), Clemente 1 (3), Smith 3 (3), Mazeroski 1 (5). **2-out RBI:** Virdon 2, Nelson 2, Clemente 1, Smith 3. **Runners left in scoring position, 2 out:** Groat 1. **GIDP:** Law, Clemente, Mazeroski. **Team LOB:** 1

NY YANKEES	IP	H	R	ER	BB	SO	HR	ERA
Turley	1	2	3	3	1	0	1	4.82
Stafford	1	2	1	1	1	0	0	1.50
Shantz	5	4	3	3	1	0	0	4.26
Coates	0.2	2	2	2	0	0	1	5.68
Terry (L, 0-2)	0.1	1	1	1	0	0	1	5.40

PITTSBURGH	IP	H	R	ER	BB	SO	HR	ERA
Law	5	4	3	3	1	0	1	3.44
Face	3	6	4	4	1	0	1	5.23
Friend	0	2	2	2	0	0	0	13.50
Haddix (W, 2-0)	1	1	0	0	0	0	0	2.45

Ground balls-fly balls: Turley 0-3, Stafford 2-0, Shantz 9-4, Coates 0-1, Terry 0-1, Law 3-12, Face 3-6, Friend 0-0, Haddix 2-1. **Batters faced:** Turley 6, Stafford 5, Shantz 18, Coates 4, Terry 2, Law 20, Face 16, Friend 2, Haddix 4. **UMPIRES:** hp—Jackowski, 1b—Chylak, 2b—Boggess, 3b—Stevens, lf—Landes, rf—Honochick **T:** 2:36 **A:** 36,683

1961 NY YANKEES DEF. CINCINNATI, 4-1

GAME 1 New York 2 Cincinnati 0
Yankee Stadium 10/04/61

CINCINNATI	AB	R	H	HR	RBI	BB	AVG
Blasingame 2b	3	0	0	0	0	0	.000
c-Lynch ph	1	0	0	0	0	0	.000
Kasko ss	4	0	1	0	0	0	.250
Pinson cf	4	0	0	0	0	0	.000
Robinson lf	2	0	0	0	0	1	.000
Post rf	3	0	1	0	0	0	.333
Freese 3b	3	0	0	0	0	0	.000
Coleman 1b	3	0	0	0	0	0	.000
D.Johnson c	2	0	0	0	0	0	.000
a-Cardenas ph	1	0	0	0	0	0	.000
Zimmerman c	0	0	0	0	0	0	.000
O'Toole p	2	0	0	0	0	0	.000
b-Gernert ph	1	0	0	0	0	0	.000
Brosnan p	0	0	0	0	0	0	.000
TOTALS	**29**	**0**	**2**	**0**	**0**	**1**	**.069**

a - Batted for D.Johnson in the 8th
b - Batted for O'Toole in the 8th
c - Batted for Blasingame in the 9th

BATTING: Runners left in scoring position, 2 out: D.Johnson 1. **Team LOB:** 3 **FIELDING: DP:** 1 (D.Johnson-Kasko-Coleman).

NY YANKEES	AB	R	H	HR	RBI	BB	AVG
Richardson 2b	4	0	3	0	0	0	.750
Kubek ss	3	0	0	0	0	1	.000
Maris cf-rf	4	0	0	0	0	0	.000
Howard c	4	1	1	1	1	0	.250
Skowron 1b	3	1	1	1	1	1	.333
Berra lf	2	0	0	0	0	2	.000
Lopez rf	2	0	0	0	0	1	.000
a-Blanchard ph	1	0	0	0	0	0	.000
Reed cf	0	0	0	0	0	0	.000
Boyer 3b	3	0	1	0	0	0	.333
Ford p	3	0	0	0	0	0	.000
TOTALS	**29**	**2**	**6**	**2**	**2**	**5**	**.207**

a - Batted for Lopez in the 8th

BATTING: HR: Howard (1, 4th off O'Toole 0 on, 0 out), Skowron (1, 6th off O'Toole 0 on, 1 out). **RBI:** Howard 1 (1), Skowron 1 (1). **Runners left in scoring position, 2 out:** Berra 2, Ford 1. **Team LOB:** 8 **BASERUNNING: CS:** Richardson (1, 2nd base off O'Toole/D.Johnson).

CINCINNATI	IP	H	R	ER	BB	SO	HR	ERA
O'Toole (L, 0-1)	7	6	2	2	4	2	2	2.57
Brosnan	1	0	0	0	1	1	0	0.00

NY YANKEES	IP	H	R	ER	BB	SO	HR	ERA
Ford (W, 1-0)	9	2	0	0	1	6	0	0.00

Ground balls-fly balls: O'Toole 4-14, Brosnan 1-1, Ford 14-7. **Batters faced:** O'Toole 30, Brosnan 4, Ford 30. **UMPIRES:** hp—Runge, 1b—Conlan, 2b—Umont, 3b—Donatelli, lf—Crawford, rf—Stewart **T:** 2:11 **A:** 62,397

GAME 2 Cincinnati 6 New York 2
Yankee Stadium 10/05/61

CINCINNATI	AB	R	H	HR	RBI	BB	AVG
Chacon 2b	4	1	1	0	0	1	.250
Kasko ss	5	0	1	0	0	0	.222
Pinson cf	5	0	1	0	0	0	.111
Robinson lf	4	2	0	0	0	1	.000
Coleman 1b	5	1	2	1	3	0	.250
Post rf	4	2	2	0	0	0	.429
Freese 3b	2	0	0	0	0	2	.000
Edwards c	4	0	2	0	2	0	.500
Jay p	4	0	0	0	0	0	.000
TOTALS	**37**	**6**	**9**	**1**	**5**	**4**	**.167**

BATTING: 2B: Post (1, Terry), Edwards (1, Arroyo), Pinson (1, Arroyo). **HR:** Coleman (1, 4th off Terry 1 on, 1 out). **RBI:** Coleman 3 (3), Edwards 2 (2). **2-out RBI:** Edwards 1. **Runners left in scoring position, 2 out:** Chacon 2, Pinson 1, Coleman 1, Jay 1. **Team LOB:** 8 **FIELDING: DP:** 2 (Chacon-Kasko-Coleman 2).

NY YANKEES	AB	R	H	HR	RBI	BB	AVG
Richardson 2b	4	0	1	0	0	0	.500
Kubek ss	4	0	1	0	0	0	.143
Maris cf	3	1	0	0	0	1	.000
Berra lf	4	1	2	1	2	0	.333
Blanchard rf	4	0	0	0	0	0	.000
Howard c	3	0	0	0	0	1	.143
Skowron 1b	3	0	0	0	0	1	.167
Boyer 3b	2	0	0	0	0	2	.200
Terry p	2	0	0	0	0	0	.000
a-Lopez ph	0	0	0	0	0	1	.000
Arroyo p	0	0	0	0	0	0	.000
b-Gardner ph	1	0	0	0	0	0	.000
TOTALS	**30**	**2**	**4**	**1**	**2**	**6**	**.169**

a - Batted for Terry in the 7th
b - Batted for Arroyo in the 9th

BATTING: HR: Berra (1, 4th off Jay 1 on, 0 out). **RBI:** Berra 2 (2). **Runners left in scoring position, 2 out:** Maris 1. **GIDP:** Skowron, Howard. **Team LOB:** 7 **FIELDING: E:** Boyer (1), Arroyo (1), Berra (1). **PB:** Howard.

CINCINNATI	IP	H	R	ER	BB	SO	HR	ERA
Jay (W, 1-0)	9	4	2	2	6	6	1	2.00

NY YANKEES	IP	H	R	ER	BB	SO	HR	ERA
Terry (L, 0-1)	7	6	4	2	2	7	1	2.57
Arroyo	2	3	2	1	2	1	0	4.50

IBB: Freese 2 (by Terry, by Arroyo). **Ground balls-fly balls:** Jay 10-10, Terry 7-8, Arroyo 2-3. **Batters faced:** Jay 36, Terry 30, Arroyo 11. **UMPIRES:** hp—Conlan, 1b—Umont, 2b—Donatelli, 3b—Runge, lf—Crawford, rf—Stewart **T:** 2:43 **A:** 63,083

GAME 3 New York 3 Cincinnati 2
Crosley Field 10/07/61

NY YANKEES	AB	R	H	HR	RBI	BB	AVG
Richardson 2b	4	0	1	0	0	0	.417
Kubek ss	4	1	1	0	0	0	.182
Maris rf	4	1	1	1	1	0	.091
Mantle cf	4	0	0	0	0	0	.000
Reed cf	0	0	0	0	0	0	.000
Berra lf	3	0	1	0	1	1	.333
Howard c	4	0	1	0	0	0	.182
Skowron 1b	3	0	0	0	0	0	.111
Boyer 3b	3	0	0	0	0	0	.125
Stafford p	2	0	0	0	0	0	.000
Daley p	0	0	0	0	0	0	.000
a-Blanchard ph	1	1	1	1	1	0	.167
Arroyo p	0	0	0	0	0	0	.000
TOTALS	**32**	**3**	**6**	**2**	**3**	**1**	**.176**

a - Batted for Daley in the 8th

BATTING: 2B: Howard (1, Purkey). **HR:** Blanchard (1, 8th off Purkey 0 on, 2 out), Maris (1, 9th off Purkey 0 on, 0 out). **RBI:** Maris 1 (1), Berra 1 (3), Blanchard 1 (1). **2-out RBI:** Berra 1, Blanchard 1. **Runners left in scoring position, 2 out:** Kubek 1. **Team LOB:** 3 **BASERUNNING: SB:** Richardson (1, 2nd base off Purkey/Edwards). **FIELDING: E:** Stafford (1).

CINCINNATI	AB	R	H	HR	RBI	BB	AVG
Chacon 2b	3	1	1	0	0	0	.286
a-Lynch ph	0	0	0	0	0	1	.000
b-Blasingame pr-2b	0	0	0	0	0	0	.000
e-Bell ph	1	0	0	0	0	0	.000
Kasko ss	4	0	2	0	1	0	.308
Pinson cf	4	0	0	0	0	0	.077
Robinson rf	4	0	1	0	1	0	.100
Coleman 1b	4	0	2	0	0	0	.333
Post lf	4	0	0	0	0	0	.273
Freese 3b	3	0	0	0	0	1	.000
Edwards c	3	1	1	0	0	0	.429
c-Cardenas ph	1	0	1	0	0	0	.500
Purkey p	3	0	0	0	0	0	.000
d-Gernert ph	1	0	0	0	0	0	.000
TOTALS	**35**	**2**	**8**	**0**	**2**	**2**	**.188**

a - Batted for Chacon in the 7th
b - Ran for Lynch in the 7th
c - Batted for Edwards in the 9th
d - Batted for Purkey in the 9th e - Batted for Blasingame in the 9th

BATTING: 2B: Robinson (1, Stafford), Edwards (2, Stafford), Cardenas (1, Arroyo). **RBI:** Kasko 1 (1), Robinson 1 (1). **2-out RBI:** Kasko 1, Robinson 1. **Runners left in scoring position, 2 out:** Bell 1, Pinson 1, Coleman 1, Purkey 2. **Team LOB:** 8 **FIELDING: PB:** Edwards. **DP:** 1 (Kasko).

NY YANKEES	IP	H	R	ER	BB	SO	HR	ERA
Stafford	6.2	7	2	2	2	5	0	2.70
Daley	0.1	0	0	0	0	0	0	0.00
Arroyo (W, 1-0)	2	1	0	0	0	2	0	2.25

CINCINNATI	IP	H	R	ER	BB	SO	HR	ERA
Purkey (L, 0-1)	9	6	3	2	1	3	2	2.00

IBB: Lynch (by Stafford). **Ground balls-fly balls:** Stafford 7-8, Daley 0-1, Arroyo 3-1, Purkey 7-16. **Batters faced:** Stafford 29, Daley 1, Arroyo 7, Purkey 33. **UMPIRES:** hp—Umont, 1b—Donatelli, 2b—Runge, 3b—Conlan, lf—Crawford, rf—Stewart **T:** 2:15 **A:** 32,589

GAME 4 New York 7 Cincinnati 0
Crosley Field 10/08/61

NY YANKEES	AB	R	H	HR	RBI	BB	AVG
Richardson 2b	5	1	3	0	0	0	.471
Kubek ss	5	0	1	0	1	0	.188
Maris rf-cf	3	2	0	0	0	2	.071
Mantle cf	2	0	1	0	0	0	.167
a-Lopez pr-rf	3	1	1	0	2	0	.200
Howard c	4	1	1	0	1	0	.200
Berra lf	2	1	0	0	0	2	.273
Skowron 1b	3	0	3	0	1	1	.333
Boyer 3b	4	0	1	0	2	0	.167
Ford p	2	1	0	0	0	1	.000
Coates p	1	0	0	0	0	0	.000
TOTALS	**34**	**7**	**11**	**0**	**7**	**6**	**.216**

a - Ran for Mantle in the 4th

BATTING: 2B: Richardson (1, O'Toole), Howard (2, Brosnan), Boyer (1, Brosnan). **RBI:** Kubek 1 (1), Lopez 2 (2), Howard 1 (2), Skowron 1 (2), Boyer 2 (2). **2-out RBI:** Kubek 1, Skowron 1. **Runners left in scoring position, 2 out:** Kubek 2, Maris 2, Skowron 1. **GIDP:** Howard, Boyer. **Team LOB:** 6 **FIELDING: DP:** 1 (Kubek-Richardson-Skowron).

CINCINNATI	AB	R	H	HR	RBI	BB	AVG
Chacon 2b	4	0	1	0	0	0	.273
Kasko ss	4	0	1	0	0	0	.294
Pinson cf	4	0	0	0	0	0	.059
Robinson rf	1	0	0	0	0	1	.091
Post lf	4	0	1	0	0	0	.267
Freese 3b	4	0	0	0	0	0	.000
Coleman 1b	4	0	0	0	0	0	.250
D.Johnson c	2	0	2	0	0	0	.500
b-Bell ph	1	0	0	0	0	0	.000
Zimmerman c	0	0	0	0	0	0	.000
O'Toole p	1	0	0	0	0	0	.000
a-Gernert ph	1	0	0	0	0	0	.000
Brosnan p	0	0	0	0	0	0	.000
c-Lynch ph	1	0	0	0	0	0	.000
Henry p	0	0	0	0	0	0	.000
TOTALS	**31**	**0**	**5**	**0**	**0**	**1**	**.182**

a - Batted for O'Toole in the 5th
b - Batted for D.Johnson in the 7th
c - Batted for Brosnan in the 8th

BATTING: Runners left in scoring position, 2 out: Post 1, Coleman 1. **GIDP:** Post. **Team LOB:** 7 **FIELDING: E:** Pinson (1). **Outfield assists:** Pinson (1). **DP:** 3 (Kasko-Chacon-Coleman, Freese-Chacon-Coleman, Coleman).

NY YANKEES	IP	H	R	ER	BB	SO	HR	ERA
Ford (W, 2-0)	5	4	0	0	0	1	0	0.00
Coates (S, 1)	4	1	0	0	1	2	0	0.00

CINCINNATI	IP	H	R	ER	BB	SO	HR	ERA
O'Toole (L, 0-2)	5	5	2	2	3	2	0	3.00
Brosnan	3	6	5	5	3	3	0	11.25
Henry	1	0	0	0	0	2	0	0.00

WP: Brosnan 1. **IBB:** Berra 2 (by Brosnan), Maris (by Brosnan). **HBP:** Robinson 2 (by Ford, by Coates). **Ground balls-fly balls:** Ford 7-6, Coates 3-7, O'Toole 5-6, Brosnan 1-3, Henry 0-1. **Batters faced:** Ford 19, Coates 15, O'Toole 21, Brosnan 16, Henry 3. **UMPIRES:** hp—Donatelli, 1b—Runge, 2b—Conlan, 3b—Umont, lf—Crawford, rf—Stewart **T:** 2:27 **A:** 32,589

GAME 5 New York 13 Cincinnati 5
Crosley Field 10/09/61

NY YANKEES	AB	R	H	HR	RBI	BB	AVG
Richardson 2b	6	1	1	0	0	0	.391
Kubek ss	6	2	2	0	0	0	.227
Maris cf-rf	5	0	1	0	1	1	.105
Blanchard rf	4	3	3	1	2	2	.400
Reed cf	0	0	0	0	0	0	.000
Howard c	5	3	2	0	0	1	.250
Skowron 1b	5	2	2	0	3	0	.353
Lopez lf	4	2	2	1	5	0	.333
Boyer 3b	3	0	2	0	1	2	.267
Terry p	1	0	0	0	0	0	.000
Daley p	1	0	0	0	1	0	.000
TOTALS	**40**	**13**	**15**	**2**	**13**	**6**	**.255**

BATTING: 2B: Howard (3, Jay), Boyer (2, Maloney), Maris (1, Maloney), Blanchard (1, Henry). **3B:** Lopez (1, Maloney). **HR:** Blanchard (2, 1st off Jay 1 on, 2 out), Lopez (1, 4th off Henry 2 on, 1 out). **S:** Terry, Lopez, Daley. **SF:** Daley. **RBI:** Maris 1 (2), Blanchard 2 (3), Skowron 3 (5), Lopez 5 (7), Boyer 1 (3), Daley 1 (1). **2-out RBI:** Blanchard 2, Skowron 1, Lopez 1, Boyer 1. **Runners left in scoring position, 2 out:** Richardson 3, Howard 1, Skowron 3, Terry 1. **Team LOB:** 10 **Outfield assists:** Maris (1).

CINCINNATI	AB	R	H	HR	RBI	BB	AVG
Blasingame 2b	4	1	1	0	0	0	.143
e-Chacon ph	1	0	0	0	0	0	.250
Kasko ss	5	1	2	0	0	0	.318
Pinson cf	5	0	1	0	0	0	.091
Robinson rf	4	1	2	1	3	0	.200
Coleman 1b	4	1	1	0	0	0	.250
Post lf	3	1	2	1	2	0	.333
Freese 3b	4	0	1	0	0	0	.063
Edwards c	4	0	1	0	0	0	.364
Jay p	0	0	0	0	0	0	.000
Maloney p	0	0	0	0	0	0	.000
K.Johnson p	0	0	0	0	0	0	.000
a-Bell ph	1	0	0	0	0	0	.000
Henry p	0	0	0	0	0	0	.000
Jones p	0	0	0	0	0	0	.000
b-Gernert ph	1	0	0	0	0	0	.000
Purkey p	0	0	0	0	0	0	.000
c-Cardenas ph	1	0	0	0	0	0	.333
Brosnan p	0	0	0	0	0	0	.000
d-Lynch ph	1	0	0	0	0	0	.000
Hunt p	0	0	0	0	0	0	.000
TOTALS	**38**	**5**	**11**	**2**	**5**	**0**	**.206**

a - Batted for K.Johnson in the 2nd
b - Batted for Jones in the 4th
c - Batted for Purkey in the 6th
d - Batted for Brosnan in the 8th e - Batted for Blasingame in the 9th

BATTING: 2B: Freese (1, Daley), Robinson (2, Daley). **HR:** Robinson (1, 3th off Terry 2 on, 1 out), Post (1, 5th off Daley 1 on, 2 out). **RBI:** Robinson 3 (4), Post 2 (2). **2-out RBI:** Post 2. **Runners left in scoring position, 2 out:** Coleman 1, Edwards 2, Bell 1. **Team LOB:** 7 **FIELDING: E:** Coleman (1), Kasko (1), Purkey (1).

NY YANKEES	IP	H	R	ER	BB	SO	HR	ERA
Terry	2.1	6	3	3	0	0	1	4.82
Daley (W, 1-0)	6.2	5	2	0	0	3	1	0.00

CINCINNATI	IP	H	R	ER	BB	SO	HR	ERA
Jay (L, 1-1)	0.2	4	4	4	0	0	1	5.59
Maloney	0.2	4	2	2	1	1	0	27.00
K.Johnson	0.2	0	0	0	0	0	0	0.00
Henry	1.1	4	5	5	2	1	1	19.29
Jones	0.2	0	0	0	0	0	0	0.00
Purkey	2	0	2	0	2	2	0	1.64
Brosnan	2	3	0	0	0	1	0	7.50
Hunt	1	0	0	0	1	1	0	0.00

WP: Brosnan 1. **IBB:** Howard (by Henry), Boyer (by Purkey). **HBP:** Post (by Daley). **Ground balls-fly balls:** Terry 2-5, Daley 8-9, Jay 0-2, Maloney 0-1, K.Johnson 0-2, Henry 1-1, Jones 1-1, Purkey 2-2, Brosnan 2-2, Hunt 2-0. **Batters faced:** Terry 13, Daley 26, Jay 6, Maloney 7, K.Johnson 2, Henry 10, Jones 2, Purkey 10, Brosnan 9, Hunt 4. **UMPIRES:** hp—Runge, 1b—Conlan, 2b—Umont, 3b—Donatelli, lf—Crawford, rf—Stewart **T:** 3:05 **A:** 32,589

1962 NY YANKEES DEF. SAN FRANCISCO, 4-3

GAME 1 New York 6 San Francisco 2
Candlestick Park 10/04/62

NY YANKEES	AB	R	H	HR	RBI	BB	AVG
Kubek ss	5	0	2	0	0	0	.400
Richardson 2b	5	1	1	0	0	0	.200
Tresh lf	5	2	2	0	0	0	.400
Mantle cf	4	0	0	0	0	1	.000
Maris rf	4	1	2	0	2	1	.500
Howard c	3	1	2	0	1	1	.667
Skowron 1b	2	0	0	0	0	1	.000
Long 1b	2	0	1	0	1	0	.500
Boyer 3b	3	1	1	1	2	0	.333
Ford p	3	0	0	0	0	1	.000
TOTALS	**36**	**6**	**11**	**1**	**6**	**5**	**.306**

BATTING: 2B: Maris (1, O'Dell). **HR:** Boyer (1, 7th off O'Dell 0 on, 0 out). **SF:** Boyer. **RBI:** Maris 2 (2), Howard 1 (1), Long 1 (1), Boyer 2 (2). **2-out RBI:** Maris 2, Howard 1. **Runners left in scoring position, 2 out:** Kubek 1, Richardson 1, Howard 1, Skowron 1, Long 1. **GIDP:** Skowron. **Team LOB:** 10 **BASERUNNING: SB:** Mantle (1, 2nd base off O'Dell/Bailey), Tresh (1, 2nd base off Miller/Orsino). **FIELDING: DP:** 2 (Richardson-Kubek-Skowron, Boyer-Richardson-Long).

SAN FRANCISCO	AB	R	H	HR	RBI	BB	AVG
Kuenn lf	5	0	0	0	0	0	.000
Hiller 2b	4	1	1	0	0	0	.250
F.Alou rf	4	0	1	0	0	0	.250
Mays cf	4	1	3	0	1	0	.750
Cepeda 1b	4	0	0	0	0	0	.000
Davenport 3b	2	0	1	0	0	2	.500
Bailey c	4	0	0	0	0	0	.000
Miller p	0	0	0	0	0	0	.000
Pagan ss	4	0	3	0	1	0	.750
O'Dell p	3	0	1	0	0	0	.333
Larsen p	0	0	0	0	0	0	.000
Orsino c	1	0	0	0	0	0	.000
TOTALS	**35**	**2**	**10**	**0**	**2**	**2**	**.286**

BATTING: 2B: Hiller (1, Ford). **SF:** Cepeda. **RBI:** Mays 1 (1), Pagan 1 (1). **2-out RBI:** Pagan 1. **Runners left in scoring position, 2 out:** Kuenn 1, O'Dell 1. **GIDP:** Cepeda, Orsino. **Team LOB:** 8 **FIELDING: DP:** 1 (Davenport-Hiller-Cepeda).

NY YANKEES	IP	H	R	ER	BB	SO	HR	ERA
Ford (W, 1-0)	9	10	2	2	2	6	0	2.00

SAN FRANCISCO	IP	H	R	ER	BB	SO	HR	ERA
O'Dell (L, 0-1)	7.1	9	5	5	3	8	1	6.14
Larsen	1	1	1	1	1	0	0	9.00
Miller	0.2	1	0	0	1	0	0	0.00

HBP: Howard (by O'Dell). **Ground balls-fly balls:** Ford 11-8, O'Dell 6-7, Larsen 1-1, Miller 1-1. **Batters faced:** Ford 37, O'Dell 34, Larsen 5, Miller 4. **UMPIRES:** hp—Barlick, 1b—Berry, 2b—Landes, 3b—Honochick, lf—Burkhart, rf—Soar **T:** 2:43 **A:** 43,852

GAME 2 San Francisco 2 New York 0
Candlestick Park 10/05/62

NY YANKEES	AB	R	H	HR	RBI	BB	AVG
Kubek ss	4	0	0	0	0	0	.222
Richardson 2b	4	0	0	0	0	0	.111
Tresh lf	3	0	1	0	0	1	.375
Mantle cf	4	0	1	0	0	0	.125
Maris rf	3	0	0	0	0	1	.286
Berra c	2	0	0	0	0	1	.000
Long 1b	3	0	0	0	0	0	.200
Boyer 3b	3	0	1	0	0	0	.333
Terry p	2	0	0	0	0	0	.000
a-Blanchard ph	1	0	0	0	0	0	.000
Daley p	0	0	0	0	0	0	.000
TOTALS	**29**	**0**	**3**	**0**	**0**	**3**	**.215**

a - Batted for Terry in the 8th

BATTING: 2B: Mantle (1, Sanford). **Runners left in scoring position, 2 out:** Maris 2. **GIDP:** Berra. **Team LOB:** 5 **BASERUNNING: SB:** Tresh (2, 2nd base off Sanford/Haller). **FIELDING: E:** Kubek (1). **Outfield assists:** Maris (1).

SAN FRANCISCO	AB	R	H	HR	RBI	BB	AVG
Hiller 2b	3	1	1	0	0	1	.286
F.Alou rf	2	0	1	0	0	1	.333
M.Alou lf	4	0	1	0	1	0	.250
Mays cf	4	0	0	0	0	0	.375
McCovey 1b	4	1	1	1	1	0	.250
Haller c	3	0	1	0	0	0	.333
Davenport 3b	3	0	0	0	0	0	.200
Pagan ss	1	0	0	0	0	0	.600
Sanford p	3	0	1	0	0	0	.333
TOTALS	**27**	**2**	**6**	**1**	**2**	**2**	**.258**

BATTING: 2B: Hiller (2, Terry). **HR:** McCovey (1, 7th off Terry 0 on, 0 out). **S:** F.Alou, Pagan. **RBI:** M.Alou 1 (1), McCovey 1 (1). **Runners left in scoring position, 2 out:** McCovey 2, Sanford 1. **Team LOB:** 6 **FIELDING: DP:** 1 (Hiller-Pagan-McCovey).

NY YANKEES	IP	H	R	ER	BB	SO	HR	ERA
Terry (L, 0-1)	7	5	2	2	1	5	1	2.57
Daley	1	1	0	0	1	0	0	0.00

SAN FRANCISCO	IP	H	R	ER	BB	SO	HR	ERA
Sanford (W, 1-0)	9	3	0	0	3	6	0	0.00

HBP: Pagan (by Terry). **Ground balls-fly balls:** Terry 6-7, Daley 1-2, Sanford 11-9. **Batters faced:** Terry 27, Daley 5, Sanford 32. **UMPIRES:** hp—Berry, 1b—Landes, 2b—Honochick, 3b—Barlick, lf—Burkhart, rf—Soar **T:** 2:11 **A:** 43,910

GAME 3 New York 3 San Francisco 2
Yankee Stadium 10/07/62

SAN FRANCISCO	AB	R	H	HR	RBI	BB	AVG
F.Alou lf	4	0	0	0	0	0	.200
Hiller 2b	3	0	0	0	0	1	.200
Mays cf	4	1	1	0	0	0	.333
McCovey rf	3	0	0	0	0	1	.143
Cepeda 1b	4	0	0	0	0	0	.000
Bailey c	4	1	1	1	2	0	.125
Davenport 3b	4	0	1	0	0	0	.222
Pagan ss	3	0	1	0	0	0	.500
Pierce p	2	0	0	0	0	0	.000
Larsen p	0	0	0	0	0	0	.000
a-M.Alou ph	1	0	0	0	0	0	.200
Bolin p	0	0	0	0	0	0	.000
TOTALS	**32**	**2**	**4**	**1**	**2**	**2**	**.213**

a - Batted for Larsen in the 8th

BATTING: 2B: Davenport (1, Stafford), Mays (1, Stafford). **HR:** Bailey (1, 9th off Stafford 1 on, 2 out). **RBI:** Bailey 2 (2). **2-out RBI:** Bailey 2. **Runners left in scoring position, 2 out:** Hiller 1, Cepeda 1, Pierce 1. **Team LOB:** 5 **FIELDING: E:** Davenport (1), F.Alou (1), McCovey (1). **DP:** 1 (Davenport-Hiller).

NY YANKEES	AB	R	H	HR	RBI	BB	AVG
Kubek ss	4	0	1	0	0	0	.231
Richardson 2b	4	0	0	0	0	0	.077
Tresh lf	4	1	1	0	0	0	.333
Mantle cf	3	1	1	0	0	0	.182
Maris rf	3	1	1	0	2	0	.300
Howard c	3	0	1	0	0	0	.500
Skowron 1b	2	0	0	0	0	0	.000
Boyer 3b	3	0	0	0	1	0	.222
Stafford p	3	0	0	0	0	0	.000
TOTALS	**29**	**3**	**5**	**0**	**3**	**0**	**.202**

BATTING: 2B: Kubek (1, Pierce), Howard (1, Pierce). **RBI:** Maris 2 (4), Boyer 1 (3). **Runners left in scoring position, 2 out:** Richardson 1. **Team LOB:** 3 **FIELDING: E:** Boyer (1).

SAN FRANCISCO	IP	H	R	ER	BB	SO	HR	ERA
Pierce (L, 0-1)	6	5	3	2	0	3	0	3.00
Larsen	1	0	0	0	0	0	0	4.50
Bolin	1	0	0	0	0	1	0	0.00

NY YANKEES	IP	H	R	ER	BB	SO	HR	ERA
Stafford (W, 1-0)	9	4	2	2	2	5	1	2.00

HBP: Skowron (by Larsen). **Ground balls-fly balls:** Pierce 3-12, Larsen 2-1, Bolin 0-2, Stafford 10-13. **Batters faced:** Pierce 23, Larsen 4, Bolin 3, Stafford 34. **UMPIRES:** hp—Landes, 1b—Honochick, 2b—Barlick, 3b—Berry, lf—Soar, rf—Burkhart **T:** 2:06 **A:** 71,434

GAME 4 San Francisco 7 New York 3
Yankee Stadium 10/08/62

SAN FRANCISCO	AB	R	H	HR	RBI	BB	AVG
Kuenn rf	3	0	0	0	0	1	.000
O'Dell p	0	0	0	0	0	0	.333
Hiller 2b	5	1	2	1	5	0	.267
Mays cf	5	0	1	0	0	0	.294
F.Alou lf	4	1	1	0	0	0	.214
Cepeda 1b	4	0	0	0	0	0	.000
Davenport 3b	2	1	0	0	0	2	.182
Haller c	4	1	2	1	2	0	.429
Pagan ss	2	0	1	0	0	0	.500
a-M.Alou ph-rf	2	2	2	0	0	0	.429
Marichal p	2	0	0	0	0	0	.000
Bolin p	0	0	0	0	0	0	.000
Larsen p	0	0	0	0	0	0	.000
b-Bailey ph	0	0	0	0	0	0	.125
c-Nieman ph	0	0	0	0	0	1	.000
d-Bowman pr-ss	1	1	0	0	0	0	.000
TOTALS	**34**	**7**	**9**	**2**	**7**	**4**	**.227**

a - Batted for Pagan in the 7th
b - Batted for Larsen in the 7th
c - Batted for Bailey in the 7th
d - Ran for Nieman in the 7th

BATTING: 2B: F.Alou (1, Ford), M.Alou (1, Coates). **HR:** Haller (1, 2nd off Ford 1 on, 2 out), Hiller (1, 7th off Bridges 3 on, 2 out). **S:** O'Dell. **RBI:** Hiller 5 (5), Haller 2 (2). **2-out RBI:** Hiller 5, Haller 2. **Runners left in scoring position, 2 out:** Hiller 2, Mays 1. **GIDP:** F.Alou. **Team LOB:** 5 **FIELDING: E:** Davenport (2). **DP:** 2 (Haller-Hiller-Cepeda-Marichal, Hiller-Cepeda).

NY YANKEES	AB	R	H	HR	RBI	BB	AVG
Kubek ss	4	1	1	0	0	1	.235
Richardson 2b	4	0	1	0	0	1	.118
Tresh lf	5	0	2	0	1	0	.353
Mantle cf	4	1	0	0	0	1	.133
Maris rf	3	1	0	0	0	1	.231
Howard c	4	0	0	0	0	0	.300
Skowron 1b	4	0	3	0	1	0	.375
Boyer 3b	4	0	2	0	1	0	.308
Ford p	2	0	0	0	0	0	.000
a-Berra ph	0	0	0	0	0	1	.000
Coates p	0	0	0	0	0	0	.000
Bridges p	0	0	0	0	0	0	.000
b-Lopez ph	1	0	0	0	0	0	.000
TOTALS	**35**	**3**	**9**	**0**	**3**	**5**	**.217**

a - Batted for Ford in the 6th
b - Batted for Bridges in the 9th

BATTING: 3B: Skowron (1, Marichal). **RBI:** Tresh 1 (1), Skowron 1 (1), Boyer 1 (4). **2-out RBI:** Tresh 1, Skowron 1, Boyer 1. **Runners left in scoring position, 2 out:** Kubek 2, Mantle 1, Boyer 1. **GIDP:** Richardson. **Team LOB:** 10 **BASERUNNING: CS:** Kubek (1, 2nd base off Marichal/Haller). **FIELDING: E:** Richardson (1). **DP:** 1 (Boyer-Richardson-Skowron).

SAN FRANCISCO	IP	H	R	ER	BB	SO	HR	ERA
Marichal	4	2	0	0	2	4	0	0.00
Bolin	1.2	4	2	2	2	1	0	6.75
Larsen (W, 1-0)	0.1	0	0	0	1	0	0	3.86
O'Dell (S, 1)	3	3	1	1	0	0	0	5.23

NY YANKEES	IP	H	R	ER	BB	SO	HR	ERA
Ford	6	5	2	2	1	3	1	2.40
Coates (L, 0-1)	0.1	1	2	2	1	1	0	54.00
Bridges	2.2	3	3	2	2	3	1	6.75

IBB: Nieman (by Bridges). **Ground balls-fly balls:** Marichal 2-5, Bolin 3-1, Larsen 1-0, O'Dell 5-4, Ford 10-4, Coates 0-0, Bridges 2-2. **Batters faced:** Marichal 15, Bolin 11, Larsen 2, O'Dell 12, Ford 23, Coates 3, Bridges 13. **UMPIRES:** hp—Honochick, 1b—Barlick, 2b—Berry, 3b—Landes, lf—Soar, rf—Burkhart **T:** 2:55 **A:** 66,607

GAME 5 New York 5 San Francisco 3
Yankee Stadium 10/10/62

SAN FRANCISCO	AB	R	H	HR	RBI	BB	AVG
Hiller 2b	3	0	1	0	1	1	.278
Davenport 3b	4	0	0	0	0	0	.133
M.Alou rf	4	0	0	0	0	0	.273
Mays cf	4	0	0	0	0	0	.238
McCovey 1b	4	1	1	0	0	0	.182
F.Alou lf	4	0	2	0	0	0	.278
Haller c	4	0	1	0	1	0	.364
Pagan ss	4	2	2	1	1	0	.500
Sanford p	2	0	1	0	0	0	.400
Miller p	0	0	0	0	0	0	.000
a-Bailey ph	1	0	0	0	0	0	.111
TOTALS	**34**	**3**	**8**	**1**	**3**	**1**	**.228**

a - Batted for Miller in the 9th

BATTING: 2B: Hiller (3, Terry), Haller (1, Terry). **3B:** F.Alou (1, Terry). **HR:** Pagan (1, 5th off Terry 0 on, 0 out). **S:** Sanford. **SF:** Pagan. **RBI:** Hiller 1 (6), Haller 1 (3), Pagan 1 (2). **Runners left in scoring position, 2 out:** Hiller 1, M.Alou 1, Haller 1, Bailey 1. **Team LOB:** 6 **FIELDING: E:** Hiller (1), McCovey (2). **PB:** Haller. **DP:** 1 (Sanford-McCovey).

NY YANKEES	AB	R	H	HR	RBI	BB	AVG
Kubek ss	4	1	2	0	0	0	.286
Richardson 2b	4	2	2	0	0	0	.190
Tresh lf	3	2	2	1	3	0	.400
Mantle cf	3	0	0	0	0	1	.111
Maris rf	3	0	0	0	0	1	.188
Howard c	4	0	0	0	0	0	.214
Skowron 1b	3	0	0	0	0	0	.273
Boyer 3b	3	0	0	0	0	0	.250
Terry p	3	0	0	0	0	0	.000
TOTALS	**30**	**5**	**6**	**1**	**3**	**2**	**.214**

BATTING: 2B: Tresh (1, Sanford). **HR:** Tresh (1, 8th off Sanford 2 on, 1 out). **S:** Tresh. **RBI:** Tresh 3 (4). **Runners left in scoring position, 2 out:** Maris 2, Skowron 1. **Team LOB:** 4 **BASERUNNING: SB:** Mantle (2, 2nd base off Sanford/Haller).

SAN FRANCISCO	IP	H	R	ER	BB	SO	HR	ERA
Sanford (L, 1-1)	7.1	6	5	4	1	10	1	2.20
Miller	0.2	0	0	0	1	0	0	0.00

NY YANKEES	IP	H	R	ER	BB	SO	HR	ERA
Terry (W, 1-1)	9	8	3	3	1	7	1	2.81

WP: Sanford 1. **Ground balls-fly balls:** Sanford 8-4, Miller 1-1, Terry 8-11. **Batters faced:** Sanford 30, Miller 3, Terry 36. **UMPIRES:** hp—Barlick, 1b—Berry, 2b—Landes, 3b—Honochick, lf—Soar, rf—Burkhart **T:** 2:42 **A:** 63,165

GAME 6 San Francisco 5 New York 2
Candlestick Park 10/15/62

NY YANKEES	AB	R	H	HR	RBI	BB	AVG
Kubek ss	4	0	1	0	1	0	.280
Richardson 2b	4	0	0	0	0	0	.160
Tresh lf	4	0	0	0	0	0	.333
Mantle cf	4	0	0	0	0	0	.091
Maris rf	3	1	1	1	1	1	.211
Howard c	3	0	0	0	0	0	.176
Skowron 1b	3	0	0	0	0	0	.214
Boyer 3b	2	1	1	0	0	1	.278
Ford p	2	0	0	0	0	0	.000
Coates p	0	0	0	0	0	0	.000
a-Lopez ph	1	0	0	0	0	0	.000
Bridges p	0	0	0	0	0	0	.000
TOTALS	**30**	**2**	**3**	**1**	**2**	**2**	**.196**

a - Batted for Coates in the 8th

BATTING: 2B: Boyer (1, Pierce). **HR:** Maris (1, 5th off Pierce 0 on, 1 out). **RBI:** Kubek 1 (1), Maris 1 (5). **2-out RBI:** Kubek 1. **Runners left in scoring position, 2 out:** Ford 1. **GIDP:** Howard. **Team LOB:** 3 **FIELDING: E:** Boyer (2), Ford (1). **DP:** 2 (Kubek-Richardson-Skowron, Howard-Kubek).

SAN FRANCISCO	AB	R	H	HR	RBI	BB	AVG
Kuenn lf	4	1	1	0	0	0	.083
M.Alou lf	0	0	0	0	0	0	.273
Hiller 2b	4	1	2	0	0	0	.318
F.Alou rf	4	1	2	0	1	0	.318
Mays cf	3	1	1	0	0	1	.250
Cepeda 1b	4	1	3	0	2	0	.188
Davenport 3b	4	0	1	0	1	0	.158
Bailey c	4	0	0	0	0	0	.077
Pagan ss	3	0	0	0	0	0	.412
Pierce p	3	0	0	0	0	0	.000
TOTALS	**33**	**5**	**10**	**0**	**4**	**1**	**.241**

BATTING: 2B: Cepeda (1, Ford). **RBI:** F.Alou 1 (1), Cepeda 2 (2), Davenport 1 (1). **2-out RBI:** Cepeda 1. **Runners left in scoring position, 2 out:** Davenport 1, Bailey 1. **GIDP:** Mays. **Team LOB:** 5 **BASERUNNING: SB:** Mays (1, 2nd base off Bridges/Howard). **CS:** Cepeda (1, 2nd base off Ford/Howard). **FIELDING: E:** Davenport (3). **DP:** 1 (Davenport-Hiller-Cepeda).

NY YANKEES	IP	H	R	ER	BB	SO	HR	ERA
Ford (L, 1-1)	4.2	9	5	5	1	3	0	4.12
Coates	2.1	0	0	0	0	2	0	6.75
Bridges	1	1	0	0	0	0	0	4.91

SAN FRANCISCO	IP	H	R	ER	BB	SO	HR	ERA
Pierce (W, 1-1)	9	3	2	2	2	2	1	2.40

IBB: Boyer (by Pierce). **Ground balls-fly balls:** Ford 7-3, Coates 4-1, Bridges 1-2, Pierce 10-15. **Batters faced:** Ford 23, Coates 7, Bridges 4, Pierce 32. **UMPIRES:** hp—Berry, 1b—Landes, 2b—Honochick, 3b—Barlick, lf—Burkhart, rf—Soar **T:** 2:00 **A:** 43,948

GAME 7 New York 1 San Francisco 0
Candlestick Park 10/16/62

NY YANKEES	AB	R	H	HR	RBI	BB	AVG
Kubek ss	4	0	1	0	1	0	.276
Richardson 2b	2	0	0	0	0	2	.148
Tresh lf	4	0	1	0	0	0	.321
Mantle cf	3	0	1	0	0	1	.120
Maris rf	4	0	0	0	0	0	.174
Howard c	4	0	0	0	0	0	.143
Skowron 1b	4	1	1	0	0	0	.222
Boyer 3b	4	0	2	0	0	0	.318
Terry p	3	0	1	0	0	1	.125
TOTALS	**32**	**1**	**7**	**0**	**1**	**4**	**.199**

BATTING: RBI: Kubek 1 (2). **Runners left in scoring position, 2 out:** Kubek 1, Richardson 1, Tresh 1. **GIDP:** Kubek, Howard. **Team LOB:** 8

SAN FRANCISCO	AB	R	H	HR	RBI	BB	AVG
F.Alou rf	4	0	0	0	0	0	.269
Hiller 2b	4	0	0	0	0	0	.269
Mays cf	4	0	1	0	0	0	.250
McCovey lf	4	0	1	0	0	0	.200
Cepeda 1b	3	0	0	0	0	0	.158
Haller c	3	0	0	0	0	0	.286
Davenport 3b	3	0	0	0	0	0	.136
Pagan ss	2	0	0	0	0	0	.368
a-Bailey ph	1	0	0	0	0	0	.071
Bowman ss	0	0	0	0	0	0	.000
Sanford p	2	0	1	0	0	0	.429
O'Dell p	0	0	0	0	0	0	.333
b-M.Alou ph	1	0	1	0	0	0	.333
TOTALS	**31**	**0**	**4**	**0**	**0**	**0**	**.226**

a - Batted for Pagan in the 8th
b - Batted for O'Dell in the 9th

BATTING: 2B: Mays (2, Terry). **3B:** McCovey (1, Terry). **Runners left in scoring position, 2 out:** McCovey 2, Cepeda 1. **Team LOB:** 4 **FIELDING: E:** Pagan (1). **DP:** 2 (Pagan-Hiller-Cepeda, Davenport-Cepeda).

NY YANKEES	IP	H	R	ER	BB	SO	HR	ERA
Terry (W, 2-1)	9	4	0	0	0	4	0	1.80

SAN FRANCISCO	IP	H	R	ER	BB	SO	HR	ERA
Sanford (L, 1-2)	7	7	1	1	4	3	0	1.93
O'Dell	2	0	0	0	0	1	0	4.38

Ground balls-fly balls: Terry 4-19, Sanford 7-10, O'Dell 4-0. **Batters faced:** Terry 31, Sanford 31, O'Dell 5. **UMPIRES:** hp—Landes, 1b—Honochick, 2b—Barlick, 3b—Berry, lf—Burkhart, rf—Soar **T:** 2:29 **A:** 43,948

1963 LOS ANGELES DODGERS DEF. NY YANKEES, 4-0

GAME 1 Los Angeles 5 New York 2
Yankee Stadium 10/02/63

LOS ANGELES	AB	R	H	HR	RBI	BB	AVG
Wills ss	5	0	0	0	0	0	.000
Gilliam 3b	4	0	1	0	0	1	.250
W.Davis cf	3	1	0	0	0	0	.000
T.Davis lf	4	0	3	0	0	0	.750
F.Howard rf	4	1	1	0	0	0	.250
Fairly rf	0	0	0	0	0	0	.000
Skowron 1b	3	1	2	0	2	1	.667
Tracewski 2b	4	1	1	0	0	0	.250
Roseboro c	4	1	1	1	3	0	.250
Koufax p	4	0	0	0	0	0	.000
TOTALS	**35**	**5**	**9**	**1**	**5**	**2**	**.257**

BATTING: 2B: F.Howard (1, Ford). **HR:** Roseboro (1, 2nd off Ford 2 on, 1 out). **S:** W.Davis. **RBI:** Skowron 2 (2), Roseboro 3 (3). **2-out RBI:** Skowron 1. **Runners left in scoring position, 2 out:** F.Howard 1, Tracewski 3. **Team LOB:** 6 **BASERUNNING: SB:** T.Davis (1, 2nd base off Williams/E.Howard).

NY YANKEES	AB	R	H	HR	RBI	BB	AVG
Kubek ss	4	1	1	0	0	0	.250
Richardson 2b	3	0	0	0	0	1	.000
Tresh lf	3	1	1	1	2	1	.333
Mantle cf	3	0	0	0	0	1	.000
Maris rf	4	0	0	0	0	0	.000
E.Howard c	4	0	1	0	0	0	.250
Pepitone 1b	4	0	2	0	0	0	.500
Boyer 3b	4	0	1	0	0	0	.250
Ford p	1	0	0	0	0	0	.000
a-Lopez ph	1	0	0	0	0	0	.000
Williams p	0	0	0	0	0	0	.000
b-Linz ph	1	0	0	0	0	0	.000
Hamilton p	0	0	0	0	0	0	.000
c-Bright ph	1	0	0	0	0	0	.000
TOTALS	**33**	**2**	**6**	**1**	**2**	**3**	**.182**

a - Batted for Ford in the 5th
b - Batted for Williams in the 8th
c - Batted for Hamilton in the 9th

BATTING: HR: Tresh (1, 8th off Koufax 1 on, 2 out). **RBI:** Tresh 2 (2). **2-out RBI:** Tresh 2. **Runners left in scoring position, 2 out:** Maris 1, Lopez 2. **Team LOB:** 7

LOS ANGELES	IP	H	R	ER	BB	SO	HR	ERA
Koufax (W, 1-0)	9	6	2	2	3	15	1	2.00

NY YANKEES	IP	H	R	ER	BB	SO	HR	ERA
Ford (L, 0-1)	5	8	5	5	2	4	1	9.00
Williams	3	1	0	0	0	5	0	0.00
Hamilton	1	0	0	0	0	1	0	0.00

IBB: Skowron (by Ford). **Ground balls-fly balls:** Koufax 3-9, Ford 7-3, Williams 3-1, Hamilton 1-1. **Batters faced:** Koufax 36, Ford 25, Williams 10, Hamilton 3. **UMPIRES:** hp—Paparella, 1b—Gorman, 2b—Napp, 3b—Crawford, lf—Venzon, rf—Rice **T:** 2:09 **A:** 69,000

GAME 2 Los Angeles 4 New York 1
Yankee Stadium 10/03/63

LOS ANGELES	AB	R	H	HR	RBI	BB	AVG
Wills ss	4	1	2	0	0	0	.222
Gilliam 3b	4	1	1	0	0	0	.250
W.Davis cf	4	1	2	0	2	0	.286
T.Davis lf	4	0	2	0	1	0	.625
F.Howard rf	3	0	0	0	0	0	.143
a-Fairly ph-rf	0	0	0	0	0	1	.000
Skowron 1b	4	1	2	1	1	0	.571
Tracewski 2b	3	0	0	0	0	1	.143
Roseboro c	4	0	0	0	0	0	.125
Podres p	4	0	1	0	0	0	.250
Perranoski p	0	0	0	0	0	0	.000
TOTALS	**34**	**4**	**10**	**1**	**4**	**2**	**.275**

a - Batted for F.Howard in the 8th

BATTING: 2B: W.Davis 2 (2, Downing, Terry). **3B:** T.Davis 2 (2, Downing, Terry). **HR:** Skowron (1, 4th off Downing 0 on, 0 out). **RBI:** W.Davis 2 (2), T.Davis 1 (1), Skowron 1 (3). **Runners left in scoring position, 2 out:** F.Howard 1, Skowron 1. **GIDP:** Roseboro, Gilliam, Skowron. **Team LOB:** 5 **BASERUNNING: SB:** Wills (1, 2nd base off Downing/E.Howard). **FIELDING: E:** Podres (1).

NY YANKEES	AB	R	H	HR	RBI	BB	AVG
Kubek ss	4	0	0	0	0	0	.125
Richardson 2b	4	0	1	0	0	0	.143
Tresh lf	4	0	2	0	0	0	.429
Mantle cf	4	0	0	0	0	0	.000
Maris rf	1	0	0	0	0	0	.000
Lopez rf	3	1	2	0	0	0	.500
E.Howard c	4	0	2	0	1	0	.375
Pepitone 1b	3	0	0	0	0	1	.286
Boyer 3b	4	0	0	0	0	0	.125
Downing p	1	0	0	0	0	0	.000
a-Bright ph	1	0	0	0	0	0	.000
Terry p	0	0	0	0	0	0	.000
b-Linz ph	1	0	0	0	0	0	.000
Reniff p	0	0	0	0	0	0	.000
TOTALS	**34**	**1**	**7**	**0**	**1**	**1**	**.194**

a - Batted for Downing in the 5th
b - Batted for Terry in the 8th

BATTING: 2B: Lopez 2 (2, Podres). **RBI:** E.Howard 1 (1). **Runners left in scoring position, 2 out:** Mantle 1, Boyer 1, Downing 1. **Team LOB:** 7 **FIELDING: DP:** 3 (Richardson-Kubek-Pepitone, Kubek-Richardson-Pepitone, Terry-Richardson-Pepitone).

LOS ANGELES	IP	H	R	ER	BB	SO	HR	ERA
Podres (W, 1-0)	8.1	6	1	1	1	4	0	1.08
Perranoski (S, 1)	0.2	1	0	0	0	1	0	0.00

NY YANKEES	IP	H	R	ER	BB	SO	HR	ERA
Downing (L, 0-1)	5	7	3	3	1	6	1	5.40
Terry	3	3	1	1	1	0	0	3.00
Reniff	1	0	0	0	0	0	0	0.00

IBB: Fairly (by Terry). **Ground balls-fly balls:** Podres 8-13, Perranoski 1-0, Downing 5-2, Terry 7-1, Reniff 1-2. **Batters faced:** Podres 32, Perranoski 3, Downing 21, Terry 12, Reniff 3. **UMPIRES:** hp—Gorman, 1b—Napp, 2b—Crawford, 3b—Paparella, lf—Venzon, rf—Rice **T:** 2:13 **A:** 66,455

GAME 3 Los Angeles 1 New York 0
Chavez Ravine 10/05/63

NY YANKEES	AB	R	H	HR	RBI	BB	AVG
Kubek ss	4	0	2	0	0	0	.250
Richardson 2b	3	0	0	0	0	0	.100
Tresh lf	4	0	0	0	0	0	.273
Mantle cf	4	0	1	0	0	0	.091
Pepitone 1b	3	0	0	0	0	0	.200
E.Howard c	3	0	0	0	0	0	.273
Blanchard rf	3	0	0	0	0	0	.000
Boyer 3b	2	0	0	0	0	1	.100
Bouton p	2	0	0	0	0	0	.000
a-Berra ph	1	0	0	0	0	0	.000
Reniff p	0	0	0	0	0	0	.000
TOTALS	**29**	**0**	**3**	**0**	**0**	**1**	**.167**

a - Batted for Bouton in the 8th

BATTING: S: Richardson. **Runners left in scoring position, 2 out:** Mantle 1, Bouton 2. **Team LOB:** 5 **FIELDING: DP:** 2 (Pepitone-Kubek-Pepitone, Richardson-Pepitone-Kubek).

LOS ANGELES	AB	R	H	HR	RBI	BB	AVG
Wills ss	4	0	0	0	0	0	.154
Gilliam 3b	2	1	0	0	0	2	.200
W.Davis cf	3	0	0	0	0	0	.200
T.Davis lf	4	0	1	0	1	0	.500
Fairly rf	1	0	0	0	0	2	.000
Skowron 1b	3	0	1	0	0	0	.500
Roseboro c	3	0	1	0	0	0	.182
Tracewski 2b	3	0	1	0	0	0	.200
Drysdale p	1	0	0	0	0	2	.000
TOTALS	**24**	**1**	**4**	**0**	**1**	**6**	**.247**

BATTING: S: W.Davis. **RBI:** T.Davis 1 (2). **2-out RBI:** T.Davis 1. **Runners left in scoring position, 2 out:** Wills 2. **GIDP:** Gilliam. **Team LOB:** 6 **BASERUNNING: CS:** Gilliam (1, 3rd base off Reniff/E.Howard). **FIELDING: E:** Wills (1).

NY YANKEES	IP	H	R	ER	BB	SO	HR	ERA
Bouton (L, 0-1)	7	4	1	1	5	4	0	1.29
Reniff	1	0	0	0	1	1	0	0.00

LOS ANGELES	IP	H	R	ER	BB	SO	HR	ERA
Drysdale (W, 1-0)	9	3	0	0	1	9	0	0.00

WP: Bouton 2. **IBB:** Boyer (by Drysdale). **HBP:** Pepitone (by Drysdale). **Ground balls-fly balls:** Bouton 8-7, Reniff 0-0, Drysdale 11-6. **Batters faced:** Bouton 28, Reniff 3, Drysdale 32. **UMPIRES:** hp—Napp, 1b—Crawford, 2b—Paparella, 3b—Gorman, lf—Rice, rf—Venzon **T:** 2:05 **A:** 55,912

GAME 4 Los Angeles 2 New York 1
Chavez Ravine 10/06/63

NY YANKEES	AB	R	H	HR	RBI	BB	AVG
Kubek ss	4	0	0	0	0	0	.188
Richardson 2b	4	0	2	0	0	0	.214
Tresh lf	4	0	0	0	0	0	.200
Mantle cf	4	1	1	1	1	0	.133
E.Howard c	4	0	2	0	0	0	.333
Lopez rf	4	0	0	0	0	0	.250
Pepitone 1b	3	0	0	0	0	0	.154
Boyer 3b	3	0	0	0	0	0	.077
Ford p	2	0	0	0	0	0	.000
a-Linz ph	1	0	1	0	0	0	.333
Reniff p	0	0	0	0	0	0	.000
TOTALS	**33**	**1**	**6**	**1**	**1**	**0**	**.171**

a - Batted for Ford in the 8th

BATTING: 2B: Richardson (1, Koufax). **HR:** Mantle (1, 7th off Koufax 0 on, 1 out). **RBI:** Mantle 1 (1). **Runners left in scoring position, 2 out:** Mantle 1, Lopez 1. **GIDP:** Kubek. **Team LOB:** 5 **FIELDING: DP:** 2 (E.Howard-Pepitone, Kubek-Richardson-Pepitone).

LOS ANGELES	AB	R	H	HR	RBI	BB	AVG
Wills ss	2	0	0	0	0	1	.133
Gilliam 3b	3	1	0	0	0	0	.154
W.Davis cf	2	0	0	0	1	0	.167
T.Davis lf	3	0	0	0	0	0	.400
F.Howard rf	3	1	2	1	1	0	.300
Fairly rf	0	0	0	0	0	0	.000
Skowron 1b	3	0	0	0	0	0	.385
Roseboro c	3	0	0	0	0	0	.143
Tracewski 2b	3	0	0	0	0	0	.154
Koufax p	2	0	0	0	0	0	.000
TOTALS	**24**	**2**	**2**	**1**	**2**	**1**	**.214**

BATTING: HR: F.Howard (1, 5th off Ford 0 on, 1 out). **SF:** W.Davis. **RBI:** W.Davis 1 (3), F.Howard 1 (1). **GIDP:** Skowron. **Team LOB:** 0 **FIELDING: DP:** 1 (Tracewski-Skowron).

NY YANKEES	IP	H	R	ER	BB	SO	HR	ERA
Ford (L, 0-2)	7	2	2	1	1	4	1	4.50
Reniff	1	0	0	0	0	0	0	0.00

LOS ANGELES	IP	H	R	ER	BB	SO	HR	ERA
Koufax (W, 2-0)	9	6	1	1	0	8	1	1.50

Ground balls-fly balls: Ford 10-5, Reniff 1-2, Koufax 10-9. **Batters faced:** Ford 23, Reniff 3, Koufax 33. **UMPIRES:** hp—Crawford, 1b—Paparella, 2b—Gorman, 3b—Napp, lf—Rice, rf—Venzon **T:** 1:50 **A:** 55,912

1964 ST.LOUIS DEF. NY YANKEES, 4-3

GAME 1 St. Louis 9 New York 5
Sportsman's Park 10/07/64

NY YANKEES	AB	R	H	HR	RBI	BB	AVG
Linz ss	4	0	0	0	0	1	.000
B.Richardson 2b	5	0	2	0	1	0	.400
Maris cf	4	0	1	0	0	1	.250
Mantle rf	5	1	2	0	0	0	.400
Howard c	4	1	2	0	0	1	.500
Tresh lf	4	1	2	1	3	1	.500
Pepitone 1b	5	0	0	0	0	0	.000
C.Boyer 3b	4	1	1	0	0	0	.250
Ford p	1	0	1	0	1	2	1.000
Downing p	0	0	0	0	0	0	.000
a-Blanchard ph	1	0	1	0	0	0	1.000
b-Hegan pr	0	1	0	0	0	0	.000
Sheldon p	0	0	0	0	0	0	.000
Mikkelsen p	0	0	0	0	0	0	.000
TOTALS	**37**	**5**	**12**	**1**	**5**	**6**	**.324**

a - Batted for Downing in the 8th
b - Ran for Blanchard in the 8th

BATTING: 2B: Tresh (1, Sadecki), Blanchard (1, Schultz). **HR:** Tresh (1, 2nd off Sadecki 1 on, 0 out). **RBI:** B.Richardson 1 (1), Tresh 3 (3), Ford 1 (1). **2-out RBI:** B.Richardson 1, Tresh 1. **Runners left in scoring position, 2 out:** Maris 1, Mantle 1, Pepitone 3. **GIDP:** Tresh. **Team LOB:** 11 **BASERUNNING: SB:** C.Boyer (1, 2nd base off Sadecki/McCarver). **FIELDING: E:** Mantle (1), C.Boyer (1). **PB:** Howard, Howard. **DP:** 1 (Sheldon-Pepitone).

ST.LOUIS	AB	R	H	HR	RBI	BB	AVG
Flood cf	5	1	2	0	2	0	.400
Brock lf	5	1	2	0	2	0	.400
Groat ss	4	0	1	0	0	1	.250
K.Boyer 3b	3	1	1	0	1	1	.333
White 1b	4	0	0	0	0	0	.000
Shannon rf	4	3	2	1	2	0	.500
McCarver c	3	1	2	0	0	1	.667
Maxvill 2b	2	0	0	0	0	0	.000
a-James ph	1	0	0	0	0	0	.000
Schultz p	1	0	0	0	0	0	.000
Sadecki p	2	0	1	0	1	0	.500
b-Warwick ph	1	0	1	0	1	0	1.000
c-Javier pr-2b	0	1	0	0	0	0	.000
d-Skinner ph	0	0	0	0	0	1	.000
e-Buchek pr-2b	0	1	0	0	0	0	.000
TOTALS	**35**	**9**	**12**	**1**	**9**	**4**	**.343**

a - Batted for Maxvill in the 6th
b - Batted for Sadecki in the 6th
c - Ran for Warwick in the 6th
d - Batted for Javier in the 8th e - Ran for Skinner in the 8th

BATTING: 2B: McCarver (1, Ford), Brock (1, Mikkelsen). **3B:** McCarver (1, Ford), Flood (1, Downing). **HR:** Shannon (1, 6th off Ford 1 on, 1 out). **SF:** K.Boyer. **RBI:** Flood 2 (2), Brock 2 (2), K.Boyer 1 (1), Shannon 2 (2), Sadecki 1 (1), Warwick 1 (1). **2-out RBI:** Flood 2, Brock 2, Sadecki 1, Warwick 1. **Runners left in scoring position, 2 out:** Flood 1, Brock 1, K.Boyer 1, Sadecki 1. **Team LOB:** 7 **FIELDING: Outfield assists:** Brock (1). **DP:** 1 (Groat-Maxvill-White).

NY YANKEES	IP	H	R	ER	BB	SO	HR	ERA
Ford (L, 0-1)	5.1	8	5	5	1	4	1	8.44
Downing	1.2	2	1	1	0	1	0	5.40
Sheldon	0.2	0	2	0	2	0	0	0.00
Mikkelsen	0.1	2	1	0	1	0	0	0.00

ST.LOUIS	IP	H	R	ER	BB	SO	HR	ERA
Sadecki (W, 1-0)	6	8	4	4	5	2	1	6.00
Schultz (S, 1)	3	4	1	1	1	1	0	3.00

IBB: Skinner (by Sheldon). **Ground balls-fly balls:** Ford 7-4, Downing 3-1, Sheldon 1-1, Mikkelsen 0-1, Sadecki 7-7, Schultz 4-4. **Batters faced:** Ford 25, Downing 7, Sheldon 4, Mikkelsen 4, Sadecki 29, Schultz 14. **UMPIRES:** hp—Secory, 1b—McKinley, 2b—Burkhart, 3b—Soar, lf—V.Smith, rf—A.Smith **T:** 2:42 **A:** 30,805

GAME 2 New York 8 St. Louis 3
Sportsman's Park 10/08/64

NY YANKEES	AB	R	H	HR	RBI	BB	AVG
Linz ss	4	2	3	1	1	1	.375
B.Richardson 2b	5	1	2	0	1	0	.400
Maris cf	5	1	2	0	0	0	.333
Mantle rf	4	2	1	0	2	1	.333
Lopez rf	0	0	0	0	0	0	.000
Howard c	4	2	1	0	0	1	.375
Pepitone 1b	4	0	2	0	1	0	.222
Tresh lf	3	0	1	0	2	1	.429
C.Boyer 3b	3	0	0	0	1	1	.143
Stottlemyre p	5	0	0	0	0	0	.000
TOTALS	**37**	**8**	**12**	**1**	**8**	**5**	**.324**

BATTING: 2B: B.Richardson (1, Gibson), Howard (1, Gibson), Pepitone (1, Gibson), Mantle (1, G.Richardson). **HR:** Linz (1, 9th off Schultz 0 on, 0 out). **SF:** C.Boyer, Tresh. **RBI:** Linz 1 (1), B.Richardson 1 (2), Mantle 2 (2), Pepitone 1 (1), Tresh 2 (5), C.Boyer 1 (1). **Runners left in scoring position, 2 out:** Maris 2, Pepitone 1, Stottlemyre 3. **Team LOB:** 10 **FIELDING: PB:** Howard. **DP:** 1 (Linz-B.Richardson-Pepitone).

ST.LOUIS	AB	R	H	HR	RBI	BB	AVG
Flood cf	4	0	0	0	1	0	.222
Brock lf	4	0	0	0	1	0	.222
White 1b	3	0	0	0	0	1	.000
K.Boyer 3b	4	0	0	0	0	0	.143
Groat ss	3	1	1	0	0	1	.286
McCarver c	4	0	1	0	1	0	.429
Shannon rf	4	1	1	0	0	0	.375
Maxvill 2b	2	0	1	0	0	0	.250
a-Warwick ph	1	1	1	0	0	0	1.000
Schultz p	0	0	0	0	0	0	.000
G.Richardson p	0	0	0	0	0	0	.000
Craig p	0	0	0	0	0	0	.000
d-James ph	1	0	0	0	0	0	.000
Gibson p	1	0	1	0	0	0	1.000
b-Skinner ph	1	0	1	0	0	0	1.000
c-Buchek pr-2b	0	0	0	0	0	0	.000
TOTALS	**32**	**3**	**7**	**0**	**3**	**2**	**.284**

a - Batted for Maxvill in the 8th
b - Batted for Gibson in the 8th
c - Ran for Skinner in the 8th
d - Batted for Craig in the 9th

BATTING: 2B: Skinner (1, Stottlemyre). **3B:** Groat (1, Stottlemyre). **S:** Gibson. **RBI:** Flood 1 (3), Brock 1 (3), McCarver 1 (1). **Runners left in scoring position, 2 out:** Brock 1, K.Boyer 1. **GIDP:** Shannon. **Team LOB:** 5

NY YANKEES	IP	H	R	ER	BB	SO	HR	ERA
Stottlemyre (W, 1-0)	9	7	3	3	2	4	0	3.00

ST.LOUIS	IP	H	R	ER	BB	SO	HR	ERA
Gibson (L, 0-1)	8	8	4	4	3	9	0	4.50
Schultz	0.1	2	2	2	0	0	1	8.10
G.Richardson	0.1	2	2	2	2	0	0	54.00
Craig	0.1	0	0	0	0	1	0	0.00

WP: Gibson 1. **IBB:** Tresh (by Gibson), Howard (by G.Richardson), C.Boyer (by G.Richardson). **HBP:** Pepitone (by Gibson). **Ground balls-fly balls:** Stottlemyre 17-4, Gibson 8-6, Schultz 0-1, G.Richardson 0-0, Craig 0-0. **Batters faced:** Stottlemyre 35, Gibson 36, Schultz 3, G.Richardson 5, Craig 1. **UMPIRES:** hp—McKinley, 1b—Burkhart, 2b—Soar, 3b—V.Smith, lf—A.Smith, rf—Secory **T:** 2:29 **A:** 30,805

GAME 3 New York 2 St. Louis 1
Yankee Stadium 10/10/64

ST.LOUIS	AB	R	H	HR	RBI	BB	AVG
Flood cf	5	0	0	0	0	0	.143
Brock lf	4	0	0	0	0	0	.154
White 1b	4	0	1	0	0	0	.091
K.Boyer 3b	4	0	0	0	0	0	.091
Groat ss	4	0	1	0	0	0	.273
McCarver c	2	1	1	0	0	2	.444
Shannon rf	3	0	1	0	0	0	.364
Maxvill 2b	3	0	1	0	0	0	.286
a-Warwick ph	0	0	0	0	0	1	1.000
Buchek 2b	0	0	0	0	0	0	.000
Simmons p	2	0	1	0	1	0	.500
b-Skinner ph	1	0	0	0	0	0	.500
Schultz p	0	0	0	0	0	0	.000
TOTALS	**32**	**1**	**6**	**0**	**1**	**3**	**.253**

a - Batted for Maxvill in the 9th
b - Batted for Simmons in the 9th

BATTING: 2B: Groat (1, Bouton), Maxvill (1, Bouton). **S:** Simmons, Shannon. **RBI:** Simmons 1 (1). **2-out RBI:** Simmons 1. **Runners left in scoring position, 2 out:** Flood 1, Brock 1, Shannon 2, Maxvill 1. **Team LOB:** 9 **FIELDING: DP:** 1 (Maxvill-Groat-White).

NY YANKEES	AB	R	H	HR	RBI	BB	AVG
Linz ss	4	0	0	0	0	0	.250
B.Richardson 2b	4	0	1	0	0	0	.357
Maris cf	4	0	0	0	0	0	.231
Mantle rf	3	1	2	1	1	1	.417
Howard c	2	1	1	0	0	1	.400
Tresh lf	3	0	0	0	0	0	.300
Pepitone 1b	2	0	0	0	0	1	.182
C.Boyer 3b	3	0	1	0	1	0	.200
Bouton p	3	0	0	0	0	0	.000
TOTALS	**28**	**2**	**5**	**1**	**2**	**3**	**.284**

BATTING: 2B: C.Boyer (1, Simmons), Mantle (2, Simmons). **HR:** Mantle (1, 9th off Schultz 0 on, 0 out). **RBI:** Mantle 1 (3), C.Boyer 1 (2). **2-out RBI:** C.Boyer 1. **Runners left in scoring position, 2 out:** Tresh 2, Bouton 2. **GIDP:** Howard. **Team LOB:** 5 **FIELDING: E:** Mantle (2), Linz (1).

ST.LOUIS	IP	H	R	ER	BB	SO	HR	ERA
Simmons	8	4	1	1	3	2	0	1.13
Schultz (L, 0-1)	0	1	1	1	0	0	1	10.80

NY YANKEES	IP	H	R	ER	BB	SO	HR	ERA
Bouton (W, 1-0)	9	6	1	0	3	2	0	0.00

IBB: McCarver (by Bouton), Howard (by Simmons). **Ground balls-fly balls:** Simmons 11-10, Schultz 0-0, Bouton 8-16. **Batters faced:** Simmons 30, Schultz 1, Bouton 37. **UMPIRES:** hp—Burkhart, 1b—Soar, 2b—V.Smith, 3b—A.Smith, lf—Secory, rf—McKinley **T:** 2:16 **A:** 67,101

GAME 4 St. Louis 4 New York 3
Yankee Stadium 10/11/64

ST.LOUIS	AB	R	H	HR	RBI	BB	AVG
Flood cf	4	1	2	0	0	0	.222
Brock lf	4	0	0	0	0	0	.118
Groat ss	4	1	1	0	0	0	.267
K.Boyer 3b	4	1	1	1	4	0	.133
White 1b	4	0	0	0	0	0	.067
Shannon rf	4	0	0	0	0	0	.267
McCarver c	3	0	1	0	0	1	.417
Maxvill 2b	3	0	0	0	0	1	.200
Sadecki p	0	0	0	0	0	0	.500
Craig p	1	0	0	0	0	0	.000
a-Warwick ph	1	1	1	0	0	0	1.000
Taylor p	1	0	0	0	0	0	.000
TOTALS	**33**	**4**	**6**	**1**	**4**	**2**	**.235**

a - Batted for Craig in the 6th

BATTING: HR: K.Boyer (1, 6th off Downing 3 on, 1 out). **RBI:** K.Boyer 4 (5). **Runners left in scoring position, 2 out:** Flood 1, Brock 1. **GIDP:** K.Boyer. **Team LOB:** 4 **Outfield assists:** Shannon (1).

NY YANKEES	AB	R	H	HR	RBI	BB	AVG
Linz ss	4	1	1	0	0	0	.250
B.Richardson 2b	4	1	1	0	1	0	.333
Maris cf	4	1	1	0	0	0	.235
Mantle rf	2	0	1	0	1	2	.429
Howard c	3	0	1	0	1	1	.385
Tresh lf	4	0	0	0	0	0	.214
Pepitone 1b	3	0	0	0	0	1	.143
C.Boyer 3b	4	0	1	0	0	0	.214
Downing p	2	0	0	0	0	0	.000
Mikkelsen p	0	0	0	0	0	0	.000
a-Blanchard ph	1	0	0	0	0	0	.500
Terry p	0	0	0	0	0	0	.000
TOTALS	**31**	**3**	**6**	**0**	**3**	**4**	**.263**

a - Batted for Mikkelsen in the 7th

BATTING: 2B: Linz (1, Sadecki), B.Richardson (2, Sadecki). **RBI:** B.Richardson 1 (3), Mantle 1 (4), Howard 1 (1). **Runners left in scoring position, 2 out:** Linz 1. **Team LOB:** 5 **BASERUNNING: CS:** Linz (1, 3rd base off Sadecki/McCarver). **FIELDING: E:** B.Richardson (1). **DP:** 1 (Linz-B.Richardson-Pepitone).

ST.LOUIS	IP	H	R	ER	BB	SO	HR	ERA
Sadecki	0.1	4	3	2	0	0	0	8.53
Craig (W, 1-0)	4.2	2	0	0	3	8	0	0.00
Taylor (S, 1)	4	0	0	0	1	2	0	0.00

NY YANKEES	IP	H	R	ER	BB	SO	HR	ERA
Downing (L, 0-1)	6	4	4	3	2	4	1	4.70
Mikkelsen	1	0	0	0	0	1	0	0.00
Terry	2	2	0	0	0	3	0	0.00

Ground balls-fly balls: Sadecki 0-0, Craig 2-3, Taylor 8-2, Downing 6-9, Mikkelsen 2-0, Terry 1-1. **Batters faced:** Sadecki 4, Craig 18, Taylor 13, Downing 25, Mikkelsen 3, Terry 7. **UMPIRES:** hp—Soar, 1b—V.Smith, 2b—A.Smith, 3b—Secory, lf—McKinley, rf—Burkhart **T:** 2:18 **A:** 66,312

GAME 5 St. Louis 5 New York 2
Yankee Stadium 10/12/64

ST.LOUIS	AB	R	H	HR	RBI	BB	AVG
Flood cf	4	1	1	0	0	1	.227
Brock lf	5	0	2	0	1	0	.182
White 1b	4	1	0	0	1	1	.053
K.Boyer 3b	4	0	1	0	0	0	.158
Groat ss	4	1	1	0	0	1	.263
McCarver c	5	1	3	1	3	0	.471
Shannon rf	5	0	0	0	0	0	.200
Maxvill 2b	5	0	1	0	0	0	.200
Gibson p	4	1	1	0	0	0	.400
TOTALS	**40**	**5**	**10**	**1**	**5**	**3**	**.238**

BATTING: HR: McCarver (1, 10th off Mikkelsen 2 on, 1 out). **RBI:** Brock 1 (4), White 1 (1), McCarver 3 (4). **Runners left in scoring position, 2 out:** White 1, McCarver 2, Maxvill 1. **GIDP:** Shannon. **Team LOB:** 9 **BASERUNNING: SB:** White (1, 3rd base off Mikkelsen/Howard). **FIELDING: E:** Groat (1). **DP:** 1 (Maxvill-Groat-White).

NY YANKEES	AB	R	H	HR	RBI	BB	AVG
Linz ss	5	0	0	0	0	0	.190
B.Richardson 2b	5	0	3	0	0	0	.391
Maris cf	5	0	0	0	0	0	.182
Mantle rf	3	1	0	0	0	1	.353
Howard c	3	0	0	0	0	0	.313
Pepitone 1b	4	0	1	0	0	0	.167
Tresh lf	3	1	1	1	2	1	.235
C.Boyer 3b	2	0	0	0	0	0	.188
a-Blanchard ph	1	0	0	0	0	0	.333
Gonzalez 3b	1	0	0	0	0	0	.000
Stottlemyre p	2	0	1	0	0	0	.143
b-Lopez ph	1	0	0	0	0	0	.000
Reniff p	0	0	0	0	0	0	.000
Mikkelsen p	0	0	0	0	0	0	.000
c-Hegan ph	1	0	0	0	0	0	.000
TOTALS	**36**	**2**	**6**	**1**	**2**	**2**	**.243**

a - Batted for C.Boyer in the 7th
b - Batted for Stottlemyre in the 7th
c - Batted for Mikkelsen in the 10th

BATTING: HR: Tresh (2, 9th off Gibson 1 on, 2 out). **RBI:** Tresh 2 (7). **2-out RBI:** Tresh 2. **Runners left in scoring position, 2 out:** Stottlemyre 2. **GIDP:** Maris. **Team LOB:** 7 **FIELDING: E:** Howard (1), B.Richardson (2). **DP:** 1 (Linz-B.Richardson-Pepitone).

ST.LOUIS	IP	H	R	ER	BB	SO	HR	ERA
Gibson (W, 1-1)	10	6	2	0	2	13	1	2.00

NY YANKEES	IP	H	R	ER	BB	SO	HR	ERA
Stottlemyre	7	6	2	1	2	6	0	2.25
Reniff	0.1	2	0	0	0	0	0	0.00
Mikkelsen (L, 0-1)	2.2	2	3	3	1	3	1	6.75

IBB: Tresh (by Gibson). **HBP:** Howard (by Gibson). **Ground balls-fly balls:** Gibson 8-9, Stottlemyre 10-5, Reniff 1-0, Mikkelsen 3-2. **Batters faced:** Gibson 39, Stottlemyre 30, Reniff 3, Mikkelsen 11. **UMPIRES:** hp—V.Smith, 1b—A.Smith, 2b—Secory, 3b—McKinley, lf—Burkhart, rf—Soar **T:** 2:37 **A:** 65,633

GAME 6 New York 8 St. Louis 3
Sportsman's Park 10/14/64

NY YANKEES	AB	R	H	HR	RBI	BB	AVG
Linz ss	5	1	1	0	0	0	.192
B.Richardson 2b	4	0	2	0	0	0	.407
Maris cf	4	1	1	1	1	0	.192
Mantle rf	3	2	1	1	1	1	.350
Howard c	4	1	1	0	1	0	.300
Tresh lf	3	2	1	0	0	1	.250
Pepitone 1b	4	1	1	1	4	0	.182
C.Boyer 3b	4	0	1	0	0	0	.200
Bouton p	4	0	1	0	1	0	.143
Hamilton p	0	0	0	0	0	0	.000
TOTALS	**35**	**8**	**10**	**3**	**8**	**2**	**.250**

BATTING: 2B: Tresh (2, Simmons). **HR:** Maris (1, 6th off Simmons 0 on, 1 out), Mantle (2, 6th off Simmons 0 on, 1 out), Pepitone (1, 8th off G.Richardson 3 on, 2 out). **S:** B.Richardson. **RBI:** Maris 1 (1), Mantle 1 (5), Howard 1 (2), Pepitone 4 (5), Bouton 1 (1). **2-out RBI:** Howard 1, Pepitone 4, Bouton 1. **Runners left in scoring position, 2 out:** Mantle 1. **Team LOB:** 3 **BASERUNNING: SB:** B.Richardson (1, 2nd base off Simmons/McCarver). **FIELDING: DP:** 2 (B.Richardson-Linz-Pepitone, Linz-B.Richardson-Pepitone).

ST.LOUIS	AB	R	H	HR	RBI	BB	AVG
Flood cf	3	2	1	0	0	2	.240
Brock lf	4	0	3	0	0	0	.269
White 1b	4	0	0	0	2	0	.043
K.Boyer 3b	4	0	0	0	0	0	.130
Groat ss	4	0	0	0	0	0	.217
McCarver c	4	0	2	0	0	0	.476
Shannon rf	4	1	1	0	0	0	.208
Maxvill 2b	2	0	0	0	0	0	.176
a-Warwick ph	1	0	0	0	0	0	.750
Buchek 2b	1	0	1	0	0	0	1.000
Simmons p	2	0	1	0	0	0	.500
Taylor p	0	0	0	0	0	0	.000
b-James ph	1	0	0	0	0	0	.000
Schultz p	0	0	0	0	0	0	.000
G.Richardson p	0	0	0	0	0	0	.000
Humphreys p	0	0	0	0	0	0	.000
c-Skinner ph	1	0	1	0	1	0	.667
TOTALS	**35**	**3**	**10**	**0**	**3**	**2**	**.246**

a - Batted for Maxvill in the 7th

b - Batted for Taylor in the 7th
c - Batted for Humphreys in the 9th

BATTING: 2B: Brock (2, Bouton). **RBI:** White 2 (3), Skinner 1 (1). **Runners left in scoring position, 2 out:** White 1, Groat 1. **GIDP:** White, Flood. **Team LOB:** 7 **FIELDING: E:** Brock (1). **DP:** 1 (Maxvill-Groat).

NY YANKEES	IP	H	R	ER	BB	SO	HR	ERA
Bouton (W, 2-0)	8.1	9	3	3	2	5	0	1.56
Hamilton (S, 1)	0.2	1	0	0	0	0	0	0.00

ST.LOUIS	IP	H	R	ER	BB	SO	HR	ERA
Simmons (L, 0-1)	6.1	7	3	3	0	6	2	2.51
Taylor	0.2	0	0	0	0	0	0	0.00
Schultz	0.2	2	4	4	2	0	0	18.00
G.Richardson	0.1	1	1	1	0	0	1	40.50
Humphreys	1	0	0	0	0	1	0	0.00

IBB: Mantle (by Schultz). **Ground balls-fly balls:** Bouton 7-12, Hamilton 1-0, Simmons 4-9, Taylor 0-1, Schultz 1-0, G.Richardson 0-1, Humphreys 2-0. **Batters faced:** Bouton 35, Hamilton 2, Simmons 26, Taylor 1, Schultz 6, G.Richardson 2, Humphreys 3. **UMPIRES:** hp—A.Smith, 1b—Secory, 2b—McKinley, 3b—Burkhart, lf—Soar, rf—V.Smith **T:** 2:37 **A:** 30,805

GAME 7 St. Louis 7 New York 5
Sportsman's Park 10/15/64

NY YANKEES	AB	R	H	HR	RBI	BB	AVG
Linz ss	5	1	2	1	1	0	.226
B.Richardson 2b	5	1	2	0	0	0	.406
Maris cf	4	1	1	0	0	0	.200
Mantle rf	4	1	1	1	3	0	.333
Howard c	4	0	1	0	0	0	.292
Pepitone 1b	4	0	0	0	0	0	.154
Tresh lf	2	0	1	0	0	2	.273
C.Boyer 3b	4	1	1	1	1	0	.208
Stottlemyre p	1	0	0	0	0	0	.125
a-Hegan ph	0	0	0	0	0	1	.000
Downing p	0	0	0	0	0	0	.000
Sheldon p	0	0	0	0	0	0	.000
b-Lopez ph	1	0	0	0	0	0	.000
Hamilton p	0	0	0	0	0	0	.000
Mikkelsen p	0	0	0	0	0	0	.000
c-Blanchard ph	1	0	0	0	0	0	.250
TOTALS	**35**	**5**	**9**	**3**	**5**	**3**	**.251**

a - Batted for Stottlemyre in the 5th
b - Batted for Sheldon in the 7th
c - Batted for Mikkelsen in the 9th

BATTING: HR: Mantle (3, 6th off Gibson 2 on, 0 out), C.Boyer (1, 9th off Gibson 0 on, 1 out), Linz (2, 9th off Gibson 0 on, 2 out). **RBI:** Linz 1 (2), Mantle 3 (8), C.Boyer 1 (3). **2-out RBI:** Linz 1. **Runners left in scoring position, 2 out:** Stottlemyre 2. **GIDP:** B.Richardson. **Team LOB:** 6 **FIELDING: E:** C.Boyer (2).

ST.LOUIS	AB	R	H	HR	RBI	BB	AVG
Flood cf	5	0	0	0	0	0	.200
Brock lf	4	1	2	1	1	0	.300
White 1b	4	1	2	0	0	0	.111
K.Boyer 3b	4	3	3	1	1	0	.222
Groat ss	3	0	0	0	1	1	.192
McCarver c	2	1	1	0	2	1	.478
Shannon rf	4	1	1	0	0	0	.214
Maxvill 2b	3	0	1	0	1	0	.200
Gibson p	4	0	0	0	0	0	.222
TOTALS	**33**	**7**	**10**	**2**	**6**	**2**	**.254**

BATTING: 2B: White (1, Stottlemyre), K.Boyer (1, Downing). **HR:** Brock (1, 5th off Downing 0 on, 0 out), K.Boyer (2, 7th off Hamilton 0 on, 2 out). **S:** Maxvill. **SF:** McCarver. **RBI:** Brock 1 (5), K.Boyer 1 (6), Groat 1 (1), McCarver 2 (6), Maxvill 1 (1). **2-out RBI:** K.Boyer 1. **Runners left in scoring position, 2 out:** Flood 2, K.Boyer 1. **Team LOB:** 6 **BASERUNNING: SB:** McCarver (1, home off Stottlemyre/Howard), Shannon (1, home off Stottlemyre/Howard). **FIELDING: E:** Groat (2). **Outfield assists:** Shannon (2). **DP:** 2 (Groat-Maxvill-White, Shannon-Groat).

NY YANKEES	IP	H	R	ER	BB	SO	HR	ERA
Stottlemyre (L, 1-1)	4	5	3	3	2	2	0	3.15
Downing	0	3	3	3	0	0	1	8.22
Sheldon	2	0	0	0	0	2	0	0.00
Hamilton	1.1	2	1	1	0	2	1	4.50
Mikkelsen	0.2	0	0	0	0	0	0	5.79

ST.LOUIS	IP	H	R	ER	BB	SO	HR	ERA
Gibson (W, 2-1)	9	9	5	5	3	9	3	3.00

Ground balls-fly balls: Stottlemyre 7-3, Downing 0-0, Sheldon 1-2, Hamilton 2-0, Mikkelsen 1-1, Gibson 7-10. **Batters faced:** Stottlemyre 19, Downing 3, Sheldon 6, Hamilton 7, Mikkelsen 2, Gibson 38. **UMPIRES:** hp—Secory, 1b—McKinley, 2b—Burkhart, 3b—Soar, lf—V.Smith, rf—A.Smith **T:** 2:40 **A:** 30,346

1965 LOS ANGELES DEF. MINNESOTA, 4-3

GAME 1 Minnesota 8 Los Angeles 2
Metropolitan Stadium 10/06/65

LOS ANGELES	AB	R	H	HR	RBI	BB	AVG
Wills ss	5	0	2	0	1	0	.400
Gilliam 3b	5	0	1	0	0	0	.200
Davis cf	4	0	1	0	0	0	.250
Fairly rf	4	1	1	1	1	0	.250
Johnson lf	4	0	1	0	0	0	.250
Lefebvre 2b	4	1	1	0	0	0	.250
Parker 1b	3	0	1	0	0	1	.333
Roseboro c	4	0	1	0	0	0	.250
Drysdale p	1	0	0	0	0	0	.000
Reed p	0	0	0	0	0	0	.000
a-Crawford ph	1	0	1	0	0	0	1.000
Brewer p	0	0	0	0	0	0	.000
b-Moon ph	1	0	0	0	0	0	.000
Perranoski p	0	0	0	0	0	0	.000
c-LeJohn ph	1	0	0	0	0	0	.000
TOTALS	**37**	**2**	**10**	**1**	**2**	**1**	**.270**

a - Batted for Reed in the 5th
b - Batted for Brewer in the 7th
c - Batted for Perranoski in the 9th

BATTING: HR: Fairly (1, 2nd off Grant 0 on, 0 out). **RBI:** Wills 1 (1), Fairly 1 (1). **2-out RBI:** Wills 1. **Runners left in scoring position, 2 out:** Wills 1, Gilliam 2, Lefebvre 1. **Team LOB:** 9 **FIELDING: DP:** 1 (Perranoski-Wills-Parker).

MINNESOTA	AB	R	H	HR	RBI	BB	AVG
Versalles ss	5	1	2	1	4	0	.400
Valdespino lf	4	1	1	0	0	0	.250
Oliva rf	4	0	0	0	0	0	.000
Killebrew 3b	3	1	1	0	0	1	.333
Hall cf	3	0	1	0	0	1	.333
Mincher 1b	3	2	1	1	1	1	.333
Battey c	4	0	1	0	2	0	.250
Quilici 2b	4	1	2	0	1	0	.500
Grant p	3	2	1	0	0	0	.333
TOTALS	**33**	**8**	**10**	**2**	**8**	**3**	**.303**

BATTING: 2B: Quilici (1, Drysdale), Valdespino (1, Drysdale), Grant (1, Brewer). **HR:** Mincher (1, 2nd off Drysdale 0 on, 2 out), Versalles (1, 3th off Drysdale 2 on, 0 out). **S:** Grant. **RBI:** Versalles 4 (4), Mincher 1 (1), Battey 2 (2), Quilici 1 (1). **2-out RBI:** Mincher 1, Battey 2, Quilici 1. **Runners left in scoring position, 2 out:** Oliva 1, Battey 1, Grant 1. **GIDP:** Battey. **Team LOB:** 5 **BASERUNNING: SB:** Versalles (1, 2nd base off Brewer/Roseboro).

LOS ANGELES	IP	H	R	ER	BB	SO	HR	ERA
Drysdale (L, 0-1)	2.2	7	7	3	1	4	2	10.13
Reed	1.1	0	0	0	0	1	0	0.00
Brewer	2	3	1	1	0	1	0	4.50
Perranoski	2	0	0	0	2	0	0	0.00

MINNESOTA	IP	H	R	ER	BB	SO	HR	ERA
Grant (W, 1-0)	9	10	2	2	1	5	1	2.00

WP: Brewer 1. **Ground balls-fly balls:** Drysdale 3-1, Reed 1-2, Brewer 3-2, Perranoski 1-4, Grant 4-18. **Batters faced:** Drysdale 17, Reed 4, Brewer 9, Perranoski 7, Grant 38. **UMPIRES:** hp—Hurley, 1b—Venzon, 2b—Flaherty, 3b—Sudol, lf—Stewart, rf—Vargo **T:** 2:29 **A:** 47,797

GAME 2 Minnesota 5 Los Angeles 1
Metropolitan Stadium 10/07/65

LOS ANGELES	AB	R	H	HR	RBI	BB	AVG
Wills ss	4	0	1	0	0	0	.333
Gilliam 3b	4	0	0	0	0	0	.111
Davis cf	4	0	0	0	0	0	.125
Johnson lf	4	0	0	0	0	0	.125
Fairly rf	4	1	2	0	0	0	.375
Lefebvre 2b	4	0	2	0	0	0	.375
Parker 1b	1	0	1	0	0	1	.500
Roseboro c	4	0	1	0	1	0	.250
Koufax p	2	0	0	0	0	0	.000
a-Drysdale ph	1	0	0	0	0	0	.000
Perranoski p	0	0	0	0	0	0	.000
Miller p	0	0	0	0	0	0	.000
b-Tracewski ph	1	0	0	0	0	0	.000
TOTALS	**33**	**1**	**7**	**0**	**1**	**1**	**.243**

a - Batted for Koufax in the 7th
b - Batted for Miller in the 9th

BATTING: S: Parker. **RBI:** Roseboro 1 (1). **Runners left in scoring position, 2 out:** Wills 3, Johnson 1, Koufax 1, Tracewski 2. **Team LOB:** 8 **FIELDING: E:** Johnson (1), Gilliam 2 (2).

MINNESOTA	AB	R	H	HR	RBI	BB	AVG
Versalles ss	5	2	1	0	0	0	.300
Nossek cf	3	0	1	0	0	0	.333
Oliva rf	4	1	1	0	1	0	.125
Killebrew 3b	3	0	2	0	1	1	.500
Battey c	4	0	1	0	0	0	.250
Allison lf	4	1	1	0	0	0	.250
Mincher 1b	4	1	1	0	0	0	.286
Quilici 2b	2	0	0	0	0	2	.333
Kaat p	4	0	1	0	2	0	.250
TOTALS	**33**	**5**	**9**	**0**	**4**	**3**	**.288**

BATTING: 2B: Oliva (1, Koufax), Allison (1, Perranoski). **3B:** Versalles (1, Perranoski). **S:** Nossek. **RBI:** Oliva 1 (1), Killebrew 1 (1), Kaat 2 (2). **2-out RBI:** Kaat 2. **Runners left in scoring position, 2 out:** Versalles 1, Oliva 1, Battey 2, Mincher 1. **Team LOB:** 8 **BASERUNNING: CS:** Quilici (1, 2nd base off Koufax/Roseboro).

LOS ANGELES	IP	H	R	ER	BB	SO	HR	ERA
Koufax (L, 0-1)	6	6	2	1	1	9	0	1.50
Perranoski	1.2	3	3	3	2	1	0	7.36
Miller	0.1	0	0	0	0	0	0	0.00

MINNESOTA	IP	H	R	ER	BB	SO	HR	ERA
Kaat (W, 1-0)	9	7	1	1	1	3	0	1.00

WP: Perranoski 1. **BK:** , Perranoski 1. **IBB:** Quilici (by Perranoski). **HBP:** Parker (by Kaat). **Ground balls-fly balls:** Koufax 3-5, Perranoski 3-2, Miller 0-1, Kaat 9-14. **Batters faced:** Koufax 25, Perranoski 11, Miller 1, Kaat 36. **UMPIRES:** hp—Venzon, 1b—Flaherty, 2b—Sudol, 3b—Stewart, lf—Vargo, rf—Hurley **T:** 2:13 **A:** 48,700

GAME 3 Los Angeles 4 Minnesota 0
Chavez Ravine 10/09/65

MINNESOTA	AB	R	H	HR	RBI	BB	AVG
Versalles ss	3	0	2	0	0	1	.385
Nossek cf	4	0	1	0	0	0	.286
Oliva rf	4	0	1	0	0	0	.167
Killebrew 3b	3	0	0	0	0	1	.333
Battey c	3	0	0	0	0	0	.182
Zimmerman c	1	0	0	0	0	0	.000
Allison lf	3	0	0	0	0	0	.143
Mincher 1b	3	0	1	0	0	0	.300
Quilici 2b	3	0	0	0	0	0	.222
Pascual p	1	0	0	0	0	0	.000
a-Rollins ph	1	0	0	0	0	0	.000
Merritt p	0	0	0	0	0	0	.000
b-Valdespino ph	1	0	0	0	0	0	.200
Klippstein p	0	0	0	0	0	0	.000
TOTALS	**30**	**0**	**5**	**0**	**0**	**2**	**.250**

a - Batted for Pascual in the 6th
b - Batted for Merritt in the 8th

BATTING: 2B: Versalles (1, Osteen). **S:** Versalles. **Runners left in scoring position, 2 out:** Nossek 1. **GIDP:** Oliva, Zimmerman. **Team LOB:** 5 **FIELDING: DP:** 1 (Zimmerman-Versalles).

LOS ANGELES	AB	R	H	HR	RBI	BB	AVG
Wills ss	4	0	1	0	1	0	.308
Gilliam 3b	4	0	1	0	0	0	.154
Kennedy 3b	0	0	0	0	0	0	.000
Davis cf	4	1	1	0	0	0	.167
Fairly rf	4	1	1	0	0	0	.333
Johnson lf	2	0	2	0	1	1	.300
Lefebvre 2b	2	1	1	0	0	0	.400
Tracewski 2b	2	0	0	0	0	0	.000
Parker 1b	3	1	1	0	0	1	.429
Roseboro c	3	0	1	0	2	0	.273
Osteen p	2	0	1	0	0	0	.500
TOTALS	**30**	**4**	**10**	**0**	**4**	**2**	**.270**

BATTING: 2B: Gilliam (1, Pascual), Johnson 2 (2, Pascual), Fairly (1, Pascual), Wills (1, Merritt). **S:** Johnson, Osteen. **RBI:** Wills 1 (2), Johnson 1 (1), Roseboro 2 (3). **2-out RBI:** Wills 1, Johnson 1. **Runners left in scoring position, 2 out:** Wills 2, Davis 1, Fairly 1, Tracewski 1, Roseboro 1. **Team LOB:** 6 **BASERUNNING: SB:** Wills (1, 2nd base off Pascual/Battey), Parker (1, 3rd base off Pascual/Battey), Roseboro (1, 3rd base off Pascual/Battey). **CS:** Johnson (1, 2nd base off Klippstein/Zimmerman). **FIELDING: E:** Kennedy (1). **DP:** 2 (Tracewski-Parker, Wills-Parker).

MINNESOTA	IP	H	R	ER	BB	SO	HR	ERA
Pascual (L, 0-1)	5	8	3	3	1	0	0	5.40
Merritt	2	2	1	1	0	0	0	4.50
Klippstein	1	0	0	0	1	1	0	0.00

LOS ANGELES	IP	H	R	ER	BB	SO	HR	ERA
Osteen (W, 1-0)	9	5	0	0	2	2	0	0.00

Ground balls-fly balls: Pascual 7-7, Merritt 0-4, Klippstein 0-1, Osteen 16-7. **Batters faced:** Pascual 24, Merritt 7, Klippstein 3, Osteen 32. **UMPIRES:** hp—Flaherty, 1b—Sudol, 2b—Stewart, 3b—Vargo, lf—Hurley, rf—Venzon **T:** 2:06 **A:** 55,934

GAME 4 Los Angeles 7 Minnesota 2
Chavez Ravine 10/10/65

MINNESOTA	AB	R	H	HR	RBI	BB	AVG
Versalles ss	4	0	1	0	0	0	.353
Valdespino lf	4	0	1	0	0	0	.222
Oliva rf	4	1	1	1	1	0	.188
Killebrew 3b	2	1	1	1	1	2	.364
Hall cf	4	0	0	0	0	0	.143
Mincher 1b	4	0	0	0	0	0	.214
Battey c	3	0	0	0	0	0	.143
Zimmerman c	0	0	0	0	0	0	.000
Quilici 2b	3	0	0	0	0	0	.167
Grant p	2	0	0	0	0	0	.200
Worthington p	0	0	0	0	0	0	.000
a-Nossek ph	1	0	1	0	0	0	.375
Pleis p	0	0	0	0	0	0	.000
TOTALS	**31**	**2**	**5**	**2**	**2**	**2**	**.228**

a - Batted for Worthington in the 8th

BATTING: HR: Killebrew (1, 4th off Drysdale 0 on, 1 out), Oliva (1, 6th off Drysdale 0 on, 2 out). **RBI:** Oliva 1 (2), Killebrew 1 (2). **2-out RBI:** Oliva 1. **Team LOB:** 4 **FIELDING: E:** Quilici (1), Worthington (1). **DP:** 1 (Battey-Versalles).

LOS ANGELES	AB	R	H	HR	RBI	BB	AVG
Wills ss	4	1	2	0	0	0	.353
Gilliam 3b	2	1	0	0	0	1	.133
a-Kennedy pr-3b	0	0	0	0	0	0	.000
Davis cf	4	1	2	0	0	0	.250
Fairly rf	4	1	1	0	3	0	.313
Johnson lf	4	1	2	1	2	0	.357
Parker 1b	4	2	2	1	1	0	.455
Roseboro c	3	0	1	0	0	1	.286
Tracewski 2b	4	0	0	0	0	0	.000
Drysdale p	3	0	0	0	0	0	.000
TOTALS	**32**	**7**	**10**	**2**	**6**	**2**	**.280**

a - Ran for Gilliam in the 7th

BATTING: HR: Parker (1, 4th off Grant 0 on, 2 out), Johnson (1, 8th off Pleis 0 on, 1 out). **RBI:** Fairly 3 (4), Johnson 2 (3), Parker 1 (1). **2-out RBI:** Parker 1. **Team LOB:** 4 **BASERUNNING: SB:** Wills (2, 2nd base off Grant/Battey), Parker (2, 2nd base off Grant/Battey). **CS:** Roseboro (1, 2nd base off Grant/Battey), Wills (1, 2nd base off Grant/Battey). **Outfield assists:** Johnson (1).

MINNESOTA	IP	H	R	ER	BB	SO	HR	ERA
Grant (L, 1-1)	5	6	5	4	1	2	1	3.86
Worthington	2	2	1	0	1	2	0	0.00
Pleis	1	2	1	1	0	0	1	9.00

LOS ANGELES	IP	H	R	ER	BB	SO	HR	ERA
Drysdale (W, 1-1)	9	5	2	2	2	11	2	3.86

WP: Grant 1. **HBP:** Gilliam (by Worthington). **Ground balls-fly balls:** Grant 5-7, Worthington 1-2, Pleis 1-2, Drysdale 8-7. **Batters faced:** Grant 21, Worthington 9, Pleis 5, Drysdale 33. **UMPIRES:** hp—Sudol, 1b—Stewart, 2b—Vargo, 3b—Hurley, lf—Venzon, rf—Flaherty **T:** 2:15 **A:** 55,920

GAME 5 Los Angeles 7 Minnesota 0
Chavez Ravine 10/11/65

MINNESOTA	AB	R	H	HR	RBI	BB	AVG
Versalles ss	4	0	0	0	0	0	.286
Nossek cf	4	0	1	0	0	0	.333
Oliva rf	3	0	0	0	0	0	.158
Killebrew 3b	3	0	1	0	0	0	.357
Battey c	3	0	0	0	0	0	.118
Allison lf	2	0	0	0	0	1	.111
Mincher 1b	3	0	0	0	0	0	.176
Quilici 2b	3	0	1	0	0	0	.200
Kaat p	1	0	0	0	0	0	.200
Boswell p	0	0	0	0	0	0	.000
a-Rollins ph	1	0	0	0	0	0	.000
Perry p	0	0	0	0	0	0	.000
b-Valdespino ph	1	0	1	0	0	0	.300
TOTALS	**28**	**0**	**4**	**0**	**0**	**1**	**.213**

a - Batted for Boswell in the 6th
b - Batted for Perry in the 9th

BATTING: GIDP: Battey, Mincher. **Team LOB:** 2

LOS ANGELES	AB	R	H	HR	RBI	BB	AVG
Wills ss	5	2	4	0	1	0	.455
Gilliam 3b	4	1	2	0	2	0	.211
Kennedy 3b	1	0	0	0	0	0	.000
Davis cf	4	1	2	0	0	0	.300
Johnson lf	5	1	1	0	1	0	.316
Fairly rf	5	1	3	0	1	0	.381
Parker 1b	4	0	0	0	0	0	.333
Tracewski 2b	3	0	1	0	0	1	.100
Roseboro c	2	1	0	0	0	2	.250
Koufax p	4	0	1	0	1	0	.167
TOTALS	**37**	**7**	**14**	**0**	**6**	**3**	**.302**

BATTING: 2B: Wills 2 (3, Kaat, Perry), Fairly (2, Kaat). **S:** Davis, Parker. **RBI:** Wills 1 (3), Gilliam 2 (2), Johnson 1 (4), Fairly 1 (5), Koufax 1 (1). **2-out RBI:** Wills 1, Koufax 1. **Runners left in scoring position, 2 out:** Wills 1, Kennedy 1, Johnson 2, Parker 2, Roseboro 1, Koufax 1. **Team LOB:** 11 **BASERUNNING: SB:** Davis 3 (3, 2nd base off Kaat/Battey, 2nd base off Boswell/Battey, 2nd base off Perry/Battey), Wills (3, 2nd base off Boswell/Battey). **CS:** Tracewski (1, 3rd base off Kaat/Battey). **FIELDING: DP:** 3 (Wills-Tracewski-Parker 2, Wills-Tracewski).

MINNESOTA	IP	H	R	ER	BB	SO	HR	ERA
Kaat (L, 1-1)	2.1	6	4	3	0	1	0	3.18
Boswell	2.2	3	1	1	2	3	0	3.38
Perry	3	5	2	2	1	3	0	6.00

LOS ANGELES	IP	H	R	ER	BB	SO	HR	ERA
Koufax (W, 1-1)	9	4	0	0	1	10	0	0.60

IBB: Roseboro (by Perry). **Ground balls-fly balls:** Kaat 4-2, Boswell 3-2, Perry 0-5, Koufax 7-7. **Batters faced:** Kaat 14, Boswell 13, Perry 15, Koufax 29. **UMPIRES:** hp—Stewart, 1b—Vargo, 2b—Hurley, 3b—Venzon, lf—Flaherty, rf—Sudol **T:** 2:34 **A:** 55,801

GAME 6 Minnesota 5 Los Angeles 1
Metropolitan Stadium 10/13/65

LOS ANGELES	AB	R	H	HR	RBI	BB	AVG
Wills ss	4	0	1	0	0	0	.423
Gilliam 3b	4	0	0	0	0	0	.174
Davis cf	4	0	0	0	0	0	.250
Fairly rf	4	1	2	1	1	0	.400
Johnson lf	4	0	1	0	0	0	.304
Parker 1b	4	0	0	0	0	0	.263
Roseboro c	3	0	1	0	0	0	.263
Tracewski 2b	3	0	1	0	0	0	.154
Osteen p	1	0	0	0	0	0	.333
a-Crawford ph	1	0	0	0	0	0	.500
Reed p	0	0	0	0	0	0	.000
b-Moon ph	1	0	0	0	0	0	.000
Miller p	0	0	0	0	0	0	.000
TOTALS	**33**	**1**	**6**	**1**	**1**	**0**	**.282**

a - Batted for Osteen in the 6th
b - Batted for Reed in the 8th

BATTING: HR: Fairly (2, 7th off Grant 0 on, 0 out). **SF:** Gilliam. **RBI:** Fairly 1 (6). **Runners left in scoring position, 2 out:** Davis 1, Roseboro 1. **Team LOB:** 5 **BASERUNNING: CS:** Roseboro (2, 2nd base off Grant/Battey). **FIELDING: E:** Tracewski (1). **DP:** 1 (Osteen-Wills-Parker).

MINNESOTA	AB	R	H	HR	RBI	BB	AVG
Versalles ss	3	0	1	0	0	1	.292
Nossek cf	4	0	0	0	0	0	.250
Oliva rf	4	0	2	0	0	0	.217
Killebrew 3b	4	0	0	0	0	0	.278
Battey c	4	1	1	0	0	0	.143
Allison lf	3	2	1	1	2	1	.167
Mincher 1b	3	0	0	0	0	1	.150
Quilici 2b	2	1	0	0	0	2	.176
Grant p	3	1	1	1	3	0	.250
TOTALS	**30**	**5**	**6**	**2**	**5**	**5**	**.211**

BATTING: 3B: Battey (1, Osteen). **HR:** Allison (1, 4th off Osteen 1 on, 0 out), Grant (1, 6th off Reed 2 on, 2 out). **SF:** Killebrew. **RBI:** Allison 2 (2), Grant 3 (3). **2-out RBI:** Grant 3. **Runners left in scoring position, 2 out:** Versalles 1, Killebrew 1, Grant 1. **GIDP:** Nossek. **Team LOB:** 6 **BASERUNNING: SB:** Allison (1, 2nd base off Reed/Roseboro). **FIELDING: E:** Killebrew (1). **DP:** 1 (Battey-Versalles).

LOS ANGELES	IP	H	R	ER	BB	SO	HR	ERA
Osteen (L, 1-1)	5	4	2	1	3	2	1	0.64
Reed	2	2	3	3	2	3	1	8.10
Miller	1	0	0	0	0	0	0	0.00

MINNESOTA	IP	H	R	ER	BB	SO	HR	ERA
Grant (W, 2-1)	9	6	1	1	0	5	1	2.74

IBB: Quilici (by Reed). **Ground balls-fly balls:** Osteen 10-3, Reed 1-2, Miller 1-2, Grant 11-11. **Batters faced:** Osteen 22, Reed 10, Miller 3, Grant 33. **UMPIRES:** hp—Vargo, 1b—Hurley, 2b—Venzon, 3b—Flaherty, lf—Sudol, rf—Stewart **T:** 2:16 **A:** 49,578

GAME 7 Los Angeles 2 Minnesota 0
Metropolitan Stadium 10/14/65

LOS ANGELES	AB	R	H	HR	RBI	BB	AVG
Wills ss	4	0	0	0	0	1	.367
Gilliam 3b	5	0	2	0	0	0	.214
Kennedy 3b	0	0	0	0	0	0	.000
Davis cf	2	0	0	0	0	0	.231
Johnson lf	4	1	1	1	1	0	.296
Fairly rf	4	1	1	0	0	0	.379
Parker 1b	4	0	2	0	1	0	.304
Tracewski 2b	4	0	0	0	0	0	.118
Roseboro c	2	0	1	0	0	2	.286
Koufax p	3	0	0	0	0	1	.111
TOTALS	**32**	**2**	**7**	**1**	**2**	**4**	**.274**

BATTING: 2B: Roseboro (1, Kaat), Fairly (3, Kaat). **3B:** Parker (1, Klippstein). **HR:** Johnson (2, 4th off Kaat 0 on, 0 out). **S:** Davis. **RBI:** Johnson 1 (5), Parker 1 (2). **Runners left in scoring position, 2 out:** Wills 2, Davis 2, Johnson 1, Fairly 2, Koufax 1. **Team LOB:** 9 **BASERUNNING: CS:** Wills (2, 2nd base off Perry/Battey).

MINNESOTA	AB	R	H	HR	RBI	BB	AVG
Versalles ss	4	0	1	0	0	0	.286
Nossek cf	4	0	0	0	0	0	.200
Oliva rf	3	0	0	0	0	1	.192
Killebrew 3b	3	0	1	0	0	1	.286
Battey c	4	0	0	0	0	0	.120
Allison lf	4	0	0	0	0	0	.125
Mincher 1b	3	0	0	0	0	0	.130
Quilici 2b	3	0	1	0	0	0	.200
Kaat p	1	0	0	0	0	0	.167
Worthington p	0	0	0	0	0	0	.000
a-Rollins ph	0	0	0	0	0	1	.000
Klippstein p	0	0	0	0	0	0	.000
Merritt p	0	0	0	0	0	0	.000
b-Valdespino ph	1	0	0	0	0	0	.273
Perry p	0	0	0	0	0	0	.000
TOTALS	**30**	**0**	**3**	**0**	**0**	**3**	**.195**

a - Batted for Worthington in the 5th
b - Batted for Merritt in the 8th

BATTING: 2B: Quilici (2, Koufax). **Runners left in scoring position, 2 out:** Nossek 1, Battey 1. **Team LOB:** 6 **FIELDING: E:** Oliva (1).

LOS ANGELES	IP	H	R	ER	BB	SO	HR	ERA
Koufax (W, 2-1)	9	3	0	0	3	10	0	0.38

MINNESOTA	IP	H	R	ER	BB	SO	HR	ERA
Kaat (L, 1-2)	3	5	2	2	1	2	1	3.77
Worthington	2	0	0	0	1	0	0	0.00
Klippstein	1.2	2	0	0	1	2	0	0.00
Merritt	1.1	0	0	0	0	1	0	2.70
Perry	1	0	0	0	1	1	0	4.50

IBB: Roseboro (by Klippstein). **HBP:** Davis (by Klippstein). **Ground balls-fly balls:** Koufax 8-9, Kaat 1-5, Worthington 2-4, Klippstein 2-1, Merritt 2-1, Perry 1-0. **Batters faced:** Koufax 33, Kaat 15, Worthington 7, Klippstein 9, Merritt 4, Perry 3. **UMPIRES:** hp—Hurley, 1b—Venzon, 2b—Flaherty, 3b—Sudol, lf—Stewart, rf—Vargo **T:** 2:27 **A:** 50,596

1966 BALTIMORE DEF. LOS ANGELES, 4-0

GAME 1 Baltimore 5 Los Angeles 2
Dodger Stadium 10/05/66

BALTIMORE	AB	R	H	HR	RBI	BB	AVG
Aparicio ss	5	0	0	0	1	0	.000
Snyder cf-lf	3	1	1	0	1	2	.333
F.Robinson rf	5	1	2	1	2	0	.400
B.Robinson 3b	5	1	1	1	1	0	.200
Powell 1b	5	0	1	0	0	0	.200
Blefary lf	3	0	1	0	0	1	.333
Blair cf	0	0	0	0	0	0	.000
D.Johnson 2b	4	1	2	0	0	0	.500
Etchebarren c	3	1	1	0	0	1	.333
McNally p	0	0	0	0	0	0	.000
Drabowsky p	2	0	0	0	0	1	.000
TOTALS	**35**	**5**	**9**	**2**	**5**	**5**	**.257**

BATTING: 2B: D.Johnson (1, Moeller), Powell (1, Miller). **HR:** F.Robinson (1, 1st off Drysdale 1 on, 1 out), B.Robinson (1, 1st off Drysdale 0 on, 1 out). **S:** McNally. **RBI:** Aparicio 1 (1), Snyder 1 (1), F.Robinson 2 (2), B.Robinson 1 (1). **2-out RBI:** Snyder 1. **Runners left in scoring position, 2 out:** F.Robinson 2, D.Johnson 1. **Team LOB:** 9

LOS ANGELES	AB	R	H	HR	RBI	BB	AVG
Wills ss	3	0	0	0	0	2	.000
W.Davis cf	4	0	1	0	0	0	.250
L.Johnson rf	3	1	0	0	0	1	.000
T.Davis lf	3	0	0	0	0	1	.000
Lefebvre 2b	3	1	1	1	1	1	.333
Parker 1b	4	0	1	0	0	0	.250
Gilliam 3b	2	0	0	0	1	2	.000
Roseboro c	4	0	0	0	0	0	.000
Drysdale p	0	0	0	0	0	0	.000
a-Stuart ph	1	0	0	0	0	0	.000
Moeller p	0	0	0	0	0	0	.000
b-Barbieri ph	1	0	0	0	0	0	.000
Miller p	0	0	0	0	0	0	.000
c-Covington ph	1	0	0	0	0	0	.000
Perranoski p	0	0	0	0	0	0	.000
d-Fairly ph	1	0	0	0	0	0	.000
TOTALS	**30**	**2**	**3**	**1**	**2**	**7**	**.100**

a - Batted for Drysdale in the 2nd
b - Batted for Moeller in the 4th
c - Batted for Miller in the 7th
d - Batted for Perranoski in the 9th

BATTING: 2B: Parker (1, McNally). **HR:** Lefebvre (1, 2nd off McNally 0 on, 0 out). **RBI:** Lefebvre 1 (1), Gilliam 1 (1). **2-out RBI:** Gilliam 1. **Runners left in scoring position, 2 out:** Wills 1, T.Davis 2, Roseboro 2. **Team LOB:** 8 **BASERUNNING: SB:** Wills (1, 2nd base off McNally/Etchebarren).

BALTIMORE	IP	H	R	ER	BB	SO	HR	ERA
McNally	2.1	2	2	2	5	1	1	7.71
Drabowsky (W, 1-0)	6.2	1	0	0	2	11	0	0.00

LOS ANGELES	IP	H	R	ER	BB	SO	HR	ERA
Drysdale (L, 0-1)	2	4	4	4	2	1	2	18.00
Moeller	2	1	1	1	1	0	0	4.50
Miller	3	2	0	0	2	1	0	0.00
Perranoski	2	2	0	0	0	1	0	0.00

IBB: Blefary (by Miller). **Ground balls-fly balls:** McNally 1-5, Drabowsky 3-6, Drysdale 0-4, Moeller 5-1, Miller 6-2, Perranoski 2-3. **Batters faced:** McNally 14, Drabowsky 23, Drysdale 12, Moeller 8, Miller 13, Perranoski 8. **UMPIRES:** hp—Jackowski, 1b—Chylak, 2b—Pelekoudas, 3b—Rice, lf—Steiner, rf—Drummond **T:** 2:56 **A:** 55,941

GAME 2 Baltimore 6 Los Angeles 0
Dodger Stadium 10/06/66

BALTIMORE	AB	R	H	HR	RBI	BB	AVG
Aparicio ss	5	0	2	0	1	0	.200
Blefary lf	5	0	0	0	0	0	.125
F.Robinson rf	3	2	1	0	0	2	.375
B.Robinson 3b	4	1	1	0	0	0	.222
Powell 1b	3	1	2	0	1	0	.375
D.Johnson 2b	4	0	2	0	2	0	.500
Blair cf	3	1	0	0	0	1	.000
Etchebarren c	3	1	0	0	1	1	.167
Palmer p	4	0	0	0	0	0	.000
TOTALS	**34**	**6**	**8**	**0**	**5**	**4**	**.246**

BATTING: 2B: Aparicio (1, Koufax). **3B:** F.Robinson (1, Koufax). **S:** Powell. **RBI:** Aparicio 1 (2), Powell 1 (1), D.Johnson 2 (2), Etchebarren 1 (1). **2-out RBI:** Aparicio 1. **Runners left in scoring position, 2 out:** Blefary 1, Palmer 2. **GIDP:** Etchebarren. **Team LOB:** 6

LOS ANGELES	AB	R	H	HR	RBI	BB	AVG
Wills ss	4	0	0	0	0	0	.000
Gilliam 3b	4	0	0	0	0	0	.000
W.Davis cf	4	0	0	0	0	0	.125
Fairly rf	3	0	0	0	0	1	.000
Lefebvre 2b	3	0	0	0	0	1	.167
L.Johnson lf	4	0	1	0	0	0	.143
Roseboro c	4	0	1	0	0	0	.125
Parker 1b	2	0	1	0	0	1	.333
Koufax p	2	0	0	0	0	0	.000
Perranoski p	0	0	0	0	0	0	.000
Regan p	0	0	0	0	0	0	.000
a-T.Davis ph	1	0	1	0	0	0	.250
Brewer p	0	0	0	0	0	0	.000
TOTALS	**31**	**0**	**4**	**0**	**0**	**3**	**.115**

a - Batted for Regan in the 8th

BATTING: 2B: L.Johnson (1, Palmer). **SF:** Gilliam. **Runners left in scoring position, 2 out:** W.Davis 1, Koufax 2. **Team LOB:** 7 **FIELDING: E:** Gilliam (1), W.Davis 2 (2), Fairly (1), Perranoski (1). **DP:** 1 (Gilliam-Roseboro-Parker).

BALTIMORE	IP	H	R	ER	BB	SO	HR	ERA
Palmer (W, 1-0)	9	4	0	0	3	6	0	0.00

LOS ANGELES	IP	H	R	ER	BB	SO	HR	ERA
Koufax (L, 0-1)	6	6	4	1	2	2	0	1.50
Perranoski	1.1	2	2	2	1	1	0	5.40
Regan	0.2	0	0	0	1	1	0	0.00
Brewer	1	0	0	0	0	1	0	0.00

WP: Palmer 1, Regan 1. **IBB:** Parker (by Palmer), Blair (by Koufax). **Ground balls-fly balls:** Palmer 8-13, Koufax 2-14, Perranoski 1-1, Regan 0-1, Brewer 1-1. **Batters faced:** Palmer 34, Koufax 26, Perranoski 7, Regan 3, Brewer 3. **UMPIRES:** hp—Chylak, 1b—Pelekoudas, 2b—Rice, 3b—Steiner, lf—Drummond, rf—Jackowski **T:** 2:26 **A:** 55,947

GAME 3 Baltimore 1 Los Angeles 0
Memorial Stadium 10/08/66

LOS ANGELES	AB	R	H	HR	RBI	BB	AVG
Wills ss	3	0	1	0	0	0	.100
Parker 1b	4	0	1	0	0	0	.300
Regan p	0	0	0	0	0	0	.000
W.Davis cf	4	0	0	0	0	0	.083
Fairly rf-1b	3	0	1	0	0	1	.143
Lefebvre 2b	4	0	0	0	0	0	.100
L.Johnson lf-rf	4	0	2	0	0	0	.273
Roseboro c	3	0	0	0	0	0	.091
Kennedy 3b	3	0	0	0	0	0	.000
Osteen p	2	0	0	0	0	0	.000
a-T.Davis ph-lf	1	0	1	0	0	0	.400
TOTALS	**31**	**0**	**6**	**0**	**0**	**1**	**.141**

a - Batted for Osteen in the 8th

BATTING: 2B: Parker (2, Bunker). **S:** Wills. **Runners left in scoring position, 2 out:** W.Davis 1, Fairly 1, Lefebvre 1. **GIDP:** L.Johnson. **Team LOB:** 6 **FIELDING: DP:** 2 (Wills-Lefebvre-Parker, Lefebvre-Wills-Parker).

BALTIMORE	AB	R	H	HR	RBI	BB	AVG
Aparicio ss	3	0	1	0	0	0	.231
Blefary lf	3	0	0	0	0	0	.091
Snyder lf	0	0	0	0	0	0	.333
F.Robinson rf	3	0	0	0	0	0	.273
B.Robinson 3b	2	0	0	0	0	1	.182
Powell 1b	3	0	1	0	0	0	.364
D.Johnson 2b	3	0	0	0	0	0	.364
Blair cf	3	1	1	1	1	0	.167
Etchebarren c	3	0	0	0	0	0	.111
Bunker p	2	0	0	0	0	0	.000
TOTALS	**25**	**1**	**3**	**1**	**1**	**1**	**.213**

BATTING: HR: Blair (1, 5th off Osteen 0 on, 2 out). **RBI:** Blair 1 (1). **2-out RBI:** Blair 1. **GIDP:** D.Johnson, Powell. **Team LOB:** 1 **FIELDING: DP:** 1 (Aparicio-D.Johnson-Powell).

LOS ANGELES	IP	H	R	ER	BB	SO	HR	ERA
Osteen (L, 0-1)	7	3	1	1	1	3	1	1.29
Regan	1	0	0	0	0	1	0	0.00

BALTIMORE	IP	H	R	ER	BB	SO	HR	ERA
Bunker (W, 1-0)	9	6	0	0	1	6	0	0.00

Ground balls-fly balls: Osteen 11-5, Regan 2-0, Bunker 10-9. **Batters faced:** Osteen 23, Regan 3, Bunker 33. **UMPIRES:** hp—Pelekoudas, 1b—Rice, 2b—Steiner, 3b—Drummond, lf—Jackowski, rf—Chylak **T:** 1:55 **A:** 54,445

GAME 4 Baltimore 1 Los Angeles 0
Memorial Stadium 10/09/66

LOS ANGELES	AB	R	H	HR	RBI	BB	AVG
Wills ss	3	0	0	0	0	1	.077
W.Davis cf	4	0	0	0	0	0	.063
L.Johnson rf	4	0	1	0	0	0	.267
T.Davis lf	3	0	0	0	0	0	.250
Lefebvre 2b	2	0	1	0	0	1	.167
Parker 1b	3	0	0	0	0	0	.231
Roseboro c	3	0	0	0	0	0	.071
Kennedy 3b	2	0	1	0	0	0	.200
a-Stuart ph	1	0	0	0	0	0	.000
Drysdale p	2	0	0	0	0	0	.000
b-Ferrara ph	1	0	1	0	0	0	1.000
c-Oliver pr	0	0	0	0	0	0	.000
TOTALS	**28**	**0**	**4**	**0**	**0**	**2**	**.142**

a - Batted for Kennedy in the 9th

b - Batted for Drysdale in the 9th
c - Ran for Ferrara in the 9th

BATTING: Runners left in scoring position, 2 out: L.Johnson 1. **GIDP:** T.Davis, Parker. **Team LOB:** 3 **BASERUNNING: CS:** Kennedy (1, 2nd base off McNally/Etchebarren). **FIELDING: DP:** 1 (Lefebvre-Wills-Parker).

BALTIMORE	AB	R	H	HR	RBI	BB	AVG
Aparicio ss	3	0	1	0	0	0	.250
Snyder cf-lf	3	0	0	0	0	0	.167
F.Robinson rf	3	1	1	1	1	0	.286
B.Robinson 3b	3	0	1	0	0	0	.214
Powell 1b	3	0	1	0	0	0	.357
Blefary lf	2	0	0	0	0	1	.077
Blair cf	0	0	0	0	0	0	.167
D.Johnson 2b	3	0	0	0	0	0	.286
Etchebarren c	3	0	0	0	0	0	.083
McNally p	3	0	0	0	0	0	.000
TOTALS	**26**	**1**	**4**	**1**	**1**	**1**	**.200**

BATTING: HR: F.Robinson (2, 4th off Drysdale 0 on, 1 out). **RBI:** F.Robinson 1 (3). **GIDP:** D.Johnson. **Team LOB:** 2 **BASERUNNING: CS:** Aparicio (1, 2nd base off Drysdale/Roseboro). **FIELDING: DP:** 3 (Aparicio-D.Johnson-Powell, B.Robinson-D.Johnson-Powell, Etchebarren-D.Johnson).

LOS ANGELES	IP	H	R	ER	BB	SO	HR	ERA
Drysdale (L, 0-2)	8	4	1	1	1	5	1	4.50

BALTIMORE	IP	H	R	ER	BB	SO	HR	ERA
McNally (W, 1-0)	9	4	0	0	2	4	0	1.59

Ground balls-fly balls: Drysdale 6-11, McNally 8-12. **Batters faced:** Drysdale 27, McNally 30. **UMPIRES:** hp—Rice, 1b—Steiner, 2b—Drummond, 3b—Jackowski, lf—Chylak, rf—Pelekoudas **T:** 1:45 **A:** 54,458

1967 ST.LOUIS DEF. BOSTON, 4-3

GAME 1 St. Louis 2 Boston 1
Fenway Park 10/04/67

ST.LOUIS	AB	R	H	HR	RBI	BB	AVG
Brock lf	4	2	4	0	0	1	1.000
Flood cf	5	0	1	0	0	0	.200
Maris rf	4	0	1	0	2	1	.250
Cepeda 1b	4	0	0	0	0	0	.000
McCarver c	3	0	0	0	0	1	.000
Shannon 3b	4	0	2	0	0	0	.500
Javier 2b	4	0	2	0	0	0	.500
Maxvill ss	2	0	0	0	0	2	.000
B.Gibson p	4	0	0	0	0	0	.000
TOTALS	**34**	**2**	**10**	**0**	**2**	**5**	**.294**

BATTING: 2B: Flood (1, Santiago). **RBI:** Maris 2 (2). **Runners left in scoring position, 2 out:** Brock 1, Maris 2, Shannon 1, B.Gibson 1. **GIDP:** Cepeda, B.Gibson. **Team LOB:** 10 **BASERUNNING: SB:** Brock 2 (2, 2nd base off Santiago/R.Gibson).

BOSTON	AB	R	H	HR	RBI	BB	AVG
Adair 2b	4	0	0	0	0	0	.000
Jones 3b	4	0	1	0	0	0	.250
Yastrzemski lf	4	0	0	0	0	0	.000
Harrelson rf	3	0	0	0	0	0	.000
Wyatt p	0	0	0	0	0	0	.000
c-Foy ph	1	0	0	0	0	0	.000
Scott 1b	3	0	2	0	0	1	.667
Petrocelli ss	3	0	0	0	0	0	.000
d-Andrews ph	1	0	0	0	0	0	.000
Smith cf	3	0	1	0	0	0	.333
R.Gibson c	2	0	0	0	0	0	.000
a-Siebern ph-rf	1	0	1	0	0	0	1.000
b-Tartabull pr-rf	0	0	0	0	0	0	.000
Santiago p	2	1	1	1	1	0	.500
Howard c	0	0	0	0	0	0	.000
TOTALS	**31**	**1**	**6**	**1**	**1**	**1**	**.194**

a - Batted for R.Gibson in the 7th
b - Ran for Siebern in the 8th
c - Batted for Wyatt in the 9th
d - Batted for Petrocelli in the 9th

BATTING: 2B: Scott (1, B.Gibson). **HR:** Santiago (1, 3th off B.Gibson 0 on, 1 out). **S:** Howard. **RBI:** Santiago 1 (1). **Runners left in scoring position, 2 out:** Jones 1, Petrocelli 1. **Team LOB:** 5 **BASERUNNING: CS:** Smith (1, 2nd base off B.Gibson/McCarver). **FIELDING: PB:** R.Gibson. **Outfield assists:** Yastrzemski (1). **DP:** 2 (Jones-Scott, Jones-Adair-Scott).

ST.LOUIS	IP	H	R	ER	BB	SO	HR	ERA
B.Gibson (W, 1-0)	9	6	1	1	1	10	1	1.00

BOSTON	IP	H	R	ER	BB	SO	HR	ERA
Santiago (L, 0-1)	7	10	2	2	3	5	0	2.57
Wyatt	2	0	0	0	2	1	0	0.00

BK: Wyatt 1. **Ground balls-fly balls:** B.Gibson 4-11, Santiago 6-7, Wyatt 0-5. **Batters faced:** B.Gibson 33, Santiago 31, Wyatt 8. **UMPIRES:** hp—Stevens, 1b—Barlick, 2b—Umont, 3b—Donatelli, lf—Runge, rf—Pryor **T:** 2:22 **A:** 34,796

GAME 2 Boston 5 St. Louis 0
Fenway Park 10/05/67

ST.LOUIS	AB	R	H	HR	RBI	BB	AVG
Brock lf	4	0	0	0	0	0	.500
Flood cf	3	0	0	0	0	1	.125
Maris rf	3	0	0	0	0	0	.143
Cepeda 1b	3	0	0	0	0	0	.000
McCarver c	3	0	0	0	0	0	.000
Shannon 3b	3	0	0	0	0	0	.286
Javier 2b	3	0	1	0	0	0	.429
Maxvill ss	2	0	0	0	0	0	.000
a-Tolan ph	1	0	0	0	0	0	.000
Bressoud ss	0	0	0	0	0	0	.000
Hughes p	2	0	0	0	0	0	.000
Willis p	0	0	0	0	0	0	.000
Hoerner p	0	0	0	0	0	0	.000
Lamabe p	0	0	0	0	0	0	.000
b-Ricketts ph	1	0	0	0	0	0	.000
TOTALS	**28**	**0**	**1**	**0**	**0**	**1**	**.177**

a - Batted for Maxvill in the 8th
b - Batted for Lamabe in the 9th

BATTING: 2B: Javier (1, Lonborg). **Runners left in scoring position, 2 out:** Tolan 1. **Team LOB:** 2 **FIELDING: E:** Shannon (1).

BOSTON	AB	R	H	HR	RBI	BB	AVG
Tartabull rf	4	1	0	0	0	1	.000
Jones 3b	5	1	2	0	0	0	.333
Yastrzemski lf	4	2	3	2	4	1	.375
Scott 1b	4	1	1	0	0	1	.429
Smith cf	3	0	0	0	0	1	.167
Adair 2b	4	0	2	0	0	0	.250
Petrocelli ss	2	0	1	0	1	1	.200
Howard c	3	0	0	0	0	1	.000
Lonborg p	4	0	0	0	0	0	.000
TOTALS	**33**	**5**	**9**	**2**	**5**	**6**	**.234**

BATTING: HR: Yastrzemski 2 (2, 4th off Hughes 0 on, 0 out, 7th off Hoerner 2 on, 0 out). **SF:** Petrocelli. **RBI:** Yastrzemski 4 (4), Petrocelli 1 (1). **Runners left in scoring position, 2 out:** Scott 1, Howard 2, Lonborg 2. **Team LOB:** 11 **BASERUNNING: SB:** Adair (1, 2nd base off Willis/McCarver).

ST.LOUIS	IP	H	R	ER	BB	SO	HR	ERA
Hughes (L, 0-1)	5.1	4	2	1	3	5	1	1.69
Willis	0.2	1	2	2	2	1	0	27.00
Hoerner	0.2	2	1	1	1	0	1	13.50
Lamabe	1.1	2	0	0	0	2	0	0.00

BOSTON	IP	H	R	ER	BB	SO	HR	ERA
Lonborg (W, 1-0)	9	1	0	0	1	4	0	0.00

IBB: Howard (by Willis). **Ground balls-fly balls:** Hughes 3-9, Willis 0-0, Hoerner 0-2, Lamabe 1-1, Lonborg 13-10. **Batters faced:** Hughes 24, Willis 5, Hoerner 5, Lamabe 6, Lonborg 29. **UMPIRES:** hp—Barlick, 1b—Umont, 2b—Donatelli, 3b—Runge, lf—Pryor, rf—Stevens **T:** 2:24 **A:** 35,188

GAME 3 St. Louis 5 Boston 2
Busch Stadium 10/07/67

BOSTON	AB	R	H	HR	RBI	BB	AVG
Tartabull rf	4	0	0	0	0	0	.000
Jones 3b	4	0	3	0	1	0	.462
Yastrzemski lf	3	0	0	0	0	0	.273
Scott 1b	4	0	0	0	0	0	.273
Smith cf	4	1	2	1	1	0	.300
Adair 2b	4	0	0	0	0	0	.167
Petrocelli ss	3	0	0	0	0	0	.125
Howard c	3	0	1	0	0	0	.167
Bell p	0	0	0	0	0	0	.000
a-Thomas ph	1	0	0	0	0	0	.000
Waslewski p	0	0	0	0	0	0	.000
b-Andrews ph	1	1	1	0	0	0	.500
Stange p	0	0	0	0	0	0	.000
c-Foy ph	1	0	0	0	0	0	.000
Osinski p	0	0	0	0	0	0	.000
TOTALS	**32**	**2**	**7**	**1**	**2**	**0**	**.229**

a - Batted for Bell in the 3th
b - Batted for Waslewski in the 6th
c - Batted for Stange in the 8th

BATTING: HR: Smith (1, 7th off Briles 0 on, 0 out). **RBI:** Jones 1 (1), Smith 1 (1). **Runners left in scoring position, 2 out:** Scott 1. **GIDP:** Yastrzemski. **Team LOB:** 4 **FIELDING: E:** Stange (1). **Outfield assists:** Yastrzemski (2). **DP:** 1 (Bell-Petrocelli-Scott).

ST.LOUIS	AB	R	H	HR	RBI	BB	AVG
Brock lf	4	2	2	0	0	0	.500
Flood cf	4	0	1	0	1	0	.167
Maris rf	4	1	2	0	1	0	.273
Cepeda 1b	4	0	1	0	1	0	.091
McCarver c	4	1	1	0	0	0	.100
Shannon 3b	3	1	2	1	2	0	.400
Javier 2b	3	0	1	0	0	0	.400
Maxvill ss	3	0	0	0	0	0	.000
Briles p	3	0	0	0	0	0	.000
TOTALS	**32**	**5**	**10**	**1**	**5**	**0**	**.223**

BATTING: 2B: Cepeda (1, Osinski). **3B:** Brock (1, Bell). **HR:** Shannon (1, 2nd off Bell 1 on, 0 out). **RBI:** Flood 1 (1), Maris 1 (3), Cepeda 1 (1), Shannon 2 (2). **2-out RBI:** Cepeda 1. **Runners left in scoring position, 2 out:** McCarver 1, Briles 1. **GIDP:** Maris. **Team LOB:** 3 **FIELDING: DP:** 1 (Javier-Maxvill-Cepeda).

BOSTON	IP	H	R	ER	BB	SO	HR	ERA
Bell (L, 0-1)	2	5	3	3	0	1	1	13.50
Waslewski	3	0	0	0	0	3	0	0.00
Stange	2	3	1	0	0	0	0	0.00
Osinski	1	2	1	1	0	0	0	9.00

ST.LOUIS	IP	H	R	ER	BB	SO	HR	ERA
Briles (W, 1-0)	9	7	2	2	0	4	1	2.00

HBP: Yastrzemski (by Briles). **Ground balls-fly balls:** Bell 2-1, Waslewski 4-2, Stange 1-5, Osinski 2-1, Briles 12-9. **Batters faced:** Bell 9, Waslewski 9, Stange 9, Osinski 5, Briles 33. **UMPIRES:** hp—Umont, 1b—Donatelli, 2b—Runge, 3b—Pryor, lf—Stevens, rf—Barlick **T:** 2:15 **A:** 54,575

GAME 4 St. Louis 6 Boston 0
Busch Stadium 10/08/67

BOSTON	AB	R	H	HR	RBI	BB	AVG
Tartabull rf	4	0	2	0	0	0	.167
Jones 3b	4	0	0	0	0	0	.353
Yastrzemski lf	4	0	2	0	0	0	.333
Scott 1b	4	0	1	0	0	0	.267
Smith cf	3	0	0	0	0	1	.231
Adair 2b	4	0	0	0	0	0	.125
Petrocelli ss	3	0	0	0	0	0	.091
Howard c	2	0	0	0	0	0	.125
Morehead p	0	0	0	0	0	0	.000
b-Siebern ph	1	0	0	0	0	0	.500
Brett p	0	0	0	0	0	0	.000
Santiago p	0	0	0	0	0	0	.500
Bell p	0	0	0	0	0	0	.000
a-Foy ph	1	0	0	0	0	0	.000
Stephenson p	0	0	0	0	0	0	.000
Ryan c	2	0	0	0	0	0	.000
TOTALS	**32**	**0**	**5**	**0**	**0**	**1**	**.211**

a - Batted for Bell in the 3th
b - Batted for Morehead in the 8th

BATTING: 2B: Yastrzemski (1, B.Gibson). **Runners left in scoring position, 2 out:** Adair 1. **Team LOB:** 6

ST.LOUIS	AB	R	H	HR	RBI	BB	AVG
Brock lf	4	1	2	0	0	0	.500
Flood cf	4	1	1	0	0	0	.188
Maris rf	4	1	1	0	2	0	.267
Cepeda 1b	4	1	1	0	0	0	.133
McCarver c	3	1	1	0	2	0	.154
Shannon 3b	3	1	0	0	0	1	.308
Javier 2b	4	0	2	0	1	0	.429
Maxvill ss	3	0	1	0	1	1	.100
B.Gibson p	3	0	0	0	0	1	.000
TOTALS	**32**	**6**	**9**	**0**	**6**	**3**	**.238**

BATTING: 2B: Maris (1, Santiago), Cepeda (2, Stephenson), Javier (2, Stephenson), Brock (1, Stephenson). **SF:** McCarver. **RBI:** Maris 2 (5), McCarver 2 (2), Javier 1 (1), Maxvill 1 (1). **2-out RBI:** Maxvill 1. **Runners left in scoring position, 2 out:** Flood 1, Cepeda 1, B.Gibson 3. **Team LOB:** 6 **BASERUNNING: SB:** Brock (3, 2nd base off Morehead/Ryan).

BOSTON	IP	H	R	ER	BB	SO	HR	ERA
Santiago (L, 0-2)	0.2	6	4	4	0	0	0	7.04
Bell	1.1	0	0	0	0	0	0	8.10
Stephenson	2	3	2	2	1	0	0	9.00
Morehead	3	0	0	0	1	2	0	0.00
Brett	1	0	0	0	1	1	0	0.00

ST.LOUIS	IP	H	R	ER	BB	SO	HR	ERA
B.Gibson (W, 2-0)	9	5	0	0	1	6	0	0.50

WP: Stephenson 1. **Ground balls-fly balls:** Santiago 0-2, Bell 1-3, Stephenson 4-1, Morehead 4-3, Brett 1-1, B.Gibson 11-10. **Batters faced:** Santiago 8, Bell 4, Stephenson 10, Morehead 10, Brett 4, B.Gibson 33. **UMPIRES:** hp—Donatelli, 1b—Runge, 2b—Pryor, 3b—Stevens, lf—Barlick, rf—Umont **T:** 2:05 **A:** 54,575

GAME 5 Boston 3 St. Louis 1
Busch Stadium 10/09/67

BOSTON	AB	R	H	HR	RBI	BB	AVG
Foy 3b	5	1	1	0	0	0	.125
Andrews 2b	3	0	1	0	0	0	.400
Yastrzemski lf	3	0	1	0	0	1	.333
Harrelson rf	3	0	1	0	1	1	.167
Tartabull rf	0	0	0	0	0	0	.167
Scott 1b	3	1	0	0	0	1	.222
Smith cf	4	1	1	0	0	0	.235
Petrocelli ss	3	0	0	0	0	1	.071
Howard c	4	0	1	0	2	0	.167
Lonborg p	4	0	0	0	0	0	.000
TOTALS	**32**	**3**	**6**	**0**	**3**	**4**	**.206**

BATTING: 2B: Yastrzemski (2, Washburn), Smith (1, Willis). **S:** Andrews, Foy, Petrocelli. **RBI:** Harrelson 1 (1), Howard 2 (2). **2-out RBI:** Harrelson 1. **Runners left in scoring position, 2 out:** Harrelson 1, Scott 1. **GIDP:** Scott. **Team LOB:** 7 **FIELDING: E:** Petrocelli (1).

ST.LOUIS	AB	R	H	HR	RBI	BB	AVG
Brock lf	4	0	0	0	0	0	.400
Flood cf	4	0	0	0	0	0	.150
Maris rf	4	1	2	1	1	0	.316
Cepeda 1b	4	0	0	0	0	0	.105
McCarver c	3	0	0	0	0	0	.125
Shannon 3b	3	0	0	0	0	0	.250
Javier 2b	3	0	0	0	0	0	.353
Maxvill ss	2	0	1	0	0	0	.167
b-Ricketts ph	1	0	0	0	0	0	.000
Willis p	0	0	0	0	0	0	.000
Lamabe p	0	0	0	0	0	0	.000
Carlton p	1	0	0	0	0	0	.000
a-Tolan ph	1	0	0	0	0	0	.000
Washburn p	0	0	0	0	0	0	.000
c-Gagliano ph	1	0	0	0	0	0	.000
Bressoud ss	0	0	0	0	0	0	.000
TOTALS	**31**	**1**	**3**	**1**	**1**	**0**	**.210**

a - Batted for Carlton in the 6th
b - Batted for Maxvill in the 8th
c - Batted for Washburn in the 8th

BATTING: HR: Maris (1, 9th off Lonborg 0 on, 2 out). **RBI:** Maris 1 (6). **2-out RBI:** Maris 1. **Runners left in scoring position, 2 out:** Gagliano 1. **Team LOB:** 3 **FIELDING: E:** Shannon (2), Maris (1). **DP:** 2 (Javier-Maxvill-Cepeda, McCarver-Javier-McCarver-Shannon-Lamabe-McCarver).

BOSTON	IP	H	R	ER	BB	SO	HR	ERA
Lonborg (W, 2-0)	9	3	1	1	0	4	1	0.50

ST.LOUIS	IP	H	R	ER	BB	SO	HR	ERA
Carlton (L, 0-1)	6	3	1	0	2	5	0	0.00
Washburn	2	1	0	0	0	2	0	0.00
Willis	0	1	2	1	2	0	0	40.50
Lamabe	1	1	0	0	0	2	0	0.00

WP: Carlton 1. **IBB:** Petrocelli (by Willis). **Ground balls-fly balls:** Lonborg 15-9, Carlton 5-8, Washburn 3-1, Willis 0-0, Lamabe 0-0. **Batters faced:** Lonborg 31, Carlton 24, Washburn 7, Willis 3, Lamabe 3. **UMPIRES:** hp—Runge, 1b—Pryor, 2b—Stevens, 3b—Barlick, lf—Umont, rf—Donatelli **T:** 2:20 **A:** 54,575

GAME 6 Boston 8 St. Louis 4
Fenway Park 10/11/67

ST.LOUIS	AB	R	H	HR	RBI	BB	AVG
Brock lf	5	2	2	1	3	0	.400
Flood cf	5	0	1	0	1	0	.160
Maris rf	4	0	2	0	0	1	.348
Cepeda 1b	5	0	1	0	0	0	.125
McCarver c	3	0	0	0	0	1	.105
Shannon 3b	4	0	1	0	0	0	.250
Javier 2b	4	1	1	0	0	0	.333
Maxvill ss	3	0	0	0	0	1	.133
Hughes p	1	0	0	0	0	0	.000
Willis p	0	0	0	0	0	0	.000
a-Spiezio ph	1	0	0	0	0	0	.000
Briles p	0	0	0	0	0	0	.000
b-Tolan ph	0	1	0	0	0	1	.000
Lamabe p	0	0	0	0	0	0	.000
Hoerner p	0	0	0	0	0	0	.000
Jaster p	0	0	0	0	0	0	.000
Washburn p	0	0	0	0	0	0	.000
c-Ricketts ph	1	0	0	0	0	0	.000
Woodeshick p	0	0	0	0	0	0	.000
TOTALS	**36**	**4**	**8**	**1**	**4**	**4**	**.212**

a - Batted for Willis in the 5th
b - Batted for Briles in the 7th
c - Batted for Washburn in the 8th

BATTING: 2B: Javier (3, Waslewski), Shannon (1, Bell). **HR:** Brock (1, 7th off Wyatt 1 on, 1 out). **RBI:** Brock 3 (3), Flood 1 (2). **2-out RBI:** Brock 1, Flood 1. **Runners left in scoring position, 2 out:** Cepeda 1, Javier 1, Ricketts 2. **Team LOB:** 9 **BASERUNNING: SB:** Brock (4, 2nd base off Waslewski/Howard).

BOSTON	AB	R	H	HR	RBI	BB	AVG
Foy 3b	4	1	1	0	1	0	.167
Andrews 2b	5	1	2	0	1	0	.400
Yastrzemski lf	4	2	3	1	1	1	.409
Harrelson rf	3	0	0	0	0	0	.111
Tartabull rf	0	0	0	0	0	0	.167
b-Adair ph	0	0	0	0	1	0	.125
Bell p	0	0	0	0	0	0	.000
Scott 1b	4	0	1	0	0	0	.227
Smith cf	4	1	2	1	2	0	.286
Petrocelli ss	3	2	2	2	2	1	.176
Howard c	4	0	0	0	0	0	.125
Waslewski p	1	0	0	0	0	0	.000
Wyatt p	0	0	0	0	0	0	.000
a-Jones ph	1	1	1	0	0	0	.389
Thomas rf	1	0	0	0	0	0	.000
TOTALS	**34**	**8**	**12**	**4**	**8**	**2**	**.232**

a - Batted for Wyatt in the 7th
b - Batted for Tartabull in the 7th

BATTING: 2B: Foy (1, Lamabe). **HR:** Petrocelli 2 (2, 2nd off Hughes 0 on, 2 out, 4th off Hughes 0 on, 2 out), Yastrzemski (3, 4th off Hughes 0 on, 0 out), Smith (2, 4th off Hughes 0 on, 2 out). **S:** Foy. **SF:** Adair. **RBI:** Foy 1 (1), Andrews 1 (1), Yastrzemski 1 (5), Adair 1 (1), Smith 2 (3), Petrocelli 2 (3). **2-out RBI:** Smith 2, Petrocelli 2. **Runners left in scoring position, 2 out:** Harrelson 1, Howard 2. **Team LOB:** 7 **FIELDING: E:** Petrocelli (2).

ST.LOUIS	IP	H	R	ER	BB	SO	HR	ERA
Hughes	3.2	5	4	4	0	2	4	5.00
Willis	0.1	0	0	0	0	0	0	27.00
Briles	2	0	0	0	1	0	0	1.64
Lamabe (L, 0-1)	0.1	2	2	2	0	0	0	6.75
Hoerner	0	2	2	2	0	0	0	40.50
Jaster	0.1	2	0	0	0	0	0	0.00
Washburn	0.1	0	0	0	1	0	0	0.00
Woodeshick	1	1	0	0	0	0	0	0.00

BOSTON	IP	H	R	ER	BB	SO	HR	ERA
Waslewski	5.1	4	2	2	2	4	0	2.16
Wyatt (W, 1-0)	1.2	1	2	2	1	0	1	4.91
Bell (S, 1)	2	3	0	0	1	0	0	5.06

IBB: Yastrzemski (by Briles), Petrocelli (by Washburn). **HBP:** Waslewski (by Briles). **Ground balls-fly balls:** Hughes 2-7, Willis 1-0, Briles 3-2, Lamabe 1-0, Hoerner 0-0, Jaster 0-0, Washburn 1-0, Woodeshick 3-0, Waslewski 9-4, Wyatt 1-4, Bell 2-4. **Batters faced:** Hughes 16, Willis 1, Briles 8, Lamabe 3, Hoerner 2, Jaster 3, Washburn 2, Woodeshick 4, Waslewski 23, Wyatt 7, Bell 10. **UMPIRES:** hp—Pryor, 1b—Stevens, 2b—Barlick, 3b—Umont, lf—Donatelli, rf—Runge **T:** 2:48 **A:** 35,188

GAME 7 St. Louis 7 Boston 2
Fenway Park 10/12/67

ST.LOUIS	AB	R	H	HR	RBI	BB	AVG
Brock lf	4	1	2	0	0	1	.414
Flood cf	3	1	1	0	1	2	.179
Maris rf	3	0	2	0	1	1	.385
Cepeda 1b	5	0	0	0	0	0	.103
McCarver c	5	1	1	0	0	0	.125
Shannon 3b	4	1	0	0	0	0	.208
Javier 2b	4	1	2	1	3	0	.360
Maxvill ss	4	1	1	0	0	0	.158
B.Gibson p	4	1	1	1	1	0	.091
TOTALS	**36**	**7**	**10**	**2**	**6**	**4**	**.223**

BATTING: 2B: McCarver (1, Lonborg), Brock (2, Lonborg). **3B:** Maxvill (1, Lonborg). **HR:** B.Gibson (1, 5th off Lonborg 0 on, 1 out), Javier (1, 6th off Lonborg 2 on, 0 out). **SF:** Maris. **RBI:** Flood 1 (3), Maris 1 (7), Javier 3 (4), B.Gibson 1 (1). **2-out RBI:** Flood 1. **Runners left in scoring position, 2 out:** Flood 1, Cepeda 1, McCarver 2. **Team LOB:** 7 **BASERUNNING: SB:** Brock 3 (7, 2nd base off Lonborg/Howard, 3rd base off Lonborg/Howard, 2nd base off Morehead/R.Gibson). **CS:** Javier (1, 2nd base off Lonborg/Howard). **FIELDING: E:** Javier (1). **DP:** 1 (Maxvill-Javier-Cepeda).

BOSTON	AB	R	H	HR	RBI	BB	AVG
Foy 3b	3	0	0	0	0	1	.133
Morehead p	0	0	0	0	0	0	.000
Osinski p	0	0	0	0	0	0	.000
Brett p	0	0	0	0	0	0	.000
Andrews 2b	3	0	0	0	0	0	.308
Yastrzemski lf	3	0	1	0	0	1	.400
Harrelson rf	4	0	0	0	0	0	.077
Scott 1b	4	1	1	0	1	0	.231
Smith cf	3	0	0	0	0	0	.250
Petrocelli ss	3	1	1	0	0	0	.200
Howard c	2	0	0	0	0	0	.111
b-Jones ph-3b	0	0	0	0	0	1	.389
Lonborg p	1	0	0	0	0	0	.000
a-Tartabull ph	1	0	0	0	0	0	.154
Santiago p	0	0	0	0	0	0	.500
c-Siebern ph	1	0	0	0	1	0	.333
R.Gibson c	0	0	0	0	0	0	.000
TOTALS	**28**	**2**	**3**	**0**	**2**	**3**	**.216**

a - Batted for Lonborg in the 6th
b - Batted for Howard in the 8th
c - Batted for Santiago in the 8th

BATTING: 2B: Petrocelli (1, B.Gibson). **3B:** Scott (1, B.Gibson). **S:** Andrews. **RBI:** Scott 1 (1), Siebern 1 (1). **Runners left in scoring position, 2 out:** Harrelson 1. **GIDP:** Harrelson. **Team LOB:** 3 **FIELDING: E:** Foy (1).

ST.LOUIS	IP	H	R	ER	BB	SO	HR	ERA
B.Gibson (W, 3-0)	9	3	2	2	3	10	0	1.00

BOSTON	IP	H	R	ER	BB	SO	HR	ERA
Lonborg (L, 2-1)	6	10	7	6	1	3	2	2.63
Santiago	2	0	0	0	0	1	0	5.59
Morehead	0.1	0	0	0	3	1	0	0.00
Osinski	0.1	0	0	0	0	0	0	6.75
Brett	0.1	0	0	0	0	0	0	0.00

WP: B.Gibson 1, Lonborg 1. **Ground balls-fly balls:** B.Gibson 8-7, Lonborg 7-7, Santiago 1-4, Morehead 0-0, Osinski 0-1, Brett 1-0. **Batters faced:** B.Gibson 32, Lonborg 29, Santiago 6, Morehead 4, Osinski 1, Brett 1. **UMPIRES:** hp—Stevens, 1b—Barlick, 2b—Umont, 3b—Donatelli, lf—Runge, rf—Pryor **T:** 2:23 **A:** 35,188

1968 DETROIT DEF. ST.LOUIS, 4-3

GAME 1 St. Louis 4 Detroit 0
Busch Stadium 10/02/68

DETROIT	AB	R	H	HR	RBI	BB	AVG
McAuliffe 2b	4	0	1	0	0	0	.250
Stanley ss	4	0	2	0	0	0	.500
Kaline rf	4	0	1	0	0	0	.250
Cash 1b	4	0	0	0	0	0	.000
Horton lf	4	0	0	0	0	0	.000
Northrup cf	3	0	0	0	0	0	.000
Freehan c	2	0	0	0	0	1	.000
Wert 3b	2	0	1	0	0	0	.500
b-Mathews ph	1	0	0	0	0	0	.000
Tracewski 3b	0	0	0	0	0	0	.000
McLain p	1	0	0	0	0	0	.000
a-Matchick ph	1	0	0	0	0	0	.000
Dobson p	0	0	0	0	0	0	.000
c-Brown ph	1	0	0	0	0	0	.000
McMahon p	0	0	0	0	0	0	.000
TOTALS	**31**	**0**	**5**	**0**	**0**	**1**	**.161**

a - Batted for McLain in the 6th
b - Batted for Wert in the 8th
c - Batted for Dobson in the 8th

BATTING: 2B: Kaline (1, Gibson). **Runners left in scoring position, 2 out:** Cash 2. **Team LOB:** 5 **BASERUNNING: CS:** Stanley (1, 2nd base off Gibson/McCarver). **FIELDING: E:** Freehan (1), Northrup (1), Cash (1).

ST.LOUIS	AB	R	H	HR	RBI	BB	AVG
Brock lf	4	1	1	1	1	0	.250
Flood cf	4	0	1	0	0	0	.250
Maris rf	3	1	0	0	0	1	.000
Cepeda 1b	4	0	0	0	0	0	.000
McCarver c	3	1	1	0	0	1	.333
Shannon 3b	4	1	2	0	1	0	.500
Javier 2b	3	0	1	0	2	1	.333
Maxvill ss	2	0	0	0	0	1	.000
Gibson p	2	0	0	0	0	0	.000
TOTALS	**29**	**4**	**6**	**1**	**4**	**4**	**.207**

BATTING: 3B: McCarver (1, McLain). **HR:** Brock (1, 7th off Dobson 0 on, 2 out). **S:** Gibson. **RBI:** Brock 1 (1), Shannon 1 (1), Javier 2 (2). **2-out RBI:** Brock 1. **Runners left in scoring position, 2 out:** Flood 1, Maris 1, Javier 1, Gibson 1. **Team LOB:** 6 **BASERUNNING: SB:** Brock (1, 2nd base off McLain/Freehan), Javier (1, 2nd base off McLain/Freehan), Flood (1, 2nd base off Dobson/Freehan). **CS:** Javier (1, 2nd base off Dobson/Freehan).

DETROIT	IP	H	R	ER	BB	SO	HR	ERA
McLain (L, 0-1)	5	3	3	2	3	3	0	3.60
Dobson	2	2	1	1	1	0	1	4.50
McMahon	1	1	0	0	0	0	0	0.00

ST.LOUIS	IP	H	R	ER	BB	SO	HR	ERA
Gibson (W, 1-0)	9	5	0	0	1	17	0	0.00

Ground balls-fly balls: McLain 4-8, Dobson 1-4, McMahon 1-2, Gibson 2-7. **Batters faced:** McLain 22, Dobson 8, McMahon 4, Gibson 32. **UMPIRES:** hp—Gorman, 1b—Honochick, 2b—Landes, 3b—Kinnamon, lf—Harvey, rf—Haller **T:** 2:29 **A:** 54,692

GAME 2 Detroit 8 St. Louis 1
Busch Stadium 10/03/68

DETROIT	AB	R	H	HR	RBI	BB	AVG
McAuliffe 2b	5	0	2	0	2	1	.333
Stanley ss-cf	5	0	1	0	0	0	.333
Kaline rf	5	2	2	0	0	0	.333
Cash 1b	5	2	3	1	1	0	.333
Horton lf	3	2	2	1	1	1	.286
Oyler ss	0	0	0	0	0	0	.000
Northrup cf-lf	5	1	1	0	0	0	.125
Freehan c	4	0	0	0	0	1	.000
Wert 3b	2	0	0	0	1	3	.250
Lolich p	4	1	2	1	2	1	.500
TOTALS	**38**	**8**	**13**	**3**	**7**	**7**	**.261**

BATTING: HR: Horton (1, 2nd off Briles 0 on, 1 out), Lolich (1, 3th off Briles 0 on, 1 out), Cash (1, 6th off Briles 0 on, 0 out). **S:** Oyler. **RBI:** McAuliffe 2 (2), Cash 1 (1), Horton 1 (1), Wert 1 (1), Lolich 2 (2). **2-out RBI:** McAuliffe 2, Wert 1, Lolich 1. **Runners left in scoring position, 2 out:** McAuliffe 2, Stanley 2, Kaline 1, Freehan 1. **GIDP:** Northrup, Stanley. **Team LOB:** 11 **FIELDING: E:** Stanley (1). **DP:** 1 (Stanley-McAuliffe-Cash).

ST.LOUIS	AB	R	H	HR	RBI	BB	AVG
Brock lf	3	1	1	0	0	1	.286
Javier 2b	4	0	2	0	0	0	.429
Flood cf	3	0	1	0	0	1	.286
Cepeda 1b	4	0	2	0	1	0	.250
Shannon 3b	4	0	0	0	0	0	.250
McCarver c	4	0	0	0	0	0	.143
Davis rf	4	0	0	0	0	0	.000
Maxvill ss	3	0	0	0	0	0	.000
Briles p	2	0	0	0	0	0	.000
Carlton p	0	0	0	0	0	0	.000
Willis p	0	0	0	0	0	0	.000
a-Gagliano ph	1	0	0	0	0	0	.000
Hoerner p	0	0	0	0	0	0	.000
TOTALS	**32**	**1**	**6**	**0**	**1**	**2**	**.197**

a - Batted for Willis in the 8th

BATTING: RBI: Cepeda 1 (1). **Runners left in scoring position, 2 out:** Flood 2, Shannon 1. **GIDP:** Shannon. **Team LOB:** 6 **BASERUNNING: SB:** Brock 2 (3, 2nd base off Lolich/Freehan). **FIELDING: E:** Shannon (1). **DP:** 2 (Maxvill-Cepeda, Javier-Maxvill-Cepeda).

DETROIT	IP	H	R	ER	BB	SO	HR	ERA
Lolich (W, 1-0)	9	6	1	1	2	9	0	1.00

ST.LOUIS	IP	H	R	ER	BB	SO	HR	ERA
Briles (L, 0-1)	5	7	4	4	1	2	3	7.20
Carlton	1	4	2	2	1	1	0	18.00
Willis	2	1	0	0	2	2	0	0.00
Hoerner	1	1	2	0	3	1	0	0.00

IBB: Freehan (by Hoerner). **Ground balls-fly balls:** Lolich 9-8, Briles 5-8, Carlton 0-2, Willis 2-0, Hoerner 1-1. **Batters faced:** Lolich 34, Briles 23, Carlton 8, Willis 7, Hoerner 8. **UMPIRES:** hp—Honochick, 1b—Landes, 2b—Kinnamon, 3b—Harvey, lf—Haller, rf—Gorman **T:** 2:41 **A:** 54,692

GAME 3 St. Louis 7 Detroit 3
Tiger Stadium 10/05/68

ST.LOUIS	AB	R	H	HR	RBI	BB	AVG
Brock lf	4	1	3	0	0	1	.455
Flood cf	4	2	2	0	1	1	.364
Maris rf	3	2	1	0	0	2	.167
Cepeda 1b	5	1	1	1	3	0	.231
McCarver c	5	1	2	1	3	0	.250
Shannon 3b	4	0	2	0	0	1	.333
Javier 2b	4	0	1	0	0	1	.364
Maxvill ss	4	0	0	0	0	1	.000
Washburn p	3	0	0	0	0	0	.000
Hoerner p	2	0	1	0	0	0	.500
TOTALS	**38**	**7**	**13**	**2**	**7**	**7**	**.253**

BATTING: 2B: Flood (1, Wilson), Maris (1, McMahon). **HR:** McCarver (1, 5th off Dobson 2 on, 2 out), Cepeda (1, 7th off McMahon 2 on, 0 out). **RBI:** Flood 1 (1), Cepeda 3 (4), McCarver 3 (3). **2-out RBI:** McCarver 3. **Runners left in scoring position, 2 out:** Maris 1, Cepeda 1, Maxvill 1, Hoerner 2. **Team LOB:** 11 **BASERUNNING: SB:** Brock 3 (6, 2nd base off Wilson/Freehan). **CS:** Brock (1, 3rd base off Wilson/Freehan), McCarver (1, 3rd base off Wilson/Freehan).

DETROIT	AB	R	H	HR	RBI	BB	AVG
McAuliffe 2b	4	2	2	1	1	0	.385
Stanley ss	3	0	0	0	0	1	.250
Kaline rf	4	1	1	1	2	0	.308
Cash 1b	3	0	0	0	0	1	.250
Horton lf	2	0	0	0	0	2	.222
Northrup cf	4	0	0	0	0	0	.083
Freehan c	3	0	0	0	0	1	.000
Wert 3b	4	0	0	0	0	0	.125
Wilson p	1	0	0	0	0	0	.000
Dobson p	0	0	0	0	0	0	.000
a-Matchick ph	1	0	0	0	0	0	.000
McMahon p	0	0	0	0	0	0	.000
Patterson p	0	0	0	0	0	0	.000
b-Comer ph	1	0	1	0	0	0	1.000
Hiller p	0	0	0	0	0	0	.000
c-Price ph	1	0	0	0	0	0	.000
TOTALS	**31**	**3**	**4**	**2**	**3**	**5**	**.220**

a - Batted for Dobson in the 5th
b - Batted for Patterson in the 7th
c - Batted for Hiller in the 9th

BATTING: HR: Kaline (1, 3th off Washburn 1 on, 2 out), McAuliffe (1, 5th off Washburn 0 on, 2 out). **RBI:** McAuliffe 1 (3), Kaline 2 (2). **2-out RBI:** McAuliffe 1, Kaline 2. **Runners left in scoring position, 2 out:** Kaline 1, Freehan 1, Wert 1. **Team LOB:** 6 **FIELDING: DP:** 2 (Freehan-Wert 2).

ST.LOUIS	IP	H	R	ER	BB	SO	HR	ERA
Washburn (W, 1-0)	5.1	3	3	3	4	3	2	5.06
Hoerner (S, 1)	3.2	1	0	0	1	2	0	0.00

DETROIT	IP	H	R	ER	BB	SO	HR	ERA
Wilson (L, 0-1)	4.1	4	3	3	6	3	0	6.23
Dobson	0.2	2	1	1	0	0	1	6.75
McMahon	1	3	3	3	0	1	1	13.50
Patterson	1	0	0	0	0	0	0	0.00
Hiller	2	4	0	0	1	1	0	0.00

Ground balls-fly balls: Washburn 8-5, Hoerner 3-6, Wilson 4-4, Dobson 0-2, McMahon 1-1, Patterson 1-2, Hiller 2-3. **Batters faced:** Washburn 23, Hoerner 13, Wilson 21, Dobson 4, McMahon 6, Patterson 3, Hiller 11. **UMPIRES:** hp—Landes, 1b—Kinnamon, 2b—Harvey, 3b—Haller, lf—Gorman, rf—Honochick **T:** 3:17 **A:** 53,634

GAME 4 St. Louis 10 Detroit 1
Tiger Stadium 10/06/68

ST.LOUIS	AB	R	H	HR	RBI	BB	AVG
Brock lf	5	2	3	1	4	0	.500
Flood cf	5	1	1	0	0	0	.313
Maris rf	5	1	0	0	1	0	.091
Cepeda 1b	4	0	1	0	0	1	.235
McCarver c	5	1	3	0	1	0	.353
Shannon 3b	5	1	2	0	2	0	.353
Javier 2b	4	1	2	0	0	1	.400
Maxvill ss	4	1	0	0	0	1	.000
Gibson p	3	2	1	1	2	1	.200
TOTALS	**40**	**10**	**13**	**2**	**10**	**4**	**.273**

BATTING: 2B: Shannon (1, McLain), Javier (1, Hiller), Brock (1, Hiller). **3B:** McCarver (2, McLain), Brock (1, Sparma). **HR:** Brock

(2, 1st off McLain 0 on, 0 out), Gibson (1, 4th off Sparma 0 on, 0 out). **RBI:** Brock 4 (5), Maris 1 (1), McCarver 1 (4), Shannon 2 (3), Gibson 2 (2). **2-out RBI:** McCarver 1, Shannon 2. **Runners left in scoring position, 2 out:** Cepeda 1, Javier 1, Maxvill 2. **Team LOB:** 7 **BASERUNNING: SB:** Brock (7, 3rd base off Dobson/Freehan). **CS:** Cepeda (1, 2nd base off Patterson/Freehan). **FIELDING: DP:** 1 (Cepeda-Maxvill).

DETROIT	AB	R	H	HR	RBI	BB	AVG
McAuliffe 2b	4	0	0	0	0	0	.294
Stanley ss	4	0	0	0	0	0	.188
Kaline rf	4	0	2	0	0	0	.353
Cash 1b	4	0	1	0	0	0	.250
Horton lf	3	0	0	0	0	1	.167
Northrup cf	4	1	1	1	1	0	.125
Mathews 3b	2	0	1	0	0	1	.333
Freehan c	3	0	0	0	0	0	.000
McLain p	1	0	0	0	0	0	.000
Sparma p	0	0	0	0	0	0	.000
Patterson p	0	0	0	0	0	0	.000
a-Price ph	1	0	0	0	0	0	.000
Lasher p	0	0	0	0	0	0	.000
b-Matchick ph	1	0	0	0	0	0	.000
Hiller p	0	0	0	0	0	0	.000
Dobson p	0	0	0	0	0	0	.000
TOTALS	**31**	**1**	**5**	**1**	**1**	**2**	**.206**

a - Batted for Patterson in the 5th
b - Batted for Lasher in the 7th

BATTING: 2B: Kaline (2, Gibson). **HR:** Northrup (1, 4th off Gibson 0 on, 1 out). **RBI:** Northrup 1 (1). **Runners left in scoring position, 2 out:** Cash 1, McLain 1. **GIDP:** Northrup. **Team LOB:** 5 **FIELDING: E:** Freehan (2), Mathews (1), Northrup (2).

ST.LOUIS	IP	H	R	ER	BB	SO	HR	ERA
Gibson (W, 2-0)	9	5	1	1	2	10	1	0.50

DETROIT	IP	H	R	ER	BB	SO	HR	ERA
McLain (L, 0-2)	2.2	6	4	3	1	3	1	5.87
Sparma	0.1	2	2	2	0	0	1	54.00
Patterson	2	1	0	0	1	0	0	0.00
Lasher	2	1	0	0	0	1	0	0.00
Hiller	0	2	4	3	2	0	0	13.50
Dobson	2	1	0	0	0	0	0	3.86

Ground balls-fly balls: Gibson 6-10, McLain 4-2, Sparma 1-0, Patterson 1-3, Lasher 2-3, Hiller 1-0, Dobson 3-3. **Batters faced:** Gibson 33, McLain 16, Sparma 3, Patterson 6, Lasher 7, Hiller 5, Dobson 7. **UMPIRES:** hp—Kinnamon, 1b—Harvey, 2b—Haller, 3b—Gorman, lf—Honochick, rf—Landes **T:** 2:34 **A:** 53,634

GAME 5 Detroit 5 St. Louis 3
Tiger Stadium 10/07/68

ST.LOUIS	AB	R	H	HR	RBI	BB	AVG
Brock lf	5	1	3	0	0	0	.524
Javier 2b	4	0	2	0	0	0	.421
Flood cf	4	1	1	0	1	0	.300
Cepeda 1b	4	1	1	1	2	0	.238
Shannon 3b	4	0	0	0	0	0	.286
McCarver c	3	0	1	0	0	1	.350
Davis rf	3	0	0	0	0	0	.000
a-Gagliano ph	1	0	0	0	0	0	.000
Maxvill ss	3	0	0	0	0	0	.000
b-Spiezio ph	1	0	1	0	0	0	1.000
c-Schofield pr	0	0	0	0	0	0	.000
Briles p	2	0	0	0	0	0	.000
Hoerner p	0	0	0	0	0	0	.500
Willis p	0	0	0	0	0	0	.000
d-Maris ph	1	0	0	0	0	0	.083
TOTALS	**35**	**3**	**9**	**1**	**3**	**1**	**.270**

a - Batted for Davis in the 9th
b - Batted for Maxvill in the 9th
c - Ran for Spiezio in the 9th
d - Batted for Willis in the 9th

BATTING: 2B: Brock 2 (3, Lolich). **HR:** Cepeda (2, 1st off Lolich 1 on, 1 out). **RBI:** Flood 1 (2), Cepeda 2 (6). **Runners left in scoring position, 2 out:** Brock 1, Maxvill 1. **Team LOB:** 7 **BASERUNNING: SB:** Flood (2, 2nd base off Lolich/Freehan). **CS:** Brock (2, 2nd base off Lolich/Freehan). **FIELDING: DP:** 1 (Shannon-Javier-Cepeda).

DETROIT	AB	R	H	HR	RBI	BB	AVG
McAuliffe 2b	4	1	1	0	0	0	.286
Stanley ss-cf	3	2	1	0	0	1	.211
Kaline rf	4	0	2	0	2	0	.381
Cash 1b	2	0	2	0	2	1	.333
Horton lf	4	1	1	0	0	0	.188
Oyler ss	0	0	0	0	0	0	.000
Northrup cf-lf	3	0	1	0	1	1	.158
Freehan c	4	0	0	0	0	0	.000
Wert 3b	3	0	0	0	0	1	.091
Lolich p	4	1	1	0	0	0	.375
TOTALS	**31**	**5**	**9**	**0**	**5**	**4**	**.222**

BATTING: 3B: Stanley (1, Briles), Horton (1, Briles). **SF:** Cash. **RBI:** Kaline 2 (4), Cash 2 (3), Northrup 1 (2). **2-out RBI:** Northrup 1. **Runners left in scoring position, 2 out:** Northrup 1, Freehan 2. **GIDP:** Horton. **Team LOB:** 7 **FIELDING: E:** Cash (2). **Outfield assists:** Horton (1).

ST.LOUIS	IP	H	R	ER	BB	SO	HR	ERA
Briles	6.1	6	3	3	3	5	0	5.56
Hoerner (L, 0-1)	0	3	2	2	1	0	0	3.86
Willis	1.2	0	0	0	0	1	0	0.00

DETROIT	IP	H	R	ER	BB	SO	HR	ERA
Lolich (W, 2-0)	9	9	3	3	1	8	1	2.00

IBB: Northrup (by Briles). **HBP:** Briles (by Lolich). **Ground balls-fly balls:** Briles 6-6, Hoerner 0-0, Willis 2-2, Lolich 10-8. **Batters faced:** Briles 27, Hoerner 4, Willis 5, Lolich 37. **UMPIRES:** hp—Harvey, 1b—Haller, 2b—Gorman, 3b—Honochick, lf—Landes, rf—Kinnamon **T:** 2:43 **A:** 53,634

GAME 6 Detroit 13 St. Louis 1
Busch Stadium 10/09/68

DETROIT	AB	R	H	HR	RBI	BB	AVG
McAuliffe 2b	2	2	0	0	0	3	.261
Stanley ss-cf	5	2	1	0	0	0	.208
Kaline rf	4	3	3	1	4	0	.440
Cash 1b	4	2	3	0	2	1	.409
Horton lf	3	2	2	0	2	1	.263
Oyler ss	0	0	0	0	0	0	.000
Northrup cf-lf	5	1	2	1	4	0	.208
Freehan c	4	0	1	0	1	1	.050
Wert 3b	3	1	0	0	0	1	.071
McLain p	4	0	0	0	0	0	.000
TOTALS	**34**	**13**	**12**	**2**	**13**	**7**	**.245**

BATTING: 2B: Horton (1, Washburn). **HR:** Northrup (2, 3th off Jaster 3 on, 0 out), Kaline (2, 5th off Carlton 0 on, 2 out). **S:** McLain. **RBI:** Kaline 4 (8), Cash 2 (5), Horton 2 (3), Northrup 4 (6), Freehan 1 (1). **2-out RBI:** Kaline 3, Cash 1, Horton 1. **Runners left in scoring position, 2 out:** Northrup 1. **GIDP:** McLain, Stanley, Northrup. **Team LOB:** 5 **FIELDING: E:** Stanley (2). **DP:** 1 (Stanley-McAuliffe-Cash).

ST.LOUIS	AB	R	H	HR	RBI	BB	AVG
Brock lf	4	0	1	0	0	0	.480
Flood cf	4	0	0	0	0	0	.250
Maris rf	4	1	2	0	0	0	.188
Cepeda 1b	4	0	2	0	0	0	.280
McCarver c	4	0	1	0	0	0	.333
Shannon 3b	4	0	1	0	0	0	.280
Javier 2b	4	0	1	0	1	0	.391
Maxvill ss	4	0	0	0	0	0	.000
Washburn p	0	0	0	0	0	0	.000
Jaster p	0	0	0	0	0	0	.000
Willis p	0	0	0	0	0	0	.000
Hughes p	0	0	0	0	0	0	.000
a-Ricketts ph	1	0	1	0	0	0	1.000
Carlton p	0	0	0	0	0	0	.000
b-Tolan ph	1	0	0	0	0	0	.000
Granger p	0	0	0	0	0	0	.000
c-Edwards ph	1	0	0	0	0	0	.000
Nelson p	0	0	0	0	0	0	.000
TOTALS	**35**	**1**	**9**	**0**	**1**	**0**	**.268**

a - Batted for Hughes in the 3th
b - Batted for Carlton in the 6th
c - Batted for Granger in the 8th

BATTING: SF: Flood. **RBI:** Javier 1 (3). **2-out RBI:** Javier 1. **Runners left in scoring position, 2 out:** Maxvill 3. **GIDP:** Shannon. **Team LOB:** 7 **FIELDING: E:** Brock (1). **DP:** 3 (Maxvill-Javier-Cepeda 2, Granger-Maxvill-Cepeda).

DETROIT	IP	H	R	ER	BB	SO	HR	ERA
McLain (W, 1-2)	9	9	1	1	0	7	0	3.24

ST.LOUIS	IP	H	R	ER	BB	SO	HR	ERA
Washburn (L, 1-1)	2	4	5	5	3	3	0	9.82
Jaster	0	2	3	3	1	0	1	0.00
Willis	0.2	1	4	4	2	0	0	8.31
Hughes	0.1	2	0	0	0	0	0	0.00
Carlton	3	3	1	1	0	2	1	6.75
Granger	2	0	0	0	1	1	0	0.00
Nelson	1	0	0	0	0	1	0	0.00

IBB: McAuliffe (by Willis). **HBP:** Wert (by Willis), Kaline (by Granger), Horton (by Granger). **Ground balls-fly balls:** McLain 4-15, Washburn 1-1, Jaster 0-0, Willis 1-0, Hughes 0-1, Carlton 2-4, Granger 3-0, Nelson 0-2. **Batters faced:** McLain 35, Washburn 12, Jaster 3, Willis 6, Hughes 3, Carlton 11, Granger 7, Nelson 3. **UMPIRES:** hp—Haller, 1b—Gorman, 2b—Honochick, 3b—Landes, lf—Kinnamon, rf—Harvey **T:** 2:26 **A:** 54,692

GAME 7 Detroit 4 St. Louis 1
Busch Stadium 10/10/68

DETROIT	AB	R	H	HR	RBI	BB	AVG
McAuliffe 2b	4	0	0	0	0	0	.222
Stanley ss-cf	4	0	1	0	0	0	.214
Kaline rf	4	0	0	0	0	0	.379
Cash 1b	4	1	1	0	0	0	.385
Horton lf	4	1	2	0	0	0	.304
a-Tracewski pr	0	1	0	0	0	0	.000
Oyler ss	0	0	0	0	0	0	.000
Northrup cf-lf	4	1	2	0	2	0	.250
Freehan c	4	0	1	0	1	0	.083
Wert 3b	3	0	1	0	1	1	.118
Lolich p	4	0	0	0	0	0	.250
TOTALS	**35**	**4**	**8**	**0**	**4**	**1**	**.242**

a - Ran for Horton in the 9th

BATTING: 2B: Freehan (1, Gibson). **3B:** Northrup (1, Gibson). **SF:** Northrup. **RBI:** Northrup 2 (8), Freehan 1 (2), Wert 1 (2). **2-out RBI:** Northrup 2, Freehan 1, Wert 1. **Runners left in scoring position, 2 out:** Lolich 2. **Team LOB:** 5 **FIELDING: E:** Northrup (3). **DP:** 1 (Stanley-Cash).

ST.LOUIS	AB	R	H	HR	RBI	BB	AVG
Brock lf	3	0	1	0	0	1	.464
Javier 2b	4	0	0	0	0	0	.333
Flood cf	4	0	2	0	0	0	.286
Cepeda 1b	3	0	0	0	0	1	.250
Shannon 3b	4	1	1	1	1	0	.276
McCarver c	3	0	1	0	0	1	.333
Maris rf	3	0	0	0	0	0	.158
Maxvill ss	2	0	0	0	0	0	.000
a-Gagliano ph	1	0	0	0	0	0	.000
Schofield ss	0	0	0	0	0	0	.000
Gibson p	3	0	0	0	0	0	.125
TOTALS	**30**	**1**	**5**	**1**	**1**	**3**	**.255**

a - Batted for Maxvill in the 8th

BATTING: HR: Shannon (1, 9th off Lolich 0 on, 2 out). **RBI:** Shannon 1 (4). **2-out RBI:** Shannon 1. **Runners left in scoring position, 2 out:** Shannon 1. **GIDP:** Maris. **Team LOB:** 5 **BASERUNNING: SB:** Flood (3, 2nd base off Lolich/Freehan).

DETROIT	IP	H	R	ER	BB	SO	HR	ERA
Lolich (W, 3-0)	9	5	1	1	3	4	1	1.67

ST.LOUIS	IP	H	R	ER	BB	SO	HR	ERA
Gibson (L, 2-1)	9	8	4	4	1	8	0	1.67

IBB: Wert (by Gibson). **Ground balls-fly balls:** Lolich 10-11, Gibson 5-14. **Batters faced:** Lolich 33, Gibson 36. **UMPIRES:** hp—Gorman, 1b—Honochick, 2b—Landes, 3b—Kinnamon, lf—Harvey, rf—Haller **T:** 2:07 **A:** 54,692

1969 NY METS DEF. BALTIMORE, 4-1

GAME 1 Baltimore 4 New York 1
Memorial Stadium 10/11/69

NY METS	AB	R	H	HR	RBI	BB	AVG
Agee cf	4	0	0	0	0	0	.000
Harrelson ss	3	0	1	0	0	1	.333
Jones lf	4	0	1	0	0	0	.250
Clendenon 1b	4	1	2	0	0	0	.500
Swoboda rf	3	0	1	0	0	1	.333
Charles 3b	4	0	0	0	0	0	.000
Grote c	4	0	1	0	0	0	.250
Weis 2b	1	0	0	0	1	2	.000
Seaver p	1	0	0	0	0	0	.000
a-Dyer ph	1	0	0	0	0	0	.000
Cardwell p	0	0	0	0	0	0	.000
b-Gaspar ph	1	0	0	0	0	0	.000
Taylor p	0	0	0	0	0	0	.000
c-Shamsky ph	1	0	0	0	0	0	.000
TOTALS	**31**	**1**	**6**	**0**	**1**	**4**	**.194**

a - Batted for Seaver in the 6th
b - Batted for Cardwell in the 7th
c - Batted for Taylor in the 9th

BATTING: 2B: Clendenon (1, Cuellar). **SF:** Weis. **RBI:** Weis 1 (1). **Runners left in scoring position, 2 out:** Swoboda 1, Gaspar 1, Shamsky 1. **GIDP:** Agee. **Team LOB:** 8 **FIELDING: E:** Weis (1).

BALTIMORE	AB	R	H	HR	RBI	BB	AVG
Buford lf	4	1	2	1	2	0	.500
Blair cf	3	0	0	0	0	1	.000
F.Robinson rf	4	0	0	0	0	0	.000
Powell 1b	4	0	1	0	0	0	.250
B.Robinson 3b	4	0	0	0	0	0	.000
Hendricks c	3	1	1	0	0	0	.333
Johnson 2b	2	1	0	0	0	1	.000
Belanger ss	3	1	1	0	1	0	.333
Cuellar p	3	0	1	0	1	0	.333
TOTALS	**30**	**4**	**6**	**1**	**4**	**2**	**.200**

BATTING: 2B: Buford (1, Seaver). **HR:** Buford (1, 1st off Seaver 0 on, 0 out). **RBI:** Buford 2 (2), Belanger 1 (1), Cuellar 1 (1). **2-out RBI:** Buford 1, Belanger 1, Cuellar 1. **Runners left in scoring position, 2 out:** Blair 2. **Team LOB:** 4 **FIELDING: DP:** 1 (Belanger-Johnson-Powell).

NY METS	IP	H	R	ER	BB	SO	HR	ERA
Seaver (L, 0-1)	5	6	4	4	1	3	1	7.20
Cardwell	1	0	0	0	0	0	0	0.00
Taylor	2	0	0	0	1	3	0	0.00

BALTIMORE	IP	H	R	ER	BB	SO	HR	ERA
Cuellar (W, 1-0)	9	6	1	1	4	8	0	1.00

Ground balls-fly balls: Seaver 6-7, Cardwell 2-1, Taylor 1-1, Cuellar 11-6. **Batters faced:** Seaver 23, Cardwell 3, Taylor 6, Cuellar 36. **UMPIRES:** hp—Soar, 1b—Secory, 2b—Napp, 3b—Crawford, lf—DiMuro, rf—Weyer **T:** 2:13 **A:** 50,429

GAME 2 New York 2 Baltimore 1
Memorial Stadium 10/12/69

NY METS	AB	R	H	HR	RBI	BB	AVG
Agee cf	4	0	0	0	0	0	.000
Harrelson ss	3	0	0	0	0	1	.167
Jones lf	4	0	0	0	0	0	.125
Clendenon 1b	3	1	1	1	1	1	.429
Swoboda rf	4	0	0	0	0	0	.143
Charles 3b	4	1	2	0	0	0	.250
Grote c	4	0	1	0	0	0	.250
Weis 2b	3	0	2	0	1	1	.500
Koosman p	4	0	0	0	0	0	.000
Taylor p	0	0	0	0	0	0	.000
TOTALS	**33**	**2**	**6**	**1**	**2**	**3**	**.188**

BATTING: 2B: Charles (1, McNally). **HR:** Clendenon (1, 4th off McNally 0 on, 0 out). **RBI:** Clendenon 1 (1), Weis 1 (2). **2-out RBI:** Weis 1. **Runners left in scoring position, 2 out:** Jones 1, Grote 1, Koosman 2. **Team LOB:** 7

BALTIMORE	AB	R	H	HR	RBI	BB	AVG
Buford lf	4	0	0	0	0	0	.250
Blair cf	4	1	1	0	0	0	.143
F.Robinson rf	3	0	0	0	0	1	.000
a-Rettenmund pr	0	0	0	0	0	0	.000
Powell 1b	3	0	0	0	0	1	.143
B.Robinson 3b	4	0	1	0	1	0	.125
Johnson 2b	2	0	0	0	0	1	.000
Etchebarren c	3	0	0	0	0	0	.000
Belanger ss	3	0	0	0	0	0	.167
McNally p	3	0	0	0	0	0	.000
TOTALS	**29**	**1**	**2**	**0**	**1**	**3**	**.136**

a - Ran for F.Robinson in the 9th

BATTING: RBI: B.Robinson 1 (1). **2-out RBI:** B.Robinson 1. **Runners left in scoring position, 2 out:** B.Robinson 1. **Team LOB:** 4 **BASERUNNING: SB:** Blair (1, 2nd base off Koosman/Grote).

NY METS	IP	H	R	ER	BB	SO	HR	ERA
Koosman (W, 1-0)	8.2	2	1	1	3	4	0	1.04
Taylor (S, 1)	0.1	0	0	0	0	0	0	0.00

BALTIMORE	IP	H	R	ER	BB	SO	HR	ERA
McNally (L, 0-1)	9	6	2	2	3	7	1	2.00

WP: McNally 1. **IBB:** Weis (by McNally). **Ground balls-fly balls:** Koosman 7-15, Taylor 1-0, McNally 11-9. **Batters faced:** Koosman 31, Taylor 1, McNally 36. **UMPIRES:** hp—Secory, 1b—Napp, 2b—Crawford, 3b—DiMuro, lf—Weyer, rf—Soar **T:** 2:20 **A:** 50,850

GAME 3 New York 5 Baltimore 0
Shea Stadium 10/14/69

BALTIMORE	AB	R	H	HR	RBI	BB	AVG
Buford lf	3	0	0	0	0	2	.182
Blair cf	5	0	0	0	0	0	.083
F.Robinson rf	2	0	1	0	0	2	.111
Powell 1b	4	0	2	0	0	0	.273
B.Robinson 3b	4	0	0	0	0	0	.083
Hendricks c	4	0	0	0	0	0	.143
Johnson 2b	4	0	0	0	0	0	.000
Belanger ss	2	0	0	0	0	2	.125
Palmer p	2	0	0	0	0	0	.000
a-May ph	0	0	0	0	0	1	.000
Leonhard p	0	0	0	0	0	0	.000
b-Dalrymple ph	1	0	1	0	0	0	1.000
c-Salmon pr	0	0	0	0	0	0	.000
TOTALS	**31**	**0**	**4**	**0**	**0**	**7**	**.133**

a - Batted for Palmer in the 7th
b - Batted for Leonhard in the 9th
c - Ran for Dalrymple in the 9th

BATTING: SF: Buford. **Runners left in scoring position, 2 out:** Blair 4, B.Robinson 1, Hendricks 1. **Team LOB:** 11 **FIELDING: E:** Palmer (1).

NY METS	AB	R	H	HR	RBI	BB	AVG
Agee cf	3	1	1	1	1	1	.091
Garrett 3b	1	0	0	0	0	2	.000
Jones lf	4	0	0	0	0	0	.083
Shamsky rf	4	0	0	0	0	0	.000
Weis 2b	0	0	0	0	0	0	.500
Boswell 2b	3	1	1	0	0	0	.333
Gaspar rf	1	0	0	0	0	0	.000
Kranepool 1b	4	1	1	1	1	0	.250
Grote c	3	1	1	0	1	1	.273
Harrelson ss	3	1	1	0	0	1	.222
Gentry p	3	0	1	0	2	0	.333
Ryan p	0	0	0	0	0	0	.000
TOTALS	**29**	**5**	**6**	**2**	**5**	**5**	**.194**

BATTING: 2B: Gentry (1, Palmer), Grote (1, Palmer). **HR:** Agee (1, 1st off Palmer 0 on, 0 out), Kranepool (1, 8th off Leonhard 0 on, 1 out). **S:** Garrett. **RBI:** Agee 1 (1), Kranepool 1 (1), Grote 1 (1), Gentry 2 (2). **2-out RBI:** Gentry 2. **Runners left in scoring position, 2 out:** Agee 1, Shamsky 1, Boswell 1, Gentry 2. **Team LOB:** 6

BALTIMORE	IP	H	R	ER	BB	SO	HR	ERA
Palmer (L, 0-1)	6	5	4	4	4	5	1	6.00
Leonhard	2	1	1	1	1	1	1	4.50

NY METS	IP	H	R	ER	BB	SO	HR	ERA
Gentry (W, 1-0)	6.2	3	0	0	5	4	0	0.00
Ryan (S, 1)	2.1	1	0	0	2	3	0	0.00

Ground balls-fly balls: Palmer 6-7, Leonhard 0-4, Gentry 6-10, Ryan 0-4. **Batters faced:** Palmer 27, Leonhard 8, Gentry 28, Ryan 10. **UMPIRES:** hp—Napp, 1b—Crawford, 2b—DiMuro, 3b—Weyer, lf—Soar, rf—Secory **T:** 2:23 **A:** 56,335

GAME 4 New York 2 Baltimore 1
Shea Stadium 10/15/69

BALTIMORE	AB	R	H	HR	RBI	BB	AVG
Buford lf	5	0	0	0	0	0	.125
Blair cf	4	0	1	0	0	1	.125
F.Robinson rf	4	1	1	0	0	0	.154
Powell 1b	4	0	1	0	0	0	.267
B.Robinson 3b	3	0	0	0	1	0	.067
Hendricks c	3	0	0	0	0	1	.100
Johnson 2b	4	0	0	0	0	0	.000
Belanger ss	4	0	1	0	0	0	.167
Cuellar p	2	0	1	0	0	0	.400
a-May ph	1	0	0	0	0	0	.000
Watt p	0	0	0	0	0	0	.000
b-Dalrymple ph	1	0	1	0	0	0	1.000
Hall p	0	0	0	0	0	0	.000
Richert p	0	0	0	0	0	0	.000
TOTALS	**35**	**1**	**6**	**0**	**1**	**2**	**.144**

a - Batted for Cuellar in the 8th
b - Batted for Watt in the 10th

BATTING: SF: B.Robinson. **RBI:** B.Robinson 1 (2). **Runners left in scoring position, 2 out:** Blair 1, F.Robinson 2. **Team LOB:** 7 **BASERUNNING: CS:** Johnson (1, 2nd base off Seaver/Grote). **FIELDING: E:** Richert (1). **DP:** 3 (Belanger-Johnson-Powell 2, Hendricks-Johnson).

NY METS	AB	R	H	HR	RBI	BB	AVG
Agee cf	4	0	1	0	0	0	.133
Harrelson ss	4	0	1	0	0	0	.231
Jones lf	4	0	1	0	0	0	.125
Clendenon 1b	4	1	1	1	1	0	.364
Swoboda rf	4	0	3	0	0	0	.364
Charles 3b	3	0	0	0	0	0	.182
a-Shamsky ph	1	0	0	0	0	0	.000
Garrett 3b	0	0	0	0	0	0	.000
Grote c	4	0	1	0	0	0	.267
b-Gaspar pr	0	1	0	0	0	0	.000
Weis 2b	3	0	2	0	0	1	.571
Seaver p	3	0	0	0	0	0	.000
c-Martin ph	0	0	0	0	0	0	.000
TOTALS	**34**	**2**	**10**	**1**	**1**	**1**	**.220**

a - Batted for Charles in the 9th
b - Ran for Grote in the 10th
c - Batted for Seaver in the 10th

BATTING: 2B: Grote (2, Hall). **HR:** Clendenon (2, 2nd off Cuellar 0 on, 0 out). **S:** Martin. **RBI:** Clendenon 1 (2). **Runners left in scoring position, 2 out:** Jones 2, Shamsky 1. **GIDP:** Jones, Seaver. **Team LOB:** 7 **BASERUNNING: CS:** Swoboda (1, 2nd base off Cuellar/Hendricks). **FIELDING: E:** Garrett (1).

BALTIMORE	IP	H	R	ER	BB	SO	HR	ERA
Cuellar	7	7	1	1	0	5	1	1.13
Watt	2	2	0	0	0	2	0	0.00
Hall (L, 0-1)	0	1	1	0	1	0	0	0.00
Richert	0	0	0	0	0	0	0	0.00

NY METS	IP	H	R	ER	BB	SO	HR	ERA
Seaver (W, 1-1)	10	6	1	1	2	6	0	3.00

IBB: Weis (by Hall). **Ground balls-fly balls:** Cuellar 11-2, Watt 3-1, Hall 0-0, Richert 0-0, Seaver 9-14. **Batters faced:** Cuellar 25, Watt 8, Hall 2, Richert 1, Seaver 38. **UMPIRES:** hp—Crawford, 1b—DiMuro, 2b—Weyer, 3b—Soar, lf—Secory, rf—Napp **T:** 2:33 **A:** 57,367

GAME 5 New York 5 Baltimore 3
Shea Stadium 10/16/69

BALTIMORE	AB	R	H	HR	RBI	BB	AVG
Buford lf	4	0	0	0	0	0	.100
Blair cf	4	0	0	0	0	0	.100
F.Robinson rf	3	1	1	1	1	1	.188
Powell 1b	4	0	1	0	0	0	.263
b-Salmon pr	0	0	0	0	0	0	.000
B.Robinson 3b	4	0	0	0	0	0	.053
Johnson 2b	4	0	1	0	0	0	.063
Etchebarren c	3	0	0	0	0	0	.000
Belanger ss	3	1	1	0	0	0	.200
McNally p	2	1	1	1	2	0	.200
a-Motton ph	1	0	0	0	0	0	.000
Watt p	0	0	0	0	0	0	.000
TOTALS	**32**	**3**	**5**	**2**	**3**	**1**	**.146**

a - Batted for McNally in the 8th
b - Ran for Powell in the 9th

BATTING: HR: McNally (1, 3th off Koosman 1 on, 0 out), F.Robinson (1, 3th off Koosman 0 on, 2 out). **RBI:** F.Robinson 1 (1), McNally 2 (2). **2-out RBI:** F.Robinson 1. **Team LOB:** 3 **FIELDING: E:** Powell (1).

NY METS	AB	R	H	HR	RBI	BB	AVG
Agee cf	3	0	1	0	0	1	.167
Harrelson ss	4	0	0	0	0	0	.176
Jones lf	3	2	1	0	0	0	.158
Clendenon 1b	3	1	1	1	2	1	.357
Swoboda rf	4	1	2	0	1	0	.400
Charles 3b	4	0	0	0	0	0	.133
Grote c	4	0	0	0	1	0	.211
Weis 2b	4	1	1	1	1	0	.455
Koosman p	3	0	1	0	0	0	.143
TOTALS	**32**	**5**	**7**	**2**	**5**	**2**	**.220**

BATTING: 2B: Koosman (1, McNally), Jones (1, Watt), Swoboda (1, Watt). **HR:** Clendenon (3, 6th off McNally 1 on, 0 out), Weis (1, 7th off McNally 0 on, 0 out). **RBI:** Clendenon 2 (4), Swoboda 1 (1), Grote 1 (2), Weis 1 (3). **2-out RBI:** Grote 1. **Runners left in scoring position, 2 out:** Jones 1, Swoboda 1. **Team LOB:** 6 **BASERUNNING: SB:** Agee (1, 2nd base off McNally/Etchebarren).

BALTIMORE	IP	H	R	ER	BB	SO	HR	ERA
McNally	7	5	3	3	2	6	2	2.81
Watt (L, 0-1)	1	2	2	1	0	1	0	3.00

NY METS	IP	H	R	ER	BB	SO	HR	ERA
Koosman (W, 2-0)	9	5	3	3	1	5	2	2.04

HBP: Jones (by McNally). **Ground balls-fly balls:** McNally 5-10, Watt 2-1, Koosman 10-12. **Batters faced:** McNally 29, Watt 6, Koosman 33. **UMPIRES:** hp—DiMuro, 1b—Weyer, 2b—Soar, 3b—Secory, lf—Napp, rf—Crawford **T:** 2:14 **A:** 57,397

1970 BALTIMORE DEF. CINCINNATI, 4-1

GAME 1 Baltimore 4 Cincinnati 3
Riverfront Stadium 10/10/70

BALTIMORE	AB	R	H	HR	RBI	BB	AVG
Buford lf	4	0	1	0	0	0	.250
Blair cf	4	1	1	0	0	0	.250
Powell 1b	3	1	1	1	2	1	.333
F.Robinson rf	4	0	0	0	0	0	.000
B.Robinson 3b	4	1	1	1	1	0	.250
Hendricks c	4	1	1	1	1	0	.250
Johnson 2b	3	0	1	0	0	1	.333
Belanger ss	3	0	1	0	0	1	.333
Palmer p	4	0	0	0	0	0	.000
Richert p	0	0	0	0	0	0	.000
TOTALS	**33**	**4**	**7**	**3**	**4**	**3**	**.212**

BATTING: 2B: Johnson (1, Carroll). **HR:** Powell (1, 4th off Nolan 1 on, 1 out), Hendricks (1, 5th off Nolan 0 on, 0 out), B.Robinson (1, 7th off Nolan 0 on, 1 out). **RBI:** Powell 2 (2), B.Robinson 1 (1), Hendricks 1 (1). **Runners left in scoring position, 2 out:** Palmer 2. **GIDP:** Powell. **Team LOB:** 5 **FIELDING: E:** B.Robinson (1), Hendricks (1).

CINCINNATI	AB	R	H	HR	RBI	BB	AVG
Rose rf	3	0	0	0	0	1	.000
Tolan cf	4	2	1	0	0	1	.250
Perez 3b	3	0	0	0	0	1	.000
Bench c	4	0	1	0	1	0	.250
May 1b	4	1	2	1	2	0	.500
Carbo lf	2	0	0	0	0	2	.000
Helms 2b	4	0	1	0	0	0	.250
Woodward ss	2	0	0	0	0	0	.000
a-Cline ph	1	0	0	0	0	0	.000
Chaney ss	0	0	0	0	0	0	.000
b-Stewart ph	1	0	0	0	0	0	.000
Nolan p	2	0	0	0	0	0	.000
Carroll p	0	0	0	0	0	0	.000
c-Bravo ph	1	0	0	0	0	0	.000
TOTALS	**31**	**3**	**5**	**1**	**3**	**5**	**.161**

a - Batted for Woodward in the 6th
b - Batted for Chaney in the 9th
c - Batted for Carroll in the 9th

BATTING: 2B: Tolan (1, Palmer). **HR:** May (1, 3th off Palmer 1 on, 2 out). **S:** Nolan. **RBI:** Bench 1 (1), May 2 (2). **2-out RBI:** Bench 1, May 2. **Runners left in scoring position, 2 out:** Rose 1, Bench 1, Carbo 1, Nolan 1. **Team LOB:** 8 **BASERUNNING: SB:** Tolan (1, 2nd base off Palmer/Hendricks). **CS:** Carbo (1, 2nd base off Palmer/Hendricks). **FIELDING: DP:** 1 (May-Woodward-May).

BALTIMORE	IP	H	R	ER	BB	SO	HR	ERA
Palmer (W, 1-0)	8.2	5	3	3	5	2	1	3.12
Richert (S, 1)	0.1	0	0	0	0	0	0	0.00

CINCINNATI	IP	H	R	ER	BB	SO	HR	ERA
Nolan (L, 0-1)	6.2	5	4	4	1	7	3	5.40
Carroll	2.1	2	0	0	2	4	0	0.00

WP: Palmer 1. **IBB:** Belanger (by Carroll). **Ground balls-fly balls:** Palmer 7-16, Richert 0-1, Nolan 4-8, Carroll 1-2. **Batters faced:** Palmer 37, Richert 1, Nolan 25, Carroll 11. **UMPIRES:** hp—Burkhart, 1b—Flaherty, 2b—Venzon, 3b—Stewart, lf—Williams, rf—Ashford **T:** 2:24 **A:** 51,531

GAME 2 Baltimore 6 Cincinnati 5
Riverfront Stadium 10/11/70

BALTIMORE	AB	R	H	HR	RBI	BB	AVG
Buford lf	4	1	2	0	0	1	.375
Blair cf	5	1	2	0	1	0	.333
Powell 1b	3	2	2	1	2	2	.500
F.Robinson rf	5	0	0	0	0	0	.000
B.Robinson 3b	4	1	1	0	1	0	.250
Hendricks c	3	0	1	0	2	1	.286
Johnson 2b	3	0	1	0	0	1	.333
Belanger ss	4	0	0	0	0	0	.143
Cuellar p	1	0	0	0	0	0	.000
Phoebus p	0	0	0	0	0	0	.000
a-Salmon ph	1	1	1	0	0	0	1.000
Drabowsky p	1	0	0	0	0	0	.000
Lopez p	0	0	0	0	0	0	.000
Hall p	1	0	0	0	0	0	.000
TOTALS	**35**	**6**	**10**	**1**	**6**	**5**	**.250**

a - Batted for Phoebus in the 5th

BATTING: 2B: Hendricks (1, Wilcox). **HR:** Powell (2, 4th off McGlothlin 0 on, 0 out). **RBI:** Blair 1 (1), Powell 2 (4), B.Robinson 1 (2), Hendricks 2 (3). **2-out RBI:** B.Robinson 1, Hendricks 2. **Runners left in scoring position, 2 out:** F.Robinson 1, Johnson 1. **GIDP:** Blair, Powell. **Team LOB:** 7 **FIELDING: E:** Belanger (1), Blair (1). **DP:** 1 (B.Robinson-Johnson-Powell).

CINCINNATI	AB	R	H	HR	RBI	BB	AVG
Rose rf	3	0	0	0	0	1	.000
Tolan cf	4	2	1	1	1	0	.250
Perez 3b	4	1	1	0	0	0	.143
Bench c	3	1	1	1	1	1	.286
May 1b	4	1	1	0	2	0	.375
McRae lf	4	0	2	0	1	0	.500
Helms 2b	4	0	0	0	0	0	.125
Woodward ss	2	0	0	0	0	0	.000
a-Cline ph	1	0	1	0	0	0	.500
Chaney ss	0	0	0	0	0	0	.000
c-Carbo ph	1	0	0	0	0	0	.000
McGlothlin p	2	0	0	0	0	0	.000
Wilcox p	0	0	0	0	0	0	.000
Carroll p	0	0	0	0	0	0	.000
b-Bravo ph	0	0	0	0	0	0	.000
Gullett p	0	0	0	0	0	0	.000
d-Stewart ph	1	0	0	0	0	0	.000
TOTALS	**33**	**5**	**7**	**2**	**5**	**2**	**.188**

a - Batted for Woodward in the 7th
b - Batted for Carroll in the 7th
c - Batted for Chaney in the 9th
d - Batted for Gullett in the 9th

BATTING: 2B: May (1, Cuellar), McRae (1, Phoebus). **HR:** Tolan (1, 3th off Cuellar 0 on, 0 out), Bench (1, 6th off Drabowsky 0 on, 0 out). **S:** Bravo. **RBI:** Tolan 1 (1), Bench 1 (2), May 2 (4), McRae 1 (1). **2-out RBI:** May 2, McRae 1. **Runners left in scoring position, 2 out:** Perez 1, McGlothlin 1. **GIDP:** May. **Team LOB:** 4 **FIELDING: DP:** 2 (Woodward-Helms-May, May-Woodward-May).

BALTIMORE	IP	H	R	ER	BB	SO	HR	ERA
Cuellar	2.1	4	4	1	1	1	1	3.86
Phoebus (W, 1-0)	1.2	1	0	0	0	0	0	0.00
Drabowsky	2.1	2	1	1	1	1	1	3.86
Lopez	0.1	0	0	0	0	0	0	0.00
Hall (S, 1)	2.1	0	0	0	0	0	0	0.00

CINCINNATI	IP	H	R	ER	BB	SO	HR	ERA
McGlothlin	4.1	6	4	4	2	2	1	8.31
Wilcox (L, 0-1)	0.1	3	2	2	0	0	0	54.00
Carroll	2.1	1	0	0	0	1	0	0.00
Gullett	2	0	0	0	3	2	0	0.00

Ground balls-fly balls: Cuellar 4-3, Phoebus 3-1, Drabowsky 3-2, Lopez 0-1, Hall 4-3, McGlothlin 6-4, Wilcox 0-1, Carroll 5-0, Gullett 2-2. **Batters faced:** Cuellar 13, Phoebus 5, Drabowsky 10, Lopez 1, Hall 7, McGlothlin 20, Wilcox 4, Carroll 7, Gullett 9. **UMPIRES:** hp—Flaherty, 1b—Venzon, 2b—Stewart, 3b—Williams, lf—Ashford, rf—Burkhart **T:** 2:26 **A:** 51,531

GAME 3 Baltimore 9 Cincinnati 3
Memorial Stadium 10/13/70

CINCINNATI	AB	R	H	HR	RBI	BB	AVG
Rose rf	5	0	2	0	1	0	.182
Tolan cf	4	0	1	0	0	0	.250
Perez 3b	3	0	0	0	0	1	.100
Bench c	4	0	0	0	0	0	.182
May 1b	3	1	1	0	0	1	.364
McRae lf	4	1	2	0	0	0	.500
Helms 2b	4	1	1	0	0	0	.167
Concepcion ss	3	0	1	0	2	0	.333
Cloninger p	2	0	0	0	0	0	.000
Granger p	0	0	0	0	0	0	.000
a-Woodward ph	1	0	1	0	0	0	.200
Gullett p	0	0	0	0	0	0	.000
b-Cline ph	1	0	0	0	0	0	.333
TOTALS	**34**	**3**	**9**	**0**	**3**	**2**	**.214**

a - Batted for Granger in the 7th
b - Batted for Gullett in the 9th

BATTING: SF: Concepcion. **RBI:** Rose 1 (1), Concepcion 2 (2). **2-out RBI:** Rose 1, Concepcion 1. **Runners left in scoring position, 2 out:** Tolan 1, Bench 1, Cloninger 1. **GIDP:** Perez. **Team LOB:** 7 **FIELDING: Outfield assists:** McRae (1). **DP:** 1 (Bench-Helms).

BALTIMORE	AB	R	H	HR	RBI	BB	AVG
Buford lf	3	2	1	1	1	1	.364
Belanger ss	4	0	0	0	0	0	.091
Powell 1b	3	1	0	0	0	1	.333
F.Robinson rf	4	2	3	1	1	0	.231
Blair cf	3	1	3	0	1	1	.500
B.Robinson 3b	4	1	2	0	2	0	.333
Johnson 2b	2	1	0	0	0	2	.250
Etchebarren c	4	0	0	0	0	0	.000
McNally p	4	1	1	1	4	0	.250
TOTALS	**31**	**9**	**10**	**3**	**9**	**5**	**.273**

BATTING: 2B: B.Robinson 2 (2, Cloninger, Granger), Blair (1, Gullett). **HR:** F.Robinson (1, 3th off Cloninger 0 on, 2 out), Buford (1, 5th off Cloninger 0 on, 1 out), McNally (1, 6th off Granger 3 on, 2 out). **RBI:** Buford 1 (1), F.Robinson 1 (1), Blair 1 (2), B.Robinson 2 (4), McNally 4 (4). **2-out RBI:** F.Robinson 1, Blair 1, B.Robinson 2, McNally 4. **Runners left in scoring position, 2 out:** B.Robinson 1, Johnson 2. **Team LOB:** 3 **BASERUNNING: CS:** Blair (1, 2nd base off Cloninger/Bench), Johnson (1, 2nd base off

Cloninger/Bench). **FIELDING: E:** Etchebarren (1). **DP:** 1 (B.Robinson-Powell).

CINCINNATI	IP	H	R	ER	BB	SO	HR	ERA
Cloninger (L, 0-1)	5.1	6	5	5	3	3	2	8.44
Granger	0.2	2	3	3	1	1	1	40.50
Gullett	2	2	1	1	1	0	0	2.25
BALTIMORE	**IP**	**H**	**R**	**ER**	**BB**	**SO**	**HR**	**ERA**
McNally (W, 1-0)	9	9	3	3	2	5	0	3.00

IBB: Johnson (by Granger). **Ground balls-fly balls:** Cloninger 4-7, Granger 1-0, Gullett 2-3, McNally 9-11. **Batters faced:** Cloninger 23, Granger 5, Gullett 8, McNally 37. **UMPIRES:** hp—Venzon, 1b—Stewart, 2b—Williams, 3b—Ashford, lf—Burkhart, rf—Flaherty **T:** 2:09 **A:** 51,773

GAME 4 Cincinnati 6 Baltimore 5
Memorial Stadium 10/14/70

CINCINNATI	AB	R	H	HR	RBI	BB	AVG
Tolan cf	3	1	1	0	0	2	.267
Rose rf	5	1	2	1	1	0	.250
Perez 3b	4	1	0	0	0	1	.071
Bench c	4	1	1	0	0	0	.200
May 1b	3	2	2	1	4	1	.429
Carbo lf	4	0	0	0	0	0	.000
Helms 2b	3	0	1	0	0	1	.200
Concepcion ss	3	0	1	0	1	0	.333
Carroll p	1	0	0	0	0	0	.000
Nolan p	1	0	0	0	0	0	.000
Gullett p	1	0	0	0	0	0	.000
Woodward ss	0	0	0	0	0	0	.200
a-Bravo ph	1	0	0	0	0	0	.000
Chaney ss	1	0	0	0	0	0	.000
TOTALS	**34**	**6**	**8**	**2**	**6**	**5**	**.220**

a - Batted for Woodward in the 7th

BATTING: 3B: Concepcion (1, Palmer). **HR:** Rose (1, 5th off Palmer 0 on, 1 out), May (2, 8th off Watt 2 on, 0 out). **RBI:** Rose 1 (2), May 4 (8), Concepcion 1 (3). **2-out RBI:** May 1, Concepcion 1. **Runners left in scoring position, 2 out:** Bench 1, Carbo 1, Nolan 1. **Team LOB:** 6 **BASERUNNING: CS:** Tolan (1, 2nd base off Drabowsky/Hendricks). **FIELDING: E:** Tolan (1), Rose (1), Perez (1). **Outfield assists:** Rose (1).

BALTIMORE	AB	R	H	HR	RBI	BB	AVG
Buford lf	4	0	0	0	0	1	.267
Blair cf	3	0	0	0	0	0	.400
Powell 1b	3	1	0	0	0	1	.250
F.Robinson rf	4	1	1	0	1	0	.235
B.Robinson 3b	4	2	4	1	2	0	.500
Hendricks c	4	0	2	0	2	0	.364
Johnson 2b	4	0	0	0	0	0	.167
Belanger ss	3	0	0	0	0	0	.071
a-Crowley ph	1	0	0	0	0	0	.000
Palmer p	3	1	1	0	0	0	.143
Watt p	0	0	0	0	0	0	.000
Drabowsky p	0	0	0	0	0	0	.000
b-Rettenmund ph	1	0	0	0	0	0	.000
TOTALS	**34**	**5**	**8**	**1**	**5**	**2**	**.263**

a - Batted for Belanger in the 9th
b - Batted for Drabowsky in the 9th

BATTING: HR: B.Robinson (2, 2nd off Nolan 0 on, 0 out). **S:** Blair. **RBI:** F.Robinson 1 (2), B.Robinson 2 (6), Hendricks 2 (5). **2-out RBI:** F.Robinson 1, B.Robinson 1, Hendricks 1. **Runners left in scoring position, 2 out:** F.Robinson 1, Hendricks 2, Belanger 1. **Team LOB:** 5

CINCINNATI	IP	H	R	ER	BB	SO	HR	ERA
Nolan	2.2	4	4	4	2	2	1	7.71
Gullett	2.2	3	1	0	0	2	0	1.35
Carroll (W, 1-0)	3.2	1	0	0	0	4	0	0.00
BALTIMORE	**IP**	**H**	**R**	**ER**	**BB**	**SO**	**HR**	**ERA**
Palmer	7	6	5	5	4	7	1	4.60
Watt (L, 0-1)	1	2	1	1	1	3	1	9.00
Drabowsky	1	0	0	0	0	0	0	2.70

Ground balls-fly balls: Nolan 4-1, Gullett 3-2, Carroll 5-3, Palmer 6-8, Watt 0-0, Drabowsky 0-2. **Batters faced:** Nolan 14, Gullett 10, Carroll 13, Palmer 31, Watt 6, Drabowsky 2. **UMPIRES:** hp—Stewart, 1b—Williams, 2b—Ashford, 3b—Burkhart, lf—Flaherty, rf—Venzon **T:** 2:26 **A:** 53,007

GAME 5 Baltimore 9 Cincinnati 3
Memorial Stadium 10/15/70

CINCINNATI	AB	R	H	HR	RBI	BB	AVG
Tolan cf	4	0	0	0	0	0	.211
Rose rf	4	1	1	0	0	0	.250
Perez 3b	4	0	0	0	0	0	.056
Bench c	4	1	1	0	1	0	.211
May 1b	4	1	1	0	0	0	.389
McRae lf	3	0	1	0	2	0	.455
c-Corrales ph	1	0	0	0	0	0	.000
Helms 2b	3	0	1	0	0	0	.222
Concepcion ss	3	0	1	0	0	0	.333
Merritt p	1	0	0	0	0	0	.000
Granger p	0	0	0	0	0	0	.000
Wilcox p	0	0	0	0	0	0	.000
a-Bravo ph	0	0	0	0	0	1	.000
Cloninger p	0	0	0	0	0	0	.000
b-Carbo ph	1	0	0	0	0	0	.000
Washburn p	0	0	0	0	0	0	.000
Carroll p	0	0	0	0	0	0	.000
TOTALS	**32**	**3**	**6**	**0**	**3**	**1**	**.213**

a - Batted for Wilcox in the 5th
b - Batted for Cloninger in the 7th
c - Batted for McRae in the 9th

BATTING: 2B: Rose (1, Cuellar), May (2, Cuellar), McRae (2, Cuellar). **RBI:** Bench 1 (3), McRae 2 (3). **2-out RBI:** Bench 1, McRae 2. **Runners left in scoring position, 2 out:** Helms 1. **GIDP:** Carbo. **Team LOB:** 3

BALTIMORE	AB	R	H	HR	RBI	BB	AVG
Belanger ss	5	0	1	0	1	0	.105
Blair cf	4	2	3	0	1	1	.474
F.Robinson rf	5	2	2	1	2	0	.273
Powell 1b	5	1	2	0	1	0	.294
Rettenmund lf	4	2	2	1	2	1	.400
B.Robinson 3b	5	0	1	0	0	0	.429
Johnson 2b	4	1	3	0	2	1	.313
Etchebarren c	3	1	1	0	0	2	.143
Cuellar p	3	0	0	0	0	0	.000
TOTALS	**38**	**9**	**15**	**2**	**9**	**5**	**.292**

BATTING: 2B: Powell (1, Granger), Johnson (2, Cloninger). **HR:** F.Robinson (2, 1st off Merritt 1 on, 1 out), Rettenmund (1, 5th off Cloninger 0 on, 1 out). **S:** Cuellar. **RBI:** Belanger 1 (1), Blair 1 (3), F.Robinson 2 (4), Powell 1 (5), Rettenmund 2 (2), Johnson 2 (2). **2-out RBI:** Belanger 1, Blair 1, Johnson 1. **Runners left in scoring position, 2 out:** Belanger 3, F.Robinson 1, B.Robinson 1, Etchebarren 1. **Team LOB:** 11 **FIELDING: DP:** 1 (Cuellar-Belanger-Powell).

CINCINNATI	IP	H	R	ER	BB	SO	HR	ERA
Merritt (L, 0-1)	1.2	3	4	4	1	0	1	21.60
Granger	0.2	5	2	2	0	0	0	33.75
Wilcox	1.2	0	0	0	0	2	0	9.00
Cloninger	2	4	1	1	2	1	1	7.36
Washburn	1.1	2	2	2	2	0	0	13.50
Carroll	0.2	1	0	0	0	2	0	0.00
BALTIMORE	**IP**	**H**	**R**	**ER**	**BB**	**SO**	**HR**	**ERA**
Cuellar (W, 1-0)	9	6	3	3	1	4	0	3.18

IBB: Etchebarren (by Cloninger). **Ground balls-fly balls:** Merritt 0-5, Granger 1-1, Wilcox 1-2, Cloninger 2-3, Washburn 2-1, Carroll 0-0, Cuellar 8-14. **Batters faced:** Merritt 9, Granger 7, Wilcox 5, Cloninger 12, Washburn 8, Carroll 3, Cuellar 33. **UMPIRES:** hp—Williams, 1b—Ashford, 2b—Burkhart, 3b—Flaherty, lf—Venzon, rf—Stewart **T:** 2:35 **A:** 45,341

1971 PITTSBURGH DEF. BALTIMORE, 4-3

GAME 1 Baltimore 5 Pittsburgh 3
Memorial Stadium 10/09/71

PITTSBURGH	AB	R	H	HR	RBI	BB	AVG
Cash 2b	4	0	1	0	1	0	.250
Clines cf	4	0	0	0	0	0	.000
Clemente rf	4	0	2	0	0	0	.500
Stargell lf	3	0	0	0	0	1	.000
Robertson 1b	3	1	0	0	0	1	.000
Sanguillen c	4	1	0	0	1	0	.000
Pagan 3b	4	0	0	0	0	0	.000
Hernandez ss	2	1	0	0	1	0	.000
b-Oliver ph	1	0	0	0	0	0	.000
Ellis p	1	0	0	0	0	0	.000
Moose p	1	0	0	0	0	0	.000
a-Mazeroski ph	1	0	0	0	0	0	.000
Miller p	0	0	0	0	0	0	.000
TOTALS	**32**	**3**	**3**	**0**	**3**	**2**	**.094**

a - Batted for Moose in the 7th
b - Batted for Hernandez in the 9th

BATTING: 2B: Clemente (1, McNally). **S:** Hernandez. **RBI:** Cash 1 (1), Sanguillen 1 (1), Hernandez 1 (1). **2-out RBI:** Cash 1. **Runners left in scoring position, 2 out:** Stargell 1, Pagan 1, Oliver 1. **Team LOB:** 5

BALTIMORE	AB	R	H	HR	RBI	BB	AVG
Buford lf	4	2	2	1	1	0	.500
Blair cf	0	0	0	0	0	0	.000
Rettenmund cf-lf	4	1	1	1	3	0	.250
Powell 1b	3	0	0	0	0	1	.000
F.Robinson rf	4	1	2	1	1	0	.500
Hendricks c	4	0	1	0	0	0	.250
B.Robinson 3b	4	0	1	0	0	0	.250
D.Johnson 2b	4	0	1	0	0	0	.250
Belanger ss	4	1	2	0	0	0	.500
McNally p	3	0	0	0	0	0	.000
TOTALS	**34**	**5**	**10**	**3**	**5**	**1**	**.294**

BATTING: 3B: Belanger (1, Moose). **HR:** F.Robinson (1, 2nd off Ellis 0 on, 0 out), Rettenmund (1, 3th off Ellis 2 on, 1 out), Buford (1, 5th off Moose 0 on, 0 out). **RBI:** Buford 1 (1), Rettenmund 3 (3), F.Robinson 1 (1). **Runners left in scoring position, 2 out:** Hendricks 1, Belanger 2, McNally 1. **Team LOB:** 6 **FIELDING: E:** Belanger 2 (2), Hendricks (1).

PITTSBURGH	IP	H	R	ER	BB	SO	HR	ERA
Ellis (L, 0-1)	2.1	4	4	4	1	1	2	15.43
Moose	3.2	3	1	1	0	4	1	2.45
Miller	2	3	0	0	0	1	0	0.00
BALTIMORE	**IP**	**H**	**R**	**ER**	**BB**	**SO**	**HR**	**ERA**
McNally (W, 1-0)	9	3	3	0	2	9	0	0.00

WP: Moose 1, McNally 1. **Ground balls-fly balls:** Ellis 4-2, Moose 3-4, Miller 3-2, McNally 9-11. **Batters faced:** Ellis 12, Moose 14, Miller 9, McNally 35. **UMPIRES:** hp—Chylak, 1b—Sudol, 2b—Rice, 3b—Vargo, lf—Odom, rf—Kibler **T:** 2:06 **A:** 53,229

GAME 2 Baltimore 11 Pittsburgh 3
Memorial Stadium 10/11/71

PITTSBURGH	AB	R	H	HR	RBI	BB	AVG
Cash 2b	5	0	0	0	0	0	.111
Hebner 3b	3	1	1	1	3	2	.333
Clemente rf	5	0	2	0	0	0	.444
Stargell lf	3	0	1	0	0	2	.167
Giusti p	0	0	0	0	0	0	.000
Oliver cf	5	0	1	0	0	0	.167
Robertson 1b	3	0	0	0	0	2	.000
Sanguillen c	5	0	1	0	0	0	.111
Hernandez ss	2	1	1	0	0	2	.250
c-May ph	1	0	0	0	0	0	.000
B.Johnson p	2	0	0	0	0	0	.000
Kison p	0	0	0	0	0	0	.000
Moose p	0	0	0	0	0	0	.000
Veale p	0	0	0	0	0	0	.000
a-Sands ph	1	0	0	0	0	0	.000
Miller p	0	0	0	0	0	0	.000
b-Davalillo ph-lf	1	1	1	0	0	0	1.000
TOTALS	**36**	**3**	**8**	**1**	**3**	**8**	**.162**

a - Batted for Veale in the 6th
b - Batted for Miller in the 8th
c - Batted for Hernandez in the 9th

BATTING: 2B: Clemente (2, Palmer). **HR:** Hebner (1, 8th off Palmer 2 on, 2 out). **RBI:** Hebner 3 (3). **2-out RBI:** Hebner 3. **Runners left in scoring position, 2 out:** Cash 2, Oliver 1, Robertson 2. **Team LOB:** 14 **FIELDING: E:** Oliver (1). **Outfield assists:** Stargell (1). **DP:** 2 (Cash-Hernandez, Stargell-Sanguillen).

BALTIMORE	AB	R	H	HR	RBI	BB	AVG
Buford lf	5	0	0	0	1	0	.222
Rettenmund cf-rf	5	1	2	0	1	0	.333
Powell 1b	5	1	1	0	0	0	.125
F.Robinson rf	4	2	3	0	0	0	.625
a-Blair pr-cf	1	1	1	0	0	0	1.000
Hendricks c	3	2	2	0	2	1	.429
B.Robinson 3b	3	2	3	0	3	2	.571
D.Johnson 2b	5	1	2	0	2	0	.333
Belanger ss	3	1	0	0	0	2	.286
Palmer p	2	0	0	0	2	2	.000
Hall p	0	0	0	0	0	0	.000
TOTALS	**36**	**11**	**14**	**0**	**11**	**7**	**.343**

a - Ran for F.Robinson in the 6th

BATTING: RBI: Buford 1 (2), Rettenmund 1 (4), Hendricks 2 (2), B.Robinson 3 (3), D.Johnson 2 (2), Palmer 2 (2). **2-out RBI:** Rettenmund 1. **Runners left in scoring position, 2 out:** Powell 1, Belanger 1, Palmer 1. **Team LOB:** 9 **FIELDING: E:** Belanger (3).

PITTSBURGH	IP	H	R	ER	BB	SO	HR	ERA
B.Johnson (L, 0-1)	3.1	4	4	4	2	1	0	10.80
Kison	0	0	0	0	2	0	0	0.00
Moose	1	5	5	5	0	0	0	11.57
Veale	0.2	1	1	1	2	0	0	13.50
Miller	2	3	1	1	0	1	0	2.25
Giusti	1	1	0	0	1	0	0	0.00
BALTIMORE	**IP**	**H**	**R**	**ER**	**BB**	**SO**	**HR**	**ERA**
Palmer (W, 1-0)	8	7	3	3	8	10	1	3.38
Hall (S, 1)	1	1	0	0	0	0	0	0.00

HBP: Hendricks (by B.Johnson). **Ground balls-fly balls:** B.Johnson 4-4, Kison 0-0, Moose 0-2, Veale 2-0, Miller 4-1, Giusti 0-3, Palmer 8-7, Hall 2-1. **Batters faced:** B.Johnson 16, Kison 2, Moose 7, Veale 5, Miller 9, Giusti 5, Palmer 40, Hall 4. **UMPIRES:** hp—Sudol, 1b—Rice, 2b—Vargo, 3b—Odom, lf—Kibler, rf—Chylak **T:** 2:55 **A:** 53,239

GAME 3 Pittsburgh 5 Baltimore 1
Three Rivers Stadium 10/12/71

BALTIMORE	AB	R	H	HR	RBI	BB	AVG
Buford lf	4	0	0	0	0	0	.154
Rettenmund cf	4	0	0	0	0	0	.231
Powell 1b	4	0	0	0	0	0	.083
F.Robinson rf	4	1	2	1	1	0	.583
Hendricks c	3	0	0	0	0	1	.300
B.Robinson 3b	3	0	1	0	0	0	.500
D.Johnson 2b	3	0	0	0	0	0	.250
Belanger ss	3	0	0	0	0	0	.200
Cuellar p	1	0	0	0	0	1	.000
Dukes p	0	0	0	0	0	0	.000
a-Shopay ph	1	0	0	0	0	0	.000
Watt p	0	0	0	0	0	0	.000
TOTALS	**30**	**1**	**3**	**1**	**1**	**2**	**.270**

a - Batted for Dukes in the 8th

BATTING: HR: F.Robinson (2, 7th off Blass 0 on, 0 out). **RBI:** F.Robinson 1 (2). **Runners left in scoring position, 2 out:** Powell 1. **Team LOB:** 4 **FIELDING: E:** Powell (1), B.Robinson (1), Cuellar (1). **DP:** 1 (B.Robinson-D.Johnson).

PITTSBURGH	AB	R	H	HR	RBI	BB	AVG
Cash 2b	4	1	1	0	0	1	.154
Oliver cf	4	0	0	0	0	1	.100
Clemente rf	4	1	1	0	1	0	.385
Stargell lf	1	1	0	0	0	3	.143
Robertson 1b	4	1	1	1	3	0	.100
Sanguillen c	4	1	2	0	0	0	.231
Pagan 3b	4	0	2	0	1	0	.250
Alley ss	2	0	0	0	0	1	.000
Hernandez ss	1	0	0	0	0	0	.200
Blass p	4	0	0	0	0	0	.000
TOTALS	**32**	**5**	**7**	**1**	**5**	**6**	**.180**

BATTING: 2B: Cash (1, Cuellar), Pagan (1, Cuellar), Sanguillen (1, Cuellar). **HR:** Robertson (1, 7th off Cuellar 2 on, 0 out). **RBI:** Clemente 1 (1), Robertson 3 (3), Pagan 1 (1). **Runners left in scoring position, 2 out:** Oliver 1, Robertson 2, Blass 3. **Team LOB:** 9

BALTIMORE	IP	H	R	ER	BB	SO	HR	ERA
Cuellar (L, 0-1)	6	7	5	4	6	4	1	6.00
Dukes	1	0	0	0	0	0	0	0.00
Watt	1	0	0	0	0	1	0	0.00
PITTSBURGH	**IP**	**H**	**R**	**ER**	**BB**	**SO**	**HR**	**ERA**
Blass (W, 1-0)	9	3	1	1	2	8	1	1.00

IBB: Cash (by Cuellar). **Ground balls-fly balls:** Cuellar 9-6, Dukes 1-2, Watt 0-2, Blass 10-9. **Batters faced:** Cuellar 32, Dukes 3, Watt 3, Blass 32. **UMPIRES:** hp—Rice, 1b—Vargo, 2b—Odom, 3b—Kibler, lf—Chylak, rf—Sudol **T:** 2:20 **A:** 50,403

GAME 4 Pittsburgh 4 Baltimore 3
Three Rivers Stadium 10/13/71

BALTIMORE	AB	R	H	HR	RBI	BB	AVG
Blair cf	4	1	2	0	0	0	.600
Belanger ss	4	1	1	0	0	0	.214
Rettenmund lf	4	1	1	0	0	0	.235
F.Robinson rf	2	0	0	0	0	1	.500
B.Robinson 3b	3	0	0	0	1	0	.385
Powell 1b	3	0	0	0	1	0	.067
D.Johnson 2b	3	0	0	0	0	0	.200
Etchebarren c	2	0	0	0	0	0	.000
Dobson p	2	0	0	0	0	0	.000
Jackson p	0	0	0	0	0	0	.000
a-Shopay ph	1	0	0	0	0	0	.000
Watt p	0	0	0	0	0	0	.000
Richert p	0	0	0	0	0	0	.000
TOTALS	**28**	**3**	**4**	**0**	**2**	**1**	**.242**

a - Batted for Jackson in the 7th

BATTING: 2B: Blair (1, Kison). **SF:** B.Robinson, Powell. **RBI:** B.Robinson 1 (4), Powell 1 (1). **Runners left in scoring position, 2 out:** Belanger 1, D.Johnson 1. **GIDP:** Etchebarren. **Team LOB:** 4 **FIELDING: E:** Blair (1). **DP:** 1 (Belanger-D.Johnson-Powell).

PITTSBURGH	AB	R	H	HR	RBI	BB	AVG
Cash 2b	4	1	1	0	0	1	.176
Hebner 3b	5	1	1	0	0	0	.250
Clemente rf	4	0	3	0	0	1	.471
Stargell lf	5	1	2	0	1	0	.250
Oliver cf	4	0	2	0	2	1	.214
Robertson 1b	4	1	1	0	0	0	.143
Sanguillen c	4	0	2	0	0	0	.294
Hernandez ss	3	0	1	0	0	0	.250
a-Davalillo ph	1	0	1	0	0	0	.500
Giusti p	0	0	0	0	0	0	.000
Walker p	0	0	0	0	0	0	.000
Kison p	2	0	0	0	0	1	.000
b-May ph	1	0	1	0	1	0	.500
c-Alley pr-ss	0	0	0	0	0	0	.000
TOTALS	**37**	**4**	**14**	**0**	**4**	**4**	**.234**

a - Batted for Hernandez in the 7th
b - Batted for Kison in the 7th
c - Ran for May in the 7th

BATTING: 2B: Stargell (1, Dobson), Oliver (1, Dobson). **RBI:** Stargell 1 (1), Oliver 2 (2), May 1 (1). **2-out RBI:** Stargell 1, Oliver 2, May 1. **Runners left in scoring position, 2 out:** Cash 1, Stargell 2, Robertson 2, Sanguillen 2. **GIDP:** Cash. **Team LOB:** 13 **BASERUNNING: SB:** Sanguillen (1, 2nd base off Dobson/Etchebarren), Hernandez (1, 2nd base off Dobson/Etchebarren). **FIELDING: PB:** Sanguillen. **DP:** 1 (Hernandez-Cash-Robertson).

BALTIMORE	IP	H	R	ER	BB	SO	HR	ERA
Dobson	5.1	10	3	3	3	4	0	5.06
Jackson	0.2	0	0	0	1	0	0	0.00
Watt (L, 0-1)	1.1	4	1	1	0	1	0	3.86
Richert	0.2	0	0	0	0	1	0	0.00
PITTSBURGH	**IP**	**H**	**R**	**ER**	**BB**	**SO**	**HR**	**ERA**
Walker	0.2	3	3	3	1	0	0	40.50
Kison (W, 1-0)	6.1	1	0	0	0	3	0	0.00
Giusti (S, 1)	2	0	0	0	0	1	0	0.00

IBB: F.Robinson (by Walker), Oliver (by Dobson). **HBP:** D.Johnson (by Kison), F.Robinson (by Kison), Etchebarren (by Kison). **Ground balls-fly balls:** Dobson 7-4, Jackson 1-1, Watt 0-3, Richert 0-1, Walker 0-0, Kison 7-8, Giusti 3-2. **Batters faced:** Dobson 28, Jackson 3, Watt 8, Richert 2, Walker 6, Kison 22, Giusti 6. **UMPIRES:** hp—Vargo, 1b—Odom, 2b—Kibler, 3b—Chylak, lf—Sudol, rf—Rice **T:** 2:48 **A:** 51,378

GAME 5 Pittsburgh 4 Baltimore 0
Three Rivers Stadium 10/14/71

BALTIMORE	AB	R	H	HR	RBI	BB	AVG
Buford lf	3	0	0	0	0	1	.125
Blair cf	4	0	0	0	0	0	.333
Powell 1b	3	0	1	0	0	0	.111
F.Robinson rf	3	0	0	0	0	0	.412
Hendricks c	2	0	0	0	0	1	.250
B.Robinson 3b	3	0	1	0	0	0	.375
D.Johnson 2b	3	0	0	0	0	0	.167
Belanger ss	3	0	0	0	0	0	.176
McNally p	1	0	0	0	0	0	.000
Leonhard p	0	0	0	0	0	0	.000
a-Shopay ph	1	0	0	0	0	0	.000
Dukes p	0	0	0	0	0	0	.000
b-Rettenmund ph	1	0	0	0	0	0	.222
TOTALS	**27**	**0**	**2**	**0**	**0**	**2**	**.213**

a - Batted for Leonhard in the 6th
b - Batted for Dukes in the 9th

BATTING: GIDP: B.Robinson, F.Robinson. **Team LOB:** 2 **FIELDING: E:** B.Robinson (2). **Outfield assists:** Blair (1).

PITTSBURGH	AB	R	H	HR	RBI	BB	AVG
Cash 2b	4	0	0	0	0	1	.143
Clines cf	3	2	1	0	0	1	.143
Clemente rf	4	0	1	0	1	0	.429
Stargell lf	4	0	1	0	0	0	.250
Robertson 1b	3	1	1	1	1	1	.176
Sanguillen c	4	1	1	0	0	0	.286
Pagan 3b	4	0	1	0	0	0	.250
Hernandez ss	3	0	2	0	0	0	.364
Briles p	2	0	1	0	1	0	.500
TOTALS	**31**	**4**	**9**	**1**	**3**	**3**	**.244**

BATTING: 3B: Clines (1, McNally). **HR:** Robertson (2, 2nd off McNally 0 on, 0 out). **S:** Briles, Briles. **RBI:** Clemente 1 (2), Robertson 1 (4), Briles 1 (1). **2-out RBI:** Briles 1. **Runners left in scoring position, 2 out:** Cash 2, Clines 1, Stargell 1, Sanguillen 2, Pagan 1. **Team LOB:** 9 **BASERUNNING: SB:** Clines (1, 2nd base off McNally/Hendricks), Sanguillen (2, 2nd base off McNally/Hendricks). **FIELDING: DP:** 2 (Hernandez-Cash-Robertson, Pagan-Cash-Robertson).

BALTIMORE	IP	H	R	ER	BB	SO	HR	ERA
McNally (L, 1-1)	4	7	4	3	2	3	1	2.08
Leonhard	1	0	0	0	1	0	0	0.00
Dukes	3	2	0	0	0	1	0	0.00
PITTSBURGH	**IP**	**H**	**R**	**ER**	**BB**	**SO**	**HR**	**ERA**
Briles (W, 1-0)	9	2	0	0	2	2	0	0.00

WP: McNally 1. **HBP:** Hernandez (by Dukes). **Ground balls-fly balls:** McNally 6-2, Leonhard 0-3, Dukes 2-5, Briles 9-14. **Batters faced:** McNally 21, Leonhard 4, Dukes 12, Briles 29. **UMPIRES:** hp—Odom, 1b—Kibler, 2b—Chylak, 3b—Sudol, lf—Rice, rf—Vargo **T:** 2:16 **A:** 51,377

GAME 6 Baltimore 3 Pittsburgh 2
Memorial Stadium 10/16/71

PITTSBURGH	AB	R	H	HR	RBI	BB	AVG
Cash 2b	5	0	1	0	0	0	.154
Hebner 3b	4	0	0	0	0	1	.167
Clemente rf	4	1	2	1	1	1	.440
Stargell lf	4	0	0	0	0	1	.200
Oliver cf	5	1	1	0	1	0	.211
Miller p	0	0	0	0	0	0	.000
Robertson 1b	4	0	2	0	1	0	.238
Sanguillen c	4	0	3	0	0	0	.360
Hernandez ss	4	0	0	0	0	0	.267
Moose p	1	0	0	0	0	0	.000
B.Johnson p	1	0	0	0	0	0	.000
Giusti p	0	0	0	0	0	0	.000
a-Davalillo ph-cf	1	0	0	0	0	0	.333
TOTALS	**37**	**2**	**9**	**1**	**2**	**3**	**.244**

a - Batted for Giusti in the 10th

BATTING: 2B: Oliver (2, Palmer). **3B:** Clemente (1, Palmer). **HR:** Clemente (1, 3th off Palmer 0 on, 1 out). **S:** Moose. **RBI:** Clemente 1 (3), Robertson 1 (5). **Runners left in scoring position, 2 out:** Cash 2, Stargell 1, Oliver 2. **Team LOB:** 9 **BASERUNNING: SB:** Cash (1, 2nd base off Dobson/Hendricks). **FIELDING: E:** Hebner (1). **DP:** 1 (Hebner-Cash-Robertson).

BALTIMORE	AB	R	H	HR	RBI	BB	AVG
Buford lf	4	1	3	1	1	1	.250
D.Johnson 2b	5	0	1	0	1	0	.174
Powell 1b	5	0	1	0	0	0	.130
F.Robinson rf	4	1	0	0	0	1	.333
Rettenmund cf	5	0	1	0	0	0	.217
B.Robinson 3b	4	0	1	0	1	0	.350
Hendricks c	4	0	0	0	0	0	.188
Belanger ss	1	1	1	0	0	3	.222
Palmer p	2	0	0	0	0	0	.000
a-Shopay ph	1	0	0	0	0	0	.000
Dobson p	0	0	0	0	0	0	.000
McNally p	0	0	0	0	0	0	.000
TOTALS	**35**	**3**	**8**	**1**	**3**	**5**	**.216**

a - Batted for Palmer in the 9th

BATTING: 2B: Buford (1, Giusti). **HR:** Buford (2, 6th off Moose 0 on, 0 out). **S:** Palmer. **SF:** B.Robinson. **RBI:** Buford 1 (3), D.Johnson 1 (3), B.Robinson 1 (5). **2-out RBI:** D.Johnson 1. **Runners left in scoring position, 2 out:** Buford 1, D.Johnson 2, Powell 1, B.Robinson 1, Palmer 1. **GIDP:** D.Johnson. **Team LOB:** 10 **BASERUNNING: SB:** Belanger (1, 2nd base off B.Johnson/Sanguillen). **Outfield assists:** Buford (1).

PITTSBURGH	IP	H	R	ER	BB	SO	HR	ERA
Moose	5	4	1	1	2	3	1	6.52
B.Johnson	1.2	1	1	1	1	2	0	9.00
Giusti	2.1	2	0	0	1	3	0	0.00
Miller (L, 0-1)	0.2	1	1	1	1	0	0	3.86
BALTIMORE	**IP**	**H**	**R**	**ER**	**BB**	**SO**	**HR**	**ERA**
Palmer	9	8	2	2	1	5	1	2.65
Dobson	0.2	1	0	0	1	1	0	4.50
McNally (W, 2-1)	0.1	0	0	0	1	0	0	2.03

IBB: Clemente (by Dobson). **Ground balls-fly balls:** Moose 7-4, B.Johnson 1-2, Giusti 2-2, Miller 1-0, Palmer 8-12, Dobson 0-1, McNally 0-1. **Batters faced:** Moose 21, B.Johnson 7, Giusti 10, Miller 4, Palmer 35, Dobson 4, McNally 2. **UMPIRES:** hp—Kibler, 1b—Chylak, 2b—Sudol, 3b—Rice, lf—Vargo, rf—Odom **T:** 2:59 **A:** 44,174

GAME 7 Pittsburgh 2 Baltimore 1
Memorial Stadium 10/17/71

PITTSBURGH	AB	R	H	HR	RBI	BB	AVG
Cash 2b	4	0	0	0	0	0	.133
Clines cf	4	0	0	0	0	0	.091
Clemente rf	4	1	1	1	1	0	.414
Robertson 1b	4	0	0	0	0	0	.240
Sanguillen c	4	0	2	0	0	0	.379
Stargell lf	4	1	1	0	0	0	.208
Pagan 3b	3	0	1	0	1	0	.267
Hernandez ss	3	0	0	0	0	0	.222
Blass p	3	0	0	0	0	0	.000
TOTALS	**33**	**2**	**6**	**1**	**2**	**0**	**.235**

BATTING: 2B: Pagan (2, Cuellar). **HR:** Clemente (2, 4th off Cuellar 0 on, 2 out). **RBI:** Clemente 1 (4), Pagan 1 (2). **2-out RBI:** Clemente 1. **Runners left in scoring position, 2 out:** Cash 1, Stargell 1. **Team LOB:** 4 **FIELDING: E:** Robertson (1). **DP:** 1 (Cash-Robertson).

BALTIMORE	AB	R	H	HR	RBI	BB	AVG
Buford lf	3	0	1	0	1	1	.261
D.Johnson 2b	4	0	0	0	0	0	.148
Powell 1b	4	0	0	0	0	0	.111
F.Robinson rf	4	0	0	0	0	0	.280
Rettenmund cf	4	0	0	0	0	0	.185
B.Robinson 3b	2	0	0	0	0	1	.318
Hendricks c	3	1	2	0	0	0	.263
Belanger ss	3	0	1	0	0	0	.238
Cuellar p	2	0	0	0	0	0	.000
a-Shopay ph	0	0	0	0	0	0	.000
Dobson p	0	0	0	0	0	0	.000
McNally p	0	0	0	0	0	0	.000
TOTALS	**29**	**1**	**4**	**0**	**1**	**2**	**.205**

a - Batted for Cuellar in the 8th

BATTING: 2B: Hendricks (1, Blass). **S:** Shopay. **RBI:** Buford 1 (4). **Runners left in scoring position, 2 out:** D.Johnson 1, Cuellar 1. **GIDP:** Belanger. **Team LOB:** 4

PITTSBURGH	IP	H	R	ER	BB	SO	HR	ERA
Blass (W, 2-0)	9	4	1	1	2	5	0	1.00
BALTIMORE	**IP**	**H**	**R**	**ER**	**BB**	**SO**	**HR**	**ERA**
Cuellar (L, 0-2)	8	4	2	2	0	6	1	3.86
Dobson	0.2	2	0	0	0	1	0	4.05
McNally	0.1	0	0	0	0	0	0	1.98

Ground balls-fly balls: Blass 12-8, Cuellar 11-7, Dobson 1-0, McNally 1-0. **Batters faced:** Blass 32, Cuellar 28, Dobson 4, McNally 1. **UMPIRES:** hp—Chylak, 1b—Sudol, 2b—Rice, 3b—Vargo, lf—Odom, rf—Kibler **T:** 2:10 **A:** 47,291

1972 OAKLAND DEF. CINCINNATI, 4-3

GAME 1 Oakland 3 Cincinnati 2
Riverfront Stadium 10/14/72

OAKLAND	AB	R	H	HR	RBI	BB	AVG
Campaneris ss	3	0	2	0	0	0	.667
Rudi lf	4	0	0	0	0	0	.000
Alou rf	3	0	0	0	0	1	.000
Epstein 1b	3	0	0	0	0	1	.000
b-Lewis pr	0	0	0	0	0	0	.000
Hegan 1b	0	0	0	0	0	0	.000
Bando 3b	4	0	0	0	0	0	.000
Hendrick cf	2	1	0	0	0	1	.000
Tenace c	3	2	2	2	3	0	.667
Green 2b	2	0	0	0	0	0	.000
a-Marquez ph	1	0	0	0	0	0	.000
Kubiak 2b	0	0	0	0	0	0	.000
Holtzman p	2	0	0	0	0	0	.000
Fingers p	0	0	0	0	0	0	.000
Blue p	0	0	0	0	0	1	.000
TOTALS	**27**	**3**	**4**	**2**	**3**	**4**	**.148**

a - Batted for Green in the 8th
b - Ran for Epstein in the 9th

BATTING: HR: Tenace 2 (2, 2nd off Nolan 1 on, 2 out, 5th off Nolan 0 on, 1 out). **S:** Campaneris. **RBI:** Tenace 3 (3). **2-out RBI:** Tenace 2. **Runners left in scoring position, 2 out:** Rudi 1. **Team LOB:** 2 **BASERUNNING: CS:** Campaneris (1, 2nd base off Nolan/Bench), Lewis (1, 2nd base off Carroll/Bench).

CINCINNATI	AB	R	H	HR	RBI	BB	AVG
Rose lf	4	0	0	0	0	1	.000
Morgan 2b	3	0	0	0	0	0	.000
Tolan cf	4	0	1	0	0	0	.250
Bench c	3	2	2	0	0	1	.667
Perez 1b	4	0	2	0	0	0	.500
Menke 3b	3	0	0	0	1	1	.000
Geronimo rf	3	0	0	0	0	0	.000
b-McRae ph	1	0	1	0	0	0	1.000
c-Foster pr	0	0	0	0	0	0	.000
Concepcion ss	2	0	1	0	1	1	.500
Nolan p	2	0	0	0	0	0	.000
Borbon p	0	0	0	0	0	0	.000
a-Uhlaender ph	1	0	0	0	0	0	.000
Carroll p	0	0	0	0	0	0	.000
d-Javier ph	1	0	0	0	0	0	.000
TOTALS	**31**	**2**	**7**	**0**	**2**	**5**	**.226**

a - Batted for Borbon in the 7th
b - Batted for Geronimo in the 9th
c - Ran for McRae in the 9th
d - Batted for Carroll in the 9th

BATTING: 2B: Bench (1, Holtzman). **S:** Concepcion. **RBI:** Menke 1 (1), Concepcion 1 (1). **Runners left in scoring position, 2 out:** Rose 1, Tolan 1, Geronimo 1, Nolan 2. **Team LOB:** 8 **BASERUNNING: CS:** Concepcion (1, 2nd base off Fingers/Tenace). **FIELDING: DP:** 1 (Morgan-Perez).

OAKLAND	IP	H	R	ER	BB	SO	HR	ERA
Holtzman (W, 1-0)	5	5	2	2	3	3	0	3.60
Fingers	1.2	1	0	0	1	3	0	0.00
Blue (S, 1)	2.1	1	0	0	1	1	0	0.00
CINCINNATI	**IP**	**H**	**R**	**ER**	**BB**	**SO**	**HR**	**ERA**
Nolan (L, 0-1)	6	4	3	3	2	0	2	4.50
Borbon	1	0	0	0	0	0	0	0.00
Carroll	2	0	0	0	2	1	0	0.00

WP: Blue 1. **IBB:** Concepcion (by Holtzman). **Ground balls-fly balls:** Holtzman 7-4, Fingers 0-1, Blue 2-3, Nolan 5-11, Borbon 3-0, Carroll 1-2. **Batters faced:** Holtzman 22, Fingers 6, Blue 9, Nolan 22, Borbon 3, Carroll 7. **UMPIRES:** hp—Pelekoudas, 1b—Honochick, 2b—Steiner, 3b—Umont, lf—Engel, rf—Haller **T:** 2:18 **A:** 52,918

GAME 2 Oakland 2 Cincinnati 1
Riverfront Stadium 10/15/72

OAKLAND	AB	R	H	HR	RBI	BB	AVG
Campaneris ss	5	0	1	0	0	0	.375
Alou rf	4	0	1	0	0	0	.143
Rudi lf	3	1	2	1	1	1	.286
Epstein 1b	2	0	0	0	0	1	.000
a-Lewis pr	0	0	0	0	0	0	.000
Hegan 1b	1	0	0	0	0	0	.000
Bando 3b	4	0	1	0	0	0	.125
Hendrick cf	4	1	1	0	0	0	.167
Tenace c	4	0	0	0	0	0	.286
Green 2b	4	0	2	0	0	0	.333
Hunter p	3	0	1	0	1	1	.333
Fingers p	0	0	0	0	0	0	.000
TOTALS	**34**	**2**	**9**	**1**	**2**	**3**	**.213**

a - Ran for Epstein in the 6th

BATTING: HR: Rudi (1, 3th off Grimsley 0 on, 1 out). **RBI:** Rudi 1 (1), Hunter 1 (1). **2-out RBI:** Hunter 1. **Runners left in scoring position, 2 out:** Campaneris 3, Hegan 1. **Team LOB:** 8 **BASERUNNING: SB:** Alou (1, 2nd base off Hall/Bench). **CS:** Lewis (2, 2nd base off Borbon/Bench). **FIELDING: E:** Hunter (1), Epstein (1). **DP:** 1 (Campaneris-Green-Epstein).

CINCINNATI	AB	R	H	HR	RBI	BB	AVG
Rose lf	4	0	1	0	0	0	.125
Morgan 2b	4	0	0	0	0	0	.000
Tolan cf	4	0	0	0	0	0	.125
Bench c	3	0	1	0	0	1	.500
Perez 1b	3	1	2	0	0	1	.571
Menke 3b	4	0	0	0	0	0	.000
Geronimo rf	4	0	0	0	0	0	.000
Chaney ss	2	0	0	0	0	1	.000
c-McRae ph	1	0	1	0	1	0	1.000
d-Concepcion pr	0	0	0	0	0	0	.500
Grimsley p	1	0	0	0	0	0	.000
a-Uhlaender ph	1	0	1	0	0	0	.500
Borbon p	0	0	0	0	0	0	.000
b-Hague ph	1	0	0	0	0	0	.000
Hall p	0	0	0	0	0	0	.000
e-Javier ph	1	0	0	0	0	0	.000
TOTALS	**33**	**1**	**6**	**0**	**1**	**3**	**.203**

a - Batted for Grimsley in the 5th
b - Batted for Borbon in the 7th
c - Batted for Chaney in the 9th
d - Ran for McRae in the 9th e - Batted for Hall in the 9th

BATTING: 2B: Uhlaender (1, Hunter). **RBI:** McRae 1 (1). **2-out RBI:** McRae 1. **Runners left in scoring position, 2 out:** Tolan 2, Geronimo 1, Grimsley 2. **GIDP:** Menke. **Team LOB:** 8 **BASERUNNING: SB:** Morgan (1, 2nd base off Hunter/Tenace). **FIELDING: Outfield assists:** Rose (1). **DP:** 1 (Bench-Chaney).

APPENDIX II

OAKLAND	IP	H	R	ER	BB	SO	HR	ERA
Hunter (W, 1-0)	8.2	6	1	1	3	6	0	1.04
Fingers (S, 1)	0.1	0	0	0	0	0	0	0.00

CINCINNATI	IP	H	R	ER	BB	SO	HR	ERA
Grimsley (L, 0-1)	5	6	2	2	0	1	1	3.60
Borbon	2	0	0	0	1	4	0	0.00
Hall	2	3	0	0	2	2	0	0.00

IBB: Chaney (by Hunter). **Ground balls-fly balls:** Hunter 6-14, Fingers 0-1, Grimsley 10-3, Borbon 0-1, Hall 1-3. **Batters faced:** Hunter 35, Fingers 1, Grimsley 20, Borbon 6, Hall 11. **UMPIRES:** hp—Honochick, 1b—Steiner, 2b—Umont, 3b—Engel, lf—Haller, rf—Pelekoudas **T:** 2:26 **A:** 53,224

GAME 3 Cincinnati 1 Oakland 0
Oakland Coliseum 10/18/72

CINCINNATI	AB	R	H	HR	RBI	BB	AVG
Rose lf	3	0	0	0	0	1	.091
Morgan 2b	3	0	0	0	0	1	.000
Tolan cf	4	0	1	0	0	0	.167
Bench c	4	0	0	0	0	0	.300
Perez 1b	3	1	1	0	0	1	.500
Menke 3b	2	0	1	0	0	1	.111
Geronimo rf	4	0	1	0	1	0	.091
Chaney ss	4	0	0	0	0	0	.000
Billingham p	4	0	0	0	0	0	.000
Carroll p	0	0	0	0	0	0	.000
TOTALS	**31**	**1**	**4**	**0**	**1**	**4**	**.179**

BATTING: S: Menke. **RBI:** Geronimo 1 (1). **Runners left in scoring position, 2 out:** Rose 2, Morgan 1, Menke 2. **Team LOB:** 8 **BASERUNNING: SB:** Rose (1, 2nd base off Odom/Tenace), Geronimo (1, 2nd base off Odom/Tenace), Tolan (1, 2nd base off Fingers/Tenace). **FIELDING: E:** Bench (1). **DP:** 1 (Morgan-Chaney-Perez).

OAKLAND	AB	R	H	HR	RBI	BB	AVG
Campaneris ss	3	0	0	0	0	1	.273
Alou rf	3	0	0	0	0	0	.100
Rudi lf	4	0	1	0	0	0	.273
Epstein 1b	2	0	0	0	0	2	.000
Bando 3b	4	0	0	0	0	0	.083
Hendrick cf	4	0	0	0	0	0	.100
Tenace c	3	0	0	0	0	0	.200
Green 2b	2	0	1	0	0	0	.375
a-Marquez ph	1	0	1	0	0	0	.500
b-Lewis pr	0	0	0	0	0	0	.000
Kubiak 2b	0	0	0	0	0	0	.000
Odom p	2	0	0	0	0	0	.000
c-Hegan ph	1	0	0	0	0	0	.000
Blue p	0	0	0	0	0	0	.000
Fingers p	0	0	0	0	0	0	.000
TOTALS	**29**	**0**	**3**	**0**	**0**	**3**	**.178**

a - Batted for Green in the 7th
b - Ran for Marquez in the 7th
c - Batted for Odom in the 7th

BATTING: S: Alou. **GIDP:** Bando. **Team LOB:** 6 **FIELDING: E:** Tenace (1), Epstein (2).

CINCINNATI	IP	H	R	ER	BB	SO	HR	ERA
Billingham (W, 1-0)	8	3	0	0	3	7	0	0.00
Carroll (S, 1)	1	0	0	0	0	0	0	0.00

OAKLAND	IP	H	R	ER	BB	SO	HR	ERA
Odom (L, 0-1)	7	3	1	1	2	11	0	1.29
Blue	0.1	1	0	0	1	0	0	0.00
Fingers	1.2	0	0	0	1	3	0	0.00

IBB: Epstein (by Billingham), Perez (by Fingers). **Ground balls-fly balls:** Billingham 11-5, Carroll 2-1, Odom 7-3, Blue 0-1, Fingers 1-1. **Batters faced:** Billingham 30, Carroll 3, Odom 27, Blue 3, Fingers 6. **UMPIRES:** hp—Steiner, 1b—Umont, 2b—Engel, 3b—Haller, lf—Pelekoudas, rf—Honochick **T:** 2:24 **A:** 49,410

GAME 4 Oakland 3 Cincinnati 2
Oakland Coliseum 10/19/72

CINCINNATI	AB	R	H	HR	RBI	BB	AVG
Rose lf	4	0	0	0	0	0	.067
Morgan 2b	3	1	0	0	0	1	.000
Tolan cf	4	0	1	0	2	0	.188
Bench c	4	0	2	0	0	0	.357
Perez 1b	4	0	2	0	0	0	.500
McRae rf	4	0	1	0	0	0	.500
Geronimo rf	0	0	0	0	0	0	.091
Menke 3b	4	0	0	0	0	0	.077
Concepcion ss	3	1	1	0	0	0	.400
Gullett p	2	0	0	0	0	0	.000
a-Javier ph	0	0	0	0	0	0	.000
Borbon p	0	0	0	0	0	0	.000
Carroll p	0	0	0	0	0	0	.000
TOTALS	**32**	**2**	**7**	**0**	**2**	**1**	**.189**

a - Batted for Gullett in the 8th

BATTING: 2B: Tolan (1, Blue). **S:** Javier. **RBI:** Tolan 2 (2). **2-out RBI:** Tolan 2. **Runners left in scoring position, 2 out:** Bench 1, Perez 2. **GIDP:** Menke. **Team LOB:** 5 **BASERUNNING: SB:** Bench (1, 2nd base off Holtzman/Tenace). **FIELDING: E:** Perez (1). **DP:** 1 (Concepcion-Perez).

OAKLAND	AB	R	H	HR	RBI	BB	AVG
Campaneris ss	4	0	0	0	0	0	.200
Alou rf	3	0	0	0	0	1	.077
Rudi lf	4	0	2	0	0	0	.333
Bando 3b	3	0	2	0	0	1	.200
Epstein 1b	3	0	0	0	0	0	.000
Hegan 1b	1	0	0	0	0	0	.000
Hendrick cf	3	0	0	0	0	0	.077
a-Marquez ph	1	0	1	0	0	0	.667
b-Lewis pr	0	1	0	0	0	0	.000
Tenace c	4	2	2	1	1	0	.286
Green 2b	3	0	1	0	0	0	.364
c-Mincher ph	1	0	1	0	1	0	1.000
d-Odom pr	0	0	0	0	0	0	.000
Holtzman p	3	0	0	0	0	0	.000
Blue p	0	0	0	0	0	0	.000
Fingers p	0	0	0	0	0	0	.000
e-Mangual ph	1	0	1	0	1	0	1.000
TOTALS	**34**	**3**	**10**	**1**	**3**	**2**	**.210**

a - Batted for Hendrick in the 9th
b - Ran for Marquez in the 9th
c - Batted for Green in the 9th
d - Ran for Mincher in the 9th e - Batted for Fingers in the 9th

BATTING: 2B: Green (1, Gullett). **HR:** Tenace (3, 5th off Gullett 0 on, 1 out). **RBI:** Tenace 1 (4), Mincher 1 (1), Mangual 1 (1). **Runners left in scoring position, 2 out:** Epstein 2, Holtzman 1. **GIDP:** Hendrick. **Team LOB:** 8 **FIELDING: E:** Holtzman (1). **DP:** 1 (Holtzman-Green-Hegan).

CINCINNATI	IP	H	R	ER	BB	SO	HR	ERA
Gullett	7	5	1	1	2	4	1	1.29
Borbon	1.1	2	1	1	0	0	0	2.08
Carroll (L, 0-1)	0	3	1	1	0	0	0	3.00

OAKLAND	IP	H	R	ER	BB	SO	HR	ERA
Holtzman	7.2	5	1	1	0	1	0	2.13
Blue	0.1	2	1	1	1	0	0	3.00
Fingers (W, 1-0)	1	0	0	0	0	1	0	0.00

IBB: Bando (by Gullett). **Ground balls-fly balls:** Gullett 7-9, Borbon 4-0, Carroll 0-0, Holtzman 13-8, Blue 0-1, Fingers 0-1. **Batters faced:** Gullett 27, Borbon 6, Carroll 3, Holtzman 28, Blue 4, Fingers 2. **UMPIRES:** hp—Umont, 1b—Engel , 2b—Haller, 3b—Pelekoudas, lf—Honochick, rf—Steiner **T:** 2:06 **A:** 49,410

GAME 5 Cincinnati 5 Oakland 4
Oakland Coliseum 10/20/72

CINCINNATI	AB	R	H	HR	RBI	BB	AVG
Rose lf	5	1	3	1	2	0	.200
Morgan 2b	3	2	0	0	0	2	.000
Tolan cf	4	0	2	0	2	0	.250
Bench c	4	0	0	0	0	0	.278
Perez 1b	4	0	1	0	0	0	.444
Menke 3b	3	1	1	1	1	0	.125
Geronimo rf	4	1	1	0	0	0	.133
Chaney ss	1	0	0	0	0	1	.000
b-Hague ph	1	0	0	0	0	0	.000
Carroll p	0	0	0	0	0	0	.000
Grimsley p	0	0	0	0	0	0	.000
Billingham p	0	0	0	0	0	0	.000
McGlothlin p	1	0	0	0	0	0	.000
Borbon p	0	0	0	0	0	0	.000
a-Uhlaender ph	1	0	0	0	0	0	.333
Hall p	0	0	0	0	0	0	.000
c-Concepcion ph-ss	2	0	0	0	0	0	.286
TOTALS	**33**	**5**	**8**	**2**	**5**	**3**	**.200**

a - Batted for Borbon in the 5th
b - Batted for Chaney in the 7th
c - Batted for Hall in the 7th

BATTING: 2B: Perez (1, Hunter). **HR:** Rose (1, 1st off Hunter 0 on, 0 out), Menke (1, 4th off Hunter 0 on, 1 out). **S:** Menke, Grimsley. **SF:** Geronimo. **RBI:** Rose 2 (2), Tolan 2 (4), Menke 1 (2). **2-out RBI:** Tolan 1. **Runners left in scoring position, 2 out:** Bench 1, Menke 1, McGlothlin 1. **Team LOB:** 6 **BASERUNNING: SB:** Tolan 2 (3, 2nd base off Fingers/Tenace, 3rd base off Fingers/Tenace), Morgan (2, 2nd base off Fingers/Tenace). **FIELDING: DP:** 1 (Morgan-Bench).

OAKLAND	AB	R	H	HR	RBI	BB	AVG
Campaneris ss	5	0	0	0	0	0	.150
Alou rf	4	0	0	0	0	0	.059
Rudi lf	3	0	0	0	0	0	.278
Epstein 1b	2	1	0	0	0	1	.000
Hegan 1b	1	0	1	0	0	0	.250
Bando 3b	3	1	1	0	0	1	.222
Hendrick cf	2	1	1	0	0	0	.133
c-Mincher ph	0	0	0	0	0	0	1.000
d-Mangual ph-cf	1	0	0	0	0	0	.500
Tenace c	2	1	1	1	3	2	.313
f-Odom pr	0	0	0	0	0	0	.000
Green 2b	1	0	0	0	0	0	.333
a-Marquez ph	1	0	1	0	1	0	.750
b-Lewis pr	0	0	0	0	0	0	.000
Kubiak 2b	2	0	1	0	0	0	.500
Hunter p	2	0	0	0	0	0	.200
Fingers p	0	0	0	0	0	0	.000
Hamilton p	0	0	0	0	0	0	.000
e-Duncan ph	1	0	1	0	0	0	1.000
TOTALS	**30**	**4**	**7**	**1**	**4**	**4**	**.214**

a - Batted for Green in the 4th
b - Ran for Marquez in the 4th
c - Batted for Hendrick in the 8th
d - Batted for Mincher in the 8th e - Batted for Hamilton in the 9th f - Ran for Tenace in the 9th

BATTING: HR: Tenace (4, 2nd off McGlothlin 2 on, 1 out). **S:** Hendrick, Fingers. **RBI:** Tenace 3 (7), Marquez 1 (1). **Runners left in scoring position, 2 out:** Campaneris 1, Mangual 1. **Team LOB:** 6 **FIELDING: E:** Alou (1), Bando (1). **Outfield assists:** Alou (1). **DP:** 1 (Alou-Tenace).

CINCINNATI	IP	H	R	ER	BB	SO	HR	ERA
McGlothlin	3	2	4	4	2	3	1	12.00
Borbon	1	1	0	0	1	0	0	1.69
Hall	2	0	0	0	0	1	0	0.00
Carroll	1.2	3	0	0	0	1	0	1.93
Grimsley (W, 1-1)	0.2	0	0	0	1	0	0	3.18
Billingham (S, 1)	0.2	1	0	0	0	0	0	0.00

OAKLAND	IP	H	R	ER	BB	SO	HR	ERA
Hunter	4.2	5	3	3	2	2	2	2.70
Fingers (L, 1-1)	3.2	3	2	2	1	4	0	2.16
Hamilton	0.2	0	0	0	0	0	0	0.00

WP: Fingers 1. **IBB:** Chaney (by Hunter), Tenace (by Borbon). **HBP:** Rudi (by McGlothlin). **Ground balls-fly balls:** McGlothlin 4-2, Borbon 0-1, Hall 3-2, Carroll 2-1, Grimsley 1-1, Billingham 0-1, Hunter 4-7, Fingers 4-3, Hamilton 0-1. **Batters faced:** McGlothlin 14, Borbon 4, Hall 6, Carroll 8, Grimsley 3, Billingham 2, Hunter 21, Fingers 16, Hamilton 1. **UMPIRES:** hp—Engel, 1b—Haller, 2b—Pelekoudas, 3b—Honochick, lf—Steiner, rf—Umont **T:** 2:26 **A:** 49,410

GAME 6 Cincinnati 8 Oakland 1
Riverfront Stadium 10/21/72

OAKLAND	AB	R	H	HR	RBI	BB	AVG
Campaneris ss	4	0	0	0	0	0	.125
Alou rf	4	0	0	0	0	0	.048
Rudi lf	4	0	1	0	0	0	.273
Epstein 1b	4	0	0	0	0	0	.000
Bando 3b	4	1	2	0	0	0	.273
Mangual cf	4	0	2	0	0	0	.500
Tenace c	4	0	1	0	0	0	.300
Green 2b	2	0	1	0	1	0	.357
a-Marquez ph	1	0	0	0	0	0	.600
Kubiak 2b	1	0	0	0	0	0	.333
Blue p	1	0	0	0	0	1	.000
Locker p	0	0	0	0	0	0	.000
b-Mincher ph	0	0	0	0	0	0	1.000
c-Duncan ph	1	0	0	0	0	0	.500
Hamilton p	0	0	0	0	0	0	.000
Horlen p	0	0	0	0	0	0	.000
TOTALS	**34**	**1**	**7**	**0**	**1**	**1**	**.213**

a - Batted for Green in the 7th
b - Batted for Locker in the 7th
c - Batted for Mincher in the 7th

BATTING: 2B: Green (2, Nolan). **RBI:** Green 1 (1). **2-out RBI:** Green 1. **Runners left in scoring position, 2 out:** Campaneris 1, Bando 1, Tenace 1, Kubiak 1. **Team LOB:** 7 **FIELDING: E:** Mangual (1).

CINCINNATI	AB	R	H	HR	RBI	BB	AVG
Rose lf	3	1	0	0	0	2	.174
Morgan 2b	5	1	2	0	1	0	.095
Tolan cf	4	2	2	0	2	0	.292
Bench c	2	2	1	1	1	2	.300
Perez 1b	3	0	1	0	1	1	.429
McRae rf	3	1	1	0	0	0	.444
Geronimo rf	1	0	1	0	2	0	.188
Menke 3b	4	0	0	0	0	0	.100
Concepcion ss	3	1	2	0	1	0	.400
Nolan p	1	0	0	0	0	0	.000
Grimsley p	1	0	0	0	0	0	.000
Borbon p	0	0	0	0	0	0	.000
Hall p	2	0	0	0	0	0	.000
TOTALS	**32**	**8**	**10**	**1**	**8**	**5**	**.219**

BATTING: 2B: Morgan (1, Blue), McRae (1, Blue). **3B:** Concepcion (1, Horlen). **HR:** Bench (1, 4th off Blue 0 on, 2 out). **SF:** Concepcion. **RBI:** Morgan 1 (1), Tolan 2 (6), Bench 1 (1), Perez 1 (1), Geronimo 2 (3), Concepcion 1 (2). **2-out RBI:** Morgan 1, Tolan 2, Bench 1, Perez 1, Geronimo 2. **Runners left in scoring position, 2 out:** Morgan 1, Bench 1, McRae 1, Menke 1. **Team LOB:** 6 **BASERUNNING: SB:** Tolan 2 (5, 2nd base off Locker/Tenace, 2nd base off Horlen/Tenace), Concepcion (1, 2nd base off Hamilton/Tenace). **CS:** Rose (1, 2nd base off Blue/Tenace).

OAKLAND	IP	H	R	ER	BB	SO	HR	ERA
Blue (L, 0-1)	5.2	4	3	3	2	4	1	4.15
Locker	0.1	1	0	0	0	0	0	0.00
Hamilton	0.2	3	4	4	1	1	0	27.00
Horlen	1.1	2	1	1	2	1	0	6.75

CINCINNATI	IP	H	R	ER	BB	SO	HR	ERA
Nolan	4.2	3	1	1	0	3	0	3.38
Grimsley (W, 2-1)	1	1	0	0	1	0	0	2.70
Borbon	1	1	0	0	0	0	0	1.42
Hall (S, 1)	2.1	2	0	0	0	1	0	0.00

WP: Horlen 1. **IBB:** Bench 2 (by Locker, by Horlen), Rose (by Hamilton). **Ground balls-fly balls:** Blue 4-7, Locker 1-0, Hamilton 0-1, Horlen 2-1, Nolan 5-6, Grimsley 1-2, Borbon 1-2, Hall 4-2. **Batters faced:** Blue 22, Locker 2, Hamilton 6, Horlen 8, Nolan 17, Grimsley 5, Borbon 4, Hall 9. **UMPIRES:** hp—Haller, 1b—Pelekoudas, 2b—Honochick, 3b—Steiner, lf—Umont, rf—Engel **T:** 2:21 **A:** 52,737

GAME 7 Oakland 3 Cincinnati 2
Riverfront Stadium 10/22/72

OAKLAND	AB	R	H	HR	RBI	BB	AVG
Campaneris ss	4	1	2	0	0	0	.179
Mangual cf	4	1	0	0	0	0	.300
Rudi lf	3	0	0	0	0	1	.240
Tenace 1b	3	0	2	0	2	0	.348
a-Lewis pr	0	1	0	0	0	0	.000
Hegan 1b	1	0	0	0	0	0	.200
Bando 3b	4	0	1	0	1	0	.269
Alou rf	3	0	0	0	0	1	.042
Duncan c	3	0	0	0	0	1	.200
Green 2b	4	0	1	0	0	0	.333
Odom p	2	0	0	0	0	0	.000
Hunter p	0	0	0	0	0	1	.200
Holtzman p	0	0	0	0	0	0	.000
Fingers p	1	0	0	0	0	0	.000
TOTALS	**32**	**3**	**6**	**0**	**3**	**4**	**.209**

a - Ran for Tenace in the 6th

BATTING: 2B: Tenace (1, Borbon), Bando (1, Borbon). **S:** Mangual, Campaneris. **RBI:** Tenace 2 (9), Bando 1 (1). **2-out RBI:** Tenace 2, Bando 1. **Runners left in scoring position, 2 out:** Hegan 1, Green 2. **Team LOB:** 8 **FIELDING: E:** Campaneris (1). **DP:** 1 (Campaneris-Tenace).

CINCINNATI	AB	R	H	HR	RBI	BB	AVG
Rose lf	5	1	2	0	0	0	.214
Morgan 2b	3	0	1	0	0	1	.125
Tolan cf	2	0	0	0	0	1	.269
Foster rf	0	0	0	0	0	0	.000
c-Javier ph	0	0	0	0	0	0	.000
d-Hague ph-rf	1	0	0	0	0	0	.000
Bench c	3	0	0	0	0	1	.261
Perez 1b	2	1	1	0	1	1	.435
Menke 3b	4	0	0	0	0	0	.083
Geronimo rf-cf	3	0	0	0	0	1	.158
Concepcion ss	3	0	0	0	0	1	.308
Billingham p	1	0	0	0	0	0	.000
a-McRae ph	0	0	0	0	1	0	.444
Borbon p	0	0	0	0	0	0	.000
Carroll p	0	0	0	0	0	0	.000
Grimsley p	0	0	0	0	0	0	.000
b-Uhlaender ph	1	0	0	0	0	0	.250
Hall p	0	0	0	0	0	0	.000
e-Chaney ph	0	0	0	0	0	0	.000
TOTALS	**28**	**2**	**4**	**0**	**2**	**6**	**.209**

a - Batted for Billingham in the 5th
b - Batted for Grimsley in the 7th
c - Batted for Foster in the 8th
d - Batted for Javier in the 8th e - Batted for Hall in the 9th

BATTING: 2B: Perez (2, Odom), Morgan (2, Holtzman). **SF:** McRae, Perez. **RBI:** Perez 1 (2), McRae 1 (2). **Runners left in scoring position, 2 out:** Rose 1, Menke 4. **GIDP:** Morgan. **Team LOB:** 8 **BASERUNNING: SB:** Bench (2, 2nd base off Fingers/Duncan). **CS:** Morgan (1, 2nd base off Odom/Duncan). **FIELDING: E:** Tolan (1), Concepcion (1).

OAKLAND	IP	H	R	ER	BB	SO	HR	ERA
Odom	4.1	2	1	1	4	2	0	1.59
Hunter (W, 2-0)	2.2	1	1	1	1	3	0	2.81
Holtzman	0	1	0	0	0	0	0	2.13
Fingers (S, 2)	2	0	0	0	1	0	0	1.74

CINCINNATI	IP	H	R	ER	BB	SO	HR	ERA
Billingham	5	2	1	0	1	4	0	0.00
Borbon (L, 0-1)	0.2	3	2	2	0	0	0	3.86
Carroll	1	0	0	0	2	1	0	1.59
Grimsley	0.1	0	0	0	1	1	0	2.57
Hall	2	1	0	0	0	3	0	0.00

WP: Hunter 1. **IBB:** Alou (by Carroll), Rudi (by Grimsley), Bench (by Fingers). **HBP:** Chaney (by Fingers). **Ground balls-fly balls:** Odom 4-5, Hunter 1-4, Holtzman 0-0, Fingers 1-4, Billingham 6-5, Borbon 1-0, Carroll 2-0, Grimsley 0-0, Hall 2-1. **Batters faced:** Odom 17, Hunter 11, Holtzman 1, Fingers 8, Billingham 18, Borbon 5, Carroll 6, Grimsley 2, Hall 7. **UMPIRES:** hp—Pelekoudas, 1b—Honochick, 2b—Steiner, 3b—Umont, lf—Engel, rf—Haller **T:** 2:50 **A:** 56,040

1973 OAKLAND DEF. NY METS, 4-3

GAME 1 Oakland 2 New York 1
Oakland Coliseum 10/13/73

NY METS	AB	R	H	HR	RBI	BB	AVG
Garrett 3b	5	0	0	0	0	0	.000
Millan 2b	4	0	1	0	0	0	.250
Mays cf	4	0	1	0	0	0	.250
Jones lf	4	1	2	0	0	0	.500
Milner 1b	4	0	2	0	1	0	.500
Grote c	4	0	0	0	0	0	.000
Hahn rf	2	0	0	0	0	1	.000
b-Kranepool ph	1	0	0	0	0	0	.000
Harrelson ss	2	0	0	0	0	1	.000
c-Hodges ph	0	0	0	0	0	1	.000
d-Martinez pr	0	0	0	0	0	0	.000
Matlack p	0	0	0	0	0	1	.000
a-Boswell ph	1	0	1	0	0	0	1.000
McGraw p	0	0	0	0	0	0	.000
e-Staub ph	0	0	0	0	0	0	.000
f-Beauchamp ph	1	0	0	0	0	0	.000
TOTALS	**32**	**1**	**7**	**0**	**1**	**4**	**.219**

a - Batted for Matlack in the 7th
b - Batted for Hahn in the 9th
c - Batted for Harrelson in the 9th
d - Ran for Hodges in the 9th e - Batted for McGraw in the 9th f - Batted for Staub in the 9th

BATTING: 2B: Jones (1, Holtzman). **3B:** Millan (1, Holtzman). **S:** Matlack. **RBI:** Milner 1 (1). **Runners left in scoring position, 2 out:** Millan 1, Mays 1, Harrelson 2. **GIDP:** Garrett. **Team LOB:** 9 **FIELDING: E:** Millan (1), Mays (1).

OAKLAND	AB	R	H	HR	RBI	BB	AVG
Campaneris ss	4	1	1	0	0	0	.250
Rudi lf	3	0	1	0	1	0	.333
Bando 3b	3	0	1	0	0	1	.333
Jackson cf-rf	3	0	0	0	0	1	.000
Tenace 1b	3	0	0	0	0	0	.000
Alou rf	3	0	0	0	0	0	.000
Davalillo cf	0	0	0	0	0	0	.000
Fosse c	3	0	0	0	0	0	.000
Green 2b	2	0	0	0	0	1	.000
Holtzman p	1	1	1	0	0	0	1.000
a-Mangual ph	1	0	0	0	0	0	.000
Fingers p	1	0	0	0	0	0	.000
Knowles p	0	0	0	0	0	0	.000
TOTALS	**27**	**2**	**4**	**0**	**1**	**3**	**.148**

a - Batted for Holtzman in the 5th

BATTING: 2B: Holtzman (1, Matlack). **S:** Rudi. **SF:** Jackson. **RBI:** Rudi 1 (1). **2-out RBI:** Rudi 1. **Runners left in scoring position, 2 out:** Jackson 2. **Team LOB:** 5 **BASERUNNING: SB:** Campaneris (1, 2nd base off Matlack/Grote). **CS:** Green (1, 2nd base off Matlack/Grote). **FIELDING: PB:** Fosse. **DP:** 2 (Holtzman-Tenace, Green-Campaneris-Tenace).

NY METS	IP	H	R	ER	BB	SO	HR	ERA
Matlack (L, 0-1)	6	3	2	0	2	3	0	0.00
McGraw	2	1	0	0	1	1	0	0.00

OAKLAND	IP	H	R	ER	BB	SO	HR	ERA
Holtzman (W, 1-0)	5	4	1	1	3	2	0	1.80
Fingers	3.1	3	0	0	1	3	0	0.00
Knowles (S, 1)	0.2	0	0	0	0	0	0	0.00

IBB: Bando (by McGraw). **Ground balls-fly balls:** Matlack 6-9, McGraw 4-0, Holtzman 5-6, Fingers 2-5, Knowles 0-2. **Batters faced:** Matlack 23, McGraw 8, Holtzman 21, Fingers 14, Knowles 2. **UMPIRES:** hp—Springstead, 1b—Donatelli, 2b—Neudecker, 3b—Pryor, lf—Goetz, rf—Wendelstedt **T:** 2:26 **A:** 46,021

GAME 2 New York 10 Oakland 7
Oakland Coliseum 10/14/73

NY METS	AB	R	H	HR	RBI	BB	AVG
Garrett 3b	6	1	1	1	1	1	.091
Millan 2b	6	0	0	0	0	1	.100
Staub rf	5	0	1	0	0	0	.200
d-Mays pr-cf	2	1	1	0	1	0	.333
Jones lf	5	3	3	1	1	1	.556
Milner 1b	6	1	2	0	0	1	.400
Grote c	6	1	2	0	0	0	.200
Hahn cf-rf	7	1	1	0	1	0	.111
Harrelson ss	6	1	3	0	1	0	.375
Koosman p	1	0	0	0	0	0	.000
Sadecki p	0	0	0	0	0	0	.000
a-Theodore ph	1	0	0	0	0	0	.000
Parker p	0	0	0	0	0	0	.000
b-Kranepool ph	0	0	0	0	0	0	.000
c-Beauchamp ph	1	0	0	0	0	0	.000
McGraw p	2	1	1	0	0	0	.500
Stone p	0	0	0	0	0	0	.000
TOTALS	**54**	**10**	**15**	**2**	**5**	**4**	**.256**

a - Batted for Sadecki in the 5th
b - Batted for Parker in the 6th
c - Batted for Kranepool in the 6th
d - Ran for Staub in the 9th

BATTING: 2B: Harrelson (1, Fingers). **HR:** Jones (1, 2nd off Blue 0 on, 0 out), Garrett (1, 3th off Blue 0 on, 2 out). **S:** McGraw. **RBI:** Garrett 1 (1), Mays 1 (1), Jones 1 (1), Hahn 1 (1), Harrelson 1 (1). **2-out RBI:** Garrett 1, Mays 1. **Runners left in scoring position, 2 out:** Staub 2, Hahn 4, Harrelson 1. **Team LOB:** 15 **FIELDING: E:** Koosman (1). **DP:** 1 (Garrett-Millan-Milner).

OAKLAND	AB	R	H	HR	RBI	BB	AVG
Campaneris ss	6	2	1	0	0	0	.200
Rudi lf	5	1	2	0	1	1	.375
Bando 3b	5	2	1	0	1	1	.250
Jackson cf	6	1	4	0	2	0	.444
Tenace 1b	3	0	1	0	1	3	.167
Alou rf	6	0	3	0	2	0	.333
Fosse c	5	0	0	0	0	1	.000
Green 2b	2	0	0	0	0	0	.000
a-Mangual ph	1	0	0	0	0	0	.000
Kubiak 2b	0	0	0	0	0	0	.000
c-Andrews ph-2b	2	0	0	0	0	1	.000
Blue p	2	0	0	0	0	0	.000
Pina p	0	0	0	0	0	0	.000
Knowles p	0	0	0	0	0	0	.000
b-Conigliaro ph	1	0	0	0	0	0	.000
Odom p	0	0	0	0	0	0	.000
d-Johnson ph	1	0	1	0	0	0	1.000
e-Lewis pr	0	1	0	0	0	0	.000
Fingers p	1	0	0	0	0	0	.000
Lindblad p	0	0	0	0	0	0	.000
f-Davalillo ph	1	0	0	0	0	0	.000
TOTALS	**47**	**7**	**13**	**0**	**7**	**7**	**.230**

a - Batted for Green in the 6th
b - Batted for Knowles in the 7th
c - Batted for Kubiak in the 8th
d - Batted for Odom in the 9th e - Ran for Johnson in the 9th f - Batted for Lindblad in the 12th

BATTING: 2B: Rudi (1, Koosman), Alou (1, Koosman), Jackson (1, McGraw), Johnson (1, McGraw). **3B:** Bando (1, Koosman), Campaneris (1, Koosman), Jackson (1, McGraw). **RBI:** Rudi 1 (2), Bando 1 (1), Jackson 2 (2), Tenace 1 (1), Alou 2 (2). **2-out RBI:** Jackson 2, Tenace 1, Alou 1. **Runners left in scoring position, 2 out:** Campaneris 2, Tenace 2, Alou 1, Green 3. **GIDP:** Tenace. **Team LOB:** 12 **BASERUNNING: SB:** Campaneris (2, 3rd base off McGraw/Grote). **CS:** Rudi (1, 2nd base off Koosman/Grote). **FIELDING: E:** Bando (1), Knowles (1), Tenace (1), Andrews 2 (2). **Outfield assists:** Rudi (1). **DP:** 1 (Rudi-Fosse).

NY METS	IP	H	R	ER	BB	SO	HR	ERA
Koosman	2.1	6	3	3	3	4	0	11.57
Sadecki	1.2	0	0	0	0	3	0	0.00
Parker	1	1	0	0	0	0	0	0.00
McGraw (W, 1-0)	6	5	4	4	3	8	0	4.50
Stone (S, 1)	1	1	0	0	1	0	0	0.00

OAKLAND	IP	H	R	ER	BB	SO	HR	ERA
Blue	5.1	4	4	4	2	4	2	6.75
Pina	0	2	2	0	0	0	0	0.00
Knowles	1.2	1	0	0	2	2	0	0.00
Odom	2	2	0	0	0	2	0	0.00
Fingers (L, 0-1)	2.2	6	4	1	0	2	0	1.50
Lindblad	0.1	0	0	0	0	0	0	0.00

IBB: Fosse (by Koosman), Millan (by Knowles). **HBP:** Grote (by Pina), Campaneris (by McGraw), Jones (by Fingers). **Ground balls-fly balls:** Koosman 3-0, Sadecki 1-0, Parker 1-1, McGraw 9-1, Stone 2-1, Blue 8-5, Pina 0-0, Knowles 2-2, Odom 1-3, Fingers 2-3, Lindblad 3-0. **Batters faced:** Koosman 16, Sadecki 4, Parker 3, McGraw 27, Stone 5, Blue 23, Pina 3, Knowles 9, Odom 8, Fingers 15, Lindblad 3. **UMPIRES:** hp—Donatelli, 1b—Neudecker, 2b—Pryor, 3b—Goetz, lf—Wendelstedt, rf—Springstead **T:** 4:13 **A:** 49,151

GAME 3 Oakland 3 New York 2
Shea Stadium 10/16/73

OAKLAND	AB	R	H	HR	RBI	BB	AVG
Campaneris ss	6	1	3	0	1	0	.313
Rudi lf	5	0	2	0	1	0	.385
Bando 3b	4	1	2	0	0	0	.333
Jackson rf	5	0	0	0	0	0	.286
Tenace 1b-c	3	0	1	0	1	2	.222
Davalillo cf-1b	5	0	1	0	0	0	.167
Fosse c	2	0	0	0	0	0	.000
a-Bourque ph-1b	2	0	1	0	0	0	.500
d-Lewis pr	0	0	0	0	0	0	.000
Lindblad p	1	0	0	0	0	0	.000
Fingers p	0	0	0	0	0	0	.000
Green 2b	2	0	0	0	0	0	.000
b-Alou ph	1	0	0	0	0	0	.300
Kubiak 2b	1	1	0	0	0	1	.000
Hunter p	2	0	0	0	0	0	.000
c-Johnson ph	1	0	0	0	0	0	.500
Knowles p	0	0	0	0	0	0	.000
e-Mangual ph-cf	2	0	0	0	0	0	.000
TOTALS	**42**	**3**	**10**	**0**	**3**	**3**	**.233**

a - Batted for Fosse in the 7th
b - Batted for Green in the 7th
c - Batted for Hunter in the 7th
d - Ran for Bourque in the 9th e - Batted for Knowles in the 9th

BATTING: 2B: Rudi (2, Seaver), Bando (1, Seaver), Tenace (1, Seaver). **S:** Bando. **RBI:** Campaneris 1 (1), Rudi 1 (3), Tenace 1 (2). **2-out RBI:** Campaneris 1, Tenace 1. **Runners left in scoring position, 2 out:** Campaneris 2, Jackson 1, Tenace 1, Davalillo 2, Fosse 1. **Team LOB:** 10 **BASERUNNING: SB:** Campaneris (3, 2nd base off Seaver/Grote). **FIELDING: E:** Hunter (1).

NY METS	AB	R	H	HR	RBI	BB	AVG
Garrett 3b	4	1	2	1	1	2	.200
Millan 2b	5	1	2	0	0	0	.200
Staub rf	6	0	2	0	0	0	.273
Jones lf	5	0	0	0	0	1	.357
Milner 1b	3	0	1	0	0	2	.385
Grote c	5	0	0	0	0	0	.133
Hahn cf	5	0	1	0	0	0	.143
Harrelson ss	5	0	2	0	0	0	.385
Seaver p	3	0	0	0	0	0	.000
a-Beauchamp ph	1	0	0	0	0	0	.000
Sadecki p	0	0	0	0	0	0	.000
McGraw p	0	0	0	0	0	0	.500
b-Mays ph	1	0	0	0	0	0	.286
Parker p	0	0	0	0	0	0	.000
TOTALS	**43**	**2**	**10**	**1**	**1**	**5**	**.248**

a - Batted for Seaver in the 8th
b - Batted for McGraw in the 10th

BATTING: 2B: Hahn (1, Hunter), Staub (1, Lindblad). **HR:** Garrett (2, 1st off Hunter 0 on, 0 out). **S:** Millan. **RBI:** Garrett 1 (2). **Runners left in scoring position, 2 out:** Staub 2, Jones 1, Milner 1, Hahn 1. **Team LOB:** 14 **FIELDING: E:** Millan (2). **PB:** Grote. **Outfield assists:** Jones (1), Hahn (1).

OAKLAND	IP	H	R	ER	BB	SO	HR	ERA
Hunter	6	7	2	2	3	5	1	3.00
Knowles	2	0	0	0	1	0	0	0.00
Lindblad (W, 1-0)	2	3	0	0	1	0	0	0.00
Fingers (S, 1)	1	0	0	0	0	0	0	1.29

NY METS	IP	H	R	ER	BB	SO	HR	ERA
Seaver	8	7	2	2	1	12	0	2.25
Sadecki	0	1	0	0	0	0	0	0.00
McGraw	2	1	0	0	1	1	0	3.60
Parker (L, 0-1)	1	1	1	0	1	1	0	0.00

WP: Hunter 1. **IBB:** Garrett (by Hunter), Jones (by Lindblad), Tenace (by McGraw). **Ground balls-fly balls:** Hunter 5-9, Knowles 3-3, Lindblad 4-2, Fingers 1-1, Seaver 5-6, Sadecki 1-0, McGraw 2-3, Parker 0-1. **Batters faced:** Hunter 29, Knowles 7, Lindblad 10, Fingers 3, Seaver 32, Sadecki 2, McGraw 8, Parker 4. **UMPIRES:** hp—Neudecker, 1b—Pryor, 2b—Goetz, 3b—Wendelstedt, lf—Springstead, rf—Donatelli **T:** 3:15 **A:** 54,817

GAME 4 New York 6 Oakland 1
Shea Stadium 10/17/73

OAKLAND	AB	R	H	HR	RBI	BB	AVG
Campaneris ss	4	0	0	0	0	0	.250
Rudi lf	4	0	1	0	0	0	.353
Bando 3b	3	1	0	0	0	1	.267
Jackson cf	4	0	1	0	0	0	.278
Tenace 1b	3	0	1	0	1	1	.250
Alou rf	4	0	0	0	0	0	.214
Fosse c	4	0	1	0	0	0	.071
Green 2b	1	0	0	0	0	0	.000
a-Mangual ph	1	0	0	0	0	0	.000
Kubiak 2b	1	0	0	0	0	0	.000
d-Johnson ph	1	0	1	0	0	0	.667
Holtzman p	0	0	0	0	0	0	1.000
Odom p	1	0	0	0	0	0	.000
Knowles p	0	0	0	0	0	0	.000
b-Conigliaro ph	1	0	0	0	0	0	.000
Pina p	0	0	0	0	0	0	.000
c-Andrews ph	1	0	0	0	0	0	.000
Lindblad p	0	0	0	0	0	0	.000
e-Davalillo ph	0	0	0	0	0	1	.167
TOTALS	**33**	**1**	**5**	**0**	**1**	**3**	**.215**

a - Batted for Green in the 5th
b - Batted for Knowles in the 5th
c - Batted for Pina in the 8th
d - Batted for Kubiak in the 9th e - Batted for Lindblad in the 9th

BATTING: RBI: Tenace 1 (3). **Runners left in scoring position, 2 out:** Campaneris 2, Jackson 1, Alou 1. **Team LOB:** 9 **FIELDING: E:** Green (1). **Outfield assists:** Rudi (2). **DP:** 4 (Bando-Green-Tenace, Green-Campaneris-Tenace, Knowles-Fosse-Tenace, Kubiak-Tenace).

NY METS	AB	R	H	HR	RBI	BB	AVG
Garrett 3b	4	2	1	0	0	0	.211
Millan 2b	5	1	1	0	0	0	.200
Staub rf	4	1	4	1	5	1	.467
Jones lf	3	0	1	0	0	1	.353
Theodore lf	1	0	0	0	0	0	.000
Milner 1b	3	0	0	0	0	1	.313
Grote c	4	0	3	0	0	0	.263
Hahn cf	4	1	1	0	0	0	.167
Harrelson ss	2	1	1	0	0	2	.400
Matlack p	3	0	1	0	0	1	.333
Sadecki p	0	0	0	0	0	0	.000
TOTALS	**33**	**6**	**13**	**1**	**5**	**6**	**.278**

BATTING: HR: Staub (1, 1st off Holtzman 2 on, 0 out). **RBI:** Staub 5 (5). **Runners left in scoring position, 2 out:** Millan 1, Matlack 1. **GIDP:** Hahn, Grote, Milner, Matlack. **Team LOB:** 10 **FIELDING: E:** Garrett (1).

OAKLAND	IP	H	R	ER	BB	SO	HR	ERA
Holtzman (L, 1-1)	0.1	4	3	3	1	0	1	6.75
Odom	2.2	3	2	2	2	0	0	3.86
Knowles	1	1	1	0	1	1	0	0.00
Pina	3	4	0	0	2	0	0	0.00
Lindblad	1	1	0	0	0	1	0	0.00

NY METS	IP	H	R	ER	BB	SO	HR	ERA
Matlack (W, 1-1)	8	3	1	0	2	5	0	0.00
Sadecki (S, 1)	1	2	0	0	1	2	0	0.00

WP: Odom 1. **IBB:** Harrelson (by Pina). **HBP:** Garrett (by Knowles), Campaneris (by Matlack). **Ground balls-fly balls:** Holtzman 1-0, Odom 6-0, Knowles 2-0, Pina 5-2, Lindblad 0-2,

Matlack 11-9, Sadecki 0-1. **Batters faced:** Holtzman 6, Odom 11, Knowles 6, Pina 13, Lindblad 4, Matlack 31, Sadecki 6. **UMPIRES:** hp—Pryor, 1b—Goetz, 2b—Wendelstedt, 3b—Springstead, lf—Donatelli, rf—Neudecker **T:** 2:41 **A:** 54,817

GAME 5 New York 2 Oakland 0
Shea Stadium 10/18/73

OAKLAND	AB	R	H	HR	RBI	BB	AVG
Campaneris ss	3	0	1	0	0	1	.261
Rudi lf	4	0	0	0	0	0	.286
Bando 3b	3	0	1	0	0	1	.278
Jackson cf	3	0	0	0	0	1	.238
Tenace 1b	1	0	0	0	0	3	.231
d-Odom pr	0	0	0	0	0	0	.000
Bourque 1b	0	0	0	0	0	0	.500
Alou rf	4	0	0	0	0	0	.167
Fosse c	4	0	1	0	0	0	.111
Green 2b	2	0	0	0	0	0	.000
a-Johnson ph	0	0	0	0	0	1	.667
b-Lewis pr	0	0	0	0	0	0	.000
Kubiak 2b	1	0	0	0	0	0	.000
Blue p	2	0	0	0	0	0	.000
Knowles p	0	0	0	0	0	0	.000
c-Mangual ph	1	0	0	0	0	0	.000
Fingers p	0	0	0	0	0	0	.000
e-Conigliaro ph	1	0	0	0	0	0	.000
TOTALS	**29**	**0**	**3**	**0**	**0**	**7**	**.197**

a - Batted for Green in the 7th
b - Ran for Johnson in the 7th
c - Batted for Knowles in the 7th
d - Ran for Tenace in the 8th e - Batted for Fingers in the 9th

BATTING: 2B: Fosse (1, Koosman). **Runners left in scoring position, 2 out:** Campaneris 2, Jackson 1, Alou 1. **GIDP:** Jackson. **Team LOB:** 9 **FIELDING: E:** Campaneris (1).

NY METS	AB	R	H	HR	RBI	BB	AVG
Garrett 3b	3	0	0	0	0	1	.182
Millan 2b	4	0	0	0	0	0	.167
Staub rf	3	0	1	0	0	1	.444
Jones lf	4	1	2	0	0	0	.381
Milner 1b	4	0	2	0	1	0	.350
Grote c	3	1	1	0	0	0	.273
Hahn cf	4	0	1	0	1	0	.182
Harrelson ss	2	0	0	0	0	2	.353
Koosman p	3	0	0	0	0	0	.000
McGraw p	1	0	0	0	0	0	.333
TOTALS	**31**	**2**	**7**	**0**	**2**	**4**	**.269**

BATTING: 2B: Jones (2, Blue). **3B:** Hahn (1, Blue). **S:** Grote. **RBI:** Milner 1 (2), Hahn 1 (2). **2-out RBI:** Hahn 1. **Runners left in scoring position, 2 out:** Staub 1, Harrelson 2, Koosman 1, McGraw 1. **Team LOB:** 10 **FIELDING: E:** Garrett (2). **DP:** 1 (Millan-Harrelson-Milner).

OAKLAND	IP	H	R	ER	BB	SO	HR	ERA
Blue (L, 0-1)	5.2	6	2	2	1	4	0	4.91
Knowles	0.1	0	0	0	1	1	0	0.00
Fingers	2	1	0	0	2	1	0	1.00

NY METS	IP	H	R	ER	BB	SO	HR	ERA
Koosman (W, 1-0)	6.1	3	0	0	4	4	0	3.12
McGraw (S, 1)	2.2	0	0	0	3	3	0	2.84

WP: Blue 1. **IBB:** Harrelson 2 (by Knowles, by Fingers). **Ground balls-fly balls:** Blue 8-6, Knowles 0-0, Fingers 4-0, Koosman 7-7, McGraw 1-4. **Batters faced:** Blue 25, Knowles 2, Fingers 9, Koosman 25, McGraw 11. **UMPIRES:** hp—Goetz, 1b—Wendelstedt, 2b—Springstead, 3b—Donatelli, lf—Neudecker, rf—Pryor **T:** 2:39 **A:** 54,817

GAME 6 Oakland 3 New York 1
Oakland Coliseum 10/20/73

NY METS	AB	R	H	HR	RBI	BB	AVG
Garrett 3b	3	0	1	0	0	1	.200
Millan 2b	4	0	1	0	1	0	.179
Staub rf	4	0	1	0	0	0	.409
Jones lf	4	0	0	0	0	0	.320
Milner 1b	4	0	1	0	0	0	.333
Grote c	4	0	1	0	0	0	.269
Hahn cf	3	0	0	0	0	0	.160
b-Kranepool ph	1	0	0	0	0	0	.000
Harrelson ss	3	0	0	0	0	0	.300
Seaver p	2	0	0	0	0	0	.000
a-Boswell ph	1	1	1	0	0	0	1.000
McGraw p	0	0	0	0	0	0	.333
TOTALS	**33**	**1**	**6**	**0**	**1**	**1**	**.257**

a - Batted for Seaver in the 8th
b - Batted for Hahn in the 9th

BATTING: RBI: Millan 1 (1). **Runners left in scoring position, 2 out:** Jones 1, Milner 1. **Team LOB:** 6 **FIELDING: E:** Garrett (3), Hahn (1). **DP:** 1 (Grote-Millan).

OAKLAND	AB	R	H	HR	RBI	BB	AVG
Campaneris ss	4	0	0	0	0	0	.222
Rudi lf	3	1	1	0	0	1	.292
Bando 3b	4	1	1	0	0	0	.273
Jackson rf-cf	4	1	3	0	2	0	.320
Tenace c-1b	3	0	0	0	0	1	.188
Davalillo cf	2	0	0	0	0	1	.125
a-Alou ph-rf	0	0	0	0	1	0	.167
Johnson 1b	4	0	1	0	0	0	.429
Fosse c	0	0	0	0	0	0	.111
Green 2b	3	0	1	0	0	0	.083
Hunter p	3	0	0	0	0	0	.000
Knowles p	0	0	0	0	0	0	.000
Fingers p	0	0	0	0	0	0	.000
TOTALS	**30**	**3**	**7**	**0**	**3**	**3**	**.202**

a - Batted for Davalillo in the 8th

BATTING: 2B: Jackson 2 (3, Seaver). **SF:** Alou. **RBI:** Jackson 2 (4), Alou 1 (3). **2-out RBI:** Jackson 2. **Runners left in scoring position, 2 out:** Bando 1, Tenace 2, Hunter 1. **Team LOB:** 7 **BASERUNNING: CS:** Tenace (1, 2nd base off McGraw/Grote).

NY METS	IP	H	R	ER	BB	SO	HR	ERA
Seaver (L, 0-1)	7	6	2	2	2	6	0	2.40
McGraw	1	1	1	0	1	1	0	2.63

OAKLAND	IP	H	R	ER	BB	SO	HR	ERA
Hunter (W, 1-0)	7.1	4	1	1	1	1	0	2.03
Knowles	0.1	2	0	0	0	1	0	0.00
Fingers (S, 2)	1.1	0	0	0	0	0	0	0.87

WP: Seaver 1. **Ground balls-fly balls:** Seaver 9-7, McGraw 0-0, Hunter 7-14, Knowles 0-0, Fingers 1-3. **Batters faced:** Seaver 30, McGraw 4, Hunter 27, Knowles 3, Fingers 4. **UMPIRES:** hp—Wendelstedt, 1b—Springstead, 2b—Donatelli, 3b—Neudecker, lf—Pryor, rf—Goetz **T:** 2:07 **A:** 49,333

GAME 7 Oakland 5 New York 2
Oakland Coliseum 10/21/73

NY METS	AB	R	H	HR	RBI	BB	AVG
Garrett 3b	5	0	0	0	0	0	.167
Millan 2b	4	1	1	0	0	0	.188
Staub rf	4	0	2	0	1	0	.423
Jones lf	3	0	0	0	0	1	.286
Milner 1b	3	1	0	0	0	1	.296
Grote c	4	0	1	0	0	0	.267
Hahn cf	4	0	3	0	0	0	.241
Harrelson ss	4	0	0	0	0	0	.250
Matlack p	1	0	0	0	0	0	.250
Parker p	0	0	0	0	0	0	.000
a-Beauchamp ph	1	0	0	0	0	0	.000
Sadecki p	0	0	0	0	0	0	.000
b-Boswell ph	1	0	1	0	0	0	1.000
Stone p	0	0	0	0	0	0	.000
c-Kranepool ph	1	0	0	0	0	0	.000
d-Martinez pr	0	0	0	0	0	0	.000
TOTALS	**35**	**2**	**8**	**0**	**1**	**2**	**.253**

a - Batted for Parker in the 5th
b - Batted for Sadecki in the 7th
c - Batted for Stone in the 9th
d - Ran for Kranepool in the 9th

BATTING: 2B: Millan (1, Holtzman), Staub (2, Holtzman). **RBI:** Staub 1 (6). **Runners left in scoring position, 2 out:** Garrett 2, Milner 2. **GIDP:** Matlack. **Team LOB:** 8 **FIELDING: E:** Jones (1).

OAKLAND	AB	R	H	HR	RBI	BB	AVG
Campaneris ss	4	2	3	1	2	0	.290
Rudi lf	3	1	2	0	1	1	.333
Bando 3b	4	0	0	0	0	0	.231
Jackson cf-rf	4	1	1	1	2	0	.310
Tenace c-1b	3	0	0	0	0	1	.158
Alou rf	1	0	0	0	0	0	.158
a-Davalillo ph-cf	3	0	0	0	0	0	.091
Johnson 1b	3	0	0	0	0	0	.300
Fosse c	1	0	1	0	0	0	.158
Green 2b	4	0	0	0	0	0	.063
Holtzman p	2	1	1	0	0	0	.667
Fingers p	1	0	1	0	0	0	.333
Knowles p	0	0	0	0	0	0	.000
TOTALS	**33**	**5**	**9**	**2**	**5**	**2**	**.212**

a - Batted for Alou in the 3th

BATTING: 2B: Holtzman (2, Matlack). **HR:** Campaneris (1, 3th off Matlack 1 on, 1 out), Jackson (1, 3th off Matlack 1 on, 2 out). **SF:** Holtzman. **RBI:** Campaneris 2 (3), Rudi 1 (4), Jackson 2 (6). **2-out RBI:** Jackson 2. **Runners left in scoring position, 2 out:** Jackson 1. **Team LOB:** 6 **FIELDING: E:** Tenace (2). **DP:** 1 (Bando-Campaneris-Green).

NY METS	IP	H	R	ER	BB	SO	HR	ERA
Matlack (L, 1-2)	2.2	4	4	4	1	3	2	2.16
Parker	1.1	0	0	0	1	1	0	0.00
Sadecki	2	2	1	1	0	1	0	1.93
Stone	2	3	0	0	0	3	0	0.00

OAKLAND	IP	H	R	ER	BB	SO	HR	ERA
Holtzman (W, 2-1)	5.1	5	1	1	1	4	0	4.22
Fingers	3.1	3	1	0	1	2	0	0.66
Knowles (S, 2)	0.1	0	0	0	0	0	0	0.00

Ground balls-fly balls: Matlack 3-2, Parker 1-2, Sadecki 1-4, Stone 2-1, Holtzman 4-7, Fingers 5-4, Knowles 0-1. **Batters faced:** Matlack 13, Parker 5, Sadecki 8, Stone 9, Holtzman 21, Fingers 15, Knowles 1. **UMPIRES:** hp—Springstead, 1b—Donatelli, 2b—Neudecker, 3b—Pryor, lf—Goetz, rf—Wendelstedt **T:** 2:37 **A:** 49,333

1974 OAKLAND DEF. LOS ANGELES, 4-1

GAME 1 Oakland 3 Los Angeles 2
Dodger Stadium 10/12/74

OAKLAND	AB	R	H	HR	RBI	BB	AVG
Campaneris ss	2	1	1	0	1	0	.500
North cf	2	0	0	0	0	1	.000
Bando 3b	4	0	0	0	0	0	.000
Jackson rf	3	1	1	1	1	1	.333
C.Washington rf	0	0	0	0	0	0	.000
Rudi lf	4	0	2	0	0	0	.500
Tenace 1b	3	0	1	0	0	0	.333
Fosse c	3	0	0	0	0	1	.000
Green 2b	3	0	0	0	0	0	.000
a-Holt ph	1	0	0	0	0	0	.000
Maxvill 2b	0	0	0	0	0	0	.000
Holtzman p	1	1	1	0	0	1	1.000
Fingers p	2	0	0	0	0	0	.000
Hunter p	0	0	0	0	0	0	.000
TOTALS	**28**	**3**	**6**	**1**	**2**	**4**	**.214**

a - Batted for Green in the 9th

BATTING: 2B: Holtzman (1, Messersmith). **HR:** Jackson (1, 2nd off Messersmith 0 on, 0 out). **S:** Campaneris, Campaneris, North, Tenace. **RBI:** Campaneris 1 (1), Jackson 1 (1). **Runners left in scoring position, 2 out:** Bando 1, Fingers 1. **Team LOB:** 6 **BASERUNNING: CS:** North (1, 2nd base off Messersmith/Yeager). **FIELDING: E:** Campaneris (1), Jackson (1). **DP:** 1 (Campaneris-Green-Tenace).

LOS ANGELES	AB	R	H	HR	RBI	BB	AVG
Lopes 2b	5	1	0	0	0	0	.000
Buckner lf	5	0	2	0	1	0	.400
Wynn cf	4	1	1	1	1	1	.250
Garvey 1b	5	0	2	0	0	0	.400
c-Paciorek pr	0	0	0	0	0	0	.000
Ferguson rf-c	3	0	0	0	0	1	.000
Cey 3b	3	0	1	0	0	1	.333
Russell ss	4	0	1	0	0	0	.250
Yeager c	3	0	1	0	0	0	.333
a-Crawford ph-rf	1	0	1	0	0	0	1.000
Messersmith p	3	0	2	0	0	0	.667
b-Joshua ph	1	0	0	0	0	0	.000
Marshall p	0	0	0	0	0	0	.000
TOTALS	**37**	**2**	**11**	**1**	**2**	**3**	**.297**

a - Batted for Yeager in the 8th
b - Batted for Messersmith in the 8th
c - Ran for Garvey in the 9th

BATTING: HR: Wynn (1, 9th off Fingers 0 on, 2 out). **RBI:** Buckner 1 (1), Wynn 1 (1). **2-out RBI:** Wynn 1. **Runners left in scoring position, 2 out:** Wynn 1, Cey 2, Russell 1, Yeager 1, Joshua 1. **GIDP:** Cey. **Team LOB:** 12 **FIELDING: E:** Cey (1). **Outfield assists:** Ferguson (1). **DP:** 1 (Ferguson-Yeager).

OAKLAND	IP	H	R	ER	BB	SO	HR	ERA
Holtzman	4.1	7	1	0	2	3	0	0.00
Fingers (W, 1-0)	4.1	4	1	1	1	3	1	2.08
Hunter (S, 1)	0.1	0	0	0	0	1	0	0.00

LOS ANGELES	IP	H	R	ER	BB	SO	HR	ERA
Messersmith (L, 0-1)	8	5	3	2	3	8	1	2.25
Marshall	1	1	0	0	1	1	0	0.00

WP: Messersmith 1. **HBP:** Ferguson (by Fingers). **Pitches-strikes:** Holtzman 71-41, Fingers 67-44, Hunter 5-3, Messersmith 127-83, Marshall 16-10. **Ground balls-fly balls:** Holtzman 6-3, Fingers 3-7, Hunter 0-0, Messersmith 7-5, Marshall 0-1. **Batters faced:** Holtzman 21, Fingers 19, Hunter 1, Messersmith 31, Marshall 5. **UMPIRES:** hp—Gorman, 1b—Kunkel, 2b—Harvey, 3b—Denkinger, lf—Olsen, rf—Luciano **T:** 2:43 **A:** 55,974

GAME 2 Los Angeles 3 Oakland 2
Dodger Stadium 10/13/74

OAKLAND	AB	R	H	HR	RBI	BB	AVG
Campaneris ss	4	0	1	0	0	0	.333
North cf	4	0	0	0	0	0	.000
Haney c	0	0	0	0	0	0	.000
Bando 3b	3	1	0	0	0	0	.000
Jackson rf	3	1	2	0	0	1	.500
Rudi lf	4	0	1	0	2	0	.375
f-H.Washington pr	0	0	0	0	0	0	.000
Tenace 1b	3	0	0	0	0	1	.167
Fosse c	2	0	0	0	0	0	.000
a-Alou ph	1	0	0	0	0	0	.000
Odom p	0	0	0	0	0	0	.000
e-Mangual ph	1	0	0	0	0	0	.000
Green 2b	2	0	0	0	0	0	.000
b-Holt ph	1	0	1	0	0	0	.500
c-Maxvill pr-2b	0	0	0	0	0	0	.000
Blue p	2	0	0	0	0	0	.000
d-C.Washington ph-cf	1	0	1	0	0	0	1.000
TOTALS	**31**	**2**	**6**	**0**	**2**	**2**	**.203**

a - Batted for Fosse in the 8th
b - Batted for Green in the 8th
c - Ran for Holt in the 8th
d - Batted for Blue in the 8th e - Batted for Odom in the 9th f - Ran for Rudi in the 9th

BATTING: 2B: Campaneris (1, Sutton), Jackson (1, Sutton). **RBI:** Rudi 2 (2). **Runners left in scoring position, 2 out:** North 1, Fosse 1. **GIDP:** Tenace, North. **Team LOB:** 5

LOS ANGELES	AB	R	H	HR	RBI	BB	AVG
Lopes 2b	4	0	0	0	0	0	.000
Buckner lf	4	0	0	0	0	0	.222
Wynn cf	3	0	0	0	0	1	.143
Garvey 1b	4	1	2	0	0	0	.444
Ferguson rf	3	1	1	1	2	1	.167
Cey 3b	3	1	0	0	0	1	.167
Russell ss	3	0	1	0	0	0	.286
Yeager c	3	0	2	0	1	0	.500
Sutton p	2	0	0	0	0	0	.000
Marshall p	0	0	0	0	0	0	.000
TOTALS	**29**	**3**	**6**	**1**	**3**	**3**	**.258**

BATTING: HR: Ferguson (1, 6th off Blue 1 on, 1 out). **S:** Sutton. **RBI:** Ferguson 2 (2), Yeager 1 (1). **Runners left in scoring position, 2 out:** Lopes 1, Buckner 1, Cey 1. **Team LOB:** 6 **BASERUNNING: SB:** Ferguson (1, 2nd base off Odom/Haney). **FIELDING: E:** Russell (1). **DP:** 2 (Sutton-Lopes-Garvey, Russell-Garvey).

OAKLAND	IP	H	R	ER	BB	SO	HR	ERA
Blue (L, 0-1)	7	6	3	3	2	5	1	3.86
Odom	1	0	0	0	1	2	0	0.00

LOS ANGELES	IP	H	R	ER	BB	SO	HR	ERA
Sutton (W, 1-0)	8	5	2	2	2	9	0	2.25
Marshall (S, 1)	1	1	0	0	0	2	0	0.00

WP: Sutton 1. **HBP:** Bando (by Sutton). **Pitches-strikes:** Blue 99-63, Odom 21-11, Sutton 136-88, Marshall 9-8. **Ground balls-fly balls:** Blue 5-10, Odom 0-1, Sutton 7-7, Marshall 0-0. **Batters faced:** Blue 29, Odom 4, Sutton 31, Marshall 3. **UMPIRES:** hp—Kunkel, 1b—Harvey, 2b—Denkinger, 3b—Olsen, lf—Luciano, rf—Gorman **T:** 2:40 **A:** 55,989

GAME 3 Oakland 3 Los Angeles 2
Oakland Coliseum 10/15/74

LOS ANGELES	AB	R	H	HR	RBI	BB	AVG
Lopes 2b	3	0	2	0	0	1	.167
Buckner lf	4	1	1	1	1	0	.231
Wynn cf	4	0	1	0	0	0	.182
Garvey 1b	4	0	1	0	0	0	.385
Crawford rf	4	1	1	1	1	0	.400
Ferguson c	3	0	0	0	0	1	.111
c-Auerbach pr	0	0	0	0	0	0	.000
Cey 3b	4	0	0	0	0	0	.100
Russell ss	4	0	1	0	0	0	.273
Downing p	1	0	0	0	0	0	.000
Brewer p	0	0	0	0	0	0	.000
a-Lacy ph	1	0	0	0	0	0	.000
Hough p	0	0	0	0	0	0	.000
b-Joshua ph	1	0	0	0	0	0	.000
Marshall p	0	0	0	0	0	0	.000
TOTALS	**33**	**2**	**7**	**2**	**2**	**2**	**.242**

a - Batted for Brewer in the 5th
b - Batted for Hough in the 7th
c - Ran for Ferguson in the 9th

BATTING: HR: Buckner (1, 8th off Hunter 0 on, 1 out), Crawford (1, 9th off Fingers 0 on, 0 out). **RBI:** Buckner 1 (2), Crawford 1 (1). **Runners left in scoring position, 2 out:** Garvey 1, Joshua 1. **GIDP:** Russell. **Team LOB:** 6 **BASERUNNING: SB:** Lopes 2 (2, 2nd base off Hunter/Fosse, 3rd base off Hunter/Fosse). **FIELDING: E:** Ferguson 2 (2).

OAKLAND	AB	R	H	HR	RBI	BB	AVG
North cf	4	1	1	0	0	0	.100
Campaneris ss	4	0	2	0	1	0	.400
Bando 3b	3	1	0	0	0	1	.000
Jackson rf	3	0	0	0	0	1	.333
C.Washington rf	0	0	0	0	0	0	1.000
Rudi lf	4	0	1	0	1	0	.333
Tenace 1b	2	0	1	0	0	2	.250
a-H.Washington pr	0	0	0	0	0	0	.000
Holt 1b	0	0	0	0	0	0	.500
Fosse c	4	0	0	0	0	0	.000
Green 2b	3	1	0	0	0	1	.000
Hunter p	2	0	0	0	0	0	.000
Fingers p	0	0	0	0	0	0	.000
TOTALS	**29**	**3**	**5**	**0**	**2**	**5**	**.193**

a - Ran for Tenace in the 8th

BATTING: 2B: Campaneris (2, Downing). **S:** Hunter. **RBI:** Campaneris 1 (2), Rudi 1 (3). **2-out RBI:** Campaneris 1, Rudi 1. **Runners left in scoring position, 2 out:** Bando 1, Jackson 1, Fosse 3. **Team LOB:** 8 **BASERUNNING: SB:** Jackson (1, 2nd base off Hough/Ferguson). **FIELDING: E:** Green (1), Campaneris (2). **DP:** 3 (Green-Campaneris, Green-Tenace, Green-Campaneris-Holt).

LOS ANGELES	IP	H	R	ER	BB	SO	HR	ERA
Downing (L, 0-1)	3.2	4	3	1	4	3	0	2.45
Brewer	0.1	0	0	0	0	1	0	0.00
Hough	2	0	0	0	1	4	0	0.00
Marshall	2	1	0	0	0	1	0	0.00

OAKLAND	IP	H	R	ER	BB	SO	HR	ERA
Hunter (W, 1-0)	7.1	5	1	1	2	4	1	1.17
Fingers	1.2	2	1	1	0	1	1	3.00

WP: Hough 1. **Pitches-strikes:** Downing 75-40, Brewer 6-3, Hough 36-22, Marshall 17-13, Hunter 96-62, Fingers 18-12. **Ground balls-fly balls:** Downing 6-2, Brewer 0-0, Hough 1-1, Marshall 3-2, Hunter 6-12, Fingers 2-1. **Batters faced:** Downing 20, Brewer 1, Hough 7, Marshall 7, Hunter 29, Fingers 6. **UMPIRES:** hp—Harvey, 1b—Denkinger, 2b—Olsen, 3b—Luciano, lf—Gorman, rf—Kunkel **T:** 2:35 **A:** 49,347

GAME 4 Oakland 5 Los Angeles 2
Oakland Coliseum 10/16/74

LOS ANGELES	AB	R	H	HR	RBI	BB	AVG
Lopes 2b	4	0	0	0	0	0	.125
Buckner lf	4	0	1	0	0	0	.235
Wynn cf	3	0	1	0	0	1	.214
Garvey 1b	4	1	2	0	0	0	.412
Ferguson rf	3	1	0	0	0	1	.083
Cey 3b	4	0	1	0	0	0	.143
Russell ss	4	0	1	0	2	0	.267
Yeager c	3	0	1	0	0	0	.444
b-Joshua ph	1	0	0	0	0	0	.000
Messersmith p	1	0	0	0	0	0	.500
a-Paciorek ph	1	0	0	0	0	0	.000
Marshall p	0	0	0	0	0	0	.000
TOTALS	**32**	**2**	**7**	**0**	**2**	**2**	**.237**

a - Batted for Messersmith in the 7th
b - Batted for Yeager in the 9th

BATTING: 2B: Buckner (1, Holtzman), Yeager (1, Holtzman), Wynn (1, Holtzman). **3B:** Russell (1, Holtzman). **S:** Messersmith. **RBI:** Russell 2 (2). **2-out RBI:** Russell 2. **Runners left in scoring position, 2 out:** Buckner 1, Garvey 1, Ferguson 1, Cey 1, Yeager 1. **GIDP:** Joshua. **Team LOB:** 6 **FIELDING: E:** Messersmith (1). **DP:** 2 (Lopes-Garvey, Russell-Lopes-Garvey).

OAKLAND	AB	R	H	HR	RBI	BB	AVG
Campaneris ss	3	0	0	0	0	0	.308
North cf	3	1	0	0	0	1	.077
Bando 3b	3	1	1	0	1	1	.077
Jackson rf	3	1	1	0	0	1	.333
Rudi 1b-lf	3	0	0	0	0	0	.267
C.Washington lf	3	1	2	0	0	1	.750
Tenace 1b	0	0	0	0	0	0	.250
Fosse c	2	0	1	0	0	0	.091
a-Holt ph	1	0	1	0	2	0	.667
b-H.Washington pr	0	0	0	0	0	0	.000
Haney c	0	0	0	0	0	0	.000
Green 2b	2	0	0	0	1	0	.000
Holtzman p	3	1	1	1	1	0	.500
Fingers p	0	0	0	0	0	0	.000
TOTALS	**26**	**5**	**7**	**1**	**5**	**4**	**.211**

a - Batted for Fosse in the 6th
b - Ran for Holt in the 6th

BATTING: HR: Holtzman (1, 3th off Messersmith 0 on, 1 out). **S:** Green, Rudi. **RBI:** Bando 1 (1), Holt 2 (2), Green 1 (1), Holtzman 1 (1). **Runners left in scoring position, 2 out:** Campaneris 2. **GIDP:** Rudi. **Team LOB:** 4 **BASERUNNING: CS:** Campaneris (1, 2nd base off Messersmith/Yeager). **FIELDING: DP:** 1 (Green-Campaneris-Tenace).

LOS ANGELES	IP	H	R	ER	BB	SO	HR	ERA
Messersmith (L, 0-2)	6	6	5	5	4	4	1	4.50
Marshall	2	1	0	0	0	2	0	0.00

OAKLAND	IP	H	R	ER	BB	SO	HR	ERA
Holtzman (W, 1-0)	7.2	6	2	2	2	7	0	1.50
Fingers (S, 1)	1.1	1	0	0	0	2	0	2.45

WP: Holtzman 1. **IBB:** C.Washington (by Messersmith). **HBP:** Campaneris (by Messersmith). **Pitches-strikes:** Messersmith 97-57, Marshall 20-12, Holtzman 104-65, Fingers 16-11. **Ground balls-fly balls:** Messersmith 6-4, Marshall 2-1, Holtzman 10-5, Fingers 1-0. **Batters faced:** Messersmith 27, Marshall 6, Holtzman 31, Fingers 4. **UMPIRES:** hp—Denkinger, 1b—Olsen, 2b—Luciano, 3b—Gorman, lf—Kunkel, rf—Harvey **T:** 2:17 **A:** 49,347

GAME 5 Oakland 3 Los Angeles 2
Oakland Coliseum 10/17/74

LOS ANGELES	AB	R	H	HR	RBI	BB	AVG
Lopes 2b	2	1	0	0	0	2	.111
Buckner lf	3	0	1	0	0	0	.250
Wynn cf	2	0	0	0	1	1	.188
Garvey 1b	4	0	1	0	1	0	.381
Ferguson rf	4	0	1	0	0	0	.125
Cey 3b	3	0	1	0	0	1	.176
Russell ss	3	0	0	0	0	0	.222
b-Crawford ph	1	0	0	0	0	0	.333
Yeager c	2	0	0	0	0	1	.364
c-Joshua ph	1	0	0	0	0	0	.000
Sutton p	1	0	0	0	0	0	.000
a-Paciorek ph	1	1	1	0	0	0	.500
Marshall p	0	0	0	0	0	1	.000
TOTALS	**27**	**2**	**5**	**0**	**2**	**6**	**.228**

a - Batted for Sutton in the 6th
b - Batted for Russell in the 9th
c - Batted for Yeager in the 9th

BATTING: 2B: Paciorek (1, Blue). **S:** Buckner. **SF:** Wynn. **RBI:** Wynn 1 (2), Garvey 1 (1). **2-out RBI:** Garvey 1. **Runners left in scoring position, 2 out:** Lopes 1, Yeager 1. **GIDP:** Russell. **Team LOB:** 6 **BASERUNNING: CS:** Lopes (1, 2nd base off Blue/Fosse). **FIELDING: E:** Yeager (1).

OAKLAND	AB	R	H	HR	RBI	BB	AVG
Campaneris ss	4	0	2	0	0	0	.353
North cf	4	1	0	0	0	0	.059
Bando 3b	3	0	0	0	1	0	.063
Jackson rf	2	0	0	0	0	1	.286
Rudi 1b-lf	3	1	2	1	1	0	.333
C.Washington lf	3	0	1	0	0	0	.571
Fingers p	0	0	0	0	0	0	.000
Fosse c	3	1	1	1	1	0	.143
Green 2b	3	0	0	0	0	0	.000
Blue p	2	0	0	0	0	0	.000
Odom p	0	0	0	0	0	0	.000
Tenace 1b	1	0	0	0	0	0	.222
TOTALS	**28**	**3**	**6**	**2**	**3**	**1**	**.211**

BATTING: HR: Fosse (1, 2nd off Sutton 0 on, 0 out), Rudi (1, 7th off Marshall 0 on, 0 out). **SF:** Bando. **RBI:** Bando 1 (2), Rudi 1 (4), Fosse 1 (1). **Runners left in scoring position, 2 out:** Bando 1, C.Washington 1. **Team LOB:** 3 **BASERUNNING: SB:** North (1, 2nd base off Sutton/Yeager), Campaneris (1, 2nd base off Marshall/Yeager). **CS:** C.Washington (1, 2nd base off Sutton/Yeager). **FIELDING: E:** North (1). **DP:** 1 (Campaneris-Green-Rudi).

LOS ANGELES	IP	H	R	ER	BB	SO	HR	ERA
Sutton	5	4	2	2	1	3	1	2.77
Marshall (L, 0-1)	3	2	1	1	0	4	1	1.00

OAKLAND	IP	H	R	ER	BB	SO	HR	ERA
Blue	6.2	4	2	2	5	4	0	3.29
Odom (W, 1-0)	0.1	0	0	0	0	0	0	0.00
Fingers (S, 2)	2	1	0	0	1	0	0	1.93

Pitches-strikes: Sutton 63-42, Marshall 41-30, Blue 95-54, Odom 4-3, Fingers 23-16. **Ground balls-fly balls:** Sutton 2-8, Marshall 3-2, Blue 6-6, Odom 1-0, Fingers 1-4. **Batters faced:** Sutton 19, Marshall 11, Blue 27, Odom 1, Fingers 7. **UMPIRES:** hp—Olsen, 1b—Luciano, 2b—Gorman, 3b—Kunkel, lf—Harvey, rf—Denkinger **T:** 2:23 **A:** 49,347

1975 CINCINNATI DEF. BOSTON, 4-3

GAME 1 Boston 6 Cincinnati 0
Fenway Park 10/11/75

CINCINNATI	AB	R	H	HR	RBI	BB	AVG
Rose 3b	4	0	0	0	0	0	.000
Morgan 2b	4	0	2	0	0	0	.500
Bench c	4	0	0	0	0	0	.000
Perez 1b	4	0	0	0	0	0	.000
Foster lf	4	0	2	0	0	0	.500
Concepcion ss	4	0	0	0	0	0	.000
Griffey rf	3	0	1	0	0	0	.333
Geronimo cf	1	0	0	0	0	2	.000
Gullett p	3	0	0	0	0	0	.000
Carroll p	0	0	0	0	0	0	.000
McEnaney p	0	0	0	0	0	0	.000
TOTALS	**31**	**0**	**5**	**0**	**0**	**2**	**.161**

BATTING: 2B: Morgan (1, Tiant), Griffey (1, Tiant). **Runners left in scoring position, 2 out:** Perez 2, Gullett 2. **Team LOB:** 6 **BASERUNNING: CS:** Foster (1, 2nd base off Tiant/Fisk). **FIELDING: Outfield assists:** Geronimo (1). **DP:** 2 (Geronimo-Bench, Perez).

BOSTON	AB	R	H	HR	RBI	BB	AVG
Evans rf	4	1	1	0	0	0	.250
Doyle 2b	3	1	2	0	0	1	.667
Yastrzemski lf	4	1	1	0	1	1	.250
Fisk c	3	1	0	0	1	1	.000
Lynn cf	4	0	2	0	0	0	.500
Petrocelli 3b	3	1	2	0	2	1	.667
Burleson ss	3	0	3	0	1	1	1.000
Cooper 1b	3	0	0	0	1	0	.000
Tiant p	3	1	1	0	0	1	.333
TOTALS	**30**	**6**	**12**	**0**	**6**	**6**	**.400**

BATTING: 2B: Petrocelli (1, Gullett). **S:** Doyle, Evans. **SF:** Cooper. **RBI:** Yastrzemski 1 (1), Fisk 1 (1), Petrocelli 2 (2), Burleson 1 (1), Cooper 1 (1). **Runners left in scoring position, 2 out:** Evans 1, Yastrzemski 1, Lynn 1, Tiant 1. **Team LOB:** 9 **BASERUNNING: CS:** Burleson (1, 2nd base off Gullett/Bench).

CINCINNATI	IP	H	R	ER	BB	SO	HR	ERA
Gullett (L, 0-1)	6	10	4	4	4	3	0	6.00
Carroll	0	0	1	1	1	0	0	0.00
McEnaney	2	2	1	1	1	1	0	4.50

BOSTON	IP	H	R	ER	BB	SO	HR	ERA
Tiant (W, 1-0)	9	5	0	0	2	3	0	0.00

BK: Tiant 1. **IBB:** Geronimo 2 (by Tiant), Burleson (by Gullett). **Pitches-strikes:** Gullett 96-56, Carroll 6-2, McEnaney 26-14, Tiant 100-65. **Ground balls-fly balls:** Gullett 4-7, Carroll 0-0, McEnaney 1-2, Tiant 7-16. **Batters faced:** Gullett 30, Carroll 1, McEnaney 8, Tiant 33. **UMPIRES:** hp—Frantz, 1b—Colosi, 2b—Barnett, 3b—Stello, lf—Maloney, rf—Davidson **T:** 2:27 **A:** 35,205

GAME 2 Cincinnati 3 Boston 2
Fenway Park 10/12/75

CINCINNATI	AB	R	H	HR	RBI	BB	AVG
Rose 3b	4	0	2	0	0	0	.250
Morgan 2b	3	1	0	0	0	1	.286
Bench c	4	1	2	0	0	0	.250
Perez 1b	3	0	0	0	1	1	.000
Foster lf	4	0	1	0	0	0	.375
Concepcion ss	4	1	1	0	1	0	.125
Griffey rf	4	0	1	0	1	0	.286
Geronimo cf	3	0	0	0	0	1	.000
Billingham p	2	0	0	0	0	0	.000
Borbon p	0	0	0	0	0	0	.000
McEnaney p	0	0	0	0	0	0	.000
a-Rettenmund ph	1	0	0	0	0	0	.000
Eastwick p	1	0	0	0	0	0	.000
TOTALS	**33**	**3**	**7**	**0**	**3**	**3**	**.188**

a - Batted for McEnaney in the 8th

BATTING: 2B: Bench (1, Lee), Griffey (2, Drago). **RBI:** Perez 1 (1), Concepcion 1 (1), Griffey 1 (1). **2-out RBI:** Concepcion 1, Griffey 1. **Runners left in scoring position, 2 out:** Concepcion 1, Eastwick 1. **Team LOB:** 6 **BASERUNNING: SB:** Concepcion (1, 2nd base off Drago/Fisk). **CS:** Morgan (1, 2nd base off Lee/Fisk). **FIELDING: E:** Concepcion (1). **DP:** 1 (Billingham-Concepcion-Bench-Rose-Bench).

BOSTON	AB	R	H	HR	RBI	BB	AVG
Cooper 1b	5	0	1	0	0	0	.125
Doyle 2b	4	0	1	0	0	0	.429
Yastrzemski lf	3	2	1	0	0	1	.286
Fisk c	3	0	1	0	1	1	.167
Lynn cf	4	0	0	0	0	0	.250
Petrocelli 3b	4	0	2	0	1	0	.571
Evans rf	2	0	0	0	0	1	.167
Burleson ss	4	0	1	0	0	0	.571
Lee p	3	0	0	0	0	0	.000
Drago p	0	0	0	0	0	0	.000
a-Carbo ph	1	0	0	0	0	0	.000
TOTALS	**33**	**2**	**7**	**0**	**2**	**3**	**.302**

a - Batted for Drago in the 9th

BATTING: 2B: Cooper (1, Billingham). **RBI:** Fisk 1 (2), Petrocelli 1 (3). **2-out RBI:** Fisk 1, Petrocelli 1. **Runners left in scoring position, 2 out:** Evans 1, Burleson 2, Lee 1. **Team LOB:** 8 **BASERUNNING: CS:** Evans (1, 3rd base off Billingham/Bench).

CINCINNATI	IP	H	R	ER	BB	SO	HR	ERA
Billingham	5.2	6	2	1	2	5	0	1.59
Borbon	0.1	0	0	0	0	0	0	0.00
McEnaney	1	0	0	0	0	2	0	3.00
Eastwick (W, 1-0)	2	1	0	0	1	1	0	0.00

BOSTON	IP	H	R	ER	BB	SO	HR	ERA
Lee	8	5	2	2	2	5	0	2.25
Drago (L, 0-1)	1	2	1	1	1	0	0	9.00

IBB: Geronimo (by Drago). **HBP:** Evans (by Billingham). **Pitches-strikes:** Billingham 88-49, Borbon 3-2, McEnaney 13-9, Eastwick 30-18, Lee 93-60, Drago 20-12. **Ground balls-fly balls:** Billingham 9-2, Borbon 0-1, McEnaney 1-0, Eastwick 0-5, Lee 10-8, Drago 2-1. **Batters faced:** Billingham 25, Borbon 1, McEnaney 3, Eastwick 8, Lee 30, Drago 6. **UMPIRES:** hp—Colosi, 1b—Barnett, 2b—Stello, 3b—Maloney, lf—Davidson, rf—Frantz **T:** 2:38 **A:** 35,205

GAME 3 Cincinnati 6 Boston 5
Riverfront Stadium 10/14/75

BOSTON	AB	R	H	HR	RBI	BB	AVG
Cooper 1b	5	0	0	0	0	0	.077
Doyle 2b	5	0	1	0	0	0	.333
Yastrzemski lf	4	1	0	0	0	1	.182
Fisk c	3	1	1	1	1	2	.222
Lynn cf	3	0	1	0	1	0	.273
Petrocelli 3b	4	1	2	0	0	0	.545
Evans rf	4	1	2	1	2	0	.300
Burleson ss	4	0	2	0	0	0	.545
Wise p	2	0	0	0	0	0	.000
Burton p	0	0	0	0	0	0	.000
Cleveland p	0	0	0	0	0	0	.000
a-Carbo ph	1	1	1	1	1	0	.500
Willoughby p	0	0	0	0	0	0	.000
Moret p	0	0	0	0	0	0	.000
TOTALS	**35**	**5**	**10**	**3**	**5**	**3**	**.296**

a - Batted for Cleveland in the 7th

BATTING: HR: Fisk (1, 2nd off Nolan 0 on, 0 out), Carbo (1, 7th off Carroll 0 on, 2 out), Evans (1, 9th off Eastwick 1 on, 1 out). **S:** Willoughby. **SF:** Lynn. **RBI:** Fisk 1 (3), Lynn 1 (1), Evans 2 (2),

Carbo 1 (1). **2-out RBI:** Carbo 1. **Runners left in scoring position, 2 out:** Cooper 1, Petrocelli 2. **GIDP:** Burleson, Fisk. **Team LOB:** 5 **FIELDING: E:** Fisk 2 (2). **DP:** 1 (Petrocelli-Cooper).

CINCINNATI	AB	R	H	HR	RBI	BB	AVG
Rose 3b	4	1	1	0	0	1	.250
Griffey rf	3	0	0	0	0	1	.200
b-Rettenmund ph	1	0	0	0	0	0	.000
Morgan 2b	4	0	1	0	2	0	.273
Perez 1b	3	1	0	0	0	1	.000
Bench c	4	1	1	1	2	0	.250
Foster lf	3	0	0	0	0	1	.273
Concepcion ss	4	1	1	1	1	0	.167
Geronimo cf	4	2	2	1	1	0	.250
Nolan p	1	0	0	0	0	0	.000
Darcy p	1	0	0	0	0	0	.000
Carroll p	0	0	0	0	0	0	.000
McEnaney p	1	0	1	0	0	0	1.000
Eastwick p	0	0	0	0	0	0	.000
a-Armbrister ph	1	0	0	0	0	0	.000
TOTALS	**34**	**6**	**7**	**3**	**6**	**4**	**.194**

a - Batted for Eastwick in the 10th
b - Batted for Griffey in the 10th

BATTING: 3B: Rose (1, Wise). **HR:** Bench (1, 4th off Wise 1 on, 2 out), Concepcion (1, 5th off Wise 0 on, 0 out), Geronimo (1, 5th off Wise 0 on, 0 out). **SF:** Morgan. **RBI:** Morgan 2 (2), Bench 2 (2), Concepcion 1 (2), Geronimo 1 (1). **2-out RBI:** Bench 2. **Runners left in scoring position, 2 out:** Perez 1, Concepcion 1. **Team LOB:** 5 **BASERUNNING: SB:** Foster (1, 2nd base off Wise/Fisk), Perez (1, 2nd base off Wise/Fisk), Griffey (1, 2nd base off Burton/Fisk). **FIELDING: Outfield assists:** Griffey (1). **DP:** 2 (Morgan-Concepcion-Perez, Morgan-Perez).

BOSTON	IP	H	R	ER	BB	SO	HR	ERA
Wise	4.1	4	5	5	2	1	3	10.38
Burton	0.1	0	0	0	1	0	0	0.00
Cleveland	1.1	0	0	0	0	2	0	0.00
Willoughby (L, 0-1)	3	2	1	0	0	1	0	0.00
Moret	0.1	1	0	0	1	1	0	0.00

CINCINNATI	IP	H	R	ER	BB	SO	HR	ERA
Nolan	4	3	1	1	1	0	1	2.25
Darcy	2	2	1	1	2	0	0	4.50
Carroll	0.2	1	1	1	0	0	1	27.00
McEnaney	1.2	1	1	1	0	2	0	3.86
Eastwick (W, 2-0)	1.2	3	1	1	0	0	1	2.45

WP: Darcy 1. **IBB:** Rose (by Moret). **Pitches-strikes:** Wise 75-44, Burton 11-4, Cleveland 15-10, Willoughby 28-22, Moret 13-6, Nolan 40-27, Darcy 37-18, Carroll 5-4, McEnaney 16-11, Eastwick 25-14. **Ground balls-fly balls:** Wise 7-5, Burton 0-0, Cleveland 1-1, Willoughby 6-2, Moret 0-0, Nolan 6-5, Darcy 4-1, Carroll 1-0, McEnaney 1-2, Eastwick 1-2. **Batters faced:** Wise 19, Burton 2, Cleveland 4, Willoughby 11, Moret 3, Nolan 15, Darcy 10, Carroll 2, McEnaney 6, Eastwick 7. **UMPIRES:** hp—Barnett, 1b—Stello, 2b—Maloney, 3b—Davidson, lf—Frantz, rf—Colosi **T:** 3:03 **A:** 55,392

GAME 4 Boston 5 Cincinnati 4
Riverfront Stadium 10/15/75

BOSTON	AB	R	H	HR	RBI	BB	AVG
Beniquez lf	4	0	1	0	1	0	.250
Miller lf	1	0	0	0	0	0	.000
Doyle 2b	5	0	1	0	0	0	.294
Yastrzemski 1b	4	0	2	0	1	1	.267
Fisk c	5	1	1	0	0	0	.214
Lynn cf	4	1	1	0	0	0	.267
Petrocelli 3b	4	0	1	0	0	0	.467
Evans rf	4	1	2	0	2	0	.357
Burleson ss	4	1	1	0	1	0	.467
Tiant p	3	1	1	0	0	1	.333
TOTALS	**38**	**5**	**11**	**0**	**5**	**2**	**.294**

BATTING: 2B: Burleson (1, Norman). **3B:** Evans (1, Norman). **RBI:** Beniquez 1 (1), Yastrzemski 1 (2), Evans 2 (4), Burleson 1 (2). **2-out RBI:** Yastrzemski 1. **Runners left in scoring position, 2 out:** Fisk 1. **GIDP:** Yastrzemski. **Team LOB:** 8 **FIELDING: E:** Doyle (1). **Outfield assists:** Lynn (1).

CINCINNATI	AB	R	H	HR	RBI	BB	AVG
Rose 3b	3	1	1	0	0	2	.267
Griffey rf	5	0	1	0	1	0	.200
Morgan 2b	3	1	0	0	0	2	.214
Perez 1b	4	0	0	0	0	0	.000
Bench c	4	0	1	0	1	0	.250
Foster lf	4	1	2	0	0	0	.333
Concepcion ss	4	1	1	0	1	0	.188
Geronimo cf	4	0	3	0	1	0	.417
Norman p	1	0	0	0	0	0	.000
Borbon p	0	0	0	0	0	0	.000
a-Crowley ph	1	0	0	0	0	0	.000
Carroll p	0	0	0	0	0	0	.000
b-Chaney ph	1	0	0	0	0	0	.000
Eastwick p	0	0	0	0	0	0	.000
c-Armbrister ph	0	0	0	0	0	0	.000
TOTALS	**34**	**4**	**9**	**0**	**4**	**4**	**.212**

a - Batted for Borbon in the 4th
b - Batted for Carroll in the 6th
c - Batted for Eastwick in the 9th

BATTING: 2B: Griffey (3, Tiant), Bench (2, Tiant), Concepcion (1, Tiant). **3B:** Geronimo (1, Tiant). **S:** Armbrister. **RBI:** Griffey 1 (2), Bench 1 (3), Concepcion 1 (3), Geronimo 1 (2). **2-out RBI:** Bench 1, Concepcion 1, Geronimo 1. **Runners left in scoring position, 2 out:** Morgan 1, Bench 2, Foster 1, Crowley 1. **Team LOB:** 8 **FIELDING: E:** Perez (1). **DP:** 1 (Morgan-Concepcion-Perez).

BOSTON	IP	H	R	ER	BB	SO	HR	ERA
Tiant (W, 2-0)	9	9	4	4	4	4	0	2.00

CINCINNATI	IP	H	R	ER	BB	SO	HR	ERA
Norman (L, 0-1)	3.1	7	4	4	1	2	0	10.80
Borbon	0.2	2	1	0	0	0	0	0.00
Carroll	2	2	0	0	0	2	0	6.75
Eastwick	3	0	0	0	1	0	0	1.35

WP: Norman 1. **Pitches-strikes:** Tiant 155-87, Norman 57-32, Borbon 12-8, Carroll 24-17, Eastwick 28-20. **Ground balls-fly balls:** Tiant 7-14, Norman 4-3, Borbon 1-2, Carroll 4-0, Eastwick 6-3. **Batters faced:** Tiant 39, Norman 17, Borbon 5, Carroll 8, Eastwick 10. **UMPIRES:** hp—Stello, 1b—Maloney, 2b—Davidson, 3b—Frantz, lf—Colosi, rf—Barnett **T:** 2:52 **A:** 55,667

GAME 5 Cincinnati 6 Boston 2
Riverfront Stadium 10/16/75

BOSTON	AB	R	H	HR	RBI	BB	AVG
Beniquez lf	3	0	0	0	0	1	.143
Doyle 2b	4	1	1	0	0	0	.286
Yastrzemski 1b	3	1	1	0	1	0	.278
Fisk c	4	0	1	0	0	0	.222
Lynn cf	4	0	1	0	1	0	.263
Petrocelli 3b	4	0	0	0	0	0	.368
Evans rf	3	0	1	0	0	0	.353
Burleson ss	3	0	0	0	0	0	.389
Cleveland p	2	0	0	0	0	0	.000
Willoughby p	0	0	0	0	0	0	.000
a-Griffin ph	1	0	0	0	0	0	.000
Pole p	0	0	0	0	0	0	.000
Segui p	0	0	0	0	0	0	.000
TOTALS	**31**	**2**	**5**	**0**	**2**	**1**	**.269**

a - Batted for Willoughby in the 8th

BATTING: 2B: Lynn (1, Gullett). **3B:** Doyle (1, Gullett). **SF:** Yastrzemski. **RBI:** Yastrzemski 1 (3), Lynn 1 (2). **2-out RBI:** Lynn 1. **Runners left in scoring position, 2 out:** Petrocelli 2. **Team LOB:** 4 **FIELDING: Outfield assists:** Beniquez (1). **DP:** 2 (Beniquez-Fisk, Burleson-Yastrzemski).

CINCINNATI	AB	R	H	HR	RBI	BB	AVG
Rose 3b	3	0	2	0	1	1	.333
Griffey rf	4	0	1	0	0	0	.211
Morgan 2b	3	1	1	0	0	1	.235
Bench c	3	2	1	0	0	1	.263
Perez 1b	3	2	2	2	4	1	.118
Foster lf	4	0	0	0	0	0	.263
Concepcion ss	2	0	0	0	1	0	.167
Geronimo cf	4	0	0	0	0	0	.313
Gullett p	3	1	1	0	0	0	.167
Eastwick p	0	0	0	0	0	0	.000
TOTALS	**29**	**6**	**8**	**2**	**6**	**4**	**.224**

BATTING: 2B: Rose (1, Cleveland). **HR:** Perez 2 (2, 4th off Cleveland 0 on, 2 out, 6th off Cleveland 2 on, 0 out). **SF:** Concepcion. **RBI:** Rose 1 (1), Perez 4 (5), Concepcion 1 (4). **2-out RBI:** Rose 1, Perez 1. **Runners left in scoring position, 2 out:** Griffey 1, Gullett 1. **Team LOB:** 5 **BASERUNNING: SB:** Morgan (1, 2nd base off Cleveland/Fisk), Concepcion (2, 2nd base off Willoughby/Fisk).

BOSTON	IP	H	R	ER	BB	SO	HR	ERA
Cleveland (L, 0-1)	5	7	5	5	2	3	2	7.11
Willoughby	2	1	0	0	0	1	0	0.00
Pole	0	0	1	1	2	0	0	0.00
Segui	1	0	0	0	0	0	0	0.00

CINCINNATI	IP	H	R	ER	BB	SO	HR	ERA
Gullett (W, 1-1)	8.2	5	2	2	1	7	0	3.68
Eastwick (S, 1)	0.1	0	0	0	0	1	0	1.29

HBP: Concepcion (by Willoughby). **Pitches-strikes:** Cleveland 69-51, Willoughby 29-16, Pole 9-1, Segui 9-5, Gullett 108-71, Eastwick 3-3. **Ground balls-fly balls:** Cleveland 3-8, Willoughby 1-3, Pole 0-0, Segui 0-2, Gullett 3-15, Eastwick 0-0. **Batters faced:** Cleveland 23, Willoughby 7, Pole 2, Segui 3, Gullett 32, Eastwick 1. **UMPIRES:** hp—Maloney, 1b—Davidson, 2b—Frantz, 3b—Colosi, lf—Barnett, rf—Stello **T:** 2:23 **A:** 56,393

GAME 6 Boston 7 Cincinnati 6
Fenway Park 10/21/75

CINCINNATI	AB	R	H	HR	RBI	BB	AVG
Rose 3b	5	1	2	0	0	0	.348
Griffey rf	5	2	2	0	2	1	.250
Morgan 2b	6	1	1	0	0	0	.217
Bench c	6	0	1	0	1	0	.240
Perez 1b	6	0	2	0	0	0	.174
Foster lf	6	0	2	0	2	0	.280
Concepcion ss	6	0	1	0	0	0	.167
Geronimo cf	6	1	2	1	1	0	.318
Nolan p	0	0	0	0	0	0	.000
a-Chaney ph	1	0	0	0	0	0	.000
Norman p	0	0	0	0	0	0	.000
Billingham p	0	0	0	0	0	0	.000
b-Armbrister ph	0	1	0	0	0	1	.000
Carroll p	0	0	0	0	0	0	.000
c-Crowley ph	1	0	1	0	0	0	.500
Borbon p	1	0	0	0	0	0	.000
Eastwick p	0	0	0	0	0	0	.000
McEnaney p	0	0	0	0	0	0	1.000
d-Driessen ph	1	0	0	0	0	0	.000
Darcy p	0	0	0	0	0	0	.000
TOTALS	**50**	**6**	**14**	**1**	**6**	**2**	**.237**

a - Batted for Nolan in the 3th
b - Batted for Billingham in the 5th
c - Batted for Carroll in the 6th
d - Batted for McEnaney in the 10th

BATTING: 2B: Foster (1, Tiant). **3B:** Griffey (1, Tiant). **HR:** Geronimo (2, 8th off Tiant 0 on, 0 out). **RBI:** Griffey 2 (4), Bench 1 (4), Foster 2 (2), Geronimo 1 (3). **2-out RBI:** Bench 1, Foster 2. **Runners left in scoring position, 2 out:** Rose 1, Concepcion 2, Geronimo 1, Driessen 1. **Team LOB:** 11 **BASERUNNING: SB:** Concepcion (3, 2nd base off Drago/Fisk). **FIELDING: Outfield assists:** Foster (1). **DP:** 1 (Foster-Bench).

BOSTON	AB	R	H	HR	RBI	BB	AVG
Cooper 1b	5	0	0	0	0	0	.056
Drago p	0	0	0	0	0	0	.000
b-Miller ph	1	0	0	0	0	0	.000
Wise p	0	0	0	0	0	0	.000
Doyle 2b	5	0	1	0	0	1	.269
Yastrzemski lf-1b	6	1	3	0	0	0	.333
Fisk c	4	2	2	1	1	2	.273
Lynn cf	4	2	2	1	3	1	.304
Petrocelli 3b	4	1	0	0	0	1	.304
Evans rf	5	0	1	0	0	0	.318
Burleson ss	3	0	0	0	0	2	.333
Tiant p	2	0	0	0	0	0	.250
Moret p	0	0	0	0	0	0	.000
a-Carbo ph-lf	2	1	1	1	3	0	.500
TOTALS	**41**	**7**	**10**	**3**	**7**	**7**	**.264**

a - Batted for Moret in the 8th
b - Batted for Drago in the 11th

BATTING: 2B: Doyle (1, Norman), Evans (1, Billingham). **HR:** Lynn (1, 1st off Nolan 2 on, 2 out), Carbo (2, 8th off Eastwick 2 on, 2 out), Fisk (2, 12th off Darcy 0 on, 0 out). **S:** Tiant. **RBI:** Fisk 1 (4), Lynn 3 (5), Carbo 3 (4). **2-out RBI:** Lynn 3, Carbo 3. **Runners left in scoring position, 2 out:** Doyle 2, Petrocelli 3. **Team LOB:** 9 **FIELDING: E:** Burleson (1). **Outfield assists:** Evans (1). **DP:** 1 (Evans-Yastrzemski-Doyle).

CINCINNATI	IP	H	R	ER	BB	SO	HR	ERA
Nolan	2	3	3	3	0	2	1	6.00
Norman	0.2	1	0	0	2	0	0	9.00
Billingham	1.1	1	0	0	1	1	0	1.29
Carroll	1	1	0	0	0	0	0	4.91
Borbon	2	1	2	2	2	1	0	6.00
Eastwick	1	2	1	1	1	2	1	2.25
McEnaney	1	0	0	0	1	0	0	3.18
Darcy (L, 0-1)	2	1	1	1	0	1	1	4.50

BOSTON	IP	H	R	ER	BB	SO	HR	ERA
Tiant	7	11	6	6	2	5	1	3.60
Moret	1	0	0	0	0	0	0	0.00
Drago	3	1	0	0	0	1	0	2.25
Wise (W, 1-0)	1	2	0	0	0	1	0	8.44

IBB: Fisk 2 (by Norman, by McEnaney). **HBP:** Rose (by Drago). **Pitches-strikes:** Nolan 31-20, Norman 22-9, Billingham 21-11, Carroll 10-7, Borbon 33-17, Eastwick 24-14, McEnaney 7-3, Darcy 29-18, Tiant 113-72, Moret 7-6, Drago 34-18, Wise 19-12. **Ground balls-fly balls:** Nolan 2-2, Norman 0-2, Billingham 2-0, Carroll 2-1, Borbon 4-1, Eastwick 0-1, McEnaney 1-1, Darcy 3-2, Tiant 6-11, Moret 2-1, Drago 3-4, Wise 0-2. **Batters faced:** Nolan 9, Norman 5, Billingham 6, Carroll 4, Borbon 9, Eastwick 6, McEnaney 3, Darcy 7, Tiant 35, Moret 3, Drago 10, Wise 5. **UMPIRES:** hp—Davidson, 1b—Frantz, 2b—Colosi, 3b—Barnett, lf—Stello, rf—Maloney **T:** 4:01 **A:** 35,205

GAME 7 Cincinnati 4 Boston 3
Fenway Park 10/22/75

CINCINNATI	AB	R	H	HR	RBI	BB	AVG
Rose 3b	4	0	2	0	1	1	.370
Morgan 2b	4	0	2	0	1	1	.259
Bench c	4	1	0	0	0	1	.207
Perez 1b	5	1	1	1	2	0	.179
Foster lf	4	0	1	0	0	0	.276
Concepcion ss	4	0	1	0	0	0	.179
Griffey rf	2	2	1	0	0	2	.269
Geronimo cf	3	0	0	0	0	0	.280
Gullett p	1	0	1	0	0	0	.286
a-Rettenmund ph	1	0	0	0	0	0	.000
Billingham p	0	0	0	0	0	0	.000
b-Armbrister ph	0	0	0	0	0	1	.000
Carroll p	0	0	0	0	0	0	.000
c-Driessen ph	1	0	0	0	0	0	.000
McEnaney p	0	0	0	0	0	0	1.000
TOTALS	**33**	**4**	**9**	**1**	**4**	**6**	**.242**

a - Batted for Gullett in the 5th
b - Batted for Billingham in the 7th
c - Batted for Carroll in the 9th

BATTING: HR: Perez (3, 6th off Lee 1 on, 2 out). **S:** Geronimo. **RBI:** Rose 1 (2), Morgan 1 (3), Perez 2 (7). **2-out RBI:** Rose 1, Morgan 1, Perez 2. **Runners left in scoring position, 2 out:** Bench 2, Perez 2, Foster 1. **GIDP:** Geronimo, Rettenmund. **Team LOB:** 9 **BASERUNNING: SB:** Morgan (2, 2nd base off Lee/Fisk), Griffey (2, 2nd base off Moret/Fisk). **FIELDING: DP:** 1 (Concepcion-Morgan-Perez).

BOSTON	AB	R	H	HR	RBI	BB	AVG
Carbo lf	3	1	1	0	0	1	.429
Miller lf	0	0	0	0	0	0	.000
b-Beniquez ph	1	0	0	0	0	0	.125
Doyle 2b	4	1	1	0	0	0	.267
c-Montgomery ph	1	0	0	0	0	0	.000
Yastrzemski 1b	5	1	1	0	1	0	.310
Fisk c	3	0	0	0	0	1	.240
Lynn cf	2	0	0	0	0	2	.280
Petrocelli 3b	3	0	1	0	1	1	.308
Evans rf	2	0	0	0	1	2	.292
Burleson ss	3	0	0	0	0	1	.292
Lee p	3	0	1	0	0	0	.167
Moret p	0	0	0	0	0	0	.000
Willoughby p	0	0	0	0	0	0	.000
a-Cooper ph	1	0	0	0	0	0	.053
Burton p	0	0	0	0	0	0	.000
Cleveland p	0	0	0	0	0	0	.000
TOTALS	**31**	**3**	**5**	**0**	**3**	**8**	**.251**

a - Batted for Willoughby in the 8th
b - Batted for Miller in the 9th
c - Batted for Doyle in the 9th

BATTING: 2B: Carbo (1, Gullett). **RBI:** Yastrzemski 1 (4), Petrocelli 1 (4), Evans 1 (5). **2-out RBI:** Petrocelli 1, Evans 1. **Runners left in scoring position, 2 out:** Yastrzemski 1, Fisk 1, Burleson 2, Lee 2. **GIDP:** Burleson. **Team LOB:** 9 **FIELDING: E:** Doyle (2). **Outfield assists:** Carbo (1). **DP:** 2 (Doyle-Burleson-Yastrzemski, Burleson-Doyle-Yastrzemski).

CINCINNATI	IP	H	R	ER	BB	SO	HR	ERA
Gullett	4	4	3	3	5	5	0	4.34
Billingham	2	1	0	0	2	1	0	1.00
Carroll (W, 1-0)	2	0	0	0	1	1	0	3.18
McEnaney (S, 1)	1	0	0	0	0	0	0	2.70

BOSTON	IP	H	R	ER	BB	SO	HR	ERA
Lee	6.1	7	3	3	1	2	1	3.14
Moret	0.1	1	0	0	2	0	0	0.00
Willoughby	1.1	0	0	0	0	0	0	0.00
Burton (L, 0-1)	0.2	1	1	1	2	0	0	9.00
Cleveland	0.1	0	0	0	1	0	0	6.75

WP: Gullett 1. **IBB:** Fisk (by Gullett). **Pitches-strikes:** Gullett 74-38, Billingham 34-18, Carroll 23-13, McEnaney 8-5, Lee 80-47, Moret 17-6, Willoughby 9-5, Burton 18-9, Cleveland 11-5. **Ground balls-fly balls:** Gullett 3-4, Billingham 2-3, Carroll 3-1, McEnaney 1-2, Lee 9-6, Moret 0-1, Willoughby 2-2, Burton 1-0, Cleveland 0-1. **Batters faced:** Gullett 21, Billingham 9, Carroll 6, McEnaney 3, Lee 25, Moret 4, Willoughby 4, Burton 5, Cleveland 2. **UMPIRES:** hp—Frantz, 1b—Colosi, 2b—Barnett, 3b—Stello, lf—Maloney, rf—Davidson **T:** 2:52 **A:** 35,205

1976 CINCINNATI DEF. NY YANKEES, 4-0

GAME 1 Cincinnati 5 New York 1
Riverfront Stadium 10/16/76

NY YANKEES	AB	R	H	HR	RBI	BB	AVG
Rivers cf	4	0	0	0	0	0	.000
White lf	4	0	1	0	0	0	.250
Munson c	4	0	1	0	0	0	.250
Piniella dh	3	1	1	0	0	0	.333
b-May ph	1	0	0	0	0	0	.000
Chambliss 1b	3	0	1	0	0	0	.333
Nettles 3b	3	0	0	0	1	0	.000
Maddox rf	2	0	1	0	0	1	.500
c-Gamble ph	1	0	0	0	0	0	.000
Randolph 2b	2	0	0	0	0	1	.000
Stanley ss	1	0	0	0	0	1	.000
a-Velez ph	1	0	0	0	0	0	.000
Mason ss	0	0	0	0	0	0	.000
TOTALS	**29**	**1**	**5**	**0**	**1**	**3**	**.172**

a - Batted for Stanley in the 7th
b - Batted for Piniella in the 8th
c - Batted for Maddox in the 9th

BATTING: 2B: Piniella (1, Gullett). **3B:** Maddox (1, Gullett). **SF:** Nettles. **RBI:** Nettles 1 (1). **Runners left in scoring position, 2 out:** Piniella 1, May 1, Randolph 1, Velez 1. **GIDP:** Nettles, Nettles. **Team LOB:** 6 **BASERUNNING: CS:** Rivers (1, 2nd base off Gullett/Bench). **FIELDING: E:** Chambliss (1). **DP:** 2 (Alexander-Randolph-Chambliss, Randolph-Stanley-Chambliss).

CINCINNATI	AB	R	H	HR	RBI	BB	AVG
Rose 3b	2	0	0	0	1	1	.000
Griffey rf	4	1	0	0	0	0	.000
Morgan 2b	4	1	1	1	1	0	.250
Perez 1b	4	0	3	0	1	0	.750
Driessen dh	4	0	0	0	0	0	.000
Foster lf	3	1	2	0	0	1	.667
Bench c	3	1	2	0	1	0	.667
Geronimo cf	3	0	1	0	0	0	.333
Concepcion ss	3	1	1	0	0	0	.333
TOTALS	**30**	**5**	**10**	**1**	**4**	**2**	**.333**

BATTING: 2B: Perez (1, Alexander), Geronimo (1, Lyle). **3B:** Concepcion (1, Alexander), Bench (1, Alexander). **HR:** Morgan (1, 1st off Alexander 0 on, 2 out). **SF:** Rose. **RBI:** Rose 1 (1), Morgan 1 (1), Perez 1 (1), Bench 1 (1). **2-out RBI:** Morgan 1, Perez 1. **Runners left in scoring position, 2 out:** Griffey 1, Foster 1. **GIDP:** Bench, Geronimo. **Team LOB:** 4 **BASERUNNING: SB:** Griffey (1, 2nd base off Alexander/Munson). **CS:** Perez (1, 2nd base off Alexander/Munson). **FIELDING: E:** Geronimo (1). **DP:** 2 (Morgan-Concepcion-Perez, Morgan-Perez).

NY YANKEES	IP	H	R	ER	BB	SO	HR	ERA
Alexander (L, 0-1)	6	9	5	5	2	1	1	7.50
Lyle	2	1	0	0	0	3	0	0.00

CINCINNATI	IP	H	R	ER	BB	SO	HR	ERA
Gullett (W, 1-0)	7.1	5	1	1	3	4	0	1.23
Borbon	1.2	0	0	0	0	0	0	0.00

WP: Lyle 1. **HBP:** Chambliss (by Gullett). **Pitches-strikes:** Alexander 95-49, Lyle 23-18, Gullett 95-59, Borbon 12-8. **Ground balls-fly balls:** Alexander 4-8, Lyle 2-2, Gullett 8-7, Borbon 2-3. **Batters faced:** Alexander 25, Lyle 8, Gullett 29, Borbon 5. **UMPIRES:** hp—Weyer, 1b—DiMuro, 2b—B. Williams, 3b—Deegan, lf—Froemming, rf—Phillips **T:** 2:10 **A:** 54,826

GAME 2 Cincinnati 4 New York 3
Riverfront Stadium 10/17/76

NY YANKEES	AB	R	H	HR	RBI	BB	AVG
Rivers cf	5	0	0	0	0	0	.000
White lf	3	0	1	0	0	1	.286
Munson c	4	1	1	0	1	0	.250
Piniella rf	4	0	2	0	0	0	.429
Chambliss 1b	4	0	2	0	0	0	.429
Nettles 3b	4	0	1	0	1	0	.143
Maddox dh	3	0	0	0	0	0	.200
a-May ph	1	0	0	0	0	0	.000
Randolph 2b	4	1	1	0	0	0	.167
Stanley ss	3	1	1	0	1	1	.250
TOTALS	**35**	**3**	**9**	**0**	**3**	**2**	**.219**

a - Batted for Maddox in the 8th

BATTING: 2B: Stanley (1, Norman). **RBI:** Munson 1 (1), Nettles 1 (2), Stanley 1 (1). **Runners left in scoring position, 2 out:** White 1, Randolph 2. **GIDP:** Maddox. **Team LOB:** 7 **FIELDING: E:** Stanley (1).

CINCINNATI	AB	R	H	HR	RBI	BB	AVG
Rose 3b	4	0	0	0	0	1	.000
Griffey rf	4	1	0	0	1	0	.000
Morgan 2b	4	0	2	0	0	1	.375
Perez 1b	5	0	2	0	1	0	.556
Driessen dh	4	1	2	0	0	0	.250
Foster lf	4	0	1	0	1	0	.429
Bench c	4	1	2	0	0	0	.571
Geronimo cf	2	1	0	0	0	2	.200
Concepcion ss	4	0	1	0	1	0	.286
TOTALS	**35**	**4**	**10**	**0**	**4**	**4**	**.308**

BATTING: 2B: Driessen (1, Hunter), Bench (1, Hunter). **3B:** Morgan (1, Hunter). **SF:** Griffey. **RBI:** Griffey 1 (1), Perez 1 (2), Foster 1 (1), Concepcion 1 (1). **2-out RBI:** Perez 1. **Runners left in scoring position, 2 out:** Morgan 1, Perez 2, Concepcion 2. **Team LOB:** 10 **BASERUNNING: SB:** Morgan (1, 2nd base off Hunter/Munson), Concepcion (1, 2nd base off Hunter/Munson). **CS:** Foster (1, 2nd base off Hunter/Munson). **FIELDING: DP:** 1 (Concepcion-Morgan-Perez).

NY YANKEES	IP	H	R	ER	BB	SO	HR	ERA
Hunter (L, 0-1)	8.2	10	4	3	4	5	0	3.12

CINCINNATI	IP	H	R	ER	BB	SO	HR	ERA
Norman	6.1	9	3	3	2	2	0	4.26
Billingham (W, 1-0)	2.2	0	0	0	0	1	0	0.00

IBB: Morgan (by Hunter). **Pitches-strikes:** Hunter 135-79, Norman 88-57, Billingham 37-24. **Ground balls-fly balls:** Hunter 3-17, Norman 5-11, Billingham 5-2. **Batters faced:** Hunter 40, Norman 29, Billingham 8. **UMPIRES:** hp—DiMuro, 1b—Williams, 2b—Deegan, 3b—Froemming, lf—Phillips, rf—Weyer **T:** 2:33 **A:** 54,816

GAME 3 Cincinnati 6 New York 2
Yankee Stadium 10/19/76

CINCINNATI	AB	R	H	HR	RBI	BB	AVG
Rose 3b	5	1	2	0	0	0	.182
Griffey rf	4	0	1	0	0	0	.083
Morgan 2b	4	1	1	0	1	0	.333
Perez 1b	4	0	0	0	0	0	.385
Driessen dh	3	2	3	1	1	1	.455
Foster lf	4	1	2	0	2	0	.455
Bench c	4	0	2	0	0	0	.545
Geronimo cf	4	1	1	0	1	0	.222
Concepcion ss	4	0	1	0	1	0	.273
TOTALS	**36**	**6**	**13**	**1**	**6**	**1**	**.327**

BATTING: 2B: Foster (1, Ellis), Driessen (2, Jackson), Morgan (1, Jackson). **HR:** Driessen (1, 4th off Ellis 0 on, 0 out). **RBI:** Morgan 1 (2), Driessen 1 (1), Foster 2 (3), Geronimo 1 (1), Concepcion 1 (2). **Runners left in scoring position, 2 out:** Perez 1, Foster 1. **GIDP:** Rose, Bench, Concepcion. **Team LOB:** 4 **BASERUNNING: SB:** Driessen (1, 2nd base off Ellis/Munson), Geronimo (1, 2nd base off Ellis/Munson). **FIELDING: E:** Zachry (1), Morgan (1). **DP:** 1 (Perez-Concepcion).

NY YANKEES	AB	R	H	HR	RBI	BB	AVG
Rivers cf	4	0	2	0	0	1	.154
White lf	3	0	0	0	0	2	.200
Munson c	5	0	3	0	0	0	.385
Chambliss 1b	5	1	1	0	0	0	.333
May dh	4	0	0	0	0	0	.000
Nettles 3b	2	0	0	0	0	2	.111
Gamble rf	3	0	1	0	1	0	.250
b-Piniella ph-rf	1	0	0	0	0	0	.375
Randolph 2b	4	0	0	0	0	0	.100
Stanley ss	1	0	0	0	0	0	.200
a-Hendricks ph	1	0	0	0	0	0	.000
Mason ss	1	1	1	1	1	0	1.000
c-Velez ph	1	0	0	0	0	0	.000
TOTALS	**35**	**2**	**8**	**1**	**2**	**5**	**.222**

a - Batted for Stanley in the 4th
b - Batted for Gamble in the 8th
c - Batted for Mason in the 9th

BATTING: HR: Mason (1, 7th off Zachry 0 on, 1 out). **RBI:** Gamble 1 (1), Mason 1 (1). **Runners left in scoring position, 2 out:** Chambliss 2, Randolph 1, Hendricks 1. **Team LOB:** 11 **FIELDING: DP:** 3 (Stanley-Randolph-Chambliss, Nettles-Chambliss, Nettles-Randolph-Chambliss).

CINCINNATI	IP	H	R	ER	BB	SO	HR	ERA
Zachry (W, 1-0)	6.2	6	2	2	5	6	1	2.70
McEnaney (S, 1)	2.1	2	0	0	0	1	0	0.00

NY YANKEES	IP	H	R	ER	BB	SO	HR	ERA
Ellis (L, 0-1)	3.1	7	4	4	0	1	1	10.80
Jackson	3.2	4	2	2	0	3	0	4.91
Tidrow	2	2	0	0	1	1	0	0.00

IBB: Driessen (by Tidrow). **Pitches-strikes:** Zachry 109-67, McEnaney 31-20, Ellis 59-40, Jackson 56-35, Tidrow 20-12. **Ground balls-fly balls:** Zachry 4-9, McEnaney 4-3, Ellis 7-1, Jackson 2-5, Tidrow 3-0. **Batters faced:** Zachry 30, McEnaney 10, Ellis 16, Jackson 14, Tidrow 7. **UMPIRES:** hp—Williams, 1b—Deegan, 2b—Froemming, 3b—Phillips, lf—Weyer, rf—DiMuro **T:** 2:40 **A:** 56,667

GAME 4 Cincinnati 7 New York 2
Yankee Stadium 10/21/76

CINCINNATI	AB	R	H	HR	RBI	BB	AVG
Rose 3b	5	0	1	0	0	0	.188
Griffey rf	5	0	0	0	0	0	.059
Morgan 2b	3	1	1	0	0	1	.333
Perez 1b	3	1	0	0	0	1	.313
Driessen dh	3	1	0	0	0	1	.357
Foster lf	3	1	1	0	1	1	.429
Bench c	4	2	2	2	5	0	.533
Geronimo cf	4	1	2	0	0	0	.308
Concepcion ss	3	0	2	0	1	1	.357
TOTALS	**33**	**7**	**9**	**2**	**7**	**5**	**.313**

BATTING: 2B: Rose (1, Figueroa), Geronimo (2, Tidrow), Concepcion (1, Tidrow). **HR:** Bench 2 (2, 4th off Figueroa 1 on, 2 out, 9th off Tidrow 2 on, 1 out). **RBI:** Foster 1 (4), Bench 5 (6), Concepcion 1 (3). **2-out RBI:** Foster 1, Bench 2. **Runners left in scoring position, 2 out:** Griffey 2, Foster 1. **Team LOB:** 4 **BASERUNNING: SB:** Geronimo (2, 2nd base off Figueroa/Munson), Morgan (2, 2nd base off Figueroa/Munson). **CS:** Foster (2, 2nd base off Figueroa/Munson), Concepcion (1, 2nd base off Figueroa/Munson). **FIELDING: E:** Morgan (2).

NY YANKEES	AB	R	H	HR	RBI	BB	AVG
Rivers cf	5	1	1	0	0	0	.167
White lf	5	0	0	0	0	0	.133
Munson c	4	1	4	0	1	0	.529
Chambliss 1b	4	0	1	0	1	0	.313
May dh	3	0	0	0	0	0	.000
b-Piniella ph	1	0	0	0	0	0	.333
Nettles 3b	3	0	2	0	0	1	.250
Gamble rf	4	0	0	0	0	0	.125
Randolph 2b	4	0	0	0	0	0	.071
Stanley ss	1	0	0	0	0	1	.167
a-Hendricks ph	1	0	0	0	0	0	.000
Mason ss	0	0	0	0	0	0	1.000
c-Velez ph	1	0	0	0	0	0	.000
TOTALS	**36**	**2**	**8**	**0**	**2**	**2**	**.222**

a - Batted for Stanley in the 6th
b - Batted for May in the 8th
c - Batted for Mason in the 9th

BATTING: 2B: Chambliss (1, Nolan). **RBI:** Munson 1 (2), Chambliss 1 (1). **2-out RBI:** Chambliss 1. **Runners left in scoring position, 2 out:** May 3. **Team LOB:** 9 **BASERUNNING: SB:** Rivers (1, 2nd base off Nolan/Bench). **FIELDING: DP:** 1 (Stanley-Nettles-Chambliss-Randolph).

CINCINNATI	IP	H	R	ER	BB	SO	HR	ERA
Nolan (W, 1-0)	6.2	8	2	2	1	1	0	2.70
McEnaney (S, 2)	2.1	0	0	0	1	1	0	0.00

NY YANKEES	IP	H	R	ER	BB	SO	HR	ERA
Figueroa (L, 0-1)	8	6	5	5	5	2	1	5.63
Tidrow	0.1	3	2	2	0	0	1	7.71
Lyle	0.2	0	0	0	0	0	0	0.00

WP: Figueroa 1. **Pitches-strikes:** Nolan 87-62, McEnaney 20-12, Figueroa 109-69, Tidrow 9-9, Lyle 4-4. **Ground balls-fly balls:** Nolan 6-14, McEnaney 2-4, Figueroa 8-11, Tidrow 0-1, Lyle 2-0. **Batters faced:** Nolan 30, McEnaney 8, Figueroa 32, Tidrow 4, Lyle 2. **UMPIRES:** hp—Deegan, 1b—Froemming, 2b—Phillips, 3b—Weyer, lf—DiMuro, rf—Williams **T:** 2:36 **A:** 56,700

1977 NY YANKEES DEF. LOS ANGELES, 4-2

GAME 1 New York 4 Los Angeles 3
Yankee Stadium 10/11/77

LOS ANGELES	AB	R	H	HR	RBI	BB	AVG
Lopes 2b	5	1	0	0	0	1	.000
Russell ss	6	1	1	0	1	0	.167
Smith rf	4	0	1	0	0	1	.250
Cey 3b	3	0	0	0	1	1	.000
Garvey 1b	4	0	1	0	0	1	.250
Baker lf	4	1	1	0	0	0	.250
Burke cf	3	0	1	0	0	0	.333
a-Mota ph	1	0	0	0	0	0	.000
Monday cf	1	0	0	0	0	0	.000
Yeager c	3	0	0	0	0	1	.000
b-Landestoy pr	0	0	0	0	0	0	.000
Grote c	1	0	0	0	0	0	.000
Sutton p	2	0	0	0	0	1	.000
Rautzhan p	0	0	0	0	0	0	.000
Sosa p	0	0	0	0	0	0	.000
c-Lacy ph	1	0	1	0	1	0	1.000
Garman p	0	0	0	0	0	0	.000
d-Davalillo ph	1	0	0	0	0	0	.000
Rhoden p	0	0	0	0	0	0	.000
TOTALS	**39**	**3**	**6**	**0**	**3**	**6**	**.154**

a - Batted for Burke in the 9th
b - Ran for Yeager in the 9th
c - Batted for Sosa in the 9th
d - Batted for Garman in the 12th

BATTING: 3B: Russell (1, Gullett). **SF:** Cey. **RBI:** Russell 1 (1), Cey 1 (1), Lacy 1 (1). **Runners left in scoring position, 2 out:** Russell 1, Garvey 1, Sutton 1. **Team LOB:** 8 **BASERUNNING: CS:** Smith (1, 2nd base off Gullett/Munson). **Outfield assists:** Smith (1).

NY YANKEES	AB	R	H	HR	RBI	BB	AVG
Rivers cf	6	0	0	0	0	0	.000
Randolph 2b	5	3	2	1	1	1	.400
Munson c	4	1	2	0	1	2	.500
Jackson rf	2	0	1	0	0	1	.500
Blair rf	2	0	1	0	1	0	.500
Chambliss 1b	5	0	1	0	1	0	.200
Nettles 3b	4	0	0	0	0	1	.000
Piniella lf	5	0	2	0	0	0	.400
Dent ss	5	0	2	0	0	0	.400
Gullett p	1	0	0	0	0	0	.000
Lyle p	2	0	0	0	0	0	.000
TOTALS	**41**	**4**	**11**	**1**	**4**	**5**	**.268**

BATTING: 2B: Munson (1, Sutton), Randolph (1, Rhoden). **HR:** Randolph (1, 6th off Sutton 0 on, 0 out). **S:** Gullett, Gullett. **RBI:** Randolph 1 (1), Munson 1 (1), Blair 1 (1), Chambliss 1 (1). **2-out RBI:** Chambliss 1. **Runners left in scoring position, 2 out:** Rivers 2, Nettles 1, Dent 2. **Team LOB:** 12 **Outfield assists:** Rivers (1).

LOS ANGELES	IP	H	R	ER	BB	SO	HR	ERA
Sutton	7	8	3	3	1	4	1	3.86
Rautzhan	0.1	0	0	0	2	0	0	0.00
Sosa	0.2	0	0	0	0	1	0	0.00
Garman	3	1	0	0	1	3	0	0.00
Rhoden (L, 0-1)	0	2	1	1	1	0	0	0.00

NY YANKEES	IP	H	R	ER	BB	SO	HR	ERA
Gullett	8.1	5	3	3	6	6	0	3.24
Lyle (W, 1-0)	3.2	1	0	0	0	2	0	0.00

IBB: Munson (by Rhoden). **HBP:** Baker (by Gullett), Jackson (by Sutton). **Pitches-strikes:** Sutton 99-61, Rautzhan 10-2, Sosa 8-6, Garman 25-17, Rhoden 10-4, Gullett 133-74, Lyle 29-21. **Ground balls-fly balls:** Sutton 6-8, Rautzhan 1-0, Sosa 1-0, Garman 5-1, Rhoden 0-0, Gullett 7-9, Lyle 4-5. **Batters faced:** Sutton 30, Rautzhan 3, Sosa 2, Garman 11, Rhoden 3, Gullett 35, Lyle 12. **UMPIRES:** hp—Chylak, 1b—Sudol, 2b—McCoy, 3b—Dale, lf—Evans, rf—McSherry **T:** 3:24 **A:** 56,668

GAME 2 Los Angeles 6 New York 1
Yankee Stadium 10/12/77

LOS ANGELES	AB	R	H	HR	RBI	BB	AVG
Lopes 2b	4	0	0	0	0	0	.000
Russell ss	4	1	1	0	0	0	.200
Smith rf	3	2	2	1	2	1	.429
Cey 3b	4	1	1	1	2	0	.143
Garvey 1b	4	1	2	1	1	0	.375
Baker lf	4	0	0	0	0	0	.125
Monday cf	3	0	1	0	0	0	.250
Burke cf	1	0	0	0	0	0	.250
Yeager c	4	1	2	1	1	0	.286
Hooton p	3	0	0	0	0	0	.000
TOTALS	**34**	**6**	**9**	**4**	**6**	**1**	**.205**

BATTING: 2B: Smith (1, Hunter). **HR:** Cey (1, 1st off Hunter 1 on, 2 out), Yeager (1, 2nd off Hunter 0 on, 2 out), Smith (1, 3th off Hunter 1 on, 1 out), Garvey (1, 9th off Lyle 0 on, 0 out). **RBI:** Smith 2 (2), Cey 2 (3), Garvey 1 (1), Yeager 1 (1). **2-out RBI:** Cey 2, Yeager 1. **Team LOB:** 2 **BASERUNNING: CS:** Garvey (1, 2nd base off Tidrow/Munson). **FIELDING: DP:** 1 (Garvey-Russell-Garvey).

NY YANKEES	AB	R	H	HR	RBI	BB	AVG
Rivers cf	4	0	0	0	0	0	.000
Randolph 2b	4	1	1	0	0	0	.333
Munson c	4	0	1	0	0	0	.375
Jackson rf	4	0	0	0	1	0	.167
Chambliss 1b	4	0	0	0	0	0	.111
Nettles 3b	2	0	1	0	0	1	.167
Piniella lf	3	0	1	0	0	0	.375
Dent ss	2	0	1	0	0	0	.429
b-Johnson ph	1	0	0	0	0	0	.000
Stanley ss	0	0	0	0	0	0	.000
Hunter p	0	0	0	0	0	0	.000
Tidrow p	1	0	0	0	0	0	.000
a-Zeber ph	1	0	0	0	0	0	.000
Clay p	0	0	0	0	0	0	.000
c-White ph	1	0	0	0	0	0	.000
Lyle p	0	0	0	0	0	0	.000
TOTALS	**31**	**1**	**5**	**0**	**1**	**1**	**.222**

a - Batted for Tidrow in the 5th
b - Batted for Dent in the 7th
c - Batted for Clay in the 8th

BATTING: RBI: Jackson 1 (1). **Runners left in scoring position, 2 out:** Rivers 1. **GIDP:** Jackson. **Team LOB:** 4

LOS ANGELES	IP	H	R	ER	BB	SO	HR	ERA
Hooton (W, 1-0)	9	5	1	1	1	8	0	1.00
NY YANKEES	**IP**	**H**	**R**	**ER**	**BB**	**SO**	**HR**	**ERA**
Hunter (L, 0-1)	2.1	5	5	5	0	0	3	19.29
Tidrow	2.2	3	0	0	0	1	0	0.00
Clay	3	0	0	0	1	0	0	0.00
Lyle	1	1	1	1	0	0	1	1.93

Pitches-strikes: Hooton 114-75, Hunter 49-33, Tidrow 41-28, Clay 32-18, Lyle 13-8. **Ground balls-fly balls:** Hooton 6-12, Hunter 5-2, Tidrow 2-3, Clay 5-4, Lyle 1-2. **Batters faced:** Hooton 32, Hunter 12, Tidrow 9, Clay 10, Lyle 4. **UMPIRES:** hp—Sudol, 1b—McCoy, 2b—Dale, 3b—Evans, lf—McSherry, rf—Chylak **T:** 2:27 **A:** 56,691

GAME 3 New York 5 Los Angeles 3
Dodger Stadium 10/14/77

NY YANKEES	AB	R	H	HR	RBI	BB	AVG
Rivers cf	5	1	3	0	1	0	.200
Randolph 2b	4	0	0	0	0	1	.231
Munson c	5	1	1	0	1	0	.308
Jackson rf	3	2	1	0	1	1	.222
Blair rf	1	0	0	0	0	0	.333
Piniella lf	3	0	2	0	1	0	.455
Chambliss 1b	4	0	1	0	1	0	.154
Nettles 3b	4	1	1	0	0	0	.200
Dent ss	3	0	1	0	0	1	.400
Torrez p	3	0	0	0	0	0	.000
TOTALS	**35**	**5**	**10**	**0**	**5**	**3**	**.243**

BATTING: 2B: Rivers 2 (2, John), Munson (2, John). **S:** Torrez. **RBI:** Rivers 1 (1), Munson 1 (2), Jackson 1 (2), Piniella 1 (1), Chambliss 1 (2). **Runners left in scoring position, 2 out:** Randolph 1, Munson 1, Blair 1, Torrez 2. **GIDP:** Chambliss. **Team LOB:** 8 **BASERUNNING: SB:** Rivers (1, 2nd base off Hough/Yeager).

LOS ANGELES	AB	R	H	HR	RBI	BB	AVG
Lopes 2b	4	0	0	0	0	1	.000
Russell ss	4	0	0	0	0	0	.143
Smith rf	3	1	1	0	0	1	.400
Cey 3b	3	0	0	0	0	1	.100
Garvey 1b	4	1	2	0	0	0	.417
Baker lf	4	1	2	1	3	0	.250
Monday cf	4	0	0	0	0	0	.125
Yeager c	4	0	2	0	0	0	.364
John p	2	0	0	0	0	0	.000
a-Davalillo ph	1	0	0	0	0	0	.000
Hough p	0	0	0	0	0	0	.000
b-Mota ph	1	0	0	0	0	0	.000
TOTALS	**34**	**3**	**7**	**1**	**3**	**3**	**.206**

a - Batted for John in the 6th
b - Batted for Hough in the 9th

BATTING: 2B: Yeager (1, Torrez). **HR:** Baker (1, 3th off Torrez 2 on, 2 out). **RBI:** Baker 3 (3). **2-out RBI:** Baker 3. **Runners left in scoring position, 2 out:** Lopes 2, Garvey 1, Baker 1. **Team LOB:** 7 **BASERUNNING: SB:** Lopes (1, 2nd base off Torrez/Munson). **FIELDING: E:** Baker (1). **DP:** 1 (Garvey-Russell-Garvey).

NY YANKEES	IP	H	R	ER	BB	SO	HR	ERA
Torrez (W, 1-0)	9	7	3	3	3	9	1	3.00
LOS ANGELES	**IP**	**H**	**R**	**ER**	**BB**	**SO**	**HR**	**ERA**
John (L, 0-1)	6	9	5	4	3	7	0	6.00
Hough	3	1	0	0	0	2	0	0.00

HBP: Piniella (by John). **Pitches-strikes:** Torrez 125-81, John 101-64, Hough 41-30. **Ground balls-fly balls:** Torrez 11-7, John 8-1, Hough 1-6. **Batters faced:** Torrez 37, John 30, Hough 10. **UMPIRES:** hp—McCoy, 1b—Dale, 2b—Evans, 3b—McSherry, lf—Chylak, rf—Sudol **T:** 2:31 **A:** 55,992

GAME 4 New York 4 Los Angeles 2
Dodger Stadium 10/15/77

NY YANKEES	AB	R	H	HR	RBI	BB	AVG
Rivers cf	4	0	1	0	0	0	.211
Randolph 2b	4	0	0	0	0	0	.176
Munson c	4	0	1	0	0	0	.294
Jackson rf	4	2	2	1	1	0	.308
Blair rf	0	0	0	0	0	0	.333
Piniella lf	4	1	1	0	1	0	.400
Chambliss 1b	3	1	1	0	0	0	.188
Nettles 3b	3	0	0	0	1	0	.154
Dent ss	3	0	1	0	1	0	.385
Guidry p	2	0	0	0	0	0	.000
TOTALS	**31**	**4**	**7**	**1**	**4**	**0**	**.239**

BATTING: 2B: Jackson (1, Rau), Chambliss (1, Rau). **HR:** Jackson (1, 6th off Rhoden 0 on, 2 out). **S:** Guidry. **RBI:** Jackson 1 (3), Piniella 1 (2), Nettles 1 (1), Dent 1 (1). **2-out RBI:** Jackson 1. **Runners left in scoring position, 2 out:** Rivers 1. **GIDP:** Munson, Piniella. **Team LOB:** 1

LOS ANGELES	AB	R	H	HR	RBI	BB	AVG
Lopes 2b	2	1	1	1	2	2	.067
Russell ss	4	0	0	0	0	0	.111
Smith cf	4	0	0	0	0	0	.286
Cey 3b	4	0	2	0	0	0	.214
Garvey 1b	4	0	0	0	0	0	.313
Baker lf	4	0	0	0	0	0	.188
Lacy rf	2	0	0	0	0	1	.333
Yeager c	3	0	0	0	0	0	.286
Rau p	0	0	0	0	0	0	.000
Rhoden p	2	1	1	0	0	0	.500
a-Mota ph	1	0	0	0	0	0	.000
Garman p	0	0	0	0	0	0	.000
TOTALS	**30**	**2**	**4**	**1**	**2**	**3**	**.190**

a - Batted for Rhoden in the 8th

BATTING: 2B: Rhoden (1, Guidry), Cey (1, Guidry). **HR:** Lopes (1, 3th off Guidry 1 on, 1 out). **RBI:** Lopes 2 (2). **Runners left in scoring position, 2 out:** Cey 1, Baker 1, Yeager 1. **Team LOB:** 4 **BASERUNNING: SB:** Lopes (2, 2nd base off Guidry/Munson). **CS:** Lopes (1, 2nd base off Guidry/Munson). **FIELDING: DP:** 2 (Russell-Lopes-Garvey, Lopes-Russell-Garvey).

NY YANKEES	IP	H	R	ER	BB	SO	HR	ERA
Guidry (W, 1-0)	9	4	2	2	3	7	1	2.00
LOS ANGELES	**IP**	**H**	**R**	**ER**	**BB**	**SO**	**HR**	**ERA**
Rau (L, 0-1)	1	4	3	3	0	0	0	27.00
Rhoden	7	2	1	1	0	5	1	2.57
Garman	1	1	0	0	0	0	0	0.00

Pitches-strikes: Guidry 120-84, Rau 12-9, Rhoden 82-51, Garman 6-4. **Ground balls-fly balls:** Guidry 8-11, Rau 1-1, Rhoden 10-5, Garman 1-1. **Batters faced:** Guidry 33, Rau 6, Rhoden 23, Garman 3. **UMPIRES:** hp—Dale, 1b—Evans, 2b—McSherry, 3b—Chylak, lf—Sudol, rf—McCoy **T:** 2:07 **A:** 55,995

GAME 5 Los Angeles 10 New York 4
Dodger Stadium 10/16/77

NY YANKEES	AB	R	H	HR	RBI	BB	AVG
Rivers cf	4	0	0	0	0	0	.174
Randolph 2b	4	0	1	0	0	0	.190
Munson c	4	1	2	1	1	0	.333
Johnson c	0	0	0	0	0	0	.000
Jackson rf	4	2	2	1	1	0	.353
Chambliss 1b	4	1	2	0	0	0	.250
Nettles 3b	4	0	2	0	1	0	.235
Piniella lf	4	0	0	0	0	0	.316
Dent ss	4	0	0	0	1	0	.294
Gullett p	1	0	0	0	0	0	.000
Clay p	0	0	0	0	0	0	.000
a-Zeber ph	1	0	0	0	0	0	.000
Tidrow p	0	0	0	0	0	0	.000
b-White ph	1	0	0	0	0	0	.000
Hunter p	0	0	0	0	0	0	.000
c-Blair ph	1	0	0	0	0	0	.250
TOTALS	**36**	**4**	**9**	**2**	**4**	**0**	**.241**

a - Batted for Clay in the 6th
b - Batted for Tidrow in the 7th
c - Batted for Hunter in the 9th

BATTING: 2B: Randolph (2, Sutton), Nettles (1, Sutton). **HR:** Munson (1, 8th off Sutton 0 on, 2 out), Jackson (2, 8th off Sutton 0 on, 2 out). **RBI:** Munson 1 (3), Jackson 1 (4), Nettles 1 (2), Dent 1 (2). **2-out RBI:** Munson 1, Jackson 1. **Runners left in scoring position, 2 out:** Munson 1, Dent 1, White 1. **Team LOB:** 5 **FIELDING: E:** Piniella (1), Nettles (1).

LOS ANGELES	AB	R	H	HR	RBI	BB	AVG
Lopes 2b	5	1	2	0	0	0	.150
Russell ss	5	1	2	0	1	0	.174
Smith cf-rf	4	2	1	1	2	1	.278
Cey 3b	4	0	0	0	0	0	.167
Garvey 1b	4	2	2	0	0	0	.350
Baker lf	4	2	3	0	2	0	.300
Lacy rf	3	1	2	0	1	0	.500
Burke cf	1	0	0	0	0	0	.200
Yeager c	2	1	1	1	4	0	.313
a-Oates ph-c	1	0	0	0	0	0	.000
Sutton p	4	0	0	0	0	0	.000
TOTALS	**37**	**10**	**13**	**2**	**10**	**1**	**.224**

a - Batted for Yeager in the 7th

BATTING: 2B: Garvey (1, Gullett). **3B:** Lopes (1, Gullett). **HR:** Yeager (2, 4th off Gullett 2 on, 1 out), Smith (2, 6th off Tidrow 1 on, 1 out). **SF:** Yeager. **RBI:** Russell 1 (2), Smith 2 (4), Baker 2 (5), Lacy 1 (2), Yeager 4 (5). **Runners left in scoring position, 2 out:** Garvey 1. **Team LOB:** 5

NY YANKEES	IP	H	R	ER	BB	SO	HR	ERA
Gullett (L, 0-1)	4.1	8	7	6	1	4	1	6.39
Clay	0.2	2	1	1	0	0	0	2.45
Tidrow	1	2	2	2	0	0	1	4.91
Hunter	2	1	0	0	0	1	0	10.38
LOS ANGELES	**IP**	**H**	**R**	**ER**	**BB**	**SO**	**HR**	**ERA**
Sutton (W, 1-0)	9	9	4	4	0	2	2	3.94

Pitches-strikes: Gullett 97-63, Clay 14-11, Tidrow 11-9, Hunter 25-16, Sutton 108-71. **Ground balls-fly balls:** Gullett 5-5, Clay 1-0, Tidrow 2-1, Hunter 2-3, Sutton 9-16. **Batters faced:** Gullett 23, Clay 4, Tidrow 5, Hunter 7, Sutton 36. **UMPIRES:** hp—Evans, 1b—McSherry, 2b—Chylak, 3b—Sudol, lf—McCoy, rf—Dale **T:** 2:29 **A:** 55,955

GAME 6 New York 8 Los Angeles 4
Yankee Stadium 10/18/77

LOS ANGELES	AB	R	H	HR	RBI	BB	AVG
Lopes 2b	4	0	1	0	0	0	.167
Russell ss	3	0	0	0	0	1	.154
Smith rf	4	2	1	1	1	0	.273
Cey 3b	3	1	1	0	0	1	.190
Garvey 1b	4	1	2	0	2	0	.375
Baker lf	4	0	1	0	0	0	.292
Monday cf	4	0	1	0	0	0	.167
Yeager c	3	0	1	0	0	0	.316
b-Davalillo ph	1	0	1	0	1	0	.333
Hooton p	2	0	0	0	0	0	.000
Sosa p	0	0	0	0	0	0	.000
Rau p	0	0	0	0	0	0	.000
a-Goodson ph	1	0	0	0	0	0	.000
Hough p	0	0	0	0	0	0	.000
c-Lacy ph	1	0	0	0	0	0	.429
TOTALS	**34**	**4**	**9**	**1**	**4**	**2**	**.231**

a - Batted for Rau in the 7th
b - Batted for Yeager in the 9th
c - Batted for Hough in the 9th

BATTING: 3B: Garvey (1, Torrez). **HR:** Smith (3, 3th off Torrez 0 on, 2 out). **RBI:** Smith 1 (5), Garvey 2 (3), Davalillo 1 (1). **2-out RBI:** Smith 1, Garvey 2, Davalillo 1. **Runners left in scoring position, 2 out:** Baker 1, Hooton 1, Lacy 1. **GIDP:** Smith, Smith. **Team LOB:** 5

NY YANKEES	AB	R	H	HR	RBI	BB	AVG
Rivers cf	4	0	2	0	0	0	.222
Randolph 2b	4	1	0	0	0	0	.160
Munson c	4	1	1	0	0	0	.320
Jackson rf	3	4	3	3	5	1	.450
Chambliss 1b	4	2	2	1	2	0	.292
Nettles 3b	4	0	0	0	0	0	.190
Piniella lf	3	0	0	0	1	0	.273
Dent ss	2	0	0	0	0	1	.263
Torrez p	3	0	0	0	0	0	.000
TOTALS	**31**	**8**	**8**	**4**	**8**	**2**	**.244**

BATTING: 2B: Chambliss (2, Sosa). **HR:** Chambliss (1, 2nd off Hooton 1 on, 0 out), Jackson 3 (5, 4th off Hooton 1 on, 0 out, 5th off Sosa 1 on, 2 out, 8th off Hough 0 on, 0 out). **SF:** Rivers, Piniella. **RBI:** Jackson 5 (9), Chambliss 2 (4), Piniella 1 (3). **2-out RBI:** Jackson 2. **Runners left in scoring position, 2 out:** Munson 1. **Team LOB:** 2 **FIELDING: E:** Dent (1). **PB:** Munson. **Outfield assists:** Piniella (1). **DP:** 2 (Dent-Randolph-Chambliss, Chambliss-Dent-Chambliss).

LOS ANGELES	IP	H	R	ER	BB	SO	HR	ERA
Hooton (L, 1-1)	3	3	4	4	1	1	2	3.75
Sosa	1.2	3	3	3	1	0	1	11.57
Rau	1.1	0	0	0	0	1	0	11.57
Hough	2	2	1	1	0	3	1	1.80
NY YANKEES	**IP**	**H**	**R**	**ER**	**BB**	**SO**	**HR**	**ERA**
Torrez (W, 2-0)	9	9	4	2	2	6	1	2.50

Pitches-strikes: Hooton 39-22, Sosa 26-14, Rau 16-11, Hough 31-20, Torrez 119-72. **Ground balls-fly balls:** Hooton 5-3, Sosa 3-1, Rau 2-1, Hough 2-1, Torrez 10-9. **Batters faced:** Hooton 13, Sosa 9, Rau 4, Hough 8, Torrez 36. **UMPIRES:** hp—McSherry, 1b—Chylak, 2b—Sudol, 3b—McCoy, lf—Dale, rf—Evans **T:** 2:18 **A:** 56,407

1978 NY YANKEES DEF. LOS ANGELES, 4-2

GAME 1 Los Angeles 11 New York 5
Dodger Stadium 10/10/78

NY YANKEES	AB	R	H	HR	RBI	BB	AVG
Rivers cf	4	0	0	0	0	0	.000
Blair cf	1	0	0	0	0	0	.000
White lf	4	0	1	0	0	1	.250
Munson c	4	1	0	0	0	0	.000
Jackson dh	4	1	3	1	1	0	.750
Piniella rf	4	2	1	0	1	0	.250
Nettles 3b	4	0	1	0	1	0	.250
Chambliss 1b	4	1	1	0	0	0	.250
Stanley 2b	2	0	1	0	0	1	.500
a-Johnson ph	1	0	0	0	0	0	.000
Doyle 2b	0	0	0	0	0	0	.000
Dent ss	4	0	1	0	2	0	.250
TOTALS	**36**	**5**	**9**	**1**	**5**	**2**	**.250**

a - Batted for Stanley in the 8th

BATTING: 2B: Stanley (1, John). **HR:** Jackson (1, 7th off John 0 on, 0 out). **RBI:** Jackson 1 (1), Piniella 1 (1), Nettles 1 (1), Dent 2 (2). **2-out RBI:** Nettles 1, Dent 2. **Runners left in scoring position, 2 out:** White 1, Chambliss 1, Johnson 1. **GIDP:** Munson. **Team LOB:** 6 **FIELDING: E:** Dent (1). **DP:** 2 (Dent-Stanley-Chambliss, Munson-Doyle).

LOS ANGELES	AB	R	H	HR	RBI	BB	AVG
Lopes 2b	5	2	2	2	5	0	.400
Russell ss	5	1	3	0	0	0	.600
Smith rf	5	0	1	0	1	0	.200
Garvey 1b	5	1	2	0	0	0	.400
Cey 3b	4	1	1	0	0	1	.250
Baker lf	4	2	3	1	1	0	.750
Monday cf	2	2	1	0	0	1	.500
a-North ph-cf	1	1	1	0	2	0	1.000
Lacy dh	3	0	1	0	1	1	.333
Yeager c	4	1	0	0	0	0	.000
TOTALS	**38**	**11**	**15**	**3**	**10**	**3**	**.395**

a - Batted for Monday in the 7th

BATTING: 2B: Monday (1, Figueroa), North (1, Lindblad), Russell (1, Tidrow). **HR:** Baker (1, 2nd off Figueroa 0 on, 0 out), Lopes 2 (2, 2nd off Figueroa 1 on, 2 out, 4th off Clay 2 on, 1 out). **RBI:** Lopes 5 (5), Smith 1 (1), Baker 1 (1), North 2 (2), Lacy 1 (1). **2-out RBI:** Lopes 2. **Runners left in scoring position, 2 out:** Garvey 1, Cey 1, Yeager 1. **GIDP:** Yeager. **Team LOB:** 6 **BASERUNNING: CS:** Smith (1, 2nd base off Tidrow/Munson). **FIELDING: E:** Lopes (1). **DP:** 1 (Lopes-Russell-Garvey).

NY YANKEES	IP	H	R	ER	BB	SO	HR	ERA
Figueroa (L, 0-1)	1.2	5	3	3	1	0	2	16.20
Clay	2.1	4	4	3	2	2	1	11.57
Lindblad	2.1	4	3	3	0	1	0	11.57
Tidrow	1.2	2	1	1	0	1	0	5.40
LOS ANGELES	**IP**	**H**	**R**	**ER**	**BB**	**SO**	**HR**	**ERA**
John (W, 1-0)	7.2	8	5	3	2	4	1	3.52
Forster	1.1	1	0	0	0	3	0	0.00

WP: Clay 1. **Pitches-strikes:** Figueroa 38-20, Clay 38-23, Lindblad 36-21, Tidrow 32-20, John 122-71, Forster 21-17. **Ground balls-fly balls:** Figueroa 1-3, Clay 4-2, Lindblad 1-5, Tidrow 1-2, John 17-2, Forster 1-0. **Batters faced:** Figueroa 10, Clay 14, Lindblad 11, Tidrow 6, John 33, Forster 5. **UMPIRES:** hp—Vargo, 1b—Haller, 2b—Kibler, 3b—Springstead, lf—Pulli, rf—Brinkman **T:** 2:48 **A:** 55,997

GAME 2 Los Angeles 4 New York 3
Dodger Stadium 10/11/78

NY YANKEES	AB	R	H	HR	RBI	BB	AVG
White lf	5	2	2	0	0	0	.333
Thomasson cf	3	0	1	0	0	0	.333
a-Blair ph-cf	1	0	1	0	0	1	.500
Munson c	4	1	1	0	0	1	.125
Jackson dh	4	0	1	0	3	0	.500
Nettles 3b	4	0	0	0	0	0	.125
Piniella rf	4	0	2	0	0	0	.375
Spencer 1b	4	0	1	0	0	0	.250
Doyle 2b	3	0	1	0	0	0	.333
b-Johnson ph	1	0	0	0	0	0	.000
Stanley 2b	0	0	0	0	0	0	.500
Dent ss	4	0	1	0	0	0	.250
TOTALS	**37**	**3**	**11**	**0**	**3**	**2**	**.274**

a - Batted for Thomasson in the 7th
b - Batted for Doyle in the 8th

BATTING: 2B: Munson (1, Hooton), Jackson (1, Hooton), Blair (1, Forster). **RBI:** Jackson 3 (4). **2-out RBI:** Jackson 2. **Runners left in scoring position, 2 out:** Jackson 2, Nettles 3, Dent 1. **GIDP:** Johnson. **Team LOB:** 10 **BASERUNNING: SB:** White (1, 2nd base off Hooton/Yeager). **CS:** Thomasson (1, 2nd base off Hooton/Yeager). **FIELDING: DP:** 1 (Nettles-Spencer).

LOS ANGELES	AB	R	H	HR	RBI	BB	AVG
Lopes 2b	4	1	1	0	0	0	.333
Russell ss	4	0	1	0	0	0	.444
Smith rf	4	2	1	0	0	0	.222
Garvey 1b	3	0	1	0	0	0	.375
Cey 3b	3	1	2	1	4	0	.429
Baker lf	3	0	0	0	0	0	.429
Monday cf	3	0	0	0	0	0	.200
North cf	0	0	0	0	0	0	1.000
Lacy dh	3	0	0	0	0	0	.167
Yeager c	3	0	1	0	0	0	.143
TOTALS	**30**	**4**	**7**	**1**	**4**	**0**	**.324**

BATTING: HR: Cey (1, 6th off Hunter 2 on, 2 out). **RBI:** Cey 4 (4). **2-out RBI:** Cey 3. **GIDP:** Baker. **Team LOB:** 2 **FIELDING: DP:** 1 (Cey-Lopes-Garvey).

NY YANKEES	IP	H	R	ER	BB	SO	HR	ERA
Hunter (L, 0-1)	6	7	4	4	0	2	1	6.00
Gossage	2	0	0	0	0	0	0	0.00
LOS ANGELES	**IP**	**H**	**R**	**ER**	**BB**	**SO**	**HR**	**ERA**
Hooton (W, 1-0)	6	8	3	3	1	5	0	4.50
Forster	2.1	3	0	0	1	3	0	0.00
Welch (S, 1)	0.2	0	0	0	0	1	0	0.00

WP: Hooton 1. **HBP:** Jackson (by Hooton). **Pitches-strikes:** Hunter 95-64, Gossage 20-12, Hooton 100-67, Forster 34-23, Welch 11-8. **Ground balls-fly balls:** Hunter 5-10, Gossage 2-4, Hooton 4-9, Forster 3-0, Welch 0-1. **Batters faced:** Hunter 24, Gossage 6, Hooton 28, Forster 10, Welch 2. **UMPIRES:** hp—Haller, 1b—Kibler, 2b—Springstead, 3b—Pulli, lf—Brinkman, rf—Vargo **T:** 2:37 **A:** 55,982

GAME 3 New York 5 Los Angeles 1
Yankee Stadium 10/13/78

LOS ANGELES	AB	R	H	HR	RBI	BB	AVG
Lopes 2b	5	0	1	0	0	0	.286
Russell ss	4	0	2	0	1	1	.462
Smith rf	4	0	1	0	0	1	.231
Garvey 1b	4	0	1	0	0	0	.333
Cey 3b	3	0	0	0	0	1	.300
Baker lf	3	0	2	0	0	1	.500
Lacy dh	4	0	1	0	0	0	.200
North cf	3	1	0	0	0	1	.250
Yeager c	1	0	0	0	0	1	.125
a-Mota ph	0	0	0	0	0	1	.000
Grote c	0	0	0	0	0	0	.000
Ferguson c	1	0	0	0	0	0	.000
TOTALS	**32**	**1**	**8**	**0**	**1**	**7**	**.300**

a - Batted for Yeager in the 6th

BATTING: 2B: Garvey (1, Guidry). **RBI:** Russell 1 (1). **2-out RBI:** Russell 1. **Runners left in scoring position, 2 out:** Lopes 2, Garvey 2, Cey 1. **GIDP:** Lacy, Lacy. **Team LOB:** 11 **BASERUNNING: SB:** North (1, 2nd base off Guidry/Munson). **CS:** Russell (1, 2nd base off Guidry/Munson).

NY YANKEES	AB	R	H	HR	RBI	BB	AVG
Rivers cf	4	0	3	0	0	0	.375
a-Blair pr-cf	0	0	0	0	0	0	.500
White lf	3	2	1	1	1	1	.333
Munson c	4	1	1	0	1	0	.167
Jackson dh	3	0	1	0	1	1	.455
Piniella rf	4	0	1	0	1	0	.333
Nettles 3b	4	1	1	0	0	0	.167
Chambliss 1b	3	0	1	0	0	1	.286
Doyle 2b	4	0	0	0	0	0	.143
Dent ss	4	1	1	0	1	0	.250
TOTALS	**33**	**5**	**10**	**1**	**5**	**3**	**.283**

a - Ran for Rivers in the 7th

BATTING: HR: White (1, 1st off Sutton 0 on, 1 out). **RBI:** White 1 (1), Munson 1 (1), Jackson 1 (5), Piniella 1 (2), Dent 1 (3). **Runners left in scoring position, 2 out:** Rivers 1, White 1, Nettles 2. **Team LOB:** 7 **BASERUNNING: SB:** Piniella (1, 2nd base off Sutton/Yeager). **CS:** Rivers (1, 2nd base off Sutton/Yeager). **FIELDING: E:** Dent (2). **DP:** 2 (Nettles-Doyle-Chambliss, Dent-Doyle-Chambliss).

LOS ANGELES	IP	H	R	ER	BB	SO	HR	ERA
Sutton (L, 0-1)	6.1	9	5	5	3	2	1	7.11
Rautzhan	0.2	1	0	0	0	0	0	0.00
Hough	1	0	0	0	0	0	0	0.00
NY YANKEES	**IP**	**H**	**R**	**ER**	**BB**	**SO**	**HR**	**ERA**
Guidry (W, 1-0)	9	8	1	1	7	4	0	1.00

Pitches-strikes: Sutton 101-66, Rautzhan 5-4, Hough 9-4, Guidry 134-79. **Ground balls-fly balls:** Sutton 7-9, Rautzhan 1-1, Hough 1-2, Guidry 11-9. **Batters faced:** Sutton 30, Rautzhan 3, Hough 3, Guidry 39. **UMPIRES:** hp—Kibler, 1b—Springstead, 2b—Pulli, 3b—Brinkman, lf—Vargo, rf—Haller **T:** 2:27 **A:** 56,447

GAME 4 New York 4 Los Angeles 3
Yankee Stadium 10/14/78

LOS ANGELES	AB	R	H	HR	RBI	BB	AVG
Lopes 2b	4	1	0	0	0	1	.222
Russell ss	5	0	2	0	0	0	.444
Smith rf	4	1	1	1	3	1	.235
Garvey 1b	4	0	0	0	0	1	.250
Cey 3b	4	0	1	0	0	0	.286
Baker lf	4	0	0	0	0	0	.357
Monday dh	2	0	1	0	0	2	.286
North cf	4	0	0	0	0	0	.125
Yeager c	3	1	1	0	0	0	.182
a-Davalillo ph	1	0	0	0	0	0	.000
Grote c	0	0	0	0	0	0	.000
TOTALS	**35**	**3**	**6**	**1**	**3**	**5**	**.267**

a - Batted for Yeager in the 9th

BATTING: 2B: Yeager (1, Figueroa). **HR:** Smith (1, 5th off Figueroa 2 on, 2 out). **RBI:** Smith 3 (4). **2-out RBI:** Smith 3. **Runners left in scoring position, 2 out:** Monday 1, Yeager 1. **Team LOB:** 7 **BASERUNNING: SB:** Garvey (1, 2nd base off Figueroa/Munson). **Outfield assists:** Smith (1).

NY YANKEES	AB	R	H	HR	RBI	BB	AVG
Blair cf	4	1	2	0	0	0	.500
b-Rivers ph	1	0	0	0	0	0	.333
White lf	3	2	1	0	0	1	.333
Munson c	3	1	2	0	1	2	.267
Jackson dh	4	0	2	0	1	0	.467
Piniella rf	5	0	1	0	2	0	.294
Nettles 3b	4	0	0	0	0	0	.125
Chambliss 1b	4	0	0	0	0	0	.182
Stanley 2b	3	0	0	0	0	0	.200
a-Spencer ph	1	0	0	0	0	0	.200
Doyle 2b	0	0	0	0	0	0	.143
Dent ss	4	0	1	0	0	0	.250
TOTALS	**36**	**4**	**9**	**0**	**4**	**3**	**.275**

a - Batted for Stanley in the 9th
b - Batted for Blair in the 10th

BATTING: 2B: Munson (2, Forster). **S:** White. **RBI:** Munson 1 (2), Jackson 1 (6), Piniella 2 (4). **2-out RBI:** Piniella 1. **Runners left in scoring position, 2 out:** Nettles 2. **Team LOB:** 8 **BASERUNNING: SB:** Munson (1, 2nd base off John/Yeager). **FIELDING: Outfield assists:** Piniella (1). **DP:** 1 (Piniella-Chambliss-Dent).

LOS ANGELES	IP	H	R	ER	BB	SO	HR	ERA
John	7	6	3	2	2	2	0	3.07
Forster	0.1	1	0	0	0	0	0	0.00
Welch (L, 0-1)	2.1	2	1	1	1	3	0	3.00
NY YANKEES	**IP**	**H**	**R**	**ER**	**BB**	**SO**	**HR**	**ERA**
Figueroa	5	4	3	3	4	2	1	8.10
Tidrow	3	2	0	0	0	4	0	1.93
Gossage (W, 1-0)	2	0	0	0	1	2	0	0.00

HBP: Jackson (by Forster). **Pitches-strikes:** John 116-70, Forster 4-4, Welch 46-31, Figueroa 88-43, Tidrow 42-32, Gossage 30-20. **Ground balls-fly balls:** John 14-4, Forster 0-0, Welch 0-4, Figueroa 2-10, Tidrow 2-3, Gossage 0-4. **Batters faced:** John 28, Forster 3, Welch 10, Figueroa 22, Tidrow 11, Gossage 7. **UMPIRES:** hp—Springstead, 1b—Pulli, 2b—Brinkman, 3b—Vargo, lf—Haller, rf—Kibler **T:** 3:17 **A:** 56,445

GAME 5 New York 12 Los Angeles 2
Yankee Stadium 10/15/78

LOS ANGELES	AB	R	H	HR	RBI	BB	AVG
Lopes 2b	4	2	2	0	0	1	.273
Russell ss	5	0	2	0	1	0	.435
Smith rf	4	0	1	0	1	0	.238
Garvey 1b	4	0	1	0	0	0	.250
Cey 3b	3	0	1	0	0	1	.294
Baker lf	4	0	0	0	0	0	.278
Monday cf	3	0	0	0	0	1	.200
Lacy dh	4	0	0	0	0	0	.143
Yeager c	2	0	1	0	0	0	.231
a-Oates ph-c	1	0	1	0	0	1	1.000
TOTALS	**34**	**2**	**9**	**0**	**2**	**4**	**.266**

a - Batted for Yeager in the 7th

BATTING: 2B: Russell (2, Beattie). **RBI:** Russell 1 (2), Smith 1 (5). **Runners left in scoring position, 2 out:** Garvey 3, Cey 2, Lacy 1. **GIDP:** Lopes. **Team LOB:** 9 **BASERUNNING: SB:** Lopes (1, 2nd base off Beattie/Munson), Russell (1, 2nd base off Beattie/Munson). **CS:** Monday (1, 2nd base off Beattie/Munson). **FIELDING: E:** Russell (1), Smith (1). **PB:** Yeager, Oates. **DP:** 2 (Russell-Lopes-Garvey, Lopes-Russell-Garvey).

NY YANKEES	AB	R	H	HR	RBI	BB	AVG
Rivers cf	5	2	3	0	1	0	.429
a-Blair pr-cf	1	1	0	0	0	0	.429
White lf	5	2	2	0	3	0	.350
Johnstone rf	0	0	0	0	0	0	.000
Munson c	5	1	3	0	5	0	.350
Heath c	0	0	0	0	0	0	.000
Jackson dh	3	0	1	0	0	2	.444
Piniella rf	4	0	1	0	1	0	.286
Thomasson lf	1	0	0	0	0	0	.250
Nettles 3b	5	0	1	0	0	0	.143
Spencer 1b	4	2	1	0	0	1	.222
Doyle 2b	5	2	3	0	0	0	.333
Dent ss	4	2	3	0	1	1	.350
TOTALS	**42**	**12**	**18**	**0**	**11**	**4**	**.310**

a - Ran for Rivers in the 7th

BATTING: 2B: Munson (3, Hough), Dent (1, Hough). **RBI:** Rivers 1 (1), White 3 (4), Munson 5 (7), Piniella 1 (5), Dent 1 (4). **2-out RBI:** White 1, Munson 3, Dent 1. **Runners left in scoring position, 2 out:** Rivers 1, Blair 2, Jackson 1, Piniella 1. **GIDP:** Piniella, Nettles. **Team LOB:** 10 **BASERUNNING: SB:** Rivers (1, 3rd base off Hooton/Yeager), White (2, 3rd base off Hooton/Yeager). **FIELDING: DP:** 1 (Nettles-Doyle-Spencer).

LOS ANGELES	IP	H	R	ER	BB	SO	HR	ERA
Hooton (L, 1-1)	2.1	5	4	3	2	1	0	6.48
Rautzhan	1.1	3	3	3	0	0	0	13.50
Hough	4.1	10	5	5	2	5	0	8.44
NY YANKEES	**IP**	**H**	**R**	**ER**	**BB**	**SO**	**HR**	**ERA**
Beattie (W, 1-0)	9	9	2	2	4	8	0	2.00

WP: Hough 1. **IBB:** Jackson (by Hooton). **Pitches-strikes:** Hooton 45-26, Rautzhan 13-9, Hough 94-61, Beattie 137-85. **Ground balls-fly balls:** Hooton 4-2, Rautzhan 3-0, Hough 3-6, Beattie 6-11. **Batters faced:** Hooton 14, Rautzhan 6, Hough 26, Beattie 38. **UMPIRES:** hp—Pulli, 1b—Brinkman, 2b—Vargo, 3b—Haller, lf—Kibler, rf—Springstead **T:** 2:56 **A:** 56,448

GAME 6 New York 7 Los Angeles 2
Dodger Stadium 10/17/78

NY YANKEES	AB	R	H	HR	RBI	BB	AVG
Rivers cf	4	0	0	0	0	0	.333
Blair cf	1	0	0	0	0	0	.375
White lf	4	1	1	0	0	1	.333
Thomasson lf	0	0	0	0	0	0	.250
Munson c	5	0	1	0	0	0	.320
Jackson dh	5	1	1	1	2	0	.391
Piniella rf	4	1	1	0	0	0	.280
Johnstone rf	0	0	0	0	0	0	.000
Nettles 3b	4	1	1	0	0	0	.160
Spencer 1b	3	1	0	0	0	1	.167
Doyle 2b	4	2	3	0	2	0	.438
Dent ss	4	0	3	0	3	0	.417
TOTALS	**38**	**7**	**11**	**1**	**7**	**2**	**.306**

BATTING: 2B: Doyle (1, Sutton). **HR:** Jackson (2, 7th off Welch 1 on, 1 out). **RBI:** Jackson 2 (8), Doyle 2 (2), Dent 3 (7). **2-out RBI:** Doyle 1, Dent 1. **Runners left in scoring position, 2 out:** Rivers 1, White 1, Jackson 1. **Team LOB:** 6 **FIELDING: DP:** 2 (Doyle-Dent-Spencer, Nettles-Doyle-Spencer).

LOS ANGELES	AB	R	H	HR	RBI	BB	AVG
Lopes 2b	4	1	2	1	2	0	.308
Russell ss	3	0	1	0	0	1	.423
Smith rf	4	0	0	0	0	0	.200
Garvey 1b	4	0	0	0	0	0	.208
Cey 3b	4	0	1	0	0	0	.286
Baker lf	3	0	0	0	0	0	.238
Monday cf	3	0	0	0	0	0	.154
Ferguson c	3	1	2	0	0	0	.500
Davalillo dh	2	0	1	0	0	0	.333
TOTALS	**30**	**2**	**7**	**1**	**2**	**1**	**.261**

BATTING: 2B: Ferguson 2 (2, Hunter). **HR:** Lopes (3, 1st off Hunter 0 on, 0 out). **S:** Davalillo. **RBI:** Lopes 2 (7). **GIDP:** Smith, Russell. **Team LOB:** 3 **BASERUNNING: SB:** Lopes (2, 2nd base off Hunter/Munson). **CS:** Russell (2, 2nd base off Hunter/Munson). **FIELDING: E:** Ferguson (1).

NY YANKEES	IP	H	R	ER	BB	SO	HR	ERA
Hunter (W, 1-1)	7	6	2	2	1	3	1	4.15
Gossage	2	1	0	0	0	2	0	0.00
LOS ANGELES	**IP**	**H**	**R**	**ER**	**BB**	**SO**	**HR**	**ERA**
Sutton (L, 0-2)	5.2	8	5	5	1	6	0	7.50
Welch	1.1	2	2	2	1	2	1	6.23
Rau	2	1	0	0	0	3	0	0.00

WP: Sutton 1. **Pitches-strikes:** Hunter 89-58, Gossage 24-17, Sutton 96-70, Welch 27-14, Rau 27-19. **Ground balls-fly balls:** Hunter 8-7, Gossage 1-2, Sutton 7-4, Welch 0-2, Rau 2-1. **Batters faced:** Hunter 26, Gossage 6, Sutton 26, Welch 7, Rau 7. **UMPIRES:** hp—Brinkman, 1b—Vargo, 2b—Haller, 3b—Kibler, lf—Springstead, rf—Pulli **T:** 2:34 **A:** 55,985

1979 PITTSBURGH DEF. BALTIMORE, 4-3

GAME 1 Baltimore 5 Pittsburgh 4
Memorial Stadium 10/10/79

PITTSBURGH	AB	R	H	HR	RBI	BB	AVG
Moreno cf	5	0	0	0	0	0	.000
Foli ss	5	1	1	0	0	0	.200
Parker rf	5	1	4	0	0	0	.800
B.Robinson lf	5	1	1	0	0	0	.200
Stargell 1b	5	1	1	1	2	0	.200
Madlock 3b	3	0	0	0	0	1	.000
Nicosia c	4	0	0	0	0	0	.000
Garner 2b	4	0	3	0	2	0	.750
Kison p	0	0	0	0	0	0	.000
Rooker p	1	0	0	0	0	0	.000
a-Sanguillen ph	1	0	0	0	0	0	.000
Romo p	0	0	0	0	0	0	.000
b-Lacy ph	1	0	0	0	0	0	.000
D.Robinson p	0	0	0	0	0	0	.000
c-Stennett ph	1	0	1	0	0	0	1.000
Jackson p	0	0	0	0	0	0	.000
TOTALS	**40**	**4**	**11**	**1**	**4**	**1**	**.275**

a - Batted for Rooker in the 5th
b - Batted for Romo in the 6th
c - Batted for D.Robinson in the 8th

BATTING: 2B: Parker (1, Flanagan), Garner (1, Flanagan). **HR:** Stargell (1, 8th off Flanagan 0 on, 0 out). **RBI:** Stargell 2 (2), Garner 2 (2). **2-out RBI:** Garner 2. **Runners left in scoring position, 2 out:** Moreno 3, Foli 1, B.Robinson 1, Stargell 1, Nicosia 1. **Team LOB:** 10 **BASERUNNING: CS:** Parker (1, 2nd base off Flanagan/Dempsey). **FIELDING: E:** Garner (1), Stargell (1). **DP:** 1 (Madlock-Garner-Stargell).

BALTIMORE	AB	R	H	HR	RBI	BB	AVG
Bumbry cf	4	1	1	0	0	0	.250
Belanger ss	3	1	0	0	0	1	.000
Singleton rf	3	0	1	0	0	1	.333
Murray 1b	2	1	1	0	0	2	.500
Lowenstein lf	4	1	0	0	1	0	.000
Roenicke lf	0	0	0	0	0	0	.000
DeCinces 3b	3	1	1	1	2	1	.333
Smith 2b	2	0	1	0	0	1	.500
a-Dauer ph-2b	1	0	1	0	0	0	1.000
Dempsey c	4	0	0	0	0	0	.000
Flanagan p	4	0	0	0	0	0	.000
TOTALS	**30**	**5**	**6**	**1**	**3**	**6**	**.200**

a - Batted for Smith in the 8th

BATTING: HR: DeCinces (1, 1st off Kison 1 on, 1 out). **S:** Bumbry. **RBI:** Lowenstein 1 (1), DeCinces 2 (2). **Runners left in scoring position, 2 out:** Singleton 1, Lowenstein 1, Dempsey 1, Flanagan 1. **GIDP:** Smith. **Team LOB:** 8 **BASERUNNING: SB:** Murray (1, 2nd base off Romo/Nicosia). **FIELDING: E:** DeCinces 2 (2).

PITTSBURGH	IP	H	R	ER	BB	SO	HR	ERA
Kison (L, 0-1)	0.1	3	5	4	2	0	1	108.00
Rooker	3.2	2	0	0	1	2	0	0.00
Romo	1	0	0	0	2	0	0	0.00
D.Robinson	2	0	0	0	1	1	0	0.00
Jackson	1	1	0	0	0	1	0	0.00
BALTIMORE	**IP**	**H**	**R**	**ER**	**BB**	**SO**	**HR**	**ERA**
Flanagan (W, 1-0)	9	11	4	2	1	7	1	2.00

WP: Kison 1. **IBB:** Smith (by Romo). **Pitches-strikes:** Kison 27-11, Rooker 56-31, Romo 24-10, D.Robinson 34-19, Jackson 15-9, Flanagan 137-100. **Ground balls-fly balls:** Kison 2-0, Rooker 5-3, Romo 0-3, D.Robinson 2-3, Jackson 1-1, Flanagan 15-7. **Batters faced:** Kison 7, Rooker 14, Romo 5, D.Robinson 7, Jackson 4, Flanagan 41. **UMPIRES:** hp—Neudecker, 1b—Engel, 2b—Goetz, 3b—Tata, lf—McKean, rf—Runge **T:** 3:18 **A:** 53,735

GAME 2 Pittsburgh 3 Baltimore 2
Memorial Stadium 10/11/79

PITTSBURGH	AB	R	H	HR	RBI	BB	AVG
Moreno cf	5	0	1	0	0	0	.100
Foli ss	4	0	1	0	0	0	.222
Parker rf	4	0	1	0	0	0	.556
Stargell 1b	4	1	1	0	0	0	.222
Milner lf	3	1	1	0	0	0	.333
b-B.Robinson ph	1	0	1	0	0	0	.333
c-Alexander pr-lf	0	0	0	0	0	0	.000
Madlock 3b	4	0	2	0	1	0	.286
Ott c	3	1	1	0	1	0	.333
Garner 2b	2	0	1	0	0	2	.667
Blyleven p	2	0	0	0	0	0	.000
a-Easler ph	0	0	0	0	0	1	.000
D.Robinson p	0	0	0	0	0	0	.000
d-Sanguillen ph	1	0	1	0	1	0	.500
Tekulve p	0	0	0	0	0	0	.000
TOTALS	**33**	**3**	**11**	**0**	**3**	**3**	**.301**

a - Batted for Blyleven in the 7th
b - Batted for Milner in the 9th
c - Ran for B.Robinson in the 9th
d - Batted for D.Robinson in the 9th

BATTING: SF: Ott. **RBI:** Madlock 1 (1), Ott 1 (1), Sanguillen 1 (1). **2-out RBI:** Sanguillen 1. **Runners left in scoring position, 2 out:** Moreno 3, Parker 1. **GIDP:** Blyleven. **Team LOB:** 7
BASERUNNING: CS: Madlock (1, 2nd base off Palmer/Dempsey), Alexander (1, 2nd base off Stanhouse/Dempsey). **FIELDING: E:** Parker (1). **Outfield assists:** Parker (1). **DP:** 3 (Madlock-Garner-Stargell, Parker-Ott, Foli-Garner-Madlock-Garner).

BALTIMORE	AB	R	H	HR	RBI	BB	AVG
Bumbry cf	5	0	0	0	0	0	.111
Belanger ss	3	0	0	0	0	0	.000
b-Crowley ph	0	0	0	0	0	1	.000
T.Martinez p	0	0	0	0	0	0	.000
Stanhouse p	0	0	0	0	0	0	.000
Singleton rf	4	1	1	0	0	0	.286
Murray 1b	3	1	3	1	2	1	.800
DeCinces 3b	4	0	0	0	0	0	.143
Lowenstein lf	3	0	1	0	0	1	.143
Smith 2b	4	0	0	0	0	0	.167
Dempsey c	3	0	1	0	0	1	.143
Palmer p	2	0	0	0	0	0	.000
a-Kelly ph	0	0	0	0	0	1	.000
Garcia ss	1	0	0	0	0	0	.000
TOTALS	**32**	**2**	**6**	**1**	**2**	**5**	**.194**

a - Batted for Palmer in the 7th
b - Batted for Belanger in the 7th

BATTING: 2B: Murray (1, Blyleven). **HR:** Murray (1, 2nd off Blyleven 0 on, 0 out). **RBI:** Murray 2 (2). **Runners left in scoring position, 2 out:** Singleton 2, DeCinces 1, Palmer 1. **GIDP:** Smith. **Team LOB:** 8 **FIELDING: E:** DeCinces (3). **DP:** 2 (Murray-Palmer, Murray-Belanger-Smith).

PITTSBURGH	IP	H	R	ER	BB	SO	HR	ERA
Blyleven	6	5	2	2	2	1	1	3.00
D.Robinson (W, 1-0)	2	1	0	0	3	2	0	0.00
Tekulve (S, 1)	1	0	0	0	0	2	0	0.00

BALTIMORE	IP	H	R	ER	BB	SO	HR	ERA
Palmer	7	8	2	2	2	3	0	2.57
T.Martinez	1	1	0	0	0	1	0	0.00
Stanhouse (L, 0-1)	1	2	1	1	1	0	0	9.00

WP: Palmer 1. **IBB:** Garner (by Palmer). **Pitches-strikes:** Blyleven 85-57, D.Robinson 40-26, Tekulve 14-11, Palmer 96-62, T.Martinez 18-12, Stanhouse 19-10. **Ground balls-fly balls:** Blyleven 9-7, D.Robinson 2-2, Tekulve 1-0, Palmer 8-6, T.Martinez 1-1, Stanhouse 0-2. **Batters faced:** Blyleven 24, D.Robinson 10, Tekulve 3, Palmer 28, T.Martinez 4, Stanhouse 5. **UMPIRES:** hp—Engel, 1b—Goetz, 2b—Tata, 3b—McKean, lf—Runge, rf—Neudecker **T:** 3:13 **A:** 53,739

GAME 3 Baltimore 8 Pittsburgh 4
Three Rivers Stadium 10/12/79

BALTIMORE	AB	R	H	HR	RBI	BB	AVG
Garcia ss	4	2	4	0	4	1	.800
Ayala lf	2	1	2	1	2	0	1.000
a-Bumbry ph-cf	2	1	1	0	0	0	.182
Singleton rf	5	0	2	0	1	0	.333
Murray 1b	4	0	0	0	0	1	.444
DeCinces 3b	5	0	0	0	1	0	.083
Roenicke cf-lf	5	0	1	0	0	0	.200
Dauer 2b	5	1	1	0	0	0	.333
Dempsey c	5	2	2	0	0	0	.250
McGregor p	3	1	0	0	0	1	.000
TOTALS	**40**	**8**	**13**	**1**	**8**	**3**	**.245**

a - Batted for Ayala in the 4th

BATTING: 2B: Garcia (1, Candelaria), Dauer (1, Candelaria), Dempsey (1, Romo). **3B:** Garcia (1, Candelaria). **HR:** Ayala (1, 3th off Candelaria 1 on, 1 out). **RBI:** Garcia 4 (4), Ayala 2 (2), Singleton 1 (1), DeCinces 1 (3). **2-out RBI:** Garcia 1. **Runners left in scoring position, 2 out:** Bumbry 1, Singleton 2, DeCinces 1, Roenicke 2. **Team LOB:** 9 **Outfield assists:** Roenicke (1).

PITTSBURGH	AB	R	H	HR	RBI	BB	AVG
Moreno cf	4	1	2	0	0	0	.214
Foli ss	4	0	0	0	0	0	.154
Parker rf	3	0	0	0	1	0	.417
B.Robinson lf	4	0	1	0	0	0	.300
Stargell 1b	4	2	2	0	0	0	.308
Madlock 3b	4	0	1	0	1	0	.273
Nicosia c	4	1	1	0	0	0	.125
Garner 2b	4	0	1	0	2	0	.500
Candelaria p	1	0	1	0	0	0	1.000
Romo p	1	0	0	0	0	0	.000
Jackson p	0	0	0	0	0	0	.000
a-Lacy ph	1	0	0	0	0	0	.000
Tekulve p	0	0	0	0	0	0	.000
TOTALS	**34**	**4**	**9**	**0**	**4**	**0**	**.290**

a - Batted for Jackson in the 7th

BATTING: 2B: Moreno 2 (2, McGregor), Garner (2, McGregor), Stargell (1, McGregor). **SF:** Parker. **RBI:** Parker 1 (1), Madlock 1 (2), Garner 2 (4). **Runners left in scoring position, 2 out:** Moreno 1, Parker 1. **Team LOB:** 4 **FIELDING: E:** Foli (1). **Outfield assists:** B.Robinson (1), Moreno (1).

BALTIMORE	IP	H	R	ER	BB	SO	HR	ERA
McGregor (W, 1-0)	9	9	4	4	0	6	0	4.00

PITTSBURGH	IP	H	R	ER	BB	SO	HR	ERA
Candelaria (L, 0-1)	3	8	6	5	2	2	1	15.00
Romo	3.2	5	2	2	1	4	0	3.86
Jackson	0.1	0	0	0	0	0	0	0.00
Tekulve	2	0	0	0	0	1	0	0.00

WP: Romo 1. **BK:** McGregor 1. **HBP:** Bumbry (by Romo). **Pitches-strikes:** McGregor 88-73, Candelaria 75-51, Romo 61-38, Jackson 3-2, Tekulve 8-5. **Ground balls-fly balls:** McGregor 7-12, Candelaria 4-3, Romo 2-5, Jackson 0-1, Tekulve 4-1. **Batters faced:** McGregor 35, Candelaria 19, Romo 18, Jackson 1, Tekulve 6. **UMPIRES:** hp—Goetz, 1b—Tata, 2b—McKean, 3b—Runge, lf—Neudecker, rf—Engel **T:** 2:51 **A:** 50,848

GAME 4 Baltimore 9 Pittsburgh 6
Three Rivers Stadium 10/13/79

BALTIMORE	AB	R	H	HR	RBI	BB	AVG
Bumbry cf	5	1	1	0	1	0	.188
Garcia ss	5	2	2	0	2	0	.600
Belanger ss	0	0	0	0	0	0	.000
Singleton rf	5	0	3	0	1	0	.412
Murray 1b	5	1	0	0	0	0	.286
DeCinces 3b	1	1	0	0	0	4	.077
Roenicke lf	3	0	0	0	0	0	.125
c-Lowenstein ph-lf	2	1	1	0	2	0	.222
Dauer 2b	3	0	1	0	0	0	.333
d-Smith ph-2b	0	1	0	0	0	1	.167
Skaggs c	3	1	1	0	0	0	.333
e-Crowley ph	1	0	1	0	2	0	1.000
f-Dempsey pr-c	0	1	0	0	0	0	.250
D.Martinez p	0	0	0	0	0	0	.000
Stewart p	1	0	0	0	0	0	.000
a-May ph	1	0	0	0	0	0	.000
Stone p	0	0	0	0	0	0	.000
b-Kelly ph	1	0	1	0	0	0	1.000
Stoddard p	1	0	1	0	1	0	1.000
TOTALS	**37**	**9**	**12**	**0**	**9**	**5**	**.266**

a - Batted for Stewart in the 5th
b - Batted for Stone in the 7th
c - Batted for Roenicke in the 8th
d - Batted for Dauer in the 8th e - Batted for Skaggs in the 8th f - Ran for Crowley in the 8th

BATTING: 2B: Garcia (2, Bibby), Singleton (1, Bibby), Lowenstein (1, Tekulve), Crowley (1, Tekulve). **RBI:** Bumbry 1 (1), Garcia 2 (6), Singleton 1 (2), Lowenstein 2 (3), Crowley 2 (2), Stoddard 1 (1). **Runners left in scoring position, 2 out:** DeCinces 1, Dauer 1. **GIDP:** Skaggs, Murray, Bumbry. **Team LOB:** 6 **BASERUNNING: SB:** DeCinces (1, 2nd base off Bibby/Ott). **FIELDING: Outfield assists:** Bumbry (1). **DP:** 2 (D.Martinez-Garcia-Murray, Dauer-Garcia-Murray).

PITTSBURGH	AB	R	H	HR	RBI	BB	AVG
Moreno cf	5	0	2	0	1	0	.263
Foli ss	4	2	3	0	0	1	.294
Parker rf	5	0	2	0	1	0	.412
Stargell 1b	5	1	3	1	1	0	.389
Milner lf	3	1	2	0	1	1	.500
D.Robinson p	0	0	0	0	0	0	.000
Tekulve p	0	0	0	0	0	0	.000
a-Easler ph	1	0	0	0	0	0	.000
Madlock 3b	3	1	2	0	0	2	.357
Ott c	5	0	1	0	2	0	.250
Garner 2b	4	1	2	0	0	0	.500
Bibby p	3	0	0	0	0	0	.000
Jackson p	0	0	0	0	0	0	.000
B.Robinson lf	1	0	0	0	0	0	.273
TOTALS	**39**	**6**	**17**	**1**	**6**	**4**	**.329**

a - Batted for Tekulve in the 9th

BATTING: 2B: Madlock (1, D.Martinez), Ott (1, D.Martinez), Stargell (2, Stewart), Milner (1, Stone), Parker (2, Stone). **HR:** Stargell (2, 2nd off D.Martinez 0 on, 0 out). **RBI:** Moreno 1 (1), Parker 1 (2), Stargell 1 (3), Milner 1 (1), Ott 2 (3). **2-out RBI:** Moreno 1, Parker 1. **Runners left in scoring position, 2 out:** Stargell 1, Ott 1, Garner 2. **GIDP:** Parker, Madlock. **Team LOB:** 10 **BASERUNNING: CS:** Madlock (2, 2nd base off Stoddard/Skaggs). **FIELDING: E:** Madlock (1). **DP:** 3 (Foli-Garner-Stargell 2, Garner-Foli-Stargell).

BALTIMORE	IP	H	R	ER	BB	SO	HR	ERA
D.Martinez	1.1	6	4	4	0	0	1	27.00
Stewart	2.2	4	0	0	1	0	0	0.00
Stone	2	4	2	2	2	2	0	9.00
Stoddard (W, 1-0)	3	3	0	0	1	3	0	0.00

PITTSBURGH	IP	H	R	ER	BB	SO	HR	ERA
Bibby	6.1	7	3	2	2	7	0	2.84
Jackson	0.2	0	0	0	0	0	0	0.00
D.Robinson	0.1	2	3	3	1	0	0	6.23
Tekulve (L, 0-1)	1.2	3	3	3	2	1	0	5.79

IBB: Milner (by Stewart), Madlock (by Stone), Smith (by Tekulve). **Pitches-strikes:** D.Martinez 27-16, Stewart 38-22, Stone 54-29, Stoddard 46-33, Bibby 117-71, Jackson 6-3, D.Robinson 20-12, Tekulve 34-17. **Ground balls-fly balls:** D.Martinez 2-0, Stewart 3-3, Stone 2-2, Stoddard 3-2, Bibby 5-6, Jackson 1-0, D.Robinson 1-0, Tekulve 4-0. **Batters faced:** D.Martinez 8, Stewart 11, Stone 12, Stoddard 12, Bibby 27, Jackson 1, D.Robinson 4, Tekulve 10. **UMPIRES:** hp—Tata, 1b—McKean, 2b—Runge, 3b—Neudecker, lf—Engel, rf—Goetz **T:** 3:48 **A:** 50,883

GAME 5 Pittsburgh 7 Baltimore 1
Three Rivers Stadium 10/14/79

BALTIMORE	AB	R	H	HR	RBI	BB	AVG
Garcia ss	4	0	0	0	0	0	.429
Ayala lf	1	0	0	0	0	1	.667
a-Bumbry ph-cf	1	0	0	0	0	1	.176
Singleton rf	4	0	0	0	0	0	.333
Murray 1b	4	0	0	0	0	0	.222
Roenicke cf-lf	4	1	1	0	0	0	.167
DeCinces 3b	4	0	2	0	0	0	.176
Dauer 2b	3	0	0	0	1	0	.250
c-Lowenstein ph	1	0	1	0	0	0	.300
Dempsey c	3	0	2	0	0	0	.333
d-Crowley ph	1	0	0	0	0	0	.500
Flanagan p	1	0	0	0	0	1	.000
b-Kelly ph	1	0	0	0	0	0	.500
Stoddard p	0	0	0	0	0	0	1.000
T.Martinez p	0	0	0	0	0	0	.000
Stanhouse p	0	0	0	0	0	0	.000
TOTALS	**32**	**1**	**6**	**0**	**1**	**3**	**.251**

a - Batted for Ayala in the 6th
b - Batted for Flanagan in the 7th
c - Batted for Dauer in the 9th
d - Batted for Dempsey in the 9th

BATTING: 2B: Roenicke (1, Rooker), Dempsey (2, Blyleven). **RBI:** Dauer 1 (1). **Runners left in scoring position, 2 out:** Garcia 1, Crowley 1, Kelly 1. **GIDP:** Dauer, Singleton. **Team LOB:** 7 **FIELDING: E:** Stoddard (1), Stanhouse (1).

PITTSBURGH	AB	R	H	HR	RBI	BB	AVG
Moreno cf	4	1	0	0	0	1	.217
Foli ss	4	2	2	0	3	1	.333
Parker rf	4	1	2	0	1	1	.429
B.Robinson lf	4	0	1	0	0	0	.267
Stargell 1b	3	1	1	0	1	0	.381
Madlock 3b	4	1	4	0	1	0	.500
Nicosia c	4	0	0	0	0	0	.083
Garner 2b	4	1	2	0	1	0	.500
Rooker p	1	0	0	0	0	0	.000
a-Lacy ph	1	0	1	0	0	0	.333
Blyleven p	1	0	0	0	0	0	.000
TOTALS	**34**	**7**	**13**	**0**	**7**	**3**	**.339**

a - Batted for Rooker in the 5th

BATTING: 2B: B.Robinson (1, Flanagan), Parker (3, T.Martinez). **3B:** Foli (1, Stoddard). **S:** B.Robinson, Blyleven. **SF:** Stargell. **RBI:** Foli 3 (3), Parker 1 (3), Stargell 1 (4), Madlock 1 (3), Garner 1 (5). **2-out RBI:** Foli 3, Parker 1, Madlock 1. **Runners left in scoring position, 2 out:** Moreno 1, B.Robinson 3, Stargell 1. **Team LOB:** 9 **FIELDING: E:** Garner (2). **DP:** 2 (Garner-Foli-Stargell, Blyleven-Garner-Foli-Stargell).

BALTIMORE	IP	H	R	ER	BB	SO	HR	ERA
Flanagan (L, 1-1)	6	6	2	2	1	6	0	2.40
Stoddard	0.2	2	2	2	0	0	0	4.91
T.Martinez	0.1	2	1	1	0	0	0	6.75
Stanhouse	1	3	2	2	2	0	0	13.50

PITTSBURGH	IP	H	R	ER	BB	SO	HR	ERA
Rooker	5	3	1	1	2	2	0	1.04
Blyleven (W, 1-0)	4	3	0	0	1	3	0	1.80

IBB: Moreno (by Stanhouse), Parker (by Stanhouse). **Pitches-strikes:** Flanagan 72-50, Stoddard 17-10, T.Martinez 9-5, Stanhouse 28-14, Rooker 74-43, Blyleven 52-37. **Ground balls-fly balls:** Flanagan 5-5, Stoddard 2-0, T.Martinez 1-0, Stanhouse 0-2, Rooker 5-7, Blyleven 5-4. **Batters faced:** Flanagan 25, Stoddard 4, T.Martinez 3, Stanhouse 8, Rooker 19, Blyleven 16. **UMPIRES:** hp—McKean, 1b—Runge, 2b—Neudecker, 3b—Engel, lf—Goetz, rf—Tata **T:** 2:54 **A:** 50,920

GAME 6 Pittsburgh 4 Baltimore 0
Memorial Stadium 10/16/79

PITTSBURGH	AB	R	H	HR	RBI	BB	AVG
Moreno cf	5	1	3	0	1	0	.286
Foli ss	5	1	2	0	0	0	.346
Parker rf	4	0	1	0	1	1	.400
Stargell 1b	4	0	0	0	1	0	.320
Milner lf	3	0	0	0	0	1	.333
Tekulve p	1	0	0	0	0	0	.000
Madlock 3b	3	0	0	0	0	1	.429
Ott c	4	1	2	0	0	0	.333
Garner 2b	3	1	2	0	0	0	.524
Candelaria p	2	0	0	0	0	0	.333
a-Lacy ph	1	0	0	0	0	0	.250
B.Robinson lf	0	0	0	0	1	0	.267
TOTALS	**35**	**4**	**10**	**0**	**4**	**3**	**.330**

a - Batted for Candelaria in the 7th

BATTING: 2B: Foli (1, Palmer), Garner (3, Palmer). **SF:** Stargell, B.Robinson. **RBI:** Moreno 1 (2), Parker 1 (4), Stargell 1 (5), B.Robinson 1 (1). **2-out RBI:** Moreno 1. **Runners left in scoring position, 2 out:** Foli 1, Milner 3, Candelaria 2. **Team LOB:** 10 **FIELDING: DP:** 2 (Madlock-Stargell, Foli-Garner-Stargell).

BALTIMORE	AB	R	H	HR	RBI	BB	AVG
Garcia ss	3	0	1	0	0	0	.412
d-Kelly ph	1	0	0	0	0	0	.333
Belanger ss	0	0	0	0	0	0	.000
Ayala lf	3	0	0	0	0	0	.333
e-Crowley ph	1	0	0	0	0	0	.333
Stoddard p	0	0	0	0	0	0	1.000
Singleton rf	4	0	3	0	0	0	.400
Murray 1b	4	0	0	0	0	0	.182
DeCinces 3b	4	0	0	0	0	0	.143
Roenicke cf	2	0	0	0	0	0	.143
a-Bumbry ph-cf	1	0	0	0	0	0	.167
Dauer 2b	2	0	1	0	0	0	.286
b-Smith ph-2b	1	0	1	0	0	0	.286
Dempsey c	3	0	1	0	0	0	.333
Palmer p	2	0	0	0	0	0	.000
c-Lowenstein ph-lf	1	0	0	0	0	0	.273
TOTALS	**32**	**0**	**7**	**0**	**0**	**0**	**.246**

a - Batted for Roenicke in the 7th
b - Batted for Dauer in the 7th
c - Batted for Palmer in the 8th
d - Batted for Garcia in the 8th
e - Batted for Ayala in the 8th

BATTING: Runners left in scoring position, 2 out: Roenicke 1. **GIDP:** Murray, Dempsey. **Team LOB:** 5 **FIELDING: E:** Bumbry (1).

PITTSBURGH	IP	H	R	ER	BB	SO	HR	ERA
Candelaria (W, 1-1)	6	6	0	0	0	2	0	5.00
Tekulve (S, 2)	3	1	0	0	0	4	0	3.52

BALTIMORE	IP	H	R	ER	BB	SO	HR	ERA
Palmer (L, 0-1)	8	10	4	4	3	5	0	3.60
Stoddard	1	0	0	0	0	0	0	3.86

HBP: Garner (by Palmer). **Pitches-strikes:** Candelaria 65-48, Tekulve 34-26, Palmer 119-77, Stoddard 9-7. **Ground balls-fly balls:** Candelaria 7-7, Tekulve 2-3, Palmer 7-10, Stoddard 1-2. **Batters faced:** Candelaria 22, Tekulve 10, Palmer 38, Stoddard 3. **UMPIRES:** hp—Runge, 1b—Neudecker, 2b—Engel, 3b—Goetz, lf—Tata, rf—McKean **T:** 2:30 **A:** 53,739

GAME 7 Pittsburgh 4 Baltimore 1
Memorial Stadium 10/17/79

PITTSBURGH	AB	R	H	HR	RBI	BB	AVG
Moreno cf	5	1	3	0	1	0	.333
Foli ss	4	0	1	0	0	0	.333
Parker rf	4	0	0	0	0	0	.345
B.Robinson lf	4	1	1	0	1	0	.263
Stargell 1b	5	1	4	1	2	0	.400
Madlock 3b	3	0	0	0	0	1	.375
Nicosia c	4	0	0	0	0	0	.063
Garner 2b	3	1	1	0	0	1	.500
Bibby p	1	0	0	0	0	0	.000
a-Sanguillen ph	1	0	0	0	0	0	.333
D.Robinson p	0	0	0	0	0	0	.000
Jackson p	1	0	0	0	0	0	.000
Tekulve p	1	0	0	0	0	0	.000
TOTALS	**36**	**4**	**10**	**1**	**4**	**2**	**.323**

a - Batted for Bibby in the 5th

BATTING: 2B: Stargell 2 (4, McGregor), Garner (4, Stoddard). **HR:** Stargell (3, 6th off McGregor 1 on, 1 out). **S:** Foli. **RBI:** Moreno 1 (3), B.Robinson 1 (2), Stargell 2 (7). **Runners left in scoring position, 2 out:** B.Robinson 1, Nicosia 1, Garner 1, Bibby 1. **GIDP:** Stargell. **Team LOB:** 10

BALTIMORE	AB	R	H	HR	RBI	BB	AVG
Bumbry cf	3	0	0	0	0	1	.143
Garcia ss	3	0	1	0	0	0	.400
d-Ayala ph	0	0	0	0	0	0	.333
e-Crowley ph	1	0	0	0	0	0	.250
Stoddard p	0	0	0	0	0	0	1.000
Flanagan p	0	0	0	0	0	0	.000
Stanhouse p	0	0	0	0	0	0	.000
T.Martinez p	0	0	0	0	0	0	.000
D.Martinez p	0	0	0	0	0	0	.000
Singleton rf	3	0	0	0	0	1	.357
Murray 1b	4	0	0	0	0	0	.154
Lowenstein lf	2	0	0	0	0	0	.231
a-Roenicke ph-lf	2	0	0	0	0	0	.125
DeCinces 3b	4	0	2	0	0	0	.200
Dempsey c	3	0	0	0	0	0	.286
f-Kelly ph	1	0	0	0	0	0	.250
Dauer 2b	3	1	1	1	1	0	.294
McGregor p	1	0	0	0	0	1	.000
b-May ph	0	0	0	0	0	1	.000
c-Belanger pr-ss	0	0	0	0	0	0	.000
TOTALS	**30**	**1**	**4**	**1**	**1**	**4**	**.232**

a - Batted for Lowenstein in the 7th
b - Batted for McGregor in the 8th
c - Ran for May in the 8th
d - Batted for Garcia in the 8th e - Batted for Ayala in the 8th f - Batted for Dempsey in the 9th

BATTING: HR: Dauer (1, 3th off Bibby 0 on, 0 out). **RBI:** Dauer 1 (2). **Runners left in scoring position, 2 out:** Bumbry 1, Murray 2. **Team LOB:** 6 **BASERUNNING: CS:** Garcia (1, 2nd base off Bibby/Nicosia). **FIELDING: E:** Lowenstein (1), Garcia (1). **DP:** 1 (Belanger-Murray).

PITTSBURGH	IP	H	R	ER	BB	SO	HR	ERA
Bibby	4	3	1	1	0	3	1	2.61
D.Robinson	0.2	1	0	0	1	0	0	5.40
Jackson (W, 1-0)	2.2	0	0	0	2	1	0	0.00
Tekulve (S, 3)	1.2	0	0	0	1	2	0	2.89

BALTIMORE	IP	H	R	ER	BB	SO	HR	ERA
McGregor (L, 1-1)	8	7	2	2	2	2	1	3.18
Stoddard	0.1	1	1	1	0	0	0	5.40
Flanagan	0	1	1	1	0	0	0	3.00
Stanhouse	0	1	0	0	0	0	0	13.50
T.Martinez	0	0	0	0	0	0	0	6.75
D.Martinez	0.2	0	0	0	0	0	0	18.00

IBB: Garner (by McGregor), Madlock (by McGregor), Singleton (by Tekulve). **HBP:** Parker (by T.Martinez), B.Robinson (by D.Martinez). **Pitches-strikes:** Bibby 44-33, D.Robinson 20-14, Jackson 37-21, Tekulve 21-12, McGregor 95-69, Stoddard 3-3, Flanagan 3-2, Stanhouse 4-3, T.Martinez 2-2, D.Martinez 4-4. **Ground balls-fly balls:** Bibby 5-3, D.Robinson 0-2, Jackson 0-7, Tekulve 1-2, McGregor 11-11, Stoddard 1-0, Flanagan 0-0, Stanhouse 0-0, T.Martinez 0-0, D.Martinez 1-0. **Batters faced:** Bibby 14, D.Robinson 4, Jackson 10, Tekulve 6, McGregor 34, Stoddard 2, Flanagan 1, Stanhouse 1, T.Martinez 1, D.Martinez 2. **UMPIRES:** hp—Neudecker, 1b—Engel, 2b—Goetz, 3b—Tata, lf—McKean, rf—Runge **T:** 2:54 **A:** 53,733

1980 PHILADELPHIA DEF. KANSAS CITY, 4-2

GAME 1 Philadelphia 7 Kansas City 6
Veterans Stadium 10/14/80

KANSAS CITY	AB	R	H	HR	RBI	BB	AVG
Wilson lf	5	0	0	0	0	0	.000
McRae dh	3	1	1	0	0	1	.333
Brett 3b	4	1	1	0	0	0	.250
Aikens 1b	4	2	2	2	4	0	.500
Porter c	2	1	0	0	0	2	.000
Otis cf	4	1	3	1	2	0	.750
Hurdle rf	3	0	1	0	0	0	.333
a-Wathan ph-rf	1	0	0	0	0	0	.000
White 2b	4	0	1	0	0	0	.250
Washington ss	4	0	0	0	0	0	.000
TOTALS	**34**	**6**	**9**	**3**	**6**	**3**	**.265**

a - Batted for Hurdle in the 8th

BATTING: 2B: Brett (1, Walk). **HR:** Otis (1, 2nd off Walk 1 on, 0 out), Aikens 2 (2, 3th off Walk 1 on, 2 out, 8th off Walk 1 on, 0 out). **RBI:** Aikens 4 (4), Otis 2 (2). **2-out RBI:** Aikens 2. **Runners left in scoring position, 2 out:** McRae 1, Hurdle 1. **GIDP:** Wathan. **Team LOB:** 4 **BASERUNNING: SB:** White (1, 2nd base off Walk/Boone). **FIELDING: E:** Leonard (1). **Outfield assists:** Wilson (1).

PHILADELPHIA	AB	R	H	HR	RBI	BB	AVG
Smith lf	4	0	2	0	0	0	.500
Gross lf	1	0	0	0	0	0	.000
Rose 1b	3	1	0	0	0	0	.000
Schmidt 3b	2	2	1	0	0	2	.500
McBride rf	4	1	3	1	3	0	.750
Luzinski dh	3	0	0	0	0	0	.000
Maddox cf	3	0	0	0	1	0	.000
Trillo 2b	4	1	1	0	0	0	.250
Bowa ss	4	1	1	0	0	0	.250
Boone c	4	1	3	0	2	0	.750
TOTALS	**32**	**7**	**11**	**1**	**6**	**2**	**.344**

BATTING: 2B: Boone 2 (2, Leonard). **HR:** McBride (1, 3th off Leonard 2 on, 2 out). **SF:** Maddox. **RBI:** McBride 3 (3), Maddox 1 (1), Boone 2 (2). **2-out RBI:** McBride 3, Boone 1. **Runners left in scoring position, 2 out:** Smith 1, Maddox 1, Trillo 1. **Team LOB:** 6 **BASERUNNING: SB:** Bowa (1, 2nd base off Leonard/Porter). **CS:** Smith (1, 2nd base off Martin/Porter). **FIELDING: Outfield assists:** Smith (1). **DP:** 1 (Bowa-Trillo-Rose).

KANSAS CITY	IP	H	R	ER	BB	SO	HR	ERA
Leonard (L, 0-1)	3.2	6	6	6	1	3	1	14.73
Martin	4	5	1	1	1	1	0	2.25
Quisenberry	0.1	0	0	0	0	0	0	0.00

PHILADELPHIA	IP	H	R	ER	BB	SO	HR	ERA
Walk (W, 1-0)	7	8	6	6	3	3	3	7.71
McGraw (S, 1)	2	1	0	0	0	2	0	0.00

WP: Walk 1. **HBP:** Rose (by Leonard), Luzinski (by Martin). **Pitches-strikes:** Leonard 70-45, Martin 68-40, Quisenberry 2-2, Walk 123-75, McGraw 27-17. **Ground balls-fly balls:** Leonard 6-1, Martin 4-5, Quisenberry 1-0, Walk 7-10, McGraw 2-1. **Batters faced:** Leonard 18, Martin 18, Quisenberry 1, Walk 31, McGraw 6. **UMPIRES:** hp—Wendelstedt, 1b—Kunkel, 2b—Pryor, 3b—Denkinger, lf—Rennert, rf—Bremigan **T:** 3:01 **A:** 65,791

GAME 2 Philadelphia 6 Kansas City 4
Veterans Stadium 10/15/80

KANSAS CITY	AB	R	H	HR	RBI	BB	AVG
Wilson lf	4	1	1	0	0	1	.111
Washington ss	4	0	1	0	0	0	.125
Brett 3b	2	0	2	0	0	1	.500
Chalk 3b	0	1	0	0	0	1	.000
a-Porter ph	1	0	0	0	0	0	.000
McRae dh	4	1	3	0	0	1	.571
Otis cf	5	1	2	0	2	0	.556
Wathan c	3	0	0	0	1	1	.000
Aikens 1b	3	0	1	0	0	1	.429
LaCock 1b	0	0	0	0	0	0	.000
Cardenal rf	4	0	0	0	0	0	.000
White 2b	4	0	1	0	0	0	.250
TOTALS	**34**	**4**	**11**	**0**	**3**	**6**	**.294**

a - Batted for Chalk in the 9th

BATTING: 2B: Otis (1, Carlton). **S:** Washington. **SF:** Wathan. **RBI:** Otis 2 (4), Wathan 1 (1). **Runners left in scoring position, 2 out:** Wilson 1, Washington 1, McRae 1, Otis 1. **GIDP:** Otis, Cardenal, White. **Team LOB:** 11 **BASERUNNING: SB:** Wilson (1, 3rd base off Carlton/Boone), Chalk (1, 2nd base off Carlton/Boone). **FIELDING: DP:** 2 (Washington-White-Aikens, Washington-White-LaCock).

PHILADELPHIA	AB	R	H	HR	RBI	BB	AVG
Smith lf	3	0	0	0	0	0	.286
a-Unser ph-lf	1	1	1	0	1	0	1.000
Rose 1b	4	0	0	0	0	0	.000
McBride rf	3	1	1	0	1	1	.571
Schmidt 3b	4	1	2	0	1	0	.500
Moreland dh	4	1	2	0	1	0	.500
Maddox cf	3	1	1	0	0	0	.167
b-Gross ph-cf	1	0	0	0	0	0	.000
Trillo 2b	2	0	0	0	1	0	.167
Bowa ss	3	0	1	0	1	0	.286
Boone c	1	1	0	0	0	2	.600
TOTALS	**29**	**6**	**8**	**0**	**6**	**3**	**.311**

a - Batted for Smith in the 8th
b - Batted for Maddox in the 8th

BATTING: 2B: Maddox (1, Gura), Unser (1, Quisenberry), Schmidt (1, Quisenberry). **SF:** Trillo. **RBI:** Unser 1 (1), McBride 1 (4), Schmidt 1 (1), Moreland 1 (1), Trillo 1 (1), Bowa 1 (1). **2-out RBI:** Bowa 1. **Runners left in scoring position, 2 out:** Smith 1. **GIDP:** Moreland, Gross. **Team LOB:** 3 **FIELDING: E:** Trillo (1). **Outfield assists:** Maddox (1). **DP:** 4 (Bowa-Trillo-Rose 2, Bowa-Trillo-Rose, Maddox-Rose-Schmidt).

KANSAS CITY	IP	H	R	ER	BB	SO	HR	ERA
Gura	6	4	2	2	2	2	0	3.00
Quisenberry (L, 0-1)	2	4	4	4	1	0	0	15.43

PHILADELPHIA	IP	H	R	ER	BB	SO	HR	ERA
Carlton (W, 1-0)	8	10	4	3	6	10	0	3.38
Reed (S, 1)	1	1	0	0	0	2	0	0.00

WP: Carlton 1. **Pitches-strikes:** Gura 85-50, Quisenberry 31-21, Carlton 164-95, Reed 26-17. **Ground balls-fly balls:** Gura 3-11, Quisenberry 5-0, Carlton 7-3, Reed 1-0. **Batters faced:** Gura 23, Quisenberry 10, Carlton 38, Reed 4. **UMPIRES:** hp—Kunkel, 1b—Pryor, 2b—Denkinger, 3b—Rennert, lf—Bremigan, rf—Wendelstedt **T:** 3:01 **A:** 65,775

GAME 3 Kansas City 4 Philadelphia 3
Royals Stadium 10/17/80

PHILADELPHIA	AB	R	H	HR	RBI	BB	AVG
Smith lf	4	0	2	0	1	1	.364
a-Gross ph-lf	0	0	0	0	0	0	.000
Rose 1b	4	0	1	0	1	2	.091
Schmidt 3b	5	1	1	1	1	1	.364
McBride rf	5	0	2	0	0	0	.500
Moreland dh	5	0	1	0	0	0	.333
Maddox cf	4	0	1	0	0	1	.200
Trillo 2b	5	1	2	0	0	0	.273
Bowa ss	5	1	3	0	0	0	.417
Boone c	4	0	1	0	0	1	.444
TOTALS	**41**	**3**	**14**	**1**	**3**	**6**	**.324**

a - Batted for Smith in the 10th

BATTING: 2B: Trillo (1, Gale). **HR:** Schmidt (1, 5th off Gale 0 on, 0 out). **S:** Gross. **RBI:** Smith 1 (1), Rose 1 (1), Schmidt 1 (2). **2-out RBI:** Rose 1. **Runners left in scoring position, 2 out:** Schmidt 4, Moreland 1, Bowa 4. **GIDP:** Trillo. **Team LOB:** 15
BASERUNNING: SB: Bowa (2, 2nd base off Martin/Porter). **FIELDING: DP:** 1 (Bowa-Trillo-Rose).

KANSAS CITY	AB	R	H	HR	RBI	BB	AVG
Wilson lf	4	1	0	0	0	1	.077
White 2b	5	0	0	0	0	0	.154
Brett 3b	4	1	2	1	1	1	.500
Aikens 1b	5	1	2	0	1	0	.417
McRae dh	4	0	2	0	1	0	.545
Otis cf	4	1	2	1	1	0	.538
Hurdle rf	4	0	2	0	0	0	.429
a-Concepcion pr	0	0	0	0	0	0	.000
Cardenal rf	0	0	0	0	0	0	.000
Porter c	4	0	0	0	0	0	.000
Washington ss	4	0	1	0	0	0	.167
TOTALS	**38**	**4**	**11**	**2**	**4**	**2**	**.292**

a - Ran for Hurdle in the 9th

BATTING: 2B: Brett (2, Ruthven). **3B:** Aikens (1, Ruthven). **HR:** Brett (1, 1st off Ruthven 0 on, 2 out), Otis (2, 7th off Ruthven 0 on, 1 out). **RBI:** Brett 1 (1), Aikens 1 (5), McRae 1 (1), Otis 1 (5). **2-out RBI:** Brett 1, Aikens 1. **Runners left in scoring position, 2 out:** Aikens 1, Hurdle 1, Washington 1. **GIDP:** Otis. **Team LOB:** 7 **BASERUNNING: SB:** Hurdle (1, 2nd base off Ruthven/Boone), Wilson (2, 2nd base off McGraw/Boone). **CS:** Washington (1, 3rd base off McGraw/Boone). **FIELDING: DP:** 2 (White-Washington-Aikens, White).

PHILADELPHIA	IP	H	R	ER	BB	SO	HR	ERA
Ruthven	9	9	3	3	0	7	2	3.00
McGraw (L, 0-1)	0.2	2	1	1	2	1	0	3.38

KANSAS CITY	IP	H	R	ER	BB	SO	HR	ERA
Gale	4.1	7	2	2	3	3	1	4.15
Martin	3.1	5	1	1	1	1	0	2.45
Quisenberry (W, 1-1)	2.1	2	0	0	2	0	0	7.71

IBB: Maddox (by Quisenberry), Rose (by Quisenberry), Brett (by McGraw). **Pitches-strikes:** Ruthven 130-83, McGraw 18-7, Gale 80-49, Martin 45-29, Quisenberry 31-16. **Ground balls-fly balls:** Ruthven 12-7, McGraw 0-0, Gale 5-5, Martin 2-6, Quisenberry 2-3. **Batters faced:** Ruthven 35, McGraw 5, Gale 23, Martin 15, Quisenberry 10. **UMPIRES:** hp—Pryor, 1b—Denkinger, 2b—Rennert , 3b—Bremigan , lf—Wendelstedt, rf—Kunkel **T:** 3:19 **A:** 42,380

GAME 4 Kansas City 5 Philadelphia 3
Royals Stadium 10/18/80

PHILADELPHIA	AB	R	H	HR	RBI	BB	AVG
Smith dh	4	0	0	0	0	0	.267
Rose 1b	4	1	2	0	0	0	.200
McBride rf	3	0	1	0	0	1	.467
Schmidt 3b	3	0	1	0	1	0	.357
Unser lf	4	0	1	0	0	0	.400
Maddox cf	4	0	1	0	0	0	.214
Trillo 2b	4	2	1	0	0	0	.267
Bowa ss	4	0	2	0	1	0	.438
Boone c	3	0	1	0	1	0	.417
TOTALS	**33**	**3**	**10**	**0**	**3**	**1**	**.319**

BATTING: 2B: McBride (1, Leonard), Trillo (2, Leonard), Rose (1, Leonard). **SF:** Boone, Schmidt. **RBI:** Schmidt 1 (3), Bowa 1 (2), Boone 1 (3). **2-out RBI:** Bowa 1. **Runners left in scoring position, 2 out:** Smith 1, Schmidt 1, Unser 1, Trillo 1, Boone 1. **GIDP:** Smith. **Team LOB:** 6 **BASERUNNING: SB:** Bowa (3, 2nd base off Leonard/Porter). **CS:** McBride (1, 2nd base off Leonard/Porter). **FIELDING: E:** Christenson (1).

KANSAS CITY	AB	R	H	HR	RBI	BB	AVG
Wilson lf	4	1	1	0	0	1	.118
White 2b	5	0	0	0	0	0	.111
Brett 3b	5	1	1	0	1	0	.400
Aikens 1b	3	2	2	2	3	1	.467
McRae dh	4	1	2	0	0	0	.533
Otis cf	4	0	2	0	1	0	.529
Hurdle rf	2	0	1	0	0	2	.444
Porter c	3	0	0	0	0	1	.000
Washington ss	4	0	1	0	0	0	.188
TOTALS	**34**	**5**	**10**	**2**	**5**	**5**	**.293**

BATTING: 2B: McRae 2 (2, Christenson, Noles), Otis (2, Christenson), Hurdle (1, Noles). **3B:** Brett (1, Christenson). **HR:** Aikens 2 (4, 1st off Christenson 1 on, 1 out, 2nd off Noles 0 on, 2 out). **RBI:** Brett 1 (2), Aikens 3 (8), Otis 1 (6). **2-out RBI:** Aikens 1. **Runners left in scoring position, 2 out:** Wilson 3, McRae 1, Otis 1, Washington 1. **Team LOB:** 10 **FIELDING: E:** White (1). **DP:** 1 (Brett-White-Aikens).

PHILADELPHIA	IP	H	R	ER	BB	SO	HR	ERA
Christenson (L, 0-1)	0.1	5	4	4	0	0	1	108.00
Noles	4.2	5	1	1	2	6	1	1.93
Saucier	0.2	0	0	0	2	0	0	0.00
Brusstar	2.1	0	0	0	1	0	0	0.00

KANSAS CITY	IP	H	R	ER	BB	SO	HR	ERA
Leonard (W, 1-1)	7	9	3	2	1	2	0	6.75
Quisenberry (S, 1)	2	1	0	0	0	0	0	5.40

WP: Saucier 1, Leonard 1. **Pitches-strikes:** Christenson 22-14, Noles 73-44, Saucier 13-3, Brusstar 19-12, Leonard 81-56, Quisenberry 23-14. **Ground balls-fly balls:** Christenson 0-1, Noles 3-5, Saucier 0-2, Brusstar 6-1, Leonard 9-7, Quisenberry 5-0. **Batters faced:** Christenson 6, Noles 21, Saucier 4, Brusstar 8, Leonard 29, Quisenberry 7. **UMPIRES:** hp—Denkinger, 1b—Rennert, 2b—Bremigan, 3b—Wendelstedt, lf—Kunkel, rf—Pryor **T:** 2:37 **A:** 42,363

GAME 5 Philadelphia 4 Kansas City 3
Royals Stadium 10/19/80

PHILADELPHIA	AB	R	H	HR	RBI	BB	AVG
Rose 1b	4	0	0	0	0	0	.158
McBride rf	4	1	0	0	0	0	.368
Schmidt 3b	4	2	2	1	2	0	.389
Luzinski lf	2	0	0	0	0	1	.000
a-Smith pr-lf	0	0	0	0	0	0	.267
b-Unser ph-lf	1	1	1	0	1	0	.500
Moreland dh	3	0	1	0	0	0	.333
Maddox cf	4	0	0	0	0	0	.167
Trillo 2b	4	0	1	0	1	0	.263
Bowa ss	4	0	1	0	0	0	.400
Boone c	3	0	1	0	0	0	.400
TOTALS	**33**	**4**	**7**	**1**	**4**	**1**	**.298**

a - Ran for Luzinski in the 7th
b - Batted for Smith in the 9th

BATTING: 2B: Unser (2, Quisenberry). **HR:** Schmidt (2, 4th off Gura 1 on, 1 out). **S:** Moreland. **RBI:** Schmidt 2 (5), Unser 1 (2), Trillo 1 (2). **2-out RBI:** Trillo 1. **Runners left in scoring position, 2 out:** McBride 1, Trillo 1. **Team LOB:** 4 **Outfield assists:** McBride (1).

KANSAS CITY	AB	R	H	HR	RBI	BB	AVG
Wilson lf	5	0	2	0	0	0	.182
White 2b	3	0	0	0	0	1	.095
Brett 3b	5	0	1	0	1	0	.350
Aikens 1b	3	0	1	0	0	2	.444
b-Concepcion pr	0	0	0	0	0	0	.000
McRae dh	5	0	1	0	0	0	.450
Otis cf	3	1	2	1	1	2	.550
Hurdle rf	3	1	1	0	0	0	.417
a-Cardenal ph-rf	2	0	0	0	0	0	.000
Porter c	4	0	2	0	0	0	.143
Washington ss	3	1	2	0	1	0	.263
TOTALS	**36**	**3**	**12**	**1**	**3**	**5**	**.301**

a - Batted for Hurdle in the 7th
b - Ran for Aikens in the 9th

BATTING: 2B: Wilson (1, Reed), McRae (3, McGraw). **HR:** Otis (3, 6th off Bystrom 0 on, 0 out). **S:** White. **SF:** Washington. **RBI:** Brett 1 (3), Otis 1 (7), Washington 1 (1). **Runners left in scoring position, 2 out:** White 1, Brett 1, Aikens 1, McRae 1, Cardenal 3, Porter 1. **Team LOB:** 13 **BASERUNNING: SB:** Brett (1, 2nd base off Bystrom/Boone). **FIELDING: E:** Brett (1). **DP:** 2 (White-Aikens-Gura, Gura-Aikens).

PHILADELPHIA	IP	H	R	ER	BB	SO	HR	ERA
Bystrom	5	10	3	3	1	4	1	5.40
Reed	1	1	0	0	0	0	0	0.00
McGraw (W, 1-1)	3	1	0	0	4	5	0	1.59

KANSAS CITY	IP	H	R	ER	BB	SO	HR	ERA
Gura	6.1	4	2	1	1	2	1	2.19
Quisenberry (L, 1-2)	2.2	3	2	2	0	0	0	5.79

IBB: Otis (by McGraw). **Pitches-strikes:** Bystrom 80-51, Reed 4-3, McGraw 47-26, Gura 77-51, Quisenberry 32-24. **Ground balls-fly balls:** Bystrom 5-5, Reed 0-1, McGraw 3-1, Gura 4-12, Quisenberry 8-0. **Batters faced:** Bystrom 26, Reed 3, McGraw 14, Gura 23, Quisenberry 12. **UMPIRES:** hp—Rennert, 1b—Bremigan, 2b—Wendelstedt, 3b—Kunkel, lf—Pryor, rf—Denkinger **T:** 2:51 **A:** 42,369

GAME 6 Philadelphia 4 Kansas City 1
Veterans Stadium 10/21/80

KANSAS CITY	AB	R	H	HR	RBI	BB	AVG
Wilson lf	4	0	0	0	0	1	.154
Washington ss	3	0	1	0	1	0	.273
Brett 3b	4	0	2	0	0	0	.375
McRae dh	4	0	0	0	0	0	.375
Otis cf	3	0	0	0	0	1	.478
Aikens 1b	2	0	0	0	0	2	.400
a-Concepcion pr	0	0	0	0	0	0	.000
Wathan c	3	1	2	0	0	1	.286
Cardenal rf	4	0	2	0	0	0	.200
White 2b	4	0	0	0	0	0	.080
TOTALS	**31**	**1**	**7**	**0**	**1**	**5**	**.290**

a - Ran for Aikens in the 9th

BATTING: SF: Washington. **RBI:** Washington 1 (2). **Runners left in scoring position, 2 out:** Wilson 2, McRae 2. **GIDP:** Wathan, Brett. **Team LOB:** 9 **FIELDING: E:** White (2), Aikens (1). **DP:** 1 (Splittorff-Washington-Aikens).

PHILADELPHIA	AB	R	H	HR	RBI	BB	AVG
Smith lf	4	2	1	0	0	0	.263
Gross lf	0	0	0	0	0	0	.000
Rose 1b	4	0	3	0	0	0	.261
Schmidt 3b	3	0	1	0	2	1	.381
McBride rf	4	0	0	0	1	0	.304
Luzinski dh	4	0	0	0	0	0	.000
Maddox cf	4	0	2	0	0	0	.227
Trillo 2b	4	0	0	0	0	0	.217
Bowa ss	4	1	1	0	0	0	.375
Boone c	2	1	1	0	1	1	.412
TOTALS	**33**	**4**	**9**	**0**	**4**	**2**	**.294**

BATTING: 2B: Maddox (2, Gale), Smith (1, Martin), Bowa (1, Splittorff). **RBI:** Schmidt 2 (7), McBride 1 (5), Boone 1 (4). **2-out RBI:** Boone 1. **Runners left in scoring position, 2 out:** Luzinski 1, Maddox 1, Bowa 1. **GIDP:** Trillo. **Team LOB:** 7 **BASERUNNING: CS:** Rose (1, 2nd base off Pattin/Wathan). **FIELDING: DP:** 2 (Bowa-Trillo-Rose, Bowa-Rose).

KANSAS CITY	IP	H	R	ER	BB	SO	HR	ERA
Gale (L, 0-1)	2	4	2	1	1	1	0	4.26
Martin	2.1	1	1	1	1	0	0	2.79
Splittorff	1.2	4	1	1	0	0	0	5.40
Pattin	1	0	0	0	0	2	0	0.00
Quisenberry	1	0	0	0	0	0	0	5.23

PHILADELPHIA	IP	H	R	ER	BB	SO	HR	ERA
Carlton (W, 2-0)	7	4	1	1	3	7	0	2.40
McGraw (S, 2)	2	3	0	0	2	2	0	1.17

Pitches-strikes: Gale 40-24, Martin 32-15, Splittorff 33-20, Pattin 12-7, Quisenberry 6-4, Carlton 110-72, McGraw 48-29. **Ground balls-fly balls:** Gale 2-4, Martin 1-6, Splittorff 3-1, Pattin 1-0, Quisenberry 1-2, Carlton 6-6, McGraw 1-2. **Batters faced:** Gale 12, Martin 9, Splittorff 8, Pattin 3, Quisenberry 3, Carlton 26, McGraw 11. **UMPIRES:** hp—Bremigan, 1b—Wendelstedt, 2b—Kunkel, 3b—Pryor, lf—Denkinger, rf—Rennert **T:** 3:00 **A:** 65,838

1981 LOS ANGELES DEF. NY YANKEES, 4-2

GAME 1 New York 5 Los Angeles 3
Yankee Stadium 10/20/81

LOS ANGELES	AB	R	H	HR	RBI	BB	AVG
Lopes 2b	3	1	0	0	0	1	.000
Russell ss	3	0	0	0	0	0	.000
c-Johnstone ph	1	0	1	0	1	0	1.000
Stewart p	0	0	0	0	0	0	.000
Baker lf	2	0	1	0	1	1	.500
Garvey 1b	4	0	1	0	0	0	.250
Cey 3b	4	0	1	0	0	0	.250
Guerrero cf	3	0	0	0	0	1	.000
Monday rf	4	0	0	0	0	0	.000
Yeager c	3	1	1	1	1	0	.333
d-Landreaux ph	1	0	0	0	0	0	.000
Reuss p	1	0	0	0	0	0	.000
Castillo p	0	0	0	0	0	0	.000
Goltz p	0	0	0	0	0	0	.000
a-Sax ph	1	0	0	0	0	0	.000
Niedenfuer p	0	0	0	0	0	0	.000
b-Thomas ph-ss	0	1	0	0	0	1	.000
TOTALS	**30**	**3**	**5**	**1**	**3**	**4**	**.167**

a - Batted for Goltz in the 5th
b - Batted for Niedenfuer in the 8th
c - Batted for Russell in the 8th
d - Batted for Yeager in the 9th

BATTING: HR: Yeager (1, 5th off Guidry 0 on, 2 out). **SF:** Baker. **RBI:** Johnstone 1 (1), Baker 1 (1), Yeager 1 (1). **2-out RBI:** Yeager 1. **Team LOB:** 5 **FIELDING: DP:** 1 (Thomas-Garvey).

NY YANKEES	AB	R	H	HR	RBI	BB	AVG
Randolph 2b	3	0	0	0	0	1	.000
Mumphrey cf	3	2	2	0	0	1	.667
Winfield lf	3	0	0	0	1	1	.000
Piniella rf	4	1	2	0	1	0	.500
Watson 1b	3	1	2	1	3	1	.667
Nettles 3b	3	0	0	0	0	1	.000
Cerone c	3	0	0	0	0	1	.000
Milbourne ss	4	1	0	0	0	0	.000
Guidry p	2	0	0	0	0	0	.000
Davis p	0	0	0	0	0	0	.000
Gossage p	0	0	0	0	0	0	.000
TOTALS	**28**	**5**	**6**	**1**	**5**	**6**	**.214**

BATTING: 2B: Piniella (1, Reuss). **HR:** Watson (1, 1st off Reuss 2 on, 2 out). **S:** Guidry. **RBI:** Winfield 1 (1), Piniella 1 (1), Watson 3 (3). **2-out RBI:** Winfield 1, Piniella 1, Watson 3. **Runners left in scoring position, 2 out:** Piniella 2, Nettles 1. **GIDP:** Milbourne. **Team LOB:** 6 **BASERUNNING: SB:** Mumphrey (1, 2nd base off Reuss/Yeager), Piniella (1, 2nd base off Castillo/Yeager). **FIELDING: PB:** Cerone. **Outfield assists:** Winfield (1).

LOS ANGELES	IP	H	R	ER	BB	SO	HR	ERA
Reuss (L, 0-1)	2.2	5	4	4	0	2	1	13.50
Castillo	1	0	1	1	5	0	0	9.00
Goltz	0.1	0	0	0	0	0	0	0.00
Niedenfuer	3	1	0	0	0	0	0	0.00
Stewart	1	0	0	0	1	0	0	0.00

NY YANKEES	IP	H	R	ER	BB	SO	HR	ERA
Guidry (W, 1-0)	7	4	1	1	2	6	1	1.29
Davis	0	0	2	2	2	0	0	0.00
Gossage (S, 1)	2	1	0	0	0	2	0	0.00

Pitches-strikes: Reuss 38-30, Castillo 36-13, Goltz 2-2, Niedenfuer 24-19, Stewart 11-7, Guidry 85-57, Davis 9-1, Gossage 33-20. **Ground balls-fly balls:** Reuss 4-2, Castillo 1-1, Goltz 0-1, Niedenfuer 1-8, Stewart 1-1, Guidry 6-8, Davis 0-0, Gossage 2-1. **Batters faced:** Reuss 13, Castillo 8, Goltz 1, Niedenfuer 10, Stewart 3, Guidry 26, Davis 2, Gossage 7. **UMPIRES:** hp—Barnett, 1b—Colosi, 2b—Cooney, 3b—Harvey, lf—Garcia, rf—Stello **T:** 2:32 **A:** 56,470

GAME 2 New York 3 Los Angeles 0
Yankee Stadium 10/21/81

LOS ANGELES	AB	R	H	HR	RBI	BB	AVG
Lopes 2b	3	0	0	0	0	0	.000
d-Monday ph	1	0	0	0	0	0	.000
Howe p	0	0	0	0	0	0	.000
Stewart p	0	0	0	0	0	0	.000
Russell ss	4	0	1	0	0	0	.143
Baker lf	4	0	0	0	0	0	.167
Garvey 1b	3	0	2	0	0	1	.429
Cey 3b	4	0	0	0	0	0	.125
Guerrero rf	4	0	0	0	0	0	.000
Landreaux cf	3	0	0	0	0	0	.000
Yeager c	2	0	0	0	0	0	.200
a-Johnstone ph	1	0	0	0	0	0	.500
Scioscia c	0	0	0	0	0	0	.000
Hooton p	2	0	0	0	0	0	.000
Forster p	0	0	0	0	0	0	.000
b-Smith ph	1	0	1	0	0	0	1.000
c-Sax pr-2b	0	0	0	0	0	0	.000
TOTALS	**32**	**0**	**4**	**0**	**0**	**1**	**.145**

a - Batted for Yeager in the 8th
b - Batted for Forster in the 8th
c - Ran for Smith in the 8th
d - Batted for Lopes in the 8th

BATTING: Runners left in scoring position, 2 out: Yeager 1. **Team LOB:** 6 **FIELDING: E:** Lopes (1), Stewart (1). **DP:** 1 (Russell-Lopes-Garvey).

NY YANKEES	AB	R	H	HR	RBI	BB	AVG
Mumphrey cf	2	0	0	0	0	2	.400
Milbourne ss	4	0	1	0	1	0	.125
Winfield lf	4	0	0	0	0	0	.000
Gamble rf	2	0	0	0	0	1	.000
b-Piniella ph	1	0	1	0	0	0	.600
c-Brown pr-rf	0	1	0	0	0	0	.000
Nettles 3b	4	1	2	0	0	0	.286
Watson 1b	4	0	2	0	1	0	.571
Cerone c	2	0	0	0	0	2	.000
Randolph 2b	2	1	0	0	1	1	.000
John p	1	0	0	0	0	0	.000
a-Murcer ph	0	0	0	0	0	0	.000
Gossage p	1	0	0	0	0	0	.000
TOTALS	**27**	**3**	**6**	**0**	**3**	**6**	**.218**

a - Batted for John in the 7th
b - Batted for Gamble in the 8th
c - Ran for Piniella in the 8th

BATTING: 2B: Milbourne (1, Hooton). **S:** John, Murcer. **SF:** Randolph. **RBI:** Milbourne 1 (1), Watson 1 (4), Randolph 1 (1). **2-out RBI:** Milbourne 1. **Runners left in scoring position, 2 out:** Winfield 1, Nettles 1, Gossage 1. **GIDP:** Milbourne. **Team LOB:** 9 **FIELDING: E:** Milbourne (1).

LOS ANGELES	IP	H	R	ER	BB	SO	HR	ERA
Hooton (L, 0-1)	6	3	1	0	4	1	0	0.00
Forster	1	0	0	0	1	0	0	0.00
Howe	0.1	2	2	2	0	0	0	54.00
Stewart	0.2	1	0	0	1	1	0	0.00

NY YANKEES	IP	H	R	ER	BB	SO	HR	ERA
John (W, 1-0)	7	3	0	0	0	4	0	0.00
Gossage (S, 2)	2	1	0	0	1	3	0	0.00

IBB: Mumphrey (by Forster), Cerone (by Stewart). **Pitches-strikes:** Hooton 100-58, Forster 6-2, Howe 9-7, Stewart 11-5, John 78-51, Gossage 30-20. **Ground balls-fly balls:** Hooton 10-7, Forster 1-0, Howe 0-1, Stewart 0-0, John 14-4, Gossage 1-2. **Batters faced:** Hooton 26, Forster 3, Howe 3, Stewart 4, John 25, Gossage 8. **UMPIRES:** hp—Colosi, 1b—Cooney, 2b—Harvey, 3b—Garcia, lf—Stello, rf—Barnett **T:** 2:29 **A:** 56,505

GAME 3 Los Angeles 5 New York 4
Dodger Stadium 10/23/81

NY YANKEES	AB	R	H	HR	RBI	BB	AVG
Randolph 2b	2	0	0	0	0	3	.000
Mumphrey cf	5	0	0	0	0	0	.200
Winfield lf	3	0	0	0	0	2	.000
Piniella rf	5	1	1	0	0	0	.400
Watson 1b	4	1	2	1	1	0	.545
Cerone c	4	2	2	1	2	0	.222
Rodriguez 3b	4	0	2	0	0	0	.500
Milbourne ss	2	0	2	0	1	2	.300
Righetti p	1	0	0	0	0	0	.000
Frazier p	1	0	0	0	0	0	.000
May p	0	0	0	0	0	0	.000
a-Murcer ph	1	0	0	0	0	0	.000
Davis p	0	0	0	0	0	0	.000
TOTALS	**32**	**4**	**9**	**2**	**4**	**7**	**.241**

a - Batted for May in the 8th

BATTING: 2B: Cerone (1, Valenzuela), Watson (1, Valenzuela). **HR:** Watson (2, 2nd off Valenzuela 0 on, 0 out), Cerone (1, 3th off Valenzuela 1 on, 2 out). **S:** Righetti. **RBI:** Watson 1 (5), Cerone 2 (2), Milbourne 1 (2). **2-out RBI:** Cerone 2. **Runners left in scoring position, 2 out:** Randolph 1, Mumphrey 1, Righetti 1, Frazier 1. **GIDP:** Piniella. **Team LOB:** 9 **BASERUNNING: CS:** Randolph (1, 2nd base off Valenzuela/Scioscia). **FIELDING: DP:** 2 (Randolph-Watson, Milbourne-Randolph-Watson).

LOS ANGELES	AB	R	H	HR	RBI	BB	AVG
Lopes 2b	4	1	2	0	0	0	.200
Russell ss	5	1	2	0	0	0	.250
Baker lf	4	0	0	0	0	0	.100
Garvey 1b	4	1	2	0	0	0	.455
Cey 3b	2	2	2	1	3	2	.300
Guerrero cf-rf	3	0	1	0	1	0	.100
Monday rf	2	0	1	0	0	1	.143
b-Thomas ph-cf	1	0	0	0	0	0	.000
Yeager c	1	0	0	0	0	0	.167
a-Scioscia ph-c	3	0	1	0	1	0	.333
Valenzuela p	3	0	0	0	0	1	.000
TOTALS	**32**	**5**	**11**	**1**	**5**	**4**	**.213**

a - Batted for Yeager in the 3th
b - Batted for Monday in the 7th

BATTING: 2B: Lopes (1, Righetti), Guerrero (1, Frazier). **HR:** Cey (1, 1st off Righetti 2 on, 2 out). **S:** Lopes. **RBI:** Cey 3 (3), Guerrero 1 (1), Scioscia 1 (1). **2-out RBI:** Cey 3. **Runners left in scoring position, 2 out:** Baker 1, Yeager 1, Scioscia 1, Valenzuela 1. **GIDP:** Scioscia, Thomas. **Team LOB:** 9 **FIELDING: E:** Lopes (2). **DP:** 2 (Russell-Lopes-Garvey, Cey-Garvey).

NY YANKEES	IP	H	R	ER	BB	SO	HR	ERA
Righetti	2	5	3	3	2	1	1	13.50
Frazier (L, 0-1)	2	3	2	2	2	1	0	9.00
May	3	2	0	0	0	2	0	0.00
Davis	1	1	0	0	0	1	0	18.00

LOS ANGELES	IP	H	R	ER	BB	SO	HR	ERA
Valenzuela (W, 1-0)	9	9	4	4	7	6	2	4.00

IBB: Milbourne 2 (by Valenzuela), Monday (by Frazier). **HBP:** Guerrero (by Righetti). **Pitches-strikes:** Righetti 62-37, Frazier 37-21, May 26-19, Davis 10-7, Valenzuela 147-92. **Ground balls-fly balls:** Righetti 1-3, Frazier 4-1, May 3-2, Davis 1-1, Valenzuela 9-8. **Batters faced:** Righetti 14, Frazier 11, May 9, Davis 4, Valenzuela 40. **UMPIRES:** hp—Cooney, 1b—Harvey, 2b—Garcia, 3b—Stello, lf—Barnett, rf—Colosi **T:** 3:04 **A:** 56,236

GAME 4 Los Angeles 8 New York 7
Dodger Stadium 10/24/81

NY YANKEES	AB	R	H	HR	RBI	BB	AVG
Randolph 2b	5	3	2	1	1	1	.167
Milbourne ss	4	1	1	0	1	0	.286
Winfield cf-lf-cf	4	0	0	0	0	1	.000
Jackson rf	3	2	3	1	1	2	1.000
Gamble lf	4	1	2	0	1	0	.333
a-Brown pr-cf	0	0	0	0	0	0	.000
b-Piniella ph-lf	1	0	0	0	0	0	.364
Watson 1b	3	0	1	0	2	1	.500
Cerone c	5	0	2	0	1	0	.286
e-Robertson pr	0	0	0	0	0	0	.000
Rodriguez 3b	4	0	2	0	0	0	.500
c-Foote ph	1	0	0	0	0	0	.000
Reuschel p	2	0	0	0	0	0	.000
May p	1	0	0	0	0	0	.000
Davis p	0	0	0	0	0	0	.000
Frazier p	1	0	0	0	0	0	.000
John p	0	0	0	0	0	0	.000
d-Murcer ph	1	0	0	0	0	0	.000
TOTALS	**39**	**7**	**13**	**2**	**7**	**5**	**.270**

a - Ran for Gamble in the 6th
b - Batted for Brown in the 8th
c - Batted for Rodriguez in the 9th
d - Batted for John in the 9th e - Ran for Cerone in the 9th

BATTING: 2B: Milbourne (2, Welch). **3B:** Randolph (1, Welch). **HR:** Randolph (1, 2nd off Goltz 0 on, 2 out), Jackson (1, 8th off Howe 0 on, 2 out). **S:** Milbourne. **SF:** Watson. **RBI:** Randolph 1 (2), Milbourne 1 (3), Jackson 1 (1), Gamble 1 (1), Watson 2 (7), Cerone 1 (3). **2-out RBI:** Randolph 1, Jackson 1, Gamble 1, Watson 1, Cerone 1. **Runners left in scoring position, 2 out:** Randolph 1, Watson 2, Cerone 2, Reuschel 2. **Team LOB:** 12 **BASERUNNING: SB:** Winfield (1, 2nd base off Forster/Scioscia). **FIELDING: E:** Jackson (1).

LOS ANGELES	AB	R	H	HR	RBI	BB	AVG
Lopes 2b	5	2	2	0	2	0	.267
Russell ss	5	0	1	0	1	0	.235
Garvey 1b	5	1	3	0	0	0	.500
Cey 3b	5	0	2	0	2	0	.333
Baker lf	5	1	1	0	0	0	.133
Monday rf	3	1	1	0	0	1	.200
Thomas cf	1	0	0	0	0	0	.000
Guerrero cf-rf	3	0	2	0	0	1	.231
Scioscia c	1	1	0	0	0	1	.250
d-Yeager ph-c	0	0	0	0	1	0	.167
Welch p	0	0	0	0	0	0	.000
Goltz p	0	0	0	0	0	0	.000
a-Landreaux ph	1	1	1	0	0	0	.200
Forster p	0	0	0	0	0	0	.000
b-Smith ph	1	0	0	0	0	0	.500
Niedenfuer p	0	0	0	0	0	0	.000
c-Johnstone ph	1	1	1	1	2	0	.667
Howe p	0	0	0	0	0	0	.000
TOTALS	**36**	**8**	**14**	**1**	**8**	**3**	**.262**

a - Batted for Goltz in the 3th
b - Batted for Forster in the 4th
c - Batted for Niedenfuer in the 6th
d - Batted for Scioscia in the 7th

BATTING: 2B: Landreaux (1, Reuschel), Garvey (1, May), Monday (1, Frazier). **HR:** Johnstone (1, 6th off Davis 1 on, 1 out). **S:** Scioscia, Howe. **SF:** Yeager. **RBI:** Lopes 2 (2), Russell 1 (1), Cey 2 (5), Yeager 1 (2), Johnstone 2 (3). **2-out RBI:** Lopes 1. **Runners left in scoring position, 2 out:** Lopes 2, Russell 1, Baker 1. **Team LOB:** 10 **BASERUNNING: SB:** Lopes 2 (2, 2nd base off Reuschel/Cerone, 3rd base off Davis/Cerone). **FIELDING: E:** Russell (1). **Outfield assists:** Guerrero (1).

NY YANKEES	IP	H	R	ER	BB	SO	HR	ERA
Reuschel	3	6	2	2	1	2	0	6.00
May	1.1	2	1	1	0	1	0	2.08
Davis	1	2	3	2	1	2	1	18.00
Frazier (L, 0-2)	0.2	2	2	2	1	0	0	13.50
John	2	2	0	0	0	2	0	0.00

LOS ANGELES	IP	H	R	ER	BB	SO	HR	ERA
Welch	0	3	2	2	1	0	0	0.00
Goltz	3	4	2	2	1	2	1	5.40
Forster	1	1	0	0	2	0	0	0.00
Niedenfuer	2	2	2	0	1	0	0	0.00
Howe (W, 1-0)	3	3	1	1	0	1	1	8.10

IBB: Jackson (by Niedenfuer), Guerrero (by Frazier). **Pitches-strikes:** Reuschel 57-32, May 16-11, Davis 26-18, Frazier 22-12, John 32-18, Welch 16-6, Goltz 59-44, Forster 26-13, Niedenfuer 35-23, Howe 33-22. **Ground balls-fly balls:** Reuschel 3-4, May 1-1, Davis 0-2, Frazier 0-2, John 1-1, Welch 0-0, Goltz 5-1, Forster 2-0, Niedenfuer 1-6, Howe 4-4. **Batters faced:** Reuschel 16, May 6, Davis 7, Frazier 5, John 8, Welch 4, Goltz 14, Forster 6, Niedenfuer 10, Howe 12. **UMPIRES:** hp—Harvey, 1b—Garcia, 2b—Stello, 3b—Barnett, lf—Colosi, rf—Cooney **T:** 3:32 **A:** 56,242

GAME 5 Los Angeles 2 New York 1
Dodger Stadium 10/25/81

NY YANKEES	AB	R	H	HR	RBI	BB	AVG
Randolph 2b	3	0	0	0	0	1	.133
Milbourne ss	4	0	1	0	0	0	.278
Winfield cf-lf	4	0	1	0	0	0	.056
Jackson rf	4	1	1	0	0	0	.571
Gossage p	0	0	0	0	0	0	.000
Watson 1b	3	0	0	0	0	1	.412
Piniella lf-rf	4	0	2	0	1	0	.400
a-Brown pr	0	0	0	0	0	0	.000
Cerone c	4	0	0	0	0	0	.222
Rodriguez 3b	3	0	0	0	0	1	.364
Guidry p	3	0	0	0	0	0	.000
Mumphrey cf	0	0	0	0	0	0	.200
TOTALS	**32**	**1**	**5**	**0**	**1**	**3**	**.247**

a - Ran for Piniella in the 9th

BATTING: 2B: Jackson (1, Reuss). **RBI:** Piniella 1 (2). **Runners left in scoring position, 2 out:** Randolph 2, Jackson 1, Rodriguez 1. **GIDP:** Cerone, Jackson. **Team LOB:** 7

LOS ANGELES	AB	R	H	HR	RBI	BB	AVG
Lopes 2b	3	0	0	0	0	1	.222
Russell ss	4	0	0	0	0	0	.190
Garvey 1b	4	0	1	0	0	0	.450
Cey 3b	2	0	0	0	0	1	.294
a-Landreaux pr-cf	0	0	0	0	0	0	.200
Baker lf	4	0	0	0	0	0	.105
Guerrero rf	3	1	1	1	1	0	.250
Yeager c	3	1	2	1	1	0	.333
Thomas cf-3b	3	0	0	0	0	0	.000
Reuss p	2	0	0	0	0	1	.000
TOTALS	**28**	**2**	**4**	**2**	**2**	**3**	**.241**

a - Ran for Cey in the 8th

BATTING: 2B: Yeager (1, Guidry). **HR:** Guerrero (1, 7th off Guidry 0 on, 1 out), Yeager (2, 7th off Guidry 0 on, 1 out). **RBI:** Guerrero 1 (2), Yeager 1 (3). **Runners left in scoring position, 2 out:** Baker 3, Reuss 1. **Team LOB:** 6 **BASERUNNING: SB:** Landreaux (1, 2nd base off Gossage/Cerone), Lopes (3, 2nd base off Gossage/Cerone). **FIELDING: E:** Lopes 2 (4). **DP:** 2 (Russell-Lopes-Garvey, Lopes-Garvey).

NY YANKEES	IP	H	R	ER	BB	SO	HR	ERA
Guidry (L, 1-1)	7	4	2	2	2	9	2	1.93
Gossage	1	0	0	0	1	0	0	0.00

LOS ANGELES	IP	H	R	ER	BB	SO	HR	ERA
Reuss (W, 1-1)	9	5	1	1	3	6	0	3.86

IBB: Rodriguez (by Reuss). **HBP:** Cey (by Gossage). **Pitches-strikes:** Guidry 99-70, Gossage 20-15, Reuss 108-74. **Ground balls-fly balls:** Guidry 3-9, Gossage 1-2, Reuss 16-5. **Batters faced:** Guidry 27, Gossage 5, Reuss 35. **UMPIRES:** hp—Garcia, 1b—Stello, 2b—Barnett, 3b—Colosi, lf—Cooney, rf—Harvey **T:** 2:19 **A:** 56,115

GAME 6 Los Angeles 9 New York 2
Yankee Stadium 10/28/81

LOS ANGELES	AB	R	H	HR	RBI	BB	AVG
Lopes 2b	4	2	1	0	0	2	.227
Russell ss	4	0	2	0	1	0	.240
Garvey 1b	4	1	1	0	0	1	.417
Cey 3b	3	1	2	0	1	0	.350
a-Thomas ph-3b	2	1	0	0	1	0	.000
Baker lf	5	2	2	0	0	0	.167
Guerrero cf-rf	5	1	3	1	5	0	.333
Monday rf	3	0	1	0	0	1	.231
Landreaux cf	1	0	0	0	0	0	.167
Yeager c	5	0	1	0	1	0	.286
Hooton p	2	1	0	0	0	1	.000
Howe p	2	0	0	0	0	0	.000
TOTALS	**40**	**9**	**13**	**1**	**9**	**5**	**.258**

a - Batted for Cey in the 6th

BATTING: 3B: Guerrero (1, Frazier). **HR:** Guerrero (2, 8th off May 0 on, 2 out). **S:** Russell. **RBI:** Russell 1 (2), Cey 1 (6), Thomas 1 (1), Guerrero 5 (7), Yeager 1 (4). **2-out RBI:** Cey 1, Guerrero 5, Yeager 1. **Runners left in scoring position, 2 out:** Garvey 1, Baker 1, Monday 1, Yeager 2, Hooton 1. **Team LOB:** 10 **BASERUNNING: SB:** Lopes (4, 3rd base off Reuschel/Cerone), Russell (1, 3rd base off Reuschel/Cerone). **CS:** Russell (1, 2nd base off John/Cerone). **FIELDING: E:** Lopes (5).

NY YANKEES	AB	R	H	HR	RBI	BB	AVG
Randolph 2b	3	1	2	1	1	2	.222
Mumphrey cf	5	0	1	0	0	0	.200
Winfield lf	4	0	0	0	0	1	.045
Jackson rf	5	0	0	0	0	0	.333
Watson 1b	5	0	0	0	0	0	.318
Nettles 3b	3	0	2	0	0	0	.400
b-Rodriguez pr-3b	1	1	1	0	0	0	.417
Cerone c	3	0	0	0	0	1	.190
Milbourne ss	2	0	0	0	0	2	.250
John p	1	0	0	0	0	0	.000
a-Murcer ph	1	0	0	0	0	0	.000
Frazier p	0	0	0	0	0	0	.000
Davis p	0	0	0	0	0	0	.000
Reuschel p	0	0	0	0	0	0	.000
c-Gamble ph	0	0	0	0	0	0	.333
d-Piniella ph	1	0	1	0	1	0	.438
May p	0	0	0	0	0	0	.000
e-Brown ph	1	0	0	0	0	0	.000
LaRoche p	0	0	0	0	0	0	.000
TOTALS	**35**	**2**	**7**	**1**	**2**	**6**	**.238**

a - Batted for John in the 4th
b - Ran for Nettles in the 6th
c - Batted for Reuschel in the 6th
d - Batted for Gamble in the 6th e - Batted for May in the 8th

BATTING: 2B: Nettles (1, Hooton), Randolph (1, Hooton). **HR:** Randolph (2, 3th off Hooton 0 on, 2 out). **RBI:** Randolph 1 (3), Piniella 1 (3). **2-out RBI:** Randolph 1. **Runners left in scoring position, 2 out:** Mumphrey 2, Jackson 3, Watson 1, Murcer 1. **Team LOB:** 12 **BASERUNNING: SB:** Randolph (1, 2nd base off Hooton/Yeager). **FIELDING: E:** Milbourne (2), Nettles (1).

LOS ANGELES	IP	H	R	ER	BB	SO	HR	ERA
Hooton (W, 1-1)	5.1	5	2	2	5	2	1	1.59
Howe (S, 1)	3.2	2	0	0	1	3	0	3.86

NY YANKEES	IP	H	R	ER	BB	SO	HR	ERA
John	4	6	1	1	0	2	0	0.69
Frazier (L, 0-3)	1	4	3	3	0	1	0	17.18
Davis	0.1	1	3	2	2	1	0	23.14
Reuschel	0.2	1	1	0	2	0	0	4.91
May	2	1	1	1	1	2	1	2.84
LaRoche	1	0	0	0	0	2	0	0.00

IBB: Milbourne (by Hooton), Garvey (by Reuschel), Monday (by Reuschel). **Pitches-strikes:** Hooton 104-59, Howe 54-37, John 48-33, Frazier 17-13, Davis 19-8, Reuschel 23-11, May 24-14, LaRoche 16-11. **Ground balls-fly balls:** Hooton 7-7, Howe 3-6, John 6-4, Frazier 0-1, Davis 0-0, Reuschel 3-0, May 2-2, LaRoche 0-1. **Batters faced:** Hooton 26, Howe 15, John 18, Frazier 7, Davis 4, Reuschel 6, May 8, LaRoche 3. **UMPIRES:** hp—Stello, 1b—Barnett, 2b—Colosi, 3b—Cooney, lf—Harvey, rf—Garcia **T:** 3:09 **A:** 56,513

1982 ST. LOUIS DEF. MILWAUKEE, 4-3

GAME 1 Milwaukee 10 St. Louis 0
Busch Stadium 10/12/82

MILWAUKEE	AB	R	H	HR	RBI	BB	AVG
Molitor 3b	6	1	5	0	2	0	.833
Yount ss	6	1	4	0	2	0	.667
Cooper 1b	4	1	0	0	0	1	.000
Simmons c	5	1	2	1	1	0	.400
Oglivie lf	4	1	0	0	0	1	.000
Thomas cf	4	0	1	0	1	1	.250
Howell dh	2	0	0	0	0	0	.000
a-Money ph	2	1	1	0	1	0	.500
Moore rf	5	2	2	0	0	0	.400
Gantner 2b	4	2	2	0	2	0	.500
TOTALS	**42**	**10**	**17**	**1**	**9**	**3**	**.405**

a - Batted for Howell in the 7th

BATTING: 2B: Moore (1, Forsch), Yount (1, Forsch). **3B:** Gantner (1, Lahti). **HR:** Simmons (1, 5th off Forsch 0 on, 1 out). **S:** Gantner. **RBI:** Molitor 2 (2), Yount 2 (2), Simmons 1 (1), Thomas 1 (1), Money 1 (1), Gantner 2 (2). **2-out RBI:** Molitor 1, Yount 2, Thomas 1, Money 1, Gantner 2. **Runners left in scoring position, 2 out:** Cooper 2, Simmons 1, Moore 2. **GIDP:** Oglivie. **Team LOB:** 10

ST.LOUIS	AB	R	H	HR	RBI	BB	AVG
Herr 2b	3	0	0	0	0	1	.000
L.Smith lf	4	0	0	0	0	0	.000
Hernandez 1b	4	0	0	0	0	0	.000
Hendrick rf	4	0	0	0	0	0	.000
Tenace dh	3	0	0	0	0	0	.000
Porter c	3	0	2	0	0	0	.667
Green cf	3	0	0	0	0	0	.000
Oberkfell 3b	3	0	1	0	0	0	.333
O.Smith ss	3	0	0	0	0	0	.000
TOTALS	**30**	**0**	**3**	**0**	**0**	**1**	**.100**

BATTING: 2B: Porter (1, Caldwell). **Runners left in scoring position, 2 out:** Herr 1, Green 1. **Team LOB:** 4 **FIELDING: E:** Hernandez (1). **DP:** 1 (Hernandez-O.Smith-Hernandez).

MILWAUKEE	IP	H	R	ER	BB	SO	HR	ERA
Caldwell (W, 1-0)	9	3	0	0	1	3	0	0.00

ST.LOUIS	IP	H	R	ER	BB	SO	HR	ERA
Forsch (L, 0-1)	5.2	10	6	4	1	1	1	6.35
Kaat	1.1	1	0	0	1	1	0	0.00
LaPoint	1.2	3	2	2	1	0	0	10.80
Lahti	0.1	3	2	2	0	1	0	54.00

HBP: Howell (by Forsch). **Pitches-strikes:** Caldwell 100-66, Forsch 88-58, Kaat 16-9, LaPoint 29-19, Lahti 13-12. **Ground balls-fly balls:** Caldwell 14-10, Forsch 10-5, Kaat 1-1, LaPoint 3-2, Lahti 0-0. **Batters faced:** Caldwell 31, Forsch 29, Kaat 5, LaPoint 9, Lahti 4. **UMPIRES:** hp—Weyer, 1b—Haller, 2b—Kibler, 3b—Phillips, lf—Davidson, rf—Evans **T:** 2:30 **A:** 53,723

GAME 2 St. Louis 5 Milwaukee 4
Busch Stadium 10/13/82

MILWAUKEE	AB	R	H	HR	RBI	BB	AVG
Molitor 3b	5	1	2	0	0	0	.636
Yount ss	4	1	1	0	1	1	.500
Cooper 1b	5	0	3	0	1	0	.333
Simmons c	3	1	1	1	1	1	.375
Oglivie lf	4	0	1	0	0	0	.125
Thomas cf	3	0	0	0	0	1	.143
Howell dh	4	1	0	0	0	0	.000
Moore rf	4	0	2	0	1	0	.444
Gantner 2b	3	0	0	0	0	1	.286
TOTALS	**35**	**4**	**10**	**1**	**4**	**4**	**.351**

BATTING: 2B: Moore (2, Stuper), Yount (2, Stuper), Cooper (1, Bair). **HR:** Simmons (2, 3th off Stuper 0 on, 2 out). **RBI:** Yount 1 (3), Cooper 1 (1), Simmons 1 (2), Moore 1 (1). **2-out RBI:** Simmons 1, Moore 1. **Runners left in scoring position, 2 out:** Oglivie 1, Gantner 1. **GIDP:** Simmons. **Team LOB:** 8 **BASERUNNING: SB:** Molitor (1, 2nd base off Stuper/Porter). **CS:** Molitor (1, 2nd base off Sutter/Porter). **FIELDING: E:** Oglivie (1).

ST.LOUIS	AB	R	H	HR	RBI	BB	AVG
Herr 2b	3	1	1	0	1	1	.167
Oberkfell 3b	3	1	2	0	1	0	.500
b-Tenace ph	1	0	0	0	0	0	.000
Ramsey 3b	0	0	0	0	0	0	.000
Hernandez 1b	3	0	0	0	0	1	.000
Hendrick rf	3	2	0	0	0	1	.000
Porter c	4	0	2	0	2	0	.571
L.Smith lf	3	0	0	0	0	1	.000
Iorg dh	2	0	1	0	0	0	.500
a-Green ph	1	0	0	0	0	0	.000
c-Braun ph	0	0	0	0	1	1	.000
McGee cf	4	1	0	0	0	0	.000
O.Smith ss	4	0	2	0	0	0	.286
TOTALS	**31**	**5**	**8**	**0**	**5**	**5**	**.180**

a - Batted for Iorg in the 7th
b - Batted for Oberkfell in the 7th
c - Batted for Green in the 8th

BATTING: 2B: Herr (1, Sutton), Porter (2, Sutton). **RBI:** Herr 1 (1), Oberkfell 1 (1), Porter 2 (2), Braun 1 (1). **2-out RBI:** Herr 1, Oberkfell 1, Porter 2. **Runners left in scoring position, 2 out:** Tenace 1, L.Smith 1, O.Smith 2. **Team LOB:** 7 **BASERUNNING: SB:** McGee (1, 2nd base off Sutton/Simmons), Oberkfell (1, 2nd base off Sutton/Simmons), O.Smith (1, 2nd base off McClure/Simmons). **FIELDING: DP:** 1 (Hernandez-O.Smith-Hernandez).

MILWAUKEE	IP	H	R	ER	BB	SO	HR	ERA
Sutton	6	5	4	4	1	3	0	6.00
McClure (L, 0-1)	1.1	2	1	1	2	2	0	6.75
Ladd	0.2	1	0	0	2	0	0	0.00

ST.LOUIS	IP	H	R	ER	BB	SO	HR	ERA
Stuper	4	6	4	4	3	3	1	9.00
Kaat	0.2	1	0	0	0	0	0	0.00
Bair	2	1	0	0	0	3	0	0.00
Sutter (W, 1-0)	2.1	2	0	0	1	1	0	0.00

WP: Stuper 2. **IBB:** Simmons (by Sutter). **Pitches-strikes:** Sutton 89-56, McClure 37-20, Ladd 14-5, Stuper 74-42, Kaat 10-6, Bair 31-21, Sutter 29-20. **Ground balls-fly balls:** Sutton 8-7, McClure 1-1, Ladd 0-1, Stuper 6-2, Kaat 0-2, Bair 0-3, Sutter 3-2. **Batters faced:** Sutton 24, McClure 8, Ladd 4, Stuper 20, Kaat 3, Bair 7,

Sutter 9. **UMPIRES:** hp—Haller, 1b—Kibler, 2b—Phillips, 3b—Davidson, lf—Evans, rf—Weyer **T:** 2:54 **A:** 53,723

GAME 3 St. Louis 6 Milwaukee 2
County Stadium 10/15/82

ST.LOUIS	AB	R	H	HR	RBI	BB	AVG
Herr 2b	5	0	0	0	0	0	.091
Oberkfell 3b	4	0	0	0	0	0	.300
Hernandez 1b	4	0	0	0	0	0	.000
Hendrick rf	2	1	1	0	0	1	.111
Porter c	4	0	0	0	0	0	.364
L.Smith lf	4	2	2	0	1	0	.182
Green lf	0	0	0	0	0	0	.000
Iorg dh	4	1	1	0	0	0	.333
McGee cf	3	2	2	2	4	1	.286
O.Smith ss	3	0	0	0	1	1	.200
TOTALS	**33**	**6**	**6**	**2**	**6**	**3**	**.181**

BATTING: 2B: L.Smith (1, Vuckovich), Iorg (1, Vuckovich). **3B:** L.Smith (1, Vuckovich). **HR:** McGee 2 (2, 5th off Vuckovich 2 on, 1 out, 7th off Vuckovich 0 on, 2 out). **RBI:** L.Smith 1 (1), McGee 4 (4), O.Smith 1 (1). **2-out RBI:** McGee 1, O.Smith 1. **Runners left in scoring position, 2 out:** Herr 2, Iorg 1. **Team LOB:** 4 **BASERUNNING: CS:** Hendrick (1, 2nd base off Vuckovich/Simmons). **FIELDING: E:** Hernandez (2). **DP:** 1 (Herr-O.Smith-Hernandez).

MILWAUKEE	AB	R	H	HR	RBI	BB	AVG
Molitor 3b	4	0	0	0	0	0	.467
Yount ss	3	1	0	0	0	1	.385
Cooper 1b	4	1	1	1	2	0	.308
Simmons c	4	0	1	0	0	0	.333
Oglivie lf	4	0	0	0	0	0	.083
Thomas cf	4	0	1	0	0	0	.182
Howell dh	2	0	0	0	0	0	.000
a-Money ph	1	0	0	0	0	1	.333
Moore rf	3	0	0	0	0	1	.333
Gantner 2b	3	0	2	0	0	0	.400
TOTALS	**32**	**2**	**5**	**1**	**2**	**3**	**.294**

a - Batted for Howell in the 7th

BATTING: 2B: Gantner (1, Andujar). **HR:** Cooper (1, 8th off Sutter 1 on, 2 out). **RBI:** Cooper 2 (3). **2-out RBI:** Cooper 2. **Runners left in scoring position, 2 out:** Yount 2, Moore 2. **GIDP:** Yount. **Team LOB:** 6 **FIELDING: E:** Cooper (1), Gantner (1), Simmons (1).

ST.LOUIS	IP	H	R	ER	BB	SO	HR	ERA
Andujar (W, 1-0)	6.1	3	0	0	1	3	0	0.00
Kaat	0.1	1	0	0	0	1	0	0.00
Bair	0	0	0	0	1	0	0	0.00
Sutter (S, 1)	2.1	1	2	2	1	1	1	3.86

MILWAUKEE	IP	H	R	ER	BB	SO	HR	ERA
Vuckovich (L, 0-1)	8.2	6	6	4	3	1	2	4.15
McClure	0.1	0	0	0	0	0	0	5.40

IBB: McGee (by Vuckovich). **Pitches-strikes:** Andujar 79-51, Kaat 11-6, Bair 6-2, Sutter 38-26, Vuckovich 122-70, McClure 2-2. **Ground balls-fly balls:** Andujar 7-8, Kaat 0-0, Bair 0-0, Sutter 2-5, Vuckovich 13-12, McClure 1-0. **Batters faced:** Andujar 22, Kaat 2, Bair 1, Sutter 10, Vuckovich 36, McClure 1. **UMPIRES:** hp—Kibler, 1b—Phillips, 2b—Davidson, 3b—Evans, lf—Weyer, rf—Haller **T:** 2:53 **A:** 56,556

GAME 4 Milwaukee 7 St. Louis 5
County Stadium 10/16/82

ST.LOUIS	AB	R	H	HR	RBI	BB	AVG
Herr 2b	4	0	0	0	2	0	.067
Oberkfell 3b	2	2	1	0	0	2	.333
b-Tenace ph	1	0	0	0	0	0	.000
Hernandez 1b	4	0	0	0	0	0	.000
Hendrick rf	4	0	1	0	1	0	.154
Porter c	3	0	1	0	0	1	.357
L.Smith lf	4	1	1	0	0	0	.200
Iorg dh	4	0	2	0	1	0	.400
a-Green pr	0	0	0	0	0	0	.000
McGee cf	4	1	1	0	0	0	.273
O.Smith ss	3	1	1	0	0	1	.231
TOTALS	**33**	**5**	**8**	**0**	**4**	**4**	**.197**

a - Ran for Iorg in the 8th
b - Batted for Oberkfell in the 9th

BATTING: 2B: Oberkfell (1, Haas), L.Smith (2, Haas), Iorg (2, Haas). **SF:** Herr. **RBI:** Herr 2 (3), Hendrick 1 (1), Iorg 1 (1). **2-out RBI:** Hendrick 1. **Runners left in scoring position, 2 out:** Herr 1, Hendrick 1, L.Smith 1. **GIDP:** Hernandez, McGee. **Team LOB:** 6 **BASERUNNING: SB:** McGee (2, 2nd base off Haas/Simmons), Oberkfell (2, 2nd base off Haas/Simmons). **FIELDING: DP:** 2 (Herr-Hernandez, O.Smith-Hernandez).

MILWAUKEE	AB	R	H	HR	RBI	BB	AVG
Molitor 3b	4	1	0	0	0	1	.368
Yount ss	4	1	2	0	2	0	.412
Cooper 1b	4	1	2	0	1	0	.353
Simmons c	2	0	0	0	0	2	.286
Thomas cf	4	0	1	0	2	0	.200
Oglivie lf	3	1	1	0	0	1	.133
Money dh	4	2	2	0	0	0	.429
Moore rf	4	0	1	0	0	0	.313
Gantner 2b	4	1	1	0	2	0	.357
TOTALS	**33**	**7**	**10**	**0**	**7**	**4**	**.296**

BATTING: 2B: Money (1, LaPoint), Gantner (2, LaPoint). **3B:** Oglivie (1, LaPoint). **RBI:** Yount 2 (5), Cooper 1 (4), Thomas 2 (3), Gantner 2 (4). **2-out RBI:** Yount 2, Cooper 1, Thomas 2, Gantner 1. **Runners left in scoring position, 2 out:** Oglivie 1, Money 3. **GIDP:** Gantner. **Team LOB:** 6 **FIELDING: E:** Gantner (2), Yount (1). **DP:** 2 (Gantner-Yount-Cooper, Gantner-Cooper).

ST.LOUIS	IP	H	R	ER	BB	SO	HR	ERA
LaPoint	6.2	7	4	1	1	3	0	3.24
Bair (L, 0-1)	0	1	2	2	1	0	0	9.00
Kaat	0	1	1	1	1	0	0	3.86
Lahti	1.1	1	0	0	1	0	0	10.80

MILWAUKEE	IP	H	R	ER	BB	SO	HR	ERA
Haas	5.1	7	5	4	2	3	0	6.75
Slaton (W, 1-0)	2	1	0	0	2	1	0	0.00
McClure (S, 1)	1.2	0	0	0	0	2	0	2.70

WP: Kaat 1, Haas 1. **IBB:** Simmons (by Lahti), Oglivie (by Lahti). **Pitches-strikes:** LaPoint 85-57, Bair 9-3, Kaat 9-3, Lahti 26-15, Haas 102-63, Slaton 28-17, McClure 15-10. **Ground balls-fly balls:** LaPoint 7-9, Bair 0-0, Kaat 0-0, Lahti 1-3, Haas 6-6, Slaton 3-2, McClure 2-0. **Batters faced:** LaPoint 27, Bair 2, Kaat 2, Lahti 6, Haas 25, Slaton 9, McClure 4. **UMPIRES:** hp—Phillips, 1b—Davidson, 2b—Evans, 3b—Weyer, lf—Haller, rf—Kibler **T:** 3:04 **A:** 56,560

GAME 5 Milwaukee 6 St. Louis 4
County Stadium 10/17/82

ST.LOUIS	AB	R	H	HR	RBI	BB	AVG
L.Smith dh	5	0	2	0	0	0	.250
Green lf	5	2	2	0	0	0	.222
Hernandez 1b	4	1	3	0	2	1	.158
Hendrick rf	5	0	3	0	2	0	.278
Porter c	5	0	1	0	0	0	.316
a-Ramsey pr	0	0	0	0	0	0	.000
McGee cf	5	0	1	0	0	0	.250
Oberkfell 3b	4	0	3	0	0	0	.438
b-Tenace ph	1	0	0	0	0	0	.000
Herr 2b	4	0	0	0	0	0	.053
O.Smith ss	3	1	0	0	0	1	.188
TOTALS	**41**	**4**	**15**	**0**	**4**	**2**	**.238**

a - Ran for Porter in the 9th
b - Batted for Oberkfell in the 9th

BATTING: 2B: Hernandez 2 (2, Caldwell), Green (1, Caldwell). **3B:** Green (1, Caldwell). **RBI:** Hernandez 2 (2), Hendrick 2 (3). **2-out RBI:** Hernandez 1, Hendrick 1. **Runners left in scoring position, 2 out:** Porter 2, Tenace 1. **GIDP:** O.Smith. **Team LOB:** 12 **BASERUNNING: SB:** L.Smith (1, 2nd base off Caldwell/Simmons). **CS:** L.Smith (1, 3rd base off Caldwell/Simmons). **FIELDING: E:** Forsch (1), Herr (1). **DP:** 2 (Porter-Herr, Oberkfell-Herr-Hernandez).

MILWAUKEE	AB	R	H	HR	RBI	BB	AVG
Molitor 3b	4	1	1	0	1	1	.348
Yount ss	4	2	4	1	1	0	.524
Cooper 1b	4	0	1	0	1	0	.333
Simmons c	3	0	0	0	1	1	.235
Oglivie lf	4	1	2	0	0	0	.211
Thomas cf	4	0	0	0	0	0	.158
Money dh	3	1	0	0	0	1	.300
Moore rf	4	1	2	0	1	0	.350
Gantner 2b	4	0	1	0	1	0	.333
TOTALS	**34**	**6**	**11**	**1**	**6**	**3**	**.301**

BATTING: 2B: Yount (3, Forsch), Moore (3, Forsch). **HR:** Yount (1, 7th off Forsch 0 on, 2 out). **RBI:** Molitor 1 (3), Yount 1 (6), Cooper 1 (5), Simmons 1 (3), Moore 1 (2), Gantner 1 (5). **2-out RBI:** Yount 1, Moore 1, Gantner 1. **Runners left in scoring position, 2 out:** Molitor 1, Simmons 1, Oglivie 3. **GIDP:** Money. **Team LOB:** 7 **BASERUNNING: CS:** Oglivie (1, 2nd base off Forsch/Porter). **FIELDING: E:** Gantner (3). **DP:** 1 (Molitor-Cooper).

ST.LOUIS	IP	H	R	ER	BB	SO	HR	ERA
Forsch (L, 0-2)	7	8	4	3	2	3	1	4.97
Sutter	1	3	2	2	1	2	0	6.35

MILWAUKEE	IP	H	R	ER	BB	SO	HR	ERA
Caldwell (W, 2-0)	8.1	14	4	4	2	3	0	2.08
McClure (S, 2)	0.2	1	0	0	0	1	0	2.25

Pitches-strikes: Forsch 118-71, Sutter 24-15, Caldwell 131-84, McClure 5-5. **Ground balls-fly balls:** Forsch 7-10, Sutter 1-0, Caldwell 17-4, McClure 0-1. **Batters faced:** Forsch 30, Sutter 7, Caldwell 40, McClure 3. **UMPIRES:** hp—Davidson, 1b—Evans, 2b—Weyer, 3b—Haller, lf—Kibler, rf—Phillips **T:** 3:02 **A:** 56,562

GAME 6 St. Louis 13 Milwaukee 1
Busch Stadium 10/19/82

MILWAUKEE	AB	R	H	HR	RBI	BB	AVG
Molitor 3b	4	0	1	0	0	0	.333
Yount ss	4	0	0	0	0	0	.440
Cooper 1b	4	0	0	0	0	0	.280
Simmons c	2	0	0	0	0	1	.211
Yost c	0	0	0	0	0	1	.000
Oglivie lf	4	0	1	0	0	0	.217
Thomas cf	3	0	0	0	0	0	.136
a-Edwards pr-cf	0	0	0	0	0	0	.000
Money dh	3	0	0	0	0	0	.231
Moore rf	3	0	1	0	0	0	.348
Gantner 2b	3	1	1	0	0	0	.333
TOTALS	**30**	**1**	**4**	**0**	**0**	**2**	**.277**

a - Ran for Thomas in the 8th

BATTING: 2B: Gantner (3, Stuper). **Runners left in scoring position, 2 out:** Oglivie 1. **GIDP:** Money, Molitor. **Team LOB:** 4 **FIELDING: E:** Yount 2 (3), Gantner 2 (5).

ST.LOUIS	AB	R	H	HR	RBI	BB	AVG
L.Smith lf	3	1	1	0	0	0	.261
Green lf	1	1	0	0	0	1	.200
Oberkfell 3b	5	1	0	0	0	0	.333
Hernandez 1b	5	2	2	1	4	0	.208
Hendrick rf	5	2	2	0	1	0	.304
Porter c	4	1	1	1	2	0	.304
Brummer c	0	0	0	0	0	0	.000
Iorg dh	4	3	3	0	0	0	.500
McGee cf	4	1	1	0	1	0	.250
Herr 2b	3	1	2	0	2	0	.136
O.Smith ss	4	0	0	0	0	0	.150
TOTALS	**38**	**13**	**12**	**2**	**10**	**1**	**.252**

BATTING: 2B: Iorg 2 (4, Sutton, Medich), Herr (2, Sutton). **3B:** Iorg (1, Sutton). **HR:** Porter (1, 4th off Sutton 1 on, 0 out), Hernandez (1, 5th off Sutton 1 on, 1 out). **S:** L.Smith, Herr. **RBI:** Hernandez 4 (6), Hendrick 1 (4), Porter 2 (4), McGee 1 (5), Herr 2 (5). **2-out RBI:** Hernandez 2, Hendrick 1, Herr 1. **Runners left in scoring position, 2 out:** O.Smith 1. **Team LOB:** 3 **BASERUNNING: SB:** L.Smith (2, 2nd base off Sutton/Simmons). **FIELDING: E:** Oberkfell (1). **DP:** 2 (Oberkfell-Herr-Hernandez, Herr-O.Smith-Hernandez).

MILWAUKEE	IP	H	R	ER	BB	SO	HR	ERA
Sutton (L, 0-1)	4.1	7	7	5	0	2	2	7.84
Slaton	0.2	0	0	0	0	0	0	0.00
Medich	2	5	6	4	1	0	0	18.00
Bernard	1	0	0	0	0	1	0	0.00

ST.LOUIS	IP	H	R	ER	BB	SO	HR	ERA
Stuper (W, 1-0)	9	4	1	1	2	2	0	3.46

WP: Medich 2, Stuper 1. **BK:** Sutton 1. **Pitches-strikes:** Sutton 67-45, Slaton 3-3, Medich 39-21, Bernard 13-10, Stuper 104-66. **Ground balls-fly balls:** Sutton 9-2, Slaton 0-2, Medich 3-4, Bernard 2-1, Stuper 9-15. **Batters faced:** Sutton 21, Slaton 2, Medich 13, Bernard 4, Stuper 32. **UMPIRES:** hp—Evans, 1b—Weyer, 2b—Haller, 3b—Kibler, lf—Phillips, rf—Davidson **T:** 2:21 **A:** 53,723

GAME 7 St. Louis 6 Milwaukee 3
Busch Stadium 10/20/82

MILWAUKEE	AB	R	H	HR	RBI	BB	AVG
Molitor 3b	4	1	2	0	1	0	.355
Yount ss	4	0	1	0	0	0	.414
Cooper 1b	3	0	1	0	1	0	.286
Simmons c	4	0	0	0	0	0	.174
Oglivie lf	4	1	1	1	1	0	.222
Thomas cf	4	0	0	0	0	0	.115
Howell dh	3	0	0	0	0	0	.000
Moore rf	3	0	1	0	0	0	.346
Gantner 2b	3	1	1	0	0	0	.333
TOTALS	**32**	**3**	**7**	**1**	**3**	**0**	**.269**

BATTING: 2B: Gantner (4, Andujar). **HR:** Oglivie (1, 5th off Andujar 0 on, 0 out). **SF:** Cooper. **RBI:** Molitor 1 (4), Cooper 1 (6), Oglivie 1 (1). **Team LOB:** 3

ST.LOUIS	AB	R	H	HR	RBI	BB	AVG
L.Smith lf	5	2	3	0	1	0	.321
Oberkfell 3b	3	0	0	0	0	0	.292
a-Tenace ph	0	0	0	0	0	1	.000
b-Ramsey pr-3b	1	1	0	0	0	0	.000
Hernandez 1b	3	1	2	0	2	2	.259
Hendrick rf	5	0	2	0	1	0	.321
Porter c	5	0	1	0	1	0	.286
Iorg dh	3	0	2	0	0	0	.529
c-Green ph	0	0	0	0	0	0	.200
d-Braun ph	2	0	1	0	1	0	.500
McGee cf	5	1	1	0	0	0	.240
Herr 2b	3	0	1	0	0	1	.160
O.Smith ss	4	1	2	0	0	0	.208
TOTALS	**39**	**6**	**15**	**0**	**6**	**4**	**.273**

a - Batted for Oberkfell in the 6th
b - Ran for Tenace in the 6th
c - Batted for Iorg in the 6th
d - Batted for Green in the 6th

BATTING: 2B: L.Smith 2 (4, Vuckovich, Haas). **RBI:** L.Smith 1 (2), Hernandez 2 (8), Hendrick 1 (5), Porter 1 (5), Braun 1 (2). **2-out RBI:** Porter 1, Braun 1. **Runners left in scoring position, 2 out:** L.Smith 2, Hernandez 1, Iorg 2, Braun 1, McGee 1. **Team LOB:** 13 **FIELDING: E:** Andujar (1). **Outfield assists:** Hendrick (1).

MILWAUKEE	IP	H	R	ER	BB	SO	HR	ERA
Vuckovich	5.1	10	3	3	2	3	0	4.50
McClure (L, 0-2)	0.1	2	1	1	1	0	0	4.15
Haas	2	1	2	2	1	1	0	7.36
Caldwell	0.1	2	0	0	0	0	0	2.04

ST.LOUIS	IP	H	R	ER	BB	SO	HR	ERA
Andujar (W, 2-0)	7	7	3	2	0	1	1	1.35
Sutter (S, 2)	2	0	0	0	0	2	0	4.70

IBB: Hernandez (by Haas). **Pitches-strikes:** Vuckovich 87-53, McClure 23-12, Haas 23-15, Caldwell 6-5, Andujar 72-52, Sutter 26-20. **Ground balls-fly balls:** Vuckovich 5-8, McClure 1-0, Haas 3-2, Caldwell 1-0, Andujar 12-6, Sutter 4-0. **Batters faced:** Vuckovich 28, McClure 4, Haas 8, Caldwell 3, Andujar 27, Sutter 6. **UMPIRES:** hp—Evans, 1b—Weyer, 2b—Haller, 3b—Kibler, lf—Phillips, rf—Davidson **T:** 2:50 **A:** 53,723

1983 BALTIMORE DEF. PHILADELPHIA, 4-1

GAME 1 Philadelphia 2 Baltimore 1
Memorial Stadium 10/11/83

PHILADELPHIA	AB	R	H	HR	RBI	BB	AVG
Morgan 2b	4	1	2	1	1	0	.500
Rose 1b	4	0	1	0	0	0	.250
Schmidt 3b	4	0	0	0	0	0	.000
Lezcano rf	3	0	0	0	0	0	.000
a-Hayes ph-rf	1	0	0	0	0	0	.000
Matthews lf	3	0	1	0	0	0	.333
Maddox cf	3	1	1	1	1	0	.333
Diaz c	3	0	0	0	0	0	.000
DeJesus ss	3	0	0	0	0	0	.000
Denny p	3	0	0	0	0	0	.000
Holland p	0	0	0	0	0	0	.000
TOTALS	**31**	**2**	**5**	**2**	**2**	**0**	**.161**

a - Batted for Lezcano in the 9th

BATTING: HR: Morgan (1, 6th off McGregor 0 on, 2 out), Maddox (1, 8th off McGregor 0 on, 0 out). **RBI:** Morgan 1 (1), Maddox 1 (1). **2-out RBI:** Morgan 1. **GIDP:** Maddox. **Team LOB:** 2 **BASERUNNING: CS:** Morgan (1, 2nd base off McGregor/Dempsey).

BALTIMORE	AB	R	H	HR	RBI	BB	AVG
Bumbry cf	4	0	1	0	0	0	.250
Stewart p	0	0	0	0	0	0	.000
Martinez p	0	0	0	0	0	0	.000
Dwyer rf	3	1	1	1	1	0	.333
c-Ford ph-rf	1	0	0	0	0	0	.000
Ripken ss	4	0	1	0	0	0	.250
Murray 1b	4	0	1	0	0	0	.250
Lowenstein lf	3	0	1	0	0	0	.333
d-Roenicke ph	1	0	0	0	0	0	.000
Dauer 2b	3	0	0	0	0	0	.000
Cruz 3b	3	0	0	0	0	0	.000
Dempsey c	2	0	0	0	0	0	.000
a-Shelby ph-cf	1	0	0	0	0	0	.000
McGregor p	2	0	0	0	0	0	.000
b-Nolan ph-c	1	0	0	0	0	0	.000
TOTALS	**32**	**1**	**5**	**1**	**1**	**0**	**.156**

a - Batted for Dempsey in the 8th
b - Batted for McGregor in the 8th
c - Batted for Dwyer in the 8th
d - Batted for Lowenstein in the 9th

BATTING: 2B: Bumbry (1, Denny). **HR:** Dwyer (1, 1st off Denny 0 on, 1 out). **RBI:** Dwyer 1 (1). **Runners left in scoring position, 2 out:** Ford 1. **Team LOB:** 4 **FIELDING: E:** Cruz (1). **DP:** 1 (Ripken-Dauer-Murray).

PHILADELPHIA	IP	H	R	ER	BB	SO	HR	ERA
Denny (W, 1-0)	7.2	5	1	1	0	5	1	1.17
Holland (S, 1)	1.1	0	0	0	0	1	0	0.00

BALTIMORE	IP	H	R	ER	BB	SO	HR	ERA
McGregor (L, 0-1)	8	4	2	2	0	6	2	2.25
Stewart	0.2	1	0	0	0	1	0	0.00
Martinez	0.1	0	0	0	0	0	0	0.00

Pitches-strikes: Denny 109-73, Holland 15-10, McGregor 85-63, Stewart 11-6, Martinez 2-2. **Ground balls-fly balls:** Denny 12-6, Holland 0-3, McGregor 7-10, Stewart 0-1, Martinez 1-0. **Batters faced:** Denny 28, Holland 4, McGregor 27, Stewart 3, Martinez 1. **UMPIRES:** hp—Springstead, 1b—Vargo, 2b—Clark, 3b—Pulli, lf—Palermo, rf—Rennert **T:** 2:22 **A:** 52,204

GAME 2 Baltimore 4 Philadelphia 1
Memorial Stadium 10/12/83

PHILADELPHIA	AB	R	H	HR	RBI	BB	AVG
Morgan 2b	4	1	1	0	0	0	.375
Rose 1b	4	0	0	0	0	0	.125
Schmidt 3b	4	0	0	0	0	0	.000
Lefebvre rf	2	0	0	0	1	0	.000
Matthews lf	3	0	1	0	0	0	.333
Gross cf	3	0	0	0	0	0	.000
Diaz c	3	0	1	0	0	0	.167
b-Samuel pr	0	0	0	0	0	0	.000
Virgil c	0	0	0	0	0	0	.000
DeJesus ss	3	0	0	0	0	0	.000
Hudson p	1	0	0	0	0	0	.000
Hernandez p	0	0	0	0	0	0	.000
a-Hayes ph	1	0	0	0	0	0	.000
Andersen p	0	0	0	0	0	0	.000
c-Perez ph	1	0	0	0	0	0	.000
Reed p	0	0	0	0	0	0	.000
TOTALS	**29**	**1**	**3**	**0**	**1**	**0**	**.133**

a - Batted for Hernandez in the 6th
b - Ran for Diaz in the 8th
c - Batted for Andersen in the 8th

BATTING: SF: Lefebvre. **RBI:** Lefebvre 1 (1). **Runners left in scoring position, 2 out:** Matthews 1. **GIDP:** Perez. **Team LOB:** 2 **BASERUNNING: SB:** Morgan (1, 2nd base off Boddicker/Dempsey).

BALTIMORE	AB	R	H	HR	RBI	BB	AVG
Bumbry cf	2	0	0	0	0	0	.167
a-Shelby ph-cf	2	1	1	0	0	0	.333
Ford rf	3	0	1	0	0	0	.250
Ripken ss	3	0	1	0	1	1	.286
Murray 1b	4	0	0	0	0	0	.125
Lowenstein lf	4	1	3	1	1	0	.571
b-Landrum pr-lf	0	0	0	0	0	0	.000
Dauer 2b	4	1	1	0	0	0	.143
Cruz 3b	4	1	1	0	0	0	.143
Dempsey c	3	0	1	0	1	1	.200
Boddicker p	3	0	0	0	1	0	.000
TOTALS	**32**	**4**	**9**	**1**	**4**	**2**	**.219**

a - Batted for Bumbry in the 5th
b - Ran for Lowenstein in the 8th

BATTING: 2B: Lowenstein (1, Hudson), Dempsey (1, Hudson). **HR:** Lowenstein (1, 5th off Hudson 0 on, 0 out). **SF:** Boddicker. **RBI:** Ripken 1 (1), Lowenstein 1 (1), Dempsey 1 (1), Boddicker 1 (1). **2-out RBI:** Ripken 1. **Runners left in scoring position, 2 out:** Murray 3, Cruz 1, Boddicker 1. **Team LOB:** 8 **BASERUNNING: SB:** Landrum (1, 2nd base off Reed/Virgil). **FIELDING: DP:** 1 (Dauer-Ripken-Murray).

PHILADELPHIA	IP	H	R	ER	BB	SO	HR	ERA
Hudson (L, 0-1)	4.1	5	3	3	0	3	1	6.23
Hernandez	0.2	0	0	0	1	1	0	0.00
Andersen	2	3	1	1	0	1	0	4.50
Reed	1	1	0	0	1	1	0	0.00

BALTIMORE	IP	H	R	ER	BB	SO	HR	ERA
Boddicker (W, 1-0)	9	3	1	0	0	6	0	0.00

IBB: Dempsey (by Reed). **HBP:** Ford (by Hernandez). **Pitches-strikes:** Hudson 66-45, Hernandez 19-13, Andersen 39-27, Reed 13-9, Boddicker 107-74. **Ground balls-fly balls:** Hudson 2-7, Hernandez 0-1, Andersen 4-1, Reed 0-2, Boddicker 15-5. **Batters faced:** Hudson 18, Hernandez 4, Andersen 9, Reed 5, Boddicker 30. **UMPIRES:** hp—Vargo, 1b—Clark, 2b—Pulli, 3b—Palermo, lf—Rennert, rf—Springstead **T:** 2:27 **A:** 52,132

GAME 3 Baltimore 3 Philadelphia 2
Veterans Stadium 10/14/83

BALTIMORE	AB	R	H	HR	RBI	BB	AVG
Shelby cf	4	0	2	0	0	0	.429
Ford rf	3	1	1	1	1	1	.286
Ripken ss	3	0	0	0	0	1	.200
Murray 1b	4	0	0	0	0	0	.083
Roenicke lf	4	0	0	0	0	0	.000
Dauer 2b	4	0	0	0	0	0	.091
Cruz 3b	3	0	0	0	0	1	.100
Dempsey c	4	1	2	0	0	0	.333
Flanagan p	1	0	0	0	0	0	.000
a-Singleton ph	1	0	0	0	0	0	.000
Palmer p	0	0	0	0	0	0	.000
b-Ayala ph	1	1	1	0	1	0	1.000
Stewart p	1	0	0	0	0	0	.000
Martinez p	0	0	0	0	0	0	.000
TOTALS	**33**	**3**	**6**	**1**	**2**	**3**	**.206**

a - Batted for Flanagan in the 5th
b - Batted for Palmer in the 7th

BATTING: 2B: Dempsey 2 (3, Carlton). **HR:** Ford (1, 6th off Carlton 0 on, 1 out). **RBI:** Ford 1 (1), Ayala 1 (1). **2-out RBI:** Ayala 1. **Runners left in scoring position, 2 out:** Ripken 1, Singleton 1. **GIDP:** Dempsey, Roenicke. **Team LOB:** 6 **Outfield assists:** Ford (1), Roenicke (1).

PHILADELPHIA	AB	R	H	HR	RBI	BB	AVG
Morgan 2b	3	1	1	1	1	1	.364
Lezcano rf	4	0	1	0	0	0	.143
Hayes rf	0	0	0	0	0	0	.000
Schmidt 3b	4	0	0	0	0	0	.000
Matthews lf	3	1	1	1	1	1	.333
Perez 1b	4	0	1	0	0	0	.200
Maddox cf	4	0	0	0	0	0	.143
Diaz c	3	0	2	0	0	0	.333
a-Lefebvre ph	0	0	0	0	0	0	.000
b-Rose ph	1	0	0	0	0	0	.111
DeJesus ss	3	0	2	0	0	1	.222
Carlton p	3	0	0	0	0	0	.000
Holland p	0	0	0	0	0	0	.000
c-Virgil ph	1	0	0	0	0	0	.000
TOTALS	**33**	**2**	**8**	**2**	**2**	**3**	**.172**

a - Batted for Diaz in the 9th
b - Batted for Lefebvre in the 9th
c - Batted for Holland in the 9th

BATTING: HR: Matthews (1, 2nd off Flanagan 0 on, 0 out), Morgan (2, 3th off Flanagan 0 on, 0 out). **RBI:** Morgan 1 (2), Matthews 1 (1). **Runners left in scoring position, 2 out:** Carlton 3. **Team LOB:** 7 **BASERUNNING: CS:** Morgan (2, 2nd base off Stewart/Dempsey). **FIELDING: E:** Schmidt (1), DeJesus (1). **DP:** 2 (DeJesus-Morgan-Perez, Schmidt-Morgan-Perez).

BALTIMORE	IP	H	R	ER	BB	SO	HR	ERA
Flanagan	4	6	2	2	1	1	2	4.50
Palmer (W, 1-0)	2	2	0	0	1	1	0	0.00
Stewart	2	0	0	0	1	3	0	0.00
Martinez (S, 1)	1	0	0	0	0	0	0	0.00

PHILADELPHIA	IP	H	R	ER	BB	SO	HR	ERA
Carlton (L, 0-1)	6.2	5	3	2	3	7	1	2.70
Holland	2.1	1	0	0	0	4	0	0.00

WP: Palmer 1, Carlton 1. **Pitches-strikes:** Flanagan 62-39, Palmer 42-20, Stewart 29-16, Martinez 11-8, Carlton 107-61, Holland 24-21. **Ground balls-fly balls:** Flanagan 5-5, Palmer 2-3, Stewart 1-1, Martinez 2-1, Carlton 10-2, Holland 1-3. **Batters faced:** Flanagan 18, Palmer 9, Stewart 6, Martinez 3, Carlton 27, Holland 9. **UMPIRES:** hp—Clark, 1b—Pulli, 2b—Palermo, 3b—Rennert, lf—Springstead, rf—Vargo **T:** 2:35 **A:** 65,792

GAME 4 Baltimore 5 Philadelphia 4
Veterans Stadium 10/15/83

BALTIMORE	AB	R	H	HR	RBI	BB	AVG
Bumbry cf	3	0	0	0	0	0	.111
e-Ford ph	1	0	0	0	0	0	.250
Stewart p	1	0	0	0	0	0	.000
Martinez p	0	0	0	0	0	0	.000
Dwyer rf	5	2	2	0	0	0	.375
Landrum rf	0	0	0	0	0	0	.000
Ripken ss	5	1	1	0	0	0	.200
Murray 1b	4	0	1	0	0	1	.125
Lowenstein lf	4	1	1	0	0	0	.455
Dauer 2b-3b	4	1	3	0	3	0	.267
Cruz 3b	2	0	1	0	0	0	.167
a-Nolan ph-c	1	0	0	0	0	1	.000
Dempsey c	1	0	0	0	0	1	.300
b-Singleton ph	0	0	0	0	1	1	.000
c-Sakata pr-2b	1	0	0	0	0	0	.000
Davis p	2	0	0	0	0	0	.000
d-Shelby ph-cf	1	0	1	0	1	0	.500
TOTALS	**35**	**5**	**10**	**0**	**5**	**4**	**.227**

a - Batted for Cruz in the 6th
b - Batted for Dempsey in the 6th
c - Ran for Singleton in the 6th
d - Batted for Davis in the 6th e - Batted for Bumbry in the 6th

BATTING: 2B: Dauer (1, Denny), Dwyer (1, Reed). **SF:** Shelby. **RBI:** Dauer 3 (3), Singleton 1 (1), Shelby 1 (1). **2-out RBI:** Dauer 1. **Runners left in scoring position, 2 out:** Ford 1, Nolan 1, Davis 2. **GIDP:** Stewart. **Team LOB:** 8 **FIELDING: E:** Lowenstein (1). **DP:** 2 (Dauer-Murray, Ripken-Sakata-Murray).

PHILADELPHIA	AB	R	H	HR	RBI	BB	AVG
Morgan 2b	5	0	0	0	0	0	.250
Rose 1b	3	1	2	0	1	1	.250
Schmidt 3b	4	0	1	0	0	0	.063
Lefebvre rf	3	0	1	0	1	0	.200
b-Perez ph	1	0	1	0	0	0	.333
c-Samuel pr	0	0	0	0	0	0	.000
Lezcano rf	0	0	0	0	0	0	.143
Matthews lf	3	0	1	0	0	1	.333
Gross cf	3	0	0	0	0	0	.000
d-Maddox ph	1	0	0	0	0	0	.125
Diaz c	4	1	2	0	0	0	.385
e-Dernier pr	0	1	0	0	0	0	.000
DeJesus ss	4	0	0	0	0	0	.154
Denny p	2	1	1	0	1	0	.200
Hernandez p	0	0	0	0	0	0	.000
Reed p	0	0	0	0	0	0	.000
a-Hayes ph	1	0	0	0	0	0	.000
Andersen p	0	0	0	0	0	0	.000
f-Virgil ph	1	0	1	0	1	0	.500
TOTALS	**35**	**4**	**10**	**0**	**4**	**2**	**.203**

a - Batted for Reed in the 7th
b - Batted for Lefebvre in the 8th
c - Ran for Perez in the 8th
d - Batted for Gross in the 9th e - Ran for Diaz in the 9th f - Batted for Andersen in the 9th

BATTING: 2B: Lefebvre (1, Davis), Diaz (1, Davis), Rose (1, Davis). **RBI:** Rose 1 (1), Lefebvre 1 (2), Denny 1 (1), Virgil 1 (1). **2-out RBI:** Rose 1, Virgil 1. **Runners left in scoring position, 2 out:** Schmidt 1, Diaz 1. **GIDP:** Gross, Matthews. **Team LOB:** 6 **FIELDING: DP:** 1 (Andersen-DeJesus-Morgan).

BALTIMORE	IP	H	R	ER	BB	SO	HR	ERA
Davis (W, 1-0)	5	6	3	3	1	3	0	5.40
Stewart	2.1	1	0	0	1	2	0	0.00
Martinez (S, 2)	1.2	3	1	1	0	0	0	3.00

PHILADELPHIA	IP	H	R	ER	BB	SO	HR	ERA
Denny (L, 1-1)	5.1	7	4	4	3	4	0	3.46
Hernandez	0.1	0	0	0	0	0	0	0.00
Reed	1.1	2	1	1	1	3	0	3.86
Andersen	2	1	0	0	0	0	0	2.25

WP: Davis 1. **BK:** , Stewart 1. **IBB:** Dempsey (by Denny), Nolan (by Denny). **Pitches-strikes:** Davis 78-51, Stewart 37-22, Martinez 27-19, Denny 88-54, Hernandez 2-1, Reed 29-17, Andersen 26-15. **Ground balls-fly balls:** Davis 4-7, Stewart 1-4, Martinez 3-1, Denny 5-7, Hernandez 0-0, Reed 0-1, Andersen 3-2. **Batters faced:** Davis 21, Stewart 9, Martinez 7, Denny 26, Hernandez 1, Reed 7, Andersen 6. **UMPIRES:** hp—Pulli, 1b—Palermo, 2b—Rennert, 3b—Springstead, lf—Vargo, rf—Clark **T:** 2:50 **A:** 66,947

GAME 5 Baltimore 5 Philadelphia 0
Veterans Stadium 10/16/83

BALTIMORE	AB	R	H	HR	RBI	BB	AVG
Bumbry cf	2	0	0	0	1	0	.091
b-Shelby ph-cf	1	0	0	0	0	0	.444
Ford rf	4	0	0	0	0	0	.167
Landrum rf	0	0	0	0	0	0	.000
Ripken ss	3	1	0	0	0	1	.167
Murray 1b	4	2	3	2	3	0	.250
Lowenstein lf	2	0	0	0	0	0	.385
a-Roenicke ph-lf	2	0	0	0	0	0	.000
Dauer 2b	4	0	0	0	0	0	.211
Cruz 3b	4	0	0	0	0	0	.125
Dempsey c	3	2	2	1	1	0	.385
McGregor p	3	0	0	0	0	0	.000
TOTALS	**32**	**5**	**5**	**3**	**5**	**1**	**.213**

a - Batted for Lowenstein in the 6th
b - Batted for Bumbry in the 8th

BATTING: 2B: Dempsey (4, Hudson). **HR:** Murray 2 (2, 2nd off Hudson 0 on, 0 out, 4th off Hudson 1 on, 0 out), Dempsey (1, 3th off Hudson 0 on, 0 out). **SF:** Bumbry. **RBI:** Bumbry 1 (1), Murray 3 (3), Dempsey 1 (2). **Runners left in scoring position, 2 out:** Ripken 1. **Team LOB:** 2 **FIELDING: DP:** 1 (Cruz-Dauer-Murray).

PHILADELPHIA	AB	R	H	HR	RBI	BB	AVG
Morgan 2b	3	0	1	0	0	1	.263
Rose rf	4	0	2	0	0	0	.313
Schmidt 3b	4	0	0	0	0	0	.050
Matthews lf	4	0	0	0	0	0	.250
Perez 1b	4	0	0	0	0	0	.200
Maddox cf	4	0	2	0	0	0	.250
Diaz c	2	0	0	0	0	1	.333
DeJesus ss	3	0	0	0	0	0	.125
Hudson p	1	0	0	0	0	0	.000
Bystrom p	0	0	0	0	0	0	.000
a-Samuel ph	1	0	0	0	0	0	.000
Hernandez p	0	0	0	0	0	0	.000
b-Lezcano ph	1	0	0	0	0	0	.125
Reed p	0	0	0	0	0	0	.000
TOTALS	**31**	**0**	**5**	**0**	**0**	**2**	**.195**

a - Batted for Bystrom in the 5th
b - Batted for Hernandez in the 8th

BATTING: 2B: Maddox (1, McGregor). **3B:** Morgan (1, McGregor). **Runners left in scoring position, 2 out:** Schmidt 1, DeJesus 1, Samuel 1. **GIDP:** DeJesus. **Team LOB:** 6 **FIELDING: E:** Diaz (1).

BALTIMORE	IP	H	R	ER	BB	SO	HR	ERA
McGregor (W, 1-1)	9	5	0	0	2	6	0	1.06

PHILADELPHIA	IP	H	R	ER	BB	SO	HR	ERA
Hudson (L, 0-2)	4	4	5	5	1	3	3	8.64
Bystrom	1	0	0	0	0	1	0	0.00
Hernandez	3	0	0	0	0	3	0	0.00
Reed	1	1	0	0	0	0	0	2.70

WP: Bystrom 1. **Pitches-strikes:** McGregor 113-83, Hudson 67-44, Bystrom 19-13, Hernandez 38-24, Reed 14-10. **Ground balls-fly balls:** McGregor 6-14, Hudson 1-8, Bystrom 2-0, Hernandez 3-3, Reed 1-2. **Batters faced:** McGregor 33, Hudson 17, Bystrom 4, Hernandez 9, Reed 4. **UMPIRES:** hp—Palermo, 1b—Rennert, 2b—Springstead, 3b—Vargo, lf—Clark, rf—Pulli **T:** 2:21 **A:** 67,064

1984 DETROIT DEF. SAN DIEGO, 4-1

GAME 1 Detroit 3 San Diego 2
Jack Murphy Stadium 10/09/84

DETROIT	AB	R	H	HR	RBI	BB	AVG
Whitaker 2b	4	1	1	0	0	1	.250
Trammell ss	5	0	2	0	1	0	.400
Gibson rf	4	0	0	0	0	1	.000
Parrish c	3	1	2	0	0	1	.667
Herndon lf	3	1	2	1	2	1	.667
Garbey dh	4	0	0	0	0	0	.000
Lemon cf	4	0	1	0	0	0	.250
Evans 1b	3	0	0	0	0	1	.000
b-Bergman pr-1b	0	0	0	0	0	0	.000
Castillo 3b	2	0	0	0	0	1	.000
a-Grubb ph	0	0	0	0	0	0	.000
c-Brookens ph-3b	1	0	0	0	0	0	.000
TOTALS	**33**	**3**	**8**	**1**	**3**	**6**	**.242**

a - Batted for Castillo in the 8th
b - Ran for Evans in the 8th
c - Batted for Grubb in the 8th

BATTING: 2B: Whitaker (1, Thurmond), Parrish (1, Thurmond). **HR:** Herndon (1, 5th off Thurmond 1 on, 2 out). **RBI:** Trammell 1 (1), Herndon 2 (2). **2-out RBI:** Herndon 2. **Runners left in scoring position, 2 out:** Whitaker 1, Herndon 1, Garbey 1, Brookens 1. **Team LOB:** 9 **BASERUNNING: SB:** Trammell (1, 2nd base off Thurmond/Kennedy). **CS:** Trammell (1, 2nd base off Thurmond/Kennedy), Gibson (1, 2nd base off Thurmond/Kennedy). **FIELDING: Outfield assists:** Gibson (1). **DP:** 1 (Whitaker-Evans).

SAN DIEGO	AB	R	H	HR	RBI	BB	AVG
Wiggins 2b	4	0	1	0	0	0	.250
Gwynn rf	2	0	1	0	0	2	.500
Garvey 1b	4	1	1	0	0	0	.250
Nettles 3b	2	1	2	0	0	1	1.000
a-Salazar pr-3b	1	0	0	0	0	0	.000
Kennedy c	4	0	2	0	2	0	.500
Brown cf	4	0	0	0	0	0	.000
Martinez lf	4	0	0	0	0	0	.000
Templeton ss	4	0	0	0	0	0	.000
Bevacqua dh	3	0	1	0	0	0	.333
TOTALS	**32**	**2**	**8**	**0**	**2**	**3**	**.250**

a - Ran for Nettles in the 6th

BATTING: 2B: Kennedy (1, Morris), Bevacqua (1, Morris). **RBI:** Kennedy 2 (2). **2-out RBI:** Kennedy 2. **Runners left in scoring position, 2 out:** Garvey 1, Kennedy 1, Brown 1, Templeton 1. **GIDP:** Garvey. **Team LOB:** 6 **BASERUNNING: SB:** Gwynn (1, 2nd base off Morris/Parrish). **CS:** Gwynn (1, 2nd base off Morris/Parrish). **FIELDING: E:** Martinez (1). **DP:** 1 (Garvey).

DETROIT	IP	H	R	ER	BB	SO	HR	ERA
Morris (W, 1-0)	9	8	2	2	3	9	0	2.00
SAN DIEGO	**IP**	**H**	**R**	**ER**	**BB**	**SO**	**HR**	**ERA**
Thurmond (L, 0-1)	5	7	3	3	3	2	1	5.40
Hawkins	2.2	1	0	0	3	0	0	0.00
Dravecky	1.1	0	0	0	0	1	0	0.00

IBB: Evans (by Hawkins). **Pitches-strikes:** Morris 135-86, Thurmond 123-69, Hawkins 44-22, Dravecky 16-10. **Ground balls-fly balls:** Morris 9-6, Thurmond 6-6, Hawkins 1-6, Dravecky 1-2. **Batters faced:** Morris 35, Thurmond 24, Hawkins 11, Dravecky 4. **UMPIRES:** hp—Doug Harvey, 1b—Larry Barnett, 2b—Bruce Froemming, 3b—Garcia, lf—Paul Runge, rf—Reilly **T:** 3:18 **A:** 57,908

GAME 2 San Diego 5 Detroit 3
Jack Murphy Stadium 10/10/84

DETROIT	AB	R	H	HR	RBI	BB	AVG
Whitaker 2b	4	1	1	0	0	0	.250
Trammell ss	4	1	2	0	0	0	.444
Gibson rf	4	1	2	0	1	0	.250
Parrish c	3	0	0	0	1	0	.333
Evans 3b-1b	4	0	1	0	1	0	.143
Jones lf	2	0	0	0	0	0	.000
a-Herndon ph-lf	2	0	0	0	0	0	.400
Grubb dh	2	0	1	0	0	0	.500
b-Kuntz ph	1	0	0	0	0	0	.000
Lemon cf	3	0	0	0	0	0	.143
Bergman 1b	2	0	0	0	0	0	.000
c-Brookens ph-3b	1	0	0	0	0	0	.000
TOTALS	**32**	**3**	**7**	**0**	**3**	**0**	**.231**

a - Batted for Jones in the 7th
b - Batted for Grubb in the 7th
c - Batted for Bergman in the 8th

BATTING: SF: Parrish. **RBI:** Gibson 1 (1), Parrish 1 (1), Evans 1 (1). **Runners left in scoring position, 2 out:** Lemon 1. **Team LOB:** 3 **BASERUNNING: SB:** Gibson (1, 2nd base off Whitson/Kennedy). **FIELDING: E:** Trammell (1), Gibson (1), Herndon (1). **DP:** 1 (Parrish-Whitaker).

SAN DIEGO	AB	R	H	HR	RBI	BB	AVG
Wiggins 2b	5	1	3	0	0	0	.444
Gwynn rf	3	0	1	0	0	1	.400
Garvey 1b	3	0	0	0	0	0	.143
Nettles 3b	1	1	0	0	1	2	.667
Kennedy c	4	1	1	0	0	0	.375
Bevacqua dh	4	2	3	1	3	0	.571
Martinez lf	3	0	0	0	0	1	.000
Templeton ss	4	0	3	0	0	0	.375
Brown cf	3	0	0	0	1	0	.000
Salazar cf	1	0	0	0	0	0	.000
TOTALS	**31**	**5**	**11**	**1**	**5**	**4**	**.302**

BATTING: HR: Bevacqua (1, 5th off Petry 2 on, 1 out). **S:** Garvey. **SF:** Nettles. **RBI:** Nettles 1 (1), Bevacqua 3 (3), Brown 1 (1). **Runners left in scoring position, 2 out:** Wiggins 2, Gwynn 1, Kennedy 2, Brown 1. **Team LOB:** 8 **BASERUNNING: CS:** Wiggins (1, 2nd base off Petry/Parrish), Gwynn (2, 2nd base off Scherrer/Parrish), Bevacqua (1, 2nd base off Bair/Parrish). **FIELDING: Outfield assists:** Gwynn (1). **DP:** 1 (Gwynn-Garvey).

DETROIT	IP	H	R	ER	BB	SO	HR	ERA
Petry (L, 0-1)	4.1	8	5	5	3	2	1	10.38
Lopez	0.2	1	0	0	1	0	0	0.00
Scherrer	1.1	2	0	0	0	0	0	0.00
Bair	0.2	0	0	0	0	1	0	0.00
Hernandez	1	0	0	0	0	0	0	0.00
SAN DIEGO	**IP**	**H**	**R**	**ER**	**BB**	**SO**	**HR**	**ERA**
Whitson	0.2	5	3	3	0	0	0	40.50
Hawkins (W, 1-0)	5.1	1	0	0	0	3	0	0.00
Lefferts (S, 1)	3	1	0	0	0	5	0	0.00

BK: Petry 1. **Pitches-strikes:** Petry 78-46, Lopez 13-9, Scherrer 15-11, Bair 14-8, Hernandez 10-8, Whitson 17-11, Hawkins 54-39, Lefferts 48-33. **Ground balls-fly balls:** Petry 5-4, Lopez 0-2, Scherrer 1-2, Bair 0-0, Hernandez 2-1, Whitson 0-1, Hawkins 5-7, Lefferts 1-3. **Batters faced:** Petry 24, Lopez 4, Scherrer 5, Bair 1, Hernandez 3, Whitson 7, Hawkins 16, Lefferts 10. **UMPIRES:** hp—Larry Barnett, 1b—Bruce Froemming, 2b—Garcia, 3b—Paul Runge, lf—Reilly, rf—Doug Harvey **T:** 2:44 **A:** 57,911

GAME 3 Detroit 5 San Diego 2
Tiger Stadium 10/12/84

SAN DIEGO	AB	R	H	HR	RBI	BB	AVG
Wiggins 2b	5	1	2	0	0	0	.429
Gwynn rf	5	1	2	0	0	0	.400
Garvey 1b	5	0	1	0	1	0	.167
Nettles 3b	2	0	0	0	1	1	.400
Kennedy c	3	0	0	0	0	1	.273
Bevacqua dh	4	0	1	0	0	0	.455
Martinez lf	4	0	1	0	0	0	.091
Templeton ss	4	0	2	0	0	0	.417
Brown cf	3	0	0	0	0	0	.000
a-Salazar ph	1	0	1	0	0	0	.333
TOTALS	**36**	**2**	**10**	**0**	**2**	**2**	**.293**

a - Batted for Brown in the 9th

BATTING: 2B: Wiggins (1, Wilcox), Garvey (1, Scherrer). **SF:** Nettles. **RBI:** Garvey 1 (1), Nettles 1 (2). **Runners left in scoring position, 2 out:** Wiggins 1, Kennedy 2, Brown 1. **Team LOB:** 10

DETROIT	AB	R	H	HR	RBI	BB	AVG
Whitaker 2b	3	1	0	0	0	2	.182
Trammell ss	3	1	2	0	1	2	.500
Gibson rf	2	0	0	0	1	2	.200
Parrish c	3	0	1	0	0	2	.333
Herndon lf	4	0	1	0	1	1	.333
Garbey dh	5	0	0	0	0	0	.000
Lemon cf	5	1	2	0	0	0	.250
Evans 1b	2	1	0	0	0	2	.111
Bergman 1b	0	0	0	0	0	0	.000
Castillo 3b	4	1	1	1	2	0	.167
TOTALS	**31**	**5**	**7**	**1**	**5**	**11**	**.229**

BATTING: 2B: Trammell (1, Lollar). **HR:** Castillo (1, 2nd off Lollar 1 on, 2 out). **RBI:** Trammell 1 (2), Gibson 1 (2), Herndon 1 (3), Castillo 2 (2). **2-out RBI:** Trammell 1, Gibson 1, Herndon 1, Castillo 2. **Runners left in scoring position, 2 out:** Parrish 3, Herndon 2, Garbey 2, Castillo 1. **Team LOB:** 14 **BASERUNNING: SB:** Gibson (2, 2nd base off Harris/Kennedy).

SAN DIEGO	IP	H	R	ER	BB	SO	HR	ERA
Lollar (L, 0-1)	1.2	4	4	4	4	0	1	21.60
Booker	1	0	1	1	4	0	0	9.00
Harris	5.1	3	0	0	3	5	0	0.00
DETROIT	**IP**	**H**	**R**	**ER**	**BB**	**SO**	**HR**	**ERA**
Wilcox (W, 1-0)	6	7	1	1	2	4	0	1.50
Scherrer	0.2	2	1	1	0	0	0	4.50
Hernandez (S, 1)	2.1	1	0	0	0	0	0	0.00

WP: Lollar 1. **HBP:** Gibson (by Harris). **Pitches-strikes:** Lollar 55-28, Booker 31-11, Harris 87-52, Wilcox 100-63, Scherrer 5-5, Hernandez 29-21. **Ground balls-fly balls:** Lollar 2-3, Booker 2-1, Harris 4-7, Wilcox 7-7, Scherrer 1-0, Hernandez 3-4. **Batters faced:** Lollar 13, Booker 7, Harris 23, Wilcox 27, Scherrer 4, Hernandez 8. **UMPIRES:** hp—Bruce Froemming, 1b—Garcia, 2b—Paul Runge, 3b—Reilly, lf—Doug Harvey, rf—Larry Barnett **T:** 3:11 **A:** 51,970

GAME 4 Detroit 4 San Diego 2
Tiger Stadium 10/13/84

SAN DIEGO	AB	R	H	HR	RBI	BB	AVG
Wiggins 2b	3	0	0	0	0	0	.353
b-Summers ph	1	0	0	0	0	0	.000
Roenicke lf	0	0	0	0	0	0	.000
Gwynn rf	4	0	1	0	0	0	.357
Garvey 1b	4	1	1	0	0	0	.188
Nettles 3b	4	0	0	0	0	0	.222
Kennedy c	4	1	1	1	1	0	.267
Bevacqua dh	3	0	1	0	0	0	.429
Martinez lf	2	0	0	0	0	0	.077
a-Flannery ph-2b	1	0	1	0	0	0	1.000
Templeton ss	3	0	0	0	0	0	.333
Brown cf	3	0	0	0	0	0	.000
TOTALS	**32**	**2**	**5**	**1**	**1**	**0**	**.260**

a - Batted for Martinez in the 8th
b - Batted for Wiggins in the 8th

BATTING: 2B: Bevacqua (2, Morris), Garvey (2, Morris). **HR:** Kennedy (1, 2nd off Morris 0 on, 1 out). **RBI:** Kennedy 1 (3). **Runners left in scoring position, 2 out:** Summers 1, Templeton 1. **Team LOB:** 3 **FIELDING: E:** Wiggins (1), Gwynn (1). **DP:** 2 (Kennedy-Nettles, Templeton-Wiggins-Garvey).

DETROIT	AB	R	H	HR	RBI	BB	AVG
Whitaker 2b	4	2	2	0	0	0	.267
Trammell ss	4	2	3	2	4	0	.563
Gibson rf	4	0	1	0	0	0	.214
Parrish c	4	0	0	0	0	0	.231
Evans 3b	2	0	0	0	0	1	.091
Brookens 3b	1	0	0	0	0	0	.000
Grubb dh	1	0	0	0	0	0	.333
a-Garbey ph	2	0	0	0	0	0	.000
Jones lf	1	0	0	0	0	0	.000
b-Herndon ph-lf	2	0	1	0	0	0	.364
Lemon cf	2	0	0	0	0	1	.214
Bergman 1b	3	0	0	0	0	0	.000
TOTALS	**30**	**4**	**7**	**2**	**4**	**2**	**.230**

a - Batted for Grubb in the 3th
b - Batted for Jones in the 4th

BATTING: 2B: Whitaker (2, Dravecky). **HR:** Trammell 2 (2, 1st off Show 1 on, 0 out, 3th off Show 1 on, 1 out). **RBI:** Trammell 4 (6). **Runners left in scoring position, 2 out:** Evans 1, Garbey 1. **GIDP:** Lemon. **Team LOB:** 4 **BASERUNNING: SB:** Gibson (3, 2nd base off Show/Kennedy), Lemon (1, 2nd base off Dravecky/Kennedy). **CS:** Lemon (1, 3rd base off Dravecky/Kennedy).

SAN DIEGO	IP	H	R	ER	BB	SO	HR	ERA
Show (L, 0-1)	2.2	4	4	3	1	2	2	10.13
Dravecky	3.1	3	0	0	1	4	0	0.00
Lefferts	1	0	0	0	0	0	0	0.00
Gossage	1	0	0	0	0	0	0	0.00
DETROIT	**IP**	**H**	**R**	**ER**	**BB**	**SO**	**HR**	**ERA**
Morris (W, 2-0)	9	5	2	2	0	4	1	2.00

WP: Morris 2. **Pitches-strikes:** Show 50-30, Dravecky 52-35, Lefferts 13-7, Gossage 7-6, Morris 102-73. **Ground balls-fly balls:** Show 4-3, Dravecky 3-1, Lefferts 1-2, Gossage 2-1, Morris 13-10. **Batters faced:** Show 14, Dravecky 12, Lefferts 3, Gossage 3, Morris 32. **UMPIRES:** hp—Garcia, 1b—Paul Runge, 2b—Reilly, 3b—Doug Harvey, lf—Larry Barnett, rf—Bruce Froemming **T:** 2:20 **A:** 52,130

GAME 5 Detroit 8 San Diego 4
Tiger Stadium 10/14/84

SAN DIEGO	AB	R	H	HR	RBI	BB	AVG
Wiggins 2b	5	0	2	0	1	0	.364
Gwynn rf	5	0	0	0	0	0	.263
Garvey 1b	4	0	1	0	1	0	.200
Nettles 3b	3	0	1	0	0	1	.250
Kennedy c	4	0	0	0	0	0	.211
Bevacqua dh	3	2	1	1	1	1	.412
Martinez lf	4	0	2	0	0	0	.176
a-Salazar pr-cf	0	0	0	0	0	0	.333
Templeton ss	4	1	1	0	0	0	.316
Brown cf-lf	2	1	1	0	1	0	.067
b-Bochy ph	1	0	1	0	0	0	1.000
c-Roenicke pr	0	0	0	0	0	0	.000
TOTALS	**35**	**4**	**10**	**1**	**4**	**2**	**.265**

a - Ran for Martinez in the 8th
b - Batted for Brown in the 9th
c - Ran for Bochy in the 9th

BATTING: 2B: Templeton (1, Petry). **HR:** Bevacqua (2, 8th off Hernandez 0 on, 2 out). **SF:** Brown. **RBI:** Wiggins 1 (1), Garvey 1 (2), Bevacqua 1 (4), Brown 1 (2). **2-out RBI:** Wiggins 1, Garvey 1, Bevacqua 1. **Runners left in scoring position, 2 out:** Gwynn 1, Kennedy 1, Bevacqua 1. **Team LOB:** 7 **BASERUNNING: SB:** Wiggins (1, 2nd base off Petry/Parrish). **CS:** Salazar (1, 2nd base off Hernandez/Parrish). **FIELDING: E:** Wiggins (2). **DP:** 1 (Garvey-Templeton).

DETROIT	AB	R	H	HR	RBI	BB	AVG
Whitaker 2b	3	1	1	0	0	1	.278
Trammell ss	4	1	0	0	0	0	.450
Gibson rf	4	3	3	2	5	1	.333
Parrish c	5	2	2	1	1	0	.278
Herndon lf	4	0	1	0	0	1	.333
Lemon cf	3	0	2	0	1	1	.294
Garbey dh	1	0	0	0	0	0	.000
a-Grubb ph	0	0	0	0	0	0	.333
b-Kuntz ph	0	0	0	0	1	0	.000
c-Johnson ph	1	0	0	0	0	0	.000
Evans 1b	4	0	0	0	0	0	.067
Bergman 1b	0	0	0	0	0	0	.000
Castillo 3b	3	1	2	0	0	1	.333
TOTALS	**32**	**8**	**11**	**3**	**8**	**5**	**.253**

a - Batted for Garbey in the 4th
b - Batted for Grubb in the 5th
c - Batted for Kuntz in the 7th

BATTING: HR: Gibson 2 (2, 1st off Thurmond 1 on, 1 out, 8th off Gossage 2 on, 1 out), Parrish (1, 7th off Gossage 0 on, 1 out). **S:** Whitaker, Trammell. **SF:** Kuntz. **RBI:** Gibson 5 (7), Parrish 1 (2), Lemon 1 (1), Kuntz 1 (1). **Runners left in scoring position, 2 out:** Trammell 2, Garbey 1, Evans 2. **GIDP:** Whitaker. **Team LOB:** 9 **BASERUNNING: SB:** Parrish (1, 2nd base off Thurmond/Kennedy), Lemon (2, 2nd base off Gossage/Kennedy). **CS:** Herndon (1, 3rd base off Hawkins/Kennedy).

SAN DIEGO	IP	H	R	ER	BB	SO	HR	ERA
Thurmond	0.1	5	3	3	0	0	1	10.13
Hawkins (L, 1-1)	4	2	1	1	3	1	0	0.75
Lefferts	2	1	0	0	1	2	0	0.00
Gossage	1.2	3	4	4	1	2	2	13.50
DETROIT	**IP**	**H**	**R**	**ER**	**BB**	**SO**	**HR**	**ERA**
Petry	3.2	6	3	3	2	2	0	9.00
Scherrer	1	1	0	0	0	0	0	3.00
Lopez (W, 1-0)	2.1	0	0	0	0	4	0	0.00
Hernandez (S, 2)	2	3	1	1	0	0	1	1.69

WP: Hawkins 1. **HBP:** Grubb (by Hawkins). **Pitches-strikes:** Thurmond 15-9, Hawkins 57-31, Lefferts 25-15, Gossage 31-23, Petry 69-39, Scherrer 9-7, Lopez 25-21, Hernandez 26-20. **Ground balls-fly balls:** Thurmond 1-0, Hawkins 1-9, Lefferts 1-1, Gossage 1-2, Petry 7-1, Scherrer 1-2, Lopez 1-2, Hernandez 1-4. **Batters faced:** Thurmond 6, Hawkins 17, Lefferts 7, Gossage 11, Petry 19, Scherrer 4, Lopez 7, Hernandez 8. **UMPIRES:** hp—Paul Runge, 1b—Reilly, 2b—Doug Harvey, 3b—Larry Barnett, lf—Bruce Froemming, rf—Garcia **T:** 2:55 **A:** 51,901

1985 KANSAS CITY DEF. ST. LOUIS, 4-3

GAME 1 St. Louis 3 Kansas City 1
Royals Stadium 10/19/85

ST.LOUIS	AB	R	H	HR	RBI	BB	AVG
McGee cf	4	0	1	0	1	0	.250
O.Smith ss	3	0	0	0	0	1	.000
Herr 2b	4	1	1	0	0	0	.250
Clark 1b	4	0	1	0	1	0	.250
Landrum lf	4	1	2	0	0	0	.500
Cedeno rf	3	0	1	0	1	0	.333
Worrell p	1	0	0	0	0	0	.000
Pendleton 3b	2	1	0	0	0	2	.000
Porter c	3	0	1	0	0	1	.333
Tudor p	1	0	0	0	0	0	.000
Van Slyke rf	2	0	0	0	0	0	.000
TOTALS	**31**	**3**	**7**	**0**	**3**	**4**	**.226**

BATTING: 2B: Landrum (1, Jackson), Cedeno (1, Jackson), McGee (1, Jackson), Clark (1, Quisenberry). **S:** Tudor. **RBI:** McGee 1 (1), Clark 1 (1), Cedeno 1 (1). **Runners left in scoring position, 2 out:** O.Smith 1, Herr 2, Porter 1, Van Slyke 2. **Team LOB:** 6 **BASERUNNING: SB:** O.Smith (1, 2nd base off Jackson/Sundberg). **FIELDING: E:** Pendleton (1). **DP:** 1 (Pendleton-Porter).

KANSAS CITY	AB	R	H	HR	RBI	BB	AVG
L.Smith lf	3	0	1	0	0	1	.333
Wilson cf	4	0	1	0	0	0	.250
Brett 3b	4	0	1	0	0	0	.250
White 2b	4	0	0	0	0	0	.000
Sundberg c	3	1	1	0	0	1	.333
Motley rf	3	0	1	0	0	0	.333
d-Sheridan ph	1	0	1	0	0	0	1.000
Balboni 1b	4	0	1	0	1	0	.250
Biancalana ss	1	0	0	0	0	1	.000
a-Jones ph	1	0	1	0	0	0	1.000
Quisenberry p	0	0	0	0	0	0	.000
Black p	0	0	0	0	0	0	.000
e-Orta ph	1	0	0	0	0	0	.000
Jackson p	2	0	0	0	0	0	.000
b-McRae ph	0	0	0	0	0	0	.000
c-Concepcion pr-ss	0	0	0	0	0	0	.000
f-Iorg ph	1	0	0	0	0	0	.000
TOTALS	**32**	**1**	**8**	**0**	**1**	**3**	**.250**

a - Batted for Biancalana in the 7th
b - Batted for Jackson in the 7th
c - Ran for McRae in the 7th
d - Batted for Motley in the 9th e - Batted for Black in the 9th f - Batted for Concepcion in the 9th

BATTING: 2B: Sundberg (1, Tudor), Sheridan (1, Worrell). **3B:** Jones (1, Tudor). **S:** Motley. **RBI:** Balboni 1 (1). **Runners left in scoring position, 2 out:** Wilson 2, Jackson 1, Iorg 1. **Team LOB:** 8 **BASERUNNING: CS:** L.Smith (1, 2nd base off Tudor/Porter). **FIELDING: PB:** Sundberg. **Outfield assists:** Wilson (1), L.Smith (1).

ST.LOUIS	IP	H	R	ER	BB	SO	HR	ERA
Tudor (W, 1-0)	6.2	7	1	1	2	5	0	1.35
Worrell (S, 1)	2.1	1	0	0	1	0	0	0.00
KANSAS CITY	**IP**	**H**	**R**	**ER**	**BB**	**SO**	**HR**	**ERA**
Jackson (L, 0-1)	7	4	2	2	2	7	0	2.57
Quisenberry	1.2	3	1	1	0	2	0	5.40
Black	0.1	0	0	0	2	1	0	0.00

IBB: Pendleton (by Black). **HBP:** McRae (by Tudor). **Pitches-strikes:** Tudor 100-61, Worrell 27-17, Jackson 91-56, Quisenberry 25-16, Black 14-5. **Ground balls-fly balls:** Tudor 4-8, Worrell 2-5, Jackson 7-5, Quisenberry 2-0, Black 0-0. **Batters faced:** Tudor 27, Worrell 9, Jackson 26, Quisenberry 7, Black 3. **UMPIRES:** hp—Don Denkinger, 1b—Billy Williams, 2b—Jim McKean, 3b—Bob Engel, lf—John Shulock, rf—Jim Quick **T:** 2:48 **A:** 41,650

GAME 2 St. Louis 4 Kansas City 2
Royals Stadium 10/20/85

ST.LOUIS	AB	R	H	HR	RBI	BB	AVG
McGee cf	4	1	1	0	0	0	.250
O.Smith ss	4	0	0	0	0	0	.000
Herr 2b	4	0	0	0	0	0	.125
Clark 1b	3	1	1	0	1	1	.286
Landrum lf	4	1	2	0	0	0	.500
Cedeno rf	3	1	0	0	0	1	.167
Lahti p	0	0	0	0	0	0	.000
Pendleton 3b	4	0	2	0	3	0	.333
Porter c	3	0	0	0	0	1	.167
Cox p	2	0	0	0	0	0	.000
a-Harper ph	1	0	0	0	0	0	.000
Dayley p	0	0	0	0	0	0	.000
b-Van Slyke ph-rf	1	0	0	0	0	0	.000
TOTALS	**33**	**4**	**6**	**0**	**4**	**3**	**.203**

a - Batted for Cox in the 8th
b - Batted for Dayley in the 9th

BATTING: 2B: McGee (2, Leibrandt), Landrum (2, Leibrandt), Pendleton (1, Leibrandt). **RBI:** Clark 1 (2), Pendleton 3 (3). **2-out RBI:** Clark 1, Pendleton 3. **Runners left in scoring position, 2 out:** Cedeno 1, Van Slyke 1. **Team LOB:** 5 **FIELDING: Outfield assists:** Landrum (1). **DP:** 3 (Herr-O.Smith-Clark 2, Cox-O.Smith-Herr).

KANSAS CITY	AB	R	H	HR	RBI	BB	AVG
L.Smith lf	4	0	2	0	0	0	.429
Jones lf	0	0	0	0	0	0	1.000
Wilson cf	4	1	2	0	0	0	.375
Brett 3b	4	1	1	0	1	0	.250
White 2b	3	0	3	0	1	1	.429
Sheridan rf	4	0	0	0	0	0	.200
Quisenberry p	0	0	0	0	0	0	.000
Sundberg c	4	0	0	0	0	0	.143
Balboni 1b	4	0	1	0	0	0	.250
Biancalana ss	1	0	0	0	0	2	.000
a-Orta ph	1	0	0	0	0	0	.000
Leibrandt p	2	0	0	0	0	0	.000
Motley rf	0	0	0	0	0	0	.333
TOTALS	**31**	**2**	**9**	**0**	**2**	**3**	**.270**

a - Batted for Biancalana in the 9th

BATTING: 2B: Brett (1, Cox), White 2 (2, Cox, Dayley). **S:** Leibrandt. **RBI:** Brett 1 (1), White 1 (1). **Runners left in scoring position, 2 out:** L.Smith 1, Sheridan 1, Sundberg 1, Balboni 2. **GIDP:** Wilson, Leibrandt, Orta. **Team LOB:** 6 **BASERUNNING: SB:** White (1, 2nd base off Cox/Porter), Wilson (1, 2nd base off Cox/Porter).

ST.LOUIS	IP	H	R	ER	BB	SO	HR	ERA
Cox	7	7	2	2	3	5	0	2.57
Dayley (W, 1-0)	1	1	0	0	0	1	0	0.00
Lahti (S, 1)	1	1	0	0	0	0	0	0.00
KANSAS CITY	**IP**	**H**	**R**	**ER**	**BB**	**SO**	**HR**	**ERA**
Leibrandt (L, 0-1)	8.2	6	4	4	2	6	0	4.15
Quisenberry	0.1	0	0	0	1	0	0	4.50

IBB: Cedeno (by Leibrandt), Porter (by Quisenberry). **Pitches-strikes:** Cox 94-57, Dayley 14-10, Lahti 11-6, Leibrandt 136-85, Quisenberry 5-1. **Ground balls-fly balls:** Cox 8-4, Dayley 2-0, Lahti 1-1, Leibrandt 12-8, Quisenberry 0-1. **Batters faced:** Cox 28, Dayley 4, Lahti 3, Leibrandt 34, Quisenberry 2. **UMPIRES:** hp—Billy Williams, 1b—Jim McKean, 2b—Bob Engel, 3b—John Shulock, lf—Jim Quick, rf—Don Denkinger **T:** 2:44 **A:** 41,656

GAME 3 Kansas City 6 St. Louis 1
Busch Stadium 10/22/85

KANSAS CITY	AB	R	H	HR	RBI	BB	AVG
L.Smith lf	5	0	2	0	2	0	.417
Jones lf	0	0	0	0	0	0	1.000
Wilson cf	5	0	2	0	0	0	.385
Brett 3b	2	2	2	0	0	3	.400
White 2b	4	2	2	1	3	1	.455
Sheridan rf	5	0	0	0	0	0	.100
Sundberg c	2	1	1	0	0	3	.222
Balboni 1b	4	0	0	0	0	1	.167
Biancalana ss	5	1	2	0	1	0	.286
Saberhagen p	3	0	0	0	0	0	.000
TOTALS	**35**	**6**	**11**	**1**	**6**	**8**	**.286**

BATTING: 2B: L.Smith (1, Andujar), White (3, Horton). **HR:** White (1, 5th off Andujar 1 on, 0 out). **S:** Saberhagen. **RBI:** L.Smith 2 (2), White 3 (4), Biancalana 1 (1). **2-out RBI:** L.Smith 2, Biancalana 1. **Runners left in scoring position, 2 out:** Wilson 1, Sheridan 2, Saberhagen 2. **GIDP:** White. **Team LOB:** 11 **BASERUNNING: SB:** Wilson (2, 2nd base off Andujar/Porter). **CS:** L.Smith (2, 2nd base off Andujar/Porter). **FIELDING: DP:** 1 (Sundberg-Brett).

ST.LOUIS	AB	R	H	HR	RBI	BB	AVG
McGee cf	4	0	1	0	0	0	.250
O.Smith ss	4	1	1	0	0	0	.091
Herr 2b	3	0	1	0	0	1	.182
Clark 1b	4	0	1	0	1	0	.273
Van Slyke rf	4	0	0	0	0	0	.000
Pendleton 3b	4	0	1	0	0	0	.300
Porter c	3	0	0	0	0	0	.111
Landrum lf	3	0	1	0	0	0	.455
Andujar p	1	0	0	0	0	0	.000
Campbell p	0	0	0	0	0	0	.000
a-Jorgensen ph	1	0	0	0	0	0	.000
Horton p	0	0	0	0	0	0	.000
b-Harper ph	1	0	0	0	0	0	.000
Dayley p	0	0	0	0	0	0	.000
TOTALS	**32**	**1**	**6**	**0**	**1**	**1**	**.198**

a - Batted for Campbell in the 5th
b - Batted for Horton in the 7th

BATTING: RBI: Clark 1 (3). **Runners left in scoring position, 2 out:** Pendleton 1. **Team LOB:** 5 **BASERUNNING: SB:** McGee (1, 2nd base off Saberhagen/Sundberg). **CS:** McGee (1, 3rd base off Saberhagen/Sundberg). **FIELDING: DP:** 1 (Herr-Clark).

KANSAS CITY	IP	H	R	ER	BB	SO	HR	ERA
Saberhagen (W, 1-0)	9	6	1	1	1	8	0	1.00
ST.LOUIS	**IP**	**H**	**R**	**ER**	**BB**	**SO**	**HR**	**ERA**
Andujar (L, 0-1)	4	9	4	4	3	3	1	9.00
Campbell	1	0	0	0	1	2	0	0.00
Horton	2	2	2	2	2	1	0	9.00
Dayley	2	0	0	0	2	2	0	0.00

BK: Horton 1. **IBB:** Brett (by Andujar), Balboni (by Horton). **Pitches-strikes:** Saberhagen 140-93, Andujar 74-40, Campbell 20-13, Horton 35-18, Dayley 45-26. **Ground balls-fly balls:** Saberhagen 8-10, Andujar 1-5, Campbell 1-0, Horton 4-1, Dayley 1-3. **Batters faced:** Saberhagen 33, Andujar 22, Campbell 4, Horton 10, Dayley 8. **UMPIRES:** hp—Jim McKean, 1b—Bob Engel, 2b—John Shulock, 3b—Jim Quick, lf—Don Denkinger, rf—Billy Williams **T:** 2:59 **A:** 53,634

GAME 4 St. Louis 3 Kansas City 0
Busch Stadium 10/23/85

KANSAS CITY	AB	R	H	HR	RBI	BB	AVG
L.Smith lf	4	0	0	0	0	0	.313
Wilson cf	4	0	1	0	0	0	.353
Brett 3b	4	0	1	0	0	0	.357
White 2b	4	0	0	0	0	0	.333
Sundberg c	4	0	1	0	0	0	.231
Motley rf	4	0	0	0	0	0	.143
Balboni 1b	2	0	1	0	0	1	.214
Biancalana ss	2	0	0	0	0	0	.222
b-McRae ph	1	0	0	0	0	0	.000
Concepcion ss	0	0	0	0	0	0	.000
Black p	1	0	0	0	0	0	.000
a-Wathan ph	1	0	0	0	0	0	.000
Beckwith p	0	0	0	0	0	0	.000
c-Jones ph	1	0	1	0	0	0	1.000
Quisenberry p	0	0	0	0	0	0	.000
TOTALS	**32**	**0**	**5**	**0**	**0**	**1**	**.254**

a - Batted for Black in the 6th
b - Batted for Biancalana in the 7th
c - Batted for Beckwith in the 8th

BATTING: 2B: Jones (1, Tudor). **Runners left in scoring position, 2 out:** Brett 1, White 1, McRae 2. **Team LOB:** 6 **FIELDING: E:** Black (1). **Outfield assists:** L.Smith (2). **DP:** 1 (Black-White).

ST.LOUIS	AB	R	H	HR	RBI	BB	AVG
McGee cf	3	1	2	1	1	1	.333
O.Smith ss	2	0	0	0	0	1	.077
Herr 2b	3	0	1	0	0	1	.214
Clark 1b	3	0	1	0	0	1	.286
Landrum lf	4	1	1	1	1	0	.400
Cedeno rf	3	0	0	0	0	0	.111
Van Slyke rf	0	0	0	0	0	0	.000
Pendleton 3b	3	1	1	0	0	0	.308
Nieto c	1	0	0	0	1	1	.000
Tudor p	3	0	0	0	0	0	.000
TOTALS	**25**	**3**	**6**	**2**	**3**	**5**	**.207**

BATTING: 2B: Herr (1, Beckwith). **3B:** Pendleton (1, Black). **HR:** Landrum (1, 2nd off Black 0 on, 1 out), McGee (1, 3th off Black 0 on, 2 out). **S:** Nieto, O.Smith. **RBI:** McGee 1 (2), Landrum 1 (1), Nieto 1 (1). **2-out RBI:** McGee 1. **Runners left in scoring position, 2 out:** O.Smith 1, Landrum 1, Cedeno 1. **Team LOB:** 5 **BASERUNNING: CS:** O.Smith (1, 2nd base off Black/Sundberg).

KANSAS CITY	IP	H	R	ER	BB	SO	HR	ERA
Black (L, 0-1)	5	4	3	3	3	3	2	5.06
Beckwith	2	1	0	0	0	3	0	0.00
Quisenberry	1	1	0	0	2	0	0	3.00
ST.LOUIS	**IP**	**H**	**R**	**ER**	**BB**	**SO**	**HR**	**ERA**
Tudor (W, 2-0)	9	5	0	0	1	8	0	0.57

WP: Quisenberry 1. **IBB:** McGee (by Black), Herr (by Quisenberry). **Pitches-strikes:** Black 72-42, Beckwith 18-13, Quisenberry 26-12, Tudor 108-80. **Ground balls-fly balls:** Black 6-3, Beckwith 2-1, Quisenberry 1-0, Tudor 8-11. **Batters faced:** Black 20, Beckwith 7, Quisenberry 5, Tudor 33. **UMPIRES:** hp—Bob Engel, 1b—John Shulock, 2b—Jim Quick, 3b—Don Denkinger, lf—Billy Williams, rf—Jim McKean **T:** 2:19 **A:** 53,634

GAME 5 Kansas City 6 St. Louis 1
Busch Stadium 10/24/85

KANSAS CITY	AB	R	H	HR	RBI	BB	AVG
L.Smith lf	4	2	2	0	0	1	.350
Jones lf	0	0	0	0	0	0	1.000
Wilson cf	5	0	2	0	2	0	.364
Brett 3b	4	0	1	0	0	1	.333
Pryor 3b	0	0	0	0	0	0	.000
White 2b	5	1	0	0	1	0	.250
Sheridan rf	5	0	2	0	1	0	.200
Balboni 1b	4	0	1	0	0	1	.222
Sundberg c	4	2	1	0	0	0	.235
Biancalana ss	3	1	2	0	1	1	.333
Jackson p	4	0	0	0	0	0	.000
TOTALS	**38**	**6**	**11**	**0**	**5**	**4**	**.262**

BATTING: 2B: Sundberg (2, Forsch), Sheridan (2, Lahti). **3B:** Wilson (1, Forsch). **RBI:** Wilson 2 (2), White 1 (5), Sheridan 1 (1), Biancalana 1 (2). **2-out RBI:** Wilson 2, Sheridan 1. **Runners left in scoring position, 2 out:** L.Smith 1, Brett 1, White 2, Sheridan 1, Balboni 1. **GIDP:** Sundberg. **Team LOB:** 9 **BASERUNNING: SB:** L.Smith (1, 2nd base off Horton/Nieto). **FIELDING: E:** Jackson (1), Brett (1).

ST.LOUIS	AB	R	H	HR	RBI	BB	AVG
McGee cf	4	0	2	0	0	0	.368
O.Smith ss	3	0	0	0	0	1	.063
Herr 2b	4	1	1	0	0	0	.222
Clark 1b	3	0	1	0	1	1	.294
Landrum lf	4	0	1	0	0	0	.368
Cedeno rf	4	0	0	0	0	0	.077
Pendleton 3b	3	0	0	0	0	1	.250
Nieto c	4	0	0	0	0	0	.000
Forsch p	0	0	0	0	0	0	.000
Horton p	1	0	0	0	0	0	.000
Campbell p	0	0	0	0	0	0	.000
a-DeJesus ph	1	0	0	0	0	0	.000
Worrell p	0	0	0	0	0	0	.000
b-Harper ph	1	0	0	0	0	0	.000
Lahti p	0	0	0	0	0	0	.000
TOTALS	**32**	**1**	**5**	**0**	**1**	**3**	**.196**

a - Batted for Campbell in the 5th
b - Batted for Worrell in the 7th

BATTING: 2B: Herr (2, Jackson), Clark (2, Jackson). **RBI:** Clark 1 (4). **2-out RBI:** Clark 1. **Runners left in scoring position, 2 out:** Herr 1, Landrum 3, Nieto 1. **Team LOB:** 7 **BASERUNNING: CS:** McGee (2, 2nd base off Jackson/Sundberg). **FIELDING: E:** O.Smith (1). **DP:** 1 (Pendleton-Herr).

KANSAS CITY	IP	H	R	ER	BB	SO	HR	ERA
Jackson (W, 1-1)	9	5	1	1	3	5	0	1.69
ST.LOUIS	**IP**	**H**	**R**	**ER**	**BB**	**SO**	**HR**	**ERA**
Forsch (L, 0-1)	1.2	5	4	4	1	2	0	21.60
Horton	2	1	0	0	3	4	0	4.50
Campbell	1.1	0	0	0	0	2	0	0.00
Worrell	2	0	0	0	0	6	0	0.00
Lahti	2	5	2	1	0	1	0	3.00

IBB: Brett (by Horton). **Pitches-strikes:** Jackson 125-80, Forsch 54-31, Horton 40-21, Campbell 15-10, Worrell 27-21, Lahti 34-23. **Ground balls-fly balls:** Jackson 11-11, Forsch 1-2, Horton 2-0, Campbell 2-0, Worrell 0-0, Lahti 5-0. **Batters faced:** Jackson 35, Forsch 11, Horton 10, Campbell 4, Worrell 6, Lahti 11. **UMPIRES:** hp—John Shulock, 1b—Jim Quick, 2b—Don Denkinger, 3b—Billy Williams, lf—Jim McKean, rf—Bob Engel **T:** 2:52 **A:** 53,634

GAME 6 Kansas City 2 St. Louis 1
Royals Stadium 10/26/85

ST.LOUIS	AB	R	H	HR	RBI	BB	AVG
O.Smith ss	3	0	0	0	0	1	.053
McGee cf	4	0	0	0	0	0	.304
Herr 2b	4	0	0	0	0	0	.182
Clark 1b	4	0	0	0	0	0	.238
Landrum lf	4	0	1	0	0	0	.348
Pendleton 3b	4	1	1	0	0	0	.250
Cedeno rf	2	0	1	0	0	1	.133
b-Van Slyke pr-rf	0	0	0	0	0	0	.000
Porter c	3	0	1	0	0	0	.167
Cox p	2	0	0	0	0	0	.000
a-Harper ph	1	0	1	0	1	0	.250
c-Lawless pr	0	0	0	0	0	0	.000
Dayley p	0	0	0	0	0	0	.000
Worrell p	0	0	0	0	0	0	.000
TOTALS	**31**	**1**	**5**	**0**	**1**	**2**	**.190**

a - Batted for Cox in the 8th
b - Ran for Cedeno in the 8th
c - Ran for Harper in the 8th

BATTING: RBI: Harper 1 (1). **2-out RBI:** Harper 1. **Runners left in scoring position, 2 out:** McGee 2. **GIDP:** O.Smith. **Team LOB:** 5 **FIELDING: PB:** Porter. **DP:** 1 (Herr-O.Smith-Clark).

KANSAS CITY	AB	R	H	HR	RBI	BB	AVG
L.Smith lf	4	0	1	0	0	0	.333
Wilson cf	3	0	1	0	0	1	.360
Brett 3b	4	0	0	0	0	0	.273
White 2b	4	0	1	0	0	0	.250
Sheridan rf	3	0	1	0	0	0	.222
a-Motley ph	0	0	0	0	0	0	.143
b-Orta ph	1	0	1	0	0	0	.333
Balboni 1b	3	0	2	0	0	1	.286
c-Concepcion pr	0	1	0	0	0	0	.000
Sundberg c	4	1	1	0	0	0	.238
Biancalana ss	3	0	1	0	0	0	.333
d-McRae ph	0	0	0	0	0	1	.000
e-Wathan pr	0	0	0	0	0	0	.000
Leibrandt p	2	0	0	0	0	0	.000
Quisenberry p	0	0	0	0	0	0	.000
f-Iorg ph	1	0	1	0	2	0	.500
TOTALS	**32**	**2**	**10**	**0**	**2**	**3**	**.270**

a - Batted for Sheridan in the 9th
b - Batted for Motley in the 9th
c - Ran for Balboni in the 9th
d - Batted for Biancalana in the 9th e - Ran for McRae in the 9th f - Batted for Quisenberry in the 9th

BATTING: 2B: L.Smith (2, Cox). **S:** Leibrandt. **RBI:** Iorg 2 (2). **Runners left in scoring position, 2 out:** L.Smith 1, White 1, Leibrandt 1. **GIDP:** Brett. **Team LOB:** 9 **BASERUNNING: CS:** White (1, 2nd base off Cox/Porter). **FIELDING: DP:** 1 (Biancalana-White-Balboni).

ST.LOUIS	IP	H	R	ER	BB	SO	HR	ERA
Cox	7	7	0	0	1	8	0	1.29
Dayley	1	0	0	0	1	2	0	0.00
Worrell (L, 0-1)	0.1	3	2	2	1	0	0	3.86
KANSAS CITY	**IP**	**H**	**R**	**ER**	**BB**	**SO**	**HR**	**ERA**
Leibrandt	7.2	4	1	1	2	4	0	2.76
Quisenberry (W, 1-0)	1.1	1	0	0	0	1	0	2.08

IBB: McRae (by Worrell). **Pitches-strikes:** Cox 99-62, Dayley 18-11, Worrell 18-11, Leibrandt 103-67, Quisenberry 16-12. **Ground balls-fly balls:** Cox 5-5, Dayley 0-1, Worrell 1-0, Leibrandt 9-9, Quisenberry 2-1. **Batters faced:** Cox 27, Dayley 4, Worrell 5, Leibrandt 28, Quisenberry 5. **UMPIRES:** hp—Jim Quick, 1b—Don Denkinger, 2b—Billy Williams, 3b—Jim McKean, lf—Bob Engel, rf—John Shulock **T:** 2:47 **A:** 41,628

GAME 7 Kansas City 11 St. Louis 0
Royals Stadium 10/27/85

ST.LOUIS	AB	R	H	HR	RBI	BB	AVG
O.Smith ss	4	0	1	0	0	0	.087
McGee cf	4	0	0	0	0	0	.259
Herr 2b	4	0	0	0	0	0	.154
Clark 1b	4	0	1	0	0	0	.240
Van Slyke rf	4	0	1	0	0	0	.091
Pendleton 3b	3	0	1	0	0	0	.261
Landrum lf	2	0	1	0	0	0	.360
Andujar p	0	0	0	0	0	0	.000
Forsch p	0	0	0	0	0	0	.000
a-Braun ph	1	0	0	0	0	0	.000
Dayley p	0	0	0	0	0	0	.000
Porter c	3	0	0	0	0	0	.133
Tudor p	1	0	0	0	0	0	.000
Campbell p	0	0	0	0	0	0	.000
Lahti p	0	0	0	0	0	0	.000
Horton p	0	0	0	0	0	0	.000
Jorgensen lf	2	0	0	0	0	0	.000
TOTALS	**32**	**0**	**5**	**0**	**0**	**0**	**.185**

a - Batted for Forsch in the 7th

BATTING: Runners left in scoring position, 2 out: Porter 1. **Team LOB:** 5 **FIELDING: DP:** 2 (Pendleton-Herr-Clark, Herr-O.Smith-Clark).

KANSAS CITY	AB	R	H	HR	RBI	BB	AVG
L.Smith lf	3	2	1	0	2	1	.333
Jones lf	1	0	0	0	0	0	.667
Wilson cf	5	1	2	0	1	0	.367
Brett 3b	5	2	4	0	0	0	.370
White 2b	4	1	1	0	1	1	.250
Sundberg c	3	1	1	0	1	2	.250
Balboni 1b	4	2	2	0	2	1	.320
Motley rf	4	1	3	1	3	0	.364
Biancalana ss	3	0	0	0	0	1	.278
Saberhagen p	4	1	0	0	0	0	.000
TOTALS	**36**	**11**	**14**	**1**	**10**	**6**	**.288**

BATTING: 2B: L.Smith (3, Lahti). **HR:** Motley (1, 2nd off Tudor 1 on, 1 out). **RBI:** L.Smith 2 (4), Wilson 1 (3), White 1 (6), Sundberg 1 (1), Balboni 2 (3), Motley 3 (3). **2-out RBI:** L.Smith 2, Wilson 1, White 1. **Runners left in scoring position, 2 out:** Balboni 2, Saberhagen 2. **GIDP:** White, Biancalana. **Team LOB:** 7 **BASERUNNING: SB:** L.Smith (2, 3rd base off Tudor/Porter), Brett (1, 3rd base off Tudor/Porter), Wilson (3, 3rd base off Campbell/Porter).

ST.LOUIS	IP	H	R	ER	BB	SO	HR	ERA
Tudor (L, 2-1)	2.1	3	5	5	4	1	1	3.00
Campbell	1.2	4	1	1	1	1	0	2.25
Lahti	0.2	4	4	4	0	1	0	12.27
Horton	0	1	1	1	0	0	0	6.75
Andujar	0	1	0	0	1	0	0	9.00
Forsch	1.1	1	0	0	0	1	0	12.00
Dayley	2	0	0	0	0	0	0	0.00
KANSAS CITY	**IP**	**H**	**R**	**ER**	**BB**	**SO**	**HR**	**ERA**
Saberhagen (W, 2-0)	9	5	0	0	0	2	0	0.50

WP: Forsch 1. **IBB:** Biancalana (by Campbell). **Pitches-strikes:** Tudor 55-31, Campbell 31-18, Lahti 23-18, Horton 1-1, Andujar 17-10, Forsch 19-12, Dayley 19-12, Saberhagen 92-64. **Ground balls-fly balls:** Tudor 1-5, Campbell 2-1, Lahti 1-0, Horton 0-0, Andujar 0-0, Forsch 1-1, Dayley 0-6, Saberhagen 7-18. **Batters faced:** Tudor 14, Campbell 9, Lahti 6, Horton 1, Andujar 2, Forsch 4, Dayley 6, Saberhagen 32. **UMPIRES:** hp—Don Denkinger, 1b—Billy Williams, 2b—Jim McKean, 3b—Bob Engel, lf—John Shulock, rf—Jim Quick **T:** 2:46 **A:** 41,658

1986 NY METS DEF. BOSTON, 4-3

GAME 1 Boston 1 New York 0
Shea Stadium 10/18/86

BOSTON	AB	R	H	HR	RBI	BB	AVG
Boggs 3b	4	0	0	0	0	0	.000
Barrett 2b	4	0	1	0	0	0	.250
Buckner 1b	4	0	1	0	0	0	.250
Stapleton 1b	0	0	0	0	0	0	.000
Rice lf	2	1	1	0	0	2	.500
Evans rf	3	0	0	0	0	1	.000
Gedman c	4	0	0	0	0	0	.000
Henderson cf	4	0	2	0	0	0	.500
Owen ss	2	0	0	0	0	2	.000
Hurst p	3	0	0	0	0	0	.000
a-Greenwell ph	1	0	0	0	0	0	.000
Schiraldi p	0	0	0	0	0	0	.000
TOTALS	**31**	**1**	**5**	**0**	**0**	**5**	**.161**

a - Batted for Hurst in the 9th

BATTING: Runners left in scoring position, 2 out: Evans 1, Hurst 1, Greenwell 2. **GIDP:** Buckner. **Team LOB:** 8 **FIELDING: DP:** 1 (Boggs-Barrett-Buckner).

NY METS	AB	R	H	HR	RBI	BB	AVG
Wilson lf	4	0	1	0	0	0	.250
McDowell p	0	0	0	0	0	0	.000
Dykstra cf	3	0	0	0	0	1	.000
Hernandez 1b	3	0	0	0	0	1	.000
Carter c	4	0	1	0	0	0	.250
Strawberry rf	2	0	0	0	0	2	.000
Knight 3b	3	0	0	0	0	1	.000
Teufel 2b	3	0	2	0	0	0	.667
a-Backman pr-2b	1	0	0	0	0	0	.000
Santana ss	2	0	0	0	0	0	.000
c-Heep ph	1	0	0	0	0	0	.000
Darling p	2	0	0	0	0	0	.000
b-Mitchell ph-lf	1	0	0	0	0	0	.000
TOTALS	**29**	**0**	**4**	**0**	**0**	**5**	**.138**

a - Ran for Teufel in the 7th
b - Batted for Darling in the 7th
c - Batted for Santana in the 9th

BATTING: S: Santana. **Runners left in scoring position, 2 out:** Wilson 1, Carter 1, Santana 2. **GIDP:** Knight. **Team LOB:** 8 **BASERUNNING: SB:** Wilson (1, 2nd base off Hurst/Gedman), Strawberry (1, 2nd base off Hurst/Gedman). **FIELDING: E:** Teufel (1). **Outfield assists:** Mitchell (1). **DP:** 1 (Teufel-Santana-Hernandez).

BOSTON	IP	H	R	ER	BB	SO	HR	ERA
Hurst (W, 1-0)	8	4	0	0	4	8	0	0.00
Schiraldi (S, 1)	1	0	0	0	1	1	0	0.00
NY METS	**IP**	**H**	**R**	**ER**	**BB**	**SO**	**HR**	**ERA**
Darling (L, 0-1)	7	3	1	0	3	8	0	0.00
McDowell	2	2	0	0	2	0	0	0.00

WP: Darling 2. **IBB:** Owen 2 (by Darling, by McDowell). **Pitches-strikes:** Hurst 126-81, Schiraldi 17-8, Darling 108-72, McDowell 31-14. **Ground balls-fly balls:** Hurst 5-9, Schiraldi 1-1, Darling 6-7, McDowell 3-2. **Batters faced:** Hurst 31, Schiraldi 4, Darling 27, McDowell 9. **UMPIRES:** hp—Kibler, 1b—Evans, 2b—Wendelstedt, 3b—Brinkman, lf—Montague, rf—Ford **T:** 0:00 **A:** 55,076

GAME 2 Boston 9 New York 3
Shea Stadium 10/19/86

BOSTON	AB	R	H	HR	RBI	BB	AVG
Boggs 3b	5	1	2	0	2	1	.222
Barrett 2b	5	0	2	0	1	1	.333
Buckner 1b	5	0	2	0	1	0	.333
b-Stapleton pr-1b	1	0	0	0	0	0	.000
Rice lf	6	2	3	0	0	0	.500
Evans rf	4	2	2	1	2	1	.286
Gedman c	5	0	1	0	0	0	.111
Henderson cf	5	2	3	1	2	0	.556
Owen ss	4	1	3	0	1	1	.500
c-Romero pr-ss	0	0	0	0	0	0	.000
Clemens p	1	1	0	0	0	0	.000
Crawford p	1	0	0	0	0	0	.000
a-Greenwell ph	1	0	0	0	0	0	.000
Stanley p	1	0	0	0	0	0	.000
TOTALS	**44**	**9**	**18**	**2**	**9**	**4**	**.307**

a - Batted for Crawford in the 7th
b - Ran for Buckner in the 8th
c - Ran for Owen in the 9th

BATTING: 2B: Boggs 2 (2, Gooden, Fernandes). **HR:** Henderson (1, 4th off Gooden 0 on, 0 out), Evans (1, 5th off Gooden 1 on, 0 out). **S:** Clemens. **RBI:** Boggs 2 (2), Barrett 1 (1), Buckner 1 (1), Evans 2 (2), Henderson 2 (2), Owen 1 (1). **Runners left in scoring position, 2 out:** Barrett 2, Buckner 2, Rice 2, Gedman 2, Henderson 1. **GIDP:** Evans. **Team LOB:** 13

NY METS	AB	R	H	HR	RBI	BB	AVG
Dykstra cf	3	0	1	0	0	1	.167
Backman 2b	3	1	2	0	1	2	.500
Hernandez 1b	4	0	1	0	1	1	.143
Carter c	4	0	1	0	1	0	.250
Strawberry rf	4	0	0	0	0	0	.000
Heep lf	2	0	0	0	0	1	.000
Aguilera p	0	0	0	0	0	0	.000
Orosco p	0	0	0	0	0	0	.000
a-Mazzilli ph	1	0	0	0	0	0	.000
Fernandes p	0	0	0	0	0	0	.000
Sisk p	0	0	0	0	0	0	.000
Johnson 3b	4	0	0	0	0	0	.000
Santana ss	4	1	2	0	0	0	.333
Gooden p	2	1	1	0	0	0	.500
Wilson lf	2	0	0	0	0	0	.167
TOTALS	**33**	**3**	**8**	**0**	**3**	**5**	**.194**

a - Batted for Orosco in the 8th

BATTING: S: Dykstra. **RBI:** Backman 1 (1), Hernandez 1 (1), Carter 1 (1). **Runners left in scoring position, 2 out:** Hernandez 1, Carter 1, Strawberry 1, Heep 1, Gooden 1. **Team LOB:** 9 **BASERUNNING: CS:** Backman (1, 2nd base off Clemens/Gedman). **FIELDING: E:** Hernandez (1). **DP:** 1 (Santana-Backman-Hernandez).

BOSTON	IP	H	R	ER	BB	SO	HR	ERA
Clemens	4.1	5	3	3	4	3	0	6.23
Crawford (W, 1-0)	1.2	1	0	0	0	2	0	0.00
Stanley (S, 1)	3	2	0	0	1	3	0	0.00
NY METS	**IP**	**H**	**R**	**ER**	**BB**	**SO**	**HR**	**ERA**
Gooden (L, 0-1)	5	8	6	5	2	6	2	9.00
Aguilera	1	5	2	2	1	1	0	18.00
Orosco	2	2	0	0	0	3	0	0.00
Fernandes	0.1	3	1	1	0	1	0	27.00
Sisk	0.2	0	0	0	1	1	0	0.00

IBB: Barrett (by Sisk). **Pitches-strikes:** Clemens 82-50, Crawford 31-19, Stanley 44-27, Gooden 91-59, Aguilera 23-15, Orosco 30-20, Fernandes 13-12, Sisk 11-4. **Ground balls-fly balls:** Clemens 2-6, Crawford 2-1, Stanley 3-3, Gooden 5-4, Aguilera 1-1, Orosco 1-1, Fernandes 0-0, Sisk 0-1. **Batters faced:** Clemens 21, Crawford 6, Stanley 12, Gooden 26, Aguilera 9, Orosco 7, Fernandes 4, Sisk 3. **UMPIRES:** hp—Evans, 1b—Wendelstedt, 2b—Brinkman, 3b—Montague, lf—Ford, rf—Kibler **T:** 0:00 **A:** 55,076

GAME 3 New York 7 Boston 1
Fenway Park 10/21/86

NY METS	AB	R	H	HR	RBI	BB	AVG
Dykstra cf	5	2	4	1	1	0	.455
Backman 2b	5	1	1	0	0	0	.333
Hernandez 1b	4	1	2	0	0	1	.273
Carter c	5	1	2	0	3	0	.308
Strawberry rf	4	1	1	0	0	0	.100
Knight 3b	4	0	1	0	1	0	.143
Heep dh	3	0	1	0	2	0	.167
a-Mitchell ph	0	0	0	0	0	0	.000
b-Mazzilli ph	1	0	0	0	0	0	.000
Wilson lf	4	0	0	0	0	0	.100
Santana ss	4	1	1	0	0	0	.300
TOTALS	**39**	**7**	**13**	**1**	**7**	**1**	**.248**

a - Batted for Heep in the 8th
b - Batted for Mitchell in the 8th

BATTING: 2B: Carter (1, Boyd), Knight (1, Sambito). **HR:** Dykstra (1, 1st off Boyd 0 on, 0 out). **RBI:** Dykstra 1 (1), Carter 3 (4), Knight 1 (1), Heep 2 (2). **2-out RBI:** Carter 2. **Runners left in scoring position, 2 out:** Carter 3, Santana 2. **GIDP:** Carter. **Team LOB:** 6 **FIELDING: DP:** 1 (Backman-Santana-Hernandez).

BOSTON	AB	R	H	HR	RBI	BB	AVG
Boggs 3b	3	0	1	0	0	1	.250
Barrett 2b	4	0	2	0	1	0	.385
Buckner 1b	4	0	0	0	0	0	.231
Rice lf	3	0	0	0	0	1	.364
Baylor dh	4	0	1	0	0	0	.250
Evans rf	4	0	0	0	0	0	.182
Gedman c	4	0	0	0	0	0	.077
Henderson cf	2	1	1	0	0	1	.545
Owen ss	3	0	0	0	0	0	.333
TOTALS	**31**	**1**	**5**	**0**	**1**	**3**	**.264**

BATTING: 2B: Baylor (1, Ojeda). **RBI:** Barrett 1 (2). **Runners left in scoring position, 2 out:** Buckner 1, Rice 1, Gedman 2. **GIDP:** Owen. **Team LOB:** 6 **FIELDING: PB:** Gedman. **DP:** 1 (Owen-Buckner).

NY METS	IP	H	R	ER	BB	SO	HR	ERA
Ojeda (W, 1-0)	7	5	1	1	3	6	0	1.29
McDowell	2	0	0	0	0	0	0	0.00
BOSTON	**IP**	**H**	**R**	**ER**	**BB**	**SO**	**HR**	**ERA**
Boyd (L, 0-1)	7	9	6	6	1	3	1	7.71
Sambito	0	2	1	1	0	0	0	0.00
Stanley	2	2	0	0	0	1	0	0.00

WP: Ojeda 1, Sambito 1. **Pitches-strikes:** Ojeda 114-64, McDowell 27-20, Boyd 107-77, Sambito 5-2, Stanley 27-19. **Ground balls-fly balls:** Ojeda 8-6, McDowell 5-1, Boyd 8-10, Sambito 0-0, Stanley 4-0. **Batters faced:** Ojeda 28, McDowell 6, Boyd 31, Sambito 2, Stanley 7. **UMPIRES:** hp—Wendelstedt, 1b—Brinkman, 2b—Montague, 3b—Ford, lf—Kibler, rf—Evans **T:** 0:00 **A:** 33,595

GAME 4 New York 6 Boston 2
Fenway Park 10/22/86

NY METS	AB	R	H	HR	RBI	BB	AVG
Dykstra cf	5	1	1	1	2	0	.375
Backman 2b	4	1	2	0	0	0	.385
Hernandez 1b	3	0	0	0	0	1	.214
Carter c	4	2	3	2	3	0	.412
Strawberry rf	4	1	2	0	0	0	.214
Knight 3b	4	0	2	0	1	0	.273
Heep dh	4	0	0	0	0	0	.100
Wilson lf	4	1	2	0	0	0	.214
Santana ss	4	0	0	0	0	0	.214
TOTALS	**36**	**6**	**12**	**3**	**6**	**1**	**.270**

BATTING: 2B: Strawberry (1, Nipper), Carter (2, Nipper). **HR:** Carter 2 (2, 4th off Nipper 1 on, 1 out, 8th off Crawford 0 on, 1 out), Dykstra (2, 7th off Crawford 1 on, 2 out). **RBI:** Dykstra 2 (3), Carter 3 (7), Knight 1 (2). **2-out RBI:** Dykstra 2. **Runners left in scoring position, 2 out:** Dykstra 1, Hernandez 1. **GIDP:** Heep. **Team LOB:** 4 **BASERUNNING: SB:** Backman (1, 2nd base off Nipper/Gedman), Wilson 2 (3, 2nd base off Crawford/Gedman, 2nd base off Stanley/Gedman). **CS:** Strawberry (1, 2nd base off Crawford/Gedman). **Outfield assists:** Wilson (1).

BOSTON	AB	R	H	HR	RBI	BB	AVG
Boggs 3b	5	0	0	0	0	0	.176
Barrett 2b	4	0	2	0	0	1	.412
Buckner 1b	5	0	0	0	0	0	.167
Rice lf	4	1	1	0	0	1	.333
Baylor dh	3	0	0	0	0	1	.143
Evans rf	3	1	1	0	1	1	.214
Gedman c	4	0	3	0	0	0	.235
Henderson cf	3	0	0	0	1	0	.429
Owen ss	1	0	0	0	0	2	.300
a-Greenwell ph	0	0	0	0	0	1	.000
b-Romero pr-ss	0	0	0	0	0	0	.000
TOTALS	**32**	**2**	**7**	**0**	**2**	**7**	**.254**

a - Batted for Owen in the 8th
b - Ran for Greenwell in the 8th

BATTING: 2B: Barrett (1, Darling), Gedman (1, Darling), Rice (1, McDowell). **SF:** Henderson. **RBI:** Evans 1 (3), Henderson 1 (3). **Runners left in scoring position, 2 out:** Boggs 2, Buckner 2, Evans 2. **Team LOB:** 11 **FIELDING: E:** Gedman (1). **Outfield assists:** Rice (1). **DP:** 3 (Buckner-Owen-Buckner, Rice-Gedman, Gedman-Barrett).

NY METS	IP	H	R	ER	BB	SO	HR	ERA
Darling (W, 1-1)	7	4	0	0	6	4	0	0.00
McDowell	0.2	3	2	2	1	0	0	3.86
Orosco (S, 1)	1.1	0	0	0	0	1	0	0.00
BOSTON	**IP**	**H**	**R**	**ER**	**BB**	**SO**	**HR**	**ERA**
Nipper (L, 0-1)	6	7	3	3	1	2	1	4.50
Crawford	2	4	3	3	0	2	2	7.36
Stanley	1	1	0	0	0	0	0	0.00

Pitches-strikes: Darling 115-68, McDowell 17-11, Orosco 16-9, Nipper 96-60, Crawford 37-29, Stanley 12-8. **Ground balls-fly balls:** Darling 4-12, McDowell 0-1, Orosco 3-0, Nipper 10-4, Crawford 1-2, Stanley 1-2. **Batters faced:** Darling 30, McDowell 6, Orosco 4, Nipper 24, Crawford 9, Stanley 4. **UMPIRES:** hp—Brinkman, 1b—Montague, 2b—Ford, 3b—Kibler, lf—Evans, rf—Wendelstedt **T:** 0:00 **A:** 33,920

GAME 5 Boston 4 New York 2
Fenway Park 10/23/86

NY METS	AB	R	H	HR	RBI	BB	AVG
Dykstra cf	5	0	1	0	0	0	.333
Teufel 2b	4	1	2	1	1	0	.571
Hernandez 1b	4	0	1	0	0	0	.222
Carter c	4	0	0	0	0	0	.333
Strawberry rf	4	0	1	0	0	0	.222
Knight 3b	4	0	1	0	0	0	.267
Mitchell dh	4	0	1	0	0	0	.200
Wilson lf	4	1	2	0	0	0	.278
Santana ss	2	0	1	0	1	1	.250
TOTALS	**35**	**2**	**10**	**1**	**2**	**1**	**.273**

BATTING: 2B: Teufel (1, Hurst), Wilson (1, Hurst). **HR:** Teufel (1, 8th off Hurst 0 on, 1 out). **S:** Santana. **RBI:** Teufel 1 (1), Santana 1 (1). **2-out RBI:** Santana 1. **Runners left in scoring position, 2 out:** Teufel 2, Hernandez 1, Carter 1, Strawberry 1. **GIDP:** Knight. **Team LOB:** 8 **FIELDING: E:** Santana (1).

BOSTON	AB	R	H	HR	RBI	BB	AVG
Boggs 3b	5	0	2	0	0	0	.227
Barrett 2b	4	0	2	0	0	1	.429
Buckner 1b	5	1	1	0	0	0	.174
Stapleton 1b	0	0	0	0	0	0	.000
Rice lf	3	1	2	0	0	1	.389
Baylor dh	3	1	1	0	1	0	.200
Evans rf	4	0	2	0	1	0	.278
Gedman c	4	0	0	0	0	0	.190
Henderson cf	4	1	2	0	1	0	.444
Owen ss	3	0	0	0	1	0	.231
TOTALS	**35**	**4**	**12**	**0**	**4**	**2**	**.272**

BATTING: 2B: Henderson (1, Fernandes), Barrett (2, Fernandes). **3B:** Henderson (1, Gooden), Rice (1, Gooden). **SF:** Owen. **RBI:** Baylor 1 (1), Evans 1 (4), Henderson 1 (4), Owen 1 (2). **2-out RBI:** Evans 1. **Runners left in scoring position, 2 out:** Boggs 2, Buckner 3, Evans 2, Gedman 1. **Team LOB:** 11 **FIELDING: DP:** 1 (Boggs-Barrett-Buckner).

NY METS	IP	H	R	ER	BB	SO	HR	ERA
Gooden (L, 0-2)	4	9	4	3	2	3	0	8.00
Fernandes	4	3	0	0	0	5	0	2.08
BOSTON	**IP**	**H**	**R**	**ER**	**BB**	**SO**	**HR**	**ERA**
Hurst (W, 2-0)	9	10	2	2	1	6	1	1.06

HBP: Baylor (by Gooden). **Pitches-strikes:** Gooden 92-58, Fernandes 60-44, Hurst 130-91. **Ground balls-fly balls:** Gooden 5-3, Fernandes 2-5, Hurst 11-8. **Batters faced:** Gooden 24, Fernandes 15, Hurst 37. **UMPIRES:** hp—Montague, 1b—Ford, 2b—Kibler, 3b—Evans, lf—Wendelstedt, rf—Brinkman **T:** 0:00 **A:** 34,010

GAME 6 New York 6 Boston 5
Shea Stadium 10/25/86

BOSTON	AB	R	H	HR	RBI	BB	AVG
Boggs 3b	5	2	3	0	0	1	.296
Barrett 2b	4	1	3	0	2	2	.480
Buckner 1b	5	0	0	0	0	0	.143
Rice lf	5	0	0	0	0	1	.304
Evans rf	4	0	1	0	2	1	.273
Gedman c	5	0	1	0	0	0	.192
Henderson cf	5	1	2	1	1	0	.435
Owen ss	4	1	3	0	0	0	.353
Clemens p	3	0	0	0	0	0	.000
a-Greenwell ph	1	0	0	0	0	0	.000
Schiraldi p	1	0	0	0	0	0	.000
Stanley p	0	0	0	0	0	0	.000
TOTALS	**42**	**5**	**13**	**1**	**5**	**5**	**.279**

a - Batted for Clemens in the 8th

BATTING: 2B: Evans (1, Ojeda), Boggs (3, Aguilera). **HR:** Henderson (2, 10th off Aguilera 0 on, 0 out). **S:** Owen. **RBI:** Barrett 2 (4), Evans 2 (6), Henderson 1 (5). **2-out RBI:** Barrett 2, Evans 1. **Runners left in scoring position, 2 out:** Buckner 3, Rice 1, Gedman 4. **GIDP:** Gedman. **Team LOB:** 14 **FIELDING: E:** Evans (1), Gedman (2), Buckner (1). **DP:** 1 (Barrett-Owen-Buckner).

NY METS	AB	R	H	HR	RBI	BB	AVG
Dykstra cf	4	0	0	0	0	0	.280
Backman 2b	4	0	1	0	0	0	.353
Hernandez 1b	4	0	1	0	0	1	.227
Carter c	4	1	1	0	1	0	.320
Strawberry rf	2	1	0	0	0	2	.200
Aguilera p	0	0	0	0	0	0	.000
d-Mitchell ph	1	1	1	0	0	0	.333
Knight 3b	4	2	2	0	2	1	.316
Wilson lf	5	0	1	0	1	0	.261
Santana ss	1	0	0	0	0	0	.235
a-Heep ph	1	0	0	0	0	0	.091
Elster ss	1	0	0	0	0	0	.000
c-Johnson ph-ss	1	0	0	0	0	0	.000
Ojeda p	2	0	0	0	0	0	.000
McDowell p	0	0	0	0	0	0	.000
Orosco p	0	0	0	0	0	0	.000
b-Mazzilli ph-rf	2	1	1	0	0	0	.250
TOTALS	**36**	**6**	**8**	**0**	**4**	**4**	**.264**

a - Batted for Santana in the 5th
b - Batted for Orosco in the 8th
c - Batted for Elster in the 9th
d - Batted for Aguilera in the 10th

BATTING: S: Dykstra, Backman. **SF:** Carter. **RBI:** Carter 1 (8), Knight 2 (4), Wilson 1 (1). **2-out RBI:** Knight 1, Wilson 1. **Runners left in scoring position, 2 out:** Dykstra 1, Strawberry 2, Wilson 1. **GIDP:** Heep. **Team LOB:** 8 **BASERUNNING: SB:** Strawberry 2 (3, 2nd base off Clemens/Gedman). **FIELDING: E:** Knight (1), Elster (1). **Outfield assists:** Wilson (2). **DP:** 1 (Backman-Elster-Hernandez).

BOSTON	IP	H	R	ER	BB	SO	HR	ERA
Clemens	7	4	2	1	2	8	0	3.18
Schiraldi (L, 0-1)	2.2	4	4	3	2	1	0	7.36
Stanley	0	0	0	0	0	0	0	0.00
NY METS	**IP**	**H**	**R**	**ER**	**BB**	**SO**	**HR**	**ERA**
Ojeda	6	8	2	2	2	3	0	2.08
McDowell	1.2	2	1	0	3	1	0	2.84
Orosco	0.1	0	0	0	0	0	0	0.00
Aguilera (W, 1-0)	2	3	2	2	0	3	1	12.00

WP: Stanley 1. **IBB:** Boggs (by McDowell), Hernandez (by Schiraldi). **HBP:** Buckner (by Aguilera). **Pitches-strikes:** Clemens 139-92, Schiraldi 55-33, Stanley 9-6, Ojeda 88-59, McDowell 45-27, Orosco 1-1, Aguilera 36-25. **Ground balls-fly balls:** Clemens 6-6, Schiraldi 1-5, Stanley 1-0, Ojeda 4-11, McDowell 2-1, Orosco 0-1, Aguilera 2-1. **Batters faced:** Clemens 26, Schiraldi 16, Stanley 1, Ojeda 28, McDowell 10, Orosco 1, Aguilera 10. **UMPIRES:** hp—Ford, 1b—Kibler, 2b—Evans, 3b—Wendelstedt, lf—Brinkman, rf—Montague **T:** 0:00 **A:** 55,078

GAME 7 New York 8 Boston 5
Shea Stadium 10/27/86

BOSTON	AB	R	H	HR	RBI	BB	AVG
Boggs 3b	4	0	1	0	1	1	.290
Barrett 2b	5	0	1	0	0	0	.433
Buckner 1b	4	1	2	0	0	0	.188
Rice lf	4	1	2	0	0	0	.333
Evans rf	4	1	2	1	3	0	.308
Gedman c	4	1	1	1	1	0	.200
Henderson cf	2	1	0	0	0	1	.400
Owen ss	3	0	0	0	0	0	.300
b-Baylor ph	1	0	0	0	0	0	.182
Nipper p	0	0	0	0	0	0	.000
Crawford p	0	0	0	0	0	0	.000
Hurst p	0	0	0	0	0	0	.000
a-Armas ph	1	0	0	0	0	0	.000
Schiraldi p	0	0	0	0	0	0	.000
Sambito p	0	0	0	0	0	0	.000
Stanley p	0	0	0	0	0	0	.000
Romero ss	1	0	0	0	0	0	.000
TOTALS	**33**	**5**	**9**	**2**	**5**	**2**	**.278**

a - Batted for Hurst in the 7th
b - Batted for Owen in the 8th

BATTING: 2B: Evans (2, McDowell). **HR:** Evans (2, 2nd off Darling 0 on, 0 out), Gedman (1, 2nd off Darling 0 on, 0 out). **S:** Hurst, Hurst. **RBI:** Boggs 1 (3), Evans 3 (9), Gedman 1 (1). **2-out RBI:** Boggs 1. **Runners left in scoring position, 2 out:** Barrett 1, Buckner 1, Baylor 1. **Team LOB:** 6 **Outfield assists:** Evans (1).

NY METS	AB	R	H	HR	RBI	BB	AVG
Wilson cf-lf	3	1	1	0	0	1	.269
Teufel 2b	2	0	0	0	0	1	.444
b-Backman pr-2b	1	1	0	0	0	1	.333
Hernandez 1b	4	0	1	0	3	0	.231
Carter c	4	0	0	0	1	0	.276
Strawberry rf	4	1	1	1	1	0	.208
Knight 3b	4	2	3	1	1	0	.391
Mitchell lf	2	0	0	0	0	0	.250
c-Dykstra ph-cf	2	1	1	0	0	0	.296
Santana ss	3	1	1	0	1	1	.250
Darling p	1	0	0	0	0	0	.000
Fernandes p	0	0	0	0	0	0	.000
a-Mazzilli ph	1	1	1	0	0	0	.400
McDowell p	0	0	0	0	0	0	.000
Orosco p	1	0	1	0	1	0	1.000
TOTALS	**32**	**8**	**10**	**2**	**8**	**4**	**.271**

a - Batted for Fernandes in the 6th
b - Ran for Teufel in the 6th
c - Batted for Mitchell in the 7th

BATTING: HR: Knight (1, 7th off Schiraldi 0 on, 0 out), Strawberry (1, 8th off Nipper 0 on, 0 out). **S:** McDowell. **SF:** Hernandez. **RBI:** Hernandez 3 (4), Carter 1 (9), Strawberry 1 (1), Knight 1 (5), Santana 1 (2), Orosco 1 (1). **Runners left in scoring position, 2 out:** Hernandez 2, Carter 1. **Team LOB:** 7 **Outfield assists:** Mitchell (2).

BOSTON	IP	H	R	ER	BB	SO	HR	ERA
Hurst	6	4	3	3	1	3	0	1.96
Schiraldi (L, 0-2)	0.1	3	3	3	0	0	1	13.50
Sambito	0.1	0	0	0	2	0	0	27.00
Stanley	0.1	0	0	0	0	0	0	0.00
Nipper	0.1	3	2	2	1	0	1	7.11
Crawford	0.2	0	0	0	0	0	0	6.23
NY METS	**IP**	**H**	**R**	**ER**	**BB**	**SO**	**HR**	**ERA**
Darling	3.2	6	3	3	1	0	2	1.53
Fernandes	2.1	0	0	0	1	4	0	1.35
McDowell (W, 1-0)	1	3	2	2	0	1	0	4.91
Orosco (S, 2)	2	0	0	0	0	2	0	0.00

WP: Schiraldi 1. **IBB:** Wilson (by Sambito), Santana (by Nipper). **HBP:** Henderson (by Darling), Wilson (by Crawford). **Pitches-strikes:** Hurst 74-48, Schiraldi 16-8, Sambito 12-4, Stanley 2-1, Nipper 18-10, Crawford 6-4, Darling 59-40, Fernandes 30-21, McDowell 17-14, Orosco 24-18. **Ground balls-fly balls:** Hurst 7-8, Schiraldi 0-0, Sambito 0-0, Stanley 1-0, Nipper 1-0, Crawford 2-0, Darling 1-7, Fernandes 0-3, McDowell 2-0, Orosco 2-2. **Batters faced:** Hurst 23, Schiraldi 4, Sambito 3, Stanley 1, Nipper 5, Crawford 3, Darling 18, Fernandes 8, McDowell 6, Orosco 6. **UMPIRES:** hp—Kibler, 1b—Evans, 2b—Wendelstedt, 3b—Brinkman, lf—Montague, rf—Ford **T:** 0:00 **A:** 55,032

1987 MINNESOTA DEF. ST.LOUIS, 4-3

GAME 1 Minnesota 10 St. Louis 1
Humphrey Metrodome 10/17/87

ST.LOUIS	AB	R	H	HR	RBI	BB	AVG
Coleman lf	4	0	0	0	0	0	.000
Smith ss	4	0	0	0	0	0	.000
Herr 2b	4	0	0	0	0	0	.000
Lindeman 1b	4	1	2	0	0	0	.500
McGee cf	3	0	2	0	0	0	.667
Pena c	3	0	0	0	1	0	.000
Lake c	0	0	0	0	0	0	.000
Oquendo rf	3	0	0	0	0	0	.000
Pagnozzi dh	3	0	1	0	0	0	.333
Lawless 3b	3	0	0	0	0	0	.000
TOTALS	**31**	**1**	**5**	**0**	**1**	**0**	**.161**

BATTING: 2B: Lindeman (1, Viola). **RBI:** Pena 1 (1). **Runners left in scoring position, 2 out:** Pena 1. **GIDP:** Pena. **Team LOB:** 3 **FIELDING: E:** Lawless (1). **Outfield assists:** McGee (1). **DP:** 1 (Lawless-Herr-Lindeman).

MINNESOTA	AB	R	H	HR	RBI	BB	AVG
Gladden lf	4	1	2	1	5	1	.500
Gagne ss	5	0	0	0	0	0	.000
Puckett cf	5	0	1	0	0	0	.200
Gaetti 3b	5	1	2	0	0	0	.400
Baylor dh	5	1	1	0	0	0	.200
Brunansky rf	3	1	1	0	0	1	.333
Davidson rf	0	0	0	0	0	0	.000
Hrbek 1b	2	2	1	0	2	2	.500
Larkin 1b	0	0	0	0	0	0	.000
Lombardozzi 2b	3	3	2	1	2	1	.667
Laudner c	3	1	1	0	1	1	.333
TOTALS	**35**	**10**	**11**	**2**	**10**	**6**	**.314**

BATTING: 2B: Gaetti (1, Forsch), Gladden (1, Horton). **HR:** Gladden (1, 4th off Forsch 3 on, 0 out), Lombardozzi (1, 5th off Forsch 1 on, 1 out). **RBI:** Gladden 5 (5), Hrbek 2 (2), Lombardozzi 2 (2), Laudner 1 (1). **2-out RBI:** Gladden 1. **Runners left in scoring position, 2 out:** Gagne 1, Puckett 1, Baylor 1, Brunansky 1, Lombardozzi 1. **GIDP:** Baylor. **Team LOB:** 7 **BASERUNNING: SB:** Gladden (1, 2nd base off Magrane/Pena). **FIELDING: DP:** 1 (Gaetti-Lombardozzi-Hrbek).

ST.LOUIS	IP	H	R	ER	BB	SO	HR	ERA
Magrane (L, 0-1)	3	4	5	5	4	1	0	15.00
Forsch	3	4	4	4	2	0	2	12.00
Horton	2	3	1	1	0	1	0	4.50
MINNESOTA	**IP**	**H**	**R**	**ER**	**BB**	**SO**	**HR**	**ERA**
Viola (W, 1-0)	8	5	1	1	0	5	0	1.13
Atherton	1	0	0	0	0	0	0	0.00

Pitches-strikes: Magrane 59-30, Forsch 46-28, Horton 28-17, Viola 101-71, Atherton 7-6. **Ground balls-fly balls:** Magrane 4-4, Forsch 5-5, Horton 3-1, Viola 13-5, Atherton 1-2. **Batters faced:** Magrane 17, Forsch 16, Horton 8, Viola 28, Atherton 3. **UMPIRES:** hp—Phillips, 1b—Weyer, 2b—Kosc, 3b—McSherry, lf—Kaiser, rf—Tata **T:** 0:00 **A:** 55,171

GAME 2 Minnesota 8 St. Louis 4
Humphrey Metrodome 10/18/87

ST.LOUIS	AB	R	H	HR	RBI	BB	AVG
Coleman lf	4	1	1	0	0	0	.125
Smith ss	4	0	1	0	0	0	.125
Herr 2b	4	0	0	0	0	0	.000
Driessen 1b	4	1	1	0	1	0	.250
McGee cf	4	0	1	0	1	0	.429
Pendleton dh	4	1	1	0	0	0	.250
Ford rf	3	1	2	0	0	1	.667
Oquendo 3b	4	0	1	0	0	0	.143
Pena c	4	0	1	0	2	0	.143
TOTALS	**35**	**4**	**9**	**0**	**4**	**1**	**.212**

BATTING: 2B: Driessen (1, Berenguer). **RBI:** Driessen 1 (1), McGee 1 (1), Pena 2 (3). **2-out RBI:** Driessen 1, McGee 1, Pena 1. **Runners left in scoring position, 2 out:** Coleman 1, Driessen 1, Pena 1. **Team LOB:** 5 **BASERUNNING: SB:** Coleman (1, 2nd base off Berenguer/Laudner).

MINNESOTA	AB	R	H	HR	RBI	BB	AVG
Gladden lf	5	0	1	0	1	0	.333
Gagne ss	4	0	1	0	1	0	.111
Puckett cf	4	1	1	0	0	0	.222
Hrbek 1b	3	1	1	0	0	1	.400
Gaetti 3b	3	2	2	1	1	1	.500
Bush dh	3	1	1	0	2	0	.333
a-Larkin ph	1	0	0	0	0	0	.000
Brunansky rf	3	1	0	0	0	1	.167
Lombardozzi 2b	3	0	0	0	0	0	.333
b-Smalley ph	1	0	1	0	0	0	1.000
c-Newman pr-2b	0	0	0	0	0	0	.000
Laudner c	3	2	2	1	3	1	.500
TOTALS	**33**	**8**	**10**	**2**	**8**	**4**	**.309**

a - Batted for Bush in the 8th
b - Batted for Lombardozzi in the 8th
c - Ran for Smalley in the 8th

BATTING: 2B: Bush (1, Cox), Gagne (1, Tunnell), Smalley (1, Worrell). **HR:** Gaetti (1, 2nd off Cox 0 on, 1 out), Laudner (1, 6th off Tunnell 0 on, 1 out). **RBI:** Gladden 1 (6), Gagne 1 (1), Gaetti 1 (1), Bush 2 (2), Laudner 3 (4). **2-out RBI:** Gladden 1, Gagne 1, Laudner 2. **Runners left in scoring position, 2 out:** Gladden 1, Puckett 2, Brunansky 1. **Team LOB:** 5 **Outfield assists:** Puckett (1).

ST.LOUIS	IP	H	R	ER	BB	SO	HR	ERA
Cox (L, 0-1)	3.2	6	7	7	2	3	1	17.18
Tunnell	2.1	3	1	1	1	1	1	3.86
Dayley	1.1	0	0	0	0	1	0	0.00
Worrell	0.2	1	0	0	1	0	0	0.00
MINNESOTA	**IP**	**H**	**R**	**ER**	**BB**	**SO**	**HR**	**ERA**
Blyleven (W, 1-0)	7	6	2	2	1	8	0	2.57
Berenguer	1	3	2	2	0	0	0	18.00
Reardon	1	0	0	0	0	0	0	0.00

WP: Cox 1. **IBB:** Brunansky (by Cox). **Pitches-strikes:** Cox 61-40, Tunnell 34-19, Dayley 14-9, Worrell 10-6, Blyleven 91-60, Berenguer 17-12, Reardon 10-6. **Ground balls-fly balls:** Cox 3-5, Tunnell 4-1, Dayley 2-1, Worrell 1-1, Blyleven 9-3, Berenguer 1-2, Reardon 1-2. **Batters faced:** Cox 19, Tunnell 10, Dayley 4, Worrell 4, Blyleven 27, Berenguer 6, Reardon 3. **UMPIRES:** hp—Weyer, 1b—Kosc, 2b—McSherry, 3b—Kaiser, lf—Tata, rf—Phillips **T:** 2:42 **A:** 55,257

GAME 3 St. Louis 3 Minnesota 1
Busch Stadium 10/20/87

MINNESOTA	AB	R	H	HR	RBI	BB	AVG
Gladden lf	4	0	1	0	0	0	.308
Gagne ss	3	1	0	0	0	1	.083
Puckett cf	3	0	1	0	0	1	.250
Gaetti 3b	4	0	0	0	0	0	.333
Brunansky rf	4	0	1	0	1	0	.200
Hrbek 1b	4	0	0	0	0	0	.222
Laudner c	3	0	2	0	0	0	.556
b-Bush ph	1	0	0	0	0	0	.250
Lombardozzi 2b	3	0	0	0	0	0	.222
Straker p	2	0	0	0	0	0	.000
a-Larkin ph	1	0	0	0	0	0	.000
Berenguer p	0	0	0	0	0	0	.000
Schatzeder p	0	0	0	0	0	0	.000
TOTALS	**32**	**1**	**5**	**0**	**1**	**2**	**.260**

a - Batted for Straker in the 7th
b - Batted for Laudner in the 9th

BATTING: 2B: Laudner (1, Tudor). **3B:** Puckett (1, Worrell). **RBI:** Brunansky 1 (1). **2-out RBI:** Brunansky 1. **Runners left in scoring position, 2 out:** Gagne 1, Gaetti 1, Hrbek 1, Straker 1. **Team LOB:** 6 **FIELDING: E:** Gagne (1). **DP:** 1 (Gagne-Lombardozzi-Hrbek).

ST.LOUIS	AB	R	H	HR	RBI	BB	AVG
Coleman lf	4	1	1	0	2	0	.167
Smith ss	4	0	2	0	1	0	.250
Herr 2b	4	0	1	0	0	0	.083
Driessen 1b	4	0	0	0	0	0	.125
Worrell p	0	0	0	0	0	0	.000
McGee cf	4	0	2	0	0	0	.455
Ford rf	4	0	1	0	0	0	.429
Oquendo 3b	3	1	1	0	0	1	.200
Pena c	2	1	1	0	0	1	.222
Tudor p	2	0	0	0	0	0	.000
a-Pendleton ph	0	0	0	0	0	0	.250
Lindeman 1b	0	0	0	0	0	0	.500
TOTALS	**31**	**3**	**9**	**0**	**3**	**2**	**.237**

a - Batted for Tudor in the 7th

BATTING: 2B: McGee (1, Straker), Coleman (1, Berenguer). **S:** Pendleton. **RBI:** Coleman 2 (2), Smith 1 (1). **Runners left in scoring position, 2 out:** Herr 1, Ford 1, Oquendo 1, Pena 1. **GIDP:** Herr. **Team LOB:** 7 **BASERUNNING: SB:** Coleman 2 (3, 2nd base off Straker/Laudner, 3rd base off Berenguer/Laudner). **CS:** Ford (1, 2nd base off Schatzeder/Laudner). **FIELDING: E:** Pena (1).

MINNESOTA	IP	H	R	ER	BB	SO	HR	ERA
Straker	6	4	0	0	2	4	0	0.00
Berenguer (L, 0-1)	0.1	4	3	3	0	0	0	33.75
Schatzeder	1.2	1	0	0	0	1	0	0.00
ST.LOUIS	**IP**	**H**	**R**	**ER**	**BB**	**SO**	**HR**	**ERA**
Tudor (W, 1-0)	7	4	1	1	2	7	0	1.29
Worrell (S, 1)	2	1	0	0	0	1	0	0.00

BK: Straker 1. **Pitches-strikes:** Straker 89-55, Berenguer 16-13, Schatzeder 17-11, Tudor 97-62, Worrell 28-20. **Ground balls-fly balls:** Straker 9-5, Berenguer 0-0, Schatzeder 2-1, Tudor 6-8, Worrell 1-4. **Batters faced:** Straker 24, Berenguer 5, Schatzeder 5, Tudor 27, Worrell 7. **UMPIRES:** hp—Kosc, 1b—McSherry, 2b—Kaiser, 3b—Tata, lf—Phillips, rf—Weyer **T:** 0:00 **A:** 0,000

GAME 4 St. Louis 7 Minnesota 2
Busch Stadium 10/21/87

MINNESOTA	AB	R	H	HR	RBI	BB	AVG
Gladden lf	5	0	1	0	0	0	.278
Newman 2b	3	0	1	0	0	1	.333
d-Baylor ph	1	0	1	0	0	0	.333
Puckett cf	4	0	1	0	1	0	.250
Gaetti 3b	3	0	1	0	0	0	.333
Brunansky rf	4	0	0	0	0	0	.143
Hrbek 1b	4	0	1	0	0	0	.231
Laudner c	3	0	0	0	0	1	.417
Butera c	0	0	0	0	0	0	.000
Gagne ss	4	1	1	1	1	0	.125
Viola p	1	0	0	0	0	0	.000
Schatzeder p	0	0	0	0	0	0	.000
a-Larkin ph	0	1	0	0	0	1	.000
Niekro p	0	0	0	0	0	0	.000
b-Smalley ph	1	0	0	0	0	0	.500
Frazier p	0	0	0	0	0	0	.000
c-Davidson ph	1	0	0	0	0	0	.000
TOTALS	**34**	**2**	**7**	**1**	**2**	**3**	**.246**

a - Batted for Schatzeder in the 5th
b - Batted for Niekro in the 7th
c - Batted for Frazier in the 9th
d - Batted for Newman in the 9th

BATTING: HR: Gagne (1, 3th off Mathews 0 on, 0 out). **RBI:** Puckett 1 (1), Gagne 1 (2). **Runners left in scoring position, 2 out:** Brunansky 3, Laudner 1, Gagne 1. **GIDP:** Laudner. **Team LOB:** 10 **BASERUNNING: SB:** Gaetti (1, 2nd base off Mathews/Pena), Brunansky (1, 2nd base off Mathews/Pena). **FIELDING: E:** Puckett (1).

ST.LOUIS	AB	R	H	HR	RBI	BB	AVG
Coleman lf	4	1	1	0	0	1	.188
Smith ss	4	1	0	0	0	1	.188
Herr 2b	3	1	2	0	0	2	.200
Lindeman 1b	4	1	2	0	2	0	.500
McGee cf	4	0	2	0	2	0	.467
Pena c	3	1	1	0	0	1	.250
Oquendo rf	4	1	1	0	0	0	.214
Lawless 3b	4	1	1	1	3	0	.143
Mathews p	1	0	0	0	0	0	.000
Forsch p	2	0	0	0	0	0	.000
Dayley p	1	0	0	0	0	0	.000
TOTALS	**34**	**7**	**10**	**1**	**7**	**5**	**.252**

BATTING: 2B: McGee (2, Schatzeder), Coleman (2, Niekro). **HR:** Lawless (1, 4th off Viola 2 on, 0 out). **RBI:** Lindeman 2 (2), McGee 2 (3), Lawless 3 (3). **2-out RBI:** Lindeman 2, McGee 2. **Runners left in scoring position, 2 out:** McGee 1, Pena 3, Lawless 1. **Team LOB:** 9 **BASERUNNING: SB:** Coleman (4, 2nd base off Schatzeder/Laudner). **FIELDING: E:** Lindeman (1). **DP:** 1 (Lindeman-Smith-Forsch).

MINNESOTA	IP	H	R	ER	BB	SO	HR	ERA
Viola (L, 1-1)	3.1	6	5	5	3	4	1	4.76
Schatzeder	0.2	2	2	2	1	1	0	7.71
Niekro	2	1	0	0	1	1	0	0.00
Frazier	2	1	0	0	0	2	0	0.00

ST.LOUIS	IP	H	R	ER	BB	SO	HR	ERA
Mathews	3.2	2	1	1	2	3	1	2.45
Forsch (W, 1-0)	2.2	4	1	1	1	3	0	7.94
Dayley (S, 1)	2.2	1	0	0	0	2	0	0.00

WP: Mathews 1. **IBB:** Herr (by Schatzeder). **HBP:** Gaetti (by Mathews), Lindeman (by Niekro), Puckett (by Forsch). **Pitches-strikes:** Viola 75-46, Schatzeder 12-7, Niekro 26-16, Frazier 19-13, Mathews 62-36, Forsch 45-26, Dayley 42-27. **Ground balls-fly balls:** Viola 3-3, Schatzeder 0-1, Niekro 3-2, Frazier 1-3, Mathews 3-5, Forsch 4-1, Dayley 4-2. **Batters faced:** Viola 19, Schatzeder 5, Niekro 9, Frazier 7, Mathews 16, Forsch 14, Dayley 9. **UMPIRES:** hp—McSherry, 1b—Kaiser, 2b—Tata, 3b—Phillips, lf—Weyer, rf—Kosc **T:** 0:00 **A:** 0,000

GAME 5 St. Louis 4 Minnesota 2
Busch Stadium 10/22/87

MINNESOTA	AB	R	H	HR	RBI	BB	AVG
Gladden lf	3	1	1	0	0	2	.286
Gagne ss	4	1	1	0	0	0	.150
e-Baylor ph	1	0	0	0	0	0	.286
Puckett cf	4	0	0	0	0	0	.200
Hrbek 1b	4	0	1	0	0	0	.235
Gaetti 3b	4	0	1	0	2	0	.316
Brunansky rf	4	0	1	0	0	0	.167
Laudner c	2	0	0	0	0	1	.357
b-Newman ph	1	0	0	0	0	0	.250
Lombardozzi 2b	2	0	1	0	0	1	.273
c-Smalley ph	0	0	0	0	0	1	.500
Blyleven p	1	0	0	0	0	0	.000
a-Larkin ph	1	0	0	0	0	0	.000
Atherton p	0	0	0	0	0	0	.000
Reardon p	0	0	0	0	0	0	.000
d-Bush ph	1	0	0	0	0	0	.200
TOTALS	**32**	**2**	**6**	**0**	**2**	**5**	**.235**

a - Batted for Blyleven in the 7th
b - Batted for Laudner in the 9th
c - Batted for Lombardozzi in the 9th
d - Batted for Reardon in the 9th e - Batted for Gagne in the 9th

BATTING: 3B: Gaetti (1, Worrell). **S:** Blyleven. **RBI:** Gaetti 2 (3). **2-out RBI:** Gaetti 2. **Runners left in scoring position, 2 out:** Gagne 1, Baylor 1, Puckett 1, Brunansky 1, Lombardozzi 1. **Team LOB:** 9 **BASERUNNING: SB:** Gladden (2, 2nd base off Cox/Pena). **FIELDING: E:** Gagne (2). **DP:** 1 (Laudner-Gaetti).

ST.LOUIS	AB	R	H	HR	RBI	BB	AVG
Coleman lf	3	2	1	0	0	1	.211
Smith ss	4	1	2	0	1	0	.250
Herr 2b	4	0	0	0	0	0	.158
Driessen 1b	3	1	1	0	0	1	.182
Dayley p	0	0	0	0	0	0	.000
Worrell p	0	0	0	0	0	0	.000
McGee cf	4	0	0	0	0	0	.368
Ford rf	4	0	1	0	2	0	.364
Oquendo 3b	4	0	2	0	0	0	.278
Pena c	4	0	3	0	0	0	.375
a-Johnson pr	0	0	0	0	0	0	.000
Lake c	0	0	0	0	0	0	.000
Cox p	2	0	0	0	0	0	.000
Lindeman 1b	1	0	0	0	0	0	.444
TOTALS	**33**	**4**	**10**	**0**	**3**	**2**	**.262**

a - Ran for Pena in the 8th

BATTING: S: Cox, Cox, Oquendo. **RBI:** Smith 1 (2), Ford 2 (2). **2-out RBI:** Ford 2. **Runners left in scoring position, 2 out:** Smith 1, McGee 1, Pena 1, Lindeman 1. **Team LOB:** 8 **BASERUNNING: SB:** Coleman 2 (6, 3rd base off Blyleven/Laudner, 3rd base off Reardon/Laudner), Smith 2 (2, 3rd base off Blyleven/Laudner, 2nd base off Reardon/Laudner), Johnson (1, 2nd base off Reardon/Laudner).

MINNESOTA	IP	H	R	ER	BB	SO	HR	ERA
Blyleven (L, 1-1)	6	7	3	2	1	4	0	2.77
Atherton	0.1	0	1	1	1	0	0	6.75
Reardon	1.2	3	0	0	0	3	0	0.00

ST.LOUIS	IP	H	R	ER	BB	SO	HR	ERA
Cox (W, 1-1)	7.1	5	2	2	3	6	0	7.36
Dayley	0.1	0	0	0	0	0	0	0.00
Worrell (S, 2)	1.1	1	0	0	2	0	0	0.00

BK: Atherton 1. **IBB:** Driessen (by Blyleven). **Pitches-strikes:** Blyleven 98-62, Atherton 11-5, Reardon 30-23, Cox 97-59, Dayley 2-1, Worrell 38-23. **Ground balls-fly balls:** Blyleven 10-3, Atherton 1-0, Reardon 0-2, Cox 9-6, Dayley 0-1, Worrell 1-3. **Batters faced:** Blyleven 26, Atherton 2, Reardon 8, Cox 30, Dayley 1, Worrell 7. **UMPIRES:** hp—Kaiser, 1b—Tata, 2b—Phillips, 3b—Weyer, lf—Kosc, rf—McSherry **T:** 0:00 **A:** 0,000

GAME 6 Minnesota 11 St. Louis 5
Humphrey Metrodome 10/24/87

ST.LOUIS	AB	R	H	HR	RBI	BB	AVG
Coleman lf	5	0	0	0	0	0	.167
Smith ss	4	1	1	0	0	1	.250
Herr 2b	5	1	3	1	1	0	.250
Driessen 1b	2	1	1	0	0	0	.231
b-Pagnozzi ph	1	0	0	0	0	0	.250
Morris rf	2	0	0	0	0	0	.000
McGee cf	4	1	2	0	1	0	.391
Pendleton dh	3	1	2	0	1	1	.429
Ford rf	1	0	0	0	0	0	.333
a-Lindeman ph-rf-1b	3	0	0	0	0	0	.333
Oquendo 3b	3	0	1	0	2	0	.286
Pena c	3	0	1	0	0	1	.368
TOTALS	**36**	**5**	**11**	**1**	**5**	**3**	**.270**

a - Batted for Ford in the 4th
b - Batted for Driessen in the 5th

BATTING: 2B: Driessen (2, Straker). **HR:** Herr (1, 1st off Straker 0 on, 2 out). **SF:** Oquendo. **RBI:** Herr 1 (1), McGee 1 (4), Pendleton 1 (1), Oquendo 2 (2). **2-out RBI:** Herr 1, McGee 1, Oquendo 1. **Runners left in scoring position, 2 out:** Coleman 1, Morris 2, Oquendo 1. **GIDP:** Morris. **Team LOB:** 8 **BASERUNNING: SB:** Pendleton 2 (2, 3rd base off Schatzeder/Laudner, 2nd base off Berenguer/Laudner). **FIELDING: E:** McGee (1), Lindeman (2). **PB:** Pena.

MINNESOTA	AB	R	H	HR	RBI	BB	AVG
Gladden lf	5	1	2	0	0	0	.308
Gagne ss	5	1	1	0	0	0	.160
Puckett cf	4	4	4	0	1	1	.333
Gaetti 3b	5	1	1	0	1	0	.292
Baylor dh	3	2	2	1	3	1	.400
a-Bush ph	1	0	0	0	0	0	.167
Brunansky rf	4	1	1	0	1	1	.182
Hrbek 1b	4	1	1	1	4	1	.238
Laudner c	5	0	0	0	0	0	.263
Lombardozzi 2b	4	0	3	0	1	0	.400
TOTALS	**40**	**11**	**15**	**2**	**11**	**4**	**.262**

a - Batted for Baylor in the 8th

BATTING: 2B: Lombardozzi (1, Tudor), Gaetti (2, Tudor). **3B:** Gladden (1, Tudor). **HR:** Baylor (1, 5th off Tudor 1 on, 0 out), Hrbek (1, 6th off Dayley 3 on, 2 out). **RBI:** Puckett 1 (2), Gaetti 1 (4), Baylor 3 (3), Brunansky 1 (2), Hrbek 4 (6), Lombardozzi 1 (3). **2-out RBI:** Baylor 1, Hrbek 4, Lombardozzi 1. **Runners left in scoring position, 2 out:** Gagne 2, Hrbek 1, Laudner 1. **Team LOB:** 9 **BASERUNNING: SB:** Puckett (1, 2nd base off Tudor/Pena). **FIELDING: DP:** 1 (Lombardozzi-Gagne-Hrbek).

ST.LOUIS	IP	H	R	ER	BB	SO	HR	ERA
Tudor (L, 1-1)	4	11	6	6	1	1	1	5.73
Horton	1	2	1	1	0	0	0	6.00
Forsch	0.2	0	2	2	2	0	0	9.95
Dayley	0.1	1	1	1	0	0	1	1.93
Tunnell	2	1	1	0	1	0	0	2.08

MINNESOTA	IP	H	R	ER	BB	SO	HR	ERA
Straker	3	5	4	4	1	2	1	4.00
Schatzeder (W, 1-0)	2	1	1	1	2	1	0	6.23
Berenguer	3	3	0	0	0	1	0	10.38
Reardon	1	2	0	0	0	0	0	0.00

IBB: Baylor (by Forsch), Hrbek (by Tunnell). **Pitches-strikes:** Tudor 65-42, Horton 18-11, Forsch 16-6, Dayley 2-2, Tunnell 29-15, Straker 54-34, Schatzeder 40-28, Berenguer 47-30, Reardon 15-11. **Ground balls-fly balls:** Tudor 5-6, Horton 1-2, Forsch 0-2, Dayley 1-0, Tunnell 4-3, Straker 4-3, Schatzeder 1-3, Berenguer 5-2, Reardon 1-2. **Batters faced:** Tudor 24, Horton 5, Forsch 4, Dayley 2, Tunnell 9, Straker 15, Schatzeder 9, Berenguer 11, Reardon 5. **UMPIRES:** hp—Tata, 1b—Phillips, 2b—Weyer, 3b—Kosc, lf—McSherry, rf—Kaiser **T:** 3:04 **A:** 55,293

GAME 7 Minnesota 4 St. Louis 2
Humphrey Metrodome 10/25/87

ST.LOUIS	AB	R	H	HR	RBI	BB	AVG
Coleman lf	4	0	0	0	0	0	.143
Smith ss	4	0	0	0	0	0	.214
Herr 2b	4	0	1	0	0	0	.250
Lindeman 1b	3	1	1	0	0	0	.333
a-Ford ph	1	0	0	0	0	0	.308
McGee cf	4	1	1	0	0	0	.370
Pena dh	3	0	2	0	1	0	.409
Oquendo rf	3	0	0	0	0	0	.250
Lawless 3b	3	0	0	0	0	0	.100
Lake c	3	0	1	0	1	0	.333
TOTALS	**32**	**2**	**6**	**0**	**2**	**0**	**.259**

a - Batted for Lindeman in the 9th

BATTING: 2B: Pena (1, Viola). **RBI:** Pena 1 (4), Lake 1 (1). **2-out RBI:** Lake 1. **Runners left in scoring position, 2 out:** Coleman 1, Lawless 1. **Team LOB:** 3 **BASERUNNING: SB:** Pena (1, 3rd base off Viola/Laudner). **CS:** Herr (1, 2nd base off Viola/Laudner). **Outfield assists:** Coleman 2 (2).

MINNESOTA	AB	R	H	HR	RBI	BB	AVG
Gladden lf	5	0	1	0	1	0	.290
Gagne ss	5	1	2	0	1	0	.200
Puckett cf	4	0	2	0	1	0	.357
Gaetti 3b	3	0	0	0	0	1	.259
Baylor dh	3	0	1	0	0	0	.385
Brunansky rf	3	2	1	0	0	1	.200
Hrbek 1b	3	0	0	0	0	1	.208
Laudner c	3	1	2	0	0	1	.318
Lombardozzi 2b	2	0	1	0	1	0	.412
a-Smalley ph	0	0	0	0	0	1	.500
b-Newman pr-2b	1	0	0	0	0	0	.200
TOTALS	**32**	**4**	**10**	**0**	**4**	**5**	**.269**

a - Batted for Lombardozzi in the 6th
b - Ran for Smalley in the 6th

BATTING: 2B: Puckett (1, Cox), Gladden (2, Worrell). **RBI:** Gladden 1 (7), Gagne 1 (3), Puckett 1 (3), Lombardozzi 1 (4). **2-out RBI:** Gladden 1, Gagne 1, Lombardozzi 1. **Runners left in scoring position, 2 out:** Gladden 1, Gagne 1, Puckett 2, Baylor 2. **Team LOB:** 10 **BASERUNNING: SB:** Gaetti (2, 2nd base off Magrane/Lake). **CS:** Puckett (1, 3rd base off Cox/Lake).

ST.LOUIS	IP	H	R	ER	BB	SO	HR	ERA
Magrane	4.1	5	2	2	1	4	0	8.59
Cox (L, 1-2)	0.2	2	1	1	3	0	0	7.71
Worrell	3	3	1	1	1	2	0	1.29

MINNESOTA	IP	H	R	ER	BB	SO	HR	ERA
Viola (W, 2-1)	8	6	2	2	0	7	0	3.72
Reardon (S, 1)	1	0	0	0	0	0	0	0.00

HBP: Baylor (by Magrane). **Pitches-strikes:** Magrane 67-41, Cox 21-7, Worrell 53-35, Viola 95-69, Reardon 16-11. **Ground balls-fly balls:** Magrane 4-5, Cox 0-0, Worrell 2-5, Viola 7-9, Reardon 1-2. **Batters faced:** Magrane 20, Cox 5, Worrell 13, Viola 29, Reardon 3. **UMPIRES:** hp—Phillips, 1b—Weyer, 2b—Kosc, 3b—McSherry, lf—Kaiser, rf—Tata **T:** 0:00 **A:** 55,376

1988 LOS ANGELES DEF. OAKLAND, 4-1

GAME 1 Los Angeles 5 Oakland 4
Dodger Stadium 10/15/88

OAKLAND	AB	R	H	HR	RBI	BB	AVG
Lansford 3b	4	1	0	0	0	1	.000
Henderson cf	5	0	2	0	0	0	.400
Canseco rf	4	1	1	1	4	0	.250
Parker lf	2	0	0	0	0	2	.000
a-Javier pr-lf	1	0	1	0	0	0	1.000
McGwire 1b	3	0	0	0	0	2	.000
Steinbach c	4	0	1	0	0	0	.250
Hassey c	0	0	0	0	0	0	.000
Hubbard 2b	4	1	2	0	0	0	.500
Weiss ss	4	0	0	0	0	0	.000
Stewart p	3	1	0	0	0	1	.000
Eckersley p	0	0	0	0	0	0	.000
TOTALS	**34**	**4**	**7**	**1**	**4**	**6**	**.206**

a - Ran for Parker in the 7th

BATTING: 2B: Henderson (1, Leary). **HR:** Canseco (1, 2nd off Belcher 3 on, 2 out). **RBI:** Canseco 4 (4). **2-out RBI:** Canseco 4. **Runners left in scoring position, 2 out:** Lansford 1, Steinbach 3, Hubbard 1. **Team LOB:** 10 **BASERUNNING: SB:** Canseco (1, 2nd base off Leary/Scioscia). **FIELDING: DP:** 1 (Lansford-McGwire).

LOS ANGELES	AB	R	H	HR	RBI	BB	AVG
Sax 2b	3	1	1	0	0	0	.333
Stubbs 1b	4	0	0	0	0	0	.000
Hatcher lf	3	1	1	1	2	1	.333
Marshall rf	4	1	1	0	0	0	.250
Shelby cf	4	0	1	0	0	0	.250
Scioscia c	4	0	1	0	1	0	.250
Hamilton 3b	4	0	0	0	0	0	.000
Griffin ss	2	0	1	0	0	1	.500
d-M.Davis ph	0	1	0	0	0	1	.000
Belcher p	0	0	0	0	0	0	.000
a-Heep ph	1	0	0	0	0	0	.000
Leary p	0	0	0	0	0	0	.000
b-Woodson ph	1	0	0	0	0	0	.000
Holton p	0	0	0	0	0	0	.000
c-Gonzalez ph	1	0	0	0	0	0	.000
Pena p	0	0	0	0	0	0	.000
e-Gibson ph	1	1	1	1	2	0.	1.000
TOTALS	**32**	**5**	**7**	**2**	**5**	**3**	**.219**

a - Batted for Belcher in the 2nd
b - Batted for Leary in the 5th
c - Batted for Holton in the 7th
d - Batted for Griffin in the 9th e - Batted for Pena in the 9th

BATTING: HR: Hatcher (1, 1st off Stewart 1 on, 1 out), Gibson (1, 9th off Eckersley 1 on, 2 out). **RBI:** Hatcher 2 (2), Scioscia 1 (1), Gibson 2 (2). **2-out RBI:** Gibson 2. **Runners left in scoring position, 2 out:** Stubbs 2. **GIDP:** Hamilton. **Team LOB:** 5 **BASERUNNING: SB:** Sax (1, 2nd base off Stewart/Steinbach), M.Davis (1, 2nd base off Eckersley/Hassey).

OAKLAND	IP	H	R	ER	BB	SO	HR	ERA
Stewart	8	6	3	3	2	5	1	3.38
Eckersley (L, 0-1)	0.2	1	2	2	1	1	1	27.00

LOS ANGELES	IP	H	R	ER	BB	SO	HR	ERA
Belcher	2	3	4	4	4	3	1	18.00
Leary	3	3	0	0	1	3	0	0.00
Holton	2	0	0	0	1	0	0	0.00
Pena (W, 1-0)	2	1	0	0	0	3	0	0.00

WP: Stewart 1. **BK:** , Stewart 1. **IBB:** McGwire (by Leary). **HBP:** Canseco (by Belcher), Sax (by Stewart). **Pitches-strikes:** Stewart 97-68, Eckersley 0-0, Belcher 70-38, Leary 43-27, Holton 20-11, Pena 0-0. **Ground balls-fly balls:** Stewart 7-11, Eckersley 0-1, Belcher 1-2, Leary 5-1, Holton 3-3, Pena 1-2. **Batters faced:** Stewart 32, Eckersley 4, Belcher 14, Leary 13, Holton 7, Pena 7. **UMPIRES:** hp—Harvey (NL), 1b—Merrill (AL), 2b—Froemming (NL), 3b—Cousins (AL), lf—Crawford (NL), rf—McCoy (AL) **T:** 3:04 **A:** 55,983

GAME 2 Los Angeles 6 Oakland 0
Dodger Stadium 10/16/88

OAKLAND	AB	R	H	HR	RBI	BB	AVG
Lansford 3b	3	0	0	0	0	1	.000
Henderson cf	4	0	0	0	0	0	.222
Canseco rf	4	0	0	0	0	0	.125
Parker lf	4	0	3	0	0	0	.500
McGwire 1b	3	0	0	0	0	0	.000
Hassey c	3	0	0	0	0	0	.000
Hubbard 2b	2	0	0	0	0	1	.333
Weiss ss	3	0	0	0	0	0	.000
S.Davis p	1	0	0	0	0	0	.000
Nelson p	0	0	0	0	0	0	.000
a-Polonia ph	1	0	0	0	0	0	.000
Young p	0	0	0	0	0	0	.000
Plunk p	0	0	0	0	0	0	.000
b-Baylor ph	1	0	0	0	0	0	.000
Honeycutt p	0	0	0	0	0	0	.000
TOTALS	**29**	**0**	**3**	**0**	**0**	**2**	**.159**

a - Batted for Nelson in the 6th
b - Batted for Plunk in the 8th

BATTING: Runners left in scoring position, 2 out: Parker 1, McGwire 1, Baylor 1. **GIDP:** McGwire, McGwire. **Team LOB:** 4 **BASERUNNING: SB:** Weiss (1, 2nd base off Hershiser/Scioscia).

LOS ANGELES	AB	R	H	HR	RBI	BB	AVG
Sax 2b	4	1	1	0	0	0	.286
Stubbs 1b	2	1	1	0	1	1	.167
a-Woodson ph-1b	1	0	0	0	0	0	.000
Hatcher lf	4	1	2	0	1	0	.429
Marshall rf	4	1	2	1	3	0	.375
Gonzalez rf	0	0	0	0	0	0	.000
Shelby cf	4	0	0	0	0	0	.125
Scioscia c	4	0	0	0	0	0	.125
Hamilton 3b	4	0	0	0	0	0	.000
Griffin ss	4	1	1	0	0	0	.333
Hershiser p	3	1	3	0	1	0	1.000
TOTALS	**34**	**6**	**10**	**1**	**6**	**1**	**.258**

a - Batted for Stubbs in the 6th

BATTING: 2B: Hershiser 2 (2, S.Davis, Young). **3B:** Marshall (1, Nelson). **HR:** Marshall (1, 3th off S.Davis 2 on, 1 out). **RBI:** Stubbs 1 (1), Hatcher 1 (3), Marshall 3 (3), Hershiser 1 (1). **Runners left in scoring position, 2 out:** Woodson 1, Hatcher 1, Hamilton 1. **Team LOB:** 5 **FIELDING: E:** Hamilton (1). **DP:** 2 (Griffin-Sax-Stubbs 2).

OAKLAND	IP	H	R	ER	BB	SO	HR	ERA
S.Davis (L, 0-1)	3.1	8	6	6	0	2	1	16.20
Nelson	1.2	1	0	0	1	1	0	0.00
Young	1	1	0	0	0	0	0	0.00
Plunk	1	0	0	0	0	3	0	0.00
Honeycutt	1	0	0	0	0	2	0	0.00

LOS ANGELES	IP	H	R	ER	BB	SO	HR	ERA
Hershiser (W, 1-0)	9	3	0	0	2	8	0	0.00

Pitches-strikes: S.Davis 66-46, Nelson 19-12, Young 11-8, Plunk 17-12, Honeycutt 14-11, Hershiser 101-64. **Ground balls-fly balls:** S.Davis 5-3, Nelson 2-2, Young 1-2, Plunk 0-0, Honeycutt 0-1, Hershiser 12-6. **Batters faced:** S.Davis 18, Nelson 7, Young 4, Plunk 3, Honeycutt 3, Hershiser 31. **UMPIRES:** hp—Merrill (AL), 1b—Froemming (NL), 2b—Cousins (AL), 3b—Crawford (NL), lf—McCoy (AL), rf—Crawford (NL) **T:** 2:30 **A:** 56,051

GAME 3 Oakland 2 Los Angeles 1
Oakland Coliseum 10/18/88

LOS ANGELES	AB	R	H	HR	RBI	BB	AVG
Sax 2b	5	0	1	0	0	0	.250
Stubbs 1b	4	0	1	0	1	0	.200
c-Woodson ph-1b	1	0	0	0	0	0	.000
Hatcher lf-rf	4	0	1	0	0	0	.364
Marshall rf	1	0	0	0	0	0	.333
a-Heep ph-lf	3	0	1	0	0	0	.250
Shelby cf	3	0	2	0	0	1	.273
M.Davis dh	2	0	0	0	0	1	.000
b-Anderson ph	1	0	0	0	0	0	.000
Scioscia c	4	0	1	0	0	0	.167
Hamilton 3b	3	1	1	0	0	1	.091
Griffin ss	3	0	0	0	0	0	.222
TOTALS	**34**	**1**	**8**	**0**	**1**	**3**	**.250**

a - Batted for Marshall in the 4th
b - Batted for M.Davis in the 8th
c - Batted for Stubbs in the 9th

BATTING: 2B: Stubbs (1, Welch), Heep (1, Welch), Hatcher (1, Nelson). **S:** Griffin. **SF:** Scioscia. **RBI:** Stubbs 1 (2). **2-out RBI:** Stubbs 1. **Runners left in scoring position, 2 out:** Hatcher 1, Heep 1, Scioscia 1, Griffin 3. **Team LOB:** 10 **BASERUNNING: SB:** Shelby (1, 2nd base off Welch/Hassey). **FIELDING: E:** Scioscia (1). **DP:** 1 (Leary-Stubbs).

OAKLAND	AB	R	H	HR	RBI	BB	AVG
Phillips lf	1	0	0	0	0	0	.000
a-Polonia ph-lf	3	0	0	0	0	0	.000
Henderson cf	4	0	0	0	0	0	.154
Canseco rf	4	0	0	0	0	0	.083
McGwire 1b	4	1	1	1	1	0	.100
Steinbach dh	3	0	2	0	0	0	.429
Lansford 3b	3	0	0	0	0	0	.000
Hubbard 2b	3	1	1	0	0	0	.333
Hassey c	1	0	1	0	1	2	.250
Weiss ss	3	0	0	0	0	0	.000
TOTALS	**29**	**2**	**5**	**1**	**2**	**2**	**.163**

a - Batted for Phillips in the 3th

BATTING: 2B: Steinbach (1, Leary). **HR:** McGwire (1, 9th off Howell 0 on, 1 out). **SF:** Weiss. **RBI:** McGwire 1 (1), Hassey 1 (1). **Runners left in scoring position, 2 out:** Henderson 1, Lansford 1. **Team LOB:** 4 **BASERUNNING: SB:** Hubbard (1, 2nd base off Leary/Scioscia).

LOS ANGELES	IP	H	R	ER	BB	SO	HR	ERA
Tudor	1.1	0	0	0	0	1	0	0.00
Leary	3.2	3	1	1	1	1	0	1.35
Pena	3	1	0	0	1	4	0	0.00
Howell (L, 0-1)	0.1	1	1	1	0	0	1	27.00

OAKLAND	IP	H	R	ER	BB	SO	HR	ERA
Welch	5	6	1	1	3	8	0	1.80
Cadaret	0.1	0	0	0	0	0	0	0.00
Nelson	1.2	2	0	0	0	1	0	0.00
Honeycutt (W, 1-0)	2	0	0	0	0	3	0	0.00

BK: Leary 1. **Pitches-strikes:** Tudor 21-15, Leary 55-30, Pena 55-35, Howell 9-7, Welch 95-58, Cadaret 2-2, Nelson 17-14, Honeycutt 22-16. **Ground balls-fly balls:** Tudor 1-2, Leary 4-5, Pena 0-5, Howell 0-1, Welch 3-3, Cadaret 0-1, Nelson 3-1, Honeycutt 1-2. **Batters faced:** Tudor 4, Leary 14, Pena 11, Howell 2, Welch 24, Cadaret 1, Nelson 7, Honeycutt 6. **UMPIRES:** hp—Froemming (NL), 1b—Cousins (AL), 2b—Crawford (NL), 3b—McCoy (AL), lf—Harvey (NL), rf—Merrill (AL) **T:** 0:00 **A:** 0,000

GAME 4 Los Angeles 4 Oakland 3
Oakland Coliseum 10/19/88

LOS ANGELES	AB	R	H	HR	RBI	BB	AVG
Sax 2b	4	1	1	0	0	1	.250
Stubbs 1b	3	1	1	0	0	0	.231
a-Woodson ph-1b	1	0	0	0	1	0	.000
Hatcher lf	4	1	1	0	0	0	.333
Marshall rf	0	0	0	0	0	0	.333
M.Davis rf	3	0	0	0	0	0	.000
b-Gonzalez ph-rf-lf	1	0	0	0	0	0	.000
Shelby cf	4	0	1	0	1	0	.267
Scioscia c	2	0	1	0	0	0	.214
Dempsey c	1	0	0	0	0	1	.000
Heep dh	4	0	1	0	0	0	.250
Hamilton 3b	4	0	1	0	0	0	.133
Griffin ss	3	1	1	0	0	1	.250
TOTALS	**34**	**4**	**8**	**0**	**2**	**3**	**.246**

a - Batted for Stubbs in the 7th
b - Batted for M.Davis in the 8th

BATTING: 2B: Stubbs (2, Stewart), Shelby (1, Cadaret). **SF:** Hatcher. **RBI:** Woodson 1 (1), Shelby 1 (1). **Runners left in scoring position, 2 out:** Hatcher 1, Scioscia 1, Heep 1. **Team LOB:** 6 **BASERUNNING: SB:** M.Davis (2, 2nd base off Stewart/Steinbach). **CS:** Heep (1, 2nd base off Stewart/Steinbach), Scioscia (1, 2nd base off Stewart/Steinbach), Griffin (1, 2nd base off Eckersley/Steinbach). **FIELDING: E:** Griffin (1). **PB:** Scioscia.

OAKLAND	AB	R	H	HR	RBI	BB	AVG
Polonia lf	5	1	1	0	0	0	.111
Henderson cf	5	1	4	0	1	0	.333
c-Javier pr	0	0	0	0	0	0	1.000
Canseco rf	3	0	0	0	1	2	.067
Parker dh	5	0	0	0	0	0	.273
McGwire 1b	3	0	0	0	0	1	.077
Lansford 3b	4	0	1	0	1	0	.071
Steinbach c	4	0	1	0	0	0	.364
Hubbard 2b	3	0	0	0	0	0	.250
a-Hassey ph	1	0	1	0	0	0	.400
b-Gallego pr-2b	0	0	0	0	0	0	.000
Weiss ss	4	1	1	0	0	0	.071
TOTALS	**37**	**3**	**9**	**0**	**3**	**3**	**.186**

a - Batted for Hubbard in the 8th
b - Ran for Hassey in the 8th
c - Ran for Henderson in the 9th

BATTING: 2B: Henderson (2, Belcher). **RBI:** Henderson 1 (1), Canseco 1 (5), Lansford 1 (1). **2-out RBI:** Henderson 1, Lansford 1. **Runners left in scoring position, 2 out:** McGwire 2, Lansford 1, Steinbach 1. **Team LOB:** 10 **FIELDING: E:** Hubbard (1), Weiss (1). **PB:** Steinbach.

LOS ANGELES	IP	H	R	ER	BB	SO	HR	ERA
Belcher (W, 1-0)	6.2	7	3	2	2	7	0	6.23
Howell (S, 1)	2.1	2	0	0	1	2	0	3.38

OAKLAND	IP	H	R	ER	BB	SO	HR	ERA
Stewart (L, 0-1)	6.1	6	4	2	3	0	0	3.14
Cadaret	1.2	1	0	0	0	3	0	0.00
Eckersley	1	1	0	0	0	1	0	10.80

Pitches-strikes: Belcher 119-74, Howell 32-19, Stewart 89-53, Cadaret 22-16, Eckersley 9-7. **Ground balls-fly balls:** Belcher 6-7, Howell 1-5, Stewart 5-14, Cadaret 1-1, Eckersley 0-1. **Batters faced:** Belcher 29, Howell 11, Stewart 28, Cadaret 6, Eckersley 3. **UMPIRES:** hp—Cousins (AL), 1b—Crawford (NL), 2b—McCoy (AL), 3b—Harvey (NL), lf—Merrill (AL), rf—Froemming (NL) **T:** 3:05 **A:** 49,317

GAME 5 Los Angeles 5 Oakland 2
Oakland Coliseum 10/20/88

LOS ANGELES	AB	R	H	HR	RBI	BB	AVG
Sax 2b	4	0	2	0	0	0	.300
Stubbs 1b	4	1	2	0	0	0	.294
Hatcher lf	4	2	2	1	2	0	.368
Gonzalez lf	0	0	0	0	0	0	.000
Marshall rf	4	0	0	0	0	0	.231
Shelby cf	3	0	0	0	0	1	.222
M.Davis dh	2	2	1	1	2	2	.143
Dempsey c	4	0	1	0	1	0	.200
Hamilton 3b	4	0	0	0	0	0	.105
Griffin ss	4	0	0	0	0	0	.188
TOTALS	**33**	**5**	**8**	**2**	**5**	**3**	**.246**

BATTING: 2B: Dempsey (1, Nelson). **HR:** Hatcher (2, 1st off S.Davis 1 on, 1 out), M.Davis (1, 4th off S.Davis 1 on, 2 out). **SF:** Hamilton. **RBI:** Hatcher 2 (5), M.Davis 2 (2), Dempsey 1 (1). **2-out RBI:** M.Davis 2, Dempsey 1. **Runners left in scoring position, 2 out:** Hatcher 1, Hamilton 1. **GIDP:** Dempsey. **Team LOB:** 4 **BASERUNNING: CS:** Sax (1, 2nd base off S.Davis/Hassey).

OAKLAND	AB	R	H	HR	RBI	BB	AVG
Javier lf	3	0	1	0	2	0	.500
Henderson cf	2	0	0	0	0	2	.300
Canseco rf	4	0	0	0	0	0	.053
Parker dh	4	0	0	0	0	0	.200
McGwire 1b	4	0	0	0	0	0	.059
Hassey c	3	0	0	0	0	1	.250
Lansford 3b	4	1	2	0	0	0	.167
Phillips 2b	3	1	1	0	0	1	.250
Weiss ss	2	0	0	0	0	0	.063
TOTALS	**29**	**2**	**4**	**0**	**2**	**4**	**.177**

BATTING: S: Weiss. **SF:** Javier. **RBI:** Javier 2 (2). **Runners left in scoring position, 2 out:** Canseco 1, Parker 2, Phillips 1. **Team LOB:** 6 **FIELDING: DP:** 1 (Weiss-Phillips-McGwire).

LOS ANGELES	IP	H	R	ER	BB	SO	HR	ERA
Hershiser (W, 2-0)	9	4	2	2	4	9	0	1.00

OAKLAND	IP	H	R	ER	BB	SO	HR	ERA
S.Davis (L, 0-2)	4.2	6	4	4	1	5	2	11.25
Cadaret	0	1	0	0	0	0	0	0.00
Nelson	3	1	1	1	2	1	0	1.42
Honeycutt	0.1	0	0	0	0	0	0	0.00
Plunk	0.2	0	0	0	0	0	0	0.00
Burns	0.1	0	0	0	0	0	0	0.00

WP: Hershiser 1. **Pitches-strikes:** Hershiser 117-75, S.Davis 81-48, Cadaret 5-3, Nelson 45-27, Honeycutt 3-3, Plunk 5-3, Burns 3-3. **Ground balls-fly balls:** Hershiser 6-10, S.Davis 6-1, Cadaret 0-0, Nelson 4-4, Honeycutt 1-0, Plunk 0-2, Burns 1-0. **Batters faced:** Hershiser 35, S.Davis 19, Cadaret 1, Nelson 12, Honeycutt 1, Plunk 2, Burns 1. **UMPIRES:** hp—Crawford (NL), 1b—McCoy (AL), 2b—Harvey (NL), 3b—Merrill (AL), lf—Froemming (NL), rf—Cousins (AL) **T:** 2:51 **A:** 49,317

1989 OAKLAND DEF. SAN FRANCISCO, 4-0

GAME 1 Oakland 5 San Francisco 0
Oakland Coliseum 10/14/89

SAN FRANCISCO	AB	R	H	HR	RBI	BB	AVG
Butler cf	4	0	0	0	0	0	.000
Thompson 2b	4	0	0	0	0	0	.000
Clark 1b	4	0	2	0	0	0	.500
Mitchell lf	4	0	2	0	0	0	.500
Williams 3b-ss	4	0	0	0	0	0	.000
Riles dh	4	0	0	0	0	0	.000
Maldonado rf	4	0	0	0	0	0	.000
Kennedy c	3	0	0	0	0	0	.000
Uribe ss	2	0	1	0	0	0	.500
a-Oberkfell ph-3b	0	0	0	0	0	1	.000
TOTALS	**33**	**0**	**5**	**0**	**0**	**1**	**.152**

a - Batted for Uribe in the 8th

BATTING: 2B: Clark (1, Stewart). **Runners left in scoring position, 2 out:** Mitchell 2, Maldonado 2. **Team LOB:** 7

OAKLAND	AB	R	H	HR	RBI	BB	AVG
R.Henderson lf	5	0	2	0	1	0	.400
Lansford 3b	5	0	1	0	0	0	.200
Gallego 2b	0	0	0	0	0	0	.000
Canseco rf	3	0	0	0	0	1	.000
Parker dh	4	1	1	1	1	0	.250
D.Henderson cf	3	1	0	0	0	1	.000
McGwire 1b	4	0	3	0	0	0	.750
Steinbach c	4	1	1	0	0	0	.250
Phillips 2b-3b	4	1	2	0	1	0	.500
Weiss ss	4	1	1	1	1	0	.250
TOTALS	**36**	**5**	**11**	**2**	**4**	**2**	**.306**

BATTING: HR: Parker (1, 3th off Garrelts 0 on, 0 out), Weiss (1, 4th off Garrelts 0 on, 0 out). **RBI:** R.Henderson 1 (1), Parker 1 (1), Phillips 1 (1), Weiss 1 (1). **Runners left in scoring position, 2 out:** Canseco 1, Parker 2. **Team LOB:** 9 **FIELDING: E:** Stewart (1). **PB:** Steinbach.

SAN FRANCISCO	IP	H	R	ER	BB	SO	HR	ERA
Garrelts (L, 0-1)	4	7	5	4	1	5	2	9.00
Hammaker	1.2	3	0	0	0	2	0	0.00
Brantley	1.1	1	0	0	1	0	0	0.00
LaCoss	1	0	0	0	0	1	0	0.00

OAKLAND	IP	H	R	ER	BB	SO	HR	ERA
Stewart (W, 1-0)	9	5	0	0	1	6	0	0.00

Pitches-strikes: Garrelts 76-47, Hammaker 32-19, Brantley 22-13, LaCoss 9-6, Stewart 138-86. **Ground balls-fly balls:** Garrelts 4-4, Hammaker 1-2, Brantley 2-2, LaCoss 2-0, Stewart 11-11. **Batters faced:** Garrelts 21, Hammaker 8, Brantley 6, LaCoss 3, Stewart 34. **UMPIRES:** hp—Garcia, 1b—Runge, 2b—Voltaggio, 3b—Rennert, lf—Clark, rf—Gregg **T:** 2:45 **A:** 49,385

GAME 2 Oakland 5 San Francisco 1
Oakland Coliseum 10/15/89

SAN FRANCISCO	AB	R	H	HR	RBI	BB	AVG
Butler cf	2	0	1	0	0	2	.167
Thompson 2b	3	0	0	0	1	0	.000
Clark 1b	4	0	0	0	0	0	.250
Mitchell lf	4	0	1	0	0	0	.375
Williams 3b-ss	4	0	0	0	0	0	.000
Riles dh	3	0	0	0	0	0	.000
Maldonado rf	3	0	0	0	0	0	.000
Kennedy c	3	0	1	0	0	0	.167
Uribe ss	2	1	0	0	0	0	.250
a-Oberkfell ph-3b	1	0	1	0	0	0	1.000
TOTALS	**29**	**1**	**4**	**0**	**1**	**2**	**.145**

a - Batted for Uribe in the 8th

BATTING: SF: Thompson. **RBI:** Thompson 1 (1). **Runners left in scoring position, 2 out:** Thompson 1, Clark 1, Mitchell 1, Maldonado 1. **GIDP:** Thompson. **Team LOB:** 4 **BASERUNNING: SB:** Butler 2 (2, 2nd base off Moore/Steinbach). **FIELDING: DP:** 2 (Williams-Thompson-Clark, Kennedy-Williams).

OAKLAND	AB	R	H	HR	RBI	BB	AVG
R.Henderson lf	3	1	3	0	0	1	.625
Lansford 3b	3	0	1	0	1	1	.250
Canseco rf	2	1	0	0	0	2	.000
Parker dh	4	1	1	0	1	0	.250
D.Henderson cf	3	1	0	0	0	1	.000
McGwire 1b	4	0	1	0	0	0	.500
Steinbach c	4	1	1	1	3	0	.250
Phillips 2b	3	0	0	0	0	0	.286
Weiss ss	3	0	0	0	0	0	.143
TOTALS	**29**	**5**	**7**	**1**	**5**	**5**	**.277**

BATTING: 2B: Lansford (1, Reuschel), Parker (1, Reuschel), McGwire (1, Downs). **3B:** R.Henderson (1, Lefferts). **HR:** Steinbach (1, 4th off Reuschel 2 on, 1 out). **RBI:** Lansford 1 (1), Parker 1 (2), Steinbach 3 (3). **Runners left in scoring position, 2 out:** Parker 1, D.Henderson 1, Phillips 1. **GIDP:** Lansford. **Team LOB:** 5 **BASERUNNING: SB:** R.Henderson (1, 2nd base off Reuschel/Kennedy). **CS:** R.Henderson (1, 3rd base off Downs/Kennedy). **FIELDING: DP:** 1 (Weiss-Phillips-McGwire).

SAN FRANCISCO	IP	H	R	ER	BB	SO	HR	ERA
Reuschel (L, 0-1)	4	5	5	5	4	2	1	11.25
Downs	2	1	0	0	0	2	0	0.00
Lefferts	1	1	0	0	1	1	0	0.00
Bedrosian	1	0	0	0	0	2	0	0.00

OAKLAND	IP	H	R	ER	BB	SO	HR	ERA
Moore (W, 1-0)	7	4	1	1	2	7	0	1.29
Honeycutt	1.1	0	0	0	0	1	0	0.00
Eckersley	0.2	0	0	0	0	0	0	0.00

WP: Moore 2. **IBB:** Canseco (by Lefferts). **Pitches-strikes:** Reuschel 76-41, Downs 26-16, Lefferts 16-10, Bedrosian 7-7, Moore 114-75, Honeycutt 9-6, Eckersley 9-5. **Ground balls-fly balls:** Reuschel 4-5, Downs 2-1, Lefferts 2-0, Bedrosian 1-0, Moore 6-7, Honeycutt 2-0, Eckersley 1-1. **Batters faced:** Reuschel 20, Downs 6, Lefferts 5, Bedrosian 3, Moore 27, Honeycutt 3, Eckersley 2. **UMPIRES:** hp—Runge, 1b—Voltaggio, 2b—Rennert, 3b—Clark, lf—Gregg, rf—Garcia **T:** 2:47 **A:** 49,388

GAME 3 Oakland 13 San Francisco 7
Candlestick Park 10/27/89

OAKLAND	AB	R	H	HR	RBI	BB	AVG
R.Henderson lf	5	1	1	0	0	1	.462
Nelson p	0	0	0	0	0	0	.000
Burns p	0	0	0	0	0	0	.000
Lansford 3b	4	4	3	1	2	1	.417
Honeycutt p	0	0	0	0	0	0	.000
b-Gallego ph-3b	1	0	0	0	0	0	.000
Canseco rf	5	3	3	1	3	0	.300
Javier rf	0	0	0	0	0	0	.000
McGwire 1b	4	0	0	0	1	1	.333
D.Henderson cf	4	2	3	2	4	0	.300
Steinbach c	4	0	1	0	1	1	.250
Phillips 2b-3b-lf	5	1	1	1	1	0	.250
Weiss ss	5	1	1	0	0	0	.167
Stewart p	3	0	0	0	0	0	.000
a-Blankenship ph-2b	2	1	1	0	0	0	.500
TOTALS	**42**	**13**	**14**	**5**	**12**	**4**	**.299**

a - Batted for Stewart in the 8th
b - Batted for Honeycutt in the 9th

BATTING: 2B: D.Henderson (1, Garrelts), R.Henderson (1, Garrelts). **HR:** D.Henderson 2 (2, 4th off Garrelts 0 on, 0 out, 5th off Downs 0 on, 1 out), Phillips (1, 4th off Garrelts 0 on, 1 out), Canseco (1, 5th off Downs 2 on, 0 out), Lansford (1, 6th off Brantley 0 on, 2 out). **RBI:** Lansford 2 (3), Canseco 3 (3), McGwire 1 (1), D.Henderson 4 (4), Steinbach 1 (4), Phillips 1 (2). **2-out RBI:** Lansford 1, D.Henderson 2, Steinbach 1. **Runners left in scoring position, 2 out:** McGwire 1, Steinbach 1, Phillips 1. **GIDP:** D.Henderson. **Team LOB:** 7 **BASERUNNING: SB:** R.Henderson 2 (3, 3rd base off Garrelts/Kennedy, 2nd base off Downs/Kennedy).

SAN FRANCISCO	AB	R	H	HR	RBI	BB	AVG
Butler cf	3	0	0	0	0	0	.111
b-Nixon ph-cf	2	1	1	0	0	0	.500
Thompson 2b	3	0	0	0	0	0	.000
c-Litton ph-2b	2	0	2	0	1	0	1.000
Clark 1b	4	1	1	0	0	1	.250
Mitchell lf	5	1	1	0	0	0	.308
Oberkfell 3b	2	1	1	0	0	2	.667
Williams ss	4	1	1	1	1	0	.083
Kennedy c	3	0	1	0	2	0	.222
Manwaring c	1	1	1	0	0	0	1.000
Sheridan rf	2	0	0	0	0	0	.000
Brantley p	0	0	0	0	0	0	.000
a-Riles ph	1	0	0	0	0	0	.000
Hammaker p	0	0	0	0	0	0	.000
Lefferts p	0	0	0	0	0	0	.000
d-Bathe ph	1	1	1	1	3	0	1.000
Garrelts p	1	0	0	0	0	0	.000
Downs p	0	0	0	0	0	0	.000
Maldonado rf	3	0	0	0	0	0	.000
TOTALS	**37**	**7**	**10**	**2**	**7**	**3**	**.192**

a - Batted for Brantley in the 7th
b - Batted for Butler in the 8th
c - Batted for Thompson in the 8th
d - Batted for Lefferts in the 9th

BATTING: 2B: Manwaring (1, Nelson), Litton (1, Burns). **HR:** Williams (1, 2nd off Stewart 0 on, 2 out), Bathe (1, 9th off Nelson 2 on, 1 out). **RBI:** Litton 1 (1), Williams 1 (1), Kennedy 2 (2), Bathe 3 (3). **2-out RBI:** Litton 1, Williams 1, Kennedy 2. **Runners left in scoring position, 2 out:** Mitchell 1, Sheridan 1. **Team LOB:** 6 **FIELDING: E:** Williams (1), Mitchell (1), Lefferts (1). **DP:** 1 (Oberkfell-Thompson-Clark).

OAKLAND	IP	H	R	ER	BB	SO	HR	ERA
Stewart (W, 2-0)	7	5	3	3	1	8	1	1.69
Honeycutt	1	1	0	0	0	1	0	0.00
Nelson	0.2	3	4	4	1	1	1	54.00
Burns	0.1	1	0	0	1	0	0	0.00

SAN FRANCISCO	IP	H	R	ER	BB	SO	HR	ERA
Garrelts (L, 0-2)	3.1	6	4	4	0	3	2	9.82
Downs	1	2	4	4	2	1	2	12.00
Brantley	2.2	1	1	1	2	1	1	2.25
Hammaker	0.2	5	4	4	0	0	0	15.43
Lefferts	1.1	0	0	0	0	0	0	0.00

HBP: D.Henderson (by Hammaker). **Pitches-strikes:** Stewart 86-60, Honeycutt 8-7, Nelson 20-9, Burns 11-4, Garrelts 52-35, Downs 29-16, Brantley 35-21, Hammaker 18-14, Lefferts 20-12. **Ground balls-fly balls:** Stewart 3-10, Honeycutt 2-0, Nelson 0-1, Burns 0-1, Garrelts 6-1, Downs 1-1, Brantley 5-2, Hammaker 1-1, Lefferts 1-4. **Batters faced:** Stewart 27, Honeycutt 4, Nelson 6, Burns 3, Garrelts 16, Downs 7, Brantley 11, Hammaker 8, Lefferts 5. **UMPIRES:** hp—Voltaggio, 1b—Rennert, 2b—Clark, 3b—Gregg, lf—Garcia, rf—Runge **T:** 3:03 **A:** 62,038

GAME 4 Oakland 9 San Francisco 6
Candlestick Park 10/28/89

OAKLAND	AB	R	H	HR	RBI	BB	AVG
R.Henderson lf	6	2	3	1	2	0	.474
Lansford 3b	4	1	2	0	1	1	.438
Canseco rf	4	1	2	0	0	1	.357
McGwire 1b	5	0	1	0	0	0	.294
D.Henderson cf	3	2	1	0	0	2	.308
Steinbach c	4	1	1	0	3	1	.250
Phillips 2b	5	0	1	0	1	0	.235
Weiss ss	3	1	0	0	0	2	.133
Moore p	3	1	1	0	2	0	.333
a-Phelps ph	1	0	0	0	0	0	.000
Nelson p	0	0	0	0	0	0	.000
Honeycutt p	0	0	0	0	0	0	.000
Burns p	0	0	0	0	0	0	.000
b-Parker ph	1	0	0	0	0	0	.222
Eckersley p	0	0	0	0	0	0	.000
TOTALS	**39**	**9**	**12**	**1**	**9**	**7**	**.301**

a - Batted for Moore in the 7th
b - Batted for Burns in the 9th

BATTING: 2B: D.Henderson (2, Robinson), Moore (1, Robinson), Phillips (1, LaCoss). **3B:** Steinbach (1, LaCoss), R.Henderson (2, Brantley). **HR:** R.Henderson (1, 1st off Robinson 0 on, 0 out). **SF:** Phillips. **RBI:** R.Henderson 2 (3), Lansford 1 (4), Steinbach 3 (7), Phillips 1 (3), Moore 2 (2). **2-out RBI:** R.Henderson 1, Steinbach 3, Phillips 1, Moore 2. **Runners left in scoring position, 2 out:** McGwire 2, Steinbach 1, Phillips 2, Moore 1. **Team LOB:** 10 **BASERUNNING: SB:** Canseco (1, 2nd base off LaCoss/Kennedy).

SAN FRANCISCO	AB	R	H	HR	RBI	BB	AVG
Butler cf	5	1	3	0	1	0	.286
Oberkfell 3b	3	0	0	0	0	0	.333
d-Thompson ph-2b	1	0	1	0	1	0	.091
Bedrosian p	0	0	0	0	0	0	.000
Clark 1b	4	1	1	0	0	0	.250
Mitchell lf	4	1	1	1	2	0	.294
Williams ss-3b	4	0	1	0	0	0	.125
Kennedy c	3	1	0	0	0	1	.167
Litton 2b-3b-2b	4	1	1	1	2	0	.500
Nixon rf	3	0	0	0	0	1	.200
Robinson p	0	0	0	0	0	0	.000
LaCoss p	1	0	0	0	0	0	.000
a-Bathe ph	1	0	0	0	0	0	.500
Brantley p	0	0	0	0	0	0	.000
Downs p	0	0	0	0	0	0	.000
b-Riles ph	0	0	0	0	0	0	.000
c-Maldonado ph	1	1	1	0	0	0	.091
Lefferts p	0	0	0	0	0	0	.000
Uribe ss	1	0	0	0	0	0	.200
TOTALS	**35**	**6**	**9**	**2**	**6**	**2**	**.209**

a - Batted for LaCoss in the 5th
b - Batted for Downs in the 7th
c - Batted for Riles in the 7th
d - Batted for Oberkfell in the 7th

BATTING: 2B: Butler (1, Honeycutt). **3B:** Maldonado (1, Honeycutt). **HR:** Mitchell (1, 6th off Moore 1 on, 2 out), Litton (1, 7th off Nelson 1 on, 0 out). **RBI:** Butler 1 (1), Thompson 1 (2), Mitchell 2 (2), Litton 2 (3). **2-out RBI:** Mitchell 2. **Runners left in scoring position, 2 out:** Nixon 1. **Team LOB:** 4 **BASERUNNING: CS:** Butler (1, 2nd base off Moore/Steinbach).

OAKLAND	IP	H	R	ER	BB	SO	HR	ERA
Moore (W, 2-0)	6	5	2	2	1	3	1	2.08
Nelson	0.1	1	2	2	1	0	1	54.00
Honeycutt	0.1	3	2	2	0	0	0	6.75
Burns	1.1	0	0	0	0	0	0	0.00
Eckersley (S, 1)	1	0	0	0	0	0	0	0.00

SAN FRANCISCO	IP	H	R	ER	BB	SO	HR	ERA
Robinson (L, 0-1)	1.2	4	4	4	1	0	1	21.60
LaCoss	3.1	4	3	3	3	1	0	6.23
Brantley	0.1	3	1	1	0	0	0	4.15
Downs	1.2	0	0	0	0	1	0	7.71
Lefferts	0.1	1	1	1	1	0	0	3.38
Bedrosian	1.2	0	0	0	2	0	0	0.00

IBB: Weiss 2 (by Robinson, by LaCoss). **Pitches-strikes:** Moore 85-56, Nelson 10-4, Honeycutt 7-6, Burns 15-10, Eckersley 4-4, Robinson 35-20, LaCoss 50-27, Brantley 15-9, Downs 13-9, Lefferts 11-6, Bedrosian 27-14. **Ground balls-fly balls:** Moore 10-4, Nelson 0-1, Honeycutt 0-1, Burns 0-4, Eckersley 2-1, Robinson 2-3, LaCoss 4-5, Brantley 0-1, Downs 1-3, Lefferts 1-0, Bedrosian 2-3. **Batters faced:** Moore 23, Nelson 3, Honeycutt 4, Burns 4, Eckersley 3, Robinson 10, LaCoss 17, Brantley 4, Downs 5, Lefferts 3, Bedrosian 7. **UMPIRES:** hp—Rennert, 1b—Clark, 2b—Gregg, 3b—Garcia, lf—Runge, rf—Voltaggio **T:** 3:07 **A:** 62,032

1990 CINCINNATI DEF. OAKLAND, 4-0

GAME 1 Cincinnati 7 Oakland 0
Riverfront Stadium 10/16/90

OAKLAND	AB	R	H	HR	RBI	BB	AVG
R.Henderson lf	5	0	3	0	0	0	.600
McGee cf	5	0	1	0	0	0	.200
Canseco rf	2	0	0	0	0	2	.000
McGwire 1b	3	0	0	0	0	1	.000
Lansford 3b	4	0	2	0	0	0	.500
Steinbach c	4	0	1	0	0	0	.250
Randolph 2b	4	0	1	0	0	0	.250
Gallego ss	4	0	0	0	0	0	.000
Stewart p	1	0	0	0	0	0	.000
a-Jennings ph	1	0	1	0	0	0	1.000
Burns p	0	0	0	0	0	0	.000
Nelson p	0	0	0	0	0	0	.000
b-Hassey ph	1	0	0	0	0	0	.000
Sanderson p	0	0	0	0	0	0	.000
Eckersley p	0	0	0	0	0	0	.000
c-D.Henderson ph	1	0	0	0	0	0	.000
TOTALS	**35**	**0**	**9**	**0**	**0**	**3**	**.257**

a - Batted for Stewart in the 5th
b - Batted for Nelson in the 7th
c - Batted for Eckersley in the 9th

BATTING: 2B: R.Henderson 2 (2, Rijo, Myers). **Runners left in scoring position, 2 out:** McGee 1, McGwire 3, Randolph 2, Gallego 2. **GIDP:** McGee. **Team LOB:** 11 **BASERUNNING: SB:** McGee (1, 2nd base off Rijo/Oliver), Lansford (1, 2nd base off Rijo/Oliver). **FIELDING: E:** Gallego (1). **DP:** 2 (Randolph-McGwire, Gallego-Randolph-McGwire).

CINCINNATI	AB	R	H	HR	RBI	BB	AVG
Larkin ss	4	1	0	0	0	1	.000
Hatcher cf	3	3	3	0	1	1	1.000
O'Neill rf	2	1	0	0	1	2	.000
Davis lf	4	2	2	1	3	0	.500
Morris 1b	4	0	1	0	0	0	.250
Sabo 3b	3	0	1	0	2	1	.333
Oliver c	4	0	1	0	0	0	.250
Duncan 2b	3	0	1	0	0	1	.333
Rijo p	3	0	1	0	0	0	.333
Dibble p	0	0	0	0	0	0	.000
a-Benzinger ph	1	0	0	0	0	0	.000
Myers p	0	0	0	0	0	0	.000
TOTALS	**31**	**7**	**10**	**1**	**7**	**6**	**.323**

a - Batted for Dibble in the 8th

BATTING: 2B: Hatcher 2 (2, Stewart, Burns). **HR:** Davis (1, 1st off Stewart 1 on, 2 out). **RBI:** Hatcher 1 (1), O'Neill 1 (1), Davis 3 (3), Sabo 2 (2). **2-out RBI:** Davis 2, Sabo 2. **Runners left in scoring position, 2 out:** Davis 1, Duncan 1. **GIDP:** Larkin, Oliver. **Team LOB:** 6 **BASERUNNING: CS:** Sabo (1, 2nd base off Stewart/Steinbach). **FIELDING: DP:** 1 (Duncan-Larkin-Morris).

OAKLAND	IP	H	R	ER	BB	SO	HR	ERA
Stewart (L, 0-1)	4	3	4	4	4	3	1	9.00
Burns	0.2	4	3	3	1	0	0	40.50
Nelson	1.1	2	0	0	1	0	0	0.00
Sanderson	1	1	0	0	0	0	0	0.00
Eckersley	1	0	0	0	0	1	0	0.00

CINCINNATI	IP	H	R	ER	BB	SO	HR	ERA
Rijo (W, 1-0)	7	7	0	0	2	5	0	0.00
Dibble	1	1	0	0	1	0	0	0.00
Myers	1	1	0	0	0	2	0	0.00

WP: Dibble 1. **Pitches-strikes:** Stewart 64-34, Burns 20-9, Nelson 21-10, Sanderson 12-7, Eckersley 6-5, Rijo 105-67, Dibble 18-10, Myers 15-11. **Ground balls-fly balls:** Stewart 4-4, Burns 1-1, Nelson 2-1, Sanderson 1-1, Eckersley 0-2, Rijo 8-7, Dibble 1-2, Myers 0-1. **Batters faced:** Stewart 18, Burns 7, Nelson 6, Sanderson 3, Eckersley 3, Rijo 29, Dibble 5, Myers 4. **UMPIRES:** hp—Pulli (NL), 1b—Roe (AL), 2b—Quick (NL), 3b—Hendry (AL), lf—Marsh (NL), rf—Barnett (AL) **T:** 2:48 **A:** 55,830

GAME 2 Cincinnati 5 Oakland 4
Riverfront Stadium 10/17/90

OAKLAND	AB	R	H	HR	RBI	BB	AVG
R.Henderson lf	4	1	1	0	0	1	.444
Lansford 3b	4	0	1	0	0	0	.375
Canseco rf	5	1	1	1	2	0	.143
McGwire 1b	4	1	2	0	0	1	.286
D.Henderson cf	4	1	2	0	0	1	.400
Steinbach c	0	0	0	0	0	0	.250
Randolph 2b	4	0	0	0	0	1	.125
Hassey c	4	0	2	0	1	0	.400
a-Bordick pr-ss	0	0	0	0	0	0	.000
Gallego ss	4	0	1	0	1	0	.125
b-Baines ph	1	0	0	0	0	0	.000
Eckersley p	0	0	0	0	0	0	.000
Welch p	3	0	0	0	0	0	.000
Honeycutt p	0	0	0	0	0	0	.000
McGee cf	0	0	0	0	0	0	.200
TOTALS	**37**	**4**	**10**	**1**	**4**	**4**	**.264**

a - Ran for Hassey in the 10th
b - Batted for Gallego in the 10th

BATTING: HR: Canseco (1, 3th off Jackson 0 on, 1 out). **S:** Lansford, Welch. **SF:** Hassey. **RBI:** Canseco 2 (2), Hassey 1 (1), Gallego 1 (1). **2-out RBI:** Gallego 1. **Runners left in scoring position, 2 out:** R.Henderson 2, D.Henderson 1, Randolph 1, Welch 1. **GIDP:** Canseco. **Team LOB:** 10 **BASERUNNING: SB:** R.Henderson (1, 2nd base off Jackson/Oliver). **FIELDING: E:** Hassey (1), McGwire (1). **Outfield assists:** R.Henderson (1).

CINCINNATI	AB	R	H	HR	RBI	BB	AVG
Larkin ss	5	1	3	0	0	0	.333
Hatcher cf	4	2	4	0	1	1	1.000
O'Neill rf	4	0	0	0	0	1	.000
Davis lf	5	0	0	0	1	0	.222
Morris 1b	3	0	0	0	0	0	.143
c-Braggs ph	1	0	0	0	1	0	.000
Dibble p	0	0	0	0	0	0	.000
d-Bates ph	1	1	1	0	0	0	1.000
Sabo 3b	5	0	3	0	0	0	.500
Oliver c	5	1	2	0	1	0	.333
Duncan 2b	3	0	0	0	0	1	.167
Jackson p	1	0	0	0	0	0	.000
Scudder p	0	0	0	0	0	0	.000
a-Oester ph	1	0	1	0	1	0	1.000
Armstrong p	0	0	0	0	0	0	.000
b-Winningham ph	1	0	0	0	0	0	.000
Charlton p	0	0	0	0	0	0	.000
Benzinger 1b	1	0	0	0	0	0	.000
TOTALS	**40**	**5**	**14**	**0**	**5**	**3**	**.338**

a - Batted for Scudder in the 4th
b - Batted for Armstrong in the 7th
c - Batted for Morris in the 8th
d - Batted for Dibble in the 10th

BATTING: 2B: Larkin (1, Welch), Hatcher 2 (4, Welch), Oliver (1, Welch). **3B:** Hatcher (1, Welch). **RBI:** Hatcher 1 (2), Davis 1 (4), Braggs 1 (1), Oliver 1 (1), Oester 1 (1). **2-out RBI:** Oester 1. **Runners left in scoring position, 2 out:** Larkin 1, O'Neill 1, Morris 2, Oliver 1. **Team LOB:** 10 **FIELDING: E:** Jackson (1), Oliver (1). **DP:** 1 (Larkin-Duncan-Benzinger).

OAKLAND	IP	H	R	ER	BB	SO	HR	ERA
Welch	7.1	9	4	4	2	2	0	4.91
Honeycutt	1.2	2	0	0	1	0	0	0.00
Eckersley (L, 0-1)	0.1	3	1	1	0	0	0	6.75

CINCINNATI	IP	H	R	ER	BB	SO	HR	ERA
Jackson	2.2	6	4	3	2	0	1	10.13
Scudder	1.1	0	0	0	2	2	0	0.00
Armstrong	3	1	0	0	0	3	0	0.00
Charlton	1	1	0	0	0	0	0	0.00
Dibble (W, 1-0)	2	2	0	0	0	2	0	0.00

IBB: Hatcher (by Honeycutt). **Pitches-strikes:** Welch 105-64, Honeycutt 31-17, Eckersley 11-11, Jackson 63-34, Scudder 22-10, Armstrong 42-25, Charlton 13-10, Dibble 30-19. **Ground balls-fly balls:** Welch 9-9, Honeycutt 3-2, Eckersley 1-0, Jackson 5-2, Scudder 1-1, Armstrong 4-2, Charlton 1-1, Dibble 1-2. **Batters faced:** Welch 31, Honeycutt 8, Eckersley 4, Jackson 17, Scudder 6, Armstrong 10, Charlton 4, Dibble 7. **UMPIRES:** hp—Roe (AL), 1b—Quick (NL), 2b—Hendry (AL), 3b—Marsh (NL), lf—Barnett (AL), rf—Pulli (NL) **T:** 3:31 **A:** 55,832

GAME 3 Cincinnati 8 Oakland 3
Oakland Coliseum 10/19/90

CINCINNATI	AB	R	H	HR	RBI	BB	AVG
Larkin ss	5	0	2	0	1	0	.357
Hatcher cf	5	1	2	0	0	0	.750
O'Neill rf	3	1	1	0	0	2	.111
Davis lf	5	1	2	0	1	0	.286
Morris dh	4	0	0	0	1	1	.091
Sabo 3b	4	2	2	2	3	1	.500
Benzinger 1b	5	1	2	0	0	0	.286
Oliver c	5	1	2	0	1	0	.357
Duncan 2b	4	1	1	0	1	0	.200
TOTALS	**40**	**8**	**14**	**2**	**8**	**4**	**.342**

BATTING: 2B: Oliver (2, Sanderson). **3B:** Larkin (1, Sanderson). **HR:** Sabo 2 (2, 2nd off Moore 0 on, 0 out, 3th off Moore 1 on, 2 out). **RBI:** Larkin 1 (1), Davis 1 (5), Morris 1 (1), Sabo 3 (5), Oliver 1 (2), Duncan 1 (1). **2-out RBI:** Larkin 1, Sabo 2, Oliver 1, Duncan 1. **Runners left in scoring position, 2 out:** Hatcher 1, Davis 1, Morris 1, Benzinger 1. **GIDP:** Hatcher, Benzinger. **Team LOB:** 9 **BASERUNNING: SB:** Duncan (1, 2nd base off Sanderson/Steinbach), O'Neill (1, 2nd base off Sanderson/Steinbach). **FIELDING: E:** Oliver (2).

OAKLAND	AB	R	H	HR	RBI	BB	AVG
R.Henderson lf	3	1	1	1	1	1	.417
Lansford 3b	3	0	0	0	0	1	.273
Canseco rf	4	0	0	0	0	0	.091
D.Henderson cf	4	1	1	0	0	0	.333
Baines dh	4	1	1	1	2	0	.200
McGwire 1b	4	0	1	0	0	0	.273
Steinbach c	4	0	0	0	0	0	.125
Randolph 2b	4	0	3	0	0	0	.333
Gallego ss	2	0	0	0	0	0	.100
a-McGee ph	1	0	0	0	0	0	.167
Bordick ss	0	0	0	0	0	0	.000
b-Blankenship ph	1	0	0	0	0	0	.000
TOTALS	**34**	**3**	**7**	**2**	**3**	**2**	**.245**

a - Batted for Gallego in the 7th
b - Batted for Bordick in the 9th

BATTING: 2B: D.Henderson (1, Browning). **HR:** Baines (1, 2nd off Browning 1 on, 0 out), R.Henderson (1, 3th off Browning 0 on, 0 out). **RBI:** R.Henderson 1 (1), Baines 2 (2). **Runners left in scoring position, 2 out:** Lansford 1, Canseco 1. **Team LOB:** 6 **BASERUNNING: SB:** R.Henderson (2, 2nd base off Browning/Oliver), Randolph (1, 2nd base off Dibble/Oliver). **FIELDING: E:** McGwire (2). **DP:** 2 (Gallego-Randolph-McGwire, Randolph-McGwire).

CINCINNATI	IP	H	R	ER	BB	SO	HR	ERA
Browning (W, 1-0)	6	6	3	3	2	2	2	4.50
Dibble	1.2	0	0	0	0	2	0	0.00
Myers	1.1	1	0	0	0	1	0	0.00

OAKLAND	IP	H	R	ER	BB	SO	HR	ERA
Moore (L, 0-1)	2.2	8	6	2	0	1	2	6.75
Sanderson	0.2	3	2	2	1	0	0	10.80
Klink	0	0	0	0	1	0	0	0.00
Nelson	3.2	1	0	0	1	0	0	0.00
Burns	1	1	0	0	1	0	0	16.20
Young	1	1	0	0	0	0	0	0.00

WP: Sanderson 1, Burns 1. **Pitches-strikes:** Browning 92-57, Dibble 21-13, Myers 24-15, Moore 60-33, Sanderson 31-15, Klink 7-3, Nelson 35-24, Burns 17-8, Young 9-6. **Ground balls-fly balls:** Browning 7-9, Dibble 1-2, Myers 2-1, Moore 6-1, Sanderson 2-0, Klink 0-0, Nelson 5-5, Burns 2-1, Young 2-1. **Batters faced:** Browning 26, Dibble 5, Myers 5, Moore 16, Sanderson 6, Klink 1, Nelson 12, Burns 5, Young 4. **UMPIRES:** hp—Quick (NL), 1b—Hendry (AL), 2b—Marsh (NL), 3b—Froemming (NL), lf—Pulli (NL), rf—Roe (AL) **T:** 3:01 **A:** 48,269

GAME 4 Cincinnati 2 Oakland 1
Oakland Coliseum 10/20/90

CINCINNATI	AB	R	H	HR	RBI	BB	AVG
Larkin ss	3	1	1	0	0	1	.353
Hatcher cf	0	0	0	0	0	0	.750
Winningham cf	3	1	2	0	0	0	.500
O'Neill rf	3	0	0	0	0	0	.083
Davis lf	0	0	0	0	0	0	.286
a-Braggs ph-lf	3	0	0	0	1	1	.000
Morris dh	3	0	0	0	1	0	.071
Sabo 3b	4	0	3	0	0	0	.563
Benzinger 1b	4	0	0	0	0	0	.182
Oliver c	4	0	1	0	0	0	.333
Duncan 2b	4	0	0	0	0	0	.143
TOTALS	**31**	**2**	**7**	**0**	**2**	**2**	**.317**

a - Batted for Davis in the 2nd

BATTING: 2B: Oliver (3, Stewart), Sabo (1, Stewart). **S:** O'Neill. **SF:** Morris, Sabo. **RBI:** Braggs 1 (2), Morris 1 (2). **Runners left in scoring position, 2 out:** Winningham 1, Duncan 1. **GIDP:** Morris. **Team LOB:** 7 **BASERUNNING: CS:** Hatcher (1, 2nd base off Stewart/Quirk). **FIELDING: E:** Oliver (3).

OAKLAND	AB	R	H	HR	RBI	BB	AVG
R.Henderson lf	3	0	0	0	0	1	.333
McGee rf	4	1	1	0	0	0	.200
D.Henderson cf	4	0	0	0	0	0	.231
Baines dh	2	0	0	0	0	1	.143
b-Canseco ph	1	0	0	0	0	0	.083
Lansford 3b	4	0	1	0	1	0	.267
Quirk c	3	0	0	0	0	0	.000
McGwire 1b	3	0	0	0	0	0	.214
Randolph 2b	3	0	0	0	0	0	.267
Gallego ss	1	0	0	0	0	1	.091
a-Hassey ph	1	0	0	0	0	0	.333
Bordick ss	0	0	0	0	0	0	.000
TOTALS	**29**	**1**	**2**	**0**	**1**	**3**	**.207**

a - Batted for Gallego in the 8th
b - Batted for Baines in the 9th

BATTING: 2B: McGee (1, Rijo). **RBI:** Lansford 1 (1). **2-out RBI:** Lansford 1. **Runners left in scoring position, 2 out:** McGee 2, Quirk 1. **Team LOB:** 4 **BASERUNNING: SB:** Gallego (1, 2nd base off Rijo/Oliver), R.Henderson (3, 2nd base off Rijo/Oliver). **FIELDING: E:** Stewart (1). **DP:** 1 (Randolph-Gallego-McGwire).

CINCINNATI	IP	H	R	ER	BB	SO	HR	ERA
Rijo (W, 2-0)	8.1	2	1	1	3	9	0	0.59
Myers (S, 1)	0.2	0	0	0	0	0	0	0.00

OAKLAND	IP	H	R	ER	BB	SO	HR	ERA
Stewart (L, 0-2)	9	7	2	1	2	2	0	3.46

IBB: Baines (by Rijo). **HBP:** Hatcher (by Stewart). **Pitches-strikes:** Rijo 114-73, Myers 11-6, Stewart 112-75. **Ground balls-fly balls:** Rijo 8-8, Myers 1-1, Stewart 11-11. **Batters faced:** Rijo 30, Myers 2, Stewart 36. **UMPIRES:** hp—Hendry (AL), 1b—Marsh (NL), 2b—Froemming (NL), 3b—Pulli (NL), lf—Roe (AL), rf—Quick (NL) **T:** 2:48 **A:** 48,613

1991 MINNESOTA DEF. ATLANTA, 4-3

GAME 1 Minnesota 5 Atlanta 2
Humphrey Metrodome 10/19/91

ATLANTA	AB	R	H	HR	RBI	BB	AVG
Smith dh	3	1	0	0	0	1	.000
Treadway 2b	3	1	1	0	0	1	.333
Pendleton 3b	4	0	0	0	0	0	.000
Justice rf	2	0	1	0	0	2	.500
Gant cf	4	0	3	0	2	0	.750
Bream 1b	4	0	0	0	0	0	.000
Hunter lf	4	0	0	0	0	0	.000
Olson c	3	0	1	0	0	1	.333
Belliard ss	1	0	0	0	0	0	.000
a-Blauser ph-ss	2	0	0	0	0	0	.000
TOTALS	**30**	**2**	**6**	**0**	**2**	**5**	**.200**

a - Batted for Belliard in the 7th

BATTING: S: Belliard. **RBI:** Gant 2 (2). **2-out RBI:** Gant 2. **Runners left in scoring position, 2 out:** Treadway 1, Bream 3. **GIDP:** Belliard, Pendleton. **Team LOB:** 7 **FIELDING: E:** Treadway (1). **Outfield assists:** Justice (1), Hunter (1). **DP:** 2 (Belliard-Treadway, Hunter-Pendleton-Olson).

MINNESOTA	AB	R	H	HR	RBI	BB	AVG
Gladden lf	2	1	0	0	0	2	.000
Knoblauch 2b	3	0	3	0	1	1	1.000
Puckett cf	4	0	0	0	0	0	.000
Davis dh	3	0	0	0	0	1	.000
Harper c	4	0	2	0	0	0	.500
Mack rf	4	0	0	0	0	0	.000
Hrbek 1b	4	2	2	1	1	0	.500
Leius 3b	2	1	1	0	0	0	.500
a-Pagliarulo ph-3b	1	0	0	0	0	0	.000
Gagne ss	3	1	1	1	3	0	.333
TOTALS	**30**	**5**	**9**	**2**	**5**	**4**	**.300**

a - Batted for Leius in the 6th

BATTING: 2B: Harper (1, Leibrandt), Hrbek (1, Leibrandt). **HR:** Gagne (1, 5th off Leibrandt 2 on, 0 out), Hrbek (1, 6th off Clancy 0 on, 1 out). **RBI:** Knoblauch 1 (1), Hrbek 1 (1), Gagne 3 (3). **2-out RBI:** Knoblauch 1. **Runners left in scoring position, 2 out:** Knoblauch 1, Davis 1. **Team LOB:** 5 **BASERUNNING: SB:** Knoblauch 2 (2, 2nd base off Leibrandt/Olson, 2nd base off Clancy/Olson), Gladden (1, 2nd base off Leibrandt/Olson). **CS:** Gladden (1, 2nd base off Wohlers/Olson). **FIELDING: E:** Gladden (1). **DP:** 2 (Gagne-Hrbek, Knoblauch-Gagne-Hrbek).

ATLANTA	IP	H	R	ER	BB	SO	HR	ERA
Leibrandt (L, 0-1)	4	7	4	4	1	3	1	9.00
Clancy	2	1	1	1	2	0	1	4.50
Wohlers	1	1	0	0	1	1	0	0.00
Stanton	1	0	0	0	0	2	0	0.00

MINNESOTA	IP	H	R	ER	BB	SO	HR	ERA
Morris (W, 1-0)	7	5	2	2	4	3	0	2.57
Guthrie	0.2	0	0	0	1	0	0	0.00
Aguilera (S, 1)	1.1	1	0	0	0	0	0	0.00

IBB: Davis (by Clancy). **Pitches-strikes:** Leibrandt 83-54, Clancy 33-17, Wohlers 18-9, Stanton 11-7, Morris 100-60, Guthrie 7-3, Aguilera 18-13. **Ground balls-fly balls:** Leibrandt 3-4, Clancy 4-2, Wohlers 1-0, Stanton 1-0, Morris 7-9, Guthrie 1-0, Aguilera 1-3. **Batters faced:** Leibrandt 18, Clancy 9, Wohlers 4, Stanton 3, Morris 29, Guthrie 2, Aguilera 5. **UMPIRES:** hp—Don Denkinger, 1b—Harry Wendelstedt, 2b—Drew Coble, 3b—Terry Tata, lf—Rick Reed, rf—Ed Montague **T:** 3:00 **A:** 55,108

GAME 2 Minnesota 3 Atlanta 2
Humphrey Metrodome 10/20/91

ATLANTA	AB	R	H	HR	RBI	BB	AVG
Smith dh	3	0	0	0	0	0	.000
Pendleton 3b	4	0	2	0	0	0	.250
Gant cf	4	0	1	0	0	0	.500
Justice rf	4	1	1	0	0	0	.333
Bream 1b	4	0	1	0	0	0	.125
Hunter lf	3	0	1	0	1	0	.143
Olson c	4	1	1	0	0	0	.286
Lemke 2b	3	0	0	0	0	0	.000
a-Gregg ph	1	0	0	0	0	0	.000
Belliard ss	2	0	1	0	1	0	.333
TOTALS	**32**	**2**	**8**	**0**	**2**	**0**	**.226**

a - Batted for Lemke in the 9th

BATTING: 2B: Bream (1, Tapani), Olson (1, Tapani). **S:** Smith. **SF:** Hunter, Belliard. **RBI:** Hunter 1 (1), Belliard 1 (1). **Runners left in scoring position, 2 out:** Justice 1, Lemke 1. **Team LOB:** 6 **FIELDING: E:** Justice (1). **DP:** 2 (Pendleton-Bream, Glavine-Lemke-Bream).

MINNESOTA	AB	R	H	HR	RBI	BB	AVG
Gladden lf	4	0	0	0	0	0	.000
Knoblauch 2b	3	1	0	0	0	1	.500
Puckett cf	4	0	0	0	0	0	.000
Davis dh	3	1	1	1	2	0	.167
Harper c	2	0	1	0	0	1	.500
Mack rf	3	0	0	0	0	0	.000
Hrbek 1b	2	0	0	0	0	1	.333
Leius 3b	3	1	1	1	1	0	.400
Gagne ss	3	0	1	0	0	0	.333
TOTALS	**27**	**3**	**4**	**2**	**3**	**3**	**.228**

BATTING: HR: Davis (1, 1st off Glavine 1 on, 2 out), Leius (1, 8th off Glavine 0 on, 0 out). **RBI:** Davis 2 (2), Leius 1 (1). **2-out RBI:** Davis 2. **Runners left in scoring position, 2 out:** Puckett 1. **GIDP:** Puckett, Leius. **Team LOB:** 3 **FIELDING: E:** Leius (1). **Outfield assists:** Gladden (1).

ATLANTA	IP	H	R	ER	BB	SO	HR	ERA
Glavine (L, 0-1)	8	4	3	1	3	6	2	1.13

MINNESOTA	IP	H	R	ER	BB	SO	HR	ERA
Tapani (W, 1-0)	8	7	2	2	0	3	0	2.25
Aguilera (S, 2)	1	1	0	0	0	3	0	0.00

BK: Glavine 1. **Pitches-strikes:** Glavine 108-66, Tapani 106-70, Aguilera 19-13. **Ground balls-fly balls:** Glavine 13-4, Tapani 9-9, Aguilera 0-0. **Batters faced:** Glavine 30, Tapani 31, Aguilera 4. **UMPIRES:** hp—Harry Wendelstedt, 1b—Drew Coble, 2b—Terry Tata, 3b—Rick Reed, lf—Ed Montague, rf—Don Denkinger **T:** 2:37 **A:** 55,145

GAME 3 Atlanta 5 Minnesota 4
Atlanta-Fulton County Stadium 10/22/91

MINNESOTA	AB	R	H	HR	RBI	BB	AVG
Gladden lf	6	1	3	0	0	0	.250
Knoblauch 2b	5	0	1	0	1	0	.364
Hrbek 1b	6	0	1	0	0	0	.250
Puckett cf	4	1	1	1	1	2	.083
Mack rf	4	0	0	0	0	0	.000
Willis p	0	0	0	0	0	0	.000
f-Sorrento ph	1	0	0	0	0	0	.000
Guthrie p	0	0	0	0	0	0	.000
h-Aguilera ph-p	1	0	0	0	0	0	.000
Leius 3b	3	0	0	0	0	0	.250
d-Pagliarulo ph-3b	1	0	0	0	0	0	.000
g-Newman ph-3b	1	0	0	0	0	0	.000
Gagne ss	5	0	0	0	0	0	.182
Ortiz c	2	0	1	0	0	0	.500
b-Harper ph-c	3	1	1	0	0	0	.444
Erickson p	1	0	0	0	0	0	.000
West p	0	0	0	0	0	0	.000
Leach p	0	0	0	0	0	0	.000
a-Larkin ph	1	0	1	0	0	0	1.000
Bedrosian p	0	0	0	0	0	0	.000
c-Davis ph	1	1	1	1	2	0	.286
Brown rf	0	0	0	0	0	0	.000
e-Bush ph-rf	2	0	0	0	0	0	.000
TOTALS	**47**	**4**	**10**	**2**	**4**	**2**	**.221**

a - Batted for Leach in the 6th
b - Batted for Ortiz in the 8th
c - Batted for Bedrosian in the 8th
d - Batted for Leius in the 9th e - Batted for Brown in the 9th f - Batted for Willis in the 10th g - Batted for Pagliarulo in the 11th h - Batted for Guthrie in the 12th

BATTING: 3B: Gladden (1, Avery). **HR:** Puckett (1, 7th off Avery 0 on, 0 out), Davis (2, 8th off Pena 1 on, 0 out). **SF:** Knoblauch. **RBI:** Knoblauch 1 (2), Puckett 1 (1), Davis 2 (4). **Runners left in scoring position, 2 out:** Hrbek 1, Mack 1, Sorrento 1, Aguilera 2, Bush 1. **Team LOB:** 10 **BASERUNNING: SB:** Knoblauch (3, 2nd base off Mercker/Olson). **FIELDING: E:** Knoblauch (1).

ATLANTA	AB	R	H	HR	RBI	BB	AVG
Smith lf	4	1	1	1	1	0	.100
Mitchell lf	2	0	0	0	0	0	.000
Pendleton 3b	4	1	0	0	0	2	.167
Gant cf	6	0	0	0	0	0	.286
Justice rf	6	2	2	1	1	0	.333
Bream 1b	3	0	1	0	0	1	.182
b-Hunter ph-1b	2	0	0	0	0	0	.111
Olson c	3	1	1	0	1	3	.300
Lemke 2b	5	0	2	0	1	1	.250
Belliard ss	3	0	1	0	1	1	.333
c-Blauser ph-ss	1	0	0	0	0	0	.000
Avery p	3	0	0	0	0	0	.000
Pena p	0	0	0	0	0	0	.000
a-Treadway ph	0	0	0	0	0	0	.333
Stanton p	0	0	0	0	0	0	.000
d-Cabrera ph	1	0	0	0	0	0	.000
Wohlers p	0	0	0	0	0	0	.000
Mercker p	0	0	0	0	0	0	.000
Clancy p	0	0	0	0	0	0	.000
TOTALS	**43**	**5**	**8**	**2**	**5**	**8**	**.210**

a - Batted for Pena in the 9th
b - Batted for Bream in the 10th
c - Batted for Belliard in the 10th
d - Batted for Stanton in the 11th

BATTING: 2B: Bream (2, Erickson), Olson (2, Guthrie). **HR:** Justice (1, 4th off Erickson 0 on, 0 out), Smith (1, 5th off Erickson 0 on, 1 out). **S:** Treadway. **RBI:** Smith 1 (1), Justice 1 (1), Olson 1 (1), Lemke 1 (1), Belliard 1 (2). **2-out RBI:** Olson 1,

Lemke 1, Belliard 1. **Runners left in scoring position, 2 out:** Gant 1, Lemke 2, Belliard 1, Blauser 1, Avery 2. **Team LOB:** 12 **BASERUNNING: SB:** Justice (1, 2nd base off Aguilera/Harper). **FIELDING: E:** Pendleton (1), Lemke (1).

MINNESOTA	IP	H	R	ER	BB	SO	HR	ERA
Erickson	4.2	5	4	3	2	3	2	5.79
West	0	0	0	0	2	0	0	0.00
Leach	0.1	0	0	0	0	1	0	0.00
Bedrosian	2	0	0	0	0	1	0	0.00
Willis	2	0	0	0	2	0	0	0.00
Guthrie	2	1	0	0	1	1	0	0.00
Aguilera (L, 0-1)	0.2	2	1	1	1	0	0	3.00

ATLANTA	IP	H	R	ER	BB	SO	HR	ERA
Avery	7	4	3	2	0	5	1	2.57
Pena	2	4	1	1	0	4	1	4.50
Stanton	2	1	0	0	1	3	0	0.00
Wohlers	0.1	1	0	0	0	0	0	0.00
Mercker	0.1	0	0	0	0	1	0	0.00
Clancy (W, 1-0)	0.1	0	0	0	1	0	0	3.86

WP: Erickson 1, Pena 1. **IBB:** Pendleton (by Willis), Puckett 2 (by Stanton, by Clancy). **Pitches-strikes:** Erickson 88-49, West 10-2, Leach 4-4, Bedrosian 25-15, Willis 27-15, Guthrie 37-21, Aguilera 17-9, Avery 84-59, Pena 41-29, Stanton 22-15, Wohlers 8-4, Mercker 8-6, Clancy 7-2. **Ground balls-fly balls:** Erickson 7-5, West 0-0, Leach 0-0, Bedrosian 3-2, Willis 1-4, Guthrie 2-3, Aguilera 0-2, Avery 5-11, Pena 1-1, Stanton 1-2, Wohlers 1-1, Mercker 0-0, Clancy 0-1. **Batters faced:** Erickson 22, West 2, Leach 1, Bedrosian 6, Willis 8, Guthrie 8, Aguilera 5, Avery 26, Pena 10, Stanton 8, Wohlers 3, Mercker 1, Clancy 2. **UMPIRES:** hp—Drew Coble, 1b—Terry Tata, 2b—Rick Reed, 3b—Ed Montague, lf—Don Denkinger, rf—Harry Wendelstedt **T:** 4:04 **A:** 50,878

GAME 4 Atlanta 3 Minnesota 2
Atlanta-Fulton County Stadium 10/23/91

MINNESOTA	AB	R	H	HR	RBI	BB	AVG
Gladden lf	4	0	0	0	0	0	.188
Knoblauch 2b	3	0	1	0	0	1	.357
Puckett cf	4	0	1	0	0	0	.125
Hrbek 1b	4	0	0	0	0	0	.188
Harper c	4	1	2	0	0	0	.462
Mack rf	4	0	0	0	0	0	.000
Pagliarulo 3b	3	1	3	1	2	0	.600
b-Leius ph-3b	1	0	0	0	0	0	.222
Bedrosian p	0	0	0	0	0	0	.000
Gagne ss	3	0	0	0	0	0	.143
Morris p	2	0	0	0	0	0	.000
a-Larkin ph	1	0	0	0	0	0	.500
Willis p	0	0	0	0	0	0	.000
Guthrie p	0	0	0	0	0	0	.000
Newman 3b	0	0	0	0	0	0	.000
TOTALS	**33**	**2**	**7**	**1**	**2**	**1**	**.219**

a - Batted for Morris in the 7th
b - Batted for Pagliarulo in the 9th

BATTING: 2B: Knoblauch (1, Smoltz), Harper (2, Smoltz). **HR:** Pagliarulo (1, 7th off Smoltz 0 on, 1 out). **S:** Mack. **RBI:** Pagliarulo 2 (2). **Runners left in scoring position, 2 out:** Hrbek 2, Gagne 1, Morris 1. **Team LOB:** 5 **BASERUNNING: SB:** Knoblauch (4, 2nd base off Stanton/Olson). **Outfield assists:** Puckett (1).

ATLANTA	AB	R	H	HR	RBI	BB	AVG
Smith lf	4	1	2	1	1	0	.214
Pendleton 3b	4	1	2	1	1	0	.250
Gant cf	3	0	1	0	0	1	.294
Justice rf	3	0	0	0	0	1	.267
Bream 1b	3	0	0	0	0	0	.143
c-Hunter ph-1b	1	0	0	0	0	0	.100
Olson c	3	0	0	0	0	1	.231
Lemke 2b	4	1	3	0	0	0	.417
Belliard ss	2	0	0	0	0	0	.250
a-Treadway ph	1	0	0	0	0	0	.250
Blauser ss	0	0	0	0	0	1	.000
Smoltz p	2	0	0	0	0	0	.000
b-Gregg ph	1	0	0	0	0	0	.000
Wohlers p	0	0	0	0	0	0	.000
Stanton p	0	0	0	0	0	0	.000
d-Cabrera ph	0	0	0	0	0	0	.000
e-Willard ph	0	0	0	0	1	0	.000
TOTALS	**31**	**3**	**8**	**2**	**3**	**4**	**.221**

a - Batted for Belliard in the 7th
b - Batted for Smoltz in the 7th
c - Batted for Bream in the 8th
d - Batted for Stanton in the 9th e - Batted for Cabrera in the 9th

BATTING: 2B: Lemke (1, Morris), Pendleton (1, Morris). **3B:** Lemke (1, Guthrie). **HR:** Pendleton (1, 3th off Morris 0 on, 2 out), Smith (2, 7th off Willis 0 on, 2 out). **S:** Pendleton. **SF:** Willard. **RBI:** Smith 1 (2), Pendleton 1 (1), Willard 1 (1). **2-out RBI:** Smith 1, Pendleton 1. **Runners left in scoring position, 2 out:** Justice 1, Bream 1, Belliard 1, Smoltz 1. **Team LOB:** 7 **BASERUNNING: SB:** Gant (1, 2nd base off Morris/Harper), Smith (1, 2nd base off Morris/Harper).

MINNESOTA	IP	H	R	ER	BB	SO	HR	ERA
Morris	6	6	1	1	3	4	1	2.08
Willis	1.1	1	1	1	0	1	1	2.70
Guthrie (L, 0-1)	1	1	1	1	1	1	0	2.45
Bedrosian	0.1	0	0	0	0	0	0	0.00

ATLANTA	IP	H	R	ER	BB	SO	HR	ERA
Smoltz	7	7	2	2	0	7	1	2.57
Wohlers	0.1	0	0	0	1	0	0	0.00
Stanton (W, 1-0)	1.2	0	0	0	0	1	0	0.00

WP: Morris 1. **IBB:** Blauser (by Guthrie). **Pitches-strikes:** Morris 94-50, Willis 17-12, Guthrie 18-8, Bedrosian 4-3, Smoltz 97-68, Wohlers 10-6, Stanton 26-17. **Ground balls-fly balls:** Morris 5-7, Willis 1-2, Guthrie 1-1, Bedrosian 0-0, Smoltz 8-5, Wohlers 1-0, Stanton 0-4. **Batters faced:** Morris 25, Willis 5, Guthrie 5, Bedrosian 1, Smoltz 27, Wohlers 2, Stanton 5. **UMPIRES:** hp—Terry Tata, 1b—Rick Reed, 2b—Ed Montague, 3b—Don Denkinger, lf—Harry Wendelstedt, rf—Drew Coble **T:** 2:57 **A:** 50,878

GAME 5 Atlanta 14 Minnesota 5
Atlanta-Fulton County Stadium 10/24/91

MINNESOTA	AB	R	H	HR	RBI	BB	AVG
Gladden lf	5	1	1	0	0	0	.190
Knoblauch 2b	3	1	1	0	0	1	.353
Bedrosian p	0	0	0	0	0	0	.000
Ortiz c	1	0	0	0	1	0	.333
Puckett cf	2	1	1	0	0	0	.167
c-Brown ph-cf	2	0	0	0	0	0	.000
Davis rf	3	2	1	0	0	1	.300
Willis p	0	0	0	0	0	0	.000
Harper c	2	0	0	0	1	1	.400
d-Bush ph-rf	1	0	0	0	0	0	.000
Leius 3b	2	0	1	0	1	1	.273
West p	0	0	0	0	0	0	.000
Newman 2b	1	0	1	0	1	0	.500
Hrbek 1b	3	0	0	0	1	0	.158
e-Sorrento ph-1b	0	0	0	0	0	1	.000
Gagne ss	4	0	1	0	0	0	.167
Tapani p	1	0	0	0	0	0	.000
a-Larkin ph	1	0	0	0	0	0	.333
Leach p	0	0	0	0	0	0	.000
b-Pagliarulo ph-3b	2	0	0	0	0	0	.429
TOTALS	**33**	**5**	**7**	**0**	**5**	**5**	**.218**

a - Batted for Tapani in the 5th
b - Batted for Leach in the 7th
c - Batted for Puckett in the 8th
d - Batted for Harper in the 8th e - Batted for Hrbek in the 8th

BATTING: 2B: Gagne (1, Glavine). **3B:** Newman (1, Clancy), Gladden (2, St.Claire). **S:** Puckett. **SF:** Davis. **RBI:** Ortiz 1 (1), Harper 1 (1), Leius 1 (2), Newman 1 (1), Hrbek 1 (2). **2-out RBI:** Newman 1. **Runners left in scoring position, 2 out:** Gladden 1, Harper 1, Gagne 3. **Team LOB:** 7 **BASERUNNING: CS:** Leius (1, 2nd base off Glavine/Olson). **FIELDING: E:** Harper (1). **DP:** 1 (Newman-Gagne-Sorrento).

ATLANTA	AB	R	H	HR	RBI	BB	AVG
Smith lf	5	1	1	1	1	0	.211
Mitchell lf	0	0	0	0	0	0	.000
Pendleton 3b	4	3	2	0	0	1	.300
Gant cf	4	3	3	0	1	1	.381
Justice rf	5	2	2	1	5	0	.300
Bream 1b	2	0	0	0	0	1	.125
b-Hunter ph-1b	2	2	2	1	2	0	.250
Olson c	5	1	3	0	0	0	.333
St.Claire p	0	0	0	0	0	0	.000
Lemke 2b	4	2	2	0	3	1	.438
Belliard ss	4	0	2	0	2	0	.333
Glavine p	2	0	0	0	0	0	.000
Mercker p	0	0	0	0	0	0	.000
a-Gregg ph	1	0	0	0	0	0	.000
Clancy p	1	0	0	0	0	0	.000
Cabrera c	0	0	0	0	0	0	.000
TOTALS	**39**	**14**	**17**	**3**	**14**	**4**	**.269**

a - Batted for Mercker in the 6th
b - Batted for Bream in the 7th

BATTING: 2B: Belliard (1, Tapani), Pendleton (2, Willis). **3B:** Lemke 2 (3, Tapani, Bedrosian), Gant (1, Willis). **HR:** Justice (2, 4th off Tapani 1 on, 0 out), Smith (3, 7th off West 0 on, 0 out), Hunter (1, 8th off Willis 0 on, 1 out). **RBI:** Smith 1 (3), Gant 1 (3), Justice 5 (6), Hunter 2 (3), Lemke 3 (4), Belliard 2 (4). **Runners left in scoring position, 2 out:** Smith 2, Olson 1, Belliard 1. **GIDP:** Lemke. **Team LOB:** 5 **BASERUNNING: SB:** Olson (1, 2nd base off Tapani/Harper), Justice (2, 2nd base off Leach/Harper). **FIELDING: E:** Pendleton (2).

MINNESOTA	IP	H	R	ER	BB	SO	HR	ERA
Tapani (L, 1-1)	4	6	4	4	2	4	1	4.50
Leach	2	2	1	1	0	1	0	3.86
West	0	2	4	4	2	0	1	0.00
Bedrosian	1	3	2	2	0	1	0	5.40
Willis	1	4	3	3	0	0	1	8.31

ATLANTA	IP	H	R	ER	BB	SO	HR	ERA
Glavine (W, 1-1)	5.1	4	3	3	4	2	0	2.70
Mercker	0.2	0	0	0	0	0	0	0.00
Clancy	2	2	1	1	1	2	0	4.15
St.Claire	1	1	1	1	0	0	0	9.00

WP: Bedrosian 1. **Pitches-strikes:** Tapani 54-34, Leach 30-19, West 14-4, Bedrosian 26-19, Willis 16-11, Glavine 84-45, Mercker 5-3, Clancy 37-22, St.Claire 6-5. **Ground balls-fly balls:** Tapani 6-1, Leach 2-3, West 0-0, Bedrosian 0-2, Willis 2-0, Glavine 9-4, Mercker 2-0, Clancy 4-0, St.Claire 1-2. **Batters faced:** Tapani 19, Leach 8, West 4, Bedrosian 6, Willis 6, Glavine 24, Mercker 2, Clancy 9, St.Claire 4. **UMPIRES:** hp—Rick Reed, 1b—Ed Montague, 2b—Don Denkinger, 3b—Harry Wendelstedt, lf—Drew Coble, rf—Terry Tata **T:** 2:59 **A:** 50,878

GAME 6 Minnesota 4 Atlanta 3
Humphrey Metrodome 10/26/91

ATLANTA	AB	R	H	HR	RBI	BB	AVG
Smith dh	3	1	0	0	0	1	.182
Pendleton 3b	5	1	4	1	2	0	.400
Gant cf	5	0	0	0	1	0	.308
Justice rf	4	0	0	0	0	1	.250
Bream 1b	4	0	1	0	0	1	.150
c-Mitchell pr-lf	0	0	0	0	0	0	.000
Hunter lf-1b	5	0	0	0	0	0	.176
Olson c	5	0	0	0	0	0	.261
Lemke 2b	4	1	2	0	0	0	.450
Belliard ss	2	0	1	0	0	0	.357
a-Gregg ph	0	0	0	0	0	0	.000
b-Blauser ph-ss	2	0	1	0	0	0	.200
TOTALS	**39**	**3**	**9**	**1**	**3**	**3**	**.262**

a - Batted for Belliard in the 7th
b - Batted for Gregg in the 7th
c - Ran for Bream in the 11th

BATTING: HR: Pendleton (2, 5th off Erickson 1 on, 1 out). **RBI:** Pendleton 2 (3), Gant 1 (4). **Runners left in scoring position, 2 out:** Justice 1, Bream 1. **GIDP:** Smith. **Team LOB:** 7 **BASERUNNING: CS:** Mitchell (1, 2nd base off Aguilera/Harper). **FIELDING: E:** Hunter (1). **DP:** 2 (Bream-Belliard-Bream, Blauser-Lemke-Bream).

MINNESOTA	AB	R	H	HR	RBI	BB	AVG
Gladden lf	4	1	0	0	0	1	.160
Knoblauch 2b	5	1	1	0	0	0	.318
Puckett cf	4	2	3	1	3	0	.273
Davis dh	4	0	0	0	0	0	.214
Mack rf	4	0	2	0	1	0	.105
Leius 3b	3	0	2	0	0	0	.357
b-Pagliarulo ph-3b	1	0	0	0	0	0	.375
Hrbek 1b	4	0	0	0	0	0	.130
Ortiz c	2	0	0	0	0	0	.200
a-Harper ph-c	2	0	0	0	0	0	.353
Gagne ss	4	0	1	0	0	0	.182
TOTALS	**37**	**4**	**9**	**1**	**4**	**1**	**.222**

a - Batted for Ortiz in the 7th
b - Batted for Leius in the 9th

BATTING: 2B: Mack (1, Avery). **3B:** Puckett (1, Avery). **HR:** Puckett (2, 11th off Leibrandt 0 on, 0 out). **SF:** Puckett. **RBI:** Puckett 3 (4), Mack 1 (1). **2-out RBI:** Mack 1. **Runners left in scoring position, 2 out:** Mack 1, Hrbek 1, Gagne 2. **GIDP:** Hrbek, Gladden. **Team LOB:** 5 **BASERUNNING: SB:** Gladden (2, 2nd base off Avery/Olson), Puckett (1, 2nd base off Stanton/Olson). **FIELDING: DP:** 2 (Gagne-Hrbek, Gagne).

ATLANTA	IP	H	R	ER	BB	SO	HR	ERA
Avery	6	6	3	3	1	3	0	3.46
Stanton	2	2	0	0	0	1	0	0.00
Pena	2	0	0	0	0	2	0	2.25
Leibrandt (L, 0-2)	0	1	1	1	0	0	1	11.25

MINNESOTA	IP	H	R	ER	BB	SO	HR	ERA
Erickson	6	5	3	3	2	2	1	5.06
Guthrie	0.1	1	0	0	1	1	0	2.25
Willis	2.2	1	0	0	0	1	0	5.14
Aguilera (W, 1-1)	2	2	0	0	0	0	0	1.80

WP: Guthrie 1. **HBP:** Smith (by Erickson). **Pitches-strikes:** Avery 83-55, Stanton 36-24, Pena 24-16, Leibrandt 4-2, Erickson 100-57, Guthrie 13-8, Willis 33-21, Aguilera 14-11. **Ground balls-fly balls:** Avery 9-5, Stanton 1-3, Pena 3-1, Leibrandt 0-0, Erickson 9-7, Guthrie 0-0, Willis 3-3, Aguilera 0-4. **Batters faced:** Avery 25, Stanton 7, Pena 6, Leibrandt 1, Erickson 26, Guthrie 3, Willis 8, Aguilera 6. **UMPIRES:** hp—Ed Montague, 1b—Don Denkinger, 2b—Harry Wendelstedt, 3b—Drew Coble, lf—Terry Tata, rf—Rick Reed **T:** 3:46 **A:** 55,155

GAME 7 Minnesota 1 Atlanta 0
Humphrey Metrodome 10/27/91

ATLANTA	AB	R	H	HR	RBI	BB	AVG
Smith dh	4	0	2	0	0	1	.231
Pendleton 3b	5	0	1	0	0	0	.367
Gant cf	4	0	0	0	0	0	.267
Justice rf	3	0	1	0	0	1	.259
Bream 1b	4	0	0	0	0	0	.125
Hunter lf	4	0	1	0	0	0	.190
Olson c	4	0	0	0	0	0	.222
Lemke 2b	4	0	1	0	0	0	.417
Belliard ss	2	0	1	0	0	0	.375
a-Blauser ph-ss	1	0	0	0	0	0	.167
TOTALS	**35**	**0**	**7**	**0**	**0**	**2**	**.253**

a - Batted for Belliard in the 10th

BATTING: 2B: Hunter (1, Morris), Pendleton (3, Morris). **S:** Belliard. **Runners left in scoring position, 2 out:** Gant 2, Olson 2. **GIDP:** Bream. **Team LOB:** 8 **FIELDING: DP:** 3 (Bream-Belliard-Bream, Belliard, Lemke-Belliard-Bream).

MINNESOTA	AB	R	H	HR	RBI	BB	AVG
Gladden lf	5	1	3	0	0	0	.233
Knoblauch 2b	4	0	1	0	0	0	.308
Puckett cf	2	0	0	0	0	3	.250
Hrbek 1b	3	0	0	0	0	1	.115
Davis dh	4	0	1	0	0	0	.222
d-Brown ph	0	0	0	0	0	0	.000
e-Larkin ph	1	0	1	0	1	0	.500
Harper c	4	0	2	0	0	0	.381
Mack rf	4	0	1	0	0	0	.130
Pagliarulo 3b	3	0	0	0	0	1	.273
Gagne ss	2	0	0	0	0	0	.167
a-Bush ph	1	0	1	0	0	0	.250
b-Newman pr-ss	0	0	0	0	0	0	.500
c-Sorrento ph	1	0	0	0	0	0	.000
Leius ss	0	0	0	0	0	0	.357
TOTALS	**34**	**1**	**10**	**0**	**1**	**5**	**.232**

a - Batted for Gagne in the 8th
b - Ran for Bush in the 8th
c - Batted for Newman in the 9th
d - Batted for Davis in the 10th e - Batted for Brown in the 10th

BATTING: 2B: Gladden 2 (2, Smoltz, Pena). **S:** Knoblauch. **RBI:** Larkin 1 (1). **Runners left in scoring position, 2 out:** Puckett 1, Pagliarulo 1, Sorrento 1. **GIDP:** Davis, Mack. **Team LOB:** 12 **FIELDING: DP:** 1 (Hrbek-Harper-Hrbek).

ATLANTA	IP	H	R	ER	BB	SO	HR	ERA
Smoltz	7.1	6	0	0	1	4	0	1.26
Stanton	0.2	2	0	0	1	0	0	0.00
Pena (L, 0-1)	1.1	2	1	1	3	1	0	3.38

MINNESOTA	IP	H	R	ER	BB	SO	HR	ERA
Morris (W, 2-0)	10	7	0	0	2	8	0	1.17

WP: Morris 1. **IBB:** Justice (by Morris), Puckett 2 (by Stanton, by Pena), Pagliarulo (by Pena), Hrbek (by Pena). **HBP:** Hrbek (by Smoltz). **Pitches-strikes:** Smoltz 104-69, Stanton 20-11, Pena 24-11, Morris 126-79. **Ground balls-fly balls:** Smoltz 7-10, Stanton 0-1, Pena 1-0, Morris 11-9. **Batters faced:** Smoltz 29, Stanton 4, Pena 8, Morris 38. **UMPIRES:** hp—Don Denkinger, 1b—Harry Wendelstedt, 2b—Drew Coble, 3b—Terry Tata, lf—Rick Reed, rf—Ed Montague **T:** 3:23 **A:** 55,118

1992 TORONTO DEF. ATLANTA, 4-2

GAME 1 Atlanta 3 Toronto 1
Atlanta-Fulton County Stadium 10/17/92

TORONTO	AB	R	H	HR	RBI	BB	AVG
White cf	4	0	0	0	0	0	.000
Alomar 2b	4	0	0	0	0	0	.000
Carter 1b	4	1	1	1	1	0	.250
Winfield rf	3	0	1	0	0	0	.333
Maldonado lf	3	0	0	0	0	0	.000
Gruber 3b	3	0	0	0	0	0	.000
Borders c	3	0	2	0	0	0	.667
Lee ss	3	0	0	0	0	0	.000
Morris p	2	0	0	0	0	0	.000
Stottlemyre p	0	0	0	0	0	0	.000
a-Tabler ph	1	0	0	0	0	0	.000
Wells p	0	0	0	0	0	0	.000
TOTALS	**30**	**1**	**4**	**1**	**1**	**0**	**.133**

a - Batted for Stottlemyre in the 8th

BATTING: HR: Carter (1, 4th off Glavine 0 on, 0 out). **RBI:** Carter 1 (1). **Runners left in scoring position, 2 out:** Lee 1. **GIDP:** Lee. **Team LOB:** 2

ATLANTA	AB	R	H	HR	RBI	BB	AVG
Nixon cf	3	0	1	0	0	1	.333
Blauser ss	4	0	0	0	0	0	.000
Belliard ss	0	0	0	0	0	0	.000
Pendleton 3b	4	0	0	0	0	0	.000
Justice rf	2	1	0	0	0	2	.000
Bream 1b	3	0	1	0	0	1	.333
Gant lf	3	1	0	0	0	1	.000
Berryhill c	4	1	1	1	3	0	.250
Lemke 2b	3	0	1	0	0	0	.333
Glavine p	2	0	0	0	0	1	.000
TOTALS	**28**	**3**	**4**	**1**	**3**	**6**	**.143**

BATTING: HR: Berryhill (1, 6th off Morris 2 on, 2 out). **SF:** Justice. **RBI:** Berryhill 3 (3). **2-out RBI:** Berryhill 3. **Runners left in scoring position, 2 out:** Blauser 1, Justice 1, Gant 2. **Team LOB:** 7 **BASERUNNING: SB:** Nixon (1, 2nd base off Morris/Borders), Gant (1, 2nd base off Morris/Borders). **FIELDING: DP:** 1 (Belliard-Bream).

TORONTO	IP	H	R	ER	BB	SO	HR	ERA
Morris (L, 0-1)	6	4	3	3	5	7	1	4.50
Stottlemyre	1	0	0	0	0	2	0	0.00
Wells	1	0	0	0	1	1	0	0.00

ATLANTA	IP	H	R	ER	BB	SO	HR	ERA
Glavine (W, 1-0)	9	4	1	1	0	6	1	1.00

WP: Morris 1. **Pitches-strikes:** Morris 98-54, Stottlemyre 13-10, Wells 16-10, Glavine 120-75. **Ground balls-fly balls:** Morris 6-5, Stottlemyre 1-0, Wells 1-1, Glavine 11-9. **Batters faced:** Morris 27, Stottlemyre 3, Wells 4, Glavine 30. **UMPIRES:** hp—Jerry Crawford, 1b—Mike Reilly, 2b—Joe West, 3b—Dan Morrison, lf—Bob Davidson, rf—John Shulock **T:** 2:37 **A:** 51,763

GAME 2 Toronto 5 Atlanta 4
Atlanta-Fulton County Stadium 10/18/92

TORONTO	AB	R	H	HR	RBI	BB	AVG
White cf	5	0	1	0	1	0	.111
Alomar 2b	4	1	1	0	0	1	.125
Carter lf	3	0	1	0	0	1	.286
Winfield rf	4	0	1	0	1	0	.286
Olerud 1b	4	0	0	0	0	0	.000
Gruber 3b	4	0	0	0	0	0	.000
Borders c	3	1	1	0	0	1	.500
Lee ss	3	1	1	0	0	0	.167
b-Bell ph	0	1	0	0	0	1	.000
Griffin ss	0	0	0	0	0	0	.000
Cone p	2	0	2	0	1	0	1.000
Wells p	0	0	0	0	0	0	.000
a-Maldonado ph	1	0	0	0	0	0	.000
Stottlemyre p	0	0	0	0	0	0	.000
Ward p	0	0	0	0	0	0	.000
c-Sprague ph	1	1	1	1	2	0	1.000
Henke p	0	0	0	0	0	0	.000
TOTALS	**34**	**5**	**9**	**1**	**5**	**4**	**.203**

a - Batted for Wells in the 7th
b - Batted for Lee in the 9th
c - Batted for Ward in the 9th

BATTING: 2B: Borders (1, Smoltz), Alomar (1, Smoltz). **HR:** Sprague (1, 9th off Reardon 1 on, 1 out). **RBI:** White 1 (1), Winfield 1 (1), Cone 1 (1), Sprague 2 (2). **2-out RBI:** White 1, Cone 1. **Runners left in scoring position, 2 out:** Alomar 1, Gruber 1, Maldonado 1. **Team LOB:** 6 **FIELDING: E:** Lee (1), Borders (1). **DP:** 2 (Lee-Olerud 2).

ATLANTA	AB	R	H	HR	RBI	BB	AVG
Nixon cf	5	0	0	0	0	0	.125
Sanders lf	3	1	1	0	0	2	.333
Pendleton 3b	4	1	1	0	0	1	.125
Justice rf	3	1	1	0	1	1	.200
Bream 1b	1	1	0	0	0	1	.250
a-Hunter ph-1b	1	0	0	0	1	0	.000
Blauser ss	3	0	1	0	0	1	.143
Belliard ss	0	0	0	0	0	0	.000
Berryhill c	3	0	0	0	0	1	.143
Lemke 2b	4	0	1	0	1	0	.286
Smoltz p	3	0	0	0	0	0	.000
Stanton p	0	0	0	0	0	0	.000
Reardon p	0	0	0	0	0	0	.000
b-L.Smith ph	0	0	0	0	0	0	.000
c-Gant pr	0	0	0	0	0	0	.000
TOTALS	**30**	**4**	**5**	**0**	**3**	**7**	**.155**

a - Batted for Bream in the 5th
b - Batted for Reardon in the 9th
c - Ran for L.Smith in the 9th

BATTING: SF: Hunter, Nixon. **RBI:** Justice 1 (1), Hunter 1 (1), Lemke 1 (1). **Runners left in scoring position, 2 out:** Pendleton 1, Justice 1, Berryhill 1. **GIDP:** Lemke, Smoltz. **Team LOB:** 8 **BASERUNNING: SB:** Justice (1, 2nd base off Cone/Borders), Blauser (1, 2nd base off Cone/Borders), Sanders 2 (2, 2nd base off Cone/Borders), Gant (2, 2nd base off Henke/Borders). **FIELDING: E:** Bream (1). **DP:** 1 (Blauser-Hunter).

TORONTO	IP	H	R	ER	BB	SO	HR	ERA
Cone	4.1	5	4	3	5	2	0	6.23
Wells	1.2	0	0	0	1	2	0	0.00
Stottlemyre	1	0	0	0	0	0	0	0.00
Ward (W, 1-0)	1	0	0	0	0	2	0	0.00
Henke (S, 1)	1	0	0	0	1	0	0	0.00

ATLANTA	IP	H	R	ER	BB	SO	HR	ERA
Smoltz	7.1	8	3	2	3	8	0	2.45
Stanton	0.1	0	0	0	0	0	0	0.00
Reardon (L, 0-1)	1.1	1	2	2	1	1	1	13.50

WP: Smoltz 2. **HBP:** L.Smith (by Henke). **Pitches-strikes:** Cone 94-48, Wells 18-11, Stottlemyre 8-6, Ward 15-8, Henke 19-12, Smoltz 117-72, Stanton 1-1, Reardon 20-12. **Ground balls-fly balls:** Cone 4-6, Wells 0-2, Stottlemyre 1-2, Ward 1-0, Henke 0-3, Smoltz 5-7, Stanton 0-1, Reardon 1-2. **Batters faced:** Cone 22, Wells 6, Stottlemyre 3, Ward 3, Henke 5, Smoltz 31, Stanton 1, Reardon 6. **UMPIRES:** hp—Mike Reilly, 1b—Joe West, 2b—Dan Morrison, 3b—Bob Davidson, lf—John Shulock, rf—Jerry Crawford **T:** 3:30 **A:** 51,763

GAME 3 Toronto 3 Atlanta 2
Skydome 10/20/92

ATLANTA	AB	R	H	HR	RBI	BB	AVG
Nixon cf	4	1	0	0	0	0	.083
Sanders lf	4	1	3	0	0	0	.571
Pendleton 3b	4	0	2	0	0	0	.250
Justice rf	3	0	1	0	1	1	.250
L.Smith dh	4	0	1	0	1	0	.250
Bream 1b	4	0	2	0	0	0	.375
a-Hunter pr-1b	0	0	0	0	0	0	.000
Blauser ss	4	0	0	0	0	0	.091
Berryhill c	4	0	0	0	0	0	.091
Lemke 2b	3	0	0	0	0	0	.200
TOTALS	**34**	**2**	**9**	**0**	**2**	**1**	**.196**

a - Ran for Bream in the 9th

BATTING: 2B: Sanders (1, Guzman). **SF:** Berryhill. **RBI:** Justice 1 (2), L.Smith 1 (1). **2-out RBI:** L.Smith 1. **Runners left in scoring position, 2 out:** Justice 1, L.Smith 2, Bream 1. **Team LOB:** 6 **BASERUNNING: SB:** Sanders (3, 2nd base off Guzman/Borders), Nixon (2, 2nd base off Guzman/Borders). **CS:** Hunter (1, 2nd base off Ward/Borders). **FIELDING: DP:** 1 (Pendleton-Lemke-Bream).

TORONTO	AB	R	H	HR	RBI	BB	AVG
White cf	4	0	0	0	0	0	.077
Alomar 2b	4	1	1	0	0	0	.167
Carter rf	3	1	1	1	1	1	.300
Winfield dh	3	0	1	0	0	0	.300
Olerud 1b	3	0	0	0	0	0	.000
a-Sprague ph	0	0	0	0	0	1	1.000
Maldonado lf	4	0	1	0	1	0	.125
Gruber 3b	2	1	1	1	1	1	.111
Borders c	3	0	1	0	0	0	.444
Lee ss	3	0	0	0	0	0	.111
TOTALS	**29**	**3**	**6**	**2**	**3**	**3**	**.204**

a - Batted for Olerud in the 9th

BATTING: HR: Carter (2, 4th off Avery 0 on, 1 out), Gruber (1, 8th off Avery 0 on, 0 out). **S:** Winfield. **RBI:** Carter 1 (2), Maldonado 1 (1), Gruber 1 (1). **Runners left in scoring position, 2 out:** White 1, Lee 1. **GIDP:** Maldonado. **Team LOB:** 5 **BASERUNNING: SB:** Gruber (1, 2nd base off Avery/Berryhill), Alomar (1, 2nd base off Wohlers/Berryhill). **FIELDING: E:** Gruber (1). **Outfield assists:** Maldonado (1). **DP:** 2 (White-Lee, Borders-Lee).

ATLANTA	IP	H	R	ER	BB	SO	HR	ERA
Avery (L, 0-1)	8	5	3	3	1	9	2	3.38
Wohlers	0.1	0	0	0	1	0	0	0.00
Stanton	0	0	0	0	1	0	0	0.00
Reardon	0	1	0	0	0	0	0	13.50

TORONTO	IP	H	R	ER	BB	SO	HR	ERA
Guzman	8	8	2	1	1	7	0	1.13
Ward (W, 2-0)	1	1	0	0	0	2	0	0.00

IBB: Justice (by Guzman), Carter (by Wohlers), Sprague (by Stanton). **Pitches-strikes:** Avery 122-80, Wohlers 5-1, Stanton 4-0, Reardon 3-3, Guzman 115-74, Ward 17-11. **Ground balls-fly balls:** Avery 8-6, Wohlers 0-0, Stanton 0-0, Reardon 0-0, Guzman 7-9, Ward 0-0. **Batters faced:** Avery 29, Wohlers 2, Stanton 1, Reardon 1, Guzman 32, Ward 3. **UMPIRES:** hp—Joe West, 1b—Dan Morrison, 2b—Bob Davidson, 3b—John Shulock, lf—Jerry Crawford, rf—Mike Reilly **T:** 2:49 **A:** 51,813

GAME 4 Toronto 2 Atlanta 1
Skydome 10/21/92

ATLANTA	AB	R	H	HR	RBI	BB	AVG
Nixon cf	4	0	2	0	0	0	.188
Blauser ss	4	0	1	0	0	0	.133
Pendleton 3b	4	0	0	0	0	0	.188
L.Smith dh	4	0	0	0	0	0	.125
Justice rf	4	0	0	0	0	0	.167
Gant lf	3	1	1	0	0	0	.167
Hunter 1b	3	0	1	0	0	0	.250
Berryhill c	3	0	0	0	0	0	.071
Lemke 2b	3	0	0	0	1	0	.154
TOTALS	**32**	**1**	**5**	**0**	**1**	**0**	**.185**

BATTING: 2B: Gant (1, Key). **RBI:** Lemke 1 (2). **Runners left in scoring position, 2 out:** Blauser 2, L.Smith 1. **Team LOB:** 4 **BASERUNNING: SB:** Blauser (2, 2nd base off Key/Borders), Nixon (3, 2nd base off Ward/Borders). **FIELDING: Outfield assists:** Gant (1). **DP:** 2 (Blauser-Lemke, Blauser-Lemke-Hunter).

TORONTO	AB	R	H	HR	RBI	BB	AVG
White cf	4	0	3	0	1	0	.235
Alomar 2b	3	0	0	0	0	1	.133
Carter rf	3	0	0	0	0	1	.231
Winfield dh	3	0	0	0	0	1	.231
Olerud 1b	3	0	2	0	0	0	.200
Maldonado lf	3	0	0	0	0	0	.091
Gruber 3b	2	1	0	0	0	1	.091
Borders c	3	1	1	1	1	0	.417
Lee ss	3	0	0	0	0	0	.083
TOTALS	**27**	**2**	**6**	**1**	**2**	**4**	**.208**

BATTING: 2B: White (1, Glavine). **HR:** Borders (1, 3th off Glavine 0 on, 0 out). **RBI:** White 1 (2), Borders 1 (1). **2-out RBI:** White 1. **Runners left in scoring position, 2 out:** White 1, Winfield 1, Maldonado 1. **GIDP:** Gruber. **Team LOB:** 5 **BASERUNNING: SB:** Alomar (2, 3rd base off Glavine/Berryhill).

ATLANTA	IP	H	R	ER	BB	SO	HR	ERA
Glavine (L, 1-1)	8	6	2	2	4	2	1	1.59

TORONTO	IP	H	R	ER	BB	SO	HR	ERA
Key (W, 1-0)	7.2	5	1	1	0	6	0	1.17
Ward	0.1	0	0	0	0	1	0	0.00
Henke (S, 2)	1	0	0	0	0	1	0	0.00

WP: Ward 1. **Pitches-strikes:** Glavine 114-67, Key 91-57, Ward 14-11, Henke 11-7. **Ground balls-fly balls:** Glavine 12-7, Key 5-11, Ward 1-0, Henke 1-1. **Batters faced:** Glavine 31, Key 27, Ward 2, Henke 3. **UMPIRES:** hp—Dan Morrison, 1b—Bob Davidson, 2b—John Shulock, 3b—Jerry Crawford, lf—Mike Reilly, rf—Joe West **T:** 2:21 **A:** 52,090

GAME 5 Atlanta 7 Toronto 2
Skydome 10/22/92

ATLANTA	AB	R	H	HR	RBI	BB	AVG
Nixon cf	5	2	3	0	0	0	.286
Sanders lf	5	1	2	0	1	0	.500
Pendleton 3b	5	1	2	0	1	0	.238
Justice rf	3	2	1	1	1	1	.200
L.Smith dh	4	1	1	1	4	0	.167
Bream 1b	4	0	0	0	0	0	.250
Blauser ss	4	0	1	0	0	0	.158
Belliard ss	0	0	0	0	0	0	.000
Berryhill c	4	0	1	0	0	0	.111
Lemke 2b	4	0	2	0	0	0	.235
TOTALS	**38**	**7**	**13**	**2**	**7**	**1**	**.222**

BATTING: 2B: Nixon (1, Morris), Pendleton 2 (2, Morris). **HR:** Justice (1, 4th off Morris 0 on, 0 out), L.Smith (1, 5th off Morris 3 on, 2 out). **RBI:** Sanders 1 (1), Pendleton 1 (1), Justice 1 (3), L.Smith 4 (5). **2-out RBI:** Sanders 1, L.Smith 4. **Runners left in scoring position, 2 out:** Pendleton 1, L.Smith 1. **Team LOB:** 5 **BASERUNNING: SB:** Nixon 2 (5, 3rd base off Morris/Borders, 2nd base off Morris/Borders). **CS:** Blauser (1, 2nd base off Morris/Borders). **FIELDING: DP:** 1 (Lemke-Blauser-Bream).

TORONTO	AB	R	H	HR	RBI	BB	AVG
White cf	4	0	0	0	0	0	.190
Alomar 2b	3	0	0	0	0	1	.111
Carter rf	4	0	1	0	0	0	.235
Winfield dh	4	0	1	0	0	0	.235
Olerud 1b	3	2	2	0	0	0	.308
a-Sprague ph-1b	1	0	0	0	0	0	.500
Maldonado lf	2	0	0	0	0	2	.077
Gruber 3b	4	0	0	0	0	0	.067
Borders c	4	0	2	0	2	0	.438
Lee ss	3	0	0	0	0	1	.067
TOTALS	**32**	**2**	**6**	**0**	**2**	**4**	**.204**

a - Batted for Olerud in the 8th

BATTING: 2B: Borders (2, Smoltz). **RBI:** Borders 2 (3). **2-out RBI:** Borders 1. **Runners left in scoring position, 2 out:** White 1, Maldonado 1, Lee 2. **GIDP:** Alomar. **Team LOB:** 7 **BASERUNNING: SB:** Carter (1, 2nd base off Stanton/Berryhill). **FIELDING: Outfield assists:** Maldonado (2). **DP:** 1 (Maldonado-Borders).

ATLANTA	IP	H	R	ER	BB	SO	HR	ERA
Smoltz (W, 1-0)	6	5	2	2	4	4	0	2.70
Stanton (S, 1)	3	1	0	0	0	1	0	0.00

TORONTO	IP	H	R	ER	BB	SO	HR	ERA
Morris (L, 0-2)	4.2	9	7	7	1	5	2	8.44
Wells	1.1	1	0	0	0	0	0	0.00
Timlin	1	0	0	0	0	0	0	0.00
Eichhorn	1	0	0	0	0	1	0	0.00
Stottlemyre	1	3	0	0	0	1	0	0.00

IBB: Justice (by Morris). **Pitches-strikes:** Smoltz 114-66, Stanton 41-28, Morris 82-54, Wells 19-13, Timlin 9-6, Eichhorn 14-12, Stottlemyre 17-11. **Ground balls-fly balls:** Smoltz 4-10, Stanton 4-3, Morris 3-5, Wells 0-4, Timlin 2-1, Eichhorn 1-1, Stottlemyre 0-1. **Batters faced:** Smoltz 27, Stanton 9, Morris 23, Wells 5, Timlin 3, Eichhorn 3, Stottlemyre 5. **UMPIRES:** hp—Bob Davidson, 1b—John Shulock, 2b—Jerry Crawford, 3b—Mike Reilly, lf—Joe West, rf—Dan Morrison **T:** 3:05 **A:** 52,268

GAME 6 Toronto 4 Atlanta 3
Atlanta-Fulton County Stadium 10/24/92

TORONTO	AB	R	H	HR	RBI	BB	AVG
White cf	5	2	2	0	0	0	.231
Alomar 2b	6	1	3	0	0	0	.208
Carter 1b	5	0	2	0	1	0	.273
Winfield rf	5	0	1	0	2	1	.227
Maldonado lf	6	1	2	1	1	0	.158
Gruber 3b	4	0	1	0	0	0	.105
Borders c	4	0	2	0	0	1	.450
Lee ss	4	0	1	0	0	0	.105
b-Tabler ph	1	0	0	0	0	0	.000
Griffin ss	0	0	0	0	0	0	.000
Cone p	2	0	0	0	0	1	.500
Stottlemyre p	0	0	0	0	0	0	.000
Wells p	0	0	0	0	0	0	.000
a-Bell ph	1	0	0	0	0	0	.000
Ward p	0	0	0	0	0	0	.000
Henke p	0	0	0	0	0	0	.000
Key p	1	0	0	0	0	0	.000
Timlin p	0	0	0	0	0	0	.000
TOTALS	**44**	**4**	**14**	**1**	**4**	**3**	**.230**

a - Batted for Wells in the 8th
b - Batted for Lee in the 10th

BATTING: 2B: Borders (3, Avery), Carter 2 (2, P.Smith, Stanton), Winfield (1, Leibrandt). **HR:** Maldonado (1, 4th off Avery 0 on, 0 out). **S:** Gruber. **SF:** Carter, Borders. **RBI:** Carter 1 (3), Winfield 2 (3), Maldonado 1 (2). **2-out RBI:** Winfield 2. **Runners left in scoring position, 2 out:** White 1, Winfield 2, Maldonado 2, Gruber 1, Bell 1. **GIDP:** Cone. **Team LOB:** 13 **BASERUNNING: SB:** White (1, 2nd base off Avery/Berryhill), Alomar (3, 2nd base off Avery/Berryhill). **FIELDING: E:** Griffin (1).

ATLANTA	AB	R	H	HR	RBI	BB	AVG
Nixon cf	6	0	2	0	1	0	.296
Sanders lf	3	1	2	0	0	0	.533
b-Gant ph-lf	2	0	0	0	0	0	.125
Pendleton 3b	4	0	1	0	1	0	.240
Justice rf	4	0	0	0	0	1	.158
Bream 1b	3	0	0	0	0	2	.200
Blauser ss	5	2	3	0	0	0	.250
Berryhill c	4	0	0	0	0	0	.091
e-Smoltz pr	0	0	0	0	0	0	.000
Lemke 2b	2	0	0	0	0	1	.211
c-L.Smith ph	0	0	0	0	0	1	.167
Belliard 2b	0	0	0	0	0	0	.000
Avery p	1	0	0	0	0	0	.000
P.Smith p	1	0	0	0	0	0	.000
a-Treadway ph	1	0	0	0	0	0	.000
Stanton p	0	0	0	0	0	0	.000
Wohlers p	0	0	0	0	0	0	.000
d-Cabrera ph	1	0	0	0	0	0	.000
Leibrandt p	0	0	0	0	0	0	.000
f-Hunter ph	1	0	0	0	1	0	.200
TOTALS	**38**	**3**	**8**	**0**	**3**	**5**	**.220**

a - Batted for P.Smith in the 7th
b - Batted for Sanders in the 7th
c - Batted for Lemke in the 9th
d - Batted for Wohlers in the 9th e - Ran for Berryhill in the 11th f - Batted for Leibrandt in the 11th

BATTING: 2B: Sanders (2, Cone). **S:** Berryhill, Belliard. **SF:** Pendleton. **RBI:** Nixon 1 (1), Pendleton 1 (2), Hunter 1 (2). **2-out RBI:** Nixon 1. **Runners left in scoring position, 2 out:** Nixon 1, Gant 2, Pendleton 2, Avery 1. **Team LOB:** 10 **BASERUNNING: SB:** Sanders 2 (5, 3rd base off Cone/Borders, 2nd base off Cone/Borders). **CS:** Nixon (1, 2nd base off Wells/Borders). **FIELDING: E:** Justice (1). **Outfield assists:** Sanders (1). **DP:** 1 (Lemke-Blauser-Bream).

TORONTO	IP	H	R	ER	BB	SO	HR	ERA
Cone	6	4	1	1	3	6	0	3.48
Stottlemyre	0.2	1	0	0	0	1	0	0.00
Wells	0.1	0	0	0	0	0	0	0.00
Ward	1	0	0	0	1	1	0	0.00
Henke	1.1	2	1	1	1	0	0	2.70
Key (W, 2-0)	1.1	1	1	0	0	0	0	1.00
Timlin (S, 1)	0.1	0	0	0	0	0	0	0.00

ATLANTA	IP	H	R	ER	BB	SO	HR	ERA
Avery	4	6	2	2	2	2	1	3.75
P.Smith	3	3	0	0	0	0	0	0.00
Stanton	1.2	2	0	0	1	0	0	0.00
Wohlers	0.1	0	0	0	0	0	0	0.00
Leibrandt (L, 0-1)	2	3	2	2	0	0	0	9.00

IBB: Borders (by Stanton). **HBP:** White (by Leibrandt). **Pitches-strikes:** Cone 103-62, Stottlemyre 11-8, Wells 4-2, Ward 16-9, Henke 33-22, Key 14-11, Timlin 2-2, Avery 60-35, P.Smith 39-27, Stanton 19-12, Wohlers 5-5, Leibrandt 34-22. **Ground balls-fly balls:** Cone 4-7, Stottlemyre 1-0, Wells 0-0, Ward 0-2, Henke 1-2, Key 4-0, Timlin 1-0, Avery 6-2, P.Smith 4-5, Stanton 1-3, Wohlers 1-0, Leibrandt 1-5. **Batters faced:** Cone 25, Stottlemyre 3, Wells 0, Ward 4, Henke 7, Key 6, Timlin 1, Avery 19, P.Smith 12, Stanton 8, Wohlers 1, Leibrandt 10. **UMPIRES:** hp—John Shulock, 1b—Jerry Crawford, 2b—Mike Reilly, 3b—Joe West, lf—Dan Morrison, rf—Bob Davidson **T:** 4:07 **A:** 51,763

1993 TORONTO DEF. PHILADELPHIA, 4-2

GAME 1 Toronto 8 Philadelphia 5
Skydome 10/16/93

PHILADELPHIA	AB	R	H	HR	RBI	BB	AVG
Dykstra cf	4	1	1	0	0	1	.250
Duncan 2b	5	2	3	0	0	0	.600
Kruk 1b	4	2	3	0	2	1	.750
Hollins 3b	4	0	0	0	0	1	.000
Daulton c	4	0	1	0	1	1	.250
Eisenreich rf	5	0	1	0	1	0	.200
Jordan dh	5	0	1	0	0	0	.200
Thompson lf	3	0	0	0	0	0	.000
a-Incaviglia ph-lf	1	0	0	0	0	0	.000
Stocker ss	3	0	1	0	0	1	.333
TOTALS	**38**	**5**	**11**	**0**	**4**	**5**	**.289**

a - Batted for Thompson in the 8th

BATTING: 3B: Duncan (1, Guzman). **RBI:** Kruk 2 (2), Daulton 1 (1), Eisenreich 1 (1). **2-out RBI:** Eisenreich 1. **Runners left in scoring position, 2 out:** Duncan 1, Kruk 2, Eisenreich 1, Jordan 1. **GIDP:** Thompson. **Team LOB:** 11 **BASERUNNING: SB:** Dykstra (1, 2nd base off Guzman/Borders), Duncan (1, 2nd base off Guzman/Borders). **FIELDING: E:** Thompson (1). **DP:** 1 (Stocker-Duncan-Kruk).

TORONTO	AB	R	H	HR	RBI	BB	AVG
Henderson lf	3	1	1	0	0	1	.333
White cf	4	3	2	1	2	0	.500
Alomar 2b	4	0	1	0	2	0	.250
Carter rf	3	1	1	0	1	0	.333
Olerud 1b	3	2	2	1	1	1	.667
Molitor dh	4	0	1	0	1	0	.250
Fernandez ss	3	0	0	0	1	1	.000
Sprague 3b	4	0	1	0	0	0	.250
Borders c	4	1	1	0	0	0	.250
TOTALS	**32**	**8**	**10**	**2**	**8**	**3**	**.313**

BATTING: 2B: White (1, West), Alomar (1, West). **HR:** White (1, 5th off Schilling 0 on, 2 out), Olerud (1, 6th off Schilling 0 on, 1 out). **SF:** Carter. **RBI:** White 2 (2), Alomar 2 (2), Carter 1 (1), Olerud 1 (1), Molitor 1 (1), Fernandez 1 (1). **2-out RBI:** White 1. **Runners left in scoring position, 2 out:** Henderson 1, Molitor 1. **GIDP:** White. **Team LOB:** 4 **BASERUNNING: SB:** Alomar (1, 3rd base off Andersen/Daulton). **CS:** Fernandez (1, 2nd base off Schilling/Daulton). **FIELDING: E:** Carter (1), Alomar (1), Sprague (1). **DP:** 1 (Fernandez-Olerud).

PHILADELPHIA	IP	H	R	ER	BB	SO	HR	ERA
Schilling (L, 0-1)	6.1	8	7	6	2	3	2	8.53
West	0	2	1	1	0	0	0	0.00
Andersen	0.2	0	0	0	1	1	0	0.00
Mason	1	0	0	0	0	1	0	0.00

TORONTO	IP	H	R	ER	BB	SO	HR	ERA
Guzman	5	5	4	4	4	6	0	7.20
Leiter (W, 1-0)	2.2	4	0	0	1	2	0	0.00
Ward (S, 1)	1.1	2	1	0	0	3	0	0.00

WP: Schilling 1, Guzman 1. **IBB:** Daulton (by Guzman), Olerud (by Andersen). **Pitches-strikes:** Schilling 99-61, West 12-8, Andersen 15-8, Mason 11-7, Guzman 121-74, Leiter 56-37, Ward 30-23. **Ground balls-fly balls:** Schilling 8-6, West 0-0, Andersen 0-1, Mason 1-1, Guzman 6-3, Leiter 5-1, Ward 0-1. **Batters faced:** Schilling 28, West 2, Andersen 3, Mason 3, Guzman 24, Leiter 13, Ward 6. **UMPIRES:** hp—Dave Phillips, 1b—Paul Runge, 2b—Mark Johnson, 3b—Charlie Williams, lf—Tim McClelland, rf—Dana DeMuth **T:** 0:00 **A:** 0,000

GAME 2 Philadelphia 6 Toronto 4
Skydome 10/17/93

PHILADELPHIA	AB	R	H	HR	RBI	BB	AVG
Dykstra cf	4	2	2	1	1	1	.375
Duncan 2b	4	1	1	0	0	1	.444
Kruk 1b	5	1	2	0	1	0	.556
Hollins 3b	4	1	2	0	1	1	.250
Batiste 3b	0	0	0	0	0	0	.000
Daulton c	5	0	1	0	0	0	.222
Eisenreich rf	4	1	1	1	3	1	.222
Incaviglia lf	4	0	1	0	0	0	.200
a-Thompson pr-lf	0	0	0	0	0	0	.000
Jordan dh	4	0	1	0	0	0	.222
Stocker ss	3	0	1	0	0	1	.333
TOTALS	**37**	**6**	**12**	**2**	**6**	**5**	**.307**

a - Ran for Incaviglia in the 8th

BATTING: HR: Eisenreich (1, 3th off Stewart 2 on, 1 out), Dykstra (1, 7th off Castillo 0 on, 0 out). **RBI:** Dykstra 1 (1), Kruk 1 (3), Hollins 1 (1), Eisenreich 3 (4). **Runners left in scoring position, 2 out:** Kruk 2, Hollins 1, Eisenreich 2, Stocker 1. **GIDP:** Eisenreich. **Team LOB:** 9 **BASERUNNING: CS:** Stocker (1, 2nd base off Stewart/Borders). **FIELDING: DP:** 1 (Stocker-Duncan-Kruk).

TORONTO	AB	R	H	HR	RBI	BB	AVG
Henderson lf	3	0	0	0	0	1	.167
White cf	4	0	1	0	0	0	.375
Molitor dh	3	2	2	0	0	1	.429
Carter rf	4	1	1	1	2	0	.286
Olerud 1b	3	0	0	0	1	0	.333
Alomar 2b	3	1	1	0	0	1	.286
Fernandez ss	3	0	2	0	1	1	.333
Sprague 3b	4	0	0	0	0	0	.125
a-Griffin pr	0	0	0	0	0	0	.000
Borders c	4	0	1	0	0	0	.250
TOTALS	**31**	**4**	**8**	**1**	**4**	**4**	**.286**

a - Ran for Sprague in the 9th

BATTING: 2B: White (2, Mulholland), Fernandez (1, Mulholland), Molitor (1, Mason). **HR:** Carter (1, 4th off Mulholland 1 on, 0 out). **SF:** Olerud, Olerud. **RBI:** Carter 2 (3), Olerud 1 (2), Fernandez 1 (2). **2-out RBI:** Fernandez 1. **Runners left in scoring position, 2 out:** Molitor 1, Sprague 1. **GIDP:** Borders. **Team LOB:** 5 **BASERUNNING: SB:** Molitor (1, 3rd base off Ma.Williams/Daulton), Alomar (2, 2nd base off Ma.Williams/Daulton). **CS:** Henderson (1, 2nd base off Mulholland/Daulton), Alomar (1, 3rd base off Ma.Williams/Daulton). **FIELDING: DP:** 1 (Sprague-Alomar-Olerud).

PHILADELPHIA	IP	H	R	ER	BB	SO	HR	ERA
Mulholland (W, 1-0)	5.2	7	3	3	2	4	1	4.76
Mason	1.2	1	1	1	0	2	0	3.38
Ma.Williams (S, 1)	1.2	0	0	0	2	0	0	0.00

TORONTO	IP	H	R	ER	BB	SO	HR	ERA
Stewart (L, 0-1)	6	6	5	5	4	6	1	7.50
Castillo	1	3	1	1	0	0	1	9.00
Eichhorn	0.1	1	0	0	1	0	0	0.00
Timlin	1.2	2	0	0	0	2	0	0.00

WP: Stewart 1. **BK:** , Stewart 1. **Pitches-strikes:** Mulholland 105-62, Mason 24-15, Ma.Williams 31-15, Stewart 122-79, Castillo 21-14, Eichhorn 16-8, Timlin 22-16. **Ground balls-fly balls:** Mulholland 4-8, Mason 1-2, Ma.Williams 2-0, Stewart 6-5, Castillo 1-2, Eichhorn 1-0, Timlin 2-0. **Batters faced:** Mulholland 25, Mason 6, Ma.Williams 5, Stewart 27, Castillo 6, Eichhorn 3, Timlin 6. **UMPIRES:** hp—Paul Runge, 1b—Mark Johnson, 2b—Charlie Williams, 3b—Tim McClelland, lf—Dana DeMuth, rf—Dave Phillips **T:** 3:35 **A:** 52,062

GAME 3 Toronto 10 Philadelphia 3
Veterans Stadium 10/19/93

TORONTO	AB	R	H	HR	RBI	BB	AVG
Henderson lf	4	2	2	0	0	0	.300
White cf	4	2	1	0	1	1	.333
Molitor 1b	4	3	3	1	3	1	.545
Carter rf	4	1	1	0	1	0	.273
Alomar 2b	5	2	4	0	2	0	.500
Fernandez ss	3	0	2	0	2	1	.444
Sprague 3b	4	0	0	0	1	0	.083
Borders c	4	0	0	0	0	1	.167
Hentgen p	3	0	0	0	0	0	.000
Cox p	1	0	0	0	0	0	.000
Ward p	0	0	0	0	0	0	.000
TOTALS	**36**	**10**	**13**	**1**	**10**	**4**	**.313**

BATTING: 2B: Henderson (1, Rivera). **3B:** Molitor (1, Jackson), White (1, Rivera), Alomar (1, Andersen). **HR:** Molitor (1, 3th off Jackson 0 on, 2 out). **SF:** Carter, Fernandez, Sprague. **RBI:** White 1 (3), Molitor 3 (4), Carter 1 (4), Alomar 2 (4), Fernandez 2 (4), Sprague 1 (1). **2-out RBI:** Molitor 1. **Runners left in scoring position, 2 out:** Sprague 2, Borders 1. **Team LOB:** 7 **BASERUNNING: SB:** Alomar 2 (4, 2nd base off Rivera/Daulton, 3rd base off Rivera/Daulton). **FIELDING: E:** Carter (2). **DP:** 2 (Alomar-Fernandez-Molitor, Molitor-Sprague-Cox).

PHILADELPHIA	AB	R	H	HR	RBI	BB	AVG
Dykstra cf	5	0	1	0	0	0	.308
Duncan 2b	5	0	2	0	1	0	.429
Kruk 1b	3	1	2	0	0	2	.583
Hollins 3b	3	0	0	0	0	1	.182
Daulton c	3	0	0	0	0	0	.167
Eisenreich rf	4	0	1	0	1	0	.231
Incaviglia lf	3	0	0	0	0	0	.125
Thigpen p	0	0	0	0	0	0	.000
b-Morandini ph	0	0	0	0	0	1	.000
Andersen p	0	0	0	0	0	0	.000
Stocker ss	4	0	1	0	0	0	.300
Jackson p	1	0	0	0	0	0	.000
a-Chamberlain ph	1	0	0	0	0	0	.000
Rivera p	0	0	0	0	0	0	.000
Thompson lf	2	2	2	1	1	0	.400
TOTALS	**34**	**3**	**9**	**1**	**3**	**5**	**.294**

a - Batted for Jackson in the 5th
b - Batted for Thigpen in the 8th

BATTING: 2B: Kruk (1, Hentgen). **HR:** Thompson (1, 9th off Ward 0 on, 0 out). **RBI:** Duncan 1 (1), Eisenreich 1 (5), Thompson 1 (1). **2-out RBI:** Eisenreich 1. **Runners left in scoring position, 2 out:** Daulton 2, Incaviglia 2. **GIDP:** Chamberlain, Hollins. **Team LOB:** 9

TORONTO	IP	H	R	ER	BB	SO	HR	ERA
Hentgen (W, 1-0)	6	5	1	1	3	6	0	1.50
Cox	2	3	1	1	2	2	0	4.50
Ward	1	1	1	1	0	2	1	3.86

PHILADELPHIA	IP	H	R	ER	BB	SO	HR	ERA
Jackson (L, 0-1)	5	6	4	4	1	1	1	7.20
Rivera	1.1	4	4	4	2	3	0	27.00
Thigpen	1.2	0	0	0	1	0	0	0.00
Andersen	1	3	2	2	0	0	0	10.80

HBP: Henderson (by Thigpen). **Pitches-strikes:** Hentgen 99-59, Cox 29-16, Ward 18-14, Jackson 89-50, Rivera 50-29, Thigpen 26-15, Andersen 29-16. **Ground balls-fly balls:** Hentgen 4-7, Cox 2-1, Ward 1-0, Jackson 5-8, Rivera 0-0, Thigpen 1-2, Andersen 2-1. **Batters faced:** Hentgen 25, Cox 10, Ward 4, Jackson 22, Rivera 10, Thigpen 6, Andersen 6. **UMPIRES:** hp—Mark Johnson, 1b—Charlie Williams, 2b—Tim McClelland, 3b—Dana DeMuth, lf—Dave Phillips, rf—Paul Runge **T:** 0:00 **A:** 0,000

GAME 4 Toronto 15 Philadelphia 14
Veterans Stadium 10/20/93

TORONTO	AB	R	H	HR	RBI	BB	AVG
Henderson lf	5	2	2	0	2	1	.333
White cf	5	2	3	0	4	1	.412
Alomar 2b	6	1	2	0	1	0	.444
Carter rf	6	2	3	0	0	0	.353
Olerud 1b	4	2	1	0	0	2	.300
Molitor 3b	4	2	2	0	2	1	.533
Griffin 3b	0	0	0	0	0	0	.000
Fernandez ss	6	2	3	0	5	0	.467
Borders c	4	1	1	0	1	1	.188
Stottlemyre p	0	0	0	0	0	1	.000
a-Butler ph	1	1	0	0	0	0	.000
Leiter p	1	0	1	0	0	0	1.000
Castillo p	1	0	0	0	0	0	.000
b-Sprague ph	1	0	0	0	0	0	.077
Timlin p	0	0	0	0	0	0	.000
Ward p	0	0	0	0	0	0	.000
TOTALS	**44**	**15**	**18**	**0**	**15**	**7**	**.343**

a - Batted for Stottlemyre in the 3th
b - Batted for Castillo in the 8th

BATTING: 2B: Henderson (2, Greene), Leiter (1, Mason), White (3, West), Molitor (2, Andersen), Carter (1, Thigpen). **3B:** White (2, Mi.Williams). **SF:** Alomar, Molitor. **RBI:** Henderson 2 (2), White 4 (7), Alomar 1 (5), Molitor 2 (6), Fernandez 5 (9), Borders 1 (1). **2-out RBI:** Henderson 2, White 4, Molitor 1, Fernandez 2. **Runners left in scoring position, 2 out:** Henderson 1, Alomar 3, Fernandez 1, Borders 3. **Team LOB:** 10 **BASERUNNING: SB:** Henderson (1, 3rd base off Mason/Daulton), White (1, 3rd base off Mason/Daulton).

PHILADELPHIA	AB	R	H	HR	RBI	BB	AVG
Dykstra cf	5	4	3	2	4	1	.389
Duncan 2b	6	1	3	0	1	0	.450
Kruk 1b	5	0	0	0	0	1	.412
Hollins 3b	4	3	2	0	0	2	.267
Daulton c	3	2	1	1	3	1	.200
Eisenreich rf	4	2	1	0	1	1	.235
Thompson lf	5	1	3	0	5	0	.500
Stocker ss	4	0	0	0	0	1	.214
Greene p	1	1	1	0	0	0	1.000
Mason p	1	0	0	0	0	0	.000
a-Jordan ph	1	0	0	0	0	0	.200
West p	0	0	0	0	0	0	.000
b-Chamberlain ph	1	0	0	0	0	0	.000
Andersen p	0	0	0	0	0	0	.000
Mi.Williams p	0	0	0	0	0	0	.000
c-Morandini ph	1	0	0	0	0	0	.000
Thigpen p	0	0	0	0	0	0	.000
TOTALS	**41**	**14**	**14**	**3**	**14**	**7**	**.307**

a - Batted for Mason in the 5th
b - Batted for West in the 6th
c - Batted for Mi.Williams in the 8th

BATTING: 2B: Dykstra (1, Leiter), Thompson (1, Leiter), Hollins (1, Castillo). **3B:** Thompson (1, Stottlemyre). **HR:** Dykstra 2 (3, 2nd off Stottlemyre 1 on, 0 out, 5th off Leiter 1 on, 2 out), Daulton (1, 5th off Leiter 1 on, 0 out). **RBI:** Dykstra 4 (5), Duncan 1 (2), Daulton 3 (4), Eisenreich 1 (6), Thompson 5 (6). **2-out RBI:** Dykstra 2, Duncan 1, Eisenreich 1, Thompson 4. **Runners left in scoring position, 2 out:** Kruk 1, Thompson 2, Stocker 1, Chamberlain 1. **Team LOB:** 8 **BASERUNNING: SB:** Dykstra (2, 2nd base off Stottlemyre/Borders), Duncan (2, 2nd base off Castillo/Borders). **Outfield assists:** Dykstra (1).

TORONTO	IP	H	R	ER	BB	SO	HR	ERA
Stottlemyre	2	3	6	6	4	1	1	27.00
Leiter	2.2	8	6	6	0	1	2	10.13
Castillo (W, 1-0)	2.1	3	2	2	3	1	0	8.10
Timlin	0.2	0	0	0	0	2	0	0.00
Ward (S, 2)	1.1	0	0	0	0	2	0	2.45

PHILADELPHIA	IP	H	R	ER	BB	SO	HR	ERA
Greene	2.1	7	7	7	4	1	0	27.00
Mason	2.2	2	0	0	1	2	0	1.69
West	1	3	2	2	0	0	0	27.00
Andersen	1.1	2	3	2	1	2	0	15.00
Mi.Williams (L, 0-1)	0.2	3	3	3	1	1	0	11.57
Thigpen	1	1	0	0	0	0	0	0.00

HBP: Molitor (by West), Daulton (by Castillo). **Pitches-strikes:** Stottlemyre 53-26, Leiter 52-31, Castillo 53-28, Timlin 8-6, Ward 14-10, Greene 66-31, Mason 38-21, West 18-12, Andersen 26-14, Mi.Williams 20-13, Thigpen 17-11. **Ground balls-fly balls:** Stottlemyre 2-3, Leiter 4-4, Castillo 3-3, Timlin 0-0, Ward 0-2, Greene 0-5, Mason 3-3, West 1-2, Andersen 1-1, Mi.Williams 1-0, Thigpen 3-0. **Batters faced:** Stottlemyre 13, Leiter 16, Castillo 14, Timlin 2, Ward 4, Greene 17, Mason 11, West 7, Andersen 7, Mi.Williams 6, Thigpen 4. **UMPIRES:** hp—Charlie Williams, 1b—Tim McClelland, 2b—Dana DeMuth, 3b—Dave Phillips, lf—Paul Runge, rf—Mark Johnson **T:** 4:14 **A:** 0,000

GAME 5 Philadelphia 2 Toronto 0
Veterans Stadium 10/21/93

TORONTO	AB	R	H	HR	RBI	BB	AVG
Henderson lf	3	0	0	0	0	1	.278
White cf	3	0	0	0	0	1	.350
Alomar 2b	3	0	1	0	0	1	.429
Carter rf	4	0	0	0	0	0	.286
Olerud 1b	4	0	0	0	0	0	.214
Molitor 3b	4	0	1	0	0	0	.474
Fernandez ss	3	0	0	0	0	0	.389
Borders c	3	0	2	0	0	0	.263
a-Canate pr	0	0	0	0	0	0	.000
Knorr c	0	0	0	0	0	0	.000
Guzman p	2	0	0	0	0	0	.000
b-Butler ph	1	0	1	0	0	0	.500
Cox p	0	0	0	0	0	0	.000
TOTALS	**30**	**0**	**5**	**0**	**0**	**3**	**.312**

a - Ran for Borders in the 8th
b - Batted for Guzman in the 8th

BATTING: Runners left in scoring position, 2 out: Alomar 1. **GIDP:** Guzman, Alomar. **Team LOB:** 6 **BASERUNNING: CS:** Alomar (2, 2nd base off Schilling/Daulton). **FIELDING: E:** Borders (1). **DP:** 1 (Fernandez-Olerud).

PHILADELPHIA	AB	R	H	HR	RBI	BB	AVG
Dykstra cf	2	1	0	0	0	2	.350
Duncan 2b	4	0	0	0	0	0	.375
Kruk 1b	3	0	1	0	1	1	.400
Hollins 3b	3	0	1	0	0	1	.278
Batiste 3b	0	0	0	0	0	0	.000
Daulton c	4	1	1	0	0	0	.211
Eisenreich rf	4	0	0	0	0	0	.190
Thompson lf	3	0	0	0	0	0	.385
Stocker ss	2	0	1	0	1	1	.250
Schilling p	2	0	1	0	0	0	.500
TOTALS	**27**	**2**	**5**	**0**	**2**	**6**	**.288**

BATTING: 2B: Daulton (1, Guzman), Stocker (1, Guzman). **S:** Schilling. **RBI:** Kruk 1 (4), Stocker 1 (1). **2-out RBI:** Stocker 1. **Runners left in scoring position, 2 out:** Duncan 2, Daulton 1, Thompson 1, Schilling 1. **GIDP:** Duncan. **Team LOB:** 8 **BASERUNNING: SB:** Dykstra (3, 2nd base off Guzman/Borders). **FIELDING: E:** Duncan (1). **DP:** 3 (Kruk-Stocker-Duncan, Daulton-Duncan, Duncan-Stocker-Kruk).

TORONTO	IP	H	R	ER	BB	SO	HR	ERA
Guzman (L, 0-1)	7	5	2	1	4	6	0	3.75
Cox	1	0	0	0	2	3	0	3.00

PHILADELPHIA	IP	H	R	ER	BB	SO	HR	ERA
Schilling (W, 1-1)	9	5	0	0	3	6	0	3.52

IBB: Dykstra (by Guzman). **Pitches-strikes:** Guzman 105-59, Cox 24-12, Schilling 155-104. **Ground balls-fly balls:** Guzman 5-8, Cox 0-0, Schilling 8-11. **Batters faced:** Guzman 29, Cox 5, Schilling 33. **UMPIRES:** hp—Tim McClelland, 1b—Dana DeMuth, 2b—Dave Phillips, 3b—Paul Runge, lf—Mark Johnson, rf—Charlie Williams **T:** 0:00 **A:** 0,000

GAME 6 Toronto 8 Philadelphia 6
Skydome 10/23/93

PHILADELPHIA	AB	R	H	HR	RBI	BB	AVG
Dykstra cf	3	1	1	1	3	2	.348
Duncan dh	5	1	1	0	0	0	.345
Kruk 1b	3	0	0	0	0	2	.348
Hollins 3b	5	1	1	0	1	0	.261
Batiste 3b	0	0	0	0	0	0	.000
Daulton c	4	1	1	0	0	1	.217
Eisenreich rf	5	0	2	0	1	0	.231
Thompson lf	3	0	0	0	0	0	.313
a-Incaviglia ph-lf	0	0	0	0	1	0	.125
Stocker ss	3	1	0	0	0	1	.211
Morandini 2b	4	1	1	0	0	0	.200
TOTALS	**35**	**6**	**7**	**1**	**6**	**6**	**.274**

a - Batted for Thompson in the 7th

BATTING: 2B: Daulton (2, Stewart). **HR:** Dykstra (4, 7th off Stewart 2 on, 0 out). **SF:** Incaviglia. **RBI:** Dykstra 3 (8), Hollins 1 (2), Eisenreich 1 (7), Incaviglia 1 (1). **2-out RBI:** Eisenreich 1. **Runners left in scoring position, 2 out:** Kruk 1, Hollins 2, Stocker 1. **Team LOB:** 9 **BASERUNNING: SB:** Duncan (3, 2nd base off Cox/Borders), Dykstra (4, 2nd base off Leiter/Borders).

TORONTO	AB	R	H	HR	RBI	BB	AVG
Henderson lf	4	1	0	0	0	1	.227
White cf	4	1	0	0	0	1	.292
Molitor dh	5	3	3	1	2	0	.500
Carter rf	4	1	1	1	4	0	.280
Olerud 1b	3	1	1	0	0	1	.235
a-Griffin pr-3b	0	0	0	0	0	0	.000
Alomar 2b	4	1	3	0	1	0	.480
Fernandez ss	3	0	0	0	0	0	.333
Sprague 3b-1b	2	0	0	0	1	1	.067
Borders c	4	0	2	0	0	0	.304
TOTALS	**33**	**8**	**10**	**2**	**8**	**4**	**.311**

a - Ran for Olerud in the 8th

BATTING: 2B: Olerud (1, Mulholland), Alomar (2, Mulholland). **3B:** Molitor (2, Mulholland). **HR:** Molitor (2, 5th off Mulholland 0 on, 1 out), Carter (2, 9th off Mi.Williams 2 on, 1 out). **SF:** Carter, Sprague. **RBI:** Molitor 2 (8), Carter 4 (8), Alomar 1 (6), Sprague 1 (2). **2-out RBI:** Alomar 1. **Runners left in scoring position, 2 out:** Borders 2. **Team LOB:** 7 **FIELDING: E:** Alomar (2), Sprague (2).

PHILADELPHIA	IP	H	R	ER	BB	SO	HR	ERA
Mulholland	5	7	5	5	1	1	1	6.75
Mason	2.1	1	0	0	0	2	0	1.17
West	0	0	0	0	1	0	0	27.00
Andersen	0.2	0	0	0	1	0	0	12.27
Mi.Williams (L, 0-2)	0.1	2	3	3	1	0	1	20.25

TORONTO	IP	H	R	ER	BB	SO	HR	ERA
Stewart	6	4	4	4	4	2	1	6.75
Cox	0.1	3	2	2	1	1	0	8.10
Leiter	1.2	0	0	0	1	2	0	7.71
Ward (W, 1-0)	1	0	0	0	0	0	0	1.93

HBP: Fernandez (by Andersen). **Pitches-strikes:** Mulholland 70-41, Mason 27-20, West 5-1, Andersen 26-16, Mi.Williams 21-11, Stewart 120-68, Cox 24-12, Leiter 21-12, Ward 7-5. **Ground balls-fly balls:** Mulholland 4-8, Mason 4-2, West 0-0, Andersen 1-1, Mi.Williams 0-1, Stewart 7-11, Cox 0-0, Leiter 1-1, Ward 1-2. **Batters faced:** Mulholland 23, Mason 8, West 1, Andersen 4, Mi.Williams 4, Stewart 28, Cox 5, Leiter 6, Ward 3. **UMPIRES:** hp—Dana DeMuth, 1b—Dave Phillips, 2b—Paul Runge, 3b—Mark Johnson, lf—Charlie Williams, rf—Tim McClelland **T:** 3:27 **A:** 0,000

1995 ATLANTA DEF. CLEVELAND, 4-2

GAME 1 Atlanta 3 Cleveland 2
Atlanta-Fulton County Stadium 10/21/95

CLEVELAND	AB	R	H	HR	RBI	BB	AVG
Lofton cf	4	2	1	0	0	0	.250
Vizquel ss	4	0	0	0	1	0	.000
Baerga 2b	4	0	0	0	1	0	.000
Belle lf	3	0	0	0	0	1	.000
Murray 1b	3	0	0	0	0	0	.000
Tavarez p	0	0	0	0	0	0	.000
Embree p	0	0	0	0	0	0	.000
Thome 3b	3	0	1	0	0	0	.333
Ramirez rf	3	0	0	0	0	0	.000
Alomar c	3	0	0	0	0	0	.000
Hershiser p	2	0	0	0	0	0	.000
Assenmacher p	0	0	0	0	0	0	.000
Sorrento 1b	1	0	0	0	0	0	.000
TOTALS	**30**	**2**	**2**	**0**	**2**	**0**	**.067**

BATTING: RBI: Vizquel 1 (1), Baerga 1 (1). **Team LOB:** 1 **BASERUNNING: SB:** Lofton 2 (2, 2nd base off Maddux/O'Brien, 3rd base off Maddux/O'Brien). **FIELDING: DP:** 1 (Vizquel-Baerga).

ATLANTA	AB	R	H	HR	RBI	BB	AVG
Grissom cf	4	0	1	0	0	0	.250
Lemke 2b	3	0	1	0	0	1	.333
Jones 3b	4	0	0	0	0	0	.000
McGriff 1b	3	2	1	1	1	1	.333
Justice rf	1	1	0	0	0	2	.000
Klesko lf	2	0	0	0	0	0	.000
a-Devereaux ph-lf	0	0	0	0	0	1	.000
O'Brien c	2	0	0	0	0	0	.000
b-Polonia ph	1	0	0	0	1	0	.000
Lopez c	0	0	0	0	0	0	.000
Belliard ss	2	0	0	0	1	0	.000
Maddux p	3	0	0	0	0	0	.000
TOTALS	**25**	**3**	**3**	**1**	**3**	**5**	**.120**

a - Batted for Klesko in the 7th
b - Batted for O'Brien in the 7th

BATTING: HR: McGriff (1, 2nd off Hershiser 0 on, 0 out). **S:** Belliard. **RBI:** McGriff 1 (1), Polonia 1 (1), Belliard 1 (1). **Runners left in scoring position, 2 out:** Maddux 1. **Team LOB:** 4 **FIELDING: E:** Belliard (1).

CLEVELAND	IP	H	R	ER	BB	SO	HR	ERA
Hershiser (L, 0-1)	6	3	3	3	3	7	1	4.50
Assenmacher	0	0	0	0	1	0	0	0.00
Tavarez	1.1	0	0	0	1	0	0	0.00
Embree	0.2	0	0	0	0	2	0	0.00

ATLANTA	IP	H	R	ER	BB	SO	HR	ERA
Maddux (W, 1-0)	9	2	2	0	0	4	0	0.00

Pitches-strikes: Hershiser 101-61, Assenmacher 5-1, Tavarez 15-9, Embree 8-6, Maddux 100-66. **Ground balls-fly balls:** Hershiser 9-1, Assenmacher 0-0, Tavarez 3-0, Embree 0-0, Maddux 20-4. **Batters faced:** Hershiser 23, Assenmacher 1, Tavarez 5, Embree 2, Maddux 30. **UMPIRES:** hp—Harry Wendelstedt, 1b—Jim McKean, 2b—Bruce Froemming, 3b—John Hirschbeck, lf—Frank Pulli, rf—Joe Brinkman **T:** 2:37 **A:** 51,876

GAME 2 Atlanta 4 Cleveland 3
Atlanta-Fulton County Stadium 10/22/95

CLEVELAND	AB	R	H	HR	RBI	BB	AVG
Lofton cf	5	1	1	0	0	0	.222
Vizquel ss	4	0	1	0	0	1	.125
Baerga 2b	4	0	0	0	0	1	.000
Belle lf	3	1	1	0	0	1	.167
Murray 1b	3	1	1	1	2	1	.167
Ramirez rf	4	0	2	0	0	0	.286
Thome 3b	3	0	0	0	0	1	.167
T.Pena c	3	0	0	0	0	0	.000
b-Sorrento ph	1	0	0	0	0	0	.000
Alomar c	0	0	0	0	0	0	.000
Martinez p	2	0	0	0	0	0	.000
Embree p	0	0	0	0	0	0	.000
a-Kirby ph	1	0	0	0	0	0	.000
Poole p	0	0	0	0	0	0	.000
Tavarez p	0	0	0	0	0	0	.000
c-Amaro ph	1	0	0	0	0	0	.000
TOTALS	**34**	**3**	**6**	**1**	**2**	**5**	**.125**

a - Batted for Embree in the 7th
b - Batted for T.Pena in the 8th
c - Batted for Tavarez in the 9th

BATTING: HR: Murray (1, 2nd off Glavine 1 on, 0 out). **SF:** Vizquel. **RBI:** Murray 2 (2). **Runners left in scoring position, 2 out:** Baerga 2, Belle 1, Thome 1. **Team LOB:** 9 **BASERUNNING: SB:** Lofton 2 (4, 2nd base off Glavine/Lopez, 2nd base off McMichael/Lopez), Vizquel (1, 2nd base off Wohlers/Lopez). **FIELDING: E:** Martinez (1), Belle (1). **DP:** 2 (Baerga-Vizquel-Murray, Vizquel-Baerga-Murray).

ATLANTA	AB	R	H	HR	RBI	BB	AVG
Grissom cf	3	1	1	0	0	1	.286
Lemke 2b	3	1	1	0	0	1	.333
Jones 3b	3	0	2	0	1	0	.286
McGriff 1b	4	0	0	0	0	0	.143
Justice rf	3	1	2	0	1	1	.500
Wohlers p	0	0	0	0	0	0	.000
Klesko lf	3	0	0	0	0	0	.000
Devereaux lf-rf	1	0	0	0	0	0	.000
Lopez c	3	1	1	1	2	0	.333
Belliard ss	4	0	0	0	0	0	.000
Glavine p	1	0	0	0	0	1	.000
a-Smith ph	1	0	1	0	0	0	1.000
McMichael p	0	0	0	0	0	0	.000
A.Pena p	0	0	0	0	0	0	.000
Polonia lf	0	0	0	0	0	0	.000
TOTALS	**29**	**4**	**8**	**1**	**4**	**3**	**.204**

a - Batted for Glavine in the 6th

BATTING: 2B: Jones (1, Martinez). **HR:** Lopez (1, 6th off Martinez 1 on, 1 out). **SF:** Jones. **RBI:** Jones 1 (1), Justice 1 (1), Lopez 2 (2). **2-out RBI:** Justice 1. **Runners left in scoring position, 2 out:** Lemke 1, Klesko 2. **GIDP:** McGriff, Belliard. **Team LOB:** 7 **FIELDING: E:** Jones (1), Devereaux (1).

CLEVELAND	IP	H	R	ER	BB	SO	HR	ERA
Martinez (L, 0-1)	5.2	8	4	4	3	3	1	6.35
Embree	0.1	0	0	0	0	0	0	0.00
Poole	1	0	0	0	0	0	0	0.00
Tavarez	1	0	0	0	0	0	0	0.00

ATLANTA	IP	H	R	ER	BB	SO	HR	ERA
Glavine (W, 1-0)	6	3	2	2	3	3	1	3.00
McMichael	0.2	1	1	0	1	1	0	0.00
A.Pena	1	1	0	0	1	0	0	0.00
Wohlers (S, 1)	1.1	1	0	0	0	1	0	0.00

WP: Glavine 1, McMichael 1. **HBP:** Grissom (by Martinez), Lopez (by Tavarez). **Pitches-strikes:** Martinez 97-57, Embree 3-1, Poole 14-9, Tavarez 5-4, Glavine 104-55, McMichael 24-10, A.Pena 16-9, Wohlers 17-12. **Ground balls-fly balls:** Martinez 8-4, Embree 0-1, Poole 1-2, Tavarez 1-1, Glavine 7-9, McMichael 1-1, A.Pena 0-2, Wohlers 1-2. **Batters faced:** Martinez 28, Embree 1, Poole 3, Tavarez 3, Glavine 25, McMichael 5, A.Pena 4, Wohlers 5. **UMPIRES:** hp—Jim McKean, 1b—Bruce Froemming, 2b—John Hirschbeck, 3b—Frank Pulli, lf—Joe Brinkman, rf—Harry Wendelstedt **T:** 3:17 **A:** 51,877

GAME 3 Cleveland 7 Atlanta 6
Jacobs Field 10/24/95

ATLANTA	AB	R	H	HR	RBI	BB	AVG
Grissom cf	6	1	2	0	0	0	.308
Polonia lf	4	1	1	0	1	1	.200
Jones 3b	3	2	1	0	0	2	.300
McGriff 1b	5	1	3	1	2	0	.333
Justice rf	5	0	0	0	1	0	.222
Klesko dh	3	1	2	1	1	0	.250
b-Devereaux ph	2	0	1	0	1	0	.333
Lopez c	5	0	0	0	0	0	.125
Lemke 2b	5	0	2	0	0	0	.364
Belliard ss	2	0	0	0	0	0	.000
a-Smith ph	1	0	0	0	0	0	.500
Mordecai ss	1	0	0	0	0	0	.000
TOTALS	**42**	**6**	**12**	**2**	**6**	**3**	**.240**

a - Batted for Belliard in the 7th
b - Batted for Klesko in the 8th

BATTING: 2B: Jones (2, Nagy), Grissom (1, Nagy). **HR:** McGriff (2, 6th off Nagy 0 on, 2 out), Klesko (1, 7th off Nagy 0 on, 0 out). **S:** Mordecai. **RBI:** Polonia 1 (2), McGriff 2 (3), Justice 1 (2), Klesko 1 (1), Devereaux 1 (1). **2-out RBI:** McGriff 2. **Runners left in scoring position, 2 out:** Jones 1. **GIDP:** Lopez, Grissom. **Team LOB:** 7 **BASERUNNING: SB:** Polonia (1, 2nd base off Assenmacher/Alomar), McGriff (1, 2nd base off Mesa/Alomar). **CS:** Grissom (1, 3rd base off Nagy/Alomar). **FIELDING: E:** Belliard (2). **DP:** 1 (Lemke-McGriff).

CLEVELAND	AB	R	H	HR	RBI	BB	AVG
Lofton cf	3	3	3	0	0	3	.417
Vizquel ss	6	2	2	0	1	0	.214
Baerga 2b	6	0	3	0	3	0	.214
b-Espinoza pr	0	1	0	0	0	0	.000
Belle lf	4	0	1	0	1	2	.200
Murray dh	6	0	1	0	1	0	.167
Thome 3b	4	0	0	0	0	1	.100
Ramirez rf	2	1	0	0	0	3	.222
Sorrento 1b	4	0	1	0	0	0	.167
a-Kirby pr	0	0	0	0	0	0	.000
Perry 1b	1	0	0	0	0	0	.000
Alomar c	5	0	1	0	1	0	.125
TOTALS	**41**	**7**	**12**	**0**	**7**	**9**	**.190**

a - Ran for Sorrento in the 8th
b - Ran for Baerga in the 11th

BATTING: 2B: Lofton (1, Smoltz), Alomar (1, Wohlers), Baerga (1, A.Pena). **3B:** Vizquel (1, Smoltz). **RBI:** Vizquel 1 (2), Baerga 3 (4), Belle 1 (1), Murray 1 (3), Alomar 1 (1). **2-out RBI:** Baerga 1. **Runners left in scoring position, 2 out:** Vizquel 1, Baerga 2, Murray 1. **GIDP:** Ramirez. **Team LOB:** 13 **BASERUNNING: SB:** Lofton (5, 3rd base off Mercker/Lopez), Ramirez (1, 2nd base off Wohlers/Lopez). **CS:** Lofton (1, 2nd base off Clontz/Lopez). **FIELDING: E:** Sorrento (1), Baerga (1). **DP:** 2 (Baerga-Vizquel-Sorrento, Baerga-Vizquel-Perry).

ATLANTA	IP	H	R	ER	BB	SO	HR	ERA
Smoltz	2.1	6	4	4	2	4	0	15.43
Clontz	2.1	1	0	0	0	1	0	0.00
Mercker	2	1	1	1	2	2	0	4.50
McMichael	0.2	1	1	1	1	1	0	6.75
Wohlers	2.2	1	0	0	3	2	0	0.00
A.Pena (L, 0-1)	0	2	1	1	1	0	0	9.00

CLEVELAND	IP	H	R	ER	BB	SO	HR	ERA
Nagy	7	8	5	5	1	4	2	6.43
Assenmacher	0.1	0	1	1	1	0	0	27.00
Tavarez	0.2	1	0	0	0	0	0	0.00
Mesa (W, 1-0)	3	3	0	0	1	3	0	0.00

IBB: Lofton 2 (by Wohlers), Belle (by A.Pena). **Pitches-strikes:** Smoltz 56-34, Clontz 32-20, Mercker 34-15, McMichael 17-11, Wohlers 40-19, A.Pena 14-7, Nagy 87-57, Assenmacher 10-5, Tavarez 3-2, Mesa 52-35. **Ground balls-fly balls:** Smoltz 3-0, Clontz 4-1, Mercker 3-1, McMichael 0-1, Wohlers 5-1, A.Pena 0-0, Nagy 9-7, Assenmacher 1-1, Tavarez 1-0, Mesa 3-1. **Batters faced:** Smoltz 15, Clontz 7, Mercker 9, McMichael 4, Wohlers 12, A.Pena 3, Nagy 29, Assenmacher 3, Tavarez 2, Mesa 12. **UMPIRES:** hp—Bruce Froemming, 1b—John Hirschbeck, 2b—Frank Pulli, 3b—Joe Brinkman, lf—Harry Wendelstedt, rf—Jim McKean **T:** 4:09 **A:** 43,584

GAME 4 Atlanta 5 Cleveland 2
Jacobs Field 10/25/95

ATLANTA	AB	R	H	HR	RBI	BB	AVG
Grissom cf	4	1	3	0	0	1	.412
Polonia lf	4	1	2	0	1	0	.333
Devereaux lf	0	0	0	0	0	1	.333
Jones 3b	4	1	0	0	0	1	.214
McGriff 1b	3	1	1	0	0	2	.333
Justice rf	5	0	1	0	2	0	.214
Klesko dh	3	1	1	1	1	1	.273
a-Mordecai ph	1	0	0	0	0	0	.000
Lopez c	5	0	2	0	1	0	.231
Lemke 2b	5	0	1	0	0	0	.313
Belliard ss	3	0	0	0	0	0	.000
TOTALS	**37**	**5**	**11**	**1**	**5**	**6**	**.256**

a - Batted for Klesko in the 9th

BATTING: 2B: Lopez 2 (2, Hill, Embree), Polonia (1, Hill), McGriff (1, Embree). **HR:** Klesko (2, 6th off Hill 0 on, 1 out). **S:** Belliard. **RBI:** Polonia 1 (3), Justice 2 (4), Klesko 1 (2), Lopez 1 (3). **2-out RBI:** Justice 2, Lopez 1. **Runners left in scoring position, 2 out:** Jones 2, McGriff 1, Justice 2, Lemke 1, Belliard 1. **Team LOB:** 12 **BASERUNNING: SB:** Grissom 2 (2, 2nd base off Hill/Alomar, 2nd base off Tavarez/Alomar). **FIELDING: E:** Lemke (1). **DP:** 1 (Jones-Lemke-McGriff).

CLEVELAND	AB	R	H	HR	RBI	BB	AVG
Lofton cf	5	0	0	0	0	0	.294
Vizquel ss	3	0	0	0	0	1	.176
Baerga 2b	4	0	1	0	0	0	.222
Belle lf	3	1	1	1	1	1	.231
Murray dh	2	0	0	0	0	2	.143
Ramirez rf	3	1	1	1	1	1	.250
Perry 1b	3	0	0	0	0	0	.000
b-Sorrento ph	1	0	1	0	0	0	.286
Espinoza 3b	2	0	1	0	0	0	.500
a-Thome ph-3b	2	0	1	0	0	0	.167
Alomar c	4	0	0	0	0	0	.083
TOTALS	**32**	**2**	**6**	**2**	**2**	**5**	**.190**

a - Batted for Espinoza in the 7th
b - Batted for Perry in the 9th

BATTING: 2B: Thome (1, McMichael), Sorrento (1, Wohlers). **HR:** Belle (1, 6th off Avery 0 on, 2 out), Ramirez (1, 9th off Wohlers 0 on, 0 out). **RBI:** Belle 1 (2), Ramirez 1 (1). **2-out RBI:** Belle 1. **Runners left in scoring position, 2 out:** Lofton 1, Vizquel 1, Murray 1, Perry 1. **GIDP:** Baerga. **Team LOB:** 8 **BASERUNNING: CS:** Espinoza (1, 2nd base off Avery/Lopez). **FIELDING: PB:** Alomar.

ATLANTA	IP	H	R	ER	BB	SO	HR	ERA
Avery (W, 1-0)	6	3	1	1	5	3	1	1.50
McMichael	2	1	0	0	0	0	0	2.70
Wohlers	0	2	1	1	0	0	1	2.25
Borbon (S, 1)	1	0	0	0	0	2	0	0.00

CLEVELAND	IP	H	R	ER	BB	SO	HR	ERA
Hill (L, 0-1)	6.1	6	3	3	4	1	1	4.26
Assenmacher	0.2	1	1	0	1	2	0	9.00
Tavarez	0.2	2	0	0	1	1	0	0.00
Embree	1.1	2	1	1	0	0	0	3.86

BK: Avery 1. **IBB:** Ramirez (by Avery), Jones (by Assenmacher). **Pitches-strikes:** Avery 111-60, McMichael 16-13, Wohlers 10-6, Borbon 11-7, Hill 94-58, Assenmacher 16-9, Tavarez 18-11, Embree 24-18. **Ground balls-fly balls:** Avery 7-7, McMichael 6-0, Wohlers 0-0, Borbon 0-1, Hill 8-10, Assenmacher 0-0, Tavarez 0-0, Embree 0-4. **Batters faced:** Avery 25, McMichael 7, Wohlers 2, Borbon 3, Hill 29, Assenmacher 4, Tavarez 5, Embree 6. **UMPIRES:** hp—John Hirschbeck, 1b—Frank Pulli, 2b—Joe Brinkman, 3b—Harry Wendelstedt, lf—Jim McKean, rf—Bruce Froemming **T:** 3:14 **A:** 43,578

GAME 5 Cleveland 5 Atlanta 4
Jacobs Field 10/26/95

ATLANTA	AB	R	H	HR	RBI	BB	AVG
Grissom cf	4	0	1	0	1	0	.381
Polonia lf	4	1	1	1	1	0	.308
Jones 3b	4	0	1	0	0	0	.222
McGriff 1b	4	1	1	0	0	0	.316
Justice rf	4	0	0	0	0	0	.167
Klesko dh	4	2	2	1	2	0	.333
Lemke 2b	4	0	0	0	0	0	.250
O'Brien c	1	0	0	0	0	0	.000
b-Lopez ph-c	1	0	0	0	0	0	.214
Belliard ss	1	0	0	0	0	0	.000
a-Smith ph	0	0	0	0	0	1	.500
Mordecai ss	1	0	1	0	0	0	.333
TOTALS	**32**	**4**	**7**	**2**	**4**	**1**	**.248**

a - Batted for Belliard in the 5th
b - Batted for O'Brien in the 7th

BATTING: 2B: Jones (3, Hershiser), McGriff (2, Mesa). **HR:** Polonia (1, 4th off Hershiser 0 on, 0 out), Klesko (3, 9th off Mesa 1 on, 2 out). **S:** O'Brien. **RBI:** Grissom 1 (1), Polonia 1 (4), Klesko 2 (4). **2-out RBI:** Klesko 2. **Runners left in scoring position, 2 out:** McGriff 1. **GIDP:** Polonia. **Team LOB:** 3

CLEVELAND	AB	R	H	HR	RBI	BB	AVG
Lofton cf	4	0	0	0	0	0	.238
Vizquel ss	3	1	1	0	0	1	.200
Baerga 2b	4	1	1	0	0	0	.227
Belle lf	3	2	1	1	2	1	.250
Murray dh	3	0	0	0	0	1	.118
Thome 3b	4	1	2	1	2	0	.250
Ramirez rf	3	0	1	0	1	0	.267
Perry 1b	1	0	0	0	0	0	.000
Sorrento 1b	3	0	0	0	0	0	.200
Kirby rf	0	0	0	0	0	0	.000
Alomar c	3	0	2	0	0	0	.200
TOTALS	**31**	**5**	**8**	**2**	**5**	**3**	**.202**

BATTING: 2B: Alomar (2, Maddux), Baerga (2, Maddux). **HR:** Belle (2, 1st off Maddux 1 on, 2 out), Thome (1, 8th off Clontz 0 on, 2 out). **RBI:** Belle 2 (4), Thome 2 (2), Ramirez 1 (2). **2-out RBI:** Belle 2, Thome 2, Ramirez 1. **Runners left in scoring position, 2 out:** Lofton 1, Sorrento 1. **Team LOB:** 5 **FIELDING: E:** Hershiser (1). **DP:** 2 (Vizquel-Baerga-Sorrento, Hershiser-Perry).

ATLANTA	IP	H	R	ER	BB	SO	HR	ERA
Maddux (L, 1-1)	7	7	4	4	3	4	1	2.25
Clontz	1	1	1	1	0	1	1	2.70

CLEVELAND	IP	H	R	ER	BB	SO	HR	ERA
Hershiser (W, 1-1)	8	5	2	1	1	6	1	2.57
Mesa (S, 1)	1	2	2	2	0	1	1	4.50

IBB: Smith (by Hershiser), Belle (by Maddux). **Pitches-strikes:** Maddux 99-62, Clontz 20-14, Hershiser 104-63, Mesa 18-15. **Ground balls-fly balls:** Maddux 7-9, Clontz 2-0, Hershiser 12-4, Mesa 1-1. **Batters faced:** Maddux 30, Clontz 4, Hershiser 29, Mesa 5. **UMPIRES:** hp—Frank Pulli, 1b—Joe Brinkman, 2b—Harry Wendelstedt, 3b—Jim McKean, lf—Bruce Froemming, rf—John Hirschbeck **T:** 2:33 **A:** 43,595

GAME 6 Atlanta 1 Cleveland 0
Atlanta-Fulton County Stadium 10/28/95

CLEVELAND	AB	R	H	HR	RBI	BB	AVG
Lofton cf	4	0	0	0	0	0	.200
Vizquel ss	3	0	0	0	0	0	.174
a-Sorrento ph	1	0	0	0	0	0	.182
Baerga 2b	4	0	0	0	0	0	.192
Belle lf	1	0	0	0	0	2	.235
Murray 1b	2	0	0	0	0	1	.105
Ramirez rf	3	0	0	0	0	0	.222
Embree p	0	0	0	0	0	0	.000
Tavarez p	0	0	0	0	0	0	.000
Assenmacher p	0	0	0	0	0	0	.000
Thome 3b	3	0	0	0	0	0	.211
T.Pena c	3	0	1	0	0	0	.167
Martinez p	1	0	0	0	0	0	.000
Poole p	1	0	0	0	0	0	.000
Hill p	0	0	0	0	0	0	.000
Amaro rf	1	0	0	0	0	0	.000
TOTALS	**27**	**0**	**1**	**0**	**0**	**3**	**.179**

a - Batted for Vizquel in the 9th

BATTING: Runners left in scoring position, 2 out: Vizquel 1. **Team LOB:** 3 **BASERUNNING: SB:** Lofton (6, 2nd base off Glavine/Lopez). **CS:** Belle (1, 2nd base off Glavine/Lopez). **FIELDING: E:** Thome (1). **DP:** 1 (Martinez-Vizquel-Baerga-Murray).

ATLANTA	AB	R	H	HR	RBI	BB	AVG
Grissom cf	4	0	1	0	0	0	.360
Lemke 2b	2	0	1	0	0	1	.273
Jones 3b	3	0	2	0	0	1	.286
McGriff 1b	4	0	0	0	0	0	.261
Justice rf	2	1	2	1	1	2	.250
Klesko lf	1	0	0	0	0	2	.313
Devereaux lf	1	0	0	0	0	0	.250
Lopez c	3	0	0	0	0	1	.176
Belliard ss	4	0	0	0	0	0	.000
Glavine p	3	0	0	0	0	0	.000
a-Polonia ph	1	0	0	0	0	0	.286
Wohlers p	0	0	0	0	0	0	.000
TOTALS	**28**	**1**	**6**	**1**	**1**	**7**	**.244**

a - Batted for Glavine in the 8th

BATTING: 2B: Justice (1, Martinez). **HR:** Justice (1, 6th off Poole 0 on, 0 out). **S:** Lemke. **RBI:** Justice 1 (5). **Runners left in scoring position, 2 out:** McGriff 1, Devereaux 2, Belliard 2. **GIDP:** Belliard. **Team LOB:** 11 **BASERUNNING: SB:** Grissom (3, 3rd base off Embree/T.Pena). **CS:** Lemke (1, 2nd base off Martinez/T.Pena).

CLEVELAND	IP	H	R	ER	BB	SO	HR	ERA
Martinez	4.2	4	0	0	5	2	0	3.48
Poole (L, 0-1)	1.1	1	1	1	0	1	1	3.86
Hill	0	1	0	0	0	0	0	4.26
Embree	1	0	0	0	2	0	0	2.70
Tavarez	0.2	0	0	0	0	0	0	0.00
Assenmacher	0.1	0	0	0	0	1	0	6.75

ATLANTA	IP	H	R	ER	BB	SO	HR	ERA
Glavine (W, 2-0)	8	1	0	0	3	8	0	1.29
Wohlers (S, 2)	1	0	0	0	0	0	0	1.80

IBB: Klesko (by Martinez), Jones (by Embree). **Pitches-strikes:** Martinez 82-44, Poole 25-18, Hill 5-2, Embree 13-5, Tavarez 16-12, Assenmacher 5-4, Glavine 109-67, Wohlers 9-6. **Ground balls-fly balls:** Martinez 5-5, Poole 3-1, Hill 0-0, Embree 0-2, Tavarez 0-2, Assenmacher 0-0, Glavine 6-9, Wohlers 0-3. **Batters faced:** Martinez 21, Poole 6, Hill 1, Embree 5, Tavarez 2, Assenmacher 1, Glavine 27, Wohlers 3. **UMPIRES:** hp—Joe Brinkman, 1b—Harry Wendelstedt, 2b—Jim McKean, 3b—Bruce Froemming, lf—John Hirschbeck, rf—Frank Pulli **T:** 3:01 **A:** 51,875

1996 NY YANKEES DEF. ATLANTA, 4-2

GAME 1 Atlanta 12 New York 1
Yankee Stadium 10/20/96

ATLANTA	AB	R	H	HR	RBI	BB	AVG
Grissom cf	5	2	2	0	1	0	.400
Lemke 2b	4	0	2	0	1	0	.500
C.Jones 3b	4	1	1	0	3	0	.250
McGriff 1b	5	2	2	1	2	0	.400
Lopez c	4	2	1	0	0	1	.250
Perez c	0	0	0	0	0	0	.000
Dye rf	5	0	1	0	0	0	.200
A.Jones lf	4	3	3	2	5	0	.750
Klesko dh	4	1	0	0	0	0	.000
Blauser ss	3	1	1	0	0	0	.333
a-Polonia ph	1	0	0	0	0	0	.000
Belliard ss	0	0	0	0	0	0	.000
TOTALS	**39**	**12**	**13**	**3**	**12**	**1**	**.333**

a - Batted for Blauser in the 8th

BATTING: HR: A.Jones 2 (2, 2nd off Pettitte 1 on, 2 out, 3th off Boehringer 2 on, 2 out), McGriff (1, 5th off Boehringer 0 on, 1 out). **S:** Lemke. **SF:** C.Jones. **RBI:** Grissom 1 (1), Lemke 1 (1), C.Jones 3 (3), McGriff 2 (2), A.Jones 5 (5). **2-out RBI:** A.Jones 5. **Team LOB:** 3 **BASERUNNING: SB:** C.Jones (1, 3rd base off Pettitte/Leyritz).

NY YANKEES	AB	R	H	HR	RBI	BB	AVG
Jeter ss	3	1	0	0	0	1	.000
Boggs 3b	4	0	2	0	1	0	.500
Williams cf	3	0	0	0	0	1	.000
Martinez 1b	3	0	1	0	0	1	.333
Fielder dh	4	0	0	0	0	0	.000
Strawberry lf	3	0	0	0	0	0	.000
Raines lf	1	0	0	0	0	0	.000
O'Neill rf	2	0	0	0	0	1	.000
Aldrete rf	0	0	0	0	0	0	.000
a-Hayes ph	1	0	0	0	0	0	.000
Duncan 2b	3	0	0	0	0	0	.000
Fox 2b	0	0	0	0	0	0	.000
b-Sojo ph	1	0	0	0	0	0	.000
Leyritz c	3	0	1	0	0	1	.333
TOTALS	**31**	**1**	**4**	**0**	**1**	**5**	**.129**

a - Batted for Aldrete in the 9th
b - Batted for Fox in the 9th

BATTING: 2B: Boggs (1, Smoltz). **RBI:** Boggs 1 (1). **2-out RBI:** Boggs 1. **Runners left in scoring position, 2 out:** Jeter 1, Williams 2, Fielder 1. **Team LOB:** 8 **FIELDING: E:** Duncan (1).

ATLANTA	IP	H	R	ER	BB	SO	HR	ERA
Smoltz (W, 1-0)	6	2	1	1	5	4	0	1.50
McMichael	1	2	0	0	0	1	0	0.00
Neagle	1	0	0	0	0	0	0	0.00
Wade	0.2	0	0	0	0	0	0	0.00
Clontz	0.1	0	0	0	0	0	0	0.00

NY YANKEES	IP	H	R	ER	BB	SO	HR	ERA
Pettitte (L, 0-1)	2.1	6	7	7	1	1	1	27.00
Boehringer	3	5	5	3	0	2	2	9.00
Weathers	1.2	1	0	0	0	0	0	0.00
Nelson	1	1	0	0	0	1	0	0.00
Wetteland	1	0	0	0	0	2	0	0.00

Pitches-strikes: Smoltz 103-57, McMichael 13-10, Neagle 10-6, Wade 5-4, Clontz 2-2, Pettitte 54-31, Boehringer 71-43, Weathers 19-10, Nelson 13-9, Wetteland 17-11. **Ground balls-fly balls:** Smoltz 5-9, McMichael 1-1, Neagle 1-2, Wade 1-1, Clontz 0-1, Pettitte 1-4, Boehringer 2-6, Weathers 2-2, Nelson 0-2, Wetteland 0-1. **Batters faced:** Smoltz 25, McMichael 5, Neagle 3, Wade 2, Clontz 1, Pettitte 14, Boehringer 15, Weathers 6, Nelson 4, Wetteland 3. **UMPIRES:** hp—Evans, Jim, 1b—Tata, Terry, 2b—Welke, Tim, 3b—Rippley, Steve, lf—Young, Larry, rf—Davis, Gerry **T:** 3:10 **A:** 56,365

GAME 2 Atlanta 4 New York 0
Yankee Stadium 10/21/96

ATLANTA	AB	R	H	HR	RBI	BB	AVG
Grissom cf	5	1	2	0	1	0	.400
Lemke 2b	4	2	2	0	0	0	.500
C.Jones 3b	3	0	1	0	0	1	.286
McGriff 1b	3	0	2	0	3	0	.500
Lopez c	4	0	1	0	0	0	.250
Dye rf	4	0	1	0	0	0	.222
A.Jones lf	3	0	0	0	0	0	.429
Pendleton dh	4	1	1	0	0	0	.250
Blauser ss	2	0	0	0	0	1	.200
a-Polonia ph	1	0	0	0	0	0	.000
Belliard ss	0	0	0	0	0	0	.000
TOTALS	**33**	**4**	**10**	**0**	**4**	**2**	**.319**

a - Batted for Blauser in the 9th

BATTING: 2B: Lemke (1, Key), Grissom (1, Key), C.Jones (1, Key), Pendleton (1, Key). **S:** Lemke. **SF:** McGriff. **RBI:** Grissom 1 (2), McGriff 3 (5). **2-out RBI:** Grissom 1, McGriff 1. **Runners left in scoring position, 2 out:** Grissom 1, Dye 2. **GIDP:** Blauser, Lopez. **Team LOB:** 7 **FIELDING: DP:** 1 (Lemke-Blauser-McGriff).

NY YANKEES	AB	R	H	HR	RBI	BB	AVG
Raines lf	4	0	2	0	0	0	.400
Boggs 3b	4	0	1	0	0	0	.375
Williams cf	4	0	0	0	0	0	.000
Martinez 1b	4	0	0	0	0	0	.143
Fielder dh	4	0	2	0	0	0	.250
a-Fox pr	0	0	0	0	0	0	.000
O'Neill rf	4	0	1	0	0	0	.167
Duncan 2b	3	0	0	0	0	0	.000
Girardi c	3	0	0	0	0	0	.000
Jeter ss	2	0	1	0	0	0	.200
TOTALS	**32**	**0**	**7**	**0**	**0**	**0**	**.175**

a - Ran for Fielder in the 9th

BATTING: 2B: O'Neill (1, Maddux). **Runners left in scoring position, 2 out:** Williams 1, O'Neill 1, Girardi 1. **GIDP:** Boggs. **Team LOB:** 6 **BASERUNNING: CS:** Raines (1, 2nd base off Maddux/Lopez). **FIELDING: E:** Raines (1). **DP:** 2 (Duncan-Jeter-Martinez, Key-Duncan-Martinez).

ATLANTA	IP	H	R	ER	BB	SO	HR	ERA
Maddux (W, 1-0)	8	6	0	0	0	2	0	0.00
Wohlers	1	1	0	0	0	3	0	0.00

NY YANKEES	IP	H	R	ER	BB	SO	HR	ERA
Key (L, 0-1)	6	10	4	4	2	0	0	6.00
Lloyd	0.2	0	0	0	0	2	0	0.00
Nelson	1.1	0	0	0	0	2	0	0.00
Rivera	1	0	0	0	0	1	0	0.00

HBP: A.Jones (by Key), Jeter (by Maddux). **Pitches-strikes:** Maddux 81-62, Wohlers 18-12, Key 98-55, Lloyd 8-6, Nelson 14-9, Rivera 15-10. **Ground balls-fly balls:** Maddux 18-2, Wohlers 0-0, Key 8-6, Lloyd 0-0, Nelson 2-0, Rivera 2-0. **Batters faced:** Maddux 29, Wohlers 4, Key 29, Lloyd 2, Nelson 4, Rivera 3. **UMPIRES:** hp—Tata, Terry, 1b—Welke, Tim, 2b—Rippley, Steve, 3b—Young, Larry, lf—Davis, Gerry, rf—Evans, Jim **T:** 2:44 **A:** 56,340

GAME 3 New York 5 Atlanta 2
Atlanta-Fulton County Stadium 10/22/96

NY YANKEES	AB	R	H	HR	RBI	BB	AVG
Raines lf	4	1	1	0	0	1	.333
Jeter ss	3	1	1	0	0	1	.250
Williams cf	5	2	2	1	3	0	.167
Fielder 1b	3	0	1	0	0	1	.273
b-Fox pr	0	1	0	0	0	0	.000
Martinez 1b	0	0	0	0	0	1	.143
Hayes 3b	5	0	0	0	0	0	.000
Strawberry rf	3	0	1	0	1	1	.167
Duncan 2b	3	0	1	0	0	0	.111
Sojo 2b	1	0	1	0	1	0	.500
Girardi c	2	0	0	0	0	1	.000
Cone p	2	0	0	0	0	0	.000
a-Leyritz ph	1	0	0	0	0	0	.250
Rivera p	1	0	0	0	0	0	.000
Lloyd p	0	0	0	0	0	0	.000
Wetteland p	0	0	0	0	0	0	.000
TOTALS	**33**	**5**	**8**	**1**	**5**	**6**	**.198**

a - Batted for Cone in the 7th
b - Ran for Fielder in the 8th

BATTING: 2B: Fielder (1, McMichael). **HR:** Williams (1, 8th off McMichael 1 on, 0 out). **S:** Jeter, Girardi. **RBI:** Williams 3 (3), Strawberry 1 (1), Sojo 1 (1). **Runners left in scoring position, 2 out:** Raines 1, Hayes 2, Cone 2, Rivera 1. **Team LOB:** 9 **FIELDING: E:** Jeter (1). **DP:** 1 (Fielder-Jeter-Fielder).

ATLANTA	AB	R	H	HR	RBI	BB	AVG
Grissom cf	4	1	3	0	0	0	.500
Lemke 2b	4	0	1	0	1	0	.417
C.Jones 3b	3	0	1	0	0	1	.300
McGriff 1b	3	0	0	0	0	1	.364
Klesko lf	3	0	0	0	1	1	.000
Lopez c	4	0	1	0	0	0	.250
A.Jones rf	4	0	0	0	0	0	.273
Blauser ss	4	0	0	0	0	0	.111
Glavine p	1	1	0	0	0	1	.000
a-Polonia ph	0	0	0	0	0	1	.000
McMichael p	0	0	0	0	0	0	.000
Clontz p	0	0	0	0	0	0	.000
Bielecki p	0	0	0	0	0	0	.000
b-Pendleton ph	1	0	0	0	0	0	.200
TOTALS	**31**	**2**	**6**	**0**	**2**	**5**	**.282**

a - Batted for Glavine in the 7th
b - Batted for Bielecki in the 9th

BATTING: 3B: Grissom (1, Rivera). **RBI:** Lemke 1 (2), Klesko 1 (1). **2-out RBI:** Klesko 1. **Runners left in scoring position, 2 out:** Lopez 2. **GIDP:** Lemke. **Team LOB:** 7 **BASERUNNING: CS:** A.Jones (1, 2nd base off Cone/Girardi), Polonia (1, 2nd base off Rivera/Girardi). **FIELDING: E:** Blauser (1). **Outfield assists:** A.Jones (1). **DP:** 1 (A.Jones-McGriff).

NY YANKEES	IP	H	R	ER	BB	SO	HR	ERA
Cone (W, 1-0)	6	4	1	1	4	3	0	1.50
Rivera	1.1	2	1	1	1	1	0	3.86
Lloyd	0.2	0	0	0	0	1	0	0.00
Wetteland (S, 1)	1	0	0	0	0	2	0	0.00

ATLANTA	IP	H	R	ER	BB	SO	HR	ERA
Glavine (L, 0-1)	7	4	2	1	3	8	0	1.29
McMichael	0	3	3	3	0	0	1	27.00
Clontz	1	1	0	0	1	1	0	0.00
Bielecki	1	0	0	0	2	2	0	0.00

IBB: Strawberry (by Clontz). **Pitches-strikes:** Cone 97-53, Rivera 35-18, Lloyd 6-5, Wetteland 24-17, Glavine 111-68, McMichael 6-5, Clontz 19-12, Bielecki 18-9. **Ground balls-fly balls:** Cone 7-6, Rivera 0-2, Lloyd 0-1, Wetteland 2-0, Glavine 8-3, McMichael 0-0, Clontz 2-0, Bielecki 1-0. **Batters faced:** Cone 24, Rivera 6, Lloyd 2, Wetteland 4, Glavine 28, McMichael 3, Clontz 5, Bielecki 5. **UMPIRES:** hp—Welke, Tim, 1b—Rippley, Steve, 2b—Young, Larry, 3b—Davis, Gerry, lf—Evans, Jim, rf—Tata, Terry **T:** 3:22 **A:** 51,843

GAME 4 New York 8 Atlanta 6
Atlanta-Fulton County Stadium 10/23/96

NY YANKEES	AB	R	H	HR	RBI	BB	AVG
Raines lf	5	1	0	0	0	1	.214
Jeter ss	4	2	2	0	0	2	.333
Williams cf	4	1	0	0	0	2	.125
Fielder 1b	4	1	2	0	1	1	.333
e-Fox pr-3b	0	0	0	0	0	0	.000
f-Boggs ph-3b	0	0	0	0	1	1	.375
Hayes 3b-1b	5	1	3	0	1	1	.273
Strawberry rf	5	0	2	0	0	1	.273
Duncan 2b	5	1	0	0	0	0	.071
Girardi c	2	0	0	0	0	0	.000
b-O'Neill ph	1	0	0	0	0	0	.143
Leyritz c	2	1	1	1	3	0	.333
Rogers p	1	0	1	0	0	0	1.000
Boehringer p	0	0	0	0	0	0	.000
a-Sojo ph	1	0	1	0	0	0	.667
Weathers p	0	0	0	0	0	0	.000
c-Martinez ph	1	0	0	0	0	0	.125
Nelson p	0	0	0	0	0	0	.000
d-Aldrete ph	1	0	0	0	0	0	.000
Rivera p	0	0	0	0	0	0	.000
Lloyd p	1	0	0	0	0	0	.000
Wetteland p	0	0	0	0	0	0	.000
TOTALS	**42**	**8**	**12**	**1**	**6**	**9**	**.225**

a - Batted for Boehringer in the 5th
b - Batted for Girardi in the 6th
c - Batted for Weathers in the 6th
d - Batted for Nelson in the 8th e - Ran for Fielder in the 9th f - Batted for Fox in the 10th

BATTING: HR: Leyritz (1, 8th off Wohlers 2 on, 1 out). **RBI:** Fielder 1 (1), Boggs 1 (2), Hayes 1 (1), Leyritz 3 (3). **2-out RBI:** Boggs 1. **Runners left in scoring position, 2 out:** Strawberry 3, Duncan 2, Martinez 1. **GIDP:** Williams. **Team LOB:** 13 **FIELDING: DP:** 1 (Jeter-Duncan-Hayes).

ATLANTA	AB	R	H	HR	RBI	BB	AVG
Grissom cf	5	0	1	0	2	0	.421
Lemke 2b	5	0	1	0	0	0	.353
C.Jones 3b-ss	3	2	1	0	0	2	.308
McGriff 1b	3	1	2	1	1	2	.429
Clontz p	0	0	0	0	0	0	.000
Lopez c	2	1	0	0	1	1	.214
Wohlers p	0	0	0	0	0	0	.000
Avery p	0	0	0	0	0	0	.000
Klesko 1b	1	0	0	0	0	0	.000
A.Jones lf	4	1	3	0	1	1	.400
Dye rf	4	0	0	0	0	0	.154
Blauser ss	3	1	1	0	1	0	.167
Belliard ss	0	0	0	0	0	0	.000
a-Polonia ph	1	0	0	0	0	0	.000
Pendleton 3b	1	0	0	0	0	0	.167
Neagle p	1	0	0	0	0	0	.000
Wade p	0	0	0	0	0	0	.000
Bielecki p	1	0	0	0	0	0	.000
Perez c	1	0	0	0	0	0	.000
TOTALS	**35**	**6**	**9**	**1**	**6**	**6**	**.275**

a - Batted for Belliard in the 8th

BATTING: 2B: Grissom (2, Rogers), A.Jones (1, Weathers). **HR:** McGriff (2, 2nd off Rogers 0 on, 0 out). **S:** Neagle, Dye. **SF:** Lopez. **RBI:** Grissom 2 (4), McGriff 1 (6), Lopez 1 (1), A.Jones 1 (6), Blauser 1 (1). **2-out RBI:** Grissom 2, A.Jones 1. **Runners left in scoring position, 2 out:** Lemke 1, Dye 3, Perez 1. **GIDP:** McGriff. **Team LOB:** 8 **FIELDING: E:** Dye (1), Klesko (1). **DP:** 1 (Blauser-Lemke-McGriff).

NY YANKEES	IP	H	R	ER	BB	SO	HR	ERA
Rogers	2	5	5	5	2	0	1	22.50
Boehringer	2	0	0	0	0	3	0	5.40
Weathers	1	1	1	1	2	2	0	3.38
Nelson	2	0	0	0	1	2	0	0.00
Rivera	1.1	2	0	0	1	1	0	2.45
Lloyd (W, 1-0)	1	0	0	0	0	1	0	0.00
Wetteland (S, 2)	0.2	1	0	0	0	0	0	0.00

ATLANTA	IP	H	R	ER	BB	SO	HR	ERA
Neagle	5	5	3	2	4	3	0	3.00
Wade	0	0	0	0	1	0	0	0.00
Bielecki	2	0	0	0	1	4	0	0.00
Wohlers	2	6	3	3	0	1	1	9.00
Avery (L, 0-1)	0.2	1	2	1	3	0	0	13.50
Clontz	0.1	0	0	0	0	1	0	0.00

BK: Weathers 1. **IBB:** McGriff (by Weathers), Williams (by Avery). **Pitches-strikes:** Rogers 52-26, Boehringer 24-17, Weathers 29-14, Nelson 35-19, Rivera 26-16, Lloyd 9-5, Wetteland 10-7, Neagle 93-50, Wade 6-2, Bielecki 34-22, Wohlers 28-22, Avery 29-12, Clontz 7-4. **Ground balls-fly balls:** Rogers 4-1, Boehringer 1-1, Weathers 1-0, Nelson 3-1, Rivera 1-1, Lloyd 1-0, Wetteland 0-2, Neagle 7-4, Wade 0-0, Bielecki 0-2, Wohlers 4-1, Avery 2-0, Clontz 0-1. **Batters faced:** Rogers 13, Boehringer 6, Weathers 6, Nelson 7, Rivera 7, Lloyd 2, Wetteland 3, Neagle 23, Wade 1, Bielecki 7, Wohlers 12, Avery 6, Clontz 2. **UMPIRES:** hp—Rippley, Steve, 1b—Young, Larry, 2b—Davis, Gerry, 3b—Evans, Jim, lf—Tata, Terry, rf—Welke, Tim **T:** 4:17 **A:** 51,881

GAME 5 New York 1 Atlanta 0
Atlanta-Fulton County Stadium 10/24/96

NY YANKEES	AB	R	H	HR	RBI	BB	AVG
Jeter ss	4	0	0	0	0	0	.250
Hayes 3b	4	1	0	0	0	0	.200
Williams cf	4	0	0	0	0	0	.100
Fielder 1b	4	0	3	0	1	0	.421
Martinez 1b	0	0	0	0	0	0	.125
Strawberry lf	3	0	0	0	0	1	.214
O'Neill rf	2	0	0	0	0	2	.111
Duncan 2b	4	0	0	0	0	0	.056
Sojo 2b	0	0	0	0	0	0	.667
Leyritz c	2	0	1	0	0	2	.375
Pettitte p	4	0	0	0	0	0	.000
Wetteland p	0	0	0	0	0	0	.000
TOTALS	**31**	**1**	**4**	**0**	**1**	**5**	**.207**

BATTING: 2B: Fielder (2, Smoltz). **RBI:** Fielder 1 (2). **Runners left in scoring position, 2 out:** Duncan 3, Pettitte 1. **Team LOB:** 8 **BASERUNNING: SB:** Leyritz (1, 2nd base off Smoltz/Lopez), Duncan (1, 2nd base off Wohlers/Lopez). **FIELDING: E:** Jeter (2). **DP:** 2 (Duncan-Jeter-Fielder, Pettitte-Duncan-Fielder).

ATLANTA	AB	R	H	HR	RBI	BB	AVG
Grissom cf	3	0	2	0	0	1	.455
Lemke 2b	4	0	0	0	0	0	.286
C.Jones 3b	4	0	1	0	0	0	.294
McGriff 1b	3	0	0	0	0	1	.353
Lopez c	4	0	0	0	0	0	.167
A.Jones lf	2	0	1	0	0	1	.412
b-Klesko ph	0	0	0	0	0	1	.000
Dye rf	3	0	0	0	0	0	.125
c-Polonia ph	1	0	0	0	0	0	.000
Blauser ss	3	0	0	0	0	0	.133
Smoltz p	2	0	1	0	0	0	.500
a-Mordecai ph	1	0	0	0	0	0	.000
Wohlers p	0	0	0	0	0	0	.000
TOTALS	**30**	**0**	**5**	**0**	**0**	**4**	**.256**

a - Batted for Smoltz in the 8th
b - Batted for A.Jones in the 9th
c - Batted for Dye in the 9th

BATTING: 2B: C.Jones (2, Pettitte). **Runners left in scoring position, 2 out:** Lemke 1, Dye 1, Polonia 1. **GIDP:** Lopez, C.Jones. **Team LOB:** 7 **BASERUNNING: SB:** A.Jones (1, 2nd base off Pettitte/Leyritz), Grissom (1, 2nd base off Pettitte/Leyritz). **CS:** A.Jones (2, 2nd base off Pettitte/Leyritz). **FIELDING: E:** Grissom (1). **DP:** 1 (McGriff).

NY YANKEES	IP	H	R	ER	BB	SO	HR	ERA
Pettitte (W, 1-1)	8.1	5	0	0	3	4	0	5.91
Wetteland (S, 3)	0.2	0	0	0	1	0	0	0.00

ATLANTA	IP	H	R	ER	BB	SO	HR	ERA
Smoltz (L, 1-1)	8	4	1	0	3	10	0	0.64
Wohlers	1	0	0	0	2	0	0	6.75

IBB: Leyritz (by Wohlers), Klesko (by Wetteland). **Pitches-strikes:** Pettitte 96-59, Wetteland 12-8, Smoltz 135-79, Wohlers 18-8. **Ground balls-fly balls:** Pettitte 13-6, Wetteland 1-1, Smoltz 6-8, Wohlers 2-1. **Batters faced:** Pettitte 31, Wetteland 3, Smoltz 31, Wohlers 5. **UMPIRES:** hp—Young, Larry, 1b—Davis, Gerry, 2b—Evans, Jim, 3b—Tata, Terry, lf—Welke, Tim, rf—Rippley, Steve **T:** 2:54 **A:** 51,881

GAME 6 New York 3 Atlanta 2
Yankee Stadium 10/26/96

ATLANTA	AB	R	H	HR	RBI	BB	AVG
Grissom cf	5	0	2	0	1	0	.444
Lemke 2b	5	0	0	0	0	0	.231
C.Jones 3b	4	0	1	0	0	0	.286
McGriff 1b	3	1	0	0	0	1	.300
Lopez c	3	0	1	0	0	1	.190
A.Jones lf-rf	3	0	1	0	0	1	.400
Dye rf	1	0	0	0	1	1	.118
a-Klesko ph-lf	2	1	1	0	0	0	.100
Pendleton dh	3	0	1	0	0	1	.222
c-Belliard pr	0	0	0	0	0	0	.000
Blauser ss	3	0	1	0	0	0	.167
b-Polonia ph	1	0	0	0	0	0	.000
TOTALS	**33**	**2**	**8**	**0**	**2**	**5**	**.254**

a - Batted for Dye in the 6th
b - Batted for Blauser in the 9th
c - Ran for Pendleton in the 9th

BATTING: 2B: Blauser (1, Key), C.Jones (3, Key). **RBI:** Grissom 1 (5), Dye 1 (1). **2-out RBI:** Grissom 1. **Runners left in scoring position, 2 out:** Lemke 2, Klesko 1. **GIDP:** Pendleton. **Team LOB:** 9 **BASERUNNING: CS:** Pendleton (1, 2nd base off Key/Girardi). **FIELDING: DP:** 2 (C.Jones-Lemke-McGriff, McGriff-Blauser-McGriff).

NY YANKEES	AB	R	H	HR	RBI	BB	AVG
Jeter ss	4	1	1	0	1	0	.250
Boggs 3b	3	0	0	0	0	0	.273
Hayes 3b	1	0	0	0	0	0	.188
Williams cf	4	0	2	0	1	0	.167
Fielder dh	4	0	1	0	0	0	.391
Martinez 1b	3	0	0	0	0	0	.091
Strawberry lf	2	0	0	0	0	1	.188
O'Neill rf	3	1	1	0	0	0	.167
Duncan 2b	1	0	0	0	0	0	.053
Sojo 2b	2	0	1	0	0	0	.600
Girardi c	3	1	2	0	1	0	.200
TOTALS	**30**	**3**	**8**	**0**	**3**	**1**	**.216**

BATTING: 2B: O'Neill (2, Maddux), Sojo (1, Maddux). **3B:** Girardi (1, Maddux). **RBI:** Jeter 1 (1), Williams 1 (4), Girardi 1 (1). **2-out RBI:** Williams 1. **Runners left in scoring position, 2 out:** Fielder 2, Girardi 1. **GIDP:** Jeter, O'Neill. **Team LOB:** 4 **BASERUNNING: SB:** Jeter (1, 2nd base off Maddux/Lopez), Williams (1, 2nd base off Wohlers/Lopez). **FIELDING: E:** Duncan (2). **DP:** 1 (Jeter-Martinez).

ATLANTA	IP	H	R	ER	BB	SO	HR	ERA
Maddux (L, 1-1)	7.2	8	3	3	1	3	0	1.72
Wohlers	0.1	0	0	0	0	0	0	6.23

NY YANKEES	IP	H	R	ER	BB	SO	HR	ERA
Key (W, 1-1)	5.1	5	1	1	3	1	0	3.97
Weathers	0.1	0	0	0	1	1	0	3.00
Lloyd	0.1	0	0	0	0	0	0	0.00
Rivera	2	0	0	0	1	1	0	1.59
Wetteland (S, 4)	1	3	1	1	0	2	0	2.08

Pitches-strikes: Maddux 103-65, Wohlers 4-4, Key 91-44, Weathers 8-4, Lloyd 3-1, Rivera 22-15, Wetteland 25-17. **Ground balls-fly balls:** Maddux 12-6, Wohlers 1-0, Key 6-7, Weathers 0-0, Lloyd 0-1, Rivera 2-3, Wetteland 0-1. **Batters faced:** Maddux 30, Wohlers 1, Key 22, Weathers 2, Lloyd 1, Rivera 7, Wetteland 6. **UMPIRES:** hp—Gerry Davis, 1b—Jim Evans, 2b—Terry Tata, 3b—Tim Welke, lf—Steve Rippley, rf—Larry Young **T:** 2:52 **A:** 56,375

1997 FLORIDA DEF. CLEVELAND, 4-3

GAME 1 Florida 7 Cleveland 4
Pro Player Stadium 10/18/97

CLEVELAND	AB	R	H	HR	RBI	BB	AVG
Roberts 2b	4	1	2	0	0	1	.500
Vizquel ss	4	0	0	0	0	0	.000
Ramirez rf	3	1	1	1	1	2	.333
Justice lf	4	0	2	0	1	1	.500
Williams 3b	5	0	1	0	0	0	.200
Thome 1b	5	1	1	1	1	0	.200
Alomar c	5	0	1	0	0	0	.200
Grissom cf	3	1	2	0	0	1	.667
Hershiser p	2	0	0	0	0	0	.000
Juden p	0	0	0	0	0	0	.000
a-Branson ph	1	0	0	0	0	0	.000
Plunk p	0	0	0	0	0	0	.000
b-Giles ph	1	0	1	0	1	0	1.000
Assenmacher p	0	0	0	0	0	0	.000
TOTALS	**37**	**4**	**11**	**2**	**4**	**5**	**.297**

a - Batted for Juden in the 6th
b - Batted for Plunk in the 8th

BATTING: 2B: Roberts 2 (2, Hernandez), Grissom (1, Hernandez), Giles (1, Powell). **HR:** Ramirez (1, 5th off Hernandez 0 on, 2 out), Thome (1, 6th off Hernandez 0 on, 1 out). **S:** Vizquel. **RBI:** Ramirez 1 (1), Justice 1 (1), Thome 1 (1), Giles 1 (1). **2-out RBI:** Ramirez 1, Giles 1. **Runners left in scoring position, 2 out:** Roberts 1, Vizquel 1, Williams 1, Thome 1, Alomar 1, Hershiser 1. **Team LOB:** 12 **FIELDING: DP:** 1 (Roberts-Vizquel-Thome).

FLORIDA	AB	R	H	HR	RBI	BB	AVG
White cf	4	0	0	0	0	1	.000
Renteria ss	4	0	0	0	1	0	.000
Sheffield rf	2	1	0	0	0	2	.000
Bonilla 3b	3	2	2	0	0	1	.667
Daulton 1b	2	1	1	0	0	0	.500
Conine 1b	2	0	1	0	1	0	.500
Alou lf	3	1	1	1	3	1	.333
Johnson c	3	1	1	1	1	1	.333
Counsell 2b	3	1	1	0	0	1	.333
Hernandez p	2	0	0	0	0	0	.000
Cook p	0	0	0	0	0	0	.000
Powell p	0	0	0	0	0	0	.000
a-Cangelosi ph	1	0	0	0	0	0	.000
Nen p	0	0	0	0	0	0	.000
TOTALS	**29**	**7**	**7**	**2**	**6**	**7**	**.241**

a - Batted for Powell in the 8th

BATTING: 2B: Counsell (1, Hershiser). **HR:** Alou (1, 4th off Hershiser 2 on, 0 out), Johnson (1, 4th off Hershiser 0 on, 0 out). **S:** Hernandez. **RBI:** Renteria 1 (1), Conine 1 (1), Alou 3 (3), Johnson 1 (1). **Runners left in scoring position, 2 out:** Sheffield 1, Hernandez 2. **GIDP:** Conine. **Team LOB:** 6 **FIELDING: E:** Sheffield (1).

CLEVELAND	IP	H	R	ER	BB	SO	HR	ERA
Hershiser (L, 0-1)	4.1	6	7	7	4	2	2	14.54
Juden	0.2	0	0	0	2	0	0	0.00
Plunk	2	1	0	0	1	1	0	0.00
Assenmacher	1	0	0	0	0	2	0	0.00

FLORIDA	IP	H	R	ER	BB	SO	HR	ERA
Hernandez (W, 1-0)	5.2	8	3	3	2	5	2	4.76
Cook	1.2	0	0	0	1	2	0	0.00
Powell	0.2	1	1	1	2	1	0	13.50
Nen (S, 1)	1	2	0	0	0	2	0	0.00

WP: Juden 1. **Pitches-strikes:** Hershiser 83-49, Juden 22-9, Plunk 22-12, Assenmacher 12-9, Hernandez 101-60, Cook 26-16, Powell 28-12, Nen 19-16. **Ground balls-fly balls:** Hershiser 6-4, Juden 2-0, Plunk 2-2, Assenmacher 1-0, Hernandez 6-5, Cook 0-3, Powell 0-1, Nen 1-0. **Batters faced:** Hershiser 23, Juden 4, Plunk 7, Assenmacher 3, Hernandez 27, Cook 6, Powell 5, Nen 5. **UMPIRES:** hp—Ed Montague, 1b—Dale Ford, 2b—Joe West, 3b—Greg Kosc, lf—Randy Marsh, rf—Ken Kaiser **T:** 0:00 **A:** 67,245

GAME 2 Cleveland 6 Florida 1
Pro Player Stadium 10/19/97

CLEVELAND	AB	R	H	HR	RBI	BB	AVG
Roberts 2b	3	0	1	0	2	0	.429
a-Fernandez ph-2b	2	0	2	0	0	0	1.000
Vizquel ss	4	1	2	0	0	1	.250
Ramirez rf	5	0	0	0	0	0	.125
Justice lf	3	0	1	0	1	1	.429
Williams 3b	4	2	2	0	0	0	.333
Thome 1b	4	0	1	0	0	0	.222
Alomar c	4	2	2	1	2	0	.333
Grissom cf	4	1	3	0	1	0	.714
Ogea p	2	0	0	0	0	0	.000
Jackson p	1	0	0	0	0	0	.000
Mesa p	0	0	0	0	0	0	.000
TOTALS	**36**	**6**	**14**	**1**	**6**	**2**	**.342**

a - Batted for Roberts in the 7th

BATTING: 2B: Vizquel (1, Brown), Fernandez (1, Heredia). **HR:** Alomar (1, 6th off Brown 1 on, 2 out). **S:** Ogea. **RBI:** Roberts 2 (2), Justice 1 (2), Alomar 2 (2), Grissom 1 (1). **2-out RBI:** Roberts 2, Justice 1, Alomar 2. **Runners left in scoring position, 2 out:** Ramirez 1, Justice 1, Jackson 1. **GIDP:** Alomar, Ramirez, Ramirez. **Team LOB:** 6 **BASERUNNING: CS:** Justice (1, 2nd base off Brown/Johnson). **FIELDING: DP:** 1 (Williams-Roberts-Thome).

FLORIDA	AB	R	H	HR	RBI	BB	AVG
White cf	5	0	2	0	0	0	.222
Renteria ss	4	1	2	0	0	0	.250
Sheffield rf	2	0	1	0	0	1	.250
Bonilla 3b	4	0	0	0	0	0	.286
Conine 1b	3	0	1	0	1	0	.400
b-Daulton ph-1b	1	0	0	0	0	0	.333
Alou lf	4	0	2	0	0	0	.429
Johnson c	3	0	0	0	0	0	.167
c-Zaun ph	1	0	0	0	0	0	.000
Counsell 2b	3	0	0	0	0	1	.167
Brown p	2	0	0	0	0	0	.000
Heredia p	0	0	0	0	0	0	.000
a-Eisenreich ph	1	0	0	0	0	0	.000
Alfonseca p	0	0	0	0	0	0	.000
d-Floyd ph	1	0	0	0	0	0	.000
TOTALS	**34**	**1**	**8**	**0**	**1**	**2**	**.238**

a - Batted for Heredia in the 7th
b - Batted for Conine in the 8th
c - Batted for Johnson in the 9th
d - Batted for Alfonseca in the 9th

BATTING: 2B: Renteria (1, Ogea), Alou 2 (2, Ogea), White (1, Ogea). **RBI:** Conine 1 (2). **2-out RBI:** Conine 1. **Runners left in scoring position, 2 out:** Renteria 1, Conine 1, Alou 1, Johnson 1. **GIDP:** Sheffield. **Team LOB:** 9 **FIELDING: DP:** 3 (Bonilla-Counsell-Conine, Counsell-Renteria-Conine, Bonilla-Counsell-Daulton).

CLEVELAND	IP	H	R	ER	BB	SO	HR	ERA
Ogea (W, 1-0)	6.2	7	1	1	1	4	0	1.35
Jackson	1.1	1	0	0	0	1	0	0.00
Mesa	1	0	0	0	1	1	0	0.00

FLORIDA	IP	H	R	ER	BB	SO	HR	ERA
Brown (L, 0-1)	6	10	6	6	2	4	1	9.00
Heredia	1	1	0	0	0	1	0	0.00
Alfonseca	2	3	0	0	0	0	0	0.00

HBP: Sheffield (by Ogea). **Pitches-strikes:** Ogea 94-61, Jackson 17-9, Mesa 12-7, Brown 95-58, Heredia 13-11, Alfonseca 18-14. **Ground balls-fly balls:** Ogea 6-9, Jackson 1-2, Mesa 2-0, Brown 8-2, Heredia 1-1, Alfonseca 2-3. **Batters faced:** Ogea 28, Jackson 5, Mesa 4, Brown 27, Heredia 4, Alfonseca 8. **UMPIRES:** hp—Dale Ford, 1b—Joe West, 2b—Greg Kosc, 3b—Randy Marsh, lf—Ken Kaiser, rf—Ed Montague **T:** 2:48 **A:** 67,025

GAME 3 Florida 14 Cleveland 11
Jacobs Field 10/21/97

FLORIDA	AB	R	H	HR	RBI	BB	AVG
White cf	5	0	1	0	0	1	.214
Renteria ss	4	2	2	0	1	2	.333
Sheffield rf	5	2	3	1	5	1	.444
Bonilla 3b	5	1	1	0	2	1	.250
Daulton 1b	4	3	2	1	2	2	.429
Conine 1b	0	0	0	0	0	0	.400
Alou lf	5	0	0	0	0	0	.250
Eisenreich dh	3	1	2	1	2	0	.500
a-Abbott ph	1	0	0	0	0	0	.000
b-Floyd ph	0	1	0	0	0	1	.000
Johnson c	5	2	3	0	0	0	.364
Counsell 2b	5	2	2	0	1	0	.273
TOTALS	**42**	**14**	**16**	**3**	**13**	**8**	**.295**

a - Batted for Eisenreich in the 8th
b - Batted for Abbott in the 9th

BATTING: 2B: Sheffield (1, Jackson). **HR:** Sheffield (1, 1st off Nagy 0 on, 2 out), Daulton (1, 4th off Nagy 0 on, 0 out), Eisenreich (1, 6th off Nagy 1 on, 2 out). **RBI:** Renteria 1 (2), Sheffield 5 (5), Bonilla 2 (2), Daulton 2 (2), Eisenreich 2 (2), Counsell 1 (1). **2-out RBI:** Sheffield 3, Bonilla 2, Eisenreich 2. **Runners left in scoring position, 2 out:** Sheffield 2, Alou 1. **GIDP:** Bonilla, Sheffield. **Team LOB:** 9 **FIELDING: E:** Leiter (1), Bonilla 2 (2). **DP:** 1 (Counsell-Renteria-Daulton).

CLEVELAND	AB	R	H	HR	RBI	BB	AVG
Roberts lf	5	1	1	0	2	0	.333
Vizquel ss	4	0	0	0	1	2	.167
Ramirez rf	5	0	1	0	2	0	.154
Justice dh	3	2	0	0	0	2	.300
Williams 3b	5	0	1	0	1	0	.286
Alomar c	3	2	2	0	1	1	.417
a-Giles ph	0	1	0	0	0	1	1.000
Thome 1b	4	3	2	1	2	1	.308
Fernandez 2b	4	0	1	0	1	0	.500
Grissom cf	3	2	2	0	1	2	.700
TOTALS	**36**	**11**	**10**	**1**	**11**	**9**	**.321**

a - Batted for Alomar in the 9th

BATTING: 2B: Roberts (3, Nen). **HR:** Thome (2, 5th off Leiter 1 on, 1 out). **S:** Roberts. **SF:** Fernandez. **RBI:** Roberts 2 (4), Vizquel 1 (1), Ramirez 2 (3), Williams 1 (1), Alomar 1 (3), Thome 2 (3), Fernandez 1 (1), Grissom 1 (2). **2-out RBI:** Roberts 2, Vizquel 1, Ramirez 2, Williams 1, Alomar 1, Grissom 1. **Runners left in scoring position, 2 out:** Vizquel 1, Ramirez 1, Justice 1, Williams 1, Thome 1. **GIDP:** Grissom. **Team LOB:** 9 **FIELDING: E:** Grissom (1), Thome (1), Fernandez (1). **DP:** 2 (Thome-Vizquel-Nagy, Vizquel-Fernandez-Thome).

FLORIDA	IP	H	R	ER	BB	SO	HR	ERA
Leiter	4.2	6	7	4	6	3	1	7.71
Heredia	2.1	0	0	0	1	0	0	0.00
Cook (W, 1-0)	1	1	0	0	0	1	0	0.00
Nen	1	3	4	4	2	1	0	18.00

CLEVELAND	IP	H	R	ER	BB	SO	HR	ERA
Nagy	6	6	5	5	4	5	3	7.50
Anderson	0.1	1	1	1	0	0	0	27.00
Jackson	0.2	2	1	1	1	0	0	4.50
Assenmacher	0.2	3	0	0	0	1	0	0.00
Plunk (L, 0-1)	0.2	2	4	3	2	1	0	10.13
Morman	0.1	0	2	0	1	1	0	0.00
Mesa	0.1	2	1	1	0	0	0	6.75

WP: Mesa 1. **IBB:** Daulton (by Jackson), Floyd (by Plunk). **Pitches-strikes:** Leiter 114-64, Heredia 34-20, Cook 17-13, Nen 43-26, Nagy 96-55, Anderson 9-6, Jackson 16-8, Assenmacher 18-12, Plunk 25-12, Morman 18-10, Mesa 12-7. **Ground balls-fly balls:** Leiter 8-4, Heredia 3-4, Cook 0-1, Nen 1-0, Nagy 7-4, Anderson 1-0, Jackson 1-1, Assenmacher 0-1, Plunk 1-0, Morman 1-0, Mesa 0-1. **Batters faced:** Leiter 27, Heredia 8, Cook 4, Nen 8, Nagy 26, Anderson 2, Jackson 5, Assenmacher 5, Plunk 6, Morman 3, Mesa 3. **UMPIRES:** hp—(unknown), 1b—Greg Kosc, 2b—(unknown), 3b—Ken Kaiser, lf—, rf—Dale Ford **T:** 4:12 **A:** 44,880

GAME 4 Cleveland 10 Florida 3
Jacobs Field 10/22/97

FLORIDA	AB	R	H	HR	RBI	BB	AVG
White cf	4	0	0	0	0	0	.167
Renteria ss	4	0	1	0	0	0	.313
Sheffield rf	3	0	0	0	0	1	.333
Bonilla 3b	4	0	0	0	0	0	.188
Daulton 1b	3	2	2	0	0	1	.500
Alou lf	3	1	1	1	2	1	.267
Eisenreich dh	2	0	2	0	1	1	.667
a-Arias ph	1	0	0	0	0	0	.000
Johnson c	4	0	0	0	0	0	.267
Counsell 2b	2	0	0	0	0	1	.231
b-Abbott ph	1	0	0	0	0	0	.000
TOTALS	**31**	**3**	**6**	**1**	**3**	**5**	**.272**

a - Batted for Eisenreich in the 9th
b - Batted for Counsell in the 9th

BATTING: 2B: Daulton (1, Wright). **HR:** Alou (2, 6th off Wright 1 on, 1 out). **SF:** Alou. **RBI:** Alou 2 (5), Eisenreich 1 (3). **Runners left in scoring position, 2 out:** Sheffield 1, Johnson 1, Counsell 1. **GIDP:** Bonilla. **Team LOB:** 6 **BASERUNNING: SB:** Counsell (1, 2nd base off Wright/Alomar). **FIELDING: E:** Saunders (1), Renteria (1).

CLEVELAND	AB	R	H	HR	RBI	BB	AVG
Roberts lf	4	0	1	0	0	0	.313
Giles lf	1	0	1	0	1	0	1.000
Vizquel ss	5	2	2	0	0	0	.235
Ramirez rf	4	2	1	1	2	1	.176
Justice dh	3	2	1	0	0	2	.308
Williams 3b	3	3	3	1	2	2	.412
Alomar c	5	0	3	0	3	0	.471
Thome 1b	4	0	1	0	0	1	.294
Fernandez 2b	5	1	2	0	1	0	.455
Grissom cf	4	0	0	0	0	0	.500
TOTALS	**38**	**10**	**15**	**2**	**9**	**6**	**.340**

BATTING: 2B: Alomar (1, Saunders), Roberts (4, Saunders). **HR:** Ramirez (2, 1st off Saunders 1 on, 1 out), Williams (1, 8th off Powell 1 on, 1 out). **RBI:** Giles 1 (2), Ramirez 2 (5), Williams 2 (3), Alomar 3 (6), Fernandez 1 (2). **2-out RBI:** Alomar 1. **Runners left in scoring position, 2 out:** Vizquel 3, Thome 3. **Team LOB:** 10 **BASERUNNING: SB:** Vizquel (1, 2nd base off Vosberg/Johnson). **CS:** Giles (1, 2nd base off Vosberg/Johnson). **FIELDING: DP:** 2 (Fernandez-Vizquel-Thome, Thome).

FLORIDA	IP	H	R	ER	BB	SO	HR	ERA
Saunders (L, 0-1)	2	7	6	6	3	2	1	27.00
Alfonseca	3	3	0	0	0	4	0	0.00
Vosberg	2	3	2	2	2	1	0	9.00
Powell	1	2	2	2	1	0	1	16.20

CLEVELAND	IP	H	R	ER	BB	SO	HR	ERA
Wright (W, 1-0)	6	5	3	3	5	5	1	4.50
Anderson (S, 1)	3	1	0	0	0	2	0	2.70

WP: Wright 1. **Pitches-strikes:** Saunders 68-33, Alfonseca 57-39, Vosberg 34-16, Powell 23-11, Wright 115-62, Anderson 37-28. **Ground balls-fly balls:** Saunders 2-2, Alfonseca 2-3, Vosberg 2-2, Powell 3-0, Wright 5-6, Anderson 2-5. **Batters faced:** Saunders 16, Alfonseca 12, Vosberg 10, Powell 6, Wright 26, Anderson 10. **UMPIRES:** hp—Greg Kosc, 1b—Randy Marsh, 2b—Ken Kaiser, 3b—Ed Montague, lf—Dale Ford, rf—Joe West **T:** 3:15 **A:** 44,887

GAME 5 Florida 8 Cleveland 7
Jacobs Field 10/23/97

FLORIDA	AB	R	H	HR	RBI	BB	AVG
White cf	4	0	2	0	2	1	.227
Renteria ss	5	0	1	0	0	0	.286
Sheffield rf	5	1	2	0	0	0	.353
Bonilla 3b	4	1	1	0	0	1	.200
a-Arias pr-3b	0	1	0	0	0	0	.000
Daulton dh	5	1	2	0	0	0	.467
Alou lf	5	2	3	1	4	0	.350
Conine 1b	5	1	1	0	0	0	.300
Johnson c	5	1	3	0	2	0	.350
Counsell 2b	2	0	0	0	0	2	.200
TOTALS	**40**	**8**	**15**	**1**	**8**	**4**	**.295**

a - Ran for Bonilla in the 9th

BATTING: 2B: Daulton (2, Hershiser), White 2 (3, Hershiser, Assenmacher), Bonilla (1, Mesa). **HR:** Alou (3, 6th off Hershiser 2 on, 2 out). **RBI:** White 2 (2), Alou 4 (9), Johnson 2 (3). **2-out RBI:** White 2, Alou 3, Johnson 1. **Runners left in scoring position, 2 out:** White 1, Renteria 4, Johnson 1. **GIDP:** Bonilla. **Team LOB:** 9 **BASERUNNING: SB:** Alou (1, 2nd base off Juden/Alomar), Daulton (1, 3rd base off Mesa/Alomar). **FIELDING: DP:** 2 (Renteria-Counsell-Conine, Hernandez-Renteria-Conine).

CLEVELAND	AB	R	H	HR	RBI	BB	AVG
Roberts 2b	3	1	0	0	0	2	.263
Vizquel ss	4	1	1	0	0	0	.238
Ramirez rf	5	0	1	0	0	0	.182
Justice dh	5	0	1	0	2	0	.278
Williams 3b	3	2	1	0	0	2	.400
Thome 1b	4	2	2	0	1	1	.333
Alomar c	5	1	2	1	4	0	.455
Giles lf	1	0	0	0	0	3	.667
Grissom cf	4	0	1	0	0	0	.444
TOTALS	**34**	**7**	**9**	**1**	**7**	**8**	**.326**

BATTING: 3B: Thome (1, Hernandez). **HR:** Alomar (2, 3th off Hernandez 2 on, 2 out). **S:** Vizquel. **RBI:** Justice 2 (4), Thome 1 (4), Alomar 4 (10). **2-out RBI:** Thome 1, Alomar 3. **Runners left in scoring position, 2 out:** Roberts 1, Vizquel 2, Justice 1, Grissom 1. **GIDP:** Alomar, Justice. **Team LOB:** 9 **FIELDING: Outfield assists:** Ramirez (1). **DP:** 1 (Roberts-Vizquel-Thome).

FLORIDA	IP	H	R	ER	BB	SO	HR	ERA
Hernandez (W, 2-0)	8	7	6	5	8	2	1	5.27
Nen (S, 2)	1	2	1	0	0	1	0	12.00

CLEVELAND	IP	H	R	ER	BB	SO	HR	ERA
Hershiser (L, 0-2)	5.2	9	6	6	2	3	1	11.70
Morman	0	0	0	0	1	0	0	0.00
Plunk	0.1	0	0	0	1	1	0	9.00
Juden	1.1	2	1	1	0	0	0	4.50
Assenmacher	0.2	1	0	0	0	1	0	0.00
Mesa	1	3	1	1	0	1	0	7.71

WP: Hernandez 1. **Pitches-strikes:** Hernandez 142-77, Nen 18-14, Hershiser 96-60, Morman 5-1, Plunk 10-5, Juden 17-11, Assenmacher 21-14, Mesa 16-11. **Ground balls-fly balls:** Hernandez 13-7, Nen 1-1, Hershiser 6-6, Morman 0-0, Plunk 0-0, Juden 1-3, Assenmacher 0-1, Mesa 0-2. **Batters faced:** Hernandez 38, Nen 5, Hershiser 26, Morman 1, Plunk 2, Juden 6, Assenmacher 3, Mesa 6. **UMPIRES:** hp—Randy Marsh, 1b—Ken Kaiser, 2b—Ed Montague, 3b—Dale Ford, lf—Joe West, rf—Greg Kosc **T:** 3:39 **A:** 44,888

GAME 6 Cleveland 4 Florida 1
Pro Player Stadium 10/25/97

CLEVELAND	AB	R	H	HR	RBI	BB	AVG
Roberts 2b	3	0	1	0	0	0	.273
Fernandez 2b	1	0	1	0	0	0	.500
Vizquel ss	4	1	1	0	0	0	.240
Ramirez rf	1	0	0	0	2	1	.174
Justice lf	4	0	0	0	0	0	.227
Williams 3b	4	1	2	0	0	0	.417
Thome 1b	3	1	0	0	0	1	.292
Alomar c	3	0	0	0	0	1	.400
Grissom cf	3	0	0	0	0	1	.381
Ogea p	2	1	2	0	2	0	.500
Jackson p	1	0	0	0	0	0	.000
Assenmacher p	0	0	0	0	0	0	.000
a-Seitzer ph	1	0	0	0	0	0	.000
Mesa p	0	0	0	0	0	0	.000
TOTALS	**30**	**4**	**7**	**0**	**4**	**4**	**.313**

a - Batted for Assenmacher in the 9th

BATTING: 2B: Vizquel (2, Brown), Ogea (1, Brown), Williams (1, Powell). **SF:** Ramirez, Ramirez. **RBI:** Ramirez 2 (7), Ogea 2 (2). **Runners left in scoring position, 2 out:** Justice 1, Seitzer 1. **GIDP:** Roberts. **Team LOB:** 5 **BASERUNNING: SB:** Vizquel 2 (3, 3rd base off Brown/Johnson, 2nd base off Powell/Johnson). **CS:** Roberts (1, 2nd base off Brown/Johnson).

FLORIDA	AB	R	H	HR	RBI	BB	AVG
White cf	5	0	3	0	0	0	.296
Renteria ss	5	0	0	0	0	0	.231
Sheffield rf	3	0	0	0	0	2	.300
Bonilla 3b	4	0	0	0	0	0	.167
Conine 1b	2	0	0	0	0	0	.250
b-Eisenreich ph-1b	1	0	0	0	0	1	.571
Alou lf	3	1	1	0	0	1	.348
Johnson c	4	0	2	0	0	0	.375
Counsell 2b	4	0	1	0	0	0	.211
Brown p	1	0	0	0	0	0	.000
a-Daulton ph	0	0	0	0	1	0	.467
Heredia p	0	0	0	0	0	0	.000
c-Cangelosi ph	1	0	1	0	0	0	.500
Powell p	0	0	0	0	0	0	.000
Vosberg p	0	0	0	0	0	0	.000
d-Floyd ph	1	0	0	0	0	0	.000
TOTALS	**34**	**1**	**8**	**0**	**1**	**4**	**.286**

a - Batted for Brown in the 5th
b - Batted for Conine in the 6th
c - Batted for Heredia in the 7th
d - Batted for Vosberg in the 9th

BATTING: 3B: White (1, Mesa). **SF:** Daulton. **RBI:** Daulton 1 (3). **Runners left in scoring position, 2 out:** Renteria 2, Sheffield 1, Bonilla 2, Johnson 2. **Team LOB:** 11 **BASERUNNING: SB:** White (1, 2nd base off Ogea/Alomar). **FIELDING: DP:** 1 (Counsell-Renteria-Conine).

CLEVELAND	IP	H	R	ER	BB	SO	HR	ERA
Ogea (W, 2-0)	5	4	1	1	2	1	0	1.54
Jackson	2	2	0	0	2	2	0	2.25
Assenmacher	1	1	0	0	0	1	0	0.00
Mesa (S, 1)	1	1	0	0	0	1	0	5.40

FLORIDA	IP	H	R	ER	BB	SO	HR	ERA
Brown (L, 0-2)	5	5	4	4	3	2	0	8.18
Heredia	2	0	0	0	0	4	0	0.00
Powell	1	2	0	0	0	1	0	10.13
Vosberg	1	0	0	0	1	1	0	6.00

IBB: Alomar (by Vosberg). **Pitches-strikes:** Ogea 71-40, Jackson 40-22, Assenmacher 12-8, Mesa 13-9, Brown 89-53, Heredia 25-19, Powell 22-13, Vosberg 18-9. **Ground balls-fly balls:** Ogea 4-9, Jackson 2-2, Assenmacher 0-2, Mesa 2-0, Brown 5-4, Heredia 1-1, Powell 1-1, Vosberg 1-1. **Batters faced:** Ogea 21, Jackson 10, Assenmacher 4, Mesa 4, Brown 21, Heredia 6, Powell 5, Vosberg 4. **UMPIRES:** hp—(none), 1b—Ed Montague, 2b—(none), 3b—Joe West, lf—(none), rf—Randy Marsh **T:** 3:15 **A:** 67,498

GAME 7 Florida 3 Cleveland 2
Pro Player Stadium 10/26/97

CLEVELAND	AB	R	H	HR	RBI	BB	AVG
Vizquel ss	5	0	1	0	0	0	.233
Fernandez 2b	5	0	2	0	2	0	.471
Ramirez rf	3	0	0	0	0	2	.154
Justice lf	5	0	0	0	0	0	.185
Williams 3b	2	0	0	0	0	3	.385
Alomar c	5	0	1	0	0	0	.367
Thome 1b	4	1	1	0	0	1	.286
Grissom cf	4	1	1	0	0	0	.360
Wright p	2	0	0	0	0	0	.000
Assenmacher p	0	0	0	0	0	0	.000
Jackson p	0	0	0	0	0	0	.000
Anderson p	0	0	0	0	0	0	.000
a-Giles ph	1	0	0	0	0	0	.500
Mesa p	0	0	0	0	0	0	.000
Nagy p	0	0	0	0	0	0	.000
TOTALS	**36**	**2**	**6**	**0**	**2**	**6**	**.291**

a - Batted for Anderson in the 9th

BATTING: S: Wright. **RBI:** Fernandez 2 (4). **2-out RBI:** Fernandez 2. **Runners left in scoring position, 2 out:** Justice 2, Giles 1. **GIDP:** Thome, Thome. **Team LOB:** 8 **BASERUNNING: SB:** Vizquel 2 (5, 2nd base off Leiter/Johnson, 3rd base off Leiter/Johnson). **FIELDING: E:** Ramirez (1), Fernandez (2). **DP:** 1 (Fernandez-Vizquel-Thome).

FLORIDA	AB	R	H	HR	RBI	BB	AVG
White cf	6	0	0	0	0	0	.242
Renteria ss	5	0	3	0	1	1	.290
Sheffield rf	4	0	1	0	0	1	.292
Daulton 1b	3	0	0	0	0	0	.389
c-Conine ph-1b	1	0	0	0	0	0	.231
Nen p	0	0	0	0	0	0	.000
e-Cangelosi ph	1	0	0	0	0	0	.333
Powell p	0	0	0	0	0	0	.000
Alou lf	5	1	1	0	0	0	.321
Bonilla 3b	5	1	2	1	1	0	.207
Johnson c	4	0	1	0	0	0	.357
d-Zaun pr-c	1	0	0	0	0	0	.000
Counsell 2b	3	1	0	0	1	1	.182
Leiter p	0	0	0	0	0	2	.000
Cook p	0	0	0	0	0	0	.000
a-Floyd ph	0	0	0	0	0	0	.000
b-Abbott ph	1	0	0	0	0	0	.000
Alfonseca p	0	0	0	0	0	0	.000
Heredia p	0	0	0	0	0	0	.000
Eisenreich 1b	1	0	0	0	0	1	.500
TOTALS	**40**	**3**	**8**	**1**	**3**	**6**	**.272**

a - Batted for Cook in the 7th
b - Batted for Floyd in the 7th
c - Batted for Daulton in the 8th
d - Ran for Johnson in the 9th e - Batted for Nen in the 10th

BATTING: 2B: Renteria (2, Wright). **HR:** Bonilla (1, 7th off Wright 0 on, 0 out). **SF:** Counsell. **RBI:** Renteria 1 (3), Bonilla 1 (3), Counsell 1 (2). **2-out RBI:** Renteria 1. **Runners left in scoring position, 2 out:** Sheffield 1, Alou 2. **GIDP:** Daulton. **Team LOB:** 12 **FIELDING: DP:** 2 (Daulton-Renteria-Daulton, Counsell-Renteria-Eisenreich).

CLEVELAND	IP	H	R	ER	BB	SO	HR	ERA
Wright	6.1	2	1	1	5	7	1	2.92
Assenmacher	0.2	0	0	0	0	1	0	0.00
Jackson	0.2	0	0	0	0	1	0	1.93
Anderson	0.1	0	0	0	0	0	0	2.45
Mesa	1.2	4	1	1	0	2	0	5.40
Nagy (L, 0-1)	1	2	1	0	1	0	0	6.43

FLORIDA	IP	H	R	ER	BB	SO	HR	ERA
Leiter	6	4	2	2	4	7	0	5.06
Cook	1	0	0	0	0	2	0	0.00
Alfonseca	1.1	0	0	0	1	1	0	0.00
Heredia	0	1	0	0	0	0	0	0.00
Nen	1.2	1	0	0	0	3	0	7.71
Powell (W, 1-0)	1	0	0	0	1	0	0	7.36

IBB: Ramirez (by Leiter), Eisenreich (by Nagy). **Pitches-strikes:** Wright 108-63, Assenmacher 11-7, Jackson 6-5, Anderson 7-5, Mesa 39-23, Nagy 21-15, Leiter 118-65, Cook 12-8, Alfonseca 15-9, Heredia 1-1, Nen 24-18, Powell 10-6. **Ground balls-fly balls:** Wright 5-7, Assenmacher 0-1, Jackson 1-0, Anderson 0-1, Mesa 2-0, Nagy 2-2, Leiter 4-5, Cook 0-1, Alfonseca 3-0, Heredia 0-0, Nen 1-1, Powell 2-0. **Batters faced:** Wright 26, Assenmacher 2, Jackson 2, Anderson 1, Mesa 9, Nagy 7, Leiter 25, Cook 3, Alfonseca 5, Heredia 1, Nen 6, Powell 3. **UMPIRES:** hp—Ed Montague, 1b—Dale Ford, 2b—Joe West, 3b—Greg Kosc, lf—Randy Marsh, rf—Ken Kaiser **T:** 4:10 **A:** 67,204

1998 NY YANKEES DEF. SAN DIEGO, 4-0

GAME 1 New York 9 San Diego 6
Yankee Stadium 10/17/98

SAN DIEGO	AB	R	H	HR	RBI	BB	AVG
Veras 2b	4	1	1	0	0	1	.250
Gwynn rf	4	1	3	1	2	0	.750
Vaughn lf	4	3	2	2	3	0	.500
Caminiti 3b	3	0	0	0	0	1	.000
Leyritz dh	4	0	0	0	0	0	.000
Joyner 1b	3	0	0	0	0	1	.000
Finley cf	4	0	1	0	0	0	.250
C.Hernandez c	3	0	0	0	0	0	.000
a-G.Myers ph	1	0	0	0	0	0	.000
Gomez ss	3	1	1	0	0	0	.333
b-VanderWal ph	1	0	0	0	0	0	.000
TOTALS	**34**	**6**	**8**	**3**	**5**	**3**	**.235**

a - Batted for C.Hernandez in the 9th
b - Batted for Gomez in the 9th

BATTING: 2B: Finley (1, Wells). **HR:** Vaughn 2 (2, 3th off Wells 1 on, 2 out, 5th off Wells 0 on, 2 out), Gwynn (1, 5th off Wells 1 on, 2 out). **RBI:** Gwynn 2 (2), Vaughn 3 (3). **2-out RBI:** Gwynn 2, Vaughn 3. **Runners left in scoring position, 2 out:** Caminiti 1, Finley 1, C.Hernandez 1. **GIDP:** Vaughn. **Team LOB:** 4 **FIELDING: E:** Vaughn (1). **Outfield assists:** Finley (1).

NY YANKEES	AB	R	H	HR	RBI	BB	AVG
Knoblauch 2b	4	1	2	1	3	0	.500
Jeter ss	4	1	1	0	0	1	.250
O'Neill rf	5	0	0	0	0	0	.000
Williams cf	4	1	0	0	0	1	.000
Davis dh	3	2	1	0	0	1	.333
Martinez 1b	3	2	1	1	4	1	.333
Brosius 3b	4	0	1	0	0	0	.250
Posada c	3	1	1	0	0	1	.333
Ledee lf	3	1	2	0	2	1	.667
TOTALS	**33**	**9**	**9**	**2**	**9**	**6**	**.273**

BATTING: 2B: Ledee (1, Brown). **HR:** Knoblauch (1, 7th off Wall 2 on, 1 out), Martinez (1, 7th off Langston 3 on, 2 out). **RBI:** Knoblauch 3 (3), Martinez 4 (4), Ledee 2 (2). **2-out RBI:** Martinez 4, Ledee 2. **Runners left in scoring position, 2 out:** Knoblauch 2, O'Neill 2, Williams 2. **Team LOB:** 7 **FIELDING: E:** Knoblauch (1). **DP:** 2 (Knoblauch-Martinez, Martinez).

SAN DIEGO	IP	H	R	ER	BB	SO	HR	ERA
Brown	6.1	6	4	4	3	5	0	5.68
Wall (L, 0-1)	0	2	2	2	0	0	1	0.00
Langston	0.2	1	3	3	2	0	1	40.50
Boehringer	0.1	0	0	0	1	1	0	0.00
R.Myers	0.2	0	0	0	0	2	0	0.00

NY YANKEES	IP	H	R	ER	BB	SO	HR	ERA
Wells (W, 1-0)	7	7	5	5	2	4	3	6.43
Nelson	0.2	1	1	0	1	1	0	0.00
M.Rivera (S, 1)	1.1	0	0	0	0	2	0	0.00

WP: Langston 1. **IBB:** Williams (by Langston). **HBP:** Knoblauch (by Boehringer). **Pitches-strikes:** Brown 106-60, Wall 4-2, Langston 21-9, Boehringer 21-10, R.Myers 8-6, Wells 113-79, Nelson 15-9, M.Rivera 25-19. **Ground balls-fly balls:** Brown 7-6, Wall 0-0, Langston 0-2, Boehringer 0-1, R.Myers 0-0, Wells 5-10, Nelson 1-0, M.Rivera 2-1. **Batters faced:** Brown 27, Wall 2, Langston 5, Boehringer 4, R.Myers 2, Wells 28, Nelson 4, M.Rivera 5. **UMPIRES:** hp—Rich Garcia, 1b—Mark Hirschbeck, 2b—Dale Scott, 3b—Dana DeMuth **T:** 3:29 **A:** 56,712

GAME 2 New York 9 San Diego 3
Yankee Stadium 10/18/98

SAN DIEGO	AB	R	H	HR	RBI	BB	AVG
Veras 2b	5	0	1	0	1	0	.222
Gwynn rf	4	0	1	0	0	1	.500
Vaughn dh	4	0	0	0	0	1	.250
Caminiti 3b	5	1	1	0	0	0	.125
Joyner 1b	2	0	0	0	0	1	.000
a-Leyritz ph-1b	1	0	0	0	0	0	.000
Finley cf	4	0	0	0	0	0	.125
VanderWal lf	3	0	2	0	0	0	.500
b-R.Rivera ph-lf	1	1	1	0	1	0	1.000
G.Myers c	3	0	0	0	0	0	.000
c-C.Hernandez ph-c	1	0	1	0	0	0	.250
Gomez ss	3	1	2	0	0	0	.500
d-Sweeney ph	1	0	1	0	1	0	1.000
Sheets ss	0	0	0	0	0	0	.000
TOTALS	**37**	**3**	**10**	**0**	**3**	**3**	**.254**

a - Batted for Joyner in the 8th
b - Batted for VanderWal in the 8th
c - Batted for G.Myers in the 8th
d - Batted for Gomez in the 8th

BATTING: 2B: Veras (1, O.Hernandez), VanderWal (1, O.Hernandez), Caminiti (1, Stanton), R.Rivera (1, Stanton). **3B:** Gomez (1, O.Hernandez). **RBI:** Veras 1 (1), R.Rivera 1 (1), Sweeney 1 (1). **2-out RBI:** Veras 1, R.Rivera 1, Sweeney 1. **Runners left in scoring position, 2 out:** Veras 1, Gwynn 1, Vaughn 2, Joyner 1. **Team LOB:** 10 **FIELDING: E:** Caminiti (1). **DP:** 3 (Veras-Gomez-Joyner, Veras-Joyner, Wall-Gomez-Joyner).

NY YANKEES	AB	R	H	HR	RBI	BB	AVG
Knoblauch 2b	3	2	2	0	0	2	.571
Jeter ss	5	1	2	0	1	0	.333
O'Neill rf	5	1	1	0	0	0	.100
Williams cf	4	1	1	1	2	1	.125
Davis dh	3	1	1	0	1	2	.333
a-Bush pr	0	0	0	0	0	0	.000
Martinez 1b	5	1	3	0	0	0	.500
Brosius 3b	5	1	3	0	1	0	.444
Posada c	4	1	1	1	2	1	.286
Ledee lf	3	0	2	0	1	1	.667
TOTALS	**37**	**9**	**16**	**2**	**8**	**7**	**.357**

a - Ran for Davis in the 8th

BATTING: 2B: Ledee (2, Ashby). **HR:** Williams (1, 2nd off Ashby 1 on, 2 out), Posada (1, 5th off Boehringer 1 on, 1 out). **RBI:** Jeter 1 (1), Williams 2 (2), Davis 1 (1), Brosius 1 (1), Posada 2 (2), Ledee 1 (3). **2-out RBI:** Williams 2, Davis 1, Brosius 1, Ledee 1. **Runners left in scoring position, 2 out:** Knoblauch 1, O'Neill 1, Davis 1, Posada 3. **GIDP:** Posada, Brosius, Jeter. **Team LOB:** 11 **BASERUNNING: SB:** Knoblauch (1, 2nd base off Ashby/G.Myers). **CS:** Ledee (1, 3rd base off Ashby/G.Myers).

SAN DIEGO	IP	H	R	ER	BB	SO	HR	ERA
Ashby (L, 0-1)	2.2	10	7	4	1	1	1	13.50
Boehringer	1.2	4	2	2	1	2	1	9.00
Wall	2.2	1	0	0	3	1	0	6.75
Miceli	1	1	0	0	2	1	0	0.00

NY YANKEES	IP	H	R	ER	BB	SO	HR	ERA
O.Hernandez (W,1-0)	7	6	1	1	3	7	0	1.29
Stanton	0.2	3	2	2	0	1	0	27.00
Nelson	1.1	1	0	0	0	2	0	0.00

Pitches-strikes: Ashby 68-44, Boehringer 48-29, Wall 43-24, Miceli 25-15, O.Hernandez 115-70, Stanton 22-14, Nelson 21-16. **Ground balls-fly balls:** Ashby 5-1, Boehringer 1-2, Wall 3-2, Miceli 1-1, O.Hernandez 4-10, Stanton 1-0, Nelson 1-1. **Batters faced:** Ashby 18, Boehringer 10, Wall 10, Miceli 6, O.Hernandez 30, Stanton 5, Nelson 5. **UMPIRES:** hp—Mark Hirschbeck, 1b—Dale Scott, 2b—Dana DeMuth, 3b—Tim Tschida **T:** 3:31 **A:** 56,692

GAME 3 New York 5 San Diego 4
Qualcomm Stadium 10/20/98

NY YANKEES	AB	R	H	HR	RBI	BB	AVG
Knoblauch 2b	4	0	1	0	0	1	.455
Jeter ss	4	0	1	0	0	1	.308
O'Neill rf	4	1	1	0	0	1	.143
Williams cf	4	0	0	0	0	0	.083
Martinez 1b	3	1	0	0	0	1	.364
Brosius 3b	4	2	3	2	4	0	.538
Spencer lf	3	1	1	0	0	0	.333
d-Ledee ph-lf	1	0	0	0	0	0	.571
Girardi c	2	0	0	0	0	0	.000
a-Posada ph-c	2	0	1	0	0	0	.333
Cone p	2	0	1	0	0	0	.500
b-Davis ph	1	0	0	0	1	0	.286
c-Bush pr	0	0	0	0	0	0	.000
Lloyd p	0	0	0	0	0	0	.000
Mendoza p	1	0	0	0	0	0	.000
M.Rivera p	0	0	0	0	0	0	.000
TOTALS	**35**	**5**	**9**	**2**	**5**	**4**	**.324**

a - Batted for Girardi in the 7th
b - Batted for Cone in the 7th
c - Ran for Davis in the 7th
d - Batted for Spencer in the 8th

BATTING: 2B: Spencer (1, Hitchcock). **HR:** Brosius 2 (2, 7th off Hitchcock 0 on, 0 out, 8th off Hoffman 2 on, 1 out). **RBI:** Brosius 4 (5), Davis 1 (2). **Runners left in scoring position, 2 out:** Martinez 2. **GIDP:** O'Neill. **Team LOB:** 7 **FIELDING: E:** O'Neill (1). **Outfield assists:** Spencer (1).

SAN DIEGO	AB	R	H	HR	RBI	BB	AVG
Veras 2b	3	2	1	0	0	1	.250
Gwynn rf	4	1	2	0	2	0	.500
a-R.Rivera pr-rf	0	0	0	0	0	0	1.000
Vaughn lf	3	0	0	0	1	0	.182
Caminiti 3b	2	0	0	0	1	1	.100
Joyner 1b	3	0	0	0	0	1	.000
Finley cf	4	0	0	0	0	0	.083
Leyritz c	2	0	0	0	0	0	.000
C.Hernandez c	2	0	1	0	0	0	.333
b-VanderWal pr	0	0	0	0	0	0	.500
Gomez ss	3	0	1	0	0	0	.444
Hoffman p	0	0	0	0	0	0	.000
c-Sweeney ph	1	0	1	0	0	0	1.000
Hitchcock p	2	1	1	0	0	0	.500
Hamilton p	0	0	0	0	0	0	.000
R.Myers p	0	0	0	0	0	0	.000
Sheets ss	2	0	0	0	0	0	.000
TOTALS	**31**	**4**	**7**	**0**	**4**	**3**	**.245**

a - Ran for Gwynn in the 8th
b - Ran for C.Hernandez in the 9th
c - Batted for Hoffman in the 9th

BATTING: 2B: Veras (2, Mendoza). **SF:** Caminiti, Vaughn. **RBI:** Gwynn 2 (4), Vaughn 1 (4), Caminiti 1 (1). **Runners left in scoring position, 2 out:** Leyritz 1, Sheets 1. **Team LOB:** 5 **BASERUNNING: SB:** Finley (1, 2nd base off Cone/Girardi). **FIELDING: E:** Caminiti (2). **PB:** Leyritz. **DP:** 2 (Gomez-Veras-Joyner, Gomez-Veras).

NY YANKEES	IP	H	R	ER	BB	SO	HR	ERA
Cone	6	2	3	2	3	4	0	3.00
Lloyd	0.1	0	0	0	0	0	0	0.00
Mendoza (W, 1-0)	1	2	1	1	0	1	0	9.00
M.Rivera (S, 2)	1.2	3	0	0	0	2	0	0.00

SAN DIEGO	IP	H	R	ER	BB	SO	HR	ERA
Hitchcock	6	7	2	1	1	7	1	1.50
Hamilton	1	0	0	0	1	1	0	0.00
R.Myers	0	0	1	1	1	0	0	13.50
Hoffman (L, 0-1)	2	2	2	2	1	0	1	9.00

Pitches-strikes: Cone 87-47, Lloyd 1-1, Mendoza 12-11, M.Rivera 22-19, Hitchcock 92-60, Hamilton 19-11, R.Myers 6-2, Hoffman 37-21. **Ground balls-fly balls:** Cone 6-7, Lloyd 1-0, Mendoza 1-0, M.Rivera 1-1, Hitchcock 4-6, Hamilton 1-1, R.Myers 0-0, Hoffman 4-2. **Batters faced:** Cone 23, Lloyd 1, Mendoza 4, M.Rivera 8, Hitchcock 25, Hamilton 4, R.Myers 1, Hoffman 9. **UMPIRES:** hp—Dale Scott, 1b—Dana DeMuth, 2b—Tim Tschida, 3b—Jerry Crawford **T:** 3:14 **A:** 64,667

GAME 4 New York 3 San Diego 0
Qualcomm Stadium 10/21/98

NY YANKEES	AB	R	H	HR	RBI	BB	AVG
Knoblauch 2b	5	0	1	0	0	0	.375
Jeter ss	4	2	2	0	0	1	.353
O'Neill rf	5	1	2	0	0	0	.211
Williams cf	4	0	0	0	1	0	.063
Martinez 1b	2	0	1	0	0	2	.385
Brosius 3b	4	0	1	0	1	0	.471
Ledee lf	3	0	2	0	1	0	.600
Girardi c	4	0	0	0	0	0	.000
Pettitte p	2	0	0	0	0	0	.000
Nelson p	0	0	0	0	0	0	.000
M.Rivera p	1	0	0	0	0	0	.000
TOTALS	**34**	**3**	**9**	**0**	**3**	**3**	**.309**

BATTING: 2B: Ledee (3, Brown), O'Neill (1, Brown). **S:** Pettitte. **SF:** Ledee. **RBI:** Williams 1 (3), Brosius 1 (6), Ledee 1 (4). **Runners left in scoring position, 2 out:** Knoblauch 1, Williams 1, Brosius 1, Girardi 1, Pettitte 2. **Team LOB:** 9 **FIELDING: DP:** 2 (Knoblauch-Jeter-Martinez, Jeter-Knoblauch-Martinez).

SAN DIEGO	AB	R	H	HR	RBI	BB	AVG
Veras 2b	3	0	0	0	0	1	.200
Gwynn rf	4	0	2	0	0	0	.500
Vaughn lf	4	0	0	0	0	0	.133
Caminiti 3b	4	0	1	0	0	0	.143
Leyritz 1b	3	0	0	0	0	1	.000
R.Rivera cf	4	0	3	0	0	0	.800
C.Hernandez c	4	0	0	0	0	0	.200
Gomez ss	2	0	0	0	0	1	.364
b-Sweeney ph	1	0	0	0	0	0	.667
Brown p	2	0	1	0	0	0	.500
a-VanderWal ph	1	0	0	0	0	0	.400
Miceli p	0	0	0	0	0	0	.000
R.Myers p	0	0	0	0	0	0	.000
TOTALS	**32**	**0**	**7**	**0**	**0**	**3**	**.239**

a - Batted for Brown in the 8th
b - Batted for Gomez in the 9th

BATTING: 2B: R.Rivera (2, Pettitte). **Runners left in scoring position, 2 out:** Leyritz 2, Brown 2. **GIDP:** Caminiti, C.Hernandez. **Team LOB:** 8

NY YANKEES	IP	H	R	ER	BB	SO	HR	ERA
Pettitte (W, 1-0)	7.1	5	0	0	3	4	0	0.00
Nelson	0.1	0	0	0	0	1	0	0.00
M.Rivera (S, 3)	1.1	2	0	0	0	0	0	0.00

SAN DIEGO	IP	H	R	ER	BB	SO	HR	ERA
Brown (L, 0-1)	8	8	3	3	3	8	0	4.40
Miceli	0.2	1	0	0	0	0	0	0.00
R.Myers	0.1	0	0	0	0	0	0	9.00

IBB: Martinez 2 (by Brown). **Pitches-strikes:** Pettitte 101-64, Nelson 5-3, M.Rivera 20-12, Brown 118-73, Miceli 13-10, R.Myers 3-1. **Ground balls-fly balls:** Pettitte 14-3, Nelson 0-0, M.Rivera 2-1, Brown 11-3, Miceli 0-2, R.Myers 0-1. **Batters faced:** Pettitte 29, Nelson 1, M.Rivera 5, Brown 35, Miceli 3, R.Myers 1. **UMPIRES:** hp—Dana DeMuth, 1b—Tim Tschida, 2b—Jerry Crawford, 3b—Rich Garcia **T:** 2:58 **A:** 65,427

1999 NY YANKEES DEF. ATLANTA, 4-0

GAME 1 New York 4 Atlanta 1
Turner Field 10/23/99

NY YANKEES	AB	R	H	HR	RBI	BB	AVG
Knoblauch 2b	4	1	0	0	0	0	.000
Jeter ss	4	1	2	0	1	1	.500
O'Neill rf	4	0	1	0	2	0	.250
B.Williams cf	2	0	0	0	0	2	.000
Martinez 1b	3	0	0	0	0	1	.000
Posada c	4	0	0	0	0	0	.000
Ledee lf	3	0	0	0	0	0	.000
c-Leyritz ph	0	0	0	0	1	1	.000
Nelson p	0	0	0	0	0	0	.000
Stanton p	0	0	0	0	0	0	.000
Rivera p	0	0	0	0	0	0	.000
Brosius 3b	4	1	3	0	0	0	.750
O.Hernandez p	1	0	0	0	0	0	.000
a-Strawberry ph	0	0	0	0	0	1	.000
b-Curtis pr-lf	1	1	0	0	0	0	.000
TOTALS	**30**	**4**	**6**	**0**	**4**	**6**	**.200**

a - Batted for O.Hernandez in the 8th
b - Ran for Strawberry in the 8th
c - Batted for Ledee in the 8th

BATTING: S: O.Hernandez, Knoblauch. **RBI:** Jeter 1 (1), O'Neill 2 (2), Leyritz 1 (1). **2-out RBI:** Leyritz 1. **Runners left in scoring position, 2 out:** Jeter 1, B.Williams 1, Ledee 1, Brosius 2. **GIDP:** Posada. **Team LOB:** 7 **BASERUNNING: SB:** Jeter (1, 2nd base off Maddux/Perez), B.Williams (1, 2nd base off Maddux/Perez). **CS:** Jeter (1, 2nd base off Remlinger/Perez).

ATLANTA	AB	R	H	HR	RBI	BB	AVG
G.Williams lf	4	0	0	0	0	0	.000
Boone 2b	4	0	1	0	0	0	.250
C.Jones 3b	2	1	1	1	1	2	.500
Jordan rf	4	0	0	0	0	0	.000
Klesko 1b	3	0	0	0	0	0	.000
Hunter 1b	0	0	0	0	0	0	.000
e-Myers ph	1	0	0	0	0	0	.000
A.Jones cf	2	0	0	0	0	1	.000
Perez c	2	0	0	0	0	1	.000
Weiss ss	2	0	0	0	0	0	.000
a-Guillen ph	0	0	0	0	0	0	.000
b-J.Hernandez ph-ss	1	0	0	0	0	0	.000
Maddux p	2	0	0	0	0	0	.000
Rocker p	0	0	0	0	0	0	.000
c-Battle ph	0	0	0	0	0	0	.000
d-Lockhart ph	1	0	0	0	0	0	.000
Remlinger p	0	0	0	0	0	0	.000
TOTALS	**28**	**1**	**2**	**1**	**1**	**4**	**.071**

a - Batted for Weiss in the 8th
b - Batted for Guillen in the 8th
c - Batted for Rocker in the 8th
d - Batted for Battle in the 8th e - Batted for Hunter in the 9th

BATTING: HR: C.Jones (1, 4th off O.Hernandez 0 on, 1 out). **RBI:** C.Jones 1 (1). **Runners left in scoring position, 2 out:** Myers 1. **Team LOB:** 4 **BASERUNNING: CS:** C.Jones (1, 2nd base off O.Hernandez/Posada). **FIELDING: E:** Hunter 2 (2). **DP:** 1 (Boone-Weiss-Klesko).

NY YANKEES	IP	H	R	ER	BB	SO	HR	ERA
O.Hernandez (W, 1-0)	7	1	1	1	2	10	1	1.29
Nelson	0.1	0	0	0	1	1	0	0.00
Stanton	0.1	0	0	0	0	1	0	0.00
Rivera (S, 1)	1.1	1	0	0	1	1	0	0.00

ATLANTA	IP	H	R	ER	BB	SO	HR	ERA
Maddux (L, 0-1)	7	5	4	2	3	5	0	2.57
Rocker	1	1	0	0	2	3	0	0.00
Remlinger	1	0	0	0	1	0	0	0.00

IBB: B.Williams (by Rocker). **Pitches-strikes:** O.Hernandez 97-62, Nelson 10-4, Stanton 5-4, Rivera 19-14, Maddux 95-58, Rocker 30-13, Remlinger 9-5. **Ground balls-fly balls:** O.Hernandez 4-6, Nelson 0-0, Stanton 0-0, Rivera 2-1, Maddux 6-8, Rocker 0-0, Remlinger 1-1. **Batters faced:** O.Hernandez 23, Nelson 2, Stanton 1, Rivera 6, Maddux 29, Rocker 6, Remlinger 3. **UMPIRES:** hp—Randy Marsh, 1b—Rocky Roe, 2b—Steve Rippley, 3b—Derryl Cousins **T:** 2:57 **A:** 51,342

GAME 2 New York 7 Atlanta 2
Turner Field 10/24/99

NY YANKEES	AB	R	H	HR	RBI	BB	AVG
Knoblauch 2b	4	1	2	0	1	1	.250
Jeter ss	5	2	2	0	0	0	.444
O'Neill rf	4	0	1	0	1	1	.250
B.Williams cf	4	1	3	0	0	1	.500
Martinez 1b	5	2	2	0	2	0	.250
Ledee lf	4	0	2	0	1	1	.286
Brosius 3b	5	1	2	0	1	0	.556
Girardi c	4	0	0	0	0	0	.000
Cone p	4	0	0	0	0	0	.000
Mendoza p	1	0	0	0	0	0	.000
Nelson p	0	0	0	0	0	0	.000
TOTALS	**40**	**7**	**14**	**0**	**6**	**4**	**.286**

BATTING: 2B: Ledee (1, Millwood), Jeter (1, Mulholland), Brosius (1, Mulholland). **S:** Girardi. **RBI:** Knoblauch 1 (1), O'Neill 1 (3), Martinez 2 (2), Ledee 1 (1), Brosius 1 (1). **2-out RBI:** Knoblauch 1, Martinez 1, Brosius 1. **Runners left in scoring position, 2 out:** Knoblauch 1, O'Neill 1, Martinez 1, Girardi 1, Mendoza 1. **GIDP:** B.Williams. **Team LOB:** 11 **BASERUNNING: SB:** Knoblauch (1, 2nd base off Millwood/Myers). **FIELDING: E:** Cone (1). **DP:** 3 (Jeter-Martinez, Brosius-Knoblauch-Martinez, Knoblauch-Jeter-Martinez).

ATLANTA	AB	R	H	HR	RBI	BB	AVG
G.Williams lf	4	0	0	0	0	0	.000
Guillen ss	4	0	0	0	0	0	.000
C.Jones 3b	3	1	1	0	0	1	.400
Jordan rf	3	0	0	0	0	1	.000
Klesko 1b	4	0	0	0	0	0	.000
Lockhart 2b	2	1	0	0	0	2	.000
Myers c	3	0	2	0	1	1	.500
A.Jones cf	3	0	0	0	0	0	.000
McGlinchy p	0	0	0	0	0	0	.000
b-Boone ph	1	0	1	0	1	0	.400
Millwood p	0	0	0	0	0	0	.000
Mulholland p	0	0	0	0	0	1	.000
a-Fabregas ph	1	0	0	0	0	0	.000
Springer p	0	0	0	0	0	0	.000
Nixon cf	2	0	1	0	0	0	.500
TOTALS	**30**	**2**	**5**	**0**	**2**	**6**	**.121**

a - Batted for Mulholland in the 5th
b - Batted for McGlinchy in the 9th

BATTING: 2B: Boone (1, Nelson). **RBI:** Myers 1 (1), Boone 1 (1). **2-out RBI:** Myers 1, Boone 1. **Runners left in scoring position, 2 out:** Jordan 1, A.Jones 1, Nixon 2. **GIDP:** Guillen, A.Jones, G.Williams. **Team LOB:** 7 **FIELDING: E:** Guillen (1). **DP:** 1 (Guillen-Klesko).

NY YANKEES	IP	H	R	ER	BB	SO	HR	ERA
Cone (W, 1-0)	7	1	0	0	5	4	0	0.00
Mendoza	1.2	3	2	2	1	0	0	10.80
Nelson	0.1	1	0	0	0	0	0	0.00

ATLANTA	IP	H	R	ER	BB	SO	HR	ERA
Millwood (L, 0-1)	2	8	5	4	2	2	0	18.00
Mulholland	3	3	2	2	1	3	0	6.00
Springer	2	1	0	0	0	1	0	0.00
McGlinchy	2	2	0	0	1	2	0	0.00

IBB: B.Williams (by Mulholland). **Pitches-strikes:** Cone 109-60, Mendoza 32-20, Nelson 8-5, Millwood 67-43, Mulholland 52-34, Springer 26-26, McGlinchy 35-24. **Ground balls-fly balls:** Cone 7-9, Mendoza 3-1, Nelson 1-0, Millwood 3-0, Mulholland 4-2, Springer 1-4, McGlinchy 3-1. **Batters faced:** Cone 26, Mendoza 8, Nelson 2, Millwood 15, Mulholland 14, Springer 7, McGlinchy 9. **UMPIRES:** hp—Rocky Roe, 1b—Steve Rippley, 2b—Derryl Cousins, 3b—Gerry Davis **T:** 3:14 **A:** 51,226

GAME 3 New York 6 Atlanta 5
Yankee Stadium 10/26/99

ATLANTA	AB	R	H	HR	RBI	BB	AVG
G.Williams lf	5	2	2	0	0	0	.154
Boone 2b	5	1	4	0	1	0	.600
a-Nixon pr	0	0	0	0	0	0	.500
Lockhart 2b	0	0	0	0	0	0	.000
C.Jones 3b	4	0	1	0	1	1	.333
Jordan rf	3	1	1	0	1	2	.100
A.Jones cf	5	1	1	0	0	0	.100
J.Hernandez dh	4	0	1	0	2	0	.200
b-Guillen ph	1	0	0	0	0	0	.000
Perez c	4	0	1	0	0	0	.167
c-Klesko ph-1b	1	0	1	0	0	0	.125
Hunter 1b	4	0	1	0	0	0	.250
d-Myers ph-c	1	0	0	0	0	0	.400
Weiss ss	4	0	1	0	0	0	.167
TOTALS	**41**	**5**	**14**	**0**	**5**	**3**	**.212**

a - Ran for Boone in the 9th
b - Batted for J.Hernandez in the 10th
c - Batted for Perez in the 10th
d - Batted for Hunter in the 10th

BATTING: 2B: Boone 3 (4, Pettitte), J.Hernandez (1, Pettitte). **3B:** G.Williams (1, Pettitte). **RBI:** Boone 1 (2), C.Jones 1 (2), Jordan 1 (1), J.Hernandez 2 (2). **Runners left in scoring position, 2 out:** G.Williams 2, A.Jones 1, J.Hernandez 2, Hunter 1. **GIDP:** Jordan. **Team LOB:** 9 **BASERUNNING: SB:** J.Hernandez (1, 3rd base off Pettitte/Girardi). **CS:** Boone (1, 3rd base off Pettitte/Girardi), Nixon (1, 2nd base off Rivera/Girardi). **FIELDING: E:** Jordan (1). **DP:** 2 (Hunter, Hunter-Weiss-Boone).

NY YANKEES	AB	R	H	HR	RBI	BB	AVG
Knoblauch 2b	4	2	2	1	2	0	.333
Jeter ss	4	0	1	0	0	0	.385
O'Neill rf	4	0	1	0	1	0	.250
B.Williams cf	4	0	0	0	0	0	.300
Davis dh	4	0	0	0	0	0	.000
Martinez 1b	4	1	1	1	1	0	.250
Brosius 3b	4	0	0	0	0	0	.385
Curtis lf	4	2	2	2	2	0	.400
Girardi c	3	1	2	0	0	0	.286
TOTALS	**35**	**6**	**9**	**4**	**6**	**0**	**.276**

BATTING: 2B: Knoblauch (1, Glavine). **HR:** Curtis 2 (2, 5th off Glavine 0 on, 2 out, 10th off Remlinger 0 on, 0 out), Martinez (1, 7th off Glavine 0 on, 1 out), Knoblauch (1, 8th off Glavine 1 on, 0 out). **RBI:** Knoblauch 2 (3), O'Neill 1 (4), Martinez 1 (3), Curtis 2 (2). **2-out RBI:** Curtis 1. **Runners left in scoring position, 2 out:** Jeter 1. **GIDP:** O'Neill. **Team LOB:** 2 **FIELDING: DP:** 1 (Jeter-Martinez).

ATLANTA	IP	H	R	ER	BB	SO	HR	ERA
Glavine	7	7	5	4	0	3	3	5.14
Rocker	2	1	0	0	0	1	0	0.00
Remlinger (L, 0-1)	0	1	1	1	0	0	1	9.00

NY YANKEES	IP	H	R	ER	BB	SO	HR	ERA
Pettitte	3.2	10	5	5	1	1	0	12.27
Grimsley	2.1	2	0	0	2	0	0	0.00
Nelson	2	0	0	0	0	2	0	0.00
Rivera (W, 1-0)	2	2	0	0	0	2	0	0.00

WP: Pettitte 1. **Pitches-strikes:** Glavine 76-47, Rocker 21-14, Remlinger 3-2, Pettitte 72-45, Grimsley 37-19, Nelson 29-18, Rivera 30-22. **Ground balls-fly balls:** Glavine 7-11, Rocker 1-3, Remlinger 0-0, Pettitte 7-2, Grimsley 2-4, Nelson 1-3, Rivera 3-0. **Batters faced:** Glavine 28, Rocker 6, Remlinger 1, Pettitte 21, Grimsley 10, Nelson 6, Rivera 7. **UMPIRES:** hp—Steve Rippley, 1b—Derryl Cousins, 2b—Gerry Davis, 3b—Jim Joyce **T:** 3:16 **A:** 56,794

GAME 4 New York 4 Atlanta 1
Yankee Stadium 10/27/99

ATLANTA	AB	R	H	HR	RBI	BB	AVG
G.Williams lf	4	0	1	0	0	0	.176
Boone 2b	3	0	1	0	1	1	.538
C.Jones 3b	4	0	0	0	0	0	.231
Jordan rf	3	0	0	0	0	1	.077
Klesko 1b	4	0	1	0	0	0	.167
Lockhart dh	4	0	1	0	0	0	.143
Perez c	2	0	0	0	0	0	.125
a-Myers ph-c	1	0	0	0	0	0	.333
A.Jones cf	3	0	0	0	0	0	.077
Weiss ss	3	1	1	0	0	0	.222
TOTALS	**31**	**1**	**5**	**0**	**1**	**2**	**.200**

a - Batted for Perez in the 8th

BATTING: RBI: Boone 1 (3). **2-out RBI:** Boone 1. **Runners left in scoring position, 2 out:** C.Jones 1. **GIDP:** Perez. **Team LOB:** 5

NY YANKEES	AB	R	H	HR	RBI	BB	AVG
Knoblauch 2b	4	1	1	0	0	0	.313
Sojo 2b	0	0	0	0	0	0	.000
Jeter ss	4	1	1	0	0	0	.353
O'Neill rf	3	0	0	0	0	1	.200
B.Williams cf	3	1	0	0	0	1	.231
Martinez 1b	3	0	1	0	2	1	.267
Strawberry dh	3	0	1	0	0	0	.333
a-Leyritz ph	1	1	1	1	1	0	1.000
Posada c	4	0	2	0	1	0	.250
Ledee lf	3	0	0	0	0	0	.200
b-Curtis ph-lf	1	0	0	0	0	0	.333
Brosius 3b	3	0	1	0	0	0	.375
TOTALS	**32**	**4**	**8**	**1**	**4**	**3**	**.270**

a - Batted for Strawberry in the 8th
b - Batted for Ledee in the 8th

BATTING: 2B: Posada (1, Mulholland). **HR:** Leyritz (1, 8th off Mulholland 0 on, 2 out). **RBI:** Martinez 2 (5), Leyritz 1 (2), Posada 1 (1). **2-out RBI:** Leyritz 1, Posada 1. **Runners left in scoring position, 2 out:** O'Neill 1, Ledee 1, Curtis 1, Brosius 1. **Team LOB:** 7 **BASERUNNING: SB:** Jeter 2 (3, 2nd base off Smoltz/Perez). **FIELDING: DP:** 1 (Brosius-Knoblauch-Martinez).

ATLANTA	IP	H	R	ER	BB	SO	HR	ERA
Smoltz (L, 0-1)	7	6	3	3	3	11	0	3.86
Mulholland	0.2	2	1	1	0	0	1	7.36
Springer	0.1	0	0	0	0	0	0	0.00

NY YANKEES	IP	H	R	ER	BB	SO	HR	ERA
Clemens (W, 1-0)	7.2	4	1	1	2	4	0	1.17
Nelson	0	1	0	0	0	0	0	0.00
Rivera (S, 2)	1.1	0	0	0	0	0	0	0.00

IBB: B.Williams (by Smoltz). **Pitches-strikes:** Smoltz 121-76, Mulholland 15-10, Springer 1-1, Clemens 103-63, Nelson 4-3, Rivera 22-14. **Ground balls-fly balls:** Smoltz 6-4, Mulholland 0-2, Springer 0-1, Clemens 16-2, Nelson 0-0, Rivera 2-2. **Batters faced:** Smoltz 30, Mulholland 4, Springer 1, Clemens 28, Nelson 1, Rivera 4. **UMPIRES:** hp—Derryl Cousins, 1b—Gerry Davis, 2b—Jim Joyce, 3b—Randy Marsh **T:** 2:58 **A:** 56,752

2000 NY YANKEES DEF. NY METS, 4-1

GAME 1 Yankees 4 Mets 3
Yankee Stadium 10/21/00

NY METS	AB	R	H	HR	RBI	BB	AVG
Perez rf	6	0	1	0	0	0	.167
Alfonzo 2b	6	0	1	0	1	0	.167
Piazza dh	5	0	1	0	0	0	.200
Zeile 1b	5	0	2	0	0	0	.400
Ventura 3b	5	0	0	0	0	0	.000
Agbayani lf	4	1	2	0	0	0	.500
McEwing lf	1	0	0	0	0	0	.000
Payton cf	5	1	1	0	0	0	.200
Pratt c	2	1	0	0	0	1	.000
Bordick ss	1	0	0	0	0	0	.000
a-Trammell ph	1	0	1	0	2	0	1.000
Abbott ss	2	0	1	0	0	0	.500
TOTALS	**43**	**3**	**10**	**0**	**3**	**1**	**.233**

a - Batted for Bordick in the 7th

BATTING: 2B: Agbayani (1, Pettitte), Zeile (1, Pettitte), Abbott (1, Rivera). **S:** Bordick. **RBI:** Alfonzo 1 (1), Trammell 2 (2). **2-out RBI:** Alfonzo 1. **Runners left in scoring position, 2 out:** Alfonzo 3, Piazza 1, Bordick 1. **Team LOB:** 8 **BASERUNNING: CS:** Piazza (1, 2nd base off Pettitte/Posada). **FIELDING: DP:** 1 (Alfonzo-Abbott-Zeile).

NY YANKEES	AB	R	H	HR	RBI	BB	AVG
Knoblauch dh	4	1	0	0	1	1	.000
Jeter ss	4	1	1	0	0	2	.250
Justice lf	4	0	1	0	2	1	.250
b-Bellinger pr-lf	0	0	0	0	0	0	.000
c-Hill ph-lf	1	0	0	0	0	0	.000
Williams cf	4	0	0	0	0	2	.000
Martinez 1b	6	1	2	0	0	0	.333
Posada c	5	0	1	0	0	1	.200
O'Neill rf	4	1	1	0	0	2	.250
Brosius 3b	3	0	1	0	0	0	.333
a-Polonia ph	1	0	1	0	0	0	1.000
Sojo 3b	2	0	0	0	0	0	.000
Vizcaino 2b	6	0	4	0	1	0	.667
TOTALS	**44**	**4**	**12**	**0**	**4**	**9**	**.273**

a - Batted for Brosius in the 9th
b - Ran for Justice in the 10th
c - Batted for Bellinger in the 11th

BATTING: 2B: Justice (1, Leiter), Posada (1, Wendell). **SF:** Knoblauch. **RBI:** Knoblauch 1 (1), Justice 2 (2), Vizcaino 1 (1). **2-out RBI:** Vizcaino 1. **Runners left in scoring position, 2 out:** Knoblauch 1, Jeter 1, Hill 2, Posada 2, Brosius 1. **GIDP:** O'Neill. **Team LOB:** 15 **BASERUNNING: CS:** Knoblauch (1, 2nd base off Leiter/Pratt). **Outfield assists:** Justice (1).

NY METS	IP	H	R	ER	BB	SO	HR	ERA
Leiter	7	5	2	2	3	7	0	2.57
J.Franco	1	1	0	0	0	0	0	0.00
Benitez	1	2	1	1	1	1	0	9.00
Cook	0	0	0	0	2	0	0	0.00
Rusch	1.2	1	0	0	2	0	0	0.00
Wendell (L, 0-1)	1	3	1	1	1	0	0	9.00

NY YANKEES	IP	H	R	ER	BB	SO	HR	ERA
Pettitte	6.2	8	3	3	1	4	0	4.05
Nelson	1.1	1	0	0	0	0	0	0.00
Rivera	2	1	0	0	0	3	0	0.00
Stanton (W, 1-0)	2	0	0	0	0	3	0	0.00

WP: Rusch 2. **IBB:** Williams (by Leiter), Posada (by Rusch), O'Neill (by Wendell). **HBP:** Pratt 2 (by Pettitte, by Rivera). **Pitches-strikes:** Leiter 126-76, J.Franco 15-9, Benitez 30-19, Cook 9-1, Rusch 31-16, Wendell 20-12, Pettitte 95-66, Nelson 19-13, Rivera 33-26, Stanton 23-18. **Ground balls-fly balls:** Leiter 8-5, J.Franco 0-3, Benitez 0-1, Cook 0-0, Rusch 2-2, Wendell 1-2, Pettitte 6-7, Nelson 0-4, Rivera 1-2, Stanton 1-2. **Batters faced:** Leiter 28, J.Franco 4, Benitez 6, Cook 2, Rusch 7, Wendell 7, Pettitte 28, Nelson 5, Rivera 8, Stanton 6. **UMPIRES:** hp—Ed Montague, 1b—Charlie Reliford, 2b—Jeff Kellogg, 3b—Tim Welke, lf—Tim McClelland, rf—Jerry Crawford **T:** 4:51 **A:** 55,913

GAME 2 Yankees 6 Mets 5
Yankee Stadium 10/22/00

NY METS	AB	R	H	HR	RBI	BB	AVG
Perez rf	4	0	0	0	0	0	.100
Alfonzo 2b	3	1	1	0	0	0	.222
Piazza c	4	1	1	1	2	0	.222
Ventura 3b	4	0	1	0	0	0	.111
Zeile 1b	4	0	2	0	0	0	.444
Agbayani lf	4	1	1	0	0	0	.375
Harris dh	4	1	0	0	0	0	.000
Payton cf	4	1	1	1	3	0	.222
Bordick ss	2	0	0	0	0	0	.000
a-Hamilton ph	1	0	0	0	0	0	.000
Abbott ss	1	0	0	0	0	0	.333
TOTALS	**35**	**5**	**7**	**2**	**5**	**0**	**.218**

a - Batted for Bordick in the 8th

BATTING: HR: Piazza (1, 9th off Nelson 1 on, 0 out), Payton (1, 9th off Rivera 2 on, 2 out). **RBI:** Piazza 2 (2), Payton 3 (3). **2-out RBI:** Payton 3. **Runners left in scoring position, 2 out:** Harris 1. **Team LOB:** 4 **FIELDING: E:** Payton (1), Bordick (1), Perez (1).

NY YANKEES	AB	R	H	HR	RBI	BB	AVG
Knoblauch dh	4	0	0	0	0	1	.000
Jeter ss	5	1	3	0	0	0	.444
Justice lf	3	1	0	0	0	1	.143
Bellinger lf	0	0	0	0	0	0	.000
Williams cf	3	1	0	0	0	2	.000
Martinez 1b	5	1	3	0	2	0	.455
Posada c	3	1	2	0	1	2	.375
O'Neill rf	4	0	3	0	1	0	.500
Brosius 3b	3	1	1	1	2	0	.333
Vizcaino 2b	4	0	0	0	0	0	.400
TOTALS	**34**	**6**	**12**	**1**	**6**	**6**	**.308**

BATTING: 2B: Martinez (1, Hampton), Jeter 2 (2, Hampton, White), O'Neill (1, Rusch). **HR:** Brosius (1, 2nd off Hampton 0 on, 0 out). **SF:** Brosius. **RBI:** Martinez 2 (2), Posada 1 (1), O'Neill 1 (1), Brosius 2 (2). **2-out RBI:** Martinez 2, Posada 1, O'Neill 1. **Runners left in scoring position, 2 out:** Justice 1, Williams 1, Posada 1, O'Neill 2, Brosius 2, Vizcaino 1. **Team LOB:** 12 **BASERUNNING: CS:** Vizcaino (1, 2nd base off Hampton/Piazza). **FIELDING: E:** Clemens (1). **PB:** Posada.

NY METS	IP	H	R	ER	BB	SO	HR	ERA
Hampton (L, 0-1)	6	8	4	4	5	4	1	6.00
Rusch	0.1	2	1	1	0	0	0	4.50
White	1.1	1	1	1	1	1	0	6.75
Cook	0.1	1	0	0	0	0	0	0.00

NY YANKEES	IP	H	R	ER	BB	SO	HR	ERA
Clemens (W, 1-0)	8	2	0	0	0	9	0	0.00
Nelson	0	3	3	3	0	0	1	20.25
Rivera	1	2	2	2	0	1	1	6.00

WP: Clemens 1. **IBB:** Posada (by Hampton), Williams (by White). **HBP:** Alfonzo (by Clemens), Justice (by Hampton). **Pitches-strikes:** Hampton 123-65, Rusch 11-8, White 23-12, Cook 4-4, Clemens 116-81, Nelson 8-7, Rivera 18-15. **Ground balls-fly balls:** Hampton 7-6, Rusch 1-0, White 2-0, Cook 1-0, Clemens 11-5, Nelson 0-0, Rivera 1-1. **Batters faced:** Hampton 31, Rusch 3, White 6, Cook 2, Clemens 28, Nelson 3, Rivera 5. **UMPIRES:** hp—Charlie Reliford, 1b—Jeff Kellogg, 2b—Tim Welke, 3b—Tim McClelland, lf—Jerry Crawford, rf—Ed Montague **T:** 3:30 **A:** 56,059

GAME 3 Mets 4 Yankees 2
Shea Stadium 10/24/00

NY YANKEES	AB	R	H	HR	RBI	BB	AVG
Vizcaino 2b	4	0	0	0	0	0	.286
c-Polonia ph	1	0	0	0	0	0	.500
Jeter ss	4	1	2	0	0	1	.462
Justice lf	3	0	1	0	1	1	.200
Williams cf	4	0	0	0	0	0	.000
Martinez 1b	3	1	1	0	0	1	.429
Posada c	4	0	0	0	0	0	.250
O'Neill rf	4	0	3	0	1	0	.583
Brosius 3b	2	0	0	0	0	0	.250
a-Hill ph	1	0	0	0	0	0	.000
Sojo 3b	0	0	0	0	0	0	.000
Hernandez p	2	0	0	0	0	0	.000
Stanton p	0	0	0	0	0	0	.000
b-Knoblauch ph	1	0	1	0	0	0	.111
TOTALS	**33**	**2**	**8**	**0**	**2**	**3**	**.288**

a - Batted for Brosius in the 8th
b - Batted for Stanton in the 9th
c - Batted for Vizcaino in the 9th

BATTING: 2B: O'Neill (2, Reed), Justice (2, Reed). **3B:** O'Neill (1, Reed). **S:** Hernandez. **RBI:** Justice 1 (3), O'Neill 1 (2). **2-out RBI:** Justice 1. **Runners left in scoring position, 2 out:** Vizcaino 2, Justice 1, Williams 2, Martinez 1, Brosius 1. **GIDP:** Posada. **Team LOB:** 10

NY METS	AB	R	H	HR	RBI	BB	AVG
Perez rf	3	0	0	0	0	1	.077
Alfonzo 2b	4	0	0	0	0	0	.154
Piazza c	4	1	1	0	0	0	.231
Ventura 3b	3	1	2	1	1	1	.250
Zeile 1b	4	1	2	0	1	0	.462
Agbayani lf	3	0	1	0	1	1	.364
b-McEwing pr-lf	0	1	0	0	0	0	.000
Payton cf	4	0	1	0	0	0	.231
Bordick ss	3	0	1	0	0	0	.167
c-Harris ph	0	0	0	0	0	0	.000
d-Trammell ph	0	0	0	0	1	0	1.000
Benitez p	0	0	0	0	0	0	.000
Reed p	1	0	1	0	0	0	1.000
a-Hamilton ph	1	0	0	0	0	0	.000
Wendell p	0	0	0	0	0	0	.000
Cook p	0	0	0	0	0	0	.000
J.Franco p	0	0	0	0	0	0	.000
e-Abbott ph-ss	1	0	0	0	0	0	.250
TOTALS	**31**	**4**	**9**	**1**	**4**	**3**	**.239**

a - Batted for Reed in the 6th
b - Ran for Agbayani in the 8th
c - Batted for Bordick in the 8th
d - Batted for Harris in the 8th e - Batted for J.Franco in the 8th

BATTING: 2B: Ventura (1, Hernandez), Piazza (1, Hernandez), Zeile (2, Hernandez), Agbayani (2, Hernandez). **HR:** Ventura (1, 2nd off Hernandez 0 on, 0 out). **S:** Reed. **SF:** Trammell. **RBI:** Ventura 1 (1), Zeile 1 (1), Agbayani 1 (1), Trammell 1 (3). **Runners left in scoring position, 2 out:** Alfonzo 1, Agbayani 1, Hamilton 2. **Team LOB:** 8 **FIELDING: DP:** 1 (Ventura-Alfonzo-Zeile).

NY YANKEES	IP	H	R	ER	BB	SO	HR	ERA
Hernandez (L, 0-1)	7.1	9	4	4	3	12	1	4.91
Stanton	0.2	0	0	0	0	1	0	0.00

NY METS	IP	H	R	ER	BB	SO	HR	ERA
Reed	6	6	2	2	1	8	0	3.00
Wendell	0.2	0	0	0	1	2	0	5.40
Cook	0.1	0	0	0	1	1	0	0.00
J.Franco (W, 1-0)	1	1	0	0	0	0	0	0.00
Benitez (S, 1)	1	1	0	0	0	1	0	4.50

HBP: Brosius (by Reed), Justice (by Cook). **Pitches-strikes:** Hernandez 134-91, Stanton 7-6, Reed 101-70, Wendell 13-8, Cook 10-3, J.Franco 9-8, Benitez 14-10. **Ground balls-fly balls:** Hernandez 2-7, Stanton 0-0, Reed 4-5, Wendell 0-0, Cook 0-0, J.Franco 1-1, Benitez 0-2. **Batters faced:** Hernandez 34, Stanton 2, Reed 26, Wendell 3, Cook 3, J.Franco 3, Benitez 4. **UMPIRES:** hp—Jeff Kellogg, 1b—Tim Welke, 2b—Tim McClelland, 3b—Jerry Crawford, lf—Ed Montague, rf—Charlie Reliford **T:** 3:39 **A:** 55,299

GAME 4 Yankees 3 Mets 2
Shea Stadium 10/25/00

NY YANKEES	AB	R	H	HR	RBI	BB	AVG
Jeter ss	5	2	2	1	1	0	.444
Sojo 2b	4	0	1	0	1	1	.167
Justice lf	5	0	0	0	0	0	.133
Bellinger lf	0	0	0	0	0	0	.000
Williams cf	4	0	0	0	0	0	.000
Martinez 1b	4	0	2	0	0	0	.444
O'Neill rf	4	1	2	0	0	0	.563
Posada c	3	0	0	0	0	1	.200
Brosius 3b	1	0	1	0	1	2	.333
Neagle p	2	0	0	0	0	0	.000
Cone p	0	0	0	0	0	0	.000
a-Canseco ph	1	0	0	0	0	0	.000
Nelson p	0	0	0	0	0	0	.000
Stanton p	0	0	0	0	0	0	.000
Rivera p	1	0	0	0	0	0	.000
TOTALS	**34**	**3**	**8**	**1**	**3**	**4**	**.276**

a - Batted for Cone in the 6th

BATTING: 3B: O'Neill (2, Jones), Jeter (1, Jones). **HR:** Jeter (1, 1st off Jones 0 on, 0 out). **SF:** Brosius. **RBI:** Jeter 1 (1), Sojo 1 (1), Brosius 1 (3). **Runners left in scoring position, 2 out:** Justice 2, Williams 2, Neagle 1, Canseco 1. **GIDP:** O'Neill. **Team LOB:** 9 **BASERUNNING: SB:** Sojo (1, 2nd base off Rusch/Piazza). **FIELDING: DP:** 1 (Nelson-Martinez).

NY METS	AB	R	H	HR	RBI	BB	AVG
Perez rf	3	1	1	0	0	0	.125
d-Abbott ph-ss	1	0	0	0	0	0	.200
Alfonzo 2b	3	0	0	0	0	1	.125
Piazza c	4	1	1	1	2	0	.235
Zeile 1b	4	0	2	0	0	0	.471
e-McEwing pr	0	0	0	0	0	0	.000
Benitez p	0	0	0	0	0	0	.000
Ventura 3b	4	0	0	0	0	0	.188
Agbayani lf	3	0	0	0	0	1	.286
Payton cf	4	0	2	0	0	0	.294
Bordick ss	2	0	0	0	0	0	.125
a-Harris ph	0	0	0	0	0	1	.000
J.Franco p	0	0	0	0	0	0	.000
M.Franco 1b	1	0	0	0	0	0	.000
Jones p	2	0	0	0	0	0	.000
Rusch p	0	0	0	0	0	0	.000
b-Hamilton ph	0	0	0	0	0	0	.000
c-Trammell ph-rf	1	0	0	0	0	0	.500
TOTALS	**32**	**2**	**6**	**1**	**2**	**3**	**.227**

a - Batted for Bordick in the 7th
b - Batted for Rusch in the 7th
c - Batted for Hamilton in the 7th
d - Batted for Perez in the 7th e - Ran for Zeile in the 8th

BATTING: HR: Piazza (2, 3th off Neagle 1 on, 1 out). **RBI:** Piazza 2 (4). **Runners left in scoring position, 2 out:** Jones 1. **Team LOB:** 6 **FIELDING: E:** Trammell (1). **DP:** 1 (Zeile-Abbott-J.Franco).

NY YANKEES	IP	H	R	ER	BB	SO	HR	ERA
Neagle	4.2	4	2	2	2	3	1	3.86
Cone	0.1	0	0	0	0	0	0	0.00
Nelson (W, 1-0)	1.1	1	0	0	1	1	0	10.13
Stanton	0.2	0	0	0	0	2	0	0.00
Rivera (S, 1)	2	1	0	0	0	2	0	3.60

NY METS	IP	H	R	ER	BB	SO	HR	ERA
Jones (L, 0-1)	5	4	3	3	3	3	1	5.40
Rusch	2	3	0	0	0	2	0	2.25
J.Franco	1	1	0	0	0	1	0	0.00
Benitez	1	0	0	0	1	0	0	3.00

IBB: Posada (by Jones), Brosius (by Jones). **Pitches-strikes:** Neagle 73-45, Cone 5-4, Nelson 23-12, Stanton 7-6, Rivera 28-20, Jones 82-46, Rusch 37-23, J.Franco 8-6, Benitez 23-14. **Ground balls-fly balls:** Neagle 4-7, Cone 0-1, Nelson 0-2, Stanton 0-0, Rivera 1-3, Jones 6-5, Rusch 2-2, J.Franco 1-0, Benitez 1-3. **Batters faced:** Neagle 20, Cone 1, Nelson 5, Stanton 2, Rivera 7, Jones 22, Rusch 9, J.Franco 3, Benitez 5. **UMPIRES:** hp—Tim Welke, 1b—Tim McClelland, 2b—Jerry Crawford, 3b—Ed Montague, lf—Charlie Reliford, rf—Jeff Kellogg **T:** 3:20 **A:** 55,290

GAME 5 Yankees 4 Mets 2
Shea Stadium 10/26/00

NY YANKEES	AB	R	H	HR	RBI	BB	AVG
Vizcaino 2b	3	0	0	0	0	0	.235
a-Knoblauch ph	1	0	0	0	0	0	.100
Stanton p	0	0	0	0	0	0	.000
b-Hill ph	1	0	0	0	0	0	.000
Rivera p	0	0	0	0	0	0	.000
Jeter ss	4	1	1	1	1	0	.409
Justice lf	4	0	1	0	0	0	.158
Bellinger lf	0	0	0	0	0	0	.000
Williams cf	3	1	2	1	1	1	.111
Martinez 1b	4	0	0	0	0	0	.364
O'Neill rf	3	0	0	0	0	1	.474
Posada c	3	1	1	0	0	1	.222
Brosius 3b	4	1	1	0	0	0	.308
Pettitte p	3	0	0	0	0	0	.000
Sojo 2b	1	0	1	0	1	0	.286
TOTALS	**34**	**4**	**7**	**2**	**3**	**3**	**.263**

a - Batted for Vizcaino in the 8th
b - Batted for Stanton in the 9th

BATTING: HR: Williams (1, 2nd off Leiter 0 on, 0 out), Jeter (2, 6th off Leiter 0 on, 1 out). **SF:** Brosius. **RBI:** Jeter 1 (2), Williams 1 (1), Sojo 1 (2). **2-out RBI:** Sojo 1. **Runners left in scoring position, 2 out:** Hill 1, Pettitte 1. **Team LOB:** 6

NY METS	AB	R	H	HR	RBI	BB	AVG
Agbayani lf	4	0	1	0	1	1	.278
Alfonzo 2b	5	0	1	0	0	0	.143
Piazza c	5	0	2	0	0	0	.273
Zeile 1b	3	0	0	0	0	1	.400
Ventura 3b	4	0	0	0	0	0	.150
Trammell rf	3	1	1	0	0	1	.400
Perez rf	0	0	0	0	0	0	.125
Payton cf	4	1	2	0	0	0	.333
Abbott ss	3	0	1	0	0	1	.250
Leiter p	2	0	0	0	0	0	.000
J.Franco p	0	0	0	0	0	0	.000
a-Hamilton ph	1	0	0	0	0	0	.000
TOTALS	**34**	**2**	**8**	**0**	**1**	**4**	**.229**

a - Batted for J.Franco in the 9th

BATTING: 2B: Piazza (2, Pettitte). **S:** Leiter. **RBI:** Agbayani 1 (2). **2-out RBI:** Agbayani 1. **Runners left in scoring position, 2 out:** Agbayani 2, Alfonzo 1, Piazza 1, Ventura 1, Leiter 1. **Team LOB:** 10 **FIELDING: E:** Payton (2).

NY YANKEES	IP	H	R	ER	BB	SO	HR	ERA
Pettitte	7	8	2	0	3	5	0	1.98
Stanton (W, 2-0)	1	0	0	0	0	1	0	0.00
Rivera (S, 2)	1	0	0	0	1	1	0	3.00

NY METS	IP	H	R	ER	BB	SO	HR	ERA
Leiter (L, 0-1)	8.2	7	4	3	3	9	2	2.87
J.Franco	0.1	0	0	0	0	0	0	0.00

IBB: Zeile (by Pettitte). **Pitches-strikes:** Pettitte 129-80, Stanton 14-9, Rivera 13-8, Leiter 142-84, J.Franco 6-3. **Ground balls-fly balls:** Pettitte 12-3, Stanton 1-1, Rivera 0-2, Leiter 9-8, J.Franco 0-1. **Batters faced:** Pettitte 32, Stanton 3, Rivera 4, Leiter 36, J.Franco 1. **UMPIRES:** hp—Tim McClelland, 1b—Jerry Crawford, 2b—Ed Montague, 3b—Charlie Reliford, lf—Jeff Kellogg, rf—Tim Welke **T:** 3:32 **A:** 55,292

2001 ARIZONA DEF. NY YANKEES, 4-3

GAME 1 Arizona 9 New York 1
Bank One Ballpark 10/27/01

NY YANKEES	AB	R	H	HR	RBI	BB	AVG
Knoblauch lf	4	0	0	0	0	0	.000
Stanton p	0	0	0	0	0	0	.000
Jeter ss	3	1	0	0	0	0	.000
Justice rf-lf	3	0	0	0	0	0	.000
c-Spencer ph	1	0	0	0	0	0	.000
B.Williams cf	4	0	1	0	1	0	.250
Martinez 1b	3	0	0	0	0	1	.000
Posada c	3	0	1	0	0	1	.333
Soriano 2b	3	0	0	0	0	0	.000
Brosius 3b	3	0	1	0	0	0	.333
Mussina p	1	0	0	0	0	0	.000
Choate p	0	0	0	0	0	0	.000
a-Wilson ph	1	0	0	0	0	0	.000
Hitchcock p	0	0	0	0	0	0	.000
b-O'Neill ph-rf	1	0	0	0	0	0	.000
TOTALS	**30**	**1**	**3**	**0**	**1**	**2**	**.100**

a - Batted for Choate in the 5th
b - Batted for Hitchcock in the 8th
c - Batted for Justice in the 9th

BATTING: 2B: B.Williams (1, Schilling), Brosius (1, Schilling). **RBI:** B.Williams 1 (1). **2-out RBI:** B.Williams 1. **Runners left in scoring position, 2 out:** Martinez 1, Mussina 1. **Team LOB:** 5 **FIELDING: E:** B.Williams (1), Brosius (1).

ARIZONA	AB	R	H	HR	RBI	BB	AVG
Womack ss	4	1	0	0	0	0	.000
Counsell 2b	4	1	1	1	1	0	.250
Gonzalez lf	5	2	2	1	2	0	.400
Sanders rf	3	2	2	0	0	1	.667
Finley cf	4	2	1	0	1	0	.250
M.Williams 3b	3	1	1	0	1	0	.333
Grace 1b	3	0	1	0	2	1	.333
Miller c	4	0	2	0	1	0	.500
Schilling p	3	0	0	0	0	0	.000
a-Bell ph	1	0	0	0	0	0	.000
Morgan p	0	0	0	0	0	0	.000
Swindell p	0	0	0	0	0	0	.000
TOTALS	**34**	**9**	**10**	**2**	**8**	**2**	**.294**

a - Batted for Schilling in the 7th

BATTING: 2B: Miller (1, Mussina), Gonzalez (1, Choate), Grace (1, Choate). **HR:** Counsell (1, 1st off Mussina 0 on, 1 out), Gonzalez (1, 3th off Mussina 1 on, 1 out). **S:** Counsell. **SF:** M.Williams. **RBI:** Counsell 1 (1), Gonzalez 2 (2), Finley 1 (1), M.Williams 1 (1), Grace 2 (2), Miller 1 (1). **2-out RBI:** Finley 1, Grace 2, Miller 1. **Runners left in scoring position, 2 out:** Miller 1, Schilling 2. **Team LOB:** 6

NY YANKEES	IP	H	R	ER	BB	SO	HR	ERA
Mussina (L, 0-1)	3	6	5	3	1	4	2	9.00
Choate	1	3	4	1	1	1	0	9.00
Hitchcock	3	1	0	0	0	6	0	0.00
Stanton	1	0	0	0	0	0	0	0.00

ARIZONA	IP	H	R	ER	BB	SO	HR	ERA
Schilling (W, 1-0)	7	3	1	1	1	8	0	1.29
Morgan	1	0	0	0	0	0	0	0.00
Swindell	1	0	0	0	1	1	0	0.00

IBB: Grace (by Mussina), Sanders (by Choate). **HBP:** Jeter (by Schilling), Womack (by Mussina). **Pitches-strikes:** Mussina 67-47, Choate 22-12, Hitchcock 39-27, Stanton 6-4, Schilling 101-68, Morgan 10-6, Swindell 14-8. **Ground balls-fly balls:** Mussina 2-2, Choate 2-1, Hitchcock 2-1, Stanton 2-1, Schilling 6-7, Morgan 1-2, Swindell 0-2. **Batters faced:** Mussina 18, Choate 8, Hitchcock 10, Stanton 3, Schilling 26, Morgan 3, Swindell 4. **UMPIRES:** hp—Steve Rippley, 1b—Mark Hirschbeck, 2b—Dale Scott, 3b—Ed Rapuano, lf—Jim Joyce, rf—Dana DeMuth **T:** 2:44 **A:** 49,646

GAME 2 Arizona 4 New York 0
Bank One Ballpark 10/28/01

NY YANKEES	AB	R	H	HR	RBI	BB	AVG
Knoblauch lf	4	0	0	0	0	0	.000
Velarde 1b	3	0	0	0	0	1	.000
Jeter ss	4	0	0	0	0	0	.000
B.Williams cf	3	0	0	0	0	0	.143
Posada c	3	0	1	0	0	0	.333
Spencer rf	3	0	1	0	0	0	.250
Soriano 2b	3	0	1	0	0	0	.167
Brosius 3b	3	0	0	0	0	0	.167
Pettitte p	2	0	0	0	0	0	.000
a-Sojo ph	1	0	0	0	0	0	.000
Stanton p	0	0	0	0	0	0	.000
TOTALS	**29**	**0**	**3**	**0**	**0**	**1**	**.102**

a - Batted for Pettitte in the 8th

BATTING: GIDP: Sojo. **Team LOB:** 3 **FIELDING: DP:** 1 (Brosius-Soriano-Velarde).

ARIZONA	AB	R	H	HR	RBI	BB	AVG
Womack ss	4	0	0	0	0	0	.000
Counsell 2b	4	0	0	0	0	0	.125
Gonzalez lf	2	0	0	0	0	0	.286
Sanders rf	3	2	1	0	0	0	.500
Bautista cf	3	1	2	0	1	0	.667
M.Williams 3b	3	1	2	1	3	0	.500
Grace 1b	3	0	0	0	0	0	.167
Miller c	3	0	0	0	0	0	.286
Finley 3b	0	0	0	0	0	0	.250
Johnson p	3	0	0	0	0	0	.000
TOTALS	**28**	**4**	**5**	**1**	**4**	**0**	**.242**

BATTING: 2B: Bautista (1, Pettitte). **HR:** M.Williams (1, 7th off Pettitte 2 on, 1 out). **RBI:** Bautista 1 (1), M.Williams 3 (4). **GIDP:** Miller. **Team LOB:** 1 **FIELDING: DP:** 1 (Finley-Counsell-Grace).

NY YANKEES	IP	H	R	ER	BB	SO	HR	ERA
Pettitte (L, 0-1)	7	5	4	4	0	8	1	5.14
Stanton	1	0	0	0	0	0	0	0.00

ARIZONA	IP	H	R	ER	BB	SO	HR	ERA
Johnson (W, 1-0)	9	3	0	0	1	11	0	0.00

HBP: Gonzalez (by Pettitte). **Pitches-strikes:** Pettitte 79-64, Stanton 12-7, Johnson 110-76. **Ground balls-fly balls:** Pettitte 10-2, Stanton 2-1, Johnson 10-5. **Batters faced:** Pettitte 26, Stanton 3, Johnson 30. **UMPIRES:** hp—Mark Hirschbeck, 1b—Dale Scott, 2b—Ed Rapuano, 3b—Jim Joyce **T:** 2:35 **A:** 49,646

GAME 3 New York 2 Arizona 1
Yankee Stadium 10/30/01

ARIZONA	AB	R	H	HR	RBI	BB	AVG
Counsell 2b	4	0	0	0	0	0	.083
Finley cf	2	1	0	0	0	2	.167
Gonzalez lf	4	0	1	0	0	0	.273
Sanders rf	3	0	0	0	0	0	.333
Durazo dh	3	0	2	0	0	1	.667
M.Williams 3b	3	0	0	0	1	0	.333
Grace 1b	3	0	0	0	0	0	.111
Miller c	3	0	0	0	0	0	.200
Womack ss	3	0	0	0	0	0	.000
TOTALS	**28**	**1**	**3**	**0**	**1**	**3**	**.200**

BATTING: SF: M.Williams. **RBI:** M.Williams 1 (5). **Runners left in scoring position, 2 out:** M.Williams 1, Grace 1. **Team LOB:** 5 **BASERUNNING: SB:** Sanders (1, 2nd base off Clemens/Posada). **CS:** Finley (1, 2nd base off Clemens/Posada). **FIELDING: E:** Womack (1), Miller (1), Grace (1). **DP:** 1 (Counsell-Grace).

NY YANKEES	AB	R	H	HR	RBI	BB	AVG
Knoblauch dh	4	0	0	0	0	0	.000
Jeter ss	4	0	1	0	0	0	.091
O'Neill rf	4	0	2	0	0	0	.400
b-Bellinger pr-lf	0	0	0	0	0	0	.000
B.Williams cf	3	1	1	0	0	1	.200
Martinez 1b	4	0	0	0	0	0	.000
Posada c	3	1	1	1	1	1	.333
Spencer lf	1	0	0	0	0	1	.200
a-Justice ph-lf-rf	2	0	0	0	0	0	.000
Brosius 3b	3	0	1	0	1	0	.222
Soriano 2b	3	0	1	0	0	0	.222
TOTALS	**31**	**2**	**7**	**1**	**2**	**3**	**.144**

a - Batted for Spencer in the 6th
b - Ran for O'Neill in the 7th

BATTING: HR: Posada (1, 2nd off Anderson 0 on, 0 out). **RBI:** Posada 1 (1), Brosius 1 (1). **2-out RBI:** Brosius 1. **Runners left in scoring position, 2 out:** B.Williams 1, Martinez 1, Soriano 3. **GIDP:** O'Neill. **Team LOB:** 8 **BASERUNNING: SB:** O'Neill (1, 2nd base off Anderson/Miller). **FIELDING: E:** Soriano (1). **DP:** 1 (Posada-Jeter).

ARIZONA	IP	H	R	ER	BB	SO	HR	ERA
Anderson (L, 0-1)	5.1	5	2	2	3	1	1	3.38
Morgan	1.1	1	0	0	0	1	0	0.00
Swindell	1.1	1	0	0	0	1	0	0.00

NY YANKEES	IP	H	R	ER	BB	SO	HR	ERA
Clemens (W, 1-0)	7	3	1	1	3	9	0	1.29
Rivera (S, 1)	2	0	0	0	0	4	0	0.00

WP: Anderson 1, Morgan 1, Swindell 1. **HBP:** Sanders (by Clemens). **Pitches-strikes:** Anderson 107-70, Morgan 17-10, Swindell 28-18, Clemens 115-72, Rivera 29-21. **Ground balls-fly balls:** Anderson 9-6, Morgan 3-0, Swindell 0-3, Clemens 6-4, Rivera 2-0. **Batters faced:** Anderson 24, Morgan 5, Swindell 5, Clemens 27, Rivera 6. **UMPIRES:** hp—Dale Scott, 1b—Ed Rapuano, 2b—Jim Joyce, 3b—Dana DeMuth, lf—Steve Rippley, rf—Mark Hirschbeck **T:** 3:26 **A:** 55,820

GAME 4 New York 4 Arizona 3
Yankee Stadium 10/31/01

ARIZONA	AB	R	H	HR	RBI	BB	AVG
Womack ss	4	0	2	0	0	1	.133
Counsell 2b	2	0	0	0	0	0	.071
Gonzalez lf	3	1	1	0	0	1	.286
Durazo dh	3	0	1	0	1	1	.500
a-Cummings pr	0	1	0	0	0	0	.000
b-Bautista ph	1	0	0	0	0	0	.500
M.Williams 3b	4	0	0	0	1	0	.231
Finley cf	4	0	1	0	0	0	.200
Sanders rf	4	0	0	0	0	0	.231
Grace 1b	3	1	1	1	1	1	.167
Miller c	3	0	0	0	0	0	.154
TOTALS	**31**	**3**	**6**	**1**	**3**	**4**	**.198**

a - Ran for Durazo in the 8th
b - Batted for Cummings in the 10th

BATTING: 2B: Womack (1, Hernandez), Durazo (1, Stanton). **HR:** Grace (1, 4th off Hernandez 0 on, 2 out). **S:** Counsell, Counsell, Counsell. **RBI:** Durazo 1 (1), M.Williams 1 (6), Grace 1 (3). **2-out RBI:** Grace 1. **Runners left in scoring position, 2 out:** M.Williams 1, Finley 2. **GIDP:** Sanders, Womack. **Team LOB:** 7 **FIELDING: DP:** 1 (Counsell-Womack-Grace).

NY YANKEES	AB	R	H	HR	RBI	BB	AVG
Jeter ss	5	1	1	1	1	0	.125
O'Neill rf	4	1	1	0	0	0	.333
B.Williams cf	4	0	1	0	0	0	.214
Martinez 1b	3	1	1	1	2	1	.100
Posada c	3	0	0	0	0	1	.250
Justice dh	4	0	1	0	0	0	.111
Spencer lf	4	1	1	1	1	0	.222
Brosius 3b	4	0	1	0	0	0	.231
Soriano 2b	4	0	0	0	0	0	.154
TOTALS	**35**	**4**	**7**	**3**	**4**	**2**	**.160**

BATTING: 2B: Brosius (2, Schilling). **HR:** Spencer (1, 3th off Schilling 0 on, 0 out), Martinez (1, 9th off Kim 1 on, 2 out), Jeter (1, 10th off Kim 0 on, 2 out). **RBI:** Jeter 1 (1), Martinez 2 (2), Spencer 1 (1). **2-out RBI:** Jeter 1, Martinez 2. **Runners left in scoring position, 2 out:** O'Neill 1, Justice 1, Spencer 1. **GIDP:** Posada. **Team LOB:** 4 **FIELDING: Outfield assists:** Spencer (1). **DP:** 3 (Jeter-Soriano-Martinez, Spencer-Posada, Soriano-Jeter-Martinez).

ARIZONA	IP	H	R	ER	BB	SO	HR	ERA
Schilling	7	3	1	1	1	9	1	1.29
Kim (L, 0-1)	2.2	4	3	3	1	5	2	10.13

NY YANKEES	IP	H	R	ER	BB	SO	HR	ERA
Hernandez	6.1	4	1	1	4	5	1	1.42
Stanton	1	2	2	2	0	0	0	6.00
Mendoza	1.2	0	0	0	0	1	0	0.00
Rivera (W, 1-0)	1	0	0	0	0	0	0	0.00

HBP: Gonzalez (by Hernandez), Miller (by Hernandez). **Pitches-strikes:** Schilling 88-63, Kim 61-36, Hernandez 96-52, Stanton 19-12, Mendoza 24-15, Rivera 13-9. **Ground balls-fly balls:** Schilling 8-3, Kim 1-2, Hernandez 4-5, Stanton 1-1, Mendoza 4-1, Rivera 3-0. **Batters faced:** Schilling 24, Kim 13, Hernandez 27, Stanton 4, Mendoza 6, Rivera 3. **UMPIRES:** hp—Ed Rapuano, 1b—Jim Joyce, 2b—Dana DeMuth, 3b—Steve Rippley, lf—Mark Hirschbeck, rf—Dale Scott **T:** 3:31 **A:** 55,863

GAME 5 New York 3 Arizona 2
Yankee Stadium 11/01/01

ARIZONA	AB	R	H	HR	RBI	BB	AVG
Womack ss	6	0	1	0	0	0	.143
Counsell 2b	6	0	0	0	0	0	.050
Gonzalez lf	4	0	0	0	0	0	.222
Bautista lf	1	0	1	0	0	0	.600
Durazo dh	4	0	1	0	0	1	.400
M.Williams 3b	4	0	0	0	0	0	.176
Finley cf	4	1	3	1	1	1	.357
Sanders rf	5	0	0	0	0	0	.167
Grace 1b	3	0	0	0	0	2	.133
Barajas c	5	1	2	1	1	0	.400
TOTALS	**42**	**2**	**8**	**2**	**2**	**4**	**.196**

BATTING: HR: Finley (1, 5th off Mussina 0 on, 0 out), Barajas (1, 5th off Mussina 0 on, 2 out). **S:** M.Williams. **RBI:** Finley 1 (2), Barajas 1 (1). **2-out RBI:** Barajas 1. **Runners left in scoring position, 2 out:** Counsell 1, M.Williams 1, Grace 2, Barajas 1. **GIDP:** Grace. **Team LOB:** 9 **BASERUNNING: SB:** Womack (1, 2nd base off Mussina/Posada). **FIELDING: DP:** 2 (Womack-Counsell-Grace, Counsell-Grace).

NY YANKEES	AB	R	H	HR	RBI	BB	AVG
Jeter ss	5	0	1	0	0	0	.143
O'Neill rf	3	0	0	0	0	2	.250
B.Williams cf	4	0	1	0	0	1	.222
Martinez 1b	5	0	1	0	0	0	.133
Posada c	5	1	1	0	0	0	.235
Spencer lf	4	0	1	0	0	1	.231
Justice dh	2	0	0	0	0	1	.091
a-Knoblauch pr	2	1	1	0	0	0	.071
Brosius 3b	4	1	1	1	2	0	.235
Soriano 2b	5	0	2	0	1	0	.222
TOTALS	**39**	**3**	**9**	**1**	**3**	**5**	**.177**

a - Ran for Justice in the 7th

BATTING: 2B: Posada (1, Kim). **HR:** Brosius (1, 9th off Kim 1 on, 2 out). **S:** Brosius. **RBI:** Brosius 2 (3), Soriano 1 (1). **2-out RBI:** Brosius 2. **Runners left in scoring position, 2 out:** Martinez 1, Posada 1, Brosius 1, Soriano 1. **GIDP:** Posada, O'Neill. **Team LOB:** 8 **BASERUNNING: CS:** Soriano (1, 2nd base off Batista/Barajas). **FIELDING: E:** Posada (1). **DP:** 1 (Soriano-Jeter-Martinez).

ARIZONA	IP	H	R	ER	BB	SO	HR	ERA
Batista	7.2	5	0	0	5	6	0	0.00
Swindell	0.1	0	0	0	0	0	0	0.00
Kim	0.2	2	2	2	0	1	1	13.50
Morgan	2.1	0	0	0	0	0	0	0.00
Lopez (L, 0-1)	0.1	2	1	1	0	0	0	27.00

NY YANKEES	IP	H	R	ER	BB	SO	HR	ERA
Mussina	8	5	2	2	3	10	2	4.09
Mendoza	1	1	0	0	0	0	0	0.00
Rivera	2	2	0	0	1	0	0	0.00
Hitchcock (W, 1-0)	1	0	0	0	0	0	0	0.00

WP: Batista 1, Mussina 1. **IBB:** Grace (by Mussina), Durazo (by Mussina), Finley (by Rivera). **Pitches-strikes:** Batista 126-71, Swindell 4-4, Kim 15-9, Morgan 29-17, Lopez 7-5, Mussina 125-82, Mendoza 11-8, Rivera 23-15, Hitchcock 10-9. **Ground balls-fly balls:** Batista 9-5, Swindell 0-1, Kim 1-0, Morgan 3-4, Lopez 0-0, Mussina 6-8, Mendoza 2-0, Rivera 3-2, Hitchcock 1-2. **Batters faced:** Batista 30, Swindell 1, Kim 4, Morgan 7, Lopez 3, Mussina 32, Mendoza 3, Rivera 9, Hitchcock 3. **UMPIRES:** hp—Jim Joyce, 1b—Dana DeMuth, 2b—Steve Rippley, 3b—Mark Hirschbeck, lf—Dale Scott, rf—Ed Rapuano **T:** 4:15 **A:** 56,018

GAME 6 Arizona 15 New York 2
Bank One Ballpark 11/03/01

NY YANKEES	AB	R	H	HR	RBI	BB	AVG
Knoblauch lf	3	0	0	0	0	1	.059
Stanton p	0	0	0	0	0	0	.000
Jeter ss	2	0	0	0	0	0	.130
Wilson ss	2	0	0	0	0	0	.000
B.Williams cf	2	1	1	0	0	2	.250
Posada c	2	0	0	0	0	0	.211
Greene c	2	1	1	0	0	0	.500
Spencer rf	4	0	1	0	1	0	.235
Martinez 1b	2	0	1	0	0	0	.176
Sojo 1b	2	0	1	0	1	0	.333
Soriano 2b	4	0	1	0	0	0	.227
Brosius 3b	4	0	0	0	0	0	.190
Pettitte p	1	0	1	0	0	0	.333
Witasick p	0	0	0	0	0	0	.000
Choate p	1	0	0	0	0	0	.000
a-Bellinger ph-lf	2	0	0	0	0	0	.000
TOTALS	**33**	**2**	**7**	**0**	**2**	**3**	**.183**

a - Batted for Choate in the 7th

BATTING: 2B: Greene (1, Johnson). **RBI:** Spencer 1 (2), Sojo 1 (1). **Runners left in scoring position, 2 out:** Posada 2, Brosius 1. **GIDP:** Greene. **Team LOB:** 7 **FIELDING: E:** Soriano (2). **Outfield assists:** Knoblauch (1). **DP:** 1 (Soriano-Martinez-Jeter).

ARIZONA	AB	R	H	HR	RBI	BB	AVG
Womack ss	6	2	3	0	2	0	.222
Bautista cf	4	0	3	0	5	0	.667
b-Finley ph-cf	1	0	0	0	0	1	.333
Gonzalez lf	4	1	2	0	2	0	.273
a-Dellucci pr-lf	2	0	1	0	0	0	.500
Colbrunn 1b	5	2	2	0	1	1	.400
M.Williams 3b	5	1	3	0	1	0	.273
Sanders rf	5	2	4	0	1	0	.304
Bell 2b	5	2	1	0	1	0	.167
Miller c	4	3	2	0	1	1	.235
Barajas c	0	0	0	0	0	0	.400
Johnson p	4	2	1	0	1	0	.143
c-Durazo ph	1	0	0	0	0	0	.364
Witt p	0	0	0	0	0	0	.000
Brohawn p	0	0	0	0	0	0	.000
TOTALS	**46**	**15**	**22**	**0**	**15**	**3**	**.258**

a - Ran for Gonzalez in the 4th
b - Batted for Bautista in the 6th
c - Batted for Johnson in the 7th

BATTING: 2B: Womack (2, Pettitte), Sanders (1, Pettitte), M.Williams 2 (2, Pettitte, Witasick), Gonzalez (2, Witasick), Miller (2, Witasick). **RBI:** Womack 2 (2), Bautista 5 (6), Gonzalez 2 (4), Colbrunn 1 (1), M.Williams 1 (7), Sanders 1 (1), Bell 1 (1), Miller 1 (2), Johnson 1 (1). **2-out RBI:** Womack 2, Bautista 1, Colbrunn 1, M.Williams 1. **Runners left in scoring position, 2 out:** Gonzalez 1, M.Williams 2, Sanders 1. **GIDP:** Gonzalez. **Team LOB:** 10 **FIELDING: DP:** 1 (M.Williams-Bell-Colbrunn).

NY YANKEES	IP	H	R	ER	BB	SO	HR	ERA
Pettitte (L, 0-2)	2	7	6	6	2	1	0	10.00
Witasick	1.1	10	9	8	0	4	0	54.00
Choate	2.2	4	0	0	0	1	0	2.45
Stanton	2	1	0	0	1	3	0	3.60

ARIZONA	IP	H	R	ER	BB	SO	HR	ERA
Johnson (W, 2-0)	7	6	2	2	2	7	0	1.13
Witt	1	0	0	0	1	1	0	0.00
Brohawn	1	1	0	0	0	1	0	0.00

WP: Witasick 1. **IBB:** Miller (by Pettitte). **Pitches-strikes:** Pettitte 62-39, Witasick 55-40, Choate 37-30, Stanton 33-19, Johnson 104-66, Witt 16-10, Brohawn 14-11. **Ground balls-fly balls:** Pettitte 4-0, Witasick 0-0, Choate 4-4, Stanton 1-2, Johnson 2-12, Witt 1-0, Brohawn 1-1. **Batters faced:** Pettitte 14, Witasick 14, Choate 13, Stanton 8, Johnson 29, Witt 3, Brohawn 4. **UMPIRES:** hp—Dana DeMuth, 1b—Steve Rippley, 2b—Mark Hirschbeck, 3b—Dale Scott, lf—Ed Rapuano, rf—Jim Joyce **T:** 3:33 **A:** 49,707

GAME 7 Arizona 3 New York 2
Bank One Ballpark 11/04/01

NY YANKEES	AB	R	H	HR	RBI	BB	AVG
Jeter ss	4	1	1	0	0	0	.148
O'Neill rf	3	0	2	0	0	0	.333
b-Knoblauch ph-lf	1	0	0	0	0	0	.056
B.Williams cf	4	0	0	0	0	0	.208
Martinez 1b	4	0	1	0	1	0	.190
Posada c	4	0	0	0	0	0	.174
Spencer lf-rf	3	0	0	0	0	0	.200
Soriano 2b	3	1	1	1	1	0	.240
Brosius 3b	3	0	0	0	0	0	.167
Clemens p	2	0	0	0	0	0	.000
Stanton p	0	0	0	0	0	0	.000
a-Justice ph	1	0	1	0	0	0	.167
Rivera p	0	0	0	0	0	0	.000
TOTALS	**32**	**2**	**6**	**1**	**2**	**0**	**.183**

a - Batted for Stanton in the 8th
b - Batted for O'Neill in the 8th

BATTING: 2B: O'Neill (1, Schilling). **HR:** Soriano (1, 8th off Schilling 0 on, 0 out). **RBI:** Martinez 1 (3), Soriano 1 (2). **Runners left in scoring position, 2 out:** B.Williams 1, Spencer 1. **Team LOB:** 3 **FIELDING: E:** Soriano (3), Rivera (1). **Outfield assists:** B.Williams (1).

ARIZONA	AB	R	H	HR	RBI	BB	AVG
Womack ss	5	0	2	0	1	0	.250
Counsell 2b	4	0	1	0	0	0	.083
Gonzalez lf	5	0	1	0	1	0	.259
M.Williams 3b	4	0	1	0	0	0	.269
Finley cf	4	1	2	0	0	0	.368
Bautista rf	3	0	1	0	1	1	.583
Grace 1b	4	0	3	0	0	0	.263
a-Dellucci pr	0	0	0	0	0	0	.500
Miller c	4	0	0	0	0	0	.190
c-Cummings pr	0	1	0	0	0	0	.000
Schilling p	3	0	0	0	0	0	.000
Batista p	0	0	0	0	0	0	.000
Johnson p	0	0	0	0	0	0	.143
b-Bell ph	1	1	0	0	0	0	.143
TOTALS	**37**	**3**	**11**	**0**	**3**	**1**	**.264**

a - Ran for Grace in the 9th
b - Batted for Johnson in the 9th
c - Ran for Miller in the 9th

BATTING: 2B: Bautista (2, Clemens), Womack (3, Rivera). **RBI:** Womack 1 (3), Gonzalez 1 (5), Bautista 1 (7). **Runners left in scoring position, 2 out:** M.Williams 1, Finley 1, Miller 1, Schilling 1. **Team LOB:** 11 **BASERUNNING: CS:** Womack (1, 2nd base off Stanton/Posada). **Outfield assists:** Bautista (1).

NY YANKEES	IP	H	R	ER	BB	SO	HR	ERA
Clemens	6.1	7	1	1	1	10	0	1.35
Stanton	0.2	0	0	0	0	0	0	3.18
Rivera (L, 1-1)	1.1	4	2	1	0	3	0	1.42

ARIZONA	IP	H	R	ER	BB	SO	HR	ERA
Schilling	7.1	6	2	2	0	9	1	1.69
Batista	0.1	0	0	0	0	0	0	0.00
Johnson (W, 3-0)	1.1	0	0	0	0	1	0	1.04

HBP: Counsell (by Rivera). **Pitches-strikes:** Clemens 114-75, Stanton 4-3, Rivera 27-21, Schilling 103-75, Batista 1-1, Johnson 17-12. **Ground balls-fly balls:** Clemens 8-2, Stanton 0-1, Rivera 2-0, Schilling 1-11, Batista 1-0, Johnson 1-2. **Batters faced:** Clemens 28, Stanton 1, Rivera 10, Schilling 27, Batista 1, Johnson 4. **UMPIRES:** hp—Steve Rippley, 1b—Mark Hirschbeck, 2b—Dale Scott, 3b—Ed Rapuano, lf—Jim Joyce, rf—Dana DeMuth **T:** 3:20 **A:** 49,589

2002 ANAHEIM DEF. SAN FRANCISCO, 4-3

GAME 1 San Francisco 4 Anaheim 3
Edison Field 10/19/02

SAN FRANCISCO	AB	R	H	HR	RBI	BB	AVG
Lofton cf	3	0	0	0	0	0	.000
Aurilia ss	4	0	0	0	0	0	.000
Kent 2b	4	0	0	0	0	0	.000
Bonds lf	3	1	1	1	1	1	.333
Santiago c	4	0	1	0	0	0	.250
Sanders rf	3	2	2	1	1	1	.667
Snow 1b	3	1	1	1	2	1	.333
Bell 3b	4	0	0	0	0	0	.000
Shinjo dh	3	0	1	0	0	0	.333
a-Goodwin ph	1	0	0	0	0	0	.000
TOTALS	**32**	**4**	**6**	**3**	**4**	**3**	**.188**

a - Batted for Shinjo in the 9th

BATTING: HR: Bonds (1, 2nd off Washburn 0 on, 0 out), Sanders (1, 2nd off Washburn 0 on, 1 out), Snow (1, 6th off Washburn 1 on, 2 out). **S:** Lofton. **RBI:** Bonds 1 (1), Sanders 1 (1), Snow 2 (2). **2-out RBI:** Snow 2. **Runners left in scoring position, 2 out:** Kent 1, Sanders 1, Bell 2. **Team LOB:** 5

ANAHEIM	AB	R	H	HR	RBI	BB	AVG
Eckstein ss	5	0	1	0	0	0	.200
Erstad cf	5	0	1	0	0	0	.200
Salmon rf	4	0	0	0	0	0	.000
Anderson lf	4	0	1	0	0	0	.250
Glaus 3b	4	2	2	2	2	0	.500
Fullmer dh	3	1	1	0	0	1	.333
Spiezio 1b	3	0	1	0	0	1	.333
a-Figgins pr	0	0	0	0	0	0	.000
Wooten 1b	0	0	0	0	0	0	.000
B.Molina c	3	0	0	0	0	0	.000
b-Palmeiro ph	1	0	0	0	0	0	.000
J.Molina c	0	0	0	0	0	0	.000
Kennedy 2b	4	0	2	0	1	0	.500
TOTALS	**36**	**3**	**9**	**2**	**3**	**2**	**.250**

a - Ran for Spiezio in the 8th
b - Batted for B.Molina in the 8th

BATTING: 2B: Kennedy (1, Schmidt), Spiezio (1, Schmidt). **HR:** Glaus 2 (2, 2nd off Schmidt 0 on, 1 out, 6th off Schmidt 0 on, 0 out). **RBI:** Glaus 2 (2), Kennedy 1 (1). **2-out RBI:** Kennedy 1. **Runners left in scoring position, 2 out:** Salmon 1, Anderson 1, B.Molina 3. **Team LOB:** 8 **BASERUNNING: SB:** Fullmer (1, 2nd base off Schmidt/Santiago).

SAN FRANCISCO	IP	H	R	ER	BB	SO	HR	ERA
Schmidt (W, 1-0)	5.2	9	3	3	1	6	2	4.76
Fe.Rodriguez	1.1	0	0	0	0	1	0	0.00
Worrell	1	0	0	0	1	1	0	0.00
Nen (S, 1)	1	0	0	0	0	1	0	0.00

ANAHEIM	IP	H	R	ER	BB	SO	HR	ERA
Washburn (L, 0-1)	5.2	6	4	4	2	5	3	6.35
Donnelly	1.2	0	0	0	0	0	0	0.00
Schoeneweis	0	0	0	0	1	0	0	0.00
Weber	1.2	0	0	0	0	2	0	0.00

Pitches-strikes: Schmidt 91-66, Fe.Rodriguez 16-11, Worrell 23-13, Nen 13-11, Washburn 106-63, Donnelly 21-11, Schoeneweis 4-0, Weber 23-15. **Ground balls-fly balls:** Schmidt 3-8, Fe.Rodriguez 1-2, Worrell 1-1, Nen 0-2, Washburn 7-4, Donnelly 3-2, Schoeneweis 0-0, Weber 2-1. **Batters faced:** Schmidt 27, Fe.Rodriguez 4, Worrell 4, Nen 3, Washburn 25, Donnelly 5, Schoeneweis 1, Weber 5. **UMPIRES:** hp—Jerry Crawford, 1b—Angel Hernandez, 2b—Tim Tschida, 3b—Mike Winters, lf—Mike Reilly, rf—Tim McClelland **T:** 3:44 **A:** 44,603

GAME 2 Anaheim 11 San Francisco 10
Edison Field 10/20/02

SAN FRANCISCO	AB	R	H	HR	RBI	BB	AVG
Lofton cf	5	0	1	0	0	0	.125
Aurilia ss	5	1	1	0	0	0	.111
Kent 2b	5	1	1	1	1	0	.111
Bonds lf	2	3	1	1	1	3	.400
Santiago c	5	1	1	0	0	0	.222
Snow 1b	4	2	2	0	2	0	.429
Sanders rf	4	1	2	1	3	0	.571
Bell 3b	4	1	2	1	2	0	.250
Dunston dh	4	0	1	0	1	0	.250
TOTALS	**38**	**10**	**12**	**4**	**10**	**3**	**.257**

BATTING: 2B: Aurilia (1, Lackey). **HR:** Sanders (2, 2nd off Appier 2 on, 1 out), Bell (1, 2nd off Appier 0 on, 1 out), Kent (1, 3th off Appier 0 on, 0 out), Bonds (2, 9th off Percival 0 on, 2 out). **RBI:** Kent 1 (1), Bonds 1 (2), Snow 2 (4), Sanders 3 (4), Bell 2 (2), Dunston 1 (1). **2-out RBI:** Bonds 1, Bell 1, Dunston 1. **Runners left in scoring position, 2 out:** Lofton 2. **Team LOB:** 4 **BASERUNNING: SB:** Sanders (1, 2nd base off Lackey/B.Molina). **FIELDING: E:** Lofton (1). **PB:** Santiago. **Outfield assists:** Sanders (1). **DP:** 1 (Bell-Kent-Snow).

ANAHEIM	AB	R	H	HR	RBI	BB	AVG
Eckstein ss	5	3	3	0	0	0	.400
Erstad cf	5	2	2	0	1	0	.300
Salmon rf	4	3	4	2	4	1	.500
Ochoa rf	0	0	0	0	0	0	.000
Anderson lf	5	1	2	0	2	0	.333
Glaus 3b	4	1	2	0	0	0	.500
Fullmer dh	3	1	2	0	1	1	.500
Spiezio 1b	3	0	1	0	2	0	.333
B.Molina c	4	0	0	0	0	0	.000
Kennedy 2b	4	0	0	0	0	0	.250
TOTALS	**37**	**11**	**16**	**2**	**10**	**2**	**.342**

BATTING: 2B: Erstad 2 (2, Ru.Ortiz, Zerbe), Glaus (1, Ru.Ortiz). **HR:** Salmon 2 (2, 2nd off Ru.Ortiz 1 on, 1 out, 8th off Fe.Rodriguez 1 on, 2 out). **SF:** Spiezio. **RBI:** Erstad 1 (1), Salmon 4 (4), Anderson 2 (2), Fullmer 1 (1), Spiezio 2 (2). **2-out RBI:** Salmon 2, Anderson 1. **Runners left in scoring position, 2 out:** Anderson 1, Fullmer 1, Kennedy 1. **GIDP:** B.Molina. **Team LOB:** 5 **BASERUNNING: SB:** Fullmer (2, home off Ru.Ortiz/Santiago), Spiezio (1, home off Ru.Ortiz/Santiago). **FIELDING: E:** Anderson (1). **DP:** 1 (Eckstein-Spiezio).

SAN FRANCISCO	IP	H	R	ER	BB	SO	HR	ERA
Ru.Ortiz	1.2	9	7	7	0	0	1	37.80
Zerbe	4	4	2	1	0	0	0	2.25
Witasick	0	0	0	0	1	0	0	0.00
Fultz	0.1	1	0	0	0	0	0	0.00
Fe.Rodriguez (L, 0-1)	1.2	2	2	2	1	0	1	6.00
Worrell	0.1	0	0	0	0	0	0	0.00

ANAHEIM	IP	H	R	ER	BB	SO	HR	ERA
Appier	2	5	5	5	2	2	3	22.50
Lackey	2.1	2	2	2	1	1	0	7.71
Weber	0.2	4	2	2	0	1	0	7.71
Fr.Rodriguez (W, 1-0)	3	0	0	0	0	4	0	0.00
Percival (S, 1)	1	1	1	1	0	0	1	9.00

IBB: Bonds (by Lackey). **Pitches-strikes:** Ru.Ortiz 46-29, Zerbe 56-35, Witasick 6-2, Fultz 3-2, Fe.Rodriguez 37-24, Worrell 2-1, Appier 48-28, Lackey 32-20, Weber 26-17, Fr.Rodriguez 26-22, Percival 14-9. **Ground balls-fly balls:** Ru.Ortiz 1-4, Zerbe 10-0, Witasick 0-0, Fultz 0-0, Fe.Rodriguez 0-5, Worrell 0-1, Appier 3-1, Lackey 2-3, Weber 1-0, Fr.Rodriguez 3-2, Percival 0-3. **Batters faced:** Ru.Ortiz 14, Zerbe 15, Witasick 1, Fultz 1, Fe.Rodriguez 8, Worrell 1, Appier 13, Lackey 9, Weber 6, Fr.Rodriguez 9, Percival 4. **UMPIRES:** hp—Angel Hernandez, 1b—Tim Tschida, 2b—Mike Winters, 3b—Mike Reilly, lf—Tim McClelland, rf—Jerry Crawford **T:** 3:57 **A:** 44,584

GAME 3 Anaheim 10 San Francisco 4
Pacific Bell Park 10/22/02

ANAHEIM	AB	R	H	HR	RBI	BB	AVG
Eckstein ss	5	1	2	0	1	1	.400
Erstad cf	6	2	3	0	0	0	.375
Salmon rf	4	2	1	0	1	2	.417
Schoeneweis p	0	0	0	0	0	0	.000
Anderson lf	6	0	1	0	1	0	.267
Glaus 3b	5	2	2	0	1	1	.462
Spiezio 1b	5	1	2	0	3	1	.364
Kennedy 2b	5	1	2	0	1	0	.308
B.Molina c	2	1	2	0	1	3	.222
Ra.Ortiz p	3	0	0	0	0	0	.000
a-Wooten ph	1	0	0	0	0	0	.000
Donnelly p	0	0	0	0	0	0	.000
b-Gil ph	1	0	1	0	0	0	1.000
Ochoa rf	0	0	0	0	0	0	.000
TOTALS	**43**	**10**	**16**	**0**	**9**	**8**	**.353**

a - Batted for Ra.Ortiz in the 6th
b - Batted for Donnelly in the 8th

BATTING: 2B: Kennedy (2, Hernandez), Erstad (3, Hernandez), Salmon (1, Fe.Rodriguez). **3B:** Spiezio (1, Hernandez). **RBI:** Eckstein 1 (1), Salmon 1 (5), Anderson 1 (3), Glaus 1 (3), Spiezio 3 (5), Kennedy 1 (2), B.Molina 1 (1). **2-out RBI:** Eckstein 1, Spiezio 1, Kennedy 1, B.Molina 1. **Runners left in scoring position, 2 out:** Erstad 1, Anderson 2, Glaus 1, Spiezio 1, Ra.Ortiz 4. **GIDP:** Spiezio. **Team LOB:** 15 **BASERUNNING: SB:** Erstad (1, 3rd base off Hernandez/Santiago), Salmon (1, 3rd base off Hernandez/Santiago). **FIELDING: DP:** 1 (Eckstein-Kennedy-Spiezio).

SAN FRANCISCO	AB	R	H	HR	RBI	BB	AVG
Lofton cf	4	1	0	0	0	1	.083
Aurilia ss	5	1	2	1	1	0	.214
Kent 2b	4	1	2	0	0	0	.231
Bonds lf	2	1	1	1	2	2	.429
Santiago c	4	0	0	0	1	0	.154
Snow 1b	4	0	1	0	0	0	.364
Sanders rf	4	0	0	0	0	0	.364
Bell 3b	1	0	0	0	0	3	.222
Hernandez p	0	0	0	0	0	0	.000
Witasick p	0	0	0	0	0	0	.000
a-Feliz ph	1	0	0	0	0	0	.000
Fultz p	0	0	0	0	0	0	.000
b-Dunston ph	1	0	0	0	0	0	.200
Fe.Rodriguez p	0	0	0	0	0	0	.000
Eyre p	0	0	0	0	0	0	.000
c-Martinez ph	1	0	0	0	0	0	.000
TOTALS	**31**	**4**	**6**	**2**	**4**	**6**	**.238**

a - Batted for Witasick in the 4th
b - Batted for Fultz in the 6th
c - Batted for Eyre in the 9th

BATTING: HR: Aurilia (1, 5th off Ra.Ortiz 0 on, 1 out), Bonds (3, 5th off Ra.Ortiz 1 on, 1 out). **S:** Hernandez. **RBI:** Aurilia 1 (1), Bonds 2 (4), Santiago 1 (1). **Runners left in scoring position, 2 out:** Lofton 1, Snow 2. **GIDP:** Bell. **Team LOB:** 7 **BASERUNNING: SB:** Lofton (1, 2nd base off Ra.Ortiz/B.Molina). **FIELDING: E:** Bell (1), Santiago (1). **DP:** 1 (Aurilia-Kent-Snow).

ANAHEIM	IP	H	R	ER	BB	SO	HR	ERA
Ra.Ortiz (W, 1-0)	5	5	4	4	4	3	2	7.20
Donnelly	2	0	0	0	2	0	0	0.00
Schoeneweis	2	1	0	0	0	2	0	0.00

SAN FRANCISCO	IP	H	R	ER	BB	SO	HR	ERA
Hernandez (L, 0-1)	3.2	5	6	5	5	3	0	12.27
Witasick	0.1	3	2	2	1	1	0	54.00
Fultz	2	3	1	1	1	0	0	3.86
Fe.Rodriguez	1	1	0	0	0	0	0	4.50
Eyre	2	4	1	0	1	1	0	0.00

IBB: Bonds (by Ra.Ortiz), B.Molina 2 (by Hernandez), Salmon (by Eyre). **HBP:** Kennedy (by Fultz). **Pitches-strikes:** Ra.Ortiz 93-50, Donnelly 34-18, Schoeneweis 16-13, Hernandez 92-47, Witasick 16-11, Fultz 28-19, Fe.Rodriguez 12-8, Eyre 28-19. **Ground balls-fly balls:** Ra.Ortiz 6-5, Donnelly 0-6, Schoeneweis 1-2, Hernandez 6-3, Witasick 0-0, Fultz 2-4, Fe.Rodriguez 0-3, Eyre 2-2. **Batters faced:** Ra.Ortiz 24, Donnelly 8, Schoeneweis 6, Hernandez 22, Witasick 5, Fultz 11, Fe.Rodriguez 4, Eyre 10. **UMPIRES:** hp—Tim Tschida, 1b—Mike Winters, 2b—Mike Reilly, 3b—Tim McClelland, lf—Jerry Crawford, rf—Angel Hernandez **T:** 3:37 **A:** 42,707

GAME 4 San Francisco 4 Anaheim 3
Pacific Bell Park 10/23/02

ANAHEIM	AB	R	H	HR	RBI	BB	AVG
Eckstein ss	3	0	0	0	1	0	.333
Erstad cf	4	0	0	0	0	0	.300
Salmon rf	4	0	1	0	0	0	.375
Anderson lf	4	1	2	0	0	0	.316
Glaus 3b	4	1	1	1	2	0	.412
Spiezio 1b	4	0	1	0	0	0	.333
Gil 2b	3	1	2	0	0	0	.750
b-Kennedy ph	1	0	1	0	0	0	.357
B.Molina c	3	0	1	0	0	0	.250
c-Fullmer ph	1	0	0	0	0	0	.429
Lackey p	2	0	1	0	0	0	.500
Weber p	0	0	0	0	0	0	.000
a-Palmeiro ph	1	0	0	0	0	0	.000
Fr.Rodriguez p	0	0	0	0	0	0	.000
TOTALS	**34**	**3**	**10**	**1**	**3**	**0**	**.340**

a - Batted for Weber in the 7th
b - Batted for Gil in the 9th
c - Batted for B.Molina in the 9th

BATTING: HR: Glaus (3, 3th off Rueter 1 on, 1 out). **SF:** Eckstein. **RBI:** Eckstein 1 (2), Glaus 2 (5). **Runners left in scoring position, 2 out:** Erstad 1, Glaus 1. **GIDP:** Glaus, B.Molina, Fullmer. **Team LOB:** 5 **FIELDING: PB:** B.Molina. **Outfield assists:** Anderson (1). **DP:** 3 (Eckstein-Spiezio, Eckstein-Gil-Spiezio, B.Molina-Gil).

SAN FRANCISCO	AB	R	H	HR	RBI	BB	AVG
Lofton cf	4	1	3	0	0	0	.250
Aurilia ss	4	1	3	0	1	0	.333
Kent 2b	3	0	0	0	1	0	.188
Bonds lf	1	0	0	0	0	3	.375
Santiago c	4	0	1	0	1	0	.176
Snow 1b	4	1	1	0	0	0	.333
Sanders rf	4	0	1	0	0	0	.333
Bell 3b	4	0	2	0	1	0	.308
Rueter p	2	1	1	0	0	0	.500
a-Goodwin ph	0	0	0	0	0	1	.000
Fe.Rodriguez p	0	0	0	0	0	0	.000
Worrell p	0	0	0	0	0	0	.000
b-Martinez ph	1	0	0	0	0	0	.000
Nen p	0	0	0	0	0	0	.000
TOTALS	**31**	**4**	**12**	**0**	**4**	**4**	**.273**

a - Batted for Rueter in the 6th
b - Batted for Worrell in the 8th

BATTING: 2B: Aurilia (2, Lackey). **SF:** Kent. **RBI:** Aurilia 1 (2), Kent 1 (2), Santiago 1 (2), Bell 1 (3). **Runners left in scoring position, 2 out:** Aurilia 1, Sanders 1, Rueter 1. **GIDP:** Santiago, Santiago. **Team LOB:** 8 **BASERUNNING: SB:** Goodwin (1, 2nd base off Weber/B.Molina). **CS:** Bell (1, 2nd base off Fr.Rodriguez/B.Molina). **FIELDING: E:** Bell (2). **DP:** 3 (Aurilia-Kent-Snow, Snow-Aurilia-Rueter, Aurilia-Snow).

ANAHEIM	IP	H	R	ER	BB	SO	HR	ERA
Lackey	5	9	3	3	3	2	0	6.14
Weber	1	1	0	0	1	0	0	5.40
Fr.Rodriguez (L, 1-1)	2	2	1	0	0	2	0	0.00

SAN FRANCISCO	IP	H	R	ER	BB	SO	HR	ERA
Rueter	6	9	3	3	0	2	1	4.50
Fe.Rodriguez	1	0	0	0	0	1	0	3.60
Worrell (W, 1-0)	1	0	0	0	0	0	0	0.00
Nen (S, 2)	1	1	0	0	0	0	0	0.00

IBB: Bonds 3 ((by Lackey, by Lackey). **Pitches-strikes:** Lackey 95-54, Weber 19-12, Fr.Rodriguez 36-21, Rueter 88-54, Fe.Rodriguez 9-6, Worrell 13-9, Nen 7-7. **Ground balls-fly balls:** Lackey 6-4, Weber 0-2, Fr.Rodriguez 1-2, Rueter 12-2, Fe.Rodriguez 1-1, Worrell 1-2, Nen 1-1. **Batters faced:** Lackey 25, Weber 4, Fr.Rodriguez 7, Rueter 26, Fe.Rodriguez 3, Worrell 3, Nen 3. **UMPIRES:** hp—Mike Winters, 1b—Mike Reilly, 2b—Tim McClelland, 3b—Jerry Crawford, lf—Angel Hernandez, rf—Tim Tschida **T:** 3:02 **A:** 42,703

GAME 5 San Francisco 16 Anaheim 4
Pacific Bell Park 10/24/02

ANAHEIM	AB	R	H	HR	RBI	BB	AVG
Eckstein ss	4	1	2	0	1	1	.364
Erstad cf	4	0	1	0	1	0	.292
Salmon rf	4	1	1	0	0	0	.350
Ochoa rf	1	0	0	0	0	0	.000
Anderson lf	5	0	1	0	0	0	.292
Glaus 3b	4	0	1	0	1	0	.381
Spiezio 1b	2	0	0	0	0	2	.294
Shields p	0	0	0	0	0	0	.000
Kennedy 2b	4	0	0	0	0	0	.278
B.Molina c	4	1	1	0	0	0	.250
J.Molina c	0	0	0	0	0	0	.000
Washburn p	1	0	0	0	0	0	.000
a-Palmeiro ph	1	1	1	0	0	0	.333
Donnelly p	0	0	0	0	0	0	.000
b-Gil ph	1	0	1	0	0	0	.800
Weber p	0	0	0	0	0	0	.000
Wooten 1b	1	0	1	0	0	0	.500
TOTALS	**36**	**4**	**10**	**0**	**3**	**3**	**.328**

a - Batted for Washburn in the 5th
b - Batted for Donnelly in the 6th

BATTING: 2B: Palmeiro (1, Schmidt), Glaus (2, Schmidt), Gil (1, Zerbe). **SF:** Erstad. **RBI:** Eckstein 1 (3), Erstad 1 (2), Glaus 1 (6). **2-out RBI:** Glaus 1. **Runners left in scoring position, 2 out:** Salmon 1, Anderson 1, Glaus 1, Kennedy 1. **Team LOB:** 9 **BASERUNNING: SB:** Eckstein (1, 2nd base off Schmidt/Santiago). **FIELDING: E:** Erstad (1), Glaus (1).

SAN FRANCISCO	AB	R	H	HR	RBI	BB	AVG
Lofton cf	6	3	3	0	2	0	.318
Eyre p	0	0	0	0	0	0	.000
Aurilia ss	6	2	2	1	3	0	.333
Kent 2b	5	4	3	2	4	1	.286
Bonds lf	4	2	3	0	1	1	.500
Santiago c	3	0	1	0	3	1	.200
Sanders rf	1	0	0	0	1	1	.313
Fe.Rodriguez p	0	0	0	0	0	0	.000
a-Dunston ph	1	0	0	0	0	0	.167
Worrell p	0	0	0	0	0	0	.000
b-Feliz ph	1	0	0	0	0	0	.000
Goodwin rf	0	0	0	0	0	0	.000
Snow 1b	4	2	2	0	0	1	.368
Bell 3b	3	2	2	0	1	1	.375
Schmidt p	1	0	0	0	0	0	.000
Zerbe p	0	0	0	0	0	0	.000
Shinjo rf-cf	2	1	0	0	0	0	.200
TOTALS	**37**	**16**	**16**	**3**	**15**	**6**	**.308**

a - Batted for Fe.Rodriguez in the 6th
b - Batted for Worrell in the 8th

BATTING: 2B: Bonds 2 (2, Washburn, Weber), Kent (1, Washburn). **3B:** Lofton (1, Weber). **HR:** Kent 2 (3, 6th off Weber 1 on, 2 out, 7th off Shields 1 on, 2 out), Aurilia (2, 8th off Shields 2 on, 2 out). **S:** Schmidt, Shinjo. **SF:** Santiago, Sanders. **RBI:** Lofton 2 (2), Aurilia 3 (5), Kent 4 (6), Bonds 1 (5), Santiago 3 (5), Sanders 1 (5), Bell 1 (4). **2-out RBI:** Aurilia 3, Kent 4, Bell 1. **Runners left in scoring position, 2 out:** Aurilia 1, Dunston 1, Snow 1, Schmidt 2. **Team LOB:** 8

ANAHEIM	IP	H	R	ER	BB	SO	HR	ERA
Washburn (L, 0-2)	4	6	6	6	5	1	0	9.31
Donnelly	1	0	0	0	0	2	0	0.00
Weber	1.1	5	5	5	1	2	1	13.50
Shields	1.2	5	5	1	0	1	2	5.40

SAN FRANCISCO	IP	H	R	ER	BB	SO	HR	ERA
Schmidt	4.2	7	3	3	3	8	0	5.23
Zerbe (W, 1-0)	1	2	1	1	0	0	0	3.60
Fe.Rodriguez	0.1	0	0	0	0	0	0	3.38
Worrell	2	1	0	0	0	2	0	0.00
Eyre	1	0	0	0	0	1	0	0.00

WP: Schmidt 1. **IBB:** Sanders (by Washburn), Bonds (by Washburn), Santiago (by Weber). **HBP:** Bell (by Weber). **Pitches-strikes:** Washburn 79-40, Donnelly 17-12, Weber 36-24, Shields 49-30, Schmidt 104-67, Zerbe 14-11, Fe.Rodriguez 4-1, Worrell 28-19, Eyre 7-6. **Ground balls-fly balls:** Washburn 2-6, Donnelly 0-1, Weber 1-0, Shields 3-2, Schmidt 3-2, Zerbe 2-1, Fe.Rodriguez 1-0, Worrell 2-2, Eyre 1-1. **Batters faced:** Washburn 23, Donnelly 3, Weber 11, Shields 11, Schmidt 24, Zerbe 5, Fe.Rodriguez 1, Worrell 7, Eyre 3. **UMPIRES:** hp—Mike Reilly, 1b—Tim McClelland, 2b—Jerry Crawford, 3b—Angel Hernandez, lf—Tim Tschida, rf—Mike Winters **T:** 3:53 **A:** 42,713

GAME 6 Anaheim 6 San Francisco 5
Edison Field 10/26/02

SAN FRANCISCO	AB	R	H	HR	RBI	BB	AVG
Lofton cf	5	2	2	0	0	0	.333
Aurilia ss	4	0	0	0	0	1	.286
Kent 2b	4	0	2	0	1	0	.320
Bonds lf	2	1	1	1	1	2	.500
Santiago c	3	0	0	0	0	1	.174
Snow 1b	4	0	1	0	0	0	.348
Sanders rf	4	0	0	0	0	0	.250
Bell 3b	4	1	1	0	0	0	.350
Dunston dh	3	1	1	1	2	0	.222
a-Goodwin ph	1	0	0	0	0	0	.000
TOTALS	**34**	**5**	**8**	**2**	**4**	**4**	**.296**

a - Batted for Dunston in the 9th

BATTING: 2B: Lofton (1, Appier). **HR:** Dunston (1, 5th off Appier 1 on, 1 out), Bonds (4, 6th off Fr.Rodriguez 0 on, 0 out). **RBI:** Kent 1 (7), Bonds 1 (6), Dunston 2 (3). **2-out RBI:** Kent 1. **Runners left in scoring position, 2 out:** Santiago 1. **GIDP:** Santiago. **Team LOB:** 6 **BASERUNNING: SB:** Lofton 2 (3, 3rd base off Fr.Rodriguez/B.Molina, 2nd base off Fr.Rodriguez/B.Molina). **FIELDING: E:** Bonds (1). **DP:** 1 (Kent-Aurilia-Snow).

ANAHEIM	AB	R	H	HR	RBI	BB	AVG
Eckstein ss	4	0	0	0	0	0	.308
Erstad cf	3	1	1	1	1	1	.296
Salmon rf	4	0	2	0	0	0	.375
b-Figgins pr	0	1	0	0	0	0	.000
Ochoa rf	0	0	0	0	0	0	.000
Anderson lf	4	1	1	0	0	0	.286
Glaus 3b	3	1	2	0	2	1	.417
Fullmer dh	4	1	1	0	0	0	.364
Spiezio 1b	3	1	1	1	3	1	.300
B.Molina c	2	0	0	0	0	0	.222
a-Palmeiro ph	1	0	0	0	0	0	.250
J.Molina c	0	0	0	0	0	0	.000
Kennedy 2b	4	0	2	0	0	0	.318
TOTALS	**32**	**6**	**10**	**2**	**6**	**3**	**.326**

a - Batted for B.Molina in the 7th
b - Ran for Salmon in the 8th

BATTING: 2B: Glaus (3, Nen). **HR:** Spiezio (1, 7th off Fe.Rodriguez 2 on, 1 out), Erstad (1, 8th off Worrell 0 on, 0 out). **S:** J.Molina. **RBI:** Erstad 1 (3), Glaus 2 (8), Spiezio 3 (8). **Runners left in scoring position, 2 out:** Salmon 1, Kennedy 2. **GIDP:** Anderson. **Team LOB:** 6 **FIELDING: E:** B.Molina (1). **DP:** 1 (Glaus-Kennedy-Spiezio).

SAN FRANCISCO	IP	H	R	ER	BB	SO	HR	ERA
Ru.Ortiz	6.1	4	2	2	2	2	0	10.13
Fe.Rodriguez	0.1	1	1	1	0	1	1	4.76
Eyre	0	1	0	0	0	0	0	0.00
Worrell (L, 1-1)	0.1	3	3	2	0	0	1	3.86
Nen	1	1	0	0	1	2	0	0.00

ANAHEIM	IP	H	R	ER	BB	SO	HR	ERA
Appier	4.1	4	3	3	3	2	1	11.37
Fr.Rodriguez	2.2	4	2	2	0	4	1	2.35
Donnelly (W, 1-0)	1	0	0	0	1	2	0	0.00
Percival (S, 2)	1	0	0	0	0	2	0	4.50

WP: Fr.Rodriguez 1. **IBB:** Bonds (by Appier), Spiezio (by Nen). **Pitches-strikes:** Ru.Ortiz 98-60, Fe.Rodriguez 16-11, Eyre 2-1, Worrell 10-7, Nen 22-13, Appier 71-36, Fr.Rodriguez 46-35, Donnelly 16-10, Percival 17-11. **Ground balls-fly balls:** Ru.Ortiz 8-8, Fe.Rodriguez 0-0, Eyre 0-0, Worrell 0-1, Nen 0-0, Appier 3-7, Fr.Rodriguez 2-2, Donnelly 0-1, Percival 0-1. **Batters faced:** Ru.Ortiz 24, Fe.Rodriguez 2, Eyre 1, Worrell 4, Nen 5, Appier 19, Fr.Rodriguez 12, Donnelly 4, Percival 3. **UMPIRES:** hp—Tim McClelland, 1b—Jerry Crawford, 2b—Angel Hernandez, 3b—Tim Tschida, lf—Mike Winters, rf—Mike Reilly **T:** 3:48 **A:** 44,506

GAME 7 Anaheim 4 San Francisco 1
Edison Field 10/27/02

SAN FRANCISCO	AB	R	H	HR	RBI	BB	AVG
Lofton cf	4	0	0	0	0	1	.290
Aurilia ss	4	0	0	0	0	0	.250
Kent 2b	4	0	0	0	0	0	.276
Bonds lf	3	0	1	0	0	1	.471
Santiago c	3	1	2	0	0	1	.231
Snow 1b	4	0	3	0	0	0	.407
Sanders rf	1	0	0	0	1	0	.238
a-Goodwin ph-rf	2	0	0	0	0	0	.000
Bell 3b	3	0	0	0	0	1	.304
Feliz dh	3	0	0	0	0	0	.000
b-Shinjo ph	1	0	0	0	0	0	.167
TOTALS	**32**	**1**	**6**	**0**	**1**	**4**	**.281**

a - Batted for Sanders in the 6th
b - Batted for Feliz in the 9th

BATTING: 2B: Snow (1, Donnelly). **SF:** Sanders. **RBI:** Sanders 1 (6). **Runners left in scoring position, 2 out:** Lofton 1, Sanders 1, Goodwin 2. **Team LOB:** 9 **FIELDING: Outfield assists:** Lofton (1). **DP:** 1 (Lofton-Kent).

ANAHEIM	AB	R	H	HR	RBI	BB	AVG
Eckstein ss	3	1	1	0	0	1	.310
Erstad cf	3	1	1	0	0	0	.300
Salmon rf	2	1	0	0	0	1	.346
Ochoa rf	0	0	0	0	0	0	.000
Anderson lf	4	0	1	0	3	0	.281
Glaus 3b	2	0	0	0	0	2	.385
Fullmer dh	4	0	0	0	0	0	.267
Spiezio 1b	3	1	0	0	0	1	.261
B.Molina c	3	0	2	0	1	0	.286
Kennedy 2b	3	0	0	0	0	0	.280
TOTALS	**27**	**4**	**5**	**0**	**4**	**5**	**.310**

BATTING: 2B: B.Molina 2 (2, Hernandez, Rueter), Anderson (1, Hernandez). **S:** Erstad. **RBI:** Anderson 3 (6), B.Molina 1 (2). **2-out RBI:** B.Molina 1. **Runners left in scoring position, 2 out:** Eckstein 1, B.Molina 1, Kennedy 1. **Team LOB:** 6

SAN FRANCISCO	IP	H	R	ER	BB	SO	HR	ERA
Hernandez (L, 0-2)	2	4	4	4	4	1	0	14.29
Zerbe	1	0	0	0	0	0	0	3.00
Rueter	4	1	0	0	1	3	0	2.70
Worrell	1	0	0	0	0	1	0	3.18

ANAHEIM	IP	H	R	ER	BB	SO	HR	ERA
Lackey (W, 1-0)	5	4	1	1	1	4	0	4.38
Donnelly	2	1	0	0	1	2	0	0.00
Fr.Rodriguez	1	0	0	0	1	3	0	2.08
Percival (S, 3)	1	1	0	0	1	1	0	3.00

IBB: Glaus (by Hernandez). **HBP:** Salmon (by Hernandez). **Pitches-strikes:** Hernandez 52-24, Zerbe 7-5, Rueter 63-35, Worrell 9-7, Lackey 86-56, Donnelly 30-21, Fr.Rodriguez 16-11, Percival 20-13. **Ground balls-fly balls:** Hernandez 0-3, Zerbe 3-0, Rueter 5-4, Worrell 1-1, Lackey 3-7, Donnelly 1-3, Fr.Rodriguez 0-0, Percival 1-1. **Batters faced:** Hernandez 14, Zerbe 3, Rueter 14, Worrell 3, Lackey 20, Donnelly 8, Fr.Rodriguez 4, Percival 5. **UMPIRES:** hp—Jerry Crawford, 1b—Angel Hernandez, 2b—Tim Tschida, 3b—Mike Winters, lf—Mike Reilly, rf—Tim McClelland **T:** 3:16 **A:** 44,598

Bibliography

Periodicals

Note: Countless issues of each of the following periodicals were used as reference material in researching the past century of baseball history while writing this book. This list is provided for readers as is in the interest of both fairness to the sources and brevity in general.

Baseball Magazine
Boston Globe
Boston Herald
Chicago Defender
Chicago Tribune
Cincinnati Enquirer
Cleveland News
Cleveland Plain Dealer
Detroit Free Press
Los Angeles Times
Louisville Times
Newark Star-Ledger
Newsday
Newsweek
New York Daily News
New Yorker
New York Clipper
New York Herald-Tribune
New York Mirror
New York Post
New York Times
Oakland Tribune
Oneonta Daily Star
Philadelphia Inquirer
Philadelphia Press
Pittsburgh Press
Reach Baseball Guide
San Francisco Examiner
Spalding Baseball Guide
Sports Collector's Digest
Sporting Life
Sporting News
Sports Illustrated
Springfield (MA) Daily News
Springfield (MA) Morning Union
St. Louis Globe-Democrat
Timeline
USA Today
USA Today Baseball Weekly
Wall Street Journal
Washington Post
Washington Star

Books

Alexander, Charles. *John McGraw.* New York: Viking, 1988.
Alexander, Charles. *Ty Cobb.* New York: Oxford, 1984.
Angell, Roger. *Five Seasons: A Baseball Companion.* New York: Simon & Schuster, 1977.
Angell, Roger. *The Summer Game.* New York: Viking Press, 1972.
Asinof, Eliot. *Eight Men Out: The Black Sox and the 1919 World Series.* New York: Henry Holt, 1987.
Browning, Reed. *Cy Young: A Baseball Life.* Amherst: University of Massachusetts Press, 2000.
Carter, Gary, with Ken Abraham. *The Gamer.* Dallas: Word, 1993.
Clark, Dick, and Larry Lester, eds. *The Negro Leagues Book.* Cleveland: Society for American Baseball Research, 1994.
Cramer, Richard Ben. *Joe DiMaggio: The Hero's Life.* New York: Simon & Schuster, 2000.
Creamer, Robert. *Babe: The Legend Comes to Life.* New York: Simon & Schuster, 1974.
Daniel, W. Harrison. *Jimmie Foxx: The Life and Times of a Baseball Hall of Famer, 1907–1967.* Jefferson, NC: McFarland, 1996.
DeValeria, Dennis, and Jeanne Burke DeValeria. *Honus Wagner: A Biography.* New York: Henry Holt, 1996.
Delsohn, Steve. *True Blue: The Dramatic Story of the Los Angeles Dodgers, Told by the Men Who Lived It.* New York: Morrow, 2001.
Dickey, Glenn. *The History of the World Series Since 1903.* New York: Stein and Day, 1984.
Feller, Bob, with Bill Gilbert. *Now Pitching, Bob Feller.* New York: Carol Group, 1990.
Ford, Whitey, with Phil Pepe. *Slick.* New York: Morrow, 1987.
Gibson, Bob, with Phil Pepe. *From Ghetto to Glory: The Story of Bob Gibson.* Englewood Cliffs, NJ: Prentice Hall, 1968.
Gibson, Kirk, with Lynn Henning. *Bottom of the Ninth.* Chelsea, MI: Sleeping Bear Press, 1997.
Gruver, Edward. *Koufax.* Dallas: Taylor, 2000.
Halberstam, David. *Summer of '49.* New York: Morrow, 1989.
Herzog, Whitey, and Jonathan Pitts. *You're Missin' a Great Game.* New York: Simon & Schuster, 1999.
Hetrick, Thomas J. *Chris Von der Ahe and the St. Louis Browns.* Lanham, MD: Scarecrow Press, 1999.
Holway, John. *The Complete Book of Baseball's Negro Leagues.* Fern Park, FL: Hastings House, 2001.
Honig, Donald. *Baseball Between the Lines.* New York: Coward, McCann & Geoghegan, 1976.
Honig, Donald. *Baseball When the Grass Was Real.* New York: Coward, McCann & Geoghegan, 1975.
Honig, Donald. *The Man in the Dugout.* Chicago: Follett Publishing Co., 1977.
Honig, Donald. *The October Heroes.* New York: Simon and Schuster, 1979.
Irvin, Monte, with James Riley. *Nice Guys Finish First.* New York: Carroll & Graf, 1996.
Jackson, Reggie, with Mike Lupica. *Reggie.* New York: Ballantine, 1985.
James, Bill. *The Bill James Historical Baseball Abstract.* New York: Villard, 1988.
Kaplan, Jim. *Lefty Grove: An American Original.* Cleveland: Society for American Baseball Research, 2000.
Lanctot, Neil. *Fair Dealing and Clean Playing: The Hilldale Club and the Development of Black Professional Baseball, 1910–1932.* Jefferson, NC: McFarland, 1994.
Lansche, Jerry. *Glory Fades Away: The Nineteenth-Century World Series Rediscovered.* Dallas: Taylor Publishing, 1991.
Lieb, Fred. *The Story of the World Series.* New York: Putnam, 1965.
Mantle, Mickey, with Mickey Herskowitz. *All My Octobers: My Memories of Twelve World Series When the Yankees Ruled Baseball.* New York: HarperCollins, 1994.
Markusen, Bruce. *Baseball's Last Dynasty: Charlie Finley's Oakland A's.* Indianapolis: Masters Press, 1998.
Markusen, Bruce. *Roberto Clemente: The Great One.* Champaign, IL: Sports Publishing, 1998.
Marichal, Juan, with Charles Einstein. *A Pitcher's Story.* Garden City, NY: Doubleday, 1967.
Neft, David, and Richard Cohen. *The World Series.* New York: St. Martin's, 1990.
Nemec, David. *The Beer and Whisky League: The Illustrated History of the American Association - Baseball's Renegade Major League.* New York: Lyons & Burford, 1994.
Peary, Danny, ed. *They Played the Game: 65 Players Remember Baseball's Greatest Era, 1947-1964.* New York: Hyperion, 1994.
Plaut, David. *Chasing October: The Dodgers-Giants Pennant Race of 1962.* South Bend, IN: Diamond Communications, 1992.
Puckett, Kirby. *I Love This Game!* New York: HarperCollins, 1993.
Rampersad, Arnold. *Jackie Robinson: A Biography.* New York: Knopf, 1997.
Riley, James A. *The Biographical Encyclopedia of the Negro Baseball Leagues.* New York: Carroll & Graf, 1994.
Ritter, Lawrence S. *The Glory of Their Times: The Story of the Early Days of Baseball Told by the Men Who Played It.* New York: Quill/William Morrow, 1992.
Robinson, Brooks, with Fred Bauer. *Putting It All Together.* New York: Hawthorn, 1971.
Robinson, Frank, with Al Silverman. *My Life Is Baseball.* New York: Doubleday, 1968.
Robinson, Jackie, as told to Alfred Duckett. *I Never Had It Made.* New York: Ecco Press, 1995.
Robinson, Ray. *Matty: An American Hero.* New York: Oxford, 1993.
Roseboro, John, with Bill Libby. *Glory Days With the Dodgers.* New York: Atheneum, 1978.
Rosenbaum, Dave. *If They Don't Win It's a Shame: The Year the Marlins Bought the World Series.* Tampa: McGregor, 1998.
Snider, Duke, with Bill Gilbert. *The Duke of Flatbush.* New York: Zebra Books, 1988.
Sowell, Mike. *One Pitch Away: The Players' Stories of the 1986 League Championships and World Series.* New York: Macmillan, 1995.
Stargell, Willie, and Tom Bird. *Willie Stargell: An Autobiography.* New York: Harper & Row, 1984.
Thomas, Henry. *Walter Johnson: Baseball's Big Train.* Lincoln: University of Nebraska Press, 1998.
Tygiel, Jules. *Baseball's Great Experiment: Jackie Robinson and His Legacy.* New York: Oxford University Press, 1983.
Torre, Joe, with Tom Verducci. *Chasing the Dream: My Lifelong Journey to the World Series.* New York: Bantam, 1997.
Veeck, Bill, with Ed Linn. *Veeck – As In Wreck: The Autobiography of Bill Veeck.* New York: Bantam, 1963.
Welch, Bob, and George Vecsey. *Five O'Clock Comes Early: A Young Man's Battle With Alcoholism.* New York: Morrow, 1982.

Archives

National Baseball Hall of Fame Library, Cooperstown, New York

Websites

www.baseball-reference.com
www.baseballlibrary.com
www.retrosheet.org

Photography Credits

AP/Wide World Photos: p. 2, 47 bottom, 54-55, 80 bottom, 84 bottom, 88 bottom, 89 bottom, 92 bottom, 94 bottom, 95, 96 bottom, 97 bottom right, 100 top, 103 top, 104 left and right, 106, 107 bottom, 120, 135, 149, 155 bottom, 159 top, 161 top, 162 bottom, 163 middle, 168 top, 169 bottom, 172 top right and bottom, 174 bottom, 180 bottom,199 bottom, 207 left and right, 211 bottom, 215 bottom, 219 bottom, 223, 231 top, 234, 240 bottom left, 242 bottom right, 247 top right, 249 top and bottom, 257 bottom, 315

Baseball Hall of Fame Library Cooperstown, N.Y.: p. 5, 8 top, 10-11, 16, 17 top and bottom, 19 bottom right, 21 bottom, 22 left and right, 23, 24 right, 25 top, 27 bottom, 28 right, 31 top and bottom, 33 bottom left and right, 35, 36 bottom, 37, 38, 40, 41 top, 42 top, 43 top, 44 bottom, 46 top and bottom, 48 left and right, 49 bottom, 50 bottom left, middle and right, 51 bottom middle, 56 left, 57 top, 58 bottom, 58 bottom, 60 top and bottom, 61bottom, 62 bottom, 64 top, 65 left and right, 67, 71 bottom, 74 right, 75 top, 76 bottom, 78 top, 79 bottom, 82 bottom, 84 middle, 86 bottom, 89 top left, 93 top, 98 top, 102, 114-115 top and bottom, 116-117 top and bottom, 124 bottom, 130 bottom, 146 top and bottom, 176 bottom, 190 bottom right, 228

Corbis: ©AFP: p. 8 bottom, 254 bottom, 255 bottom right, 256 bottom left; ©Bettmann: p. 12 bottom, 14-15, 20, 26 bottom right, 32 left and right, 51 bottom left and right, 52 left, 58 top, 62 bottom, 66, 69 bottom, 70 bottom, 74 left, 77 top and bottom, 78 bottom, 79 top, 83 top and bottom, 86 middle, 87, 93 bottom, 97 bottom left, 99 bottom, 100 bottom, 101 bottom, 105, 111 left and right, 112 bottom right, 113, 118 left and right, 119 bottom right, 121 top right and bottom, 122 left and right, 123, 124 top, 125 bottom left, 126 left and right, 127 top and bottom, 128, 129 top and bottom, 131 left and right, 132 top, 133 bottom, 134 bottom, 135 (4 inset photos), 139, 141, 144 left and right bottom, 145 top, 148 bottom, 150 left and right, 151 top, 152-153, 163, 165 top, 166 bottom, 170 top; 175 bottom, 177, 179 bottom, 180 top left, 183, 184, 185 bottom left, 188-189, 190 top, 191 top, 194 bottom, 197, 203 bottom right, 206 , 208 top left and bottom, 212, 213 right, 214, 215 top, 218 top, 226 left; ©Neal Preston: p. 198 bottom left and right, 200 top right; ©Richard Hamilton Smith: p. 192-193; ©Reuters NewMedia Inc.: p. 90, 230 bottom, 255 top, 257 top, 258; ©Underwood & Underwood: p. 29 bottom, 32 left and right, 52 right, 56 bottom right, 57 bottom, 68, 84 bottom

George Brace Collection: p. 72 bottom left

Globe Newspaper Company, Inc.: ©1986: p. 216 top

Getty Images: ©Jeff Gross: p. 238-239

Library of Congress: p. 13 top

Major League Baseball: p. 232 right, 241, 243 bottom right, 244, 246 top, 250 bottom; ©Rich Pilling: p. 182 top, 205 bottom, 213 left, 218 bottom, 222 bottom, 223bottom, 226 right, 228 bottom, 231 bottom, 233 bottom; ©Ron Vesley: p. 232 left, 236 (full page image)

Transcendental Graphics: p. 12 top, 13 bottom, 18, 19 top and bottom left, 21 top, 24 left, 25 bottom, 26 top and bottom left, 27 top, 28 left, 29 top, 30 top and bottom, 33 top, 34 top and bottom, 36 top, 39 top, 41 bottom, 42 bottom, 43 bottom, 44 top and bottom, 45 top, 46 top, 48 top, 49 top, 50 top, 51 top, 52 bottom, 53, 56 top, 58 top, 61 top, 62 top, 63 top, 64 bottom, 65 top, 69 top, 71 top, 72, 74 top, 75 bottom, 76 top, 77 top, 80 top, 81 top and bottom, 82 top, 84 top, 86 top, 88 top, 89 top right, 92 top, 94 top, 96 top, 98, 100 top, 101 top, 104 top, 105 top, 107 top, 108-109, 110 top and bottom, 112 top and bottom left, 119 top and bottom left, 121 top left, 121 top left, 124 top and bottom right, 125 top and bottom right, 130 top, 132 bottom, 133 top, 134 top, 136 top and bottom left, 138, 140 top right, 142 top right, 143, 144 top, 148 top left and right, 149 top, 154 top and bottom, 158 top, 160 top, 165 top, 167 top, 170 bottom, 171 top and bottom right, 173 top, 178 bottom, 179 top, 182 top left, 185 top, 187 top, 194 top, 195 top, 198 top, 199 top, 203 top, 204 top, 205 top, 207 top, 208 top right, 211 top, 215 top left, 217 top, 218 top, 222 top, 228 top left, 229 top, 240 top, 242 top, 245 top, 246 top left, 253 top, 256 top, front and back endpapers

Sports Illustrated: ©John Biever: p. 6-7, 259 top and bottom; ©John McDonough: p. 247 bottom, 256 bottom right; ©James Drake: p. 160; 162 top, 163 bottom, 166 top, 200 top left; ©Jacquiline Duvoisin: p. 220 bottom; ©John D. Hanion: p. 216 bottom right; ©John Iacono: p. 210, 216 bottom left, 223 top, 224-225, 235 bottom, 236 inset, 243 top and bottom left, 246 bottom, 253 bottom; ©Walter Iooss Jr.: p. 9, 158, 161 bottom, 168 bottom, 180 top right, 181, 185 bottom right, 196 left, 202 bottom right, 203 left, 208 bottom; ©Mark Kauffman: p. 136 bottom right, 137; ©Heinz Kluetmeier: p. 186 top and bottom, 187 bottom, 190 bottom, 201, 204 bottom, 220 top; ©Neil Leifer: p. 155 top, 157 top, 196 right; ©V. J. Lovero: p. 228 top right, 242 bottom left, 248, 252 bottom left, 254 top, 255 bottom left; ©Richard Mackson: p. 230 top; ©Manny Millan: p. 202 bottom left; ©Ron Modra: p. 209 bottom, 229 bottom, 245 bottom ; ©Marvin E. Newman: p. 151 bottom, 159 bottom; ©Hy Peskin: p. 142 bottom, 150 top left; © Art Rickerby: p. 150 bottom; ©Herb Scharfman: p. 164, 167 bottom, 171 bottom left, 173, 175 top, 178 top, 182 bottom; ©Chuck Solomon: p. 232 top, 241 bottom right; 251 middle; ©George Tiedemann: p. 200 bottom; ©Al Tielemans: p. 251 bottom, 252 bottom right; ©Tony Tomsic: p. 217 bottom; ©Tony Triolo: p. 174 top, 176 top, 191 bottom; ©John G. Zimmerman: p. 140 top and bottom, 142 top, 145 bottom, 147, 195 bottom

United Feature Syndicate, Inc.: p. 157, PEANUTS cartoon reprinted by permission

LEFT: In 1982, Robin Yount became one of a handful of shortstops in baseball history to lead his league in OPS (on-base plus slugging), the single best measure of offensive performance. Yount collected twelve hits in that year's World Series, including four in the game pictured here, but it wasn't enough as the Brewers lost to St. Louis, four games to three.

INDEX

INDEX

INDEX

AT BAT
POS.SS
BALL
STRIKE
OUT